Cyclopedia
of
LITERARY
CHARACTERS

Cyclopedia

of

LITERARY

CHARACTERS

Revised Edition

Volume One
Aaron's Rod–dem

---

edited by
A. J. Sobczak

original editions edited by
Frank N. Magill

associate editor
Janet Alice Long

SALEM PRESS, INC.
Pasadena, California   Englewood Cliffs, New Jersey

Editor in Chief: Dawn P. Dawson
Managing Editor: Chris Moose
Project Editor: A. J. Sobczak
Acquisitions Editor: Mark Rehn
Research Supervisor: Jeffry Jensen
Research: Jun Ohnuki
Production Editor: Janet Alice Long
Layout: William Zimmerman

Copyright © 1963, 1990, 1998, by SALEM PRESS, INC.

The Revised Edition includes *Cyclopedia of Literary Characters*, 1963 (first edition); *Cyclopedia of Literary Characters II*, 1990; and material new to this edition.

∞ The paper used in these volumes conforms to the American National Standard for Permanence of Paper for Printed Library Materials, Z39.48-1984.

Library of Congress Cataloging-in-Publication Data
Cyclopedia of literary characters / edited by A. J. Sobczak ; associate editor, Janet Alice Long. — Rev. ed.
    p. cm.
"This comprehensive revised edition of Cyclopedia of literary characters combines all the titles from the original Cyclopedia of literary characters and from Cyclopedia of literary characters II . . . adds character descriptions from titles included in Masterplots (revised second edition, 1996) and the Masterplots II sets covering African American literature (1994), women's literature (1995), and American fiction (supplement, 1994) . . . 3,300 titles [in all]."—Publisher's note.
    Includes index
1. Literature—Stories, plots, etc. 2. Literature—Dictionaries. 3. Characters and characteristics in literature. I. Sobczak, A. J. II. Long, Janet Alice.
PN44.M3 1998
809'.927—dc21
ISBN 0-89356-438-9 (set)   97-45813
ISBN 0-89356-439-7 (vol. 1)   CIP

SECOND PRINTING
PRINTED IN THE UNITED STATES OF AMERICA

PUBLISHER'S NOTE

In 1963, Salem Press presented its *Cyclopedia of Literary Characters*, two volumes collecting more than sixteen thousand character descriptions from some thirteen hundred novels, plays, epics, and other classics of world literature, arranged alphabetically by title of work. The list of works from which these characters were selected was developed from the original *Masterplots* series, which provided plot summaries of the world's greatest literature. The *Cyclopedia of Literary Characters* offered readers the opportunity to become familiar with both famous and less well-known personalities from classic fiction: Major characters were presented in write-ups of one hundred to one hundred fifty words; supporting and minor characters were described in fewer words, according to their importance.

In 1986, Salem Press brought out the first volumes in a new survey of literature, *Masterplots II*, American Fiction Series, which covered novels of twentieth century North and Latin America that were not treated in previous *Masterplots*. *Cyclopedia of Literary Characters II*, published in 1990, collected those new characters who made their appearance in the following series in *Masterplots II*: American Fiction, British and Commonwealth Fiction, World Fiction, and Drama. In addition, twenty works from the Short Stories series, generally qualifying as novellas, were chosen for character coverage. In total, 1,437 works were represented in those four volumes.

Masterplots II has since grown to a total of fifty-eight volumes, thirty-four of which (encompassing novel-length fiction and drama) are covered by *Cyclopedia of Literary Characters, Revised Edition*. (Not covered are ten volumes surveying short fiction, four volumes surveying great works of literary nonfiction, four volumes surveying biographies written for young adults, and six volumes surveying poetry.) This whole new generation of literary characters prompted publication of a revised edition of *Cyclopedia of Literary Characters*.

This comprehensive revised edition of *Cyclopedia of Literary Characters* combines all the titles from the original *Cyclopedia of Literary Characters* and from *Cyclopedia of Literary Characters II*. In addition, it adds character descriptions from titles included in *Masterplots Revised Second Edition* (1996) and the *Masterplots II* sets covering African American Literature (1994), Women's Literature (1995), and American Fiction (Supplement, 1994). Character analyses for these books are completely new. In total, this revised edition covers 3,300 titles, adding 574 titles to the previous coverage, replacing 84 of the previously published articles to provide more complete coverage, and updating dozens more articles. Books by a given author that commonly are studied together are treated in a single article, allowing the user to study character development across the books. Heavily cross-referenced indexes allow easy access to all titles covered. *Cyclopedia of Literary Characters, Revised Edition* can be used both on its own and as a companion set to *Masterplots II*, in which plot summaries and analyses complement the character descriptions found here.

Articles are arranged alphabetically by title of work, volume 1 beginning with *Aaron's Rod* by D. H. Lawrence and volume 5 concluding with *Zuleika Dobson* by Max Beerbohm. Each article starts with some standard ready-reference top matter, expanded from the earlier volumes. This top matter includes each book's title, foreign title if originally published in a language other than English, author's name with birth and death years, date of first publication (sometimes first production for drama and first transcription for early works), genre (novel or novels, novella, drama, poetry, short fiction), locale, time of action, and plot type. The characters are arranged by order of importance within each article. As in the first two *Cyclopedia of Literary Characters* sets, the central or key characters receive lengthy descriptions; supporting and minor figures receive less extensive treatment. Not every character who may have made an appearance in the works is represented; most contributors, however, made an effort to list more characters than appeared in the listing of "Principal Characters" found in the counterpart article from a *Masterplots* or *Masterplots II* set.

Pronunciation guides are provided for character names that are most likely to be mispronounced (primarily foreign-language names), especially in cases in which the spelling of the name would not prompt a reasonable facsimile of correct pronunciation from an English-language speaker. The intention was not to provide pronunciation automatically for all foreign-language names (many of which, such as Heinz or Jacques, will be familiar to most readers); nor was the intention to instruct the reader in the subtleties of foreign-language pronunciation. Rather, pronunciation is offered where the editors believe that the original spelling would present an obstacle to oral discussion of these characters. A Key to Pronunciation is found in the front matter of each volume. This pronunciation guide is phonetic, avoiding symbols that could be unfamiliar to the users of *Cyclopedia of Literary Characters, Revised Edition*.

Three indexes, found at the back of volume 5, are designed to help the user more readily access the text. First, there is a complete list of titles, including cross-references. Second, an Author Index lists titles by author; again cross-references are included. Finally, the alphabetical Character Index lists the more than twenty thousand characters herein described, using last names if those appear in the original works or using first names or descriptions. The Character Index is a valuable aid in locating the author and work or works with which a particular character is associated.

The editors wish to thank a long list of contributors. The names of contributors to *Cyclopedia of Literary Characters II* and of contributors of articles new to *Cyclopedia of Literary Characters, Revised Edition* will be found, along with their affiliations, both in the front matter to the first volume and appended to the articles themselves; contributors to the original *Cyclopedia of Literary Characters* were anonymous. The efforts of all contributors in compiling the descriptions are greatly appreciated.

PREFACE TO THE ORIGINAL EDITION

Imagination is the stock in trade of the storyteller. The characters he creates are the vehicles by means of which he transmits his imagination and insight to his audience. If he is a keen observer and a clever commentator on what he has observed, it is likely that his characters will seem lifelike and identifiable and will make a lasting impression on his readers.

It has been said that the greatest compliment an author can pay a predecessor is to try and emulate his characterizations. We have had innumerable *Milites Gloriosi* and Falstaffs down through the years. Shakespeare, and Dickens, too, supplied enough original character material to keep generations of authors hard at work for a lifetime trying to emulate them. Yet emulation is not always undesirable, for new insights cast new lights. And it is these new lights that make incisive fiction so rewarding. One excuse nonreaders of fiction give for avoiding the medium and devoting their reading time to nonfiction is that reading "make-believe" is a waste of time. Unfortunately for them, this group misses the whole point of character development, an artistic process that enables a wise and skillful author to probe a given "personality" with much greater accuracy and insight than would ever be possible with a complex living organism, including even himself. For example, Flem Snopes could not be any one particular individual in real life. But through him, Faulkner could give us a composite personality that followed a straight line to a sure end. Thus we could be instructed without being impeded by the unpredictable but realistic drawbacks of divergent human responses that are bound to occur in real life.

Cyclopedia of Literary Characters comprises a collection of more than sixteen thousand characters from some thirteen hundred novels, dramas, and epics drawn from world literature. Within this vast collection are the great names from fiction and drama, familiar characters whose exploits have entertained countless generations of readers. Though the cast of Aeschylus' *The Suppliants* forms the oldest extant characters in European dramatic literature, tribal tales and Oriental literature had their well-developed fictional heroes and villains long before a Greek playwright formalized such figures for the stage.

In this book major characters receive a substantial writeup of perhaps one hundred or one hundred fifty words in which an assessment of the character is given, a critical evaluation with regard to psychological motivation, development, possible flaws, and related matters. Lesser characters receive less space but they too are analyzed. Identification and relationships are given for even the most minor characters.

Characters in each book appear together, in the order of diminishing importance. Book titles are arranged alphabetically in the text but a special character index of fifty pages will be found at the end of the text, in which characters are listed alphabetically. Thus, a character may be located readily regardless of whether the title of the book in which he appears is known. Following the alphabetical character index will be found an author index which lists all authors whose works are represented in *Cyclopedia of Literary Characters*.

The alphabetical character index is a massive collection of names containing 11,940 listings. To keep the index even within this limit certain abbreviations were employed. For example, *etc.*, following a name indicated that other characters of the same family name also appear in the article referred to. Thus, the listing *Babbitt, George F., etc., 72* means that other Babbitts (Myra, Verona, Ted) will also be found in the article on page 72 that includes George. Obviously, many names appear several times in a collection of this size. The name Antonio, for example, appears often in Shakespeare and more than a dozen times throughout this book. In such cases all page numbers on which the name appears are shown in the alphabetical character index.

Pronunciation is given for names likely to be mispronounced and for unfamiliar foreign names. A key to pronunciation with a guide for certain foreign sounds is included.

The preparation of this book has been a long and arduous task and as the project progressed it grew in complexity and scope. But despite the demands, it has been a pleasure to deal intimately for so long with the world's leading literary characters. The substantial writing staff and our tireless proofreaders join me in hoping that this collection will serve a useful purpose for those who are interested in studying the ways in which the master storytellers went about the job of making their characters compelling and timeless.

Frank N. Magill

CONTRIBUTING REVIEWERS

Hardin Aasand
Dickinson State University

Michael Adams
Horrmann Library, Wagner College
Fairleigh Dickinson University

Patrick Adcock
Henderson State University

C. M. Adderley
University of South Florida

Amy Adelstein
Independent Scholar

Jacob H. Adler
Purdue University

Kerry Ahearn
Independent Scholar

C. D. Akerley
U.S. Naval Academy

Yasuko Akiyama
Independent Scholar

A. Owen Aldridge
University of Illinois

Betty Alldredge
Angelo State University

Arthur Tilo Alt
Duke University

Daniel Altamiranda
Arizona State University

Emily Alward
Greenwood, Indiana, Public Library

Christopher L. Anderson
University of Tulsa

Raymond M. Archer
Indiana University at Kokomo

Stanley Archer
Texas A&M University

Frank Ardolino
University of Hawaii at Manoa

Christopher M. Armitage
University of North Carolina at Chapel Hill

Dorothy B. Aspinwall
University of Hawaii at Manoa

Philip Auslander
Georgia Institute of Technology

Addell Austin
State University of New York College
at Oneonta

Charles Avinger
Washtenaw Community College

Marie-Denise Boros Azzi
Rutgers, State University of New Jersey

Raymond Bach
Texas A&M University

James Baird
University of North Texas

JoAnn Balingit
Independent Scholar

Judith L. Barban
Winthrop University

Laura Stone Barnard
University of Wisconsin—Milwaukee

Henry J. Baron
Calvin College

David Barratt
University of North Carolina at Asheville
Chester College, England

Lindon Barrett
University of California, Irvine

Thomas F. Barry
Himeji Dokkyo University

Melissa E. Barth
Appalachian State University

Sally Bartlett
University of South Florida

Kate M. Begnal
Utah State University

Carol F. Bender
Alma College

Robert M. Bender
University of Missouri—Columbia

Joe Benson
AT&T State University

Richard P. Benton
Trinity College

Cynthia Breslin Beres
Independent Scholar

Mary G. Berg
Harvard University

Jennifer E. Berkley
Independent Scholar

Donna Berliner
Southern Methodist University

Robert L. Berner
University of Wisconsin—Oshkosh

Dorothy M. Betz
Georgetown University

Cynthia A. Bily
Siena Heights College
Adrian College

Margaret Boe Birns
New York University

Nicholas Birns
The New School for Social Research

Scott Blackwell
Ball State University

Elizabeth Bleicher
University of Southern California

Harriet Blodgett
Stanford University

Harold Blythe
Eastern Kentucky University

Pegge Bochynski
Salem State College

Janice M. Bogstad
University of Wisconsin—Eau-Claire

Brinda Bose
Boston University

Wendy Bousfield
Syracuse University

Seth Bovey
University of New Mexico

James H. Bowden
Indiana University Southeast

Robert Bowie
Miami University

Marion Boyle
Bloomsburg University

Jerry W. Bradley
New Mexico Institute of Mining and
Technology

Patrick Brady
University of Tennessee

John Braeman
University of Nebraska, Lincoln

Gerhard Brand
California State University, Los Angeles

Philip Brantingham
Loyola University of Chicago

Francis J. Bremer
Millersville University of Pennsylvania

Chris Breyer
Independent Scholar

Susan Briziarelli
Washington University

J. R. Broadus
University of North Carolina at Chapel Hill

Robert R. Brock
University of Montana

David Bromige
Sonoma State University

Diane Brotemarkle
Aims Community College

Laura Browder
Boston College

Keith H. Brower
Dickinson College

Alan Brown
Livingston University

Elizabeth Brown-Guillory
University of Houston

Carl Brucker
Arkansas Tech University

Maurice P. Brungardt
Loyola University, New Orleans

David D. Buck
University of Wisconsin—Milwaukee

Paul Budra
Simon Fraser University, Ontario, Canada

Jeffrey L. Buller
Loras College
Georgia Southern University

David L. Bullock
Kansas State University

Lori Hall Burghardt
University of Tennessee

Cherelyn Bush
West Chester University

Roland E. Bush
California State University, Long Beach

Rebecca R. Butler
Dalton College

Anne Callahan
Loyola University of Chicago

Thomas J. Campbell
Pacific Lutheran University

Edmund J. Campion
University of Tennessee

Pamela Canal
Independent Scholar

Byron D. Cannon
University of Utah

Kenneth D. Capers
West Georgia College

Thomas Carmichael
University of Toronto

David A. Carpenter
Eastern Illinois University

Irene Campos Carr
Northeastern Illinois University

Warren J. Carson
University of South Carolina—Spartanburg

Ron Carter
Rappahannock Community College

Sonya H. Cashdan
East Tennessee State University

Leonard Casper
Boston College

Jocelyn Creigh Cass
Fraser Valley College

Thomas J. Cassidy
University of Wisconsin-Steven's Point
South Carolina State University

Lauren Chadwick
Northwestern State University

Susan Chainey
Sacramento City College

Lila Chalpin
Massachusetts College of Art

Edgar L. Chapman
Bradley University

Patricia T. Cheves
Appalachian State University

John Steven Childs
Polytechnic University

Balance Chow
San Jose State University

Dennis C. Chowenhill
Chabot College

C. L. Chua
California State University, Fresno

Michael Cisco
Independent Scholar

Patricia Clark
University of Tennessee

Karen M. Cleveland
Independent Scholar

Greta McCormick Coger
Northwest Mississippi Community College

Julian W. Connolly
University of Virginia

Bernard A. Cook
Loyola University, New Orleans

Will H. Corral
Stanford University

Alan Cottrell
University of Missouri at Kansas City

Virginia Crane
California State University, Los Angeles

Frederic M. Crawford
Middle Tennessee State University

Lee B. Croft
Arizona State University

W. Gordon Cunliffe
University of Wisconsin—Madison

Jeff Cupp
University of Charleston

Erik D. Curren
University of California, Irvine

Su A. Cutler
Kalamazoo Valley Community College

Noel Daigle
Independent Scholar

Donald A. Daiker
Miami University

Anita P. Davis
Converse College

Dale Davis
Northwest Mississippi Community College

Jane Davis
Cornell University

Jo Culbertson Davis
Williams Baptist College

Jocelyn Roberts Davis
Independent Scholar

Mary Virginia Davis
California State University, Sacramento

Matthew K. Davis
Independent Scholar

Timothy C. Davis
University of South Florida

Kwame S. N. Dawes
University of South Carolina at Sumter

Frank Day
Clemson University

Dennis R. Dean
Independent Scholar

Jodi Dean
Hobart and William Smith Colleges

Michael P. Dean
University of Mississippi

Mary Jo Deegan
University of Nebraska, Lincoln

Bill Delaney
Independent Scholar

Linda C. DeMeritt
Allegheny College

Francine Dempsey
College of Saint Rose

Scott Denham
Davidson College

Apryl Lea Denny
Viterbo College

John Deredita
Independent Scholar

Don DeRose
Independent Scholar

James I. Deutsch
George Washington University

James E. Devlin
*State University of New York College
    at Oneonta*

Ikenna Dieke
Allen University

Gene Doty
University of Missouri—Rolla

Randi A. Drubin
Ball State University

Sarah Smith Ducksworth
Kean College of New Jersey

Virginia Dumont-Poston
Lander University

Joyce Duncan
East Tennessee State University

Gweneth A. Dunleavy
*Augustana College
University of Louisville*

Paul F. Dvorak
Virginia Commonwealth University

Karen Dwyer
Purdue University

Stefan Dziemianowicz
Independent Scholar

K Edgington
Towson State University

Bruce L. Edwards
Bowling Green State University

Clifford Edwards
Fort Hays State University

William Eiland
University of Georgia

Janet Mason Ellerby
University of North Carolina at Wilmington

Robert P. Ellis
Independent Scholar

Penelope J. Engelbrecht
DePaul University

Thomas L. Erskine
Salisbury State University

Donald T. Evans
Trenton State College

Thomas H. Falk
Michigan State University

Jo N. Farrar
San Jacinto College

James Feast
New York University

Tom Feller
Independent Scholar

Gaston F. Fernandez
University of Arkansas

Jaime Ferrán
Syracuse University

Joseph A. Feustle, Jr.
University of Toledo

Donald M. Fiene
University of Tennessee

John W. Fiero
University of Southwestern Louisiana

Daniel D. Fineman
Occidental College

Edward Fiorelli
St. John's University

David Marc Fischer
Independent Scholar

Ruth D. Fisher
Kutztown University

Louise Flavin
University of Cincinnati

Kay Kenney Fortson
Phillips University

Ronald Foust
Loyola University, New Orleans

Thomas C. Fox
Washington University

Carol Franks
Portland State University

Thomas B. Frazier
Cumberland College

Maureen Fries
*State University of New York College
    at Fredonia*

Ronald H. Fritze
Lamar University

Mary Pierce Frost
Independent Scholar

Kelly Fuller
Claremont Graduate School

Constance M. Fulmer
Pepperdine University

James Gaasch
Humboldt State University

Frank Gado
Union College

Robert L. Gale
University of Pittsburgh

Louis Gallo
Radford University

Charles E. Gannon
University of Liverpool

Ann Davison Garbett
Averett College

Daniel H. Garrison
Northwestern University

Michael Wm. Gearhart
University of South Florida

Marshall Bruce Gentry
University of Indianapolis

Philip Gerard
University of North Carolina at Wilmington

Dana Gerhardt
Independent Scholar

Donna Gerstenberger
University of Washington

Jill B. Gidmark
University of Minnesota

Donald Gilman
Ball State University

Jonathan A. Glenn
Holy Cross Junior College

Beaird Glover
Independent Scholar

Jacqueline L. Gmuca
*University of South Carolina
    Coastal Carolina College*

Donald Gochberg
Michigan State University

Hazel Gold
Northwestern University

Marc Goldstein
Independent Scholar

Lucy Golsan
Independent Scholar

Richard J. Golsan
Texas A&M University

Margaret Bozenna Goscilo
Johnson State College

Karen Gould
Independent Scholar

Sandra Y. Govan
University of North Carolina at Charlotte

Kenneth B. Grant
*University of Wisconsin
Center—Baraboo/Sauk*

Eleanor H. Green
Ohio Northern University

James Green
Arizona State University

John L. Grigsby
Tennessee Technological University

M. Katherine Grimes
Ferrum College

L. M. Grow
Broward Community College

M. Martin Guiney
Kenyon College

Mark Haag
University of California, Los Angeles

Angela Hague
Middle Tennessee State University

Steven L. Hale
Morris Brown College

Elsie Galbreath Haley
Metropolitan State College of Denver

Jay L. Halio
University of Delaware

James C. Hall
University of Illinois at Chicago

Yasmine Yong Hall
Elms College

Barbara J. Hampton
Independent Scholar

Paul Hansom
Independent Scholar

Natalie Harper
Simon's Rock of Bard College

E. Lynn Harris
University of Illinois at Chicago

Sandra Hanby Harris
Tidewater Community College

Suzan Harrison
Eckerd College

Jack Hart
University of Rio Grande

A. Waller Hastings
Northern State University

John C. Hawley
Santa Clara University

Melanie C. Hawthorne
Texas A&M University

Mark Allen Heberle
University of Hawaii at Manoa

Ruth J. Heflin
Oklahoma State University

Elyce Rae Helford
Middle Tennessee State University

Peter B. Heller
Manhattan College

Terry Heller
Coe College

Vicki Due Hendricks
Broward Community College

Joyce E. Henry
Ursinus College

John Higby
Appalachian State University

Richard A. Hill
Taylor Univerity

Michael Craig Hillmann
University of Texas at Austin

Rebecca Stingley Hinton
*Clermont College
Indiana University East*

Arthur D. Hlavaty
Independent Scholar

Eric H. Hobson
University of Tennessee

James L. Hodge
Bowdoin College

Heidi J. Holder
University of Massachusetts at Amherst

William H. Holland, Jr.
Middle Tennessee State University

Michael Hollister
Portland State University

Anna R. Holloway
Fort Valley State College

John R. Holmes
Franciscan University of Steubenville

Glenn Hopp
Howard Payne University

Pierre L. Horn
Wright State University

Eric Howard
Independent Scholar

Anne Howells
Occidental College

Ruth Hsu
University of Southern California

Amy E. Hudock
University of South Carolina

Steven R. Huff
Oberlin College

David E. Huntley
Appalachian State University

E. D. Huntley
Appalachian State University

Geraldine L. Hutchins
East Tennessee State University

Allen E. Hye
Wright State University

Archibald E. Irwin
Indiana University Southeast

Nalini Iyer
Purdue University

John Jacob
*North Central College
Northwestern University*

Terry Hays Jackson
East Tennessee State University

Shakuntala Jayaswal
University of New Haven

Alphine W. Jefferson
College of Wooster

W. A. Johnsen
Michigan State University

Kathleen A. Johnson
Lake Forest College

Mary Johnson
University of South Florida

Sheila Golburgh Johnson
Independent Scholar

Yvonne Johnson
Collin County Community College

Eunice Pedersen Johnston
North Dakota State University

CONTRIBUTING REVIEWERS

Douglas A. Jones
Andrews University

James W. Jones
Central Michigan University

Jane Anderson Jones
Manatee Community College

Sharon Lynette Jones
University of Georgia

Michael Scott Joseph
Rutgers University Libraries

B. A. Kachur
University of Missouri-St. Louis

Anne K. Kaler
Gwynedd-Mercy College

Albert E. Kalson
Purdue University

Leela Kapai
University of the District of Columbia

Ludmila Kapschutschenko-Schmitt
Rider University

Daven M. Kari
California Baptist College

Bettye Choate Kash
Tennessee Technological University

Richard S. Keating
U.S. Air Force Academy

Richard Keenan
University of Maryland—Eastern Shore

Katherine Keller
University of Central Florida

Steven G. Kellman
University of Texas at San Antonio

Richard Kelly
University of Tennessee

Viktor R. Kemper
Western Illinois University

W. P. Kenney
Manhattan College

Martin Kich
Lehigh University

Christine Kiebuzinska
Virginia Polytechnic Institute and State University

N. Jacquelyn Kilpatrick
Governors State University

Cassandra Kircher
University of Iowa

Susan S. Kissel
Northern Kentucky University

Paul Kistel
Los Angeles Pierce College

Wm. Laird Kleine-Ahlbrandt
Purdue University

James Knippling
University of Delaware

Grove Koger
Boise Public Library

Kathleen L. Komar
University of California, Los Angeles

Tom Koontz
Ball State University

Paula Kopacz
Eastern Kentucky University

Stephanie Korney
Independent Scholar

Steven C. Kowall
Independent Scholar

Kenneth Krauss
College of Saint Rose

Susan Kress
Skidmore College

Marlies Kronegger
Michigan State University

Lolette Kuby
Akron University

Mildred C. Kuner
Independent Scholar

Katherine C. Kurk
Northern Kentucky University

Linda L. Labin
Husson College

William LaHay
Independent Scholar

Joseph Laker
Wheeling Jesuit College

Carole J. Lambert
Azusa Pacific University

David W. Landrum
Cornerstone College

James B. Lane
Indiana University Northwest

P. R. Lannert
Independent Scholar

David H. J. Larmour
Texas Tech University

Eugene S. Larson
Los Angeles Pierce College

Terry Lass
Columbia College, Missouri

Ellen M. Laun
Pennsylvania State University, Fayette

Katherine G. Lederer
Southwest Missouri State University

Linda Ledford-Miller
University of Scranton

A. Robert Lee
University of Kent at Canterbury

Penelope A. LeFew
Rock Valley College

Bruce H. Leland
Western Illinois University

Lagretta T. Lenker
University of South Florida

Leon Lewis
Appalachian State University

Leslie W. Lewis
Indiana University, Bloomington

Terrance L. Lewis
Clarion University

Sherry Lee Linkon
Youngstown State University

T. M. Lipman
Independent Scholar

Laurie Lisa
Arizona State University

Thomas Lisk
North Carolina State University

Donald E. Livingston, Jr.
Arizona State University

James L. Livingston
Northern Michigan University

Shirley W. Logan
University of Maryland

Richard Logsdon
Community College of Southern Nevada

Helen Lojek
Boise State University

R. M. Longyear
University of Kentucky

Barbara A. Looney
University of South Florida

Janet Lorenz
Independent Scholar

Michael Loudon
Eastern Illinois University

Barbara Lounsberry
University of Northern Iowa

Philip H. Lutes
University of Montana

R. C. Lutz
University of California, Santa Barbara
University of the Pacific

Sara McAlpin
Clarke College

Janet McCann
Texas A&M University

Joanne McCarthy
Tacoma Community College

Janie Caves McCauley
Bob Jones University

Robert McClenaghan
Independent Scholar

Arthur F. McClure
Central Missouri State University

Robert McColley
University of Illinois at Urbana-Champaign

Jean McConnell
University of New Mexico

Philip McDermott
Independent Scholar

Andrew Macdonald
Loyola University, New Orleans

Gina Macdonald
Loyola University, New Orleans
Tulane University

William J. McDonald
Baylor University

Gregory McElwain
University of New Mexico

Ron McFarland
University of Idaho

Richard D. McGhee
Kansas State University

Edythe M. McGovern
Los Angeles Valley College

S. Thomas Mack
University of South Carolina at Aiken

Nancy A. Macky
Westminster College

Joseph McLaren
Hofstra University

John L. McLean
Morehead State University

Alan L. McLeod
Rider College

Marian B. McLeod
Trenton State College

David W. Madden
California State University, Sacramento

Paul Madden
Hardin-Simmons University

Gordon Robert Maddison
Broward Community College

Coleen Maddy
University of Iowa

Helga Stipa Madland
University of Oklahoma

Philip Magnier
Independent Scholar

Mary E. Mahony
Wayne County Community College

Edward A. Malone
University of Missouri at Rolla

Martha Manheim
Siena Heights College

B. P. Mann
University of San Diego

Donna Maples
Howard Payne University

Lois Marchino
University of Texas at El Paso

Louis Markos
Houston Baptist University

Chogollah Maroufi
California State University, Los Angeles

Joss Lutz Marsh
California Institute of Technology

Liz Marshall
Independent Scholar

Hubert M. Martin, Jr.
University of Kentucky

Charles E. May
California State University, Long Beach

Laurence W. Mazzeno
U.S. Naval Academy
Ursuline College

Kenneth W. Meadwell
University of Winnipeg

Patrick Meanor
State University of New York College
at Oneonta

Leslie Mellichamp
Virginia Polytechnic Institute and State
University

Ann A. Merrill
Emory University

Vasa D. Mihailovich
University of North Carolina at Chapel Hill

Jane Ann Miller
Dartmouth College

Pat Miller
Valdosta State University

Randall M. Miller
Saint Joseph's University

Kathleen Mills
Baldwin-Wallace College

Maureen W. Mills
Central Michigan University

Michele Mock-Murton
Indiana University of Pennsylvania

Christian H. Moe
Southern Illinois University at Carbondale

Fritz Monsma
Independent Scholar

Robert A. Morace
Daemen College

Gwendolyn Morgan
Montana State University

Bernard E. Morris
Independent Scholar

Daniel Charles Morris
Harvard University

Robert E. Morsberger
California State Polytechnic University,
Pomona

Charmaine Allmon Mosby
Western Kentucky University

James V. Muhleman
Hawaii Loa College

N. Samuel Murrell
College of Wooster

John M. Muste
Ohio State University

Eunice Myers
Wichita State University

Susan V. Myers
University of New Mexico

Mary Henry Nachtsheim
College of St. Catherine

D. Gosselin Nakeeb
Pace University

William Nelles
Northwestern State University of Louisiana

Elizabeth R. Nelson
Saint Peter's College

John S. Nelson
Saint Mary of the Plains College

J. W. Newcomb
Memphis State University

CONTRIBUTING REVIEWERS

Terry Nienhuis
Western Carolina University

Donald R. Noble
University of Alabama

Marjorie J. Oberlander
Mercy College

George O'Brien
Georgetown University

Rafael Ocasio
Agnes Scott College

Aileen O'Catherine
Independent Scholar

Lawrence J. Oliver
Texas A&M University

Kathleen O'Mara
*State University of New York College
  at Oneonta*

Robert M. Otten
Assumption College

Lisa Paddock
Independent Scholar

Lucille Izzo Pallotta
Onondaga Community College

Janet Taylor Palmer
Caldwell Community College

Matthew Parfitt
Boston University

David Patterson
Oklahoma State University

D. G. Paz
Clemson University

David Peck
California State University, Long Beach

Robert W. Peckham
Sacred Heart Major Seminary

V. Penelope Pelizzon
University of California, Irvine

William E. Pemberton
University of Wisconsin—La Crosse

Thomas D. Petitjean, Jr.
University of Southwestern Louisiana

Marion Boyle Petrillo
Bloomsburg University

Helmut F. Pfanner
University of Nebraska—Lincoln

R. Craig Philips
Michigan State University

William L. Phillips
University of Washington

H. Alan Pickrell
Emory & Henry College

Susan L. Piepke
Bridgewater College

Karen Ann Pinter
Sauk Valley College

Steven L. Piott
Clarion University

Rosaria Pipia
*Queens College of the City University
  of New York*

David W. Pitre
Episcopal School of Baton Rouge

Mary Ellen Pitts
Memphis State University

Marjorie Podolsky
*Pennsylvania State University at Erie
  The Behrend College*

Ann L. Postlethweight
University of South Florida

Clifton W. Potter, Jr.
Lynchburg College

John F. Povey
University of California, Los Angeles

Andrew B. Preslar
Lamar University at Orange

Verbie Lovorn Prevost
University of Tennessee at Chattanooga

Cliff Prewencki
Independent Scholar

Marian Price
University of Central Florida

Victoria Price
Lamar University

Karen Priest
Lamar University at Orange

David Pringle
University of South Florida

Charles Pullen
Queen's University, Ontario, Canada

Diane Quinn
Independent Scholar

Josef Raab
University of Southern California

Josephine Raburn
Cameron University

Gregory J. Racz
*Princeton University
Parsons School of Design*

Elizabeth L. Rambo
Biola University

Inez L. Ramsey
James Madison University

James H. Randall
Coe College

Tom Rash
Asheville-Buncombe Community College

John D. Raymer
Indiana University at South Bend

Jere Real
Lynchburg College

Peter J. Reed
University of Minnesota

Rosemary M. Canfield Reisman
Troy State University

Clark G. Reynolds
College of Charleston

Rodney P. Rice
U.S. Air Force Academy

Betty Richardson
Southern Illinois University at Edwardsville

Jochen Richter
Allegheny College

Jerome J. Rinkus
Pomona College

Claire J. Robinson
Independent Scholar

James W. Robinson, Jr.
Chaminade University

Vicki K. Robinson
State University of New York at Farmingdale

Mark William Rocha
Glassboro State College

Gisela Roethke-Makemson
Dickinson College

Kim Dickson Rogers
Independent Scholar

Peter S. Rogers
Loyola University, New Orleans

Mary Rohrberger
University of Northern Iowa

Douglas Rollins
Dawson College

Jill Rollins
Trafalgar School, Quebec, Canada

Carl Rollyson
Baruch College, City University of New York

Evelyn Romig
Howard Payne University

Paul Rosefeldt
University of New Orleans

Delgado Community College

Joseph Rosenblum
University of North Carolina at Greensboro

Natania Rosenfeld
Princeton University

Sidney Rosenfeld
Oberlin College

Stella P. Rosenfeld
Cleveland State University

Cheri Louise Ross
Pennsylvania State University—Mont Alto

Robert L. Ross
University of Texas at Austin

Gabrielle Rowe
McKendree College

Elizabeth A. Rubino
Northwestern State University of Louisiana

Nancy E. Rupprecht
Middle Tennessee State University

Susan Rusinko
Bloomsburg University

Dennis Ryan
University of South Florida

Chaman L. Sahni
Boise State University

Gregory Salyer
Huntingdon College

John Scheckter
C. W. Post College, Long Island University

Leda Schiavo
University of Illinois at Chicago

Gary D. Schmidt
Calvin College

Carol E. Schmudde
Eastern Illinois University

Thomas C. Schunk
Quincy College

Jo C. Searles
*Pennsylvania State University,
    University Park*

Millicent Sharma
Independent Scholar

Julie Sherrick
Independent Scholar

John C. Sherwood
University of Oregon

Agnes A. Shields
Chestnut Hill College

Thelma J. Shinn
Arizona State University

T. A. Shippey
St. Louis University

R. Baird Shuman
University of Illinois at Urbana-Champaign

Anne W. Sienkewicz
Independent Scholar

Charles L. P. Silet
Iowa State University

Caren S. Silvester
Bob Jones University

Rennie Simson
Syracuse University
*State University of New York
    College of Agriculture and Technology at
    Morrisville*

Carl Singleton
Fort Hays State University

Amy Sisson
Independent Scholar

Genevieve Slomski
Independent Scholar

Marjorie Smelstor
University of Wisconsin—Eau Claire

Gilbert Smith
North Carolina State University

Pamela J. Olubunmi Smith
University of Nebraska at Omaha

Ira Smolensky
Monmouth College

Marjorie Smolensky
Monmouth College
Carl Sandburg College

Traci S. Smrcka
University of Southwestern Louisiana

Katherine Snipes
Eastern Washington University

A. J. Sobczak
Independent Scholar

Stephen F. Soitos
University of Massachusetts at Amherst

Janet L. Solberg
Kalamazoo College

Marcia J. Songer
East Tennessee State University

George Soule
Carleton College

Madison U. Sowell
Brigham Young University

Thomas D. Spaccarelli
University of the South

Hartley S. Spatt
*State University of New York Maritime
    College*

Brian Stableford
Independent Scholar

Tony J. Stafford
University of Texas at El Paso

Isabel B. Stanley
East Tennessee State University

Sandra K. Stanley
California State University, Northridge

Lisa S. Starks
University of South Florida

Helen Winter Stauffer
Kearney State College

Larry L. Stewart
College of Wooster

Ingo R. Stoehr
Kilgore College

Louise M. Stone
Bloomsburg University

H. R. Stoneback
*State University of New York College
    at New Paltz*

Richard Stoner
Broome Community College

Gary Storhoff
University of Connecticut at Stamford

Gerald Strauss
Bloomsburg University

Ian Stuart
University of California, Santa Barbara

James Sullivan
California State University, Los Angeles

Charlene E. Suscavage
University of Southern Maine

Catherine Swanson
Oxford University

Roy Arthur Swanson
University of Wisconsin—Milwaukee

Susan Elizabeth Sweeney
Holy Cross College

Charles Sweet
Eastern Kentucky University

Alice L. Swensen
University of Northern Iowa

Thomas J. Taylor
Independent Scholar

Charlotte Templin
University of Indianapolis

CONTRIBUTING REVIEWERS

Terry Theodore
University of North Carolina at Wilmington

Marcelle Thiébaux
St. John's University, New York

Allen Thiher
University of Missouri—Columbia

Betty Taylor Thompson
Texas Southern University

Lloyd R. Thompson
University of New Haven

Lou Thompson
New Mexico Institute of Mining and Technology

Evelyn Toft
Fort Hays State University

Charles P. Toombs
California State University, San Diego

John P. Turner, Jr.
Humboldt State University

John Merritt Unsworth
North Carolina State University

Luiz Fernando Valente
Brown University

Russell Valentino
University of California, Los Angeles

Elizabeth Vander Meer
Independent Scholar

George W. Van Devender
Hardin-Simmons University

J. K. Van Dover
Lincoln University

Dennis Vannatta
University of Arkansas

Donald Vanouse
State University of New York College at Oswego

Anita M. Vickers
Pennsylvania State University—Schuylkill

Mary E. Virginia
Independent Scholar

Emil Volek
Arizona State University

Albert Wachtel
Pitzer College

Sue Brannan Walker
University of South Alabama

Jaquelyn W. Walsh
McNeese State University

Kelly C. Walter
Southern California College

Gordon Walters
DePauw University

Qun Wang
California State University, Monterey Bay

Gladys J. Washington
Texas Southern University

John C. Watson
University of Oregon

Patricia L. Watson
University of Georgia

Linda S. Watts
Drake University

H. J. Weatherford
Georgia Southern College

James Michael Welsh
Salisbury State University

John Whalen-Bridge
University of Southern California

Susan Whaley
Independent Scholar

Cynthia Jane Whitney
University of South Florida

Barbara Wiedemann
Auburn University at Montgomery

Clarke L. Wilhelm
Denison University

Thomas Willard
University of Arizona

Ray Willbanks
Memphis State University

Sandra Willbanks
Maharishi International University

Bettye J. Williams
University of Arkansas Pine Bluff

Lori Williams
Independent Scholar

Philip F. Williams
Arizona State University

Robert J. Willis
East Stroudsburg University

John Wilson
Independent Scholar

Johnny Wink
Ouachita Baptist University

Michael Witkoski
Independent Scholar

Susan Wladaver-Morgan
Independent Scholar

Leigh Woods
Independent Scholar

Shawn Woodyard
Independent Scholar

Martin Morse Wooster
American Enterprise Institute

Karin A. Wurst
Michigan State University

Jennifer L. Wyatt
Southern Illinois University at Edwardsville

Robert E. Yahnke
University of Minnesota

Vincent Yang
Pennsylvania State University, University Park

Marlene Youmans
State University of New York College at Potsdam

Mary Young
The College of Wooster

Laura M. Zaidman
University of South Carolina at Sumter

Michael Zeitlin
University of Toronto

Laura Weiss Zlogar
University of Wisconsin—River Falls

Harry Zohn
Brandeis University

John Zubizarreta
Columbia College, South Carolina

CONTENTS

Key to Pronunciation xxvii

Aaron's Rod 1
The Abbé Constantin 1
The Abbess of Crewe 2
The Abduction 2
Abe Lincoln in Illinois 3
Abel Sánchez 3
Abraham and Isaac 4
Absalom, Absalom! 5
Absalom and Achitophel 6
The Absentee 6
Absurd Person Singular 7
The Abyss 7
The Accident 8
Accidental Death of an Anarchist 9
The Accidental Tourist 10
The Acharnians 10
The Acolyte 11
Acquainted with Grief 11
Across 12
Across the River and into the Trees 12
Ada or Ardor 13
Adam Bede 14
The Adding Machine 15
The Admirable Crichton 16
Adolphe 17
The Adventures of Augie March 17
The Adventures of Hajji Baba of Ispahan . 18
Adventures of Huckleberry Finn 18
The Adventures of Roderick Random 19
The Adventures of Tom Sawyer 20
The Aeneid 21
The Aerodrome 22
Aesop's Fables 23
The Affected Young Ladies 23
After Many a Summer Dies the Swan 24
After the Banquet 25
After the Fall 25
Afternoon Men 26
The Afternoon of a Faun 27
Against the Grain 27
The Age of Innocence 28
The Age of Wonders 28
Agents and Patients 29
Agnes Grey 30
The Agony and the Ecstasy 30

L'Aiglon 31
Ajax 31
Alburquerque 32
Alcestis 33
The Alchemist 34
Aleck Maury, Sportsman 34
The Alexandria Quartet 35
Alice Adams 37
Alice's Adventures in Wonderland 37
All-Bright Court 38
All Fall Down 39
All Fools 39
All for Love 40
All God's Chillun Got Wings 41
All Green Shall Perish 41
All Hallows Eve 42
All Men Are Brothers 42
All Men Are Enemies 43
All My Sons 44
All Our Yesterdays 45
All Quiet on the Western Front 46
All That Fall 46
All the King's Men 47
All the Pretty Horses 48
All's Well That Ends Well 48
Almanac of the Dead 49
Almayer's Folly 49
Alnilam 50
Alton Locke 50
Amadeus 51
Amadís of Gaul 52
The Ambassadors 52
Ambiguous Adventure 53
Amelia 54
America Hurrah 55
The American 55
American Buffalo 56
The American Dream 56
An American Dream 57
An American Tragedy 58
Amerika 58
Among Women Only 59
Amores 60
Amphitryon 60
Amphitryon 38 61
Anabasis 61
Anancy's Score 62

The Anatomy Lesson 63
The Ancient Child 63
And Quiet Flows the Don 64
Andorra 64
Andria 65
Andromache *(Euripedes)* 66
Andromache *(Racine)* 66
The Andromeda Strain 67
Ángel Guerra 68
Angel Pavement 68
Angels Fall 69
Angels in America 70
Angels on Toast 71
Angle of Repose 71
Anglo-Saxon Attitudes 72
Animal Dreams 73
Animal Farm 73
Anna Christie 74
Anna Karénina 74
Anna of the Five Towns 75
Annals of the Parish 76
Anne of the Thousand Days 76
Annie John 77
Anniversaries 77
Another Country 79
Another Life 79
Anthony Adverse 80
Antigone *(Anouilh)* 81
Antigone *(Sophocles)* 81
The Antiquary 82
Antony and Cleopatra 82
Anywhere but Here 84
The Apes of God 84
The Apostle 86
Appalachee Red 87
The Apple in the Dark 87
The Apple of the Eye 88
Appointment in Samarra 88
The Apprenticeship of Duddy Kravitz 89
The Arabian Nights' Entertainments 90
The Arbitration 90
Arcadia 90
The Architect and the Emperor of Assyria 92
Argenis 92
Der arme Heinrich 93
The Armies of the Night 93
Arms and the Man 94
Arne 94
Around the World in Eighty Days 95
Arrow of God 95

Arrowsmith 96
Artamenes 97
The Artamonov Business 98
Arturo's Island 98
As a Man Grows Older 99
As for Me and My House 99
As I Lay Dying 100
As the Crow Flies 101
As You Like It 101
Ashes 102
Ashes and Diamonds 103
The Asiatics 104
The Aspern Papers 104
The Assistant 105
Astrophil and Stella 105
Asya 106
At Play in the Fields of the Lord 107
At Swim-Two-Birds 108
At the Sign of the Reine Pédauque 109
At Weddings and Wakes 109
Atala 110
Atalanta in Calydon 110
Atlas Shrugged 111
Attachments 111
Aucassin and Nicolette 112
August 1914 112
Aunt Dan and Lemon 114
Aunt Julia and the Scriptwriter 114
The Aunt's Story 115
Aura 116
Aurora Leigh 116
Auto-da-Fé 117
The Autobiography of Alice B. Toklas . . . 118
The Autobiography of an Ex-Coloured Man 118
The Autobiography of Miss Jane Pittman 119
The Autumn of the Patriarch 120
Avalovara 121
Awake and Sing! 122
The Awakening 123
The Awkward Age 123
The Axe 124

Baal 126
Babbitt 126
Babel-17 127
The Bacchae 128
The Bachelors 129
Back to Methuselah 129
Badenheim 1939 131
Baga 132

CONTENTS

Bailey's Café 132
The Balcony 133
The Bald Soprano 134
The Balkan Trilogy 134
The Ballad of Peckham Rye 135
The Ballad of the Sad Café 136
Bambi 137
Banana Bottom 137
Bang the Drum Slowly 138
Banjo 139
Barabbas 139
The Barber of Seville 140
Barchester Towers 140
Barefoot in the Head 141
Barefoot in the Park 142
The Bark Tree 142
Barnabo of the Mountains 143
Barnaby Rudge 144
Barometer Rising 145
The Baron in the Trees 145
Baron Münchausen's Narrative of His
    Marvellous Travels and Campaigns in
    Russia 146
The Barracks 147
The Barracks Thief 148
Barren Ground 148
Barrio Boy 149
Barry Lyndon 150
Bartholomew Fair 150
The Basic Training of Pavlo Hummel 152
The Bass Saxophone 152
Bastard Out of Carolina 153
The Bathhouse 153
Batouala 154
The Battle of Pharsalus 154
The Bay of Silence 155
The Beach of Falesá 156
Beachmasters 156
The Bean Trees 156
Bearheart 157
Beauchamp's Career 158
The Beautiful and Damned 158
Beauty and Sadness 159
The Beautyful Ones Are Not Yet Born 160
The Beaux' Stratagem 160
The Beaver Coat 161
Because It Is Bitter, and Because It Is My
    Heart 161
Becket 162
The Bedbug 163

The Beet Queen 164
Beetlecreek 164
A Beggar in Jerusalem 165
Beggar on Horseback 166
The Beggars' Bush 167
The Beggar's Opera 167
Bel-Ami 168
Belinda 168
The Bell 169
A Bell for Adano 170
The Bell Jar 171
The Bellarosa Connection 171
Bellefleur 172
Beloved 173
A Bend in the River 173
Bend Sinister 174
Benefactors 175
Ben-Hur 176
Benito Cereno 176
Beowulf 177
Bérénice 178
Berlin Alexanderplatz 178
Betrayal 179
Betrayed by Rita Hayworth 179
The Betrothed 180
Betsey Brown 181
Between the Acts 181
Bevis of Hampton 182
Beyond Our Power 182
Beyond the Bedroom Wall 182
The Big Knife 184
The Big Rock Candy Mountain 185
The Big Sky 185
The Big Sleep 186
Billiards at Half-Past Nine 187
Billy Bathgate 188
Billy Budd, Foretopman 189
Billy Phelan's Greatest Game 189
Biloxi Blues 190
Bird at My Window 191
The Birds 191
The Birds Fall Down 192
The Birthday King 193
The Birthday Party 193
The Black Arrow 194
Black Boy 194
The Black Hermit 195
Black Mischief 196
The Black Prince 196
Black Robe 197

The Black Swan 198
Black Thunder 198
Black Valley 199
Black Water 199
The Blacker the Berry 200
The Blacks 201
Bleak House 202
Bless Me, Ultima 203
Bless the Beasts and Children 204
Blithe Spirit 205
The Blithedale Romance 205
The Blood Knot 206
Blood Meridian 207
The Blood of the Lamb 207
Blood Wedding 208
A Bloodsmoor Romance 208
Bloody Poetry 209
A Blot in the 'Scutcheon 210
The Blue Bird 210
Blue Boy 211
The Blue Mountains of China 212
The Blue Room 212
Bluebeard 213
Blues for Mister Charlie 214
The Bluest Eye 215
The Boarding-House 215
Boesman and Lena 216
Bogmail 217
The Bohemians of the Latin Quarter 217
The Bond 218
The Bondman 218
The Bonds of Interest 219
Bone 219
The Bone People 220
Bonecrack 220
The Bonfire of the Vanities 221
Bonjour Tristesse 222
The Book of Bebb 222
A Book of Common Prayer 223
The Book of Laughter and Forgetting 224
The Book of Lights 225
The Book of the Courtier 225
Book of the Duchess 226
The Book of the Ladies 227
The Book of Theseus 227
Borderline 228
Boris Godunov 229
Born Brothers 229
Born in Captivity 230
The Borough 230
Bosnian Chronicle 231
The Bostonians 232
Botchan 232
Bouvard and Pécuchet 233
The Boy Without a Flag 233
The Boys in the Band 234
The Bracknels 235
The Braggart Soldier 235
Brand 236
Brave New World 236
Bread and Wine 237
Bread Givers 237
Break of Noon 238
Brendan 238
The Brick People 239
The Bridal Canopy 240
The Bride 240
The Bride of Lammermoor 241
Brideshead Revisited 241
The Bridge of San Luis Rey 242
The Bridge on the Drina 242
A Brief Life 243
Brief Lives 244
Bright Shadow 245
A Brighter Sun 245
Brighton Beach Memoirs 246
Brighton Rock 247
Britannicus 248
Broad and Alien Is the World 248
Broadway Bound 248
The Broken Jug 249
The Bronze Horseman 249
Brother Ass 250
The Brothers 251
The Brothers Ashkenazi 251
The Brothers Karamazov 252
Brown Girl, Brownstones 252
The Browning Version 253
Bruno's Dream 254
The Brushwood Boy 254
Brut 255
Buchanan Dying 256
Buddenbrooks 256
The Bull from the Sea 258
Bullet Park 258
Bullivant and the Lambs 259
The Bulwark 260
The Burden of Proof 260
Burger's Daughter 261
Buried Child 262

CONTENTS

Burmese Days 262
The Burn 263
Burning Water 264
A Burnt-Out Case 265
Burr 266
Bus Stop 267
Bussy d'Ambois 268
Butley 268
By Love Possessed 269

The Cabala 270
The Cabin 270
Cadmus 270
Caesar and Cleopatra 271
Caesar or Nothing 271
Cain 272
The Caine Mutiny 272
Cakes and Ale 273
Caleb Williams 273
Caliban's Filibuster 274
Caligula 274
The Call 275
Call It Sleep 275
The Call of the Wild 276
Calm Down Mother 276
Cambridge 277
Camel Xiangzi 278
Camille 279
Campaspe 279
Cancer Ward 280
Candida 282
Candide 282
Cane 283
Cannery Row 283
The Cannibal 284
The Canterbury Tales 285
A Canticle for Leibowitz 286
Capricornia 287
Captain Blackman 288
Captain Horatio Hornblower 289
Captain Singleton 289
The Captain with the Whiskers 290
Captains Courageous 290
The Captain's Daughter 291
The Captives 291
The Caretaker 292
Carmen 292
The Case of Sergeant Grischa 293
Cass Timberlane 293
Cassandra 294

Caste 294
The Castle 295
The Castle of Crossed Destinies 295
The Castle of Fratta 296
The Castle of Otranto 297
Castle Rackrent 297
Casuals of the Sea 298
The Cat 298
Cat and Mouse 299
Cat on a Hot Tin Roof 299
Catch-22 300
The Catcher in the Rye 301
Catherine Carmier 301
Cathleen ni Houlihan 302
Catiline 302
Cat's Cradle 303
The Caucasian Chalk Circle 304
Caught 305
Cavalleria Rusticana 305
Cawdor 306
Cecilia 306
Celestina 307
The Cenci *(Artaud)* 307
The Cenci *(Shelley)* 308
The Centaur 308
Ceremonies in Dark Old Men 309
Ceremony 310
Ceremony in Lone Tree 310
The Ceremony of Innocence 311
César Birotteau 312
The Chain of Chance 313
A Chain of Voices 313
The Chainbearer 314
The Chairs 314
Chaka 315
The Chaneysville Incident 316
A Change of Heart 316
A Change of Skin 317
The Changeling 318
Changing Places 318
The Changing Room 319
The Chant of Jimmie Blacksmith 320
Charles Demailly 321
Charles O'Malley, the Irish Dragoon . . . 321
The Charterhouse of Parma 322
A Chaste Maid in Cheapside 322
Chéri *and* The Last of Chéri 323
Cherokee 324
The Cherokee Night 325
The Cherry Orchard 325

The Chevalier de Maison-Rouge 326
Chevengur 326
Cheyenne Autumn 327
Chicken Soup with Barley 328
The Chickencoop Chinaman 329
Child of God 330
Childe Byron 330
Childe Harold's Pilgrimage 331
Childhood, Boyhood, Youth 331
Childhood's End 332
Children of a Lesser God 333
Children of God 333
The Children of Heracles 334
Children of the Ghetto 335
Children of Violence 335
The Children's Hour 336
China Boy 337
The Chinaberry Tree 337
The Chinese Wall 338
Chips with Everything 339
Chita 339
A Chocolate Soldier 340
The Chosen 340
The Chosen Place, the Timeless People 341
The Chouans 342
Christ Stopped at Eboli 342
A Christmas Carol 343
Chronicle of a Death Foretold 343
The Cid 344
The Cider House Rules 345
Cinna 346
Cinq-Mars 346
The Circle 346
The Circle of Chalk 347
The Citadel 348
Cities of Salt 348
The City and the House 349
The City and the Pillar 350
The City Builder 351
City of Night 352
the CIVIL warS 352
Clarissa 352
Claudius the God and His Wife Messalina . . . 353
The Clayhanger Trilogy 354
Clear Light of Day 355
Cligés 355
A Clockwork Orange 356
The Cloister and the Hearth 357
The Closed Garden 357
Closely Watched Trains 358

Clotel 358
Cloud Nine 359
The Clouds 360
The Cloven Viscount 360
The Clown 361
Cock-a-Doodle Dandy 362
The Cocktail Party 363
A Coffin for Dimitrios 363
The Coffin Tree 364
A Coin in Nine Hands 365
Cold Comfort Farm 366
Cold Storage 366
The Collector 367
The Collegians 367
Colomba 368
Color of Darkness 368
The Color Purple 369
Colours in the Dark 370
Come Back, Little Sheba 370
The Comedians 371
The Comedy of Errors 371
The Comforters 372
Coming Up for Air 373
Company 373
The Company of Women 374
The Complete Tales of Uncle Remus 375
The Compromise 376
Comrades 376
Comus 377
Concluding 377
Concrete 378
The Concubine 379
A Confederacy of Dunces 379
A Confederate General from Big Sur 380
Confederates 381
The Confession of a Fool 382
Confessions of a Mask 382
Confessions of Felix Krull, Confidence Man 383
The Confessions of Nat Turner 383
Confessions of Zeno 384
The Confidence Man 385
The Confidential Clerk 385
The Conformist 386
Coningsby 387
The Conjure-Man Dies 387
The Conjure Woman 388
A Connecticut Yankee in King Arthur's
    Court 388
The Connection 389
The Conscience of the Rich 390

CONTENTS

The Conscious Lovers 390
The Conservationist 391
Consuelo 391
Contending Forces 392
The Contractor 392
Conversation in the Cathedral 393
Coonardoo 393
The Copperhead 394
Coriolanus 395
The Corn Is Green 395
The Cornerstone 396
Coronation 397
Correction 397
Corregidora 398
The Corsican Brothers 398
Cosmos 399
The Cossacks 400
The Count of Monte-Cristo 400
The Counterfeiters 402
The Counterlife 402
The Countess Cathleen 403
The Countess de Charny 404
The Country Doctor 404
A Country Doctor 405
The Country Girls Trilogy and Epilogue 405
The Country House 406
The Country of the Pointed Firs 407
Country Place 407
The Country Wife 407
The Coup 408
Coup de Grâce 409
Couples 410
The Courtesan 411
The Courtship of Miles Standish 412
Cousin Bazilio 412
Cousin Bette 413
Cousin Pons 414
The Cowards 416
The Coxcomb 416
Cracking India 417
The Cradle Song 417
Cranford 418
The Cream of the Jest 418
Crime and Punishment 419
The Crime of Sylvestre Bonnard 420
Crimes of the Heart 420
The Crisis 421
The Critic 421
The Crock of Gold 422
Crome Yellow 422

Crotchet Castle 423
The Crucible 423
The Cruise of the Cachalot 423
Crusoe's Daughter 424
Cry, the Beloved Country 425
The Crying of Lot 49 426
The Crystal World 426
Cudjo's Cave 427
Cupid and Psyche 427
Curse of the Starving Class 428
The Custom House 428
The Custom of the Country 429
The Cutter 430
The Cuttlefish 430
Cyclops 431
Cymbeline 432
The Cypresses Believe in God 433
Cyrano de Bergerac 433
Cyropaedia 434

Da 436
Daddy Was a Number Runner 436
The Dahomean 437
Daisy Miller 437
Dame Care 438
The Damnation of Theron Ware 438
A Dance in the Sun 439
The Dance of Death 439
A Dance of the Forests 440
A Dance to the Music of Time 441
Dancing at Lughnasa 441
Dangerous Acquaintances 442
Dangling Man 442
Daniel Deronda 443
Daniel Martin 444
Danton's Death 445
Daphnis and Chloë 446
The Dark Child 446
The Dark Half 447
The Dark Journey 448
Dark Laughter 448
Darkness at Noon 449
Darkness Visible 449
Daughter of Earth 450
Daughters 451
David Copperfield 451
David Harum 454
Davita's Harp 454
A Day in the Death of Joe Egg 455
The Day of the Locust 455

Days of the Turbins 456
The Dead 457
The Dead Class 458
Dead Man Leading 458
Dead Souls 459
The Dean's December 460
Dear Brutus 461
Dear Diego 461
Dear Rafe 462
Death and the King's Horseman 462
Death Comes for the Archbishop 463
A Death in the Family 465
Death in Venice 465
The Death of a Beekeeper 466
Death of a Hero 467
Death of a Salesman 467
The Death of Artemio Cruz 467
The Death of Bernadette Lefthand 468
The Death of Empedocles 468
The Death of Ivan Ilyich 469
Death of the Fox 470
The Death of the Gods 470

The Death of the Heart 471
The Death of Virgil 471
Death on the Installment Plan 471
The Death Ship 472
Deathwatch 473
Debit and Credit 473
The Debut 474
The Decameron 475
Decline and Fall 476
Deephaven 476
The Deerslayer 477
The Defense 477
Deirdre (Stephens) 478
Deirdre (Yeats) 479
Deirdre of the Sorrows 479
Delia's Song 480
A Delicate Balance 480
Deliverance 481
Delphine 481
Delta Wedding 482
dem 482

KEY TO PRONUNCIATION

As an aid to users of the *Cyclopedia of Literary Characters, Revised Edition*, guides to pronunciation have been provided for particularly difficult character names. These guides are rendered in an easy-to-use phonetic manner. Stressed syllables are indicated by small capital letters. Letters of the English language, particularly vowels, are pronounced in different ways depending on the context. Below are letters and combinations of letters used in the phonetic guides to represent various sounds, along with examples of words in which those sounds appear.

Symbols	Pronounced As In
a	answer, laugh, sample, that
ah	father, hospital
aw	awful, caught
ay	blaze, fade, waiter, weigh
ch	beach, chimp
ee	believe, cedar, leader, liter
eh	bed, head, said
ew	boot, lose
g	beg, disguise, get
i	buy, height, lie, surprise
ih	bitter, pill
j	digit, edge, jet
k	cat, kitten, hex
[n]	bon (French "silent" n)
o	cotton, hot
oh	below, coat, note, wholesome
oo	good, look
ow	couch, how
oy	boy, coin
rr (rolled r)	guerrilla (Spanish pronunciation)
s	cellar, save, scent
sh	champagne, issue, shop
uh	about, butter, enough, other
ur	birth, disturb, earth, letter
y	useful, young
z	business, zest
zh	seizure, vision

Cyclopedia
of
LITERARY
CHARACTERS

AARON'S ROD

Author: D. H. Lawrence (1885-1930)
First published: 1922
Genre: Novel

Locale: England and Italy
Time: December 24, 1919, to November, 1920
Plot: Tragicomedy

Aaron Sisson, a well-educated young man who decides not to teach but instead to return to the coal mine as a secretary to a miners' union. He leaves behind the oppressive responsibility of his wife and three daughters to become an orchestra flutist in London and then leaves London for Italy, following Lilly. He finds Lilly in Florence, seeking him out to discuss a new modus vivendi.

Lottie Sisson, his beautiful wife, with whom he has a contest of wills. She half desires and half resists his attempts to return home.

Millicent Sisson, the oldest of their three daughters, who inherits the struggle of wills from her parents. At Christmas, she tries the patience of her father by testing the strength of a family tree decoration; it breaks.

Jim Bricknell, a war veteran, the son of the local mine owner. He takes up Aaron as an interesting acquaintance who represents the real working class in his superficial commitment to cultural revolution. Bricknell repeatedly proclaims his need to be loved.

Josephine Ford, his fiancée, an artist. She has a short affair with Sisson in London.

Rawdon Lilly, an English gentleman whose cottage Bricknell visits on the strength of his own invitation. When Lilly criticizes Bricknell too severely, Bricknell knocks him breathless. Later, Aaron arrives drunk and feverish at Lilly's Covent Garden flat, to be nursed back to health. He also breaks with Lilly. Lilly knows that he is expected to save his friends by telling them some unique truth. At the end of the novel, in a long discussion, he tells Sisson that modern men and women must either love or rule.

Francis Dekker, a traveling Australian painter whose privileged means and manner contrast with Aaron's background as they ride the train to Florence together.

Angus Guest, a traveling Welsh painter who forms part of the English-speaking artistic set in Florence.

James Argyle, a traveling English writer, another visiting member of the Anglo community in Florence.

Manfredi, the Marchese del Torre, a colonel in the Italian army. He befriends Sisson as a fellow musician despite his awareness of the relationship that Sisson is forming with his wife.

Nan, the Marchesa del Torre, his wife. She draws Sisson into an affair by displaying her smoldering passion, which transforms into a childlike dependency after they become lovers.

— *W. A. Johnsen*

THE ABBÉ CONSTANTIN
(L'Abbé Constantin)

Author: Ludovic Halévy (1834-1908)
First published: 1882
Genre: Novel

Locale: France
Time: 1881
Plot: Love

The Abbé Constantin, the elderly curé of the parish near the Chateau Longueval. He is a kindly, thoughtful man. Among his good works is the rearing of the son of an army friend who was killed in battle. The priest is saddened when the nearby chateau is sold to a wealthy American woman, for he is sure that the new owner will not be a Catholic and will not be interested in his work. He is delightfully surprised to find that he is wrong and that the new owners are a blessing to him and his village.

Mrs. Scott, the wealthy new owner of the chateau, an American. As a Catholic, she is pleased to help the old curé. She tells the priest of her childhood spent in poverty and of the lawsuit that made her a millionaire.

Bettina Percival, Mrs. Scott's young sister. She is a wealthy woman tired of proposals from men who want only her fortune. She falls in love with the curé's godson, Jean Reynaud. When he proves too bashful to ask her to marry him, she arranges, with the abbé's help, to tell the man of her love.

Jean Reynaud, a brave, charitable, thoughtful young army officer, the abbé's godson. His bashfulness and his deep love for Bettina keep him from declaring himself as the young woman's suitor.

Paul de Lavardens, a spendthrift young Frenchman from a well-to-do family. He courts Bettina brashly, but to no avail.

Mme de Lavardens, Paul's mother. A good woman, she is one of the abbé's parishioners.

THE ABBESS OF CREWE: A Modern Morality Tale

Author: Muriel Spark (1918-   )
First published: 1974
Genre: Novel

Locale: Crewe, England
Time: Early 1970's
Plot: Satire

Alexandra, the recently elected Abbess of Crewe, a Roman Catholic Benedictine abbey in the English Midlands. Tall and slender, with white skin and light eyes, the forty-two-year-old abbess bears herself with a clear consciousness of her aristocratic lineage. In her quest for power, she will stop at nothing. To win the election, she bugged the abbey and the grounds, entered into a secret pact with the Jesuits to commit a burglary, and even accused her rival of being a bourgeoise instead of a lady. When she is exposed, Alexandra casts the blame on her loyal aides. She is last seen en route to the pope to be exonerated. In the parallel Watergate scandal, she represents President Richard M. Nixon.

Sister Felicity, Alexandra's unsuccessful rival for the position of abbess. A tiny, red-haired woman, usually breathless and disorganized, Felicity is a crusader for change, justice, freedom, and love, demonstrating her principles in a sizzling liaison with a Jesuit named Thomas. In her headquarters of the sewing room, however, she is very tidy; therefore, she notices immediately the theft of her thimble from her workbox. When she later finds Jesuit seminarians stealing love letters from the same box, she calls the police. After fleeing the abbey with Thomas, she exposes Alexandra and her aides. Felicity represents Senator George McGovern as well as presidential counsel John Dean.

Sister Walburga, the prioress. A long-faced, middle-aged woman from a wealthy family, she developed her mind with a series of intellectual lovers. She has subordinated her own ambitions to those of Alexandra, however, and is Alexandra's chief of staff. Realizing Alexandra's vulnerability, she insists that the abbess pretend to be ignorant of any wrongdoing in the election process. When the scandal breaks, Sister Walburga is sent to serve in an infirmary at a distant abbey. Sister Walburga represents Nixon's White House chief of staff, H. R. Haldeman.

Sister Mildred, a novice mistress and Alexandra's second in command. A pretty, blue-eyed woman with an appealing heart-shaped face, she is thirty-six years old. Timid by nature, she is contented with her subordinate position. When the police are called, Sister Mildred becomes very nervous; however, she remains loyal to Alexandra and is willing to assume the blame to shield her. She is sent to the infirmary with Walburga. Mildred represents Nixon's domestic affairs adviser, John D. Ehrlichman.

Sister Winifrede, a third aide. Tall and fair, with a round face, she looks more like a British matron than a nun. Although she is stupid, she is completely loyal and, therefore, useful for menial tasks, such as preparing refreshments during planning sessions. Anticipating possible disasters, Alexandra forces Winifrede to sign a blanket confession before her final mission, in which she tries to deliver hush money to the seminarians in the men's room of the British library and is arrested. Winifrede represents White House lawyer Charles W. Colson as well as John Dean.

Sister Gertrude, the abbey's foreign missionary. A Machiavellian in outlook and Germanic in accent, she communicates with Alexandra from the Congo or Tibet, where she is constantly rearranging local governments. Although she remains aloof from local abbey politics, once the scandal breaks, she points out Alexandra's errors. Gertrude represents Secretary of State Henry Kissinger.

Father Baudouin, a Jesuit priest and friend of Alexandra. A heavy, middle-aged man with gray hair, he is particularly attractive to Sister Walburga. After his role in organizing the burglary becomes known, he is sent to America to give seminars in demonology.

Father Maximilian, a Jesuit priest and Father Baudouin's coconspirator. He is a fine-featured, distinguished-looking man. Despite his obvious intelligence, he is easily persuaded to help Alexandra. Because of his part in the theft of Felicity's letters, he, too, is sent to America.

— *Rosemary M. Canfield Reisman*

THE ABDUCTION

Author: Maxine Kumin (1925-   )
First published: 1971
Genre: Novel

Locale: The northeastern United States
Time: The 1960's
Plot: Psychological realism

Lucy Starr, a forty-two-year-old educational consultant, teacher, and social activist. Lucy is the reader's point-of-view character for most of the novel, excepting those elements told through Theodore's interior monologue. Lucy is a member of the cultured, highly educated, white upper middle class whose social and political liberalism dominated the major cities of the Northeast for many years. Lucy has been successful in her career, but her personal life remains oddly unre-

solved. A committed, self-conscious liberal flourishing amid the upheavals of the 1960's, Lucy finds all of her certainties jeopardized by the sudden entrance into her life of two disparate individuals, Berndt Hoffman and Theodore. Lucy is altruistic and well-intentioned; she is inspired by ethical ideals stemming from deep moral convictions that perhaps developed in connection with her Jewish ethnic background. Lucy has trouble understanding what she really wants in life. The tensions between her public and private goals are illustrated by the way she employs her personal relationships as comments on the racial and cultural divisions within the United States of her era. Lucy is a good person and does not mean to hurt anyone or hurt herself, and her motives in abducting Theodore come from nothing but the highest ideals. Because of her essential confusion, she often ends up in situations beyond her control.

Theodore, a ten-and-a-half-year-old African American boy who is kidnapped by Lucy Starr. He grew up in an underprivileged background in the ghettos of Washington, D.C. His family is originally from the rural South. His father is dead, and his mother has abandoned him, leaving him to be brought up by his Aunt Alberta. Theodore is precocious and intelligent, and his family and school are inadequate for him, considering his potential. He is too young, though, to understand that Lucy has abducted him from his family and to comprehend the motives for the action. Theodore has a unique and spirited intelligence, and he is the focal point of the novel.

Berndt Hoffmann, a German-born college professor who has an affair with Lucy Starr. His identity was formed during World War II, in which he was too young to fight on the German side. Ruthless, assured, charismatic, and able to seduce women easily, Berndt seems to provide the authoritative presence that will be the solution to Lucy's myriad emotional dilemmas, but he is in fact unreliable (a fact portended by his infidelity to his wife, Susan) and sadistic. He seizes on Lucy's vulnerabilities and fails to supply her with anything loving and permanent in return.

Aunt Alberta, Theodore's aunt. Alberta epitomizes the older woman who often is the glue of impoverished urban families. She is probably the only person who loves Theodore for himself. She occasionally feels overwhelmed and fears that she cannot give him all he needs.

Dan Gibbs, an African American man whom Lucy Starr meets in the context of her work with the Washington, D.C., educational system. There is an erotic interest between Dan and Lucy, tempered by the racial taboos still lingering in this era. Unlike Berndt, Dan cares about Lucy's welfare and wants to do something to help her in her psychological crisis.

Mrs. Poston, Theodore's teacher in the fifth grade. A pillar of the educational establishment, she represents the "business as usual" approach to Theodore's upbringing that is one of the motivating factors behind Lucy's abduction of him.

Cindy Starr, Lucy's daughter by her marriage to Mortimer Starr, a Jewish intellectual. Cindy lives in Germany as a student with a boyfriend, Dieter. Although Cindy and Lucy love each other, there is tension in their relationship. Cindy is more assured and self-confident than her mother, and this creates distance between them.

— *Margaret Boe Birns*

ABE LINCOLN IN ILLINOIS

Author: Robert E. Sherwood (1896-1955)
First published: 1939
Genre: Drama

Locale: New Salem and Springfield, Illinois
Time: 1831-1861
Plot: Historical

Abe Lincoln, who, at the age of twenty-two in 1831, is an awkward, melancholy young backwoodsman with no particular ambition. By 1861, he is a man of dedicated political principles whose personality and career have been shaped by friendship, love, loss, marriage, his reactions to the Dred Scott decision, and the great debates with Stephen A. Douglas.

Ann Rutledge, Lincoln's great love, who agrees to marry him after her engagement to another man has been broken. She dies of a sudden fever.

McNeil, Ann's fiancé, who is unable to return from his home in New York State to marry Ann.

Mary Todd, an ambitious young woman who sees in Lincoln the means of fulfilling her own frustrated desires. After their marriage, she bears four children, but her jealousy and tantrums make his life so miserable that he is forced to shut her out of his election triumph.

Seth Gale, Lincoln's friend. When the possible death of his son Jimmie threatens the Gales' plans to move west, Lincoln, seeing in his friend's predicament a symbol of what could happen to his countrymen's hopes after the Dred Scott decision, finds his political convictions shaped and strengthened.

Mentor Graham, the New Salem schoolmaster who taught Lincoln grammar and encouraged his love of poetry and oratory.

Ninian Edwards, Lincoln's political mentor and Mary Todd's brother-in-law. Admiring Lincoln, he urges him to become a candidate for the Illinois State Assembly.

Judge Bowling Green, the New Salem justice of the peace.

Joshua Speed, a New Salem merchant.

Berry, Lincoln's whiskey-drinking partner in a general store. His drinking bankrupts the partnership and leaves Lincoln with a debt of fifteen hundred dollars.

Judge Stuart, with whom Lincoln opens a law office in Springfield.

William H. Herndon, Lincoln's law partner.

Stephen A. Douglas, Lincoln's political opponent.

Jimmie Gale, Seth's young son.

ABEL SÁNCHEZ
(Abel Sánchez: Una historia de pasión)

Author: Miguel de Unamuno y Jugo (1864-1936)
First published: 1917
Genre: Novel

Locale: Spain
Time: Indeterminate
Plot: Psychological

Joaquín Monegro (wah-KEEN mohn-AY-groh), a physician and scientist, an accomplished orator, and a lifelong friend and secret enemy of Abel Sánchez. In this parable of contrasts and moral ambiguities, Joaquín is the dark personality, like the biblical Cain, consumed by jealousy and hatred of his closest companion. Even as a child, Joaquín believed that Abel had robbed him of everything he ever wanted, effortlessly usurping his friends and the admiration of adults. Actually, having chosen this role, Joaquín often arranged accidents that promoted his preconceptions. When he fell passionately in love with the beautiful Helena, for example, he arranged for Abel to paint her portrait, fully aware of Abel's easy success with women. When Abel and Helena became lovers, Joaquín believed that he had proved once more that Abel had betrayed him. He becomes more sly and circumspect in his zeal to outdo and even to destroy Abel. Although he is considered a cold man, Joaquín despises himself for his continual malice and actually fights off some temptations to harm Abel. After Abel and Helena are married and are expecting a child, he refuses to attend Helena in childbirth, lest he strangle the child at birth. He marries a tender and compassionate woman. When his wife has a baby girl, he hopes that he can find salvation through the love of a child. He even becomes fond of Abel's son, who wants to become a doctor, not a painter like his father. Although Joaquín takes Abel's son, Abelin, into his household as an apprentice, originally with the malicious goal of displacing Abel as parent, he grows to love the boy and becomes a good mentor, teaching him his healing arts. Neither the love of his patient wife nor the devotion of the young people, however, can root out the ancient malice. When Abel becomes enthralled with Joaquín's grandson, born to Abelin and Joaquín's daughter, the old jealousy arises. In an argument, Joaquín reaches for Abel's throat, but Abel dies of a heart attack on the spot. The wretched Joaquín dies soon afterward, mourning that he had killed Abel and that he had never loved anyone.

Abel Sánchez (ah-BEHL SAHN-chehs), a famous painter. Although he is devoid of malice and envy, Abel is hardly a candidate for sainthood. His character is extraordinarily flat, lacking any depth of reflection, sorrow, or passion. He is egotistical and self-serving, though not offensively so. He sometimes disagrees with Joaquín regarding the nature of art. He paints the surface of things and insists that a man is no different on the inside from what he appears to be on the outside. That is one reason that Joaquín and even young Abelin are dissatisfied with his art, even though he is very skillful in producing surface effects. Only Abelin has suffered from his father's lack of warmth. Joaquín is probably correct that Abel does not want his son to follow in his footsteps as a painter, because that might dilute or even displace the father's fame. Joaquín ardently seeks truth as the highest good; Abel pursues art and beauty rather dispassionately. His marriage to Helena is thus very appropriate, though he is unfaithful to her when other beautiful women are available.

Helena Sánchez (eh-LEH-nah), Abel's wife. Abel met his match in Helena, a woman who seems to be all surface. She became enamored of Abel mostly because his portrait made her a famous beauty. She, too, seems lacking in malice or ulterior motives. Although well aware of Joaquín's passion for her, she did not lead him on or promise him any favors. She is sometimes called a peacock or a "professional beauty." She seems to have no impact on her son, nor does she appear to suffer from Abel's infidelities.

Antonia Monegro, Joaquín's wife. She personifies motherliness, tenderness, and compassion. She is drawn to Joaquín because of the sickness of his soul. A religious person, she prays for his salvation and tries to bring him back into the light through the power of unselfish love. Joaquín recognizes and seems at times to respond to her devotion. He repudiates his old infatuation with Helena, realizing the real superiority of Antonia. He welcomes the daughter she gives him as a new opportunity to learn love instead of hate. Even his satisfaction with his daughter, however, is tainted with the desire to keep pace with Abel, who had sired a son. Ultimately, the long-suffering Antonia receives a final emotional wound from the remorseful Joaquín when, on his deathbed, her husband mourns that he never loved her.

Abelin Sánchez (ah-beh-LEEN), Abel's son, who idealizes Joaquín for his devotion to the science of healing. Although Joaquín always preferred pure scientific research to actually helping people, he pursued the practice of medicine as more lucrative. The idealistic Abelin, who offers to organize and publish Joaquín's many recorded observations and brilliant insights about his patients, ensures that Joaquín's talent will have a benevolent effect. His work feeds Joaquín's neurotic desire for a fame to rival Abel's.

Joaquína Monegro Sánchez (wah-KEEN-ah), Joaquín's daughter, who inherits her mother's temperament and her desire to win salvation for her tortured father. When she desires to become a nun and spend her life in prayer for that very reason, Joaquín hastily redirects her energies, begging her to marry Abelin and thus heal the rift between the two families.

Joaquiníto Sánchez (wah-keen-EE-toh), the grandchild. His name was chosen not by anyone in the Monegro family but by Abel, the father-in-law, who becomes a regular visitor at the physician's house. The aging Abel lavishes on his grandson the affection he never accorded to his own son. The child responds to the endless drawings that Abel makes for him and soon loves Abel much more than he does his more somber grandfather. When the elder Joaquín is about to die, he has the child brought to his bedside and begs his forgiveness. The child gives it readily enough, though he understands nothing about the dying man's distress.

— *Katherine Snipes*

ABRAHAM AND ISAAC

Author: Unknown
First performed: The fifteenth century
Genre: Drama

Locale: Beersheba
Time: Biblical antiquity
Plot: Mystery and miracle play

Abraham, the willing servant of God. In spite of internal conflict, on the angel's command he prepares to sacrifice his beloved young son. His long speeches and prayers disclose his misery over losing his favorite child, but no complaint against God's command passes his lips. He is tender and frank in his explanation to Isaac about the necessity for the sacrifice.

Isaac, an appealing human child. He is terrified at the prospect of a violent death and asks if beating would not be sufficient punishment for any unwitting misdemeanor he has committed. Finding that God has ordered the sacrifice, he accepts the situation meekly, but he does say that God might have given him a better fate if it had been His will. He asks that his mother not be told about his death, for he hates to see her grieve. First pleading for delay, he changes his mind and requests prompt relief from the terrible suspense. After his reprieve by the angel, he blesses the sheep that is substituted for him and prays thankfully to the Holy Trinity. During the preparations for the sacrifice of the ram, he still fears Abraham's sword and asks if he is not to be struck while his eyes are averted.

Deus, God, who commands the testing of Abraham and the saving of Isaac.

An angel, the messenger of God. He brings the order to Abraham for the sacrifice of Isaac and later furnishes the ram for the substitute sacrifice.

The doctor, who appears at the end to elaborate on the text and explain its meaning.

ABSALOM, ABSALOM!

Author: William Faulkner (1897-1962)
First published: 1936
Genre: Novel

Locale: Mississippi
Time: 1807-1910
Plot: Psychological realism

Thomas Sutpen, the owner of Sutpen's Hundred in Yoknapatawpha County, Mississippi. Born of a poor white family in the mountains of Western Virginia, he grows up to become an ambitious man of implacable will. After his arrival in Mississippi, he thinks he can win his neighbors' respect by building a huge mansion and marrying the daughter of a respectable merchant. When he is not driving his wild African slaves and a kidnapped French architect to finish construction of his magnificent house, he seeks relaxation by fighting his most powerful slaves. Wishing to found a family dynasty, he wants, more than anything else, to have a male heir. When one son is killed and the other disappears, Sutpen, now aging, fathers a child by Milly, the granddaughter of Wash Jones, one of his tenants. After learning that the child is a girl, he rejects and insults Milly. Because of his callous rejection, old Wash Jones kills him.

Ellen Coldfield, the wife chosen by Thomas Sutpen because he believes she is "adjunctive" to his design of founding a plantation family. A meek, helpless woman, she is completely dominated by her husband.

Henry Sutpen, the son born to Thomas and Ellen Sutpen. Unlike his sister Judith, he faints when he sees his father fighting with slaves. At first, not knowing that Charles Bon is also Sutpen's son, impressionable Henry idolizes and imitates that suave young man. Later, after their return from the Civil War, he learns Bon's true identity and kills him to keep Judith from marrying her half brother, who is part black.

Charles Bon, Thomas Sutpen's unacknowledged son by his earlier marriage in Haiti. A polished man of the world, he forms a close friendship with the more provincial Henry, whom he meets at college, and he becomes engaged to Judith Sutpen. When the two return from the Civil War, Bon's charming manner does not prevent him from being killed by Henry, who has learned that his friend and sister's suitor is part black.

Judith Sutpen, Thomas Sutpen's daughter. After Charles Bon has been killed and Henry flees, she vows never to marry. She dies of smallpox contracted while nursing Charles Bon's wife.

Goodhue Coldfield, a middle-class storekeeper in the town of Jefferson, the father of Ellen and Rosa Coldfield. When the Civil War begins, he locks himself in his attic and disdainfully refuses to have any part in the conflict. Fed by Rosa, who sends him food that he pulls up in a basket, he dies alone in the attic.

Wash Jones, a squatter on Thomas Sutpen's land and, after the Civil War, his drinking companion. While his employer is away during the Civil War, Wash looks after the plantation. Ignorant, unwashed, but more vigorous than others of his type, he serves Sutpen well until the latter rejects Milly and her child. Picking up a scythe, a symbol of time and change, Wash beheads Sutpen.

Rosa Coldfield, Goodhue Coldfield's younger daughter. She is an old woman when she tells Quentin Compson that Sutpen, whom she calls a ruthless demon, brought terror and tragedy to all who had dealings with him. A strait-laced person, she recalls the abrupt, insulting fashion in which Sutpen had proposed to her in the hope that she would be able to bear him a son after his wife's death. Never married, she is obsessed by memories of her brother-in-law.

Clytemnestra Sutpen, called Clytie, Thomas Sutpen's former slave, who hides Henry Sutpen in the mansion when he returns, old and sick, years after the murder he committed. Fearing that he will be arrested, she sets fire to the house and burns herself and Henry in the conflagration, which destroys the dilapidated monument to Thomas Sutpen's pride and folly.

Milly Jones, the granddaughter of Wash Jones. She and her child are killed by Wash after Sutpen's murder.

Charles Etienne de Saint Velery Bon, the son of Charles Bon and his octoroon mistress. He dies of smallpox at Sutpen's Hundred.

Jim Bond, the half-witted son of Charles Etienne de Saint Velery Bon and a full-blooded black woman. He is the only survivor of Sutpen's family.

Quentin Compson, the anguished son of a decaying Southern family. Moody and morose, he tells the story of the Sutpens to his uncomprehending roommate at Harvard.

Driven by personal guilt, he later commits suicide. Before leaving for Harvard, he learns about Thomas Sutpen from Rosa Coldfield.

Shrevlin McCannon, called Shreve, a Canadian student at Harvard and Quentin Compson's roommate. With great curiosity but without much understanding, he listens to Quentin's strange tale of Southern passions and tragedy.

ABSALOM AND ACHITOPHEL

Author: John Dryden (1631-1700)
First published: 1681
Genre: Poetry

Locale: London, England
Time: Late seventeenth century
Plot: Satire

David, the king of Israel, a poetic representation of Charles II, king of England. Many dissatisfied Jews (Whigs) wish to rebel against him and secure the succession of his illegitimate son, Absalom (the duke of Monmouth), to the throne. The wiser Jews (Tories) see no cause for revolt against a just ruler.

Absalom, the illegitimate son of David, king of Israel, and a poetic representation of the duke of Monmouth, illegitimate son of Charles II, king of England. The dissident Jews (Whigs) seek to make him heir to his father's throne.

Achitophel, the chief of the rebellious Jews (Whigs) and a poetic representation of the earl of Shaftesbury, who attempts to persuade Absalom (the duke of Monmouth) to seize his father's throne.

Zimri (Buckingham),
Shimei (sheriff of London), and
Corah (Titus Oates), rebellious Israelite (Whig) chieftains whose characters are sketched by the poet.
Barzillai (the duke of Ormond),
Zadoc (the archbishop of Canterbury),
The Sagan of Jerusalem (the bishop of London),
Adriel (the earl of Mulgrave),
Jotham (the marquis of Halifax),
Hushai (Laurence Hyde), and
Amiel (Edward Seymour), loyal Israelite (Tory) chieftains who convince King David (Charles II) that his son Absalom (the duke of Monmouth) is being used as a tool by Achitophel (the earl of Shaftesbury).

THE ABSENTEE

Author: Maria Edgeworth (1767-1849)
First published: 1812
Genre: Novel

Locale: England and Ireland
Time: Early nineteenth century
Plot: Social realism

Lord Clonbrony, an owner of large estates in Ireland who absents himself to live in London. He is ignored in fashionable circles, travels with questionable associates, and gets into embarrassing financial circumstances.

Lady Clonbrony, an Irishwoman who apes English manners and speech. She makes herself ridiculous in London. Her chief desire is to see her son marry an heiress.

Sir Terence O'Fay, an impecunious sponger who attaches himself to Lord Clonbrony.

Lord Colambre, son of Lord Clonbrony, a student at Cambridge. He loves Grace Nugent, whom he marries. An honest, level-headed young man, he straightens out his father's financial affairs.

Grace Nugent, a distant relative of the Clonbronys. A beautiful, talented, and well-mannered girl, she eventually becomes Lord Colambre's wife.

Miss Broadhurst, a sensible young woman and an heiress whom Lady Clonbrony hopes to have as a daughter-in-law. Because she is not attracted to Lord Colambre, she eventually marries Arthur Berryl.

Arthur Berryl, a friend of Lord Clonbrony. He falls in love with and marries Miss Broadhurst.

Sir John Berryl, Arthur's father. He almost ends in debtors' prison because he has borrowed money from Mr. Mordicai. He dies, leaving his family penniless.

Mr. Mordicai, a coachmaker and money lender.

Sir James Brooke, a British official in Dublin.

Nicholas Garraghty, Lord Clonbrony's agent. He is dishonest and hated by the nobleman's tenants. When he is found out, he is dismissed.

Dennis Garraghty, Nicholas' dishonest brother.

Mrs. Raffarty, Nicholas' sister, a silly, affected woman.

Lady Dashfort, an Irish noblewoman who wants Lord Colambre as a son-in-law.

Lady Isabel, Lady Dashfort's daughter, a malicious flirt.

Lord Kilpatrick and
Lady Killpatrick, examples of what is worst in the Irish nobility.

Count O'Halloran, Lord Colambre's friend. He loves his native Ireland.

Lord Oranmore and
Lady Oranmore, examples of what is best in the Irish nobility.

Mr. Burke, an honest agent hired by Lord Clonbrony.

Mrs. O'Neill, one of Lord Clonbrony's tenants.

Brian O'Neill, Mrs. O'Neill's son.

Captain Reynolds, Grace Nugent's dead father. His papers reveal that his daughter is legitimate.

Mr. Reynolds, the Captain's father, Grace's grandfather. He is delighted to have the girl turn out to be his rightful heir.

ABSURD PERSON SINGULAR

Author: Alan Ayckbourn (1939-   )
First published: 1974
Genre: Drama

Locale: England
Time: The 1970's
Plot: Farce

Sidney Hopcroft, an up-and-coming businessman in his thirties who starts out running a general store but successfully expands into real estate development. He sports a thin mustache and, when first seen, wears a dated but well-kept suit. He is small in stature, dapper, very cheerful, and exuberant. His bustling energy, which the more urbane Brewster-Wrights find boring and gauche, suits his wife perfectly. An irrepressible handyman, he loves do-it-yourself projects and household repairs. He constantly fidgets and, when not under a sink fixing the plumbing, flits about nervously. His Christmas gift to his wife, a deluxe washing machine, is indicative of his no-nonsense, unromantic nature. Although serenely oblivious to the emotional state of others, his goodwill seems genuine and infectious. He is a spark plug, always trying to get others to have fun, even in the most unlikely situations. Much of the play's hilarity springs from Hopcroft's inappropriate activity for the circumstances, especially in act 2, when Eva Jackson repeatedly attempts suicide while Sidney tries to clean out her kitchen-sink trap.

Jane Hopcroft, Sidney's wife, also in her thirties. Called "Admiral" by Sidney, she has an obsessive need to clean and scrub. In her delight with such tasks, she seems to parody the typical wife of television commercials. She has the habit of breaking into song when busy with domestic chores, making her seem silly and inane. Like her husband, she lacks imagination and sensitivity when it comes to others. She is not as gregarious as Sidney and does not like parties or drinking, accepting her role as hostess more as a grim domestic duty than a pleasure. With dust rag in hand, she is effusive and cheerful but otherwise rather stiff and apprehensive. In the final scene, however, fortified with several drinks, she unwinds and joins in the fun with atypical abandon.

Ronald Brewster-Wright, a bank officer. A well-bred man in his forties, he is fairly imposing in appearance but not particularly distinguished. Although capable of wry observations, he is rather stuffy, deliberate, and reserved, in striking contrast to Sidney Hopcroft. Now in his second marriage, he admits that women are incomprehensible to him. Belonging to the managerial class and thus relying on servants and tradesmen, he is incompetent as a handyman. He comes close to electrocuting himself while attempting to repair a light fixture in the Jacksons' flat.

Marion Brewster-Wright, Ronald's wife, somewhat younger than him. Cosmopolitan and sophisticated, she has a patronizing attitude toward those she considers beneath her. She is also two-faced, exuding charm and warmth when face to face with the Hopcrofts but making unkind comments behind their backs. On the weary and bored side, she drinks excessively, presumably to cope with life's disenchantments. Ultimately, she is incapacitated by her alcoholism, becoming an increasing embarrassment to her husband.

Geoffrey Jackson, an architect. He is a handsome man in his mid-thirties and is a self-styled "sexual Flying Dutchman" who womanizes shamelessly. He has a rather arrogant self-esteem but is not the creative genius he imagines himself to be. He is humbled somewhat when the ceiling of a building he designed caves in and his professional prospects diminish. Ironically, in the building's ruins, his marriage begins to be rebuilt. He finally learns to value the emotional support and loyalty his wife offers him.

Eva Jackson, Geoffrey's wife, also in her thirties. Initially, she is distraught and desperately unhappy in her marriage. She feels abandoned by her husband and uses tranquilizers to cope with her misery. Fear of madness and the numbing effect of drugs make it difficult for her to socialize or perform simple household chores, and she becomes as untidy and careless as Jane Hopcroft is neat and orderly. When Geoffrey announces that he is moving out to take up with another woman, Eva, at an emotional ebb, makes an ineffectual attempt to kill herself. As if spiritually refortified by her seriocomic failure at suicide, she begins to put her life in order. In the last act, strengthened by the new demeanor of her husband, she reveals remarkable good sense and emotional stability.

— John W. Fiero

THE ABYSS
(L'Œuvre au noir)

Author: Marguerite Yourcenar (Marguerite de Crayencour, 1903-1987)
First published: 1968
Genre: Novel

Locale: Europe
Time: 1510-1569
Plot: Historical realism

Zeno (zeh-NOH), an alchemist, physician, and philosopher. At the beginning of the novel, Zeno is a wildly attractive twenty-year-old student of theology, tall and slim, pale, and haggard, with fiery eyes. Being illegitimate, he feels the hypocrisy of social morals; furthermore, he acquires early a thirst for truth, which leads him to travel and meet all the important scientists and philosophers in his quest for knowledge and in his search for himself. A true skeptic, this Humanist challenges established orthodoxy. He is passionately interested in all human and scientific pursuits and experiences, often at the risk of prison or the stake. In middle age, gaunt, gray, and frugal, he hides under the alias of **Sebastian Theus** in his hometown of Bruges, Belgium, where he is appointed physician at a church-run hospice. As confidant to several monks, he learns of their orgies and fears for his own freedom. He decides to stay, however, because his life or death no longer matters to him. Indirectly implicated, he is arrested and tried (under his real name) for all his past activities and books and condemned to die, although he can obtain a pardon if he recants all his writings. He refuses and, at the age of fifty-eight, kills himself.

Henry Maximilian Ligre (lih-greh), a soldier of fortune, Zeno's cousin and a banker's son. At the age of sixteen, he is tall and angular of face, with tawny hair, in love with life and poetry. He joins France's armies to conquer the world of arms and women. Considered a brilliant soldier, for twenty-five years he leads the rude existence of a mercenary, often penniless, always cheerful and fearless, charming women to whom he writes sonnets, and enjoying the pleasures of wine and song. He dies during a sortie, as a captain. The pages of his manuscript are buried with him in a ditch.

Henry Justus Ligre, a merchant and banker. This corpulent and lusty Fleming loves his son Henry Maximilian and tolerates his nephew Zeno. Enjoying the pleasures of food, drink, and female company, the newly widowed and increasingly rich and influential Ligre marries a trader's daughter with whom he has a son, Philibert.

Jean-Louis de Berlaimont (behr-leh-MAHN), the prior of a monastery. More than sixty years old, he is gentle and compassionate, refined and sophisticated, and devout and tolerant. A former courtier and diplomat, he enjoys discussing politics and theology with Zeno. During these talks, he sides with the Patriots against Spanish rule; torn between the presence of evil and God's inherent goodness, he sometimes doubts his own faith. He dies of a throat polyp after advising his friend to flee from the Inquisition.

Alberico de' Numi (ahl-beh-REE-koh deh NEW-mee), a prelate. A handsome and attentive young nobleman, he seduces Hilzonda Ligre, whom he later abandons to pursue his political and clerical ambitions. He receives the cardinal's hat at the age of thirty, although he continues to lead a rogue's existence and is murdered after an orgy.

Hilzonda Ligre, a bourgeois woman, Henry Justus' sister. Slender and not very pretty, when young and naïve, she fell in love with Alberico, with whom she had Zeno. Ashamed of her sin, she is finally consoled by her brother's friend and business associate, whom she eventually marries and with whom she has a daughter, Martha. All three leave for Munster, renamed the City of God. There, she becomes one of the ruler's mistresses in mystical euphoria. After the imperial troops recapture the city, she is beheaded.

Simon Adriansen, a merchant. He is a God-fearing older gentleman, bearded and wrinkled. In his conduct with all, he is charitable and kind. He is successful in his business and investments, and he is related to the Fuggers of the famous banking house. After his death following the Munster rebellion, he is buried in a Catholic cemetery, his strong Anabaptist faith notwithstanding.

Martha Adriansen, a bourgeois woman. As a little girl, she is thin and sickly, more intellectual than her cousin Benedicta Fugger, with whom she is reared after her parents die. Although a Calvinist, she lacks true fervor; during the plague of 1549, she reveals to her half brother Zeno a cowardice of the spirit that is worse than any physical cowardice.

Benedicta Fugger (few-GEHR), the daughter of Martin and Salome Fugger, a pretty girl of the same age as her cousin Martha. Martha and Benedicta are best friends and learn French, music, and drawing together; in addition, both secretly study Reformed liturgy and tenets. She dies of the plague, despite Zeno's treatment.

Bartholomew Campanus, a canon. Thirty years old but appearing much older, Campanus is Zeno's affectionate uncle and tutor. He is scholarly in his interest in languages and philosophy, which he teaches his pupil. At the end of the novel, he is eighty years old and infirm. Although his life has been peaceful and innocent, he is desolate over Zeno's past and his probable end.

Philibert Ligre, a banker. The second son of Henry Justus Ligre, he is fat and physically unassuming. Deeply interested in money and finance, he is very astute and ferocious in his business dealings. He is at first engaged to Benedicta, but when she dies, he marries his cousin Martha. He and Martha become fabulously wealthy and powerful. They live in ostentatious luxury and yet refuse to help Zeno (his cousin and her half brother) after Zeno's indictment.

Cyprian, a monk. He is Zeno's handsome and affable eighteen-year-old aide who, though superstitious, hardly educated, and lazy, has a certain nursing ability. He is involved in theologically inspired sex orgies with several other monks. After his arrest, under torture he confesses all and dies at the stake, along with his friends.

Idelette de Loos, a noble girl. This fifteen-year-old maiden, appropriately called the Fair One by the monks, is very beautiful, with blonde hair and blue eyes, and always well dressed. Daring, coquettish, and headstrong, she is the center of orgiastic and sexual rituals. Being an "angel," she supposedly cannot conceive; when she becomes pregnant and gives birth, she strangles her baby. At her trial, she implicates her accomplices. Found guilty, she is beheaded.

Sign Ulfsdatter (EWLFS-dah-tuhr), a healer and herbalist. Referred to as the Lady of Froso, she is tall, fair, beautiful, generous, and hospitable. She is one of Zeno's few peers and the only woman he truly loves.

— *Pierre L. Horn*

THE ACCIDENT
(Le Jour)

Author: Elie Wiesel (1928-)
First published: 1961
Genre: Novel

Locale: New York City
Time: The 1950's
Plot: Psychological realism

Eliezer, the narrator, a journalist of Eastern European birth. After losing his entire family in the Holocaust, Eliezer has immigrated to Paris, then to New York. He is haunted by his past, by the guilt of having survived, and by a deeply felt responsibility to bear witness on behalf of the dead. His mind is flooded with dreams, images, symbols, and memories, especially of his grandmother, whom he loved devotedly. He finds it impossible to live in the present: He is cynical, detached, and inexpressive. When he does speak, it is often in metaphors, philosophical assertions, and enigmas. He has been drawn to Kathleen since the moment they met, but ultimately he pities her faithfulness and her need to be deceived. Similarly, he feels disdain for Dr. Russel's inability to comprehend despair. Eliezer is weary of the suffering of life and longs to encounter death; the accident he survives is an expression of that longing.

Kathleen, a charming young woman who is Eliezer's lover. Kathleen believes strongly in the omnipotence of love. From an affluent background, she is confident and decisive and not accustomed to losing battles. She is blind with illusions about the goodness of the world and cannot fathom Eliezer's obsession with the past. Through their tumultuous and often cruel affair, she learns about suffering. Later, after he has left her, she is spiritually deadened by marriage to a man for whom she feels no passion.

Eliezer's grandmother, an Eastern European woman who was killed in the Holocaust. Eliezer's grandmother lives vividly in his memories and in his basic philosophy of life. She was a simple and pious elderly Jewish woman with soft white skin and an enormous black shawl. She often protected the young Eliezer from his father's temper and always treated him with compassion.

Dr. Paul Russel, the young resident who cares for Eliezer in the hospital after the accident. Russel is wise and perceptive beyond his years, and he sees in Eliezer the depth of an intense spiritual struggle. He is affable and informal at the patient's bedside but not afraid to be direct. Ultimately, his ideals and strong belief in the value of life render him unable to understand Eliezer's anguish.

Nurse, the young woman who assists in Eliezer's care. She is patient and attentive to Eliezer but commands authority when necessary. She is honest with him and responds openly to his moods and challenges. Her humor brings a much-needed lightness to his recuperation.

Sarah, a prostitute with whom Eliezer spent an evening in Paris shortly after his liberation. At the age of twelve, Sarah was forced into prostitution in a Nazi concentration camp. She became the favorite toy of the German officers. She feels shame about her manner of survival and guilt in the knowledge that sometimes she even felt pleasure in such reprehensible sexual encounters. With no pretensions about her moral stature, she is fearless, even proud. She is unpredictable, moody, and, to Eliezer, elusive.

Gyula, a Hungarian painter and friend to Eliezer. Gyula is tall and robust in his build, and rebellious and mocking in his spirit; in all ways, he is a powerful and intimidating figure. He alone understands Eliezer's despair; he alone, arrogant and energetic, is able to inspire the wounded man. Gyula has no patience for sentimentality and suffering: He refuses to hear Eliezer's confession but rather insists on painting a portrait that ultimately helps Eliezer see himself more clearly.

— *B. P. Mann*

ACCIDENTAL DEATH OF AN ANARCHIST
(Morte accidentale di un anarchico)

Author: Dario Fo (1926-   )
First published: 1970
Genre: Drama

Locale: Milan, Italy
Time: 1970
Plot: Social satire

Maniac, a shabbily dressed man with wild hair, thin spectacles, and a goatee. The Maniac is an inventive and unpredictable subversive who has been arrested twelve times for illegal impersonations. His disguises and personae include a magistrate, Professor Marco Maria Malpiero, and—perhaps his true identity—Paulo Davidovitch Gandolpho, Prose Pimpernel of the Permanent Revolution and sports editor of *Lotta Continua*, a Jewish conspiracy newspaper. The Maniac's revolutionary fervor is grounded in a deep knowledge of fields as diverse as railroads, grammar, explosives, and psychology. He is not only a disciple of Sigmund Freud but also proud to be a certified psychotic. His manner is light and cheerful, suffused with delightful mimicry and a sharply sardonic wit. His hobby is the theater, and in the police station he is at once scenarist, actor, and audience, alternately manipulating, observing, and cooperating with the police buffoons. He chatters endlessly and distractingly but is capable of stating the truth in boldly direct terms: He is both jester and seer, a wise fool. When the discussion turns to political theory, the Maniac becomes didactic and dogmatic, a seemingly disembodied voice of communist ideology. In his subtle way, he is a moral catalyst, forcing the policemen to expose the truth about the anarchist's death and maneuvering Felleti into an inescapable moral dilemma. The Maniac does not offer to sacrifice his own life senselessly but rather seems to hover above both the action and the moral questions it presents.

Francisco Giovanni Batista Giancarlo Bertozzo (bah-TEES-tah jahn-KAHR-loh behr-TOHZ-zoh), an inspector with the Milan police, an explosives and ballistics expert. Despite his simplicity and downright stupidity, Bertozzo is supercilious, arrogant, and stubborn. His devotion to the proper conduct of official business makes him an easy target of ridicule. He simply misses the subtleties of the social and political drama in which he is involved, neither knowing how to play along with pretenses nor recognizing when he is being humored or gulled.

Bellati (beh-LAH-tee), the superintendent of the Milan police. Bellati is a loud and vulgar oaf with a quick and explosive temper. He is more brash and more confident than his fastidious subordinates. Although he makes an effort to maintain protocol and appearances, his sense of humor and play overcome him, and he gets caught up in the Maniac's games and diversions.

Pissani (pee-ZAH-nee), an inspector with the Milan police, from the political branch. Pissani is a weak, cautious, and basically unintelligent man who is baffled by irony and susceptible to the least suggestion or intimidation. Throughout the Maniac's investigation, Pissani insists unrelentingly that all the circumstances surrounding the anarchist's death were aboveboard.

Maria Felleti (feh-LEH-tee), a journalist from *L'Unita*, one of Milan's major mainstream newspapers. Felleti is a direct, challenging, and confrontational reporter; devoted to exposing the truth, she does not respect or defer to the official authority of the police. She is a sensible reformist who believes deeply in the existing institutions of Italian law and democracy; therefore, she does not believe that she can or should take justice into her own hands. When put to an immediate decision once the truth about the anarchist's death is known, however, she is willing to risk her life for her beliefs.

Constables, a pair of dutiful and efficient police officers. The constables are basically fearful and remain detached, by choice or ineptitude, from the investigation. On occasion, however, they inappropriately interject personal reflections and opinions.

— *B. P. Mann*

THE ACCIDENTAL TOURIST

Author: Anne Tyler (1941-   )
First published: 1985
Genre: Novel

Locale: Baltimore, Maryland
Time: The 1980's
Plot: Psychological realism

Macon Leary, the protagonist and narrator. Macon Leary works as a travel writer for a series of books each containing "The Accidental Tourist" in the title. He hates traveling, but he enjoys writing about travel because he can manipulate descriptions into neatly controlled paragraphs. This need to control everything becomes more obsessive. Eventually, Macon withdraws from the world around him when he loses his son and his wife.

Sarah Leary, Macon Leary's wife. Sarah is an English teacher who listened to rock music in the "old days" to keep up with her students. According to Macon, she is sloppy and disorganized. She is at first amused by Macon's systems and finds his moods mysterious, but when their son Ethan dies, she becomes tired of Macon's orderliness. She looks to Macon for comfort, and when Macon cannot comfort her, she leaves him to grieve on her own.

Ethan Leary, Macon and Sarah Leary's twelve-year-old son. Although he is not an active character in the novel, his violent and mindless death is what finally ends his parents' already strained marriage. He is described as a trusting child who loved people; when nervous, he would bounce on the balls of his feet.

Edward, Ethan's nervous and temperamental Welsh Corgi. After Ethan dies, Edward starts to turn on Macon's family and friends. He gets harder to control as the novel progresses, and Macon is forced to seek help.

Muriel Pritchett, an extremely vibrant woman who works three jobs to support her son. She works as a self-employed errand girl, at The Meow-Bow Animal Hospital, and as a dog trainer. She is outspoken and fiercely independent. She first convinces Macon to hire her to train Edward, then actively pursues him as a father for her ten-year-old son, Alexander.

Rose Leary, the youngest of the Leary clan. Rose acts as a mother to her three older brothers. She cooks, cleans, and alphabetizes the kitchen so that the Leary system will function smoothly. Although Rose is in her thirties, she wears dresses that make her appear much older. She is more active than her brothers. She helps the elderly neighbors by bringing them meals and taking them grocery shopping.

Charles Leary, the oldest of the Leary brothers. He works in the family machine factory. He is divorced and childless. He is described as having a childish face. He lives in the Leary house and enjoys playing a card game called Patience that only the Leary family understands.

Porter Leary, Macon's older brother. He is the best looking of the Leary brothers. He is also divorced, and he has three children, a sixteen-year-old boy and two girls. He works in the machine factory with Charles.

Julian Edge, Macon Leary's boss. He is in his thirties and lives in a singles apartment complex. He meets Rose when he visits the Leary home, and he falls in love with her. He is disorganized, and his cluttered office reflects this.

— *Randi A. Drubin*

THE ACHARNIANS
(Acharnēs)

Author: Aristophanes (c. 450-c. 385 B.C.E.)
First performed: 425 B.C.E.
Genre: Drama

Locale: Athens
Time: 431-404 B.C.E.
Plot: Satire

Dicaeopolis (dih-kee-AH-poh-lihs), an Athenian farmer whose name means "honest citizen," a shrewd, earthy man who has had enough of deceptions wrought in the name of patriotism and who wants peace with the Spartans at practically any price. Although he is a loyal Athenian, he recognizes that the Spartans cannot be blamed for all the misfortunes of his homeland. When the assembly refuses to discuss measures for ending the war, he concludes a separate peace and opens a market where all enemies of Athens may trade. Before a chorus of Acharnian charcoal burners, who wish to stone him as a traitor, he eloquently defends the cause of peace. His wisdom is shown even more plainly near the end of the play when he, in the company of two courtesans, makes ready for the Feast of the Cups, while the pompous militarist Lamachus dons his armor to march away to defend the border.

Lamachus (LA-muh-kuhs), a general who is determined to fight the Spartans to the end. A mighty boaster, he at last receives his wounds, not at the hands of the enemy but while leaping a ditch.

Euripides (yew-RIH-pih-deez), the tragic poet, who lends Dicaeopolis rags worn by Telephus, one of the most unfortunate of the playwright's heroes, so that Dicaeopolis will appeal to the pity of the Acharnians when he defends the cause of peace before them. Dicaeopolis takes not only the rags but also other accessories, such as a beggar's staff and a broken cup, until Euripides complains that he has parted with enough material for an entire tragedy.

Amphitheus (am-FIH-thih-uhs), a friend of Dicaeopolis. Although he claims immortality, he suffers from hunger because of the deprivations of war and arranges a truce with the Spartans for Dicaeopolis.

A Megarian, a resident of a city near Athens but allied to Sparta. Also suffering from hunger, he resolves to barter his daughters, disguised as pigs, to Dicaeopolis for garlic and salt. Dicaeopolis' examination of the wares leads to a bawdy exchange between the buyer and the seller.

A Boeotian, who gives his wares to Dicaeopolis in exchange for Nicharus, an Athenian informer.

A husbandman and

a bridesmaid, who try to obtain from Dicaeopolis some of his precious balm of peace. The former is refused, but when the latter explains that she wants the substance so that the bride can keep her husband home from the war, Dicaeopolis gives it to her, exclaiming that women should not suffer as a result of the war.

The chorus of Acharnian elders, veterans who have fought at Marathon, made angry when they hear Dicaeopolis sacrificing to Bacchus after his truce is concluded. They have suffered from Spartan raids and are in no mood to tolerate pacifists. Dicaeopolis, dressed in the costume he has obtained from Euripides, speaks so tellingly for peace that the chorus is divided in sentiment and does not act against him.

An ambassador, returned from a mission sent to seek aid from the king of Persia. He escorts Pseudartabas, a supposed emissary from the Persian monarch, and two disguised Athenian citizens posing as eunuchs.

Pseudartabas (sew-DAHR-teh-buhs), the King's Eye, who pretends to bring Dicaeopolis a message from the King of Persia.

Theorus (thee-OH-ruhs), an envoy sent on a mission to Thrace. He returns with a group of ragamuffins who, he announces proudly, are the host of the Odomanti, the most warlike soldiers in Thrace, sent to aid the Athenians. Dicaeopolis is disgusted by his boasting and pretense.

THE ACOLYTE

Author: Thea Astley (1925-   )
First published: 1972
Genre: Novel

Locale: Australia
Time: Early 1950's to late 1960's
Plot: Allegory

Jack Holberg, a blind musician who becomes Australia's major composer. In his early forties by the time the novel concludes, Holberg is a handsome, powerfully built man whose blindness seems to enhance his presence. A complex character, he is both gifted and obsessed, both kind and cruel. The novel's events and the other characters' lives revolve around his rise from an itinerant pianist in country towns to a composer of international reputation.

Paul Vesper, the "acolyte" to Holberg. In his twenties when he meets Holberg, the novel's first-person narrator subordinates his own personality to focus on the composer's story. He insists on portraying himself as an ordinary and dull-witted man, fit only to serve the extraordinary and brilliant Holberg. Through the narrative's ironic stance, however, Vesper emerges as witty, likable, and sensitive in his own right, even as he bears the insults and humiliation of serving as an "acolyte" before the dubious altar of artistic genius.

Sadie, Holberg's aunt and former guardian. Sadie is a lively seventy-year-old woman who, in a red wig and outlandish clothes, gambles and frolics at Australia's noted resort, Surf-

er's Paradise. Although she is a comic character to an extent, her relation to Holberg assumes significance, for, unlike the others, she does not forgo her individuality to feed his egotism.

Jamie, Holberg's young son, actually the child of his wife's sister. A sensitive and handsome boy, he struggles to discover his identity amid the members of the odd household, the conflicting family relationships, and his father's coldness.

Hilda, Holberg's wife. A colorless and unattractive woman in her thirties, she devotes herself entirely to Holberg and his work, even though she understands neither the man nor the art he produces. She patiently bears his cruelty and indifference, along with his frequent infidelities, and remains humble and servile, even to the point of feigning blindness at times.

Ilse, Hilda's sister and Jamie's mother. Common in appearance and personality like her sister, and generally inept as well, Ilse takes a perverse delight in suffering at the hands of Holberg. Like the others, she has let her own life fall into a kind of paralysis so that Holberg's genius might flourish.

— *Robert L. Ross*

ACQUAINTED WITH GRIEF
(La cognizione del dolore)

Author: Carlo Emilio Gadda (1893-1973)
First published: 1938-1941
Genre: Novel

Locale: The mythical city of Pastrufazio in Maradagàl, South America
Time: 1925-1933
Plot: Antistory

Gonzalo Pirobutirro de Eltino (gohn-ZAH-loh pee-roh-bew-TEE-rroh day ehl-TEE-noh), a middle-aged engineer and writer. Gonzalo carries a grudge against everything and everyone, including his mother, father, and brother (the latter two are dead). He often abandons himself to bouts of anger and makes all kinds of violent accusations: He accuses the peons of thievery, the middle class of being society's disgrace, the rich of having taken advantage of the war to make money, and the military of being irresponsible warmongers. Often, Gonzalo not only insults and yells at his mother but also batters her. The last heir of the Pirobutirro family, Gonzalo basically is a misanthrope.

Elisabetta Francois Pirobutirro, Gonzalo's mother. Señora Elisabetta lives in a world of illusion. She believes that the family is still wealthy, and she is more concerned with the appearance of their social status than with the emotional problems of her son Gonzalo. She is obsessed with the memory of her son who died in the war.

Doctor Higueroa (hee-gway-ROH-ah), the Pirobutirro family's physician. Doctor Higueroa, through his thoughts, symbolizes society's point of view in its perception of Gonzalo's personality and behavior, especially the way that Gonzalo treats his mother, Señora Elisabetta.

Cavaliere Trabatta (trah-BAHT-tah), Gonzalo's neighbor. Cavaliere Trabatta is the victim of a burglary after refusing the protection of the Nistitúo, a vigilante group. He hires mercenaries to be his guards instead, and it is they who find Señora Elisabetta after she is attacked.

— *Rosaria Pipia*

ACROSS
(Der Chinese des Schmerzes)

Author: Peter Handke (1942-   )
First published: 1983
Genre: Novel

Locale: A suburb of Salzburg, Austria
Time: Early 1980's
Plot: Philosophical

Andreas Loser, a teacher of ancient languages at a high school in a suburb of Salzburg, Austria, and an amateur archaeologist who specializes in the excavation of doorways and entryways. He is in early middle age, recently separated from his wife and two children, and on a leave of absence from his teaching post. Loser is a highly introspective man in the middle of a life crisis, searching for a meaning to his existence. He is plagued by the feeling that he is merely an observer of life, rather than a participant. Near the beginning of the novel, he deliberately knocks down a man walking in Salzburg, and this act serves to bring his situation to full awareness. He is concerned intensely with nature and the simple objects around him. Later in the novel, his desire to participate in life emerges, again in the form of a violent act. While walking at night over Monchberg Mountain to play cards with several friends, he sees an old man who is spray painting swastikas on the trees and rocks. He mortally wounds the man with a rock and pushes him over the side of the cliff. Loser feels that, for once in his life, he has acted decisively and experiences no remorse for his act of murder. The next day, he contemplates death and his estrangement from life. At the end of the work, he wanders around the Salzburg area and then travels to Italy to visit the bucolic landscapes portrayed by his favorite writer, the ancient Roman poet Vergil.

The old man, whose identity is unknown. He probably is a neofascist and is approximately in his late sixties. His act of defacing nature by spray painting swastikas on the mountainside prompts the narrator's violent response.

— *Thomas F. Barry*

ACROSS THE RIVER AND INTO THE TREES

Author: Ernest Hemingway (1899-1961)
First published: 1950
Genre: Novel

Locale: Venice, Italy, and the surrounding area
Time: Winter, 1949
Plot: Realism

Richard Cantwell, a colonel in the U.S. Army Infantry who is dying of heart failure after fighting in World War II. A battered and much-decorated fifty-one-year-old professional soldier with cold steel eyes and wild boar blood, he returns to Venice, Italy, the city he loves most, to hunt ducks before he dies. In addition to a breaking heart, he has an injured leg, a crippled right hand that still cracks open, a broken nose, head wounds, and scars on his face. He defended Venice as a lieutenant in the Italian army and has many friends. Most recently, he fought in the invasion of Normandy, helped to liberate Paris, was made a brigadier general, and was later unjustly demoted to colonel. In his life, he has lost three battalions and three women. When he falls in love with Renata, a refined Venetian girl, he is able to surrender command and follow her spiritual authority. In turn, he educates her and calls her Daughter. He is a rough yet cultured man and shares with Renata excellent taste in paintings, literature, people, food, and wine. Very critical of himself, he always tries to be just to others but is inclined by nature and experience in war to be impatient, angry, and brutal. Condemning bad leadership in World War II that cost many lives, he calls himself Mister Dante. Renata brings out his saving nature and helps him purge his bitterness, fight against brutality, and die a graceful death.

Renata, a countess from an old Venetian family, in love with Richard Cantwell. Nearly nineteen years old, she is tall and graceful, with silky dark hair, almost olive-colored skin, a heartbreaking face, qualities of a gentle cat, and a delicate low voice that reminds Cantwell of Pablo Casals playing the cello. She is honest, brave, loyal, poetic, very intelligent, and independent; she does not care what people think of her, and her culture and spirit embody the values that Cantwell has fought for throughout his life. She respects his trade as a soldier, calls him Richard the Lionhearted, and fell in love with him because of his ability to transcend pain and enjoy life fully. Throughout the novel, she bravely faces the fact that he will soon be dead and makes the best of what they have in the short time remaining to them.

The Gran Maestro, the headwaiter at the Gritti Palace Hotel, an old soldier and Cantwell's best friend in Venice. Handsome from the inside out, he has a loving face; a long straight nose; kind, gay, truthful eyes; white hair; ulcers; and, like the colonel, a breaking heart. The two men fought together for Italy in World War I and share traits such as realism, practicality, integrity, dedication to duty, and the rare ability to enjoy life despite suffering. In jest and hatred of all those who profit by war, they belong to an organization with only five members, the Order of Brusadelli, named for a notorious profiteer and laughingstock. At the end of the novel, the Gran Maestro honors Renata by making her a member of the order.

Ronald Jackson, the colonel's driver, a common soldier. A sad boy from Wyoming whose brother was killed in the Pacific, he thinks the colonel is a "mean son of a bitch" who can be good-hearted and generous. In Venice, Cantwell unburdens him of duty and tells him to go and have fun. At the end of the novel, the colonel adds to Jackson's dignity by paraphrasing to him the last words of General Stonewall Jackson and lessens his inconvenience by climbing into the backseat to die.

— *Michael Hollister*

ADA OR ARDOR: A Family Chronicle

Author: Vladimir Nabokov (1899-1977)
First published: 1969
Genre: Novel

Locale: Antiterra or Demonia
Time: 1850-1965
Plot: Parody

Ivan (Van) Veen (ih-VAHN), the fastidious, rakish scion of an aristocratic family. He matures from schoolboy to scholar of psychiatry to retired traveler. Although he has many sexual partners, his life is dominated by a love affair, lasting more than eighty years, with Ada, who is said to be his cousin but actually is his sister. Fourteen-year-old Van, who earns local fame for his unusual skill at walking on his hands, meets twelve-year-old Ada in the idyllic setting of her putative father's country estate, Ardis. There they fall in love, but Van also attracts the lifelong, obsessive love of his and Ada's half sister, Lucette. A second summer at Ardis, four years later, reaffirms Van's love for Ada, but this time the idyll is shattered by Van's discovery of Ada's unfaithfulness. Van is wounded in a duel and recovers at the nurturing hands of a family friend, Cordula de Prey, in her Manhattan apartment. Eventually Van and Ada are reunited in the apartment (now Van's), but a winter of love is interrupted by the abrupt entrance of their father, Demon, who demands that the lovers part. Van spends his adult life in the study and practice of psychiatry, with a special interest in time, space, and insanity. During a transatlantic ocean voyage, Van is surprised to learn that Lucette has contrived to become his fellow passenger. When Van, out of conscientious scruples, rebuffs her advances, she jumps overboard to her death. Van and Ada meet again, in their thirties, in Switzerland, and resume their affair, although Ada is now married. The illness of Ada's husband forces another separation, but the lovers reunite again in their fifties and spend a happy and active old age together, traveling around the world from one fabulous home to another.

Adelaida (Ada) Veen (ah-deh-lah-EE-dah), a pale, dark-haired beauty who is a precocious twelve-year-old with interests in botany and entomology when she first meets and falls in love with Van. As she matures, her sensuality blossoms, and she has many male lovers, as well as, eventually, a bisexual intimacy with her troubled half sister, Lucette. Van is most angered by her brief romances with Lucette's music teacher, Philip Rack, and with Cordula de Prey's cousin, Percy. After both men die, Ada spends her young adult years in a tepid career as a film actress. In between her periodic romantic reunions with Van, Ada is married and spends much of her middle age on a ranch in Arizona with her husband. Eventually, she returns to Van and spends her old age traveling with him, photographing butterflies, and helping to edit the story of their life together.

Dementiy (Demon) Veen (deh-MEHN-tee), a fabulously wealthy, black-haired womanizer who sires both Van and Ada with his mistress, Marina Durmanov, an actress. He is married to Marina's mentally ill sister, Aqua. He is the father of record of Van only, with whom he enjoys a warm relationship. The bond is damaged when Demon inadvertently discovers that his two children are lovers. As an older man, Demon enjoys female lovers of steadily diminishing age (ending with a difficult nymphet of ten) and finally dies in a plane crash.

Marina Durmanov Veen (mah-REE-nah DUR-mah-nov), a faded, red-haired stage and film actress of mediocre gifts. She marries Daniel Veen but carries on a stormy love affair with his cousin Demon. As a result, Marina is the mother of Demon's daughter Ada, Dan's daughter Lucette, and Demon's son Van, though all involved pretend that Van was born instead to Marina's sister Aqua. Marina runs Dan's country estate, Ardis, and occasionally plays the role of doting mother while combining her acting career with a series of love affairs. Marina, who is looked upon with contempt by both Van and Ada, resolutely ignores the evidence that the siblings are lovers until she reaches her deathbed from cancer.

Aqua Durmanov Veen, Marina's twin sister, who is married to Demon Veen and claims to be Van's mother, though Van actually is Marina's child by Demon. Aqua's life is plagued by an escalating series of episodes of mental illness, culminating with her suicide before the age of forty.

Daniel Veen, a dull, stodgy art dealer of independent means. He is married to Marina Durmanov, and he is the father of Lucette and the putative father of Ada. He visits Ardis on weekends and has very formal, limited relationships with his wife and family.

Lucinda (Lucette) Veen, a beautiful, troubled redhead, a half sister to Van and Ada. Teased as a youngster by close proximity to Van and Ada's romance, she comes to love both half siblings obsessively, enjoying sexual intimacy with Ada but finding herself frustrated in her overtures to Van. On one occasion, all three have a brief sexual encounter in Van's bed. When Lucette's frantic final attempt to engage Van on board an ocean liner fails, she jumps overboard to her death.

Ida Larivière, (lah-rih-vih-EHR), young Ada and Lucette's governess. She continues in this position even after achieving unexpected literary success with her plays and short stories. She is somewhat in awe of Ada, and her characteristic failure to observe keeps her from perceiving the romantic nature of Ada and Van's relationship.

Percy de Prey, one of Ada's lovers, a heavyset, hot-tempered rival of Van, and a cousin of Cordula de Prey. He is killed in military service.

Cordula de Prey, a young school friend of Ada. She remains close to Van and Ada all their lives. She nurses Van back to health after he is wounded in a duel, gives him the Manhattan apartment where he and Ada spend a memorable winter, and arranges for Lucette to procure last-minute reservations on the ocean liner from which she plunges to her death.

Philip Rack, Lucette's music teacher and another of young Ada's lovers. A thin, self-effacing man, he eventually is poisoned by his wife and dies in the same hospital where Van is brought after being wounded in a duel.

Andrey Vinelander, a simple Russian with a ranch in Arizona. He marries Ada after Demon surprises and separates Ada and Van. Ada remains loyal, if not faithful, to Andrey during a lengthy illness that eventually leads to his death, allowing Ada at last to return to Van.

Dorothy Vinelander, Andrey's sister, a prissy, annoying pseudointellectual who is despised by both Van and Ada. In spite of her intrusiveness and inquisitiveness during a family trip to Switzerland, she fails to grasp the true nature of Van and Ada's relationship.

— *Laura Stone Barnard*

ADAM BEDE

Author: George Eliot (Mary Ann Evans, 1819-1880)
First published: 1859
Genre: Novel

Locale: England
Time: 1799
Plot: Domestic realism

Adam Bede, an intelligent young carpenter respected by everyone in the village of Hayslope. He is honored when Arthur Donnithorne, the young heir to Donnithorne Chase, has him put in charge of managing the woods on the estate. Three weeks later, however, he sees Arthur kissing Hetty Sorrel, the young woman Adam loves. Knowing that Arthur will never marry Hetty, Adam becomes angry and fights with Arthur. Arthur leaves to join his regiment, and Hetty, deserted and pregnant, promises to marry Adam. When Hetty runs off, Adam is in despair. He stands by Hetty through her trial for the murder of her child. A man who has judged others—his drunken father, Arthur, and Hetty—harshly, Adam learns tolerance and forgiveness. Later he falls in love with Dinah Morris and marries her.

Dinah Morris, a young Methodist preacher, niece of Mrs. Poyser, a farmer's wife in Hayslope. A compassionate young woman, she aids those who are ill or in trouble. When not needed by friends or her family in Hayslope, she preaches at Snowfield, a grimy industrial town twenty miles away. Seth Bede, Adam's younger brother, proposes to her several times, but she says that her religious dedication takes precedence over any private emotion. She sympathizes with Hetty Sorrel and gets Hetty to confess that she had abandoned her illegitimate baby. Dinah later falls in love with Adam Bede and recognizes the claim of private emotions by marrying him.

Captain Arthur Donnithorne, the pleasant and impulsive young heir to Donnithorne Chase who tries to forward Adam Bede's career. Attracted to Hetty Sorrel, he does not intend to marry her. After he learns that she has given birth to and abandoned his baby, he recognizes that his acts can have fateful consequences for other people. In disgrace, he leaves Hayslope, not to return for seven years.

Hester (Hetty) Sorrel, the niece of Mr. Poyser, a dairy farmer. Fond of jewels and petty finery, Hetty is an easy prey for young Donnithorne. When she realizes that he will not marry her, she becomes engaged to Adam Bede; however, in the later stages of her pregnancy, she goes to Windsor to find Donnithorne, only to learn that his regiment has been shipped to Ireland. She then tries to find Dinah Morris, but on the way her baby is born. In confusion, she abandons the child, who is discovered dead. She is tried, found guilty, and sentenced to death, but Donnithorne, just back from Ireland, manages to have her sentence changed to deportation. She dies a few years later while on her way back to Hayslope.

Mrs. Rachel Poyser, a bustling and efficient farmer's wife. Although meddling and talkative, Mrs. Poyser is generous and loyal. She also stands up for her rights and refuses to let old Squire Donnithorne impose a new farming arrangement on her and her husband. She is pleased when her niece Dinah marries Adam Bede.

Martin Poyser, her husband, the owner and manager of prosperous Hall Farm. A genial and understanding man, Poyser is regarded as the leader of the farmers and tradesmen in Hayslope. He is fond of Adam Bede and feels strongly about the deceit practiced by Hetty and Arthur Donnithorne.

Seth Bede, Adam's younger brother. Although more dreamy, less efficient, and less powerful than Adam, Seth is a fine and generous young man. A Methodist, he is in love with Dinah.

Jonathan Burge, Adam's employer, the owner of a firm of carpenters and builders. Burge makes Adam his partner.

Mrs. Lisbeth Bede, the cantankerous yet devoted mother of Adam and Seth. She is strongly partial to Adam and encourages him to marry Dinah Morris.

The Reverend Adolphus Irwine, the rector of Broxton and vicar of Hayslope. He is a genial Anglican clergyman, little interested in doctrine or conversion, who is friendly with both Arthur Donnithorne and Adam Bede. Shocked by Arthur's desertion of Hetty, he does all he can for her at the trial.

Bartle Massey, the intelligent, misogynous local schoolmaster. He values Adam as his prize pupil and teaches him mathematics in night school.

Matthias Bede, the father of Adam and Seth. Once a skillful carpenter, he has become an indolent drunkard. While drunk, he falls into a creek and drowns.

Squire Donnithorne, Arthur's aged and parsimonious grandfather, the owner of Donnithorne Chase. He dies just before Hetty's trial.

Joshua Rann, a shoemaker of Hayslope who also serves as parish clerk and strongly supports the Anglican Church.

Ben Cranage, a carpenter who works in Burge's firm. An iconoclastic man and a spirited dancer, he is the only villager who prefers Seth to Adam.

Jim Salt, another carpenter who works for Burge.

Mum Taft, a silent carpenter who works for Burge.

Chad Cranage, Ben's cousin, a blacksmith who is strongly opposed to Methodism.

Bess Cranage, called **Chad's Bess**, his daughter, a young woman fond of wearing finery. She is intermittently converted to Methodism.

Bess Salt, called **Timothy's Bess**, her cousin, the wife of Jim Salt.

Will Maskery, the Hayslope wheelwright and one of the few local Methodists.

Mr. Casson, the rubicund landlord of the Donnithorne Arms.

Mary Burge, the daughter of Jonathan Burge. The townspeople expect her to marry Adam Bede.

Mrs. Irwine, Mr. Irwine's attractive and sophisticated mother.

Miss Lydia Donnithorne, Arthur's aunt and the daughter of old Squire Donnithorne. Adam's insistence on just payment for a screen he made for her causes the old squire to become antagonistic to him.

Sarah Stone, a widow of Stoniton who takes in Hetty Sorrel and helps her when the baby is born.

John Olding, the farm laborer who discovers Hetty's dead child.

Marty Poyser, the Poysers' oldest, literal-minded son.

Tommy Poyser, the Poysers' second son, dependent and fond of his mother.

Charlotte "Totty" Poyser, the Poysers' spoiled young daughter.

Martin Poyser, Sr., the old father of Marty Poyser.

Alick, a shepherd on the Poyser farm.

Pym, Arthur Donnithorne's trusted servant.

Satchell, the Donnithorne steward, who suffers a stroke.

Mrs. Pomfret, a lady's maid at Donnithorne Chase who teaches Hetty to mend lace.

Mrs. Best, the housekeeper at Donnithorne Chase.

Mr. Craig, a gardener at Donnithorne Chase who is in love with Hetty.

Dolly, the Burge housekeeper.

Miss Kate Irwine, the older daughter of Mrs. Irwine.

Miss Anne Irwine, her younger sister, frequently subject to headaches.

Lisbeth Bede, the daughter of Dinah and Adam Bede.

Adam Bede, Jr., the son of Dinah and Adam Bede.

THE ADDING MACHINE

Author: Elmer Rice (Elmer Leopold Reizenstein, 1892-1967)
First published: 1923
Genre: Drama

Locale: The United States
Time: Early 1920's
Plot: Expressionism

Mr. Zero, a small, thin, sallow, and partially bald man in his late forties or early fifties. For twenty-five years, he has worked as a bookkeeper in a large department store, where he adds up the day's receipts after arranging sales figures in columns. For his dedicated work, he expects a raise, not having received one in seven years, but instead he learns that he is to be replaced by an adding machine. His mind is preoccupied with figures, and he reveals all the prejudices of the lower middle class, though by temperament he is stolid and subdued. He is a henpecked husband, and his marriage leaves much to be desired. For diversion, he peers at a scantily clad prostitute who lives in a nearby apartment until his wife forces him to report her to the police. Following his execution for murdering the Boss, he comes to understand that he has a slave mentality and temperament that he will never escape.

Mrs. Zero, Mr. Zero's wife for twenty-five years. She is forty-five years old, unkempt, and shapeless, with graying hair. A chronic complainer and gossipy housewife, she amuses herself with Western and romantic films. She nags Zero constantly for his lack of ambition and possesses attitudes of petty bourgeois respectability.

Daisy Diana Dorothea Devore, a plain, middle-aged woman. She is Zero's assistant bookkeeper and calls out figures for him to write down. Like Zero, she wears a green eyeshade and paper sleeve protectors while working. Her affection for Zero is masked by her quarrelsome nature. She is chronically unhappy and talks of suicide, an act she carries out after Zero's execution. In the afterlife, their romance, separated from their work, achieves a brief but futile second chance.

The Boss, a middle-aged, stoutish, bald, well-dressed manager of the department store where Zero works. Dedicated to strict business principles and efficiency, he attempts to inform Zero of his termination.

Mr. One,
Mr. Two,
Mr. Three,
Mr. Four,
Mr. Five, and
Mr. Six, friends of the Zeros, about their age, who are guests at an evening party in their apartment. They are dressed like Zero in every detail. They converse about the weather

and denounce woman suffrage, foreign agitators, minorities, Catholics, and Jews. They form half the jury that finds Zero guilty.

Mrs. One,

Mrs. Two,

Mrs. Three,

Mrs. Four,

Mrs. Five, and

Mrs. Six, wives of the male guests of the Zeros. They are all dressed alike except that each has a dress of a different color. They talk of films, gossip about a recent divorce, complain about men, and explore the illnesses of their acquaintances. They form half the jury that convicts Zero.

Guide, a man in a peaked cap and blue uniform who leads curious tourists past Zero's prison cell, delivering a lecture on him as an example of a North American murderer, explaining his pending execution, and selling photograph folders portraying his criminal life to the tourists.

The Fixer, an allegorical figure with wings suggesting an angel, but one who clips his fingernails, reads comics, and smokes a pipe. Zero expects him to prevent his execution, but the Fixer declines, pointing out that Zero's life has been worthless.

Shrdlu, an apparition from the grave, shabbily dressed, wearing silver-rimmed spectacles, and smoking a cigarette. Despondent over his unmotivated murder of his mother while the minister Dr. Amarath was present at Sunday dinner, he bears a greater burden of guilt than Zero. He relives the episode and confesses his crime to Zero. He has come to accept Dr. Amarath's fatalistic pronouncement that he has a criminal nature.

Lieutenant Charles, a middle-aged man, somewhat corpulent, barefooted, dressed in red tights, and wearing a Panama hat. He conveys an air of world-weariness, pessimism, and nonchalance. An immortal, he functions in the place where souls are prepared for reincarnation and is charged with dispatching Zero back to earth, where he will operate an incredibly advanced adding machine. He reveals information about Zero's previous incarnations.

— *Stanley Archer*

THE ADMIRABLE CRICHTON

Author: Sir James M. Barrie (1860-1937)
First published: 1914
Genre: Drama

Locale: Loam House, Mayfair, England; and a desert island
Time: Early twentieth century
Plot: Satire

William (Bill) Crichton, the butler to the earl of Loam. Stuffy, honest, and efficient, Crichton has one complaint about his master: He is not contemptuous enough of his inferiors. While in England, Crichton believes that the established social order is absolutely correct. Stranded on an island, however, he believes in the natural selection of leaders. When everyone realizes how efficient he is, Crichton takes command; he is stern, fair, and almost regal in his deportment.

The earl of Loam, a peer of the realm and Crichton's liberal master. In theory, the earl believes in the equality of all members of society. Once a month, he has his servants in for tea. When he has an opportunity to practice his theories in fact, he becomes an ardent believer in the supremacy of the aristocracy. When the yachting party of which he is host is cast away on a Pacific island, he proves completely ineffectual. For a time, he is his pompous self, until he realizes his utter incapability of leading the stranded party. After Crichton assumes command, the other castaways call him "Daddy," and he seems quite happy doing odd jobs around the camp.

The Hon. Ernest Woolley, a nephew of the earl of Loam and a maker of brilliant epigrams. Ernest is a cheerful, egotistical young man about town with enough shrewdness to avoid work entirely. In London, he idles away his time making witty remarks. Soon after being stranded on the island, however, his talent for wit gets him into trouble with Crichton, now the leader of the party. With every epigram that Ernest makes, Crichton dips his head into a bucket of cold water, thus curing Ernest of a useless habit. Proving himself to be very adaptable, he becomes a diligent worker. After returning to England, however, he reverts to type, and between epigrams he manages to write a book about his island experience, making himself the hero of the adventure. In the book, the contributions of the rest of the party, including Crichton, are dealt with summarily.

Lady Mary, the oldest daughter of the earl of Loam. A part of a useless aristocracy, she is haughty, proud, and languorous. After the shipwreck, she shows herself to be adaptable and courageous. Unlike her former self in England, she becomes a useful member of the island society. The hunter of the group, she has the opportunity to wait on the "Gov." (Crichton). If a rescue ship had not arrived, she would have been chosen to become Crichton's wife.

Agatha and

Catherine, younger daughters of the earl of Loam. After being on the island for a time, they also learn to do things for themselves, and no longer do they depend on maids to answer their every whim. At first, the lack of domestic help is trying to them.

Lord Brocklehurst, the man Mary has chosen to be her husband. He is a complete nonentity, a mother's boy, humorless, pompous, correct, cold, and useless.

Treherne, a pleasant and athletic young clergyman. He is the first to realize that Crichton is the natural leader of the group on the island.

Tweeny, in England the "between" maid. When the earl of Loam decrees that the three sisters can have only one maid among them, she goes with them, mainly to be near Crichton. On the island, she proves to be a useful helper.

Lady Brocklehurst, Lord Brocklehurst's formidable, domineering mother. After the return of the seafarers, she tries to learn what really happened on the island.

Rolleston, the valet to the earl of Loam.

Fisher, Lady Mary's maid, who refuses to go on the cruise.

ADOLPHE

Author: Benjamin Constant (1767-1830)
First published: 1816
Genre: Novel

Locale: Germany and Poland
Time: Late eighteenth and early nineteenth centuries
Plot: Psychological realism

Adolphe, a precocious young man, the narrator. Influenced by his constrained relationship with his father and the strong, unconventional opinions of an older woman of whom he has been a protégé, he finds himself in conflict with himself and with the highly conventional, mediocre society of a small German principality. He sets about the conquest of Ellenore and finally succeeds in winning her away from Count P———. Even while basking in the joys of love, he is annoyed by its constraints. This conflict brings much unhappiness both to him and to Ellenore and ends only when he is freed by her death, which leaves him desolate.

Ellenore, the mistress of Count P——— and later of Adolphe. After sharing Count P———'s life for ten years, she gives in to Adolphe's suit and becomes his mistress. Although she is soon aware of his resentment over the constraints that such an affair inevitably places on its participants, she tries desperately to hold on to his love. Unable to prevent the final deterioration of their relationship, she becomes mortally ill.

Count P———, Ellenore's lover of ten years and the acknowledged father of her children. Even after her flight with Adolphe, he offers to settle her again in suitable circumstances, only to have his offer refused.

Baron T———, a friend of Adolphe's father who is asked to influence the young man to make a final break with Ellenore.

THE ADVENTURES OF AUGIE MARCH

Author: Saul Bellow (1915-   )
First published: 1953
Genre: Novel

Locale: Primarily Chicago, Illinois
Time: The 1920's-the 1940's
Plot: Picaresque

Augie March, the narrator and main character of the story, which tells about his childhood and youth and about learning what it is to be a man. His final discovery is that there is no finality; to be involved with life and people means to hold on to such principles as freedom, fairness, and personal integrity, but it also means that one must constantly adjust the application of these principles to daily circumstances that challenge and change a person. Augie becomes involved in scratching out a living in the hard streets of Chicago, his home. During his adolescence, he takes a series of odd jobs, none of which appears to get him anywhere in a career. Augie is not interested in a career but in experience itself. He works as a distributor of handbills, a newspaper delivery boy, a janitor at a dime store, an elf in a department store at Christmastime, and a florist's deliverer, among other positions. When the Depression begins to squeeze everyone, he resorts to occupations that are outside the law, but his sense of basic morality is always strong. Augie serves in World War II. At the end of the story, he is living in Europe, where his wife, Stella, works in the film industry.

Simon March, Augie's older brother, who takes a different path and provides a contrast that places Augie's adventures in perspective. Augie's wanderings might appear to be haphazard and pointless but for the example of Simon, whose safe, correct choices lead him into a dull existence and a loveless marriage. At first, Augie appears to be a fool for refusing to yield to society's conventions, but at the end of the novel, it is clear that Simon, even though he is successful financially, is the one who squandered his life.

Georgie March, Augie and Simon's retarded brother, who is sent to a home when he gets old enough to cause trouble. Although Georgie had been a burden, when he leaves, the March family begins to fall apart. From Georgie, Augie learns how to sympathize with and care for others with handicaps, something that is important when he meets William Einhorn.

Grandma Lausch, not really Augie's grandmother but a longtime boarder at his parents' house. She tries to teach Augie about life and succeeds in acting more like a parent to him than do Augie's mother and father.

William Einhorn, an early employer of Augie who becomes one of his mentors. Although Einhorn is confined to a wheelchair, he and the rest of his family are among the biggest real estate brokers in Chicago. Einhorn runs his many business affairs, some of them illegal, from a poolroom that he owns and where Augie works as his assistant. The Wall Street crash of 1929 wipes out Einhorn.

Mister Kreindl, a neighbor of the March family who often is involved in Augie and Einhorn's business dealings.

Thea Fenchel, the great love of Augie's young manhood. She is fascinated with an eagle and convinces Augie to go with her to Mexico, where the bird can be trained more easily. When Augie angrily confesses that he is working with the eagle and making the trip only to please her, she is hurt and shocked. She thought that he loved the eagle as she does and drops Augie.

Mr. Renling, Augie's coworker at a department store, who takes him in and gives him room and board when he attends City College. Mrs. Renling also takes an interest in Augie, treats him as her son, and tries to refine him with scathing comments about most of the people they encounter.

Joe Gorman, whom Augie first spurns when Gorman asks him to take part in a robbery. Gorman later involves Augie in smuggling illegal immigrants from Canada. Gorman gets arrested, and Augie has to leave town.

Manny Padilla, one of Augie's classmates at college. He is a book thief, a skill he teaches to Augie.

Mimi Villars, a girl who lives in one of Augie's rooming houses. She nearly dies after a botched abortion. Although

Augie is not the father of her baby, he helps her as he had helped Georgie, Einhorn, and Mrs. Renling, demonstrating his basic humanity.

Grammick, a labor organizer who helps Augie start a career as a union agitator.

Stella Chesney, a girl Augie helps escape from her lover in Mexico. She later becomes Augie's wife. One of the main ironies of the novel is that Augie goes to Mexico because he loves Thea; during the trip, he is rejected by her and meets the woman he will marry.

— *Jim Baird*

THE ADVENTURES OF HAJJI BABA OF ISPAHAN

Author: James Justinian Morier (1784-1849)
First published: 1824
Genre: Novel

Locale: Persia
Time: Early nineteenth century
Plot: Picaresque

Hajji Baba, the son of a barber of Ispahan, who learns his father's trade and many Persian tales and quotations. He becomes an early nineteenth century Persian picaro whose training in thievery and trickery eventually prepares him admirably for a career in diplomatic intrigue at the Shah's court.

Osman Agha, a wealthy Turkish merchant who invites Hajji to entertain him on a buying trip to Meshed. They are captured by Turcoman robbers. Later they combine in a profitable enterprise in Constantinople.

Dervish Sefer, who buys Hajji's adulterated tobacco, then admiringly invites him to become a dervish. Before he can do so, however, Hajji is arrested and beaten until unconscious for selling adulterated tobacco.

The Court Physician, who is persuaded by stolen credentials to give Hajji a position of confidence.

Zeenab, a slave of the physician who gives her favors to Hajji and is condemned to death when the Shah discovers she is pregnant.

Mollah Bashi, whose accidental drowning gives Hajji a chance to put on the priest's clothing and collect money owed to the priest.

Mollah Nadan, a priest who gets Hajji's help in an illegal marriage market. When he forces Hajji to give him the clothes stolen from the dead Mollah Bashi, he is himself accused of Bashi's murder.

ADVENTURES OF HUCKLEBERRY FINN

Author: Mark Twain (Samuel Langhorne Clemens, 1835-1910)
First published: 1884
Genre: Novel

Locale: Mississippi
Time: Mid-nineteenth century
Plot: Adventure

Huckleberry Finn, a small-town boy living along the banks of the Mississippi River before the American Civil War. Perhaps the best-known youthful character in world fiction, Huck has become the prototype of the boy who lives a life that all boys would like to live; he also helped to shape such diverse characters as Ernest Hemingway's Nick Adams and J. D. Salinger's Holden Caulfield. He makes an adventurous voyage with the slave Jim, drifting down the Mississippi on a raft. When he contrasts himself with his flamboyant and wildly imaginative friend Tom Sawyer, Huck feels somewhat inadequate, but deep inside he has a triumphant reliance on the power of common sense. Thus the world of Huck's reality—his capture by and escape from old drunken Pap; the macabre pageant of his townsfolk searching the Mississippi for his supposedly drowned body; his encounters with the King and the Duke, two preposterous swindlers; his stay among the feuding Grangerfords and Shepherdsons; and his defense of the pure, benighted Wilks sisters—is proved to be far more imaginative than Tom Sawyer's imagination. Yet Huck is not some irresponsible wanderer through adolescence; he has a conscience. He knows it is illegal to be harboring a runaway slave, but his friendship with Jim makes him defy the law. His appreciation of the ridiculous allows him to go along with the lies and swindles of the King and the Duke until they seem ready to bring real harm to the Wilks sisters, and he himself will fib and steal to get food

and comfort; but his code of boyhood rebels at oppression, injustice, hypocrisy. Mark Twain has created in Huckleberry Finn a magnificent American example of the romanticism that rolled like a great wave across the Atlantic in the nineteenth century.

Jim, the black slave of Miss Watson. Believing that he is about to be sold down the river for eight hundred dollars, he runs away and hides on Jackson's Island, where Huck also takes refuge after faking his own murder in order to escape from Pap. Ignorant, superstitious, gullible, Jim is nevertheless, in Huck's words, "most always right; he had an uncommon level head, for a nigger." He will laugh at everything comical, but he suffers poignantly when he thinks of the family he has left in bondage. He protects Huck physically and emotionally, feeling that the boy is the one white person he can trust, never suspecting that Huck is struggling with his conscience about whether to turn Jim in. When the two companions encounter the King and the Duke, Jim is completely taken in by their fakery, though at one point he asks, "Don't it 'sprise you, de way dem kings carries on, Huck?" Typically, Jim is subservient to and patient with whites. Even when Tom Sawyer arrives at the Phelpses, where Jim has been caught and held, he goes through Tom's complicated and romantic ritual of escape with grumbling good nature. Jim is a sensitive, sincere man who seems to play his half-comic, half-tragic role in life because he is supposed to play it that way.

Tom Sawyer, Huck's friend, who can, with a lively imagination stimulated by excessive reading, turn a raid by his gang on a Sunday school picnic into the highway robbery of "a whole parcel of Spanish merchants and rich A-rabs . . . with two hundred elephants, and six hundred camels, and over a thousand 'sumter' mules, all loaded down with di'monds. . . ." He is a foil to the practicality of Huck; he is the universal boy-leader in any small town who can sway his gang or his pal into any act of fancy, despite all grumbling and disbelief. His ritual for the rescue of the captured Jim (who he knows has already been set free by Miss Watson's last will) is a masterful selection of details from all the romantic rescues of fact and fiction.

Pap, Huck's father and the town drunkard. When he learns that Huck has been awarded in trust a share of the money derived from the box of gold found in the robber's cave, he shows up one night at Huck's room at the Widow Douglas'. He takes the pledge and stays in the widow's spare room. Finding that Huck's share of the money is legally beyond his reach, he breaks the pledge and creates such havoc in the room that "they had to take soundings before they could navigate it." Pap kidnaps his son, keeping him prisoner in an old cabin. He then proceeds to go on a classic drunk, followed by a monumental case of delirium tremens: snakes in abundance crawl all over him, and one bites his cheek, though Huck, of course, can see nothing. The boy finally makes his escape from Pap by killing a pig and leaving bloody evidence of a most convincing murder. Pap's end in life is discovered by Jim: a dead body in a flooded boat on the Mississippi.

The King and

The Duke, two rapscallions and confidence men with whom Huck and Jim join up on their trip down the Mississippi. Their so-called play, "The Royal Nonesuch," finally leads to their just deserts: tarring, feathering, and riding out of town on a rail.

The Widow Douglas and

Miss Watson, unsuccessful reformers of Huck after he comes into his fortune.

Aunt Polly, Tom Sawyer's relative, who at the end of the story sets straight the by-now complicated identities of Huck and Tom.

The Grangerfords and

The Shepherdsons, two feuding families. Huck spends some time with the Grangerfords, who renew the feud when a Grangerford daughter elopes with a young Shepherdson.

Mr. Phelps and

Mrs. Phelps, at whose farm the captured Jim is confined until Tom arrives to effect his "rescue."

Mary Jane,

Susan, and

Joanna Wilks, three sisters whom the King and the Duke set out to bilk; Huck thwarts the connivers.

Judge Thatcher, "the law" who protects Huck's interests.

THE ADVENTURES OF RODERICK RANDOM

Author: Tobias Smollett (1721-1771)
First published: 1748
Genre: Novel

Locale: England
Time: The eighteenth century
Plot: Picaresque

Roderick Random, familiarly called **Rory**, a reckless and restless young man whose experiences parallel to a certain extent those of the author himself. Rory's mother dies when he is born, and his father, disinherited by his family because he had married a poor relation and a domestic, leaves England. The libertine and unscrupulous Random goes through all the stages of the eighteenth century picaresque hero. As a boy, he is mistreated by alienated relatives; he is befriended and educated (in medicine) by a sympathetic one. His life is a series of assumed identities, leading to whirlwind courtships and attempted marriages to a number of wealthy women. Robbed by a rascally friar in France, he enlists in the army of King Louis XIV. When things seem to be going too well or too badly for Random, an antagonist or a protagonist appears to change the course of his life. Sea voyages and escapades in foreign countries seem to be Random's plight, until in Buenos Aires he meets a wealthy English trader who proves to be his father. After a series of events making for an unsettled, nomadic life, Random is established, happily married, on his father's estate, from which he was evicted as a youngster. Although he often acts without scruples, Random is likable, and in the end he is a personable young man.

Tom Bowling, Random's uncle, a lieutenant aboard HMS *Thunder*. Appearing early in the story, he becomes Random's benefactor. His first move is to get Random away from mean relatives and into school. As unsettled as his nephew, Bowling fights duels on sea and land, is robbed, loses and regains command of ships, and suffers at the hands of ingrates he has befriended. Always the old salt, especially in avoiding interference in others' personal affairs, he makes his will in favor of Random and goes to sea again after seeing his young relative comfortable financially and happy maritally.

Hugh Strap, a schoolmate of Random. Like Bowling, Strap appears propitiously now and again to save Random from disaster or death. At times, Strap's good deeds lead to further involvements for his friend. Strap, an imaginative, romantic figure, curries the favor of a French nobleman to secure employment and an inheritance from his master. As the moneyed M. d'Estrapes, he grooms Random as a fine gentleman so that the scapegrace can make a wealthy marriage in England. His kindnesses are repaid when Random comes into money and acquaints Strap with the latter's wife to be.

Narcissa, the niece of the eccentric bluestocking to whom Random hires out as a footman. Narcissa falls in love with Random and he with her. Despite both her relatives and fate working against her and Random, the beautiful, clever Narcissa remains faithful to him, avoids marriage with any of her many suitors, and in the end becomes his wife.

Don Roderigo, the wealthy English trader whom Random meets in Buenos Aires. Don Roderigo, who has made a fortune through the favors of a Spanish grandee, proves to be Random's father. Don Roderigo buys his paternal estate from a debt-ridden heir, and the Random family settles once more in Scotland.

Nancy Williams, a prostitute to whom Random gives medical care after she is taken ill on the street. Their recurring contacts lead to Williams becoming Narcissa's attendant. She marries Strap.

The Squire, Narcissa's drunken, fox-hunting brother. His disposition is best described by his aunt, who refers to him as the Savage. The Squire's chief function in the plot is to contend against Random and to urge his sister toward other suitors.

Sir Timothy Thicket, one of Narcissa's suitors, whom Random beats with a cudgel for forcing his attentions on Narcissa.

Melinda Goosetrap, a young woman of fortune whom Random courts. He fails in his suit because Melinda's mother sees through his disguise as a person of means. Melinda even wins at cards with Random as he is trying to get some of her money through gambling. She exposes him when she finds him pursuing other wealthy girls.

Miss Snapper, a witty, wealthy, and deformed young woman also courted by Random after he saves her and her mother from highwaymen. He neglects her after meeting Narcissa in Bath.

Lord Quiverwit, another of Narcissa's suitors, favored by her brother. Random defeats him in a duel.

Lieutenant Crampley, the commander of the *Lizard*, one of the ships on which Random serves. Crampley appears to hound Random in an effort to right an old wrong.

Jack Ratlin,

Thomson, and

Captain Oakhum, members of ships' crews. They are representative of the many individuals involved in Random's experiences.

Launcelot Crab, the surgeon who lends Random money. Crab is only one of innumerable doctors, on land and at sea, who affect Random's fortunes.

Banter,

Chatwell, and

Bragwell, three of the wide circle of young men, in London and Bath, who are friends or foes of Random.

Mrs. Sagely, a kind old woman who befriends and takes care of Random after he has been seriously injured in a fight.

An eccentric bluestocking lady, Narcissa's aunt, whom Mrs. Sagely persuades to hire Random as a footman. Random's employer, an authoress of sorts, takes to Random because of his interpretation of her writing. She offsets some of the Squire's antagonism throughout Random's pursuit of Narcissa.

Frère Balthazar, a Scottish priest, referred to as the **Capuchin**. As are many churchmen in eighteenth century writing, the Capuchin is debauched. Among his misdeeds is the theft of Random's money, a loss that forces him to enlist in the French army.

THE ADVENTURES OF TOM SAWYER

Author: Mark Twain (Samuel Langhorne Clemens, 1835-1910)
First published: 1876
Genre: Novel

Locale: St. Petersburg, Missouri
Time: The 1840's
Plot: Adventure

Tom Sawyer, the mischievous ringleader of countless boyish adventures, who almost drives his long-suffering aunt to distraction with his pranks. When not fighting with other village urchins, the indolent boy plans numerous romantic and impractical escapades, many of which cost him hours of conscience-stricken torment. If he is not planning misdemeanors on the high seas, he is looking for buried treasure. Although unthinking, he is not really a bad boy; he is capable of generosity and occasionally surprises even himself with magnanimous acts.

Aunt Polly, Tom's warm, tenderhearted aunt. Sometimes this simple scripture-quoting old soul does not understand her mischievous charge. She uses Tom's brother Sid as an example of a model youth. Her frequent admonitions, emphasized by repeated thumps on the head with a thimble, fail to have a lasting effect on Tom. Believing herself endowed with subtle guile, she often tries to trap the boy into admitting his pranks. Rarely, however, is she successful. Tom usually manages to outwit her if Sid does not call her attention to certain inexactnesses in Tom's excuses.

Huckleberry Finn, one of Tom's best friends and a social pariah to the village mothers, but not to their sons. In the self-sufficient outcast, the boys see everything they want to be. They long for his freedom to do as he pleases. Sometimes, to

their regret, the other boys try to emulate their individualistic hero. Carefully, they mark the way he smokes strong tobacco in smelly old pipes and sleeps in empty hogsheads. Although he is not accepted by the mothers, Huck, even if he is vulgar, is a decent, honest lad. Happy only when he can sleep and eat where he pleases, Huck feels uncomfortable when the Widow Douglas takes him into her home.

Becky Thatcher, Tom's sweetheart. With her blue eyes, golden hair, and winsome smile, she captures his rather fickle heart at their first meeting. A little coquette, she, like Tom, alternately suffers from and enjoys their innocent love. Tom proves his generosity and love for her when he admits to the schoolteacher a crime he did not commit, thus astounding the rest of the class by his incredible folly.

Injun Joe, a half-breed, a murderous, sinister figure who lurks mysteriously in the background. The savagely vindictive killer stabs young Dr. Robinson and is subsequently exposed by Tom. Injun Joe, who had leaped from the courtroom window during Muff Potter's trial, almost has his revenge against the boy in a cave. Finally, he pays for his many crimes when he is trapped in the cave and dies of starvation.

Muff Potter, a local ne'er-do-well and town drunk, a crony of Pap Finn. After helping Injun Joe and Dr. Robinson rob a grave, Muff Potter is accused of killing the doctor and almost pays with his worthless life. Had Tom not belatedly intervened, he would have been hanged and Injun Joe would have gone free. When the boys see a stray dog howling at the newly released Potter, asleep in a drunken stupor, they know that he is still doomed.

Sid, Tom's half brother and one of the model boys in the community. A quiet, rather calculating child, he exposes Tom's tricks whenever possible. When Tom is presumed drowned, however, Sid manages a few snuffles. To Tom, Sid's behavior is reprehensible; he keeps clean, goes to school regularly, and behaves well in church.

Mary, Tom's cousin. She is a sweet, lovable girl who often irritates him by insisting that he wash and dress carefully for church.

Judge Thatcher, Becky's pompous but kindhearted father and the local celebrity.

Joe Harper, who runs away with Tom and Huck to Jackson's Island. Pretending to be pirates, they remain there for several days while the townspeople search for their bodies.

THE AENEID

Author: Vergil (Publius Vergilius Maro, 70-19 B.C.E.)
First transcribed: c. 29-19 B.C.E.
Genre: Poetry

Locale: The Mediterranean
Time: After the Trojan War
Plot: Epic

Aeneas (ee-NEE-uhs), the legendary progenitor of the Roman rulers whose son Ascanius, in fulfillment of a prophecy, founded Alba Longa and whose later descendants, Romulus and Remus, founded Rome. The son of Venus and of Anchises, the king of Dardanus, Aeneas is somewhat more diffident than the warrior heroes of other ancient epics, and he displays the Latin virtues of moderation and filial devotion. Only occasionally does he indulge in righteous indignation. Twice during the siege of Troy, he is saved from death by the intervention of his divine mother. After the fall of the city, he flees, carrying his aged father on his shoulders and leading his son Ascanius by the hand. In the confusion, his devoted wife Creusa is lost. Aeneas searches for her in vain until her shade appears to tell him that he will find his destiny in a distant land. After long wandering, Aeneas and his small band of followers arrive in Italy, where he engages in warfare with the people of Latium and Rutuli. Eventually, a truce is arranged and he marries Lavinia, the daughter of King Latinus. In her honor, he founds the city of Lavinium.

Anchises (an-KI-seez), the king of Dardanus, King Priam's ally in the Trojan War, and the father of Aeneas. A man of great wisdom, he guides his son through many dangers during the wanderings of Aeneas and his followers from Troy to Sicily, where Anchises dies. From the underworld, he foretells the greatness of Rome and commands Aeneas to end his travels at the place where he will eat his tables. Although he appears only as a shade within the poem, the old man figures as a sage patriarch in the recital of earlier events.

Ascanius (as-KA-nih-uhs), sometimes called **Iulus**, the son of Aeneas. He fulfills Anchises' prophecy of the place to settle when he declares, while the Trojans are eating food heaped on large pieces of bread, that they are eating their tables. He takes part in one battle, in which he acquits himself with bravery befitting the future founder of a city and a kingdom.

Creusa (kree-EW-suh), Aeneas's wife. After she becomes separated from her husband and son during the flight from Troy, Aeneas searches for her despairingly until her shade appears to tell him that she is lost to Troy forever and that in Italy an empire awaits him.

Dido (DI-doh), the queen of Carthage, whose love for Aeneas causes her death. When Jupiter sends Mercury, the messenger of the gods, to remind Aeneas of his mission, the hero prepares to continue his wanderings, in spite of the vows he has sworn and Dido's pathetic pleas that he remain with her. On the pretext of burning the love tokens he gave her, Dido prepares a funeral pyre and, lamenting her betrayal, kills herself after the departure of Aeneas and his band. Considered one of the most wronged women in all literature, Dido has beauty, charm, and character, though the latter she sacrifices to the whims of Venus.

Anna, Queen Dido's sister and confidante.

Latinus (leh-TI-nuhs), the king of Latium. Because the oracles have foretold that a stranger will appear, marry his daughter, and rule his kingdom, Latinus befriends Aeneas and promises him the hand of Lavinia, the royal princess, in marriage. The prophecy is not immediately fulfilled, however, for Juno, the enemy of Aeneas, sends the Fury Alecto to turn Amata, the wife of Latinus, against Aeneas. Amata finds a confederate in Turnus, the leader of the Rutulians, her choice as a husband for Lavinia. Bewildered and grieved by this dissension, Latinus goes into retirement. Turnus takes command of the Latiums and Rutulians in the war with the Trojans and their allies.

Lavinia (leh-VIH-nih-uh), the beautiful young daughter of King Latinus and his wife Amata. Loved by Turnus but betrothed to Aeneas, she becomes the prize for which the leaders contend in a bloody tribal war. She becomes the bride of Aeneas after the hero has killed Turnus in single combat and peace has been restored.

Turnus, the leader of the Rutulians and the enemy of Aeneas. A giant of a man and the favorite of Queen Amata for the hand of Lavinia, Turnus is a braggart warrior who makes good his boasts. Aided by Juno, he is almost successful in defeating the Trojan warriors led by Aeneas. When Turnus is decoyed away from the battle, Aeneas pursues and kills him. After the death of Turnus, according to the decision of the gods, Aeneas and his followers abandon Trojan ways and accept the customs of Latium.

Amata (uh-MAH-tuh), Latinus' wife. Goaded by the Fury Alecto, she is moved to hate Aeneas and to plot against him.

Camilla (kuh-MIH-luh), a warrior maiden of the Rutulians brought up in the worship of Diana. She dies in battle, her exposed breast pierced by a Trojan spear, and her death incites Turnus to frenzied rage and even greater efforts against the warriors of Aeneas.

Aruns (A-ruhns), the slayer of Camilla.

Opis (OH-pihs), the nymph charged by Diana to look over Camilla and protect her. Opis kills Aruns to avenge the death of the warrior maiden.

Evander (eh-VAN-dehr), the leader of an Arcadian colony and the ruler of the city of Pallanteum, built on the site of later Rome. In a dream, Tiber, the stream god, directs Aeneas to seek the help of Evander in the coming battle with the Latium and Rutulian forces under Turnus. The Arcadian leader welcomes Aeneas to his city and sends a band of warriors, under the leadership of his son Pallas, to aid the Trojans.

Pallas (PAL-uhs), the son of Evander. During a hard-fought battle, Pallas, while trying to rally his followers, meets Turnus in single combat and is killed by the Rutulian. His death causes great grief among the Trojans, and Evander is heartbroken. In the conflict between Aeneas and Turnus, Aeneas is about to spare his enemy's life when he sees that Turnus is wearing a gold-studded sword belt stripped from the body of Pallas. Proclaiming that Pallas really strikes the blow, Aeneas drives his sword through Turnus and kills the Rutulian leader.

Euryalus (yew-RIH-uh-luhs) and

Nisus (NI-suhs), valiant young Trojan warriors. During the absence of Aeneas, who has gone to Pallanteum to ask Evander for aid, the two leave the beleaguered Trojan camp and steal into the tents of the besieging enemy. There, they kill a number of the Latin soldiers and collect trophies of their exploits before they are surrounded and killed. The followers of Turnus parade the heads of the dead heroes before the Trojan camp.

Anius (A-nih-uhs), the king of Ortygia, where Aeneas and his followers sail after the ghost of Polydorus has warned them not to settle in Thrace. At Ortygia, the priest of Apollo prophesies that the descendants of Aeneas will rule over a world empire if the wanderers will return to the ancient motherland of Troy. Anchises mistakenly declares that the Trojans had come from Crete.

Celaeno (seh-LEE-noh), the queen of the Harpies. When the Trojans land in the Strophades, they unknowingly offend her, and she threatens them with famine.

Acestes (eh-SEHS-teez), the son of a Trojan maiden and a river god. He rules over that part of Sicily where Aeneas and his followers go ashore to hold funeral games in observance of Anchises' death. Aeneas awards Acestes first prize in the archery contest because he is "the favorite of the gods."

Nautes (NOH-teez), the wisest of the Trojan band. He advises Aeneas to leave the aged and infirm behind with Acestes when the Trojans continue their wanderings.

Palinurus (pa-lih-NEW-ruhs), the helmsman drowned shortly after the Trojans sail away from the kingdom of Acestes. Venus has offered his life as a sacrifice if Neptune will grant safe convoy to her son and his followers.

THE AERODROME: A Love Story

Author: Rex Warner (1905-1986)
First published: 1941
Genre: Novel

Locale: An English village
Time: Shortly after the beginning of World War II
Plot: Allegory

Roy, the supposed son of the Rector and his wife. Roy (though athletic and educated at home) is a typical village inhabitant of undeveloped character. At his twenty-first birthday dinner party (a British rite of passage to adulthood), he is told that he is adopted; he responds by getting drunk. He is ambivalent about the village (representing muddling tradition) and the aerodrome (representing modern efficiency). He is both sensual and thoughtful. Although he loses and regains his desire to see the world in realistic terms, he sees that he can neither reshape nor avoid it. The story is his autobiographical narrative of the events of the year following his birthday party; the climax is his discovery that the Air Vice-Marshal is his father.

The Flight-Lieutenant, an officer at the aerodrome, also twenty-one years old. He represents the link between the past and the future, between tradition and modernity. He has tight, yellow curls, keen eyes, and a forward-thrusting jaw; he is considered handsome and charming. Although he is often moody, bitter, and vindictive, he is admired by Roy and is successful as a seducer. He is knowledgeable, irrepressible, and a practical joker. He usually speaks with a cold voice, and he is often deeply critical of the village. He has the virtues and graces absent in Roy, though he kills both the Rector and the Air Vice-Marshal, his father, who had seduced and abandoned his mother, the Squire's sister, Florence.

The Rector, Roy's guardian and putative father. At the age of thirty, when a theological student, he planned the murder of a fellow student (brighter and more handsome) who had won the affections of the girl he loved and the appointment that he wanted. Anthony, the friend, survived, left the church, and became Air Vice-Marshal. The Rector had a child, Bess, by his housekeeper, Eva, the innkeeper's wife. He is racked by guilt and remorse, annually confessing his guilt in his prayers for forgiveness. He is now fifty-two, and his contrition is extreme, though he loves Roy and knew of his wife's pregnancy by Anthony before they were married. He has a pale face, a black beard, thin lips, and fierce, penetrating eyes, yet he is "the gentlest of men." His eternal torture, he recognizes, is the consequence of jealousy, which has brought dissimulation, deceit, and disquiet.

The Rector's Wife, a pale-faced woman with thin yellow hair and an expansive white forehead. She rarely exhibits any feelings except placidity and contentment, though when she overhears her husband's confession, her look suggests both triumph and contempt. Her closest friend is the Squire's sister, Florence. Only in her confrontation with the Air Vice-Marshal, in which she aims to protect Roy, does she show any strength of character.

The Air Vice-Marshal, the effaced theological student **Anthony**, who always has had tremendous ambition. He is a man of great intellectual gifts and of impressive physique and upright carriage. He is noted for his concentration, certainty, and self-control as well as for his lack of nervousness, his authoritative (and cold) voice, and his "small cordiality." He is opposed to inefficiency, waste, and stupidity, as well as to sentiment and spontaneity. His motto, "That the world may be clean," is his constant motivation. The news of the Rector's marriage may well have been the factor that determined his character. Hatred, pride, and ambition cause him to order the death of one son (the Flight-Lieutenant) and to kill his mother; only his "accidental" death saves Roy and his mother.

The Squire, the symbol of the traditional ways of the village, who has been in declining health since his lands were confiscated to allow for the building of the aerodrome. He seems very old: His face appears small and pale, with the skin dragged back from the bones, and his deeply pitted eyes are accented by great eyebrows. He is amiable and exudes aristocratic confidence and persuasive kindliness. He and his sister, Florence, shared mutual gratitude and devoted friendship. On his deathbed, he wishes to see Roy; he says only "Your father," then "Florence," before becoming silent. Roy infers that the Rector is not his actual father.

Florence, the Squire's sister and mother of the Flight-Lieutenant. She is a tall, thin woman with remarkably clear gray eyes and is interested in charities. The best friend of the Rector's wife, she was seduced and abandoned by Anthony.

Dr. Faulkner, a physician. A friend of both the Rector and Anthony, he rescued Anthony after a mountain-climbing accident and nursed him back to health, but he kept this a secret (to allow Anthony to lead a new life) and even went through a funeral for him, thus allowing the Rector to marry Anthony's pregnant girlfriend and to obtain his benefice. Dr. Faulkner is a short, fat man with an almost bald head and is the personification of the genial village doctor and mentor. His poise and authority in the confrontation between the Air Vice-Marshal and his antagonists at the end of the novel provide elucidation and credibility.

— *Alan L. McLeod*

AESOP'S FABLES
(Aesopea)

Author: Aesop (c. 620-c. 560 B.C.E.)
First published: Fourth century B.C.E.
Genre: Short fiction

Locale: Undefined
Time: Antiquity
Plot: Fable

The fox, who appears the most frequently of all the animals in Aesop's fables. Although usually representing cunning, deceit, or treachery, the fox also occasionally serves as a more general figure when a basic representative of humanity is needed. Although the fox is often successful because of his trickery, he should not be seen as a hero in the traditional sense. The fox's slyness usually is accompanied by cowardice, disloyalty, greed, or dishonesty. These negative qualities often prove to be the fox's undoing at the end of the story. In "The Swollen Fox," for example, the fox cleverly crawls into the hollow of an oak to eat the food left there by a group of shepherds. He ends up being too clever for his own good, however, because the meal renders him too fat to escape by the same route that he had used to enter.

The ass, who represents stupidity and frequently is either killed or ridiculed in the fable. In "The Ass in the Lion's Skin," for example, this character frightens other animals by wrapping himself in the skin of a dead lion. When his own foolishness leads him to bray rather than roar, he reveals his true nature and becomes the laughingstock of the other animals. In "The Ass in Office," the ass carries the statue of a god on his back in a religious procession. When all the people of the city bow down in reverence before the statue, the ass foolishly believes that he is the one being honored. He slows down to receive their homage, and the resulting blows of his master's stick shatter his illusions.

The goat, a foolish character similar to the ass, although he is slightly more gullible than stupid. The goat's naïveté often leads him to fall into the fox's traps. In "The Fox and the Goat," for example, the fox lures the goat into a well so that the fox can be boosted to safety. When the goat then demands this same favor in return, the fox merely dismisses him by uttering the moral "Next time, look before you leap."

The lion, who represents ferocity and is the most feared character in Aesop's fables. In "The Vain Wolf and the Lion," a wolf is admiring his own shadow, which, because of the late afternoon sun, is immense, extending down the slope of an entire valley. While the wolf's attention is thus distracted, a lion attacks him and eats him, proving that the lion's own might is more than a mere illusion. At times, Aesop introduces the lion as a symbol for royalty. In "The Lioness," for example, various animals boast of how many children they have. When it comes time for the lioness to boast of all her children, she admits that she has had only one. "But that one," the lioness concludes, "was a lion."

The wolf, who represents rapacity. He is as fierce as the lion but lacks the latter's noble stature. For example, in "The Wolves and the Sheep," the wolves persuade the sheep that there can be peace between them if only the dogs stop inciting them to endless strife. When the sheep foolishly accept this proposal and dismiss the dogs who were protecting them, the entire flock falls prey to the wolves. In "The Wolf and the Shepherds," a wolf blames a group of shepherds for their ferocity in killing a lamb, forgetting that he would have done the same thing if only he had had the chance.

— *Jeffrey L. Buller*

THE AFFECTED YOUNG LADIES
(Les Précieuses ridicules)

Author: Molière (Jean-Baptiste Poquelin, 1622-1673)
First published: 1660
Genre: Drama

Locale: Paris, France
Time: The seventeenth century
Plot: Comedy of manners

Magdelon (mahg-duh-LOH[N]) and

Cathos (kah-TOH), two romantic young ladies from the country, visiting in Paris. They are very affected, in the manner current in their day, and are full of coquetry and artificiality. Being so artificial themselves, they are completely taken in by two gentlemen's valets who pass themselves off to the girls as a marquis and a viscount. The girls' language is at times so affected as to be practically incomprehensible.

La Grange (lah grah[n]zh) and

Du Croisy (dew krwah-ZEE), two young men who pay court to the romantic young ladies. They are so disgusted with the affectations of the girls that they connive to have their valets disguise themselves as gallants and call on the ladies. After a time, they expose the valets and strip off their finery, telling the young ladies that if they are so beguiled by the servants, they must love them just as much without their masters' clothes.

The Marquis de Mascarille (mah-skah-REE) and

Viscount Jodelet (zhoh-deh-LAY), valets to La Grange and Du Croisy, respectively. Delighted to pass themselves off to the romantic young ladies as men of quality, they call attention to their perfumed finery, compose absurd verses and songs, recount imaginary battle heroics, and boast of their noble connections. At the height of a dancing party, their masters enter, expose the ruse, and strip the valets of their fine clothes.

Gorgibus (gohr-zhee-BEWS), Magdelon's father and Cathos' uncle. He is completely confused and befuddled by the affectations of the two young ladies and cannot understand their insistence that La Grange and Du Croisy are too sincere and dull. He is angry and mortified to learn that the valets have tricked the two girls. Feeling disgraced by the trick, he curses foolishness, affectation, and romantic nonsense.

AFTER MANY A SUMMER DIES THE SWAN

Author: Aldous Huxley (1894-1963)
First published: 1939
Genre: Novel

Locale: Southern California
Time: Late 1930's
Plot: Satire

Jeremy Pordage, an Englishman hired to work for six months in California cataloging the Hauberk papers, twenty-seven crates of fragments of English history relating to the Hauberk family. He has blue eyes and a bald spot on the top of his head, and he wears spectacles; he looks the scholar and gentleman that he is. He is amazed by the vulgarity of California and of his employer, Jo Stoyte, a self-made millionaire. Pordage is a bachelor tied to an emotionally devouring mother. He is a civilized observer and, according to William Propter, a potential victim.

Jo Stoyte, once the local fat boy called **Jelly-Belly**, now a California millionaire who lives in a castle. His numerous business holdings include farmland with orange groves on it and the Beverly Pantheon cemetery. He stands to make more millions buying land in the San Felipe Valley when he gets a tip that irrigation water is coming to the valley. A small, thickset man with a red face and a mass of snow-white hair, Stoyte is called Uncle Jo by the patients in his Home for Sick Children. He boasts that he had no education, and although he fills his castle with expensive European art works, he has a library with no books in it. At sixty years old, Stoyte has had a stroke and is terrified of death. Stoyte's love for the curvaceous Ginny is a mixture of concupiscence and fatherly affection.

William Propter, a large, broad-shouldered man with brown hair turning gray. He is a philosopher trying to make sense of the world. He is the author of *Short Studies in the Counter Reformation*, a book that Jeremy Pordage knows and respects. Propter talks to Jeremy and to Peter Boone about his ideas concerning reality and human behavior. A reformer, Propter puts his ideas into action, building cabins for the migrant workers working for Stoyte and using simple machines that will make him and the migrants self-sufficient. Propter knew Stoyte from his school days and befriended him then. Propter feels guilty that he might have contributed to Pete's death, though he did not.

Virginia (Ginny) Maunciple, a twenty-two-year-old woman with auburn hair, wide-set eyes, and a small, impudent nose. Her most characteristic feature is her short upper lip, which gives her face a look of childlike innocence. Through much of the novel, as Stoyte's mistress, she lives happily in the present with no long-range desires. She is fond of Stoyte and calls him Uncle Jo. She thinks herself virtuous because since she has been with him, she has not had sex with any other man, only with two female friends. A Catholic, Ginny has had Stoyte build a shrine to the Virgin Mary on the grounds of his estate. She also has a small shrine in her bedroom with a costumed Mary doll in it. When Ginny begins a degrading affair with Dr. Obispo, she is thrown into confusion and guilt. She acts as if she has been drugged by the sexual experience. She uses her new attentiveness to Pete to make Stoyte jealous, deflecting his attention from Obispo.

Sigmund Obispo, a dark-haired, dapper man with a handsome face who put Stoyte back on his feet after Stoyte suffered a stroke. Interested in research and not in patient care, Dr. Obispo has become Stoyte's personal physician as a means of getting a laboratory funded. For Stoyte, Obispo is trying to discover the secret of longevity. Obispo has only contempt for religion and philosophy (and for most other human beings), and he puts his hope in science. He is a Don Juan who insults Ginny (and everyone else) with his sarcasm, wanting her sexually but on his unromantic terms. When he gets her and when Stoyte jealously tries to kill Obispo, the doctor gets the upper hand, controlling Stoyte, Ginny, and probably the millions of dollars.

Peter Boone, Obispo's assistant in the research laboratory, an athletic young giant of a man. He is enthusiastic about liberty and justice, but he has inadequate language with which to express his feelings. He fought in the International Brigade in the Spanish Civil War in 1937, and he still feels loyalty and affection for the men with whom he fought. He is naïve, thinking that Ginny is pure and loving her. He thinks that he is unworthy of her. Idealistically, he tries to understand Propter's philosophy, and he seems willing to change his life when he is convinced. He worries whether the work that Obispo is doing in the laboratory is good. When Ginny changes from treating him like a brother to seeming to show a romantic interest, he is confused. He loses his life in the rivalry between Stoyte and Obispo, trying to comfort Ginny.

Herbert Mulge, the principal of Tarzana College. Contemptuous of the rich men he solicits, Mulge works tirelessly to obtain their money to expand the college. Mulge is a large, handsome man with a sonorous voice who uses pulpit eloquence to charm Stoyte into making contributions.

Mr. Hansen, the agent for Jo Stoyte's estates in the valley. He gives worse than average treatment to the migrant workers, making the young children work all day for two or three cents an hour and providing vermin-infested housing for the workers. Although he is a decent, kindly man in his private life, he is cruel in his service on the estates. Propter tries to make him understand the workers' needs, but Hansen does not want to know about them.

Charlie Habakkuk, the manager at the Beverly Pantheon. He tries to convince Stoyte to make improvements and extensions to the cemetery, especially by adding catacombs. When Stoyte refuses some of his suggestions, Habakkuk becomes angry, feeling that his ideas have made the cemetery popular while Stoyte reaps the profits. Charlie has made the cemetery successful by injecting sex appeal into death.

The Fifth Earl of the Hauberk family, who held the title for more than half a century and was believed to die at the age of ninety under William IV. He was the author of a notebook that Jeremy Pordage reads and catalogs. The earl collected the pornography that is part of the Hauberk Collection. Jeremy and then Dr. Obispo discover that the earl ate fish guts to prolong his life. He fathered three illegitimate children at the age of eighty-one. He faked his death and with his housekeeper Kate went underground into the subterranean passages of his house. Dr. Obispo says that slowing the development rate of an animal is possible, but the older the anthropoid, the less intelligent it is. When the doctor finds the earl and Kate still alive under the Hauberk house, he finds two stupid anthropoids.

— *Kate M. Begnal*

AFTER THE BANQUET
(Utage no ato)

Author: Yukio Mishima (Kimitake Hiraoka, 1925-1970)
First published: 1960
Genre: Novel

Locale: Tokyo, Japan
Time: Late 1950's
Plot: Satire

Kazu Fukuzawa, owner of the After the Show Retreat in Setsugoan. Kazu lives remote from civilized and noisy life, on the high grounds in the hills near Tokyo. In both her garden and her restaurant, every detail is calculated to please and soothe the eye. Seeking to combine rustic simplicity with elegance and aesthetic sense, Kazu hopes that her garden conveys a sense of detachment from worldly pleasures. Her natural state is ecstatic wonder, and she exudes love as the sun gives out heat. Her energy is an eternal delight to her visitors. Her harmonious life is challenged when she marries Noguchi. Although at times she identifies herself so deeply with the political views of her husband's party as to forget herself as an independent individual, she gradually becomes like an actress playing a role in a play based on the ideology of the radical party. In the end, however, she chooses not to submit to the dictates of society, politics, or even her husband. Instead, she returns to her sources of spiritual solace: her garden and restaurant.

Yuken Noguchi, an intellectual of the radical party. Although he is married to the peaceful Kazu Fukuzawa, Noguchi seems to be in total disharmony with himself, with society, and with nature. He hides behind an ambiguous smile, laconic conversations, artificial attitudes, cold manners, acidulous reactions, and expressionless eyes. His stingy frugality indicates his choked emotional world, and his frigidity results from sexual desires undermined by prejudices. He is blinded by righteousness; he fails to see the essence of things. His absentmindedness in relation to everyone is in tune with the cold air and gloomy atmosphere around him, whatever the season. Noguchi is enterprising and calculating. He believes that he must organize his party rationally to show a favorable balance of profits and costs. He seems to object to life rather than be subject to it. His wish still to be young contradicts his aged house, his clothing, and the comb that he has owned for thirty years.

Totsuka, a radical pamphleteer. He is stubborn in his beliefs and distorts the truth with brutal directness and uses irresponsible lies in a political pamphlet in order to secure forcefully the victory of his party.

Soichi Yamazaki, Noguchi's campaign manager for the radical party. He takes painstaking care in maintaining a devout and faithful friendship with both Noguchi and Kazu Fukuzawa. He is sincere about his promise to assist Kazu at any time.

Genki Nagayama, an old conservative politician. His indulgences in lust and power, and in money and sex, push him to prevent an auction of Kazu's property. He is disappointed that she will not sell herself to him.

— *Marlies Kronegger*

AFTER THE FALL

Author: Arthur Miller (1915-   )
First published: 1964
Genre: Drama

Locale: New York City
Time: The 1950's
Plot: Expressionism

Quentin, a lawyer who agonizes over his past—the failure of his two marriages, unhappy childhood experiences, the political witch-hunts in the 1950's, and the extent to which he bears personal responsibility for what happened to his close friends and his two wives. Quentin views these past events from the perspective of the present. He has met Holga, with whom he has fallen in love. She is European and brings with her a sense of the European past, including that of World War II, of mass destruction and the concentration camps. Quentin reacts to this grim history in terms of his own life, questioning his motives; his selfishness; his rejection of his first wife, Louise; and his inability to help his tormented second wife, Maggie. Although Quentin is not able to resolve all the conflicts within himself, with Holga's help he does come to understand better his own implication in the sufferings of others.

Holga, Quentin's fiancée, who helps him come to terms with his guilt over his previous marriages. Having suffered greatly herself during the war, she has had to deal with the issues of responsibility that Quentin addresses. Her calm, abiding presence throughout the play bespeaks a sensibility that has grown with experience and is able to accept the worst that Quentin can confess about his own character.

Louise, Quentin's first wife, who has been his mainstay for many years. In several flashback scenes, Quentin explores his estrangement from her. She is unable to understand Quentin's dissatisfaction with his own life and with their marriage. Her main complaint is that Quentin does not really talk to her, that he does not know how to interact with women, and that their growing separation is largely a matter of his inability to share himself with others.

Maggie, Quentin's second wife, a beautiful, sensuous woman who becomes a major recording star. When she first meets him, however, she lacks confidence and responds warmly to his encouragement and sensitivity. He makes her feel like a whole human being. At the same time, her exuberant spirit makes him, for a time, a much warmer and more giving person. As Maggie tears herself apart, a victim of self-doubt, she begins to view Quentin as a burden in her life, as someone who has used her. Although he tries to help her, he also withdraws from her as she becomes hysterical. She eventually commits suicide.

Felice, one of Quentin's devoted clients, who appears as almost a fantasy figure. She worships Quentin and does not see the cold side of him that makes Maggie turn against him.

Mother, who dominates Quentin's family in the childhood flashback scenes. When Quentin's father loses his money in the stock market crash of 1929, she turns against him, blaming him for the family's troubles. She recurs on stage as a figure in Quentin's mind, a part of his remembrance of his difficult childhood, playing the part of the accusing woman, which reminds him of his first wife, Louise.

Lou, one of Quentin's lawyer friends whose career is ruined by his testimony before the House Committee on Un-American Activities. His radical political background has put him in a vulnerable position, especially because he admits that he lied in one of his books about life in Soviet Russia. He has asked Quentin to defend him; Quentin takes on the task with mixed feelings, worried about his reputation and concerned that his heart is no longer in defending his colleagues.

Mickey, one of Quentin's lawyer friends who has saved Lou once before, when his academic career was threatened by charges that he had been a subversive. Mickey devastates Quentin when he admits that he is going to "name names," that is, tell the House committee about his friends who were active in radical politics.

— Carl Rollyson

AFTERNOON MEN

Author: Anthony Powell (1905-   )
First published: 1931
Genre: Novel

Locale: The Soho area of London, England
Time: The 1920's
Plot: Social satire

William Atwater, the protagonist, a young museum official. He has straw-colored hair, sometimes wears tortoiseshell-rimmed spectacles, and has long, slender legs. His father is a retired civil servant, but he has twice failed to win a Foreign Office post. He is one of the "Bright Young People" of the London Soho district, witty but bored and enervated. He secured his museum position through influence. He spends his evenings in talk, and he drifts from one situation to another.

Raymond Pringle, Atwater's friend, a painter. He is twenty-eight years old, has red hair, and affects a manner of dress that combines a workman's shirt with patent-leather shoes. He lives on a comfortable inheritance, with which he is rather tightfisted. He is a bad painter, but his study in Paris has given his work a certain slickness that allows him occasionally to sell a painting. He has a beach cottage, which is the setting for the novel's climactic scene.

Harriet Twining, Pringle's occasional mistress. She has fair hair and dark skin and is a staple of the London party scene. She attracts men, and many want to marry her immediately. She tires of them, wears them out, or spends all of their money before romance can proceed to the matrimonial stage.

Susan Nunnery, a young woman desired by Atwater. He meets her at a party early in the novel. She has a quality, at least in the protagonist's perceptions, that sets her apart from the other "Bright Young People." Her large, expressive eyes are her best feature.

Lola, a model and frequent Soho partygoer. The name she bears is her own invention. She looks like an early drawing by Augustus John. She purports to read Bertrand Russell when she requires inspiration.

Hector Barlow, another struggling artist. He is stockily built and has light eyes and black, stubbly hair that grows low onto his forehead. He wears sack-colored clothes and sucks a pipe. He was with Pringle in Paris. He has an assertive nature but is fretting over which of several girls to marry; all the alliances seem equally unlikely.

Fotheringham, an unsuccessful journalist. He is a heavily built, pink-cheeked young man who has had a temporary job for the past five years as subeditor with a spiritualist paper. He is responsible for the advertisement pages. He dislikes spiritualists as a group and complains of how they keep his nose to the grindstone. He longs for a new occupation and especially desires to go to America.

Undershaft, a young man who is a phantom presence in the novel. He has gone to America, thus escaping the pointless life the others are leading in London. For this action, he is variously admired, envied, and blamed. He is rumored to be in New York, prospering as a piano player and living with a woman of indeterminate race.

Naomi Race, a patroness of the arts. No one knows her age or anything about her late husband. She is like the dowager of drawing-room comedy. She has Atwater to dinner about once every two months.

George Nunnery, Susan's father. He is characterized by his daughter as a retired failure, a curious small man with a walrus mustache. He still discusses finance, but his bankruptcy, or something, has left him somewhat vacant.

Verelst, a wealthy Jew. He is dark, with bags under his eyes and a thick nose. He is almost good-looking and almost distinguished-looking. Susan goes off to America with him at the end of the novel.

— *Patrick Adcock*

THE AFTERNOON OF A FAUN
(L'Aprés-midi d'un faune)

Author: Stéphane Mallarmé (1842-1898)
First published: 1876
Genre: Poetry

Locale: Indeterminate
Time: Indeterminate
Plot: Fable

The Faun, the hero and narrator. The faun of mythological antiquity, half man and half goat, was associated with bucolic settings and lascivious sexual appetites, so the Faun of this work is imagined to be a creature of considerable sensual indulgence. His sexuality links him to fundamental human desire, but his intellectual probing reflects the continuing human preoccupation with self-definition. In this way, he seems remote from his animal half. Through both his aesthetic and his physical preoccupations, the Faun presents himself as essentially a romantic hero. He seeks to dominate his surroundings both to find answers and to create his songs. He lives in a pastoral setting and creates a literal harmony with it through his songs. The Faun's major role is as a representation of the poet himself. Throughout the poem, he speaks of the music he plays on panpipes, and his dreams either create or transform his encounter with the nymphs, depending on which percep-

tion of reality the reader accepts. Because the nymphs appear only through the musings of the Faun, they seem to be entirely his creatures. If the encounter with them is taken to be a literal event, the Faun has only a limited perception of the nymphs, illustrating the difficulty of finding poetic insight, something as difficult to capture as the nymphs themselves.

The nymphs, the only two other characters in the poem. They remain only partially revealed. Each is rendered specific by contrast with the other; one is younger and naïve, the other more sophisticated and aggressive. In their similarity and variety, they serve as emblems of the Faun's desire and the poet's ideal. In their variety, they encompass all women and all beauty, but described only obliquely, without realistic detail. They serve as an idealized focus for any specific concept of beauty the reader may bring to the poem.

— *Dorothy M. Betz*

AGAINST THE GRAIN
(À rebours)

Author: Joris-Karl Huysmans (1848-1907)
First published: 1884
Genre: Novel

Locale: A villa overlooking Fontenay-aux-Roses in Paris
Time: The 1880's
Plot: Black humor

Jean Des Esseintes (day zeh-SAHNT), the last descendant of a family of French aristocrats that has long been in decline, having fallen prey to the hereditary enfeeblement that—according to a common belief of the nineteenth century—was brought on by continued intermarriage and love of luxury. At the age of thirty, he is anemic, "neurasthenic" (a term replaced in modern parlance by such phrases as "highly strung"), and prey to all manner of real and imaginary illnesses. He already has indulged his appetite for commonplace pleasures and ordinary vices to the limit and now desires to become a recluse, surrounding himself with the best of everything that human artifice has to offer. He intends to live in splendid isolation, and although he retains two servants to do the housework and regularly consults his doctor, he remains the only authentic character in the narrow realm of his existence. In selecting the

objects with which he intends to embellish and glorify his privacy, Des Esseintes always prefers the artificial to the natural and the fantastic to the representational. He prefers hothouse flowers to those that can stand exposure to the elements, and he has a particular affection for carnivorous plants. He prefers perfumes carefully designed by human artificers; these have the capacity to induce an orgiastic ecstasy in him. His favorite painter is Gustave Moreau, who delighted in depicting exotic femmes fatales in gorgeously elaborate surroundings. His favorite poets are Charles Baudelaire, the great pioneer of what Théophile Gautier called the "Decadent style," and Stéphane Mallarmé, who carried that style into the new era of Symbolism. Des Esseintes considers the prose poem to be the ideal literary form, but among longer prose works, he favors those that take such delight in opposing or slyly subverting common notions of propriety that they become "satanic," like the works of Jules-Amédée Barbey d'Aurevilly. Des Esseintes' own moral views are calculatedly perverse, and he is fond of arguing against every position taken for granted by conventional moralists. Although he is able to furnish his new villa according to his tastes, gradually bringing it to maturity as a utopia in miniature, Des Esseintes' pleasure in his project is undermined by the fact that his health continues to trouble him. He is warned by his doctor that continued indulgence of his luxurious tastes will kill him, but when the doctor's prescription for a dietary supplement of beef tea is mistaken for a recipe for an enema, Des Esseintes is delighted to discover yet another form of perversity: that of taking one's nourishment into the wrong end of the alimentary canal. This is, however, his last defiant attempt to go "against the grain" of convention; he accepts thereafter that he must change his habits. He decides to enter a monastery but conserves his perversity to the end in maintaining that he is reconciled to the church not because its dogmas are true but because they are so utterly and magnificently impossible.

Mme Des Esseintes, his mother, a recluse who dreads light and spends her life secluded in her darkened bedroom. She dies while her son is young.

M. Des Esseintes, Jean's father. He lives in Paris and seldom visits his wife and child. He dies while Jean is young.

— *Brian Stableford*

THE AGE OF INNOCENCE

Author: Edith Wharton (1862-1937)
First published: 1920
Genre: Novel

Locale: New York City
Time: Late nineteenth century
Plot: Social realism

Newland Archer, a young lawyer who is a member of New York's high society. Married to May Welland, a girl from his own class, he falls in love with Ellen Olenska and for a time considers running away with her. He never does so because he is bound by his ties of marriage and convention.

Countess Ellen Olenska, a New York girl of good family who has married a Polish nobleman but now wishes a divorce from him. Intelligent and beautiful, she comes back to New York, where she tries to fit into the life she had known before her marriage. She falls in love with Newland Archer. When the young attorney, persuaded by her family, urges her not to seek a divorce, she leaves for Europe without him. Years later, Archer's son visits Ellen in Paris.

May Welland Archer, Newland's wife, a typical New York socialite with all the restrictions and forms adopted by that class. She triumphs over Ellen Olenska and saves her marriage with the announcement that she is to become a mother.

Mr. Welland and
Mrs. Welland, May's parents. Rich, conservative, puritanical, they are somewhat shocked by the discovery that their relative, Ellen, plans to divorce her husband. Clannishly, however, they give in her honor a party at which they announce the engagement of their daughter to Newland Archer.

Mrs. Catherine Mingott, May's grandmother, the mother of Mrs. Welland and a proud old aristocrat who dominates the clan.

Medora Mingott, May's aunt and Ellen's former chaperone. Flighty but good-natured, she brings Ellen back to the family home in New York after Ellen and her husband have separated.

Mr. van der Luyden and
Mrs. van der Luyden, members of the old, conservative aristocracy. They generously offer to receive Ellen after she has been snubbed by others of her class.

Julius Beaufort, a successful New York businessman. Married, he carries on affairs on the side. Eventually he goes bankrupt.

Mrs. Beaufort, his wife, a fat, pleasant woman tolerant of her husband's philanderings.

Fanny Beaufort, the daughter of Julius by one of his mistresses. She marries Dallas Archer.

Dallas Archer, the son of May and Newland Archer. He manages to cut the ties of formal society which have held his father captive for so long, marries Fanny Beaufort, and leads a more relaxed and happier life than his father's.

Ned Winsett, one of Newland Archer's friends, a journalist who tries to win Archer over to a less restrictive life.

Reggie Chivers and
Mrs. Chivers, Newland Archer's fashionable but understanding friends. They entertain him when he is trying to have a rendezvous with Ellen.

Jane Archer, Newland's wise and clever little sister. She has an ear for gossip and spends much time talking over tidbits of information with her mother.

Mrs. Archer, Newland's widowed mother. She intercedes for Ellen with the van der Luydens and manages to persuade them to give a dinner party for her after she has been snubbed by the rest of New York society.

Mrs. Lemuel Struthers, a lively, fat woman much interested in musicians and artists. She is considered quite vulgar by the "better" families.

Mr. Letterblau, the senior partner of the law firm for which Newland Archer works. He directs the young attorney to handle the Olenska divorce case.

Lawrence Lefferts, a society friend of the Archers and the Wellands.

THE AGE OF WONDERS
(Tor-ha-pela'ot)

Author: Aharon Appelfeld (1932-   )
First published: 1978
Genre: Novel

Locale: Provincial Austria
Time: 1938-1969
Plot: Social morality

Bruno A., called **the Son**, who in 1938 is a twelve-year-old schoolboy. He looks on helplessly and with only partial comprehension as his family and their comfortable existence fall to pieces in a world of jarring anti-Semitism. Aching for love and warmth from his estranged parents, the boy has intimations of decay and doom that intensify as he is shunted from provincial home to country resort and back again. In the second part of the novel, he is a middle-aged man. He returns to confront childhood ghosts after the breakup of his marriage in Jerusalem.

Father, an Austrian writer and literary critic. His successes bring joy neither to him nor to his family. A tired, absent-minded, surly man, he succumbs to bitterness and paranoia as he is attacked for the sickly Jewish spirit of his writing. His hatred of petit bourgeois Jews and ragged *Ostjuden* (Eastern European Jews) is second only to his fear of being regarded as one of them. As anti-Semitism blocks his career and destroys his self-respect, he soothes his soul with alcohol and impossible dreams of a literary and cultural renaissance. This delusion leads him to abandon his family for a baroness in Vienna.

Mother, a tall, tight-lipped, unhappy woman. She bears her husband's physical and spiritual distance in stoic fashion and strives to preserve an atmosphere of normalcy and dignity even as Jewishness makes her family an object of derision and loathing. A woman with strong philanthropic impulses, she devotes herself frantically to charitable institutions as her personal life deteriorates. After her husband runs off to Vienna, she dutifully responds to a call from the local rabbi to join the Jews assembling in the synagogue. That night, she is imprisoned with her son and adopted daughter.

Theresa, Bruno's aunt and Mother's younger sister. She is a diligent university student. Tall like her sister and radiating her inner life, she has the air of a priestess. After a fit of depression lands her in Saint Peter's sanatorium, she emerges for a family vacation only to be stricken by another fit of otherworldly melancholy. Her psychosis leads her to convert to Christianity with a sacrificial gesture, and soon thereafter she dies suddenly and mysteriously within the walls of Saint Peter's.

Brum, a onetime friend of Bruno's parents. He transforms himself from a thin, ascetic, cowering person into a bold and blunt character, renouncing his Judaism along the way. In the second part of the novel, he is an old, bitter anti-Semite. He receives a beating from Bruno yet never owns up to his Jewish past.

Stark, a sculptor. Born of a Jewish mother but reared at an "Aryan" military academy, he transmutes the anti-Semitism he encounters into a passionate yearning for his mother's faith. Much to the horror of Father, this strong-spirited man and erstwhile champion of the family's dignity has himself circumcised and submits to the squalor of a Jewish almshouse.

Salo, Father's brother. Flamboyant and vigorous, he aims to shock his conventional family. He and his mistress are a breeding ground for scandal. Salo belongs to the merchant class that Father detests.

Danzig, Bruno's violin teacher. His attempts to root out the imperfections in his playing have made him a nervous wreck. Plagued by an inferiority complex and an uncontrollable twitching of his left shoulder, he leaves for Australia.

Louise, a nubile maid, the only vibrant and sensual element in the otherwise icy household. With her rustic innocence and high spirits, she captivates Bruno and his male relatives. Bruno later discovers that Louise, who becomes fat and devoid of charm, once prostituted herself to his uncles.

Helga, an orphan adopted by Bruno's family. She gradually loses her untamed, fearless spirit and becomes docile and domesticated.

Suzi, the illegitimate daughter of Salo and his mistress. Bruno meets her and her lesbian lover upon his return to Austria. The turmoil and conflicts within her bastard psyche may be regarded as typical of the postwar generation.

— *Harry Zohn*

AGENTS AND PATIENTS

Author: Anthony Powell (1905-   )
First published: 1936
Genre: Novel

Locale: London, England; Paris, France; and Berlin, Germany
Time: The 1930's
Plot: Picaresque

Blore-Smith, a young law student. He has big brown eyes, huge ears, a shapeless face, and a speech impediment; he is naïve and inexperienced. He recently graduated from Oxford University and is in search of glamour and excitement. In London, he meets a pair of artist-intellectuals who are little better than confidence men. They exploit him mercilessly and whisk him away to absurd adventures in Paris and Berlin.

Oliver Chipchase, an art critic and amateur psychoanalyst. He has an emaciated physique and wears a severe expression. He has a history of sordid love affairs, which are the sort of love affairs he says he likes. He has a large number of eccentric acquaintances, both in London and on the Continent. He easily convinces Blore-Smith that the young man is in need of his psychiatric treatment.

Peter Maltravers, a friend of Chipchase and a dabbler in scriptwriting and filmmaking. He is tall and distinguished looking, but his appearance gives no hint of intellectual aptitude. He wishes to do a film in cinema verité style, portraying an assemblage of intellectuals as they respond to a provocative situation. Because such a venture is commercially unpromising, he desperately needs financing that will not require repayment. This he finds in the person of Blore-Smith.

Mrs. Mendoza, the owner of a flower shop in a fashionable part of London. A tall, fair-haired, beautiful woman, she combines a tweedy appearance with a bohemian lifestyle. She is variously known as Mrs. M. and Mendie.

Commander Hugo Venables, a retired naval officer who is courting Mrs. Mendoza. He is about fifty, heavily built, and purple-faced. He is a somewhat vacant man who finds it difficult to please his beloved.

Sarah Maltravers, Peter's wife, a woman of languid manner. The Maltraverses have a "modern" marriage, except that Peter becomes angry when Sarah goes out with other men. Blore-Smith develops a crush on her.

Schlumbermayer, a dealer in art objects and another eccentric friend of Chipchase and Maltravers. He is a tall, bespectacled man of about forty-five, going gray and tending toward fatness. He hosts the making of Maltravers' film. He has business cards printed in several different names.

— *Patrick Adcock*

AGNES GREY

Author: Anne Brontë (1820-1849)
First published: 1847
Genre: Novel

Locale: England
Time: Mid-nineteenth century
Plot: Domestic realism

Agnes Grey, the pious, sheltered daughter of a clergyman. She takes employment as a governess when her family's financial situation becomes desperate.

Richard Grey, Agnes' father, a poor person who loses his patrimony in a disastrous speculation.

Mrs. Grey, Agnes' mother.

Mary Grey, Agnes' sister.

Mrs. Bloomfield, mistress of Wellwood. Agnes' first employer, she is convinced that her incorrigible children, Agnes' charges, are angels.

Tom Bloomfield,

Mary Bloomfield, and

Fanny Bloomfield, Agnes' arrogant, disobedient charges.

Mr. Bloomfield, the stern father of Tom, Mary Ann, and Fanny. He blames Agnes when the children misbehave.

Uncle Robson, Mrs. Bloomfield's brother. His encouragement of Tom's cruel behavior brings forth a protest from Agnes and causes her dismissal.

Mrs. Murray, mistress of Horton Lodge, Agnes' second employer.

Rosalie Murray, Agnes' pretty, flirtatious charge at Horton Lodge. At sixteen, she is interested only in making a good match.

Matilda Murray, Agnes' younger charge at Horton Lodge, who is interested only in horses.

Edward Weston, the pious, sincere curate at Horton Lodge. He later becomes Agnes' husband.

Mr. Hatfield, the pompous rector of Horton and the rejected suitor of Rosalie Murray.

Harry Meltham, and

Mr. Green, suitors of Rosalie.

Sir Thomas Ashby, the wealthy, boorish owner of Ashby Park, with whom Rosalie makes an unhappy marriage.

Nancy Brown, an old widow at Horton visited by Agnes and Edward Weston during the development of their romance.

THE AGONY AND THE ECSTASY: A Novel of Michelangelo

Author: Irving Stone (1903-1989)
First published: 1961
Genre: Novel

Locale: Italy, particularly Florence and Rome
Time: 1487-1564
Plot: Biographical

Michelangelo Buonarroti (mi-kehl-AN-gehl-oh bwon-ah-ROH-tee), a skinny, unsociable thirteen-year-old who, as the action of the novel begins, wishes he could redraft his facial features with a crayon. He reflects on the death of his mother when he was only six years old and his consequent loneliness and hunger for love. First trained as a stonecutter and then sent away to school for three years, young Michelangelo prefers drawing to the study of Latin and Greek. It is not until he becomes a student at the Medici sculpture garden at the age of fourteen, having spent a year at Ghirlandaio's studio, that he comes to know happiness again and forms lasting friendships. Tutored by the Plato Four, he develops a love for ancient culture and a familiarity with classical texts; at the same time, he begins working seriously in marble. A beating permanently disfigures his face, and he never overcomes his insecurity about his own ugliness. He becomes a victim of his own drive for artistic perfection. Carving as long as twenty hours a day, he persists for months without adequate food or sleep. At one time, he sleeps in his clothes for a month; when he finally removes his boots, the skin of his feet comes off with them. Working on the ceiling frescoes for the Sistine Chapel, he becomes racked from the position in which he must work and almost blind from the dripping paint. In addition to experiencing the agony of working and of being treated as a mere laborer by his patron, Pope Julius II, Michelangelo suffers the agony of producing great art only to have it destroyed. Rioting Florentines break an arm off his *David*, and the Bolognese melt down a bronze statue of Julius that took fifteen months to create, recasting the metal as a cannon. He is stoned by the rock cutters of Carrara because Pope Leo insists that he use marble from Pietrasanta instead of theirs. Because Michelangelo feels an inner compunction to complete a significant body of works, he has no time for social niceties or a love relationship. He shares his father's pride in family, but he believes that as a mendicant artist working for long periods in self-imposed isolation, he cannot have a family of his own. Even as an elderly man, he retains the sense of the artist's responsibility to convey human emotion and the very meaning of life instilled in him long ago by the Medici circle. Although he becomes increasingly subject to multiple infirmities, he experiences little diminishing of his artistic powers. Viewing his works in his mind's eye, he feels the ecstasy of a long lifetime of work well done as his soul soars through the gaping hole that will become the dome of St. Peter's.

Lodovico di Lionardo Buonarroti Simoni (loh-doh-VEE-koh dee leeoh-NAHR-doh bwon-ah-ROH-tee see-MOH-nee), Michelangelo's father, a man tottering on the edge of social ruin who invests his hopes for reestablishing the family fortune on Michelangelo, the only one of his five sons ever to earn money. Lodovico, who went into despair after the death of his first wife, never showed any affection or understanding to Michelangelo as a child. From the time of the boy's apprenticeship, he controls his earnings, over the years taking eighty percent of Michelangelo's commissions while his son lives sacrificially and eats little. Never satisfied with Michelangelo's contracts, he complains and dogs him to earn more money to buy farms for him and to set his brothers up in business. When Lodovico dies on his ninetieth birthday, Michelangelo realizes his love for his father in spite of the hardships he has endured for him. He is satisfied to have been the means to the recovery of the family name.

Lorenzo de' Medici (MEH-dee-chee), called **Il Magnifico**, the untitled ruler of Michelangelo's Florence, a patron of artists and intellectuals, and a poet. The wealthy, powerful Lorenzo wants to liberate the human mind by fostering a renaissance in learning and the arts. After Lorenzo's untimely death at the age of forty-three, Michelangelo realizes that he owes all that he is to this ideal ruler-scholar whom he knew for only three years.

Contessina de' Medici, the daughter of Lorenzo de' Medici, whose youthful romance with Michelangelo is stillborn because of their social differences. After her brother Piero makes arrangements for Contessina to marry Ridolfi, she is not permitted to see Michelangelo again. They retain their feelings of affection and loyalty for many years, however, and Michelangelo attempts to intervene with Florentine authorities on her behalf during her family's eight years in exile and poverty. She eventually is restored to favor and assumes a large role in Vatican politics when her brother becomes pope. Michelangelo, greatly shaken by her sudden illness and death, maintains a lifelong relationship with her offspring.

Clarissa Saffi, a cobbler's daughter and the mistress of a Bolognese nobleman. Michelangelo is passionately attracted to her when they are both nineteen years old. Twelve years later, they have a brief affair, but after a few months she leaves him because he is too preoccupied with making wax models to give enough of himself to her.

Vittoria Colonna, the daughter of a powerful Italian family, the Marchesa di Pescara. She is a beautiful, regal, and kind Renaissance woman whom Michelangelo meets when he is sixty-one years old. They exchange his drawings and her poetry, and Michelangelo falls deeply in love with her. She is devoted to convent life and reform within the Roman Catholic church, however, and never offers him romantic love.

Tommaso de Cavalieri (kah-vah-lee-EH-ree), an elegant and handsome Roman. He is Michelangelo's assistant architect for St. Peter's and his inseparable companion during his last seventeen years.

— *Janie Caves McCauley*

L'AIGLON

Author: Edmond Rostand (1868-1918)
First published: 1900
Genre: Drama

Locale: Austria
Time: 1830-1832
Plot: Historical

Franz, the duke of Reichstadt, called **L'Aiglon**, Napoleon's son, a weak and idealistic youth. He dreams of returning to France as emperor, but he is in delicate health. He plans an escape from his ever-present guards, but his plot is discovered, and he is stopped while trying to get away. He realizes that he is not strong enough or brave enough to make the sacrifices necessary to become another Napoleon. Death from pulmonary tuberculosis soon overcomes him.

Prince Metternich, the Austrian statesman who is Franz's official jailer. He makes it his business to keep Franz closely guarded at all times and discovers his plan to escape. He provides tutors for Franz who never speak Napoleon's name in any of their lessons. He taunts Franz by pointing out to him how unlike his father he is.

Seraphin Flambeau (say-rah-FA[N]-flahm-BOH), an old soldier in Napoleon's army. He encourages Franz in his dreams of returning to France and helps him in his plan to escape. When the plan is discovered, he kills himself rather than face a firing squad.

Marie-Louise, the mother of Franz and daughter of the Austrian emperor. She does not greatly regret her husband's death and would be very happy in the Austrian court if Franz were not so grief-stricken.

Countess Camerata (ka-mehr-AH-tuh), Franz's cousin, who appears in Austria as a fitter from Paris. She is an accomplice in the plot for Franz's escape. She wears a uniform exactly like his to a fancy dress ball and, when she and Franz exchange cloaks, the guards follow her instead of him, temporarily allowing him to escape.

The archduchess, Franz's aunt, who makes Franz promise that he will ask the emperor to allow him to go back to France before he makes any plans with his friends.

Emperor Franz, Franz's grandfather, who, when Franz appears in a disguise at court and asks permission to go to France, grants it to him without realizing who Franz is.

Thérèse de Lorget (teh-REHZ deh lohr-ZHAY), Franz's beloved and a French exile.

Fanny Elssler, a dancer who helps in Franz's escape plot.

Count Sedlinsky, who is in charge of the police guard that spies on Franz.

AJAX
(Aias)

Author: Sophocles (c. 496-406 B.C.E.)
First performed: Early 440's B.C.E.
Genre: Drama

Locale: Phrygia, before Troy
Time: During the Trojan War
Plot: Tragedy

Ajax (AY-jaks), the son of Telamon and, excepting Achilles, the strongest and bravest of the Greeks who fought to win Troy. After Achilles was killed, his armor was claimed both by Ajax and by Odysseus; on the testimony of Trojan prisoners that Odysseus had been the more formidable foe, the Greeks awarded the coveted armor to him. Enraged and envious, Ajax left his tent by night, stealthily, to kill not only Odysseus but Agamemnon and Menelaus as well. The goddess Athena cast a madness upon him so that, thinking them Greek leaders, he massacred the flocks and herds. The play begins when Ajax is at the height of his delirium. After the fit has passed, he is seen to be immoderate and proud, but at the same time he commands sympathy not only because of his greatness of spirit but also because he has been, however deservedly, the victim of Athena's terrible wrath. His magnificent sense of personal honor demands that his scheme be eradicated by suicide, an action he carries out in spite of the pleas of Tecmessa and the Chorus. He is a man of such colossal inner strength, nobility, and self-sufficiency that he is not only alienated from his fellow men but also brought into conflict with the gods themselves.

Odysseus (oh-DIH-see-uhs), a resourceful leader of the Greeks at Troy. Ingenious in action and skillful in speech, he is a foil to Ajax. Whereas Ajax is the type of the hero, Odysseus is the type of the enlightened, reasonable man. Although he is an enemy of Ajax, he is horrified when Athena shows him the hero insanely torturing the animals. After the suicide of Ajax, Odysseus persuades Agamemnon to let Teucer give his corpse an honorable burial and, having befriended Teucer, nobly offers to assist at the funeral. While Ajax was alive, he and Odysseus had been at cross purposes, but after Ajax's death, Odysseus justly pays tribute of respect to the dead hero's greatness.

Teucer (TEW-sur), an archer, the son of Telamon and a captive princess. He is a half brother of Ajax. He is absent on a raid during Ajax's madness and subsequent suicide. On his return to the Greek camp, he is first taunted by enemies of Ajax because of his brother's shame and then warned by Calchas, the seer, that Ajax's safety depends on his remaining within his tent for the rest of the day. By the time Teucer reaches Ajax's tent, the hero has left for the scene where his suicide occurs. There is evidently a deep measure of trust and devotion between the brothers. Defying both Menelaus and Agamemnon, Teucer insists that Ajax be buried properly.

Tecmessa (tehk-MEE-sah), a captive, the devoted concubine of Ajax and mother of his son Eurysaces.

Menelaus (mehn-eh-LAY-uhs), the king of Sparta and the deserted husband of Helen. He is pictured as blustering and pusillanimous, eager to defame his dead enemy Ajax by forbidding burial and leaving his body to scavengers.

Agamemnon (ah-geh-MEHM-non), the commander in chief of the Greek forces and brother of Menelaus. When he denies permission to bury Ajax, Teucer defies him. He at last permits the funeral, quite ungraciously, after the intervention of Odysseus.

Eurysaces (ew-RIH-seh-seez), the young son of Ajax and Tecmessa, who receives his father's great shield from Ajax's own hand.

ALBURQUERQUE

Author: Rudolfo A. Anaya (1937-   )
First published: 1992
Genre: Novel

Locale: Albuquerque, New Mexico
Time: 1992
Plot: Magical Realism

Abrán González (ah-BRAHN gohn-SAH-lehs), a twenty-one-year-old boxer from the barrio who has given up fighting because he feels responsible for the death of a sparring partner. Abrán learns that he was adopted and that his mother was Cynthia Johnson, a talented painter. She dies from cancer shortly after Abrán discovers the truth about his birth. He sets out to discover the identity of his father. He agrees to return to the ring in exchange for information about his father and is thus drawn into the world of Albuquerque wealth and politics. Two women are attracted to him: the mayor, who represents the power and glamour that can be his as a successful fighter, and a poor nurse from a small village in the mountains, who represents a simple life of service to others and the traditional Mexican values of family and land. In the end, Abrán discovers that it is not through biology that one gains one's identity; rather, he learns, one defines oneself through the choices one makes.

Ben Chávez (CHAH-vehs), Abrán's biological father, a writer and teacher at the University of New Mexico. A poor boy from the barrio, Ben fell in love with Cynthia Johnson, an Anglo girl and the mother of Abrán, but her father insisted that the baby be put up for adoption, and she never revealed the identity of her lover to anyone. Even though he learns that Abrán is his son, he respects Cynthia's silence. Ben is an observer with a compulsion to write, rather than a man of action. He represents the artist in society, and through his stories he tells people who they are; his art enables them to understand themselves and their values.

Frank Dominic, a wealthy attorney running for mayor of Albuquerque. Although he was a high-school classmate of Ben and Cynthia, Dominic is unaware that Ben was Cynthia's lover. He promises to find out who Abrán's father was—if Abrán will return to the ring for a fight that will be the centerpiece in the celebration kicking off Dominic's campaign. Running on a platform of urban development that envisions the Albuquerque of the future as a gambling and entertainment center of canals and casinos, Dominic conceals his ruthlessness and hunger for power behind a good-old-boy façade. He is interested in using Abrán to further his political plans, but those plans are doomed to failure because they have not grown out of the character of the city but out of Dominic's insatiable ego.

Lucinda Córdova (lew-SEEN-dah KOHR-doh-vah), a nurse from a small village in northern New Mexico who befriends Abrán after the death of his mother. She represents the traditional ideal of womanhood: She is selfless and devoted to family, and she wants to devote her life to healing. When she learns that Abrán has been unfaithful to her, she breaks off their relationship. On the night of the fight, however, she realizes that she has no future without him, and she rushes to ringside to be near him. Her presence inspires him, enabling him to make a comeback and win the match.

Marisa Martínez (mahr-EE-sah mahr-TEE-nehs), the beautiful, competent, honest mayor of Albuquerque. She represents the new woman: She is divorced and lives alone, devoting herself to her work. When she meets Abrán, she is attracted to him and invites him to her home, and they make love. A detective hired by Dominic takes photographs, which Dominic then uses to try to make Marisa withdraw from the mayoral race. She is determined to see it through, however, and her courage and devotion to the city will probably be rewarded by reelection.

Jose Calabasa (hoh-SEH kah-lah-BAH-sah), a Santa Domingo Indian and loyal friend of Abrán. A Vietnam veteran who has not been able to escape the evils of the war, Jose is a student at the university and has lost touch with his pueblo and family. When Dominic attempts to buy the pueblo's water rights, Jose returns home to try to prevent the sale. He is unsuccessful, but he discovers that his future lies in helping his people. He discovers that Ben is Abrán's father when he recognizes a picture of Ben in one of Cynthia's paintings.

Walter Johnson, a wealthy businessman and also a candidate for mayor. Johnson represents Anglo business interests and bigotry. He never learns that his wife had an affair with her gynecologist and that Cynthia was not his daughter. He enters the race for mayor to oppose Dominic, whom he hates, and he wants nothing to do with Abrán after Abrán learns that Cynthia was his mother.

ALCESTIS
(Alkēstis)

Author: Euripides (c. 485-406 B.C.E.)
First performed: 438 B.C.E.
Genre: Drama

Locale: Pherae, in ancient Greece
Time: Remote antiquity
Plot: Tragicomedy

Admetus (ad-MEE-tus), of Pherae, the king of Thessaly. Because of his fair and friendly treatment of Apollo, placed at Admetus' mercy for punishment by Zeus, Admetus has been allowed to escape the appointed hour of his death if someone else will die in his place. His wife Alcestis has given her pledge to die for him, and the play opens on the day of her death. Admetus sincerely loves his wife, but he lacks the courage to die as he should instead of letting his wife die for him. Admetus is weak but is not a coward, and because he realizes his own baseness he gains in stature as the play proceeds. He advances from sincere but self-conscious lamentations to deeply moving and completely honest sorrow over his wife's sacrifice. He is saved by his one virtue: He is the best of friends and hospitality is almost an obsession with him. He welcomes Herakles, hides the fact that his wife is dead, and insists that the great hero remain as a guest. When Herakles discovers the truth, he wrestles with Thanatos—the god of death—and saves Alcestis.

Alcestis (al-SEHS-tihs), Admetus' wife. Her offer to die for her husband when all others refuse glorifies the self-sacrificing devotion of a wife. She is also the devoted mother who dies to ensure her children's safety and to preserve the kingdom for her son. On stage, she appears rather cold and reserves her passion for her children, but only because, though she loves her husband deeply, she has come to realize that his love is not of the same quality. After Herakles rescues her from Death, she is led in veiled. She is forbidden to speak for three days, until her obligations to the gods of the underworld have been fulfilled.

Herakles (HEHR-a-kleez), the son of Zeus. He is the Greek prototype of great physical strength. He stops at the house of Admetus on his way to capture the man-eating horses of Diomedes. Presented as a jovial, ingenuous boaster, he accepts Admetus' hospitality and drinks until he becomes quite merry. When told the truth about the death of Alcestis, he is stricken with remorse for his conduct and repays Admetus by rescuing

Alcestis from Death. He provides comic relief when he is drinking and when, in the final scene of the play, he presents the veiled Alcestis to Admetus. He insists that Admetus take the woman into his household, even though Admetus has sworn to Alcestis that he will never remarry. Thus, Admetus is made to refuse at first to take back Alcestis.

Pheres (FEE-rees), the aged father of Admetus. Presented as a horrible old man who refuses to sacrifice his life for his son, he is smug and complacent. He serves to make Admetus realize how ugly his conduct appears to others.

Apollo (uh-POL-oh), the god befriended by Admetus. He speaks the prologue, and in his conversation with Death he foreshadows the victory of Herakles over Death.

Thanatos (THAN-a-tohs), the god of death. Unrelenting in his right to take Alcestis, he is defeated by Herakles.

A maid, an attendant of Alcestis. She describes Alcestis' preparations for death to the Chorus and helps to reveal Alcestis' love for Admetus.

Chorus of men, citizens of Pherae. Loud in their praise of the devotion of Alcestis, they hold forth hope that Admetus' hospitality will prove a virtue to save him. Although they do not sympathize with Pheres, they realize that it is not Admetus' place to condemn him and that Admetus breaks one of the most sacred of all rules, to honor one's parents. They rejoice at the rescue of Alcestis.

Eumelus (ew-MEE-luhs), the son of Admetus and Alcestis. He breaks into lamentation as Alcestis dies and emphasizes vividly the child motive in Alcestis. The characterization is not a happy one, for the boy is far too much a miniature adult.

A servant to Admetus, who supposes Herakles to be fully aware of Alcestis' death and complains bitterly of the hero's unseemly conduct. He tells Herakles the truth. Later, he declares that if there had been no death in the family, Herakles' conduct would not have been objectionable.

THE ALCHEMIST

Author: Ben Jonson (1573-1637)
First published: 1612
Genre: Drama

Locale: London, England
Time: Early seventeenth century
Plot: Comedy of manners

Subtle, the Alchemist, a moldy, disreputable cheat. Joining forces with Jeremy Butler and Dol Common, he uses his fund of scientific and pseudo-scientific jargon to fleece the gullible. He promises large returns from transmutation of metals, astrological prophecies, physical nostrums, or whatever seems most likely to entrap his victims. When the master of the house returns, he is forced to take flight without his gains.

Face (Jeremy Butler), Subtle's contact man, who furnishes his master's house as the Alchemist's headquarters. He is a resourceful, quick-witted improviser. Disguised as a rough, blunt captain, he entices victims to the house. When his master, Lovewit, returns home unexpectedly, he arranges a marriage between Lovewit and the Widow Pliant, thereby escaping punishment.

Dol Common, the third of the tricksters, the common mistress of the other two. Her dominant personality keeps her quarrelsome cohorts in line. She can act various roles, such as an exotic lady or the Queen of the Fairies, to carry out Subtle's various schemes. Along with Subtle, she is forced to flee with the jeers of Face following her.

Sir Epicure Mammon, a fantastic voluptuary. He is a veritable fountain of lust and imagined luxury, and he seeks the philosopher's stone to help him to unbounded self-indulgence. When his investment is wiped out by the explosion of the Alchemist's furnace, planned and well-timed by Subtle, Sir Epicure confesses that he has been justly punished for his voluptuous mind.

Abel Drugger, a small-time tobacconist ambitious for commercial success. Engaged to the Widow Pliant, he takes her and her brother Kastril to the Alchemist. He is tricked not only out of his money but also out of the widow.

Kastril, an angry boy, brother of the Widow Pliant. He has come to London to learn to smoke and quarrel. Face uses him to get rid of the skeptic, Surly. He is much taken with old Lovewit, who quarrels well, and consents to his sister's marriage to him.

Pertinax Surly, a sour skeptic who prides himself on being too astute to be tricked. First coming to the Alchemist's as a friend of Sir Epicure, he returns disguised as a Spanish don, planning to save the Widow Pliant from Subtle and Face and to marry her. He is driven away by Kastril and loses the widow to Lovewit.

Tribulation Wholesome, an oily Puritan hypocrite from Amsterdam. Being quite willing to compromise his conscience for profit, he has difficulty restraining his uncompromising companion, Deacon Ananias.

Ananias, a deacon, a hot-tempered zealot who considers even the word "Christmas" a papist abomination. Quarrelsome at first, he finally agrees that counterfeiting is lawful if it is for the benefit of the faithful. Along with Tribulation, he is driven away by Lovewit.

Dame Pliant, an easygoing, attractive young widow, affianced to Drugger but perfectly willing to accept another husband. Subtle and Face both hope to marry her, but the latter decides that it is safer to hand her over to Lovewit, his master.

Lovewit, the master of the house, who has left London because of the plague. His absence sets up the plot, and his return resolves it. He drives away Subtle, Dol, and their victims, but he forgives Jeremy Butler (Face) when Butler arranges a marriage between his master and the rich young widow, Dame Pliant.

ALECK MAURY, SPORTSMAN

Author: Caroline Gordon (1895-1981)
First published: 1934
Genre: Novel

Locale: Virginia, Tennessee, Mississippi, and Missouri
Time: Late nineteenth and early twentieth centuries
Plot: Social realism

Aleck Maury, a Southern sportsman. Trained in the classics by his father and his aunt and further educated at the University of Virginia, he becomes a teacher in several small schools and colleges. His principal loves, however, are fishing and hunting, which he cultivates as fine arts.

James Morris, his uncle, a Virginia planter who introduces Aleck to fox hunting.

Victoria (Aunt Vic) Morris, his aunt, a rigorous disciplinarian and learned woman who broadens and stimulates Aleck in his studies.

Julian Morris, his cousin, who hates studies and loves sports.

Doug Fayerlee, owner of Merry Point.

Sarah Fayerlee, his wife.

Molly Fayerlee, the Fayerlees' younger daughter, whom Aleck marries. She dies a number of years later after an operation.

Richard Maury, Aleck and Molly's son. He enjoys swimming and wrestling rather than hunting and fishing. He is accidentally drowned.

Sarah (Sally) Maury, Richard's younger sister.

Steve, Sarah's husband, a scholar and author.

Rafe, a handyman in the Maury home, a giant black man who teaches young Aleck to hunt raccoons.

Mr. Jones, a mill owner who takes young Aleck fishing and instills in him a lifelong love of the sport.

Harry Morrow, Aleck's assistant at the seminary and later his superior as president of Rodman College.

William Mason, a friend from whom Aleck gets a hunting dog.

Colonel Wyndham, a fishing expert and friend of Aleck.

Jim Buford, a friend with whom Aleck lives for two years after Molly's death.

THE ALEXANDRIA QUARTET

Author: Lawrence Durrell (1912-1990)
First published: 1962
Genre: Novels

Locale: Alexandria, Egypt, and its environs; and an island in
the Cyclades
Time: From shortly before to shortly after World War II
Plot: Psychological realism

Justine, 1957

The narrator, identified as **L. G. Darley** later in the quartet. All the events in this book are filtered through Darley's understanding. After the central events recounted in the novel, Darley moves to an island (with Justine, the daughter of Melissa Artemis and Nessim Hosnani) and begins the write the narrative of *Justine*. He uses his own memories, Justine Hosnani's diary, and another book, *Moeurs*, written about Justine by Justine's former husband, the Albanian-French Jacob Arnauti. Darley recounts how he, a poor schoolteacher and later minor British War Office official and spy, began to have an affair with Justine, grew obsessed with her, and worried that Nessim, Justine's husband, was going to have him killed. Darley experiences guilt over cheating on his lover, Melissa Artemis, and on his friend Nessim. He also believes that Justine loves him. In one memorable sequence, he goes with Nessim to help Justine leave a child brothel, where they find her nearly hysterical.

Justine Hosnani, the title character. Attractive to all, multifaceted, wildly promiscuous, impressionable, and intelligent, Justine is also a staple of literature, the deceptive fatal woman. She begins an affair with Darley after hearing him deliver a lecture on poet C. P. Cavafy. She tells of being raped as child. It appears that her sexual escapades are attempts to re-enact that experience. Before marrying Nessim, she was very poor and apparently lost her one child, a daughter, perhaps as a result of kidnapping. She is Jewish, although she converted to Coptic Christianity upon marrying her second husband, Nessim. She takes part in the Cabal, a study group of the ancient religion of gnosticism. She goes to a kibbutz in Palestine after Paul Capodistria is killed.

Nessim Hosnani, an extremely rich and influential Copt from an old family. Nessim is quiet, efficient, businesslike, and Oxford-educated. He seems to tolerate Justine's many affairs, but Darley grows worried when he sees that Nessim is under great stress. Darley is invited to a duck shoot at Lake Mareotis that Nessim arranges. Justine tells Darley that he may be killed in a shooting "accident."

Balthazar, 1958

S. Balthazar, a Jewish doctor and leader of the Cabal. He narrates approximately half of the novel. Darley sends him the manuscript of *Justine*, and Balthazar returns it with commentary, referred to in the novel as the Great Interlinear. The central events of *Justine* are not as Darley interpreted them. Balthazar argues that Justine did not love Darley; she began the affair with Darley, with the prior consent of Nessim, as a means of spying. The Hosnanis hoped that Darley could inform them if the British knew of the Hosnani conspiracy for the Zionist cause, traitorous in Egypt. The Cabal, with its open meetings and religious focus, was the cover for a cabal of Zionists. Balthazar was the doctor called to the scene of Pursewarden's suicide, which he describes. Nessim arrived before

Melissa Artemis, a Greek cabaret dancer. Although her life is generally sordid, she remains comparatively innocent (as reflected by her ironic last name). In some of her aspects, she is a stock character, the poor but honest prostitute who dies. The former mistress of Cohen, a rich man, she becomes Darley's lover and is deeply distressed by his emotional unfaithfulness, of which she is aware from the start. Later, she has an affair with Nessim and has a child by him, whom Darley adopts. Suffering from malnutrition and other health problems, she dies alone at the end of the novel, of tuberculosis.

George Gaston Pombal, Darley's French flatmate, also a minor consular official.

S. Balthazar, a Jewish doctor and leader of the Cabal, the group that studies gnostic metaphysics.

Clea Montis, an ascetic painter who devotes her life to her craft. She is blonde, benign, and calm, unlike most of the characters in the novel.

Paul Capodistria, an ugly, rich lecher and evidently the man who raped Justine as a child. He is also referred to in the novel as **Da Capo**. He, not Darley, is killed at the duck shoot.

Joshua Scobie, an old British imperialist and ostensibly minor Egyptian police official. He is an alcoholic and a crossdressing homosexual. In his official police capacity, he hires Darley to spy on the Cabal, warning Darley that its members are involved in a conspiracy that will result in war. Darley finds this laughable, knowing that the Cabal is merely a group studying religious metaphysics, but he keeps a straight face and takes the job because he needs the money.

Percy Pursewarden, a successful novelist and minor official. He irritates the blocked writer Darley. Before committing suicide, Pursewarden wills Darley five hundred pounds, which Darley uses to quit teaching, move to an island in the Cyclades where he can live cheaply, and begin to write *Justine*. Darley is mystified by the suicide of Pursewarden, who had seemed content and was successful.

Balthazar and hastily erased a message about the Cabal that Pursewarden had written on his mirror. Balthazar caught sight of a word or two but did not fully understand, being innocent of the conspiracy although aware of Nessim's having political interests and secrets.

Justine Hosnani, who made her flight to the kibbutz to avoid arrest—not, as Darley first supposed, for psychological reasons. Justine is revealed as a political, more than sexual, creature, with a yearning for power and an absolute commitment to the creation of Israel.

Narouz Hosnani, Nessim's younger brother. He is ugly (with a harelip), passionate, fanatical in politics and religion, impulsive, and unwesternized. Narouz falls in love with Clea, who is almost a complete stranger to him. She, virginal, is repulsed. Narouz is violent and skilled with weapons, especially his whip. At a street fair, Narouz falls into a spell under the influence of a fanatic Muslim preacher and sees in a vision what happened to Justine's child: She drowned. Narouz tells this to Nessim, who tells Narouz never to tell Justine.

Percy Pursewarden, who, Balthazar recounts, had an affair with Justine, who doted on him. The novel ends with an old letter from Pursewarden to Clea in which he advocates, in his own satirical way, mercy, understanding, and kindness.

Joshua Scobie, now an important, if secret, public official. He asks Darley's help in maintaining appearances. Scobie asks Darley to take his dress away; he is determined to forgo his

"tendencies." Scobie is later kicked to death at the docks, where he goes, in drag, to cruise for sex. Balthazar, called because he is a doctor, helps remove the dress from the corpse before the press arrives. Scobie is buried with honors according to the story that is concocted about his death; namely, that he fell down some stairs while on official duties.

Leila Hosnani, the mother of Narouz and Nessim, among the first Coptic women to abandon the veil. When young, she dreamed of a Western education and a Western woman's freedoms. After the death of her rich old husband, Falthaus Hosnani, smallpox blights her face, and she returns to the veil and a secluded life.

Mountolive, 1958

Sir David Mountolive, the British ambassador. A conventional third-person limited-omniscient narration follows Mountolive through his diplomatic career, concentrating on his stays in Alexandria. A proper, repressed, and well-mannered young Englishman beginning a career in diplomacy, he goes to Alexandria to improve his Arabic and stays with the Hosnani family. Mountolive is entranced by the overwhelming beauty of Alexandria and Egypt. He becomes close friends with Narouz and Nessim. Mountolive also begins an affair with Leila. Although socially adept and intelligent, he is also callow and inexperienced, and he regrets betraying his host. Leila tells him that her husband, an aged invalid, gave her permission to have an affair with the young man. He is surprised to learn that Leila's attraction to him is based on her comically bookish, romanticized view of the British. At dinner with the family one evening, Mountolive commits a gaffe for which he, a diplomat-in-training, berates himself: He calls the family Muslims. Later, Mountolive leaves Egypt for service elsewhere. He returns as ambassador at a time roughly contemporaneous with the events in *Justine*. He is soon made aware of the Hosnani conspiracy and finds himself torn between duty, which calls for him to ask the Egyptian government to kill Nessim, and friendship with Nessim. Mountolive does not waver: He pressures the Egyptian government to kill Nessim. The king is deathly ill, however, and Nessim, aware of the danger he is in, is able to play for time by bribing the Egyptian minister of the interior, Memlik Pasha.

Falthaus Hosnani, the family patriarch. On hearing Mountolive refer to the Hosnanis as Muslims, he begins a long denunciation of the British. Mountolive receives a history lesson on how the Copts (who are Christians) were, since ancient times, great leaders in Egypt, until the British removed the Copts from power. The old man makes a convincing argument that the British, still harboring the ignorance and prejudice of their crusader forebears, who hated the Copts, distrusted a Christian denomination able to live in peace with Muslims. Thus, the old man's passionate hatred of the British springs from the British colonial policy of excluding Copts from public service. It is clear that Nessim shares his father's views.

Percy Pursewarden, whose story is revealed. Before committing suicide, he not only wrote a message uncovering the conspiracy on his mirror but also wrote a letter describing the Hosnani conspiracy that reaches Mountolive, along with documents from Palestine about arms shipments. Pursewarden had found himself caught between duty to state and friendship with Nessim; he opted to kill himself rather than continue his betrayal of Nessim.

Melissa Artemis, who unwittingly proved to be the link from Cohen to Pursewarden that contributed to the discovery of the conspiracy. Cohen, who loved her pathetically, told her, to impress her, that he was buying German arms and selling them to the Jews of Palestine. Cohen was a member of the Cabal. Presumably unaware of the information's significance, she related it Pursewarden during a tryst.

Narouz Hosnani, who has grown resentful of Nessim's position as the family's man of the world, largely as the result of his falling in love with Clea (who represents to him life beyond the Hosnani country estates). He begins to involve himself in politics, braying revolutionary excesses at secret meetings. Word reaches Nessim that Narouz's wild statements are likely to reach the wrong ears, and Nessim goes to the estate to tell Narouz to be silent. Narouz, drunk, refuses to obey his older brother. Nessim, nearly mad with rage, nevertheless promises himself that he will not harm his brother. One day, however, Narouz goes out for a ride on his horse, mildly surprised that his servant is absent. He becomes aware that someone is trailing him. Confident of his powers, he turns and waits with pistol and whip ready. He is gunned down by assassins. Nessim, at the house, hears the shots and finds Narouz, whose repeated last request is to see Clea.

Memlik Pasha, the minister of the interior, who is put under pressure to kill Nessim but is able to delay as long as the king is too ill to order him to do so. Memlik wishes to delay because Nessim is paying him bribes. Eventually, an aide gives Memlik the idea that Memlik, as leader of the domestic investigation, should "discover" that the British have the wrong Hosnani—that the outspoken Narouz, not Nessim, is the conspirator. By sacrificing Narouz, Memlik is able to satisfy the powers above him and continue to take bribes from Nessim.

Clea, 1960

L. G. Darley, who returns to Alexandria from his island retreat in the last year of World War II. Mnemjian, a barber and

minor character in all the novels, tells Darley what has happened. The conspiracy has collapsed: Justine is under house arrest, and Nessim, who is working as an ambulance driver for the duration, has become poor. Darley visits Justine and discovers his passion for her is gone.

George Gaston Pombal, the sensualist, who has fallen in love with Fosca but not gone to bed with her, a novelty he finds delightful. She is killed when their sailboat comes too close to a warship, and they are fired upon from the ship with a rifle.

Sir David Mountolive, who also has fallen in love, with Liza, Pursewarden's blind sister. Mountolive considers rejecting her because of the impropriety of having a blind ambassadress at social functions, but eventually he accepts his love for her.

S. Balthazar, who is in disgrace for being associated with the Cabal. After a nearly successful suicide attempt resulting from the unrequited love of a worthless actor, he is helped by his friends, especially Mountolive, to return to life and society.

Paul Capodistria, who, it is revealed, faked his own death. He did so because the conspiracy, in which he was involved, was becoming known, and he wished to escape arrest. He has left Egypt.

Clea Montis, who, with a sense of joyful destiny, becomes Darley's lover. They find their love rehabilitating. While on a boating excursion, Balthazar accidentally fires a spear gun. The spear pins Clea's right hand to a submerged wreck. Darley dives in and is forced, to save her, to cut her hand open with a knife. Her hand proves too damaged to be saved, and she is fitted with a prosthesis. She adjusts to it in her usual accepting manner, even with some pleasure when she finds that she is able to paint well with it.

Percy Pursewarden, whose notebooks come into Darley's hands. He finds more satirical attacks on himself. Pursewarden's troubled genius is revealed in the notebooks, and Darley finds himself inspired and enlightened by them. According to Pursewarden's record, Justine's lost daughter was found dead, in a child brothel. The incident was recorded, from Darley's point of view, in *Justine*. Darley reluctantly helps Liza burn Pursewarden's marvelous letters to her, in part to keep the secret that the two lived in incest for some time.

Joshua Scobie, the British imperialist homosexual drunkard, now dead. As a result of confusion in the neighborhood of his name with that of a local Muslim holy figure, Scobie has become a saint, and his bathtub a shrine.

— *Eric Howard*

ALICE ADAMS

Author: Booth Tarkington (1869-1946)
First published: 1921
Genre: Novel

Locale: A small Midwestern town
Time: Early twentieth century
Plot: Social

Alice Adams, a dreamer whose family is not rich enough to send her to college. She tries to attract attention by affected mannerisms. Disappointed in every ambition, she finally stops daydreaming and, reluctantly, enrolls in Frincke's Business College.

Virgil Adams, her father, an employee of the Lamb Wholesale Drug Company and part discoverer of the formula for a special glue. The co-discoverer has died. The failure of Virgil's project to manufacture the glue causes him to have a stroke.

Mrs. Adams, Alice's socially ambitious mother, who nags her husband to make more money but ends up taking in boarders.

Walter Adams, their son, who has stolen three hundred dollars from his employer. He is more interested in gambling with waiters than in dancing with his sister at Mildred's party.

Mildred Palmer, Alice's best friend.

Frank Dowling, a fat, unpopular boy who is the only one attentive to Alice at the dance.

Arthur Russell, a distant relative of the Palmers who is momentarily interested in Alice, then finds her repulsive.

Mr. Lamb, who builds his own glue factory and destroys Virgil Adams' prospects.

Charley Lohr, who brings the Adamses news that the absconding Walter has left town.

ALICE'S ADVENTURES IN WONDERLAND

Author: Lewis Carroll (Charles Lutwidge Dodgson, 1832-1898)
First published: 1865
Genre: Novel

Locale: The dream world of an imaginative child
Time: Victorian era
Plot: Fantasy

Alice, a curious, imaginative, strong-willed, and honest young English girl. She falls asleep by the side of a stream in a meadow and dreams that she follows a White Rabbit down his hole. She has many adventures in a Wonderland peopled by all kinds of strange characters and animals.

The White Rabbit, anxious, aristocratic, dandified. Alice follows him down his hole, which leads to an enchanted house and garden. The White Rabbit is a prime minister of sorts in Wonderland, for he has close contact with the royalty there and carries out their orders, although he does not institute policy.

The Queen of Hearts, the ill-tempered Queen of Wonderland. She constantly demands that everyone who crosses her be beheaded. Fond of croquet, she orders Alice to take part in a game in which flamingoes are used for mallets and hedgehogs for balls. She issues an order for Alice's execution at the end of the book, but the order is never carried out because Alice accuses the Queen and all her company of being only a pack of cards, an assertion that turns out to be true.

The King of Hearts, a timid, kindly man. Although he is completely under his wife's power because of her temper, he manages to pardon all her victims surreptitiously.

The Duchess, another member of royalty in Wonderland, a platitude-quoting, moralizing, ugly old woman who lives in a chaotic house. Deathly afraid of the Queen, she is ordered to be beheaded, but the sentence is never carried out.

The Cook, the Duchess' servant. She flavors everything with pepper, insults her mistress, and throws cooking pans at her.

The Cheshire Cat, the Duchess' grinning cat. Continually vanishing and reappearing, he is a great conversationalist, and he tells Alice much of the gossip in Wonderland.

The Duchess' Baby, a strange, howling, little infant. The baby turns into a pig when the Duchess entrusts it to Alice's care.

The Knave of Hearts, a timid, poetry-writing fellow accused of stealing some tarts that the Queen has made.

The March Hare, the rude host of a mad tea party to which Alice invites herself and then wishes that she had not.

The Mad Hatter, a riddle-making, blunt, outspoken guest at the tea party. He is a good friend of the March Hare, and at the party, the two try to prove to Alice that she is stupid.

The Dormouse, another guest at the tea party. He is a sleepy creature, aroused long enough to recite for Alice and then pushed headfirst into the teapot.

The Gryphon, a mythical creature, half bird, half animal, who escorts Alice to the home of the Mock Turtle so that she may hear the recital of the Turtle's life story.

The Mock Turtle, an ever-sobbing animal. He recites his life's story to Alice and everyone else within earshot.

The Caterpillar, a hookah-smoking insect who perches on the top of a magic mushroom. Officious and easily offended, he tests Alice's intelligence with a series of ridiculous riddles.

Bill, The Lizard, an unfortunate fellow picked by the other animals to go down the chimney of the White Rabbit's house and try to force out Alice, who has assumed gigantic proportions after drinking a magic potion she found on the table.

The Mouse, who greets Alice in the pool of tears that she has made by crying while she was of gigantic size. Now of minute proportions, she is almost overwhelmed by the Mouse, a creature easily offended.

The Lorry,

The Duck,

The Dodo,

The Eaglet,

The Crab, and

The Baby Crab, creatures whom Alice meets in the pool of her tears and who swim around with her.

Father William and

Father William's Son, characters in a poem that Alice recites. The old man, a former athlete, can still balance an eel on his nose, much to the amazement of his curious and impertinent son. The poem is a parody of Robert Southey's "The Old Man's Comforts."

The Pigeon, a bird Alice meets after she has made herself tall by eating part of the Caterpillar's mushroom.

The Fish Footman, the bearer of a note from the Queen inviting the Duchess to play croquet.

The Frog Footman, the impolite servant of the Duchess; his wig becomes entangled with that of the Fish Footman when the two bow in greeting each other.

The Puppy, a playful animal Alice meets while she is in her small state.

The Flamingo, the bird Alice uses for a croquet mallet in the game with the Queen.

The Hedgehog, the animal that acts as the ball in the croquet game.

Five,

Two, and

Seven, three quarrelsome gardeners of the Queen. When Alice meets them, they are painting all the white roses in the garden red, to obliterate the mistake someone had made in ordering white ones.

Elsie,

Lacie, and

Tillie, three sisters in the Dormouse's story. They live at the bottom of a well and exist solely on treacle.

Dinah, Alice's pet cat in real life.

Alice's Sister, the wise older sister who is charmed by Alice's tales of her adventures in Wonderland.

ALL-BRIGHT COURT

Author: Connie Porter (1959-   )
First published: 1991
Genre: Novel

Locale: Lackawanna, New York
Time: The 1960's and 1970's
Plot: Realism

Samuel Taylor, an African American man from Tupelo, Mississippi, who goes north in search of personal freedom and economic betterment. Samuel is a hardworking man, a devoted husband, and a loving father. When he finally admits to himself that his own dreams will never come true, he transfers his hopes to his children.

Mary Kate Bell Taylor, Samuel's wife, also from Tupelo. The daughter of a cook who was a friend and adviser to Samuel, Mary Kate is a caring, dependable person whose love for her husband enables him to face his disappointments. Nevertheless, in the early years of the marriage, when she is physically exhausted from childbearing, trapped in the house, and desperately lonely, Mary Kate very nearly has a mental breakdown. She is saved by her friendship with Venita Reed.

Michael (Mikey) Taylor, their oldest son. Intelligent like both of his parents, he has the benefit of their tutelage and their example. From them, he absorbs high standards of conduct, along with compassion toward the less fortunate. After he is sent to Essex Academy, a school primarily for privileged whites, Mikey finds it hard to relate to the people of All-Bright Court and even to his family.

Venita Reed, a young woman from Mississippi who is Mary Kate's neighbor in All-Bright Court. Heartsick over her failure to bear children, Venita retreats into herself, emerging only when Mary Kate becomes her friend. Twice Venita invests her emotions in children placed in her care, but when she loses both of them, she again retreats, losing contact even with her husband.

Moses Reed, Venita's husband, a hardworking, decent man who loves his wife but is unable to comprehend the depth of her unhappiness. Moses' easygoing, uncomplaining ways cause Samuel to dismiss him contemptuously as an "Uncle Tom." After many years, Moses finally confronts Samuel and forces him to admit how similar the two men and their lives really are. As a result, Moses and Samuel become friends.

— *Rosemary M. Canfield Reisman*

ALL FALL DOWN

Author: James Leo Herlihy (1927-1993)
First published: 1960
Genre: Novel

Locale: Cleveland, Ohio
Time: The late 1950's
Plot: Bildungsroman

Clinton Williams, the viewpoint character and narrator of portions of the story through his journal. He is approximately sixteen years old during most of the action in the novel. Like Holden Caulfield, the protagonist of J. D. Salinger's *The Catcher in the Rye* (1951), he is perceptive and articulate, but he is far more idealistic and gullible. Clinton, a romantic, experiences emotional liberation through his painful epiphany. Although he wants to be a writer, he cannot produce anything except verbatim transcriptions of other people's speech and correspondence because he has not yet learned how to synthesize his experience. The story primarily concerns his liberation from bondage to illusions, accomplished through his insights into his brother Berry-berry's true character. There is a strong suggestion that Clinton's adoration of Berry-berry has homosexual overtones and that the story really is about the disenchanted protagonist's attainment of freedom to form a wholesome heterosexual relationship when he finds an appropriate love object.

Ralph Williams, Clinton's father, who was a political activist and dynamic personality in his youth. He appears to have been emasculated by a dull marriage and his effort to maintain middle-class respectability. He deals in real estate but does not do well at it because of his anticapitalist sentiments and his chronic depression. He is a heavy solitary drinker. He feels despised and rejected because both Clinton and his wife, Annabel, have directed all their love toward the rebellious, charismatic Berry-berry. Ralph stands in sharp contrast to Berry-berry, who has no respect for convention or middle-class morality.

Annabel Williams, Clinton's mother, a drab, unimaginative housewife with an unhealthy emotional attachment to her older son. There is a strong suggestion that she may even have had an incestuous relationship with Berry-berry. At any rate, he loathes and fears her. She is the most symbolic of all the characters in the novel; she represents an unfavorable image of American middle-class women in general. Annabel's unwholesome possessiveness is largely responsible for Berry-berry's cruelty to women and his dread of forming a permanent relationship with a woman. Clinton escapes the same destructive influence because most of his mother's affection is directed at his older brother, who can be regarded as a victim as well as a victimizer.

Berry-berry Williams, Clinton's handsome, predatory older brother, who is about twenty-three years old when most of the events of the novel take place. His unusual first name suggests "beriberi," a serious disease. He is self-centered and incapable of realizing that other people have feelings or exist as independent entities. Berry-berry can be very likable and can project an illusion of human sympathy and affection. It is precisely because he is completely lacking in normal human emotions that he is so fascinating to women: He has learned to mimic affection and sympathy through a natural flair for imitation common to psychopathic personalities. Although Berry-berry is not the hero or the viewpoint character, he is the sun around whom all the other characters revolve, or perhaps a "disease" with which all the other characters are infected.

Echo O'Brien, a virgin in her early thirties. Because she has lived a sheltered life as her invalid mother's nurse and constant companion, she has remained sweet and innocent. Her alarmingly childlike trust in the essential goodness of everyone she encounters makes her a prime target for tragedy. Her wholesomeness provides a striking contrast to the sickness of the members of Clinton's dysfunctional family. Her first name, Echo, suggests that she possesses an instinctive responsiveness and authentic ability to relate to other people, something Berry-berry only projects through mimicry. She is a mirror in which the other characters view their own hypocrisy and unworthiness. Most important, she is the catalyst directly responsible for the change in the relationship between Clinton and Berry-berry.

Shirley, a young prostitute who introduces Clinton to sex and begins the boy's long process of disillusionment with Berry-berry by telling him cold facts about his older brother's parasitical and sadistic behavior. This gentle, generous young woman serves as the novel's only concrete example of the kind of women Berry-berry habitually exploits.

— *Bill Delaney*

ALL FOOLS

Author: George Chapman (c. 1559-1634)
First published: 1605
Genre: Drama

Locale: Italy
Time: The sixteenth century
Plot: Comedy

Gostanzo, a stern Florentine gentleman. He believes his son Valerio to be a shy, industrious farmer and contrasts his virtues with the supposed aberrations of Fortunio, counseling strong punishment for the filial ingratitude of the latter. He is unexpectedly won over by the elaborate schemes of the young people.

Valerio, his son, known to all but his father as a notorious gambler, drinker, and lover. He revels in schemes to gull Gostanzo and Cornelio, who once succeeded in duping him.

Marc Antonio, a mild-tempered gentleman who is ready to forgive his own son for his supposed secret marriage and is quick to intercede wherever he feels others are being too harsh or unjust.

Fortunio, Marc Antonio's older son, a gallant who is enamored of Gostanzo's daughter Bellonora. He is party to all the schemes in the air, although he initiates none of them.

Rinaldo, Fortunio's cynical brother, the intriguer who arranges the elaborate deceptions that enable Fortunio and Valerio to be with their mistresses.

Cornelio, an upstart courtier who appears to be consumed with jealousy of his young wife.

Gratiana, Valerio's bride, a beautiful but penniless young woman.

Bellonora, Fortunio's sweetheart. Her strict father, Gostanzo, keeps her under close watch, until he falls into Rinaldo's trap and gives her the much-desired opportunity to be with her lover.

Gazetta, Cornelio's wife. Chafing under her husband's jealousy, she confesses envy of the young women who have not yet settled down to married life. She entertains herself with Cornelio's friends.

ALL FOR LOVE: Or, The World Well Lost

Author: John Dryden (1631-1700)
First published: 1678
Genre: Drama

Locale: Alexandria, Egypt
Time: The first century B.C.E.
Plot: Tragedy

Mark Antony, a Roman triumvirate who, in his role of leader, is caught between concern for his people and his love for a woman. Antony shows various human traits as he tries to recapture his position of leadership against invading forces, as he accepts the friendship of his faithful officers, as he considers reconciliation with his wife and family, as he is duped by clever antagonistic individuals, and as he is shown incapable of adapting to these various relationships because of his devotion to Cleopatra, his mistress. Not strong enough or discerning enough to determine her motives, Antony dies a failure.

Cleopatra (klee-oh-PA-truh), the queen of Egypt and mistress of Antony. Steadfast in her love, as she convinces him before his death, she is deluded by some of her servants and shows the vulnerability of the great at the hands of the crafty. Cleopatra is victorious over her peers, in that she averts Antony's return to his family. She takes her life to avoid the celebration of victory over Antony's troops, a defeat that prompts Antony's suicide. Cleopatra glories in imminent death as the poison of the asp she has applied to her arm flows through her body.

Alexas (eh-LEHK-suhs), Cleopatra's eunuch, opposed to his queen's and Antony's love. Scheming Alexas uses flattery, chicanery, and lies to influence people. Knowing that Antony's troops are about to be attacked, he encourages the troops to celebrate in honor of Antony's birthday. Learning that Antony has been persuaded by his own officers to defend his position, Alexas connives to have Antony intercepted by Cleopatra as he leaves the city. Alexas also conspires to arouse Antony's jealousy and to cast doubt on Cleopatra's fidelity, and he lies when he tells Antony that Cleopatra has taken her life. Alexas is brought to justice for his perfidy.

Ventidius (vehn-TIH-dee-uhs), Antony's general and faithful follower. Seeing through Alexas' devices, he is able to circumvent some of the disaster intended for his leader. Doubting Cleopatra's motives, Ventidius tries to divert Antony's attention from her. Although he is discerning, Ventidius becomes the tool of Alexas in one of his tricks. Feeling that he has unwittingly betrayed his leader, he tries to make amends

too late. Ventidius takes his own life when he sees Antony dying.

Dolabella (doh-leh-BEH-luh), Antony's friend, who, although faithful, is banished because Antony fears that Cleopatra may fall in love with the handsome young Roman. Dolabella, dedicated to the Roman cause, attempts a reconciliation between Antony and his family. His affinity to Rome and Antony are reflected also in his willingness to see Cleopatra and to say farewell to her for Antony, who, realizing his lack of will, does not see his mistress before he attempts to renew his fight against the invaders. Dolabella's effort to serve is in vain: Antony believes, despite their denials, that Cleopatra and his young follower are in love.

Octavia (ok-TAY-vee-uh), Antony's wife and sister to Octavius, another of the triumvirate. Although she is a woman of charm and determination, Octavia is no match for Cleopatra in the fight for Antony's love. Octavia's announcement that Octavius will withdraw his army if Octavia and Antony are reunited and the sight of his two daughters cause Antony to give serious consideration to a reconciliation, but his contemplation is relatively short-lived. Octavia accepts the failure of her mission and returns to the Roman camp.

Charmion (KAHR-mih-ehn) and

Iras (I-rehs), Cleopatra's maids. Loyal to their queen, they are frequent emissaries to Antony in behalf of Cleopatra. Unwilling to face life without her, Charmion and Iras follow the queen's example and allow themselves to be bitten by the asp that already has poisoned her.

Serapion (seh-RAY-pee-ehn), a priest of Isis. Although involved in the action of the play, he is principally a spokesman for the author. He opens the play with an announcement of the ill omens and what they portend for Egypt; he also speaks last in pronouncing the valediction over Antony and Cleopatra.

Agrippina (a-grih-PI-nuh) and

Antonia, Antony and Octavia's daughters. Their appearance before their father and their delight in seeing him move him momentarily to consider returning to his family.

Myris (MI-rihs), another priest. He discusses with Serapion the events that bode no good.

ALL GOD'S CHILLUN GOT WINGS

Author: Eugene O'Neill (1888-1953)
First published: 1924
Genre: Drama

Locale: Lower Manhattan, New York
Time: Late 1890's to 1915
Plot: Tragedy

Jim Harris, an African American who dreams of becoming a lawyer. The play introduces him at the age of nine and follows his development over the next fifteen years. In the opening scene, he is already in love with Ella Downey, whom he later marries. Jim is ashamed of his race, and his feeling of inferiority prevents him from succeeding.

Ella Downey, a white girl one year younger than Jim. As a child of eight, she admires Jim, but later she reveals a hatred of black people. Although she realizes that Jim is morally superior to her white associates, she can never fully accept her marriage to him. As much as part of her wants Jim to succeed so that he can prove his true worth, another part of her wants him to fail and thus to confirm her belief that African Americans are inferior to whites. This ambivalence drives her insane. Feeling tainted because of her interracial marriage, she refuses to associate with whites, and her bigotry drives potential black friends away.

Hattie Harris, Jim's sister, a teacher in a black school. Proud of her race, Hattie tries to accept Ella and nurse her when she becomes ill, but Ella's racism drives Hattie away. Hattie is somewhat prejudiced and is reluctant to associate with whites.

Mrs. Harris, Jim's mother. Believing in the separation of the races, she regrets Jim's marriage to a white girl. She and Hattie move from lower Manhattan to the Bronx to live exclusively among black people.

Mickey, a white prizefighter the same age as Ella. They are childhood friends and then lovers. Mickey abandons her after she becomes pregnant with his child.

Shorty, a white gangster and another member of the crowd that played with Jim, Joe, and Ella when they were children together. Shorty, who is a pimp, offers to add Ella to his stable of prostitutes when she is struggling financially.

Joe, a black gangster. He cannot understand why his friend Jim is trying to become a lawyer, because he sees them both as suited only for a life on the streets. He underestimates the abilities of black people. He recognizes that Jim wants to use money and education not, like Hattie, to prove that black people are equal to whites but rather somehow to escape from his black heritage.

— Joseph Rosenblum

ALL GREEN SHALL PERISH
(Todo verdor perecerá)

Author: Eduardo Mallea (1903-1982)
First published: 1941
Genre: Novel

Locale: Argentina
Time: The 1930's and early 1940's
Plot: Existentialism

Ágata Cruz (AH-gah-tah krews), the protagonist, a once strikingly beautiful, fair-skinned, dark-haired woman, grown pallid and harder-featured from the frustration of her barren fifteen years of married life on unproductive farms in southern Argentina. She was reared in a similarly drab setting by her widowed father, developed a need to escape, and for that purpose accepted the marriage proposal of Nicanor, whom she did not love. Life with Nicanor is even less sociable than it was with her father, stifling her inner passion. When she is thirty-five years old, Ágata's anguish reaches a point of crisis. Seeking to end it all, she spends a freezing winter night outdoors and leaves doors and windows open during winter when Nicanor is inside delirious with fever. After his death from freezing, she falls into a brief affair with Sotero. With him, Ágata is able to get out of her intense, tortured subjectivity and thereby knows fleeting happiness. When Sotero callously discards her, though, she again takes up her doomed quest for self. It leads her back to the town in which she was reared, where she ends up as a street person, roaming in closed concentration on her personal void. Ágata's suicidal tendencies are restrained by the fear that the emptiness of her earthly existence will persist after death.

Nicanor Cruz (nee-KAH-nohr), a dry, unimaginative landowner who has sunk into defeat and resentment. A failure as a farmer, Nicanor has to abandon his estate for a smaller, even less productive farm. He is passionless and uncommunicative as a husband, and his relationship with Ágata breeds only bitterness. Nicanor grows dark-skinned from contact with the sun and soil, and he seems as sterile as his land. His stoic attitude brings on his final illness, pneumonia, as he walks over his dead land obsessively for an entire day in a chilling rain.

Dr. Reba (reh-bah), Ágata's father, an inept medical practitioner. He was a reader of the Bible and a sententious reciter of its proverbs but was nevertheless an atheist. A Swiss immigrant, Dr. Reba married an Argentine woman who died at the birth of Ágata, their only child. He never remarried, and he lived a life of solitude alleviated less by his poor professional efforts than by his exercise as a tavern conversationalist. He communicated better with his tavern companions than with his daughter, who loved him despite the gulf that separated them. In later life, Dr. Reba drank heavily. He died some years before the action of the novel.

Dr. Sotero (soh-TEH-roh), a worldly, opportunistic lawyer who seduces Ágata when she is a widow living in a coastal city of Bahía Blanca. Handsome, deep-voiced, good-humored, and self-assured, Sotero claims to like diffident women such as Ágata, who completely subordinates herself to him. Sotero's mysterious business dealings for a Buenos Aires entity called the Organization take him out of Bahía

Blanca and give him an excuse to leave Ágata.

Ema de Volpe (EH-mah deh VOHL-peh), a frivolous but also strong-willed woman who attaches herself to Ágata in Bahía Blanca. She is open about her own promiscuous life and does her best to wheedle intimate information out of the reticent Ágata. Conceited, perpetually overdressed, and having an exotic air about her, Ema calls herself a courtesan. She spends her evenings with Sotero, his business associate Romo, and three sisters, who are glib and slack like herself. She intro-duces Ágata to this group and encourages her to join them in their soirees.

Dr. Romo (ROH-moh), a short, heavy, sarcastic lawyer and associate of Sotero. Romo addresses everyone in an insinuat-ing tone, and he habitually and cryptically calls Sotero "Syco-phant" in front of the others. Romo visibly disdains Ágata for her docility. He is vulgar and has a taste for off-color jokes.

— *John Deredita*

ALL HALLOWS EVE

Author: Charles Williams (1886-1945)
First published: 1945
Genre: Novel

Locale: London, England
Time: October, 1945
Plot: Allegory

Lester Furnival, who lives beyond the grave. At the age of twenty-five, Lester, Richard's wife, is killed in a freak acci-dent. Newly dead, she haunts the earthly London in its inter-twining with the Eternal City. Lester's earthly marital love had been marred by occasional bitterness and anger, which she now must recognize and reform. Although she is not a com-mitted Christian, her romantic nature, including her passion and the will to love, carry over to the next life sufficiently so that she can repent and develop her spiritual powers. When her once-scorned schoolmate, Betty Wallingford, is nearly victim-ized in a murder plot, Lester substitutes herself to save her friend. Ultimately, her love proves powerful enough to destroy the evil Simon the Clerk and assist her husband in foiling Simon's conspiracy to achieve world domination.

Betty Wallingford, a timid and docile woman who seems merely the puppet of her evil parents, Simon the Clerk and the adulteress Lady Sara Wallingford. Her parents practice black magic, using Betty's lucid dreams, out-of-body experiences, and automatic speech as an intelligence service between the worlds of the living and the dead. There is an assertive, spir-ited, joyful side to Betty, the outcome of her secret Christian baptism by a saintly nurse. When Jonathan Drayton falls in love with her, Betty finds in her own loving reciprocity the will to resist and eventually to overcome the demoniac forces that conspire to ruin her and keep her and Jonathan apart.

Jonathan Drayton, a master painter, controversial colorist, and Christian artist. He is a type of romantic visionary. Like Dante's metaphors of light, which provide mediation between the physical and intellectual realms of animal nature and spirit, Jonathan's colors are the incarnation of heavenly light. His ardent love for Betty and religious faith enable him to see Simon's true nature and assist in Betty's deliverance from his evil spells.

Simon the Clerk, a type of Antichrist and necromancer. He lusts for absolute power and earns himself a number of mind-less, idolatrous human disciple-slaves, the insects of Jonathan's insightful painting. Finally, he and his tyrannical hopes are drowned in a mysterious rain, symbolic of the com-bined power of human and divine love.

Evelyn Mercer, another victim of the freak accident that kills Lester. She accompanies Lester through the dimly illumi-nated streets of the London/Eternal City habitat of the newly dead. Evelyn (a name evoking "evil") possesses no loving nature upon which to flourish. Her incessant, meaningless chatter, her devotion to malicious gossip, and her petty games of one-upmanship against the meek Betty mark Evelyn as belonging to the paltry and boring dredges of the demoniac powers. Drawn to the illusory glory of service to Simon, Evelyn betrays Lester and is destroyed by the flood of grace at the novel's climax.

Richard Furnival, the bereaved husband of Lester, a friend and astute critic of artist Jonathan Drayton. He had been a considerate husband but was insensitive to the sacrificial na-ture of love. Richard holds an important post in the govern-ment. His ever expanding consciousness of the forces of good and evil in the lives of Jonathan, Simon, Betty, and his ghost-wife Lester empower him to foil Simon's conspiracy to achieve world domination.

— *Diane Brotemarkle*

ALL MEN ARE BROTHERS
(Shui-hu chuan)

Author: Unknown; associated with Shih Nai-an (c. 1290-1365)
First transcribed: c. fifteenth century
Genre: Novel

Locale: China
Time: Thirteenth century or earlier
Plot: Adventure

Sung Chiang, the greatest of the warrior chiefs and the principal instrument for uniting the many robber bands. A scribe and a poet, he receives divine inspiration and becomes the sworn leader of 107 other chieftains. While he avenges wrongs done him by warring chieftains, he is not as blood-thirsty as are the pagan robbers.

Commander Kao and
Commander Kao's Son, the chief antagonists of Sung Chiang and the other robber chiefs. The commander and his son are evil, dictatorial, and lascivious usurpers. The son lusts

for a magistrate's wife, and because of this another man is falsely accused, branded, and exiled. The bands finally unite to overthrow their military oppressors.

Wu Sung, a giant of a man who kills a tiger in hand-to-hand combat. His brother's wife tries to seduce him. Later, she takes a lover and murders her husband. Wu Sung then kills the two lovers.

Ch'ai Chin, a lord of one of the four provinces who befriends the most valorous of the robber chiefs and protects them from Kao. When captured, he is saved by magic.

Li K'uei, the most loyal of all the chieftains as well as the most vengeful. Gentle in some ways, he insists that his aged mother be brought to their lair, mourns her death from a tiger attack, and bravely kills all the tigers. He causes his commander a great deal of trouble because of his headstrong nature. He often rights wrongs and saves his friend Ch'ai Chin.

Lu Ta, who in protecting a girl is forced to become the priest Lu Chi Shen. He causes his abbot so much trouble that he is deported, largely because of his drunkenness, but he helps bring together the village lord and the robber chief, Li Chung. He opposes Kai and prevents the execution of a military instructor. He is much admired by village lords, robber chiefs, and military leaders.

Ch'ao Kai, one of the most resourceful and shifty of the robber chiefs, himself a lord. He starts his career by stealing birthday gifts from his governor, with the help of a teacher and a magician. He flees his territory and sets up as chief among robbers, and he takes in refugees. When his band is attacked by the hated Chun family, Ch'ao Kai is killed. The robbers later conquer the Chun family and avenge his death. Sung Chiang follows Ch'ao Kai as chieftain.

Tai Chung, a jailer who has the ability to walk three hundred miles a day. He befriends the captured Sung Chiang and manages to forge release papers for him. Through a mixup, he gets his own death papers; he is freed by his friends the robbers, whom he promptly joins as a valuable scout.

Shi Wen Kung, a military instructor in the employ of the hated Chun family, chief antagonists after the death of Kao. A braggart warrior, he eludes the band and nearly succeeds in killing the robber leader, but he is finally captured by Lu Chun I.

Kung Sun Sheng, a hermit magician twice called to aid in the bandit coalition. He joins in the conspiracy to rob Governor Liang, drugging the guard so that Ch'ao Kai can steal the treasure. Later, by countermagic, he enables Ch'ai Chin to escape a magic spell.

ALL MEN ARE ENEMIES

Author: Richard Aldington (1892-1962)
First published: 1933
Genre: Novel

Locale: England, Italy, Austria, and France
Time: 1900-1914, 1919, and 1926-1927
Plot: Bildungsroman

Antony Clarendon, a sensitive, idealistic youth. He was reared in a traditional English upper-class home, its values so secure he assumed that this contented and harmonious world would be eternal. During European travels, he falls in love with Katha, an Austrian girl, whose innocent passion satisfies his quest for beauty. All of his idyllic expectations are shattered by his experiences as an officer during the terrible battles of 1916. Overwhelmed by postwar conditions and in despair that he cannot find Katha, he becomes cynical and self-destructive. He resolves, without love, to marry Margaret, a sophisticated woman of his own class, and pretends to enjoy the social round expected of him. Her father makes him the well-paid director of the family company. Soon his whole nature rebels against this empty routine, which thwarts his spiritual principles. He separates from his wife and wanders idly, until by chance he again encounters Katha. In the mutuality of their renewed love, he finds contentment.

Margaret Clarendon, Antony's wife. She is a typical product of her class, elegant and superficial. Completely fulfilled by her role as wife and hostess, she never questions the values of her upbringing. Her unthinking acceptance of the social patterns she has inherited strikes Antony as selfish arrogance. Insensitively, she cannot comprehend why he does not relish the wealthy comfort she provides. When she cannot and will not appreciate his aesthetic yearning for simpler, less materialistic virtues, he rejects her and the world she exemplifies.

Katharina (Katha), an Austrian girl who meets Antony on a romantic Italian island, where they have a passionate youth-

ful affair and plan a loving future. Their plans are disrupted by the declaration of war. During the war and the economic dislocation of its aftermath, she suffers such poverty that she is driven to prostitution until she finds a wretched, low-paying job. She retains her romantic dreams of being reunited with Antony and rediscovering their love. She personifies Antony's idealism and love of beauty and lives to share his yearning for a life free from the dictates of the snobbery of the business world.

Henry Clarendon, Antony's father. He is a dedicated amateur scientist and an atheist. His affection is limited by a cold pedantic manner and his grievance that his son is opposed to the scientific studies in which he delights. Antony receives guidance in religion and art from his mother. Her early death leaves both men bereft.

Henry Scrope, a wealthy neighbor whose distinguished family has served England at the highest levels of government for generations. He is too independent to follow that path, preferring independent explorations in remote regions. He has a major influence on Antony; his cavalier attitudes and extravagant ideas represent to Antony a valuable part of the human spirit that is endangered by modernity.

Stephen Crang, a gifted man with a brilliant mind. His family poverty is too extreme to allow him the education he deserves, so he accepts a subordinate teaching post. This unfairness so embitters him that he becomes viciously militant and condemns the entire capitalist system, which he blames for his deprivation. The war gives him the opportunity to escape the constrictions imposed by class. He changes his beliefs, modifies his accent, and becomes a willing beneficiary of the system he once rejected.

Robin Fletcher, an optimistic and idealistic young novelist who befriends Antony in Paris. Imprisoned during the war for his pacifist beliefs, he becomes a rabid Communist. He spitefully repudiates all traces of behavior that he can excoriate as "bourgeois." He changes Crang's life.

Richard Waterton, a disabled soldier. His war wound prevents him from returning to the stage or developing his skill as a sculptor, but, without despairing, he retains his generous and gentle spirit. He goes with Antony on a trip to North Africa, during which his kindly manner and quiet good sense guide Antony toward his decision to reject his marriage and his London life.

Walter Cartwright, a high-ranking civil servant who would have made an ideal husband for Margaret, because he shares her social values completely. He is handsome, somewhat pompous, openly ambitious, and utterly incapable of comprehending Antony's objections to the business world and its attendant social pretensions that satisfy him so well. He calls Antony's decision to escape "childish folly."

Julian, Margaret's young brother. Antony at first is drawn to him, believing there exists in Julian a potential for a genuine appreciation of life in its most humane mode. As he grows up, Julian, to Antony's dismay, willingly accepts the standards of his peers and becomes a typical member of his class, his only priorities being earning money and promotion, because these are the measures of success.

Evelyn, Antony's cousin. As an adolescent, she stays with his family, and her youthful, slim body wakens him to his first experience of gently tender sexuality. She remains Antony's sweetest memory until she returns to London after years in India as the wife of a senior army officer. To Antony's horror, she has taken on all the superior racist attitudes of a bigoted and self-satisfied colonial settler. Her manner appalls him and betrays the old dream, which she has long forgotten.

Babbo,

Mama, and

Filomena, the Italians who own the hotel in Aeaea where the love between Antony and Katha begins and is rediscovered. They are immensely loving, eager, and attentive toward the young couple and become, for a time, a kind of chorus as the lovers' passion develops.

— John F. Povey

ALL MY SONS

Author: Arthur Miller (1915-   )
First published: 1947
Genre: Drama

Locale: An American town
Time: Late 1940's
Plot: Psychological realism

Joe Keller, a middle-aged factory owner of working-class background. He is a plain, inarticulate man with a certain peasant shrewdness. His values are simple: work and family. His purpose in life is to pass on his business to his surviving son, Chris. His moral simplicity, however, is his undoing. During World War II, he knowingly authorized the shipment of cracked cylinder heads to the Army air force; the defective parts caused the deaths of twenty-one pilots. Although imprisoned and brought to trial, he avoided conviction by shifting the blame to his hapless partner, Steve Deever. Although he is accepted by his neighbors, they do not doubt his guilt, nor did his son Larry, who, ashamed of his father's actions, committed suicide during the war. Only his son Chris believes he is innocent. Joe is forced to face his responsibility when Larry's former girlfriend, Ann Deever, now about to marry Chris, gives the Kellers Larry's suicide letter. Realizing that his actions caused Larry's death and that the twenty-one pilots are as much his sons as Larry (he refers to them as "all my sons" in his last speech), Joe shoots himself.

Kate Keller, the fiftyish wife of Joe Keller. She superstitiously clings to the hope that her son Larry, who disappeared during the war and is assumed to be dead, will return. This false hope complicates her surviving son's plan to marry Ann Deever. To Kate, accepting the marriage means that Larry will never come back; she therefore opposes the marriage and tries to get rid of Ann. Her denial of Larry's death is rooted in her knowledge of her husband's guilt. In her mind, Larry's death is linked to the pilots' deaths; denying the reality of his death is her way of denying her husband's responsibility for the deaths

of the others. Her denial is shattered by Ann, who, to save her future happiness with Chris, reluctantly shows her Larry's suicide note.

Chris Keller, Joe's thirty-two-year-old, sensitive, and intellectual son. He works for his father's company, which someday will be his. A World War II veteran whose combat experience has left him with a strong sense of responsibility for others, he is an idealist, though rather naïve. He loves his father, causing him to ignore his suspicions about his father's guilt. He loves his mother, which casts a shadow over his desire to marry Ann. He is forced to choose between family responsibility and his moral idealism, which transcends family concerns. Unlike his father, he acknowledges obligations beyond the family. When confronted with his father's guilt, his moral idealism demands that he reject his father, which drives Joe to suicide.

Ann Deever, the attractive, twenty-six-year-old daughter of Joe's former partner and neighbor, Steve Deever, whom she has not seen since his imprisonment. She was once Larry's girlfriend but now is in love with Chris, who invited her back to her old neighborhood so he could propose to her. Her desire to marry him over Kate's objections causes her to reveal Larry's suicide note to Kate as a means of proving that he is dead.

Jim Bayliss, a doctor and the Kellers' neighbor. His idealism is periodically encouraged by Chris. Like Chris, he must choose between family responsibilities and other, greater, values. He would like to do medical research but cannot support his family on the salary it would pay; although he is a successful doctor, he has compromised his idealism. A close friend of the Kellers and particularly of Chris, he has guessed Joe's guilt.

Sue Bayliss, Jim's wife. A practical, witty woman approaching middle age, she is threatened by Jim's stifled idealism. She too is aware of Joe's guilt and finds Chris's idealism shallow. She asks Ann to not live close to them after she marries Chris, so Chris will no longer encourage her husband's interest in medical research.

George Deever, Ann's impulsive and short-tempered brother. A lawyer, he comes to the Kellers' home after visiting his embittered father in prison and realizing that Joe has destroyed his father. He tries to dissuade Ann from marrying Chris. He is almost reconciled with the Kellers, but Kate inadvertently reveals that Joe authorized the shipment of defective parts. He again asks Ann not to marry into the family that destroyed their family; when she refuses, he leaves.

Lydia Lubey, a onetime girlfriend of George Deever and the wife of Frank. She is a vibrant, beautiful woman who laughs easily. Her brief reunion with George at the Kellers shows how she too has settled for less than the ideal. She is a living reminder to George of what he lost when he went away to war; George is her reminder that she has married someone foolish and second-rate.

Frank Lubey, a foolish, insensitive, and balding haberdasher who is Lydia's husband. Although only thirty-two years old, he managed to avoid military service in the war. He foolishly encourages Kate's superstition-fueled hope of Larry's return by presenting her with a horoscope "proving" that Larry did not die because the stars were "favorable" to him the day he was reported missing. His marriage to the vivacious Lydia during the war reveals that he, like Joe Keller, profited while others died.

— Lloyd R. Thompson

ALL OUR YESTERDAYS
(Tutti i nostri ieri)

Author: Natalia Ginzburg (1916-1991)
First published: 1952
Genre: Novel

Locale: Italy
Time: Late 1930's through the end of World War II
Plot: Domestic realism

Anna, a plump, pale girl of fourteen, the younger girl in her family. On the day her father dies, she meets Giuma, the boy across the street. Although she ostensibly prefers playing with her girlfriends, she is drawn to this social superior and begins to play with him, or rather becomes the object of his imaginative play, every day. He talks to her, tells her endless fascinating stories, and even ties her to a tree. In later years, she enjoys hearing him recite poems by Eugenio Montale and eating ice cream with him at the Paris café. They imagine themselves part of the revolution, shooting and escaping over rooftops. At the age of sixteen, Anna finds herself pregnant, but Giuma refuses to marry her because of her youth and the war. Instead, he gives her one thousand lire, which he has saved to buy a boat, for an abortion. Frightened, she tells her plight to Cenzo Rena, an old family friend, who offers to keep her secret and marry her. Anna thus becomes the wife of the savior of the southern village of Borgo San Costanzo, where she gives birth to a daughter and gradually becomes sympathetic to the hard life of the peasants. She supports her husband's revolutionary activities and nurses him through a life-threatening illness. After he finally gives his life for the peasants, she, like her friends and family members, faces the future at the end of the war with courage and hope.

Cenzo Rena (CHIHN-zoh RAY-nah), a country gentleman, world traveler, and friend of Anna's father. A tall, big man with a hairy face and graying mustache, he is almost forty-eight at the time he marries Anna. A practical and generous man, he lives in an old family home high on a hill above a peasant village in southern Italy. The peasant men seek his company and advice as a revered friend and protector. He works for the improvement of their living conditions and teaches them that in a war there are no real winners. After a fugitive hiding in his cellar shoots a German, he gives himself to the Nazis and Fascists to obtain the release of ten hostages. He is shot in the village square, but he leaves to the villagers a legacy of fervor for political equality and the desire to end their cycle of poverty and misery.

Giuma (jee-EW-mah), Anna's childhood friend and the father of her child, a boy with wolflike teeth who is spoiled and rich. After having gone to school in Switzerland, he returns to Italy at the beginning of the war, a handsome and healthy seventeen-year-old. Although he despises Fascism, he will risk going to war. To everyone's surprise and his own disgrace, he fails his high school examinations and returns to school a gloomy and silent young man who reads the works of Søren Kierkegaard rather than those of Montale. Later, in Turin, he studies commercial sciences and pursues philosophy on his own. He contemplates suicide but miraculously escapes death during an air raid shortly after having apologized to Anna for making her suffer. After the war, he overcomes his guilt through psychoanalysis and marries an American physician whom he meets in Switzerland. Together, they propose to bring about socialist reforms at the soap factory he has inherited from his father.

Ippolito (ihp-POHL-ih-toh), Anna's brother and the loyal son of a revolutionary theorist who dies of lung cancer before the war begins. As an adolescent, he keeps a flea-ridden dog at the family's summer home and roams the countryside carrying a gun. He has a dry, smooth, thin, white face and a look of world-weariness. He does not like girls or the ordinary pleasures of youth. During his father's illness, he serves him as a slave, taking dictation, typing memoirs, reading *Faust* to him, and caring for his physical needs in the face of verbal abuse. After his father's death, he develops a close friendship with his neighbor Emanuele, the elder son of a soap manufacturer. They become pedantic provincial intellectuals who secretly read subversive works and talk about revolution. Expecting a police raid one evening, they furtively burn a bundle of newspapers but never hear from the authorities concerning their vague ideology. When Italy enters the war on Germany's side after the fall of France, Ippolito, sitting in the public gardens, commits suicide with his father's revolver.

Giustino (jih-ews-TEE-noh), Anna's younger brother, who ultimately fights with the partisans in Russia.

Concettina (kon-cheh-TEE-nah), Anna's older sister, who has many suitors but marries a Fascist and flees Italy to protect her baby during the war.

— *Janie Caves McCauley*

ALL QUIET ON THE WESTERN FRONT
(Im Westen nichts Neues)

Author: Erich Maria Remarque (Erich Paul Remark, 1898-1970)
First published: 1929; serial form, 1928
Genre: Novel

Locale: France and Germany
Time: World War I
Plot: Historical realism

Paul Bäumer (powl BOY-mehr), a nineteen-year-old soldier in the German army during World War I. Because he has been drafted so young, he wonders what he will be able to do to earn a living if he ever becomes a civilian again. In a battle, he stabs a French soldier and then, filled with remorse, tries to relieve the dying man's pain. When his conscience hurts him afterward, his comrades tell him that he has committed no crime. As the war drags on and more of his comrades fall, Paul becomes lonely and philosophical, but the meaning of the war still eludes him. One day in October, 1918, a quiet day on the Western front shortly before the war's end, he is killed by a stray bullet.

Albert Kropp, a German soldier, one of Paul's comrades. He loses a leg and is jealous of Paul, who, though wounded, loses no limbs.

Müller (MYEWL-ur), a German soldier, a comrade of Paul. He gets Kemmerich's boots when the man is killed. Later, at his death, the boots go to Paul.

Leer, a German soldier, one of Paul's comrades.

Stanislaus Katczinsky (STAH-nihs-lows kaht-SHIHNS-kee), a German soldier nicknamed **Kat**. When he is wounded, Paul tries to rescue him, only to have Kat killed just before they reach safety.

Tjaden (TJAH-dehn), a German soldier. He is punished for insulting Corporal Himmelstoss but feels that the chance to insult the corporal was well worth the punishment.

Haie Westhus (HI-a WAST-hews), a German soldier killed while Paul is on leave.

Detering (DAY-teh-rihng), one of Paul's comrades, a farmer before the war.

Kemmerich, one of Paul's comrades. He has a fine pair of boots that his friend Müller takes when he dies.

Corporal Himmelstoss (HIHM-mal-stohs), a petty martinet who treats his soldiers cruelly.

Frau Bäumer, Paul's mother. She saves her son's favorite foods from her meager rations so that he can have them when he is on leave. She is dying of cancer.

Herr Bäumer, Paul's father.

Erna Bäumer, Paul's sister.

ALL THAT FALL

Author: Samuel Beckett (1906-1989)
First published: 1957
Genre: Drama

Locale: County Dublin, Ireland
Time: The 1950's
Plot: Absurdist

Mrs. Rooney, a woman in her seventies in poor health, weighing more than two hundred pounds. Mrs. Rooney's trip to meet her husband at the railway station on his birthday is a long, slow journey full of chance meetings with a variety of characters. She represents the human condition, and her dragging feet suggest the difficulty of making one's way through life. Mrs. Rooney mourns the loss of her child Minnie, and she is philosophical about the brevity of existence in her remarks about the chicken killed on the road. She tries to converse with the various people she meets but ends up estranging them, suggesting modern people's inability to communicate. Mrs. Rooney is obsessed with sex, and many of her remarks carry sexual innuendo. She is caring and concerned for the health and well-being of those she meets. She announces the source of the play's title in Psalm 145, which provides the text for the Sunday service: "The Lord upholdeth all that fall and raiseth up all those that be bowed down." The quotation prompts laughter in Mr. and Mrs. Rooney, showing

their skepticism that they, as the "bowed down," will someday be raised up.

Mr. Rooney, the blind husband of Mrs. Rooney. Always in bad humor, Mr. Rooney is surprised by his wife's appearance at the train station on his birthday. He is preoccupied with counting, which he sees as one of the few satisfactions in life. When he and his wife are taunted by children on the road, he confesses an urge to kill a child, especially Jerry, the boy who guides him home from the station. His job is mundane and repetitious, and he expresses a desire to leave it. Chronically ill, he represents an urge toward death, unsure of how old he is and whether he will be alive on Monday.

Christy, a carter who meets Mrs. Rooney on the road. He is walking beside a cartload of dung, which he offers to Mrs. Rooney, suggesting that the ride down the road of life may be like a ride on a dung cart. Mrs. Rooney tells Christy that she speaks only in simple words but often thinks that her way of speaking is bizarre.

Mr. Tyler, a retired bill-broker. He meets Mrs. Rooney on the road and stops when he realizes that his bicycle tire has gone flat, suggesting that for him, too, the journey down the road of life is difficult. Mrs. Rooney falls into a fit of mourning for her dead child, but when he attempts to console her, she interprets his consolation as a sexual advance, and he rides away.

Mr. Slocum, clerk of the racecourse. Mrs. Rooney calls him an old admirer. He offers her a lift in his motorcar, but they are barely able to fit her inside. Mr. Slocum's dry wit responds to Mrs. Rooney's suggestive remarks with literal answers. He carelessly runs over a chicken on the road, prompting Mrs. Rooney's remark on life's brevity and foreshadowing the death of the child under the wheel of the train.

Tommy, a porter at the railway station. He helps Mrs. Rooney out of the Slocum motorcar, a maneuver that intimates parturition.

Mr. Barrell, the stationmaster, who is nearing retirement. He is impatient with Tommy and irritable with Mrs. Rooney, who questions him about the lateness of the train.

Miss Fitt, a lady in her thirties who professes to be very religious. She recognizes people only in church, and her charity is limited; she has to be coaxed to help Mrs. Rooney up to the platform. She describes herself as dark and "alone with her maker." She represents the inability of religious people to function in the world.

Jerry, a small boy who is hired by Mr. Rooney to lead him home from the train station. He runs after Mr. Rooney to return the ball he believes was left by him on the train. From Jerry, Mrs. Rooney learns that a child was killed on the tracks, causing the train's delay.

Female Voice and

Dolly, a woman and her daughter at the train station. They laugh at Mrs. Rooney and Miss Fitt.

— Louise Flavin

ALL THE KING'S MEN

Author: Robert Penn Warren (1905-1989)
First published: 1946
Genre: Novel

Locale: The Southern United States
Time: Late 1920's and early 1930's
Plot: Social realism

Willie Stark, called "**the Boss**," the governor of the state. A relentless, unyielding man, Willie has the capacity and the will to break anyone who opposes him. Often ruthless, he is not entirely bad, but his dictatorial powers grow until he is the leader of a powerful political machine. Nevertheless, he does more for the ordinary people of his state than did his more aristocratic predecessors. By improving schools, roads, and hospitals, he leaves these things behind him as monuments after his death. At last, even Jack Burden realizes that there was a streak of greatness in Stark.

Jack Burden, the narrator and Willie Stark's factotum. Although a capable man, Burden has spells he calls the "Great Sleep." During these periods, he becomes completely indifferent to what he is doing at the time. While attempting to finish his Ph.D. dissertation, he went into the "Great Sleep"; as a result, the degree was never completed. A cynical man, he realizes after Willie's death the hidden greatness in the "Boss's" character. Somehow, this realization makes Jack feel better about himself and the rest of humankind.

Anne Stanton, Jack Burden's former sweetheart and the daughter of an earlier governor. After meeting Willie Stark, Anne becomes his mistress, thus bringing destruction to him and to her brother Adam. After Stark's death, she marries Burden.

Adam Stanton, Anne's idealistic brother. A famous, dedicated surgeon, Adam represents, in many ways, the aristocratic past. His work is his life; money and fame mean little to him. Feeling that his sister has been ruined by a ruthless dictator, Adam shoots Willie and loses his own life in the process.

Judge Irwin, Jack Burden's real father. A hawk-visaged, still handsome old man, he has made one major error in his

life: Through bribery, he managed to obtain a high-paying job; in this way, he was able to pay off pressing debts, at the same time causing the death of the man whom he replaced. By doing so, he paved the way for his own downfall. When Jack discovers this indiscretion, the seemingly incorruptible old man commits suicide.

Sadie Burke, Governor Stark's hard-bitten, profane secretary. Feeling betrayed by Willie, the jealous woman has Tiny Duffy tell Adam Stanton about Stark's affair with Stanton's sister. No longer able to tolerate Willie's amorous dalliance with other women, she causes the death of two men—Adam and Willie.

Robert "Sugar-Boy" O'Sheean, Willie Stark's devoted chauffeur and bodyguard. He causes Jack many uneasy moments because of his fast, though expert, driving. He kills Adam after the latter shoots Willie.

Tiny Duffy, the shrewd lieutenant governor and Willie Stark's rotund foil. Biding his time, Tiny tells Adam that Anne Stanton is Willie's mistress. In this way, the grossly fat Duffy gets revenge for years of ridicule. Although he becomes governor after Stark's death, Tiny's political future is in doubt.

Sam MacMurfee, Willie Stark's slick political opponent.

Tom Stark, Willie's arrogant, football-playing son, who repays his father's pride with disdain.

Lucy Stark, Willie's long-suffering wife, a former schoolteacher.

Mrs. Ellis Burden, Jack's mother and Judge Irwin's mistress.

Miss Littlepaugh, the sister of the man whose job at the power company Judge Irwin got through bribery, thereby causing the man to commit suicide.

ALL THE PRETTY HORSES

Author: Cormac McCarthy (1933-   )
First published: 1992
Genre: Novel

Locale: East Texas and Mexico
Time: 1949
Plot: Western

John Grady Cole, the novel's protagonist, who grows up on an East Texas ranch. When his grandfather dies, he decides to seek a life of adventure in Mexico, taming horses and living free. Cole has a strong sense of the dignity of life and of his own integrity. These qualities are strongly challenged when he falls in love with a young Mexican woman; her family forbids him to court her. When he does so anyway, he is hunted down as a criminal, becoming involved in a case of alleged horse theft. Sorely challenged by men who share neither his reverence for life nor his hardy self-reliance, Cole manages to maintain his humanity and to survive largely on his own terms.

Rawlins, Cole's cousin and close friend. They team up to explore Mexico. Rawlins is something of a cowboy-philosopher, constantly asking Cole his views on the nature of life. Whereas Rawlins is loquacious, Cole is taciturn, exhibiting his ideas in action rather than in dialogue. Rawlins, like Cole, is a young man testing his convictions in an alien environment. Although he does not always agree with Cole, he sticks by his friend, valuing loyalty more than any other virtue.

Blevins, a young boy whom Cole and Rawlins meet on the road to Mexico. Rawlins is suspicious of Blevins, who keeps following him and Cole. Cole seems indifferent to Blevins but defends him when Rawlins attacks the boy for various indiscretions and reckless behavior. Both Cole and Rawlins suspect that Blevins is a runaway, and Rawlins is certain that Blevins

stole a horse and is on the run. As Blevins' fate becomes closely tied to that of Cole and Rawlins, Blevins' hapless behavior becomes Cole's problem and an index of his tolerance and humanity.

Duena Alfonsa, the aunt of Alejandra, the young Mexican woman with whom Cole falls in love. Duena Alfonsa admires Cole, whose good manners and respectful demeanor convince her that he will listen to her warning to stay away from Alejandra. Duena Alfonsa confides in Cole her own disappointments, explaining at the same time much of the history of modern Mexico, the efforts to reform it, and the corruption it has not been able to control. Her words are meant to warn Cole that he is dealing with a culture that has no respect for his own principles.

Alejandra, the strong-willed Mexican girl who falls in love with Cole. She realizes that she and Cole are taking a big risk and that her family will never approve of him, even though he has served them faithfully and wants to do the right thing by her. She is powerless to prevent Cole's conflict with her family, and she is forced to promise not to see him again. Cole endures enormous physical and mental torment, separating him from Alejandra. He braves a return to the Mexican ranch, and she breaks her vow and sees him again, acknowledging his uncompromising pursuit of his love.

— *Carl Rollyson*

ALL'S WELL THAT ENDS WELL

Author: William Shakespeare (1564-1616)
First published: 1623
Genre: Drama

Locale: France and Italy
Time: The sixteenth century
Plot: Comedy

Helena (HEHL-eh-nuh), the orphaned daughter of Gerard de Narbon, a distinguished physician, and the ward of the countess of Rousillon. She at first regards her love for Bertram, the countess' son, as hopeless; then, with the independence characteristic of the heroines of William Shakespeare's comedies, she resolves to try to win him with her father's one legacy to her, a cure for the ailing king's mysterious malady. Her charm and sincerity win the love and admiration of all who see her except Bertram himself. Hurt but undaunted by his flight from her on their wedding day, she mourns chiefly that she has sent him into danger in the Florentine war and deprived his mother of his presence. She leaves the countess without farewell, hoping at least to free her husband to return to his home if she is not successful in fulfilling his seemingly impossible conditions for a reconciliation. She contrives through an ingenious trick, substituting herself for the Florentine girl he is trying to seduce, to obtain his ring and conceive his child. She thus wins for herself a loving and repentant husband.

Bertram, Count Rousillon, a rather arrogant, self-satisfied, and impulsive young man. Proud of his noble blood, he feels degraded by the king's command that he marry Helena, and

after the ceremony he flees with his dissolute companion Parolles to the army of the duke of Florence to escape such ignomiy. He wins fame as a soldier, but he fares less well in his personal relationships. First, Parolles' essential cowardice and disloyalty are exposed by his fellow soldiers to the young count who had trusted him. Then, his attempt to seduce Diana brings about the very end he is trying to escape, union with his own wife. His antagonism for Helena melts when he hears reports of her death and recognizes the depth of the love he has lost, and he is willingly reconciled to her when she is restored to him.

The Countess Rousillon, Bertram's mother, a wise and gracious woman who is devoted to both Bertram and Helena and welcomes the idea of their marriage. Her son's callous rejection of his virtuous wife appalls her, and she grieves deeply for his folly, in spite of her protest to Helena that she looks on her as her only remaining child. After Helena's reported death and Bertram's return, she begs the king to forgive her son's youthful rebelliousness.

Parolles (pay-ROHL-ehs), Bertram's follower and fellow soldier, who has no illusions about his own character. His romantic illusions are nonexistent. He encourages Bertram to be off to the wars with him, and he aids and abets the attempted seduction of Diana. The quality of his loyalty to his patron becomes all too obvious in the hilarious drum scene when he, blindfolded, insults and offers to betray all his countrymen to free himself from the enemies into whose hands he thinks he has fallen.

The king of France, a kindly old man who has almost resigned himself to the fact that his illness is incurable when Helena comes to court with her father's prescription, which heals him. He believes her the equal of any man in the kingdom and readily agrees to reward her service to him by letting her choose her husband from the noblemen of the kingdom. Only the pleas of Lafeu and the countess, along with Bertram's late recognition of Helena's virtues, prevent him from punishing the young man severely for his rebellious flight.

Lafeu (LAH-few), an old lord, counselor to the king and the countess' friend. He is as much captivated by Helena's grace as is his king, but he blames Parolles chiefly for Bertram's ungentle desertion of his wife. Out of friendship for the countess, he arranges a marriage between Bertram and his own daughter in an attempt to assuage the king's anger against the count.

Lavache (lah-VAHSH), the countess' servant, a witty clown who is expert in the nonsensical trains of logic spun by characters such as Touchstone and Feste.

Diana Capilet (KAP-ih-leht), the attractive, virtuous daughter of a Florentine widow. She willingly agrees to help Helena win Bertram when she hears her story, and she wins a rich husband for herself as a reward from the king for her honesty.

Diana's mother, a widow who is concerned about the honor of her daughter and her house.

Violenta (vee-oh-LEHN-tah) and

Mariana (mah-ree-AH-nah), the widow's honest neighbors.

The duke of Florence, the general whose army Bertram joins.

Rinaldo (rih-NAHL-doh), the countess' steward, who first tells her of Helena's love for Bertram.

ALMANAC OF THE DEAD

Author: Leslie Marmon Silko (1948-   )
First published: 1991
Genre: Novel

Locale: Arizona, Mexico, and Colombia
Time: Late twentieth century
Plot: Social realism

Leche (LAY-chay), the mother of Ferro, and sister of Zeta. She is a celebrated psychic and keeper of the sacred Lakota text of the almanac. Initially in drug-dependent retirement, she ends up identifying herself with visionary, militant ecologists. Her complicated evolution is one of the novel's main structures.

Sterling, the gardener in Leche's compound, exiled from his Pueblo home on mistaken grounds of cultural violation. His safe return to his native place is an understated counterpart of the more global nature of Leche's ultimate commitment. He attempts to retain his integrity and self-respect.

Seese, Sterling's opposite number in Leche's household. She has a guilty past. If Sterling's problems have ethnic origins, Seese's originate in her gender and in her helpless involvement with an exploitative male world of drugs and sex.

Menardo (may-NAHR-doh), a Mexican entrepreneur. He illustrates the destructive and dehumanizing nature of personal greed and the international economic order that fosters it. His rise and fall has darkly comic as well as more sinister elements. His story can be read as a parodic treatment of the novel's other shape-changing motifs.

David, a photographer, Seese's lover and the father of her child. His reckless treatment of both these dependents has its moral payoff in his involvement with pornography and Nazi-style futurists. These developments are not only a critique of David's disregard for Seese and the subsequent obscene exploitation of their child but also contrast vividly with the nurturing character of Leche's commitment.

— *George O'Brien*

ALMAYER'S FOLLY: A Story of an Eastern River

Author: Joseph Conrad (Jósef Teodor Konrad Nałęcz Korzeniowski, 1857-1924)
First published: 1895
Genre: Novel

Locale: The Dutch East Indies
Time: Late nineteenth century
Plot: Social realism

Kaspar Almayer, an unsuccessful Dutch trader in Malaya. His ambition is to take a large profit from a secret gold mine and return with his daughter Nina to Amsterdam. He fails to find the mine, is deserted by his wife, and is disappointed by his daughter's elopement with a Malay. Friendless and addicted to opium, he lives out the last of his life in an unfinished house named Almayer's Folly.

Mrs. Almayer, a Malay. Her husband loses the prospering business her adopted father had left her. She despises her husband and all white men. She wants her daughter to remain a Malay and wants to remain a Malay herself. After her daughter's marriage, Mrs. Almayer returns to her own people.

Captain Lingard, a prosperous trader who adopted Mrs. Almayer as a child and made her his heir.

Nina, the Almayers' daughter, educated as a European despite her mixed blood. She returns to the little settlement of her girlhood because of her mistreatment by whites in Singapore. Although she is attractive to white men because of her beauty, she marries Dain Maroola, a Malay, with whom she is more certain she can retain her dignity and self-respect.

Dain Maroola, a Malay. He and Nina fall in love with each other and are married. He is a great man among his own people, being the son of a rajah.

Lakamba, the Rajah of Sambir, Almayer's enemy. He befriends Dain when the young man runs afoul the Dutch authorities, and he later becomes Mrs. Almayer's protector.

Babalatchi, Lakamba's chief aide.

ALNILAM

Author: James Dickey (1923-1997)
First published: 1987
Genre: Novel

Locale: Peckover, North Carolina
Time: The 1940's
Plot: Philosophical realism

Frank Cahill, a fifty-four-year-old carpenter and amateur body builder recently blinded by a rare form of adult diabetes. Unpredictably energized by the challenges imposed by this condition, Cahill travels from the small amusement park he built in Atlanta, Georgia, to the Air Corps training facility where his son Joel has been declared missing after his plane crashed in a farmer's field. Accompanied by his wolflike dog Zack, Cahill tries to piece together a picture of the son he has never met; he and his wife separated shortly before Joel's birth. Himself subject to a form of egotism marked by a deep reliance on instinctual response, Cahill reacts positively to what he learns about Joel's self-confidence and faith in personal impulse, but he also comes to realize the destructive potential of such willful individualism when it is converted to political ends.

Joel Cahill, a nineteen-year-old cadet pilot who becomes the center of a student cult by the strength of his inherent charisma, physical attractiveness, and symbolic cast of mind. Informed by his reading of science fiction and nineteenth century Romantic poetry, especially the works of such idealistic believers in the transforming power of the imagination as English poets Percy Bysshe Shelley and James Thomson, Joel has constructed a personal brand of mysticism aimed at mastering the machine in order eventually to transcend its physical limitations and become one with the elements. Joel transmits his ideas to other specially chosen cadets and labels their secret confederacy "Alnilam" after the star in the center of the constellation of Orion. His hold over his followers is strengthened by his mysterious disappearance and by the fulfillment of his prediction that his father would arrive at the base to witness what he has set in motion.

McClintock McCaig (Double Mac), a former crop duster turned civilian flight instructor who serves as Frank Cahill's principal guide and companion at the North Carolina base. McCaig offers Cahill an opportunity to fly a plane, and this event gives Frank insight into his son's experiences in the air

and a sense of his personal ability to find his own individual balance without the use of sight. Ironically, McCaig has volunteered for active duty in England and for training with the new invention of radar, which can be said to be a mechanical variation on the skills developed by sightless people in the detection of unseen objects.

Lennox Whitehall, a navigation instructor and veteran of the Pacific War who offers one of the two principal interpretations of Joel's status. Whitehall applauds Joel's mathematical and astronomical interests and his special ability to tap his full physical and intellectual potential, and he sympathizes with the Alnilam movement to the extent that it offers an imaginative outlet for the unconscious rebellious desires of the young and an antidote to the formulas of military bureaucracy.

Bruno Iannone, an articulate, practical-minded flight surgeon who provides Cahill with a more troubling spin on the significance of Joel's achievement. He sees Joel as the opportunistic nucleus of a fanatical group akin to the Nazis or the Ku Klux Klan, whose adherents blindly follow leaders who tell them that they are destined for some special fate.

Hannah Pelham, an Appalachian textile mill worker. By providing Joel with an opportunity to exercise his sadistic sexual fantasies, she offers evidence of the dark side of Joel's power over others. Hannah also grants Frank Cahill the comforts of her kitchen and bedroom.

Malcolm Shears, Joel's principal disciple and heir apparent. He is the keeper of Joel's undergraduate literature anthology, replete with the young man's gnomic marginalia, which the Alnilam cadets recite from memory during their secret ceremonies. With his knack for organization, Shears takes Joel's vision and imposes upon it his own sense of discipline. In the group's first collective action, a choreographed graduation-day runway traffic snarl, they intentionally destroy a number of aircraft and heedlessly cause the death of one pilot.

— *S. Thomas Mack*

ALTON LOCKE: Tailor and Poet

Author: Charles Kingsley (1819-1875)
First published: 1850
Genre: Novel

Locale: London and Cambridge, England
Time: The 1840's
Plot: Social realism

Alton Locke, a poor London tailor, self-taught poet, and political radical. Apprenticed to a tailor with the help of his rich uncle, Alton begins questioning both his widowed mother's strict Baptist faith and the political system that oppresses the poor. His coworker John Crosthwaite introduces him to Chartism, a movement to give political rights to the

working classes, and Sandy Mackaye, a philosopher and owner of a used book shop, encourages him to write. Through his rich cousin George, Alton meets and falls in love with Lillian Winnstay, whose father helps him publish his poetry. Frustrated because his low social status is a barrier to his love, Alton throws himself into political activism despite the warnings of Sandy Mackaye. When Lillian marries George and the Chartist movement collapses, Alton despairs, but a legacy from Mackaye allows him and Crossthwaite to move to Texas. Alton dies the evening their ship arrives in the New World.

John Crossthwaite, a political activist among the tailors. He is an honest man seduced by the chimera of political solutions. He introduces Alton to political thought and encourages him to believe that the plight of the workers can be improved only by means of class warfare. Under Crossthwaite's influence, Alton attends rallies and becomes a public speaker. When the Chartist movement fails, Crossthwaite helps nurse Alton back to health.

Saunders (Sandy) Mackaye, a shrewd but benevolent Scottish philosopher who takes an interest in Alton's intellectual and moral development. Under Sandy's guidance, Alton learns to write about the daily conditions of the working classes. Sandy believes in reconciliation between the classes, rather than conflict, and so discourages Alton from pinning too many hopes on Chartism. He recognizes Crossthwaite's good qualities despite the latter's excessive commitment to politics. Hoping to save Alton and Crossthwaite from their own mistakes, Sandy leaves them funds, in his will, that will allow them to move to Texas.

George Locke, Alton's rich cousin, an ambitious, self-centered, middle-class man who is attending Cambridge University to learn the ways of the gentry. He is friendly to Alton, although he wishes Alton would conceal his working-class origins. Despite his lack of interest in religion, he becomes a clergyman because of the security and the social standing associated with the position. After marrying Lillian, he contemptuously spurns Alton.

Lillian Winnstay, the beautiful, selfish friend (and later wife) of George Locke. She looks upon Alton as a pet or novelty but cannot see beyond his working-class background to appreciate his merits. She marries the less worthy George because he is of the right background and has the right income. Neither she nor George is interested in the betterment of the poor. The couple meet their just reward as the result of buying coats from exploited tailors: The coats turn out to be infected with a fever. George dies, and Lillian loses her beauty.

Eleanor Staunton, a friend of George and Lillian. She is a less attractive and vivacious, but more worthy, person. She debates politics with Alton, arguing for cooperation among the classes rather than conflict and stressing the importance of Christian charity in order to alleviate problems of the social order. When she marries an aristocrat with a social conscience, she puts her words into practice on his estates. After his death, she dedicates her life to improving the lot of the London tailors. Although she nurses Alton back to health, she cannot accompany him to Texas because her own health is declining. She wishes him goodbye and prays for a peaceful social order in England.

— *D. G. Paz*

AMADEUS

Author: Peter Shaffer (1926-   )
First published: 1980
Genre: Drama

Locale: Vienna, Austria
Time: 1781-1823
Plot: Fantasy

Antonio Salieri (sahl-YEHR-ee), a court composer and later Imperial Kappellmeister to Joseph II, emperor of Austria. He has dedicated his life and his talents to the greater honor and glory of God and has obtained fame, reputation, and the emperor's favor. Salieri belongs to a clique of Italians who have culturally colonized the court. His composure is shaken when Mozart, an upstart Austrian prodigy from Salzburg, comes to Vienna and makes a favorable impression on the emperor. Although he never questions Mozart's talent, Salieri becomes insanely jealous, schemes to ruin Mozart's career, and ultimately confesses to having killed Mozart before insanely attempting suicide. Salieri is an evil-minded, satanic figure, proud, vain, and humiliated by Mozart. He is the main player and narrator in a parable demonstrating the sin of envy.

Wolfgang Amadeus Mozart (VOHLF-gahng ah-mah-DAY-ews MOHT-zahrt), the genius composer, presented as a crude, vulgar, and tactless young egotist who has absolutely no modesty with regard to his talent. The victim of the drama, Mozart is innocent and naïve in the devious world of court politics, too tactless to veil his contempt for the court Italians and Salieri's music and too naïve to recognize Salieri as his most dangerous enemy.

Constanze Weber, the daughter of Mozart's landlady in Vienna and, later, Mozart's wife. She is well-intentioned, innocent, and tolerant of her husband's behavior, but she shares his vulgarity. She drives a wedge between Mozart and his father, Leopold, who later dies in Salzburg. She secretly visits Salieri when the couple needs money to survive, taking original manuscripts, but later she is suspicious of Salieri. She loves her husband but is unable to help him at the end, when she returns from Baden to find him, dying, in the company of Salieri.

Joseph II, the emperor of Austria, Mozart's patron, who loves music but is too dense to fully appreciate Mozart's talents. Essentially a man of mediocre intelligence and taste, he prefers Salieri to Mozart and is therefore easily influenced by Salieri. He appoints Mozart to replace Gluck as chamber composer after Gluck's death, but, on Salieri's advice, at only one-tenth of Gluck's salary.

Baron Gottfried Van Swieten (GOT-freed fan SWEE-tehn), the prefect of the Imperial Library and an ardent Freemason who helps to support Mozart and his family after Mozart becomes a Mason, until Mozart writes *The Magic Flute* and alienates his benefactor by utilizing Masonic rituals (at Salieri's suggestion) and revealing Masonic secrets in that opera. Because of his old-fashioned musical preferences, he is known as "Lord Fugue." He pays for Mozart's pauper's funeral.

Count Johann von Strack (YOH-hahn fon SHTRAK), the royal chamberlain, who conveys the emperor's orders to commission Mozart to write a comic opera in German, which further alienates the court Italians.

Count Franz Orsini-Rosenberg, the director of the Imperial Opera and part of the Italian faction. He argues against opera that is non-Italian and criticizes Mozart for employing "too many notes." He believes that "all prodigies are hateful."

The "Venticelli" (VEHN-tee-CHEH-lee), or **"Little Winds,"** which serve as "purveyors of information, gossip, and rumor" and function as a chorus to the action.

— *James Michael Welsh*

AMADÍS OF GAUL
(Amadís de Gaula)

Author: Attributed to Vasco de Lobeira (c. 1360-c. 1403)
First published: 1508
Genre: Novel

Locale: France, England, and the rest of Europe
Time: First century
Plot: Romance

Amadís de Gaul (ah-mah-DEES duh gawl), the natural son of King Perion of Gaul and Elisena, daughter of King Garinter of Lesser Britain. To be worthy of his beloved, Oriana, the daughter of the king of England, and to win her hand, he becomes a knight and passes through many brave adventures.

King Perión of Gaul (pehr-ee-OHN), the father of Amadís de Gaul.

Princess Elisena (eh-lee-SEHN-nah), the mother of Amadís de Gaul.

Galaor (gah-lah-OHR), the brother of Amadís de Gaul.

Lisuarte (lee-SWAHR-teh), the king of England and the father of Oriana.

Brisena (bree-SEH-nah), the queen of England and the mother of Oriana.

Oriana (ohr-ee-AH-nah), the daughter of King Lisuarte and Queen Brisena. She is loved by Amadís de Gaul, who wins her hand after many knightly adventures.

Urganda (ewr-GAHN-dah), an enchantress, the protector of Amadís de Gaul.

Arcalaus (ahr-kah-LOWS), a wicked magician.

King Garinter (gah-reen-TEHR), the grandfather of Amadís de Gaul.

Darioleta (dahr-ee-oh-LEH-tah), Elisena's attendant. She hides the infant Amadís de Gaul, along with his father's ring, in an ark and sets him afloat.

Gandales (gahn-DAH-lehs), a knight who finds Amadís de Gaul in the sea and rears him.

Gandalín (gahn-dahl-EEN), the son of Gandales.

Languines (lahn-GWEEN-ehs), the king of Scotland, who takes Amadís de Gaul to his court.

Abies (AH-bee-ehs), the king of Ireland and the enemy of King Perion.

Galpano (gahl-PAH-noh), a haughty robber who is overcome by Amadís de Gaul.

Barsinan (bahr-SEE-nahn), a traitor to King Lisuarte.

Apolidón (ah-pohl-lee-DOHN), the son of the king of Greece.

King Aravigo (ah-rah-VEE-goh), an enemy of King Lisuarte and Amadís de Gaul.

Gasquilán (gahs-kee-LAHN), the king of Sweden, who is overthrown in single combat by Amadís de Gaul.

Esplandián (ehs-plahn-dee-AHN), a messenger.

THE AMBASSADORS

Author: Henry James (1843-1916)
First published: 1903
Genre: Novel

Locale: Paris, France
Time: c. 1900
Plot: Psychological realism

Lambert Strether, the chief ambassador of Mrs. Newsome, his betrothed. Strether is sent to summon Mrs. Newsome's son Chad back from Paris to the family business in Wollett, Massachusetts. The fifty-five-year-old editor of a review, Strether has all the tact and diplomacy necessary to accomplish his task, but his sensitivity will not allow him either to complete it or to take advantage of Chad's situation to gain his own ends. He sees Chad as immeasurably better off in Paris and himself as somehow changed and strengthened by his sojourn abroad, though he will not allow himself to stay in Europe after having failed his benefactress. His heady experiences renew his earlier impressions, and he forms friendships, visits cathedrals, and lives easily for the first time since his wife died while bearing their son, also dead. His delicacy—in approaching young Newsome and his mistress, Mme. de Vionnet; in handling Chadwick's sister, brother-in-law, and childhood sweetheart, and in breaking off from Maria Gostrey, who loves him—is the more remarkable when one considers that his own hopes of a rich marriage and great influence have been shattered by his actions.

Chadwick (Chad) Newsome, the handsome, twenty-eight-year-old successor to a family business and the heir to a modest income from another source. Candid and open-hearted, the graying young man has been so improved by his years in Europe, largely under the tutelage of Mme de Vionnet, that no thought of his return can really be habored by anyone who has seen him. Although he himself is willing to return for a visit and to consider taking over the advertising and sales promotion of the business, his proposed marriage to Mamie Pocock is unthinkable. His greatest triumph comes as the result of his mannerly presentation of his sister's group of ambassadors to his Parisian friends, while his saddest duty is to allow his good friend Lambert Strether to return to face the consequences of a diplomatic failure.

Maria Gostrey, a self-styled introducer and tour director and a chance acquaintance of Lambert Strether. A sensitive, genial, and understanding woman, she proves to be the agent through whom the ambassador discovers the irony of Chad Newsome's situation. Her generosity and devotion to her new friend first touch him and then move him deeply when he sees her loyalty and love unencumbered by desire for personal gain.

Mme Marie de Vionnet (mah-REE deh vee-oh-NAY), the beautiful comtesse whose religion and social position will not allow her to divorce an unloved and faithless husband. Gravely lovely and charming, she has educated young Chad Newsome in the social graces and has won his heart and soul. Called a "virtuous connection" by intimate friends, the arrangement seems shabby to Mr. Waymarsh and Mrs. Pocock, typically closed-minded Americans. Through the efforts of good friends, especially Lambert Strether, Mme de Vionnet is allowed to retain her younger lover in spite of the fact that they have no future beyond their immediate happiness. Her daughter, who was believed by some to be in love with Chad Newsome, settles on a marriage more reasonable and agreeable to all.

John Little Bilham, called **Little Bilham**, an American expatriate artist and Chad Newsome's close friend. A perceptive, bright young man, he becomes the confidant of the ambassadors and, along with a friend, Miss Barrace, their interpreters of social and artistic life in Paris.

Miss Barrace, a shrewd, witty, understanding woman living in Paris. She asks Lambert Strether not to force the issue of Chad Newsome's return home.

Mr. Waymarsh, an American lawyer residing in England, Lambert Strether's friend. He accompanies Strether to Paris and directly involves himself in Chad Newsome's affairs when he writes a letter informing Mrs. Newsome that her ambassador is not fulfilling his mission.

Sarah Newsome Pocock, Chad Newsome's older sister. She, her husband, and her sister-in-law are also dispatched as Mrs. Newsome's ambassadors to make certain that Chad returns to America. She and Mr. Waymarsh join forces to separate Chad and Mme de Vionnet.

James Pocock, Sarah's husband, who during Chad Newsome's absence is in control of the Newsome mills. He enjoys his trip to Paris, sympathizes with Chad, and becomes Lambert Strether's tacit ally.

Mamie Pocock, James Pocock's younger sister, the girl Mrs. Newsome has selected as a suitable wife for her son. Although she accompanies her brother and his wife on their mission to persuade Chad Newsome to return, she loses her personal interest in the young man after meeting John Little Bilham. Little Bilham's announced intention of marrying Mamie helps Chad solve his own problems of loyalty and love in his affair with Mme de Vionnet.

Jeanne de Vionnet, Mme de Vionnet's daughter. For a time, society assumed that Chad Newsome might be in love with the daughter. Jeanne becomes engaged to M. de Montbron.

M. Gloriani, a sculptor, Mme de Vionnet's friend, famous in the artistic and fashionable circles of Parisian society.

Mme Gloriani, his lovely wife.

AMBIGUOUS ADVENTURE
(L'Aventure ambiguë)

Author: Cheikh Hamidou Kane (1928-   )
First published: 1961
Genre: Novel

Locale: Senegal and Paris, France
Time: Mid-twentieth century
Plot: Philosophical realism

Samba Diallo, a young man of the Diallobé aristocracy who is perceived by all to represent the future of his people. For this reason, the older generation of the Diallobé people struggles to influence the course of his life. As a child, Samba evinces a profound sense of the spiritual beauty of Islam and of the Koran, the words of which he repeats without understanding them. When it is decided that he will attend a French school, he becomes enamored with the Western alphabet, philosophy, and scientific method, all of which suggest that everything can be expressed, analyzed, and mastered. Undertaking university studies in philosophy in Paris, he suffers deeply over the loss of the spiritual plenitude he had known before his contact with the West. As he discusses philosophical, spiritual, and political issues with those he meets, he realizes that in the course of his "ambiguous adventure" he has internalized aspects of both cultures and is no longer completely at ease in either. Recalled to Africa by his worried father, he seems to seek out his own demise and apparently experiences a return of faith at the moment of his death.

Thierno (tee-EHR-no), a teacher of Islam in the Koranic school and spiritual master of the Diallobé people. The fragility and stiffness of his aging body make a vivid contrast with the ethereal joy in his soul. Thierno declines to help the Diallobé decide whether to send their children to the colonial schools. With his preferred successor, Samba, away in Paris, he designates Demba, a pragmatic youth of peasant stock, whose first official act is to allow the Diallobé children to attend the French school.

The Knight, Samba's father, so dubbed by a school friend of Samba (Jean Lacroix) because of his stature and noble bearing. Although he works at a civil service post in the colonial administration, his contact with the West has not altered his deep faith. Indeed, he asserts that Africa's urgent mission is to restore a sense of spirituality to an impoverished Western civilization obsessed with scientific and technological progress.

The Chief of the Diallobé, the secular leader of his people, brother of the Most Royal Lady, and Samba's cousin. The Chief represents a middle ground, a locus of indecisiveness in an era in which important decisions must be made. A lucid and profoundly human character, he clearly feels inadequate to play the role assigned him by his historical era.

The Most Royal Lady, Samba's aunt and the Chief's sister. Sixty years old but looking twenty years younger, she radiates the beauty and strength of the Diallobé aristocracy. Her principal role in the novel is to exhort her people to attend the French school. In an eloquent speech, she acknowledges that the consequences of this decision cannot be predicted; precious elements of cultural or spiritual heritage may be lost, but the Diallobé must move forward.

The Fool, a friend of Thierno. His daring gaze, strange clothing, odd speech, and marginalized position in Diallobé society have earned for him this title. His reasons for having visited the West are unclear, but he seems to have fought in World War I and to have been permanently traumatized by his experiences. The West he describes to Thierno is a cold, hard, mechanized, dehumanized world, and he opposes any contact with it. He is grief-stricken at Thierno's death, and his efforts to force Samba to pray on the holy man's grave precipitate Samba's apparent death at the end of the novel.

Paul Lacroix (lah-KRWAH), a colleague of the Knight. His principal importance is as a participant in a conversation with the Knight as the two men observe a magnificent African sunset; that sight causes them to reflect on "the end of the world." The men represent two radically different belief systems. Lacroix fears the end of the world, feeling that it could only signify human failure and would end the infinite continuation of enlightenment and scientific progress. The Knight looks forward to the end of the world as the moment when all questions and uncertainties will be resolved.

Paul Martial, a middle-aged Protestant pastor. A sympathetic and enlightened Westerner, he discusses philosophy with Samba. As a young man, he dreamed of going to Africa as a missionary. He perceived such a mission as only a spiritual exchange between cultures and would have refrained from the Westerner's frequent practice of combining proselytizing with "gifts" of medicine and technology.

Lucienne Martial, Paul's daughter, a university classmate of Samba. She advocates a political (Marxist) solution to the social crisis in Africa. Samba admires her fervent commitment, observing that she has followed the road to Damascus in the opposite direction from that taken by the apostle Paul, that is, away from her Christian upbringing. Samba does not experience a similar conversion. He recognizes that for him the resolution of conflict lies in faith rather than in politics.

— *Janet L. Solberg*

AMELIA

Author: Henry Fielding (1707-1754)
First published: 1751
Genre: Novel

Locale: England
Time: The 1740's
Plot: Domestic realism

Amelia Harris Booth, a beautiful and virtuous young Englishwoman whose troubles begin when she marries William Booth, a young army officer, against her mother's wishes. After the Gibraltar campaign, when her husband is on half-pay in an inactive status, Amelia's life becomes a constant struggle against genteel poverty. Her beauty complicates matters, for several high-ranking men who might help her husband acquire a new command pursue her in hopes that she will capitulate to them in return for the help they can give. Amelia also faces the problem of her husband's gambling and philandering. She bears all her tribulations with patience and humility; her virtue is rewarded by the inheritance of her mother's estate.

William Booth, a British captain and Amelia's husband. Although he is a meritorious junior officer who served well at Gibraltar, incurring two wounds, he has trouble securing a new command because he is too poor to buy a commission and without sufficient political influence to gain one. He loves his wife deeply, but he has weaknesses for gambling and women.

Dr. Harrison, a benevolent Anglican clergyman who regards Amelia almost as a daughter. His kindness and help save Amelia and her family from disaster several times. He lends them his house and advances them money, and his discoveries eventually place Amelia in possession of her inheritance.

Colonel Robert James, a fellow officer of William Booth during his active military duty. Unlike Booth, he remains in the military service, having the money and influence to rise in the military hierarchy and become a member of Parliament. He extends help many times to the Booths through the years, but only because he is secretly desirous of having Amelia as his mistress.

Colonel Bath, another fellow officer. Always conscious of his honor and ready to fight a duel or encourage someone else to fight one, he forces a quarrel on Booth, who wounds him.

Mrs. James, Colonel James's wife and Colonel Bath's sister. She is a great friend to Amelia until the latter's poverty causes that friendship to cool.

Betty Harris, Amelia's sister, a selfish, malicious woman who spreads lies about Amelia and enters into a complicated plot of forgery to deprive Amelia of her rightful inheritance.

Mr. Robinson, a shady character who is in and out of prison. His deathbed confession to Dr. Harrison reveals the plot to keep Amelia from her inheritance.

Mr. Murphy, a dishonest lawyer. He plots with Betty Harris to deprive Amelia of her fortune. Eventually apprehended by Dr. Harrison, he is tried, found guilty, and hanged.

Mrs. Ellison, the Booths' landlady in London. Although she seems an honest and well-meaning woman, she serves as bawd to an unnamed nobleman, procuring for him a series of women. Amelia's friends prevent her from being so victimized.

Mrs. Bennet, an unfortunate young widow who becomes Amelia's friend. Having been an earlier victim of Mrs. Ellison and the unnamed nobleman, she is able to help Amelia save herself from the plot against her virtue. Mrs. Bennet is loved by Sergeant Atkinson and becomes his wife.

Joseph Atkinson, the son of Amelia's nurse and, in a sense, her foster brother. He enlists in the army in order to be with William Booth and afterward remains in the service. Loyal to Amelia and her husband, he helps in every way he can to keep disaster from overtaking the Booths. He falls in love with Mrs. Bennet, marries her, and buys a commission with their pooled resources.

Fanny Matthews, a handsome, amoral woman who loves William Booth and tries to become his mistress. She is also Colonel James's mistress at the time. She and Booth renew their acquaintance while both are in prison.

AMERICA HURRAH

Author: Jean-Claude van Itallie (1935 or 1936-   )
First published: 1967
Genre: Drama

Locale: A subway, an office, and a motel room
Time: Mid-1960's
Plot: Allegory

First Applicant, **Jack Smith**, an unemployed house painter. He is proud of his profession, his union membership, and his Italian heritage. He recounts an occasion when, lacking direction in his life, he mentioned to his priest that he might like to join a monastery but received no reply.

Second Applicant, **Jane Smith**, an unemployed floor washer. She is of Jewish-Irish descent and has been washing floors for twenty years. She feels abandoned by her deceased husband.

Third Applicant, **Richard Smith**, an unemployed bank president. During his job interview, he flaunts his education, social status, and previous employment. Later, he reveals that he lost his job because of an unexplainable and uncontrollable feeling of panic that has incapacitated him.

Fourth Applicant, **Mary Smith**, an unemployed lady's maid. During her job interview, she brags about her family origins and the aristocratic families for whom she has worked. On the city streets, however, she becomes completely disoriented and unable to find her way.

Hal, a television ratings service employee in his late twenties or early thirties. He is cynical in outlook and enjoys tormenting George, his supervisor, with whom he feels himself to be in competition. He wants to begin a relationship with his coworker, Susan.

Susan, a television ratings service employee in her early twenties. She is engaged in an affair with her supervisor, George, who is married, but flirts with Hal. After she agrees to go to a movie with Hal, she still treats George with excessive tenderness. She is given to inexplicable fits of hysterical laughter and is in therapy.

George, a television ratings service supervisor, forty-three years old. He competes with Hal for Susan's affections, drawing attention to his greater tact and life experience, but calls off his affair with Susan after she decides to go out with Hal. He telephones his wife to tell her that he will be coming home after all, only to be greeted with incredulity. Immediately after calling off his assignation with Susan, he chokes on a chicken bone. When he recovers, he returns to his competitive stance with respect to Hal and tries to insinuate himself into Hal's date with Susan.

The Motel-Keeper, who is represented on stage by a giant papier-mâché puppet. She spouts clichés about how "homey" the rooms of her motel are and describes in great detail the various consumer catalogs from which she has ordered its decorations.

The Man and

The Woman, guests staying at the motel, also represented by giant puppets. They undress, use the bathroom, make love, dance, and destroy their room to the accompaniment of the television set and loud rock music. After attacking the Motel-Keeper herself and ripping off her arms and head, they exit through the theater's aisles.

— Philip Auslander

THE AMERICAN

Author: Henry James (1843-1916)
First published: 1877
Genre: Novel

Locale: Paris, France
Time: Mid-nineteenth century
Plot: Psychological realism

Christopher Newman, a young American millionaire who is looking for more in life than a business career. He goes to Paris to experience European culture, and he hopes to find a wife who can aid in developing his natural abilities. Both modest and astute, he has a depth of integrity that is recognized by both men and women. He is also generous in his response to the qualities of others. When he meets Claire de Cintré though his friend, Mrs. Tristram, he is drawn to her noble character and touched by her adverse situation. In his relationship with the Bellegarde family, Newman's innate decency stirs some of them to admiration and others to a desire to exploit Newman's naïveté. Newman is refused Claire, who retires to a convent. Because he has evidence showing that Claire's father was murdered by his wife, Newman is tempted to bargain for Claire, but his innate decency leads him to destroy the incriminating evidence.

Claire de Cintré (sahn-TRAY), née **Bellegarde** (behl-GAHRD), a young French woman locked in the rigid confines of her mother's domination. When she was forced into marriage with a worldly old man, her invalid father could not save her; a few years later, however, her husband's death released her. This is the woman Newman meets and loves. Seeing in Newman a sensitive and reliable man, she responds to his goodness. She is just beginning to feel strength and freedom when the Bellegardes withdraw their permission for her marriage to Newman. She is further distressed when her amiable younger brother dies in a duel. She knows intuitively of her mother's crime of murder, but there seems no way out of her dilemma. She chooses the only path open to her—the convent—where she can at least escape her family. One senses that sorrow has taught her only to endure; she does not know the enormity of her sacrifice in giving up Newman.

Mr. Tristram, Newman's somewhat boisterous American friend.

Mrs. Tristram, a woman much more perceptive than her husband. Her warmth is a kind of sisterly affection for Newman.

Madame de Bellegarde, a French aristocrat, a hard woman with neither morality nor integrity.

The Marquis de Bellegarde, the elder son in the family; he is like his mother in character.

Valentin de Bellegarde (vah-lan[n]-TAN), the younger son. He is a man of wit and kindliness who loves his sister. He dies in Switzerland as the result of a duel motivated by his affair with Mlle Nioche.

Mrs. Bread, the Bellegardes' servant. She goes to work for Newman after Valentin's dying words instruct her to re-veal Madame de Bellegarde's secret.

M. Nioche (nee-OHSH), an elderly French shopkeeper whose age and experience permit him some philosophical observations.

Mlle Nioche, his daughter. An indifferent artist, she is able to support herself by her physical charms. She is last seen in London escorted by Valentin's distant cousin, Lord Deepmere.

AMERICAN BUFFALO

Author: David Mamet (1947-   )
First published: 1976
Genre: Drama

Locale: Don's Resale Shop in an unspecified city
Time: The 1970's
Plot: Psychological realism

Don Dubrow, a man in his late forties, the owner of the junk shop called Don's Resale Shop. He unknowingly sells a rare American buffalo nickel for what he assumes must have been too little. He believes that by tricking him, the buyer achieved an unwarranted dominance over him. Don intends to get even by planning a robbery, one in which he will not participate but that will involve the nickel being restolen. This dream-fantasy of the robbery restores to Don the sense of power that he lost with the nickel's sale. When the play opens, Don is berating the dependent Bob for leaving the house he had been sent to stake out. He emphasizes his dominance by making Bob apologize for that action. Don's need for family is expressed by his fatherly friendship and concern for slow-witted Bob, whom he tries to teach the difference between friendship and business but whom he betrays out of mistrust of his own convictions and the strength of Teach's arguments. He holds the offstage character Fletch up to Bob as an example of a guy who can think on his feet, but he becomes totally demoralized when he learns through Teach that Fletch cheated him, a friend as well as a business associate. Don turns violent when frustrated. His whole life seems to exist only within his resale shop.

Walter Cole, called **Teach**, an overreactive friend and associate of Don who is unsure of his actions, although he puts up a good front by using bold language infused with positivism. His unsureness is echoed in his innate suspicion of others, and he believes that everyone is motivated by self-interest. Business in his world is necessary, and the means used in its execution are self-justifying. Deceit, physical violence, and assault are merely business tactics, and friendship is nothing more than a means of gain. Teach lacks the courage of his convictions, however, and there is a great gulf between his words and his deeds. His suspicions allow him to terrorize Bob physically, and even though these thoughts turn out to be erroneous, he is never anxious or questioning of his actions. Teach utilizes moral principles that justify his cynical outlook. His great robbery never takes place; Teach is a bungler as well as a misogynist. Offstage female characters illustrate his lack of control in his world.

Bob, a slow-witted junkie who works as a gofer for Don. He emphasizes the superiority Don feels. Bob is cheated out of participation in an abortive robbery but ironically may have done the cheating. Bob is dependent on Don for the cash to feed his drug habit. Participation in the robbery will temporarily bring him the cash he needs and perhaps inspire praise from Don. Because of his habit, however, Bob must also be committing small types of crimes, and it could be that he committed the crime that Teach accuses him of—getting the buffalo nickel from the customer in some foul way. Don's calls to the hospitals in the area prove that Don does not trust Bob. Throughout the play, Bob, in repeating much of what Don tells him, uses a type of low-language slang that indicates his low intelligence and his inability to progress outside Don's Resale Shop.

— *Marjorie J. Oberlander*

THE AMERICAN DREAM

Author: Edward Albee (1928-   )
First published: 1961
Genre: Drama

Locale: United States
Time: Late twentieth century
Plot: Absurdist

Mommy, the head of the household, who dominates the play. She complains about poor service in the department store and, in general, is fixated on her role as a consumer. Mommy's main interest is to remain in control and make life convenient for herself, which means, among other things, getting rid of outspoken and quarrelsome Grandma, who has become a nuisance. Mommy and Daddy apparently have a child who some-how disappointed them. They hope that the visit from Mrs. Barker will result in disposition of Grandma, getting a new child, and restoring their sense of domestic bliss. Mommy does not seem to notice that she often contradicts herself. At the end of the play, she welcomes the appearance of the Young Man, who seems familiar to her, even though she cannot identify him.

Daddy, who acts in most ways as Mommy's subordinate. He is a whiner and complains about how difficult it is to get anything fixed in the apartment. His comments seem infantile, and he doubts himself, so that Mommy has to keep propping him up by praising his masculinity. Like Mommy, he antici-pates the arrival of a new adopted child as if it were a product from the department store. Almost never thinking for himself, he is quite willing to have Mommy or Mrs. Barker suggest the right course of action. He is inept, so that Mommy often repeats herself to make sure that he understands her. He even has trouble finding Grandma's bedroom.

Grandma, an old and feeble but still sharp-minded woman. She knows that Mommy and Daddy are trying to get rid of her, and her sarcastic comments about their plans are astute and humorous. Grandma seems much more realistic than Mommy or Daddy and does not use their euphemisms to disguise what she says. Grandma often interrupts conversations among Mommy, Daddy, and Mrs. Barker and interprets what they say. It is Grandma, for example, who reveals that Mommy and Daddy have made a botch of their adoption of a little boy and now want a replacement for him. It is also Grandma who dubs the Young Man who arrives as "the American dream," for he is meant to function as the fulfillment of Mommy and Daddy's hopes and illusions about perfect family life in America. Grandma, in short, is the only character who knows how to speak her mind.

Mrs. Barker, a visitor to Mommy and Daddy's home who announces herself to be the chairman of Mommy's women's club. This is a surprise to Mommy, who claims to have trouble recognizing her in the artificial light. Mrs. Barker acts like one of the authorities that Mommy and Daddy have been expecting. She is more uninhibited than the other characters; for example, she takes off her dress to be more comfortable. She speaks vaguely about a number of important activities and wonders whether she has come to pick up Grandma's boxes. Eventually, Mrs. Barker learns from Grandma that she has really come to pick up Grandma.

The Young Man, a handsome and athletic man who arrives at Mommy and Daddy's apartment. He is rather dumb and without much emotion. He refers to his identical twin, who is evidently the young child that Mommy and Daddy had previously adopted. With no real motivation of his own, the Young Man seems merely to be there in order to fulfill Mommy and Daddy's desire for the perfect child.

— Carl Rollyson

AN AMERICAN DREAM

· *Author:* Norman Mailer (1923-   )
First published: 1965
Genre: Novel

Locale: New York City
Time: 1962
Plot: Symbolism

Stephen Richard Rojack, the narrator and protagonist, a war hero, former congressman, professor of existential psychology, television personality, and murderer. On a late-night visit to his estranged wife, Deborah, Rojack strangles her after enduring her taunts. She challenges his manhood, and Rojack feels particularly vulnerable because he has had doubts about his character. Although he has achieved some notoriety, he has not lived up to his own heroic image of himself. He weathers the police interrogation well, even though the police suspect him of throwing Deborah's body out the window to make her death look like suicide. Rojack is determined to act as his own man, which means confronting his hostile father-in-law, Barney Kelly, and fighting for his new love, Cherry. At the end of the novel, he leaves town on a quest westward, hoping to develop a better character based on what he has learned from murdering his wife and having to fight for his survival.

Deborah, Rojack's wife, the daughter of Barney Kelly. Although her early years with Rojack were stimulating, she obviously has lost much respect for him and goads him into killing her at precisely the moment when he is looking for help. Deborah is beautiful, but she is cold and self-involved. She seems to have none of Rojack's vulnerabilities. She dies at the beginning of the novel, but her character and her judgments of Rojack tend to dominate his thinking about himself.

Barney Kelly, a millionaire with connections to the Mafia who suspects Rojack of murdering his daughter. The cool and collected Kelly does not reveal his emotions until the moment when Rojack—determined to prove his courage through some physical feat—decides to walk the parapet outside Kelly's apartment. As Rojack makes a turn around the building, Kelly tries to trip him. Rojack's step is steady, however, and he is able to cope with this crucial moment, giving him enough courage to get through the traumatic night of Deborah's murder.

Ruta, Deborah's German maid, who is in the house the night Rojack strangles Deborah. On an impulse, Rojack invades Ruta's room after murdering Deborah and finds Ruta ready for his sexual advances. Rojack's taking of this woman is associated in his mind with his newfound energy. He asks Ruta not to mention this episode to the police, and she complies. Only later does he suspect her of having some special connection with Barney Kelly, who may have set up Ruta to keep an eye on things in the house.

Cherry, a nightclub singer with whom Rojack has an affair. She is blonde and beautiful, and she has a modest talent. Rojack appreciates her toughness and willingness to befriend him when he first meets her at a table surrounded by gangsters. Cherry becomes Rojack's inspiration. She is the woman for whom he is willing to fight, the woman who can support him in precisely the ways Deborah was unwilling to do.

Roberts, a detective who investigates Deborah's murder. Although he is certain that Rojack is her murderer, he does not have enough evidence to prove it. Instead, he tries to work on Rojack's anxieties, hoping he will confess. At the same time, Roberts has a certain admiration for Rojack's toughness.

Shago Martin, a black man with sexual prowess who has been Cherry's lover and who becomes a television replacement for Rojack. At one point, Rojack has to fight Shago for Cherry. Although the men share certain values—especially their antiestablishment bias—their feelings about Cherry divide them. In a particularly brutal scene, Rojack kicks Martin down the stairs. Although Rojack feels some compassion for his rival, he feels compelled to fight for this new woman and for his new sense of himself. Martin, on the other hand, behaves like a burned out case, trying to frighten Rojack with a knife but without the force to call him to account.

— Carl Rollyson

AN AMERICAN TRAGEDY

Author: Theodore Dreiser (1871-1945)
First published: 1925
Genre: Novel

Locale: Kansas City, Chicago, and Lycurgus, New York
Time: Early twentieth century
Plot: Naturalism

Clyde Griffiths, the tragic hero. The son of itinerant evangelists, he was reared in poverty amid an atmosphere of narrow-minded religiosity. He has thus always longed for the things that money can buy. At sixteen, he gets a job as a bellboy in a Kansas City hotel and uses his unexpectedly large earnings for his own pleasure rather than to help his family. When his sister is left penniless and pregnant, he contributes only a small sum; he is buying a coat for Hortense Briggs, a shopgirl whom he is trying to seduce. Because of a wreck in a stolen car, he has to leave Kansas City. In Chicago, he meets his rich uncle, Samuel Griffiths, who gives him a job in his factory at Lycurgus, New York. The job is an unimportant one, and Clyde is resented by his cousins, particularly by Gilbert. Clyde is forbidden to associate with the factory girls, but out of loneliness he becomes friendly with one of them, Roberta Alden, whom he persuades to become his mistress. Meanwhile he is taken up by Sondra Finchley, the daughter of a wealthy family, who wishes to spite Gilbert. They fall in love, and Clyde dreams of a rich marriage. Roberta, however, becomes pregnant and demands that he marry her, thus shattering his hopes. When their attempts at abortion fail, Clyde, inspired by a newspaper account of a murder, plans to murder Roberta. Though he intends to kill her, her death is actually the result of an accident. A long trial ensues; but in spite of all efforts, Clyde is convicted, and the story ends with his electrocution.

Roberta Alden, Clyde's mistress. A factory girl and the daughter of poor parents, she falls in love with Clyde, whom she meets at the factory. In spite of her moral scruples, she becomes his mistress. When she finds herself pregnant, she tries to force him to marry her, though she knows that he no longer loves her. This situation leads to her accidental death at Clyde's hands.

Titus Alden, Roberta's shiftless father.

Sondra Finchley, a wealthy girl who takes up with Clyde to spite his cousin Gilbert. She falls in love with him and is planning to marry him when he is arrested for murder.

Asa Griffiths, Clyde's father, a poverty-stricken itinerant evangelist.

Elvira Griffiths, Clyde's mother, the strongest member of the family.

Hester (Esta) Griffiths, Clyde's sister, who is seduced and abandoned by an actor.

Samuel Griffiths, Clyde's uncle, a rich manufacturer who gives Clyde a job in his factory.

Elizabeth Griffiths, Samuel's wife.

Gilbert Griffiths, their son, a pompous young man who resents Clyde.

Myra Griffiths and

Bella Griffiths, daughters of Samuel and Elizabeth.

Hortense Briggs, a crude, mercenary shopgirl whom Clyde tries to seduce. She is interested only in what she can persuade him to spend on her.

Thomas Ratterer, a bellboy who works with Clyde and introduces him to fast life.

Willard Sparser, the boy who steals the car and causes the accident that drives Clyde from Kansas City.

Orville Mason, a ruthless and politically ambitious district attorney who prosecutes Clyde.

Burton Burleigh, Mason's assistant. In the morgue, he threads some of Roberta's hair into Clyde's camera to provide the evidence necessary for conviction.

Alvin Belknap and

Reuben Jephson, defense attorneys.

Governor Waltham, the governor of New York, who rejects Clyde's plea for commutation of his sentence.

The Reverend Duncan McMillan, an evangelist who brings Clyde spiritual comfort just before the execution.

AMERIKA

Author: Franz Kafka (1883-1924)
First published: 1927
Genre: Novel

Locale: Primarily New York City
Time: Early twentieth century
Plot: Magical Realism

Karl Rossman, a fifteen- or sixteen-year-old youth who leaves his native Prague to seek his fortune in America. A sensitive, naïve adolescent who has been treated unfairly by his parents, Karl arrives in America with little money and few possessions but with a strong determination to triumph over circumstances. He is hardworking, eager to learn, and willing to make sacrifices—in many ways, it would seem, the ideal immigrant. His first experiences in America, however, are nightmarish, comically so in their reversal of the immigrant's dreams. Karl sees justice travestied, is himself falsely accused and beaten, and becomes a fugitive, finding a place only among the outcast. After a hiatus in the narrative (perhaps several years), however, Karl regains

hope and responds to a poster advertising jobs with the Theatre of Oklahoma (apparently a government project on a fantastic scale). In a spirit of rejoicing, Karl leaves on a rail journey across America, secure in the belief that in Oklahoma he will at last realize his dreams for himself in the New World.

Senator Edward Jacob, Karl's wealthy uncle, a proud, stuffy, self-made man. Karl meets this red-faced gentleman with a thin bamboo cane in the ship's office. The owner of Jacob Despatch Agency in New York, he has acquired American citizenship and severed all ties to his European past. Jacob exults in saving his nephew from a life of wretchedness, doing so partly because of pity and partly because of his strong dislike for his own relatives who have set the boy adrift. He takes him into his lavish surroundings, supporting and advising him and indulging the youth in every modern advantage. At the same time, he tyrannizes over him, expecting Karl to seek his unconditional approval in every situation. Without a word of warning, he castigates Karl for unintentionally going against his wishes. Convinced that nothing good can come from Karl's family, Jacob disappears from Karl's life just as unexpectedly as he entered it.

The Stoker, a ship employee. A huge, brawny man who confines Karl in a tiny compartment below the decks of the ship in New York Harbor so as to have an audience for his complaints against his superior, Schubal, who, he says, bullies him. Although Karl argues for him before the captain, the Stoker loses his case, because Schubal has fifteen noisy witnesses to support him.

Grete Mitzelbach (GREH-teh MIHT-zehl-bahkh), the fifty-year-old manageress of the Hotel Occidental. Herself an immigrant from Vienna, she benignly takes on Karl as her protégé but finds herself powerless to defend him against the Head Waiter's charges of dereliction.

Therese Berchtold (teh-RAY-zeh BEHRKH-tohlt), an eighteen-year-old Pomeranian girl who serves as Grete Mitzelbach's typist. Having warned Karl to stay away from Robinson and Delamarche, she is grief-stricken at his dismissal from the Hotel Occidental.

Brunelda, a wealthy, fat singer, the former wife of a cocoa manufacturer. She keeps Delamarche in her suburban flat with Robinson as their servant. She spends most of her time lying on a filthy couch in her red gown.

Robinson, an Irishman who attaches himself to Karl and ultimately causes him to lose his job as lift boy. He becomes a lazy drunk who lies on the balcony at Brunelda's flat and attempts to get Karl to perform the housework so that he can care for Brunelda personally.

Delamarche (deh-lah-MAHRSH), a Frenchman who succeeds in the New World by binding himself to Brunelda as her kept man.

— *Janie Caves McCauley*

AMONG WOMEN ONLY
(Tra donne sole)

Author: Cesare Pavese (1908-1950)
First published: 1949
Genre: Novel

Locale: Turin, Italy
Time: Late 1940's
Plot: Symbolic realism

Clelia Oitana (kleh-lee-ah oh-ih-TAH-nah), the narrator, a successful couturiere, who moves from Rome to Turin, Italy, to open a fashion house. Clelia, who had escaped from the Turin working-class quarter seventeen years before, returns, at the age of thirty-four, as an attractive, experienced woman. She had been driven by ambition to get ahead but is now aware that the life she has created is largely empty. Clelia moves among the elite young people of postwar Turin and finds them to lead frivolous, meaningless lives, escaping from boredom by engaging in slumming expeditions and vicious gossip about one another. Clelia is not very happy with her life, but her work, at least, brings her satisfaction. Fulfilling work is something that her friends do not have.

Rosetta Mola, the twenty-three-year-old daughter of a rich, proper Turin family. Rosetta, a serious, naïve woman, is fed up with the meaningless existence of her social group and yet unable to find an alternative. She attempts suicide the night Clelia returns to Turin. Clelia meets her and realizes that she is in trouble but has no answer to Rosetta's fundamental question: When life and love teach you who you are, as Clelia has assured her it would, what do you do with what you have learned? The book closes with Rosetta's death by suicide.

Momina (moh-MIH-nah), a rich, well-educated, former baroness. The fresh-faced and attractive brunette, slightly younger than Clelia, is the center of the group of elite young Turinians, with all activities revolving around her. Momina is cynical, discontented, and disgusted with life and with everyone and everything. Although she can live with the emptiness of her life and dismisses it with a cynical shrug, she feeds the nihilistic void within Rosetta. Momina is dangerous, perhaps deadly, to Rosetta.

Gisella (gee-zehl-lah), the keeper of a small shop and an old friend of Clelia. Gisella is a thin, gray woman with a bony, resentful face, in whom Clelia sees herself if she had not escaped the working-class quarter. Momina's group offers little to Clelia, but neither does Gisella or others from Clelia's past.

Morelli, an older friend of Clelia, whom she met in Rome and who provides a means for her to enter the elite circles and salons of Turin. Morelli seems to lead the same unproductive life as the other members of the Turin leisure class, but he possesses more substance. He enjoys life and points out to Clelia that she has turned work into a vice that controls her and into a criterion that she uses to judge the worth of other people. He describes to her the accomplishments of the parents of the young people that Clelia meets in Turin and shares her disgust at the aimless existence of the young, including their inability to enjoy life.

Febo (FAYB-oh), an architect who designs Clelia's fashion house. An attractive, young man who possesses a talent and who works; he is a frivolous, irrepressible womanizer and playboy. Clelia sleeps with him on one occasion out of boredom and to stop him from pestering her.

Becuccio (beh-KEW-chee-oh), the foreman of the crew reconstructing Clelia's fashion house. He is a young, competent, muscular, curly-haired man with an attractive smile; he appeals to Clelia. She sleeps with him out of attraction, not boredom, but recognizes, as he does, that their ways of life are too different to allow any more than a passing affair. Becuccio, a Communist and skilled worker, seems to suffer none of the emptiness of his "betters."

— *William E. Pemberton*

AMORES

Author: Ovid (Publius Ovidius Naso, 43 B.C.E. -17 C.E.)
First published: c. 20 B.C.E. (English translation c. 1597)
Genre: Poetry

Locale: Rome
Time: Augustan Age
Plot: Erotic

The speaker, who is never named; some argue that he should be distinguished from Ovid. This first-person narrator is a Roman poet born in Sulmo, as Ovid was, and in several poems he argues the case for the erotic elegy. The speaker or persona in the poems is a young man who enjoys making love and playing at love, but he is not serious about much of anything, except, presumably, his poetry, in which he has considerable confidence. He is a sexual athlete, but he is frank about his shortcomings. His romantic liaisons often are thwarted by a mistress's husband, other lovers, servants (gate-keepers), and in one case by an old witch named Dipsas, whom he overhears advising his mistress to hold out for money. Perhaps because he is promiscuous himself, he is suspicious of his mistresses. He seems most devoted to Corinna, but she is clearly not his only love, and like the other women in his life, she occasionally frustrates him by playing hard to get, so that he is forced into the conventional role of the woeful, unrequited lover. How much of Ovid's actual experience and personality are vested in the speaker is impossible to say. Those who focus on the relationship between these poems and the love poems of Propertius regard the speaker as a playful and fun-loving version of the Propertian speaker, who is generally more serious and sometimes bitter over the frustrations that come with the game of love. Ovid's speaker is much more willing to play and to enjoy the game as a game.

He is witty and audacious, in good humor even when he is lamenting his inability to get through to one mistress or another. When he declares that love has made him thin, readers do not take him so seriously as to be concerned for his health.

Corinna, the only other character of note to appear in the poems, though a few others are mentioned by name. She is the speaker's most significant, but not his only, mistress. She never speaks for herself but is always portrayed by the speaker; she is seen only from his point of view. The speaker considers her to have been his best sexual partner, and she understands how to manipulate him. It is not clear if Corinna is the mistress he beats, but it is she for whom he composes the famous elegy on the death of a pet parrot. He also expresses genuine concern over Corinna's ocean voyage. In general, Corinna appears to be the focus of the speaker's more sincere love poems, and even though he asserts that "beauty makes Corinna hard," he claims that he will remain devoted to her. He laments his loss of Corinna, whom he describes as his "sole inspiration," because others have fallen in love with his depiction of her beauty. The speaker turns on the reader by insisting on her role as a literary character: "My praise of Corinna should have been read as fiction./ You are my trouble—you, uncritical reader."

— *Ron McFarland*

AMPHITRYON
(Amphitruo)

Author: Plautus (c. 254-184 B.C.E.)
First published: c. 185 B.C.E.
Genre: Drama

Locale: Thebes
Time: Second century B.C.E.
Plot: Comedy

Amphitryon (am-FIHT-ree-uhn), a Theban general. Having defeated his enemies, Amphitryon is eager to return to his home and his wife. When she says that she already has seen him, he first thinks her unfaithful or mad. Confronted by a man who looks like him and insists he is indeed Amphitryon, he begins to think that he himself has lost his mind. When he breaks down the door to his house, he is insulted by Mercury, who is disguised as Sosia, then rebuked by his wife, and finally confronted with someone who looks just like him. On his way to kill everyone inside the house, Amphitryon is knocked down by one of Jupiter's thunderbolts. Coming back to consciousness, he is assured that his wife is innocent of any wrongdoing, and he bows to the will of Jupiter.

Alcmena (alk-MEE-nuh), the faithful wife of Amphitryon, who left her pregnant when he went to war. She believes that she has spent the night with her husband, and she has the golden cup he gave her to prove it. When he turns up again, with another golden cup, she is stunned. All she can do is deny his accusations of infidelity and conclude that he is mad. Alcmena goes into labor. She invokes the gods and, with much thunder but without pain, she produces twins, one of whom

jumps up and kills two snakes. Jupiter explains that he is the father of the stronger son.

Jupiter, the chief Roman god. Desirous of Alcmena, he takes the form of her husband, spends the night with her, and impregnates her. To make the night last as long as possible, he arranges for the stars to stop in place. Jupiter returns to the house in part to tease Amphitryon; more important, he wishes to make sure that Alcmena comes to no harm, either from Amphitryon or in childbirth. He explains matters to both husband and wife and assures them of his friendship in the future.

Mercury, a Roman god, Jupiter's son and his messenger. Disguised as the slave Sosia, he addresses the audience in the prologue, explaining the situation and pointing out that both he and Jupiter will be actors in this story. When Sosia arrives, Mercury argues with him, beats him, and sends him back to Amphitryon. Later, summoned by Jupiter, Mercury appears as Sosia. This time, pretending to be drunk, he empties a pail of water over the head of the real Amphitryon.

Sosia (SOH-see-uh), the slave whom Amphitryon took along when he went off to war. Afraid of everyone and everything, Sosia is easily intimidated, and between Mercury's arguments and his blows, he comes to doubt his own identity. When he returns to the house, he tells his master that Alcmena must be mad. Later, he dutifully obeys Jupiter's command and brings the ship's pilot to the house, thus setting up the scene in which Amphitryon and Jupiter, in the guise of Amphitryon, accuse each other of being impostors.

— *Rosemary M. Canfield Reisman*

AMPHITRYON 38

Author: Jean Giraudoux (1882-1944)
First published: 1929
Genre: Drama

Locale: Thebes, Greece
Time: Antiquity
Plot: Mock-heroic

Alcmena (alk-MEE-nuh), the wife of Amphitryon, known for both her beauty and her fidelity. Although she is flattered by the fact that Jupiter wishes to mate with her, she is determined to remain faithful to her husband. She is not interested in adventure or passion, and she uses all of her wiles and wit to remain constant rather than to deceive her husband. When she begins to suspect that Jupiter already has come to her bed disguised as Amphitryon, she demands the truth but quickly accepts his false assurances rather than disrupt the peace of her life with her husband. In her verbal skirmishes with Jupiter, she is always victorious, refusing to allow him to reveal himself as a god who is only posing as her husband. Eventually, she forces him to choose her friendship rather than her love. She is adamant in her preference for the frailties of humanity over the powers and the abilities of the gods, refusing Jupiter's offer of immortality or an opportunity to look into the future.

Jupiter, the supreme god in Roman mythology. His Greek counterpart is Zeus. He is lecherous, and when the mood seizes him, he seduces various mortal women who attract him. As chief god, he believes that this is his right. When he desires Alcmena, he uses his supreme power to create a war so that Amphitryon will be called away to battle. Jupiter then tricks Alcmena into taking him to her bed by disguising himself as her husband. Once in human form, he is amazed at how much more masterful he feels than when he was a god. Jupiter, hoping to return to Alcmena for a second night, has heavenly voices announce that he is going to become Alcmena's lover in the night to come, but she eventually convinces him to accept her friendship instead. He allows himself to be satisfied with this, knowing that she already is impregnated with his child, Hercules. His final gift to the couple enables them to forget the events of the play.

Mercury, the messenger of the gods in Roman mythology. His Greek name is Hermes. Clever, cynical, and eloquent, he acts as Jupiter's agent in the seductions. It is he who enables Jupiter to shed his godly characteristics and imitate the mortal Amphitryon so perfectly that he is able to deceive the perceptive Alcmena. His role is as a stage manager in the affair, advising and directing. He provides an ironic commentary on the behavior of both the gods and humankind.

Amphitryon (ahm-FEE-tree-ohn), the prince of Thebes, a warrior who is devoted to his wife. He tells Jupiter that he would die before willingly giving Alcmena to the god. He retains his innocence, unaware that Alcmena and Jupiter have had intercourse and that he has slept with Leda. He believes that the child soon to be born is his; he is convinced that naming the baby Hercules and allowing the crowd to believe that Jupiter and Alcmena have been lovers is simply a way for the god to save face.

Leda (LEE-duh), who is visited by Jupiter in the form of a swan. As soon as she hears that Jupiter is to visit Alcmena, she comes to rejoice with her. Unlike Alcmena, Leda was delighted by a godly visitation. She agrees to disguise herself as Alcmena when Jupiter comes, so that she can again experience that joy. Unfortunately, it is Amphitryon who appears rather than Jupiter.

Ecclissa, Alcmena's nurse. She reflects the views of the citizens of Thebes, who are thrilled that Jupiter has honored their town by choosing to seduce the wife of their prince. She is proud that Alcmena will be remembered for all time as Jupiter's love. Ecclissa is excited by her connection to this fame and by the fact that she will have the privilege of helping to raise a demigod. She is unable to understand Alcmena's reluctance to accept her destiny.

Sosios (SOH-sih-uhs), a slave. Like Mercury, he provides ironic commentary on the actions of the gods and humans. He warns that if Alcmena is successful in resisting Jupiter, chaos will descend on Thebes and Amphitryon will be stoned by his own subjects. He accuses her, like other tedious and faithful women, of putting honor before her husband's welfare.

— *Mary E. Mahony*

ANABASIS
(Anabase)

Author: Saint-John Perse (Alexis Saint-Léger Léger, 1887-1975)
First published: 1924
Genre: Poetry

Locale: The East
Time: Indeterminate
Plot: Allegory

The Leader, the central character, an unidentified man. He is the speaker who recites in epic fashion the entirety of *Anabasis*. He is a nomad who symbolizes the legendary and frequent migratory movements on horseback westward from Asia, heroic travels that bring discovery and adventure and that culminate in the foundation of new civilizations. The

Leader is an introspective man whose ancestry, physical traits, and age are not described. He is, in this way, the incarnation of humankind in action, struggling between the desire to create an organized society and the wish to depart in search of new lands. Ultimately, in canto 8, the Leader heeds the call to depart, yielding thus to the anabasis, humankind's march, and to the deep-rooted restlessness of which he is a living example. At times, the Leader becomes preoccupied with the oppressive influences of death, but because of the somewhat mystical inspiration he receives in dreams and that encourages him to pursue adventure, his spiritual dimension leads him to affirm the power of life, and, consequently, the importance of not becoming immobile through the contemplation of death. This spiritual aspect of the Leader is the sole characteristic that is evoked. In essence, he reveals himself through his interior existence, his thoughts, and, especially, through the sometimes felt conflict between sedentary and nomadic ways of life. The Leader is an exceptional individual who at times scorns the men who follow him blindly but who, ultimately, feels an abiding camaraderie with them.

The Stranger, a wanderer and unidentified man who appears in the first song of *Anabasis* and who offers bitter-tasting berries, which produce euphoria, to the Leader. He speaks of far-off provinces and instills in the Leader the desire to depart on a quest for conquest and discovery. His presence in canto 5 reawakens in the Leader the need to pursue further conquests. Enigmatic and ambiguous, the Stranger is symbolic of humanity's nomadic spirit.

The Women, a group of young women, representative of a people without men, who greet the Leader and his horsemen as the latter travel westward. These women embody the sensuality desired by men and offer them physical pleasure. Such a union is capable of producing a new society, for it brings completeness to the women as well as to the men.

The Men, a variety of men serving to represent the diversity of individuals who form a complex society. They are described by the Leader at the end of *Anabasis*. Among this group are insect eaters, vendors of sugar and cinnamon, craftsmen of leather goods, the juggler, the man who gathers pollen in a wooden jar, he who sees his soul reflected in a sword blade, the man with the falcon, the lustful, the man learned in sciences, the storyteller, and horsemen bearing letters of alliance. Such a diversity of human activity forms the mosaic of life's experiences in a collectivity.

— *Kenneth W. Meadwell*

ANANCY'S SCORE

Author: Andrew Salkey (1928-   )
First published: 1973
Genre: Short fiction

Locale: West Africa and the Caribbean
Time: Creation to the Vietnam War era
Plot: Fable

Anancy, a "spider individual person" who respects no one, human or beast. Much like his African-Caribbean counterpart, Anancy is a trickster figure, one who transcends natural and cultural boundaries. As a trickster, Anancy symbolizes primal creativity and a pathological bent toward destruction. He is both childlike and ruthlessly self-absorbed. Anancy is a marked creature in both worlds, viewed often as a pest but in the later stories almost as a savior for the Caribbean peoples. He can be a womanizer and a con artist while exhibiting an almost innate nobility. Anancy, a changeling, at one point calls himself "Peacefulness." As Peacefulness, Anancy becomes a romancer of women, much to the despair of the villagers. Other forms Anancy uses are Hope, Peace Meal, Atomic Horse, Vietnam Anancy, Spider Preacher, and Sweet Love-Powder Merchant. At the end, he undergoes a remarkable transformation into New Man Anancy, a potential leader in the land of the C. World.

Anancy's wife, an astute female creature, more than a match in wits for her trickster mate. Anancy's wife is often characterized by her overwhelming sexuality and good sense. In the Creation, Anancy and his wife become one spider individual person. In this capacity, Anancy's cunning ways are attributed to the ways of his wife, who is locked within his arachnid body. In other stories, it is not clear whether Anancy and his wife are one creature or two.

Brother Tiger, the philosopher/sage in Anancy's world. Anancy consults with Brother Tiger, depending on the tiger's wisdom to untangle dilemmas.

Brother Dog, the critic person, somewhat surly and cynical. In the Beginning, Brother Dog is described as a warmonger, goading others to wreak havoc. Sometimes he is called **Ge Bon**.

Brother Snake, a serpent. As in the Judeo-Christian Creation story, the snake offers the woman (in this case, Anancy's wife) a delicious fruit and bids her to eat it, which she does. Unlike the Garden of Eden serpent, Brother Snake is a positive figure, the harbinger of change. When Anancy and his wife become fearful of the animals, they flee the forest. During their flight, they stop to appeal to Brother Snake for assistance. Brother Snake consequently becomes their savior, transforming them into a singular spider that shares Brother Snake's power of change and magic.

Brother Tacuma, Anancy's sometime traveling companion outside the village. Also a spider individual, Brother Tacuma exerts a calming, rational influence over the impetuous Anancy.

Brother Oversea, the self-identified narrator in the short story "Anancy, the Spider Preacher." This is the only story in the collection in which the narrator is identified.

Sister Mysore Cow, Anancy's friend, who reserves judgment until she can survey the whole picture. Anancy tends to misread Sister Mysore Cow's cautiousness as a lack of faith in him and the new world order.

— *Anita M. Vickers*

THE ANATOMY LESSON

Author: Philip Roth (1933-　　)
First published: 1983
Genre: Novel

Locale: Primarily New York City and Chicago, Illinois
Time: 1973
Plot: Comic realism

Nathan Zuckerman, the protagonist, a successful writer and author of the notorious best-selling novel *Carnovsky*. For eighteen months, he has been suffering inexplicably from extreme neck and back pains that prevent him from extensive reading and even from writing, though he feels he has nothing left to write about. To make matters worse, he has turned forty. He lives alone, and to help ease his pain he not only drinks and smokes marijuana but also has a bevy of four girlfriends who visit him at different times and cater to his needs, including his sexual needs. Finally, in desperation, he decides to give up writing and become a doctor.

Robert (Bobby) Freytag, Nathan's college chum who is now a successful anesthesiologist in Chicago. Nathan flies to Chicago to consult with him about applying to medical school. Bobby's mother died three weeks earlier, and at the cemetery with Bobby's aggrieved father, Nathan loses his head (he has been taking too much Percodan and drinking vodka), attacks the old man, and falls on a gravestone, fracturing his skull and sustaining other injuries.

Henry Zuckerman, Nathan's younger brother, who believes that *Carnovsky* was a terrible affront to American Jews in general and to the Zuckerman family in particular. He holds Nathan responsible for hastening the death of their father, whose dying breath sounded like a curse on his older son. A year later, their adoring mother also dies, but Nathan does not arrive in time to hear her last words. Before her death, she scribbles the word "holocaust" on a scrap of paper, which Nathan carries with him, trying to figure out what she meant.

Milton Appel, a professor and literary critic whose severe criticism of *Carnovsky* and his other fiction Zuckerman finds it impossible to forgive. The criticism rankles still more when Appel wants Zuckerman to help defend Israeli interests by writing something "uplifting" about the country and its ideals.

Jaga, a Polish émigré who works as a receptionist in the office of Nathan's trichologist (among his other ailments, Nathan is suffering from hair loss). At first, she plays hard to get, but eventually she yields to Nathan's charms and becomes one of his four playmates. During their lovemaking, she utters long monologues about herself and her hopeless existence as a woman and an exile.

Gloria, the wife of Nathan's accountant and another of the female comforters who visit him. She enjoys making rice pudding for him and wearing a G-string.

Jenny, a painter who lives in Vermont and tries to lure Nathan away from New York to the country, where they could live a healthy life and eat fresh vegetables.

Diana, a rich heiress and the youngest of Nathan's four lovers and comforters. A student at Finch College, she tries to help Nathan by appealing to the Protestant work ethic. She also tries to convince him to stop hating Appel and write the essay.

Ricky, the female chauffeur who drives Nathan from the airport in Chicago to his hotel. En route, Nathan assumes the identity of Milton Appel, whom he describes as an arch pornographer. He tries hard to entice Ricky, but he is no match against her sturdy independence and healthy mental state. Finally, after long enduring his tirades and propositions, she tells him off.

— *Jay L. Halio*

THE ANCIENT CHILD

Author: N. Scott Momaday (1934-　　)
First published: 1989
Genre: Novel

Locale: An Indian reservation in Oklahoma and San Francisco, California
Time: Late 1980's
Plot: Mythic

Locke "Set" Setman, a forty-four-year-old artist of Kiowa descent. Orphaned when he is seven years old, he is sent to a Catholic boarding school and is subsequently adopted. As an adult, he is a successful painter, living a sophisticated life in San Francisco. He receives an enigmatic telegram summoning him to the funeral of Kope'mah, an Indian relative he never met. Intrigued, he travels to the Oklahoma reservation where she lived. While he is there, Grey gives him a bundle that contains the powerful bear medicine. Set politely accepts it, not realizing that from it emanates a magic power that will transform him, body and soul. When he returns to the city, his life gradually falls apart. Although he continues to paint, the tone of his paintings changes. Originally valued for their vivid color, his paintings take on a darker aspect that reveals his growing inner turmoil. Set tries to hide his despair by carrying on as if his life is unchanged. He travels to Paris to exhibit his work but is suddenly called back home because of the death of his adoptive father. His father's death and his growing obsession with the medicine bundle lead to Set's further psychological deterioration, and he finally experiences a complete breakdown. He is found in his paint-stained studio, sitting in front of the open medicine bundle. After being committed to a psychiatric hospital for several weeks, he is released. Lola drives him to Oklahoma and places him in Grey's care. Grey takes charge of his healing and drives him to Lukachukai, a Navaho reservation and her childhood home. Surrounded by Grey's family, he continues his recovery and begins to paint again. He and Grey marry, and they soon expect their first child. Before their baby is born, Set undertakes a vision quest on which he fulfills his destiny as a shaman and is transformed into the Bear.

Grey, a nineteen-year-old Navajo/Kiowa girl who becomes a powerful medicine woman. Grey is a natural visionary who possesses a rich imagination. The focus of her fantasies is Billy the Kid; she imagines herself to be his lover. She is also the disciple of her grandmother, Kope'mah, from whom she learns that Set will become the Bear. Grey is the one who sends Set the telegram summoning him to the reservation after Kope'mah's death, thus setting into motion the events instigating Set's transformation. After Grey gives Set the medicine bundle, she begins a transformation from a girl to a medicine woman. She gradually gives up her vivid fantasies about Billy the Kid and becomes immersed in preparations for her new calling. Her growing powers alert her to the time when Set will again enter her life. Finally, when Lola brings Set to the reservation, Grey is ready to take on her role as Set's healer and wife.

Kope'mah, a powerful medicine woman and Grey's grandmother. More than one hundred years old, Kope'mah lies dying and is attended by Grey. She bequeaths her power to Grey and tells her about Set's destiny as the Bear. Even after her death, Kope'mah's spirit directs Grey and teaches her.

Lola Bourne, a divorcée, consultant, and musician. A knowledgeable student of art, she meets Set at one of his exhibits. They are lovers for four years, but as Set's mental state deteriorates, their relationship does as well. Still in love with him, Lola is grief-stricken when she witnesses the change in his personality. She realizes that she must let him go and drives him to the reservation to place him in Grey's care.

Bent Sandridge, a philosopher and retired academic who adopts Set and provides him with a loving, stable, and stimulating environment in which to grow.

Alais Sancerre, owner of a Parisian art gallery where Set exhibits his paintings. She points out to him that the theme of transformation is prevalent in his work. It is an important observation and foreshadows his ultimate transformation into the Bear.

Billy the Kid, whose real name is **Henry McCarty**, the notorious outlaw who is the subject of Grey's fantasies. She finds compelling his love for adventure as well as his wild and violent, yet ironically gentlemanly, nature.

— *Pegge Bochynski*

AND QUIET FLOWS THE DON
(Tikhii Don)

Author: Mikhail Sholokhov (1905-1984)
First published: 1928
Genre: Novel

Locale: Tatarsk, Russia
Time: 1913-1918
Plot: Historical realism

Gregor Melekhov (GREH-gohr MEH-leh-khov), a native of the Don basin in Russia. He is married to one woman but openly goes about with another. His father whips him, and he leaves home. He joins the army and distinguishes himself in action. When the Soviet Socialist Republic is established and civil war breaks out, Gregor joins the Red Army and is made an officer. When the Red Army is beaten, Gregor, after denouncing the cruelty of Podtielkov, his old revolutionary leader who is about to be executed, returns to his village.

Piotra Melekhov (PYOH-trah), Gregor's elder brother, who is in the army with him. When the revolutionary troops advance on Tatarsk, their home village, Piotra is named commander of the villagers, who are organized by a counterrevolutionary officer.

Natalia Melekhova (nah-TAH-lyah MEH-leh-khoh-vah), Gregor's wife. When she realizes that Gregor does not love her, she tries to commit suicide. After Gregor discovers that his

mistress has been unfaithful to him, Natalia and Gregor are reconciled, and she bears him twins.

Aksinia Astakhova (ak-SEE-nya as-TA-khoh-vah), Gregor's mistress, married to Stepan Astakhov, who mistreats her. Her affair with Gregor becomes a village scandal. She goes away with him, and they become servants to a wealthy landowning family. When Gregor goes away to join the army, she is unfaithful to him with Eugene Listnitsky, the son of the family. The affair is broken off by Gregor, who whips her and goes home to his wife.

Ilia Bunchuk (eel-YA boon-CHOOK), a revolutionary leader and the chief agitator in his company. He deserts the company before he can be handed over to the authorities. He joins the revolutionary troops as a machine gunner and is prominent in the administration of the local revolutionary government. He falls in love with Anna Poodko, a woman machine gunner who is killed.

ANDORRA

Author: Max Frisch (1911-1991)
First published: 1961
Genre: Drama

Locale: Andorra, an imaginary small state
Time: The 1950's
Plot: Social criticism

Andri, a twenty-year-old who was brought up in Andorra (not the small European country but a "model") in the belief that he is a Jew whom his foster father, the teacher, rescued from persecution by the "blacks" across the border. Since then, the Andorrans have forced him into the role of an outsider and to behave like their stereotypical notion of a Jew—a rootless, greedy, lustful, heartless, oversensitive coward. Learning that

he is not a Jew exacerbates his confusion and anguish. Having been ferreted out by the totalitarian "Jew-detector," Andri finally is dragged to his doom by the invading blacks while his fellow Andorrans look on passively.

The teacher, named **Can**, a man who drinks heavily in an attempt to drown his sorrow over the stupidity, cupidity, and hypocrisy of his fellow Andorrans. As a young, idealistic gadfly and firebrand, he called his pupils' attention to the many untruths in their textbooks. Now, however, the man who cravenly disowned his son Andri has a chilling sense of doom and attempts in vain to atone for his cowardice and deception. He is the only Andorran who offers resistance to the nightmarish invaders, but eventually he feels compelled to hang himself in his schoolroom.

Barblin, the teacher's teenage daughter. She falls in love with Andri without realizing that their union would be incestuous. Barblin suffers the trauma of being raped by the brutish soldier, Peider. In the end, the half-demented girl, the only Andorran who has nothing to whitewash, senselessly splashes white paint on the town's cobblestones and speaks of saving Andri's shoes for his possible return.

The señora, a mysterious woman from across the border. She confronts her erstwhile lover, the teacher, and accuses him of cowardice in not acknowledging their son. She is suspected of being a spy for the blacks and is killed by a stone; Andri is falsely accused of having thrown it.

Father Benedict, a priest who is more sensitive and insightful than his fellow citizens, yet even he is not free from prejudice. He is the only one who really acknowledges his guilt: He enchained Andri, as it were, by fashioning for himself a fixed image of him.

The mother, the teacher's wife and Barblin's mother. She strives in vain for a peaceful atmosphere in the family.

Ferrer, the new medical officer of Andorra, widely traveled and yet a narrow-minded, frustrated Jew baiter.

Prader, a carpenter who believes that Andri should not be his apprentice but instead should become a salesman or a stockbroker. He charges the teacher an exorbitant sum for training Andri.

Peider, a soldier. He is a quintessential bully, drunken braggart, chauvinist, and anti-Semite.

The innkeeper, who is as hypocritical as his fellow citizens. He employs Andri as a kitchen boy.

Fedri, an opportunist who is too weak to oppose his master's trickery in the carpenter's shop when the chair he has made proves inferior to Andri's.

— *Harry Zohn*

ANDRIA

Author: Terence (Publius Terentius Afer, c. 190-159 B.C.E.)
First performed: 166 B.C.E.
Genre: Drama

Locale: Athens
Time: The second century B.C.E.
Plot: Comedy

Simo (SIH-moh), an aged Athenian. An outspoken, philosophical man, Simo has arranged a marriage between his son Pamphilus and Philumena, the daughter of his friend Chremes. Chremes breaks the engagement when it is discovered that Pamphilus is enamored of Glycerium, the sister of a courtesan. To test his son's fidelity, Simo goes ahead with preparations for the wedding. Advised of this ruse, Pamphilus pretends to agree to the marriage, but to his distress, Chremes renews the offer of his daughter's hand. Chremes then discovers that Glycerium has borne Pamphilus' son and again breaks the engagement. Simo is berating his son for disgracing the family name when Crito, an Andrian, reveals that Glycerium is the long-lost daughter of Chremes. Overjoyed, Simo and Chremes order the marriage of Pamphilus and Glycerium to proceed.

Pamphilus (PAM-fih-luhs), Simo's agreeable and moderate young son. He has fallen in love with Glycerium, made her pregnant, and promised to marry her. Simo's abrupt order that he marry Chremes' daughter leaves Pamphilus facing a dilemma: He must either disobey his father or betray his beloved Glycerium.

Davus (DAH-vuhs), Simo's servant. Deciding that his love for Pamphilus is stronger than his fear of Simo, Davus, in spite of Simo's warnings, tries to disrupt the marriage plans. When Pamphilus, acting on Davus' advice, finds himself in a dilemma, Davus cleverly contrives to inform Chremes that Glycerium has borne Pamphilus' child. Simo has Davus imprisoned for his effrontery, but he is freed when all turns out well.

Sosia (SOH-see-uh), a former slave whom Simo had freed in appreciation of Sosia's faithfulness. Simo reveals to Sosia his plan to test his son's character.

Glycerium (glih-SEE-ree-uhm), Chremes' daughter, originally named Pasibula. Shipwrecked with her uncle in Andros,

Glycerium had grown up there as the daughter of an Andrian family.

Chremes (KRAY-meez), a wealthy Athenian and Simo's friend. He is the father of both Glycerium and Philumena.

Chrysis (KREE-sihs), a beautiful young Andrian who had become a courtesan after her arrival in Athens. Glycerium, reared as Chrysis' sister, had come to Athens with her. On her deathbed, Chrysis had made Pamphilus swear to marry Glycerium.

Charinus (ka-RI-nuhs), a young Athenian in love with Philumena. Pamphilus promises he will try to win Philumena for Charinus.

Crito (KRI-toh), a native of Andros who comes to Athens to attend to the estate of his dead cousin, Chrysis. After a sharp exchange with Simo, who thinks Crito is a confidence man, Crito convinces Simo and Chremes that Glycerium is really Chremes' daughter.

Byrrhia (BIH-ree-uh), Charinus' servant. Overhearing Pamphilus agree to marry Philumena, Byrrhia thinks his master is being betrayed.

Philumena (fih-luh-MEE-nuh), Chremes' daughter.

Mysis (MEE-sihs), Glycerium's maidservant. Davus stages an argument with Mysis to reveal to Chremes that Glycerium has borne Pamphilus' child.

Lesbia (LEHS-bee-uh), the tippling midwife who is called to attend Glycerium.

Dromo (DROH-moh), a servant called by Simo to carry off Davus.

Phania (FA-nee-uh), Chremes' brother. Pasibula, later named Glycerium, had been entrusted to Phania's care at the time of the shipwreck. He died in Andros.

ANDROMACHE
(Andromachē)

Author: Euripides (c. 486-406 B.C.E.)
First performed: 426 B.C.E.
Genre: Drama

Locale: The temple of Thetis in Thessaly
Time: About a decade after the Trojan War
Plot: Tragedy

Andromache (an-DRO-muh-kee), the widow of Hector, allotted at the fall of Troy as a slave to Neoptolemus, son of Achilles. The prologue, spoken by Andromache, gives the necessary background. Andromache has borne a son, Molossus, to Neoptolemus; he then married a Spartan princess, Hermione, who blames her own sterility on the machinations of Andromache. For this reason, Hermione wishes to kill both Andromache and her son and has called her father, King Menelaus, from Sparta to help her. Andromache has hidden her son and taken refuge at the altar of Thetis, for Neoptolemus has gone to Delphi to atone for his insolence to Apollo. The speech is restrained and dignified; Andromache, though a slave, is still the daughter of a great people. Hermione appears to see if her enemy will leave the sanctuary to face death. Andromache refuses and answers the accusations of Hermione directly, displaying the pride that at times gets the better of her discretion. Menelaus appears and reveals that he has found Andromache's son and that she must either surrender herself to be killed or sacrifice the child. In her pride, she cannot resist insulting Menelaus as an example of undeserved reputation, but she does give a reasoned and effective plea for her life and that of her child. Menelaus then reveals that the son will be surrendered to Hermione to do with as she likes. Betrayed, Andromache delivers a violent tirade against Spartans and ends with a dignified statement that she will never flatter the Spartans with a plea for mercy. Peleus appears, however, and saves both mother and child, who then disappear from the play.

Hermione (hur-MI-eh-nee), the daughter of Menelaus and Helen, wife of Neoptolemus. Proud of her Spartan heritage and independent of her husband, she attributes her sterility to Andromache. She states a major theme of the play, that a man who wishes to live happily should have only one wife, but this fact does not excuse the jealousy, cruelty, and impiety resulting from her sterility. Andromache rightfully accuses her of the lustfulness of her mother, Helen. When Menelaus leaves without her, she becomes hysterical and immodest and attempts suicide. Her fear of death is wild, and no one sympathizes with her. Orestes, Hermione's former suitor, appears. She leaves with him, feeling no remorse over the change of husbands.

Peleus (PEE-lews), the father of Achilles and grandfather of Neoptolemus. His rescue of Andromache is possible because of his rank as ruler of Pharsalia, but his attack on Menelaus as a general who has received far more credit than he deserved and on the Spartans and the causes of the Trojan War is an effective debasement of that "glorious war." He learns later of Orestes' plan to kill Neoptolemus. He is too late to prevent the murder but is assured by his former wife, the goddess Thetis, that Andromache's children will carry on the royal line and that she will take him to live with her eternally.

Menelaus (meh-neh-LAY-uhs,) the king of Sparta and father of Hermione. Brutal, cynical, and self-satisfied, he appears glorious, Andromache points out, only because he has the power of wealth. He bases his interference in Hermione's struggle against Andromache on the fact that a woman must rely on her kinsmen and on the sophists' argument that he has the right to dispose of what belongs to Neoptolemus, because they are friends.

Orestes (oh-REHS-teez), the son of Agamemnon and Clytemnestra, formerly betrothed to Hermione. Knowing that the murder of Andromache was attempted, he takes Hermione from Phthia. He reveals his plot to have Neoptolemus killed at Delphi because of Neoptolemus' refusal to give up his claim to Hermione.

Molossus (mo-LOS-uhs), the son of Andromache and Neoptolemus. Andromache's blessing in the person of a son emphasizes her contrast with the sterility of Hermione.

A slave woman, formerly the serving maid of Andromache in Troy. She emphasizes the first impression of the dignity of Andromache.

A nurse, the servant of Hermione. She reveals Hermione's reaction to the failure of her plan to kill Andromache.

Thetis, a goddess, chief of the Nereids and wife of Peleus. She commands that the body of Neoptolemus be buried at the Phthian temple and promises that Peleus will be transformed into a god.

A Chorus of Phthian women, who sympathize with Andromache, though they point out at times that she is hardly modest. They show only fear of Hermione and have not a word to say for her; they praise Peleus and disapprove of Menelaus because of his use of power to pervert justice. They speak of the disasters resulting from the Trojan War and wonder that the gods allowed that struggle.

ANDROMACHE
(Andromaque)

Author: Jean Racine (1639-1699)
First performed: 1667
Genre: Drama

Locale: Epirus
Time: Shortly after the Trojan War
Plot: Tragedy

Andromaque (ahn-dro-MAHK), the widow of Hector, the Trojan hero, and mother of his small son Astyanax. Andromaque, now a slave of the Greek hero Pyrrhus, spurns his advances; she has promised to be true to her dead husband. Pyrrhus does nothing to bring Andromaque to a real understanding of her situation as his slave. Frantic with love for her,

Pyrrhus threatens to kill her son if she will not marry him, but he counters his extravagant threats against the boy's life with equally extravagant promises for the future of Andromaque and her son. Pyrrhus actually fosters Andromaque's capacity to live in a dream, in a world of words, of codes, of courtly manners, until her mind is filled with a view of her past estate so incurably romantic that she cannot comprehend her present condition. Pyrrhus finally abandons hope of marrying Andromaque and repledges himself to Hermione, whereupon Andromaque begs Hermione to spare the life of Astyanax. Still jealous of Andromaque, Hermione rejects her plea. Andromaque, to save the life of her son, consents to marry Pyrrhus, but she remains full of unrealistic contrivance. Having obtained Pyrrhus' promises to guard her child forever, she plans to kill herself immediately after the wedding rites. Andromaque is still on this high note of idealistic foolhardiness when Pyrrhus is killed by the soldiers of Oreste.

Pyrrhus (peer-REWS), the king of Epirus, Achilles' son, betrothed to Hermione. He has come to regret his exploits in the Trojan War because they may have cost him Andromaque's love. He tries to move Andromaque by threatening to kill her son. He is so wild with love that, like Oreste, he becomes unreasonable and unmanly. Aristocratic and demanding, he must have his way with Andromaque, whatever the cost and despite his pledge to Hermione, who also must have her way. Caught in a situation designed to reveal the follies of a passion out of control and out of bounds, Pyrrhus is not so much a character as passion's ruin, although there are glimpses of the regal man he might be when rational.

Hermione (hehr-MYOHN), the daughter of Menelaus and Helen of Troy. Oreste loves her, she loves Pyrrhus, and Pyrrhus loves Andromaque, who has solemnly vowed to be true to her dead husband Hector. This situation brings out the worst in the four lovers. Each seeks his or her own satisfaction so that not a single altruistic action is born from the love of one for another, and tragedy ensues. While Pyrrhus vacillates between his promise to marry Hermione and his desire to wed his slave, the beautiful Andromaque, haughty Hermione vacillates be-

tween loving and hating Pyrrhus. Hermione rejects Oreste to accept the hand of Pyrrhus, encourages Oreste when Pyrrhus turns from her, rejects Oreste and triumphs over Andromaque when Pyrrhus returns to her, recalls Oreste to her side when Pyrrhus again rejects her, and arranges with Oreste the murder of Pyrrhus. After the death of Pyrrhus, the proud and wretched Hermione spurns Oreste once again. She admits to him at last that she has always loved Pyrrhus and that she lied when she told Oreste she could not marry him because she was betrothed by her father and bound by her duty as a Greek princess to Pyrrhus. Although cruel and treacherous, Hermione is also pitiful in her plight. She commits suicide after viewing Pyrrhus' body.

Oreste (oh-REHST), the son of Agamemnon, sent to Epirus to demand the death of Astyanax. Oreste morbidly longs for his own death. He is melancholic, self-centered, adolescent, and driven to frenzy whenever his passions are thwarted. Oreste believes himself born to be a living example of the wrath of the gods. For Hermione's sake, he forsakes the course that his honor and his reason suggest to him. Careless of honor and duty, he arranges the murder of Pyrrhus on Pyrrhus' wedding day, only to have Hermione reject him because he has murdered the man she loves. Wild with disappointment, Oreste takes leave of his senses and in madness is borne from the stage.

Pylade (pee-LAHD), Oreste's good friend. He provides the voice of reason to balance Oreste's passion, but his friendship leads him to conspire in the wild plot to kill Pyrrhus.

Cléone (klay-OHN), Hermione's handmaiden. She counsels reason and self-control.

Céphise (say-FEEZ), Andromaque's good friend and counselor, another voice of practical good sense and duty in the midst of the emotional storms that agitate the characters in this drama.

Phoenix (fay-NEEKS), the old man who counsels Pyrrhus. Phoenix's wise advice is ultimately an instrument for furthering the tragedy. The tides of passion cannot be stemmed in the young by the advice of the rational and the old.

THE ANDROMEDA STRAIN

Author: Michael Crichton (1942-   )
First published: 1969
Genre: Novel

Locale: Flatrock, Nevada
Time: 1967
Plot: Science fiction

Jeremy Stone, a professor of bacteriology at the University of California, Berkeley. He is a Nobel Prize winner, a lawyer, and a federal government consultant whose paper on the possibilities of a bacterial or viral invasion led to his Project Wildfire, a $22 million underground containment laboratory in the Nevada desert. It is at this laboratory that any extraterrestrial enemy is to be studied and countermeasures developed. Stone's papers on bacteriology and mutant reversion have led him to be compared to Albert Einstein. His insistence on a nuclear device to destroy the lab if the alien disease threatens to escape is the key to the project and to the plot. He is a thin, balding man with a prodigious memory, a sense of humor, and an overpowering impatience that leads him to interrupt speakers and to finish conversations. Four times married, this imperious man alienates colleagues but is unquestionably an intel-

lectual power. Stone views the disaster at Piedmont, Arizona, as a confusing but challenging puzzle and the survivors as the central clues.

Peter Leavitt, a clinical microbiologist and epidemiologist specializing in parasitology. He is the chief of bacteriology at the same hospital as Hall and responsible for recruiting Hall. Leavitt's research, conducted worldwide, is famous, but ill health made him give up research abroad. He suffers from epilepsy and is hypnotized by blinking lights. This carefully hidden vulnerability has potentially disastrous consequences when a flashing alarm renders him unconscious.

Charles Burton, a fifty-four-year-old pathologist who accompanies Stone to Piedmont and then to the Wildfire lab. Burton held a professorship at Baylor Medical and served as consultant to the NASA Manned Spaceflight Center in Houston. His specialty is the effects of bacteria on human tissues. His unruly and untidy appearance puts Stone off, but his expertise is undeniable. Burton accompanies Stone on his initial investigation of the Piedmont disaster and later is trapped in a lab with the virus after it is released by a failed seal.

Mark Hall, a surgeon Stone reluctantly enlisted in the Wildfire team when another was unable to come. Known by associates as "swift, quick-tempered, and unpredictable," he operates rapidly, laughing and joking while cutting, and becomes irritable when work becomes slow and difficult. He is called out of surgery to join the team and initially is not particularly welcome as a useful member (except for his knowledge of electrolytes and his unmarried status). In an intuitive leap, however, he comes to a final understanding of the terrifying disease. He describes his experiences as "horrifying" and "unfamiliar." The alien invader finally succumbs from common earthly causes, making Hall's discovery moot, but in the meantime, as the "Odd Man" of the Wildfire instruc-

tion manual, he is the only one who can stop the nuclear self-destruct mechanism.

Major Arthur Manchek, the Project Scoop duty officer, an engineer who reacts to the mysterious cutoff in transmission of the satellite recovery team sent to Piedmont. He decides to call an alert and set up flybys, scans, and laboratory studies. Manchek is a quiet, heavyset man with labile hypertension. He is unable to lose the extra pounds necessary for promotion. Previously in charge of experiments in spacecraft landing methods at the Wright Patterson facility in Vandenberg, Ohio, Manchek had developed three new capsule shapes that were promising. He hates administrative work and was happiest working at the wind tunnels of Wright Patterson. He notices the aged survivor on the flyby films, declares a state of emergency, and calls in the experts. Manchek disappears from the novel early but reappears near the end, when he finds out about the crash of a plane that invaded Piedmont airspace and pushes for nuclear destruction of Piedmont and Wildfire.

— Andrew Macdonald

ÁNGEL GUERRA

Author: Benito Pérez Galdós (1843-1920)
First published: 1890-1891
Genre: Novel

Locale: Spain
Time: Late nineteenth century
Plot: Psychological realism

Ángel Guerra (AHN-hehl GEH-rrah), an idealistic widower of thirty whose unhappy childhood causes him to turn revolutionist. Defying his wealthy, domineering mother, he chooses the company of the violent, unsavory Babel family. In spite of his later reformation, the Babel family finally causes his death.

Doña Sales (DOHN-yah SAH-lehs), Ángel Guerra's rich, overbearing mother. Her attempts to force her son into submission drive him to take up with the criminal Babel family.

Encarnación (Ción) (ehn-kahr-nah-see-OHN), Ángel Guerra's beloved little daughter.

Lorenza (loh-REHN-sah), sometimes called **Leré** (leh-REH), Encarnación's twenty-year-old tutor. On the death of her charge, she enters a convent in Toledo where, in his loneliness, Ángel Guerra follows her. Through her influence, he seeks the comfort of the church.

Arístides García Babel (ah-REES-tee-dehs gahr-SEE-ah bah-BEHL-) and
Fausto García Babel (FOW-stoh), dishonest brothers, who, in an attempt to flee justice, demand money of Ángel Guerra. They stab him in a quarrel over his refusal to pay.

Dulcenombre (Dulce) Babel (dewl-seh-NOHM-breh), Ángel Guerra's mistress. She later enters a convent.

Padre Casado (PAH-dreh kah-SAH-doh), a priest who is preparing Ángel Guerra for holy orders.

Captain Agapito Babel (ah-gah-PEE-toh), an ex-slaver.

Matías Babel (mah-TEE-ahs) and
Policarpo Babel (poh-LEE-kahr-poh), unsavory children of Captain Agapito Babel.

Dr. Maquis (MAH-kees), physician to Doña Sales.

ANGEL PAVEMENT

Author: J. B. Priestley (1894-1984)
First published: 1930
Genre: Novel

Locale: London, England
Time: Late 1920's, during the Great Depression
Plot: Social realism

James Golspie, the protagonist, a canny, blunt, vulgar, persuasive con man who easily takes advantage of the naïve Howard Brompart Dersingham and brings financial ruin to the firm of Twigg & Dersingham, dealers in veneer and inlays for furniture makers. Returning to England after a long absence, Golspie is looking for an outlet for his inexpensive wood products from the Baltic area. He is intrigued by the Angel Pavement address of Dersingham's firm, descends on the unsuspecting group, and literally takes charge. He demands and gets his commissions in advance. Everything Golspie does affects the lives of those connected with the firm for good, at first, but eventually for evil. Medium in height, powerfully

built, and nearly bald, Golspie has thick, bushy eyebrows and a huge drooping mustache. He repels and attracts simultaneously.

Howard Brompart Dersingham, the owner, by inheritance, of Twigg & Dersingham, a firm that is slowly failing, primarily because of his incompetence. In his late thirties, he is a poor product of the English public school system. His greed, gullibility, and ineptness make easy Golspie's destruction of the company.

"Pongo" Dersingham, his wife, in her early thirties. She is the mother of two young children. She pretends to live an exciting and full social life but in fact is rather dull. She does create an optimistic outlook at the end, seeing hope in the financial disaster her husband has created.

Harold Turgis, the junior clerk in the firm, in his early twenties. A sallow, shallow, poorly dressed, and physically unattractive young man, he has dreams of romance, spawned mostly through films and magazines. He fantasizes about romantic interludes with beautiful women. He meets Lena Golspie, who teases, torments, frustrates, and then dismisses him. He tries, in a fit of anger, to kill her, but he is as unsuccessful at that as he is at most things. Like the others, he loses his job as the firm fails.

Lena Golspie, the young, very attractive daughter of James Golspie. She is a flirt and a spendthrift. This well-traveled and popular young lady has main characteristics of selfishness and disregard for others' feelings.

Herbert Norman Smeeth, the cashier and senior clerk of the firm, approximately in his fifties. Apprehensive by nature and conservative by habit, he is continually concerned about his and his family's future financial status. The temporary business success brought about by Golspie only slightly modifies his attitude, which is a cautious approach to life and business not shared by his family or his employer.

Edie Smeeth, his wife, in her early forties. She has two grown children and an obnoxious cousin, Fred Mitty, who irritates her husband. An eternal optimist, she is hopeful about the future despite the firm's failure.

George Smeeth, their twenty-year-old son, a mechanic. He lives a relaxed life that Herbert Smeeth cannot understand.

Edna Smeeth, their eighteen-year-old daughter. She lives for films and cannot hold a job because of her inability to resist complaining.

Lilian Matfield, the typist for the firm of Twigg & Dersingham. Aloof and cold to her fellow workers, she dominates them all, even though she is relatively new to the firm and only in her late twenties. She lives at the Burpenfield Club, a residence for working girls and women. Her relationships with her fellow boarders reveals much about her thinking. Incurably romantic, a dreamer of perfection, she is at first annoyed by Golspie, then fascinated by him. She dates him but refuses to spend a weekend at the coast with him. She later agrees to go, only to be left waiting in Victoria Station as he sails for South America.

Poppy Sellers, who is hired as an assistant typist when the business expands under Golspie's direction. She shows an interest in Harold Turgis and is probably his salvation as the novel ends.

Stanley Poole, a fifteen-year-old office boy at Twigg & Dersingham who fantasizes about aviation adventures and about becoming a detective.

Mrs. Pelumpton, Turgis' landlady, who is short, broad, constantly busy, and much taken by her own sacrifices in an exasperating world. She is, however, kind to Turgis.

Mr. Pelumpton, her husband, a garrulous, rheumatic old busybody who deals in secondhand, thirdhand, and fourthhand goods. He frequently offers Turgis advice.

Mr. and Mrs. Walter Pearson, friends and neighbors of the Dersinghams. Mr. Pearson is retired from business in Singapore.

Miss Verever, Mrs. Dersingham's mother's cousin, a forty-five-year-old, acid-tongued professional virgin.

T. Benenden, Herbert Smeeth's tobacconist at Angel Pavement. He warns Smeeth about the future. At the hospital after being hit by an automobile, he learns that his injuries are the least of his health problems. Smeeth visits him and is shocked by what he sees and hears.

Fred Mitty, Mrs. Smeeth's cousin, a loud, brash, self-proclaimed comic. His antics infuriate Herbert Smeeth and amuse almost no one.

— *William H. Holland, Jr.*

ANGELS FALL

Author: Lanford Wilson (1937-   )
First published: 1982
Genre: Drama

Locale: New Mexico
Time: The 1980's
Plot: Problem

Father William Doherty, a sixty-five-year-old mission priest who controls his flock with wit, deception, and persistent hope to elevate their lives. He displays a brittle, self-effacing humor, masking a strong will that results in his major conflict with Don Tabaha. A romantic who is fond of quoting romantic verse, Father Doherty sees the world as transitory and humans by nature as good; he has always maintained a "willing suspension of disbelief" about his life's role that makes him sympathetic to artists. These attitudes allow him to dismiss nuclear catastrophes that occur a few miles away. His great fault is his vanity in wanting Don, his surrogate son, to follow him in his mission.

Don Tabaha, a half Indian in his mid-twenties who was reared by his aunt (the mission's caretaker) and Father Doherty. Don is split in half by more than his racial background. Although he realizes his duty to help the American Indians as their doctor, he also is aware that he could venture into the city as a research specialist. To complicate matters, Don has a love/hate relationship with Father Doherty, his father figure. All this tension has made Don surly, yet he exhibits a natural inclination to doctor: He tries to go to the mine to treat the injured, he correctly diagnoses Niles Harris' hypoglycemia, and he warns Zappy about getting arthritis from lying on the floor. His name, Tabaha, means "by-the-river" in Navajo; it fits Don, who is at a major crossing point in his life between duty to those he loves and self-fulfillment.

Niles Harris, a fifty-six-year-old neurotic art historian and professor from Rhode Island on his way to a private sanatorium in Arizona. Niles Harris' wit is matched by that of Father Doherty, who is his counterpart in many respects. Harris, borrowing from Samuel Taylor Coleridge, announces early in the play that he has lost his ability to continue a "willing suspension of disbelief." He also quotes Blaise Pascal in French that makes him sound almost pedantic; he is rescued from pedantry by his own self-deprecation. Although he says that the source of his despair is his lost faith in his writing and teaching, later in the play he reveals that he suffered a severe loss when his brightest student committed suicide. Harris shares Father Doherty's fault of investing his vanity in a protégé. By the play's end, Harris appears improved as a result of Don Tabaha's ministrations and his argument with Father Doherty over Don's decision that allows him insight into his own problems.

Vita Harris, the thirty-year-old, strikingly handsome wife of Niles Harris. True to her first name, she is a life source for Niles. She helps him to cope with his anguish in a quiet way that counteracts the abrasiveness of the other characters. Vita comments on the actions of the others but does not judge them. Rather, she shares Father Doherty's view that the world is transitory and that such problems as nuclear disasters and disposing of her dead father's many antiques are not on the same level of importance as saving Niles's sanity or rebelling against the status quo. Vita was Niles's student and now is a writer of children's books, so she understands both sides of the debate between Father Doherty and Niles. At the end, Vita, a lapsed Catholic, remains to hear Mass.

Marion Clay, an attractive art gallery owner in her early forties. She is undergoing a major change in her life because of the death of her artist husband, Branch. Unlike Niles or Don, Marion handles change without the problem of betraying her calling. Always the realist, she encourages others but knows that her career is to be their caretaker. Her affair with Zappy is almost motherly. Marion Clay is as basic as her last name implies, but with a dignity that Father Doherty admires. Like Vita, Marion offers support to others who need it without claim of return, because she has sure faith in herself and her calling.

Salvatore "Zappy" Zappala, a twenty-one-year-old tennis pro and Marion Clay's lover. At first, Zappy appears to be the comic relief to the play. Nervous and hypochondriac, he goes into a near faint as Don relates the illnesses that the American Indians get. Fear of drinking the local water forces him to drink a thermos of martinis and get progressively more drunk. Living up to the meaning of his first name, Salvatore, he supplies the saving revelations in the play. He hears the status of the uranium mine disaster and the road's accessibility on his radio and informs the others. He supplies a vivid example for Father Doherty's lesson on vocation by narrating his discovery of a natural talent at tennis. Zappy is Don's counterpart to the degree that he is following his calling without a quandary.

— Richard Stoner

ANGELS IN AMERICA: A Gay Fantasia on National Themes

Author: Tony Kushner (1956-   )
First published: Part 1, 1992; part 2, 1994
Genre: Drama

Locale: New York City
Time: Mid-1985 to 1990
Plot: Political

Prior Walter, a thirty-one-year-old man with AIDS. When his illness becomes serious, he is abandoned by his lover, Louis Ironson. A member of a very old American and British family, he is chosen by the Angels to become a prophet and tell humankind to stop changing and progressing, to give up trying to answer impossible questions. After wrestling with the Angel, Prior is allowed to visit heaven, where he tells the angelic counsel that he will not be their prophet and that humankind cannot stop striving. He asks the Angels to let him live, for no matter how painful life is, he wants more of it.

Louis Ironson, a word processor for the Second Court of Appeals in Brooklyn and Prior Walter's lover. Devoted to Marxism and idealistic leftist politics, Louis tends to intellectualize things. He cannot face Prior's illness and abandons his lover. He has an affair with Joe Pitt and tries to accept Joe's justification for selfishness. When he learns that Joe has been the power behind a number of right-wing court decisions, he goads Joe into attacking him physically and beating him. He returns to Prior begging for forgiveness, but even though Prior loves Louis, he will not take him back.

Roy M. Cohn, a character based upon the actual lawyer of the same name. He is a powerful figure in conservative and right-wing politics. Cohn is an aggressive, ferocious, and sometimes charming man who is not afraid of anything, including breaking the law. Cohn was a prosecutor in the 1950's treason trial of Ethel and Julius Rosenberg, who were found guilty of selling secrets to the Soviet Union. Cohn illegally lobbied the judge to give Ethel Rosenberg the death penalty. Cohn is dying of AIDS, though he keeps his illness and homosexuality secret. Because of his unethical acts, the New York State Bar is trying to take away Cohn's license to practice law. Cohn is determined to die as a lawyer and wants his protégé, Joe Pitt, to take a government job in Washington so he can protect Cohn. Cohn is haunted by the ghost of Ethel Rosenberg, but he fights her to the end. After he dies, Cohn becomes God's lawyer.

Joseph Porter Pitt, chief clerk for a federal appeals court judge who has Joe write his decisions. A Mormon from Salt Lake City, Utah, Joe believes in conservative values, individual freedom, and individual responsibility. He struggles to suppress his homosexual desires. He loves his wife, Harper, but feels no desire for her. He also feels responsible for her emotional problems. He falls in love with Louis Ironson and leaves Harper to be with him. He admires Roy Cohn but cannot be as ruthless and unethical as his mentor. In the end, Joe is alone, abandoned both by Louis and Harper.

Harper Amaty Pitt, Joe's wife, who suffers from agoraphobia and a mild addiction to Valium. She often escapes into dreams and fantasies, where she meets Prior Walter. She loves Joe completely but cannot forgive him. In the end, she leaves for San Francisco determined to find a life of her own.

Hannah Porter Pitt, Joe's mother, a hard-nosed, common-sense Mormon woman with few prejudices. When Joe tells her that he is a homosexual, Hannah abandons her life in Salt Lake City and goes to New York, where she cares for Harper and Prior. She helps Prior understand his visions and, in the end, stays with him in New York.

Belize, an African American nurse. A former drag queen and lover of Prior, Belize takes care of both Prior and Roy Cohn. As much as he hates everything Cohn stands for, Belize helps Cohn because he is a gay man dying of AIDS. When Cohn dies, Belize insists that Louis sing the Kaddish, the Jewish prayer for the dead.

The Angel, also called the **Continental Principality of America**, the representative of heaven. Since God, fascinated by the way that humankind evolves, dreams, progresses, and changes, abandoned heaven in 1908, heaven has been falling apart. The Angel wants Prior to tell humankind to stop changing, to stop striving and evolving, in the hope that God might then return.

— Chris Breyer

ANGELS ON TOAST

Author: Dawn Powell (1897-1965)
First published: 1940
Genre: Novel

Locale: New York City, Chicago, Miami, Washington, D.C., and rural Connecticut
Time: 1938
Plot: Satire

Lou Donovan, one of two philandering businessmen who are the focus of the novel. The forty-one-year-old's activities in the hotel business keep him traveling almost constantly, primarily between his Chicago base and New York City. At home, he is mostly faithful to his aristocratic wife, Mary. On the road, he consorts with party girls before becoming entangled with the manipulative Trina Kameray. Lou is also haunted by the compromising presence of Francie, his first wife, whom he has kept secret from Mary. Lou grows during the course of the novel, becoming cynical about both business and romance.

Jay Oliver, Lou's comrade in business and adultery. Nagged at home by the shrewish Flo, he relaxes in New York with the more worldly, glamorous Ebie. When one of Lou's ventures fails to be realized and Jay's business suffers, he leaves Flo for Ebie.

Ebie Vane, a successful commercial artist. She once intended to be a serious artist but turns her back on Greenwich Village for the comforts of Park Avenue. Bored by the sameness of her bohemian friends, she is drawn to Jay, despite his vulgarity, because he is different. She eventually settles for a life of leisure in rural Connecticut, giving up her identity to serve Jay's wishes.

Mary Harrod Donovan, Lou's wife and mother of their small daughter. Twelve years younger than her husband, the plain, rather severe Mary is attracted to her social and psychological opposite for complex reasons and chooses to ignore his indiscretions. Impulsively accompanying Lou and the Olivers to a nightclub, she becomes more aware of the type of woman to whom he is attracted and shocks everyone by becoming such a person. Mary exhibits the extremes to which a wife will go when she loves a husband who neglects her.

Trina Kameray, an earthy, sophisticated European refugee. She seems to embody everything that both Lou's wife and girlfriends lack. She torments Lou by refusing to hide her affairs with his business associate and others. Trina uses her intelligence, ambition, and sexuality to get what she wants.

Flo Oliver, Jay's harridan wife. Despite her many flaws, Flo inspires sympathy because of the ways Jay ignores and mistreats her.

Francie, Lou's first wife, emblematic of Lou's meager beginnings and bad taste. She comes to Chicago with her gambler husband to beg Lou for a loan.

— Michael Adams

ANGLE OF REPOSE

Author: Wallace Stegner (1909-1993)
First published: 1971
Genre: Novel

Locale: California, the Dakotas, Colorado, Idaho, and Mexico
Time: The 1860's to 1970
Plot: Historical realism

Lyman Ward, a retired University of California history professor and past winner of the Bancroft Prize. Lyman, in his late fifties and suffering from a degenerative bone disease that confines him to a wheelchair, has been abandoned by his adulterous wife, Ellen Hammond Ward. To pass the time, he begins researching the personal history of his grandparents, Oliver Ward and Susan Burling Ward, who spent most of their adult lives in the American West, his academic specialty. He is extremely opinionated, and his attitudes toward the social experiments of the 1960's could not be more negative. He begins with a strong bias against his grandmother, who probably also committed adultery. Lyman is a protagonist and also the novel's narrator; during the telling of the multigenerational saga, he encounters much evidence that exposes his need for self-serving conclusions. He finds that history challenges him to be a more sympathetic and forgiving human being than the subjects of his study: He must consider allowing his estranged wife Ellen to return.

Susan Burling Ward, an Easterner and a magazine illustrator with ambitions to be an artist. Born in 1848 and reared in a small New York town, she fails to attract an aristocratic New York City husband and so marries Oliver Ward, a mining engineer, and accompanies him to California, Mexico, Colorado, Idaho, and other parts of the West. Her snobbishness and desire to return to the East prevent her from judging her husband by criteria other than those of New York City salons. After her dreams of wealth and gentility clash repeatedly with the realities of their married life, she considers leaving, and at the very least she flirts with Frank Sargent, one of Oliver's assistants. After several separations, she returns to the marriage, but it has degenerated into a kind of truce, and it never improves.

Oliver Ward, an engineer and a practical visionary. Initially, to Lyman, he is the bearer of all virtues, a strong, energetic man too large to tolerate the conventional social scene of the East and not sympathetic to its economics. He is a builder, not an exploiter. He has the knack for thinking "big ideas twenty years ahead of their time," such as a formula for cement or an irrigation scheme too large for private funding. His principles cost him several jobs, but his skills earn the respect of experts such as John Wesley Powell and Clarence King. His stubbornness, however, does not allow him to be a sufficiently sympathetic husband, and in Lyman's speculation, the Oliver-Susan marriage was loveless from 1890 until their deaths almost fifty years later.

Shelly Rasmussen, a young woman hired for the summer of 1970 to care for Lyman and to act as his scribe. Shelly is a young and candid California woman of the 1960's, extremely liberal, and a constant foil to Lyman. Her impertinent questions expose many of Lyman's contradictions and biases, and her politics elicit much preaching from him.

Augusta Drake, a New York City socialite and friend of Susan Ward. Augusta is Susan's ideal: Eastern, wealthy, and polished. The rather stuffy letters she sends Augusta from the West provide Lyman with much evidence for his historical narrative.

Frank Sargent, an assistant to Oliver Ward at the Idaho irrigation project. Young and handsome, Frank is for Susan a beautiful compromise between masculine energy and social grace. He kills himself after the drowning of the Wards' daughter Agnes and confirms for Oliver the suspicion of adultery.

Rodman Ward, a sociology professor and the son of Lyman and Ellen. A cocky and ironic man, Rodman finds his father hopelessly out of touch. His sociological methods, both personal and academic, define for Lyman the superficiality of the 1960's.

Ollie Ward, Lyman's father. Born in 1877, he grows up to be a bitter man, alienated by the Eastern education to which Susan sent him. He returns the favor by taking no part in the rearing of Lyman himself.

Ellen Hammond Ward, Lyman's estranged wife. Ellen, a shadowy presence, has run off with the surgeon who amputated Lyman's leg. In the end, she seeks a reconciliation and presents Lyman with what he sees as the ultimate test for his moral philosophy: Can he be a better man than his grandfather?

— *Kerry Ahearn*

ANGLO-SAXON ATTITUDES

Author: Angus Wilson (1913-1991)
First published: 1956
Genre: Novel

Locale: Primarily London and rural England
Time: Late 1950's
Plot: Social realism

Gerald Middleton, a retired Oxford professor of medieval history and author of the definitive study of Canute. Middleton, despite the respect of many of his peers, considers himself to be a personal and professional failure and lives in a state of mild depression. His conscience forces him to make a series of decisions that set him in search of truth and revitalize him as a man and as a historian. Though ultimately successful professionally, he fails to rebuild meaningful relationships with his family.

Ingeborg Middleton, Gerald's wife, whom he married when he was turned down by Dollie. Tall and of ample figure, she likes to be surrounded by gaiety. She tries to manage things and people around her and demands affection from her family. Inge ignores events and other things that she finds unpleasant, including an affair between Gerald and Dollie.

Robin Middleton, the eldest son of Gerald and Inge. He is a company director of the family firm from which Gerald and the rest of the family derive much of their wealth. He is unhappy in his marriage to the social-climbing Marie-Hélène, who is a Catholic and will not consider a divorce. He is carrying on an affair with his brother John's secretary, Elvira Portway.

John Middleton, the younger son of Gerald and Inge. He is a radio celebrity and journalist with political ambitions. John is making a name for himself by conducting an exposé of the persecution of a small-market gardener by the civil service. John is homosexual and develops a relationship with Larrie Rourke, an Irishman with a criminal background. John's secretary, Elvira Portway, tries to get Gerald to bring John to his senses, but Gerald fails. Rourke, on the run from the police, goes to France, with John accompanying him. A car crash kills Larrie and causes John to lose a leg.

Dollie Stokesay, née **Armstrong**, the wife of Gilbert Stokesay, an essayist and poet. Gilbert was a ruthless Nietzschean who exulted in the outbreak of World War I, in which he was killed in action. Dollie, who had rejected Gerald's marriage proposal because she found him too solemn, does have an affair with him but then drops out of his life until he looks her up as part of his investigation of the Melpham dig. The two get along well, and though a permanent relationship is out of the question, there is likelihood of a continuing close friendship.

Sir Edgar Iffley, the president of the Historical Society of Medievalists and a friend of Gerald Middleton. He has been urging Middleton to accept the general editorship of a new series of books on medieval history, which Middleton has been reluctant to do. Middleton's decision to accept the post is tied to his determination to discover the truth about Melpham and represents a turning point in his life and career. Iffley supports Middleton's challenge to the authenticity of the Melpham find.

Lionel Stokesay, who is deceased at the time of the book's action but is an important figure in the earlier events that Middleton is trying to unravel. He was Regius Professor of English History at Oxford and Gerald's tutor. He also was responsible for the Melpham dig and was too eager to accept the authenticity of the pagan idol that, it turns out, his son planted. When he discovered the truth, he concealed it to protect his son's memory.

Canon Reginald Portway, a local clergyman and antiquarian who was involved with Professor Stokesay in the Melpham dig. His granddaughter is Elvira Portway, who is John Middleton's secretary and Robin Middleton's mistress. Portway had doubts about the authenticity of the Melpham find but did not make them public. A discovery of a conscience-stricken letter that Portway sent to Lionel Stokesay is the final proof Gerald needs that the find was a fraud.

— Francis J. Bremer

ANIMAL DREAMS

Author: Barbara Kingsolver (1955-   )
First published: 1990
Genre: Novel

Locale: Grace, Arizona
Time: The 1980's
Plot: Bildungsroman

Cosima Noline, the protagonist and narrator. Cosima, who goes by the nickname Codi, is in her early thirties but is still searching for her life's work and a sense of belonging. She trained to be a medical doctor but quit during her internship. She has since worked as a scientific researcher and as a convenience store clerk. Emotionally scarred by the death of her mother and her own miscarriage at the age of fifteen, Codi is cautious about forming attachments. Her strongest bond is with her sister Hallie.

Homero Noline, Codi's father, the only doctor in Grace. Codi calls him Homer. He is the protagonist of several sections of the novel. Because he suffers from Alzheimer's disease, Homer's thinking moves fluidly between past and present. Although he has maintained distance from his daughters and his community, he cares deeply about both. He deliberately established himself and his daughters as outsiders in Grace, hiding the fact that both he and their mother grew up in the town. He denies his own illness and, like Codi, insists on remaining independent and separate through most of the novel.

Loyd Peregrina, a Native American of Apache and Navajo descent. He is a railroad engineer and Codi's lover. Loyd dated Codi briefly in high school and was the father of the baby she miscarried, although he does not find out about the incident until nearly the end of the novel. He guides Codi through the landscape surrounding Grace, helps her learn to understand herself, and offers the security and sense of belonging that Codi both seeks and fears.

Emelina Domingos, Codi's best friend. Emelina provides Codi with a home, a surrogate family, and a means of reconnecting with the people of Grace. She is instrumental in getting Codi together with Loyd.

Viola Domingos, Emelina's mother-in-law. As one of the leaders of the Stitch and Bitch club, Viola gets Codi involved in attempts to save the town from economic or environmental ruin. As one of the community women who helped care for Codi when she was a child, Viola also helps Codi remember much of what she has forgotten from her childhood.

Hallie Noline, Codi's sister. During the course of the novel, Hallie is in Nicaragua, helping residents with agricultural problems. Although Hallie is not an active character in the plot, she is important because of Codi's strong attachment to her and because she represents, for Codi, an ideal model of political activism and selflessness.

— Sherry Lee Linkon

ANIMAL FARM

Author: George Orwell (Eric Arthur Blair, 1903-1950)
First published: 1945
Genre: Novel

Locale: England
Time: Mid-twentieth century
Plot: Satire

Mr. Jones, the owner of Manor Farm. After getting drunk on Midsummer's Eve, Mr. Jones fails to return in time to feed his animals. They have been thinking about rebellion anyway, and they take this opportunity to chase away Mr. Jones, Mrs. Jones, and the human farmworkers. In his ineptness, Mr. Jones is analogous to the czar of Russia, who was unable to hold Russia together during the stress of World War I.

Old Major, a boar previously exhibited as Willingdon Beauty. He is the prize boar whose dream inspires the Animalist Revolution on Manor Farm. Modeled on Vladimir Ilich Lenin, Old Major is highly respected in the barnyard, a capable orator, and an uncompromising ideologue for the Animalist cause. He dies in his sleep before the rebellion can take place.

Snowball, a young boar whose chief rival is Napoleon. Snowball is modeled on Leon Trotsky and so represents intelligence and organizational ability rather than brute force. It is Snowball, for example, who writes the Seven Commandments on the barnyard wall, who has the idea of building the windmill, and who studies the books left behind by Mr. Jones to see what practical benefit he can extract from them. Like Trotsky, Snowball is exiled after the revolution and is falsely made out to be the chief villain of Animal Farm.

Napoleon, a young boar who ousts Snowball and assumes complete power over the other animals. While Snowball is studying human science, Napoleon trains a litter of dogs to become his secret police force. Napoleon corresponds to Joseph Stalin, who ousted Trotsky after the death of Lenin and who then led bloody purges against possible and imagined dissenters.

Squealer, also a young boar. Squealer is the most clever with language and is Napoleon's propagandist and chief misinformation officer. He is said to be able to turn black into white, meaning that he can convince most animals of things that are patently false.

Boxer, a cart horse who always works hard. His two mottos are "Napoleon is always right" and "I will work harder." When he gets a split hoof, he is sent off to the glue factory, though

Squealer claims he is sent to a hospital. He is a good friends of Benjamin.

Clover, a maternal, hardworking cart horse. Boxer and Clover are the most faithful disciples of the pigs who run Animal Farm. They are not intelligent, and so they are easily fooled by Napoleon and Squealer. Boxer and Clover represent both the main strengths and the main weaknesses of the working class.

Benjamin, a cynical donkey. He alone among Animal Farm animals is not fooled by Squealer's lies. Benjamin is not exactly an intellectual but rather represents the sort of barnyard wisdom that prefers not to announce itself publicly. Benjamin, however, cries out when Boxer is taken to the glue factory.

Mollie, a young, foolish mare. She cannot forget the niceties of farm life that were lost with the revolution; she misses decorative ribbons and the occasional lump of sugar. She runs away to a farm where she is pampered.

Moses, a raven who claims the existence of Sugarcandy Mountain. He is a spy for Mr. Jones and, in his insistence on otherworldly rewards, appears to represent institutionalized religion.

Mr. Pilkington, a human enemy of Animal Farm who comes to do business with the animals.

Frederick, a farmer from Pinchfield. Although he is an enemy of the farm, he comes to buy leftover timber. He pays with forged currency. Frederick represents Adolf Hitler, who, despite much distrust, formed the Non-Aggression Pact with the Soviet Union and then broke it.

— *John Whalen-Bridge*

ANNA CHRISTIE

Author: Eugene O'Neill (1888-1953)
First published: 1923
Genre: Drama

Locale: Johnny the Priest's saloon, New York City, and Provincetown harbor
Time: Early twentieth century
Plot: Social realism

Anna Christopherson, a girl abandoned by her seagoing father and, after the death of her mother, reared by farmer relatives in Minnesota. She is a buxom, attractive girl who learns from farm boys the facts of life. In St. Louis, she becomes a prostitute. She goes to New York to join her father, who now is skipper of a coal barge. When her father fights a man who has resolved to get Anna for his own, Anna realizes that men regard women as their property. At the end, Anna, her father, and her lover are reconciled, and Anna is to be married at last.

Chris Christopherson, Anna's father, a man whose family has paid a dreadful toll in lives to the sea. Chris loves his daughter and sailing ships; he hates steam vessels and especially hates the men who stoke the furnaces in them. He opposes Anna's lover because he follows the sea in a steamship.

Mat Burke, Anna's lover, who is rescued from the sea one night when the *Simeon Winthrop* rides at anchor in the outer harbor of Provincetown, Massachusetts. Burke's Irish glibness both attracts Anna and makes her suspicious. When Burke, one night after a fight with Chris, learns that Anna has been a prostitute, he calls her names and storms out of her life. When he returns and talks with Anna, however, they realize that they are in love.

Marthy Owen, an old prostitute who lives on the coal barge with Chris. When Chris learns that Anna is leaving St. Louis for New York, he asks Marthy to leave. She consents to move on to someone else because, as she says, Chris had always been good to her.

ANNA KARÉNINA

Author: Leo Tolstoy (1828-1910)
First published: 1875-1877
Genre: Novel

Locale: Russia
Time: Nineteenth century
Plot: Social realism

Anna Karénina (AH-nah kah-REH-nee-nah), Karénin's beautiful, wayward wife. After meeting the handsome Count Vronsky, she falls completely in love with him, even though she realizes what the consequences of this act of infidelity may be. In spite of love for her child, she cannot give up Vronsky. Estranged from her husband, this unhappy woman, once so generous and respected, has an illegitimate child, runs off with Vronsky, and finally, when his love seems to wane, commits suicide by throwing herself in front of an approaching railway engine.

Count Alexey Kirilich Vronsky (ah-lehk-SAY kee-REE-lihch VROHN-skihy), a wealthy army officer who eagerly returns Anna Karénina's love. He is not a bad man; in fact, he is thoughtful and generous in many ways, as he proved when he gave part of his inheritance to his brother. Yet he thinks nothing of taking Anna away from her husband. Actually, such behavior is part of his code, which approves patronizing his inferiors. After Anna's death, he becomes a gloomy seeker after death.

Alexei Karénin (ah-lehk-SAY kah-REH-neen), a public official and a cold-blooded, ambitious man whose main desire is to rise in government service. Seemingly incapable of jealousy or love (except self-love), he allows Anna to see Vronsky. He is afraid only that his reputation will be blemished by his wife's infidelity. In spite of his cold temperament, he is a good official who knows how to cut red tape and bureaucratic inefficiency.

Sergey Alexeyich Karénin (sehr-GAY ah-lehk-SEH-ihch), called **Serezha** (sehr-EH-zhah), Anna Karénina's bewildered young son. Recognizing the schism between his father and mother, he is often distraught by what he senses but does not understand.

Konstantine Levin (kohn-stan-TEEN LEE-vihn), a prosperous landowner. A fine, decent man, he intensely dislikes all forms of chicanery and hypocrisy. With his generous spirit and democratic outlook, he wants to help his peasants by giving them larger profits from their work on his estate. In return, he believes they will work better in his behalf. Forgetting his pride, he finally marries Kitty Shtcherbatskaya, and together they work hard to make his agricultural theories succeed.

Prince Stepan Oblonsky (steh-PAHN oh-BLON-skihy), a high government official and Anna's brother. With his strong, well-fed body, he is the very picture of robust energy. A kind, often guilt-ridden man, he has a bachelor's temperament, and he finds it practically impossible to be true to his unattractive, jealous wife. After each affair, he strongly feels his guilt and tries to make amends, only to be smitten by the next pretty face he sees. He is so cheerful and happy that people like to be around him.

Princess Darya Oblonskaya (oh-BLON-skah-yah), called **Dolly**, Oblonsky's long-suffering and unattractive wife. Faced with her husband's infidelity, she finds solace in her six children. Although she often threatens to leave him, she never does, and she becomes partly reconciled to his philandering.

Princess Catharine Shtcherbatskaya (shchehr-BAHT-skah-yah), called **Kitty**, Dolly's younger sister, who cannot choose between sober, generous Konstantine Levin and the more dashing Count Vronsky. When she learns that Vronsky obviously is not interested in marriage, she knows she has made an error in refusing Levin's proposal. After a short period of despondency, she realizes that the future is not completely gloomy, and she marries Levin.

Prince Alexander Shtcherbatsky (shchehr-BAHT-skihy), a bluff, hardy man, the father of Kitty and Dolly. He likes Levin as Kitty's suitor because he is often suspicious of Vronsky's intentions toward his daughter. His cheerfulness lifts the spirits of his associates.

Princess Shtcherbatskaya, Dolly and Kitty's ambitious mother. At first, she hopes that Kitty will marry Vronsky. Later, she is willing to accept Levin as Kitty's husband.

Nicholas Levin, Konstantine's brother. A rather pitiful figure, he is aware of his approaching death from tuberculosis. Dreading his fate, he is a somber man, subject to violent rages and childish behavior.

Sergius Ivanich Koznyshev (SUR-gee-uhs ee-VAHN-ihch kos-NIHY-shehv), Konstantine Levin's half brother, a noted novelist and philosopher whose favorite pastime is debating the issues of the day. Although he has many convincing arguments, it is doubtful that he understands the peasants as well as his less articulate brother does.

Countess Vronskaya (VROHN-skah-yah), Count Vronsky's mother. An emaciated old woman, she tries to keep her favorite son under close watch. Failing in this effort, she withholds his allowance.

Mary Nikolavna (nee-koh-LAH-ehv-nah), called **Masha**, Nicholas Levin's mistress. She looks after the sick man as she would a child, even though he does not seem to appreciate her attempts to help him.

Tanya Oblonskaya, Prince Oblonsky's daughter.

Grisha, Oblonsky's son.

Princess Elizabeth Fëdorovna Tvershaya (FYOH-doh-rov-nah TVEHR-shah-yah), called **Betsy**, who acts as a go-between for Vronsky and Anna. Like many women in her social set, Betsy has a lover.

Agatha Mikhaylovna (mee-KHAY-lov-nah), Levin's trusted housekeeper and confidante.

Princess Myagkaya (MYAG-kah-yah), who likes to gossip and has a sharp, vituperative tongue.

Lieutenant Petritsky (peh-TRIH-tskihy), Count Vronsky's friend, a hard-drinking gambler. His commanding officer often threatens to expel him from the regiment.

Prince Yashvin (YAH-shvihn), Vronsky's friend. Like Petritsky, he is a hard drinker and an inveterate gambler.

Kuzma (kewz-MAH), Levin's manservant.

Mikhail and

Piotr (pyohtr), Vronsky's servants.

Piotr Ivanovich, a professor.

Petrov (peh-TROHV), an invalid artist dying of tuberculosis. He is infatuated with Kitty.

Anna Pavlovna (PAHV-lov-nah), Petrov's jealous wife.

Sappho Stolz (SA-foh shtohltz), a full-blown actress.

Lisa Merkalova (mehr-KAH-loh-vah), Betsy Tvershaya's friend. A beautiful, charming girl, she always has a number of ardent admirers following her.

Nicholas Ivanich Sviyazhsky (SVYAZH-skihy), a wealthy landowner and a marshal of the nobility.

Mlle Varenka (vah-REHN-kah), Kitty's friend. She is wholesome and pure, and her greatest pleasure is caring for the sick.

Mme Stahl, Mlle. Varenka's malingering foster mother.

Annushka (AH-new-shkah), Anna Karénina's maid.

ANNA OF THE FIVE TOWNS

Author: Arnold Bennett (1867-1931)
First published: 1902
Genre: Novel

Locale: The Potteries, England
Time: Late nineteenth century
Plot: Domestic realism

Anna Tellwright, a young woman who is deprived of love and money in her childhood. She inherits fifty thousand pounds from her mother's estate upon reaching twenty-one. The money makes little difference in her life, for she turns it over to her father and, later, her fiancé to manage for her. She discovers that she really loves Willie Price, but she is already engaged to Henry Mynors, and she refuses to break her betrothal.

Henry Mynors, Anna's fiancé. A sound businessman, he knows the value of money. He teaches in the Sunday school, thus acquiring the approval of Anna's father. He dominates Anna as her father does.

Ephraim Tellwright, Anna's father, a wealthy, miserly ex-preacher. A stern Wesleyan, he rears his daughters most frugally. He gives his children little love.

Beatrice Sutton, Anna's friend. She brings Anna into society and shows her that a little money well spent can make life far pleasanter. When Beatrice is seriously ill, Anna nurses her competently and lovingly.

Willie Price, a young man in love with Anna. After his father's business failure, he decides to start afresh in Australia. When he discovers the extent of his love for Anna (and its hopelessness) and also learns that his father was a thief, he commits suicide by throwing himself into the shaft of an abandoned mine.

Agnes Tellwright, Anna's half sister. She is the daughter of Ephraim and his second wife, also dead.

Titus Price, Willie's father and a one-time tenant of Anna. His business fails, and he is proved to be a thief. He hangs himself.

Mrs. Sutton, Beatrice's mother, a social leader.

ANNALS OF THE PARISH: Or, The Chronicle of Dalmailing

Author: John Galt (1779-1839)
First published: 1821
Genre: Novel

Locale: Scotland
Time: 1760-1810
Plot: Social

The Reverend Micah Balwhidder, who is appointed to the Presbyterian church in the village of Dalmailing in western Scotland. Appointed without the approval of the congregation, he is harshly rebuffed at first, but the resentment soon dies, and he is accepted. He fights earnestly against smuggling and drinking. He also fights a losing battle against the appearance of other church groups in his parish. He serves his congregation for fifty years, from 1760 to 1810. He decides to retire when he finds himself deaf and forgetful.

Betty Lanshaw, a distant cousin of Balwhidder. He marries her because he feels that a minister can best serve his people when he is married. She dies a few years after their marriage.

Lord Eaglesham, a nearby nobleman who becomes Balwhidder's close friend and helps him in his good works.

Thomas Thorl, a dour Scot. He is the most outspoken of the people who resent the appointment of Balwhidder. He is, however, the first to relent.

Mrs. Malcolm, a widow with five children. Balwhidder does a great deal to help her and her family.

Charles Malcolm, one of the Widow Malcolm's sons. He becomes a successful officer in the merchant marine. His death in a naval battle saddens Balwhidder, who has come to regard him almost as a son.

Lizy Kibbock, Balwhidder's second wife, who gives the congregation a good example by her industry and thrift, making her family independent of her husband's salary.

Mr. Cayenne, an American Tory who sets up a weaving mill in Dalmailing.

Mrs. Nugent, a widow of good reputation who becomes Balwhidder's third wife.

Mr. Heckletext, a visiting minister who embarrasses Balwhidder by turning out to be the parent of an illegitimate child in Dalmailing.

Lady MacAdam, a domineering woman of the parish who is sometimes a problem for Mr. Balwhidder.

ANNE OF THE THOUSAND DAYS

Author: Maxwell Anderson (1888-1959)
First published: 1948
Genre: Drama

Locale: England
Time: 1526-1536
Plot: Historical

Anne Boleyn, the mistress and, later, wife of King Henry VIII. She was executed in 1536. Anne is first seen in the Tower of London, awaiting death. Her life with Henry is then told in flashbacks. Anne, in 1526 a not altogether innocent girl, is passionately in love with Lord Percy, Duke of Northumberland, to whom she is engaged, but she has attracted the attention of Henry, who separates the lovers. Embittered by his actions, she denounces the king's person and talents. With her world empty following the loss of her lover and with her parents applying pressure, Anne allows herself to be drawn to Henry, although she arrogantly refuses to go the way of her sister, whose reputation was stained and whose children were illegitimate. Anne demands marriage, believing that Henry cannot meet this demand because he already is married to Katharine of Aragon. When Henry seeks an annulment for that marriage, Anne is flattered by the length to which Henry will go to win her. When Henry makes her his queen, she surrenders completely, denouncing her new power and status and pleading only for Henry's love. This causes Henry's love for her to wane; he increasingly turns his attention to Jane Seymour, who, like Anne earlier, is not easily won. Threatened and insecure, Anne grows more strident in her demands. Before she will try to have another child with Henry, she insists on the death of Sir Thomas More and those others who will not accept Henry as the supreme religious authority in England and who deny the legitimacy of their marriage. Henry meets this final demand, but their son is born dead, and Anne thus loses her hold over Henry. He allows false charges of adultery to be brought against her, and Anne falls victim to the bloodshed that she herself, as she recognizes in the Tower, has let loose upon the land.

Henry VIII, king of England from 1509 to 1547. Henry has been attracted to all three Boleyn women: Elizabeth, later the mother of Anne and Mary, and both daughters. Elizabeth remembers him as innocent and naïve; Mary recalls him as insecure, unwilling to court any woman who might reject him. By the time Henry pursues Anne, he has been corrupted by his own power, mistaking his own will for God's. He speaks of courting favor among his people but, in reality, derives pleasure from imposing his own will, whether upon his courtiers, his populace, or an unwilling woman. For Henry, the chase and capture are everything; to his courtiers, he admits that he sees no difference in this respect between deer and women. When Henry first courts Anne, this brutality is only latent within him, but her defiance and the challenges she sets him bring his brutality to the surface. Once Henry has proven capable of murdering friends such as Sir Thomas More to acquire Anne, he proves equally capable of murdering Anne to acquire a new love. Henry's excuses (England's need for a male heir and God's wrathful judgment on his marriages to Katherine and Anne) are merely that, excuses that only superficially conceal the profound desire for power that, in middle age, is the core of his character.

Cardinal Thomas Wolsey, the Lord Chancellor. Wolsey compromises his religious duties to keep himself in Henry's favor and to enrich himself at the expense of the church. He arranges Henry's liaison with Anne but is horrified at their proposed marriage. He is undermined by Thomas Cromwell, who has learned amorality from him, and fails in body and spirit when he turns his palace over to Anne.

Thomas Cromwell, an adviser to Wolsey and later to Henry. Admittedly without scruples, Cromwell acquires Henry's favor by arranging the marriage with Anne but is equally willing to arrange her death, obtaining evidence against her through torture.

Sir Thomas More, a statesman, author, and, later, saint. More dies rather than renounce his allegiance to Rome, confident in the faith that, in the long run, an ultimate justice governs the universe, bringing men and women the destinies they merit. His faith is validated by the fall of Wolsey and the death of Anne.

— *Betty Richardson*

ANNIE JOHN

Author: Jamaica Kincaid (Elaine Potter Richardson, 1949-   )
First published: 1985
Genre: Novel

Locale: Antigua, West Indies
Time: The mid-1950's to the mid-1960's
Plot: Bildungsroman

Annie Victoria John, a smart, sensitive young black girl growing up in Antigua, in the British West Indies. Annie identifies with her mother and has a hard time separating herself, but she is a bright, imaginative, high-spirited girl who has a hard time following her mother's instructions and orders. She leaves home at the age of seventeen.

Annie John, Annie's mother, who married a carpenter much older than herself. She gave birth to Annie at the age of thirty. Annie's point of view is so intently focused on how her mother deals with her that it is hard to get a precise sense of who the mother is. Her attempts to discipline Annie and force her to grow cause Annie to be hurt and confused.

Alexander John, Annie's father, a carpenter who makes coffins for the local community. He is considerably older than his wife and is presented as somewhat distant from Annie. He is important in her life but outside the close bond of Annie and her mother.

Gweneth Joseph, Annie's best friend. When Annie and Gwen meet, they immediately fall in love and make promises to love each other forever. Shortly after Annie begins menstruating, she falls out of love with Gwen. The two of them remain friends, though not close friends, until Annie leaves home.

Ma Chess, Annie's grandmother, a powerful healer. When Annie falls ill and a medical doctor is not able to find anything wrong with her, it is Ma Chess who brings Annie back to health.

The Red Girl, Annie's name for a friend on whom she develops a powerful crush, at about the time she falls out of love with Gwen. Annie's mother intervenes, however, because she discovers Annie has been lying to her. The Red Girl moves away with her parents for reasons unrelated to Annie.

— *Thomas J. Cassidy*

ANNIVERSARIES: From the Life of Gesine Cresspahl
(Jahrestage: Aus dem Leben von Gesine Cresspahl)

Author: Uwe Johnson (1934-1984)
First published: 1970-1983
Genre: Novel

Locale: New York City; Mecklenburg, East Germany; and Richmond, England
Time: 1931-1968
Plot: Historical realism

Gesine Cresspahl (gay-ZEE-neh KREHS-pahl), who was born in 1933 in the province of Mecklenburg, Germany. She immigrated to New York in 1961 and has worked in a bank there since 1964. She lives in a modest apartment with her daughter, Marie, with whom she conducts frank conversations about her own and her parents' lives. Her thoughts are committed to a diary that extends from August, 1967, to August, 1968, and that mingles the present with the past. From 1939 to 1945, she underwent the normal education of a German child under the Nazis. After 1945, she spent more than three years in the Russian zone of postwar Germany, where she studied dili-

gently after the Russians arrested her father. She learned to behave cautiously but nevertheless clashed with a malicious bureaucracy. From Halle University, in East Germany, she fled to West Germany, where Marie was born. The child's father, Jakob, an East German railway official, was killed before they could be married, and Gesine, resolving to stay unmarried, emigrated. In New York, unhappy memories of her German past make her an impassioned opponent of the Vietnam War and of racial prejudice. For all her enlightened views, she spares no expense in sending Marie to a Catholic private school to avoid the squalor of public education. She finds consolation in the honest, old-fashioned truthfulness of *The New York Times* (which she calls "Auntie"). The paper is full of reports of the Vietnam War and of violence in American cities (including the death of Martin Luther King, Jr.). Such reports confirm Gesine's dislike of violence, but she is growing attached to New York, influenced by Marie's enthusiasm. She discusses her life and recent German history with a highly critical Marie. She is making good progress in her bank career. She rejects D. E.'s offers of marriage and earns the approbation of her unpleasant boss. She is learning Czech to add to her other languages, with a view to working in Prague.

Marie Cresspahl, the daughter of Gesine, born in July, 1957, in West Germany and brought to New York in 1961. At first, she hates the city, but now she would not live anywhere else and even dislikes speaking German or going to foreign restaurants. She wears a Vietnam War button in her conservative school and looks after a black girl from a nearby slum who is enrolled in the school as a token of integration. She finds the task onerous and takes part in a wild Halloween party to avoid having to invite the girl home. Enlightened principles prevail, so that she and Gesine do take the girl in for a short period. Marie's teachers are disturbed by her vehement opposition to the Vietnam War, which leads her to address an inopportune and gravely naïve question on the matter to the president of Gesine's bank. A polite child, she is highly critical of Gesine's and Germany's past.

Heinrich Cresspahl (HIN-rihkh), Gesine's father, who was born in 1888. He was a cabinetmaker in Jerichow, Mecklenburg, and, for a time, the manager of a workshop in Richmond, near London. He met his future wife, Lisbeth, on a trip to Mecklenburg. They settled in Jerichow when Gesine was born in 1933, in a Germany celebrating Adolf Hitler's rise to power. He joined the Nazi Party although he disliked the regime and had, while in England, helped German refugees. His behavior at times appeared unorthodox: He consorted with a Jewish veterinarian and, after his wife's death in 1938, took an extended tour of Denmark and England, where he had an illegitimate child. During the war, he spied for the British, reporting aircraft movements. He became mayor of Jerichow for a time during the British and Russian occupations. He fell foul of the Russian authorities, was arrested, and returned broken in health. He died in 1962. There is talk of naming a street in his honor.

Dietrich Erichson (D. E.) (DEE-trikh EH-rikh-zohn), who was born in 1928, the son of a baker in Mecklenburg, Germany. He is now a professor of physics and chemistry in the United States and does secret work for the U.S. Air Force. He arrived in the United States in 1960, after defying the East German authorities, and met Gesine in a refugee camp. A skilled technician and a mediocre lecturer, he lives with his mother in a former farmhouse in New Jersey, where Gesine and Marie visit him. He no longer regards his German past as reality. He wishes to marry Gesine and is liked by Marie. He finally gives up his courtship and is killed in a plane crash in the course of duty.

Lisbeth Papenbrock Cresspahl (PAH-pehn-brok), Gesine's mother. She was from a well-to-do Mecklenburg family with aristocratic pretensions. She followed Heinrich to England and was eager to please him. After their marriage, however, she found herself unable to settle down or to discuss her difficulties. She returned to Jerichow for the birth of her child, and Heinrich eventually joined her permanently. Uneasy in her conscience, she attempted suicide by drowning and even seemed willing to let Gesine drown in a barrel (her father rescued her, saying nothing). Lisbeth died in mysterious circumstances in a fire in 1938.

Hilde Papenbrock Paepke (HIHL-deh PAH-pehn-brok PAYP-keh), Lisbeth's sister. She married a shiftless lawyer who squandered her dowry. Her three children were Gesine's favorite cousins, and Heinrich liked her. Although she was no friend to the Nazis, she died with her children while fleeing from the advancing Russians in 1945.

Louise Papenbrock, Lisbeth's mother. Fanatically religious (she demanded more fervor in the pastor's sermons), she ruled her family. When Lisbeth returned to Jerichow, she was ready to receive her, excluding Heinrich.

Albert Papenbrock, Lisbeth's father, a shrewd businessman with aristocratic claims he could not sustain. He refused to help his son Horst with his Nazi stormtroopers and unexpectedly welcomed Heinrich as a son-in-law.

Horst Papenbrock, Lisbeth's brother, born in 1900. After his brother Robert, a violent man, vanished in 1914, he had hopes of inheriting his father's estate. He was a loyal member of the local Nazi Party and was secretly engaged to another member. According to rumor, he had a hand in local atrocities. He tried unsuccessfully to display authority as manager of his father's granary. His father sent him to Brazil to look for his brother and to get him out of mischief. He was quieter on his return. He died at Stalingrad.

Robert Papenbrock, Lisbeth's brother and Albert's son and heir. He left home abruptly but returned in 1935 to become a Gestapo official. During the war, as a "special leader" he was responsible for atrocities in the Ukraine. He turned up in the Cresspahl house after the war, left when ordered to, and escaped to West Germany.

Jakob Abs (YAH-kohp ahps), Marie's father, a refugee, with his mother, in the Cresspahls' house in 1945. He later became a railway dispatcher. After Heinrich's arrest, his mother looked after Gesine, helped by Jakob, whose strength combined with gentleness were remarkable in the postwar corruption and brutality. Returning from a visit to Gesine in Dusseldorf, he was killed, before Marie was born, under mysterious circumstances while crossing a marshaling yard in East Germany.

Mrs. Ferwalter (FEHR-vahl-tehr), a stockily built Ruthenian Jewish countrywoman, born in 1922. She was an inmate in the Mauthausen concentration camp and now lives in New York. She is the first to befriend Gesine in New York and admires her European manners. She is unable to sleep soundly and wears, Gesine imagines, a permanently disgusted expression.

Anita Grantlik (GRANT-likh), called **Anita the Red**, a refugee from Eastern Europe of Polish-German origins. She was Gesine's schoolmate. She had been raped by a Russian soldier at the age of eleven, was condemned to fieldwork, and was abandoned by her father, a policeman. She succeeded in becoming a Russian interpreter and in earning a new Swedish bicycle. She fled to the West and still corresponds with Gesine.

Karsch, a figure from the past of Gesine and D. E., now working for the United Nations and writing a book on the

American Mafia. On a visit to New York from Milan, he is kidnapped but is rescued through Gesine and D. E.'s efforts.

Annie Killainen Fleury (FLEW-ree), a friend to Gesine who lives in Vermont with her husband, a translator for the French. She abruptly leaves him, taking their three children to live for a time in Gesine's apartment, explaining that she has quarreled with him over the Vietnam issue.

Uwe Johnson, who makes a brief appearance addressing the Jewish American Congress in New York on the topic of postwar Germany, with Gesine in the audience. His reception is unfriendly.

— *W. Gordon Cunliffe*

ANOTHER COUNTRY

Author: James Baldwin (1924-1987)
First published: 1962
Genre: Novel

Locale: New York and France
Time: The 1950's
Plot: Social realism

Rufus Scott, a jazz drummer. Handsome, talented, and black, Rufus is the pivotal character in the novel, although he commits suicide at the end of the first chapter. He meets his girlfriend, Leona, a white woman from the South, while playing a gig. Their unstable relationship is torn apart by racial and other tensions between them. He beats her until his friend, Vivaldo Moore, intercedes. Rufus' ensuing depression results in his suicide: He walks out onto the George Washington Bridge and jumps. Rufus' struggle initiates the questions the novel explores, concerning the pain of sexual and racial identity.

Leona, Rufus' lover. A divorcée who lost the custody of her son, she has moved north to start a new life. Rejected and beaten by Rufus, she has a breakdown and is committed to Bellevue until she is released in the custody of her brother, who takes her back south.

Vivaldo Moore, an aspiring writer. He is an Italian American and Rufus' closest friend; he is haunted by the thought that he could have been a closer, more sensitive friend to Rufus. He falls in love with Ida Scott, Rufus' younger sister, and she eventually moves in with him. When she begins an affair with Steve Ellis, a television producer, he tries to ignore it but eventually takes some solace in a one-night affair with Eric Jones, a white Southern man with whom Rufus once had a brief, stormy affair. At the end of the novel, Ida and Vivaldo commit themselves emotionally to each other, but it is not clear that they can overcome the racial and emotional forces that have been tearing them apart.

Ida Scott, Rufus' very attractive younger sister, an aspiring singer. When Rufus dies, Ida promises herself never to let anyone take advantage of her emotionally the way she thinks people always treated her brother. Although she genuinely loves Vivaldo, she is determined to be successful as a singer. She has an affair with Steve Ellis, a television producer she meets at a party hosted by Cass and Richard Silenski. She hopes the affair will advance her singing career. She is angry at herself for her behavior and at Vivaldo for putting up with it, but also for not seeing the racial and social forces that drive her and that led her brother to kill himself. She berates Vivaldo

often before finally ending her affair with Ellis and discussing her harsh feelings and actions with Vivaldo.

Clarissa (Cass) Silenski, a white middle-class housewife. Sensitive to other people and emotional, she begins to feel estranged from her husband, Richard Silenski, a writer who is becoming financially successful while remaining artistically unsuccessful. In her frustration, she initiates an affair with Eric Jones, though she knows he prefers men. When her husband accuses her of having an affair with Vivaldo, she denies it but confesses to her affair with Eric. He leaves, threatening to divorce her and take the children, Paul and Michael.

Eric Jones, a white actor. A homosexual who grew up in the South, Eric is returning to New York from France, to which he had fled in the wake of his affair with Rufus. Lonely for his lover Yves, Eric agrees to an affair with Cass, assuming that it will last only until Yves arrives from France. The night Cass tells Richard about her affair with Eric, which is the same night Ida decides to stop seeing Steve Ellis, Eric and Vivaldo have a mutually fulfilling sexual encounter, which they both understand is only for one night.

Richard Silenski, a writer, Vivaldo's former English teacher. After years of aspiring to be a writer, though without exhibiting much talent, Richard finally becomes somewhat successful writing mysteries. Richard's involvement with this suspect type of success leads Cass to her affair with Eric. He leaves Cass when he learns about her affair with Eric and threatens to win custody of their sons.

Yves, Eric's French lover. A prostitute in his youth, Yves feels jealous of Eric when Eric goes back to America but hopes their lives will be able to continue together. The novel ends with Eric greeting Yves at the airport in New York, amid much doubt for both of them about what their future together holds.

Steve Ellis, a television producer. Sleazy, opportunistic, and self-justifying, he believes in Ida's talent as a singer but also wants to take advantage of her sexually, at least partly to assert his power over both her and Vivaldo, who has snubbed Ellis on several occasions.

— *Thomas J. Cassidy*

ANOTHER LIFE
(Drugaya zhizn')

Author: Yuri Trifonov (1925-1981)
First published: 1975
Genre: Novel

Locale: Moscow, the Soviet Union
Time: Early 1970's
Plot: Social realism

Olga Vasilievna (vah-see-LYEHV-nah), a recently widowed research biologist. After the early death of her husband, Sergei Afanasievich, she reconstructs by way of flashbacks their life together in an attempt to understand what went wrong and to assuage her guilt feelings about her husband's demise. In the end, she realizes that she is not to blame, that their marriage was doomed to failure through forces beyond their control, and that they both unknowingly had yearned for a life other than their own, which eventually led to misunderstandings and the tragic end. Although she has many acquaintances and female friends, gets on well with people, and is not afraid of life's complexities, she finds that she is psychologically overly dependent on other people and is therefore unable to attain happiness by living independently.

Sergei Afanasievich (sehr-GAY ah-fah-NAH-syeh-vihch), Olga's husband, a brilliant historian who dies prematurely at the age of forty-two without accomplishing much. Capricious and of unstable character, lacking dedication and willpower, and always in trouble at the institute where he works, he nevertheless knows how to make friends, especially among women, and ostensibly how to keep his marriage from falling apart. His main problem is a strong dependence on his mother's opinion and moods; he is compelled to explain and justify himself to her. He adores his mother and stands in awe before her for "making history" during the Russian Revolution. Because of his subservience to his mother and his fear of disappointing her high expectations of him, he is ashamed to admit failure and to make necessary changes in his behavior. Instead of accepting Olga's help, he walks away from difficulties whenever they threaten to overwhelm him. He never finishes his dissertation, spending most of the time pursuing his theory about the unbroken thread running from generation to generation, which manifests itself in a seething, bubbling urge to dissent. Although it is true that the society in which he lives saps his talents and thwarts his desire to be different, he is doomed to destruction by his emotional ineptitude and a compulsion to do only what pleases him, as were his ancestors.

Alexandra Prokofievna (proh-KOH-fyehv-nah), Sergei's mother, a retired lawyer. Having chosen to live with Sergei and Olga, she wreaks havoc in their lives through her compulsive need to domineer. She is able to dominate her son because of his weak will, whereas Olga escapes her clutches. The result is the deterioration of their marriage and the early death of Sergei. At difficult moments, she always assumes an air of dignified authority, by which she tries to make herself indispensable. She shows gross insensitivity toward her son's difficulties, as well as toward her daughter-in-law, blaming her for Sergei's death.

Irinka (ee-REEN-kah), Sergei and Olga's daughter. As a teenager, she is caught in the battle of wills among her mother, father, and grandmother. She inherited many traits from her father, including pliancy, instability, secretiveness, occasional thoughtlessness, and insensitivity. She is the true victim of the family disintegration, as she is torn between the will of her father and that of her grandmother, while her mother stands by helpless. After her father's death, she finds some rapport with her mother, yet both realize that valuable time has been lost.

Galina Yevgenievna (gah-LEE-nah yehv-GEH-nyehv-nah), Olga's mother. Unable to have any influence on her daughter's life, she spends her love and energy on her second husband, with whom she achieves a remarkable symbiosis. She lives only for his problems and illnesses and has no time for anyone else.

Georgii Maximovich (gee-OHR-gee mak-SEE-moh-vihch), Olga's stepfather, an artist. A kind and well-educated man, he was once an avant-garde painter, but he has sacrificed his principles for the secure and profitable life of a mediocre landscape artist.

Gennady (Gena) Vitalevich Klimuk (geh-NAH-dee vee-TAH-leh-vihch KLEE-mook), Sergei's colleague. A typical social climber and bureaucrat, he is largely responsible for Sergei's demise by making his life miserable in the institute and by refusing to show any understanding for his old friend.

— *Vasa D. Mihailovich*

ANTHONY ADVERSE

Author: Hervey Allen (1889-1949)
First published: 1933
Genre: Novel

Locale: Western Europe, Africa, and North America
Time: Late eighteenth and early nineteenth centuries
Plot: Picaresque

Anthony Adverse, the illegitimate son of Denis Moore and Maria; grandson and heir of John Bonnyfeather, under whom he serves as an apprentice. Anthony becomes a slave trader in Africa and a banker, businessman, and plantation owner in New Orleans. Successively captured by Indians and by soldiers, he is imprisoned in Mexico and later bleeds to death after an accident there. Anthony is more a romantic, daring man of action than an intellectual. In the variety of his adventures, he resembles the heroes of picaresque fiction, but he has neither their low-caste background nor their roguish character.

Don Luis (lew-EES), the Marquis da Vincitata (veen-see-TAH-tah), the arrogant husband of Anthony's mother and landlord of Casa Bonnyfeather. He fails in an attempt to murder Anthony and Vincent Nolte. Later governor at Santa Fe, Don Luis dies of a stroke after sentencing Anthony to prison.

Maria Bonnyfeather, daughter of John Bonnyfeather, mother of Anthony, and wife of Don Luis. She dies in childbirth.

John Bonnyfeather (secretly the Jacobite Marquis of Aberfoyle), Anthony's grandfather, a prominent merchant of Leghorn.

Faith Paleologus (pah-leh-oh-LOH-gews), Mr. Bonnyfeather's lustful housekeeper, who seduces young Anthony. She becomes Don Luis' mistress and afterward his wife.

Angela Guiseppe (jew-SEHP-peh), Faith's daughter and Anthony's mistress and mother of his son. She is later a mistress to Napoleon.

Florence Udney, Anthony's first wife. She is burned to death with Maria, her young daughter by Anthony.

Dolores de la Fuente (FWEHN-teh), Anthony's second wife, a relative of Don Luis de la Casas. She bears Anthony two children.

Vincent Nolte (NOHL-teh), Anthony's friend, a banker.

Sandy McNab, Mr. Bonnyfeather's chief clerk.

Denis Moore, an Irish-French nobleman, Maria's gallant lover, who is killed by her husband.

Captain Jorham, skipper of an American ship.

Father Xavier (hah-vee-EHR), a Jesuit priest, Anthony's childhood guardian, who tells him of his origin and of his status as Mr. Bonnyfeather's heir.

Gallego (gah-YEH-goh), a slave trader who owes money to Mr. Bonnyfeather. He dies in Africa.

Don Luis de la Casas (KAH-sahs), captain-general in Havana.

Father François (frahn-SWAH), a compassionate monk shipped from Cuba to Africa for aiding and comforting slaves.

Ferdinando (fehr-dee-NAHN-doh), Gallego's representative in Africa, who is crucified by Mnombibi.

Mnombibi (nahm-BEE-bee), an African witch doctor.

Neleta (neh-LEH-tah), Ferdinando's half-breed sister and Anthony's mistress, whom he deserts.

Captain Bittern, skipper of the "Unicorn."

M. Ouvrard (oh-VRAHRD), a French financier.

David Parish, husband of Florence Udney, whom Anthony marries after David's death.

Anna Frank, the cousin of Vincent Nolte and guardian of Anthony's son.

Mary Jorham, the young niece of Captain Jorham.

ANTIGONE

Author: Jean Anouilh (1910-1987)
First published: 1946
Genre: Drama

Locale: Thebes
Time: c. 600-500 B.C.E.
Plot: Tragedy

Antigone (an-TIH-guh-nee), the daughter of Oedipus and Jocasta, engaged to marry Haemon, son of King Creon and Queen Eurydice of Thebes. After Oedipus' death, Oedipus' son Eteocles ascended to the throne, but after one year he broke an agreement with his brother Polynices to share power with him. This action provoked a civil war in which both brothers were killed. Creon then became king. He ordered that the body of Polynices not be buried in order to discourage further rebellion. Antigone realized that Creon's decree violated Greek religious law, which required that a body be buried before a soul could cross the River Styx. Were she to obey Creon's arbitrary law, Antigone would violate her religious beliefs. She risks her life to observe a higher moral code. Creon offers to spare her life if she promises not to try again to bury Polynices. Antigone refuses, however, to compromise her moral principles. Creon then condemns her to death. Antigone's death provokes the suicides of both Haemon and Eurydice.

Creon, Oedipus' brother, an uncle to both Antigone and Ismène. He is a cynical dictator who demands blind obedience to his laws from others but grants absolute powers to himself. He affirms that social order has nothing to do with moral and political freedom. He treats Antigone condescendingly and does not want to understand Antigone's refusal to compromise her moral beliefs. Antigone correctly predicts that his abuse of power will alienate Creon from his family and his subjects. After the suicides of his son, Haemon, and his wife, Eurydice, Creon is alone, but no one feels pity for him.

The Nurse, a middle-aged woman who has cared for Antigone for many years. She wants Antigone to be happy. She relates that Antigone left home very early in the morning, but she does not imagine that it was to bury Polynices. Like all the other characters, she cannot predict that the serious but vulnerable Antigone will risk her life to remain faithful to her religious beliefs.

Ismène (ihs-MEE-nee), Antigone's older sister, a vain and unsympathetic character. Ismène is excessively concerned with clothing and her physical appearance; only marriage and social success are important to her. She tells Antigone that young women should be indifferent to political and moral problems. Although Ismène claims to love her sister, she, like Creon, treats Antigone condescendingly. Ismène's superficial arguments have no effect on Antigone.

Haemon, the son of Creon and Eurydice, a young adult. He and Antigone share a profound love for each other, and they look forward to having children together. When Haemon learns that Creon has condemned Antigone to death, he confronts his father. He rejects Creon's specious assertion that maturity requires Haemon to accept unjust and amoral laws. Like Antigone, Haemon adheres to a higher moral code. Near the end of this play, both Haemon and his mother, Eurydice, commit suicide offstage.

The chorus and

The prologue, roles traditionally interpreted by the same actor. Both comment regularly on the moral and psychological significance of the actions in this tragedy. The chorus and the prologue express ethical reactions to Antigone's self-sacrifice and to the suffering caused by Creon's abuse of power.

The three guards, decent people exploited by their military and political superiors. They do not understand why Creon so adamantly opposes burying Polynices. The guards carry out their orders to watch over Polynices' body out of their fear of Creon.

— *Edmund J. Campion*

ANTIGONE
(Antigonē)

Author: Sophocles (c. 496-406 B.C.E.)
First performed: 441 B.C.E.
Genre: Drama

Locale: Thebes
Time: Remote antiquity
Plot: Tragedy

Antigone (an-TIHG-eh-nee), the daughter of Oedipus and sister of both Eteocles (who defends Thebes) and Polynices (an exile from the city who attacks it). After Eteocles and Polynices have killed each other in battle, Creon, Antigone's uncle and now king of Thebes, decrees that Eteocles' body shall be buried with honors befitting a national hero but that Polynices' body shall be left unburied, a prey to scavengers. Divine law, Greek custom, and simple humanity demand, however, that Antigone see her brother buried; she must choose, therefore, between obedience to the temporal rule of Creon and the duty she owes to a brother she had loved. Although she knows that her fate will be death, she chooses to bury the body of her brother. She is undoubtedly strong-willed and defiant. Having been apprehended by the guards posted to prevent the burial, she replies to Creon's wrathful accusations of treason with an equal ferocity. She emerges as immensely heroic, for she alone seems clearly to understand that the king's law is inferior to divine law and that if sacrifice is required to follow the right, such sacrifice must be made. She is always aware of the glory of her deed and dies for love in the largest sense of the word, but her concurrent awareness of her youth and her loss of earthly love humanize her and make her a profoundly tragic figure.

Creon (KREE-on), the king of Thebes. Although he gives lip service to the necessity for order and for obedience to the law, he is a tyrant who has identified the welfare of the state with his own self-interest and self-will. He commits hubris through his violent misuse of his temporal power; he too has a duty to bury the dead, and his unjust condemnation of Antigone to death is murder of a near relative, although he changes her sentence from stoning to burial alive to avoid the formal pollution that would accompany such a deed. He has a regard for the external forms of religion but no understanding of its essential meaning. When Tiresias brings the gods' curse on his actions, he relents, but too late to save Antigone or his son.

Haemon (HEE-mon), Creon's son, who is engaged to wed Antigone. He attempts to placate his father. Failing in this, he declares his fidelity to Antigone. When Creon comes to release Antigone from the cave in which she has been entombed, he finds that she has hanged herself and that Haemon is embracing her suspended body. Haemon attempts to kill his father, then falls on his own sword.

Ismene (ihs-MEE-nee), Antigone's sister, as gentle and timid as Antigone is high-minded and strong. She pleads a woman's weakness when Antigone asks her to help with Polynices' burial, yet her love for her sister makes her willing to share the blame when Antigone is accused.

Eurydice (ew-RIHD-ih-see), Creon's wife. She kills herself when she is informed of Haemon's death.

Tiresias (ti-REE-see-uhs), a prophet who brings to Creon a warning and a curse that cause him belatedly to revoke his decision to execute Antigone. He is the human in closest affinity with the divine; his intercession is therefore equivalent to divine sanction for Antigone's deeds.

THE ANTIQUARY

Author: Sir Walter Scott (1771-1832)
First published: 1816
Genre: Novel

Locale: Scotland
Time: Late eighteenth century
Plot: Fiction of manners

Lovel (Major Neville), a wealthy young man of undetermined background who is forced to fight a duel and then go into hiding because he thinks he has mortally wounded his opponent. By a stroke of luck, he overhears a conversation that helps him act to save the fortune of the nobleman whose daughter, Isabella, he wishes to marry. Because of his uncertain parentage, he gives him no encouragement. Eventually, however, he is proved to be an aristocrat. His proper background established, he and Isabella are married.

Edie Ochiltree, a beggar and Lovel's friend. Ochiltree is instrumental in helping Lovel save Sir Arthur from financial ruin. Ochiltree leads Sir Arthur to a cave on his property where Lovel, supposedly abroad, has hidden a chest of money. When Ochiltree "discovers" the money, the aristocrat's financial troubles are ended.

Jonathan Oldbuck of Monkbarns, an antiquarian and a friend of Lovel and Sir Arthur. It is through his good offices that Sir Arthur discovers the chest of money in the cave and Lovel and Isabella finally can marry.

Dousterswivel, a charlatan who extorts money from innocent people; in return for a fee, he promises to find minerals or treasure, for example, on their property. Dousterswivel meets his match in Ochiltree, for the latter embarrasses him and also gives him a good scare.

The earl of Glenallan, who is told by a spiteful mother that his wife is his sister. Thus, when his wife bears a son, he is distraught. The boy's mother takes her own life. It is learned that the baby, whisked away by a servant, is actually Lovel, whose benefactor had been the earl's brother.

Captain Hector M'Intyre, Oldbuck's nephew, who forces Lovel to duel. Because Lovel thinks he has killed Hector, he goes into hiding. Hector recovers, but Lovel does not learn the truth until much later.

Sir Arthur Wardour, a nobleman whose daughter is loved by Lovel. Restored to financial security by Lovel's efforts, Sir Arthur blesses the marriage of Isabella and Lovel.

Miss Isabella Wardour, Sir Arthur's daughter, who eventually becomes Lovel's wife.

ANTONY AND CLEOPATRA

Author: William Shakespeare (1564-1616)
First published: 1623
Genre: Drama

Locale: Egypt and parts of the Roman Empire
Time: c. 30 B.C.E.
Plot: Tragedy

Mark Antony, also called **Marcus Antonius**, the majestic ruin of a great general and political leader, a triumvir of Rome. Enthralled by Cleopatra, he sometimes seems about to desert her for her real and dangerous rival, Rome. He marries Caesar's sister Octavia for political reasons but returns to Cleopatra. His greatness is shown as much by his effect on others as by his own actions. His cynical, realistic follower Enobarbus is deeply moved by him, his soldiers adore him even in defeat, his armor-bearer remains with him to the death, and even his enemy Octavius Caesar praises him in life and is shocked into heightened eulogy when he hears of his death. Antony is capable of jealous fury and reckless indiscretion, but he bears the aura of greatness. He dies by his own hand after hearing the false report of Cleopatra's death, but he lives long enough to see her once more and bid her farewell.

Cleopatra (klee-oh-PA-truh), the queen of Egypt. As a character, she has the complexity and inconsistency of real life. Like Antony, she is displayed much through the eyes of others. Even the hard-bitten realist Enobarbus is moved to lavish poetic splendor by her charm and beauty. Only Octavius Caesar, of all those who come in contact with her, is impervious to her charms, and the nobility of her death moves even him. She is mercurial and self-centered, and there is some ambiguity in her love of Antony. It is difficult to be certain that her tragic death would have taken place had cold Octavius Caesar been susceptible to her fascination. She is most queenly in her death, which she chooses to bring about in "the high Roman fashion," calling the dead Antony "husband" just before she applies the asp to her bosom.

Octavius Caesar (ok-TAY-vee-uhs SEE-zur), a triumvir of Rome, Antony's great rival. His youthfulness is set off against Antony's age, his coldness against Antony's passion, and his prudence against Antony's recklessness. The result, from a dramatic point of view, is heavily in Antony's favor. Caesar's affection for his sister Octavia is almost the only warm note in his character. His comments on the deaths of Antony and Cleopatra show unexpected generosity and magnanimity.

Domitius Enobarbus (doh-MIHSH-yuhs ee-noh-BAHR-buhs), Antony's friend and follower, a strong individual. Although given to the disillusioned cynicism of the veteran soldier, he has a splendid poetic vein that is stimulated by Cleopatra. He knows his master well and leaves him only when Antony seems to have left himself. Miserable as a deserter, Enobarbus is moved so deeply by Antony's generosity that he dies of grief. He serves as a keen, critical chorus for about three-fourths of the play.

Marcus Aemilius Lepidus (MAHR-kuhs ee-MIHL-ee-uhs LEHP-ih-duhs), the third triumvir, a "poor third," as Enobarbus calls him. He tries to bring together Antony and Octavius and to quell the thunderstorms that their rivalry frequently engenders. He is the butt of some teasing by Antony while they are both drinking heavily on Pompey's galley. After the defeat of Pompey, Octavius Caesar destroys Lepidus, leaving himself and Antony to fight for control of the world.

Sextus Pompeius (SEHKS-tuhs pom-PEE-yuhs), called **Pompey** (POM-pee), the son of Pompey the Great. Ambitious and power-hungry, he has a vein of chivalric honor that prevents his consenting to the murder of his guests, the triumvirs, aboard his galley. He makes a peace with the triumvirs, largely because of Antony, but is later attacked and defeated by Caesar and loses not only his power but also his life.

Octavia, the sister of Octavius Caesar. A virtuous widow, fond of her brother and strangely fond of Antony after their marriage, she serves as a foil to Cleopatra. She is not necessarily as dull as Cleopatra thinks her. There is pathos in her situation, but she lacks tragic stature.

Charmian, a pert, charming girl who attends Cleopatra. Gay, witty, and risque, she rises under the stress of the death of her queen to tragic dignity. She tends Cleopatra's body, closes the eyes, delivers a touching eulogy, and then joins her mistress in death.

Iras, another of Cleopatra's charming attendants. Much like Charmian, but not quite so fully drawn, she dies just before Cleopatra.

Mardian, a eunuch servant of Cleopatra. He bears the false message of Cleopatra's death to Antony, which leads Antony to kill himself.

Alexas, an attendant to Cleopatra. He jests wittily with Charmian, Iras, and the Soothsayer. After deserting Cleopatra and joining Caesar, he is hanged by Caesar's orders.

A soothsayer, who serves two functions: He makes satirical prophecies to Charmian and Iras, which turn out to be literally true, and warns Antony against remaining near Caesar, whose fortune will always predominate. The second prophecy helps Antony to make firm his decision to leave Octavia and return to Egypt.

Seleucus (seh-LEW-kuhs), Cleopatra's treasurer. He betrays to Caesar the information that Cleopatra is holding back the greater part of her treasure. She indulges in a public temper tantrum when he discloses this, but because the information apparently lulls Caesar into thinking that the queen is not planning suicide, perhaps Seleucus is really aiding, not betraying, her.

A clown, who brings a basket of figs to the captured queen. In the basket are concealed the poisonous asps. The clown's language is a mixture of simple-minded philosophy and mistaken meanings.

Ventidius (vehn-TIHD-ee-uhs), one of Antony's able subordinates. A practical soldier, he realizes that it is best to be reasonably effective but not spectacular enough to arouse the envy of his superiors. He therefore does not push his victory to the extreme.

Eros (EE-ros), Antony's loyal bodyguard and armor-bearer. He remains with his leader to final defeat. Rather than carry out Antony's command to deliver him a death stroke, he kills himself.

Scarus (SKAH-ruhs), one of Antony's tough veterans. Fighting heroically against Caesar's forces in spite of severe wounds, he rouses Antony's admiration. In partial payment, Antony requests the queen to offer him her hand to kiss.

Canidius (ka-NIHD-ee-uhs), Antony's lieutenant general. When Antony refuses his advice and indiscreetly chooses to fight Caesar's forces on sea rather than on land, then consequently meets defeat, Canidius deserts to Caesar.

Dercetas (DEHR-keh-tuhs), a loyal follower of Antony. He takes the sword stained with Antony's blood to Caesar, announces his leader's death, and offers either to serve Caesar or to die.

Demetrius (deh-MEE-tree-uhs) and

Philo (FI-loh), followers of Antony. They open the play with comments on Antony's "dotage" on the queen of Egypt.

Euphronius (ew-FROH-nee-uhs), Antony's old schoolmaster. He is Antony's emissary to Caesar asking for generous terms of surrender. Caesar refuses his requests.

Silius (SIHL-yuhs), an officer in Ventidius' army.

Menas (MEE-nas), a pirate in the service of Pompey. He remains sober at the drinking bout on board Pompey's galley and offers Pompey the world. He intends to cut the cable of the galley and then cut the throats of the triumvirs and their followers. Angered at Pompey's rejection of his proposal, he joins Enobarbus in drunken revelry and withdraws his support from Pompey.

Menecrates (mehn-EHK-reh-teez) and

Varrius (VA-ree-uhs), followers of Pompey.

Maecenas (mee-SEE-nuhs), Caesar's friend and follower. He supports Agrippa and Lepidus in arranging the alliance between Caesar and Antony.

Agrippa (eh-GRIHP-uh), Caesar's follower. He is responsible for the proposal that Antony and Octavia be married to cement the alliance. His curiosity about Cleopatra leads to Enobarbus' magnificent description of her on her royal barge.

Dolabella (dohl-ah-BEHL-uh), one of Caesar's emissaries to Cleopatra. Enchanted by her, he reveals Caesar's plan to display her in a Roman triumph. This information strengthens her resolution to take her own life.

Proculeius (proh-kew-LEE-uhs), the only one of Caesar's followers whom Antony advises Cleopatra to trust. She withholds the trust wisely, for Proculeius is sent by Caesar to lull her into a false sense of security.

Thyreus (THI-ree-uhs), an emissary of Caesar. Antony catches him kissing Cleopatra's hand and has him whipped and sent back to Caesar with insulting messages.

Gallus (GAL-uhs), another of Caesar's followers. He captures Cleopatra and her maids in the monument and leaves them guarded.

Taurus (TOH-ruhs), Caesar's lieutenant general.

ANYWHERE BUT HERE

Author: Mona Simpson (1957-   )
First published: 1986
Genre: Novel

Locale: Bay City, Wisconsin, to Hollywood, California
Time: The 1930's to the 1970's
Plot: Domestic realism

Ann August, the narrator of four sections. Ann, the daughter of Adele August, recalls moments from her youth, especially the tensions in her relationship with her mother over a period of several years.

Adele August, the narrator of the last chapter. Mother to Ann, daughter to Lillian, and sister to Carol, Adele possesses lofty ambitions. She foists those desires on Ann, dragging her across America in search of a glamorous identity for both of them in Hollywood. Adele rarely sees beyond surface impressions and allows her myopic view to dominate and control her life and her daughter's.

Carol, the narrator of three sections, all of which are addressed to Ann. Sister to Adele, wife to Jimmy, and mother to

Benny (who died in his late teens) and Hal, Carol is eleven years older than Adele. She worked as a teletype operator for the WACs during World War II, and she secretly married a French Jew who attempted to kill Adolf Hitler. Because he died on the train returning with Carol to Wisconsin, Carol did not tell her family that she had a husband before Jimmy. She finally tells Ann.

Lillian, the narrator of one chapter, which is addressed to Ann. Lillian, Adele and Carol's mother, describes her unplanned pregnancy with Carol, her relationships with both young women, and her experiences with sexual relations, which she ultimately finds repugnant.

— *Ruth J. Heflin*

THE APES OF GOD

Author: Wyndham Lewis (1882-1957)
First published: 1930
Genre: Novel

Locale: London, England
Time: Spring, 1926
Plot: Social satire

Horace Zagreus, born **Horace Follett**, a tall albino now between sixty and sixty-four years old. He is the favorite grandnephew of Lady Fredigonde Follett. He takes up young men as companions of "genius" and instructs them in the philosophy of Pierpoint. Famous as a practical joker, he is employed by Lord Osmund to provide entertainment at his Lenten Freak Party. In phallic costume, he gathers Daniel Boleyn, Julius Ratner, and Archie Margolin to present a magic show. After the disastrous failure of the Vanish, he leads his followers out onto Lord Osmund's lawn, carrying a large door, where he plays a flute while his followers dance. He dismisses Dan as the cause of his troubles at the party and puts Margolin in place as his newest genius.

Daniel Boleyn, a dull-witted young Irishman of nineteen drifting about London. He is taken up as a "genius" by Horace Zagreus, who sends him to study the "apes of god." He is self-consciously very tall, impoverished, and easily baffled. He blushes frequently and weeps easily when he thinks Horace slights him, and his nose bleeds at inopportune times. Dressed to perform as a yogi in Horace's magic show at Lord Osmund's party, his trousers catch fire, and he has to change into a woman's frock. He gets drunk on champagne and ruins the Vanish act. After Horace dismisses him in favor of Archie Margolin, Dan wanders through the General Strike in London until he is retrieved by Michael for Melanie Blackwell in France.

Dick Whittingdon, a thirty-six-year-old educated at Winchester and Sandhurst. He is the six-foot, two-inch, suntanned grandnephew of Lady Fredigonde and Sir James Follett. He competes with Horace Zagreus for approval and money from the Folletts, though he is not liked by Lady Fredigonde. Separated from his wife, he keeps a house called Grotian Walk with ten studios for his painting. He is a famous collector of whips.

Pierpoint, a painter turned philosopher, from a prominent Welsh-Irish family. He never appears in the novel except by name but is the source of many persons' ideas, especially Horace Zagreus, his contemporary in age. His analysis of relationships between society and art and artists provides the notion of "apes of god" as those wealthy persons who ape art and therefore trivialize its importance.

Julius Ratner, a special kind of "ape." He is a Jewish author and publisher with an obsession of analyzing psychological complexes. He married an heiress before the war and settled in Chelsea, but she ran off with a lover, and he turned to publishing. He is a source of money for Horace, and he publishes for Pierpoint. He is costumed as a "Split Man" by Horace for the magic show at Lord Osmund's party, to produce the illusion of cutting him in half. During the Vanish act, he is knocked from the stage by Blackshirt, who intensely dislikes Ratner. In consequence, he is hurt and threatens legal action, though he dances on the door to the tune of Horace's flute.

Archibald (Archie) Margolin, a small, twenty-year-old Jewish youth from the slums of London's East End. Taken on by Horace Zagreus as one of his young geniuses, he accompanies the magic show to the party of Lord Osmund, where he spends most of his time flipping matchsticks at party guests. He subsequently displaces Dan Boleyn as Horace's genius.

Lady Fredigonde Follett, the ninety-six-year-old great-aunt of Horace and Dick, and the wife of Sir James Follett. She is glad to move her head on a body otherwise rigid as plaster. She fantasizes about her collection of caps. When Sir James dies, she tells Horace that he can expect money from her and offers herself, in a scene of surrealistic madness, as his bride.

Matthew Plunkett, a small, middle-aged man with an obsessive interest in shells. He was psychoanalyzed in Zurich by Dr. Frumpfsusan, who advised him to choose his friends small and learn how to bully. He walks through Bloomsbury to a pub for his midday snack before his assignation with Betty Bligh at his flat. He is accosted by Dan Boleyn, the son of his Dublin cousin. Impatiently, Matthew allows Dan to rest in his apartment. He returns to meet Betty, fantasizes his sexual assault, and fails because Dan is lying in the bed to which he carries Betty.

Melanie Blackwell, a wealthy painter from St. Louis, the daughter of Irish immigrant parents. She married an Irish landowner and lived on his estate before he died. A thin woman, older than Dan, she lives with her dogs in London studios. She tries to lure Dan away from Horace by babying him, undressing him, and putting him to bed. After Dan is dumped by Horace at the end, she sends Michael to bring him to her in Azay-le-Promis.

The Lesbian-Ape, the artist into whose studio Dan Boleyn accidentally stumbles. Dan is made to pose in the nude until he faints from shame; he is awakened by the sound of her and her friend Borstie laughing at him.

Lionel (Li) Kein, a wealthy novelist of silly books. He has an obsessive interest in Marcel Proust. Beardless, but with a military mustache, he looks like a spectacled Sigmund Freud. He has known Horace Zagreus for seventeen years. When Horace insults him and his wife at a dinner party, he orders Horace out and tells him never to return.

Isabel Kein, the handsome wife of Lionel. She presides over a dinner party for seventeen guests, at which she openly gossips about her own guests, including Horace.

Lord Osmund Willoughby Finnian Shaw, the middle-aged son of the Marquis of Balbriggan, whom he, his brother, and his sister call **Cockeye**. He is more than six feet tall and fat, and he has a goatlike profile. An author of free verse, plays, novelettes, and novels, he is the master-ape. He blames his father as one of the old men who sent young men off to the Great War, though Osmund spent only a fortnight in the trenches. He is the host of the great Lenten Freak Party at his weekend country estate, Jays Mill Manor Farm.

Lord Phoebus Finnian Shaw, Osmund's six-foot, three-inch brother, who left Harrow to become a hussar but was too ill to go to the trenches in the Great War. He is the historian of the family. At the party, he shows childhood toys to guests.

Bertram Starr-Smith, called **Blackshirt**, Pierpoint's political secretary and business manager. A young, dark-faced, solemn Welshman, he wears the costume of a Fascist Blackshirt to Lord Osmund's party, where he rescues Dan Boleyn from the advances of an old man. He kicks an old colonel in the rear, takes Dan to the American Bar, where he gets drunk, and displays the Finnian Shaw library. Because he is editing an anthology of postwar verse, the Finnian Shaws are anxious to please him.

Bridget, Lady Fredigonde's maid, who combs the lady's hair each morning and helps her choose a cap.

Sir James Follett, the ancient husband of Lady Fredigonde. He dislikes his wife of more than fifty years. He spends his time lifting heavy books and looking at tigers' heads in his library. He dies of a stroke.

Francis Dallas, a forty-year-old, tanned man with a mustache. Once a favorite, he accosts Horace at the edge of Hyde Park.

Zulu Blades, a man of mixed race and black skin. He lives below Matthew Plunkett. He entertains many women night and day, arousing jealous hatred in Plunkett.

Betty Bligh, the bowlegged, four-foot, ten-inch companion chosen by Matthew Plunkett as therapy for his inferiority complex.

Michael, a small man who blows smoke through his nose. He is a Bolshevik who does odd jobs for Melanie Blackwell.

Willie Service, an attractive, mustached homosexual, assigned by Horace to chauffeur Dan Boleyn. An avid fan of Edgar Wallace detective stories, he views the world as crime-ridden.

Mrs. Lochore, Julius Ratner's housekeeper, who enters some of his fantasies about himself as a great writer and publisher.

Siegfried Victor, a young, Oxford-bred man above six feet in height, with a handsome Greek profile. He sucks a black pipe. He is a business associate of Julius Ratner, planning an anthology with Pickwort to be called "Verse of the Under-Thirties."

Hedgepinshot Mandeville Pickwort, a small man with blond hair who sucks a pipe and is an Oxford colleague of Siegfried Victor.

Cubbs, Dick Whittingdon's servant at Grotian Walk.

Bloggie, a midget Polish lesbian with money. She is a guest of Dick Whittingdon at Grotian Walk.

Richard, a small, bald millionaire renowned as a painter of sea pictures. He is a guest at Grotian Walk, where he examines Dick's paintings and disputes with his wife whether one of the paintings has too much red in it.

Jenny, Richard's wife, a guest at Grotian Walk. She puffs cigarettes and discusses colors in Dick's paintings.

Clemmie Richmond, a large-nosed friend who visits Pammie Farnham at teatime. She drips liqueur onto her dress from a chocolate candy.

Pamela (Pammie) Farnham, the hostess for tea in her Kensington flat. She entertains several guests, including Dan Boleyn, whom she insults as a thing made by Horace Zagreus.

Lady "Snotty" Briggs, one of Pammie Farnham's guests. She gossips about the notoriety of Horace Zagreus as a practical joker before the war.

David Novitsky, a Jewish-Russian, bearded guest at Pammie Farnham's tea. He is very sociable and the grinning opposite of Arthur Wildsmith.

Arthur Wildsmith, a guest of Pammie Farnham. He has a gray, goatlike face and wears eyeglasses. Detached and aloof, he is contemptuous of Novitsky's amiability.

Jimmie, a nineteen-year-old who is the focus of attention at Pammie Farnham's tea. He defends Dan Boleyn when Pammie insults him.

Hassan, a tall, dark young man in a black jacket and black trousers, with plum-black eyes and long eyelashes. He is Lionel Kein's butler, speaks with a deep cockney accent, and exudes a troubling perfume.

Kalman, a guest at the Keins' party. He sits next to Isabel and tells stories of a hardworking middle-aged journalist with a reputation for writing about youth. Kalman is an elderly man with yellow skin, a Charlie Chaplin mustache, a large nose, and thick lips. He is taunted by Horace Zagreus into a Socratic dialogue on the meaning of "eminence."

Horty, an American novelist who attends the Keins' dinner party. He sports side-whiskers and writes about himself.

Vernede, a guest at the Keins' dinner party who departs early. Small, stocky, demure, and childlike, he wears an old-fashioned, loose bow tie. He dislikes Kein, who once promised and then failed to set him up in a bookshop.

Lady Robinia Finnian Shaw, the wife of Lord Osmund for two years. She is a musician. Five feet tall, she has a narrow, colorless face and flaxen hair. During the party, she drifts about, staring distractedly at nothing.

Eustace Mulqueen, the six-foot, three-inch cousin of Lord Osmund. He stands beside Lord Phoebus behind Osmund during the dinner that begins the Lenten Freak Party. Otherwise, he contributes little.

Lady Harriet Finnian Shaw, a sister of Lord Osmund and Lord Phoebus who writes verse. She is about forty years old and very fashionable. She arrives late for the party with her companion Miss Dyott, but she contributes to the stories of old Cockeye.

Kanoot, or **Knut**, **The Finn**, a loud-mouthed guest at Lord Osmund's party. He recites passages of French poetry by Nicolas Boileau until hushed by a bored Lord Osmund. Worn out by his recitations, he falls into a deep sleep.

Sib, an old woman who is veiled and muffled. She sits beside Lord Osmund to supply him with gossip. Her specialty is people from the wicked 1890's, including the Wildes, Beardsleys, and Whistlers.

Mrs. Bosun, a housekeeper/nanny for Lord Osmund's family. She finds a frock for Dan to wear after his costume is destroyed by fire. She rushes with a medicine chest to administer to Lord Osmund when she hears that he is wounded.

Jonathan Bell, an author, costumed for Osmund's party as "Democracy" from a masque by John Dryden. He talks with Ratner about complexes and making love with fat women.

— *Richard D. McGhee*

THE APOSTLE

Author: Sholem Asch (1880-1957)
First published: 1943
Genre: Novel

Locale: The Roman Empire
Time: Shortly after the Crucifixion
Plot: Religious

Saul of Tarshish, or Tarsus, afterward known as **Paul**. A devout Jew but intellectually a searcher, he at first resents the Messianist followers of Yeshua, and he becomes a zealous spy and a persecutor of them. Troubled by Istephan's dying prayer of forgiveness of his slayers, Paul has a mystic vision that causes him to become an apostle of the Messiah, who appears to him several times. He believes himself to be divinely appointed to bring the word of Yeshua to the gentiles. As Paul, he establishes several churches. Arrested for accepting gentiles, he demands a trial as a Roman before Caesar and is finally beheaded.

Simon bar Jonah, called **Peter**. Imprisoned for healing in Yeshua's name, he is miraculously released. Imprisoned again, he is freed after eloquently defending his doctrine. He founds the church at Antioch, where he accepts gentiles as members. After working with Paul in Rome, he is crucified.

Joseph bar Naba of Cyprus, or **Barnabas**, Saul's friend, an early convert who had known Yeshua before his crucifixion.

Reb Istephan, or **Stephen**, a famous Jewish preacher.

Reb Jacob, a strict Jew, son of Joseph and younger brother of Yeshua, who leads the Messianist cult in Jerusalem after Yeshua's disappearance.

Yeshua of Nazareth, Jesus.

Nehemiah, a cripple healed by Simon in the name of Yeshua.

Jochanan, or **John**, Simon's follower, who is imprisoned with Simon and, like him, miraculously released.

Titus, Saul's first convert, a Greek.

Lukas, or **Luke**, a Greek physician, minister, and scholar who writes the life of Yeshua.

Nero, the Roman Emperor, who imprisons Paul. Nero burns Rome and blames the Christians, many of whom die forgiving their persecutors.

Seneca, a Roman through whose intervention Nero frees Paul.

Gabelus, a gladiator who becomes a Christian.

APPALACHEE RED

Author: Raymond Andrews (1934-1991)
First published: 1978
Genre: Novel

Locale: Appalachee, Muskhogean County, Georgia
Time: 1918-1963
Plot: Social morality

Appalachee Red, owner of a café and gambling house. "Red" wanders into the town of Appalachee on Thanksgiving Day, 1945, and soon captivates the town and its residents, both black and white. Appalachee Red, as he comes to be called by the locals, is the son of Little Bit Thompson and her white employer, the wealthy landowner John Morgan. Red has returned to Appalachee to claim his birthright and to exact revenge on those who have wronged him most. Red is tall and broad-shouldered, and he appears Caucasian, with long, flowing black hair. He is quiet, mysterious, and moves soundlessly and deliberately, like a cat. In little time, Red acquires ownership of the house built for his mother by her white lover; its owner, Sam Wallace, dies mysteriously and wills the property to Red. Red also seduces the black mistress of Appalachee's white, racist police chief and soon acquires controls of all the town's vice—gambling, liquor, and prostitution. He becomes the fear and envy of Appalachee. On November 22, 1963, eighteen years to the day after he returned to Appalachee, Red leaves the town, after the funeral of his mother, but not before killing the sheriff and being joined by his half sister, white socialite Roxanne Morgan. He is not heard from again.

Baby Sweet Jackson, Red's live-in lover, also called the **Black Peach**. Baby Sweet's sensuous dancing brings about the wrath of her father, overseer Poor Boy Jackson, and the lustful intentions of the boss, Edward Turner. Knowing that she is powerless to fight Turner's advances, Baby Sweet runs away to Appalachee. At the age of fifteen, she reluctantly becomes the mistress of police chief Clyde "Boots" White. She is liberated by Appalachee Red. She becomes his lover and manages the restaurant and liquor sales on the first floor of Red's Café.

Clyde "Boots" White, Appalachee's police chief and later county sheriff. He terrorizes the black residents of Appalachee after he joins the police force in 1931. One of his most heinous acts occurs on Easter Sunday, 1936, when he shoots "Big

Man" Thompson and kicks Thompson's wife, Little Bit (Red's mother), thus forcing the premature birth of her second son, Blue. Boots is killed by Appalachee Red on the day Red disappears.

Little Bit Thompson, Appalachee Red's mother. She is married to Big Man Thompson but carries on a prolonged affair with wealthy landowner John Morgan. This affair results in the birth of Appalachee Red while Big Man is serving time in prison for a crime he did not commit. Little Bit allows her older sister to take the baby to Chicago. In 1936, Little Bit is kicked senseless by Boots White as she tries to protect her husband, who has been shot by the police chief. For the next twenty-seven years, Little Bit lives in a state of insanity.

John Morgan, the heir to the large Morgan estate. As a young man, he falls in love with the new family maid, Little Bit Thompson. He fathers Appalachee Red by her and builds a home for his concubine before beginning his legitimate family. Morgan remains devoted to Little Bit for the remainder of her life and is grieving at her funeral when Appalachee Red absconds with Morgan's daughter, Roxanne, who secretly is in love with Red.

Blue Thompson, the second son of Little Bit Thompson and half brother to Appalachee Red. He is born prematurely on the day his father is killed, as a result of his mother being kicked by Boots White. He is taken under the wing of his elder half brother, who pays for Blue's education at the University of Michigan. After he is graduated from college, the best job Blue can find as a young black man is as a postal worker. Frustrated and angered by this lack of opportunity, Blue resigns his job and joins the Civil Rights movement. He returns to Appalachee and is arrested for trying to integrate Appalachee's most exclusive eatery. Tall, lanky, and defiant, Blue attends his mother's funeral under police escort.

— *Warren J. Carson*

THE APPLE IN THE DARK
(A Maçã no Escuro)

Author: Clarice Lispector (1925-1977)
First published: 1961
Genre: Novel

Locale: A remote farming region of Brazil
Time: Late 1950's
Plot: Didactic

Martim (mahr-TEEM), a middle-aged statistician from São Paulo. A heavyset, blue-eyed man, he is in hiding because he believes that he killed his wife in a jealous rage. He hides out for two weeks in a hotel in central Brazil that is occupied only by a German and a servant. When he thinks they have gone to report his presence to the police, he flees overland and finds a job doing manual labor on a small farm in exchange for board

and room. He spends a long time on the farm, which is owned and run by Vitória. He is involved for a while with Ermelinda, Vitória's younger cousin. Most of the action takes place in Martim's mind, as he tries to understand who he is and how he relates to his circumstances.

Vitória (vee-TOHR-ee-ah), a tough woman in her fifties who inherited a farm from an aunt and uncle whom she had visited in childhood. She spent her youth caring for her father, and only after his death has she been free to choose to move out to the country and run the farm herself. The farm is an isolated one, and until Martim appears, Vitória has lived with only the company of her cousin Ermelinda, Francisco the hired man, and a female mulatto cook and her small daughter. Attracted to Martim, Vitória is impelled to explain her life to him and, in the process, come to a better understanding of herself. At first, she is afraid of living and of being loved.

Ermelinda (ehr-meh-LEEN-dah), a young woman from Rio de Janeiro who has come to live on her cousin Vitória's farm after being widowed three years before Martim appears. Her sensuous indolence and vague spiritualism are attributed

to her bedridden childhood and consequent overindulgence. Ermelinda falls in love with Martim, is sexually involved with him for a time, then falls out of love and distances herself from him again. Opposite in personality from her cousin Vitória, who works hard on the farm and continually barks out orders to Martim and Francisco, Ermelinda drifts about eating candied almonds. She is sentimental and idle, and she believes in her vague presentiments about the future.

The professor, who arranges for the authorities to pick up Martim. He is a surrogate for society as a whole, and he brings the willing martyr back to reality.

— *Mary G. Berg*

THE APPLE OF THE EYE

Author: Glenway Wescott (1901-1987)
First published: 1924
Genre: Novel

Locale: Rural Wisconsin
Time: Twentieth century
Plot: Regional

Hannah Madoc, a natural, primitive young woman. Orphaned and penniless after her drunken father dies from a fall occasioned by Hannah's pushing him off a porch in self-defense, Hannah goes to work in a store. Falling in love with Jule Bier, she rejects the attentions of others. Jule's father wants him to marry someone else, however, and the grief-stricken Hannah goes away and becomes a prostitute. Jule goes to bring her home at last. The prematurely broken and bitter Hannah dies as the result of a fall.

Jule Bier, a young farmhand. In love with Hannah, he nevertheless follows his father's orders and marries a wealthy girl. He acquires a wonderful understanding of life, and as an old man advises his wife's nephew to accept the simple values, like Hannah's, rather than the warped, false values of people whose religion masks a fear of life.

Selma Duncan, Jule's wife, daughter of a wealthy farmer. She brings up her daughter to fear love and sex, with disastrous results. When the daughter's body is found, the news is kept from the ailing Selma.

Rosalia Bier, the daughter of Jule and Selma. Seduced, she is tormented by feelings of guilt, though she hides her fear from her lover. After her lover leaves, she is convinced that a baby is her inevitable punishment. She runs away in

a snowstorm; her body is found the following spring in a swamp and quietly buried there by Jule, his nephew, and a neighbor.

Mike Byron, a robust, zestful young man who works on Jule's farm. He loves Rosalia and becomes her lover. Jule tells him that he would not object to the marriage, but Mike feels trapped and leaves.

Dan Strane, Selma's nephew. A frustrated adolescent brought up in ignorance of sex by his tight-lipped mother, he is torn between curiosity and feelings of shame. Mike instructs Dan, telling him that life's processes are not obscene but wonderful. Mike is Dan's idol, but after Rosalia's desertion and death, Dan hates the memory of Mike. A talk with the understanding Jule reconciles the conflicts Dan feels. At the story's close, Dan is preparing to enter the state university.

Mrs. Strane, Selma's sister, Dan's straitlaced mother.

Mr. Bier, Jule's father, cold and calculating. He orders his son to court Selma.

Mrs. Boyle, in whose store the orphaned Hannah works.

Mr. Boyle, her husband. Hannah leaves the store to go to work on a farm near Jule's home after Mr. Boyle tries to make love to her.

APPOINTMENT IN SAMARRA

Author: John O'Hara (1905-1970)
First published: 1934
Genre: Novel

Locale: Pennsylvania
Time: 1930
Plot: Naturalism

Julian English, an automobile dealer who drinks too much. He picks fights with his friends and benefactors, gets publicly drunk, drives his wife to seek a divorce, and chases after a bootlegger's woman. When his acts add up and life becomes too complicated for him, he commits suicide.

Caroline English, a woman as superficial as her husband. When she decides to seek a divorce from her husband, she acts like a heroine in melodrama, cancelling a big party on short notice.

Harry Reilly, a wealthy Irish Catholic. At a party, Julian

throws a drink in his face, despite the fact that Reilly has befriended him and lent him the money needed to keep his Cadillac agency solvent. Julian seems a bit surprised when Reilly holds a grudge.

Helene Holman, a nightclub singer and bootlegger's woman. She and Julian get together while drunk at a Christmas celebration.

Ed Charney, a bootlegger. Though a family man, he keeps Helene as his mistress and is resentful of the favors she shows other men. He becomes angry at his aide, Al

Grecco, for letting Helene become involved with Julian.

Al Grecco, a small-time gangster who becomes angry at Charney's insults and vows to kill him.

Froggy Ogden, Caroline English's one-armed cousin, who tries to goad Julian into a fight after reproaching him for his conduct.

Dr. English, Julian's father, who looks for moral weakness in his son because his own father was an embezzler and a suicide.

Father Creedon, a priest who agrees with Julian that Harry Reilly is a bore. He refuses to take the incident of Julian's insulting Reilly seriously.

THE APPRENTICESHIP OF DUDDY KRAVITZ

Author: Mordecai Richler (1931-   )
First published: 1959
Genre: Novel

Locale: Montreal and New York City
Time: Late 1940's or 1950's
Plot: Bildungsroman

David "Duddy" Kravitz, a Montreal-born Jewish teenager and second-generation Canadian. Motherless and growing up in the shadow of his favored elder brother, Lennie, the dark, nervous Duddy feels closest to his *zeyda* (grandfather), Simcha Kravitz. Early in Duddy's life, Simcha admonishes him, "A man without land is nobody. Remember that, Duddel." Duddy works for material success and admiration by buying land in the growing resort area of the Laurentian mountains north of Montreal. His laudable goal is to provide a farm for his *zeyda* and various philanthropic benefits for the Jewish community. Duddy's more questionable values, derived from his bleak immediate environment and developed in part as a defense against the anti-Semitism he encounters in the larger French- and English-Canadian society, lead him to pursue his goals with admirable perseverance, self-sacrifice, and zeal but also with deeply ingrained ruthlessness. By the age of nineteen, having weathered bankruptcy and a nervous breakdown, he has struggled, ingratiated, and cheated his way into being the sole owner of about 440 arpents (about 375 acres) of prime Laurentian land, but at the cost of the love and respect of those few who have tried to give him the admiration and emotional security he craves. Instead, he has allied himself by choice and by deed with the moral bankrupts around him.

Simcha Kravitz, Duddy's grandfather, an immigrant Polish Jew and a shoemaker. A pious and scrupulously honest though unbending man, Simcha is trusted and honored in the community. Hurt by his elder son, Benjy, and contemptuous of his younger son, Max, Simcha tries to nurture in Duddy the principles he himself reveres. Advising his grandson that a man without land—by which he means a place where he belongs—is nobody, he inadvertently plants in Duddy the insatiable desire to acquire property, whatever the moral costs.

Max Kravitz, the middle-aged father of Lennie and Duddy, a widower, taxi driver, pimp, and big talker. His hopes and love are lavished on Lennie; his admiration, indicative of his own inability and questionable values, is reserved for the likes of the Boy Wonder, Jerry Dingleman. He takes little notice of lonely Duddy, whom he tolerates with casual affection at best and understands not at all. When Duddy acquires his land and thereby achieves spurious prominence, Max delights in this new opportunity to brag and dream.

Lennie Kravitz, Duddy's older brother. Driven by the family's expectations, Lennie is studying to achieve the apogee of success for a poor Jewish boy as a McGill University-trained medical doctor. Longing for acceptance among gentiles, he agrees to perform an abortion on a gentile socialite, bungles it,

and flees. He must be saved from disgrace by Duddy, who is thus introduced to Montreal's English-speaking gentile elite, embodied in Hugh Thomas Calder.

Benjamin Kravitz, Duddy's uncle, a wealthy textile factory owner and pseudosocialist. His childless, failed marriage to his now-alcoholic wife, Ida, has made him a bitter recluse. He paid for Lennie's education and has always perceived Duddy as grasping and deceitful, but when he is dying of cancer, he finally comes to perceive Duddy's inherent integrity. Hoping to encourage Duddy's finer qualities, Benjy wills Duddy his Outremont mansion, but his appreciation comes too late.

Yvette Durelle, Duddy's French-Canadian girlfriend, who is in her early twenties. Yvette alienates her Roman Catholic, anti-Semitic family by moving in with Duddy as his secretary and lover. Because Duddy is a minor and a Jew, she buys Duddy's land in her name. Loving and patient, she endures Duddy's boorishness and lack of respect, deserting him finally when he destroys Virgil.

Virgil Roseboro, an American in his early twenties, sweet-tempered, naïve, and epileptic. Doggedly loyal to Duddy, he allows Duddy to use him mercilessly at the expense of his precarious health and all of his money.

Jerry Dingleman, the Boy Wonder, in his late thirties and crippled by polio. Once handsome, he is now greasily florid of face, his large body dwindling to sticklike legs. A local boy, he has rocketed to flamboyant wealth and power in the American and Canadian underworlds. Now the owner of a sleazy Montreal gambling joint, he uses an impressionable, ignorant Duddy to carry heroin for him across the United States-Canadian border. Having eventually earned Duddy's contempt, he tries to circumvent Duddy's land acquisition and fails.

Mr. Cohen, a wealthy, influential, middle-aged scrap-metal merchant. He takes a fatherly interest in Duddy's career, giving him financial support and excusing, indeed encouraging, the ruthlessness and self-interest that eventually come to dominate Duddy's personality.

John MacPherson, a middle-aged, Scottish-born socialist, failed idealist, and alcoholic. A burned out teacher at Duddy's high school, he is victimized by the students. Duddy probably is responsible, through a prank, for the death of MacPherson's invalid wife. MacPherson's sardonic parting remark to Duddy, "You'll go far, Kravitz. You're going to go very far," dogs Duddy throughout his relentless search for success.

— Jill Rollins

THE ARABIAN NIGHTS' ENTERTAINMENTS
(Alf layla wa-layla)

Author: Unknown
First published: Fifteenth century
Genre: Short fiction

Locale: India, China, Persia, and Arabia
Time: Legendary past
Plot: Folklore

Shahriar, Emperor of Persia and India. Convinced of the unfaithfulness of all women, he vows to marry a new woman every day and have her executed the next morning.

Scheherazade, his wise and beautiful bride. On the night of their wedding, she begins to tell him a tale that so fascinates him that he stays her execution for a day so that he can learn the end of the story. The stories are continued for a thousand and one nights. Then, convinced of her worthiness, he bids her live and makes her his consort. The following are characters in some of her stories:

The King of the Black Isles, who nearly kills the lover of his unfaithful queen. She gets revenge by turning her husband's lower half into marble and his town and all its people into a lake of fish. A neighboring sultan kills the lover and deceives the queen into undoing all her enchantments; then she too is killed.

Sindbad the Sailor, who, in the course of his voyages, visits an island that is really the back of a sea monster; a valley of diamonds; an island inhabited by cannibal dwarfs and black one-eyed giants; and an underground river.

The Caliph Harun-al-Rashid of Baghdad, Sindbad's ruler.

Houssain,

Ali, and

Ahmed, sons of the Sultan of India. They compete for the hand of their father's ward; after an archery contest, Ali is proclaimed the winner, though Ahmed's arrow has gone so far that no one can find it.

Periebanou, a fairy living in a mountain, at whose door Ahmed finds his arrow. He marries her and with her help performs unreasonable tasks for his father, who has been persuaded by courtiers to be suspicious of his son, now secretive about his life and apparently rich and powerful. The sultan is killed by Periebanou's annoyed brother, and Ahmed succeeds him as sultan.

Princess Nouronnihar, the ward of the sultan. She is sought in marriage by the brothers. Ali wins her.

Ali Baba, a Persian woodcutter who happens upon a thieves' cave filled with riches.

Cassim, his greedy brother, who forgets the password, "Open Sesame," and so cannot get out of the cave. The thieves kill him.

Morgiana, Ali Baba's beautiful slave. She discovers that the thieves are hiding in oil jars brought by their disguised captain to Ali Baba's house. Morgiana kills the robbers, is rewarded with her freedom, and becomes Ali Baba's son's wife.

Aladdin, a young vagabond in China who gets possession of a magic lamp and, through the power of its genie, gains incredible wealth and wins the sultan's daughter as his wife.

THE ARBITRATION

Author: Menander (c. 342-c. 291 B.C.E.)
First performed: After 304 B.C.E.
Genre: Drama

Locale: A suburb of Athens
Time: The fourth century B.C.E.
Plot: Comedy of manners

Pamphila (PAM-fih-luh), Smicrines' daughter. She is ravished by an unknown, drunken young man who leaves his signet ring at the scene. She later marries her ravisher, Charisius, and bears his child. The baby is left exposed in the hills, along with the signet ring. The baby, found by peasants, is identified by the ring and returned to its rightful parents.

Charisius (kay-RIH-see-uhs), an upright young Athenian. During a drunken revel, he ravishes Pamphila, whom he later marries without remembering her as his victim. Disavowing the child he learned was born to his wife during his absence, he leaves home and spends his substance on the slave girl, Habrotonon. He is reunited with his wife after Habrotonon identifies Pamphila as his companion at the revel of a year before.

Smicrines (SMIH-krih-neez), Pamphila's father.

Habrotonon (ha-BROH-teh-non), a pretty slave woman who turns out to be Smicrines' long-lost daughter. As companion of Charisius after he learns that his wife has born a child whom he disclaims, she brings about the reunion of the husband and wife by identifying Pamphila as Charisius' victim on the night of the revel. She marries Chaerestratus.

Onesimus (oh-NEH-sih-muhs), Charisius' slave.

Chaerestratus (kee-REHS-treh-tuhs), Charisius' friend, who marries Habrotonon.

Sophrona (SOH-freh-nuh), Pamphila's nurse.

Davus (DA-vuhs), a goatherd who discovers Pamphila's baby in the hills.

Syriscus (sih-RIHS-kuhs), a charcoal burner who adopts Pamphila's baby.

Carion (KAY-ree-uhn), a vain, prying cook.

ARCADIA

Author: Sir Philip Sidney (1554-1586)
First published: 1590; revised, 1593, 1598
Genre: Novel

Locale: Arcadia, Greece
Time: Classical antiquity
Plot: Pastoral

Pyrocles (PI-rohk-leez), Prince of Macedon. Journeying with his cousin Musidorus, he fights on the side of justice in many countries before he reaches Arcadia and falls in love with a picture of the Princess Philoclea. He disguises himself as an Amazon, Zelmane, to be near his lady, only to find himself tormented by the passion of both her parents.

Musidorus (mew-sih-DOH-ruhs), his cousin and loyal friend, Prince of Thessalia. He masquerades as Dorus, a shepherd, and pretends to court the homely Mopsa in order to win the hand of the noble Princess Pamela, who is finally persuaded to run away with him.

Basilius (beh-SIH-lih-uhs), the ruler of Arcadia, who takes his Queen and their daughters into the country to prevent the fulfillment of an oracle's prophecy, which he fears portends disaster for him. He betrays both his age and his dignity in his passion for his daughter's companion, Zelmane.

Gynecia (jih-NEE-shih-uh), his young wife, who suffers agonies of conscience for the desire and jealousy she feels for Pyrocles, whose disguise she has penetrated. Resenting his attentions to Philoclea, she is freed from her passion only after she has almost killed her husband with a love potion intended for Zelmane.

Pamela, their stately, reserved older daughter, who is wooed and, after much resistance, won by Musidorus.

Philoclea (fih-lohk-LEE-uh), her sweeter, more submissive sister. She responds quickly to Pyrocles' love, but she lacks the strength with which Pamela meets difficulties.

Amphialus (am-FI-eh-luhs), Basilius' warrior nephew, who is spurred on by his ambitious mother and by his love for Philoclea to kidnap the princesses and take over the kingdom. Although he deeply regrets the deaths he causes, he cannot restrain his desire for fighting.

Cecropia (seek-ROH-pih-uh), Amphialus' ruthless mother, who spurs him on his ambitious path to overthrow her hated brother Basilius.

Philanax (fih-LA-naks), regent of Arcadia, a man of intelligence and integrity.

Dametas (day-MEE-tuhs), a foolish, arrogant shepherd, Pamela's guardian.

Miso (MI-soh), the sharp-tongued, jealous wife of Dametas.

Mopsa (MOP-suh), their homely daughter. Her stupidity makes her a useful cover for the blossoming romance between Musidorus and Pamela.

Argalus (AHR-guh-luhs), a worthy young lord and a devoted lover and husband. He dies defending the rights of his cousins, Pamela and Philoclea, against Amphialus.

Parthenia (pahr-THEE-nih-uh), Argalus' gracious wife. Grief-stricken at his death, she arms herself and fights a fatal duel with Amphialus, unwilling to live without her husband.

Demagoras (deh-MA-guh-ruhs), her vengeful rejected suitor.

Evarchus (eh-VAHR-kuhs), King of Macedon, who is judge in the trial after Basilius' apparent death. He is deeply grieved to learn that he has condemned his son Pyrocles and his nephew Musidorus, but he insists that he must endure his own suffering and uphold law and order.

Helen, Queen of Corinth. Enamored of Amphialus, she pursues him over the countryside while adoring his picture. She comes to heal his wounds after his combat with Musidorus.

Philoxenus (fih-lehk-ZEE-nuhs), a suitor of Helen. Jealous of her attentions to his foster brother, Amphialus, he challenges his rival and dies in the ensuing duel.

Timotheus (tih-MOH-thih-uhs), the father of Philoxenus.

Kalander (kah-LAN-dur), an Arcadian gentleman who shelters Musidorus after he has been shipwrecked.

Clitophon (KLI-tuh-fon), his son.

Ismenus (ihs-MEE-nuhs), Amphialus' devoted squire, killed in a battle with Philanax.

Phalantus (fuh-LAN-tuhs), a Corinthian knight who is persuaded by his selfish lady to defend the supremacy of her beauty against all challengers.

Artesia (ahr-TEE-shih-uh), Phalantus' disdainful lady, who spurns him after he loses a battle. Cecropia makes her a tool in her plot against Basilius and finally has her beheaded.

The King of Paphlagonia (pa-fluh-GOH-nee-uh), the model for Gloucester in Shakespeare's *King Lear*; a ruler blinded and exiled by his bastard son and aided by his more loyal child.

Leonatus (lee-uh-NAY-tuhs), his devoted son.

Plexirtus (plehk-SUR-tuhs), the bastard usurper, who tries to kill his virtuous brother.

Tydeus (TI-dih-uhs) and

Telenor (teh-LEE-nur), allies of Plexirtus.

Erona (eh-ROH-nuh), a Lydian princess who defies her father to marry the son of her nurse.

Antiphilus (an-TIH-fih-luhs), her selfish, treacherous husband.

Tiridates (ti-rih-DAY-teez), the cruel king of Armenia, rejected by Erona.

Artaxia (ahr-TAK-sih-uh), his sister and successor.

Plangus (PLAN-guhs), the son of the king of Iberia. He joins Telenor's army after an unfortunate affair with a married woman. When he returns, he finds her wedded to his father. He later takes refuge in Arcadia.

Andromana (an-DROH-muh-nuh), his wanton stepmother.

Pamphilus (PAM-fih-luhs), a knight despised for his inhuman treatment of women.

Dido (DI-doh), one of his victims.

Chremes (KRAY-meez), her miserly father.

Palladius (puh-LA-dih-uhs), Plangus' half brother, the unlucky lover from whom Musidorus took his pseudonym.

Zelmane (zehl-MAY-nee), his sweetheart, who adored Pyrocles and followed him, in the disguise of a page, until her death.

Clinias (KLIH-nih-uhs), a smooth-tongued, crafty shepherd in Cecropia's service.

Anaxius (eh-NAK-shih-uhs), a powerful, gigantic knight who fought with Amphialus' army.

Zoilus (ZOY-luhs) and

Lycurgus (li-KUR-guhs), his brothers, leaders of Amphialus' army after he is wounded.

Timautus (tih-MOH-tuhs), an ambitious nobleman who attempts to oust Philanax.

Sympathus (SIHM-puh-thuhs), Philanax's articulate supporter.

Kalodulus (kuh-LOH-joo-luhs), a devoted friend of Musidorus.

Dorilaus (doh-rih-LAY-uhs), Musidorus' father, killed in battle.

THE ARCHITECT AND THE EMPEROR OF ASSYRIA
(L'Architecte et l'Empereur d'Assyrie)

Author: Fernando Arrabal (1932-   )
First published: 1967
Genre: Drama

Locale: A desert island
Time: Late 1960's
Plot: Surrealism

The Emperor, the only survivor of an airplane crash on a small, almost deserted island. During the first act, the Emperor re-creates some of the principal characters of his former, "civilized" society; he plays a dictator, priest, nun, fiancée, soldier at war, doctor, and woman giving birth. In successive roles, he frenetically mimes the ceremony, pomp, and ritual that define these characters. Exhausted by his own theatricality, the Emperor suffers an apparent heart attack. Shortly after this, in a long self-reflective monologue, he says that he embraces the solitude of island life, a life without films, newspapers, or Coca-Cola. Addressing a scarecrow that he has placed on a throne, the Emperor speaks, in perhaps a rare moment of candor, of another life, of a job with a good salary and a wife who was happy when he finally received a raise. Painfully, before the scarecrow, he reviews his whole life and its main characters: his wife who cheated, his mother who no longer loved him, and his friends who, for the most part, envied him. He talks of his dreams of becoming the Emperor of Assyria one day and of writing like Voltaire.

The Architect, the only other inhabitant of the island, the "savage" and future pupil of the Emperor. Although ignorant of the rudiments of architecture, the Architect possesses special magical powers over the forces of nature. As if a stage director, he creates light and darkness at will and even is able to command, through the magic of words, the island's animals. He yearns to have knowledge of society's institutions and manners: What is a dictator? What is love? What is a mother? In a series of sadomasochistic games, role reversals, and acted-out sexual fantasies, the Architect is instructed by the Emperor in the ways of civilization. The Architect, in a recurring gesture of cruelty, threatens to abandon the Emperor by rowing to another island in his canoe. At one point, the Architect recounts a dream to the Emperor. In his dream, he was alone on a small island and an airplane fell, creating a terrible panic. Much of the interaction between the only two characters in the play depends on re-created events, ceremonies reenacted in an erotic and cruel atmosphere of panic.

— *James Gaasch*

ARGENIS

Author: John Barclay (1582-1621)
First published: 1621
Genre: Novel

Locale: Europe
Time: The Hellenistic Era
Plot: Allegory

Argenis (ahr-JEE-nihs), a beautiful, resourceful priestess of Pallas Athena and the daughter of Meleander, king of Sicily; she also symbolizes the throne of France. Having met Poliarchus, a hero in the Sicilian rebellion, she can never return the love of Archombrotus, a suitor favored by her father, or that of Radirobanes, king of Sardinia, who insists on pressing his suit and attempts to blackmail her for meeting her beloved in secret. She thwarts Radirobanes' designs, appeases her father's wrath, discovers that Archombrotus is her half brother, and marries the man of her choice.

Poliarchus (po-lih-AHR-kuhs), in reality Prince Astioristes of France, allegorically King Henry IV of Navarre, a warrior-hero in chivalric disguise. As a daring fighter for King Meleander, the young knight insists on a firm peace rather than a truce, and he thereby alienates his loved one's father and makes an enemy of the rebel leader, Lycogenes. An outcast, Poliarchus assumes female disguise and calls himself Theocrine in order to enter the heavily guarded castle where Argenis and her maidens have been sent by Meleander after Lycogenes has threatened to abduct the princess; Poliarchus' purpose is to see for himself whether Argenis is as beautiful as she is reported. The two meet and fall deeply in love. The adventures of Poliarchus include routing pirates, slaying a Sardinian interloper in single combat, and succeeding to the throne of France, as well as marrying Argenis.

Archombrotus (ahr-kom-BROH-tuhs), Poliarchus' good friend, in reality Hyempsal, prince of Mauritania and King

Meleander's favorite warrior. The first to know of his friend's deep love for Argenis, he too is smitten and presses his suit for the lovely Princess. He is above reproach, however, in his attentions, and he truly merits her hand after he kills Lycogenes, the rebel leader, in single combat, thereby ending the revolt. His bravery is rewarded when his friend Poliarchus helps to defend Mauritania and aids Queen Hyanisbe in successfully routing the invaders. In the end, Archombrotus is revealed as the royal son of King Meleander by his first wife, the sister of the queen of Mauritania.

Meleander (meh-lee-AN-dur), king of Sicily, the father of Argenis and Archombrotus. A cautious, often mistaken, but always generous man, he is unable to subdue an insurrection until two foreign knights, Poliarchus and Archombrotus, come to his aid. His friendship for the latter, who rescues him from drowning and defeats the rebel leader, and his antagonism toward the other complicate the plot. When it looks as if his kingdom will be lost, he finally takes the initiative. By leading his ships to victory and his daughter to the altar, he rights wrongs and rewards the deserving.

Radirobanes (ra-dih-roh-BAY-neez), the king of Sardinia, at first the ally of King Meleander but later his antagonist for the hand of his daughter. Though brave in war, Radirobanes is a dastard in love. He bribes a maid in order to learn of a rendezvous of the hero and heroine, attempts blackmail to win the hand of the princess, and schemes to abduct her. Thwarted in both love and war, he falls victim to Astioristes, the new king of France.

Lycogenes (li-KOH-jeh-neez), a traitorous nobleman who almost succeeds in unseating King Meleander but whose breaking of a truce brings about his deserved death at the hands of Archombrotus.

Timoclea (tih-moh-KLEE-uh), a wise and loyal matron of Sicily who becomes the chief lady of King Meleander's household after she uncovers Selenissa's part in the plot to abduct Argenis. The devoted friend of Poliarchus as well, she hides him after his banishment, acts as his agent, and consoles Argenis.

Arsidas (AHR-sih-dehs), the governor of Messana, a Sicilian nobleman loyal to the crown. He acts as a comforter to Argenis when rumors of her beloved's death are received, as an arbiter to the king, and as the confidant of the two lovers.

Selenissa (see-lee-NIHS-uh), Argenis' nurse and companion, who commits suicide after the failure of the plan to have her mistress abducted by Radirobanes.

Gobrias (GOH-bree-uhs), the commander of the war fleet sent by the king of France to invade Sicily. He rescues shipwrecked Arsidas and tells him the story of King Astioristes' adventures in Sicily while disguised as Poliarchus. Overjoyed to learn that the knight he knew as Poliarchus still lives, Arsidas offers his aid in reuniting the lovers.

Gelanorus (jee-leh-NOH-ruhs), the French nobleman who attends Poliarchus in Sicily and acts as his servant.

Nicopompus (nihk-uh-POM-puhs), the court poet who composes the epithalamium for the wedding of Argenis and Poliarchus, now revealed as Astioristes, the king of France.

Hyanisbe, queen of Mauritania.

DER ARME HEINRICH

Author: Hartmann von Aue (c. 1160/1164-c. 1210/1220)
First transcribed: c. 1195
Genre: Poetry

Locale: Germany
Time: Late twelfth century
Plot: Didactic

Heinrich von Aue (HIN-rihsh fon OW-eh), a Swabian knight. He is wealthy, handsome, and of noble birth; purity and honor are the marks of his life; and fulfillment of the obligations of knighthood is his goal. Suddenly, all is changed by the terrible knowledge that he is a leper. In search of a remedy, he finally learns that his only cure lies in finding a virgin who, out of love, will yield her heart's blood. When a peasant girl begs Heinrich to allow her to make the sacrifice, he gives in to her pleas, but at the moment before the opera-

tion, he cannot accept her offering. On the way home, God's healing grace restores Heinrich to health. He and the girl are wed amid the rejoicings of his people.

A peasant girl, the daughter of the family with whom Heinrich lives as a leper. Deeply moved by Heinrich's suffering, and for the eternal life that will be her reward, she willingly offers her heart's blood for his cure. After the knight's refusal of her sacrifice and his miraculous cure, she and Heinrich are married.

THE ARMIES OF THE NIGHT: History as a Novel, the Novel as History

Author: Norman Mailer (1923-   )
First published: 1968
Genre: Novel

Locale: Washington, D.C., Virginia, and New York
Time: October, 1967
Plot: New journalism

Norman Mailer, a famous American novelist, journalist, social critic, historian, and candidate for mayor of New York City. Variously described in the third-person narrative as Mailer, **the Novelist**, or **the Historian**, Mailer is the focal character, a principal witness to the historic events the novel recounts and analyzes. A literary genius who has just published a novel, *Why Are We in Vietnam?*, Mailer is a reluctant participant in public demonstrations against the war in Vietnam; he believes his own literary work is his only real answer to the war. A self-described Left Conservative, he is soon persuaded to lend his extraliterary efforts to the antiwar effort and is arrested during the massive protest march to the steps of the Pentagon in October, 1967.

Robert Lowell, a much-admired rival of Mailer. He is considered to be the most talented and most distinguished poet in America. A man of great personal attractiveness, Lowell makes speeches, reads his poetry, and marches with the protesters. Along with Mailer, Dwight Macdonald, Paul Goodman, and Ed de Grazia, Lowell is a speaker at the Ambassador Theater in Washington on the Thursday night before the Saturday march on the Pentagon.

Dwight Macdonald, a gregarious, massive, and bearded literary critic. He is a speaker at the Ambassador Theater and a participant in the march. He is admired by Mailer, but their relations are touchy because Macdonald is currently at work on a review of Mailer's *Why Are We in Vietnam?*

Paul Goodman, a speaker at the Ambassador Theater who is disliked though respected by Mailer. Goodman is a social critic and essayist for *Dissent*, a socialist quarterly.

Mitchell Goodman, a former Harvard classmate of Mailer. He wrote a war novel for which Mailer wrote a blurb. A member of the antiwar group Resist and a principal organizer of a demonstration at the Department of Justice in support of students refusing the draft, Goodman telephones Mailer and invites him to speak at the Ambassador Theater.

David Dellinger, a principal organizer of the march, chairman of the National Mobilization to End the War in Vietnam, and editor of the anarchist-pacifist magazine *Liberation*.

Jerry Rubin, a principal organizer of the march. He is a creative, unpredictable, militant, hippie-oriented leader of the New Left and an organizer of the first mass protest of the war at the Berkeley campus of the University of California. Rubin once appeared at a House Committee on Un-American Activities hearing wearing an American revolutionary war uniform.

Ed de Grazia, a leading lawyer for the legal defense committee of the National Mobilization to End the War in Vietnam and an old friend of Mailer.

William Sloane Coffin, Jr., the chaplain at Yale. He is a man of great personal integrity and force who participates in the march.

Hirschkop, the masterful chief counsel for the demonstrators, confident and powerfully built. He successfully defends Mailer in a brilliant courtroom encounter with Commissioner Scaife.

Commissioner Scaife, an impressive Virginia judge who attempts to hold Mailer in jail but who is outmaneuvered by Hirschkop and thus compelled to free Mailer without bail.

Fontaine, a documentary maker who records the events of the march and interviews Mailer on camera.

Leiterman, a cameraman who assists Fontaine.

Heiss, a sound man who assists Fontaine.

Walter Teague, who is arrested during the march and held in a large holding cell with Mailer. A Leninist, Teague is a tireless caller for militant antiwar activities.

Noam Chomsky, a brilliant linguist at the Massachusetts Institute of Technology. He is arrested during the march and held in the same cell as Mailer.

Dr. Benjamin Spock, a famous pediatrician. He is a speaker at and participant in the march.

— *Michael Zeitlin*

ARMS AND THE MAN: An Anti-Romantic Comedy

Author: George Bernard Shaw (1856-1950)
First published: 1898
Genre: Drama

Locale: Bulgaria
Time: November, 1885, to March, 1886
Plot: Comedy

Catherine Petkoff, the mother of Raina and wife of Major Petkoff. The Petkoffs are an upper-class Bulgarian family. As the play opens, Catherine rushes into Raina's bedroom in the late evening to tell her the news that Raina's fiancé, Sergius Saranoff, led a victory in battle in the Russian-Austrian War, with the Bulgarians on the side of the Russians. Both women are thrilled, and both are very romantic in their attitudes.

Raina Petkoff, a twenty-three-year-old who idealistically believes herself to be in love with Sergius, to whom she is engaged. As the play develops, a series of shocks and learning experiences, such as seeing Sergius with his arm around Louka, move her away from idealism and toward realism.

Louka, a servant in the household who is engaged to another servant, Nicola. She comes in to tell Catherine and Raina that the windows and shutters are to be closed and fastened because the enemy is being chased through the town by Bulgarian soldiers. Catherine tells Raina to close them and leave them closed, then leaves to take care of the rest of the household; Raina, however, prefers the windows open, so Louka closes them in such a way that Raina can open them and then leaves.

Captain Bluntschli, a Swiss mercenary soldier of about thirty-five years. He is running away after his company lost the battle to Sergius. His father owns a chain of hotels in Switzerland. Although Bluntschli is in many ways a realist, his choice of the life of a soldier, a choice not forced upon him, is unrealistic. He startles Raina when she hears him climbing up to her balcony and coming into her room after she had blown out her candle in fright; he orders her not to expose him. She goes back and forth between treating him as an enemy and feeling sorry for him. When a Russian officer arrives searching for him, she hides and protects him, and eventually he falls asleep in her bed. Though shocked, Catherine and Raina finally allow him to sleep, and presumably he leaves safely the next morning.

Nicola, a servant engaged to Louka. They have a conversation at the beginning of act 2, as they do again later, and it becomes clear that they will almost surely never marry. Louka bitterly resents being a servant, but Nicola respects his role as a servant and respects the family, viewing them as a source of patronage when he saves enough money to open a shop.

Major Paul Petkoff, a commander of the Bulgarian army who is about fifty years old. He arrives home in March, 1886, immediately after the servants' conversation.

Major Sergius Saranoff, who arrives soon after Petkoff has greeted his servants and his wife in the garden. Raina makes a dramatic entrance, and when the others leave them, Sergius and Raina express their highly romantic (and false) idea of love for each other. When Raina returns to the house, Sergius attempts to make love to Louka. Bluntschli arrives to return Petkoff's coat, which Raina had lent him. During a series of comical interludes, it is revealed that Sergius' "heroism" was a stupid mistake that turned out luckily. It turns out that Sergius will marry Louka and that Bluntschli will marry Raina (with the approval of her parents, once they learn of his wealth); both couples feel genuine love, not false romanticism.

— *Jacob H. Adler*

ARNE

Author: Bjørnstjerne Bjørnson (1832-1910)
First published: 1859
Genre: Novel

Locale: Sweden
Time: Early nineteenth century
Plot: Pastoral

Arne, the illegitimate son of Margit and Nils. As he grows up, Arne is weaned away from his mother by his father. After the father's death, he takes up drinking, as had his father. He becomes a carpenter and also interests himself in Norwegian folklore and music. Falling in love with Eli, the daughter of his father's enemy, he marries her, thus ending a feud of many years' standing.

Nils, a tailor who fiddles for country dances. He is also a drunkard. He suffers a broken back in a fight with Baard Böen and is nursed by Arne's mother, whom he later marries. A gloomy, frustrated, morose man, he finally dies in drunken violence.

Margit, Arne's thrifty, solid, peasant mother. She hopes her son will not turn out like his father. She is pleased when the young man marries Eli Böen. Before the marriage, she shows the girl the treasures she has accumulated for her son and his bride. She believes Eli can save Arne from a dissolute and wasted life.

Eli Böen, daughter of Baard Böen, Nils' enemy. She falls in love with Arne and marries him.

Baard Böen, Nils' enemy, with whom Nils has the fight in which his back is broken. Years later, Baard tries to explain what happened. He finds, trying to tell Arne, that he cannot clearly recollect the cause of the quarrel that resulted in life-long enmity.

Kristian, Arne's friend who has gone to America. He writes to Arne in hopes that Arne can be persuaded to join him in America.

AROUND THE WORLD IN EIGHTY DAYS
(Le Tour du monde en quatre-vingts jours)

Author: Jules Verne (1828-1905)
First published: 1873
Genre: Novel

Locale: A tour of the world
Time: October 2-December 21, 1872
Plot: Adventure

Phileas Fogg (FIHL-ee-uhs), an English gentleman living in London. A tall, well-built man about forty years old, with light brown hair and a beard, he lives a quiet life of great regularity. Being independently wealthy, he spends most of his day at the Reform Club reading, taking his meals, and playing whist. Apparently having lived a life of travel and adventure some years earlier, he is a man of honor and integrity. Challenged by his whist partners to prove his contention that it is possible to travel around the world in eighty days, he agrees to make the trip in that amount of time and wagers twenty thousand pounds, his entire fortune. Along the way, he delays his journey to rescue Princess Aouda from death and later falls in love with her. Encountering numerous other delays and adversities in completing the trip, he remains imperturbable and loyal to his traveling companions, even when faced at the end with the loss of his remaining fortune.

Jean Passepartout (zhahn pas-par-tew), Fogg's French manservant. A middle-aged man of pleasant and honest appearance, with brown hair and blue eyes, he possesses a portly but muscular build. Prior to serving Fogg, he led a life of travel and uncertainty; as a result, the steady and methodical lifestyle of his new master appealed to him. It is a shock to him when it is announced that they will be traveling around the world out of a carpetbag. During the course of the journey, he shows himself to be brave and resourceful. His impersonation of the dead rajah makes the rescue of Aouda possible. His actions also sometimes cause delays for his master, such as when he is arrested for violating the sanctity of a Hindu temple and when he is captured by the Sioux after he saves a train. Through all these challenges, a relationship of mutual respect and affection develops between him and Fogg.

Fix, a detective. Small, slightly built, and nervous, he is a man of some intelligence. Coming across Fogg at Suez, he decides that Fogg matches the description of the man who recently robbed the Bank of England of fifty-five thousand pounds. He follows Fogg's party to India and then to Hong Kong, seeking to throw various obstacles in their way until arrest warrants arrive. After leaving English territory, he begins to aid the travelers in their passage to England. On arrival at Liverpool, he promptly and mistakenly arrests Fogg, causing a delay that makes it seem that the wager has been lost.

Aouda (ow-ew-duh), the widow of an Indian rajah. This dark-haired, light-complected young Parsee beauty received a thorough English education that rendered her more European than Indian. After her rescue from the suttee, Fogg plans to drop her off with a relative in Hong Kong. Arriving there, it is discovered that her relative had moved to The Netherlands. As a result, she continues to accompany Fogg on his journey, and the two fall in love. When they arrive in London and it appears that Fogg has lost his wager, Aouda proposes marriage. That suggestion reveals the twenty-four-hour miscalculation resulting from crossing the international date line and allows Fogg to win his bet by appearing at the Reform Club in the nick of time.

Sir Francis Cromarty, a British army officer. A tall, fair man of fifty, he is traveling to Benares to join his troops. After becoming acquainted with Fogg through playing whist during the train ride across India, he joins Fogg and Passepartout on the elephant ride and assists in the rescue of Aouda.

Colonel Stamp Proctor, a large, red-bearded American who almost comes to blows with Fogg during a political rally in San Francisco, California. Later, they meet on a train and are about to duel when the Sioux attack, and Proctor is severely wounded.

Captain Andrew Speedy, the English captain of the *Henrietta*, an irascible man of fifty with red hair and a growling voice. Fogg is forced to buy passage to Bordeaux on his vessel for an exorbitant price. Once aboard, he bribes the crew to lock up Speedy and sail to Liverpool. He later buys the *Henrietta* from Speedy and burns its wooden superstructure for fuel.

— Ronald H. Fritze

ARROW OF GOD

Author: Chinua Achebe (1930-   )
First published: 1964
Genre: Novel

Locale: Nigeria
Time: The 1920's
Plot: Social realism

Ezeulu (eh-zuh-EW-lew), a haughty, old chief priest of Ulu in the six villages, including his own Umuachala, that compose the federation of Umuaro. He sees himself and his god as beset by two dangers: the growing influence of a nearby Christian mission and the machinations of Ezidemili, a priest of Idemili who aspires to replace Ulu with his own god as paramount deity of Umuaro. Through pride and a misunderstanding, he angers the English district officer and is imprisoned for thirty-two days. Believing everything to be part of Ulu's design for destroying Idemili, he refuses after his release to declare the New Yam festival that allows harvesting; he thus causes incipient famine. When his favorite son dies, he goes mad.

Captain T. K. Winterbottom, a fifteen-year veteran of service in Africa whose pride and unbending principles have kept him a district officer. His district headquarters is in Okperi, the land neighboring Umuaro and home of Ezeulu's mother. He admires Ezeulu as the only witness, on either side of a land dispute between Okperi and Umuaro, who spoke the truth. When Umuaro and Okperi went to war, Winterbottom intervened decisively and became known as the "Destroyer of Guns." He now intends to appoint Ezeulu as paramount chief of Umuaro and summons the old priest to Okperi, which leads to perceived insult on both sides and to Ezeulu's imprisonment. Winterbottom's sudden attack of malaria leaves the matter largely in the hands of his assistant, Tony Clarke.

Nwaka (NWAH-kah), the leader of a prosperous family of Umuachala's rival village, Umunneora. He is one of the three citizens of Umuaro who has taken the highest possible (self-awarded) honorific title. He is the lifelong friend and tool of Ezidemili and speaks openly against Ezeulu whenever he has the chance. He incites the desire for war against Okperi and later instigates criticism of Ezeulu's original reply to Winterbottom's summons.

Obika (oh-bee-KAH), Ezeulu's fiery, rowdy, hard-drinking favorite son. He is generally regarded as the most handsome and most accomplished young man of Umuachala. His whipping for tardiness by Wright, the public works officer in charge of building a road through the area, sets the tone of hostility in which Ezeulu later receives the summons from Winterbottom. Defying a fever brought on by the hardship of the delayed yam harvest, Obika fulfills the role of "runner" in a funeral ritual and dies.

Oduche (oh-DEW-cheh), the son whom Ezeulu sends to the mission church/school to learn the ways of Christianity and discover the secrets of its power. He is so far converted as to trap a sacred python and put it in a trunk to suffocate.

Moses Unachukwu (ew-nah-CHEW-kwew), a convert and the first successful missionary to his people in Umuaro. His amazed outburst when Obika attempts to attack Wright for the whipping gives rise to suspicion that he has made derogatory comments to Wright about Obika's family. He fails in attempts to combat Goodcountry's inflammatory exhortations to kill the pythons.

John Goodcountry, a zealous convert from the Niger delta area who advocates Christians' killing of sacred pythons. Later, he capitalizes on Ezeulu's harvest ban by offering immunity from Ulu's anger in exchange for an even larger yam tribute.

John Nwadika (nwah-DEE-kah), a resident of Okperi, Winterbottom's servant. He guides the messenger to Ezeulu. During Ezeulu's imprisonment, he and his wife supply food, drink, and companionship.

Okeke Akukalia (oh-KAY-kay ah-kew-KAH-lee-uh), the son of a "mixed marriage" between Umuaro and Okperi natives. He speaks for the ultimatum and delivers it to Okperi. Ascending insults lead him to destroy a local man's *ikenga*, a fetish that is broken only after death. He is killed, and the war begins.

Ogbuefi Akuebue (og-bew-EH-fee ah-kew-eh-BEW-eh), a friend and confidant of Ezeulu. In his presence, Ezeulu unbends enough to laugh and to argue without anger, yet even he finds Ezeulu ultimately unknowable.

Edogo (ay-DOH-goh), Ezeulu's eldest son. He fears that Ezeulu has sent Oduche to the Christians in order to remove him from consideration as the next high priest. His fears are met with gentle contempt by Akuebue.

Ugoye (ew-GOH-yay) and

Matefi (mah-TAY-fee), Ezeulu's younger and older wives, respectively. Matefi is jealous of Ugoye's favored treatment, and Ugoye feels harassed by her rival's disapproving comments and actions.

— *James L. Hodge*

ARROWSMITH

Author: Sinclair Lewis (1885-1951)
First published: 1925
Genre: Novel

Locale: The United States and the West Indies
Time: Early twentieth century
Plot: Social realism

Martin Arrowsmith, a doctor chiefly interested in bacteriological research. As a medical student, he falls under the influence of Dr. Gottlieb, who gives him an inkling of the excitement of pure science as opposed to the practical side of medicine. After a brief engagement to Madeline Fox, a graduate student in English, Martin marries Leora Tozer, and his marriage forces him to give up his bacteriological research for general medicine study. After graduation, he establishes himself as a general practitioner in Leora's home town of Wheatsylvania, North Dakota. He becomes acting head of the Department of Public Health there, but his honesty makes him unpopular, and he joins the staff of Dr. Pickerbaugh in Nauti-

lus, Iowa. Pickerbaugh is a fake; the job leaves Martin no time for research, and again his honesty makes enemies. He next moves to Chicago as a pathologist in the Rouncefield Clinic. Through his old teacher, Gottlieb, he next joins the McGurk Institute in New York, an organization more interested in publicity than in pure science. He works on a cure for bubonic plague; when a plague is reported on an island in the West Indies, he goes there with Leora and Dr. Sondelius. With scientific detachment, he promises Gottlieb to test the antitoxin by giving it to only half the population, using the others as controls. After Sondelius and Leora both die of the plague, Martin, in his grief, gives the antitoxin to everyone, thus ruining the value of his experiment. On his return to the McGurk Institute, Martin marries Joyce Lanyon, a wealthy and fashionable widow. The marriage is unhappy; he cannot enter her social world, and she will not leave him time for his research. Resigning from the Institute and leaving Joyce, he joins Terry Wickett in the Vermont woods, where, in a crude laboratory, they begin the work that they both want to do.

Madeline Fox, Martin's first fiancée, a graduate student in English. She is pretentiously intellectual but fascinating to the crude Martin.

Leora Tozer, Martin's first wife, whom he marries while a student. Though not very intelligent, she is warm-hearted and kind and adores Martin. She dies in the West Indies of the plague.

Joyce Lanyon, a wealthy widow, Martin's second wife. The marriage fails because she finds Martin crude and uncultivated and can never understand his devotion to research.

Professor Max Gottlieb, a German-born professor of immunology at the University of Winnemac. He represents pure science, unconcerned with practical results. His intellectual arrogance and uncompromising honesty make it difficult for him to hold a position, and his career is a failure. He gives Martin the ideal of the scientist: a man dedicated to truth.

Terry Wickett, a scientist. As rough and uncouth as Martin, he is devoted to his work. He and Martin finally establish a laboratory in the Vermont woods.

Gustaf Sondelius, a dynamic Swedish fighter against diseases all over the world. He goes to the West Indies with Martin to combat the plague, is infected, and dies.

Cliff Clawson, a vulgar, clowning, but generous fraternity brother at the university. He reappears later when Martin is married to Joyce. He has become a slick salesman of fake oil stock.

Dr. Almus Pickerbaugh, Martin's colleague in the Public Health Service. He is a complete fake, a high-pressure salesman rather than a doctor, interested only in publicity. Martin tries to work under him but is much too honest to succeed. Pickerbaugh eventually becomes a congressman.

Orchid Pickerbaugh, his nineteen-year-old daughter, who has a brief flirtation with Martin.

Dr. Rippleton Holabird, head of the Department of Physiology at the McGurk Institute. He is an example of the pseudoscientist, interested only in personal advancement.

Angus Duer, a mercenary classmate under whom Martin later works at the fashionable Rouncefield Clinic.

Dean Silva, who exerts a good influence on Martin at medical school.

ARTAMENES: Or, The Grand Cyrus
(Artamène: Ou, Le Grand Cyrus)

Author: Madeleine de Scudéry (1607-1701)
First published: 1649-1653
Genre: Novel

Locale: Asia Minor
Time: 500 B.C.
Plot: Sentimental

Artamène, in reality **Cyrus the Great**, the son of the king of Persia. Given as a child to a shepherd to be killed because of an ill omen, the boy is reared by the shepherd. As Artamène, he becomes a great general. He falls in love with Mandane, a beautiful princess, and, along with numerous others, pursues her endlessly and against great odds. After conquering many of the kingdoms of Asia while in pursuit of Mandane, Artamène finds his princess still alive and safe, and they are wed.

Cyaxares (si-AK-suh-reez), king of Cappadocia and Media. Artamène becomes his best general and falls in love with his daughter.

Mandane, the daughter of King Cyaxares. Her hand is sought by numerous kings and princes, but she loves only Artamène. She is the object of the Queen of Scythia's jealousy. When captured by the queen, she is marked for murder; by mistake, a maid of honor is killed in her place. Rescued by Artamène, she marries him at last.

Philidaspes, king of Assyria, who is in love with Mandane. He abducts her and takes her to Babylon but there loses her to a rival.

Mazare, the prince of Sacia, who also loves Mandane. While Philidaspes is locked in a tower, Mazare takes Mandane away.

The King of Pontus, also in love with Mandane. He captures her when she and Mazare are shipwrecked near his fortress. When his fortress is threatened by Artamène, he carries Mandane away.

Anaxoris, in reality **Aryante**, prince of the Massagetae and Queen Thomyris' brother. Anaxoris also loves Mandane. Entrusted with Mandane's safety by his friend Philidaspes, he turns her over to Thomyris to keep her away from Artamène.

Thomyris, the powerful queen of Scythia. In love with Artamène, her jealousy causes her to order Mandane's death. A maid of honor is killed by mistake, and before Thomyris can act again, Mandane is rescued by Artamène.

Spargapises, Thomyris' son, who commits suicide in disgrace because he is not recognized when captured in battle.

Araminta, the sister of the queen of Pontus. Mandane is jealous of her because she mistakenly thinks Artamène is enamored of her.

Spithridates, Araminta's suitor, who resembles Artamène and thus causes Mandane to think it is Artamène who is pursuing Araminta. He is killed in battle and, still being mistaken for Artamène, his head is presented to Thomyris.

Prince Phraortes (fray-OHR-teez), who abducts Araminta, leaving Spithridates desperate.

Panthea, the wife of Abradantes, who, along with Araminta, is taken as a hostage by Artamène at Sardis.

Abradantes, one of the rulers whom Artamène fights in his siege of Sardis.

Martesie, Mandane's maid of honor.

The Queen of Corinth, who forms a platonic attachment for Artamène and sends her fleet to help him capture Cumae, to which the king of Pontus has fled with Mandane.

Metrobate, a traitor.

THE ARTAMONOV BUSINESS
(Delo Artamonovykh)

Author: Maxim Gorky (Aleksey Maksimovich Peshkov, 1868-1936)
First published: 1925
Genre: Novel

Locale: Russia
Time: c. 1862-1918
Plot: Family

Ilia Artamonov (ih-LYAH ahr-TAH-meh-nov), a dictatorial stranger who builds a factory in Dromov. His business and power continue to grow despite increased resentment against him.

Peter Artamonov, Ilia Artamonov's eldest son and the heir to his business. Blind to the changes time has made in the attitude of his workers, he ends his days as a prisoner of the revolutionists.

Nikita Artamonov (ni-KIH-teh), Ilia Artamonov's hunchbacked son. Failing in his efforts to become a good monk, he leaves the religious life and is seen frequently in the company of the revolutionary Vialov.

Alexey Artamonov (ah-lehk-SAY), Ilia Artamonov's adopted son and business representative.

Ilia, Peter Artamonov's elder son. Indifferent to the affairs of the factory, he leaves home to become a historian and, later, a revolutionary.

Yakov (YAH-kehf), Peter Artamonov's younger son and the heir to his father's place in the factory. Fearing for his life among the increasingly restless workers, he flees, only to be killed by robbers on the train to Moscow.

Tikhon Vialov (TIH-hehn VYAH-lehf), a worker-philosopher in the Artamonov factory. As a soldier of the revolution, he becomes Peter Artamonov's jailer.

Natalia Baimakov (nah-TAH-lih-yeh bi-MAH-kehf), Peter Artamonov's wife.

Uliana Baimakov (ew-lih-AH-neh), the wife of Evgeny Baimakov, and, as his widow, the mistress of Ilia Artamonov.

Evgeny Baimakov (ehv-GEH-nihy), the mayor of Dromov.

Elena (eh-LEH-neh), the daughter of Peter Artamonov.

Miron (MIH-rehn), Alexey Artamonov's son.

Pauline, the mistress of Yakov Artamonov.

ARTURO'S ISLAND
(L'isola di Arturo)

Author: Elsa Morante (1918-1985)
First published: 1957
Genre: Novel

Locale: The island of Procida, near Naples
Time: 1922-1939
Plot: Psychological realism

Arturo Gerace (ahr-TEWR-oh geh-RAH-chay), the narrator of the tale, who tells the story of his life up to the age of seventeen. He was born and reared on the island of Procida, in the Bay of Naples. His father, Wilhelm Gerace, was illegitimate, the product of an affair between an immigrant Italian and a German schoolteacher. Arturo seeks affection from this moody and distant man, who is often away. Arturo's mother died shortly after his birth. When his father returns one day with a new wife, Nunziata, Arturo is dismayed. The new wife is young, barely older than Arturo. At first, the boy dislikes her, but he gradually falls in love with her. In the end, Arturo is disillusioned by his father, who turns out to be far from the romantic, heroic person Arturo has imagined him to be.

Wilhelm Gerace, Arturo's father, who grew up hating women and disliking the fishing folk of Procida. He inherited a house from a blind eccentric who befriended him and took his first wife there. She gave birth to Arturo at the age of eighteen and died shortly thereafter. Wilhelm seldom is home, leaving Arturo in the hands of various persons. His second wife, the youthful Nunziata, represents an attempt to recapture the image of his first wife, also a young woman. Nunziata is afraid of him. Wilhelm is attracted to a convict, Stella, who is in the penitentiary on the island, and he brings her home, thereby losing forever the loyalty of his son.

Nunziata (newn-ZEEAH-tah), Wilhelm's second wife, a poor girl from the slums of Naples. She arouses resentment, then affection, in Arturo. She becomes pregnant with Wilhelm's child, but for most of her pregnancy, her husband is gone. Rather prim for her age, she looks on Arturo as a strange, emotional boy and repulses his signs of affection. When Arturo injures himself while staging a suicide attempt, she nurses him back to health, earning his devotion.

Assuntina (ah-sewn-TEE-nah), a widow of Procida who becomes Arturo's mistress. She is a willing partner to his advances and sees in him a poor romantic boy who gives her true love. She is, in a way, a surrogate for Arturo's real love, Nunziata. It is through making love to Assuntina that Arturo comes to understand that his true love is for his father's second bride.

Silvestro, a youth not much older than Arturo who is engaged by Wilhelm to watch over the boy while Wilhelm is away on his many trips. He swims and plays with Arturo, and he tries to shepherd him responsibly, not always succeeding. Silvestro is conscripted into the army, however, leaving Arturo on his own. He introduces Arturo to the many beauties and recreations of Procida, helping him appreciate the uniqueness of the island.

— *Philip Brantingham*

AS A MAN GROWS OLDER
(Senilità)

Author: Italo Svevo (Ettore Schmitz, 1861-1928)
First published: 1898
Genre: Novel

Locale: Trieste, Austria
Time: The 1890's
Plot: Psychological realism

Emilio Brentani (eh-MIHL-ih-oh brehn-TAH-nee), a clerk in an insurance office. The Italian title *Senilità* (senility) must refer to him but cannot be taken literally, for he is only thirty-five years old; metaphorically, it seems not inappropriate, because his lack of energy and enterprise suits a much older man. He is content to live in a shabby apartment with his pale sister and "to go cautiously through life, avoiding all its perils, but also renouncing all its pleasures." He neither pursues a literary career (he has published one novel) nor translates his liberal political opinions into action. He might seem to be pursuing life's pleasures in his affair with Angiolina Zarri, but his irresolution and capacity for self-deception bring defeat in the end. Although he is unwilling to marry, he expects fidelity from Angiolina and blinds himself to evidence of her promiscuity. After she deserts him and his sister Amalia dies, he yields to senility, looking back with "enchanted wonder" to the period of his affair and blending Angiolina and Amalia into one splendid symbol.

Angiolina Zarri (ahn-gee-oh-LEE-nah ZAH-ree), a lower-class girl of striking beauty and vibrant health. She treats Emilio with warmth and affection, but from the first her conduct is disquieting. Aside from her engagement to Volpini, there is evidence of other affairs, not only during the past but also during her relationship with Emilio. Angiolina usually is adept at covering up, but sometimes the ruse is too transparent. She is perhaps self-deceived as well as deceitful; she gets little in return for her youth and beauty and in the end elopes with an embezzler.

Amalia Brentani (ah-MAHL-ee-ah), Emilio's sister and housekeeper. Thin and colorless, she seems to Balli to have been born gray. Her attitude toward Emilio seems almost maternal. Her suppressed romantic longings are brought to the surface by Emilio's tales of Angiolina and by Balli's visits; when she falls ill and becomes delirious, her love for Balli becomes obvious. When she dies, Emilio learns that she has been taking ether.

Stephano Balli, a sculptor, Emilio's friend and confidant. Though not without talent, he has had more success with women than with sculpture. He accepts Emilio because, like the women, he is easily dominated. He attempts to advise Emilio about Angiolina but ends up falling under her spell. He behaves decently with Amalia, however, and attends her during her last illness.

Margherita, Balli's mistress. She appears meek and submissive but turns out to have cuckolded Balli; in fact, she supports her family by prostitution.

Elena Chierici (kee-ehr-EE-chee), a widow with an unhappy past. She is a neighbor of Emilio and unselfishly volunteers to nurse Amalia in her final illness.

Volpini (vohl-PEE-nee), a middle-aged tailor to whom Angiolina becomes engaged, perhaps to cover a possible pregnancy.

Sorniani (sohr-nee-AH-nee), a shriveled little creature, a ladies' man and a malicious gossip who gives Emilio information about Angiolina.

— *John C. Sherwood*

AS FOR ME AND MY HOUSE

Author: Sinclair Ross (1908-   )
First published: 1941
Genre: Novel

Locale: Horizon, a town on the Canadian prairie
Time: The Great Depression
Plot: Psychological realism

Mrs. Bentley, the wife of Philip Bentley; her first name is never given. She narrates the novel through the journal she keeps during two years of their life in Horizon. She is pale, with dark shadows under her eyes, wears no makeup, and often mentions that her clothes are shabby. She is a loyal, loving, and protective wife but also a frustrated artist, having given up her study of the piano to follow Philip. She records her despair at Philip's growing alienation from her and from his work, her guilt at not being able to have children after giving birth to a stillborn son a year after their marriage, and her resentment of the conditions of spiritual and physical poverty in which they are forced to live. As an educated and sensitive outsider, she despises the pettiness and mean-spiritedness of many of her husband's parishioners but is careful not to offend them; she is reserved and makes few friends. Recognizing her husband's unhappiness, she takes an aggressive role in collecting his back salary from the towns where he pre-

viously preached, saving money so that he can afford to leave the church. She also takes the lead in trying to resurrect their faltering marriage, supporting her husband's ill-fated attempt to adopt Steve Kulanich, an abandoned teenager from the wrong side of the tracks, and finally accepting Philip's illegitimate child as an adoptive son when the child's mother dies in childbirth.

Philip Bentley, a United Church minister, the illegitimate son of a waitress and a young preacher who aspired to be a painter and died before his son's birth. Philip is thirty-six years old, a strong, handsome man despite his tired eyes and the haggard look caused by poverty and unhappiness. He entered the church to receive the education he could not otherwise afford, planning to repay his loans with a year or two of preaching; he now finds himself trapped financially and unable to escape to pursue a career as a painter. Solitary since childhood, Philip becomes even more withdrawn and defensive. Guilty over his lack of faith and his inability to help his parishioners, or to improve his own financial situation, he is barely tactful with his congregation and repeatedly rejects his wife's attempts at intimacy. His only outlet is his drawing, which often takes the form of bitter, satirical portraits of the town and its people. Initially passive toward his wife's attempts to enable them to escape from Horizon, he becomes more hopeful after they decide to adopt his illegitimate son.

Paul Kirby, a schoolteacher and self-described philologist, smaller and less handsome than Philip. Paul befriends both Bentleys and is clearly infatuated by Mrs. Bentley. Although he is educated and sensitive to the larger life outside Horizon, he is at peace with his surroundings and serves the Bentleys as a bridge between the small town and the completely rural countryside from which he comes. He brings Steve into their lives and provides them with the means for a brief vacation at his brother's ranch. Paul's open admiration of Mrs. Bentley finally forces a confrontation between Philip and his wife that serves to place them on a more honest footing with each other.

Judith West, the daughter of a farm family from the hills north of town. She has returned to Horizon after taking a commercial course in the city. Failing to find work there, she now assists the town clerk in his office and also works as a servant in his home. She has striking looks; she is pale, with attractive eyes and a lively smile. The matrons of the congregation tolerate her because of her contribution to the choir but are otherwise suspicious of her independence. Mrs. Bentley befriends her cautiously, recognizing the potential danger of Judith's feelings for Philip. With the birth of her son and her own death, Judith provides the Bentleys with the means to begin healing their broken marriage.

Steve Kulanich, who comes to live with the Bentleys when his father and his live-in lover are forced to leave town, abandoning the twelve-year-old boy. He is quick-tempered and accustomed to fighting with the respectable boys who taunt him about his parents. His temper, which leads him into several fights with the twin sons of the influential Mrs. Finley, and his persistent Catholicism, even after he is adopted by the United Church minister, disturb the congregation. The Catholic orphanage authorities are called in and take Steve away.

Mrs. Finley, the president of the Ladies Aid and "first lady" of the congregation. She represents much of what is petty and mean-spirited in Horizon. She is a thin woman, concerned with her status and power, who manages everything. She increases Mrs. Bentley's feelings of inadequacy in her roles as housekeeper and parson's wife.

— *Katherine Keller*

AS I LAY DYING

Author: William Faulkner (1897-1962)
First published: 1930
Genre: Novel

Locale: Mississippi
Time: Early twentieth century
Plot: Psychological realism

Anse Bundren, an ignorant and poor white man. When his wife dies, he is determined to take her body to Jefferson, as he had promised, even though the town is forty miles away. In a rickety old wagon, he and his sons must get across a flooded river that has destroyed most of the nearby bridges. Ostensibly, the shiftless and unlucky man is burying his wife there because of the promise. After a long trip with her unembalmed corpse, now dead more than a week, he arrives in Jefferson, pursued by a flock of buzzards that, like a grim chorus, hang apparently motionless against a sultry Mississippi sky. On reaching Jefferson, his family learns Anse's true reason for the trip: a set of false teeth and a "duck-shaped woman" whom he marries, to the surprise of his children.

Addie Bundren, Anse's overworked wife. Though dying, she wants to see her coffin finished. Anse does not know it, but she has always thought him to be only a man of words, and words, she thinks, are useless. Feeling isolated from him and her children, she has always tried to break through the wall of isolation surrounding her, but despairing, she never finds any meaning in her grinding existence. To her, sexual relationship means only violation, whereas, to Anse, it means love. Before her death, she believes her father's words to be true: "The reason for living was to get ready to stay dead a long time."

Darl Bundren, Addie's strange son, thought by his family to be feebleminded. Unlike the others, he seems to have the gift of second sight. Knowing the true reasons why Anse and the others are going to Jefferson, he tries to burn the barn that houses his mother's body. For this act of attempted purifica-

tion, his family declares him insane, and he is taken to the asylum at Jackson.

Jewel Bundren, Preacher Whitfield's illegitimate son. A violent young man, he loves only his horse, which costs him many long hours of labor at night. Although devoted to the animal, he allows Anse to trade it to Snopes for a badly needed team of mules. Like the rest of the Bundrens, he tenaciously hauls his mother on the long, eventful trip, all the while cursing and raging at his brothers. When Darl tries to burn the corpse, it is Jewel who manages to save her body for burial.

Cash Bundren, Anse's son, a carpenter. While his mother is dying, he busily saws and hammers away at her coffin, just outside her window. Carefully beveling the wood (he hates shoddy work) and showing his mother each board before nailing it in place, he finishes the job shortly after Addie's death. At the flooded river, he desperately tries to save his treasured tools when the wagon overturns. His leg broken on the trip, he stoically endures the pain, even after his father uses cement to plaster the swollen and infected leg.

Vardaman Bundren, Anse's son who constantly repeats to himself, "My mother is a fish."

Dewey Dell Bundren, Anse's daughter. A well-developed girl of seventeen, she has a reason for going to Jefferson: She is pregnant and wants to buy drugs that she hopes will cause a miscarriage.

Dr. Peabody, a fat, seventy-year-old country doctor. During his long practice, he has ministered to many poor families like the Bundrens. He intends to retire when his unpaid bills reach fifty thousand dollars.

Vernon Tull, Anse's helpful neighbor. He does what he can to help Bundren on his ghoulish journey.

Cora Tull, Vernon's fundamentalist wife. Constantly pray-ing and singing hymns, she tries to make Addie repent.

Preacher Whitfield, Addie's former lover, the father of Jewel.

AS THE CROW FLIES: A Lyric Play for the Air

Author: Austin Clarke (1896-1974)
First published: 1943
Genre: Drama

Locale: Near the River Shannon in western Ireland
Time: Seventh century
Plot: Poetic

Father Virgilius, a middle-aged monk and guide for the younger brothers. His primary function at the monastery of Clonmacnoise is working in the scriptorum, copying ancient manuscripts. As a devoted man of God, he interprets all phenomena in a specifically Christian context. He trusts in divine providence, even in the face of the gigantic storm in which they find themselves caught. He can see the operations of nature only as divine symbols and attempts to teach both Manus and Aengus that lesson.

Brother Aengus, a brother-novice in his late teens or early twenties. More venturesome than Brother Manus, he discovers the ancient cave of a holy man, a hermit, and feels his spiritual presence very keenly. Although frightened by the stormy violence around him, he is capable of great spiritual serenity because he is open to visionary experiences. Such experiences threaten both Father Virgilius and Brother Manus. Brother Aengus' attunement to the energies of the natural and spiritual worlds makes him capable of delving into regions of the unconscious and articulating the ancient and often destructive memories found there. He alone knows why the eagle, at the play's conclusion, is beating herself against the rocks in agony over the loss of her eaglets.

Brother Manus, a naïve novice in his late teens or early twenties. He is full of fear and apprehension about everything that happens to them. Impatient and insecure, he demands that Father Virgilius explain the dangers they are undergoing in a rational way. He does not understand what is happening in either a religious or a naturalistic framework. The voices that he does hear, he immediately interprets as demonic.

The Eagle of Knock, a mythic figure from ancient Irish folklore. She is propelled into action by the persistent question that her eaglets put to her: Has there ever been a more violent and destructive storm than the one now occurring? Her nest is invaded by a harmless-looking ancient crow seeking rest and relief from the tempest; the crow turns out to be the evil Crow of Achill and destroys the eaglets once the Eagle of Knock ventures north to seek the answer from the wise Salmon of Assaroe.

The eaglets, the young, helpless children of the Eagle of Knock. Their persistent question about the comparative sever-ity of the raging tempest becomes the call to adventure of their mother, as she foolishly takes the advice of the Crow of Achill and flies to the dangerous north.

The Crow of Achill, an ancient Irish folkloric figure, the embodiment of fatality and betrayal. She begs to be sheltered by the Eagle of Knock from the raging storm and blames an injured leg for her inability to continue her journey. She claims to have been a messenger of the Hag of Dingle and to have been present at the Hag's metamorphosis into a beautiful young woman. The crow suggests that the ferocity of the storm may be caused by the Hag's latest transformation. The crow's ability to move between human and animal life makes her the most dangerous of creatures.

The Stag of Leiterlone, a figure out of ancient Irish folklore. Like most heroes in traditional mythology, the stag recites tales of his epic escapes from other Irish mythological heroes such as Bran and Flann. His entire life has consisted of being hunted by men and their dogs; his only consolation is that he ran many of them to death.

The Blackbird of Derrycairn, a character from Celtic folklore. The blackbird tells of how she was heard and revered by such heroes as Patric and Fionn and of how they used her song to foretell the coming of dawn and her feathers to disclose the knowledge hidden in sacred trees.

The Salmon of Assaroe, the embodiment of wisdom and knowledge in Irish folklore. Like the Crow of Achill, he is both human and animal, but he uses his powers for good rather than evil. All immediately recognize him as the only authority who can answer the eaglets' persistent question. The salmon derives his power and authority from being present at the creation of the world. He witnessed the violent evolutionary formulations of all the species. To escape the terrifying trauma of such consciousness, he descended into a primal sleep in which he can remember the formation of the animal world. He also answers the eaglets' question: The worst tempest that ever occurred was the great Flood itself, which he witnessed. Because of his privileged position in the evolutionary scale, he recognizes the reappearance of the fatal woman now under the guise of the Crow of Achill, but too late to save the eaglets.

— *Patrick Meanor*

AS YOU LIKE IT

Author: William Shakespeare (1564-1616)
First published: 1623
Genre: Drama

Locale: The Forest of Arden, France
Time: The Middle Ages
Plot: Comedy

Rosalind (ROHZ-eh-lihnd), who is disguised as **Ganymede** (GAN-eh-meed) in the forest scenes, the daughter of the banished Duke Senior. A witty, self-possessed young woman, she accepts whatever fortune brings, be it love or exile, with gaiety and good sense. She is amused by the ironic situations arising from her disguise as a youth, and she wryly recognizes the humorous aspects of her growing love for Orlando, whose passion she pretends to be curing. Her central place in the lives of her companions is epitomized in the final scene, in which she sorts out the tangled skeins of romance and, with Orlando, joins three other couples before Hymen, the god of marriage.

Orlando (ohr-LAN-doh), the youngest son of Sir Rowland de Boys, the late ally of Rosalind's father. Although his elder brother mistreats him and neglects his education, he reveals his gentle birth in his manner and appearance. His love for Rosalind provokes extravagantly romantic gestures, but the deeper feeling of which he is capable is evident in his concern for his faithful old servant Adam, as well as in his fidelity to his sweetheart.

Celia (SEE-lee-uh), Rosalind's gentle cousin, who refuses to let her depart alone for the Forest of Arden. She, too, is gay and witty, ready to exchange quips with Touchstone and tease Rosalind about her love for Orlando. When she meets Orlando's brother Oliver, however, she succumbs to Cupid even more rapidly than did her cousin.

Touchstone, Duke Frederick's clever fool, who accompanies his master's daughter Celia and Rosalind into the Forest of Arden, much to the amusement of Jaques and to the consternation of the old shepherd Corin, who finds himself damned for never having been at court, according to Touchstone's logic. The fool, more than any of the other characters, remains at heart a courtier, even in Arcadia, but he returns from the forest with a country wench as his bride.

Jaques (JAY-kweez), a hanger-on of Duke Senior's court in Arden, a professional man of melancholy who philosophizes on the "seven ages of man." He is fascinated by the presence in the forest of a "motley fool," and he delights in Touchstone's explanations of court formalities. He remains in the forest when his lord recovers his dukedom, and he goes off to observe and comment on the unexpected conversion of Duke Frederick.

Oliver, Orlando's greedy, tyrannical brother, who tries to deprive him of both wealth and life. Sent by Duke Frederick to find his brother or forfeit all his lands, he is rescued by Orlando from a lioness. This kindness from his mistreated brother gives him new humanity, and he becomes a worthy husband for Celia.

Duke Frederick, Celia's strong, self-centered father, the usurper. Fearing her popularity with the people, he arbitrarily sends Rosalind away to her exiled father. Later, equally unreasonably, he banishes Orlando for being the son of an old enemy and then sets Oliver wandering in search of the brother he despises. He is reported at the end of the play to have retired from the world with an old hermit.

Duke Senior, Rosalind's genial father, banished by his brother Duke Frederick. He holds court under the greenwood trees, drawing amusement from hunting, singing, and listening to Jaques' melancholy philosophy in the golden world of Arden.

Silvius (SIHL-vee-uhs), a lovesick young shepherd. He asks Ganymede to help him win his scornful sweetheart Phebe.

Phebe (FEE-bee), a disdainful shepherdess. Rebuked by Ganymede for her cruelty to Silvius, she promptly becomes enamored of Ganymede. She promises, however, to wed Silvius if she refuses Ganymede; she does so once Rosalind reveals her identity.

Audrey, Touchstone's homely, stupid, and good-hearted country wench.

William, Audrey's equally simpleminded rustic suitor.

Corin (KOHR-ihn), a wise, well-meaning old shepherd. He gives good counsel to William and expresses the virtues of the simple life in his cross-purposes discussion of court and country with Touchstone.

Adam, a faithful old servant of Orlando's family. He accompanies his young master into the forest.

Jaques, the brother of Orlando and Oliver. He brings the news of Duke Frederick's retirement to the forest.

Sir Oliver Martext, a "hedge-priest" hired by Touchstone to marry him to Audrey in somewhat dubious rites.

Le Beau (leh boh), Duke Frederick's pompous attendant.

Charles, a champion wrestler challenged and defeated by Orlando.

Amiens (AY-mee-ehnz), one of Duke Senior's lords.

Dennis, Oliver's servant.

Hymen (HI-mehn), the god of marriage.

ASHES
(Popioły)

Author: Stefan Żeromski (1864-1925)
First published: 1904
Genre; Novel

Locale: Poland and Spain
Time: 1796-1812
Plot: Historical

Raphael Olbromski, adventurous son of an aristocratic Polish landowner. As a boy, he is thrown out of school for an escapade and then is cast out of the family by his strict father for bringing disgrace upon his name. Befriended by a nobleman, Raphael settles down and spends some time in school. After working four years as a laborer on his father's land, he serves for a time as secretary to his benefactor, Prince Gintult. Following a tragic escapade with the girl he loves, Raphael joins the forces of Napoleon and fights bravely with the French armies.

Prince Gintult, a Polish nobleman who befriends Raphael. He treats the young man almost as a member of his family, pays for the youth's education, and makes him his private secretary. Raphael later saves the prince's life in battle.

Elizabeth, the prince's sister. A haughty young woman, she strikes Raphael with her riding crop when he kisses her after rescuing her from a runaway horse. Later, she helps him escape from Austrian-held Poland to join the French forces led by Napoleon.

Helen, a beautiful young woman who loves Raphael and is loved by him for many years. Meeting after years of separation, she and Raphael flee to the country, but the lovers are set upon by bandits, who bind Raphael and rape Helen. To escape her tormentors, Helen jumps off a cliff and is killed.

Christopher Cedro, a longtime friend of Raphael. The two are schoolmates and later serve together under Napoleon. Like Raphael, Christopher is an adventurous boy and, later, a brave soldier.

Nardzevski, Raphael's uncle, a landowner who fiercely adheres to the old ways and mistreats his peasants as they were mistreated in feudal times. He will not acknowledge the Aus-

trian occupation of Poland and refuses to pay the taxes levied by Austria.

Casper, a huntsman who is Nardzevski's only loyal friend.

Peter Olbromski, Raphael's older brother. He, too, is cast out of the family by the boys' stern father. He befriends Raphael until his untimely death.

ASHES AND DIAMONDS
(Popiół i diament)

Author: Jerzy Andrzejewski (1909-1983)
First published: 1948
Genre: Novel

Locale: Ostrowiec, Poland
Time: May 5-8, 1945
Plot: Political

Stefan Szczuka (SHCHEW-kah), the son of a tailor, trained as an engineer. He becomes a member of the Communist Party in the period before the war and spends several years in prison for subversive activities. During the occupation, he is arrested again, this time by the Germans, and is sent to the concentration camp at Gross-Rosen. With the liberation of Poland by the Red Army, he becomes the head of the Communist Party Area Committee in the Southeast. Now in his mid-forties, he is ready to help build Communism in Poland. This, he believes, must be done according to the Soviet example, although through reconciliation, not revenge and repression. His credo is that a man lives in order to shape both his own country and history. His wife, Maria, was killed at Ravensbruck, and he is driven to find out details of her death. When he meets someone who will give him such information, however, he realizes that this knowledge is less important than knowing that she comforted her fellow prisoners, helping to protect them from doubts and despair. He is thus able to lay the past to rest, but this happens ironically just prior to his own death by an assassin's bullet.

Antoni Kossecki, a "stubborn, honest, and ambitious" magistrate in Ostrowiec, a moderately sized town one hundred miles south of Warsaw. He is not a man of exceptional talents but has managed to rise through hard work and perseverance. He is arrested by the Germans early in the war and sent to the concentration camp at Gross-Rosen, where, under the name of Rybicki, he becomes a camp orderly, participating in the control and beating of other prisoners. He judges this collaboration necessary for survival. The price is a guilty conscience and fear of discovery. He reconciles himself to this evil chapter in his life by consciously cutting it out from the years of peace. Now, in his fifties, he believes that he may be able still to achieve peace of mind by making a positive contribution to society.

Frank Podgorski, a former law clerk of Antoni Kossecki, now the secretary of the local committee of the Communist Party in Ostrowiec. He returns from the war, in which he fought as a member of the underground, with a strong desire to create a new social order in conformity with Marxist historical rectitude. He expects this transformation to have the support and cooperation of the Polish people, but he has doubts. He asks himself if he is capable of making the necessary sacrifices that "the world demands." He is pessi-

mistic that the hopes of the dead and the living will ever be fulfilled. His attitude becomes more doctrinaire after the murder of his older mentor, Szczuka. He hardens into a party operative, abandoning shades of gray for a strict party code of right and wrong. Whereas, earlier, he could view Kossecki's weakness in the face of death with sympathy, he now turns him over to the Security Police to be tried for war crimes.

Andrew Kossecki, Antoni's twenty-one-year-old son. He served in the Polish underground while still in his teens, rising to the rank of lieutenant. His former struggle against Nazi Germany has now become one against the Communist government implemented by the Russians. His present assignment is to assassinate Communist Party boss Szczuka, a man he does not know and has no reason for wanting dead. He questions the necessity of carrying out the mission but in the end decides to obey the orders of his superiors.

Alexander Kossecki, the timid, seventeen-year-old younger brother of Andrew. He is involved in his own war. He is a member of a teenage gang that has vague goals of fighting Poland's enemies, whoever they might be. Alexander's diffidence and lack of resolution, typical of others in his generation, eventually are offset by a determination to start his own troop of fighters, all presumably possessing the same predilection and attraction toward violence.

Julius Szretter (SHREHT-tuhr), the leader of the teenage gang of which Alexander is a member. He is tall, slender, and cruel, a great bully. He kills one of the boys in his gang because he believes that the boy would betray them and is later proud that such an act helped to steel his resolve and demonstrate his worth as a leader.

Michael Chelmicki, a friend of Andrew and a conspirator in the plot to assassinate Szczuka. The first failed attempt resulting in the death of two strangers makes him brood about the lack of justification for such violence. When he falls in love with a young woman named Christina, he wants to quit altogether because continued participation in a right-wing death squad seems obscene next to an ordinary relationship of life without violence. His fear at letting down Andrew, however, overcomes his reservations and prompts him to carry out the murder by himself.

— *Wm. Laird Kleine-Ahlbrandt*

THE ASIATICS

Author: Frederic Prokosch (1908-1989)
First published: 1935
Genre: Novel

Locale: Asia, from Beirut to Hong Kong
Time: The 1920's
Plot: Picaresque

The narrator, a nameless seeker after knowledge of the world, on a pilgrimage from Beirut to Hong Kong. A twenty-two-year-old American, he is strongly built and apparently attractive. He reveals little of his background, but it is clear that he is well read and open to experience. He becomes at times weary of the betrayals of his passing companions and considers a monkish withdrawal from the world, but he realizes finally that he must remain vulnerable to the world's shocks if he is to benefit from his observations of humanity. He makes no effort to shape his life, remaining a passive register of events. He is perhaps an innocent from the New World who deliberately seeks out the most shocking and degraded elements of the old civilizations through which he journeys.

Antoine Samazeuilh (AN-twahn sahm-a-zwee), a roguish vagabond from Rouen, France. The handsome Samazeuilh is twenty-six or twenty-seven years old, muscular, and blessed with curly blond hair. He is a faithless friend, accustomed to using friends of both sexes and abandoning them at a whim. He disappears while hiking through Syria with the narrator, only to turn up again improbably in Phnom-Penh before vanishing for good in Hue.

Feodor Krusnayaskov (FYOH-dohr krew-snah-YAHS-kof), a middle-aged Russian whom the narrator meets in Turkey. He is arrested with the narrator in Erzurum, and they spend two months together in a foul prison before escaping.

He hides the narrator in his home, but the narrator flees in the night when he learns that Krusnayaskov is a dedicated Communist.

Hans de Hahn, a Dutch adventurer of dubious background. He is a fellow prisoner with the narrator in Erzurum, and they join up again in Peshawar. De Hahn is traveling with a beautiful young woman, Ursule, and the hastily assembled *ménage à trois* collapses under sexual stress. The narrator later meets Ursule by accident in Saigon and travels with her and Samazeuilh to Hue, where de Hahn appears once more, only to die at the novel's end.

Mme de Chamellis, a beautiful, sophisticated Frenchwoman whom the narrator meets in Teheran, where she conducts a salon. She reappears in Rangoon and accompanies the narrator on a trip up the Irrawaddy River that results in her death.

Dr. Ainger, a French physician whom the narrator first meets at Mme de Chamellis' salon. They are separated after the crash of the plane in which they are flying to Meshed. The narrator finds Ainger again in an outpost near Penang, where Ainger is providing medical care to the natives. He becomes one of the most interesting and psychologically complex figures in the novel, but he dies under the pressures of his grim jungle vocation.

— *Frank Day*

THE ASPERN PAPERS

Author: Henry James (1843-1916)
First published: 1888
Genre: Novella

Locale: Venice, Italy
Time: Late nineteenth century
Plot: Psychological realism

The narrator, an unnamed, well-to-do American literary scholar. He is obsessed by a desire to learn everything possible about the life and works of the long-dead American poet Jeffrey Aspern and is willing to do almost anything to appropriate Aspern's papers. He has heard that the papers are in the possession of Juliana Bordereau, Aspern's former mistress, who is now living reclusively in Venice. Using a false name and pretending to be a writer, the narrator rents rooms in her run-down palazzo, improves her neglected garden, and in time mentions Aspern in chats, first with her niece Tita and then with Juliana, who does not mind throwing the narrator and Tita together. One night, Juliana, now quite sick, catches the unprincipled scholar rifling her old mahogany desk and collapses. Humiliated, he leaves Venice for several days. He returns to learn that Juliana has died and is buried, and he finds Tita in supposed possession of the papers, which she hints can be his only if he becomes a member of the family. The narrator leaves in consternation, sleeps on what seems to him to be Tita's proposal of marriage, and returns half resigned to agree; Tita, however, greets him with the news that she has burned the Aspern papers.

Juliana Bordereau, an American who has long resided in Venice and is Aspern's former mistress. She is now shrunken and puckered with age and sickness, constantly masks her once-celebrated eyes with a green eyeshade, and supposedly possesses a treasure trove of Aspern papers. The narrator views her as sarcastic, cynical, profane, and even witchlike. She is certainly avaricious and rude, overcharging him for rent, demanding payment months in advance, and accepting his flowers ungratefully. She teases him by offering to sell him a small oval portrait of Aspern for an exorbitant price and by encouraging him to see more of her niece Tita Bordereau, for whom she may want him to care. Juliana's discovery of the narrator rifling her desk hastens her death. The character is modeled partly on Clare Clairmont, one of the long-lived mistresses of George Gordon, Lord Byron.

Tita Bordereau, Juliana's tall, thin, pale, faded, untidy American niece (or possibly grandniece). She is middle-aged, mild, gauche, and seemingly callow. When the narrator broaches the subject of Aspern, she timidly agrees to try to help him obtain the papers. Encouraged by Juliana, the two get into his gondola to sample decorous Venetian nightlife. After

Juliana dies, Tita cannot decide whether to respect the domineering old woman's privacy or to aid the narrator, evidently the one attractive man in her life. When he rebuffs her implicit proposal, she seems to enjoy telling him that she burned the papers "one by one." The narrator, seeing her in a new light, concludes that she is "plain, dingy, elderly" and yet not "hard or vindictive." In the 1908 revision, Tita is named Tina.

Mrs. Prest, the narrator's confidante, expatriated from the United States for some fifteen years in Venice. She urges the narrator to lay siege to Juliana Bordereau by renting rooms from her and bombarding her with flowers. Mrs. Prest helps him rationalize when he feels hypocritical and duplicitous. The character is modeled partly on James's socialite friend Katherine De Kay Bronson, long a resident in Venice.

John Cumnor, a British editor and an admirer of Aspern's works. Cumnor does not appear in the story; however, he is a motivating force, because he encourages the narrator to seek the Aspern papers by any available means.

Pochintesta, the Bordereaus' Venetian lawyer friend.

— Robert L. Gale

THE ASSISTANT

Author: Bernard Malamud (1914-1986)
First published: 1957
Genre: Novel

Locale: Brooklyn, New York
Time: The 1930's
Plot: Social realism

Frank Alpine, a young Italian drifter. Tall and bearded, with eyes haunted by a profound loneliness and a deep spiritual sadness, Frank wants to escape a past full of mistakes and broken promises. Fascinated by the stories of Saint Francis that he heard in the orphanage where he was reared, he continually aspires to a life of good but finds himself unable to keep himself on the right track. After robbing the Bobers' grocery store, his guilt is so strong that he returns to the store and helps the old shopkeeper without pay. When Morris Bober falls ill, he volunteers to work as the storekeeper's assistant and stays on even after Morris' health returns. He brings in more business and is responsible for saving the store from the brink of bankruptcy. He falls in love with Helen Bober, Morris and Ida's daughter, and cautiously woos her. His struggle between doing right and doing wrong continues throughout the novel: He steals from the Bobers, lies, and rapes Helen just as she begins to warm to him; he also puts back the money he steals, saves Morris' life, and confesses to his crimes. When Morris dies, Frank puts on the grocer's apron and takes his place in the small grocery store.

Morris Bober, a sixty-year-old Russian Jewish immigrant who runs a small, failing grocery store. A heavyset man with sloping shoulders and bushy gray hair that needs trimming, Morris is the epitome of the long-suffering Jew. He is as unlucky as he is honest. Morris believes that it is his heritage to suffer. As the novel opens, he watches one of his former customers sneaking down the street with groceries bought somewhere else. He learns that a new delicatessen will soon be opening across from him; that night, he is attacked and robbed. Later, his generosity toward the drifter Frank is repaid by the assistant's theft from him. His attempts to kill himself and to burn down his store for the insurance money both fail. At the end of the novel, Morris dies of a heart attack.

Helen Bober, Morris' twenty-three-year-old daughter. Slender and attractive, Helen still lives at home with her parents, providing them with the necessary income from her job. An avid reader of novels, her heart is always set on some big future that she secretly despairs will never arrive. She longs for a college education, if not for herself, then for the man she will marry. She dreams of a man with a bright future who will fall in love with and marry her, but her brief affair with Nat Pearl leaves her feeling bitter and devalued. She warms very slowly to Frank, who betrays her.

Ida Bober, Morris' nagging wife. Fifty-one years old, with thick black hair, a lined face, and legs that hurt when she walks, Ida is as stingy and suspicious as Morris is generous and trusting. Her greatest fear is that her daughter will become romantically involved with a man who is not a Jew. Primarily for this reason, she wants Frank to leave the store, setting various dates for his departure, but she also finds that she enjoys the extra income he brings in.

Ward Minogue, the criminal son of the local detective. Violent and anti-Semitic, Ward engineers the crime that brings Frank to the store; it is Ward who hits Morris on the head with the gun. Later, when Helen is waiting in the park for Frank, Ward attacks her. He dies in the fire that takes Karp's store.

Nat Pearl, a Columbia University law student whose sister is Helen's best friend. Intelligent and handsome, Nat seems to hold the bright future Helen wants in a man, but Helen senses that he is unwilling to make a commitment to her. To his puzzlement, after a brief affair she spurns his advances.

Julius Karp, the Bobers' landlord. A highly successful liquor salesman, Karp seems to have all the luck that Morris has never enjoyed. It is Karp's store that Ward originally plans to rob, but he steals from the Bobers' store instead. Karp's store burns down instead of Morris', so it is Karp who collects the insurance money.

Poilisheh, a small, sour-faced woman who buys a three-cent unseeded hard roll from the store every morning. She is unfriendly and anti-Semitic. Her faithful appearance at the store signals the relentless beginning of each new day.

— Dana Gerhardt

ASTROPHIL AND STELLA

Author: Sir Philip Sidney (1554-1586)
First published: 1591
Genre: Poetry

Locale: England
Time: Sixteenth century
Plot: Love

Astrophil, the young lover in whose voice the sonnets and songs are cast. Although Stella is married and he describes her as virtuous, he still pursues her, begging her to love him. Whether the sonnets express the true feelings of their author, Sir Philip Sidney, the character of Astrophil clearly is meant to represent him. The last syllable of "Astrophil" echoes the name "Philip"; sonnet 30 identifies Astrophil's father as the governor of Ireland, the post Sidney's father held; and sonnet 65 describes Astrophil's coat of arms, which matches in every detail the Sidney family crest. Astrophil considers himself superior to other writers of love poetry, to whom he frequently contrasts himself: They imitate one another, and only he is original, because his inspiration is his beloved Stella. He presents himself as the servant not only of Stella but also of love, personified as the boy Cupid.

Stella, Astrophil's beloved, to whom the sonnet sequence is addressed. She differs from the stock character of the Petrarchan sonnet sequence in two key respects. First, her rejection of the lover's advances is not attributed to coldheartedness, the standard complaint of the Petrarchan sonneteer, but to her virtue, as she is married to another. Second, although her hair is the standard Petrarchan gold, her eyes are not the standard blue, but rather black. This is probably because the author of the sonnets, Sir Philip Sidney, had a real lady in mind: Penelope Devereux, who by the time the sonnets were written was married to Lord Robert Rich. After Astrophil steals a kiss, Stella admits some feeling for him,

though virtue still forbids her to encourage him. Although Petrarchan sonnet sequences normally speak only in the voice of the young man, Stella's own voice is heard in several of the songs.

Stella's husband, Astrophil's rival for Stella's love, who appears only obliquely in the sonnet sequence. He is referred to as a "rich fool," a pun on the name of his original, Lord Rich, who married Penelope Devereux, the original of Stella, in 1581. His marriage to Stella is, to Astrophil, "foul abuse" of Stella's beauties. He is ignorant of Stella's "high treasures," Astrophil maintains.

Love or **Cupid**, the personification of the force that dominates Astrophil. The two names, Love and Cupid, are used interchangeably. The traditional Renaissance iconography of Cupid is used in Love's first appearance, in sonnet 2: He "wounds" Astrophil with his golden arrows, which make him fall in love with Stella. Although Love rules Astrophil's heart, sonnet 5 reveals a rival power, virtue. Astrophil acknowledges that virtue rather than love ought to be his goal, yet he cannot stop loving Stella. Sonnet 8 recounts Love's flight from his birthplace in Greece to live in Stella's face, but although Love gets Stella's face, he will never have her heart. Love is exclusively physical, rather than a higher love. Although he knows that he will never know this kind of love with Stella, Astrophil still serves love rather than virtue.

— John R. Holmes

ASYA

Author: Ivan Turgenev (1818-1883)
First published: 1858
Genre: Novella

Locale: A small town on the Rhine in Germany
Time: Mid-nineteenth century
Plot: Psychological realism

N. N., a middle-aged Russian country landowner who narrates the story of his unhappy love affair many years earlier. In his story, he is twenty-five years old, financially secure, and without responsibility. He travels throughout Europe anxious to experience life. He finds himself more fascinated by faces than by places. Although he possesses all the skills to move gracefully through society, he nevertheless is awkward around women; he has difficulty asserting his affection for them and is easily hurt by coquetry or rejection. A sensitive, self-conscious man, he seeks out natural landscapes that mirror his moods. When he meets two fellow Russians, a man his age and a younger woman, he is intrigued by their personalities and their relationship. He notes how different they are in looks and temperament, and he cannot believe that they are brother and sister, as they profess to be. His friendship with the man ripens quickly, and his awkwardness around the young woman becomes infatuation. His increasing social intimacy with the brother soon collides with his increasing emotional intimacy with the sister. The moment at which he must choose between etiquette and passion is the climax of the story.

Gagin (GAH-gihn), a former Guardsman, now a gentleman of leisure after inheriting the estate of his father, who passed away four years earlier. Twenty-four years old, tall, slim, and well-groomed, Gagin neither looks nor acts like

(according to N. N.) the typical Russian on the Grand Tour in Europe. He spends his time showing his sister the towns and villages of the Continent and attempting to become an artist. He begins many drawings but finishes none of them; he ruefully concurs in N. N's judgment that he is a "regular Russian soul," simple and filled with noble thoughts, but without ardor and unable to bring a great task to conclusion. Gagin shares N. N.'s delight in the countryside and, when the two become friends, confides the secret of his sister's birth. His feelings toward the girl are mixed: He loves her and cares for her, yet he feels ashamed of her origin. This latter feeling makes it impossible for him to believe that N. N. could indeed love his sister enough to marry her. Gagin brought his sister to Europe because her existence made his life in Russian society awkward. He precipitates the flight that separates the lovers forever.

Anna Nikolayevna (nee-koh-LAH-ehv-nah), called by her nickname **Asya**, an emotional young woman who falls passionately in love with N. N. Short in stature and graceful in figure, Asya is seventeen years old. Her character is mercurial, one moment prankish, the next moment melancholy. She is physically active and daring. She runs when Gagin and N. N. walk, and she saunters on ledges where they fear to tread. The revelation of her parentage is the central mystery and problem of the plot. She is Gagin's half sister, born of the love match between his father and a peasant woman after the death of Gagin's mother. When the elder Gagin died, he enjoined his twenty-one-year-old son to take care of the girl. Asya proves too much of a problem for the young soldier, who can neither understand nor control her varied moods. She does not have a typical Russian soul: She possesses an inward passion that dares to strive toward completion and fulfillment.

Frau Luise (frow lew-EE-seh), a German widow who befriends Asya. She is an elderly, wizened woman whose appearance strikes N. N. as odd and slightly malevolent. Asya visits her frequently, much to Gagin's chagrin. Gagin is sure that Asya's affection for the widow is only an affectation. Luise's house is Asya's refuge, however; it is there that she escapes the leisurely, indecisive pace of a gentleman's life. There, too, N. N. and Asya have their final, tragic interview.

— *Robert M. Otten*

AT PLAY IN THE FIELDS OF THE LORD

Author: Peter Matthiessen (1927-   )
First published: 1965
Genre: Novel

Locale: Oriente State, a fictional province in South America
Time: Early 1960's
Plot: Adventure

Meriwether Lewis Moon, a Cheyenne veteran of World War II, now a soldier of fortune in quest of a significant purpose for his life equivalent to the spiritual relationship of his Indian ancestors with the natural world. Moon is an alienated rebel, driven by a combination of fierce pride and guilt about being an Indian. After fleeing the college to which he had been sent as a representative of his people, he wandered the world and now finds himself in a fictional South American country in the Amazon jungle. In need of gasoline for their airplane, he and his sidekick, Wolfie, agree to bomb a village of the local unchristianized Niaruna Indians, who are hindering the progress of cutting down the forest. Moon's affinity with the Indians is kindled during a reconnaissance flight, when an Indian defiantly shoots an arrow at his plane. Shortly thereafter, forsaking the ways of civilization, he joins the Niaruna to aid them in their battle against annihilation.

Martin Quarrier, a Christian missionary in his thirties, from the Dakotas. He is sent to aid in the "civilizing" of the Niaruna Indians. Martin's interest in anthropology, as well as in religion, makes him more sympathetic to the Indians than the other missionaries. After the death of his son, Martin becomes more interested in understanding and protecting the Indians than in converting them. He is a good, if clumsy, man whose religious beliefs are tempered by his experience. He abandons the mission, and his wife, in a futile, sacrificial attempt to save the Niaruna.

Commandante Rufino Guzmán (koh-mahn-DAHN-tay rew-FEE-noh gewz-MAHN), the prefect (principal local government authority), head of the military police, and main property owner of the province. An intelligent but coarse person, more interested in his own well-being than that of the people he governs, he is a dangerous man, ruthless in his exercise of power. Guzmán is eager to bomb the Niaruna to advance his career. Holding the passports of Moon and Wolfie, he demands that they help him destroy the Indians by bombing the village from their plane. He tolerates the Protestant missionaries because as they Christianize the Indians, they also "tame" them.

Hazel Quarrier, the ungainly, unhappy wife of Martin, an uncritical believer in her religion and in their purpose as evangelists. Psychologically ill-equipped to cope with the reality of the jungle environment, she suffers a mental breakdown after the death of their son and comes to see the jungle as the home of the devil.

Billy Quarrier, the nine-year-old son of Martin and Hazel. He adapts quickly to his new environment. His innocence, bravery, and boyish acceptance of his new world endear him to the local people. His death from blackwater fever triggers Martin's religious skepticism and Hazel's mental breakdown.

Leslie (Les) Huben, the leader of the Protestant missionaries. An athletic Christian, egotist, and coward at heart, he is able to present failure as if it were success and thereby acquires monetary support from the mission board at home. His primary interest seems to be his own fame. Toward this end, he is willing to sacrifice the Indians and anyone else. He offends Martin by speaking of Billy's death as a positive act of God.

Andy Huben, née **Agnes Carr**, the young, attractive wife of Les. She is capable of more compassion than any of the other characters. Both Martin and Moon are attracted to her. Her kiss with Moon is the means of transmitting influenza to the Niaruna.

Wolfie, Moon's companion mercenary. A wandering New York Jew, he is, like Moon, a strong, good fighter, but unlike Moon he is not in control of himself. He is extremely vulgar in action and speech, and ultimately his acts are self-defeating. Wolfie attacks the village for Guzmán even as Moon is trying to protect the Indians.

Father Xantes (ZAHN-tehs), the Catholic priest who precedes the Protestants in the attempt to convert the Indians to Christianity. A sophisticated, resilient man, confident with the history of the Catholic church behind him, he knows the Protestants are doomed to failure, and he has the patience to outlast them.

Aeore (ay-ee-OHR-ee), the most heroic of the Niaruna. He is defiant and intelligent enough to see through Moon's masquerade as a god. He is a natural leader. He shoots an arrow at Moon's plane, thereby unknowingly instigating Moon's commitment to the Niaruna.

Boronai (boh-ROHN-ay), the old chief of the Niaruna. He has the wisdom born of experience but is losing his ability to control his people in the face of white people's destruction of the natural world. When he dies of influenza, Moon and Aeore compete for control.

Pindi (PEEN-dee), a pretty, young Indian girl who is a wife of Boronai. Her husband gives her to Moon, and she bears the child of Aeore.

Uyuyu (ew-YEW-yew), or **Yoyo**, an Indian convert reared by Father Xantes as a Catholic. He went over to Huben when his materialistic prayers went unanswered. He has become an exploiter of his own people and is instrumental in the tragic conclusion of the conflict between the Indians and the whites.

— *William J. McDonald*

AT SWIM-TWO-BIRDS

Author: Flann O'Brien (Brian O'Nolan, 1911-1966)
First published: 1939
Genre: Novel

Locale: Dublin, Ireland
Time: Mid-1930's
Plot: Fantasy

The narrator, unnamed, a none-too-diligent young university student in Dublin who is writing a novel about another author, Dermot Trellis. The narrator tells about his carping uncle, his fellow students, and his drinking and wasting of time. He reads from and comments on his developing novel.

Dermot Trellis, a character in the novel that the narrator is writing. Trellis is himself writing a novel to demonstrate the consequences of immorality. Trellis is a pimply and neurotic recluse who chooses to spend most of his time in bed. In the narrator's story, the characters of Trellis' novel rebel against the roles that Trellis has assigned to them, play out their own stories, and eventually attempt to kill Trellis. Trellis is saved when his servant, Teresa, enters his room, picks up some sheets of paper from the floor, and throws those pages that sustain the existence of the rebel characters into the fire.

John Furriskey, an original character concocted by Dermot Trellis. Furriskey, a well-built, dark, and clean-shaven man of medium height, is intended by the author to be the embodiment of immorality and rakishness, but he rebels. He marries the servant, Peggy, whom Trellis intended that he dishonor. Peggy has discovered that Trellis' control over his characters is suspended when he sleeps. Furriskey conspires with the other characters first to drug Trellis so that they can live independently of him while he sleeps and finally to torture and kill Trellis.

Orlick Trellis, the illegitimate son of Dermot Trellis and Sheila Lamont, one of Trellis' characters. Sheila was to have been a girl of virtue and refinement, whose honor is destroyed by Furriskey. Trellis, however, is so taken with the beauty and refinement of his literary creation, Sheila, that he assaults her. Their offspring, Orlick, came into the world full grown. Sharing his father's writing talent as well as his pimples, Orlick, who comes under the influence of the evil Pooka, is recruited by the other rebel characters to write a novel in which Dermot Trellis is grossly abused and then, as a preliminary to his execution, placed on trial before all the characters.

The Pooka Fergus MacPhellimey, an Irish devil conjured up by Trellis as a character in his novel. The Pooka, like Trellis' other characters, has a will of his own. By besting the Good Fairy in a game of cards, the clubfooted Pooka wins the right to influence Orlick Trellis, whose inherited talent for writing is turned against Dermot Trellis. In Orlick's story, the Pooka serves as the prosecutor at Dermot's trial.

Finn MacCool, a legendary hero of Irish folklore who is "hired" by Dermot Trellis for use as an elderly character in his novel. He was intended by Trellis to be an elderly father outraged at the violation of his daughter, Peggy, by the villain Furriskey. The rebellious character Finn MacCool, however, forces himself on Peggy.

King Sweeny, the subject of a tale told by Finn MacCool. King Sweeny of Dal Araidhe assaults a saintly cleric by the name of Ronan, who then invokes a curse on him. Sweeny is transformed into a bird man, fated to fly from roost to roost around Ireland, eating wild crest and acorns. In MacCool's tale, Sweeny composes an epic describing his physical and mental anguish.

Paul Shanahan and

Antony Lamont, minor characters borrowed by Trellis for his novel. Shanahan is an older man who appeared in many of the writer William Tracy's romantic Westerns. Lamont is Sheila's brother, who was to demand satisfaction from Furriskey after he had taken advantage of her. Shanahan and Lamont do not play the roles assigned to them but instead become principal conspirators against Trellis. They relish his physical torments and are simultaneously judges, jurors, and accusers of Trellis in the story written by Orlick.

Slug Willard and

Shorty Andrews, two tough cowboys borrowed from the Westerns of William Tracy by Dermot Trellis as minor characters in his novel. They also serve as accusers and judges in Orlick's story.

The Good Fairy, a character drawn from Irish folklore by Dermot Trellis for his novel. The Good Fairy, an invisible pocket-sized creature, is intended by Dermot Trellis to contrast with the evil of the Pooka. Escaping the control of Trellis, the Good Fairy gives up the right to influence the newborn Orlick to the Pooka, who had beaten the penniless fairy at poker.

Peggy, a domestic servant created by Trellis as one of his characters. Trellis intended for Furriskey to take advantage of her and betray her. In fact, Furriskey behaves honorably toward her, and they are married.

Jem Casey, a workingman's bard who joins the other characters for the trial of Trellis.

Brinsley, the narrator's friend and fellow student. Brinsley is the narrator's drinking partner and the audience and critic for his developing manuscript.

Uncle, the narrator's penurious and rather small-minded, but well-intentioned, uncle, with whom he lives in Dublin. Uncle is fat, with a red complexion and coarse and irregular features. A third-class clerk at Guinness and a commonplace man, he is deeply concerned about his unstudious nephew's apparent slothfulness. He is appropriately pleased when his nephew passes his final examination with honor and presents him with a used watch.

— *Bernard A. Cook*

AT THE SIGN OF THE REINE PÉDAUQUE
(La Rôtisserie de la Reine Pédauque)

Author: Anatole France (Jacques-Anatole-François Thibault, 1844-1924)
First published: 1893
Genre: Novel

Locale: France
Time: Eighteenth century
Plot: Satire

Jacques Ménétrier (zhahk may-nay-tray-YAY), a carefree young scholar and lover who becomes a respectable citizen. Born of poor parents, he is educated by clerics and philosophers. Having lived a dissolute life, Jacques finally settles down as a bookseller who supports his kindly mother and father in their declining years.

Jael (zhay-EHL), an attractive young Jew who abandons her elderly lover, an uncle, to accept Jacques, only to abandon him to accept another who entices her with a gift of silver plate. Jael, however, is not peevish or vindictive. While she loves one, she likes the other man for whom she has once had the grand passion.

Catherine, a young lace-maker turned courtesan. She moves in and out of Jacques' life with predictable consistency. Though she accepts the gifts of wealthy men, her love for Jacques is constant.

Maître Jérôme Coignard (MAY-tr zhay-ROHM kwahn-YAHR), an abbé, a Greek and Latin scholar who is Jacques' tutor and who appreciates the joys of the flesh. He is killed by Jael's outraged lover, Mosaïde, who mistakenly believes that he has stolen Jael's affections.

Hercule d'Astarac (ehr-KYEWL dah-stah-RAHK), a wealthy philosopher, a student of the occult, who maintains a broken-down estate where scholars are free to pursue meta-physical delights. He comes to an unfortunate end when his home catches fire and he dies in the flames.

Brother Ange (ahnzh), a secular member of a begging order who teaches Jacques the alphabet, spends some time in jail for engaging in drunken brawls, and secretly sighs for Catherine. He eventually runs away with her.

Maurice d'Anquetil (dahnk-TEEL[DAnquetil, Maurice), a nobleman who loves Catherine and also steals Jael from Jacques. He is carefree, takes chances, and lives by his wits. He and Jacques are good friends.

De la Guéritaude (gay-ree-TOHD), a prosperous tax collector who keeps Catherine in a fine house. He is in a perpetual fit of rage because Catherine treats him outrageously with other men. He is finally seriously injured when, locked out of his own house, he causes a disturbance and is set upon by the revelers Catherine is entertaining.

Mosaïde (moh-zah-EED), a Jewish banker who fled Spain, taking his niece Jael with him as his mistress, after killing a Christian. He pretends to be a student of Hebraic texts and lives at d'Astarac's estate to do scholarly work. When d'Astarac's estate burns, Mosaïde, running from the holocaust, stumbles into a swamp and drowns.

Jeannette (zhah-NEHT), a tavern hurdy-gurdy woman who initiates Jacques in the rites of love.

AT WEDDINGS AND WAKES

Author: Alice McDermott (1953-   )
First published: 1992
Genre: Novel

Locale: Brooklyn and suburban Long Island
Time: The 1960's
Plot: Social realism

Robert Dailey,
Margaret Dailey, and
Maryanne Dailey, children who are the focus of the narration. Robert, at age twelve, is the oldest. An altar boy, he is well groomed, polite, unselfish, and studious. Margaret, the middle child, identifies more readily with Maryanne. Neither has aspirations to be a nun matching Robert's goal of becoming a priest. Both look up to Robert and try to emulate his behavior. The children are presented more forcefully as a group than as individuals.

Lucy Towne Dailey, the children's mother. She makes twice-weekly trips to Brooklyn to visit her stepmother and sisters, and she spends most of her time complaining about her husband. For about twenty years, she is the only one of the four sisters to be married. She seems never to have broken the ties with her family sufficiently to allow a happy marriage.

Bob Dailey, Lucy's husband and the children's father. He tries to provide the family with at least two weeks of something different from the trips to Brooklyn. A patient man, he does not object to his wife's constant visits "home." He has come to like the Towne women, and he willingly helps them with such matters as taxes and insurance.

Momma Towne, Lucy's stepmother, who married Lucy's father after the death of Lucy's mother following the birth of Veronica. As a seventeen-year-old recent immigrant from Ireland, she learned quickly how to be a mother to children who missed their birth mother and how to be a wife to a contentious widowed husband. A beautiful woman in her old age, she rules the homes of her daughters and remains the central figure in their lives.

May Towne, one of Lucy's three sisters, a former nun who left the nunnery because she had come to love her life as a nun so much that she could not consider her duties as a sacrifice. Enamored of Lucy's children, she takes them for walks and always has little treats or gifts for them. Her wedding and her wake are the major actions in the novel.

Agnes Towne, another sister, a successful businesswoman with cultivated tastes for music and the arts, for decor, and for personal style. She chooses the church outside their parish for May's wedding because it would make a better setting. Agnes also is in charge of the reception and other social functions.

Veronica Towne, the fourth sister, an "unfortunate" one whose facial lesions were mistreated in her youth, causing a worsening of the problem. After her first and only job (secured by Agnes) is terminated, she becomes a kind of hermit, closed up in her room until she comes out for cocktails and dinner. Her solitary drinking is tolerated by Momma Towne.

David Towne, Momma's only birth child, was spoiled in his youth and later summarily dismissed by his mother, whose iron will keeps him away from her home except for brief visits at Christmas. The Dailey children meet David's wife and two children for the first time at May's wedding.

Fred, a middle-aged mail carrier who finds May in her middle age and marries her, only to lose her four days after the wedding.

— *Mary Rohrberger*

ATALA

Author: François-Auguste-René de Chateaubriand (1768-1848)
First published: 1801
Genre: Novel

Locale: Louisiana
Time: Early eighteenth century
Plot: Philosophical realism

Atala, a young Native American woman and convert to Christianity who falls in love with Chactas, a Native American of an enemy tribe and religion. Together, she and Chactas escape into the forest and come on a mission where they think they will be safe. On Atala's birth, her mother had so feared for the child's life that she swore to the Queen of Angels an oath of virginity for Atala if the child survived. When Atala is about to succumb to Chactas, she kneels in prayer, and virtue overcomes passion. Ultimately, Atala poisons herself because she believes that if she marries Chactas, her mother will be damned. Thus, her struggle is between passion and duty. As a Romantic heroine, she remains pure and unattainable, yet passionate. Atala dies in the arms of Chactas and is buried in the Indian cemetery. In her death, which is caused by religious duty misunderstood, there is an implicit criticism of missionary zeal.

Chactas, a young, melancholic Natchez brave who remains faithful to ancient Indian tradition. He had at one time been exiled to France, and from the very beginning of his story he is shown in a state of continuous exile. Having lost his father in the wars against the Muskogees, he is captured by the enemy tribe and is to be tortured and put to death; however, Atala rescues him. He tells his tale of his flight from exile and his love for Atala. Chactas refuses to flee certain death unless

Atala accompanies him. He rages against the Christianity of Atala, because it appears to contradict nature, yet he admires the beauty and passion of her beliefs. His is a poetic struggle between natural love versus Christian notions of virtue and propriety.

Father Aubry, a wrathful missionary who rescues Atala and Chactas in a storm. He scornfully reproaches Chactas for complaining about Christianity when Chactas has not earned the right to judge providence through either his virtues or his suffering. Atala and Chactas perceive religion first as an expression of Father Aubry's compassion, then as a "civilizer." Father Aubry states that Atala's religion (incorrectly understood) led her to try to repress natural desire; when repression proved impossible, it led to her suicide. The religious rites he performs in the story are described against a backdrop of rose and golden colors, but the splendor of these rites ultimately is undercut and even annihilated, and virtue is regarded with regret at the end of the story. The mission, attacked and ravaged by the Cherokees, lies in ruins; its beauty is fleeting and vulnerable. Father Aubry dies at the hands of hostile Native Americans.

René, a young French exile to whom Chactas tells his tale. He and Chactas both have suffered estrangement.

— *Genevieve Slomski*

ATALANTA IN CALYDON

Author: Algernon Charles Swinburne (1837-1909)
First published: 1865
Genre: Poetry

Locale: Greece
Time: Remote antiquity
Plot: Tragedy

Œneus (EE-news), the king of Calydon. He has neglected his sacrifice to Artemis, goddess of the hunt. The wild boar sent by Artemis into Calydon, in punishment, is the object of the fateful hunt. Finally, after much tragedy, Œneus rules alone in Calydon.

Althæa (ahl-THEE-uh), his wife, a woman of strong will. To avert a prophecy that her newborn son would live and prosper until the brand on the hearth was consumed, she extinguished the brand and hid it. Years later, after her son has

slain her brothers, she returns the brand to the fire to be consumed. After her son's death, she dies of sorrow.

Meleager (meh-LEE-gur), the son of Œneus and Althæa. Strong and valiant, he is afflicted with great pride and lacks a proper submission to fate. He slays the boar and gives the spoils of the hunt to Atalanta. This results in a fight in which Meleager, protecting Atalanta, kills his uncles. He dies hoping his name will live among men.

Atalanta (a-tuh-LAN-tuh), an Arcadian maiden of great

beauty and a priestess of Artemis. She joins the hunt, and Meleager, though strongly warned against an infatuation, falls in love with her. Her laugh of pleasure on being given the spoils of the hunt is misinterpreted as a taunt by the Calydonians, who attack her. At last, hailing Meleager's greatness, she returns to Arcadia.

Toxeus (TOK-sews) and

Plexippus (plehk-SIH-puhs), Althæa's brothers, who are slain by Meleager.

Leda, Althæa's sister.

The Chorus, whose philosophizing on life and love, and comments on the action, illuminate the poem.

ATLAS SHRUGGED

Author: Ayn Rand (Alice Rosenbaum, 1905-1982)
First published: 1957
Genre: Novel

Locale: Primarily New York City and the state of Colorado
Time: Unspecified; approximately the 1950's
Plot: Social morality

Dagny Taggart, the head of operations of Taggart Transcontinental, a railroad company. She is described as beautiful, but with a face that is too cold and eyes that are too intense. Her brother, James Taggart, accuses her of having no feelings. Dagny is willing to tell people what to do and to take responsibility, qualities that become important as society collapses during the course of the story.

James Taggart, her brother, who recently has become president of Taggart Transcontinental. He is thirty-nine years old but appears to be fifty. James is concerned about social responsibilities, both his own and those of others.

Henry (Hank) Rearden, a steel magnate. He is forty-five years old and has been told that his face is ugly because it is unyielding and is cruel because it is expressionless. Like Dagny, he does not feel pity. Hank admires Dagny and enjoys competing with her concerning the prices they charge each other. After the successful first run of the John Galt Line, they become lovers.

Lillian Rearden, Hank's wife. She is beautiful but disappointing because of her eyes, which are vaguely pale, neither gray nor quite brown, and empty of expression. She tells Hank that it is egotistical for him to believe in right versus wrong because no one can know what is right.

Eddie Willers, Dagny's assistant. Eddie likes to look in store windows to see the products of work; he enjoys the sight of a prosperous street. As a child, he had spent summers on the Taggart estate with Dagny and James. Asked what he would do

when he grew up, he answered, "Whatever is right." At the end of the novel, he refuses to give up hope of keeping Taggart Transcontinental running as it used to.

Francisco d'Anconia, a wealthy playboy and copper magnate. He was Dagny's lover when they were teenagers. He destroys his fortune with the intent of ruining those who try to profit by his efforts.

Ragnar Danneskjöld, a pirate with pure gold hair and a face with no feeling. He seizes ships containing relief supplies.

John Galt, a rebel and mythic figure. He leads the "strike" of intellectuals against the "looters" who attempt to live on their efforts.

Ellis Wyatt, a Colorado oilman served by the Rio Norte Line of Taggart Transcontinental. He switches to a competing line because of its more reliable service, prompting James Taggart to push for the "anti-dog-eat-dog rule" for the railroads.

Philip Rearden, Hank's brother, always in precarious health but for no apparent reason. He is chronically weary and insists that Hank works too hard. He acts on behalf of various social causes and gets Hank to donate money anonymously, as he does not want Hank's name, as a greedy capitalist, to appear on contributor lists.

Wesley Mouch, Hank Rearden's representative in Washington. He becomes a powerful bureaucrat.

— A. J. Sobczak

ATTACHMENTS

Author: Judith Rossner (1935-   )
First published: 1977
Genre: Novel

Locale: Los Angeles, New York City, and Bootsville, New Hampshire
Time: The 1950's to the 1960's
Plot: Bildungsroman

Nadine, the protagonist and narrator. The only child of an exclusively devoted couple, Nadine feels isolated and yearns to be a Siamese twin, so that she might be forever attached to someone else. She is fascinated by newspaper and magazine accounts of Amos and Eddie Smith, twins joined at their abdomens by an extra band of liver. In her twenties, she meets the twins, marries Amos, and bears his two children. The only developing character, Nadine spends her youth and early adulthood frantically trying to make sense of the chaotic world in which she lives, frequently screaming in disbelief at the blindness of others. She is the only one who seems aware of

ludicrous or dangerous situations.

Dianne Shapiro, a child prodigy, later a lawyer, and Nadine's best friend. Unlike Nadine, Dianne protects herself by living a lie. She lies to herself that she will be perfectly happy as a full-time mother, withholds from her obstetrician the fact that her husband is a Siamese twin, and insists that her daughter's friends are "nice, quiet kids" when in reality they are school dropouts and drug addicts. Because of her self-deception, Dianne is able to maintain her equanimity.

Amos Smith and

Eddie Smith, Siamese twins and the husbands of Nadine

and Dianne, respectively. Abandoned by their widowed father at the age of four, the twins grew up in a foster home. They later joined a side show, from which they retired in wealth to live in Beverly Hills. In personality, the twins are opposite. When their bodies are surgically separated, their characters reverse. Like Dianne, Amos and Eddie are unaware of the true nature of conditions around them.

Carly, the daughter of Dianne and Eddie. Nadine tends Carly during Dianne's long and debilitating postpartum depression, and she continues to do so after Dianne recovers and returns to work. When Nadine has her own child, however, she unwittingly neglects Carly, except in seeing to her basic physi-

cal needs. As an adolescent, Carly experiments with marijuana and eventually runs away. Nadine blames herself for that catastrophe.

Marianne Story, a professor at Bard College, where Nadine acquires most of her postsecondary education. Although Dr. Story appears only in the beginning of the novel, she is significant as a potential role model for Nadine. When she learns that Dr. Story is dying of cancer, Nadine becomes completely disoriented and leaves college in the middle of her last year.

— *Rebecca Stingley Hinton*

AUCASSIN AND NICOLETTE
(Aucassin et Nicolette)

Author: Unknown
First published: Early thirteenth century
Genre: Novel

Locale: Provence, France
Time: Twelfth century
Plot: Historical realism

Aucassin (oh-kah-SAN), the son of Count Garin de Beaucaire. He loves Nicolette, a slave girl bought from the Saracens by a captain who has reared her as his own daughter. Aucassin's father is relentlessly opposed to the marriage, and both Aucassin and Nicolette are imprisoned in the course of the proceedings. At last they run away together and live happily for a time, until they are captured by Saracens. A storm scatters the ships, and the one on which Aucassin is a prisoner drives ashore at Beaucaire, of which he is now count, his parents having died.

Nicolette (nee-koh-LEHT), Aucassin's lover. After the lovers are separated by the Saracens, she reaches Carthage and there learns that she is the daughter of the King of Carthage.

He wants her to marry a king of the Saracens, but she remains true to Aucassin. She makes her way to Beaucaire, where they are married at last.

Count Garin de Beaucaire (gah-RAN duh boh-KEHR), father of Aucassin. He is opposed to Nicolette as a daughter-in-law.

Count Bougars de Valence (boo-GAHR deh vah-LAHNS), at war with Count Garin. Having his father's promise to let him see Nicolette on his return from battle, Aucassin fights so fiercely that he captures Count Bougars. When his father refuses to keep the bargain, Aucassin releases Count Bougars and is cast temporarily into a dungeon.

The King of Carthage, who proves to be Nicolette's father.

AUGUST 1914
(Avgust chetyrnadtsatogo)

Author: Aleksandr Solzhenitsyn (1918-   )
First published: 1971
Genre: Novel

Locale: Russia
Time: August, 1914
Plot: Historical realism

Alexander Vasilich Samsonov (vah-SEE-lihch sahm-SOH-nov), a fifty-five-year-old general in the cavalry. After a number of years of steady, but generally uneventful service with the cossack regiments, he is called, only three weeks before the outbreak of war, to command the Russian Second Army on the Polish-German front. This responsibility makes him uneasy, because he has not seen serious operational duty for at least seven years. Samsonov attempts to fulfill his tasks with military professionalism, choosing subordinates on the basis of military records, not connections. He soon realizes that powers higher up are not aware of the situation near the front. His dealings with supreme commander Zhilinsky are plagued by erroneous or contradictory orders and a personal relationship that is not between military colleagues but between a "bullying cattle drover" and a powerless but ultimately responsible subordinate. Samsonov is pursued continuously by a fear of failing to act when necessities, not orders, demand. His frustration mounts as repeated miscalculations by the Rus-

sian High Command lead to the loss of thousands of Second Army soldiers. Unable to bear the weight of responsibility for disastrous military moves he has been obliged to implement, Samsonov commits suicide, giving the High Command an excuse to condemn him for "excessively independent" operations, running counter to orders.

Georgii Mikhalych Vorotyntsev (geh-OHR-gee mih-KHAH-lihch voh-roh-TIHN-tsehv), a general staff colonel who, following duty in the Russo-Japanese war, had seemed content with gradual professional advancement and the security of marriage. Now, embroiled in the events of August, 1914, he is particularly conscious of the responsibility of commanding miserable peasants. He imagines that their reward, if they survive war, is simply staying alive. Vorotyntsev is perplexed over his position in life, not knowing what reward might be his if he survives the coming events. Throughout his life, Vorotyntsev has believed that people should do their best to assist their country. That belief turns to despair time and again as he witnesses the harmful effects of incompetence, especially in positions of authority. In a number of high-pressure situations during the August, 1914, campaign, Vorotyntsev shows resiliency and an ability to call on reserves of physical and psychological strength to salvage whatever is possible in the face of extremely adverse conditions.

Arsenii (Senka) Blagodaryov (ahr-SEH-nee blah-goh-DAHR-yov), a strong, rough-hewn, twenty-five-year-old peasant soldier. Although Senka is somewhat clumsy because of his size, he possesses a sharp intellect. He is appointed as Colonel Vorotyntsev's orderly. In this post, he shows a remarkable ability to see the consequences of others' decisions in advance. This ability, coupled with his willingness to accept dangerous assignments, earns him compliments from his commanding officer. Seen from Senka's somewhat naïve perspective, the task of fighting is a grim but necessary reality that he hopes can be concluded at least by October 1, the traditional date of village feasts. His dedication to Vorotyntsev's and the army's service is unconnected with any higher principles of glory or patriotism.

Sasha Lenartovich (leh-NAHR-toh-vihch), a twenty-four-year-old platoon commander who believes that Russia and the world will someday be transformed as a result of a great event. Earlier, he viewed the abortive 1905 revolution in Russia as a call to his student generation to join the oppressed classes' struggle to break the chains of czarist tyranny. Thus, when he is drafted in August, 1914, Sasha is driven by an overwhelming despair that he should not be on the front but instead serve the real cause of revolution elsewhere. The ignorant troops of his platoon appear to be completely unaware, not only of class struggle but also of their own fate as pawns "driven forcibly to fight against another and equally unfortunate mass of men." He considers various routes of escape from the senselessness of his situation: court-martial and expulsion from the army as a political agitator, or even surrender to the enemy. While attempting to desert his regiment, Sasha ironically falls into the entourage of Colonel Vorotyntsev, who, no longer able to marshal an effective fighting force, is reduced to attempting to break through the German lines to seek safety for a heterogeneous body of loyal survivors.

Isaakii (Sanya) Lazhenitsyn (ee-SAH-kee SAH-nyah lah-zheh-NIH-tsihn), the most intellectual of the characters. Isaakii is one of only two students from the steppe village of Sablya. He clings to the ideal of maintaining ties with traditional village values while cultivating new ideas as a student. The novelty of his ideas, especially on necessary social change in Russia, earns for him the nickname of Narodnik (stargazer). He is so inspired by the example of Leo Tolstoy that he travels to the latter's estate, meets with the great writer, and professes his loyalty as an intellectual disciple. In spite of this high idealism, when the war breaks out and Russia is attacked, Sanya feels that he has a responsibility to go to the assistance of his country. With a fellow student and covolunteer on the way through Moscow to join the army, Sanya encounters an enigmatic itinerant scholar (Varsonofiev). Their discussions wrestle with the shortcomings of *narodnik* idealism.

Zakhar Tomchak (zah-KHAHR tom-CHAK), the owner of a prosperous northern Caucasus estate near Rostov, as well as extensive lands in the Kuban. Descendant of a family of mi-

grants who originally came to the Ukraine as hired laborers, Tomchak, with his "craggy features" and "gargoyle-like" nose, still reflects his rough origins. When he goes into the city of Rostov wearing a formal suit, he strikes a somewhat comical figure. This rusticity does not keep Tomchak from using his native intelligence to further the productive goals of his agricultural domain. Many of his ideas, like the most up-to-date machinery he purchases, come from abroad or are borrowed from the German colonists whose labors have produced visibly superior results in Russia. Tomchak views Russia's declaration of war against Germany to be a great mistake. Out of fear that mass conscription will harm the effective running of his estates, he uses his influence to secure military exemptions for his son Roman and for all foremen, laborers, and cossacks in his service.

Irina (Orya) Tomchak (ee-REE-nah), Roman's wife. Irina is a tall, erect woman with an elaborate coiffure. Although she is accustomed to urban standards of elegance, she avoids displays of finery in the presence of her father-in-law. By ingratiating herself with the stern Tomchak patriarch, Irina escapes the continual reprimands that plague other members of the family. Her favored position is reflected in the fact that Tomchak relies on her reading of the *Novoe Vremya* newspaper, to the exclusion of all other sources, to learn news of Russia and the world. Irina spends long hours lost in dreams that, through their romantic content, help her remove herself psychologically from the rough conditions and unpleasant associations that surround her.

Roman Tomchak, Zakhar's son. Roman reflects the idleness of privilege. His main concern for the future is to secure the best possible conditions of inheritance. In the meantime, he concentrates on filling the role of a future estate owner, paying particular attention to his elegance. Roman is no friend of the declining Russian monarchy, nor does he subscribe to orthodox conceptions of religion. For propriety's sake, however, he keeps outward appearances of Christian faith and patriotism. This hypocrisy serves to distort even more the purchased privilege of military exemption arranged for him by his father.

Xenia Tomchak (ZEE-nyah), the youngest of the Tomchak children. With the questionable exception of her brother Roman (who is seventeen years older), Xenia is the only member of the family to profess progressive political views. She reads widely from different Western European literatures and is tempted to abandon a standard university education to pursue a career in ballet, irrespective of the effect this switch could have on her status as an heir to the Tomchak estate. Through the special efforts of her father, Xenia enters a private provincial high school known for its "left-wing liberalism" and befriends the head mistress' family. Xenia's intervention saves the daughter of the head mistress from ostracism as a result of an awkward marriage situation. Xenia herself chafes under her father's insistent pressures to marry her off. Even though her educational experiences promise to provide an opening for her into Muscovite society, she comes to realize that she has most in common with her adopted family, which has espoused liberalism out of conviction, not convention.

— *Byron D. Cannon*

AUNT DAN AND LEMON

Author: Wallace Shawn (1943-   )
First published: 1985
Genre: Drama

Locale: London and Oxford, England
Time: The 1950's to the 1980's
Plot: Play of ideas

Leonora, called **Lemon**, Susie and Jack's daughter. A sickly young woman living alone in London, Lemon sits in her apartment and subsists on bread, fruit, and vegetable juices. Lately, her time has been spent sleeping, masturbating, and reading books about the Nazi death camps. During her childhood, Lemon would lie in bed and listen to the stories told by Aunt Dan. Lemon later explains that when she was eighteen, she felt physically attracted to Aunt Dan, but because Aunt Dan was sick at the time, she did not make an advance. Lemon's defense of the Nazis and their cruelty appears to have been influenced by Aunt Dan's beliefs that governments will survive only through the use of violence.

Danielle (Aunt Dan), an American academic living in England who is a friend of Jack and Susie. As a young woman, Danielle became friends with Susie and later introduced her to Jack. She is nicknamed Aunt Dan by the eleven-year-old Lemon. At night, she would tell Lemon stories about the great man Henry Kissinger. According to Aunt Dan, the former American secretary of state carried the problems of an entire nation on his shoulders. She defends every decision that Kissinger made during the Vietnam War, for she understands that governments must use force if they are to survive. Aunt Dan has an affair with the prostitute Mindy after Mindy kills a man for sexual thrills.

Jack, Lemon's father, an American who went to England to study at Oxford. After marrying Susie, Jack went to work in an auto parts manufacturing company. Never wanting to admit that he is wrong in his actions, Jack, now the owner of his own auto parts business, feels compelled to defend his own work against that done by intellectuals in the universities, perhaps as a way of assuring himself that leaving Oxford after marrying Susie was the right thing to do. Cold and impersonal in his feelings, Jack argues that Susie and her anxieties are the causes of Lemon's eating disorder.

Susie, Lemon's mother, an Englishwoman. Loving and kind, Susie is also an emotionally sensitive woman. She becomes distraught about young Lemon's eating disorder. Her anxieties worsen when Jack tells her that her worrying is the cause of the problem. Susie opposes Aunt Dan's defense of Henry Kissinger and his decision-making involvement concerning the Vietnam War, as well as Aunt Dan's ideas that nations must exert violent force so that others do not have to. Susie tells Aunt Dan that, although she does not know Kissinger, she is certain that there are some people who cannot curb their violent natures. Susie's opposition to Aunt Dan ultimately causes a falling out between them.

Mindy Gatti, a London prostitute. Blonde and attractive, Mindy is an amoral and violent woman. Mainly for thrills, she strangles and kills Raimondo, a foreign drug dealer, after engaging in oral sex with him. After she kills him, Mindy wraps the body in a plastic sack and hides it in the trunk of a car. Later, she tells Aunt Dan about the murder, and the two make love; Aunt Dan finds herself emotionally and sexually attracted to Mindy while listening to the story. Mindy's act of murder exemplifies Aunt Dan's idea that violence is necessary in order to survive. The two begin an affair that lasts only a week. Aunt Dan breaks off the affair before her feelings for Mindy sour.

— *Dale Davis*

AUNT JULIA AND THE SCRIPTWRITER
(La tía Julia y el escribidor)

Author: Mario Vargas Llosa (1936-   )
First published: 1977
Genre: Novel

Locale: Lima, Peru
Time: The 1950's
Plot: Comic realism

Mario, also called **Varguitas** (vahr-gew-EE-tahs) and **Marito** (mah-REE-toh), the narrator-protagonist, a confident college student who is underemployed as a radio newswriter. He is waiting for the chance to devote himself completely to a literary life, preferably in Paris. Hardly anything distinguishes Mario—indiscriminately and purposely called by the author's nicknames as a young man—from the real Mario Vargas Llosa. Mario comically and romantically serializes his courtship of Julia, an aunt by his uncle's marriage, and his apprenticeship as a writer under the guidance of Pedro Camacho, a scriptwriter for radio soap operas. Mario's "autobiography" is an exercise in indiscretion at the literary and empirical level, even though his depiction of himself as an intelligent, tall, dark, and handsome extrovert is rendered truthful by the other characters. Mario sees marriage alternately as a challenge or as an adventure, all of which can be turned into literature, specifically short stories. As the narrator of the final chapter, he summarizes in one page how he reunites with Julia to share a life that would last eight years.

Aunt Julia, fourteen years older than Mario, a divorced Bolivian who cannot bear children. Physically attractive, she dazzles the young Mario with what he perceives to be healthy cunning and spontaneity. Close family ties prevent their ever getting together, but Julia is decisive and ultimately responsible for their union. She is warm and brave, and she has a wonderful sense of humor, which is what really allows her to continue, despite her awareness that their relationship will not last. The story of her divorce, ending a marriage that lasted three more years than she expected, is told strictly from Mario's point of view.

Pedro Camacho (PEH-droh kah-MAH-choh), who like Julia is a Bolivian working in Peru. He is brought in by the radio station in which Varguitas works to organize and produce the soap operas it broadcasts. Introverted and rather mechanical, he thinks only in catastrophic terms. His stories rely on extensive melodramas that are so repetitive and lacking in imagination that at times he loses characters or switches them from one program to another, without knowing he is doing so. It is implied that Pedro has a certain madness. Marito, echoing the real Vargas Llosa, attributes his own ability to organize a narrative's totality to Camacho's type of truly professional, even if perverse, influence.

— *Will H. Corral*

THE AUNT'S STORY

Author: Patrick White (1912-1990)
First published: 1948
Genre: Novel

Locale: Meroë, near Sydney, Australia; the French Riviera; and the United States
Time: Early decades of the twentieth century, particularly shortly before World War II
Plot: Psychological symbolism

Theodora Goodman, an unmarried woman in her forties. Theodora has devoted much of her adult life to caring for her difficult, antagonistic mother. Once old Mrs. Goodman dies, Theodora decides to travel. She journeys first to pre-World War II Europe and then to America. Before leaving, she recounts the story of her youth to her young niece and soulmate, Lou Parrott. Theodora was decidedly unfeminine as a girl, all bones and angles. She would say startling things and preferred going hunting with her beloved father to practicing the piano. Although clever and perceptive, Theodora has few friends; men in particular are repulsed by her. Except for occasional illuminating encounters with fellow individualists such as Moraïtis, Theodora has led a quiet life with her domineering mother. Following her tour through the Old World, Theodora lingers at the Hôtel du Midi, where her own fragile identity and grip on reality start to unravel as she comes into contact with other eccentric guests. For one (a Russian general), she takes on the role of his deceased sister Ludmilla. Theodora becomes increasingly confused, and as her sense of self begins to disintegrate, the other characters come to seem merely projections of her fervid imagination. Tensions mount in the hotel, and it self-combusts; Theodora escapes and resurfaces in the New World. She rides a train across the United States and gradually divests herself of all of her worldly possessions. It is only once she encounters Holstius that the healing process begins: He speaks to Theodora's higher self, helping her to gather the pieces of her fractured spirit. Like the characters in the hotel, Holstius seems not to exist except in Theodora's imagination. Eventually, she is taken away to an asylum by concerned, well-meaning people.

Frank Parrott, Theodora's brother-in-law, a beefy and inarticulate man. He and Theodora were good friends at one time.

Fanny Parrott, Theodora's younger sister. Married to Frank and mother to Lou, Fanny is vapid and materialistic.

Lou Parrott, Theodora's only niece. Young Lou is clever and sensitive like her aunt; they see things the same way. The one thing Theodora prizes above all is her relationship with her niece.

George Goodman, the father to Theodora and Fanny, and husband to Julia Goodman. George is a well-meaning, kind, and educated man who is naïve when it comes to financial matters. He sells off his estate bit by bit in order to satisfy his wife's desire to travel to exotic places. He understands and loves Theodora and encourages her individualism.

Julia Goodman, the mother of Theodora and Fanny. Julia prefers her plump, rosy daughter Fanny to her plain, difficult, older girl. A vain and selfish woman, Mrs. Goodman dominates her eldest daughter throughout their lives.

Moraïtis (moh-ri-ih-tihs), a visiting Greek cellist. A small, dark, sad man, he also sees beyond the superficial and conventional in life. He and Theodora recognize each other at once as kindred spirits. Although unmusical herself, Theodora attends one of Moraitis' recitals and emerges profoundly moved by his music.

Huntly Clarkson, a dilettante friend of Theodora. Huntly is a social somebody, a refined, well-to-do bachelor who collects art for its value and people for their idiosyncrasies. Although frequently repulsed by shabby, abrupt Theodora, Huntly cultivates her as a friend because she has a knack for cutting through social hypocrisy.

General Alyosha Sergei Sokolnikov,
Elsie Rapallo, and
Katina Pavlou, respectively a retired Russian military man, a wealthy American, and a young girl, all fellow guests at the Hôtel du Midi. There is some doubt that these characters are who they say they are: Throughout their stay in the hotel, each antagonizes and argues with the others, hurling accusations about others' identities. Theodora becomes the general's confidante, but she also plays friend to Mrs. Rapallo and aunt to Katina. These characters appear only in the second section of the novel. They say and do remarkable things throughout, but their speech and actions (like Theodora's) become increasingly disjointed and bizarre.

Holstius, a treelike man with whom Theodora communes in the third section of the novel. They encounter each other in an abandoned shack in the middle of nowhere in the United States. Theodora, having shed all traces of her former identity, looks to Holstius to help her reconcile and reunite the disparate halves of being such as joy and sorrow, illusion and reality, and life and death. He advises her simply to accept the whole and to love elementary things such as chairs and tables. Despite Theodora's perception of Holstius as real, his presence goes undetected by others, who in turn apprehend Theodora for seeing him.

— *Susan Whaley*

AURA

Author: Carlos Fuentes (1928-   )
First published: 1962
Genre: Novel

Locale: Mexico City, Mexico
Time: Early 1960's
Plot: Fantasy

    Felipe Montero (feh-LEE-peh mohn-TEH-roh), a young historian and part-time teacher in a private school. Bored with his present job of teaching "useless facts" to "sleepy pupils," he desires a change from his daily routine, and he is drawn to an advertisement that seems addressed personally to him. Restless and curious, he is particularly susceptible to the strange events and relationships that he encounters when he accepts the job of translating the memoirs of Señora Consuelo Llorente's dead husband. Felipe leaves the known outer world and enters Consuelo's dark, moldy home; in this mysterious, gothic setting he meets Aura, the ancient woman's niece. Gradually, he is drawn into a series of bewildering, grotesque occurrences that suggest the fantastic bond between the two women. His growing desire for Aura is consummated when he makes love to her and swears, "Nothing can separate us." Eventually, Felipe realizes that this "sterile conception" engenders another self, his own double, the embodiment of Consuelo's late husband General Llorente; through his sexual union with young Aura and his promise of undying love, Felipe completes his role in Consuelo's morbid scheme to perpetuate her youth and passionate marriage to the general. Felipe is too bewitched to protest; as he caresses Aura, he knows she is an image created by the withered, exhausted Consuelo, but he embraces her in shadowed moonlight and accepts his dark destiny.

    Señora Consuelo Llorente (kohn-SWEH-loh yohr-EHN-tay), Aura's strange, eccentric aunt, whom Felipe figures is about 109 years old. Obsessed with prolonging her youth and unwilling to relinquish the past, Consuelo dabbles in the occult, keeping odd medicines in her decrepit house, growing exotic herbs and plants in a dank garden, and performing obscure rituals and bizarre communion feasts before dim candles and a tortured black Christ. She married General Llorente at the age of fifteen and was widowed thirty-four years later in 1901, but she has remained ageless through her illusory double, Aura, waiting for the fated reappearance of her beloved groom.

    Aura (OW-rah), Consuelo's young niece. Pale and beautiful, with loose black hair and astonishing green eyes, Aura seduces Felipe, luring him into the old widow's plot to re-create her dead husband and preserve their love forever by mating Felipe with the young girl. Aura is lovely, provocative, and spectral. Felipe sees her only in shadows; he senses her more than he actually feels her, although she inflames his desire for her and he does possess her. In loving her, Felipe loses himself, for Aura is merely Consuelo's imagined self, a materialization of the old woman's past. Aura's role is to open herself sexually and "like an altar" to Felipe until he is spent and drained of his own will, his animus submerged in the dark anima figure, whose "fleshless lips" he kisses at the end.

— John Zubizarreta

AURORA LEIGH

Author: Elizabeth Barrett Browning (1806-1861)
First published: 1856
Genre: Poetry and novel

Locale: Italy and England
Time: Mid-nineteenth century
Plot: Bildungsroman

    Aurora Leigh, a heroic woman who dares to defy contemporary and traditional attitudes toward women, female writers in particular. Bravely, she rejects the security of Romney's proposed "bequest" and offer of marriage to live alone in London, pursuing her career as a poet on very limited funds. She asserts that women can be artists and accepts the loneliness of a single life rather than surrender into the role of a submissive wife. She befriends Marian and offers to take her to Italy as her companion and "sister." She accurately evaluates Lady Waldmar's evil character and berates her for her villainy, but she is strangely imperceptive of Romney's real feelings and his hints about his blindness. He tells her that she never really knew him if she could really believe he would marry Lady Waldmar. Her quest in search of her identity is triumphantly rewarded when a chastened Romney agrees to marriage on Aurora's terms, a partnership in poetry and social reform.

    Romney Leigh, Aurora's cousin, who first appears as a paternal figure as heir of the Leigh estate and as a brother figure to his teenage cousin. His social conscience causes him to dedicate his life to social reform, following some of the

typical theorists of the day. Aurora tries unsuccessfully to convince him that reform must come from within the individual. After Aurora refuses to marry him (because his proposal apparently was made without love), he generously offers to marry Marian Erle and thus rescue one poor seamstress from poverty. His generosity is rejected, thwarted by the schemes of Lady Waldmar. After a mob burns his ancestral home, the now blinded Romney arrives in Italy for his last quest as knight-errant, marriage to the socially rejected Marian. Through the efforts of Aurora and Marian, he happily acknowledges Aurora's "superiority" as poet and inspiration for social reform, thus breaking with traditional views on marriage and the role of women.

    Marian Erle, an idealized victim of society and circumstance. She escapes from abusive parents—her mother had intended to "sell" her to the local squire—and eventually is rescued by Romney from a life of destitution. Although socially "inferior," she agrees to marry him so that she can be his servant and assistant. When she is raped in a Paris brothel, she loses her reputation but insists that because she was an unwilling participant in this sexual act, she retains her purity. She intends to devote her life to rearing the child born as a result of the rape and accepts Aurora's offer of a home with dignity and gratitude. She refuses Romney's gallantry in trying to rescue her again, insisting that she never loved him but had only wanted to repay his generosity by her submission to his life and work. Marian is no longer a victim; with Aurora's help, she emerges as a serene, integrated woman.

Lady Waldmar, a selfish, manipulative, coldhearted woman who represents the worst of the members of the upper class. She ruins Romney's plan to marry Marian by convincing Marian that Romney would be degraded by this alliance. She offers Marian a new start in Australia, but either deliberately or through negligence she causes Marian to be taken to a Paris brothel and raped. Although she denies that this had been her intention, her conduct toward Marian is criminal. She is ostentatious in flaunting her beauty to attract men, presenting an almost bare bosom accented by a heavy rope of pearls at Lord Howe's home. She is not amoral, however, because she accepts the loss of Romney as "punishment" for her treatment of Marian. She writes to Aurora to express her hatred for the winner in the contest for Romney, insisting that she might have become a better woman had she married him. She is further punished by being "erased" from the consciousness of the man she had loved and admired and by being doomed to an empty social life without him.

Lord Howe, an example of the "better" part of the aristocracy, in that he has a social conscience and is particularly kind to Aurora, saving her from the riot created by the mob at Marian's aborted wedding. He is, however, ineffectual; although he is gracious and liberal, he "floats" on various social theories and "could never be anything complete." He entrusts an important letter for Aurora, explaining Romney's predicament after the mob burns Leigh Hall, to Sir Blaise Delorme, who snubs Aurora in Florence and fails to deliver the important news. He is well intentioned but not dependable.

Sir Blaise Delorme, an example of a Roman Catholic gentleman. He disapproves of Lady Waldmar's exhibition of herself and remarks that wives should be chosen for their virtues and not for display. He also seems to disapprove of Aurora in her alliance with Marian, because he deliberately snubs her in Florence, acknowledging her with only half a bow. He proves untrustworthy as Howe's emissary. His neglect causes Aurora considerable pain as she envisions Romney married to the unworthy Lady Waldmar.

Vincent Carrington, a supportive fellow artist and friend who remains loyal to Aurora throughout her difficulties. He can understand her commitment and discuss art with her. He marries one of Aurora's "disciples," Kate Ward, who has become a "feminist" because of her admiration for Aurora. Carrington asks for news of Aurora and sends her news of the success of her latest book. He admires her independence and commitment.

— *Elizabeth R. Nelson*

AUTO-DA-FÉ
(Die Blendung)

Author: Elias Canetti (1905-1994)
First published: 1935
Genre: Novel

Locale: Vienna, Austria, and Paris, France
Time: Probably the 1930's
Plot: Parody

Dr. Peter Kien (keen), a world-renowned sinologist. Kien is a forty-year-old recluse who wants to live only for his scholarly work in his private library of twenty-five thousand books. His life is completely regulated, and his library is cared for by his housekeeper Therese, whom he decides to marry in order to ensure the continuance of this good care. The marriage, however, changes this misogynist's life into a nightmarish existence. In searching for his bankbook and will, Therese makes Kien's life so unbearable that he is forced to leave his home and library. Kien is rescued by Benedikt Pfaff, who in turn imprisons Kien and brutalizes him. Eventually, Kien's brother George comes from Paris to rescue him. George reestablishes the original order of Peter's life by removing Therese and Benedikt from his home and restoring his library. Believing that everyone is satisfied, George returns to Paris. At this point, however, Peter Kien has a complete breakdown. Fantasizing that all (including his books) are plotting against him, Peter sets fire to his library and hurls himself onto the flaming pyre.

Therese Krumbholz (teh-RAY-zeh KREWM-hohlts), Peter Kien's housekeeper, a fifty-six-year-old unmarried woman who is seeking material wealth and security for her old age. Mistakenly believing that Peter Kien has considerable wealth, she sets out to obtain his bankbook and to become his sole heir after they are married. Her vicious greed and her merciless babbling of unbearable clichés and platitudes drive Kien from his home. Therese also has an absurd view of her physical and sexual charm; she is in fact a repulsive hag. This obsession, for example, leads her to mistake the flattery of a furniture salesman (referred to as "that superior young man") for amorous advances, to be followed by an encounter in the showroom of the store, where she removes her skirt and tries to embrace him with her fat and ugly body, much to the amusement of the crowd of shoppers. Whereas Kien's insanity leads him to bookishness, Therese's mania makes her pursue her greed and sexual frustrations. When George Kien tries to help his brother reestablish his life, he provides Therese with a small dairy-produce shop on the outskirts of the city on the condition that she never return to Peter Kien's home.

Fischerle (FIH-shehr-leh), also known as **Siegfried Fischer** (ZEEG-freed FIHSH-uhr), a hunchbacked dwarf whose mania drives him to imagine that he can become the world's chess champion. He exploits Peter Kien's psychosis, first by being his assistant while "unpacking" his imaginary books from his head, and then by organizing a group of four friends who "sell" books to Kien at the municipal pawn shop (the Theresianum), while Fischerle makes off with most of Kien's money.

Benedikt Pfaff (pfahf), a retired policeman and caretaker of the apartment house where Kien lives. He lives in a cellar apartment, from which he exploits and brutalizes everyone who enters or leaves the house. After Therese has driven Peter Kien out of his home and library, Pfaff becomes her lover. Together they set out to sell the library to the municipal pawn shop. Pfaff rescues Kien from the police, who think he has murdered Therese, only to incarcerate him in a dungeonlike room of his cellar apartment, where Kien is then subjected to physical harassment and brutality while Pfaff enjoys life upstairs with Therese. After Peter Kien's brother arrives, Pfaff is set up in business near Therese in another part of town.

George Kien, Peter Kien's younger brother, a psychiatrist and director of an asylum for the insane in Paris. Although George may be the only sane character, he too is portrayed as suffering a touch of madness in his unorthodox methods of treating his patients. It is obvious that his analysis of his brother's mental condition is incorrect, as it leads quickly to Peter Kien's demise.

— Thomas H. Falk

THE AUTOBIOGRAPHY OF ALICE B. TOKLAS

Author: Gertrude Stein (1874-1946)
First published: 1933
Genre: Novel

Locale: Paris, France
Time: 1903-1932
Plot: Historical realism

Gertrude Stein, a real person and a fictional character in her book. Because the reader is to assume that the autobiography was written by Alice, much can be said about Gertrude that she could not very well say about herself. For example, at the beginning of the story the general tone of the book is set. Alice announces, "The three geniuses of whom I wish to speak are Gertrude Stein, Pablo Picasso and Alfred Whitehead." It is unfortunate that readers are never informed of the topics discussed by these geniuses. As a real and a fictional character, Gertrude can express her personal opinions on the work of other artists, if she is so inclined. She was fond of Sherwood Anderson, Thornton Wilder, and Virgil Thomson and expressed her admiration for them without reservation. With the young Ernest Hemingway, it was different. When he first arrived in Paris in 1922, he sought Gertrude's help, and she gladly assisted him. When Hemingway became famous and failed to pay proper homage to his mentors, Gertrude and Sherwood Anderson in particular, she showed how bitter and vitriolic she could be toward this upstart whom she had to teach the fundamental concept that "remarks are not literature." There are many stories so filled with humor that readers can only believe them to be fiction. For example, when Gertrude and Alice were performing volunteer work with the American Fund for the French Wounded, they had to supply their own car and driver. Because Gertrude did not know how to drive, she took lessons from a Paris taxi driver, who never taught her how to drive in reverse. Consequently, all her driving during the war, whether in the city or the countryside, was directed with this limitation in mind.

Alice B. Toklas, a real person and a fictional character. While Gertrude constantly stands at the center of the artistic and literary world, Alice stands at the periphery and glances in Gertrude's direction, ensuring that no one can steal the spotlight from Gertrude. To be successful in this role, Alice devises a complicated scheme for an imaginary book, titled *The Wives of Geniuses I Have Sat With*. This idea is elaborately developed to categorize all possible persons. For example, there are real wives of real geniuses or of nongeniuses, wives who are not wives of geniuses or only near geniuses or even would-be geniuses. This system of ordering made it possible to mention by name the many people who attended the Saturday evenings at 27, rue de Fleurus, showing the immensely important role Gertrude played in Paris at that time, but without letting Gertrude be overwhelmed by the crowd. Alice plays another important role: She must express Gertrude's biased and negative views on many people. For example, Fernande Olivier, Picasso's mistress, is dismissed as being "not the least amusing" because her conversations were limited to "talk about hats and perfume." Alice's voice provides the tone and cadence for the entire novel. Her narration, which might be described as rambling, does not suggest a forgetful mind but instead represents a character anxious to tell a story complete in all of its many details. At the same time, Alice is determined to provide prominence to Gertrude.

— Thomas H. Falk

THE AUTOBIOGRAPHY OF AN EX-COLOURED MAN

Author: James Weldon Johnson (1871-1938)
First published: 1912
Genre: Novel

Locale: Southern United States, New York City, and Europe
Time: Primarily early twentieth century
Plot: Psychological realism

The narrator, a musician and composer who is not named in the novel. The son of a mulatto woman and a rich white father, the narrator moves from Georgia to Connecticut at an early age. He is extremely light-skinned, and the truth of his race is kept from him; his discovery that he is black is a traumatic one. Having been reared by his mother, he develops into an extremely sensitive adult. He is well read, has good manners, and exhibits considerable culture. He is, however, also naïve and somewhat cowardly. The latter trait is most clearly seen when, after witnessing the lynching and burning of another black man in the rural South, the narrator elects to pass for white. Even after he becomes moderately successful and comfortable, he sometimes regrets his decision to leave the black race but is much too afraid to live as a black man, based on the lynching experience.

The narrator's mother, a seamstress, a mulatto former servant who has a child by her white employer. He arranges for her and the child to move to Connecticut. She is well read and possesses considerable knowledge of black life and history, which she passes on to her son. She also barters her services as a seamstress to secure tutors and music teachers for him. She is the major force in his life. She dies shortly after his graduation from high school.

Shiny, a boyhood friend of the narrator whose nickname derives from his extremely dark complexion. Shiny is the smartest person in the class and delivers the valedictory address on Toussaint-Louverture. This speech kindles in the narrator a love and appreciation for black history and culture. Shiny works his way through the University of Massachusetts at Amherst and goes on to become a professor at Fisk University. A chance meeting between Shiny and the narrator in New York leads the narrator to disclose his race to his white girlfriend.

Red, a boyhood friend of the narrator, so called because of his red hair and freckles. Red is not disposed to become a

scholar. The narrator helps him through school, and they become fast friends after Red comforts him following his discovery of his black heritage. After high school graduation, Red's ambition is to work in a bank.

The millionaire, the narrator's benefactor. The millionaire encounters the narrator while frequenting a club where the narrator plays ragtime. He hires the narrator to perform at his private parties and later takes him to Europe. When the narrator elects to return to the United States, the millionaire provides generously for his expenses.

The Cuban exile, a cigar factory worker. He befriends the narrator upon his arrival in Jacksonville. The narrator rooms with the Cuban and his wife, and the Cuban helps him get a job at the cigar factory. He also schools the narrator on the Cuban revolution, which broadens the narrator's awareness of the plight of people of color throughout the world.

— *Warren J. Carson*

THE AUTOBIOGRAPHY OF MISS JANE PITTMAN

Author: Ernest J. Gaines (1933-   )
First published: 1971
Genre: Novel

Locale: Rural southern Louisiana
Time: Early 1860's to early 1960's
Plot: Historical realism

Miss Jane Pittman, a former slave and lifelong agricultural laborer and domestic. She is small but wiry, perhaps 110 years old at the time of the narrative. Miss Jane is a living repository of the American black experience in the Deep South. Jane has survived a long life of neglect, abuse, and oppression through a combination of endurance, tenacity, and necessary forbearance. She weathers the brutality and dehumanizing effects of institutionalized racism and the grief of personal loss with a wisdom and vitality that affects even her white social superiors. Her autobiography reflects her personality and attitude, and she shapes the novel with an eyewitness' sense of historical immediacy. At the end of the novel, in a culmination of her life, she asserts her independence and freedom by staring down a white plantation owner as she leaves for town to lend her support to a civil rights protest.

Ned Douglass, Miss Jane's adoptive son, a Spanish-American War veteran, schoolmaster, and community leader. In his late thirties at the time of his murder, Ned is tall and powerfully muscled, with intense eyes and a natural orator's persuasive ability. As a small child, Ned is unofficially adopted by Jane, herself barely more than a child, after his mother and infant sister are murdered by nightriders shortly after emancipation. Ned is the child Jane can never have biologically. His departure to the North at the age of seventeen or eighteen devastates her. He is killed because of his independent thinking and his campaigning for civil rights for black citizens.

Joe Pittman, Jane's common-law husband, a widower with two daughters and an expert breaker of wild horses. Joe accepts Jane's inability to bear children with compassion. His expertise as a horse tamer leads him to seek employment on a ranch in western Louisiana, where he becomes locally renowned for his courage and ability. Joe is killed trying to tame a huge black stallion. The seven or eight years Jane and Joe spend together are the most carefree and peaceful of Jane's life.

Jimmy Aaron, a young civil rights worker born on the Samson plantation. He is shot dead by white racists in the nearby town of Bayonne. Tall and thin, with serious eyes, Jimmy is from birth considered a savior figure in the black community. He is constantly identified as "the One" upon whom black hopes rest for a leader. Jimmy's intelligence and oratorical skills lead him neither to the pulpit—as universally hoped among the black community—nor to the teacher's lectern, but into civil rights action after the example of Dr. Martin Luther King, Jr. After successfully motivating black citizens to attend a protest in Bayonne, Jimmy dies a martyr's death.

Jules Raynard, an elderly white man, godfather to Tee Bob Samson and "like a second father" to Robert Samson, Sr. Jules, a big man with white hair and a red face, apparently an asthmatic, intervenes in the crisis triggered by Tee Bob's suicide. A man of intelligence and compassion, Jules speaks truths with Jane about the insidious effects of institutional racism on modern young people. Jane respects Jules more than any other white person.

Albert Cluveau, a Cajun ne'er-do-well and paid assassin who murders Ned Douglass. Pock-faced and bowlegged, with patchy, unkempt white hair and watery blue eyes, Cluveau admits dispassionately to Jane to killing numerous people, both black and white. Oddly attracted to Jane, Cluveau seeks her company, runs errands for her, and sips coffee and fishes with her. He shows neither hesitation nor remorse about shooting Ned, even knowing that Jane loves Ned as her son. Believing afterward that Jane has put a curse on him, Cluveau dies terrified, in a delusion of being attacked by demons.

Robert Samson, Sr., the owner of the Samson plantation and father of Tee Bob. He defends the values and attitudes of the Old South. Robert is a tall, thin man with brown hair and gray eyes. Like his natural son, Timmy Henderson, Robert is high-spirited and loves practical jokes. Robert is part of the racist status quo. He is not personally vicious, but he lacks any sympathy for black civil rights.

Tee Bob, the name by which **Robert Samson, Jr.**, is called. He is the legal heir and only child of Robert Samson, Sr. He commits suicide after falling deeply in love with the mulatto schoolteacher on his father's plantation. Childlike in appearance (though a college student), with a soft red mouth; large, sorrowful eyes; and fair, smooth skin and a beardless face, Tee Bob's love for Mary Agnes LeFabre transcends racial boundaries and social mores. His love is rebuked by the adults, both black and white, as well as by his closest friend, leading Tee Bob to take his own life.

Mary Agnes LeFabre, the mulatto teacher on the Samson plantation and the object of Tee Bob's love. Beautiful, of medium height, fair-skinned, and with long black hair, Mary Agnes resembles the people of Italian and Sicilian descent living in the Bayonne area. Mary Agnes perceives Tee Bob's basic decency and enjoys his boyish attention from a respectful distance, but she rejects Tee Bob after he confesses his love for her; she knows that they cannot be together. She is forced to leave the state in anonymity after Tee Bob's suicide.

Timmy Henderson, Robert Samson, Sr.'s, natural child by a black woman, Verda Henderson. Tall and thin, with reddish-brown hair and brown eyes, Timmy even has his father's hook nose. Beyond the striking physical resemblance, Timmy has his father's personality. His confusing identity and confused social status lead Timmy into a violent confrontation with a jealous white overseer. For Timmy's own safety, Robert sends him away from the plantation. Timmy's character and story powerfully convey the destructive effects of the South's institutionalized racism.

Amma Dean Samson, Robert Sr.'s wife, the mistress of Samson plantation. Mrs. Samson comes across as the domestic heart of the Samson enterprise, worrying about the supervision of the black staff and keeping a nervous watch over Tee Bob. She is resigned to the existence of Timmy Henderson and allows him to be Tee Bob's playmate and companion. She is devastated by Tee Bob's suicide, even though Jane tried to warn her of his love for Mary Agnes.

The narrator, a black history teacher who travels to the Samson plantation to interview Miss Jane in 1962. Although more a presence than a developed character, the narrator provides the frame story for Jane's dramatic autobiography. The narrator also establishes the importance of Jane's life and story as the oral history of all black Americans in the South.

— *David W. Pitre*

THE AUTUMN OF THE PATRIARCH
(El otoño del patriarca)

Author: Gabriel García Márquez (1928-   )
First published: 1975
Genre: Novel

Locale: An unnamed Caribbean country
Time: Late nineteenth and early twentieth centuries
Plot: Parable

The patriarch, also called **the general**, the **"All Pure,"** the **"Magnificent,"** and so on, an unnamed Latin American dictator who is somewhere between the ages of 107 and 232. At one point, he writes a note to himself reading "my name is Zacarias" (sah-kah-REE-ahs), but because this event occurs after his senility has progressed, the writing of the note, like many other events in the novel, is suspect. Superstitious, paranoid, and ruthless, illiterate but peasant-shrewd, he rules from a palace that has been converted into a marketplace. It is overrun with soldiers, prostitutes, cows, and lepers seeking miraculous cures to be bestowed by the patriarch. The state of his palace is that of the nation, and the decrepitude of both palace and nation results from and mirrors the patriarch's deteriorating mental state. The general has the huge flat feet of an elephant, a herniated testicle that whistles at night, and no lines on his smooth hands (rendering him immune to prophecy). In a sense, he is the only character in the novel, because all other characters are rendered in relation to him and the novel fluctuates between third-person reports of his actions, first-person statements made to the patriarch, and first-person interior monologue of the general's responses to characters and events. He is the history of his nation, and as he becomes increasingly senile, he even remembers the arrival of Europeans in the New World. These memories are never convincingly proven or refuted. The novel begins with and repeatedly returns to the discovery of his body, mutilated beyond recognition by vultures in the presidential palace.

Manuela Sánchez (mahn-WEH-lah SAHN-chehs), a woman from an impoverished background whose supernatural beauty astounds the nation. The patriarch dances a waltz with her out of ceremonial obligation, then gradually becomes obsessed with her to the extent that he has reveille played at three in the morning and changes the nation's clocks to distract him from his nocturnal fascination with her. The patriarch courts her in the traditional manner, going to her house with presents, but also rebuilds entire neighborhoods to elevate her slum origins. She disappears during a total eclipse of the sun, and the general's agents are unable to locate her, although rumors abound.

Bendición Alvarado (behn-dee-see-OHN ahl-vah-RAH-doh), the patriarch's mother by an unknown father, a former prostitute who paints common birds in order to sell them as exotic songbirds. During most of her son's reign, she lives frugally in a house in the suburbs of the capital city, coming to the palace to clean up after and criticize her son. She serves to keep him in touch with his peasant roots, deflating much of the pomp and ceremony that grows about the general's person. He nurses her during her fatal illness, washing her pustulated sores with various quack remedies. After her death, her son has her embalmed and sends her corpse on a tour of the provinces. Rumors of her miraculous preservation lead to his insistence on her sainthood. This demand results in his expulsion of the Catholic church from the nation, the expropriation of church property, and the institution of Bendición Alvarado as a "civil saint." She persists in his increasingly senile memory as the last person other than himself he remembers.

Leticia Mercedes María Nazareno (leh-TEE-see-ah mehr-SEH-dehs mah-REE-ah nah-sah-REH-noh), the patriarch's wife, a former nun. A stocky girl, she is noticed, in a crowd of nuns, by the patriarch during the exodus of the church from the nation. His notice of her is enough to convince his agents to kidnap her and ship her back, stripped, to his bedchamber. He keeps her there for two years before they consummate their affair, after which she becomes the power behind his throne. With much difficulty, she teaches the patriarch to read. As a result of her influence, the cult of his mother is overthrown in favor of a reinstitution of the Catholic church; yet flowers wilt, vegetables rot, and meat festers at her touch. During the Catholic marriage ceremony that will legitimate the heir she carries, she gives birth at the altar just as the archbishop asks for the bride's response. As time passes, she gradually becomes less spiritual; as she yields to the material benefits of being the patriarch's concubine, her passion is spent in shopping at the expense of the government's credit (a ritual that is controlled by the actions of the presidential guard, who occupy the bazaar before she can arrive). Her extravagance in shopping threatens to bankrupt the already insolvent government. In a plot laid by a cabal of the ruling junta, she is torn to pieces in the marketplace, along with the patriarch's son and heir, by dogs trained to attack her outfit and the heir's uniform. A purge ensues.

Patricio Aragonés (pah-TREE-see-oh ah-rah-gohn-EHS), the general's perfect double, who is arrested in the provinces for impersonating the leader and purveying spurious miracle cures. He loyally serves the general as a stand-in (after having his feet flattened with a mallet), but his naturally lighthearted and outgoing personality gradually transforms into the taciturn and brutal nature of the general. His services hasten the growth of the general's reputation for ubiquity, a major part of the general's mystique that eventually will confound any attempts to make sense of the nation's history. When Aragonés is fatally poisoned (relatively early in the patriarch's reign), he castigates the general in a deathbed speech; the general uses the confusion following the fake state funeral to launch another of his political purges. Aragonés' death presages and becomes confused with that of the patriarch, further muddling efforts by the general's countrymen to make sense of events.

General Rodrigo de Aguilar (rrohd-REE-goh deh ah-gee-LAHR), an artilleryman and academy graduate, the general's right-hand man who serves as minister of defense, director of state security, and commander of the presidential guard. His loyalty and friendship to the patriarch make him a stable reference point in the swirl of conspiracy and cabal that surrounds the government; he even has been granted the privilege of beating the patriarch at dominoes after losing his right arm to a would-be assassin's bomb. During a period of political unrest, he is late for a palace dinner held in honor of the high command; his arrival is to signal the final revolt against the dictator. After the officers fret for a while, General Rodrigo de Aguilar is brought in on a silver tray, cooked and stuffed; the general doles out equal portions to each officer present.

José Ignacio Saenz de la Barra (hoh-SAY eeg-NAH-see-oh sayns deh lah BAH-rrah), sometimes called **Nacho** (NAH-choh), a sadistic torturer. Described as a "dazzling and haughty man" and an impeccable dresser who always travels with a huge Doberman on a leash, he emerges late in the general's rule to bring the patriarch's realm into the twentieth century of systematic (rather than arbitrary) torture and totalitarian government. To fill the bags full of human heads that he insists on bringing the general, he butchers the patriarch's adversaries, friends, and those who are neutral, seemingly impartially, as he assumes full control of the new secret police that will, in time, come to dominate the government. The rise of de la Barra, as a representative of the old aristrocratic classes, is the final movement in the process that has brought the patriarch's revolution full circle: Any reforms or changes brought by the revolution have been gradually effaced by time and events. Nacho himself is killed in a popular uprising, instigated by the patriarch to forestall a military coup; the torturer's body is mutilated and strung up in a public square.

Emanuel (eh-mahn-WEHL), the patriarch's infant son. At birth, he is appointed a major general "with jurisdiction and command"; he shows an uncanny aptitude for politics, ceremony, and diplomacy that belies his years. He is killed with his mother by dogs trained to attack his uniform.

— *David Pringle*

AVALOVARA

Author: Osman Lins (1924-1978)
First published: 1973
Genre: Novel

Locale: Pompeii; France; Holland; Italy; Germany; England; and São Paulo, Recife, and Rio Grande do Sul, Brazil
Time: 200 B.C., 1908-1940, and 1938-1970
Plot: Existentialism

Abel (ah-BEHL), a writer from Northeastern Brazil, where he was born in 1935. He is a student in Paris at the age of twenty-seven, then a cashier at the Brazilian Fiscal Commission in Recife. He makes love with three women at different times in his life. He is married but separated from a woman who kills herself. He is murdered by Hayano.

Anneliese Roos (Rose), his German lover in Paris, where she has been since 1951, though she has worked as a receptionist in Amsterdam. She leaves Abel for her husband, who is in a Lausanne sanatorium.

Cecília (seh-SEE-lee-ah), Abel's androgynous Brazilian lover in Recife. She works for hospital social services. Her brothers, one a policeman, beat her and Abel. Pregnant by Abel, she dies in an accident.

Ⱶ, his twenty-three- or thirty-two-year-old lover in São Paulo. Reared by her grandparents, she married Hayano when she was still in school and attempted suicide on her wedding night. Her lovemaking with Abel is rendered in strong physical detail. During lovemaking, she recalls her previous life of first love, husband, grandparents, and feeling for the bird Avalovara. She is killed with Abel by her husband, who finds them in sexual embrace.

The Fat Woman, Abel's mother, who had been a prostitute since 1929, when she was fifteen years old. She was married to

The Treasurer at the age of nineteen but refused to give up sleeping with other men; she has mothered many children by different men.

Raul Nogueira de Albuquerque e Castro (rah-EWL noh-GAY-rah deh AHL-bew-kehr-keh eh CAHS-troh), called **The Treasurer**, who is married to The Fat Woman. He helped care for her children while working for a bank. He is killed by a truck, and it is unknown whether it was suicide or an accident.

Publius Ubonius (PEW-blee-uhs ew-BOH-nee-uhs), a Pompeiian merchant in 200 B.C. He offers Loreius freedom if he invents a phrase that can be read left to right and backward.

Loreius (loh-RAY-uhs), a slave of Publius Ubonius who discovers the mysterious phrase that unites the novel. He kills himself after his phrase is stolen.

Tyche (TI-kee), a Pompeiian courtesan who steals the mystical phrase from Loreius and sells it to Ubonius.

Julius Heckethorn, a German clockmaker, mathematician, harpsichordist, and expert on Mozart, born in 1908. His father was British and his mother German. He was shot as a traitor in 1939 by Germans in Holland. He makes the clock, which he began constructing in 1933, found in the room where ♀ and Abel make love. It was brought to Brazil from Europe by the wife of the Brazilian ambassador after the war.

Heidi Lampl, who marries Julius Heckethorn in 1930.

Olavo Hayano (oh-LAH-voh HAY-ah-noh), the husband of ♀, whom he met when they were both children. According to ♀, he is a "yolyp," or sterile freak of nature. A Brazilian soldier, he commands a detachment during the funeral for Natividade and murders his wife and Abel.

Natividade (nah-tee-vee-DAH-deh), a black maid in the Hayano household, a virgin when she dies at the age of seventy-five. Her funeral procession winds through the streets of São Paulo during the novel.

Hermelinda (ehr-meh-LEEN-dah) and

Hermenilda (ehr-meh-NEEL-dah), old women of Recife. Though not twins, they do look alike. They sew, surrounded by cats, and introduce Cecília to Abel.

— *Richard D. McGhee*

AWAKE AND SING!

Author: Clifford Odets (1906-1963)
First published: 1935
Genre: Drama

Locale: The East Bronx, New York
Time: Early 1930's
Plot: Social criticism

Bessie Berger, a working-class Jewish American housewife struggling to hold her family together during the Great Depression of the 1930's. Bessie values the appearance of respectability above all else. Her greatest fear is that she and her family might be put out of their home and thrown into the street, as an old lady who lived near them has been. Bessie is domineering and self-righteous. She does not think deeply. Her life is centered on her family, three generations of which live in a cramped apartment in the Bronx.

Myron Berger, Bessie's husband, a follower rather than a leader. Myron is a broken man, completely controlled by Bessie, who is much stronger than he is. He once studied law at night school but did not complete his studies. He tries innocently to overcome the hardships of the Depression by buying chances on the Irish Sweepstakes and by betting a few dollars on a horse, convinced that the government would not let such enterprises be crooked. His chances of winning are his only tangible hopes for the future.

Ralph Berger, Myron and Bessie's idealistic son, who scrapes by on the sixteen dollars a week he earns only by living at home. He contributes much-needed funds to the family coffers. He has a girlfriend, Blanche, but cannot entertain any realistic idea of marrying her because of his financial situation. Bessie's moral posture, the appearance of respectability at any price, appalls Ralph, a decent person who has never had an even break. When he was a child, there was never money to have his teeth fixed or to buy him a pair of roller skates he wanted. Now that he is earning money, little has changed. He still barely survives economically, and he still cannot live his own life.

Hennie Berger, Myron and Bessie's daughter, who has a streak of independence in her, although she is slowly being crushed by the same economic forces and insecurities that threaten the rest of the family. When the family's boarder, Moe Axelrod, gets Hennie pregnant, Bessie, to preserve the appearance of respectability, forces Hennie into a marriage with the unsuspecting immigrant Sam Feinschreiber, whom Hennie does not love. She finally abandons her family and compromises her child's future by running away with Moe, thereby asserting her independence but also demonstrating her self-centered willfulness.

Jacob, Bessie's father, who lives with the family. He and Ralph share a philosophical kinship. Jacob quotes the sayings of Karl Marx, using Marx to support his contention that families such as this one should not exist. Jacob and Bessie are at opposite poles, with Jacob the almost total idealist and Bessie the pragmatist. Jacob finally commits suicide by plunging off the roof of the Bergers' apartment building, having written his small insurance policy over to Ralph so that Ralph can have a new beginning.

Uncle Morty, Bessie's affluent, cigar-smoking, womanizing brother and Jacob's son. He comes to the Bergers' apartment so that his father can cut his hair. He represents the practical businessman who has ceased to be a person. He is what the people he does business with require him to be. He is loud, rich, and insensitive, a character corrupted by the very capitalistic system that has made him affluent. He refers to Jacob as a nut.

Moe Axelrod, the Bergers' sexually tempting boarder, a ladies' man who lost one leg in the war and now lives on a decent disability pension. Moe is no more sensitive than Uncle Morty. He may not be rich, but he has the security of his pension, which is important in the bleak days of the Depression. Having impregnated Hennie and refused to marry her, he proceeds to destroy the marriage her mother arranged for her by virtually forcing her to leave her husband and baby to run off with him to an uncertain—and likely not very enduring—future.

Sam Feinschreiber, a lonely immigrant with whom Myron works. Myron brings Sam home to dinner to meet Hennie, who has no interest in him. Sam, however, is the vehicle through which Bessie can preserve her family's respectability after Hennie becomes pregnant.

Schlosser, the superintendent of the building in which the Bergers live. He informs the family of Jacob's suicide.

Schlosser is German. His wife ran away with another man twenty years earlier, leaving Schlosser to rear their daughter, as Hennie is about to do. The daughter did not turn out well, and Schlosser has lived a life of desperation and frustration for two decades.

— *R. Baird Shuman*

THE AWAKENING

Author: Kate Chopin (1851-1904)
First published: 1899
Genre: Novel

Locale: New Orleans, Louisiana, and vicinity
Time: Late nineteenth century
Plot: Domestic realism

Edna Pontellier (pohn-tehl-YAY), a sensitive, impressionable twenty-eight-year-old who feels out of place in the French-Creole society into which she has married. She has two small children whom she loves, although she feels temperamentally unsuited for the confining roles of wife and mother, which are the only roles available to women of her social class in the late nineteenth century. She has regarded sex as an unenjoyable if not actually unpleasant wifely duty and has been unaware of her repressed sexuality until the time that the novel opens. Her whole life is changed by her physical and psychological "awakening."

Léonce Pontellier (lay-OHNS), Edna's husband, who is forty years old, kind, and attentive, as well as being an exceptionally good provider for her and her two children. He is absorbed in business affairs, however, and prefers to associate with men. He is often smoking, drinking, and going off to play cards with cronies. He does not understand his wife; he regards her as a valuable possession, a sex object, and the mother of his children.

Adèle Ratignolle (ah-DEHL ra-tee-NYOHL), a beautiful young married woman who is Edna's friend and confidante. She serves as a foil to Edna because she is perfectly content in her role of wife and mother of three children. She thoroughly understands Robert Lebrun's flirtatious playacting as a *cavalier servente* but fears that Edna, who is not of Creole extraction, will take it too seriously. Adèle also serves as a spokesperson for the strict mores of Creole society. At the onset of her "awakening," Edna feels a sexual attraction to Adèle before falling passionately in love with Robert.

Robert Lebrun, a handsome and emotional man, twenty-

six years old, who enjoys the company of women and can communicate with them much better than men like Léonce Pontellier because he shares feminine interests in culture and natural beauty. He likes to play at the game of love with married women and is allowed to do so because it is taken for granted that he, as well as the women involved, will conform to the strict rules of chaste behavior of their conservative Creole society. Unlike the passionate Edna Pontellier, Robert is unable to defy the moral laws of his society. When he realizes that his playacting at romance has involved himself and Edna in a terrible spiritual crisis, he flees, leading to Edna's suicide.

Alcée Arobin (al-SAY ah-roh-BA[N]), a handsome young man of fashion who is cheerful and likable but "not overburdened with depth of thought or feeling." He functions as a foil to Robert Lebrun. Alcée also is in love with Edna but is far more aggressive in his courtship behavior and apparently seduces her, although the author limits her description of such interludes to some kissing and fondling, leaving the rest to the reader's imagination. Edna does not love Alcée but puts up with him as a substitute for Robert, who is absent in Mexico during much of the novel.

Mademoiselle Reisz (rayz), a fine pianist who has dedicated her life to her art. She lives alone and has few friends.

Dr. Mandelet (man-deh-LAY), the retired Pontellier family doctor, better known for his insights into human nature than for his professional skills. He recognizes that Edna is troubled and invites her confidence. He understands the plight of women.

— *Bill Delaney*

THE AWKWARD AGE

Author: Henry James (1843-1916)
First published: 1899
Genre: Novel

Locale: London, England, and outlying estates
Time: The 1890's
Plot: Social realism

Mr. Longdon, a man in his fifties who has spent most of his life remembering the great love of his youth, Lady Julia. When he discovers that Lady Julia's granddaughter, Nanda Brookenham, is almost a reincarnation of his beloved, he determines to befriend her. Doing so causes him to become immersed in the affairs of Nanda's family and her social circle, which Longdon considers morally corrupt. He schemes to convince Nanda to leave her parents' home in London and come to live with him at his country estate.

Fernanda (Nanda) Brookenham, a nineteen-year-old woman who has developed a sense of independence and an appreciation for the ways of the world despite efforts of her mother and others to keep her ignorant of the intrigues of the adults around her. She insists on choosing her own friends and establishing her own adult relationships. Her love for Gus Vanderbank ends unhappily when she discovers that he is unwilling to settle into a conventional marriage, forgoing a lifestyle that includes an affair with her mother. Eventually, she finds in Mr. Longdon a person who seems to be above the pettiness and self-centeredness of her mother and her mother's friends.

Mrs. Brookenham, Nanda's mother and the daughter of the woman Mr. Longdon has loved for years. She is at the center of a social circle where old-fashioned moral values are held in contempt. Intent on preserving her relationship with the handsome young bachelor Gus Vanderbank, she conspires with the Duchess and others to arrange partnerships among members of her set that will permit each of them to satisfy personal desires while maintaining a façade of respectability. Her enigmatic relationship with her daughter Nanda, who is also in love with Vanderbank, drives her to an arrangement with Longdon to separate Nanda from the man both of them desire.

Gustavus Vanderbank, a handsome bachelor considered by most a highly prized catch for the right young woman. Though attracted to Nanda, he is unable to make a commitment to marry her, principally because doing so would force him to give up a lifestyle he finds comfortable. Part of that lifestyle includes engagement in an affair with Mrs. Brookenham, though the details of that arrangement are never made clear to either the other characters in the novel or to the reader.

The Duchess (Cousin Jane), a cousin to Mr. Brookenham and close friend of his wife. Together with Mrs. Brookenham, she arranges and promotes the many liaisons among the members of her social set. She is determined to find an appropriate match for her niece Aggie and manipulates the younger members of her group until she is able to convince Mr. Mitchett to marry the girl. She is engaged in a long-standing affair with Lord Petherton, but few discuss this matter except with extreme discretion.

Agnesina (Aggie), the niece of the Duchess, a sixteen-year-old ingenue who has been brought to England from Italy. Naïve, passive, and quiescent, she allows herself to be man-aged by her aunt, finally marrying Mr. Mitchett to please both the Duchess and Nanda, who actively promotes the match.

Harold Brookenham, the Brookenhams' dissolute son. Infected with *ennui*, he has no interest in life and no ambition to succeed in any profession. He is content to rely on the kindness of friends such as Mr. Mitchett and on the sympathy of his mother for his support. Knowing that his mother cannot dismiss him from her life, he takes advantage shamelessly of her devotion to keep from having to pay back his debts or to become a useful member of society.

Edward Brookenham, husband of Mrs. Brookenham and father of Nanda and Harold. A spineless figure, he seems self-conscious of his inferior social status and exceptionally accommodating of his wife's intrigues as a matchmaker and go-between in the affairs of her male and female associates.

Mr. Mitchett (Mitchy), a well-to-do young man who is in love with Nanda. Although he pursues her in vain, he is willing to be guided by her directives, even to the point of marrying Aggie to please Nanda. Because he is rich, others like Harold Brookenham and Lord Petherton attach themselves to him to sponge off his largesse.

Lord Petherton, a degenerate nobleman who depends on Mr. Mitchett for income. He has been the lover of the Duchess but eventually turns his interest to Aggie after she marries Mr. Mitchett.

Tishy Gendron, a friend of Nanda who is considered unacceptable by many in the Brookenhams' social circle. Mrs. Brookenham and others fear that Nanda is being corrupted through her association with Tishy, who invites socially questionable characters to her home and who permits the young Nanda to engage in such reprehensible acts as reading lurid novels.

— *Laurence W. Mazzeno*

THE AXE
(Olav Audunssøn i Hestviken *and* Olav Audunssøn og hans børn)

Author: Sigrid Undset (1882-1949)
First published: 1925
Genre: Novel

Locale: Norway
Time: Late thirteenth century
Plot: Historical

Olav Audunsson, the master of Hestviken, who is betrothed to Ingunn Steinfinnsdatter from infancy. After slaying a kinsman of hers in a quarrel, Olav is proclaimed an outlaw, and thus is unable to marry Ingunn, though he has been sleeping with her. Returning home much later, he finds her pregnant by another man. He kills the man in secret—a deed he can never confess, lest disclosure of his motive result in Ingunn's shame.

Steinfinn Toresson, the father of Ingunn and foster father of Olav. In love with a woman promised to another, he steals her away. They live together until everyone is reconciled to their wedding, at which time their daughter Ingunn is three years old.

Ingebjorg Jonsdatter, Steinfinn's wife. Her rejected suitor comes years afterwards to take revenge on Steinfinn, whom he shames before his household. Steinnfinn swears not to sleep with his wife until he gets vengeance; the first opportunity comes years later, and Steinfinn kills his rival in combat. Ingebjorg dies in her sleep that very night, and Steinfinn later dies of his wounds.

Ingunn Steinfinnsdatter, betrothed to Olav. Her child by another man is given to a forester's wife at birth, and at last Ingunn and Olav are married.

Arnvid Finnsson, Steinfinn's kinsman. He gives much help to the romance between Ingunn and Olav.

Kolbein Toresson, Steinfinn's gloomy half brother. He is relentlessly opposed to Ingunn's marrying Olav.

Einar Kolbeinsson, who is killed by Olav in a quarrel between the Kolbeinssons and Arnvid and Olav. As a result, Olav is outlawed and must leave Ingunn.

Teit, an Icelander and a merry, pert clerk. Ingunn succumbs to him during Olav's absence. He fathers her child and is killed by Olav.

Eirik, the illegitimate son of Teit and Ingunn.

Tore Toresson, the father of Steinfinn. He sends his son to the royal bodyguard at Bergen, where Steinfinn first sees Ingebjorg.

Queen Ingebjorg, with whom Ingebjorg Jonsdatter came from Denmark.

King Magnus, who has promised Ingebjorg to Mattias.

Mattias Haraldsson, Ingebjorg's rejected promised bridegroom. He takes revenge by shaming Steinfinn, who later kills him in combat.

Tora Steinfinnsdatter, Ingunn's sister.

Hallvard Steinfinnsson and

Jon Steinfinnsson, younger brothers of Ingunn.

Audun Ingolfsson, of Hestviken, the father of Olav. Told he is soon to die, he holds Steinfinn to an agreement made during a drinking bout that Olav and Ingunn shall marry. The orphaned Olav is then reared by Steinfinn.

Haakon Gautsson, the husband of Tora.

Bishop Thorfinn, a stern but just man. Were it not for Olav's slaying of Einar, the bishop might have succeeded in helping Olav and Ingunn to marry, despite her kinsmen's opposition.

Earl Alf Erlingsson, Queen Ingebjorg's liegeman, in whose train Olav returns briefly to make peace with the Kolbeinssons. Upon the queen's death, her son proclaims Alf and his men outlaws.

Lady Magnhild, who gives Ingunn's child to a foster mother.

B

BAAL

Author: Bertolt Brecht (1898-1956)
First published: 1922
Genre: Drama

Locale: Augsburg, Germany, and the surrounding region
Time: c. 1911
Plot: Tragedy

Baal (bahl), a poet, named for a Semitic-Phoenician god. He embodies the vitality and amorality of the fertility principle the god represented. The god's association with storms and with the life-giving properties of water is reflected in the violence and fleetingness of Baal's passions. In the moral sphere, Baal is exploitive, murderous, and prone to drunkenness. He is tied to no human or ethical obligation. In the natural sphere, he insists on enjoying the pleasures and richness of the world.

Ekart (EH-kahrt), a composer, a bear of a man who entices Baal to follow him into the forest and become his lover. Although it is his animalistic nature that attracts Baal, he is vulnerable to social ties, as evidenced by his sympathy for and desire to care for Sophie and his commitment to composing a Mass. His resistance to Baal's domination inevitably provokes the rage in which Baal murders him.

Johannes Schmidt (yoh-HAHN-nehs shmiht), Baal's friend, a young man bound by convention and propriety. He cannot consummate his desire for Johanna because he is afraid of her innocence and the social consequences. After her death, he fades into a drunken wraith of his former self.

Johanna Reiher (yoh-HAHN-nah RI-hehr), Johannes' fiancée, a seventeen-year-old virgin. She is at once repulsed by and drawn to Baal. Overcome by shame and fear after Baal seduces her and then tells her that she means no more to him than any other woman's body, she runs from his room and drowns herself in the river Laach.

Sophie Barger, another virgin, who is dragged by Baal into his room. Although she protests his advances, she is unable to resist his allure. While pregnant, she follows Baal and Ekart into the woods. When Ekart offers to care for her if she will deny her love for Baal, she refuses and is abandoned in the forest. She is almost totally defined by her sensuality, which lures her into Baal's arms, provokes her into pregnancy, and prohibits her from repudiating her love for Baal.

Mech, a timber tycoon and publisher who is interested in financing the publication of Baal's poems until Baal begins to seduce his wife, Emily. Mech's exploitation of nature—especially his destruction of trees, which are a symbol of life in the play—and his gluttonous consumption of food indicate that his interest in Baal's poetry is an attempt to devour his energy.

Emily Mech, his wife, who attracts Baal's attention with her beautiful white arms, which she shows off to advantage when she plays the harmonium. Although Baal treats her with contempt once he is tired of her, she remains enthralled by her desire for him.

Dr. Piller, a critic who brings Baal together with Mech. Although appreciative of Baal's poetry, he is repulsed by his behavior.

Mjurk (myurk), who owns the Night Cloud, a small café. He hires Baal to sing, but when he refuses to supply the poet with any more brandy, Baal breaks his contract by escaping through the toilet. Mjurk's inability to maintain any control over Baal parallels Mech's earlier failure to co-opt the poet.

— *Jane Anderson Jones*

BABBITT

Author: Sinclair Lewis (1885-1951)
First published: 1922
Genre: Novel

Locale: Zenith, a fictional Midwestern town
Time: The 1920's
Plot: Social satire

George F. Babbitt, a prosperous real-estate dealer in Zenith, a typical American city. He is the standardized product of modern American civilization, a member of the Boosters' Club, hypnotized by all the slogans of success, enthralled by material possessions, envious of those who have more, patronizing towards those who have less, yet dimly aware that his life is unsatisfactory. His high moment comes when, after delivering a speech at a real-estate convention, he is asked to take part in a political campaign against Seneca Doane, a liberal lawyer who is running for mayor. As a result of his campaign efforts, Babbitt is elected vice-president of the Boosters. His self-satisfaction is shattered when his one real friend, Paul Riesling, shoots his nagging wife and is sent to prison. For the first time, Babbitt begins to doubt the values of American middle-class life. He has a love affair with a client, Mrs. Judique, and becomes involved with her somewhat bohemian friends; he publicly questions some of the tenets of Boosterism; he refuses to join the Good Citizens' League. But the pressure of public opinion becomes too much for him; when his wife is taken ill, his brief revolt collapses, and he returns to the standardized world of the Boosters' Club.

Myra Babbitt, his colorless wife, whom he married because he could not bear to hurt her feelings. She lives only for him and the children.

Verona Babbitt, their dumpy daughter. Just out of college, she is a timid intellectual whose mild unconventionality angers her father. He is relieved when she marries Kenneth Escott.

Theodore (Ted) Babbitt, their son. A typical product of the American school system, he hates study and the thought of college. He elopes with Eunice Littlefield, thus winning his father's secret admiration, for he has at least dared to do what he wanted.

Paul Riesling, Babbitt's most intimate friend since college days. With the soul of a musician, he has been trapped into a lifetime of manufacturing tar-roofing, and he is burdened with a shrewish wife. Goaded to desperation, he shoots her; although she lives, he is sent to prison.

Zilla Riesling, Paul's nagging wife. With a vicious disposition that is made worse by having too much time on her hands, she finally prompts Paul to shoot her.

Mrs. Daniel "Tanis" Judique, a widow with whom Babbitt has a brief affair as a part of his revolt against conventionality.

Seneca Doane, a liberal lawyer, the anathema of all the solid businessmen of Zenith.

William Washington Eathorne, a rich, conservative banker. He represents the real power in Zenith.

Charles McKelvey and

Lucille McKelvey, wealthy members of Zenith's smart set. The Babbitts are hopeful of being accepted socially by the McKelveys but do not succeed.

Ed Overbrook and

Mrs. Overbrook, a down-at-the-heels couple. They are hopeful of being accepted socially by the Babbitts but do not succeed.

The Reverend Dr. John Jennison Drew, the efficient, high-powered pastor of Babbitt's church.

Vergil Gunch, a successful coal dealer. He is prominent in all the civic organizations to which Babbitt belongs.

T. Cholmondeley "Chum" Frink, a member of Babbitt's social group. He is a popular poet whose work is syndicated throughout the country.

Howard Littlefield, Babbitt's next-door neighbor. An economist for the Zenith Street Traction Company, he can prove to everyone's satisfaction that Zenith is the best of all possible worlds.

Eunice Littlefield, his flapper daughter. She elopes with Ted Babbitt, to the public surprise and indignation of both families but to Babbitt's secret delight.

Kenneth Escott, a newspaper reporter. After a tepid courtship, he finally marries Verona Babbitt.

BABEL-17

Author: Samuel R. Delany (1942-   )
First published: 1966
Genre: Novel

Locale: Aboard various spaceships and on several planets of the Alliance
Time: Distant future
Plot: Science fiction

Rydra Wong, the protagonist, the most famous poet in five galaxies. Although she is only twenty-six years old, she already is considered to be the voice of her age. In addition to writing poetry, Rydra is a skilled cryptographer, a linguist, and an interstellar captain. These fields of accomplishment, as diverse as they seem, are all aided by Rydra's total verbal recall. She always had this talent to some degree but developed it rapidly after a severe illness in her youth. Rydra also is telepathic and frequently knows what people will say before they say it. Her own assessment of this skill, however, is that she is merely "reading" the expressions of others with great precision. By the time that she was twelve, Rydra had learned seven Earth languages and five extraterrestrial tongues. In the intervening years, Rydra studied many other forms of communication, including six languages used by the Invaders. She is considered very beautiful and has high cheekbones, copper-colored pupils, and East Asian features. Her hair is long and frequently cascades over her shoulders. Five years earlier, Rydra was part of a triple, a form of marriage among three people. One of the partners has died and another, suffering from an incurable illness, has been placed in suspended animation. She is enlisted by the military of the Alliance to break the secret code called Babel-17. She discov-

ers that the language is a version of the enemy within, a parasitical system of signification that causes the human host to become a saboteur against the Alliance. Her improved version of the language, Babel-18, shifts the balance of power to the Alliance.

Dr. Markus T'Mwarba (Mocky), a psychologist and teacher. When Rydra was twelve, she was sent to T'Mwarba for treatment in psychotherapy and neurotherapy. Since that time, they have become close friends. T'Mwarba holds a black belt in Aikido and is the one person in whom Rydra places complete trust.

Danil D. Appleby, a customs official who helps Rydra assemble the crew of the *Rimbaud*. With his crew-cut red hair and wire-rimmed glasses, Appleby is, at first, the very image of the punctilious bureaucrat. After meeting Rydra, however, he develops a new sense of confidence and humor, coming to enjoy wrestling matches and ultimately even undergoing cosmetisurgery to have a mechanical dragon implanted in his shoulder as a decoration.

General Forester, the officer supervising the deciphering of Babel-17. Forester is a large man in his fifties; he is authoritarian and has a brisk and efficient manner. He falls in love with Rydra almost immediately upon meeting her.

Mollya Twa, the Navigator-One on the twenty-one-person crew of Rydra's spaceship, the *Rimbaud*. An attractive woman from Pan Africa, Mollya had committed suicide (being placed in suspended animation) seven years earlier, when her two conavigators were killed. Rydra, in need of a Navigator-One, has Mollya restored to life for the mission. Mollya has short, graphite-colored hair. Initially, she speaks only Kiswahili, but she learns English quickly.

Calli, the Navigator-Two on the *Rimbaud* crew. Calli seems rough and threatening upon first acquaintance, but he is competent and good-hearted. His face is heavily pockmarked, and he has mechanical lights implanted all over his chest, shoulders, arms, and legs.

Ron, the Navigator-Three. A small, thin man of about nineteen, Ron was the youngest member of an earlier triple, which had also included Calli. As a result, he is the one who grieves most deeply over the loss of their former Navigator-One, Cathy. Towheaded and sapphire-eyed, Ron has muscles that are sharply defined. His only cosmetisurgery is a rose that emerges from his shoulder.

Brass, who is half human and half animal. He is the pilot of the *Rimbaud*. Brass is very muscular, with brass claws, yellow plush paws, golden eyes, and a mane. While walking, he prefers to move about on all fours. Cosmetisurgically implanted fangs have left Brass unable to pronounce the sound of the letter *p*. He is chosen as pilot for the *Rimbaud* after Rydra watches him wrestle, a skill that illustrates the reflexes of potential pilots.

The Slug, a fat man whose eyes, hair, and thin beard are all black. The Slug moves slowly but thinks quickly and performs a number of supervisory functions on the *Rimbaud*, including that of ship's medic.

Jebel, the pirate captain of the spaceship *Jebel Tarik* ("Jebel's mountain"). Jebel commands a "shadow ship" that hides in the Specelli Snap. He lives by hijacking the ships of the Invaders and, when necessary, those of the Alliance. Jebel is craggy faced and wears outmoded clothing, including a plastic garment that automatically contours to his body like armor. He drapes a deep-piled black cloak over one shoulder and wears high-laced sandals. Jebel's cosmetisurgery includes false silver hair and metallic eyebrows. One thick silver ring hangs from a distended earlobe.

Nyles Ver Dorco, called **The Butcher**, one of the most important crew members on the *Jebel Tarik*. The Butcher is a mysterious figure who has no knowledge of his own past and does not understand the terms (or concepts of) "I" and "you." He is muscular and round-shouldered and wears only a breechcloth. Cocks' spurs, used as brass knuckles, have been grafted onto his wrists and heels. His hair is amber but has been closely shaved. The Butcher is branded with the convicts' mark from the penal caves of Titin. The mission to decipher Babel-17 eventually becomes a mission to determine the Butcher's identity. After he was captured by the Invaders, Babel-17 was implanted in his mind. Following his discovery by Rydra Wong, he is given a new identity that helps him counteract the effects of linguistically induced schizophrenia.

— *Jeffrey L. Buller*

THE BACCHAE
(Bakchai)

Author: Euripides (c. 485-406 B.C.E.)
First performed: c. 405 B.C.E.
Genre: Drama

Locale: Thebes, in Boeotia
Time: Remote antiquity
Plot: Tragedy

Dionysus (di-eh-NI-suhs), also called **Bromius**, **Evius**, and **Bacchus** (BA-kuhs). He is a god of the general fertility of nature and especially of wine. He has been traveling through the world spreading his teachings but has met with opposition at Thebes, where he appears disguised as his own prophet to take measures on the human level to overcome his opponents. He has driven his mother's sisters (he was the son of Semele by Zeus) to frenzy because they refused to recognize him as a god, and they now revel as thyrsus-bearing Bacchantes with the other women of Thebes on the slopes of Mount Cithaeron. Chief of the god's foes was young King Pentheus, who refuses to recognize Dionysus as a god. Appearing at first as the friend of mortals, he is joyful and willing to reason with the young king, even when Pentheus imprisons him in the royal stables. He frees himself and makes one last attempt to convince Pentheus that he must acknowledge Dionysus' divinity and power. Only when Pentheus determines to drive the Bacchantes from the hills by force does Dionysus reveal the opposite aspect of his character. Becoming cruel, ruthless, and cunning, he establishes control over the mind of Pentheus and leads him, disguised as a woman, through the streets of Thebes to Cithaeron, where he is torn apart by the maddened women of his own city, led by Pen-

theus' mother, Agave. At the end of the play, after Agave has returned and has realized what she has done, Dionysus appears to pass the sentence of exile on the family of Pentheus. The most terrible aspect of his character emerges as he extends Pentheus' fate to include the suffering of the old and the innocent.

Pentheus (PEHN-thews), the young, still beardless king of Thebes. He is a puritan with something in his own mind that prevents his seeing any but the extreme aspects, the supposed sexual excesses, of the worship of Dionysus. His opposition to the god is adamant. He imprisons some of the women who follow Dionysus and even the disguised Dionysus himself. When the imprisoned women are miraculously released, he remains angry and scornful. After he determines to move with armed force against the Bacchantes, Dionysus exerts control over him and the young king appears beastly drunk, losing all self-control and self-respect. Disguised as a woman, he is led off by Dionysus to spy, as he thinks, on the Bacchantes. The maddened women fall on him and tear him to pieces.

Agave (uh-GAY-vee), the mother of Pentheus. In a frenzy, she leads the Bacchantes as they tear her son limb from limb under the delusion that he is a lion. Still under her delusion, she first appears carrying her son's mangled head affixed to her thyrsus like a trophy. She praises the gods for guiding her in the deed, inquires after her father, Cadmus, and calls out to Pentheus to come and receive the trophy she has brought. When Cadmus slowly and painfully brings her back to sanity, dazed and perplexed, she realizes what she has done. She is condemned to exile by Dionysus.

Cadmus (KAD-muhs), the father of Agave. He first appears on his way to worship Dionysus, whom he has conventionally accepted as a god for the good of the family, because Dionysus is reputed to be the cousin of Pentheus. He urges his grandson to do the same but is refuted. He next appears, after gathering the mangled remains of his grandson from the slopes of Cithaeron, to bring Agave back to sanity. He

is condemned to exile by Dionysus, even though he protests that such action is too severe.

Tiresias (ti-REE-see-uhs), the blind prophet of Thebes. He appears with Cadmus as they prepare to worship Dionysus. He has cleverly accepted Dionysus while retaining his old beliefs. He is proud of his good sense; he has not reasoned dangerously. He urges Pentheus to do the same.

Ino (I-noh) and

Autonoë (oh-TOHN-oi-ih), Agave's sisters, who help her tear apart Pentheus' body.

Chorus of Asian Bacchae, followers of Dionysus. Their odes in praise of Dionysus present a picture of Dionysus worship in its purer form and contrast with Pentheus' warped ideas.

THE BACHELORS

Author: Muriel Spark (1918-   )
First published: 1960
Genre: Novel

Locale: London, England
Time: Mid-twentieth century
Plot: Social satire

Ronald Bridges, the assistant curator of graphology at a small London museum. As a handwriting expert, he has earned a considerable reputation in the detection of forgeries and occasionally is consulted by the police or asked to appear in court as an expert witness. An epileptic, he is subject to frequent fits. At one point in his life, he sought relief from the disease by volunteering as a subject in a drug test. Unfortunately, his case was one of the few for which the drug was ineffective. During his testimony in the trial of Patrick Seton, he has a seizure.

Martin Bowles, the lawyer who is prosecuting Patrick Seton's case. He lives with his aging mother but also spends time with Isobel Billows, a wealthy widow. His performance in court leads to the guilty verdict in Patrick's case.

Patrick Seton, a spiritualist medium charged with fraudulent conversion and forgery. A thin, pale, anxious-looking man in his mid-fifties, he lives with Alice, who is pregnant with his child. His ability to go into a trance and evoke the spirits of the dead has endeared him to wealthy widows despite the air of suspicion that surrounds his activities. He fakes his devotion to Alice; in reality, he plans to kill her if he is acquitted. His trial reveals that he is indeed a con man, interested only in swindling rich people.

Alice Dawes, a young woman who is a diabetic and is pregnant with Patrick's baby. Enamored with the spiritual atmosphere of Patrick's group, she works as a waitress, hoping for a better life after the baby is born and the trial is over.

Elsie Forrest, a waitress friend of Alice who tries to convince her of Patrick's real nature. Her theft of a forged letter

plays a crucial part in the events leading to the trial.

Freda Flower, a wealthy widow interested in spiritualism. A letter supposedly written by her, authorizing Patrick to use her financial donation, is the central piece of evidence in the trial.

Marlene Cooper, another wealthy widow interested in spiritualism who has formed a special "inner circle" within the spiritualists' group.

Tim Raymond, her nephew, always under her thumb for fear of being cut out of her will and having to go to work for himself.

Ewart Thornton, a teacher who uses his students' examination papers as an excuse for avoiding any involvement more serious than gossip about spiritualism and the affairs of the others.

Walter Prett, an art critic with one set lecture that covers all the art of the Western world.

Matthew Finch, the London correspondent of an Irish newspaper. After an evening spent with Elsie, he falls deeply in love with Alice.

Mike Garland, another clairvoyant, whose spiritual and other activities are highly suspect.

T. W. Sockett, a spiritualistic clergyman, ordained by unusual methods, who gives testimony against Patrick at the trial.

Francis Eccles, a British Council lecturer.

Detective-Inspector Fergusson, the policeman who receives all the random bits of information from the principals in the case. He testifies at the trial.

— *Louise M. Stone*

BACK TO METHUSELAH: A Metabiological Pentateuch

Author: George Bernard Shaw (1856-1950)
First published: 1921
Genre: Drama

Locale: The Garden of Eden, the Middle East, and Britain
Time: The beginning of time to A.D. 31,920
Plot: Play of ideas

"In the Beginning: B.C. 4004"

Adam, the first man, created by the splitting of Lilith into male and female. Adam is dull and plodding, the tradition-

bound agrarian who adheres to conventional morality solely from a lack of curiosity.

Eve, who eagerly eats the Forbidden Fruit to trade the agonies of individual immortality for racial immortality. Eve, the eternally curious, has a compulsion to create. Dissatisfied by both Adam's passivity and Cain's senseless hunger for glory, she yearns for something better.

The Serpent, a wise and beneficent female serpent. She frees Adam and Eve from the burden of immortality and tells them that their wills have the power to create anything they desire.

"The Gospel of the Brothers Barnabas: A.D. 1920"

Franklyn Barnabas, a clerical English gentleman of about fifty.

Conrad Barnabas, Franklyn's brother, a professor of biology. He and Franklyn are preparing to publish their proposal that human life be extended to three hundred years. Their belief is that this change is necessary if humanity is not to destroy itself.

Mr. Joyce Burge, a fifty-year-old former Liberal prime minister.

Lubin, a patriarch of seventy years of age, prime minister before Burge. Lubin and Burge are obvious demonstrations

"The Thing Happens: A.D. 2170"

The archbishop, actually William Haslam of the previous section. Now 283 years old, he still looks 45. His longevity, which he had concealed by faking drowning accidents, is accidentally discovered.

Mrs. Lutestring, the domestic minister. She is actually the parlor maid, now 274 years old. She and the archbishop discuss the difficulty of living in a world without grownups in it. They agree to marry and have long-lived children.

Burge-Lubin, the president of England, a composite of the two politicians in the previous section but hardly an improvement on either of them.

"Tragedy of an Elderly Gentleman, A.D. 3000"

Joseph Popham Bolge Bluebin Barlow, O.M., the **Elderly Gentleman**, a descendant of Burge-Lubin. The British Isles are now reserved for the long-livers. Visitors from the Empire, which now has its capital in Baghdad, visit the British Isles to consult with them. The Elderly Gentleman is at Galway with a party that has come to consult the Oracle. His tragedy is his realization of the infinite foolishness of his own society. Unable to bear returning to his own world and too immature to remain in Britain, he is at last put mercifully to death by the Oracle.

Zoo, a "girl of fifty" who resembles Savvy of Part II. Acting as Barlow's nurse, she is so enraged at his manner that she announces her conversion to the party of Colonizers, who wish to exterminate the short-livers.

Napoleon I, **Cain Adamson Charles**, "the man of des-

Cain, the archetype of the ruling-class man: the destroying man and the exploiting man. Cain demonstrates that it is "the Voice of God" that makes him kill, while it is "the Voice of the Devil" that tells Adam, "Thou shall not kill."

Enoch, the intellectual who, while young, manufactures doctrines to justify Cain's rapacity. Fortunately, Enoch lives long enough to understand "the Voice" more clearly and to repudiate Cain.

Lua, Eve's daughter and Cain's wife. For her own greedy ends, she encourages Cain's conquests.

that short-lived men are too inexperienced to rule rationally. Both dismiss the Barnabas' scheme when they cannot see how it can win votes in the next election.

Cynthia, Franklyn's eighteen-year-old daughter. Because she has grown up without bourgeois manners, she is known as "Savvy," short for "Savage."

William Haslam, a boyish clergyman who is to marry Cynthia. He is one of those destined to live three hundred years.

A parlor maid, who is leaving Franklyn's employ to marry the village woodsman. Although she speaks ironically of only one life to live, she too is to live three hundred years.

Barnabas, the accountant-general, a younger and more commonplace version of Conrad Barnabas. He threatens the long-lived ones with extinction because he fears them and because they upset his actuarial tables.

Confucius, one of the Chinese civil servants who govern England in 2170. He takes stoically the fact that long-livedness is confined to the English race.

The Negress, the minister of health, with whom Burge-Lubin has been carrying on a flirtation via television. The chance that he, too, may be long-lived makes him turn down a rendezvous with her.

tiny." He is a great general who fights because he has no other talents. He asks the Oracle how he can stop being a general without losing his glory. The Oracle quite logically takes his pistol from him and tries to shoot him.

The British envoy,

his wife, and

their daughter, conventional and uncomprehending Britishers who act as chorus. The envoy is **Badger Bluebin**, son-in-law of the Elderly Gentleman.

The Pythoness, who is 170 years old. She is so advanced beyond the "mortals," although only half-grown herself, that her gaze is enough to cow Napoleon and to kill the Elderly Gentleman.

Zozim, a very young "adult." His and Zoo's bored and mocking manner, as they attend the Oracle, offend the visitors.

"As Far as Thought Can Reach: A.D. 31,920"

Strephon and

Acis, two youths.

Chloe and

Ecrasia, two nymphs. With Strephon and Acis, they frolic in a glade before a temple in the style of Greece in the fifth

century B.C. They watch the birth of a nymph and the tragedy that grows out of the sculptors' competition.

Amaryllis, a beautiful nymph delivered from her egg while the children watch.

A She-Ancient, who delivers Amaryllis from her egg.

Arjillax and

Martellus, two sculptors. Martellus claims that he has discovered the greatest of artists, Pygmalion.

Pygmalion, a squarish, benevolent, and somewhat pedantic man who has captured the Life Force and sculptured a living man and woman. When Pygmalion tries to keep the female figure from killing the male, she bites him. Her being is so gross in comparison to Pygmalion's that he dies on the spot.

Ozymandias and

Cleopatra-Semiramis, the male and female figures. As primitive as humans of today, they pompously proclaim mystical claptrap and, after Pygmalion dies, plead human nature and beg for mercy.

A He-Ancient, who is called to decide the creatures' fate. He humanizes them to the point of wishing to die for each other, then allows them to die. The Ancients' evolutionary goal, he tells the young people, is complete freedom from the flesh, existence as a state of pure intelligence.

The Ghost of Adam,
the Ghost of Eve,
the Ghost of the Serpent, and
the Ghost of Cain, who all appear as the children drift off. They puzzle over the meaning of all that has happened.

Lilith, the Universal Mother. She appears to pronounce a benediction over humanity's history. Humankind has redeemed itself from sin and violence. Best of all, humans are not yet satisfied.

BADENHEIM 1939
(Badenheim, 'ir nofesh)

Author: Aharon Appelfeld (1932-   )
First published: 1975
Genre: Novel

Locale: Badenheim, Austria
Time: 1939
Plot: Parable

Dr. Pappenheim, a hotel "impresario" and director of the summer festival of performing arts at the Badenheim resort. Encouraging and accommodating, he works very hard at providing the hotel guests with the best entertainment. His attitude is quite positive, and when the Jews face deportation to Poland, he looks forward to a new and exciting life in a new land, feeling that no real life remains in Badenheim.

Trude, the pharmacist's wife. She is a sickly woman who worries constantly that her son-in-law Leopold beats her daughter Helena. Haunted by a hidden fear, she fades into hallucinations about ferocious wolves. Her hallucinations are replaced by childhood memories of Poland, and she believes that all will be well when she, her husband, and her daughter reach Poland.

Martin, the pharmacist. He is a sorrowful man who constantly looks after his sick wife, to the point of ultimately absorbing her sickness. He is forever promising her that all will be well, despite his own anxieties.

Leon Samitzky, a Polish musician who has wonderful memories of his childhood in Poland. He longs to return to his homeland and stirs feelings of melancholy and nostalgia in Dr. Pappenheim with his stories of his childhood. A heavy drinker who is always in debt, he looks forward to deportation to Poland.

Professor Fussholdt, a vacationer at the resort and a famous historian. Hostile to everything Jewish, he denounces such figures as Theodor Herzl and Martin Buber. His entire stay in Badenheim is spent reviewing the proofs for his latest book.

Mitzi Fussholdt, the very young wife of Professor Fussholdt. A vain and unfaithful woman, she is interested only in clothes and cosmetics, and she understands nothing of her husband's work. She is saddened at finding no friends or lovers in Badenheim and develops nightmares as a result of her fear of deportation.

Frau Zauberbilt, an escapee from a nearby sanatorium. She is divorced. She is happy until she falls ill; she then begins to cling to her belief in an afterlife.

Dr. Schutz, a vacationer and mathematician who lives off his mother's money. He is boyish and loved by all. He chases after a young schoolgirl.

A schoolgirl, the delicate, frail girlfriend of Dr. Schutz. She wants him to take her away from Badenheim and becomes pregnant with his child. Once she is pregnant, she rarely speaks to her lover, but she has no fears and no regrets.

Karl, a divorced vacationer who terrorizes people and has a fascination for the fish in the hotel aquarium. Forever thinking about his sons in a military academy, he takes up with a married woman and invites her to go to Poland with him.

Lotte, Karl's girlfriend, who is married to an agent for a large business firm. She is filled with sorrow and feels as if her life is over.

Two poetry readers, identical twins, tall and thin with a monkish look. They carry a dark secret, eat nothing, and go into seclusion. They have a passion for the poet Rainer Maria Rilke.

Princess Milbaum, the patroness of the twins. Tall and elegant, she believes that there is a conspiracy against her because people avoid her. She soon shuts herself into her room, where she writes letters complaining of how the *Ostjuden* (Eastern European Jews) have spoiled Badenheim. In the end, she is a body without a soul.

Nahum Slotzker, a *yanuka*, or boy singer, from Poland. Frightened and spoiled, he grows fat at the resort and loses his voice, as well as his innocence.

Salo, a traveling salesman who grew up in Poland and looks forward to going back. Capricious and given to drink, he delights in living off his expense account.

Gertie and

Sally, prostitutes of ages forty and forty-two, respectively. Inseparable friends, they are kind and generous. They take care of Nahum.

Peter, the pastry shop owner. Hostile and indignant, he refuses to let Sally and Gertie in his shop. He hates Dr. Pappenheim and most of the hotel guests.

Professor Mandelbaum, a master violinist who is sent to Badenheim because he is a Jew. He forces his trio to practice constantly as they await deportation.

An old rabbi, sick and confined to a wheelchair. He is forever asking questions in a mixture of Yiddish and Hebrew, and his eyes are filled with an ancient grief.

Dr. Langmann, an angry man who denies his Jewishness and dislikes Jews.

— *David Patterson*

BAGA

Author: Robert Pinget (1919-1997)
First published: 1958
Genre: Novel

Locale: Fantoine and Agapa
Time: Indeterminate
Plot: Fantasy

Architruc, the narrator. He is king of Fantoine and Agapa. He describes himself as fat, with varicose veins, a flat head, pimples, sandy-colored hair, a nose like a potato, and cauliflower ears. When Architruc is fifteen years old, his father is killed in a revolt, and his mother assumes the regency until the youth comes of age. He mopes about the palace, delighting only in a garden that he plants with lily of the valley and crowfoot. He falls in love with Baga, who is also the lover of Architruc's mother; as soon as Architruc becomes king, he names Baga as his prime minister. At first Architruc travels about his kingdom to dispense justice, but eventually he becomes bored with this practice and, like his father, cloisters himself within the palace. For him, each day is identical: He arises at noon, performs a few simple exercises, and examines his collections of pebbles, shells, leaves, eyeglasses, and watches. Then his barber arrives to shave him. Afterward, Architruc waters his plant, Ducky, and sponges its leaves. Dressed in white, the king next appears at lunch, his chief delight, and always eats beef, an omelette, and cheese before he retires to his room once more. War with Novocardia disrupts this pattern. Following his victory, he retires for a century to a hut in the forest. When he returns to the palace, a visit from Queen Conegrund again upsets his routine. While overseeing the construction of a castle in the valley of Rouget, he wanders off to join a small convent and becomes a woman for a time.

Baga, Architruc's prime minister. Baga appears subservient, bringing Architruc his morning tea and chamber pot, carrying the king's umbrella, planning the royal menu, and helping the monarch dress. Baga also conducts foreign and economic policy without consulting Architruc, converting his country into the world's leading exporter of rat pelts and building up an arsenal for eventual war with neighboring Novocardia.

Corniflet, the royal barber and part-time molecatcher. About thirty years old, he has red hair and blue eyes.

Piston and

Vielle, the royal musicians. The cornetist once had long hair, but now he and the hurdy-gurdy player are both bald. One formerly had worked as overseer in a print shop, the other as a milkboy, but Architruc's father trained them to their present occupation. Although they are sixty years old, they look eighty. They live in the forest in a one-room house that formerly was a hunting lodge. Each day, the king sends a car to bring them to the palace to play the banquet overture.

Sister Louise, a godly woman who lives on prayer and vegetables. For a time, Architruc shares her house.

Mary, a pretty young woman who joins the convent of Architruc and Sister Louise. She and Architruc sleep together until he recovers his masculinity.

Queen Conegrund, the ruler of Doualia. Fat and red-faced, she wears a red wig and a diamond crown. A voracious eater and lover, she tries to bed Architruc, but she accepts a black dishwasher in his stead. Her visit to Architruc strains the treasury, but her purchase of the dishwasher for a thousand rupees helps replenish the coffers.

Rara, an orphan adopted by Architruc to become his heir. Between ten and twenty years old, Rara is pale, blue-eyed, tall, and frail. He is a voracious reader.

King Gnar, a cave dweller who receives the letters that Architruc writes while living in the forest. Gnar may be the real power behind the throne: When Gnar tosses a dirty sock in the direction of Architruc's palace, the king at once decides to open a sock shop. Gnar has a serpent for an adviser.

Mougre, Baga's predecessor as prime minister.

— *Joseph Rosenblum*

BAILEY'S CAFÉ

Author: Gloria Naylor (1950-   )
First published: 1992
Genre: Novel

Locale: A street with different locations depending on the character
Time: The summer of 1948 to the summer of 1949
Plot: Psychological realism

Bailey, as the owner of Bailey's Café is called, a black veteran of World War II whose two great loves are baseball and his wife, Nadine. After the atom bomb was dropped on Hiroshima and Nagasaki, Bailey was overcome by guilt and despair. He was rescued by Nadine, who installed him in the café, where he can talk to the customers and speculate about life.

Nadine, also called **Deenie**, a tall, beautiful African American woman. At the time of the story, she has been married to Bailey for twelve years. Nadine is a self-controlled person who seldom talks or laughs. During their courtship, she won Bailey's respect by holding him at arm's length until she could be sure that he thought of her as an individual, not merely a sexual object.

Sadie, an aging wino and prostitute. Born only because her mother had botched an abortion, Sadie spent forty years of her life trying to find approval and love, first from her mother, then from an elderly husband. After losing the home that had become her reason for existing, Sadie began to drink. Her wine dreams have become so fulfilling that when she finally is offered love, she chooses illusion instead.

Eve, the owner of the boardinghouse-bordello near Bailey's Café. Turned out by the rigid preacher who reared her, Eve traveled on foot to New Orleans, where she made a fortune and also learned to love flowers. A cold but charitable woman, she provides a safe home for her tenants, even requiring their customers to present them with the flowers she raises and sells.

Sweet Esther, a resident of Eve's house, known as the woman who hates men. When she was still a child, Esther was sold by her brother to his depraved employer, who used her for his pleasure in a dark cellar. At Eve's, she lives in darkness, providing the same kind of services but in complete control of the situation and of her clients.

Mary, also called **Peaches**, another of Eve's tenants. Her internal conflicts made her so desperate that she slashed her own face, in hopes that if she were ugly, she would not be tempted to give in to her promiscuous impulses. Although Peaches refuses to see the father who comes seeking her, Eve assures him that his daughter eventually will find her way back home.

Jesse Bell, one of Eve's residents. Rejected and humiliated by the snobbish family into which she married, Jesse turned to lesbian lovers, alcohol, and heroin. Eve has forced her to quit taking drugs and helped her to regain her self-respect.

Mariam, a fourteen-year-old Jewish girl from Ethiopia who has been expelled from her village because, though a virgin, she is pregnant. After being discovered in Addis Ababa by the Jewish pawnbroker Gabriel, Mariam is brought to Bailey's Café and there has a son.

Stanley Beckwourth Booker T. Washington Carver Maple, Eve's housekeeper and bouncer. Born to a family of wealthy black landowners who were pioneers in Southern California, the serious, conscientious young man got a Ph.D. only to discover that because of his race, he could not get the kind of job for which he was qualified. Substituting comfortable dresses for his business suits, he lives at Eve's. He has made a fortune winning advertising contests.

— Rosemary M. Canfield Reisman

THE BALCONY
(Le Balcon)

Author: Jean Genet (1910-1986)
First published: 1956
Genre: Drama

Locale: Spain
Time: The 1930's
Plot: Absurdist

Irma, called **The Queen**, the proprietress of the Grand Balcony, a brothel specializing in role-playing games. Approximately forty years old, she wears severe clothing and jewelry that reflect her bent for business matters and the riches they bring. Predisposed to calling her wealthy customers "visitors" instead of "clients," she fears a workers' revolt that would threaten her establishment. Although she appears to have some genuine affection for one of her employees, Carmen, as well as for the Chief of Police, George, her good standing with them seems largely predicated on their usefulness to her. In scene 8, she becomes The Queen, wearing an ermine cloak and, on her brow, a diadem.

The Chief of Police, a man named **George**, a cigar smoker who wears a heavy fur-lined coat and hat. He wishes that "Chief of Police" would become one of the figures portrayed at the Grand Balcony. A politically ambitious freemason, he dreams of being enshrined in a tomb by the subjects of an empire he aspires to command. In scene 8, he becomes **The Hero**; later in the play, he seems to have achieved his goals. It is also revealed that he wears a toupee.

The Bishop and

The Judge, clients at the Grand Balcony who first appear in versions of their customary garb, wearing garish makeup, twenty-inch tragedian's cothurni, and other accoutrements that make them seem unusually large. Later in the play, they appear to have actually assumed their roles in Irma's regime.

The General, another client, a retiring-looking gentlemen who is first shown being dressed in a complete general's uniform by The Girl, an employee of the Grand Balcony. He, too, appears to assume his role in Irma's government.

Carmen, an employee, favored by Irma, who is in charge of bookkeeping at the Grand Balcony. Possibly the daughter of a cavalry colonel, she talks of bringing toys and perfumes to her own daughter, who lives at a nursery in the country. Proud of her skills, she is particularly attracted to playing female saints and other religious heroines. She uses her familiarity with clients and other employees to spy for Irma.

Chantal, a former employee who has left the Grand Balcony to join her lover, Roger. Her acting ability is coveted by the revolutionaries, who desire a fiery woman who will inspire their followers. She leaves Roger's side to join them, only to be assassinated in a plot devised by The Bishop.

Roger, Chantal's lover, who admires her spirit but also wishes to control her. After her death, he becomes the first client at the Grand Balcony to play the role of Chief of Police. Interrupting the fantasy by asking Carmen if she knew Chantal, he then appears to castrate himself.

The Executioner, a man named **Arthur**, a physically intimidating employee of the Grand Balcony who helps enact The Judge's fantasy. At heart a retiring soul who clings to the security of his job and his sycophantic relationship with Irma, he is shot in the head at the end of scene 5.

The Envoy, who wears an embassy uniform styled as a tunic and speaks enigmatically of The Queen in his first appearance in scene 7. Unaffected by the revolt, he advises Irma on matters of state once she assumes the role of The Queen.

The Man, a nervous and sloppily dressed client who stands before three mirrors as he awaits the whip and louse-infested wig that are his costume props. His reflections are played by three actors. As **The Beggar**, he cries "Long Live the Queen" in scene 8; as **The Slave**, he partakes in Roger's fantasy at the Grand Balcony.

The Woman, also called **Rosine, The Penitent, The Thief**, and

The Girl, young female employees who interact with The Bishop, The Judge, and The General and The Man, respectively.

Three Men with Machine-Guns, rebels who lead Chantal away from Roger in scene 6.

Three Photographers, earnest young men dressed in black leather jackets and blue jeans who take profile shots of The Bishop, The General, and The Judge in act 7.

— *David Marc Fischer*

THE BALD SOPRANO

Author: Eugène Ionesco (1912-1994)
First published: 1954
Genre: Drama

Locale: London, England
Time: Late 1940's or early 1950's
Plot: Absurdist

Mr. Smith, an utterly boring, illogical husband living in the suburbs of London. He discusses inconsequential trivia with his wife and with their guests, the Martins, then subsequently with the fire chief. Mr. Smith does not engage in genuine communication with his wife; they do not listen to each other. His absence of rational arguments and his numerous fallacies are satirized. These include sweeping generalization, ignoring the question, circular reasoning, faulty argument by analogy, non sequitur, oversimplification, and faulty assumptions. He frequently makes contradictory statements. His reference to all the members—both men and women—of a large, extended family having the name Bobby Watson satirizes lack of individuality and the blurring of sex lines. He refers to someone as a "living corpse," reflecting the author's view that the characters in the play are, indeed, living corpses.

Mrs. Smith, a middle-class housewife married to Mr. Smith. She opens the play by discussing the three helpings she and her husband each had at dinner, gluttony thus being satirized. She often misuses words. Her topics of conversation are utterly trivial. She turns the conversation quickly to death. She, like her husband, abounds in illogical arguments. She criticizes men as effeminate only to have Mr. Smith counter that women are doing masculine things, such as drinking whiskey.

Mary, the maid at the Smiths' house. She enters, stating the obvious, that she is their maid, as if they did not know. Having been given permission by Mrs. Smith to go out for the afternoon, she, on returning, finds the Smiths' dinner guests at the door, waiting for Mary to return home: They did not dare enter by themselves. When the Smiths leave to change into dinner clothes, she invites the Martins in. She uses faulty logic to "prove" that Mr. and Mrs. Martin are not who they say they are. When the fire chief arrives later, she embraces him, glad to see him again at last. She insists on reading to the guests her poem, "The Fire," which is woefully repetitious and atrocious verse. Through Mary, the author satirizes amateur poets.

Donald Martin, a middle-class friend of the Smiths and husband to Elizabeth. As the Martins wait in the living room for the Smiths to enter, Mr. Martin reveals that he does not know where he has met Mrs. Martin, as if they are strangers. They make so little impression on each other that they cannot even remember being together. They finally deduce that they sleep in the same bed. The author, through the Martins, satirizes marriage as lacking real unity. Mr. Martin's conversation when the Smiths appear is preposterously banal. At the end of the play, the dialogue begins to repeat from the beginning, but with the Martins speaking the lines previously spoken by the Smiths.

Elizabeth Martin, a middle-class woman married to Mr. Martin. Both are rather embarrassed and timid. She reports seeing a man on the street bend down to tie his shoelaces, a hardly believable sight; the ordinary seems to her extraordinary. Her class prejudice against Mary is also satire.

The fire chief, who has come on official business to ascertain if there is a fire in the house because he has orders to extinguish all fires in the city. He complains that his business is poor now because there are few fires; he notes that his profits on output are very meager, an attack on commercialism in public service. The fire chief points out that he does not have the right to extinguish clergymen's fires. This ties in with Mrs. Smith's comment that a fireman is also a confessor. That is, she sees him in a religious light, in that fire involves warmth, which is related to life and also to love, which religion aims to foster. Thus, the fire chief is like a priest and hears confessions. Mrs. Smith inverts the relationship, however, seeing the fire chief as the confessor. Mrs. Smith earlier had misused the word "apotheosis," which refers to exaltation to the rank of a god. The author's irony indicates that these people are degraded instead. When Mary enters, she embraces the fire chief. He observes that she had extinguished his first fires, implying, perhaps, a previous hot relationship. The fire chief refers to a bald soprano, from which term the play takes its title; the reference implies a lack of something customary and desirable, such as hair.

— *E. Lynn Harris*

THE BALKAN TRILOGY

Author: Olivia Manning (1911-1980)
First published: 1981
Genre: Novels

Locale: Bucharest, Romania; and Athens, Greece
Time: 1939-1941
Plot: Bildungsroman

The Great Fortune, 1960

Guy Pringle, who is at first a lecturer and then is in charge of the English Department at the University of Bucharest. He is a large, bearlike, physically and metaphorically nearsighted twenty-three-year-old. He is a committed English Marxist. He seems to ignore the realities around him and his marriage, preferring to give vent to his compulsive gregariousness and his camaraderie. He naïvely sees the best in everyone and imagines that generosity always will be repaid.

Harriet Pringle, Guy's twenty-two-year-old wife. They were married only a few weeks before both traveled to Bucharest from England. Harriet was an unwanted child of divorced parents and was reared by an aunt who considered her to be a nuisance. She looks to Guy for security but does not find it, partly because Romania is about to fall to German-Romanian Fascists but especially because her husband seems more interested in his Marxist idealism and how it will save the soon-to-be war-engulfed world, his teaching and theatrical projects, and the eccentrics he brings home than on striving to adjust to

his more down-to-earth wife while she tries to protect him from his opportunistic, self-serving coterie.

Prince Yakimov, called **Yaki**, a White Russian who frequently is unemployed. A former society playboy, he is now impoverished. An opportunist and weakling, he gracefully sponges on those he knows but will betray any friend or cause for the luxuries he still craves.

Sophie Oresanu, a pretty, opportunistic Romanian law student, partly Jewish, who clearly is intent on pursuing Guy and resents Harriet's presence in Bucharest. Sophie's major interest in life appears to be finding a husband, preferably one who can provide her with a British passport.

Clarence Lawson, a self-loathing young Englishman in charge of Polish refugees in Bucharest. He is attracted to strong women like Harriet, who rejects his advances. He eventually marries Sophie Oresanu, who, on acquiring her British passport, leaves him for a series of more affluent men.

The Spoilt City, 1962

Guy and

Harriet Pringle, whose marriage deteriorates further. She feels increasingly lonely. Guy is still entranced by his work and is oblivious to or unconcerned about the entrenchment of German-Romanian Iron Guard control. The Pringles let Prince Yakimov have their spare room in exchange for Yaki acting in Guy's Shakespearean production. Yaki is disappointed with

the board offered by the Pringles, especially the drinks, and becomes disloyal to Guy. Because of this, Guy's name appears on a Gestapo hit list. One day, the Pringles' apartment is raided in their absence, and they return to find that a Jewish student whom they had harbored is gone. Their days in the spoilt city, which has lost both its fortune and its soul, clearly are numbered.

Friends and Heroes, 1965

Guy Pringle, who escapes to Athens after Harriet does. Guy has difficulty landing a job in Athens. He finds the intrigues and other jealous maneuvers for advancement and power repugnant but is inclined to submit to them rather than to fight. Eventually, he finds a job arranging a show for the British military in Greece. Even as the German advance acquires momentum in the spring of 1941, Guy continues to retreat from reality, exhibiting what a hopeless romantic and irrepressible optimist he is and using Marxist philosophy to preserve his moral strength regardless of its applicability to actual events.

Harriet Pringle, who feels increasingly alienated from Guy. She is exasperated by him but still finds his innocence endearing. She nearly has an affair with Second Lieutenant Charles Warden, an upper-class British army officer on a mysterious assignment in Greece. Even as the Germans are about

to swamp the last Allied foothold in Europe, Harriet's greatest concern seems to be to scrounge around for food for a stray cat. She has become even more painfully aware of the greed, duplicity, and selfishness of people who are little ennobled by their war experiences.

Prince Yakimov, who eventually is fired from his job as a delivery man for a British newssheet and dies when the Athens police accidentally shoot him for lighting a cigarette during a blackout.

Alan Frewen, a middle-aged British information officer. He is a withdrawn loner who becomes close to Harriet Pringle at one point before returning to his true loves: His dog and Greece, where he plans to hide out after the Germans take over.

— *Peter B. Heller*

THE BALLAD OF PECKHAM RYE

Author: Muriel Spark (1918-   )
First published: 1960
Genre: Novel

Locale: Peckham Rye, England, near central London
Time: Late 1950's
Plot: Social satire

Dougal Douglas, a new employee of the English textile firm Meadows, Meade & Grindley. A twenty-three-year-old Scot with a deformed shoulder, a captivating smile, and a complete disregard for convention, Dougal is hired in the vaguely defined position of "Arts man" by virtue of his M.A. from the University of Edinburgh. Later, under another name, he takes a similar position with a rival firm. Because he is able

to play any role that occurs to him, Dougal can adjust himself to almost all the characters he meets, and as a result, he elicits their secrets, draws them into his whimsical plans, and complicates their lives. Finally, he leaves for Africa, later appearing in a monastery and eventually choosing a career as a writer.

Humphrey Place, a refrigeration engineer who lives in the same rooming house as Dougal. Handsome but weak-willed,

Humphrey is fascinated with Dougal and takes his opinions as gospel. Under Dougal's influence, Humphrey rejects his fiancée, Dixie Morse, in mid-ceremony. Two months later, however, when Dougal is no longer present, he marries her.

Trevor Lomas, an electrician and a gang leader. Tall, strong, and quarrelsome, he is jealous of Dougal, who has attracted Trevor's girl. Convinced that Dougal is either the leader of a rival gang or a police agent, Trevor and his thugs threaten and attack Dougal's friends. During his escape, Dougal is ambushed by Trevor but disarms and defeats him.

Dixie Morse, Humphrey's fiancée, a typist at Meadows Meade. A tall, attractive, dark-eyed, black-haired woman of seventeen, Dixie ruins the engagement period by her insistence on making and saving every penny she can, so that she can have a perfect wedding and a fully furnished home. Devastated by Humphrey's rejection, she nevertheless recovers enough to marry him later, when Dougal's influence has dissipated.

Leslie Crewe, Dixie's half brother. Although only thirteen years old, he is a member of Trevor Lomas' gang. When Dougal refuses to pay him blackmail to keep quiet about the two jobs, Leslie becomes his bitter enemy.

Merle Coverdale, the head of the typing pool at Meadows Meade. At the age of thirty-seven, she has tired of her long-term relationship with her married employer but finds that she cannot extricate herself. Because of her friendship with Dougal, she is murdered by her lover.

Vincent R. Druce, the managing director of Meadows Meade. Trapped in his miserable marriage to a well-off wife, he has set up a permanent relationship with Merle Coverdale. After he hears rumors that Dougal is a police agent, he is so nervous about business misdeeds that he plans to flee the country. Before he can make his plans, however, he snaps mentally, accuses his mistress of informing on him, stabs her to death with a corkscrew, and is later arrested.

Maria Cheeseman, a retired actress and singer. Dougal, who is writing her autobiography, incorporates bits of the stories told to him by the residents of Peckham Rye, as if they were part of her experience.

Jinny Ferguson, Dougal's girlfriend and fellow student at the University of Edinburgh. After he deserts her when she is ill, she breaks off their relationship and marries someone else. Dougal's tears over Jinny's rejection bring him the sympathy of his female fellow workers.

Richard Willis, the managing director of a competing textile firm. A Scot, he sees Dougal as a possible ally, hires him for a vague research job, and makes plans to place him on the firm's board of directors.

— *Rosemary M. Canfield Reisman*

THE BALLAD OF THE SAD CAFÉ

Author: Carson McCullers (1917-1967)
First published: 1943
Genre: Novella

Locale: Central Georgia
Time: The 1930's
Plot: Domestic

Amelia Evans, the owner of the sad café, a tall, powerful, independent woman with crossed eyes. A solitary child reared by her widowed father, she inherits the largest store in the tiny town and becomes the richest woman for miles around. With uncommon industry, as a shrewd businesswoman, a self-educated doctor, a determined litigant, a carpenter, a meat packer, and a moonshiner, she turns things to profit. She is ill at ease with most people in town, and they take keen interest in her scandalous relations with Marvin Macy and Cousin Lymon. Shortly after her father's death, she had married Marvin, only to storm out of the bedroom on their wedding night. Within ten days, she had run him off her premises and acquired title to all of his property. Years later, she falls in love with a diminutive hunchback who appears out of nowhere, claiming to be a distant cousin. Mellowed by this new love, her heart warms to the community as she gradually converts the store to a café. Her café brings the townspeople a new pride, for there they can forget the cheapness of their lives and let her liquor reveal the secrets of their souls that are obscured by drudgery and petty routine. Amelia's newfound happiness is ruined, however, when Marvin comes back from prison. She is mortified by Lymon's fondness for him. Her usual resolve dissolves in emotional confusion. She makes no move to curb Lymon, even when he invites Marvin to move in with them. She tries to poison Marvin once, but the plates get switched and her plan is foiled. After losing a fight to Marvin and Lymon, Amelia turns in on herself. She raises the price of everything in the café. Business falls off, and the place is boarded up. Passersby only occasionally see her grief-ridden face gazing out of the shuttered window.

Cousin Lymon Willis, a hunchbacked stranger who becomes Amelia's beloved. Standing only about four feet tall on his crooked legs, he shows up one day claiming kinship with Amelia. Frail, moody, and prone to crying fits, he nevertheless possesses an uncanny ability to relate to strangers. Thus, he penetrates her loneliness and engages the townspeople's emotions, helping to make the café a success. When Marvin comes back from prison, Lymon evinces a weird affinity for the man, following him around in public, tugging at his pants leg, and wiggling his ears to attract Marvin's attention, though he is violently rebuffed. Lymon precipitates a crisis by bringing Marvin into Amelia's living quarters. Later, with a flying tackle, he saves Marvin from being beaten in a fair fight with Amelia, and the two men run off together after wrecking the café. Lymon demonstrates the author's idea that the quality of human love depends on the lover's ardor rather than the characteristics of the beloved.

Marvin Macy, Amelia's husband, the most handsome man in the region. An abused and abandoned child, he grows up wild, wicked, bold, fearless, and cruel, seducing young girls for laughs, fighting, stealing, and probably killing. His character undergoes a brief reversal during his courtship of Amelia, but he fails to bed her on their wedding night, and the marriage lasts only ten days. She winds up with all of his property, including ten acres of land and a gold watch. After spending years in prison for robbing three gas stations, he comes back to town. There befriended by Lymon, he draws dangerously closer to her by visiting the café, taking meals with her, and eventually rooming with Lymon in her upstairs living quarters. His love-hate relationship with Amelia culminates in a bare-knuckled fight between them in the café, which he would have lost except for Lymon, who intervenes before she can strangle him. After stealing the gold watch and wrecking the café, the two men leave town together.

— *John L. McLean*

BAMBI: A Life in the Woods
(Bambi: Eine Lebensgeschichte aus dem Walde)

Author: Felix Salten (Siegmund Salzmann, 1869-1945)
First published: 1923; serial form, 1922
Genre: Novel

Locale: A forest
Time: Indeterminate
Plot: Fable

Bambi, a deer who as a fawn longs to be with his mother and his cousins, who asks many questions of his forest friends and learns much through their answers and his own observations, and who at last in maturity learns to stay by himself.

The Old Prince, a wise old stag who befriends Bambi, gives him much sage advice, saves him once from Man, and, after Bambi has been wounded by a hunter, instructs him about herbs that will heal him.

Bambi's Mother, who lovingly cares for young Bambi and teaches him forest lore and how to protect himself from Man. Before Bambi grows his new antlers, she disappears forever.

Faline, Bambi's lovely cousin, with whom he plays when they are fawns and whom he later loves.

Gobo, her small, delicate brother, who is caught by Men, kept as a pet until full-grown, and then released. Foolishly trusting all Men, he is killed when he goes to talk with a hunter.

Ena, the mother of Faline and Gobo.

Man, a puzzling and dangerous creature with a black stick that sends out thunder, fire, and death, even to his own kind.

Ronno, a stately stag who escaped after a hunter wounded him in the foot. The following year, he ceases his pursuit of Faline when Bambi challenges and defeats him in battle before the admiring Faline.

Karus, an older stag who attempts to interfere with Bambi when he wishes to play with Faline. Karus flees when attacked by Bambi.

Nettla, an old doe, self-sufficient and with her own ideas about everything. She regards Man with disgust.

Marena, a young, half-grown doe who predicts that Man will someday be as gentle as the deer themselves.

BANANA BOTTOM

Author: Claude McKay (1889-1948)
First published: 1933
Genre: Novel

Locale: Jubilee and Banana Bottom, both in Jamaica
Time: The early 1900's
Plot: Psychological realism

Tabitha (Bita) Plant, a Jamaican village girl adopted and educated by the Craigs, who are British missionaries. At the age of twelve, she had her first sexual experience, to which she was a willing partner; propriety required that it be represented as rape. Accordingly, when adopted, she is sent to Europe for seven years to be transformed into a dark-skinned Briton of Calvinist outlook, a proper model for the local villagers. She rejects hypocrisy, enjoys sensuality, identifies with folk institutions and beliefs, and adopts a philosophy and lifestyle that are amalgams of Caribbean and continental cultures, of colonial and metropolitan ways. She is the quintessential woman of the West Indies: physical, intellectual, and attuned to island life.

Malcolm Craig, a Calvinist minister of the mission church in Jubilee. His grandfather founded the mission. Well-built, frank, and hearty, he grew up in the village and loved the countryside; however, his religion was unforgiving, confining, and joyless. His true motive in adopting and educating Bita was to demonstrate his theory that natives could be transformed into civilized individuals and weaned from the joys of the flesh.

Priscilla Craig, one of only two ordained clergywomen in the colony. She is a middle-aged, small woman full of high-class anxiety, a feminist related to British suffragettes. Her face flushes with beatific light whenever she sings in church. Her son is a disabled, mentally impaired adult, and she is unable to agree to her husband's wish to adopt a boy as a possible successor. She nevertheless agrees to adopt Bita, whom she wishes to rear as "an exhibit." Like her husband, she denigrates affection and intimacy. She is generous in her expenditure of resources for Bita's education, but she is niggardly in her expenditure of love.

Crazy Bow Adair, a descendant of a Scots settler who had bought the vast mountain estate of Banana Bottom and married one of the blackest slaves whom he liberated. Precocious, intellectual, and the color of a ripe banana, he was schooled for a white-collar job; he was competent as a musician, able to play bamboo flute, guitar, banjo, and fiddle, even the school piano. He and Bita romped in the riverbank grasses, and, although he was twenty-five years old, he was considered harmlessly light-headed. Bita succumbed to his music, caressed him, and, with passion, induced her own seduction. As an educated, musical, older, and physical man, he represented those things that Bita admired in life.

Hopping Dick, a fine-strutting dandy. On her return from Europe, Bita meets him at a local market. She is impressed by his undisguised and acknowledged physicality, by his dancing and romancing. He is a follower of the primitives' god Obeah and is anti-intellectual, yet he attracts Bita for a time, for he represents that aspect of her that the Craigs have attempted to expunge. His backing out of their engagement, conversion to Christianity, and forsaking of folkways leaves Bita disillusioned and frustrated.

Herald Newton Day, a theology student. The elder son of Deacon Day, he was being groomed to succeed the Craigs in the Free Church at Jubilee. Local belief was that the Craigs intended that he should marry Bita. Mrs. Craig describes him as a worthy young man, but he is essentially proud, affected, sanctimonious, and lacking in any racial identification and self-esteem. He is an absolute hypocrite: His joy in preaching is in hearing his own voice; his sermon on the sufficiency of God's love is negated by his defiling himself with a nanny goat. He is an example of the failure to transform human nature; he is not the herald of the new town or the new day that his name suggests.

Squire Gensir, a freethinking British settler of aristocratic mien and background who is a serious student of Jamaican culture and an advocate of black self-esteem. He is an opponent of the Craigs and their philosophy; he is instrumental in having Bita accompany him to a "tea meeting," at which she dances with skill and enthusiasm, recognizing her affinity with the folk of Jamaica. According to one local preacher, Gensir is decadent because he collects folklore; however, Gensir stands firm against discrimination in accommodations. He is given to simple dress and loves the island and its common people. His high intellect, however, precludes him from being wholly submerged in the austere simplicity of village life. He is essentially "a lonely man living a lonely life," but he is the catalyst for Bita's transformation and ultimate self-fulfillment.

Jubban, the elderly drayman of Jordan Plant, Bita's father. He is thoughtful, hardworking, and an emotional, responsive, and responsible lover and husband. He is serious, strong, and proud of his race and of his own accomplishments as a worker. He is the true complement of Bita and the foundation of her contentment.

— *Marian B. McLeod*

BANG THE DRUM SLOWLY

Author: Mark Harris (Mark Harris Finkelstein, 1922-   )
First published: 1956
Genre: Novel

Locale: Perkinsville and New York, New York; Rochester, Minnesota; and Bainbridge, Georgia
Time: 1955
Plot: Social realism

Henry "Author" Wiggen, the narrator, the star left-handed pitcher of the New York Mammoths and author of a novel, *The Southpaw*. He chronicles the final months in the life of his friend, the Mammoths' third-string catcher, Bruce Pearson. Henry is Bruce's constant companion; he holds out for a contract that stipulates that Bruce can be traded or released only if Henry receives the same treatment. He protects Bruce from Katie, and he tries to keep their teammates from making Bruce the butt of their jokes and tricks, keeping Bruce's condition a secret from everyone except Holly and two teammates. While doing all these things, he pitches the Mammoths to the pennant and a World Series championship.

Bruce Pearson, a journeyman catcher who is told by doctors at the Mayo Clinic that he has Hodgkin's disease and only a few months to live. Bruce is stupid and slow, but under the threat of death, he begins to appreciate life more, taking each day as it comes. He even plays better, helping the Mammoths in their difficult drive for a pennant and becoming more of a student of the game. The divided team comes back together for the pennant race when Bruce's condition becomes generally known; the knowledge breaks down the animosities that grew during the season. Bruce catches the pennant-clinching game and collapses on the field at the end. He returns from the hospital for the start of the World Series, then his father takes him home. He dies, back home in Georgia, shortly after the end of the World Series.

Holly Webster Wiggen, Henry Wiggen's wife, who gives birth to a daughter late in the season. She does Henry's taxes, handles his finances, and supports him in his efforts to help Bruce and keep Bruce's insurance money out of Katie's hands.

"Dutch" Schnell, the manager of the Mammoths. His team does not perform up to its capabilities, causing him great frustration, which he tries to take out on Henry. He knows that something is wrong but cannot figure it out, even after hiring a private detective to find out what secret Henry and Bruce share. He is tough, threatening to release Bruce or trade him for a better catcher, but when he eventually finds out about Bruce's illness, he keeps him in the lineup.

Katie, an expensive prostitute. Bruce has been in love with her, but she has fended him off. When she figures out that he is dying and that he has a large insurance policy, she agrees to marry him if she is made the beneficiary, but Henry prevents this.

"Goose" Williams, an aging catcher who at first rides Bruce unmercifully. He is the first player Henry tells about Bruce's illness, and thereafter he is protective of Bruce.

Joe Jaros, a coach with the Mammoths and Henry's partner in a kind of con game called Tegwar, in which the rules change all the time. He rejects Henry because of the latter's insistence on letting Bruce play the game, which Bruce does not understand.

"Red" Traphagen, a retired catcher and Henry's mentor, now a college professor. He returns to the team as a coach and counselor during the final weeks of the season.

"Piney" Woods, a rookie catcher for the Mammoths who is sent back to the minors but recalled near the end of the season. He plays the guitar and sings the dirge "Streets of Laredo," which contains the words of the book's title.

— *John M. Muste*

BANJO: A Story Without a Plot

Author: Claude McKay (1889-1948)
First published: 1929
Genre: Novel

Locale: Marseilles, France
Time: Early 1920's
Plot: Social realism

Lincoln Agrippa Daily (Banjo), a black vagabond from the South who has skipped the ship that took him to Marseilles. He is a wastrel, a womanizer, a dreamer, and a loafer whose improvidence leads him to depend for his survival on instinctive actions and chance encounters. He is essentially trusting and basically generous. He is philosophical when he is tricked out of his banjo, which he values above all. He is seldom sober, though wine affords him decreasing pleasure. His charismatic personality allows him to become the leader of the small band that he organizes from the polyglot beach boys of the port. He deprecates black people who attempt to "pass" as white; he stresses racial pride, being influenced by Ray, with whom he decides to continue his vagabondage in Europe rather than return to the West Indies as a crewman on a tramp steamer. His pervasive melancholy is muted by Latnah, who cares for him after a hospitalization; in fact, she is the instrument of his metamorphosis. He is the cohesive element of his group.

Ray, a would-be writer and an educated West Indian beach boy. A drifter who has absconded from his family responsibilities to follow his own interests and whims, he regards happiness as the highest good and difference as the greatest charm of life. Moderate in his views (except for being rather strident in his antiwhite sentiments), he is dependable insofar as his immediate colleagues are concerned. He rediscovers his African roots and is proud of belonging to a race that has been "weighed and tested." Finding life in the Ditch (the Marseilles black slums) palling, he opts for an itinerant working life.

Latnah, an Earth Mother type of lover, a prostitute who offers succor to Banjo and his colleagues. She was born in Aden of a Sudanese or Abyssinian mother and an unknown father; she is "not young and far from old" and has enviable physical attributes, though she is small. Her complexion is olive-toned, she runs like a gazelle, and she is as graceful as a serpent. She is caring, energetic, and sensual, and when she swims nude in the ocean, her beauty excites her companions, for she is lovely, limber, and sinewy. She regards herself as superior to the other female denizens of the Ditch, and her difference from them is obvious. Her compassion for her companions is generous. Ray and Banjo find it difficult to leave her for their new life as migrant workers.

Bugsy, a small, wiry, aggressive boy who is dull black in complexion. He was given his nickname because his companions thought him to be "bughouse," or mentally incompetent. He is delighted with the name. He is sardonic, he dislikes French food (especially wine and horsemeat), and he is the most sober of the group. Ray describes him as "the toughest black boy I ever knew," but Banjo criticizes him for being "the meanest monkey-chaser I evah seen" (in other words, vehemently antiwhite).

Taloufa, a Nigerian who has been in Wales and the United States and is a supporter of Marcus Garvey's back-to-Africa movement. He was educated out of his native ways by Christian missionaries and is opposed to "coon stuff." He represents the blacks who have been cut off from African village life but not made part of Western urban life. Like the others, he is broke but not broken.

Buchanan Malt Avis (Malty), the best drummer on the waterfront. He is an ebullient, indefatigable West Indian who led the band of beach boys before Banjo arrived. He received his name from the trade names on boxes of goods found in the kitchen where his mother worked. He started life as a "boy" on Caribbean fishing boats; he then sailed as a "boy" to New Orleans and became a full-time seaman. He never returned home. Skilled on the guitar, ukelele, and mandolin, and possessed of a "shining, black, big-boned, plump, jolly face," he is a close friend of Ray and Latnah and accompanies them on their grape-picking excursion. Like Claude McKay, he is a versatile, irrepressible companion of both men and women.

Goosey, a "high yellow" black man from South Carolina who has lived in New Jersey and obtained a high school diploma. An aggressive person, he has had contretemps with his ship's officers and has been paid off in Marseilles with his friend Talpufa, the guitar player. Goosey, a flute player, is thoughtful and a pseudophilosopher on race relations. Ray thinks him a bonehead given to sophomoric musings. Goosey is naïve and is tricked out of his money almost immediately after his landing. A child of the Cotton Belt, he is no cosmopolite. He prefers the piano, harp, and violin to the banjo, which he sees as a symbol of bondage. He adheres to the uplift philosophy of the Harlem Renaissance intellectuals. He is mainly a foil to the sophistication of the longtime black beach boys of the Ditch.

Ginger, a long-term Ditch inhabitant, a former seaman and former convict. He is chestnut colored and has drab, brown, curly hair. He lost his seaman's papers and stole someone else's. He has become proficient in French. He always advises taking the line of least resistance, and he has ponderous opinions on all topics. When the others consider leaving the Ditch, Ginger prefers to stay and take his chances. He has succumbed to the familiar and is not cut out for the vagabond life.

— *Alan L. McLeod*

BARABBAS

Author: Pär Lagerkvist (1891-1974)
First published: 1950
Genre: Novel

Locale: Palestine, the Near East, and Rome
Time: The first century
Plot: Moral

Barabbas, a convicted robber who is freed so that Jesus Christ might be crucified in his stead. Puzzled by the events of the Crucifixion, he wanders about the earth and is finally enslaved in a Roman mine. Concealing the true nature of his relationship with the crucified Jesus, Barabbas poses as a Christian, but when confronted by the Roman governor, he readily renounces his "faith" and is taken to Rome. One night, seeing flames, he imagines that Christ has returned to save the world and destroy the city. He seizes a burning brand and is arrested and imprisoned with the Christians, who tell him that it is Caesar, not Christ, who has set the fires. Barabbas is crucified for his "crime," saying, ambiguously, as he dies, that he delivers his soul "to thee."

Barabbas' mistress, the mother of his dead child. She becomes a Christian and is stoned to death for her beliefs.

Eliahu, Barabbas' father, the leader of a robber band. Barabbas kills him in order to take over leadership of the robbers.

Sahak, Barabbas' fellow slave in the Roman mines, crucified for his faith in Christ.

Mary, the Mother of Jesus, who disturbs Barrabbas with her look of silent reproach as he leaves the Crucifixion.

Peter, the Apostle, of whom Barabbas asks questions about Christ. They are imprisoned and crucified together after the fire in Rome.

Lazarus, raised from the dead; he tells Barabbas that, once one has died, life and death are nothing.

THE BARBER OF SEVILLE: Or, The Useless Precaution
(Le Barbier de Séville: Ou, La Précaution inutile)

Author: Pierre-Augustin Caron de Beaumarchais (1732-1799)
First published: 1775
Genre: Drama

Locale: Seville, Spain
Time: The eighteenth century
Plot: Comedy

Figaro (FEE-gah-roh), the barber of Seville. Figaro is a gay and not overly scrupulous barber and apothecary who does not hesitate to be of help to Count Almaviva in his pursuit of marriage with Rosine. Full of stratagems, he multiplies false identities, to the confusion of everyone. His own vein of comment reveals that he is the foe of the old and their heavy, unjustified wielding of authority. His malice, however, is only skin deep.

Count Almaviva (ahl-mah-VEE-vah), a Spanish grandee from Madrid. The conventional ardent lover, he is thoroughly determined to achieve his goal, marriage with the beautiful Rosine. Lacking the intelligence and guile to achieve his purposes, he enlists the aid of Figaro. At Figaro's suggestion, he assumes two other identities. He first pretends to be Lindor, a soldier enamored of Rosine. When this plan fails, he becomes Alonzo, a pretended music teacher and a substitute for Don Bazile, Rosine's real music teacher. Almaviva finally quiets an outraged local authority through an appeal to his rank.

Doctor Bartholo (bahr-TOH-loh), Rosine's elderly guardian, a man suspicious of all young persons and new ideas. Fearful of losing his ward and the money she represents, he keeps her locked away from all suitors and allows her only the

company of an elderly music teacher, Don Bazile. Because of increasing suspicion, he plans to marry Rosine himself and thus keep control of her property. He is foiled, however, by the strategies of Figaro and the revealed prestige of Count Almaviva.

Don Bazile (bah-ZEEL), a slanderous music teacher and Doctor Bartholo's tool. It is he who makes arrangements for the secret marriage between Rosine and Doctor Bartholo. Although he has brought the notary to Bartholo's house, he accepts a bribe from Almaviva and deserts his former patron.

Rosine (roh-ZEE-neh), the object of Almaviva's love, an innocent, oppressed young woman. She is, however, capable of prudent suspicion about the pretended music teacher Alonzo and can be convinced that Alonzo is preparing to sell her to the count. When the identity of Alonzo as the count is revealed, Rosine faints, but she recovers in time for a happy marriage and the frustration of her guardian.

The notary, the performer of the marriage between Almaviva and Rosine. Although he is brought to the house to perform a marriage that will link Rosine and Bartholo forever, Figaro is able to convince him that it is Count Almaviva and Rosine who should be married.

BARCHESTER TOWERS

Author: Anthony Trollope (1815-1882)
First published: 1857
Genre: Novel

Locale: Barchester, a fictional English cathedral town
Time: Mid-nineteenth century
Plot: Social satire

Eleanor Bold, younger daughter of the Reverend Septimus Harding, the "Warden," and wealthy widow of John Bold. She lives with her baby son and her sister-in-law, Mary Bold. Much of the novel revolves around Eleanor's choice of one of her three suitors: Mr. Slope, Bertie Stanhope, and Mr. Arabin. Throughout a large portion of the novel, most of her ecclesiastical friends and relatives assume that she will choose Mr. Slope.

Dr. Proudie, the clergyman who becomes Bishop of Barchester after the death of Archdeacon Grantly's father. Dr. Proudie is a vain but weak man, dominated by his wife and by Mr. Slope. Although all Barchester expects him to offer the wardenship of Hiram's Hospital to Mr. Harding, Dr. Proudie allows Mr. Slope's chicanery to gain the appointment for Mr. Quiverful.

Mrs. Proudie, the aggressive and domineering wife of the

Bishop of Barchester. She attempts to control Barchester by championing evangelical and Low Church causes, awarding church patronage, and manipulating people through the offices of Mr. Slope. She antagonizes the established ecclesiastical society in Barchester.

The Reverend Obadiah Slope, the Bishop's chaplain. An evangelical clergyman, Mr. Slope antagonizes most of the chapter with his initial fiery sermon at Barchester Cathedral. He first acts as Mrs. Proudie's agent, but, after he supports the claims of Mr. Harding in an attempt to gain favor with Eleanor Bold, Mrs. Proudie scorns him. Unable to win Eleanor or the post of Dean of Barchester, he returns to London.

The Reverend Theophilus Grantly, the Archdeacon of Barchester and rector of Plumstead Episcopi. He strongly supports the claims of Harding, his father-in-law, to be reinstated as warden of Hiram's Hospital. When the nearby living of St. Ewold's becomes vacant, he goes to Oxford to obtain the post for the Reverend Francis Arabin. He also fears that his sister-in-law, Eleanor, will marry Slope.

Susan Grantly, wife of Archdeacon Grantly and the elder daughter of Mr. Harding. She generally follows her husband's lead, but she attempts to mitigate his anger at her sister.

The Reverend Septimus Harding, former warden of Hiram's Hospital. He desires his former charge but is denied it through the machinations of Mr. Slope and Mrs. Proudie, who make his appointment conditional on his assuming extra duties and administering evangelical Sunday Schools. Later, he is offered the deanship of Barchester Cathedral, but he refuses the post because of his advanced age.

The Reverend Francis Arabin, a scholarly High Church clergyman from Oxford who is brought into the living at St. Ewold's to strengthen forces against Bishop Proudie and Mr. Slope. He eventually becomes Dean of Barchester and marries Eleanor Bold.

Dr. Vesey Stanhope, holder of several livings in the Barchester area who has spent the preceding twelve years in Italy. He is summoned to Barchester by Dr. Proudie, through Slope, but has little interest in the political or ecclesiastical affairs of Barchester.

Mrs. Stanhope, his wife, interested chiefly in dress.

Charlotte Stanhope, the oldest daughter of the Stanhopes, who manages the house and the rest of the family with efficiency and intelligence. A friend of Eleanor, she urges her brother to propose to Eleanor.

La Signora Madeline Vesey Neroni, née Stanhope, the great beauty of the Stanhope family, who has been crippled in a short, disastrous marriage to a brutal Italian. Although confined to her sofa, she attracts men easily. One of her victims is Mr. Slope, whose hypocrisy she exposes, but she is sufficiently generous to encourage Eleanor to marry Mr. Arabin.

Ethelbert "Bertie" Stanhope, the amiable son of the Stanhopes, who has dabbled in law, art, and numerous religions. His family wishes to settle him with Eleanor and her money, but Bertie's proposal fails, and he is sent back to Carrara by his father.

Mr. Quiverful, the genial clergyman and father who is persuaded to accept the preferment at Hiram's Hospital in addition to his living at Puddingdale.

Mrs. Letty Quiverful, his wife and the mother of fourteen children, who begs Mrs. Proudie to bestow the preferment at Hiram's Hospital on her husband.

Miss Thorne of Ullathorne, the member of an old family at St. Ewold's, who gives a large party at which both Mr. Slope and Bertie Stanhope propose to Eleanor. Miss Thorne, however, favors Arabin and invites both Arabin and Eleanor to stay until the engagement is settled.

Wilfred Thorne, the younger brother of Miss Thorne, a bachelor and an authority on tradition and geneology.

Dr. Gwynne, Master of Lazarus College, Oxford, the man instrumental in securing the deanship for Mr. Arabin.

Olivia Proudie, the daughter of the Proudies, briefly thought to be engaged to Mr. Slope.

Mary Bold, the sister-in-law and confidante of Eleanor Bold.

Johnny Bold, the infant son of Eleanor and the late John Bold.

Griselda Grantly, the pretty daughter of Archdeacon Grantly.

Dr. Trefoil, Dean of Barchester Cathedral, who dies of apoplexy.

The Bishop of Barchester, the father of Archdeacon Grantly. He dies at the very beginning of the novel.

Dr. Omicron Pi, a famous doctor from London.

BAREFOOT IN THE HEAD: A European Fantasia

Author: Brian W. Aldiss (1925-   )
First published: 1969
Genre: Novel

Locale: Europe
Time: Near future
Plot: Science fiction

Colin Charteris, the main character, a Serbian. After the psychedelic wars, he does resettlement work for the Italian government. Seeking stability, he drives north to Metz, where he has a vision of the multiple paths of human life. His visionary powers lead him to England, where he becomes a popular messiah figure. Later, he preaches his brand of multilogic through England and then arrives in Ostend. On the way to Brussels, he switches cars with Banjo Burton, who crashes into a truck. Because Charteris survives, people think that he has risen from the dead. When the movement gets dictatorial, he resigns and wanders eastward with Angeline.

Phil Brasher, a young psychedelic who survives an airplane crash and believes himself to be a savior. He resents Charteris' coming. During a fight, Charteris pushes him in front of a car.

Angeline, Brasher's wife. After his death, she becomes Charteris' mistress and his most loyal follower. She bears his child and is the only one faithful to the end.

Banjo Burton, a hitchhiker whom Charteris picks up in Great Britain. He is a member of a rock group and introduces Charteris to Phil Brasher.

Army Burton, Banjo's brother, also a musician, who enthusiastically encourages Charteris to become the leader of the world.

Robbins, a young musician and disciple of Brasher. He turns to Charteris after Brasher's death.

Ruby Dymond, another musician who is in love with Angeline and writes songs for her. He never becomes her lover.

Greta, a groupie who is distraught after Brasher's death.

Featherstone-Haugh, another musician.

Cass, a disciple of Charteris who wants him to become a world leader. When Laundrei comes along, he teams up with him, abandoning Charteris.

Ranceville, a prop man for Boreas. He is so moved by the accident that kills Banjo that he wants to be in the car, otherwise populated by mannequins, during the filming of the crash.

Elsbeth, a young Jewish girl who temporarily becomes Charteris' mistress.

Jan Koningrijk (yahn kohn-ihn-kreek), the chief of the rescue squad for the Belgian freeway system. He is called to the accident that kills Banjo Burton in Charteris' car, leading people to believe that Charteris has risen from the dead.

Marta Koningrijk, the young schizophrenic wife of Jan who becomes Charteris' mistress after the accident.

Nicholas Boreas, a Belgian film director, middle-aged and fat, who partakes of questionable sexual activities. He wants to make a film on the life of Charteris. He re-creates the accident scene.

Kommandant Laundrei, a local military chief, middle-aged and pompous, always dressed in a splendid uniform with many medals. He arrests Charteris for loitering and then tries to get Charteris to help him become the leader of Germany by teaching him self-control, but Charteris refuses.

Hirst Wechsel (huhrst VEHK-zuhl), an aide to Kommandant Laundrei. He introduces Charteris to Laundrei. Later, he seems to turn into a bird.

Angelina, a young waitress who works at the hotel in Metz. She refuses to sleep with Charteris and is not heard from again.

— *Robert W. Peckham*

BAREFOOT IN THE PARK

Author: Neil Simon (1927-   )
First published: 1964
Genre: Drama

Locale: New York City
Time: Several days in February in the early 1960's
Plot: Comedy

Corie Bratter, a newlywed, married only six days at the beginning of the play. She is young, pretty, and full of enthusiasm for the future. Impulsive and fun-loving, she considers herself a doer, not a watcher. Her impetuosity is not shared, at first, by her mother or husband, and they are aghast when she cheers the crazy antics of Victor, a neighbor. Corie eventually learns to appreciate dependability and quiet strength.

Paul Bratter, Corie's husband, a twenty-six-year-old attorney in his first job. Both his dress and his outlook are very conservative. Extremely proper and dignified, he always knows the right thing to say. He is levelheaded and practical, and he keeps his emotions in check, perhaps too much so. After Corie accuses him of lacking playfulness, he shows her that he, too, is capable of walking barefoot in the park.

Ethel Banks, Corie's mother. She is in her late forties. Although she is still pretty, she has fallen out of step with the fashions. She lives alone in West Orange, New Jersey. Con-

sciously or unconsciously, she has adopted a narrow image of herself as someone with a sensitive stomach, a bad back, and no need for romance. It takes a wild evening out with Victor for Ethel to rediscover her carefree and spontaneous self.

Victor Velasco, the Bratters' upstairs neighbor. Fifty-eight years old, he is a colorful character. Although capable of looking positively natty in a double-breasted pinstriped suit, he also wears Japanese kimonos and berets. He is vain, flamboyant, and without shame when it comes to letting someone else pick up a tab. Married three times, he is a terrific flirt. He is also a gourmet cook; Paul refers to him as the "Hungarian Duncan Hines." There are signs that Victor is beginning to slow down. After an exhilarating evening of his own creation, he suffers a broken toe and an upset stomach.

Harry Pepper, a telephone repairman. He witnesses, to his mortification, a fight between Corie and Paul.

— *Liz Marshall*

THE BARK TREE
(Le Chiendent)

Author: Raymond Queneau (1903-1976)
First published: 1933
Genre: Novel

Locale: The outskirts of Paris, France
Time: Early twentieth century
Plot: Antistory

The narrator, a shadowy figure who often seems to be following the other characters, though he never reveals more than that about himself.

Étienne Marcel (ay-TYEHN), a Parisian bank employee. Étienne is at first a one-dimensional character, but after being observed by Pierre Le Grand, he acquires three dimensions and begins to question things. He is a typical Parisian

who works in the center of the city and returns every day by train to his house in the suburbs. He is married, has a son, and eats a disgusting meal every day in a cafeteria. This routine is broken after Pierre sees him nearly run over in front of a train station. Étienne then stops at a suburb, Blagny, where, in a café, he meets the other characters and becomes embroiled in the question of the treasure behind Old Taupe's door. Étienne becomes a near-philosopher as he awakens to questions about the world (such as the reason for two rubber ducks swimming in a shop window), especially with the help of Pierre. At the novel's end, he is drafted into the army when the French and Etruscans declare war on each other, leaving his wife to disappear and his son in the hands of the evil Bébé Toutout.

Pierre Le Grand, an observer and thinker. He is an enigmatic character who, upon being asked if he is a novelist, declares that he is a character. He is the only character conscious of Étienne's transformations and may appear under other names in the novel, such as Pierre Troc. He is something of a philosophical midwife to Étienne in helping him to learn to think. He also is involved in the comic misunderstanding when people begin to believe that Old Taupe has a fortune hidden behind his door.

Madame Sidonie Cloche (see-doh-NEE kohsh), a midwife and an abortionist. She is another observer, taking special pleasure in seeing people run over. She is instrumental in fostering the belief that Old Taupe has a fortune and gets the young servant girl Ernestine to marry him for his supposed money. A meddling old woman who is vaguely criminal, she shows up at the end of the novel during the French-Etruscan War as Queen of the Etruscans. She is unhappy about being a character in a novel.

Dominique Belhôtel (doh-mee-NEEK behl-oh-TEHL), a café proprietor, a brother of Madame Cloche. He owns the café in which Étienne stops one day for French fries. Another rather dubious figure, he achieves his ambition when he buys a brothel in order to have enough money for his son Clovis to become an engineer when he grows up.

Saturnin Belhôtel (sat-tur-NAN), a brother of Madame Cloche who works as a concierge. He has ambitions of being a writer and confides in Narcense, who lives in his hotel.

Old Taupe (tohp), a bum. Taupe clearly has no means of support except selling junk. He lives by a railroad track where he has placed a door, behind which the others believe he has a fortune. He marries the young servant girl Ernestine in a wedding feast at the café.

Narcense (nahr-SAWNS), a musician and would-be writer. Narcense is unemployed and spends most of his time pursuing women in the street. Alberte, Étienne's wife, attracts him to their suburb, where he spends time trying to meet her.

Bébé Toutout, (bay-BAY tew-TEW), a parasitic dwarf. He imposes himself on the Marcel household and goes to live there. Another figure associated with evil, the dwarf helps set up a brothel in the house after Étienne leaves for the war.

Théo (tay-OH), Étienne's son. A typical adolescent in some respects, he prefers looking at obscene photographs to reading philosophy and is interested primarily in sex. He befriends Bébé Toutout and tries to thwart Narcense.

Alberte (al-BEHRT), Étienne's wife. She is very attractive and has men pursuing her constantly, especially Narcense.

Madame Pigeonnier (pee-zheeohn-YAY), a neighbor of Étienne. She is attractive and interested in Théo.

Jupiter, a dog. This poor pet has the misfortune of leaping onto a coffin during a funeral and is hanged.

— *Allen Thiher*

BARNABO OF THE MOUNTAINS
(Bàrnabo delle montagne)

Author: Dino Buzzati (Dino Buzzati Traverso, 1906-1972)
First published: 1933
Genre: Novella

Locale: Near the village of San Nicola, Italy
Time: Early twentieth century
Plot: Psychological

Barnabo (bahr-NAH-boh), a young forester and the only one of his guard not called by a last name. Although proud and somewhat quick-tempered, Barnabo is also sensitive and considerate, as demonstrated by his pretense of allowing another forester (Pietro Molo) to win a fight rather than be humiliated. Later, he stops to help a wounded crow, not having the heart to kill it, unlike his comrades, who kill and pluck crows to be cooked for dinner. Barnabo is disgraced and his career ruined when cowardice overcomes him and he is unable to help his fellow foresters in a battle with the brigands. His only solace in exile is his special relationship with the crow that he rescued shortly before the battle. When Barnabo does have a chance to redeem himself many years later, he finds himself once again unable to kill, though for a different reason: It is not cowardice but compassion that makes Barnabo allow the brigands to escape.

Giovanni Berton, another young forester and Barnabo's friend. The son of a carpenter, Berton is fascinated by the mountains and can spend hours merely watching them. It is he who sees the smoke of the brigands in the mountains and convinces Barnabo to join him in an expedition in search of the bandits. Berton covers up for Barnabo when Barnabo is accused of cowardice, saying that Barnabo was not near the scene of the battle. Many years later, he urges Barnabo to return to San Nicola from exile and resume his life there, though not as a forester.

Antonio Del Colle (kohl-lay), the commander of the foresters when the novella begins. He is a short, elderly man who is still sprightly enough to carry heavy loads and hike through the mountains, and his eyes are still keen enough that, when he shoots his rifle, he does not miss a target at a hundred meters. He is murdered by the brigands, and his body is buried on the same mountain where another forester, Darrìo, died. It is Del Colle's death that sparks the foresters' obsession with capturing the brigands. Del Colle is succeeded as commander by Giovanni Marden.

Angelo Montani, another forester. A suspicious and dour man, Montani neither likes nor trusts Barnabo. Montani is very efficient and regimented, and he does not talk much. Sometime after Barnabo leaves in disgrace, Montani has a run-in with a bandit who, astonishingly, knows Montani's name. Obsessed with this mysterious stranger, Montani returns several times to the mountains to try to either capture or kill the bandits, but he never succeeds.

— *T. M. Lipman*

BARNABY RUDGE: A Tale of the Riots of 'Eighty

Author: Charles Dickens (1812-1870)
First published: 1841
Genre: Novel

Locale: England
Time: 1775-1780
Plot: Historical

Barnaby Rudge, the title character but a figure of lesser importance than a number of other personages in the novel. Born on the night of his father's supposed murder, he is, in his twenties, half-witted, physically strong, and grotesque, almost unearthly, in appearance because of his shock of red hair. At the same time, his sensitivity to beauty, his near idolatry of Hugh, the hostler at the Maypole Inn, and his devotion to Grip, his tame, talking raven, reveal his simple, good nature. Pardoned after being arrested and condemned to death for rioting, he becomes his mother's stay and comfort in later years.

Mrs. Rudge, his mother, whose life has been one of hardship and sorrow. Her efforts to support her mentally disordered son and to protect him from the tribulations that befall the weak-minded are rewarded after the riots, when she and Barnaby go to live at the restored Maypole Inn under the protection of kindhearted Joe Willet and his wife Dolly.

Rudge, a savage, violent man, the former steward at The Warren. He becomes a fugitive from justice after murdering his employer, Reuben Haredale, and a gardener, whose mutilated body is mistaken for Rudge's. Returning twenty-two years later, he lives a life of skulking and crime, his identity known only to his wife. Recognized while taking part in anti-Catholic riots, he is sentenced to death and hanged. Before his death, his wife makes futile efforts to get him to repent.

Emma Haredale, the daughter of the murdered Reuben Haredale. She is the victim of an agreement between her guardian-uncle and her fiancé's father that she shall not marry Edward Chester, because of their different religious beliefs and because John Chester desires a grander alliance for his son. Eventually, she and Edward are married, and he rebuilds The Warren, which is looted and burned by rioters.

Geoffrey Haredale, a Roman Catholic country squire, Emma Haredale's uncle and guardian, and a victim of mob violence during the riots. A kind-hearted man, he is especially solicitous for the welfare of Barnaby Rudge and his mother. Planning to leave England, he revisits the ruins of The Warren. There, he encounters Sir John Chester and kills him in a duel. Haredale dies several years later in a religious establishment in Italy.

Edward Chester, Emma Haredale's fiancé, who defies his father's wishes that he marry a Protestant heiress. Disowned, he goes to the Indies. He returns to become a hero at the time of the riots, saves Emma from her abductors, and marries her after her uncle withdraws his objection to the match.

John Chester, later Sir John, an egocentric man completely lacking in compassion and concerned only with his own importance and advancement. His career of selfish intrigue is ended when Geoffrey Haredale kills him in a duel. His character is modeled after that of Philip Dormer Stanhope, Lord Chesterfield.

John Willet, the landlord of the Maypole Inn, near Epping Forest. An obstinate, domineering man, he treats his grown son Joe as if he were still a boy. He never fully recovers from the mob's abuse when the inn is plundered during the rioting, but he spends his last days peacefully in a cottage, where he entertains his cronies in a miniature replica of the Maypole bar.

Joe Willet, the landlord's son. Bullied by his father and unhappily in love with Dolly Varden, he runs away and joins the army. After losing an arm while fighting in the American Revolution, he returns to England at the time of the riots and, with Edward Haredale, displays great heroism. For his services, he receives a silver snuffbox from the king. He and Dolly, whom he rescues after she and Emma Haredale have been abducted, are comfortably married and settled at the restored Maypole Inn, where old soldiers are always treated well by the landlord and his plump, cheerful wife.

Gabriel Varden, an honest, good-hearted locksmith, abducted by the rioters and ordered to open the great lock when the mob storms Newgate Prison. His defiance of the mob is only one instance of his goodness, a trait recognized and respected by all who know him.

Dolly Varden, his daughter, loved by Joe Willet. Plump, naïve, garrulous, she is the antithesis of Emma Haredale, with whom she is abducted during the riots. Rescued by Joe, she leaves no doubt as to her love for him.

Mrs. Varden, a woman of uncertain temper and changeable moods.

Hugh, the hostler at the Maypole Inn and a leader in the riots. A paradoxical character, he is a mixture of kindness and bitterness. His better side shows in his kindness to Barnaby Rudge and in his loyalty to those he trusts. Embittered by the execution of his mother, a gypsy hanged at Tyburn, he is vituperative in his attitude toward society. Condemned to die, he attributes his contempt for society and his indifference to death to his parentage. Before his execution, he divulges the fact that Sir John Chester is his father. Sir John refuses to acknowledge the relationship and abandons Hugh to his fate.

Simon Tappertit, also called **Sim** and **Simmun**, Gabriel Varden's apprentice, Joe Willet's rival for the love of Dolly Varden, and a leader of the rioters. During the confusion, he and Dennis, a hangman, abduct Dolly and Emma Haredale. His legs are crushed during the violence. His former master helps to set him up in business as a bootblack, and he is so successful that he is able to marry the widow of a rag collector. On occasion, he beats his wife; she retaliates by removing his wooden legs, exposing him to the derision of street urchins.

Miss Miggs, a servant in the Varden household, in love with Simon Tappertit. During the riots, she forsakes the Vardens to follow and look after the apprentice. She always insists that her own virtue makes her a soul-saver, and she eventually finds her proper place as a female turnkey at the County Bridwell, where she shows no mercy to women prisoners who have proved themselves weak in virtue.

Ned Dennis, a former hangman and one of the ringleaders of the riots. He is a composite of undesirable traits. Sadistic, he treats prisoners with violence; audacious, he is also traitorous; cowardly, he snivels when he is faced with his own execution.

Lord George Gordon, the fanatical instigator of the riots. Arrested on a charge of treason, he is imprisoned in the Tower. He is later acquitted when the offense with which he is charged cannot be proved.

Gashford, Lord George Gordon's toadying secretary. He deserts his employer when the nobleman is arrested.

John Grueby, Lord George Gordon's servant.

Solomon Daisy, a parish clerk and sexton,

Tom Cobb, a chandler and post-office keeper, and

Phil Parkes, a ranger, John Willet's cronies who frequent the Maypole Inn.

Mr. Langdale, a vintner. He hides Geoffrey Haredale in his house during the riots. Joe Willet and Edward Chester save them when the mob storms the house.

BAROMETER RISING

Author: Hugh MacLennan (1907-1990)
First published: 1941
Genre: Novel

Locale: Halifax and Nova Scotia, Canada
Time: December 2-10, 1917
Plot: Social realism

Neil Macrae, the twenty-eight-year-old orphaned nephew of Geoffrey Wain and unknowing father of his cousin Penelope Wain's daughter Jean. At the French Front, Geoffrey Wain, commander of Neil's regiment, had been preparing to court-martial his nephew for failing to carry out an impossible order when shelling had occurred. Wounded and temporarily amnesiac, Neil was mistakenly identified as a British private. Using his false identity, Neil has returned to Halifax to clear his own name. Still in poor health, Neil does not at first show his strength of character. This sometimes impulsive son of Jamsie Wain, rebellious daughter of the British loyalist Wain family, and John Macrae, a respected Cape Breton craftsman, embodies the best of a new breed of Canadians forged out of World War I and freed of colonialist dependence on England. An M.I.T.-trained engineer who excels in the new field of submarine design, Neil now knows exactly what he seeks. During the eight days that include the horrendous, historic Halifax explosion, this modern Odysseus is freed of Geoffrey Wain, reunited with Penelope, and aided by his true friends in clearing his name. He finds a focus for his restless energy in the monumental rescue work following the explosion. The novel's conclusion finds the uncompromising Neil facing a bright future.

Penelope (Penny) Wain, Geoffrey Wain's twenty-nine-year-old daughter, a woman of strong character and great ability with a deceptively fragile appearance. A reserved woman, Penny suffers quietly the loss of Neil and her false relationship with her daughter Jean, adopted for propriety's sake by her uncle and aunt. Penny sustains herself with her successful career as a talented ship designer; she also provides her young brother Roddie with the love and guidance the motherless boy needs. Almost ready, like the mythical Penelope, to succumb to a persistent suitor, Penny finds her patience and hope rewarded when Neil returns and they find their love undiminished.

Colonel Geoffrey Wain, a tall, broad-shouldered, impressive-looking man in his middle fifties. His military appearance is enhanced by his close-cut silver hair and black mustache. Temporarily relieved of his command at the French Front,

Wain is reluctantly home in the city and country he contemptuously regards as a colonial backwater. He does enjoy his family's traditional social superiority. Hereditary head of the booming Wain shipyards, Wain exudes authority but actually has led a life of few challenges. He is obsessed with hatred for Neil, especially when he hears that Neil is alive in Halifax, thus threatening to dash Wain's hope of resuming a military command. Wain passes some time in a desultory affair with his petite, ambitious, and vulgar young secretary, Evelyn Phillips. In the explosion, Wain dies at Evelyn's apartment, his tawdry death belying his lifetime of presumed superiority.

Doctor Angus Murray, a widower in his late forties, the medical officer in Geoffrey Wain's battalion in France. He is currently home on leave, recovering from shrapnel wounds. Tired and disreputable looking, Murray fights loneliness and impending despair with frequent bouts of drinking. He is a sensitive, self-aware man with deeply felt ideas about Canada and its future. Galvanized by the explosion, he sets up a hospital in the Wain house and completes his rehabilitation, both physical and mental, with ceaseless surgical work. Deeply in love with Penny, he gracefully relinquishes her to Neil and indeed champions Neil, seeing to the practical details of his vindication and yielding to Neil as the New Canadian.

"Big" Alec Mackenzie, a craggy Nova Scotian Highlander in his mid-forties, married and the father of three children. He misses his Cape Breton life but now makes a better living in wartime Halifax. A corporal in Wain's battalion in France, Mackenzie was privy to the fiasco involving Neil and Wain. Unaware that his job at the Wain shipyards is a bribe for his silence, Mackenzie is the best wharf foreman Wain ever had, bringing to his job the diligence and integrity with which he approaches life. An inarticulate man born to carry out orders, Mackenzie always gives his best. In the explosion, he supports—with brute strength—beams from his wrecked home, saving his wife but dooming himself when a spike pierces his lung. Rescued by Neil and Murray, Alec survives long enough to give Murray the vital testimony needed to clear Neil's name.

— *Jill Rollins*

THE BARON IN THE TREES
(Il barone rampante)

Author: Italo Calvino (1923-1985)
First published: 1957
Genre: Novel

Locale: Ombrosa, an estate in northern Italy
Time: Late eighteenth century
Plot: Fantasy

Cosimo Piovasco di Rondò (koh-ZEE-moh peeoh-VAHS-koh dee rohn-DOH), who is twelve years old at the narrative's outset. He is the eldest son in the Piovasco family and successor as baron of the Ombrosa estate. Cosimo is energetic and determined, an idealist who insists on acting on his principles. The central figure in the story, he sets the main action going when he refuses to eat a meal of snails prepared by his sister. Sent from the table, he climbs into a holm oak on his family's estate and vows never to descend from the trees. Cosimo eventually develops instincts and senses different from other humans as a result of living in the wild and having to be ever watchful and alert. This vigilance becomes "his natural state, as if his eyes had to embrace a horizon wide enough to understand all." Despite his arboreal life, he becomes studious and well read in the philosophy of the Enlightenment; as a reader as well as a tree dweller, he acquires, virtually and literally, a bird's-eye view of his era.

Biaggio Piovasco di Rondò (bee-AHJ-jee-oh), Cosimo's brother, eight years old at the outset of the action. He narrates the tales of Cosimo's extraordinary life. Though at first regarded by Cosimo as weak because of his failure to resist their father, Biaggio is a close friend and confidant to Cosimo. Biaggio takes his brother food and supplies when needed and keeps Cosimo informed of events that Cosimo cannot observe. Throughout the narrative, Biaggio maintains an attitude of wonder and awe at his brother's exploits.

Violante (Viola) Ondariva (veeoh-LAHN-teh on-dah-REE-vah), a neighbor to the Piovasco family and member of the rival Ondariva family, which has claim to some of the same lands as the Piovasco family. Approximately Cosimo's age, Viola is attractive, blonde, capricious, and independent. She meets Cosimo shortly after he enters the trees, when she is swinging in her garden and he greets her from a tree. She attracts Cosimo immediately with her teasing coyness and the fact that she is a member of the family his father has declared as sworn enemies. She occasionally assists a youthful gang of fruit thieves, who know her as **Sinforosa**, by alerting them to the location of ripe fruit and sending them an alarm when danger is near. At every chance, Cosimo attempts to impress her; according to Biaggio, this is partly to demonstrate to her

his strong will. Later, after being widowed, Viola becomes Cosimo's lover.

Arminio Piovasco di Rondò (ahr-MEE-nee-oh), the baron of Ombrosa and father of Cosimo, Biaggio, and Battista. A dreamer aspiring unrealistically to higher nobility, Arminio dresses in a powdered wig and formal French court attire, in the outdated style of Louis XIV. His response to the turbulence of his age is that of a reactionary, attempting to regain a lapsed dukedom. His otherwise harmless pretensions disgust Cosimo, whose first impulse to live in the trees is an act of rebellion against his father's authority. Arminio's principal reaction to his eldest son's rebellion is to become too embarrassed to go out or to face his friends among the nobility.

Corradino di Rondò (kohr-rah-DEE-noh), formerly **Konradine von Kurtewitz** and also called **the Generalessa**, the wife of Arminio and mother of Cosimo, Biaggio, and Battista. She is called the Generalessa by her children because of her martial bearing and her preoccupation with military matters, which she learned from her father, a general who had commanded Empress Maria Theresa's troops and took his daughter with him from camp to camp. The Generalessa is domineering and strict but protective of her children. Like her husband, she is absentminded in rearing her children, so that her sons grow up left to their own devices, enjoying much freedom. With Cosimo, she is solicitous and caring. She is one of the first to accept Cosimo's decision to live in the trees.

Battista di Rondò (bah-TEES-tah), Cosimo and Biaggio's sister. Battista's countenance is compared by Biaggio to a rodent's; she has staring eyes, narrow teeth, yellowish skin, and starched hair. She became confined to her home, dressed as a nun, after she attacked the young son of a noble family visiting her father. Battista's main interest as a youth is cooking bizarre, revolting dishes, including rats' livers, pigs' tails, and porcupines. She is the cook of the infamous meal of snails that her brother Cosimo refuses to eat. Battista eventually marries the young count of Estomac, thus ensconcing herself in the self-aggrandizing aristocratic life that Cosimo has devoted himself to protesting.

— *Dennis C. Chowenhill*

BARON MÜNCHAUSEN'S NARRATIVE
OF HIS MARVELLOUS TRAVELS AND CAMPAIGNS IN RUSSIA

Author: Rudolf Eric Raspe (1737-1794)
First published: 1785
Genre: Novel

Locale: Russia and many other parts of the world
Time: Late eighteenth century
Plot: Farce

Hieronymus, Baron Münchausen (MEWNK-how-zehn), a German nobleman who narrates an account of his journey to Russia and the adventures that followed his acceptance of a commission in the Russian army, in whose ranks he fought against the Turks. The baron explains that while he was en route to Russia, he had several unlikely experiences, and that after he joined the army, his misadventures continued, reaching a climax when he reached the moon by climbing a giant beanstalk and then had to improvise a means of returning to Earth. In the original version of his adventures (which concluded at this point), the baron is a laconic character who

retails his anecdotes in a matter-of-fact fashion, seemingly expecting that no one could possibly doubt the word of a man of his standing. Later versions, however, have him speaking in a far more elaborate and pompous fashion, so that he becomes a manifest liar whose tales are rather risqué as well as frankly preposterous. In the later editions of his story, the catalog of his adventures is expanded far beyond the limits of the original, so that he becomes a rather cartoonish figure frequently to be found in the company of legendary beings and characters borrowed from myths and fanciful literary works. The original baron is essentially a sportsman, and many of his tales concern incidents of the kind commonly reported by huntsmen, but the baron of the later versions is a cavalier braggart and man of ludicrous ambition whose dealings with various inhabitants of the far corners of the globe are usually violent and grotesquely comical. In the later phases of the final version, he becomes the general of a veritable army of imaginary characters whom he leads into battle against various enemies, including Beelzebub himself. By virtue of this extraordinary elasticity, the baron is an unusually difficult character to pin down and analyze, but that is not entirely inappropriate for a person whose name has come to symbolize gross deception and essential unreliability.

The Grand Signior of Constantinople, a Turkish aristocrat encountered more than once in the course of the baron's adventures. His attitude toward the baron is rather inconsistent: At one point he gives the baron free access to his seraglio, but at another he orders the baron's execution.

Hilaro Frosticos, a friend of the baron in the English court who helps him to mount his expedition to the interior of Africa and frequently offers his advice and opinions as to the best means of conquering that mysterious territory.

Lord Viscount Gosamer, an associate of the baron who is unwise enough to employ his spurs while riding the Sphinx in the vanguard of one of the baron's expeditions.

Don Quixote, a knight of La Mancha. He attempts to interrupt one of Münchausen's expeditions but is confounded by the baron's allies, who include, at this time, the giants Gog and Magog, the Sphinx, Merlin, and Dick Whittington.

— *Brian Stableford*

THE BARRACKS

Author: John McGahern (1935-   )
First published: 1963
Genre: Novel

Locale: Western Ireland; Dublin, Ireland; and London, England
Time: Late 1940's
Plot: Social realism

Elizabeth Reegan, a former nurse, forty years old, now married to a sergeant in the Irish police force. She is stepmother to his three children. After a nursing career in London during World War II and a passionate love affair that does not work out, Elizabeth returns to western Ireland and marries against her family's advice. The novel covers the year during which she suspects, confirms, and fails to live through cancer. The real issue, however, is not Elizabeth's physical cancer but the cancer of her growing conviction that life is essentially without meaning. Her confrontation with death merely confirms and emphasizes her conviction that the human condition is inherently one of isolation. Although she continues to rejoice in natural beauty and human kindness, she is sustained only by the endless routine of repetitive tasks that make up her life, repetitions echoed by the police rounds her husband makes and by the rounds of the seasons. The barracks within which the Reegans make their home is a microcosm of the world, for both barracks and world would fall into chaos without the cycles of duty and year to impose a hint of order.

Sergeant Reegan, Elizabeth's husband, who is fifty years old. A member of the freedom forces that achieved Irish independence in 1921, Reegan was rewarded with a position in the newly formed police force. After thirty years as a sergeant, however, he tastes the increasing bitterness of his position. Independence has made no real change in Ireland, but it has changed his life. Without it, he would have either stayed on the farm, which he loved, or immigrated to the United States. Constantly at odds with his superintendent, he dreams and plans for the day when he can buy a farm and work only for himself. He is moody and occasionally irascible, but he is also kind to Elizabeth, generous, and even sensitive. He does not begrudge the expense of her illness, though it puts off achievement of his dream. He is aware that he does not really know his wife (who never calls him by his first name, or by any name for that matter) and that they will end their days caring for each other but still essentially alone.

Michael Halliday, a London doctor, about thirty-five years old, with whom Elizabeth has an affair. Michael introduces Elizabeth (who is deeply in love with him) to an unfamiliar world of books, concerts, fancy restaurants, and ideas. Eventually, however, he confesses that he no longer loves her and that all along he has been using her to stave off his growing sense of the meaninglessness of life and his growing tendency toward suicide. He still wants her to marry him, but Elizabeth refuses. It is his cynicism that affects and infects her the most, and increasingly during the course of the novel she finds herself echoing ideas he formulated for her years before. She ends by wondering whether Reegan has not been to her what she was to Halliday, a device to postpone the suicide that is the ultimate result of such cynicism.

John James Quirke, a police superintendent about fifty years old, Reegan's supervisor. A small-minded authoritarian, he spends much of his time sneaking around and spying on the guards to be sure that they are fulfilling the exact letter of their responsibilities (which they frequently are not). He is a capricious, often vicious man whose lack of reason in the use of authority echoes the apparent lack of reason in whatever authority governs the world.

Teresa Casey, the childless wife of Ned Casey. A bit at loose ends without the routine responsibilities that sustain Elizabeth, she delightedly takes over care of the children when Elizabeth falls ill. They give her life structure, meaning, and focus; her experience thus echoes Elizabeth's and Michael's, for only routine and activity can ward off despair.

Willie,

Una, and

Sheila, Reegan's children by his first wife; they are ages twelve, eleven, and nine. They like Elizabeth, and she likes them. They are good to her, and she cares for them, yet there is no close emotional bond or genuine understanding. Indications that they can do without her threaten her sense of purpose and coherence.

— *Helen Lojek*

THE BARRACKS THIEF

Author: Tobias Wolff (1946-   )
First published: 1984
Genre: Novel

Locale: Fort Bragg, North Carolina
Time: 1967
Plot: Character study

Lewis, a young army recruit from Lawton, Kentucky, who is training as part of the Eighty-second Airborne Division at Fort Bragg. He is one of three new soldiers chosen to guard an ammunition dump in a woods outside the fort on the Fourth of July. The soldiers are instructed by the duty officer to shoot any nonmilitary personnel who come near the dump. When the local sheriff and a civilian try to convince them to leave the dump because they are in danger from a nearby forest fire, the three soldiers, led by Lewis, dutifully chase them off at gunpoint. The act forges a bond of friendship among the three new recruits, but Lewis' macho display masks his personal insecurities. Lewis is homesick and lonely. His attempts to fit in with his fellow soldiers through brash and compulsive talk alienates those around him. He brags incessantly about his sexual prowess but is mortified when a sergeant calls him "Tinkerbell" because he cannot complete a rugged training maneuver. One night, a civilian teacher at the post tends to Lewis' wounded hand, and Lewis is disturbed by the pleasure he feels from close physical contact with the man. He decides to prove his masculinity to himself by picking up a prostitute in a local bar, but the woman humiliates him when she finds out that he does not have enough money. Lewis vows to return with the appropriate sum and the next day steals the wallet of a soldier in his barracks. The ease with which he commits the theft magnifies his contempt for his barracks mates, and he enjoys the feeling of power over them that the theft gives him. Lewis' need to steal becomes a psychologically complex compulsion. He is nearly caught taking the wallet of a soldier in the shower room and eludes capture only by punching the anonymous victim in the face. When he discovers that the man he punched was Hubbard, one of the two soldiers with whom he guarded the ammunition dump, he is struck with shame. He plans to turn over a new leaf but before he can, incriminating evidence leads to his identification as the barracks thief, resulting in his emotional breakdown and dishonorable discharge from the Army.

Philip Bishop, the most aloof and urbane of the three new recruits in the Eighty-second Airborne. He is in the Army only because the Marine recruiting station was closed the day he went to enlist. Philip enlisted to escape his broken family and rebuild his damaged self-esteem. When he was in high school,

his father left his mother for another woman, and this deeply upset him. As a teenager, he vented his anger through juvenile acts of vandalism and harsh treatment of his emotionally withdrawn brother, with whom he previously enjoyed a happy relationship. He looks to the military as a means to attain personal independence and a bright future. Although he is a loner, he enjoys the camaraderie he shares with Hubbard and Lewis. He considers their standoff at the ammunition dump as a test of personal mettle that he passed, but the self-assurance it gives him is shaken by other experiences, including a confrontation with antiwar protesters outside the base and the thefts in the barracks. He feels compelled to tell Hubbard that he is not responsible for the thefts, even though no one suspects him. When Lewis is identified as the barracks thief, Philip feels betrayed and schemes with other soldiers to give him a ritual beating. He is surprised to find Hubbard contemptuous of their plan, and although the beating takes place, he does not participate. Shortly afterward, he is called up for duty in Vietnam.

Hubbard, a sensitive young man who was gulled into enlisting in the Army by a recruiter who visited his high school. He is discouraged by his experiences in basic training and frightened by the prospect of fighting in Vietnam. Initially, he is incredulous at Lewis' behavior at the ammunition dump, but he falls in with Lewis and Philip to follow orders. Shortly afterward, he is crushed to hear that the same day he was guarding the ammunition dump, his two best friends back home were killed in a drunk driving accident. He is crying in the showers over the news when Lewis steals his wallet, breaking Hubbard's nose in the process. Hubbard eventually identifies Lewis as the barracks thief after the letter his mother wrote him telling him about his friends' deaths is found in Lewis' possession. These events completely change Hubbard's outlook on life. He is called up for service in Vietnam the same day that Philip is but flees to Canada.

Guy Bishop, Philip's father, whose midlife crisis crystallizes the dissatisfaction with their traditional roles that the other men in the story feel.

— *Stefan Dziemianowicz*

BARREN GROUND

Author: Ellen Glasgow (1873-1945)
First published: 1925
Genre: Novel

Locale: Rural Virginia
Time: Late nineteenth and early twentieth centuries
Plot: Social realism

Dorinda Oakley, the daughter of a poor white Virginia farmer. Tall, dark-haired, and radiant-eyed, she is not pretty, but when she smiles, her eyes and mouth reveal an inner warmth. A vein of iron in her enables her to survive Jason's desertion of her, his marriage to Geneva Ellgood, her own attempt to kill him, the loss of her baby in an accident, the deaths of her parents and of Nathan, and the years of

hard work necessary to maintain and improve her dairy farm.

Josiah Oakley, her brother, a personification of futility who seems to Dorinda to ooze failure from the pores of his skin.

Rufus Oakley, another brother who, accused of murdering a neighboring farmer, is saved by his mother's lying statement that he was at home when the shooting occurred.

Jason Greylock, the last member of an old Virginia family. Red-haired and slightly freckled, he is charming to young Dorinda. An inner weakness leads him to desert the pregnant Dorinda and marry Geneva. The same weakness takes him on the road his father has followed, a road to death through drink.

Geneva Ellgood, later Jason's wife. She ages rapidly from living with Jason; her mind begins to fail, and she eventually drowns herself.

Nathan Pedlar, a country farmer and merchant. A tall, lank, homely man of unimpressive personality, Nathan has an instinctive knowledge of wise farm practices. He wisely advises Dorinda in the development of her dairy farm and later marries her. He is killed while trying to save the lives of passengers in a train wreck and is given a hero's funeral.

Dr. Greylock, Jason's father. Formerly a man of prominence and owner of a fine farm, he has been for some years drinking his life away and letting the farm go to ruin.

Eudora Abernethy Oakley, Dorinda's mother, who after her husband's death reveals a suppressed religious mania.

After her lie saves Rufus, her conscience drives her insane. She dies in her sleep.

Dr. Faraday, a physician who saves Dorinda's life after an accident in New York. He later hires her to look after his office and his children.

Aunt Mehitable Green, an old conjure woman and midwife in whose home Dorinda becomes ill and learns she is pregnant.

Elvira Oakley, Josiah's wife, a scold who is as much a failure as her husband.

John Abner Pedlar, Nathan's crippled son, who helps Dorinda farm.

Matthew Fairlamb, a retired carpenter, a vigorous and talkative old man.

James Ellgood, the owner of Green Acres, a flourishing stock farm.

Joshua Oakley, Dorinda's father, a good, industrious, but ineffectual man.

Rose Milford, Nathan's sick wife, a former schoolteacher who faces death by pretending it is not near.

BARRIO BOY: The Story of a Boy's Acculturation

Author: Ernesto Galarza (1905-1984)
First published: 1971
Genre: Novel

Locale: Mexico and California
Time: 1910-1920
Plot: Autobiographical

Ernesto Galarza (ehr-NEHS-toh gah-LAHR-zah), a child of single mother, Doña Henriqueta, who moves him from place to place to avoid the Mexican Revolution but, nevertheless, manages to give him a sense of security. Ernesto's earliest memories are of Jalcocotán (Jalco), a Mexican village where he, his mother, and his mother's brothers, José and Gustavo, moved after her divorce. The four move in with their Lopez relatives. As a toddler, Ernesto learns the importance of work by running errands and looking after the family's chickens. When armed soldiers visit the village, Ernesto's mother flees with her son, José, and Gustavo, first to Tepic, then to Acaponeta, then to Mazatlán. From his mother, Ernesto learns to read and write. After an arduous journey by train to the United States, Ernesto and his mother rejoin José and Gustavo in Sacramento, California. In the multiethnic barrio, Ernesto finds odd jobs that introduce him to various Americans, including Hindus, Chinese, and people of other nationalities. Ernesto learns English in first grade and becomes a translator for barrio residents. Doña Henriqueta remarries, and the family buys a house in an American neighborhood. After Gustavo and Henriqueta die of influenza, Ernesto moves back to the barrio with his Uncle José. Ernesto is fired as a farmworker when he files a complaint about polluted water in the migrant camp. The novel's ending suggests that Ernesto will continue both his schooling and his activities as a labor organizer.

Doña Henriqueta (DOHN-yah ehn-ree-KEH-tah), a single mother. She was divorced by her husband when her son, Ernesto, was an infant. With the baby and her brothers, José and Gustavo, she moves in with her sister's family in Jalco. She helps to support the family as a seamstress. As they travel from place to place to avoid the Mexican Revolution, Henriqueta makes her young son feel that each move is an adventure. She teaches Ernesto to read and write and insists that he respect others. In Sacramento, Henriqueta marries another Mexican immigrant. When the family buys a house in an American neighborhood, she feels isolated. Henriqueta and her second husband have two girls and a boy before she dies of Spanish influenza.

José Galarza (hoh-SEH), Doña Henriqueta's brother, twelve years older than his nephew Ernesto. José likes to joke and is impatient with authority figures. In Jalco, he makes up comic versions of the Latin liturgy, ending his career as an altar boy. When the family's beloved Nerón gets rabies, José kills the dog with a stick. José must hide from the *rurales* when they come to Jalco searching for recruits. As the family move from place to place, José displays great ingenuity in finding odd jobs. While an employee of the Southern Pacific Railway, he takes Ernesto for a ride on a handcar. When José shouts "Viva Madero" at a group of men, they respond with shots. In Mazatlán, José is hired to build stone markers. To avoid paying him, the foreman tries to murder José on the way home. José's confrontation with the *patrón* precipitates the family's flight to the United States. José takes care of the family when they are stricken by influenza. After Henriqueta dies, he and Ernesto return to the barrio. He provides his nephew with food and lodging on the condition that Ernesto pay for his school expenses.

Gustavo Galarza (gews-TAH-voh), Ernesto's uncle and Doña Henriqueta's brother. Gustavo precedes the family to Tepic and sends for them when he has found a job and lodging. He and José move ahead of the family to Mazatlán, where the brothers find work with the Southern Pacific Railway. In Sacramento, Gustavo dies of Spanish influenza.

Don Catarino Lopez (kah-tah-REE-noh LOH-pehs), the husband of Doña Henriqueta's sister (Ernesto's Aunt Esther) and father of two sons, Jesús and Catarino, Jr. For Ernesto, Don Catarino is the embodiment of the authoritarian *jefe de familia* (head of the family). When Henriqueta and her brothers and son move northward, the Lopez family remains in Jalco. The Lopezes sail to San Francisco in an attempt to rejoin the rest of the family in Sacramento, but they are detained at Angel Island because of an irregularity in their papers. They return to Jalco.

Mrs. Dodson, the owner of the boardinghouse in the Sacramento barrio where Doña Henriqueta and her family live. She helps the family navigate an unfamiliar culture and introduces young Ernesto to the victrola, pancakes with Karo syrup, and comic strips.

Miss Ryan, Ernesto's beautiful, energetic first-grade teacher. She gives Ernesto private tutoring in English, praising each step in his mastery of the language.

— *Wendy Bousfield*

BARRY LYNDON

Author: William Makepeace Thackeray (1811-1863)
First published: 1852; serial form, 1844
Genre: Novel

Locale: England, Ireland, and elsewhere in Europe
Time: Eighteenth century
Plot: Picaresque

Redmond Barry, later **Redmond Barry Lyndon**, the boastful and petulant narrator. He is a corrupt bully; throughout his many adventures, he behaves with consistent dishonor. At the novel's end, suffering from delirium tremens, he dies in the Fleet Prison.

The Widow Barry, his mother, who was deprived of wealth and estates by relatives. She devotes herself to the rearing of her son until his Uncle Brady persuades her to let him take the boy to Brady Castle. Much later, after Barry's marriage, Widow Barry lives with her son and aids him in his nearly successful attempt to drive his wife mad.

Lady Honoria Lyndon (ohn-oh-REE-ah), who holds the former Barry lands. Immediately upon learning of her husband's death, Barry begins an underhanded and relentless courtship that at last wears down her resistance. So brutal a husband is he that Lady Lyndon's natural haughtiness is thoroughly subdued. Kept virtually a prisoner by Barry and his mother, she is almost driven mad before her former suitor and her indignant relatives contrive to free her from Barry's custody.

Lord Bullingdon, Lady Lyndon's son and heir. Barry does his best to deplete Lord Bullingdon's future property in order to live in style and to provide for his own son, who will have no rights of inheritance. Lord Bullingdon is driven by his stepfather to run off to fight the rebels in America. He is reported killed but shows up again just in time to keep his weak-willed mother from succumbing once more to her now-estranged husband.

Bryan Lyndon, the son of Lady Lyndon and Barry, a boy overindulged by his father. Thrown from his horse, he is killed. His mother's anguish over his death causes a report that she is mad.

Uncle Brady, who invites the young Barry to Castle Brady and treats him kindly.

Nora Brady, Barry's cousin. He falls in love with her when he is fifteen and she twenty-four. In a fit of jealousy, and with characteristic selfishness, Barry fights a duel with the man she loves and whom her family wants her to marry.

Captain John Quinn, loved by Nora. Believing he has wounded Quinn, Barry flees to Ireland. Later he finds that the dueling pistols were loaded with tow and that Captain Quinn, far from dead, is married to Nora.

Mrs. Fitzsimons, a highway robbery victim whom Barry befriends on the road to Dublin. Visiting at her castle, he attempts to make a lavish impression. When his money is gone, his host and hostess are glad to see him leave.

Chevalier Balibari (ba-lee-bah-REE), suspected of being an Austrian agent by the Prussians. Having deserted from the British Army to the Prussians, Barry, now in Berlin, is sent to spy on Balibari, whom he discovers to be his own father's brother, Barry of Ballybarry, now an elderly gambler. Barry, in disguise, leaves the Prussian service and goes to Dresden with this uncle.

Countess Ida, a wealthy heiress whom Barry dislikes but courts.

Chevalier De Magny (deh mag-NYEE), the fiancé of Countess Ida. Barry wins from him, in gambling, all his possessions, including his claim to the hand of Countess Ida. Involvement in a court intrigue, however, foils the matrimonial scheme when Barry is forced to leave the duchy.

Lord Charles Lyndon, the husband of Lady Honoria Lyndon. Barry becomes acquainted with them at a spa and resolves to marry Lady Lyndon as soon as the sickly Lord Lyndon is dead.

Lord George Poynings, Lady Lyndon's former suitor, who helps in freeing her from Barry's custody.

Mick Brady, Barry's cousin. He persecutes young Barry during the latter's stay in Brady Castle.

Mrs. Brady, the wife of Uncle Brady. She hates Barry.

Frederick the Great, of Prussia. He sends Barry to spy on the Chevalier Balibari.

The Duke of X———, at whose court Barry pursues the Countess Ida.

BARTHOLOMEW FAIR

Author: Ben Jonson (1573-1637)
First published: 1631
Genre: Drama

Locale: Smithfield, London, England
Time: Early seventeenth century
Plot: Satire

Bartholomew Cokes, a foolish, prodigal young gentleman of Harrow. He is made of the stuff without which fairs and carnivals cannot succeed; fortunately for them, his kind is supposed to be born at the rate of one a minute. A trinket-buyer, he is carried away by the trifles in the booths, and he is an easy victim for pickpockets and confidence men. Blessed with a lovely, well-to-do fiancée, he neglects and loses her.

John Littlewit, a petty official with a pretty wife and a mother-in-law with Puritan leanings. He takes great pride in the fair, especially in the puppet show, for which he has written the script. He and his wife have some difficulty persuading the mother-in-law to go to the fair, but they finally succeed.

Win-the-Fight Littlewit, John's wife, Dame Purecraft's daughter. As simpleminded as her husband, she falls in with his plans to go to the fair and convinces her mother and Zeal-of-the-Land Busy that she should go to satisfy her longing for pork. She is deceived by Captain Whit into putting on a green gown (a badge of harlotry) and letting him offer her favors to a gentleman at the fair. She escapes the fate her foolishness almost brings on her.

Dame Purecraft, John Littlewit's mother-in-law. Hesitating between two suitors, Rabbi Busy and Ned Winwife, she is troubled by a prophecy that she is to marry a madman. When she meets the insane Troubleall at the fair, she pursues him, thinking it is her fate to marry him. She finally consents to marry Tom Quarlous, in disguise, believing him to be Troubleall.

Zeal-of-the-Land Busy, a Puritan divine. Filled with thunderous rhetoric against the foul fair, papistry, and other abominations, he is a gluttonous hypocrite. He manages to get himself into the stocks for disturbing the peace and at the fair is bested in an argument with a puppet.

Ned Winwife, first the suitor of Dame Purecraft, then the successful suitor of Grace Wellborn. He is a sensible foil to many of the foolish characters.

Tom Quarlous, Winwife's friend. He is the chief mover of the action, employing Edgeworth to steal Cokes's license, disguising himself as Troubleall to marry Dame Purecraft, and showing up Justice Overdo to prevent a cloud of punishments on all the inhabitants of the fair.

Humphrey Waspe, called **Numps**, Cokes's servant and tutor. A small man of demonic fury and with a foul and stinging tongue that he uses freely, he constantly rebukes his young master for irresponsibility. He himself is discomfited by losing the strongbox with the wedding agreement and by being put in the stocks.

Adam Overdo, a meddling justice of the peace, the guardian of Grace Wellborn. Thinking himself a sort of English Haroun al-Raschid, he disguises himself to seek out evil and good at the fair, in the hope of righting wrongs and punishing "enormities." His reforming zeal, misdirected by poor judgment, leads him to beatings and to the stocks. Completely discountenanced when he finds his wife in the green gown of a prostitute, squired by a pimp, he gives up his crusade of stern justice and treats the motley horde to a supper.

Dame Overdo, Adam's foolish wife. She becomes intoxicated, threatens to commit a riotous group to prison in the king's name and her husband's, and is persuaded, like Win Littlewit, to put on a green gown and wear it to the puppet play, where she gets sick.

Grace Wellborn, Cokes's fiancée, an attractive and intelligent woman. She is so much annoyed by Cokes's behavior that she offers to marry either Winwife or Quarlous. Each is to choose a fictitious name and show it to the mad beggar Troubleall, his pick to determine her husband. He chooses Winwife's pseudonym.

Lanthorn Leatherhead, a versatile operator in the fair. He runs a booth selling hobbyhorses and doubles as a puppet master. Speaking through one of his puppets, he successfully confutes Busy's blasts at the theater.

Joan Trash, a gingerbread woman. She runs a booth near Leatherhead's. When Busy turns over her booth with all the gingerbread (the gingerbread figures were idols, in his opinion), she has him arrested and put in the stocks.

Troubleall, a madman. He has an obsession that nothing is legal or suitable without a warrant from Justice Overdo. His violence at the stocks allows Busy, Numps, and the disguised Overdo to escape. Dame Purecraft wishes to marry him so that she can have a real madman for a husband in accord with the prophecy, but she mistakes Quarlous for him and marries Quarlous.

Ezekiel Edgeworth, a proficient cutpurse. A handsome young man, he draws the attention of justice Overdo, who seeks to give him advice on the danger of bad companions and to rescue him before he goes wrong. To save himself from disclosure, he steals the strongbox from Numps and turns it over to Quarlous.

Nightingale, a ballad singer. He and Edgeworth work together: Nightingale attracts a crowd and distracts their attention while Edgeworth picks their pockets. They customarily squander their gains at Ursula's at the end of the day.

Ursula, a pig-woman. She sells pork and ale and has some less savory sidelines. An enormous, greasy, bawdy, and quarrelsome woman, she is something of a she-Falstaff, lacking his essential wit.

Alice, a harlot. Angry at the competition professionals receive from amateurs, she quarrels savagely with Dame Overdo, whom she suspects of being a rival.

Dan Jordan Knockem, a horse trader.

Val Cutting, a roaring bully.

Captain Whit, a male bawd.

Puppy, a wrestler.

Northern, a clothier. All five are members of the noisy crew that hangs around Ursula's booth.

Mooncalf, Ursula's tapster.

Solomon, Littlewit's man.

Haggis and

Bristle, members of the watch.

Pocher, a beadle.

Filcher and

Sharkwell, doorkeepers at Leatherhead's puppet show.

THE BASIC TRAINING OF PAVLO HUMMEL

Author: David Rabe (1940-   )
First published: 1973
Genre: Drama

Locale: Georgia, New York, and Vietnam
Time: 1965-1967
Plot: Expressionism

Pavlo Hummel, an army private and medic during the Vietnam War. Pavlo has red hair and green eyes, is five feet, ten inches tall, and weighs 152 pounds. Estranged from his family, Pavlo has had his name legally changed from Michael to spite the father whose identity he has never known. He worries about whether to hug his mother when he returns home. Although he grew up in New York City, Pavlo is inexperienced and innocent; his street-smart persona is an act, and the other men see through it easily. Neurotically obsessed with the impression others have of him, Pavlo lies about his sexual exploits and his experiences in crime. He claims to have stolen twenty-three cars and to have had an uncle who was executed at San Quentin prison for killing four people. He never suspects or realizes that the other men know he is lying and that they are laughing at him. Pavlo thinks that he can win friends by being a good soldier, so he resorts to flattering sergeants and volunteering for difficult tasks. When he realizes that no number of push-ups will win the friendship and respect he craves, Pavlo swallows one hundred aspirin, but he is saved by the squad leader, Pierce. Pavlo is determined to prove himself in the infantry, but he is assigned to be a medic. He follows his orders to the letter but is ashamed of his job and repeatedly asks to be transferred to the battlefield. At one point, Pavlo talks Sergeant Brisbey out of committing suicide, but his efforts lack sincerity. Parham is wounded by Vietcong and cries out for Pavlo's help while Pavlo is asking for transfer. Pavlo carries Parham's body to safety, more out of a desire to impress others with his bravery than out of any concern for Parham. Finally, Pavlo is assigned to the fighting. He is wounded three times and earns the Purple Heart before he wants out, but ironically his request is refused. Pavlo is killed in a senseless incident arising from a fight over a prostitute. A grenade rolls into the room, and Pavlo scoops it up and is holding it when it explodes. He takes several days to die. Despite the changes in Pavlo as he becomes harder and more cynical, the young man never acquires any real insight.

Ardell, a soldier Pavlo creates in his fantasies. A black man in sunglasses and a strange uniform with black ribbons and medals, Ardell enters and exits throughout the play to advise Pavlo. Ardell's is an experienced and prophetic voice; the soldier teaches Pavlo about the Army and war. Ardell says that Pavlo is black inside, hiding such intense pain that the young man cannot even see himself clearly.

Sergeant Tower, the drill sergeant. A tough black man, Tower singles out Pavlo and makes him do punitive push-ups on the first day of basic training. Throughout the play, Tower gives instructions on combat and first aid. He tells the soldiers what to do when they are lost.

Kress, one of the men in Pavlo's unit. Large and muscular, Kress does not understand much. He flunks the proficiency test and has to repeat basic training. Kress constantly complains about being cold, even in the furnace room. Kress despises Pavlo.

Yen, a Vietnamese prostitute. Dressed in purple silk pajamas, Yen is the first woman with whom Pavlo has sex; he visits her regularly.

Pierce, the squad leader. Pierce does not participate in the harassment of Pavlo, but he understands why the other men dislike him. Pierce's main concern is his responsibility as leader. He is afraid of how violent incidents will reflect on him, tarnishing his military record.

Sergeant Wall, a friend of Sergeant Brisbey. After being beaten in a fight with Pavlo over Yen, Wall throws a grenade into the room.

Sergeant Brisbey, one of Pavlo's patients. Brisbey stepped on a mine and as a result lost his testicles, both legs, and one arm. He is bitter and wants to kill himself.

Mickey, Pavlo's half brother. Tougher than Pavlo, Mickey does not care what others think. He is a womanizer and heavy drinker and is disrespectful of their mother.

Mrs. Hummel, Pavlo's mother. A small, dark-haired, plump, fashionably dressed woman, Mrs. Hummel appears distracted when Pavlo returns home. She recounts a story of a mother who learns that her son was killed in Vietnam.

— *Lou Thompson*

THE BASS SAXOPHONE
(Bassaxofon)

Author: Josef Škvorecký (1924-   )
First published: 1967
Genre: Novella

Locale: A hotel in Kostelec, a Czech town in the Protectorate
     of Bohemia and Moravia
Time: The 1940's
Plot: Satire

The narrator, a male jazz musician in Kostelec, a small town in Nazi-occupied Czechoslovakia. The eighteen-year-old Czech dandy and jazz saxophonist is swept into a band concert for the Nazi occupation forces by his fascination with a beautiful rare bass saxophone. Wearing a false mustache to escape recognition by other Czechs, he dons the green, purple, and orange costume of Lothar Kinze's German orchestra in order to play the bass saxophone. His personal passion for music overcomes his fear of political reprisals. Interrupted and unmasked, he flees the hotel concert hall, but the secret experience remains for him an emblem of his youth and the mysteries of life.

Horst Hermann Kühl, a Nazi official in Kostelec. Kühl once confiscated one of the narrator's jazz records when it was accidentally broadcast in the cinema. Although the narrator suffered no prosecution for his offense, he continues to suffer from fear of Kühl and his power. Kühl attends the concert by Kinze's orchestra.

Lothar Kinze, the leader of and violin player for a small German orchestra traveling by bus through occupied territo-

ries. A seedy refugee from circus performances, Kinze recruits the narrator to replace his ill saxophonist.

The man on the gilded bed, the regular bass saxophone player in Lothar Kinze's orchestra. Interrupting the narrator's performance, he takes the stage in a stirring performance that elicits the ire of Kühl and burns itself into the memory of the narrator, a moment of pain that shakes complacency.

— Virginia Crane

BASTARD OUT OF CAROLINA

Author: Dorothy Allison (1949-   )
First published: 1992
Genre: Novel

Locale: Greenville County, South Carolina
Time: The late 1950's and early 1960's
Plot: Bildungsroman

Bone, the protagonist and narrator, whose real name is **Ruth Anne Boatwright**. She is called Bone because at birth she was "no bigger than a knuckle-bone." Her mother, Anney, was fifteen years old and unmarried when she gave birth to Bone, following a car accident brought about by her brother Travis' drunk driving.

Anney Boatwright, Bone's mother. Hardworking and poor, Anney hates the "illegitimate" stamp placed on Bone's birth certificate. To her, it puts authority behind the labels of "no good," "lazy," and "shiftless" that others have attached to her and her family all her life. When Bone is four, Anney marries the sweet, pretty Lyle Parsons and has another daughter, Reese. After Lyle dies when his truck spins off the road, she takes a job as a waitress in the White Horse Café. She meets her third husband, Glen Waddell, at the café when he comes in to eat with her brother Earle.

Glen Waddell, Anney's third husband. The youngest son of the well-off Waddell family, owners of the Sunshine Dairy, Glen is full of insecurities and self-doubt. Although his oldest brother is a respected lawyer and another brother is a dentist, Glen can barely hold a job and moves from one low-paying

truck-driving position to another. Glen is neglected by his father, whom he wants to shock and, paradoxically, earn respect from by marrying into the disreputable Boatwright family and proving himself as a man who carries a knife and embraces violence. Despite a small, thin appearance, Glen is known for his enormous hands and his extreme, sudden temper.

Reese, Bone's younger sister. A pretty child who is never mishandled or abused by Glen, Reese is Bone's sometime ally and playmate.

Shannon Pearl, Bone's friend. A short, fat, half-blind albino, Shannon carries with her a rage and resentment not unlike Bone's. Although her parents pet and adore her, most others find her repulsive.

Raylene Boatwright, Bone's aunt. A short, stocky, broadshouldered woman with closely cropped hair and an affinity for masculine dress, Aunt Raylene lives apart from the rest of the family, alone in a house on the river outside town. The one love of her life, a woman she met while working at the carnival, left Raylene for the sake of her child.

— Jodi Dean

THE BATHHOUSE: A Drama in Six Acts with a Circus and Fireworks
(Banya)

Author: Vladimir Mayakovsky (1893-1930)
First published: 1930
Genre: Drama

Locale: Moscow, the Soviet Union
Time: The late 1920's
Plot: Satire

Chudakov (chuh-dah-KOV), a Soviet inventor. He is a visionary who wants to build a time machine that will enable people to extend moments of joy and contract periods of sorrow. Single-minded, serious, hardworking, and without government support, he succeeds in making contact with the future. At the end of the play, his invention carries him and many others a hundred years into the future.

The Phosphorescent Woman, an emissary from the year 2030 who is contacted by Chudakov's invention. She comes from a time when Communism has triumphed worldwide. Articulate and authoritative, she intends to bring into the perfect state those twentieth century citizens most responsible for building it. Her Communism is humanitarian rather than ideological, commonsensical rather than doctrinaire.

Pobedonosikov (poh-bee-doh-NOH-see-kov), the chief of

the Federal Bureau of Coordination. He is a Soviet bureaucrat in love with power. Although he speaks the jargon of an egalitarian people's revolution, he delights in acquiring privileges and pulling rank. He maintains authority by reminding everyone of his (self-inflated) role in the 1917 Revolution. When the Phosphorescent Woman arrives to carry the best Communists into the future, he tries to control the operation but instead is left behind.

Velosipedkin (veh-loh-see-PEHD-kihn), an official from the Young Communist League. A worker dedicated to socialism, he is practical, aggressive, and savvy. At first skeptical of Chudakov's invention, he later becomes its strongest advocate. He battles bureaucrats in the attempt to get government support and, after the arrival of the Phosphorescent Woman, helps choose the best Communists for transportation to the future.

Optimistenko (op-tee-MEE-stehn-koh), Pobedonosikov's secretary. The quintessential bureaucrat, he shields his boss from the petitions of ordinary citizens. He is dedicated to following procedures rather than to achieving results. For each petitioner in the long queue, he has a different excuse why his boss cannot help. While worrying if the time machine has food service, he is left behind.

Polya (POH-lyah), Pobedonosikov's wife. Tired of her husband's marital arrogance and extramarital affairs, she is a secret supporter of the time machine. Ironically, she secures money from an embezzler in Pobedonosikov's office to finance a key phase of Chudakov's experiment. She convinces the Phosphorescent Woman that she belongs in the future, when married couples will be more honest and more affectionate.

Isaac Belvedonsky (behl-veh-DOHN-skih), a painter and photographer. He lacks artistic ability and artistic integrity. He sells his work to Pobedonosikov by catering to the bureau chief's ego and acquisitiveness. He specializes in bourgeois objects with a revolutionary twist, for example, a Louis Quatorze sofa decorated with hammer-and-sickle fabric.

Pont Kich (kihch), a British visitor who is in Russia to admire Soviet achievements. He speaks a kind of fractured Russian, mixing English vocabulary and Russian syntax. He indiscriminately praises what he sees and uncritically accepts what his bureaucratic guides tell him, that the Soviets have already achieved the Communist ideal.

Madame Mezalyansova (meh-zah-LYAN-tsoh-vah), an interpreter who escorts Pont Kich. She is Pobedonosikov's mistress and flaunts her status in front of Polya.

The Director of the Play, who becomes a character for one scene. Close to exasperation, he reasons with the actors who perform the roles of bureaucrats when they threaten to abandon their parts. The actors complain that they portray ignoble, unworthy social types. Desperate to save the play, he convinces them to continue the performance by introducing an uplifting, ideological pantomime into the play.

— *Robert M. Otten*

BATOUALA
(Batouala, véritable roman nègre)

Author: René Maran (1887-1960)
First published: 1921
Genre: Novel

Locale: Ubangi-Shari and French Equatorial Africa
Time: c. 1910
Plot: Social realism

Batouala (bah-TEW-ah-la), a chief of many villages in French Equatorial Africa. Vigorous and strong of limb, his prowess in the hunt, in love, and in war is a legend across his domain. He is a jealous, violent, and vengeful man. He honors Bissibingui with particular esteem until he becomes aware of the young man's desire for his favorite wife, Yassiguindja. From then on, he uses his friendship as a cloak for his jealousy and quietly plans revenge on his rival. On a hunt, he hurls a javelin at Bissibingui but misses his target and is himself ripped open by a panther's paw. As Batouala lies dying, Yassiguindja yields to Bissibingui's desire, and the two flee into the night.

Bissibingui (bee-see-BEEN-gwee), a desirable young man. Having received from eight of Batouala's nine wives proofs of their admiration and affection, he now desires his chief's ninth and favorite wife, Yassiguindja. He finally possesses her as Batouala lies dying.

Yassiguindja (yah-see-GWEE-njah), the favorite among Batouala's nine wives. Though she desires Bissibingui, she is aware of Batouala's jealousy and violence, and she will not give herself to his rival until she feels safe from discovery. She finally becomes Bissibingui's as Batouala lies dying.

Indouvoura (ihn-dew-VEW-rah), another of Batouala's wives.

THE BATTLE OF PHARSALUS
(La Bataille de Pharsale)

Author: Claude Simon (1913-   )
First published: 1969
Genre: Novel

Locale: Paris, France; on board a train in Europe; and Greece
Time: The 1960's and the ancient past
Plot: Antistory

O., the narrator and principal character in a series of events that are not told chronologically but are instead presented as the free play of his memory, which acts as a kind of "mobile," circling and changing position around a few fixed points, the most important events of his life. O.'s profession is never stated, but he is a classical scholar of sorts, and he is fascinated by the Battle of Pharsalus, about which he read as a schoolboy and the exact location of which, as an adult, he has tried to find in the north of Greece. His translations of Caesar, however, are awkward, and his interest in Roman history is limited to this battle and to Caesar's profile on the coins and bills of the countries he visits on a train trip through Europe. O. is not a writer, but he is interested in the multiple meanings of words.

Lists of Latin words, with their French meanings, are scattered throughout the narrative. The visual possibilities of letters fascinate him—the *A* in the word pantalon in an advertisement for a clothing store becomes a pair of pants. O. is not an artist, although he is writing an essay on a painting in a German museum and greatly admires battle paintings by Nicolas Poussin, Piero Della Francesca, and Paolo Uccello. Only briefly is O. seen in an office, which is probably in the old home on the family estate in southern France. He counts out small piles of money in it, just as Uncle Charles used to do, to pay the dirty, shadowy men waiting outside in the dark hallway. He still lives in this place, with a wife whom he does not love and two children whom he does.

Odette, O.'s lover, an artist's model with dark eyes and a cloud of black hair. Her child's face is made up like a "poisonous flower." She sometimes lies among cushions, surrounded by porcelain and vases of flowers, wearing a Japanese kimono, after posing for the painter, Van Velden. Sometimes, she is with O., wearing a cheap street dress and chipped fingernail polish. Her promiscuity is well known and drives O. to behavior of which he is later ashamed.

Uncle Charles, a relative whom O. remembers as being in the office, which smells of old wine and tobacco, seated at his desk, holding a half-smoked cigar in his bony hand, wearing eyeglasses that reflect the light. He is correcting, and often ridiculing, the young O.'s translation of Caesar's account of the battle of Pharsalus.

O.'s grandmother, a matriarchal figure in her old-fashioned clothes of serge or dark silk, with a high collar and small tucks across the bodice, a cameo at her throat. There is majesty and importance in her position and her age. To the young boy, she represents death.

— *Lucy Golsan*

THE BAY OF SILENCE
(La bahía de silencio)

Author: Eduardo Mallea (1903-1982)
First published: 1940
Genre: Novel

Locale: Buenos Aires, Argentina; Paris, France; Brussels, Belgium; and Como, Italy
Time: Late 1920's or 1930's
Plot: Psychological realism

Martín Tregua (mahr-TEEN TRAY-gwah), the narrator, a law student living in a boarding house in Buenos Aires. Disaffected with law school, he quits to devote himself to writing. He publishes a book of poems and becomes deeply involved with the publication of a new and provocative journal, titled *Enough*. When the patron of the review closes it down, Martín spends several years in isolation, living and writing while supporting himself on an inheritance from his father. He has one serious relationship with a woman, Mercedes Miró, that fizzles out. He deeply admires Señora de Cárdenas, whom he idealizes and observes only from afar. After spending some time in Europe, he returns to Buenos Aires, where he develops an odd but serious relationship with Gloria Bambil, a librarian whose listlessness challenges Martín to enliven her and to make her happy. At the novel's end, Martín is once again alone; Gloria has taken her own life. Señora de Cárdenas remains his inspiration and his model, his ideal, and he remains a solitary writer.

Señora de Cárdenas (see-NYOH-rah day CAHR-day-nahs), a mysterious character referred to only as "you" for most of the novel. Her identity is revealed gradually by the accretion of details throughout the text, in which her life history is interwoven. Born into an aristocratic family dating from colonial times, she is both noble and rich. She rejects the model prescribed by her social status and marries below her station, out of pity and rebellion, not out of love. Her husband comes to resent her status and wealth. His sense of inferiority leads him to drink, to womanize, and to sell his influence to the highest buyer; in short, he disgraces himself. Through it all, and through the birth of two sons, one of whom dies in a horseback riding accident, Señora de Cárdenas maintains her dignity and grace. Although she speaks to Martín only once, it is to her that his text, which is this novel, is addressed.

Jiménez (hee-MEHN-ehz), a close friend of Martín who lives at the boarding house and works on *Enough*. He has an affair with the sympathetic Inés Boll, whose estranged husband beats him about the head with his cane, breaking Jiménez's glasses on his face, lacerating his eyes. He is partially blinded as a result.

César Acevedo (SEH-sahr ah-seh-VEH-doh), the organizer and patron of *Enough*. After several numbers, he closes the review because of a lack of financial support and the apathy of the Argentine people toward their own political situation. He reappears late in the novel, an embittered man whose second marriage has gone poorly.

Mercedes Miró (mee-ROH), an intriguing young woman with whom Martín has an affair of some duration. Despite her captivating personality and intellect, he calls off the affair.

Inés Boll (ee-NEHS), a quiet and sad woman living in the boarding house. She is separated from her husband and begins an affair with Jiménez that ends tragically.

Dr. René Ferrier, a physician with whom Martín stays while in Brussels. Although he is the victim of a liver ailment, he suffers from existential angst and drinks from morning until night. He confesses to treating patients for the money it brings him, whether or not he is competent to treat them.

Cesare Antoriello (cheh-ZAH-ray AHN-toh-ree-EHL-loh), a biologist who immigrated from Italy to escape the Fascist sentiment on the rise there. He devotes his days to editing his dead son Ezio's socialist papers and spends his evenings hosting political discussions among other anti-Fascists.

Gloria Bambil (bahm-BEEL), a librarian with whom Martín has his longest and most serious relationship. The death of her mother when she was very young, followed by the lengthy illness of her manipulative, destructive father, made Gloria an isolated person who thinks poorly of herself. Her perennial sadness and distance challenge Martín, who spends much time trying to bring her happiness. She complains that she is damaging to him; he disagrees. Because he abandons his writing for long periods or at inopportune times so that he can be with her, there is some truth to what she says. She tries to force him to break off their relationship, but he refuses. She suggests that they spend a week together at the seashore. She seems very happy, but she is emaciated by the end of the week. Though never explicitly stated, it is clear that Gloria commits suicide shortly after their final week together.

— *Linda Ledford-Miller*

THE BEACH OF FALESÁ

Author: Robert Louis Stevenson (1850-1894)
First published: 1892
Genre: Novel

Locale: Falesá, a South Sea island
Time: Nineteenth century
Plot: Adventure

Wiltshire, a rough, uneducated, but courageous trader who has just come to Falesá. His predecessors having been killed or driven away by Case, a rival trader, Wiltshire immediately finds himself the object of Case's villainy. Pretending friendship, Case persuades him to marry a native girl who is under a taboo. As a result, not a single native will trade with Wiltshire.

Case, a rival who plays on the superstitions of the natives. In order to control the island, he pretends to be in league with a powerful devil. When discovered, he shoots and wounds both Wiltshire and Uma; Wiltshire then kills him with a knife.

Uma, a modest islander married in a false ceremony to Wiltshire. Because she is under a taboo, the natives will not trade with Wiltshire. Her mother is a producer of copra.

Tarleton, the missionary who marries Wiltshire and Uma.

Captain Randall, the supposed owner of a trading post and a friend of Case.

Black Jack, Case's confederate.

Maea, the most powerful chief of Falesá, who eventually gives his trade to Wiltshire in order to break Case's hold on the natives.

Vigours, an earlier trader frightened away by Case.

John Adams, another trader, who dies insane.

BEACHMASTERS

Author: Thea Astley (1925-   )
First published: 1985
Genre: Novel

Locale: Kristi, a South Pacific island
Time: Early 1980's
Plot: Social morality

Tommy Narota, the leader of a rebellion on a tiny South Pacific island. The son of a native woman and a British planter, Narota, who is approximately fifty years old, is a gentle and naïve sort, not at all a typical revolutionary. His firmly held belief in the native people's right to govern themselves on their own island inspires them to revolt, albeit unsuccessfully, against the European powers that have so long dominated them.

Gavi Salway, a teenage boy who learns at the rebellion's start that he is a half-caste. He had been reared believing that he was the child of British planters. Possessing a keen sensitivity and awareness, Gavi sets out to grasp the significance of this discovery. During the short-lived rebellion, he makes his passage into manhood.

District Agent Cordingley, the island's major British official. In appearance, speech, and actions, the middle-aged Cordingley is a near caricature of British colonial administrators. Typically, he responds to the rebellion in a bumbling, cowardly manner.

Bonser, a crude, bigoted, and exploitative Australian expatriate who works as a mechanic on the island. The rebellion to him simply provides a way to make money through gun smuggling.

Père Leyroud, an aging Roman Catholic priest who has spent forty years on the island. The rebellion serves to heighten his sense of failure and his disillusionment with the religion he preaches.

Salway, a British planter and Gavi's grandfather, who has been an island resident for fifty years. Wise and gentle, he sees the rebellion as a sign of a passing era and the end of deception concerning Gavi's true parentage.

Woodful, the school's middle-aged headmaster, who displays more understanding of the natives than most of his fellow Anglo-Saxons on the island. Woodful realizes that the rebellion has undone all of his years of well-intended struggle, and he accepts that truth.

Chloe of the Dancing Bears, an aging prostitute of British descent. A minor character, Chloe stands out as a representative of several such decadent colonial types portrayed briefly in the novel. Having long used the island as a retreat from shattered lives that they cannot face, they ignore the revolution as well.

Letty Trumble, the middle-aged wife of a minor British official. Prudish, pretentious, racist, and sexually frustrated, Trumble represents a typical kind of woman that colonialism produced.

Belle Cordingley, the American wife of District Agent Cordingley. She is a brassy blonde whose responses and actions border on the comic as she expresses bitterness and disappointment over her husband's past failures and his pathetic behavior during the rebellion.

— *Robert L. Ross*

THE BEAN TREES

Author: Barbara Kingsolver (1955-   )
First published: 1988
Genre: Novel

Locale: Tucson, Arizona
Time: Late 1980's
Plot: Social realism

Taylor Greer, the protagonist and narrator. Born and reared in rural Pittman, Kentucky, she vows not to get pregnant and live the rest of her life in Pittman. After graduating from high school and working for five years in a hospital lab, she buys an old Volkswagen and drives west. She acquires an abandoned Native American child, whom she names Turtle, in

Oklahoma. Taylor and Turtle end up in Tucson, Arizona, where Taylor struggles to rear a child by herself and earn a living. She becomes involved in the sanctuary movement for Central American refugees. Tough-minded and resilient, Taylor meets these challenges with humor, optimism, and courage.

Turtle Greer, Taylor's adopted Native American daughter. When Taylor leaves Kentucky to drive west, a young Native American woman leaves the two-year-old Turtle in Taylor's car. Turtle has been severely abused and does not begin to speak until six months after her arrival in Tucson. Taylor knows nothing about Turtle's parents or her background.

Lou Ann Ruiz (née Logan), who also is originally from Kentucky. She lives in Tucson with her infant son Dwayne Ray. After her husband, Angel Ruiz, leaves her, she advertises for a roommate, and Taylor and Turtle move in with her. Lou Ann is more traditionally domestic—and more pessimistic—than Taylor, but she provides Taylor with friendship and support, and Taylor works to bolster Lou Ann's self-esteem.

Mattie, the widowed proprietor of Jesus Is Lord Used Tires. She is both an accomplished mechanic and an important figure in Tucson's underground sanctuary movement. When Taylor and Turtle first come to town, Mattie helps them, including later giving Taylor a job at the tire shop. She becomes a role model for Taylor, teaching her about both motherhood and political activism.

Estevan (ay-STAY-vahn), formerly an English teacher in his native Guatemala, is now a refugee living in Tucson with his wife, Esperanza. He works at a Chinese restaurant as a dishwasher. Estevan and Taylor are attracted to one another, but they develop only a close friendship.

Esperanza (ay-spay-RAHN-zah), Estevan's wife. She does not speak much English. Both she and Estevan were active in a teacher's union in Guatemala, and the anti-union government forces abducted their daughter, Ismene, in an attempt to get them to reveal the names of other union members. The loss of their daughter has deeply affected them both; Esperanza has attempted suicide several times.

Virgie Mae Parsons, who lives next door to Taylor and Lou Ann. She is an elderly woman who lives with her companion, Edna Poppy. Opinionated and bigoted, Mrs. Parsons often helps Taylor and Lou Ann with child care while the younger women are at work.

Edna Poppy, Virgie Mae Parsons' housemate. She is also elderly, and blind. Much more sweet-tempered and good-natured than Mrs. Parsons, Edna also helps take care of Turtle and Dwayne Ray.

Alice Jean Stamper Greer, Taylor's mother, who still lives in Kentucky. Her first husband left before Taylor was born, and Alice reared Taylor by herself, supporting them by cleaning other people's houses. She has always been proud and supportive of Taylor.

— *Ann A. Merrill*

BEARHEART: The Heirship Chronicles

Author: Gerald Vizenor (1934-   )
First published: 1978
Genre: Novel

Locale: The central and western United States
Time: The future
Plot: Dystopian

Proude Cedarfair, the fourth of the Proude Cedarfairs, a shaman of mixed white and Chippewa (*anishinaabe*) blood. The nation's economy has been destroyed, and the reservation agents and corrupt tribal officials are cutting the last of the Cedar Circus Reservation cedar trees. Proude leads a group of unusual pilgrims on a trek toward the vision window at Pueblo Bonito, where he believes he can lead his troupe into the fourth world.

Rosina, Proude's wife. At the end of the journey, she comes over the desert with the sun and is identified with Changing Woman. She is one of three people who enter the fourth world.

Benito Saint Plumero, or **Bigfoot**, one of the pilgrims. He is a mixed-blood clown/trickster whose major source of pride is a gigantic and very active penis, dubbed President Jackson. He is canonized and made a "double saint" on the journey.

Pio Wissakodewinini, another pilgrim, who has been charged erroneously with rape and was sentenced to a sex change, which was not entirely successful. He/she shifts identities and gender often during the journey.

Inawa Biwide, a sixteen-year-old pilgrim rescued by the church from federal reservation housing. Inawa quickly becomes an apprentice shaman and eventually will follow Proude Cedarfair into the fourth world.

Bishop Omax Parasimo, who rescued Inawa. He wears metamasks that allow him to become **Sister Eternal Flame** and other characters of all genders. He is obsessed with the romantic image of Indianness of the type propagated by Hollywood.

Belladonna Darwin-Winter Catcher, a pilgrim, the daughter of a Lakota shaman and a white anthropologist. She was conceived and born at Wounded Knee, South Dakota, and has very rigid views. She holds what the author calls "terminal creeds." In the walled city of Orion, inhabited by the descendants of hunters and bucking horse breeders, she is asked about Indian values. She responds to a hunter's question about what an Indian "is" with a diatribe that reinforces all the clichés about Indian culture and behavior. She is identified as an "invented Indian," and as a result, she gets her "just desserts," a cookie laced with poison.

Little Big Mouse, a "small whitewoman with fresh water blue eyes" who rides in foot holsters at the waist of the giant Sun Bear Sun. She is attacked and torn apart by a mob of victims of chemical and cosmetic poisons because she insists on seeing them as victims.

Sun Bear Sun, the largest pilgrim, weighing three hundred pounds and standing seven feet tall. He is the son of a utopian tribal organizer by the name of Sun Bear.

Lillith Mae Farrier, a white woman and pilgrim who travels with her two boxers. She began her sexual ménage with the two dogs while teaching on an Indian reservation. She is the first to gamble with The Evil Gambler, and because she does not know the rituals of balance and power, she loses and destroys herself.

Bearheart, a mixed-blood shaman who, as a child, achieved a vision of a bear while imprisoned in a Bureau of Indian Affairs closet while the offices were being ransacked by radical members of the American Indian Movement (AIM). He is ill-tempered, especially toward "terminal creeds" and American culture. He tells a young AIM member wearing "chicken feathers and plastic beads" to read the novel in the closet, a novel of "tribal futures, futures without oil and governments to blame for personal failures." She asks what it is about, and he responds, "Sex and violence. . . . Travels through terminal creeds and social deeds escaping from evil into the fourth world where bears speak the secret languages of saints." The novel she finds is *Bearheart: The Heirship Chronicles*.

Sir Cecil Staples, called **The Evil Gambler**, the proprietor of the What Cheer Trailer Ruins. He gambles with passersby.

He bets gasoline, a necessity for the pilgrims' purloined postal truck, against the life of the bettor. He believes in chance, which Proude does not, and when Proude plays with him and wins, The Evil Gambler is destroyed. Kidnapped from a shopping mall and reared in a big-rig trailer on the road, he is pale and hairless as the result of prolonged exposure to insecticides.

Justice Pardone Cozener, a pilgrim and illiterate law school graduate, one of the "bigbellies" who are fleecing the tribes and the government. He is in love with Doctor Wilde Coxwaine.

Doctor Wilde Coxwaine, a pilgrim and bisexual tribal historian. He and Justice Pardone Cozener are entranced by the Bioavaricious Word Hospital and leave the remaining pilgrims to remain there.

Matchi Makwa, a minor pilgrim who complains about the loss of Indian racial purity.

— *N. Jacquelyn Kilpatrick*

BEAUCHAMP'S CAREER

Author: George Meredith (1828-1909)
First published: 1876; serial form, 1874-1875
Genre: Novel

Locale: England
Time: Nineteenth century
Plot: Political realism

Nevil Beauchamp (neh-VIHL boh-SHAWM), a young man who is eager to reform the world. He starts out as a naval officer but later decides to run for Parliament as a Liberal candidate. He falls in love with the sister of a French officer whose life he has saved, but she marries a man her father has chosen for her. Nevil loses the election, but the daughter of a Tory friend falls in love with him. When he proposes and she refuses him because of her father's demands, he falls ill. He marries Jenny Denham, who has nursed him during his illness. His death by drowning while trying to rescue a child ends his reformer's career.

Renée Rouaillout (ruh-NAY rew-ay-YEW), née **Renée de Croisnel** (kwah-NEHL), a rather fickle young Frenchwoman with whom Beauchamp falls in love. She refuses to marry him because she has promised her father that she will marry Rouaillout. After her marriage, she sends for Nevil because she has wagered with a friend that he will come if she sends for him. Renée leaves her husband and goes to Nevil, but he is no longer in love with her, and he effects a reconciliation between her and her husband.

Colonel Halkett, a friend of Beauchamp who is also a Tory and deplores Beauchamp's political views.

Cecelia Halkett, the colonel's daughter, who falls in love with Beauchamp because she admires his courage and thinks he is a man of high honor, in spite of his politics. She remains loyal to him through his various difficulties with Renée, but she finally bows to her father's wishes and marries a more stable young man.

Dr. Shrapnel, a wild political radical who is supposed to be helping Beauchamp with his campaign for Parliament, but who is really ruining his chances by giving him unstable ideas and advice. He is horsewhipped by Beauchamp's Uncle Everard when the uncle reads a letter that Shrapnel has written to Beauchamp that is full of radical advice.

Jenny Denham, Shrapnel's ward, who nurses Beauchamp back to health after his illness and finally marries him. She is loyal and steadfast through all of his troubles.

Everard Romfrey, Beauchamp's uncle, a conservative Englishman. He approves of an alliance between Cecelia and Beauchamp and hates Dr. Shrapnel. Romfrey's beating of Shrapnel causes a break between him and Beauchamp, but they are reconciled when Romfrey apologizes to Shrapnel.

Rosamund Culling, Romfrey's housekeeper, whom he finally marries.

THE BEAUTIFUL AND DAMNED

Author: F. Scott Fitzgerald (1896-1940)
First published: 1922
Genre: Novel

Locale: New York City and environs, and near a military training camp in South Carolina
Time: 1913-1921
Plot: Satire

Anthony Patch, a playboy and dilettante. Most of the novel is narrated from the point of view of this good-looking, intelligent, and fundamentally decent man and concerns his moral deterioration between the ages of twenty-five and thirty-three. He stands to inherit the lion's share of his grandfather's estate, worth about $75 million. This inheritance has a debilitating

effect on Anthony because it stifles any motive to do anything for himself, although he continues to entertain notions of writing about history. His parents died when he was a child, as did his paternal grandmother, who was rearing him in their stead. These tragedies left him with a chronic paranoid anxiety and help to explain why he is passive, immature, and lacking the aggressiveness to carve out a career for himself. With nothing serious to occupy his mind, he takes to drinking and becomes a hopeless alcoholic.

Gloria Gilbert Patch, Anthony's wife, three years his junior. Just as Anthony has never had to develop any strength of character because of his grandfather's riches, Gloria has never had to develop any strength of character because of her remarkable beauty. She is spoiled, selfish, and narcissistic. She believes that her beauty conveys a certain nobility upon her, so that she does not have to do anything; she merely has to be. Gloria is the worst possible wife for Anthony because she is as feckless and incompetent as he. She is Fitzgerald's model of a flapper: She is one of the first socialites to bob her hair and wear daring fashions. When her beauty begins to fade with age and dissipation, she becomes a lost soul.

Adam Patch, a millionaire and philanthropist, Anthony's grandfather. In his prime, Patch was a ruthless businessman, but in his old age, with death staring him in the face, he suddenly develops a conscience and begins trying to reform the world. He advocates hard work and sobriety, virtues that his grandson completely lacks. When Anthony learns upon the old man's death that he has been disinherited for his wild conduct, he and Gloria are thrown into desperate straits. Anthony continues squandering the meager capital he inherited from his mother and becomes involved in a seemingly endless lawsuit to overturn his grandfather's will.

Richard Caramel, Gloria's cousin and Anthony's best friend, a successful novelist. Pudgy and unattractive but talented and warmhearted, Caramel graduated from Harvard with his head full of ideals about "service to humanity." His first novel was a sincere work of art, but he gradually became corrupted by literary fame and the need to keep making money. His later works are potboilers, but he does not recognize them as such.

Maury Noble, another of Anthony's friends from Harvard days. This handsome, brilliant young man might have made important contributions to some branch of human thought but he can find no meaning in a mechanistic universe. He goes into business and becomes hardened and cynical while growing prosperous. He is another illustration of Fitzgerald's thesis that the blind forces of nature have countless ways of corroding innocence and beauty.

Joseph Bloeckman, a Jewish motion picture producer. He is in love with Gloria but loses her to Anthony, who appears to have more to offer in terms of wealth and social prestige. Bloeckman serves as a foil to Anthony: Through his brains and ambition, he acquires money, power, and even the upper-class polish that he initially lacked. His success in spite of disadvantages highlights Anthony's weakness of character.

Dorothy Raycroft, Anthony's mistress during World War I. Anthony is sent to training camp in South Carolina, where he meets this pretty, unsophisticated country girl of nineteen. After the war ends, she follows him to New York and causes him to have a nervous breakdown by demanding his love when he is in the final stages of his character disintegration and has nothing left to give anyone.

— *Bill Delaney*

BEAUTY AND SADNESS
(Utsukushisa to kanashimi to)

Author: Yasunari Kawabata (1899-1972)
First published: 1961-1963
Genre: Novel

Locale: Kyoto and Kamakura, Japan
Time: 1961
Plot: Psychological realism

Toshio Oki, a fifty-four-year-old novelist. He is a sentimental man, in the ascetic and reserved manner of the Japanese aesthetic. When Toshio was thirty years old and newly married, he had an affair with a fifteen-year-old girl. He later fictionalized this affair, and the resulting book became his best, most acclaimed, and most enduring novel. He sets the present-time action of the novel going with an impulsive action: He arranges to meet his former mistress and to listen with her to the tolling of temple bells at midnight on New Year's Eve. Instead of resulting in the hoped-for insight and perspective, the meeting brings more involvement; Toshio finds himself starting a romance, parallel to his first affair, with his former mistress's young protegée, meeting the same dilemmas and making the same flawed choices.

Otoko Ueno, a traditional Japanese painter who, at the age of fifteen, was Toshio's mistress. A reflective woman, she spends much of her time reminiscing, musing about her life and the poignant, never-to-be-spoken feelings that became the subjects of her paintings. Although she has a firmly established career and a new lover, her affair with Toshio, their love, the stillborn baby they conceived, and her eventual mental breakdown and hospitalization are still the foremost events in her life. Otoko wonders whether she should attribute the hold that the affair has over her to the power of art rather than to an enduring grand passion. Toshio's novel, although idealized, has kept their affair alive in the memory of the public. Otoko herself has forged an attachment to her lost baby by working on an idealized portrait, a picture of a child she never saw. Although she had been Toshio's saucy young lover, the main mark of her character is reflection. She is largely passive as her unreserved young companion undertakes to complete the story of Toshio and Otoko's affair.

Keiko Sakami, Otoko's student, companion, and lover. She is young, full of passionate energy, and without reserve, even ruthless, in her actions. She is beautiful, reminding many of the young Otoko. Although she asserts that she hates men, she has no reservations about using her powers of seduction against them. To Otoko's horror, she announces her plan to avenge Otoko on Toshio and his family. It may be that the revenge is directed as much against Otoko as for her benefit. Although she does cause Toshio some trouble with his wife, she does nothing against him that she might not have done had she merely wanted to be his lover. Later, however, she seduces his shy son, Taichiro. Knowing that he cannot swim, she entices him into a motorboat. She survives an apparent accident, and he dies by drowning.

Fumiko, Toshio's wife. Formerly an office typist, she is now established in the life and sentiments of an Oriental wife and mother. Newly married and in her early childbearing years when Toshio started his affair, she reacted sometimes with jealous rage and sometimes with displays of tragedy. In one of the latter, she had endangered the health of her baby, the young Taichiro. When she read Toshio's novel about the affair, she suffered a miscarriage. Still later, she became reconciled to the affair, even saying that she should have given Toshio his freedom. In the present time of the novel, Fumiko's rage and tragic pathos have muted, and she and Toshio have made a kind of peace over the affair. It is neither forgotten nor an open rift between them.

Taichiro, Toshio's son, a university professor specializing in traditional Japanese literature. Shy and scholarly, and still living with his parents, he has not, despite his advanced position, become fully his own man. He is a committed antiquarian, knowledgeable and enthusiastic about Japanese history and literature, subjects he is afraid may die from inattention. He is taken aback by Keiko's ignorance of her own heritage; nevertheless, he is easy prey for her seduction. In her company, he makes progress toward adulthood. As she leads him to take steps away from his family, however, she is only accomplishing her plan of revenge and arranging his seemingly accidental death.

— *Fritz Monsma*

THE BEAUTYFUL ONES ARE NOT YET BORN

Author: Ayi Kwei Armah (1939-   )
First published: 1968
Genre: Novel

Locale: A coastal city in Ghana
Time: 1965-1966
Plot: Social realism

The man, deliberately given the generality of anonymity, a clerk who works for the nationalized railway system in Ghana. He and his wife, Oyo, and their children live in comparative poverty because of the man's unflinching determination not to accept bribes but to live on his inadequate salary in a society that finds such behavior incomprehensible. In spite of the temptations that come to him from every side, the constant nagging of his bitter wife, and his own awareness of the hardships his honesty imposes upon his children, he maintains his unalterable moral stance. His determination is in some measure justified when a coup destroys the regime and the corrupt are arrested, but as he begins to rejoice in the vigorous national purge of corruption, he witnesses the same old crookedness immediately reactivated. The man represents, to an exaggerated degree, an idealized portrait of a truly noble man in a degraded society.

Oyo, the man's wife. She has no sympathy for her husband's honesty and all but despises him for it. Indifferent to the principles involved, she can only see how well others are managing as a result of their acquiescence to wrongdoing. She has a deep envy of the successful and yearns for the luxuries that other women enjoy. Only at the end does she commend her husband when she sees the painful consequences of corruption that come when the criminals are arrested.

Koomson, a government minister who epitomizes the grossly corrupt African politician of the postindependence years. He has come up the hard way, starting out as a tough dockworker. He is gross and vulgar but can convincingly assume a cheerful, hearty public manner that appeals to voters. He distributes bribes freely, indulging his family with all the most visibly ostentatious material things, invariably from Europe, for in Ghana only expensive foreign imports are evidence of success; local products are for failures. Koomson swindles the man's mother in a tax-evasion dodge to buy a boat, which he uses for his escape from the police when the new regime orders his arrest. At the end, he is a frightened and defeated fugitive, using his last banknotes to bribe his way to safety.

Estella, Koomson's wife, an egregious snob who embodies the pretensions of the nouveau riche. Ironically, her behavior is patterned after the arrogance of the white colonials from whom her country has been liberated politically but not yet culturally. When her husband escapes into exile, the new administration does not prosecute her, and she survives to live on in Ghana in reduced circumstances.

The teacher, another generalized figure, the man's teacher, guide, counselor, and guru. The teacher supplies him with the intellectual rationalization for his search for moral order in a delinquent and disintegrating society, reinforcing the man's personal determination with philosophic precedent. The teacher plays no active part in the events of the novel, but his long conversations and debates with the man allow the author to air his angry response to the overwhelming corruption that festers within his country.

— *John F. Povey*

THE BEAUX' STRATAGEM

Author: George Farquhar (1678?-1707)
First published: 1707
Genre: Drama

Locale: Litchfield, England
Time: Early eighteenth century
Plot: Comedy of manners

Charles, Viscount Aimwell, a gentleman who, being low in funds, is traveling in disguise, hoping to attract a country heiress. He finds her in the person of Dorinda, but consummating the union takes considerable doing. Being a second son, he is at first without the title that, upon his brother's death, comes to him shortly before he marries the heiress. In their pretended commonness, Aimwell and Archer are a source of perpetual amusement.

Francis Archer, Esq., also a gentleman out of funds, masquerading as Aimwell's servant. The men take turns, by the month, at being master and servant. Archer's initial idle flirtation with Cherry develops into true love. Because of their secretive behavior—the result of their assumed roles—Archer and Aimwell are falsely suspected of being highwaymen, adding to the havoc created by their pursuits of wealthy ladies.

Cherry, the vivacious daughter of Bonniface, an innkeeper. She is privy to the highwaymen's activities and her father's alliance with them. Prompted by her father, she spies on Aimwell and Archer, but she falls in love with Archer and he with her. Cherry contributes greatly to the comic spirit and humor of the play.

Dorinda, the modest, reserved daughter of Lady Bountiful. Hearing Dorinda spoken of as the finest woman in the country and a prospective heiress, the calculating Aimwell sets out to win her for her money. When he acquires his title and wealth, he marries her for love.

Bonniface, an innkeeper, Cherry's father, about fifty-eight years old. He has, according to his word, subsisted mainly on ale his entire life. An unscrupulous rogue, he does not hesitate to offer his daughter to an unworthy suitor when he thinks the arrangement might aid his purposes. It is finally revealed that he has run away in fear of reprisal from the other rogues.

Sullen, Dorinda's brother, a country blockhead. He is rude, stupid, and frequently drunk. He speaks little and thinks and acts even less. Although he is a man of property and is idolized by his influential mother, he is generally disliked and disregarded.

Mrs. Sullen, his wife. Unhappy in her marriage, she is frank in saying so. Paradoxically, she admits that she would endure the rude Sullen if only his manner were tempered with a little kindness. Sarcastic and abusive, she is really gentler than she sounds. With romantic scheming, she rids herself of one husband and gets another.

Scrub, Sullen's crude, comical servant. He carries the secrets of the ladies and the beaux as circumstances require.

Lady Bountiful, the mother of Sullen and Dorinda. She is reputed to be the wisest and kindest nurse in Litchfield, and to have cured more people—although by strange methods—in ten years than the doctors have killed in twenty.

Count Bellair, a French officer held prisoner in Litchfield, with whom Mrs. Sullen begins a flirtation to arouse Sullen's jealousy. The scheme merely increases Sullen's indifference. The Sullens are divorced by mutual agreement, and Mrs. Sullen will marry the count.

Sir Charles Freeman, a gentleman from London. Arriving to rescue Mrs. Sullen, his sister, from her unfortunate marriage, he brings news of Aimwell's newly granted title.

Foigard (fwah-GAHR), an Irishman pretending to be the priest and chaplain of the French officers. He provides comedy with his lack of understanding and poor command of spoken English. Finally, he is unmasked.

Gibbet, a highwayman, an emissary between Bonniface and the gang.

Hounslow and

Bagshot, highwaymen who contribute to the development of the subplot.

THE BEAVER COAT
(Der Biberpelz)

Author: Gerhart Hauptmann (1862-1946)
First published: 1893
Genre: Drama

Locale: The outskirts of Berlin
Time: The nineteenth century
Plot: Satire

Frau Wolff, a washerwoman and the ringleader of a gang of dealers in stolen goods. Protected by her reputation as an honest woman, she sets about stealing from her daughter's employer, Krüger, a load of wood and a beaver coat for delivery to the fence, Wulkow. By virtue of her own wit, the false testimony of other witnesses, and the incompetence of the justice of the peace, von Wehrhahn, the innocent in the affair are made to appear guilty, and Frau Wolff emerges as the soul of honor.

Julius Wolff, Frau Wolff's husband, a shipwright and ferry captain who uses his nautical activities as a front for his real business in life, the illegal snaring of game.

Leontine (LAY-ohn-tee-neh), the elder daughter of Julius and Frau Wolff. She is hired out to Krüger but returns home complaining that he sends her after wood late at night. Her flight is used by Frau Wolff as an opportunity to steal the wood.

Udelheid (OO-dehl-hid), Julius and Frau Wolff's younger daughter. She is used by her family as a verifier of invented evidence.

Wulkow (VOOL-koh), a boatman and a receiver of stolen goods. When he makes known his desire for a fur, his request is cheerfully filled by Frau Wolff, who delivers to him, for a price, Krüger's beaver coat.

Krüger (KREW-gur), Leontine's well-to-do employer, who is relieved by her thieving family of his load of wood and his beaver coat.

Von Wehrhahn (VAYR-hahn), the justice of the peace. He is so taken up with rigging evidence against Dr. Fleischer for a supposed slight that he cannot see to it that justice is done in his court.

Doctor Fleischer (FLI-shur), Krüger's friend, a liberal democrat who incurs the wrath of von Wehrhahn and, unwittingly, blocks the path of justice.

Motes, an informer and giver of false evidence.

BECAUSE IT IS BITTER, AND BECAUSE IT IS MY HEART

Author: Joyce Carol Oates (1938-   )
First published: 1990
Genre: Novel

Locale: A small town in western New York State
Time: The 1950's and early 1960's
Plot: Psychological realism

Iris Courtney, the daughter of troubled parents. She is a striving young teenager determined to move up in the world. On the surface, she is a good student and a happy, normal teenager; underneath is a roiling, overheated inner world of desires and compulsions. She papers over this side of herself with an agreeable persona, but as a result she becomes increasingly false and duplicitous; her outer being does not bear any resemblance to the churning libidinous, even suicidal, secret self. After the murder of Little Red Garlock by Jinx Fairchild, who has been drawn into the role of Iris' protector, she develops an obsessional erotic attachment to Jinx, and possibly to black men in general, which she keeps hidden from the outside world. Iris' name is ironic because she is not the fragile flower she appears to be. Using her strength, her intellect, and a single-minded ruthlessness, Iris moves up the social and economic ladder. She crosses into affluent America and will marry the patrician son of one of her college professors, but this success seems to have been purchased at the expense of her sexual feelings. In spite of her sweet good looks and surface charm, her continued duplicity makes her surprisingly bitter and cynical.

Jinx Fairchild, a teenager from a struggling black family who has a chance to succeed in the respectable white world. He is a star high school basketball player, but his sports nickname is also a metaphor for his unlucky life, which takes a terrible turn when he is impressed into defending Iris Courtney against Little Red Garlock's repulsive sexual advances. Although, like Iris, Jinx never reveals his role in the murder to the police, the crime has a serious effect on him. He cannot trust the white community of Hammond to give him a fair trial, and he becomes increasingly alienated from the world that once seemed to promise him great opportunities. He is also trapped in a pact of silence with Iris, a secret bond that continues to haunt them both. Jinx undergoes a fragmentation of his identity, developing a side filled with turbulent and inchoate feelings; he is no longer clear about himself. Trusting and idealistic as a youth, he becomes increasingly bitter and cyni-

cal, and his guilt feelings lead to a self-punishing "accident" on the basketball court that ruins his career as an athlete. His hopes and dreams crushed, Jinx gives up his college ambitions and eventually dies in the Vietnam War.

Persia Courtney, the mother of Iris and wife of Duke. A free spirit whose name evokes the Orient, she carries an aura of both the erotic and the exotic, but she is often intoxicated and eventually succumbs to insanity and alcohol. There is a deep bond between her and her daughter. They both become involved with black men, and both are drawn into behavior that transgresses the conventions of their society.

Duke Courtney, Iris Courtney's father. His name indicates his identity as a "sporting gent," and he eventually gives himself over to gambling, neglecting his wife and daughter.

Mr. Savage, a cultured, intellectual college professor who exudes social confidence and an elite liberalism. His family is not part of the grubby world of Hammond; it belongs to a cultivated, wealthy, upper-class world.

Mrs. Savage, a kind and handsome woman with a beautiful home and fine family. Estranged from her daughter, who has fled to New York and a less conventional life, Mrs. Savage becomes a second mother to Iris. For all her graciousness, there is an empty, unfulfilled, lonely side to Mrs. Savage, as if all her wealth and social dominance have not brought her any real happiness.

Alan Savage, the weak but agreeable son of the Savages, a secretive young man who may be homosexual. It is clear that Alan has denied his desires in order to accede to his family's wish that he marry Iris. Like Iris, he has a hidden side of his nature that he attempts to repudiate.

Little Red Garlock, a violent and demented young man, the product of Hammond's poor white underclass. He has been brought up badly by his racist mother, whose life is one of squalor and mental instability. He uses poor judgment in making sexual overtures to Iris Courtney and picking a fight with her defender, Jinx Fairchild, who eventually murders him.

— *Margaret Boe Birns*

BECKET: Or, The Honor of God
(Becket: Ou, L'Honneur de Dieu)

Author: Jean Anouilh (1910-1987)
First published: 1959
Genre: Drama

Locale: England, France, and Rome
Time: 1154-1189
Plot: Historical

Henry II, the high-strung Norman king of England, who defines his power in terms of his relationship with his friend, adviser, and eventual adversary Thomas Becket. Henry's demeanor, as well as his age, changes as he goes from young optimistic monarch to disillusioned sovereign. Initially, he believes that all he has to do to accomplish something is to give the order and have it obeyed. This simplistic attitude changes as he discovers that vested interests are formidable bulwarks. Furthermore, people develop different priorities as circumstances change; their attitudes in life alter as their roles in life differ. Henry becomes more withdrawn and isolated; he feels deserted by everybody and realizes that he must learn to be alone. In his desperation, he cries out for others to save him, thus preparing the way for the play's ultimate tragedy.

Thomas à Becket, a Saxon of common birth whose love of luxury and desire to elevate himself from his despised origins lead him into a friendship with King Henry, with whom he helps pass the time drinking and wenching. Henry appoints him chancellor of England and then Archbishop of Canterbury. In doing so, he precipitates Becket's transformation from a servant of the crown to a servant of God, putting him on a collision course with the authority of the monarch. Becket regains his honor and atones for having cheated his way into the ranks of the conquerors of his people through his martyrdom.

Gilbert Folliot, the bishop of London, "a thin-lipped, venomous man" who is led more by his antipathies than by his principles. Loyalty to the church proves less durable than his hatred of Becket. He is not without courage, although predisposed to believing that the interests of church and state are one, making it easy for him to become an agent for the condemnation of Becket.

Gwendolen, Becket's young Welsh mistress. He acquires her as a spoil of war, but she grows to love him. She becomes a symbol of Becket's devotion to Henry when Henry demands that she be delivered to his bed as a favor. Gwendolen goes without protest, but when Henry tries to embrace her, she commits suicide.

The Four English Barons, whom Henry calls his "four idiots" and his "faithful hounds." Their unswerving loyalty to the crown gives him reassurance of his own worth. These men are so willing to please that they respond to the royal will even without a direct order. They symbolize the triumph of the ethical state that has no higher goal than loyalty to itself, and they serve it even should their path lead to murder.

The Archbishop of Canterbury, Becket's elderly predecessor, an old-time server who tries to reach an accommodation with the state by appealing to reason. When that fails, he is not above using his office to get his way. He knows that he is too old for a confrontation with the king over the issue of taxation of the church, and he urges circumspection, hoping that Becket will, in time, prove to be an ally.

Louis, king of France, "a burly man with intelligent eyes" who shows that the nature of his position is to make things as difficult for England as possible. He is not averse to becoming involved in the struggles between the English Catholic church and the state. He grants Becket his royal protection, at least until the political climate might change. Louis knows that there is no principle in politics, save inconsistency.

The Pope, a thin, fidgety, small man with a problem: He needs money but believes that if he takes it from the king of England, he cannot give support to Becket, who is fighting for the rights of the church. He wants to survive in a world of high intrigue and apparently will make any kind of deal as long as he can hold on to a good reputation.

Cardinal Zambelli, the swarthy and somewhat grubby adviser to the pontiff, who tells the Pope that he should play a double game: relieve Becket of his functions as primate and then immediately reappoint him, thus scoring points against both him and the king of England. In this world of high papal politics, epitomized by this cardinal and pope, everything is a game played by constantly changing rules.

The Queen Mother, who believes that if her son Henry had only listened to her, he would not be in the mess he is in now.

The Young Queen, Henry's wife. She is a constant object of his abuse. She is naturally disturbed that her husband prefers debauchery with his friend Becket to attending to his duties as a father and husband. In her bitterness, she becomes a nag.

Henry and

Richard, Henry's young sons. He treats them with great contempt as his family generally becomes the object of his scorn and ire.

— *Wm. Laird Kleine-Ahlbrandt*

THE BEDBUG: An Extravaganza in Nine Scenes
(Klop)

Author: Vladimir Mayakovsky (1893-1930)
First published: 1929
Genre: Drama

Locale: Tambov, Soviet Union
Time: 1929 and 1979
Plot: Satire

Ivan Prisypkin (prih-SIHP-kihn), alias **Pierre Skripkin**, a former worker and Communist Party member. A man with philistine values and tastes, intent on improving his social status, Prisypkin pretentiously adopts the French name Pierre and abandons his working-class girlfriend, Zoya, to marry Elzevira, a member of the petit bourgeoisie. Amid the drunken revelry of his wedding celebration, the house burns down. All the bodies of the wedding party are recovered except Prisypkin's. Fifty years later, when Prisypkin's frozen body is discovered in an ice-filled cellar, he is unfrozen. The boisterous, vulgar Prisypkin, who curses, drinks, sings, and plays the guitar, finds himself out of place in a sterile, rationally planned, regimented futuristic society. Placed in a cage in a zoo when other citizens are infected by his contagious behavior and begin to imitate him, he is put on display along with the bedbug resurrected with him as a specimen and relic of the bourgeois past. In the final scene of the play, Prisypkin, alone and dismayed, suddenly turns to the audience and joyfully recognizes the spectators as fellow human beings who share his weaknesses and vices.

Zoya Berezkina (ZOH-yah beh-RYOZ-kih-nah), a working girl. A simple, modest, unpretentious young woman in love with Prisypkin, Zoya is driven to despair when she is jilted by Prisypkin. She shoots herself but survives the suicide attempt and reappears fifty years later as a professor's assistant who witnesses the resurrection of Prisypkin. Confronted again with Prisypkin, she realizes her folly in having attempted suicide over such a vulgarian.

Elzevira Davidovna Renaissance (ehl-zeh-VEE-rah dah-vih-DOHV-nah), a manicurist and cashier of a beauty parlor. Elzevira, Prisypkin's fiancée, is an attractive young woman who fusses over Prisypkin and lavishes him with kisses and endearing nicknames. During the drunken revelry at her wedding, she is pushed onto the stove, her veil catches fire, and she perishes in the blaze.

Rosalia Pavlovna Renaissance a hairdresser, Elzevira's mother. Rosalia is an enterprising, energetic woman eager to have her daughter marry Prisypkin to obtain the privileges that come with Prisypkin's labor union membership. Protective of her interests, she curses and threatens Zoya when Zoya claims Prisypkin as her own.

Oleg Bayan (BAH-yan), an eccentric house owner. A clever, witty man and amateur poet, he comments ironically on Prisypkin's behavior, pointing out his shortcomings. He acts as Prisypkin's companion and mentor, attempting to educate Prisypkin and to raise him to a higher cultural level. Slightly intoxicated, he delivers the main toast at Prisypkin's wedding.

The Zoo Director, who orders that Prisypkin be used as a source of nourishment for the bedbug and has them both placed in a glass case to be exhibited to the public. He pompously delivers the major address at the ceremonies unveiling the resurrected Prisypkin and the bedbug, denouncing both as parasites.

A Professor, an elderly scholar, knowledgeable about the past, who supervises the unfreezing of Prisypkin and explains Prisypkin's anachronistic speech and behavior to the doctors who assist him.

The Master of Ceremonies, who coordinates activities at the celebration to present the resurrected Prisypkin to the public.

The Chairman of the City Council, who warns citizens about the cultural danger of Prisypkin's anachronistic behavior.

A Speaker, the president of the Institute for Human Resurrection. He polls the country and records the vote to resurrect Prisypkin.

David Osipovich Renaissance (oh-SEE-poh-vihch), a hairdresser, Elzevira's father, who plays a minimal role in the play, appearing only at Elzevira's wedding.

— *Jerome J. Rinkus*

THE BEET QUEEN

Author: Louise Erdrich (1954-   )
First published: 1986
Genre: Novel

Locale: Primarily Argus, North Carolina; Minneapolis; Florida; and a Chippewa reservation
Time: 1932-1972
Plot: Domestic realism

Mary Adare, daughter of the novel's principal family. Abandoned by their mother, Adelaide, she and her brother Karl flee Minneapolis, she to her Aunt Fritzie and Uncle Pete's butcher shop in Argus, which she eventually takes over. Her rivalry with her cousin Sita is balanced by her lifelong friendship and work-partnership with Celestine, the half-Indian mother of Dot by Karl. As her fierce motherliness focuses on Dot, she grows into a formidable, eccentric, and occasionally mystical woman.

Karl Adare, a bisexual man who wanders across the Midwest. He occupies a series of jobs—most in sales—and has brief but momentous affairs with Celestine and with Wallace Pfef. Although his periodic communications, bizarre gifts, and returns to Argus punctuate the book, he remains an enigmatic presence. At the end, he rescues and reunites with Wallace, realizing what he has missed.

Celestine James, the daughter of Dutch and Regina. Regina belongs to the Kashpaw clan, among the most important Indian families in Erdrich's multinovel North Dakota saga. Originally Sita's friend, she is a strong, tall, hardworking woman. She also is the mother of the eponymous Beet Queen, whose upbringing becomes the only major conflict in her friendship with Mary.

Sita Kozka, the daughter of Pete and Fritzie Adare Kozka. Beautiful and unstable, she is the particular target of her cousin Mary's malice. She marries and divorces entrepreneur Jimmy Bohl, then civil servant Louis Tappe. Working first as a

department store model and then as a (failed) restaurateur, she declines into a dissatisfied homebody and—at first periodically, then irrevocably—into madness. She meets a bizarre death.

Wallace Pfef, the chief promoter of the Argus sugar beet phenomenon and a closet homosexual. His brief affair with Karl Adare and his deep love for Dot represent the only emotional releases in a life dominated by Babbittry and a largely successful societal conformity.

Dot Adare, the daughter of Celestine and Karl, who have a token marriage. She is a strange, unattractive, and difficult child, with much of her Aunt Mary in her makeup. Disliked by her schoolmates and manipulative of the adults around her—Celestine, Mary, and Wallace Pfef—she becomes Beet Queen by the chicanery of the latter.

Russell Kashpaw, Celestine's Indian half brother. Wounded and horribly scarred in both World War II and the Korean War, he is North Dakota's most decorated hero. He dwindles from being a high school football star into a depressed and (eventually) jobless man. Surviving a stroke and paralysis, he rides in ironic parallel to the unlovely Dot in the Sugar Beet Festival parade.

Father Jude (Adare) Miller, the younger brother of Mary and Karl. Kidnapped from them after Adelaide's desertion, he is reared by the Millers and becomes a priest. A clue to his real parentage does not lead to reunion.

— *Maureen Fries*

BEETLECREEK

Author: William Demby (1922-   )
First published: 1950
Genre: Novel

Locale: Beetlecreek, West Virginia
Time: The Depression era
Plot: Social realism

Johnny Johnson, a black teenager. Johnny goes to Beetlecreek, West Virginia, from Pittsburgh to live with his uncle, David Diggs. His mother is severely ill and has been placed in the county home and cannot care for him. Johnny arrives too late in the year to enter school, so he lounges around his aunt and uncle's house until school is dismissed; he then associates with the Nightriders, a group of four other black youths his age. As the story opens, a white hermit, Bill

Trapp, chases the gang from his property because they are stealing apples. Johnny is trapped in a tree, but Trapp invites him down and into the house for cider. Johnny becomes friends with the old man, and they pass many interesting times together. Later, as part of his initiation into the Nightriders and as part of their retaliation against Trapp for a crime that he did not commit, Johnny burns the old man's house to the ground.

Bill Trapp, a white recluse. Having grown up as an adopted child, along with his sister, Hilda, Trapp always has been melancholy and withdrawn. To attain the kind of respectable life that his sister always wanted for him, he worked a variety of jobs in a blacksmith shop, in a garage, and as a handyman for a traveling carnival, the Harry Simcoe Continental Show. After tiring from the rigors of the traveling show, Trapp purchased the May farm on the outskirts of Beetlecreek. He keeps to himself, venturing into town only to buy supplies and drinking heavily to ease the pain of loneliness. Trapp comes to life again after becoming friends with Johnny Johnson and his uncle, David Diggs. Trapp gives a cartload of pumpkins to the two Tolley sisters for the fall carnival, and he gives a party to which he invites the young black and white girls in order to encourage friendship between the races. At this party, one white girl, who was not invited, tears a picture from one of Trapp's anatomy books and fabricates a story that portrays him as a child molester. This rumor turns both the black and white communities against him. Trapp collapses at the sight of his burning house.

David Diggs, a sign painter. A tall, slender man, at thirty-two years of age he is frustrated, having dropped out of college to marry a young woman whom he had gotten pregnant while on a visit to Beetlecreek in pursuit of Edith Johnson (who is no relation to Johnny). He has no drive, no ambition, and no job, except for occasional work painting signs. When he goes to rescue his nephew from Trapp, he finds the old man to be an interesting and genuinely likable person, and they become friends. When Edith returns to Beetlecreek to attend her adopted mother's funeral, David is renewed. At her invitation, he leaves Beetlecreek for Detroit with Edith on the night of the fire and the fall carnival.

Mary Phillips Diggs, a maid, David's wife. Mary became a pious woman after her child was born dead. She wraps herself in her job as maid for the Pinkertons, a prominent white family, and in her church activities, principally with the Women's Missionary Guild, of which she aspires to be president. Although a passionate young girl when she first met David, she has become unkempt, uninteresting, and unattractive. She has a successful night selling gingerbread at the fall carnival, completely unaware that her husband has left town with another woman and that his nephew has set fire to Bill Trapp's house.

Edith Johnson, a city girl. A former resident of Beetlecreek and a college classmate of David Diggs, Edith returns to Beetlecreek to attend the funeral of her adopted mother, whom she hated. At the age of twenty-seven, she is attractive, well-dressed, and schooled in the ways of the city. The people of Beetlecreek assume that she is a prostitute, and Edith has nothing but the deepest contempt for them. After settling her mother's affairs, she returns to Detroit with David Diggs, whom she encourages to leave Beetlecreek.

The Leader, a Beetlecreek teenager. He is the callous, insensitive leader of a youth gang called the Nightriders. The gang meets in a secret hideaway to smoke, tell dirty jokes, look at pornography, and masturbate, all of which Johnny Johnson finds disgusting. When the Leader offers to make him a member, however, he jumps at the chance. The Leader issues the condition for membership on the night of Johnny's initiation: Johnny must burn Trapp's house as an act of reprisal for Trapp's alleged molestation of the Tolley girls.

Pokey, a white girl who was not invited to Trapp's party. She tears a picture from one of his anatomy books and fabricates the story that Trapp molested the girls at the party.

Telrico, a café owner. As an Italian, Telrico tries to stay out of the comings and goings of Beetlecreek because he is keenly aware that he is an outsider. His café serves as a meeting place for the men of the town. David Diggs takes Trapp to Telrico's for a drink on the night he first meets him, and Edith and David also meet regularly there.

Sarah Tolley and

Mary Ellen Tolley, two young Beetlecreek sisters. They ask Trapp for pumpkins for the fall carnival. Later, they are invited to Trapp's party, where the molestation is alleged to have occurred. The girls know that Trapp is innocent but are not allowed by their mother to tell the truth.

Mr. Tolley, a barber, Sarah and Mary Ellen's father. His barbershop is the gathering place for the town and the center for discussion of all the important business in Beetlecreek.

— *Warren J. Carson*

A BEGGAR IN JERUSALEM
(Le Mendiant de Jérusalem)

Author: Elie Wiesel (1928-   )
First published: 1968
Genre: Novel

Locale: Jerusalem
Time: 1967
Plot: Impressionistic realism

David ben Sarah, a wanderer and first-person narrator of the novel. A survivor of the Holocaust, the forty-year-old David is rebellious and skeptical of any value in a world that has lost its innocence. He is filled with memories of his childhood and spends much of his time exchanging tales and testimonies with a group of beggars in Jerusalem. At the outbreak of the Six-Day War, he joins a tank unit commanded by an old friend. Soon after meeting Katriel, another member of the unit, David makes a pact with him that if one of them should survive the war, he will bear witness for the other. David's tale, then, is a process of bearing witness for Katriel, a man whom he envies for his compulsion to magnify humanity in an inhuman world.

Katriel, a teacher who goes back into the army to fight in the Six-Day War at the insistence of his father, a blind rabbi from Safed. Tall, slim, and quiet, Katriel knows how to tell tales and how to listen to them. He loves life and the mystery of life, despite the death of his child Sasha. He is distinguished by his power to affirm the dearness of life, and in this lies his importance to David. At the time of the war, he has been married for twenty years. The one thing that most disturbs him during the war is that he has had to kill others.

When the war is over, he is missing in action, leaving David to tell his story.

Malka, Katriel's wife, a strong and beautiful woman. She met Katriel when both of them were serving in the army in their youth. An orphan and a widow, she seeks out David so that he may tell her about her husband's last days. When the beggars see her, they take her for a divine apparition. To David, she represents every woman he has ever loved, and she stirs in him a hunger for love and forgiveness. She is very much attracted to him.

Lieutenant Colonel Gad, the head of David's tank unit and a friend from David's years in postwar Europe. As young men, he and David had long conversations about life and its meaning. He is a career soldier who refuses to believe in defeat. Aggressive and courageous, he leads his men to the Western Wall only to be killed shortly thereafter.

Gdalia, a Yeminite Jew in David's tank unit who serves as a mediator between Katriel and the other soldiers. Talkative and jovial, he is schooled in philosophy and likes to interpret Katriel's tales.

Dan the Prince, a beggar who constantly writes reports to politicians and journalists. Once a historian in Europe, he claims to be the emissary of a mysterious king. His friends know him to be dignified, melancholy, intelligent, and compassionate, yet they regard him at various times as a psychotic, a rogue, and an embezzler.

Velvel, a beggar, a dwarf with only one eye. He is a gambler who knows how to rejoice and how to mock authority, even—or especially—the authority of reason.

Anshel, a street hustler who sells postcards in the Old City of Jerusalem. Having served in three wars, he is ridden with guilt.

Yakov the Timid, a beggar and former schoolteacher who plays war games with children, teaching them not to be afraid. He is known as a peacemaker.

— *David Patterson*

BEGGAR ON HORSEBACK

Authors: Marc Connelly (1890-1980) with George S. Kaufman (1889-1961)
First published: 1925
Genre: Drama

Locale: New York City
Time: The 1920's
Plot: Satire

Neil McRae, a pianist and composer. At about age thirty, he seems to be without prospects because his impracticality borders on the irresponsible. He is, however, personable and engaging, and his apparent indifference to material well-being springs more from his artistic creed than from sloth or carelessness. Wholly dedicated to his music, he lives an independent, quasi-bohemian life that is much too quixotic to suit the Cady clan. Although not in love with Gladys, Neil proposes to her when his need to be "subsidized" is pressed by Dr. Rice and Cynthia Mason. In a dream induced by sleeping pills, Neil envisions a nightmarish future with Gladys and his potential in-laws. He wakes up a wiser man, in love with Cynthia, the proper person, and determined to reject all that the Cadys represent, including the prostitution of his art.

Dr. Albert Rice, a long-standing friend to Neil and of the same age. He is humorous and amiable, and he is considerably more practical than Neil. He has a genuine concern for his friend's health, material welfare, and artistic future. In addition to providing the pills that put Neil to sleep, he enlists Cynthia's help in convincing Neil to propose to Gladys. As do the other characters, he appears in other guises in Neil's dream, first as the minister who marries Neil and Gladys, then as a reporter at Neil's trial.

Cynthia Mason, Neil's neighbor, also a musician, about twenty-five years old. Initially, she seems too motherly toward Neil, taking him to task for his wasteful behavior and forgetfulness. Her concern, however, springs from love and great respect for Neil's talent. More practical than Neil, at first she is willing to suppress her own desires to advance his career, but then, fortuitously, she has second thoughts. In the dream vignettes, it becomes clear that she is much better suited to Neil than is Gladys.

Gladys Cady, Neil's only piano student, presumably of Cynthia's age. She is on the spoiled and flighty side, determined to keep life amusing and fun. Thanks to her father's wealth and her shallowness, this is quite possible. Her tastes are entirely wrong for Neil, but it is only in his nightmarish dream, in which they are married, that he comes to realize it. It is fortunate for both of them that Gladys encounters an old flame and wants to cancel their engagement.

Mr. Cady, a no-nonsense businessman and patriarch of the Cady family. Bossy and brusque, he is a cultural philistine who believes that art, like any commodity, is good only if it can be sold at a profit. He is dedicated to two things: making money and playing golf. In Neil's dream, he is caricatured first as a crude and blustering but extremely rich manufacturer of "widgets," then as the hanging judge at Neil's murder trial.

Mrs. Cady, the mother of Homer and Gladys. She is a rather vapid woman caught up in small-town speculations and gossip. Like her daughter, she is shallow and silly, traits that become exaggerated in her depiction in Neil's dream. Her pampering of Homer helps explain his unpleasant nature.

Homer Cady, Gladys' brother. He is a surly and suspicious young man who is no more refined than his father. Although he claims to be delicate, he is a recalcitrant and loutish hypochondriac who takes issue with anything said. His appalling lack of taste is reflected by his garish yellow tie, which, in Neil's dream, grows larger and larger. Increasingly Neil's nemesis, in the dream trial he becomes the prosecuting attorney.

Jerry, an obliging young porter in Neil's apartment house. Affable and polite, he appears as a jack-of-all-roles in Neil's dream, assuming identities ranging from elevator boy to ticket taker at the murder trial to executioner.

— *John W. Fiero*

THE BEGGARS' BUSH

Authors: John Fletcher (1579-1625) and Philip Massinger (1583-1640)
First published: 1647
Genre: Drama

Locale: The Netherlands
Time: The Renaissance
Plot: Comedy

Florez, also called **Goswin**, the rightful heir, through his mother, to the earldom of Flanders. When Wolfort took over the government of the country, Florez's father entrusted his young son to the care of a wealthy merchant, and the boy grew up ignorant of his real identity. He is widely known as a talented, fortunate merchant and a generous benefactor to all who need help. He often bestows gifts on Clause, an old beggar to whom he feels drawn by a peculiar bond. Ever conscious of his honor, he is distressed at the prospect of falling prey to his debtors when his ships fail to appear. Even his love cannot withstand the strength of his sense of obligation to Clause, who has relieved him of his financial burdens, and he agrees to forsake his promised bride at the beggar's request.

Gerrard, his father, who disguises himself as **Clause**, king of the beggars, to escape death at the hands of Wolfort. He is a leader in the tradition of Robin Hood, cozening rich fools and protecting honest men in difficulties, while he keeps a watchful eye on the affairs of his son. He reluctantly halts Florez's proposed marriage, because he believes that the girl's lineage is too humble to make her a suitable wife for a duke.

Hubert, a bold, honest young courtier who bravely accuses Wolfort of crime and treason before he flees the usurper to search for his lost sweetheart, Gerrard's daughter Jacqueline. He joins the beggars' band as a hunter and plans the elaborate trap, set for Wolfort and his men, to restore Florez to his earldom.

Wolfort, the proud usurping earl. When Hubert confronts him with his guilt, he feigns a reformation, hoping to persuade the young man to reveal the whereabouts of Gerrard and his supporters, but he continues his wicked course until his fall. He refuses to repent, even after he has been captured, and chooses instead to laugh at the clever plot by which he was betrayed.

Captain Hempskirke, Wolfort's henchman. Unaware of Florez's identity, he is indignant at the young man's presumptuous courtship of the girl whom he claims as his niece. With-out any of Florez's honorable scruples, he callously accepts his rival's challenge, then hires ruffians to capture him at the appointed meeting place. Taken prisoner by the beggars, he falls blindly into Hubert's trap, leading himself and his master, Wolfort, into the hands of Gerrard's men and the loyal burghers.

Vandunke, a good-hearted, practical burgher who makes no secret, among his friends, of his opposition to the usurper and brings forces to aid in deposing him. A jovial romantic, he looks with favor on the love of Florez and his ward Bertha, and he prepares elaborate festivities to celebrate their wedding.

Margaret, his dutiful, quiet wife.

Frances, their daughter, a gracious young woman who is obviously a favorite with her father's friends.

Bertha, the daughter of the duke of Brabant. Kidnaped by Wolfort, she has been placed in Vandunke's care as Hempskirke's niece. A sensible, forthright girl, she reassures her cowardly guide when he trembles with terror at sights and sounds in the forest, and she accepts Florez's puzzling decisions with a minimum of feminine hysteria.

Jacqueline or **Jaculin**, Gerrard's daughter, who wanders with him in the beggar band, calling herself **Minche**. She is delighted to be reunited with Hubert, her fiancé, but she insists that he help her conceal her identity.

Herman, a courtier, sympathetic to Florez and Gerrard's cause.

Higgen,
Ferret,
Prig, and
Snaps, merry beggars who revel in their vagabond existence. The prospect of honest work, offered by Gerrard, so appalls them that they flee to England to continue practicing their trades, juggling, singing, peddling, and stealing.

Lord Arnold and
Lord Costin, loyal nobles who joined the beggars with Gerrard.

Vanlock, an old Flemish merchant who comes to celebrate Florez's wedding.

THE BEGGAR'S OPERA

Author: John Gay (1685-1732)
First published: 1728
Genre: Drama

Locale: London, England
Time: Early eighteenth century
Plot: Social satire

Captain Macheath (mak-HEETH), the swashbuckling leader of a band of highwaymen. A great lover of the ladies, he wins Polly Peachum with protestations of sincere and virtuous affection, privately commenting, "What a fool is a fond wench," as he prepares to entertain his favorite group of London prostitutes. Thrown into prison by Peachum and Lockit, he plays on the feelings of another "fond wench," Lucy Lockit, the jailer's daughter. He soon finds himself in the midst of a stormy quarrel between Lucy and Polly, each of whom believes herself to be his wife. In the farcical conclusion, when he is forced to pick a spouse from the large group of ladies who claim the role, he dances away with Polly.

Polly Peachum, the gay, buxom daughter of one of Macheath's colleagues. She disgraces her family by marrying and thus ruining her prospects for wealth and advancement. She staunchly defends her rights as Macheath's wife against Lucy with tirades and malicious sweetness, not at all deceived by her rival's proffered friendship.

Peachum, her father. He dispenses the stolen goods of the robber band and increases his fortune by betraying members of the troop to the police. Determined to leave his daughter free and to prevent her from revealing his double-dealing to her husband, he has Macheath arrested as soon as he hears of Polly's marriage.

Mrs. Peachum, his wife, who assists him in his shady dealings. She, too, is distressed at the prospect of Polly's singleminded devotion to Macheath and laments her daughter's inability to be as fickle as the rest of her sex.

Lucy Lockit, the jailer's daughter, who, like Polly, falls victim to Macheath's charms and helps him escape from prison. She is violently jealous of Polly and even tries to poison her, but the two are reconciled by the realization that they have both been duped.

Lockit, her father, who shares with Peachum the profits that come from the arrest of the highwaymen.

Filch, Mrs. Peachum's favorite, a skillful pickpocket and errand boy for Peachum.

Diana Trapes, one of Peachum's customers, a bawd who buys stolen finery to adorn her "ladies."

Jemmy Twitcher,
Crook-Fingered Jack,
Wat Dreary,
Robin of Bagshot,
Nimming Ned,
Harry Padington,
Matt of the Mint, and
Ben Budge, members of Macheath's gang.

Mrs. Coaxer,
Dolly Trull,
Mrs. Vixen,
Betty Doxy,
Jenny Diver,
Mrs. Slammekin,
Suky Tawdry, and
Molly Brazen, Macheath's favorite "ladies of easy virtue," who betray him for Peachum.

BEL-AMI

Author: Guy de Maupassant (1850-1893)
First published: 1885
Genre: Novel

Locale: Paris and Cannes, France
Time: c. 1885
Plot: Naturalism

Georges Duroy (zhohrzh dew-RWAH), also called **Bel-Ami** (behl-ah-MEE), an ambitious young reporter and M. Walter's employee. A complete rascal, he later assumes the more aristocratic name of **Georges du Roy de Cantel** (dew rway duh kawn-TEHL), and he shrewdly manipulates his acquaintances as he continues to rise in prominent social circles. With the help of Madeleine Forestier, whom he marries after her husband's death, he receives an editorial position. Luckily for him, most women find the dashing ex-army officer irresistible; even the somewhat aloof Madame Walter is unable to resist his charms. At the opportune moment, Duroy accuses his wife of infidelity and wins a divorce, thus leaving him free to marry Suzanne, M. Walter's lovely and wealthy young daughter.

Madeleine Forestier (mahd-LEEN foh-rehs-TYAY), Duroy's wife after the death of her husband. A rather cool and calculating woman, she has the ability to evaluate accurately ambitious young men like Duroy. Knowing many prominent people, she shows him how to advance professionally and socially. But in him she finds her match. Before their divorce, he manages to assuage his "grief" with five hundred thousand francs from her fortune. Not one to look back in regret, Madeleine quickly discovers an ambitious young man to take Duroy's place.

Clotilde de Marelle (kloh-TEELD deh mah-REHL), Duroy's mistress. She, like most women, immediately falls under his hypnotic spell. Even when he neglects her, she is unable to stay away from him. After Suzanne's marriage to

Duroy, Clotilde presses his hand warmly to indicate her continuing love for him.

Charles Forestier, Duroy's former brother officer and the editor who befriends him. Blessed with an intelligent wife and doomed by weak lungs, Forestier helps Duroy get a job as a reporter for M. Walter's newspaper. After the former's death and before his body is cold, Duroy proposes marriage to the dead man's wife.

M. Walter, the owner of the newspaper for which Duroy works. Using his powerful connections, this shrewd, avaricious man has become one of the wealthiest men in France, but he is unaware that he is a cuckold. When he learns of Duroy's intentions to marry his daughter, he dissents violently. Later, he realizes that Duroy has enough information to ruin him, and he consents readily to the marriage.

Basile Walter (bay-ZEEL), M. Walter's wife. Falling desperately in love with Duroy, she offers him anything in her power. All she desires is a little affection in return, even though she knows that he is increasingly bored with her. When she learns of Duroy's plans to marry her daughter, she almost goes insane from jealousy. As the marriage approaches, she is still unable to reconcile herself to losing her lover.

Suzanne Walter, Basile Walter's daughter. After Duroy wins his divorce from Madeleine, the naïve young girl is quite prepared to elope with him, even over the strenuous objections of her mother. She remains completely unaware of his numerous intrigues with other women.

BELINDA

Author: Maria Edgeworth (1767-1849)
First published: 1801
Genre: Novel

Locale: London and southern England
Time: Late eighteenth century
Plot: Social

Belinda Portman, an inexperienced young woman when the novel begins. Her character is strengthened rather than corrupted by her exposure to fashionable society. She resists her aunt's effort to cast her in the role of husband hunter and tries to guard against her feelings of attraction to Clarence Hervey when she is made wary by the inconsistency of his behavior toward her. As an independent-minded woman and a thoughtful reader of serious literature, she rejects superficial measures of social status. When judging others, she looks for evidence of sincere feeling, consideration for others, and educated intellect. She is able to discern the potential for reformation in both Lord and Lady Delacour and help them become their better selves.

Lady Delacour (deh-lah-KEWR), a brilliant success in fashionable London because of her wit and energy. She is emotionally impulsive and a slave to her obsessions: her need for male admirers, her hatred for her rival Mrs. Luttridge, her contempt for her husband, and her fear of the disease she believes is killing her. Behind her social mask is a desperate woman in need of the nurturing support she receives first from Belinda and then from her daughter, her husband, and a few friends.

Clarence Hervey, a young man about town and follower of Lady Delacour. He at first seems infatuated with his own superiority, but he and Belinda soon recognize each other's strengths of mind and character. Although he falls in love with Belinda, he feels committed to marry Virginia St. Pierre, his ward, and thinks he must keep his distance from Belinda. Only Lady Delacour's production of Virginia's secret love can release him from his commitment.

Lord Delacour, Lady Delacour's husband, her inferior in intellect, with an even greater lack of self-control. He has degenerated into an alcoholic boor, frustrated by her lack of respect for him, manipulated emotionally by her flirtations with other men (one of whom, Colonel Lawless, he has shot in a duel), and determined to hang on to whatever husbandly power he can by denying money for his wife's extravagances. When Belinda treats him kindly, he turns out to be a warmhearted gentleman who stops drinking excessively, loves his wife and daughter, and can carry on an intelligent conversation. His valet, Champfort, fearing loss of control over his master, is revealed to have been responsible for various plots, including the misinformation that aroused Lady Delacour's jealousy of Belinda.

Harriet Freke (frehk), formerly Lady Delacour's favorite companion and inciter of her wilder escapades. She delights in "frolics," risky behavior on or over the edge of propriety, and frequently appears in male clothing. Having allied herself with Lady Delacour's enemy Mrs. Luttridge, she tries to persuade Belinda to abandon Lady Delacour and the Percivals. She is caught spying on Lady Delacour at Twickenham, where Lady Delacour has retired for her operation and where Harriet suspects her of receiving a lover.

Mr. Percival and

Lady Anne Percival, a couple devoted to each other and their children and free from the false values of fashionable society. Both Clarence Hervey and Belinda are drawn to them and to the model their marriage represents. When Lady Delacour's jealousy forces Belinda to leave her household, the Percivals welcome Belinda at their country home. Lady Anne lectures Belinda about the dangers of clinging to the memory of a first love and urges her acknowledgment of the virtues of Mr. Vincent as a rational basis for love and marriage.

Mr. Vincent, heir to a West Indian fortune, Mr. Percival's protégé, and Belinda's suitor. Unknown to the Percivals, he is addicted to gambling. It is easy for Mrs. Luttridge, who seeks to injure Lady Delacour and Belinda, to draw him into play that costs him his fortune. He is saved from major losses by Clarence Hervey, who threatens Mrs. Luttridge with exposure. Belinda discovers his gambling when she finds in his chambers a Jew from whom he is trying to borrow money.

Virginia St. Pierre, also known as **Rachel Hartley**, Clarence Hervey's ward. Wishing to save her from repeating her mother's experience of seduction and abandonment, her grandmother brought her up in forest seclusion where she would never see a man. By accident, though, she saw a portrait of a man whose image she connected with the heroes of the romances that became her favorite reading. She longed for such a hero despite her belief that she owed love to Clarence Hervey, who renamed her and took charge of her education after her grandmother died. At the end of the novel, her life becomes a romance when Hervey finds her long-lost father, now a wealthy man, and Lady Delacour produces Captain Sunderland, the original of the portrait. He has loved Virginia ever since he spied on her in the forest.

— *Anne Howells*

THE BELL

Author: Iris Murdoch (1919-   )
First published: 1958
Genre: Novel

Locale: England
Time: The 1950's
Plot: Philosophical realism

Michael Meade, the undistinguished-looking founder and unofficial leader of Imber Court, a place next to a convent that is home to a community of religious laypersons. A good man who awaits a religious call, Michael is caught between the conflicting demands of leadership and compassion, of spiritual and sensual love. Now thirty-nine years old, he had been a schoolmaster. Despite his homosexuality, he hoped to become a priest. Led by his pupil Nick Frawley into a comparatively innocent love relationship, he was dismissed when Nick lied to

the headmaster, thus preventing Michael from becoming a priest. Later, he was inspired by Abbess to found the Imber community. He plans a ceremony of dedication for a new bell to get needed publicity. When Nick arrives at Imber, Michael keeps his distance but tries to help him. Michael is attracted to Toby and kisses him, then apologizes. After the bell ceremony is ruined, he is embraced by Catherine. When told of Toby's confession, he thinks mistakenly that it represents Nick's revenge. He finds Nick's dead body. After the community is dissolved, he remains at Imber Court, thinking of his love for Nick and feeling guilty for not expressing his love. Cared for by Dora, he regains some composure and leaves for London.

Dora Greenfield, a woman of about twenty-four years of age who came from London. Imaginative, impulsive, and careless, she offers an independent perspective on Imber Court. Because she is bored with her life and afraid of her husband, Paul, she leaves him. She has an affair with Noel Spens, then joins Paul at Imber Court, where her natural happy impulses are reproved. She is appalled by the idea of nuns shutting themselves away from the world. She briefly escapes to London but returns. When Toby tells her of the ancient bell in the lake, she realizes its importance and plans to raise it to surprise onlookers at the blessing ceremony. When she overhears Nick tell Noel about it, she makes the old bell ring and wakes up the neighborhood. The next day, she follows Catherine; when she tries to stop her from drowning, she is almost drowned herself. She stays behind when Paul goes to London, learns to swim, and cooks for Michael. When he leaves, she departs to take a job as an art teacher.

Paul Greenfield, Dora's husband, an art historian who is about thirty-seven years old. He comes from a German banking family and is a rich and violent man. He is passionately in love with Dora but treats her harshly. He works on medieval manuscripts at Imber Court and is jealous of both Toby and Noel. He is fascinated by the inscriptions on the antique bell. He returns to London without Dora.

Toby Gashe, a slim, tall, innocent young man of about eighteen years of age. He is bound for Oxford University. At Imber Court, he lives in a separate house with Nick Fawley. After Michael kisses him, he is enlightened and confused. He scales the abbey walls and is escorted out. Attracted to Dora, he tells her of discovering the bell in the lake. He kisses her and with her raises the bell. After Nick tells him that he knows about both of Toby's relationships, he betrays Michael to James and is sent home. At the end, he is happy at Oxford.

Nick Fawley, Catherine's twin brother. At the age of fourteen, he initiated a homosexual relationship with his schoolmaster, Michael; his lies to the headmaster resulted in Michael being dismissed. Later, he became dissolute and was persuaded to come to Imber Court. Melancholy and irascible at the age of twenty-eight, he lives apart with a dog named Murphy. He helps maintain machinery. He detains Toby by force and accuses him of destroying the faith of Michael, a religious man. He gives Noel the facts about Dora's plans for the old bell. He saws through bridge supports to ruin the bell ceremony and thereby to stop his sister from entering the convent. He kills himself.

Catherine Fawley, Nick's twin sister, a beautiful, religious young woman who is preparing to enter Imber Abbey and who surprisingly can drive a truck. After the bell debacle, she tries to drown herself, then reveals her love when she throws herself into Michael's arms. She is sent to London, where she receives therapy.

James Tayper Pace, a man about forty years old who unofficially ranks second at Imber Court. A handsome, masculine man with a simple faith and rigid opinions, he is a natural leader. He receives Toby's confession and judges Michael harshly. With Abbess, he dissolves the Imber Court community, then leaves.

Abbess, the head of Imber Abbey. She inspired Michael to start the Imber Court community. She acts as Michael's conscience, for she seems to know about his relations with Nick. She helps decide to dissolve the community.

Margaret Strafford, known as **Mrs. Mark**, the middle-aged, gentle enforcer of the community's rules and an arranger of concerts. At the end, she attends Catherine in London.

Noel Spens, a shallow London journalist who is a friend and lover of Dora. At Imber Court, he gets news of the old bell from Nick. He writes a sensational, derisive news feature about Imber Court events that helps destroy the community.

— *George Soule*

A BELL FOR ADANO

Author: John Hersey (1914-1993)
First published: 1944
Genre: Novel

Locale: Adano, Italy
Time: 1943
Plot: Social realism

Major Victor Joppolo (joh-POH-loh), the first military governor of Adano after the Americans have retaken Italy in World War II. He is sincerely interested in restoring the dignity of the people there, and consequently he is willing to suffer what many military men would consider a lack of respect for their position. He succeeds in replacing the bell, the town's most prized possession, which the Fascists had taken.

Sergeant Borth, an outspoken aide to Major Joppolo. He is in complete sympathy with what the major is trying to do in the town, if not with the methods he uses.

Captain Purvis, the officer in charge of the military police in Adano. Adhering rigidly to military regulations, he is careful to report any infractions of orders, including the major's countermand of General Marvin's order to keep all carts out of Adano.

General Marvin, the overbearing commander-in-chief of the American forces in Italy. He cares nothing about the Italian people or their needs and is far too conscious of his own position and the respect he feels is due him.

Giuseppe (jee-ew-SEH-peh), Major Joppolo's interpreter, who is quite proud of his position close to the major.

Tomasino (toh-mah-SEE-noh), a fisherman. He distrusts all authority and firmly believes in the dignity of the individual.

Gargano (gahr-GAH-noh), an ex-Fascist policeman whom Joppolo restores to a position of authority.

Lieutenant Trapani (trah-PAH-nee), Captain Purvis' subordinate. He is not afraid of the military and is willing to take some liberty with regulations when the outcome may be helpful.

Colonel Middleton, General Marvin's aide.

THE BELL JAR

Author: Sylvia Plath (as Victoria Lucas, 1932-1963)
First published: 1963
Genre: Novel

Locale: New York City and New England
Time: 1953
Plot: Psychological realism

Esther Greenwood, a bright college student who aspires to be a writer. At the age of nineteen, brown-eyed and brown-haired, Esther feels somewhat out of place in the world of high fashion and money to which she is introduced as a result of winning a fashion magazine contest. She enters her prestigious college on a scholarship. Esther is not one to sit in the corner feeling insecure; instead, she meets the world with a lively touch of sarcasm that colors her description of New York City, her friends, and herself. After her month in the city working as an intern on the magazine, however, her sense of daring becomes coupled with a feeling of disappointment over life. She attempts suicide and has a nervous breakdown, which is followed by recuperation in a series of hospitals and sanatoriums.

Buddy Willard, a medical student whom Esther has dated. He is an only child, and his parents encourage his relationship with Esther. Buddy has a fairly realistic view of life. Although he prides himself on his health, as a first-year medical student he contracts tuberculosis and must spend time in a sanatorium. When Esther visits him, he proposes to her, but by this time she has lost interest. Later, he visits her in the sanatorium, but by now there is nothing but curiosity about their relationship and a lurking fear that he may have contributed to her emotional condition.

Mrs. Greenwood, Esther Greenwood's widowed mother. She tries to let Esther alone and not pressure her too much. After the death of Esther's father ten years earlier, she reared Esther alone and supported the two of them by teaching business courses at a city college in Boston. She refuses at first to recognize Esther's mental illness.

Doreen, another winner in the competition that Esther won. Doreen comes from a finishing-type school in the South. She is a striking young woman, with white hair and deep blue eyes. She is much more sophisticated and daring than Esther, who is quite taken with her. Doreen does not feel any need to follow the schedule set for the girls or to worry about doing the work assignments. She takes Esther to places where, alone, she would never have thought to go; her behavior and outlook suggest to Esther a new and different approach to the world.

Jay Cee, the famous editor under whom Esther was assigned to work during her special one-month internship. She tries to help Esther learn the work and consider her future and her opportunities, but at this point in her life, Esther has another agenda.

Philomena Guinea, a novelist and alumna of the college that Esther attends. She provided the scholarship that made it possible for Esther to attend the private women's college in Massachusetts. She continues to assist Esther after her breakdown by financing a move from a public mental institution to a more exclusive, and more expensive, private one.

Dr. Nolan, a female psychiatrist who treats Esther at the hospital where she is recuperating. She administers shock treatments, but they are not as grueling to Esther as the shock treatments administered by Dr. Gordon earlier.

Joan Gilling, an acquaintance of Esther. She becomes more important in Esther's life when they find themselves at the same mental institution and have a gentle rivalry regarding privileges, freedom, and ultimately release. She is a former girlfriend of Buddy Willard. She seems to recover more quickly than Esther, but eventually she hangs herself.

— *Paula Kopacz*

THE BELLAROSA CONNECTION

Author: Saul Bellow (1915-   )
First published: 1989
Genre: Novel

Locale: New York and Jerusalem
Time: Late 1950's and the 1980's
Plot: Social realism

The narrator, who is never named. He tells the story because he is looking at a picture of Harry and Sorella Fonstein. The narrator cannot forget them, not only because they are the central figures of an interesting story but also because he cannot forget anything. He is the founder of Philadelphia's Mnemosyne Institute, which trains people in techniques for improving their memories. The narrator has made millions in this business. At the time he tells the story, he has retired from the institute but retains his perfect memory. The narrator meets the Fonsteins in the United States and again in the 1950's in Jerusalem. Thirty years later, he gets a call from a rabbi who says that an old man in his congregation claims to be related to Harry Fonstein, whom he thinks is rich. The rabbi asks the narrator to help him find Fonstein. The narrator, after many false starts, finally telephones the Fonsteins' house. A house

sitter informs him that the Fonsteins were killed in a wreck and that their son Gilbert, a memory expert, is now working the casinos in Las Vegas. The narrator realizes that his whole life has been taken up with memory, not only of facts and information but also of relationships; however, he has been able to understand little of what has happened. The narrator represents any Jew who tries to remember and understand the Jewish role in history, even the conflicts that Jews have among themselves.

Harry Fonstein, a disabled European Jew trapped in Italy during World War II. He was about to be turned over to the Nazis when he was rescued by Billy Rose's agents, who wanted to do something to help members of his ethnic group. When Fonstein arrives in America, he wants to thank Rose for his help, but on the one occasion when Fonstein encounters

Rose, Rose turns away from him. Fonstein is so insulted by this behavior that he does not want to see Rose, thereby mimicking Rose's own rudeness.

Sorella Fonstein, Harry's wife, who is not willing to let Rose alone. She has obtained the personal journal of Rose's secretary, Deborah Hamet. The Fonsteins and the narrator are in Jerusalem (the narrator is there to open a branch of his memory training institute) when Rose arrives to establish a memorial. Sorella, who is not only a relentless woman but also a physically large one, meets with Rose and threatens to reveal the contents of Hamet's journal unless Rose meets with her husband. When Rose meets Sorella, he makes her so angry that she throws Hamet's journal at him, and it goes out the window. Rose has it retrieved and no longer has anything to fear from Sorella. Sorella's inability to control her anger against Rose is her downfall.

Billy Rose, who in reality was a famous producer and the husband of Fanny Brice; he is a fictional character in this story. The novel takes its title from a mispronunciation of his name. He does not want to see Fonstein because he thinks that it was enough to save him; he does not want to get involved in his life. The narrator suggests that Rose wants to be free to pursue his pain of trying to attract beautiful women and being rejected by them. The Fonsteins represent the ancient suffering of the Jewish people. Rose's life shows that suffering has to be re-created in the new world, if only by each Jew in his or her own life.

— James Baird

BELLEFLEUR

Author: Joyce Carol Oates (1938-   )
First published: 1980
Genre: Novel

Locale: A mythical region resembling the Adirondacks, and Mount Blanc
Time: Mid-sixteenth century to late twentieth century
Plot: Gothic

Leah Bellefleur, the daughter of Della Pym. She marries her first cousin Gideon. A dominating figure in the family who is believed to have the power to control events, Leah is beautiful, energetic, and passionate. Her youthful sexual hunger develops into an obsession with winning the release of convicted mass-murderer Jean-Pierre Bellefleur II and reuniting the 3-million-acre Bellefleur empire.

Gideon Bellefleur, the son of Noel Bellefleur. He marries his first cousin Leah. Gideon is strikingly handsome, emotionally reserved, and physically reckless. Although he is a gambler and womanizer, Gideon often is the stable personality that holds the Bellefleur family together. After the death of his friend Nicholas Fuhr and his alienation from Leah, Gideon becomes increasingly distant. He is the one who destroys the family by crashing a bomb-laden airplane into the mansion.

Jedediah Bellefleur, Leah and Gideon's great-great-grandfather, a hermit who seeks God on Mount Blanc but discovers only madness, hallucinations, and murder. After years in seclusion, he learns that his brother Louis has been murdered, and he returns to marry Louis' widow, Germaine, and continue the Bellefleur line.

Germaine Bellefleur, Leah and Gideon's daughter, who seems to possess magical powers. She is a precocious and withdrawn child who suffers through the gradual dissolution of her parents' marriage. Germaine is saved from the destruction of her family, which occurs on her fourth birthday, when her father reneges on his promise to take her on a birthday ride in his airplane.

Raphael Lucien Bellefleur, Leah and Gideon's great-grandfather, who builds the Bellefleur mansion. Frustrated in his efforts to win political power, Raphael leaves a bizarre will that demands that his remains be skinned and made into a cavalry drum.

Felix (Lamentations of Jeremiah) Bellefleur, Leah and Gideon's grandfather, who is shamed when his grandiose plan to raise silver foxes concludes disastrously, losing most of the fortune that Raphael had accumulated. Felix, who was re-named Lamentations of Jeremiah by his father, drowns in a storm while desperately trying to save his remaining horses.

Jean-Pierre Bellefleur II, Leah and Gideon's uncle, who is sentenced to life in prison for murder. After Leah wins his release, Jean-Pierre commits another murder.

Noel Bellefleur, Gideon's father. Noel is an outwardly ordinary man who secretly keeps a small jeweled vial of cyanide on his person.

Della Pym, the daughter of Felix who marries an ambitious young bank clerk named Stanton Pym. Pym dies in a toboggan race on which several of the Bellefleur men have wagered. Della never forgives the family for the senseless death of her husband.

Hiram Bellefleur, Leah and Gideon's uncle, plagued by sleepwalking. He survives numerous close calls during his nighttime rambles, including a wartime walk that takes him through enemy lines. In the end, he dies from an infected cat scratch.

Ewan Bellefleur, Gideon's brother. Ewan, less physically attractive than Gideon, is similarly reckless. He becomes the bullying county sheriff, leading a violent and corrupt life until he is gunned down in his mistress' bed. After his remarkable recovery from his numerous gunshot wounds, Ewan repents his former sinful life and leaves the Bellefleurs to join a religious order.

Samuel Bellefleur, Leah and Gideon's great-uncle, who vanishes in the Bellefleur mansion's Turquoise Room when he is abducted by spirits that come to him out of a large mirror. The family nails the room shut after Samuel's disappearance.

Vernon Bellefleur, Hiram's son and the family poet. An iconoclastic coward, Vernon rebels against the Bellefleur power and status, persisting in reading his proletarian poetry in country taverns and mills. He is finally bound and thrown into a river by some drunken workmen; however, there is mysterious evidence that he may have survived the murder attempt.

Bromwell Bellefleur, Gideon and Leah's son. Painfully intellectual, Bromwell is sent off to a private school that he cannot stand. He runs away and gains admittance to a distant research institution, where he produces a mammoth volume on the existence of antimatter.

Jean-Pierre Bellefleur, the American founder of the Belle-fleur family. He was banished from France by Louis XV because of his radical ideas. Jean-Pierre managed to purchase nearly 3 million acres of wilderness that became the basis for the Bellefleur fortune.

Raphael Lucien Bellefleur II, the son of Ewan who is nearly drowned in Mink Pond by a local farm boy. Raphael has a symbiotic relationship with the pond throughout his life and disappears mysteriously when the pond finally dries up.

Nicholas Fuhr, Gideon's best friend, who dies in a horse racing accident that seems to be brought on by Leah's myste-rious powers.

Garnet Hecht, one of Gideon's mistresses. She bears his child. Conceived on the night of Germaine's birth, the illegiti-mate infant is stolen by a giant predatory bird. After failing in a suicide attempt, Garnet marries an English lord.

The Varrells, a family of low-born, poorly educated people with whom the Bellefleurs carry on a lengthy and bloody feud.

— *Carl Brucker*

BELOVED

Author: Toni Morrison (1931-   )
First published: 1987
Genre: Novel

Locale: Kentucky and Ohio
Time: 1850-1874
Plot: Historical realism

Sethe, a fugitive slave woman. She killed one of her four children eighteen years earlier, when she saw her former owner come to capture them. This happened a month after she escaped to Ohio, where her mother-in-law resided. After the incident, she alienated herself in the community while living with her youngest child in a house occupied by a ghost spirit. The dead daughter, Beloved, returns as a ghost. Sethe enjoys their reunion and responds to all of her demands. When Be-loved's demands increase, she exhausts herself physically and psychologically.

Beloved, a bodily ghost of Sethe's baby. Having died at the age of two, her throat cut with a handsaw by Sethe, she reappears as a woman of twenty. She calls herself Beloved, the only word carved on her tombstone. She is eager to listen to Sethe's stories, demands her attention, and accuses Sethe of forsaking her. She disappears with the singing of thirty women in the community.

Denver, Sethe's youngest child. Denver was born in a river while Sethe was escaping to Ohio as a runaway slave. She was named for a white woman who helped Sethe's delivery. When Beloved appears, Denver soon recognizes that she is the ghost whom she had seen as a child and welcomes her company. Witnessing her mother's exhaustion from meeting Beloved's demands, she asks for help from the community, from which she and Sethe had been isolated since Sethe's murder of her

child. Eventually, she is offered a job working for a white family.

Paul D, a former slave. He comes to Cincinnati to look for Sethe and her mother-in-law, Baby Suggs, after eighteen years of absence. He used to belong to the plantation where Sethe was enslaved. The last time he had seen Sethe was during a failed escape attempt. After his sale to a new plantation, he was moved to a camp, joined the army, stayed with a woman, and continued his journey north. Upon their reunion, Paul D and Sethe rejoice, but he is soon chased away by Beloved and informed of Sethe's actions. Following that revelation, he avoids her. Later, he reconsiders and assures Sethe that he wants to spend his life with her.

Baby Suggs, Sethe's mother-in-law. Her son, Halle, earned her freedom in return for years of his extra labor. She had seven other children, fathered by different men, and did not know where they were sold. As soon as she arrives in Ohio, she enjoys a sense of possessing her own body. She preaches to the community that they too should love their own bodies. Sethe's murder of Beloved occurs on the following day, when Baby Suggs provides a huge banquet for the community, an action that invites their anger. She dies after pondering colors for her last eight years.

— *Yasuko Akiyama*

A BEND IN THE RIVER

Author: V. S. Naipaul (1932-   )
First published: 1979
Genre: Novel

Locale: The African interior
Time: Late 1960's to mid-1970's
Plot: Psychological realism

Salim, the narrator. Born and reared on the eastern coast of Africa, Salim does not feel himself to be a true African be-cause his ancestors were Hindus of northwestern India. From an early age, Salim detached himself from his familiar com-munity and now feels insecure and uncertain about his future in postcolonial Africa. Although nominally a Muslim, he lacks the religious sense of his family. When Nazruddin, a Europeanized Muslim and family friend, offers to sell him his shop in an unidentified country in central Africa, Salim ac-cepts and drives there to take over the business. Racked by

recently won independence, military coups, and civil war, the town is not at all what Salim expected based on Nazruddin's enthusiastic descriptions. Gradually, the town comes back to life, business improves, and Salim becomes acquainted with a few of the non-African townspeople. Disorder returns to the town, however, and Salim again decides to break with his community. He travels to England to see Nazruddin's daugh-ter, to whom he has been engaged informally for many years. By mutual agreement, they end the engagement. Salim returns to the town, but, in his absence, it has become radicalized, and

Salim's shop has been taken over by a state trustee. Salim is betrayed and arrested for illegally possessing ivory, but he escapes. At the end of the novel, Salim leaves the town by steamer, presumably for Europe, moving down the river in darkness, away from the last scene of battle.

Ferdinand, a boy of fifteen or sixteen when he first comes from his isolated village. He is entrusted to Salim by his mother, Zabeth, one of Salim's principal traders who also is a sorceress. Ferdinand is ignorant, proud, and diligent. Eventually he becomes an official of the government. One of the "new Africans," he knows that he, too, is doomed by the turmoil and treachery of his countrymen. He helps Salim escape after Salim is betrayed by his assistant, Metty, and jailed for illegally possessing ivory.

Metty, the half-African boy who had been a slave in Salim's family compound and who comes to live and work with him. Their relationship is uneasy and ambivalent. During the course of the novel, Metty grows up, fathers a family secretly, and betrays Salim, who has protected and cared for him.

Father Huismans, a Belgian priest who teaches at the *lycée* that Ferdinand attends as a boy. An ardent lover of African art and culture, Father Huismans is senselessly killed by enraged bushmen during one of his collecting trips.

Raymond, a scholarly, reclusive European who is also an expert on Africa, in its political and historical aspects. He serves as an adviser to the president until the insurrection. Salim meets him at a party, but the two do not really become friends. Raymond is abandoned by the president and disappointed in his hopes but does not leave the town.

Yvette, Raymond's glamorous young wife, with whom Salim has a passionate affair. When she insults him by comparing him to Raymond, Salim beats her in uncontrolled fury, and the affair ends as she returns to her husband.

Mahesh and

Shoba, an elderly Indian couple who become Salim's closest friends. Deserted by their family, they live and act as if they were still at home in India. During the boom, they establish a Bigburger Shop, which brings them out of their self-imposed seclusion; the shop is a novelty in the town and very successful. When Salim leaves, he cannot bring himself to say goodbye to them.

— *Natalie Harper*

BEND SINISTER

Author: Vladimir Nabokov (1899-1977)
First published: 1947
Genre: Novel

Locale: An unnamed European country
Time: First half of the twentieth century
Plot: Surrealism

Adam Krug (krewg), a world-famous philosopher living in a small Eastern European country where the language is a blend of Germanic and Slavic roots. A portly, arrogant man, forty years old, Krug is contemptuous of those with lesser intellectual powers. Not interested in politics, he assumes, rather naïvely, that he has nothing to fear from the Ekwilists, who have taken over his country and instituted a police state. In a benumbed state of mind because of the recent death of his wife, he vacillates, postponing his departure abroad. His colleagues at the university and his friends are arrested one after another. Krug finally attempts to flee, but it is too late.

Olga Krug, Adam's thirty-seven-year-old wife. She dies at a hospital in the first chapter of the book.

David Krug, their son, eight years old. He is a bright, engaging child whom Krug loves inordinately. The Ekwilists eventually realize that Krug can be forced to support their oppressive policies if they take David as hostage. They seize him but then bungle everything and allow him to be murdered by a group of deranged persons participating in an experiment in group psychology.

Paduk, nicknamed (by Krug) **The Toad**, Krug's former schoolmate who becomes leader of the Ekwilist Party and later dictator of the country. A bully as a boy, the fat, powerful Krug used to torment the unpopular Paduk by tripping him and then sitting on his head. Paduk apparently is homosexual and in love with Krug. His political philosophy emphasizes the virtues of collectivity and a total equality that will reduce everyone to the lowest common denominator. His Party of the Average Man is based on a somewhat distorted version of Fradrik Skotoma's works.

Ember, Krug's friend and fellow scholar. He has translated the works of William Shakespeare into his native language.

Along with many others among Krug's acquaintances, he is arrested by the Ekwilists.

Azureus, a university president who submits immediately to the demands of the new police state and tries to influence all the professors to do the same.

Dr. Alexander, the assistant lecturer in biodynamics. He doubles as an informer and secret police functionary for the Ekwilists.

Professor Edmond Beuret (French literature),

Professor Gleeman (medieval poetry),

Professor Yanovsky (Slavic scansion),

Professor Hedron (mathematics),

Professor Rufel (political science), and

Professor Orlik (zoology), all of whom eventually are arrested, and some of whom are murdered.

Fradrik Skotoma, a political philosopher who was famous in the 1860's. He is still alive. His philosophy advocates redistribution of human consciousness so as to make all persons absolutely equal in brains, talent, and the like. His quixotic Ekwilism, impossible to realize in any practical sense, is transformed by Paduk's police state into a political doctrine attempting to enforce spiritual uniformity.

Mr. Etermon and

Mrs. Etermon, (Everyman), mindless cartoon characters roughly resembling Blondie and Dagwood Bumstead of the American comic strip *Blondie*. Paduk makes them the symbol of his Ekwilism and models his own dress and behavior for a time on that of Mr. Etermon.

Hustav and

Linda Bachofen, secret police officers who arrest Ember.

Mac, a beefy thug who arrives, with Linda Bachofen, to arrest Krug.

Mariette Bachofen, the younger sister of Linda Bachofen. She is a police spy who is sent to work as a maid for Krug and, probably, to seduce him.

Dr. Amalia von Wytwyl, the eldest of the three Bachofen sisters, who is in charge of the experiment in communal psychology that leads to the murder of David Krug. Characters such as Amalia suggest that the methods of Freudian psychology are compatible with forced collectivism and police-state brutality.

Phokus, a student, apparently the leader of the conspiracy against the Ekwilists.

Peter Quist, the owner of an antique shop who offers to help smuggle Krug and David abroad. He is an agent provocateur.

Crystalsen and

Schamm, government officials in the Paduk bureaucracy. Schamm had been another tormented schoolmate of Krug.

The narrator, a problematic character resembling the author. He frequently blends with Adam Krug, in that certain passages may refer to Krug, to the narrator, or to both. Toward the end of the book, the narrator slides down a beam of light and relieves the tormented Krug of his sanity. The final passages describe the narrator getting up from his manuscript, stretching himself, and observing the hawk moth that keeps hammering against the screen of his window.

— *Robert Bowie*

BENEFACTORS

Author: Michael Frayn (1933-   )
First published: 1984
Genre: Drama

Locale: London, England
Time: The 1970's and 1980's
Plot: Play of ideas

David Kitzinger, an architect and father of three. David is a dreamer and a schemer, a man of vision who gets caught up in ideas and concepts, especially his own. He loves architecture for the thrill of creating concrete reality from scratch and the challenge of overcoming practical obstacles. He conceives a plan to build high-rise public housing on a tract of slum land on Basuto Road in southeastern London, but the scheme grows and expands until it becomes overwhelmingly unpopular. Accepting the defeat of his plan breaks his spirit. David is concerned with helping others, but his concern is seldom responsive to their particular tangible needs. His mathematical mind is reflected in his moral attitudes: To him, independence—the integrity of things or people—is a supreme virtue. His desire to be fair and objective, to respect everyone's rights and desires and never to take sides, results in a kind of moral blindness. His purported magnanimity often is only a form of arrogance and egotism, most clearly evident in the patronizing attitude and pity he exhibits toward Colin and Sheila.

Jane Kitzinger, David's wife. Jane is a former anthropologist who has been helping with David's architectural practice and eventually becomes a caseworker with a housing trust in southwestern London. Jane is a realist who retains a healthy perspective on life and accepts things exactly as they are. She plays devil's advocate to her husband's schemes when necessary, but generally she is an extremely supportive wife and assistant. Intelligent, organized, and industrious, Jane is capable and often takes on more than her share of problems and responsibilities, never begrudgingly. She truly enjoys accommodating others, generously and diplomatically, and works hard to make things run smoothly for everyone in her life. When pushed, however, she can become fiercely possessive and territorial; having a strong sense of herself, she will fight for her own needs. She begins with an ironic awareness of economic injustice and, as a result of her involvement in both Basuto Road and the Molyneuxs' domestic life, ultimately arrives at a truer sense of social mission.

Colin Molyneux (COL-ihn mol-ee-NOH), David's friend and neighbor and a father of two. Colin, a former classical scholar, works on a women's magazine and is editing an encyclopedia of sexual terminology. Eventually, he leaves his job and his home to become a squatter in Basuto Road and organizes its poor inhabitants against the skyscraper scheme, which he considers a vulgar expression of David's maleness. Colin is a dark personality, a man full of anger and hatred, who adopts a sardonic attitude and cold reserve toward everything he encounters. He is intelligent and perceptive to the point of prescience, and he enjoys commenting on what is happening as it happens, creating a jarring social self-consciousness. His actions are often without motivation: He likes to mock others and to provoke arguments, and he considers kindness and sentiment to be crimes. He never shows tenderness, and, when his jaded veneer drops and he really becomes angry, he is absolutely ruthless. Having married Sheila out of pity and paternity, Colin is now bored and frustrated with her, as he is with the complete mediocrity his life has assumed. In breaking away over the Basuto Road scheme, he discovers a refreshing simplicity of mind and the positive energy to fight fervently for a modest cause.

Sheila Molyneux, Colin's wife and Jane's friend. Sheila is a quiet, simple, innocent soul virtually lacking in ego and confidence. She is a housewife who looks after her children, Matt and Lizzie, rather awkwardly and tentatively; later, she takes a job at the Kitzingers' house as David's secretary and assistant. Self-assured people like David and Jane terrify her, and she envies their clarity of purpose and apparent happiness. Her simplicity allows her to find a rich and spontaneous joy in simple experiences and poetic ideas, and she truly admires and delights in David's creative vision without fully understanding it. Sheila aspires to be a person who helps others, but she is hopelessly dependent on those around her for her emotional and practical needs. Intent on pleasing Colin, she is more often thwarted and baffled by him. She feels guilty for holding him back and terrified that he will leave her. Once she takes the children and leaves him, she expresses deep hatred for him, and her accumulated rage explodes in a horrible act of blind and sudden violence.

— *B. P. Mann*

BEN-HUR: A Tale of the Christ

Author: Lew Wallace (1827-1905)
First published: 1880
Genre: Novel

Locale: Jerusalem, Antioch, and the Mediterranean Sea
Time: The lifetime of Jesus Christ
Plot: Religious

Judah Ben-Hur, the son of a wealthy Jewish merchant. After accidentally injuring Valerius Gratus, the imperial governor of Judea, he is sentenced to life as a galley slave while his mother and sister are entombed in a prison tower. On his way to the sea, he is given water by a young boy, Jesus. He spends three years rowing in the galleys. When Quintus Arrius is given command of the Roman fleet, he is dismayed after he hears the story of the unjust treatment of Ben-Hur and his family. When Ben-Hur rescues Arrius during a sea battle, he is freed and made the son and heir of the rich Roman. After the death of Arrius, Ben-Hur uses his new wealth to search for his family and seek revenge against the treacherous Messala. While he works to accomplish these goals, his life becomes interwoven with the life of Jesus Christ.

Messala (muh-SAH-luh), a Roman raised in Jerusalem, Ben-Hur's boyhood friend. After being educated in Rome, he returns to Jerusalem full of contempt for all things Jewish. When Ben-Hur challenges these attitudes, their friendship turns to hatred. After the tragic accident, he refuses to help Ben-Hur and his family, encouraging and even profiting from their destruction. Eventually Ben-Hur destroys him, both physically and financially, during a chariot race. Messala continues to plot, unsuccessfully, against Ben-Hur.

Simonides (sih-MAH-nih-deez), a servant of Ben-Hur's father. After the family was destroyed, he salvaged what he could of their fortune, refusing to reveal its location even under the questioning of the Roman torturers. He prospered as a merchant in Antioch, saving the wealth he amassed for the family he had once served. When Ben-Hur returns, he gives him the money. Simonides believes that the King of the Jews will come as a mighty warrior who will restore the glory of Israel. He encourages Ben-Hur to form an army in the wilderness in preparation for the messiah who is soon to come.

Balthazar (bahl-THA-sehr), an Egyptian, one of the three magi who visited the Christ child in his manger. He has spent his life waiting for the child to fulfill his destiny. Balthazar is one of the few who realize that the kingdom the child repre-

sents is a spiritual, rather than a physical, one. He is unable to convey this message to his companions. His entire life revolves around the birth and death of Christ. When Christ dies on the cross, he also dies.

Esther, Simonides' daughter, also a servant of Ben-Hur's family. She is virtuous and wise. She loves Ben-Hur, but he is torn between her gentle nature and the seductive beauty of Iras. She eventually marries Ben-Hur.

Iras (I-ruhs), Balthazar's daughter, who is fascinated by the power of Rome and the wealth and glamour that Messala represents. She is beautiful and uses her seductive power to betray Ben-Hur. She is contemptuous of the meek manner and simple dress of Christ.

Tirzah (TIHR-zuh), Ben-Hur's sister. After the accident that destroys Ben-Hur's family, the Romans take revenge by walling up Tirzah and her mother in a prison cell. After Pilate acquires control of the country, he demands an examination of the prisons. At this point, Tirzah and her mother are released. Unfortunately, they had contracted leprosy and are now imprisoned by their disease, forced to beg on the outskirts of towns and avoid all human contact. Eventually, they are miraculously cured, and the family of Hur is reunited.

Sheik Ilderim, the greatest ruler in all the desert east of Syria. He is called "the Generous" because of his good deeds. He concealed the wise men from the wrath of Herod. He hates the Romans, who wish to steal his land and strip him of his power and wealth. He owns the horses that Ben-Hur uses to defeat Messala in the chariot race. His influence helps Ben-Hur in many ways.

Quintus Arrius (KWIHN-tuhs AY-rih-uhs), the Roman leader sent to defeat the pirates who have been attacking Roman ships in the Mediterranean. During the battle, Ben-Hur saves him; the two are the only survivors of the battle. In gratitude, he adopts Ben-Hur, who later inherits his wealth and power.

— Mary E. Mahony

BENITO CERENO

Author: Herman Melville (1819-1891)
First published: 1856
Genre: Novella

Locale: The harbor of St. Maria, off the coast of Chile, and Lima, Peru
Time: 1799
Plot: Adventure

Amasa Delano (ah-MAH-soh deh-LAH-noh), an American sea captain. Off the coast of Chile, he sees a ship in distress and sets out with food and water for its company. He finds a Spanish merchantman carrying slaves. Ship and crew are in deplorable condition, and their captain suffers from what appear to be severe mental disorders. A series of strange and sinister events lead Captain Delano to

the knowledge that the Spanish captain is a prisoner of the slaves. He is able to rescue the captive and take him ashore.

Don Benito Cereno (beh-NEE-toh seh-REH-noh), the captain of a Spanish slave ship. His human cargo mutinies and makes him a prisoner, forced to witness atrocities on and murders of the Spanish crew. After his rescue by Captain Delano, he gives testimony concerning the mutiny and dies broken in mind and spirit.

Babo (BAH-boh), a slave. He poses as the devoted servant of Captain Cereno and attempts to deceive Captain Delano concerning Cereno's true condition. Failing in this attempt, he is captured and hanged on Captain Cereno's testimony.

Don Alexandro Aranda (ah-RAHN-dah), owner of the cargo of the Spanish slave ship. He is killed and mutilated by the slaves.

Raneds (RRAH-nehds), the slave ship's mate, murdered by the slaves.

BEOWULF

Author: Unknown
First transcribed: c. 1000
Genre: Poetry

Locale: Denmark and southern Sweden
Time: The sixth century
Plot: Epic

Beowulf (bay-eh-woolf), the nephew and thane of King Hygelac of the Geats. A warrior who proves his superhuman strength and endurance in his struggle with the monster Grendel, he exemplifies the ideal lord and vassal, rewarding his own men generously and accomplishing glorious deeds to honor his king, while he fulfills all the forms of courtesy at Hrothgar's court.

Hrothgar (HROHTH-gahr), the aging lord of the Danes, a good and generous ruler deeply distressed by Grendel's ravaging visits to Heorot, his great hall. He adopts his savior, Beowulf, as his son and parts with him tearfully in a moving scene; he knows that he will not see the young warrior again.

Wealhtheow (WEE-ahl-thay-oh), his queen, a gracious, dignified hostess to the visiting Geats. She, too, grows fond of Beowulf and commends the welfare of her young sons into his hands.

Unferth (EWN-fahrth), Hrothgar's adviser, typical of the wicked counselors of folklore. Envious of Beowulf and heated with wine, he taunts the Geat with his failure to defeat Breca in a youthful swimming match. He is won over by Beowulf's victory against Grendel and lends the hero his sword, Hrunting, for the undersea battle against Grendel's mother.

Grendel (GREHN-duhl), one of the monstrous descendants of Cain, condemned to wander alone in the wastelands of the world. Given pain by the light and merriment in Hrothgar's hall, he visits it and regularly carries off warriors to devour until he is mortally maimed in a struggle with Beowulf.

Grendel's Mother, another monster. She invades Heorot to avenge her dead son and is herself killed by Beowulf after a long and difficult combat in her underwater cave.

Hygelac (HE-guh-lahk), Beowulf's lord, the wise ruler of the Geats. He is killed while leading a raid in the Rhineland.

Hygd (hihj), his young, accomplished, and intelligent queen. She offers the throne of her young son to Beowulf after Hygelac's death.

Hrothmund (HROHTH-mewnd) and

Hrethric (HRAYTH-reek), the sons of Hrothgar and Wealhtheow.

Hrothulf (HROHTH-oolf), Hrothgar's nephew and ward. Although Wealhtheow professes trust in his care of her children, there are hints of his subsequent treachery to them.

Freawaru (FRAY-ah-wah-rew), Hrothgar's daughter, about to be betrothed to Ingeld of the Heathobards as a political pawn. Beowulf prophesies that only unhappiness will arise from this alliance.

Wiglaf (WEEG-lahf), the last of Beowulf's kinsmen and his heir. He alone helps the old hero in his last fight against a ravaging dragon, and he later berates his companions for their cowardice.

Heardred (HEH-ahrd-rayd), Hygelac's son, who succeeds his father as king of the Geats. Beowulf serves as his regent until the boy reaches maturity and replaces him after Heardred is killed in battle with the Swedes.

Ongentheow (OHN-yuhn-thee-oh), the Swedish king, slain by the Geats at the battle of Ravenswood.

Onela (OHN-eh-luh),

Ohthere (OHT-ehr-uh),

Eanmund (AY-ahn-moond), and

Eadgils (AY-ahd-gihls), members of the Swedish royal family.

Wulfgar (WOOLF-gahr), Hrothgar's messenger, famous for wisdom and courtesy.

Hrethel (HRAYTH-uhl), Hygelac's father, who trained his grandson Beowulf.

Haethcynn (HATH-kihn) and

Herebeald (HEHR-uh-bay-ahld), his sons, who brought tragedy to their father through Herebeald's accidental killing of Haethcynn.

Eofor (AY-uh-fohr), a warrior of the Geats, the slayer of Ongentheow.

Aeschere (EHSH-hehr-uh), Hrothgar's thane, a victim of Grendel and his mother.

Scyld (sheeld) and

Beowulf, legendary Danish kings.

Breca (BREHK-uh), a prince of the Brondings, Beowulf's companion in a swimming marathon.

Daeghraefn (DAY-rayf-uhn), a Frankish warrior whom Beowulf crushes in his powerful grip.

Finn, the Frisian ruler in a minstrel's legend.

Hildeburh (HIHL-duh-bewr), his queen.

Sigemund (SIHG-eh-mewnd) and

Fitela (FIHT-uh-luh), the legendary Volsungs, uncle and nephew, whose valor is compared to Beowulf's.

Heremod (HEHR-uh-mohd), the minstrel's example of an evil, oppressive ruler.

Offa (OHF-fuh), the king of the Angles, another figure from an illustrative legend.

BÉRÉNICE

Author: Jean Racine (1639-1699)
First published: 1671
Genre: Drama

Locale: Rome
Time: A.D. 79
Plot: Tragedy

Bérénice (bay-ray-NEES), the beautiful queen of Palestine, deeply in love with Titus, who has succeeded Vespasian, his father, as emperor of Rome. This love obliterates everything about her and makes her neglectful and unfair in her treatment of Antiochus, the king of Commagene, who also loves her and who seems better fated than Titus to answer her passion. When Titus learns that Bérénice, as empress, would be unacceptable to the people of Rome, he realizes that he cannot tell her the truth. Blaming his father's death for the delay in announcing his plan to marry her, he asks Antiochus to explain to Bérénice that the emperor is preparing to sacrifice his love out of duty to his people. At first, Bérénice refuses to believe Antiochus, and she accuses him of speaking and acting because of jealousy. In a last interview with Titus, she expresses her anger and despair, but when she is certain that the emperor still loves her, she finds strength enough in her own love to give up all thought of happiness. She asks Antiochus to renounce the love he feels for her as well, and she leaves behind her in Rome the two men whose love she can, in her difficult situation, neither accept nor return.

Titus (tee-TEWS), the emperor of Rome. As a monarch, he is majestic, conscientious, and even clever, but as a man he suffers because of the unhappiness he must inflict on himself and others. To overcome his understandable weakness of will because of his love for Bérénice and his friendship with Antiochus, he must look constantly to the great examples of history as models for his own conduct. In parting with Bérénice, he must lose the person who has given him the most help in discovering his own virtues as a man and as a prince.

Antiochus (an-TI-eh-kuhs), the king of Commagene. A considerate friend and war companion of Titus and a chivalrous lover of Bérénice, he becomes the devoted and tortured confidant of the two lovers. He suffers to see Bérénice unhappy because of a rival who is also his friend. In this difficult position, he reveals an impulsive and anxious nature. He is easily blinded by the smallest hint of hope and depressed by any disgrace, and he would gladly sacrifice himself if he could be sure of the happiness of the woman he loves without hope. He contemplates suicide until Bérénice strengthens him through her own nobility of deed and firmness of will.

Paulin (poh-LA[N]), the confidant of Titus. He represents the point of view of Rome, both the Senate and its people, when he explains that Titus cannot make Bérénice his wife without arousing public protest. Paulin's belief is that a hero should be able to master his passions.

Arsace (ahr-SAHS), the confidant of Antiochus. He tries to remain optimistic and to comfort Antiochus in his distress. Although Arsace's arguments are logical, Antiochus, deeply in love with Bérénice, knows that love has no logic.

Phénice (fay-NEES), the confidante of Bérénice. She tries to plead the cause of Antiochus.

Rutile (rew-TEEL), a Roman citizen, representing on stage the people of Rome.

BERLIN ALEXANDERPLATZ: The Story of Franz Biberkopf
(Berlin Alexanderplatz: Die Geschichte vom Franz Biberkopf)

Author: Alfred Döblin (1878-1957)
First published: 1929
Genre: Novel

Locale: Berlin
Time: 1928-1929
Plot: Social realism

Franz Biberkopf (BIH-behr-kopf), an unskilled laborer and convicted criminal. Approximately thirty years old and of stocky build, Biberkopf has been a cement worker, furniture mover, tie-pin hawker, newspaper vendor, notions peddler, burglar, fence, pimp, and assistant doorkeeper. After his release from Tegel prison, where he spent four years for the involuntary killing of Ida, his fiancée, Biberkopf is at a loss as to what to do with his life and suffers from a sense of disorientation. He resolves to begin a new life as an honorable man, but he finds that after four years in prison, his real punishment is yet to come. Ida, whom he killed in a fit of jealous rage, had a sister, Minna, who is married to Karl, a locksmith. Franz is drawn to the place of his crime. He visits Minna and, on an impulse, rapes her. As a criminal convicted of a violent crime, Biberkopf receives official notice of his imminent expulsion from Berlin. The prison welfare association, however, intervenes, and he is allowed to remain in the city. He manages to stay on the path of blamelessness and earn his livelihood peddling notions, though he spends his evenings in the bars around Alexander Square in the city's center, a slum with high rates of crime. He soon becomes involved in racketeering.

Mieze (MEE-tseh), whose real name is **Emilie Parsunke** (pahr-ZEWN-keh) and who is also called **Sonia**. She is an attractive prostitute under twenty years of age. Eva introduces her to Franz Biberkopf, and she becomes his third mistress after his release from Tegel prison. Mieze has a gentleman friend of means, and Biberkopf becomes her pimp. Mieze and Eva are friends and, to make Biberkopf happy, she suggests to Eva that Eva bear him a child, because of Eva's continued feelings for Franz. Eventually, Eva has a miscarriage. Biberkopf and Mieze are in love; after her murder by Reinhold, Biberkopf loses his inhibitions concerning him and seeks to avenge her murder.

Eva (AY-vah), whose real name is **Emilie**, a prostitute and the lover of Herbert Wischow, her pimp. Eva was in love with Biberkopf before his imprisonment and still is after his release. She and Herbert are instrumental in sending Biberkopf to a private hospital outside the city (in Magdeburg) after he is pushed from a car by Reinhold and in seeing to it that no awkward questions are asked about his crushed arm. Eva and Herbert pay for Biberkopf's recovery in their apartment, and Eva nurses him back to health. She sets him up as Mieze's pimp. Eva is expecting a child by Franz but has a miscarriage. When Franz is sought by the police, she hides him in her uptown apartment in the borough of Wilmersdorf.

Reinhold (RIN-hohlt), a member of Herr Pums's gang of burglars, a man in his thirties. Seemingly sickly (he is hollow-cheeked and has a "yellow face"), he stutters and wears a shabby army coat. Because of Reinhold's friendliness toward Biberkopf and Biberkopf's fascination with Reinhold's views on politics and life, he succeeds in involving Biberkopf in his affairs with women. Biberkopf shares the girlfriends of whom Reinhold has tired in exchange for certain gifts. Because Biberkopf protests his innocence and was not a willing member of the gang, he is pushed by Reinhold from a moving car. Reinhold therefore is responsible for crippling Biberkopf, who loses his right arm. Reinhold betrays Biberkopf a second time when he falsely accuses him of having helped him murder Mieze. Reinhold is tried and convicted, but because of mitigating circumstances, he is sentenced to only ten years in prison.

Herbert Wischow (VIH-show), a pimp and petty thief. He and Biberkopf were friends before the imprisonment of the latter. Herbert and Eva help Franz get medical attention and recuperate. Eventually, Wischow is arrested and sentenced to two years in prison for a number of property crimes.

Karl Matter, a tinsmith and member of Pums's gang. He has a falling out with Pums over profits and is befriended by Mieze. He is implicated in her murder because he and Reinhold had taken her on an excursion to Freienwalde. Eventually, he and the "wheelwright" commit their own burglaries and thus become independent. Karl informs on Reinhold once he establishes that he will not be prosecuted for his role in Mieze's murder. Karl and the "wheelwright" are caught and sent to prison.

Lina Przyballa (LEE-nah priht-sih-BAHL-lah), called **Polish Lina**, Biberkopf's first girlfriend after his release from prison. She came from Czernowitz, and her father, Stanislaus, was a farmer. She had two miscarriages.

Otto Lüders (LEW-dehrz), Lina's uncle, who peddles shoelaces. He rapes and robs a young widow whom Biberkopf had befriended.

Gottlieb Meck (GOT-leeb), a member of the cattle dealers' association and Biberkopf's friend. He tries to get Biberkopf a job.

Herr Pums (pewmz), the leader of the burglary gang that Biberkopf joins. He and Biberkopf meet in a bar.

Cilly (SIH-lee), Biberkopf's second girlfriend after his release from Tegel, one of Reinhold's former mistresses. She returns to Reinhold when she is pressured by him to abandon Biberkopf.

Willy (VIH-lee), a former convict and a pickpocket. He meets Biberkopf in a bar and takes him to political meetings. Willy is described as young and cocky.

— Arthur Tilo Alt

BETRAYAL

Author: Harold Pinter (1930-   )
First published: 1978
Genre: Drama

Locale: England
Time: The 1970's
Plot: Representational

Emma, Robert's wife. Thirty-eight years old at the beginning of the play, which moves backward in time, Emma is dissatisfied in her marriage and ready to separate from her husband. Her marriage has failed because of an affair she had with her husband's friend Jerry, a writer. Emma apparently also has been intimate with another writer, Roger Casey. Emma is angry because she believes that Robert has been unfaithful to her, yet she ascribes little importance to the fact that she has betrayed both Robert and Jerry. This obliviousness to the consequences of her own actions is a main facet of her character.

Jerry, a forty-year-old writer. Jerry is inherently a romantic, and it is this impulse that leads him to betray Robert, his best friend. Jerry's affair with Robert's wife, Emma, also betrays his own wife, Judith. Jerry instigated the affair with Emma while a party was in progress at Robert's house in 1968; he made a drunken pass at her. Jerry is the more roman-

tic of the two men and the more naïve. He does not realize that Robert discovered the affair at least as early as 1973. Jerry comes to understand the situation four years later, when the play begins.

Robert, the cuckolded husband of Emma, also forty years old in 1977. He is a publisher; in fact, he publishes the work of both of Emma's lovers, Jerry and Roger. He is a realist and something of a detective; he seems to be the play's most clever character. He discovers Emma's infidelity while on holiday with her in Venice in 1973, when he finds a letter Jerry has written to her. From that point on, he has the upper hand. He baits Jerry with insinuations that the unsuspecting Jerry is incapable of understanding. Jerry does not discover until 1977 that Robert has been observing him for years with this knowledge of betrayal.

— James Michael Welsh

BETRAYED BY RITA HAYWORTH
(La traición de Rita Hayworth)

Author: Manuel Puig (1932-1990)
First published: 1968
Genre: Novel

Locale: Vallejos, a provincial town in Argentina
Time: 1933-1948
Plot: Bildungsroman

José Casals (hoh-SEH kah-SAHLS), also called **Toto**, the main character. The novel follows him from infancy in the small provincial town of Vallejos, Argentina, to the age of fifteen, when he is at George Washington High School, a boarding school in Merlo, a suburb of Buenos Aires. Bright and inquisitive but self-centered and spoiled, he grows up being the best student in his class and having his own way. He matures into adolescence and is exposed to an ever-widening world in which he is not always the center of attention, although intellectually he has a competitive advantage over others. Hungry for knowledge, experience, and power, he continually seeks the company of older students and adults who possess these attributes. He is confused about his own sexuality and the more intimate details of sex, and his own sexual predilections are still to be determined. As a child, he fantasizes about the romantic images of the world that come to him principally through Hollywood films, novels, and the influence of his doting mother. As he grows up, he is forced away from her protective feminine world and has to face a harsher, nastier reality. There, too, he wants to be first. He manipulates people in his search for power and prestige, which to him are the signs of success in this larger world. What is in doubt is how his search will be resolved: whether he will prefer males or females, and whether he will be abusive and exploitative in his use of the power that probably will be his.

Mita (MEE-tah), Toto's mother. A college graduate, she marries Berto, a man with less education who reminds her of an Argentine film star with whom she once danced. She works first in the hospital and then in the pharmacy. When the family is financially secure, Berto forces her to resign and devote herself to family. She consents and has a second child, who dies still unnamed. A third child, rarely mentioned, also is born. She rears her husband's nephew Héctor, dresses down, uses little makeup, gains weight, and accepts the matronly role assigned by her husband. She fantasizes and escapes her small-town existence through novels, films, and her son Toto.

Berto (BEHR-toh), Toto's father, a proud Spaniard who struggles through a difficult childhood in Spain that brings the early death of his mother and the tyranny of his brother. When he is pulled out of school to work in his brother's factory, he is deprived of an education. When his brother sells the factory, he is forced to immigrate to Argentina. There, haunted by his earlier misfortunes, he steels himself in the ways necessary to become successful. He marries above himself yet refuses to accept help from his wife's family in La Plata. He keeps his family in Vallejos and, through great effort and sacrifice,

gradually becomes a successful businessman. He makes sure his family has more than enough. He even takes his brother's son, Héctor, and rears him, although not with the attention he lavishes on Toto. He avoids the womanizing and roguish tendencies of his brother. He opts for business and familial rectitude as the appropriate strategy for success.

Héctor (EHK-tohr), Toto's cousin. He lives with Toto's family until he is twelve years old, then is sent away to a boarding school near Buenos Aires. Except for a vocational school, Vallejos has nothing beyond the sixth grade, and Héctor's Aunt Mita is afraid he will be nothing more than a mechanic if he does not go away to school. Héctor returns to Vallejos during school breaks and summer vacation. He is moved by the thrill of girls and soccer. The handsome boy seduces three bookish but good-looking women—the young schoolteacher Mari, Pug-nose, and Corky—in one summer. His dreams of the future are to leave the boarding school and return to Vallejos to play in local soccer matches, become a sports star, and seduce women. Many of the older female students interact with Toto because they are attracted to his cousin Héctor.

Paquita (pah-KEE-tah), a lower-class schoolmate of Toto in Vallejos who is three years older. Her father is an impoverished Spanish immigrant from Galicia who is a tailor. She dreams of her sexual encounters with Raúl Garcia but is tormented by guilt and her fear of mortal sin. At the end of the novel, her wedding is being planned.

Esther (ehs-TEHR), a student from a humble Buenos Aires suburb. She wins a scholarship to George Washington High School, where she becomes a classmate of Toto. She is enamored of Héctor and eagerly awaits an encounter arranged by Toto. Toto has designs on her, however, and has used Héctor as bait. When she protests his change of plans and tries to maneuver him out of the picture, Toto snubs her by referring to her lower-class origins. She sees that she is not accepted socially and begins to see the logic of the class consciousness and worker solidarity of the people from her own background, who are committed to the Peronista labor movement.

Cobito (koh-BEE-toh), a schoolmate of Toto. He is vulgar, crude, and mean. He resents school, study, and the prospects of returning to his hometown of Paraná and working behind the counter of the family store run by his brother. Envious of the intelligence, wealth, and success of Toto, he twice tries to sodomize him.

— *Maurice P. Brungardt*

THE BETROTHED
(I promessi sposi)

Author: Alessandro Manzoni (1785-1873)
First published: 1827; revised, 1840-1842
Genre: Novel

Locale: Milan, Italy
Time: The seventeenth century
Plot: Historical

Lorenzo, a young Italian peasant whose wedding is interrupted by the whim of a wicked nobleman, Don Rodrigo. Lorenzo and his betrothed seek safety by separating temporarily. He goes to Milan but is banished from the city for taking part in a famine riot. After a year, he returns to Milan and there

finds Lucia ill of the plague. At last she recovers, and they are married.

Lucia (lew-CHEE-ah), Lorenzo's betrothed. The object of Don Rodrigo's lust, she is kidnapped by his henchmen. She vows to enter a convent if rescued from her kidnappers. Fra

Cristoforo tells her that her betrothal vow takes precedence over her vow to the Church, and so Don Abbondio marries her to Lorenzo.

Don Rodrigo (rohd-REE-goh), an arrogant nobleman who, on a bet, plans to seduce Lucia. He dies of the plague while searching for her.

Don Abbondio (ah-bohn-DEE-oh), the cowardly parish priest ordered by Don Rodrigo not to marry Lorenzo and Lucia.

Fra Cristoforo (krihs-toh-ROH-roh), a saintly Capuchin who provides sanctuary for Lucia.

A nun, who is blackmailed into sending Lucia out of the sanctuary.

The Un-named, a powerful outlaw nobleman indebted to Don Rodrigo. His men kidnap Lucia, but her innocence persuades the noble outlaw to protect her from Don Rodrigo.

Cardinal Federigo (feh-deh-REE-goh), another protector of Lucia.

BETSEY BROWN

Author: Ntozake Shange (Paulette Williams, 1948-   )
First published: 1985
Genre: Novel

Locale: St. Louis, Missouri
Time: 1959
Plot: Domestic realism

Betsey Brown, the thirteen-year-old protagonist. The oldest child in a black middle-class family, Betsey struggles with the frustrations and fears of adolescence, compounded by attending a mostly white school. Because she is the oldest child, her parents have given her much of the responsibility for controlling the chaos created by her three siblings and younger cousin. This sets her apart from the other children, yet she knows she is not like her parents, and they do not understand her. Her most comforting moments are in the early morning, which she has claimed as her own. Frequently, she awakes before anyone else, seeks out one of the porches on the family's large house, and watches the sunrise. During the daytime, she finds peace and quiet by climbing a large tree in her yard. In this solitude, she is most at ease.

Greer Brown, Betsey's father, a physician. Greer wants his children to grow up proud, so he begins every morning with African drumming and chanting about black heritage, followed by a quiz about black history and culture. Under Greer's influence, Betsey comes to appreciate the blues and other styles of music that her mother considers unsuitable for people of their social class. When Greer announces his plans to involve the children in a civil rights demonstration, then further refuses to join the family in prayer, he precipitates a crisis in his marriage.

Jane Brown, Betsey's mother, a social worker who treats mentally ill patients in a segregated hospital. Jane has given up trying to manage the five children in her household, relying instead on her aging mother and a series of housekeepers. Her passion for her husband is fading, largely because his ideas about "Africanizing" his children conflict with her wishes to see them reared with the manners and tastes of their social class. Resentful of the long hours her husband puts in at the hospital and in his private practice, she amuses herself in the evenings by playing cards and polishing her nails. She leaves the family temporarily.

Vida Murray, Betsey's grandmother, who lives with the family. Vida disapproves of Greer, of modern music, and of modern women who wear lipstick. Her only comfort comes from memories of Frank, her late husband, and from rocking on the porch and praying.

Mrs. Maureen, the owner of a beauty parlor. As Betsey sees her, Mrs. Maureen is confident, worldly, and able to support herself with an honest trade. When Betsey runs away from home hoping to work in the beauty parlor, she learns that Mrs. Maureen also runs a bordello.

Carrie, the housekeeper. Although Carrie dresses strangely (she wears two housedresses at the same time, tied with a rope) and carries on a romance with the gardener behind Vida's back, she brings order to the household for the first time. She teaches the children proper manners and useful homemaking skills. Most important, she earns the love and respect of Betsey and is able to guide her through the perils of adolescence.

— *Cynthia A. Bily*

BETWEEN THE ACTS

Author: Virginia Woolf (1882-1941)
First published: 1941
Genre: Novel

Locale: England
Time: June, 1939
Plot: Psychological realism

Bartholomew Oliver, retired from civil service and the disgruntled owner of Pointz Hall, where a historical pageant is being held.

Giles Oliver, Bartholomew's son, a stockbroker who has longed to be a farmer. Recently on rather chilly terms with his wife, he is engaged in an affair with Mrs. Manresa.

Isa Oliver, Giles's wife, secretly a writer of poetry. She suspects her husband's unfaithfulness and fancies herself in love with Rupert Haines.

Mrs. Lucy Swithin, Bartholomew's widowed sister. In her imagination, she lives in England's historic past.

Mrs. Manresa, a cheerful, vulgar, and uninvited guest of the Olivers. She is carrying on an affair with Giles.

William Dodge, an uninvited and unwanted guest brought to the Olivers by Mrs. Manresa. Talking with Isa, he finds solace in his rejection and loneliness, as does she in hers.

Miss La Trobe, the lonely, frustrated writer and director of the historical pageant being presented at Pointz Hall.

Rupert Haines, a married gentleman farmer with whom Isa fancies herself in love.

George and

Caro, grandchildren of Bartholomew.

Eliza Clark,

Albert,

Mrs. Otter, and

Mr. Budge, villagers who act in the pageant.

BEVIS OF HAMPTON

Author: Unknown
First transcribed: c. 1200-1250
Genre: Poetry

Locale: England, the Holy Land, and Western Europe
Time: c. the tenth century
Plot: Romance

Bevis, a knight and the heir to the estate of Hampton. When he is seven years old, his father is murdered by his mother's lover. The assassin is beaten into senselessness by the child, whose mother, fearing further disturbances, sells him to slave merchants who take him to a Saracen court. Favorably impressing the Saracen king, he receives many honors. As a knight, he passes through a series of remarkable exploits before he marries the king's daughter, wins several kingdoms, and regains his rightful inheritance.

Josyan, the daughter of Bevis' Saracen master. She marries Bevis after his many brave knightly adventures.

Ermyn, a Saracen king, Josyan's father, into whose court Bevis goes as a slave.

Sir Murdour, the murderer of Bevis' father and usurper of Hampton.

Ascapard, the giant who becomes Bevis' page boy after the knight has subdued him.

Saber, a knight, the uncle and ally of Bevis.

Inor and

Bradmond, Saracen kings and enemies of Bevis.

Guy and

Mile, sons of Bevis of Hampton and Josyan.

King Edgar, the enemy of Bevis and Saber. To end a savage war, he agrees to give his daughter in marriage to Bevis' son, Mile.

BEYOND OUR POWER
(Over ævne, annet stykke)

Author: Bjørnstjerne Bjørnson (1832-1910)
First published: 1895
Genre: Drama

Locale: Norway
Time: Late nineteenth century
Plot: Social criticism

Rachel Sang, a wealthy young Norwegian liberal who tries to spread social enlightenment through use of a fortune inherited from an American aunt. She establishes a hospital and a newspaper. She cannot understand why the workingmen resort to violence.

Elias Sang, Rachel's brother, also a liberal. Under the influence of the demagogic Bratt, he comes to believe in sensational means to achieve the workers' ends. He tells his sister that death is the only way to a new life. He commits suicide by staying in Holger's castle when he knows it will be blown up.

Bratt, an extremist union leader and a former preacher. The workers led by him plant explosives under Holger's castle and blow it up during a meeting of industrialists there.

Pastor Falk, an idealist who preaches that social conditions can best be improved by exercising Christian patience and forbearance. He is ineffectual as an influence among the working people.

Holger, an industrialist and something of a philanthropist. He turns his mansion over to Rachel to be made into a workers' convalescent hospital.

Credo Holger, Holger's nephew, the son of Summer, Holger's liberal brother, now dead. Guided by Rachel, he dedicates his life to inventions that may make life easier and more pleasant.

Spera Holger, Holger's niece, Credo's sister. Under Rachel's influence, she decides to spend her life bringing greater freedom to women.

Maren Haug, a worker's wife who, while drunk, kills her two children and herself as an expression of the futility of life for the workers.

Halden, a young architect. Sympathizing with the workers, he helps them plant the explosives under Holger's castle, even though, as it is later discovered, he is Holger's son.

BEYOND THE BEDROOM WALL: A Family Album

Author: Larry Woiwode (1941-   )
First published: 1975
Genre: Novel

Locale: North Dakota, Illinois, and New York City
Time: 1881 to the mid-1960's
Plot: Family

Otto Neumiller, the patriarch of a German Catholic family. He immigrates to North Dakota in 1881, when he is twenty-four years old, marries Mary Reisling, and fathers Lucy, Augustina, and Charles. Energetic and civic-minded, he farms,

donates to the church, and serves on the county commission and the school and grain elevator boards. Concerned for the welfare of others, he loses all but his original homestead in a failed attempt to keep the elevator operating during an economic downturn. His rise in life and subsequent decline are recalled by his son, who travels to Mahomet in 1935 to bury him on his homestead, as he requested.

Charles John Christopher Neumiller, a carpenter, farmer, and school janitor, born in 1891 to Otto and Mary. He is dedicated, solemn and taciturn, generous, community-oriented, and a conscientious Catholic. With his wife, Marie, he fathers Martin, Elaine, Vince, Fred, Jay, Emil, Rose Marie, Tom, and Davy. A controlled man, he tenderly, but in a businesslike manner, prepares his father for burial in a homemade coffin. He feels chastened by the open expression of affection written in a birthday letter from his oldest son to his deceased father, and he wonders why he seldom thinks of the past. He admits that he can best express emotion in song, and his children remember his deep bass voice and wish for a pipe organ in their church. When he sells the North Dakota farm in 1938 and moves Marie and the younger children, his attachment to his farm animals prevents him from watching the sale. He has to be busy, frequently consults his watch, and with sons Fred and Tom operates a contracting company in Illinois. His grandson Jerome recalls that he always seemed prepared for any situation that arose. Together with his father, he represents the root and potential of a family from which later generations draw strength, but from which they also drift.

Marie Neumiller, the wife of Charles, described by her grandson Jerome as "such a bulwark of authority it seemed she was carrying within her a part of the country of Germany and a great deal of the Catholic church." Proud that her family produced a cardinal and a scholar of ecclesiastical law, she cannot tolerate the drunken behavior of Ed Jones, whose daughter her son Martin marries.

Augustina Neumiller, a sister of Charles, born in 1888. Out of fear, she never marries. She is high-strung, terrified of strangers, subject to spells, and tirelessly devoted to her father. Following his death, she remains on the North Dakota farm with hired man Clarence Popp.

Martin Neumiller, a teacher, principal, life insurance salesman, plumber, and handyman, born in 1913 to Charles and Marie. In the late 1930's, he marries a non-Catholic, Alpha Jones, with whom he has five children: Jerome, Charles, Timothy, Marie, and Susan. He shares his father's work ethic but is more introspective, enjoys telling stories of his past, and hopes to write a book about his life. He practices his faith more loosely than do his parents, and without compunction he promotes life insurance by using a picture of the holy family. He ignores Alpha's questions about faith, preferring simply to believe. Although he is talented and diligent, his life is more disappointing than successful. To earn more money, he gives up his principalship and eventually follows his parents to Illinois, where financial considerations force him to move his family into his parents' basement, then into an old garage, which he converts into a home between jobs as a plasterer. The move contributes to his wife's death, at which time he contemplates suicide. His resolve to keep his family together ultimately sustains him. Eventually, he remarries and moves to Eglington, Illinois, to work as a guidance counselor. His own life experiences call into question his ability to guide; although he keeps his children together, they grow up haphazardly, and four of them suffer terribly from the loss of their mother. Emblematic of Martin's inability to fully manage his life is his

struggle to make sense of it by writing about it; he feels overwhelmed by all the material that he wants to include.

Alpha Jones, Martin's wife, born in 1916. Big-boned and slightly overweight, she labors on her father's farm like a hired hand. Her life as a schoolteacher and years dating Martin are chronicled in a diary. She dies giving birth at the age of thirty-four. Her brief diary and children's recollections of her are the primary means of establishing her character. Deeply troubled by the suicide death of her talented brother, she names her first son after him. Her sensuality is neither fully understood nor appreciated by her husband. She converts to Catholicism only after several years of instruction, when she decides that its rituals tie her to a more ordered past. Her questions about faith and religious practice explore one of the novel's themes.

Ed Jones, Alpha' father, an alcoholic farmer born in 1871. Napoleonic in stature and demeanor, he speaks crudely and roughly but actually regrets his inability to relate well to Alpha. With his wife Electra, he fathers Elling, Conrad, Alpha, Jerome, Bernice, Kristine, and Lionell. Threatened by his wife's poise, beauty, and height, he reacts churlishly. As a former baseball catcher, dancing instructor, and Shakespearean actor who still wears his worn, hand-tailored suits and shirts, he seems ill-suited to farming. For financial reasons, he sends his two oldest sons to labor for relatives and his two youngest daughters to live with maiden aunts. As he ages, his physical ailments render him almost totally dependent on his wife. His crude humor and jokes contrast with the seriousness of the Neumiller family.

Electra Jones, the wife of Ed and mother of Alpha. Tall and attractive, with long hair, she is frail and plagued by psychosomatic illnesses. Although she is righteous and moral, she tolerates her husband's vulgarity and possesses some blatant prejudices about life and people.

Jerome Jones, a brother of Alpha, born in 1921. Unattractive, skinny, and reclusive, he is an avid reader and extremely precocious. His interest in flowers and animals leads him, without success, to form a wildlife club. Following his graduation and valedictory speech, he commits suicide by drowning himself at a class picnic. His sensitivity links him to nephews he never meets, Alpha's sons Charles and Timothy.

Jerome Neumiller, a doctor and the oldest son of Alpha and Martin, more confident and secure than his siblings. Jerome's interest in psychology leads him to perform a battery of tests on his brother Charles. Upon the death of his grandfather, his analysis of his family helps to establish the nature of several characters within the novel. No longer practicing a faith, he represents his generation's distance from the strong Catholic doctrine that directed their great-grandfather, Otto, and grandfather, Charles.

Charles Neumiller, an actor, the second son of Martin and Alpha. He marries Katherine and has a daughter. As a child, he seeks his mother's approval and is traumatized by her death. A dream about trying to reach her and communicate with her provides one source for the novel's title. His uncle Lionell, with whom he spends summers, relates to him only by criticizing him. Lionell forces Charles to masturbate him. This relationship produces in Charles unpredictable behavior and savage energy that confuse and worry his father and siblings. Jerome determines that Charles is a borderline psychotic.

When older and living in New York, Charles reacts with surprise when his father admires his voice and approves of his work doing television voice-overs. Typical of the missed communications in his life is his touching letter to his grandmother, Electra Jones, which arrives after her death.

Timothy (Tim) Neumiller, a poet and teacher, the third son of Martin and Alpha. He marries Cheri and has three children. When his mother dies, he loses his serene nature and retreats into his own world of concocted languages and voice imitations, and he calls himself Tinvalin, a name that only his wife will use. His life becomes more stable when he lives temporarily with his mother's relatives. As an adult, his recollections of the Neumiller family keep him awake at night. Paradoxically, he freely accepts his family's description of him as being apathetic, self-indulgent, and neglectful. Tim's generation is united by shared experiences, but its members do not feel the solidarity of a generation earlier, when the Neumiller business flourished and Martin moved to live closer to his parents.

Marie Neumiller, the fourth child and oldest daughter of Martin and Alpha. She never marries. Although she is a handsome child who hums and sings, Marie is heavy, and her spendthrift ways and disorganized room anger her father. Sensitive and quiet, she likes candles, cries over soap operas, carefully decorates the house for Christmas, and majors in special education. While still too young to be embarrassed, both she and Susan permit themselves to be fondled by their sexually curious brothers.

Susan Neumiller, the fifth child and youngest daughter of Martin and Alpha. She quits college to marry and works as a bookkeeper for a physician. She provides a first-person description of her stepmother, Laura. While her father dates Laura, Susan resentfully stays home and grades his school papers. She admits that the family piano is unattractive, but she feels threatened by Laura's desire to abandon it and move to Chicago. Considered by her brothers and sisters to be bright and carefree, Susan represents the element within the family that seeks to preserve common ties. Having little to no recollection of her mother, she claims that she has heard enough to see her mother however she pleases.

Laura, Martin's second wife, a devout Catholic, former music teacher, executive secretary, and private bookkeeper. When she marries Martin, she and her daughter, Ginny, move into the Pettibone, Illinois, house. An organized and careful planner, she never overcomes the discomfort that she feels in Martin's home, and she urges him to move. Her death from breast cancer brings the family together and closes the novel, just as Otto Neumiller's death opens it.

Father Schimmelpfennig, a Catholic priest in North Dakota. He hosts weekly card parties at which players drink beer and place bets. He ministers to the Neumiller family and travels to Illinois to deliver Alpha's eulogy. Sensing the instability in young Charles's life, he takes Charles and Lionell Jones on a fishing trip during a summer when Charles stays with his uncle. His periodic appearances function as a reminder of the family's geographic and religious origins in North Dakota and in the Catholic church.

— *Barbara A. Looney*

THE BIG KNIFE

Author: Clifford Odets (1906-1963)
First published: 1949
Genre: Drama

Locale: Beverly Hills, California
Time: Late 1940's
Plot: Naturalism

Charlie Castle, a film star of considerable renown. He is rich, ruggedly handsome, virile, charming, frequently cynical, and dependably candid in dealing with people. Charlie's studio is pressuring him to renew his contract, which he does not want to sign, although it is for fourteen years at four million dollars a year. One skeleton lurks in Charlie's closet: Once, when he was driving drunk, he had an accident in which someone was killed. He permitted Buddy Bliss to take the blame and to go to jail for vehicular manslaughter. The studio uses this information in its attempt to blackmail Charlie into signing his new, extended contract. Instead, he commits suicide.

Marion Castle, Charlie's wife. Disenchanted with the falseness of life in Hollywood, she is living apart from her husband and vows that she will return to him only if he refuses to commit himself to the long-term contract his studio is trying to inveigle him into signing. Marion is a completely honest person. She has discovered that honesty is a liability in the society in which she has been forced to travel as a star's wife, but this quality is too ingrained in her nature for her to change now.

Patty Benedict, a Hollywood gossip columnist whose loyalty is strictly to herself. She is a powerful woman who rules by intimidation and communicates by innuendo. She knows Charlie's dark secret and uses this knowledge in her attempts to manipulate him. She is as deceitful as Marion is honest. The two have a strained relationship, generally civil but little more.

Buddy Bliss, Charlie's agent. He is humorless, loyal, stubborn, and not very bright. He goes to jail after Charlie's accident, willingly covering for Charlie to spare the film idol the embarrassment and public humiliation to which he would have been subjected had the truth surfaced. Buddy is an innocent; he is dazzled by Charlie's success and by his prowess with people. He tries to save him from all unpleasantness and from doing anything that might tarnish his manufactured image. Buddy is the sort of person born to be exploited.

Marcus Hoff, the pudgy, self-assured head of the studio to which Charlie is under contract. The middle-aged Hoff is bright, able, and manipulative. He dresses the part of someone who runs a studio, attired in suave, expensive, tailor-made suits of subdued colors. He frequently puffs on choice Havana cigars. He is imperious, capable of observing all the amenities but then of turning full circle and destroying anyone who gets in his way.

Coy Smiley, Hoff's lean toady. He does Hoff's bidding deftly and unquestioningly. He is competent and calculating, cynical, calm, and unfailingly courteous. His Irish lineage is evident in his face and demeanor. He essentially is detached and alone, unlikely ever to be considered as anyone's friend.

Nat Danziger, a man in his sixties, the agent acting as middleman between the studio and Charlie. Nat is basically good, kind, and fatherly, although the system within which he lives is corrupt. He is sentimental and religious in the broadest sense. Although he is competent in his business dealings, he seems a misfit among the jackals of the film industry.

Connie Bliss, Buddy's wife, a lissome blonde on whom clothes look superb. She has about her a hardness, mitigated slightly by her desire to please. She has a good mind.

Hank Teagle, a fifty-year-old friend of Charlie. He limps slightly and is unpretentious, quiet, and mature. He has an undeviating devotion to Charlie.

Dixie Evans, a woman who escaped her poor Boston family and her department store job four years earlier to work in Hollywood. Despite her overindulgence in liquor, she puts up a good front of brightness and competence.

Ralph, the Castles' black butler, through whom one comes to see glimmerings of the real Charlie Castle.

Dr. Frary, the Castles' next-door neighbor and friend.

— *R. Baird Shuman*

THE BIG ROCK CANDY MOUNTAIN

Author: Wallace Stegner (1909-1993)
First published: 1943
Genre: Novel

Locale: North Dakota, Washington, Saskatchewan, Montana, Utah, and Nevada
Time: 1905-1932
Plot: Historical realism

Harry "Bo" Mason, a bootlegger, a man who is always looking for greener pastures. When Elsa Norgaard first meets him, he is running an illegal bar in North Dakota. Although he can be charming, he has a nasty temper and sometimes becomes violent. He falls in love with Elsa and marries her. He is energetic but impatient. Simply earning a living is not enough; he wants to make a fortune quickly. When one plan does not work out, he moves his family somewhere else. The longest the Mason family stays in one place is the five years they spend homesteading in Saskatchewan, but the land is too poor to support them. Bo has little regard for the law, and because bootlegging offers the most potential to make money in a hurry, he gives up all pretense at other occupations and becomes a full-time bootlegger. When Elsa is stricken with cancer, he cannot deal with her illness and finds a mistress. After her death, he begins to feel old. His moneymaking schemes fail, leaving him virtually penniless. His mistress rejects him. When he has no more hope or plans for the future, he kills his mistress and then himself.

Elsa Norgaard Mason, Bo's wife. When Elsa's mother died, her father married Elsa's best friend, a situation with which she could not live. Elsa leaves home when she turns eighteen to live with her uncle in North Dakota. There she meets Bo and is attracted by his dangerous sort of charm, though she feels uneasy about his temper. When her father learns of the romance and disapproves, she marries Bo. Elsa's main desires in life are to have a family, a home, and a stable life in a community with friends. With Bo, she gets none of these. Elsa is worn out from work at an early age. She must be the buffer between her husband and her sons. The one stable force that holds the family together, she sacrifices herself for the others. She succumbs to breast cancer before turning fifty.

Chester (Chet) Mason, Bo and Elsa's older son. Chet is big and strong, like his father, and he aspires to become a major league baseball player, like his father. He is uncomfortable with Bo's bootlegging activities. When he is only seventeen years old, he elopes with Laura Betterton, who is twenty-one, against his parents' wishes. When the Depression hits, he loses his job and must move home. Washed up at the age of twenty-three, he dies of pneumonia.

Bruce Mason, Bo and Elsa's younger son. Bruce is smaller than Chet and not as athletic, but he is much more gifted academically. As a small child, he clings to his mother in fear, a characteristic that makes Bo angry. Bo's anger makes Bruce more fearful. As a boy living on a homestead in Saskatchewan, he hunts gophers passionately and admires his father's skill with a gun, but he is more drawn to books. Deeply attached to his mother, he tries to reject his father. After graduating from high school at the age of fifteen, Bruce escapes to college and eventually to law school. The one survivor of the Mason family, he is the one who reflects on the meaning of the family experience.

Nels Norgaard, Elsa's father. Originally from Norway, he and his wife immigrated to Minnesota because her family disapproved of their marriage because he was beneath her social station. He was strict, not even allowing card games to be played in his house. When Elsa's mother died, he married a woman young enough to be his daughter.

Karl Norgaard, Elsa's uncle, a storekeeper in Hardanger, North Dakota. Less pious than his brother, he is friendly with all kinds of people, including bootleggers and gamblers.

Laura Betterton, Chet's wife. She is four years older than Chet and looking for a way to escape from her parents. After Chet becomes unable to support her, she leaves him.

— *Eunice Pedersen Johnston*

THE BIG SKY

Author: A. B. Guthrie, Jr. (1901-1991)
First published: 1947
Genre: Novel

Locale: Western United States
Time: 1830-1843
Plot: Adventure

Boone Caudill, a young mountain man, strong, reticent, moody, quick to anger, and savage when crossed. Like an Indian, he wears his long hair braided. He loves the open country and the independent life of a hunter, and he resents the settlement of the West by eastern immigrants. Stubborn and brave, he is less a thinker than a doer. Having set his mind on marrying Teal Eye, he is unceasing in his search until he finds her. Once the suspicion about the source of his son's red hair has been put into his mind, he broods on it until he finds the suspicion apparently confirmed, and he kills innocent Jim Deakins, whom he had once saved. After learning that his son could have inherited his red hair through Boone himself, he is deeply troubled. Yet he appears to regard the shooting of Jim not as a crime but only as a grave injustice to his best friend.

Teal Eye, his Indian wife, the young daughter of a Blackfoot chief. As a child she was captured by Crows, escaped, was rescued, and was taken to St. Louis. While being returned to her people so that she may be used as a basis for a friendship to be established between Jourdonnais and the Blackfoot Indians, she escapes in Blackfoot territory. Found long afterward with her people by Boone, she happily accepts him as her husband, and she bears his son. Though he deserts her when he suspects the baby's paternity, he is at the story's end on his way back to Teal Eye, in whose faithful love he now believes.

Jim Deakins, Boone's red-haired, talkative friend, who enjoys companionship, joking, drinking, and bedding down with women. Restless, he never likes to stay anywhere for long, especially away from the communities where he can enjoy associating with men and women. He is shot to death by Boone, who suspects him of having fathered Teal Eye's reddish-haired son.

Dick Summers, an old hunter, long-chinned with a lined, lean, and humorous face. He lives much in the past. Realizing that he is too old to continue the life of a mountain man, he returns east, marries, and becomes a farmer.

Jourdonnais, a French keelboat captain ambitious to build a trading post and establish his own company. He is killed in an Indian attack on his new fort.

Poordevil, a half-witted Blackfoot, ugly, tousle-haired, long-nosed, and gap-toothed. He loves whiskey and is often amusing with his rough trapper-talk English.

Elisha Peabody, a Yankee speculator who envisons hordes of Americans pushing westward and himself or his agents profiting from their passage.

McKenzie, an American Fur Company trader, cold-eyed, broad-faced, something of a dandy, and a deceitful bargainer. He loses his job because of whiskey-making.

Uncle Zeb Calloway, an old-time mountain man, brother of Serena Caudill. He is grizzled, long-nosed, and bushy-browed; he drinks heavily.

John Caudill and

Serena Caudill, Boone's parents.

Red Horn, brother of Teal Eye. He succeeds his father, Heavy Otter, as chief after smallpox kills most of the Piegans, a tribe of Blackfoot Indians.

Jonathan Bedwell, a thief who steals Boone's rifle.

Streak, a hunter killed by Boone in a fight after Streak threatens to kill Poordevil.

Nancy Litsey, a foolish and forward young girl whom Boone takes sexually on one occasion on his return home.

Dan Caudill, Boone's younger brother.

Cora Caudill, Boone's sister-in-law.

Punk Caudill and

Andy Caudill, Boone's two young nephews.

THE BIG SLEEP

Author: Raymond Chandler (1888-1959)
First published: 1939
Genre: Novel

Locale: Los Angeles, California
Time: The 1930's
Plot: Detective and mystery

Philip Marlowe, a private detective. Tall, dark, and rugged, with a poker face and a quick wit, he is attractive to women but wary of them and of all entanglements. Though cynical and hard-boiled, and a heavy drinker capable of violence, Marlowe is idealistic, even puritanical. Contemptuous of money, he is an honest loner in a corrupt world. Hired to deal with a blackmail threat, Marlowe is embroiled in a more deadly game by Sternwood's two spoiled daughters, whose advances he spurns. Independent to the point of insubordination, he refuses to stop investigating the case, even after Sternwood pays him off.

General Guy de Brisay Sternwood, an oil millionaire. Crippled and cadaverous, he subsists on little more than heat. A survivor, he is a man with no moral code, but he respects and admires the independence he sees in Marlowe and his son-in-law, Rusty Regan. At the beginning of the novel, he hires the detective to protect his younger daughter, but he turns out to be just as interested in finding his missing son-in-law.

Vivian Sternwood Regan, the general's older daughter. Tall and rangy, with black wiry hair and black eyes, she looks

like trouble to Marlowe but turns out to have her sister's and father's interests at heart. Spoiled and bored, she spends much of her time at Mars's casino, gambling away her allowance. Her attempts to manipulate Marlowe and throw him off the track instead point him in the right direction.

Carmen Sternwood, the general's younger daughter. Coy but cruel, she is an unsettling blonde with drugged, expressionless, slate-gray eyes and an alluring body that she likes to expose. Expecting men to respond to her charms, she can be deadly when they do not. Her unexpected appearances throughout the novel complicate the plot, leading finally to her exposure as Regan's killer.

Terence "Rusty" Regan, Vivian's missing husband, a tough former bootlegger and officer in the Irish Republican Army who returned Sternwood's respect. His mysterious disappearance disturbs the general.

Eddie Mars, a gambler and gangster, owner of the Cypress Club. A gray, sporty man with official connections, he is followed everywhere by his henchman but is not quite as tough as he thinks. Suspected of killing Regan, he is interested primarily in keeping his wife (and the truth) hidden in order to blackmail Vivian.

Mona Mars, Eddie's wife, blue-eyed, with a platinum wig and a silver voice. This former singer left Rusty for Eddie. As the novel begins, she supposedly has run off with Regan, but Marlowe tracks her down, giving her the chance to save him from Canino's clutches.

Norris, the Sternwood butler. Old and gravely polite, with acid-blue eyes, he is secretive and extremely protective in his role as the general's factotum and go-between with Marlowe.

Owen Taylor, the Sternwood chauffeur. Dark and boyish, he is in love with Carmen and kills Geiger. He takes a glass photographic negative to protect her before ending up, along with the car, on the ocean floor.

Arthur Gwynn Geiger, a pornographer and blackmailer, a soft man with a fat face and a Charlie Chan mustache. His bookstore is only a front, and his attempt at blackmailing the general precipitates the book's action. He is shot while taking a photograph of the drugged and naked Carmen.

Agnes Lozelle, Geiger's secretary and Brody's girlfriend. A sexy green-eyed blonde, she always ends up with the half-smart guys, such as Brody and Jones. She leaves town with the $200 that Marlowe pays to learn where Mrs. Mars is.

Joe Brody, a blackmailer and Agnes' boyfriend. He takes over Geiger's stock of pornography and tries to blackmail Vivian with the photograph of Carmen.

Carol Lundgren, Geiger's homosexual lover. This dark, handsome young punk kills Brody in the mistaken belief that he is Geiger's murderer.

Harry Jones, a small-time hood. A small man with brilliant eyes, he is not as tough as he pretends when he approaches Marlowe to sell information on Mrs. Mars's whereabouts. He later has the courage to protect Agnes at the cost of his own life.

Lash Canino, Mars's hired killer and Mona's guard. A short, heavy-set man, always dressed in brown, he is a ruthless killer who poisons Jones and is shot by Marlowe.

Bernie Ohls, the district attorney's chief investigator, Marlowe's friend and official connection. He takes Marlowe along to see Taylor's body, a favor reciprocated whenever Marlowe has anything to give the police.

Captain Al Gregory, chief of the Missing Persons Bureau. This burly, slow-moving man maintains friendly relations with Mars but, claiming to be as honest as he can be in a corrupt system, provides Marlowe with background information on Rusty.

— Philip McDermott

BILLIARDS AT HALF-PAST NINE
(Billard um halbzehn)

Author: Heinrich Böll (1917-1985)
First published: 1959
Genre: Novel

Locale: West Germany
Time: September 6, 1958
Plot: Social realism

Robert Fähmel (FAY-mehl), or **Faehmel**, a forty-three-year-old architect, demolitions expert, and widower. He is a distinguished looking gentleman with a red scar on the bridge of his nose. His days are spent according to a strict routine that stresses an almost total withdrawal from public life. Even his business associates and former army buddies do not, as a rule, see him. His secretary, Leonore, sees him only for an hour every business day. Robert inherited his father's architectural firm. On the day of the novel's plot, he reminisces about his life. His father had built the abbey of St. Anton, and, Robert had demolished it in the closing days of the war. He had done so on a military pretext; his real reason, however, was revenge. The monks and their abbot had partaken of "the sacrament of the buffalo"; that is, they had supported the Nazis. Robert has managed to keep his culpability a secret; not even his son, Joseph, who rebuilt the monastery, knows. Only his father suspects. Robert, as a young man, had resisted Nazism, and he was persecuted for it, even as a schoolboy. He and another of his classmates, Alfred Schrella, had to seek refuge in Amsterdam. Robert's mother, who was acquainted with the administrative head of the province, intervened and secured his amnesty in exchange for the promise that her son never again meddle in politics. Robert spent the war years as a demolitions expert in the army. He rose to the rank of captain. Since his return to his hometown, he has hewed closely to a rigid and intensely private routine. Every day at half-past nine, he

plays billiards in the Prince Heinrich Hotel. Only Hugo, the bellboy, is allowed in the room. It is to him that he tells his life's story. In the end, he adopts Hugo as his son and signs over to him his landholdings. He adopts him in lieu of a son that his wife, Edith, might have borne him if she had not been killed in an air raid. Robert seeks to come to terms with his own past and with that of his country, and he seeks to avoid or to punish all those whom he knows to be tarnished by their Nazi past. He has given strict instructions to Leonore not to allow anyone near him, excepting his family and Alfred Schrella.

Heinrich Fähmel (HIN-rihkh), Robert's father, an eighty-year-old architect and privy councillor. He is slim and robust, the son of a peasant. He is the founder of a well-known and respected architectural firm. At the age of thirty, he won a competition for best design of a monastery and was propelled into the forefront of architects in town. He cultivates a public image of an unusual man and artist by adhering to a rigid daily routine that includes a special breakfast at the Café Kroner. He married Johanna Kilb, the daughter of the attorney who supervised the competition. He served as a captain with the army engineers in World War I. He won two Iron Crosses, which he later discards as a token of his antiwar and anti-imperialist sentiments. He lost one of his sons to the Nazis, because he permitted him to admire military power, and he wishes to avoid that in the future for the sake of his grandchildren. Heinrich and Johanna had seven children, of whom Robert is the sole survivor. Heinrich tells his life's story to Leonore, whom he has hired for the day to tidy up his office. His eightieth birthday is about to be celebrated in the Café Kroner when he learns of his wife's arrival at the Prince Heinrich Hotel. The party at the café is cancelled; it takes place in his office instead.

Johanna Fähmel (yoh-HAH-nah), Heinrich's wife, a seventy-year-old patient in a mental hospital. She is a resolute and principled woman, although obsessive at times. In her unswerving opposition to power and privilege, to lies and terror, she refuses any advantage that might accrue to her because of her husband's prominence. She gives away bread, butter, and honey from the abbey and forces her family to subsist on its official food rations alone. Her losses during the war, Otto's allegiance to the Nazis and his death at the front, and Robert's persecution have taken their toll: She had a nervous breakdown. Once committed to a mental hospital, she finds it convenient to feign continued illness, allowing her to oppose the regime with impunity. On her husband's eightieth birthday, she resolves to kill Ben Wackes, a former Nazi and persecutor of her son who now leads the "blue-tunics," a neo-Nazi group. She contrives to steal a pistol from the hospital gardener. Instead of Wackes, however, she shoots a minister

of the government at the hotel. The man is wounded, but he survives.

Alfred Schrella, a childhood friend of Robert and his brother-in-law. Alfred and Robert were in Amsterdam together as refugees from Nazi persecution. Schrella, however, continues in exile until September 6, 1958. He has returned to his hometown after twenty-two years abroad in Holland and Britain. He is now stateless. He tells Robert that he will not stay, because he cannot live in a country that does not "tend its lambs and breeds wolves" instead.

Joseph Fähmel (YOH-sehf), Robert's twenty-seven-year-old son, an architect. Although he is only a young and reluctant architect, he has been given the task of rebuilding the abbey of St. Anton. Even at the dedication ceremony, he is ignorant of his father's role in its destruction. He is married to Marianne, a victim of her parents' Nazism. She was reared by foster parents after the war. Heinrich Fähmel likes her and looks upon her as a worthy successor to Johanna, one who will ensure the continuity of the family. Joseph, just as his father and grandfather before him, does not seek wealth and power and hence is undecided about continuing in the family tradition of serving the region as a prominent architect.

— Arthur Tilo Alt

BILLY BATHGATE

Author: E. L. Doctorow (1931-   )
First published: 1989
Genre: Novel

Locale: New York City, Onondoga, and Sarasota, New York
Time: The 1930's
Plot: Historical realism

Billy Bathgate, a fifteen-year-old boy from the Bronx who attracts the attention of gangster Dutch Schultz as he juggles outside Schultz's warehouse. A quick-witted, clever young man, he makes himself useful enough to secure a place on the fringes of the gang, running errands for Dutch, working as a busboy at his club, and eventually accompanying him on his odyssey to the country in preparation for his tax evasion trial. Billy, who never knew his father and whose mother teeters on the edge of sanity, discovers in Dutch's gang a surrogate family that both attracts and repulses him. A brave young man with a gift for pleasing adults, he senses that his association with the gang makes him part of history, but also that it places his life in jeopardy. He joins Dutch as the renowned gangster is losing his grip on his dominion, pursued by both the government and rival gangs. As Billy becomes a more integral part of the gang, he witnesses the horrific death of Schultz's lieutenant Bo Weinberg, the casually brutal murder of a window washer, and the slaughter of a hapless fire inspector who arrives at an inopportune moment. He realizes that he knows too much for his own safety. Through use of his own intelligence, he manages not only to be the only member to survive when the gang is wiped out by rivals but also to locate the gang's hidden fortune and emerge years later as a prominent and successful member of society.

Dutch Schultz, born Arthur Flegonheimer, a renowned gangster no longer at the height of his powers. In his thirties, the short-necked, solid Schultz always appears badly dressed, even in expensive clothes. The head of a complex operation with a large payroll, he surrounds himself with

admirers and dependents, always feeling like the wronged party, the victim of a double-cross. As his empire begins to decline, besieged both by rival gangs and by the government, Dutch becomes more volatile. His temper flares easily, and he murders increasingly out of rage rather than as a "business" decision. Dutch's life of crime finally catches up with him when he and his closest associates are gunned down by a rival gang.

Bo Weinberg, Schultz's handsome, well-dressed, glamorous chief henchman, who is proud of his ability to make a "clean kill." Weinberg's betrayal of Schultz results in his own gruesome death when Dutch buries his feet in concrete and pushes him overboard, in the fabled gangster tradition.

Drew Preston, Bo Weinberg's "moll," a beautiful, spoiled Park Avenue socialite who is not much older than Billy. Drew's marriage to a wealthy man allows her the freedom to "socialize" with known gangsters while he picks up young men. In self-preservation, she shifts her allegiance to Schultz after having the misfortune to witness his murder of Weinberg. Dutch is infatuated with her for a time, but when he appoints Billy to keep her company, the young man falls in love with her as well. The two have a brief affair before Billy recruits her husband to rescue her from Dutch's revenge.

Otto "Abbadabba" Berman, the brains of Schultz's operation. He controls the flow of money and the numbers racket while simultaneously attempting to control the increasingly erratic Schultz. A humpback with glasses, soft-spoken and well dressed, he takes Billy under his wing to share with him his passion for numbers.

Lulu Rosenkrantz, one of Dutch's chief henchmen. Lulu has an oversized head of unkempt hair, a broken nose, and a pockmarked face. He remains loyal to Dutch despite his increasingly erratic behavior.

Mary Behan, Billy's mother, a tall, majestic woman with long gray hair who has reared Billy on her own. She wavers in and out of sanity, caring nothing for her own appearance or for making friends but managing to keep her job in a laundry.

Arnold Garbage, Billy's junk-collecting friend from the neighborhood orphanage. Arnold stashes the spoils of Schultz's empire in his junk-strewn basement until Billy feels safe spending it.

— *Mary Virginia Davis*

BILLY BUDD, FORETOPMAN

Author: Herman Melville (1819-1891)
First published: 1924
Genre: Novel

Locale: Aboard a British man-of-war
Time: 1797
Plot: Symbolic realism

Billy Budd, a youthful member of the crew of the merchantman *Rights-of-Man*, who is impressed into service aboard H.M.S. *Indomitable* during the last decade of the eighteenth century. Billy is twenty-one, "welkin-eyed," and possessed of great masculine beauty; he has no idea who his father and mother were, having been left a foundling in a basket on the doorstep of a "good man" in Bristol, England. Billy was a cheerful, stabilizing influence on the rough crew of the merchantman; when he is taken aboard the "Indomitable," he is popular with all the officers and crew except John Claggart, the master-at-arms, who is envious of Billy's almost perfect physique and personality. Claggart falsely accuses Billy of fomenting a mutiny aboard the ship. When he repeats the charges in the Captain's quarters while Billy is present, the young man (who stutters under stress and sometimes suffers a total speech block) can say nothing in his own defense and hits Claggart on the forehead with his fist. Claggart falls and dies. In the subsequent trial, at which the Captain is the sole witness, there can be no leniency because of the recent Great Mutiny in the fleet. Billy is sentenced to hang. At the execution his last words are, "God bless Captain Vere!" Honest, refreshing, ingenuous, uncomplaining—these adjectives may be applied to Billy Budd, who represents an innocent youth trapped by the brutality of fleet regulations or, perhaps, truth and beauty trapped by the wickedness of the world.

Captain Edward Fairfax Vere, of the *Indomitable*. He is known in the fleet as "Starry" Vere to distinguish him from a kinsman and officer of like rank in the navy. The nickname is a misnomer, however, for Captain Vere, a bachelor of about forty, is a quiet, brooding intellectual who reads a great deal. He is also a fine commander, but he lacks the flamboyance of the more famous Horatio Nelson. He suffers greatly at having to testify before the three-man court against Billy Budd, whom he recognizes as an efficient, attractive, impulsive seaman. He, too, seems trapped by regulations (tightened during the Great Mutiny), which state that striking an officer is a capital offense. When Claggart comes to Captain Vere with his foggy, unsubstantiated charges that Billy is mutinous, the Captain summons Billy to his quarters to prove that Claggart is a false witness.

John Claggart, the master-at-arms of the ship. His duties are mainly to oversee the crew and its work. When Claggart observes Billy Budd, he quickly becomes envious of the personal beauty of the young man. The only basis for the charges Claggart makes against Billy is that an afterguardsman, a troublemaker, tries to be friendly and confidential with the foretopman. Because he joined the navy for no apparent reason and because he never makes any reference to his previous life ashore, Claggart is a man of mystery about whom many rumors are circulated on the ship.

The Dansker, an old veteran who serves as mainmast-man in his watch. He likes Billy from the start and is the one who nicknames him "Baby." When Billy comes to him for counsel and to ask why his petty mistakes are getting him into trouble, the Dansker astutely remarks that "Jimmy Legs" (meaning the master-at-arms) is down on him.

The Afterguardsman, a troublemaking sailor. He approaches Billy and tries to tempt him to join an incipient mutiny. Billy angrily rebuffs him but does not report the incident to any officer.

Lieutenant Ratcliffe, the officer who goes aboard the *Rights-of-Man* and selects Billy for impressment.

BILLY PHELAN'S GREATEST GAME

Author: William Kennedy (1928-   )
First published: 1978
Genre: Novel

Locale: Albany, New York
Time: 1938
Plot: Regional

William (Billy) Phelan, a young gambler and bookmaker. Billy Phelan is a pool hustler and a familiar figure among Albany's shadowy nighttime crowd. A gambler with a gift for sizing up his opponents, he earns his living on the fringes of society but in the center of a netherworld in which he moves comfortably and securely. He operates as a bookie with the permission of the powerful McCall family. When the McCalls ask him to perform a service for them that would violate his personal code of ethics, Billy must decide where his allegiance lies.

Martin Daugherty, a newspaper columnist and Billy's friend. Martin has spent his life in Albany and grew up next door to Billy's father. A journalist in the Damon Runyon tradition, he is at ease with mobsters, gamblers, and prostitutes. He sometimes has accurate visions and premonitions. He is the son of a successful playwright, and he struggles throughout the book with his conflicting feelings toward his father. Martin plays a central role in Billy's story, both by placing a bet with him that leaves Billy sorely in need of money and by chronicling the events surrounding Billy's confrontation with the McCalls.

Francis Phelan, Billy's father, an alcoholic drifter. Francis abandoned his family when Billy was nine. His reappearance in Albany after years of aimless drifting forms one of the book's important subplots. Billy grew up without his father's guidance, and his meeting with Francis provides him with an opportunity to measure himself against the man whose absence shaped the course of his life. What he finds is an alcoholic vagrant, battered and ill from his life on the road and little more than a shell of the man Billy remembers.

Morrie Berman, an acquaintance of Billy. Morrie is a shady figure on the fringes of Albany's criminal underworld. He is a former pimp, a gambler, and a grave disappointment to his family of tailors and political radicals. The McCall family suspects him of having a part in the kidnapping of Charlie McCall and asks Billy to spy on him. Billy's conflict over where his loyalties lie makes Morrie a crucial factor in his story.

Charlie McCall, the son of the city's most powerful family. Charlie is a likable young man grown soft from a life of indulgence. His kidnapping sets the story in motion.

Bindy McCall, Charlie's father. Bindy runs all the gambling in Albany. He exercises absolute control over access to the town's clubs and the right to take bets.

Patsy McCall, Bindy's brother and Charlie's uncle. Patsy and his brother Matt are the most powerful men in the city. Patsy is a ruthless behind-the-scenes manipulator who controls Albany's political life. To free his nephew, he will use all of his considerable influence.

Melissa Spencer, an actress and Martin's former lover. As a young woman, Melissa had been the lover of Martin's father and the inspiration for his best-known play, in which she is now appearing in Albany. A beautiful, sensual woman, she has been an odd link between Martin and his father.

Edward Daugherty, a playwright and Martin's father. Although he appears only near the end of the book, his presence is felt throughout the segments focusing on his son. Now senile and in a nursing home, he was once a man capable of turning the scandal that drove his wife mad into a successful play.

Emory Jones, the editor of Martin Daugherty's paper, the *Times-Union*. When Charlie McCall is kidnapped, it falls to him to convince the rest of the press to delay printing the story until the McCalls approve its publication.

— *Janet Lorenz*

BILOXI BLUES

Author: Neil Simon (1927-   )
First published: 1986
Genre: Drama

Locale: Biloxi, Mississippi
Time: 1943
Plot: Comedy

Eugene Morris Jerome, an Army recruit from Brooklyn, New York. Eugene is a young Jewish man who aspires to be a writer. He fervently records his deepest thoughts and impressions in his journal, often leaving himself more an observer than a participant in human interactions. He does have principles—respect, compassion, and open-mindedness—but he is hesitant to act on them. He always sees the lighter side of life, and he enlists his quick and acerbic wit to ease him through difficult situations. Having lived a sheltered life, Eugene is eager and determined to lose his virginity and fall in love. At least at the beginning of the play, he does not quite know the difference.

Arnold Epstein, an Army recruit from Queens, New York. Epstein is a stubborn Jewish intellectual who has very strong principles and absolutely refuses to compromise them. He has a nervous stomach and resents being in basic training, and he cannot understand why rigorous discipline and blind obedience are considered superior to respect and compassion in the shaping of soldiers. He immediately identifies Toomey as his enemy and squares off for a fierce battle. To Epstein, life is serious business, a continuous moral quandary. He is clever and sardonic, but rarely light-spirited. When humiliated, and even when beaten on his own terms, he accepts defeat stoically.

Joseph Wykowski, a recruit of Polish background from Bridgeport, Connecticut, with a stomach of steel and an irrepressible sex drive. Wykowski accepts the rigors of Army discipline without question: To him it is a game that, like any

game, he can win. He is decidedly nonintellectual and occasionally anti-Semitic, and he has no patience for moral ruminations. He is the self-proclaimed leader of the platoon. His simple strength and basic clear vision validate his arrogance.

Roy Selridge, a recruit from Schenectady, New York. Selridge is a young man with an engaging, though often overbearing, sense of humor. He falls in behind Wykowski as a coarse masculine voice in the group but ultimately lacks the courage to speak out or stand alone. Though his bravado is often hollow, his spirit is always generous and optimistic.

Donald Carney, a recruit from Montclair, New Jersey. Carney loves to sing—he sings in his sleep—and dreams of becoming a recording star. He is basically honest and good-natured but thoughtful to a fault: He has a hard time making decisions. He is faithful to his fiancée in Albany but views the prospect of marriage with serious trepidation.

James Hennesey, another recruit. He is a timid young man, relatively innocent and humorless. He misses his family but seems to be adapting well enough to Army life until he is discovered in a homosexual liaison with another soldier.

Merwyn J. Toomey, the sergeant overseeing the platoon's basic training. Toomey is a hard-boiled Southern military man who knows how to deal with trickery and back talk. He pits the recruits against one another to subjugate them to Army discipline. He accepts the special challenge that Epstein directs at him and determines to win the battle of wills. He has a steel plate in his head, a souvenir from the North African campaign, that accounts for his wholehearted commitment to the rigorous treatment of his soldiers, his sublimated sense of sadness and doom, and, ultimately, his premature retirement from active duty.

Rowena, a Biloxi prostitute. Rowena is direct and realistic: She is a happily married woman whose business is satisfying the sexual needs of young soldiers and peddling perfume and lingerie for them to send home to their girlfriends.

Daisy Hannigan, a local Catholic schoolgirl. Daisy is friendly, pretty, innocent, and dutiful. The daughter of a journalist from Chicago, she likes books and is enchanted with Eugene's literary aspirations.

— *B. P. Mann*

BIRD AT MY WINDOW

Author: Rosa Guy (1928-   )
First published: 1966
Genre: Novel

Locale: Harlem, New York, and Paris, France
Time: The 1920's to the 1950's
Plot: Naturalism

Wade Williams, the protagonist, a virile, attractive, light-skinned African American male who is "thirty-eight and never married yet never free." His life is bound up in his family and his neighborhood, and his natural intelligence and intermittent attempts at personal freedom are hampered by the conditioning of those two forces.

"Big Willie" Williams, Wade's father, a physically powerful, half-white man who lives with a bullet in his heart for one year after he is shot in a card game. It is his unfinished business, his pledge to avenge himself against the Southern whites who forced him to seek shelter in the North, that keeps Big Willie going.

Evelyn Williams, the family matriarch. Saved by her husband from a life of labor in the cotton fields of the American South, "Mumma" reluctantly shares Big Willie's exile in the North. Hers is a life of fear, complaint, and Christian hypocrisy.

Faith Williams, Wade's sister, whose devotion to her brother is nearly absolute. They share "every joy, every grief." Faith is so much a part of Wade that her eventual death at his hands signals the ultimate disintegration of his personality.

Willie Earl Williams, the eldest of the three Williams siblings, a "natural-born slickster." His tightfistedness and attendant deception further restrict Wade's options in life.

Uncle Dan Williams, Big Willie's brother, whose loyalty to the Williams clan is subordinate only to his dependence on alcohol.

Professor Jones, a one-person crusade for justice and equality. Described as a little man with a portfolio, the professor is more than willing to take on the bureaucracy at various times in Wade's life to create opportunities for the young man and the Williams family.

Clovis Rockford, Jr., Wade's friend and intellectual confidant in junior high school. The two boys share excitement at exploring the world of ideas and discovering the elasticity of their own exceptional minds. Wade's relationship with "Rocky" also is marked by his ambivalent sexual feelings and a sense of protectiveness resulting from Rocky's smallness and delicacy.

Gay Sommers, a lab technician who offers Wade a way out of Harlem through marriage, fatherhood, and a move to the Bronx. Their relationship eventually is spoiled by his despair and resentment of her confidence, which cause him to want to "grind her into the dust" and "make her as low as he felt."

Gladys, an "exquisitely ugly" woman whose life has been full of abuse. Wade is drawn to her pain, but their life together is characterized by hate as much as by need. Gladys is the personification of Wade's loneliness, and he represents to her all the men who have used and abandoned her. In the end, however, Gladys shows an inner strength that Wade does not possess.

— *S. Thomas Mack*

THE BIRDS
(Ornithes)

Author: Aristophanes (c. 450-c. 385 B.C.E.)
First performed: 414 B.C.E.
Genre: Drama

Locale: Athens and Nephelo-Coccygia, the city of the birds
Time: 431-404 B.C.E.
Plot: Social satire

Pisthetærus (pihs-theh-TI-ruhs), an old man of Athens who has left his native city in disapproval because of the corruption, especially the litigiousness, of his countrymen. High-spirited, comically fantastic, and sometimes even vulgar, he nevertheless has an underlying vein of hardheaded good sense that makes him despise hypocrites and frauds. He uses his oratorical skill to convince the birds that they are the superiors of the gods, and he proposes the creation of Nephelo-Coccygia, or "Cloud Cuckoo Land," the strategic location of which will give the birds power over both gods and men. For his pains, he is awarded wings and a position of respect in the land of the birds. He adopts a very casual attitude toward the gods who come to negotiate a peace, and through shrewd dealing he wins not only the scepter of Zeus for the birds but also the hand of Basileia, or "Sovereignty," and celestial bounty for himself.

Euelpides (ew-EHL-pih-deez), another old Athenian, Pisthetærus' companion and foil. Not as sharply individualized, he is, like Pisthetærus, disgusted with Athenian life and ready to cooperate in his friend's schemes. He too has a broadly comic wit and a keen eye for a pretty courtesan.

Epops (EH-pops), the hoopoe. Now King of the Birds, he was once Tereus, a king of Thrace and the son of Ares. After his marriage to Procne, he violated Procne's sister Philomela and cut out her tongue so that she could not tell of the deed. All three were transformed by the gods: Tereus became a hoopoe (in the version of the myth followed by Aristophanes), Procne a nightingale, and Philomela a swallow. Epops is reunited with Procne in the land of the birds, where he has special status because he has human as well as bird knowledge. He is delighted with Pisthetærus' suggestion regarding the foundation of Nephelo-Coccygia.

Trochilus (TROH-kih-luhs), the wren, a servant to Epops.

Phoenicopterus (fee-nih-KOP-tur-uhs), the flamingo, who attends the council of birds that votes to establish Nephelo-Coccygia.

A priest, who, after the establishment of Nephelo-Coccygia, makes sacrifices to all the bird gods and goddesses.

A poet, who addresses some rather bad verses to the new city.

A prophet,

Meton, a geometrician and astronomer,

an inspector of tributary towns, and

a dealer in decrees, who also arrive for the inaugural ceremonies but are driven away by Pisthetærus, who knows them to be frauds.

Iris (I-rihs), the messenger of Zeus who wanders into Nephelo-Coccygia on her way to command humankind to offer sacrifices to the gods. She is denied passage and treated impolitely because she has failed to get a safe conduct from the birds. She carries the news to Olympus that communication between gods and humans has been cut off.

A parricide,

Cinesias, a dithyrambic poet, and

an informer, who come to Nephelo-Coccygia seeking wings to aid them in attaining their various objectives. The first is sent to Thrace to fight; the second and third are beaten.

Prometheus (proh-MEE-thee-uhs), the Titan, who tells Pisthetærus that the gods are ready to come to terms with the birds because the smoke of sacrifices has been cut off and the Olympians are starving.

Poseidon (poh-SI-dehn), the god of the sea,

Herakles (HEH-reh-kleez), the demigod, and

Triballus (trih-BA-luhs), a barbarian god, who negotiate a truce with the birds by bargaining away the power of Zeus to Pisthetærus.

THE BIRDS FALL DOWN

Author: Rebecca West (Cicily Isabel Fairfield, 1892-1983)
First published: 1966
Genre: Novel

Locale: London, Paris, a French train, and a provincial French town
Time: Early twentieth century
Plot: Political

Laura Rowan, an eighteen-year-old woman who is half English and half Russian. Beautiful, intelligent, and quiet, Laura is a perceptive observer of the people around her and is responsible beyond her years. When she accompanies her grandfather on a train and hears Chubinov's declaration that Kamensky is a traitor, her imagination runs wild with scenes of Kamensky killing her because she knows the truth. These imaginings, it is later revealed, are warranted. She must decide how to deal with Chubinov's information and his scheme to murder Kamensky. At the novel's end, she decides to leave London and live with her mother in Russia.

Count Nikolai Nikolaievitch Diakonov (nih-koh-LAY nih-koh-LAY-eh-vihch dya-KOH-nov), a former minister in the czar's government, living in exile in Paris for reasons of which he is unaware. A tall, broad, elderly man, he is stubborn and cantankerous despite his failing health. His death, halfway through the novel, is caused in part by Chubinov's revelation that Kamensky is a traitor and spy.

Countess Sofia Andreievna Diakonova (SOH-fyah ahn-DREH-ehv-nah dya-KOH-noh-vah), his wife. Once beautiful, the small, slight countess is now ugly and weak, partly because of her age and partly because of a serious illness, presumably cancer. In an attempt to hide her radium treatments from her husband, Sofia convinces him to take a trip to the coast to visit relatives.

Tania Rowan, Laura's mother, the count's daughter, who lives in London. Unusually good looking, Tania is tormented throughout the novel because her marriage is failing. Although distracted, she is nevertheless a caring mother to her daughter and a devoted daughter to her aging parents. At the novel's

end, she decides not only to leave her husband but also to return to Russia, thus abandoning her sons and her life in London.

Edward Rowan, Laura's father, a young member of Parliament. Handsome and somewhat celebrated for his position in the British government, Edward seems interested only in Susie Stainton, his wife's former protegée, with whom he is presumably having an affair. Although he goes to France when Laura summons him by telegram, he is distracted and cold toward his family.

Vassili Iulevitch Chubinov (vah-SEE-lee YEW-leh-vihch chuh-BIH-nov), the son of a minor Russian aristocrat who knew Diakonov when they were both living in Russia. A middle-aged, middle-sized, unkept man, Chubinov has dedicated his life to revolutionary activities. After tailing Laura and her grandfather onto the train, he confronts them and speaks at length about his past associations with Diakonov. Finally, he reveals that Kamensky is a spy, an allegation that the count tries to deny but that greatly upsets him. At the end of the novel, Chubinov shoots Kamensky in the street because he believes that Kamensky intends to kill Laura.

Alexander Gregorievitch Kamensky (greh-GOHR-yeh-vihch KAH-mehn-skih), also known as **Gorin**, **Kaspar**, and **Sasha**, the count's secretary and confidant. A small Russian man in his early forties, Kamensky is a superb confidence artist. For years, he has worked for Diakonov, endearing himself to both the count and his wife. If Chubinov's story is correct, Kamensky actually was spying against them. He is murdered by Chubinov.

— Cassandra Kircher

THE BIRTHDAY KING

Author: Gabriel Fielding (Alan Gabriel Barnsley, 1916-1986)
First published: 1962
Genre: Novel

Locale: Bavaria, East Prussia, and Berlin
Time: August, 1939, and November, 1941-July, 1945
Plot: Historical

Ruprecht Waitzmann (VITS-mahn), the second son of a wealthy widow who owns Waitzmann Industries, a conglomerate that operates pulp and textile mills. He is an ambitious, worldly young man who is hindered from taking over the business by his religious elder brother Alfried. To further his ambitions, he cultivates the friendship of Carin von Hoffbach, a promiscuous, gossipy woman who is the wife of a baron. Her machinations in favor of Ruprecht lead to the imprisonment and torture of Ruprecht's brother, much to the shame of all concerned.

Alfried Waitzmann, the eldest son of Frau Waitzmann. He is torn between his love of the German aristocracy and his religious calling. An unsuccessful affair with a German woman who wants to be a nun in the United States does not solve his dilemma. He refuses his vocation to the priesthood, and he is finally imprisoned in a concentration camp and tortured. When the torture fails to break him, he is made a medical aide in the camp, in which position he reports to the American commander after the war.

Wilhelmina Waitzmann, an aging, nearly blind widow who is the mother of Ruprecht and Alfried. She runs Waitzmann Industries during the war, waiting for her favorite son, Alfried, to decide whether he wants to take her place. Her role is a passive one in regard to the story. She waits and hopes that her family will come out of the war intact.

Baron Nicholas von Hoffbach (HOHF-bahk), a wealthy German nobleman in his fifties who operates as liaison between Waitzmann Industries and the Nazi government. He continually upholds the ideal of the old German aristocracy in the face of what he considers Nazi barbarism. When he finds that his wife's indiscretion has led to the imprisonment of his friend Alfried, he refuses to cooperate any longer and takes part in a plot to assassinate Adolf Hitler.

Carin von Hoffbach, the baron's promiscuous French-Prussian wife, who cultivates younger men. Her affair with Ruprecht leads her to insinuate accusations against his brother Alfried to a local Schutzstaffel (SS) man, ending in Alfried's imprisonment and torture. She tries in vain to prevent her husband from getting involved with the plot to assassinate Hitler.

Leo von Hoffbach, the son of the baron and Carin. He seems interested only in his family's forest holdings and spends his entire life in the woods hunting. He briefly falls in love with the young Alexandra von Boehling, but she turns down his proposal of marriage.

Eva de Luce, the mother of Carin von Hoffbach. She is a senile elderly woman who appears in only one scene, showing the same petulant sensuality as her daughter, titillated by the "advances" of Hubertus Grunewald and Ruprecht Waitzmann.

Onkle Fritz, a cousin of Ruprecht and Alfried Waitzmann. He is a member of the board of directors of Waitzmann Industries and a good friend to Frau Waitzmann. His role in the story is that of the wise and helpful confidant.

Alexandra von Boehling (BOOH-lihng), a young lady from a noble German family living in Italy. She is visiting with the von Hoffbachs as a way to make her way toward a good marriage. She is drawn toward both Leo von Hoffbach and Ruprecht Waitzmann, neither of whom she seems to love. Her innocent passivity is a foil to the ambition of Ruprecht and to the cruel barbarism of the Nazis.

Felix Grunewald (GREWN-eh-vahlt), a middle-aged member of the SS who is in charge of a concentration camp. He prides himself on his rational and cultured approach to his prisoners. He is attracted to Alfried Waitzmann when the latter is imprisoned in his camp. He eventually has Alfried, as a trustee, do work around the commandant's house. When the Russians enter the city, he commits suicide in obedience to the Führer.

Gudrun Grunewald (GEW-druhn), a neurotic and withdrawn woman, Felix Grunewald's wife. She believes that her husband is not treating her properly. When Alfried arrives, she comes out of her cell, devoted to the Nazi cause. She commits suicide with her husband.

Hubertus Grunewald, the son of Gudrun and Felix. He is even more caught up in the Nazi mystique, writing a diary of his Nazi feelings. He chooses life over suicide when the time comes.

— Robert W. Peckham

THE BIRTHDAY PARTY

Author: Harold Pinter (1930-   )
First published: 1959
Genre: Drama

Locale: England
Time: The 1950's
Plot: Absurdist

Stanley Webber, a boarder at a seedy seaside home. In his late thirties and unkempt, he indulges in fantasies about exotic cities in which he had performed as a concert pianist. In Kafkaesque fashion, he speaks of a career that was ended by persons he refers to as "them." Filling his landlady's need for a lodger and a surrogate son, he is comfortably ensconced as a member of the household until his position is threatened by the

arrival of two strange, surrealistic guests, Goldberg and McCann. He suggests that the two have come to cart away Meg, his landlady, in a wheelbarrow. In the climactic scene, at his birthday party, Stanley beats the drum Meg has given him as a present, the tempo savagely increasing as he marches around the room. During a game of blindman's buff, the lights go out. When the lights come back on, he is standing, with his glasses broken, over Lulu, who lies spread-eagled on a table. The next morning he appears in striped trousers, black jacket, white collar, and bowler hat, and is carted away by Goldberg and McCann to a mysterious healer, "Monty," for treatment.

Meg Boles, the wife of Petey, with whom she operates a rundown boarding house. A mothering person in her mid-sixties who dislikes going out, she devotes her time to Petey's meals and comfort. She dotes on Stanley, their boarder, as a surrogate son. The surrogacy, however, takes on an Oedipal cast. Although Stanley protests to the contrary, Meg insists that it is his birthday, whereupon Goldberg suggests that a birthday party be held. At the end, seemingly unaware of Stanley's departure, she is enjoying reminiscing about being "the belle of the ball."

Nat Goldberg, a menacing new guest in his late fifties, a "smooth operator" who takes charge of things, including his accomplice, McCann, with whom he quarrels at one point. In the form of cryptic questions about their pasts, their beliefs, and the forces that shaped their lives, Goldberg attacks first Lulu, then Stanley. He is a surrealistic, allegorical figure symbolizing the destructive impersonality of the modern world and its guilt-producing threat to the sensitive individual.

Dermot McCann, a thirty-year-old man who serves Goldberg in the nefarious activities in which they conspire. He makes an indelible impression with his neat, precise tearing of a sheet of newspaper, column by column. McCann, who is Irish-Catholic, and Goldberg, who is Jewish, suggest the Judaic-Christian influence that has shaped the modern Western world.

Petey Boles, a man in his sixties, Meg's husband. A compliant husband, he functions in the story primarily to exchange breakfast banalities with Meg or with Stanley, their boarder. His blandness puts into sharp focus the strange behavior of Meg and Stanley and the menacing threats of McCann and Goldberg. He returns from work one day to announce the arrival of their two new guests. At the end, he returns to his routines as husband and deck-chair attendant as though nothing unusual has happened.

Lulu, a woman in her twenties. She appears mysteriously with a package. After flirting with both Stanley and Goldberg, she departs the next morning after being interrogated accusingly by Goldberg and savagely ordered by the puritanical "unfrocked" McCann to confess.

— *Susan Rusinko*

THE BLACK ARROW: A Tale of the Two Roses

Author: Robert Louis Stevenson (1850-1894)
First published: 1888
Genre: Novel

Locale: England
Time: The fifteenth century
Plot: Adventure

Sir Daniel Brackley, a villainous knight who fights on both sides during the fifteenth century Wars of the Roses. He adds to his own lands by becoming the guardian of children orphaned by war. He is killed by Ellis Duckworth.

Richard Shelton, called **Dick**, the orphaned son of Sir Harry Shelton of the Moat House estates. Sir Daniel is suspected of murdering Sir Harry in order to become the boy's guardian. After many difficulties, Dick marries Joanna Sedley.

Joanna Sedley, the orphaned heiress of Kettley, intended by Sir Daniel as a wife for Dick. She first meets Dick while disguised as a boy. Held prisoner by Sir Daniel, she is almost forced into marriage with Lord Shoreby, but at the church he is slain by a black arrow.

Lord Foxham, Joanna's legal guardian and the enemy of Sir Daniel.

Alicia Risingham, Joanna's friend, the niece of a powerful Lancastrian lord.

Lord Shoreby, who tries to force Joanna to marry him.

Richard of York, the Duke of Gloucester. He is saved from bandits by Dick, whom he knights after the Battle of Shoreby, in which the Lancastrians are defeated.

The Earl of Risingham, the judge of Dick and Lawless when they are denounced by Sir Oliver Oates.

Nick Appleyard, a veteran of Agincourt, killed at Moat House by a black arrow.

Bennet Hatch, Sir Daniel's bailiff at Moat House.

Sir Oliver Oates, Sir Daniel's clerk, who is accused by the outlaws of causing the death of Sir Harry Shelton.

Ellis Duckworth, who was ruined by Sir Daniel and is now the leader of a band of outlaws. He calls himself

John (Jon) Amend-All, and uses only black arrows for weapons. Eventually he kills his enemy, Sir Daniel.

Will Lawless, one of the outlaws and a friend of Dick. He finally takes orders and dies a friar.

BLACK BOY: A Record of Childhood and Youth

Author: Richard Wright (1908-1960)
First published: 1945
Genre: Nonfiction

Locale: Mississippi; Elaine, Arkansas; Memphis, Tennessee; and Chicago, Illinois
Time: 1912-1937
Plot: Autobiography

Richard Wright, the narrator of the autobiography and the black boy who is the subject of the story. Richard begins his narrative when he is four years old, describing an incident in which he attempts to set his house on fire out of boredom and frustration with his restricted life within his family. He traces his life from that point on, describing numerous adventures

and challenges that mark his journey to young adulthood. These challenges include physical ones, including the hunger that the poverty-stricken Wrights experience when Mr. Wright abandons his wife and two sons, and spiritual ones, including the search for himself within an environment that is racially charged and hostile to a young black boy growing up in

America. Ultimately, Wright goes to Chicago, Illinois, where he joins the Communist Party before learning that his calling in life is to be a solitary individual, not a member of an organized group, and to be a writer whose weapons will be the words he uses.

Ella Wright, Richard's mother, whose physical weakness makes it difficult for her to care for and even love her sons Richard and Leon. She moves her sons from place to place, temporarily housing them in an orphanage, as she tries to survive and provide for the boys, whom her husband abandoned when he left her and them for another woman.

Nathan Wright, Richard's father, who abandons his family to poverty and a hunger that stalks Richard throughout his life. He ends his life as a sharecropper in Mississippi, working the land of a white plantation owner.

Granny Wilson, Richard's grandmother, whose religious fanaticism and intolerance of what she sees as the frivolity of literature frustrate her grandson, who is both rebelling against religion and seeking the joys of reading and writing.

Aunt Maggie and
Uncle Hoskins, Ella Wright's sister and her husband. These relatives provide a welcome refuge for Ella and her sons after they are abandoned by Nathan Wright and after their brief, unhappy stay with Granny Wilson. For the first time in his life, Richard experiences security and is given all the food and love that had been deprived him earlier. Aunt Maggie is a supportive relative, and Uncle Hoskins, a saloon owner, is a tolerant man, unflappable even when his noisy nephews seem to take over the house. Uncle Hoskins is murdered by whites who want his saloon, abruptly terminating the Wrights' brief sojourn with their caring relatives.

Aunt Jody and
Uncle Clark, Richard's other aunt and uncle. Unlike Maggie and Hoskins, Jody and Clark, with whom Richard lives for a short time, are neither understanding nor supportive of their nephew. Clark beats Richard, ostensibly for Richard's bad language, and he and his wife cannot live up to Richard's hope that they will be surrogate parents for him.

Ross, a member of the Communist Party in Chicago. He is tried as a traitor, and his indictment becomes a symbol of the unqualified loyalty to the party that Richard is unable to give.

— *Marjorie Smelstor*

THE BLACK HERMIT

Author: Ngugi wa Thiong'o (James Ngugi, 1938-   )
First published: 1968
Genre: Drama

Locale: A Kenyan village and Nairobi
Time: The 1960's
Plot: Naturalism

Remi (RAY-mee), a youth of the Maura tribe who is sent to the city to attend the university and return to his village as a political and social leader for his people in the government of a newly independent country. As a student activist, he has convinced his small tribe to support the Africanist Party, which now governs. He has stayed on in the city as a clerk in an oil company rather than returning to his village, as was expected. Before his departure from home, his father and the elders of the village prevailed upon him to marry the widow of his brother, recently killed in an accident. Because he has secretly loved her and believes that she could not have loved him and married his brother, he goes through with the ceremony but flees the reality of the marriage by staying on in the city and becoming the lover of Jane, a white South African student. When he returns home with a friend from another tribe, he decries racism and tribalism, and he spurns his wife.

Nyobi (NYOH-bee), a devout Christian convert, the mother of Remi and confidante and supporter of his wife, Thoni. Her concern for Thoni and longing to see Remi prompt her to bless the mission of the elders, undertaken in the name of the old religion. Repenting, she adjures the pastor of the Christian church to go on the same mission.

Thoni (DHOH-nee), the legal wife of Remi. She has loved him from the first but has no socially acceptable way of telling him until she leaves him a note before committing suicide.

The leader of the elders, a spokesman for the religious conservatives who believe that Christianity has been taking the best men of the tribe. Remi's father was brought back to his ancestors' religion only by his imminent death, when he appealed to the elders for help in convincing Remi to do the traditional thing and marry his brother's widow. He and the other elders chafe at local administrators who are not of their tribe. They want Remi to return and do his duty as their educated citizen by forming a political party.

The pastor, a strict interpreter of morals according to the Christian view. He sees Nyobi's task as completing Thoni's conversion, and he views Remi's continued absence as a defection from the church to do the devil's work of the Africanist Party. Only Nyobi's flattering pleas convince the pastor to go to the city himself. When Remi agrees to return, the pastor feels sure that Christ has won a victory.

Jane, a white South African student at the university. She has been Remi's lover and companion in a year of frenetic partygoing. She learns of his marriage shortly before he returns home.

Omange (oh-MAHN-jee), Remi's friend and fellow activist. He is much more skeptical of the new government than Remi seems to be, and he fears the repressive possibilities of tribal politics. When he hears Remi's story of his thwarted love for Thoni, he urges Remi to go home.

The elders, who accompany their leader to the city to convince Remi to return.

The woman, who meets Thoni leaving the village. She fears what Thoni intends but cannot convince her to stay.

The first neighbor, who announces Remi's arrival. This neighbor emphasizes the freedom and political advantage to be gained from his return.

The second neighbor, who reports on Remi's speech, the effect of which was that of a stinging rebuke to the elders.

— *James L. Hodge*

BLACK MISCHIEF

Author: Evelyn Waugh (1903-1966)
First published: 1932
Genre: Novel

Locale: The mythical empire of Azania, an island off Africa
Time: Early 1930's
Plot: Satire

Seth, the newly crowned emperor of Azania. He is the twenty-four-year-old grandson of Amurath, the first emperor of this polyglot East African country. He has a naïve faith in the future and in progress, and he is determined to modernize the country at all costs. His progressive impulses are constantly at war with his tribal background and superstitious nature. He acquired enough information while at Oxford to prove Alexander Pope's famous maxim that a little learning is a dangerous thing; his efforts are largely ineffectual. He gives boots to his barefoot army, and the soldiers eat them. He shows films on birth control all across the country, but they evoke only sympathy from the audiences for the unfortunate man on the screen who has so few sons.

Basil Seal, an adventurer and one of the "Bright Young People." He is handsome, charming, opportunistic, and unscrupulous. He once had Seth to lunch at Oxford. This tenuous association has lured him to Azania, where he finds himself high commissioner and comptroller general of the ministry of modernization.

Sir Samson Courteney, the British minister to Azania. He is eccentric, inattentive, and comparatively unsuccessful in diplomatic life. The interminable assassinations, coups, and wars that characterize Azanian political life never touch him. He regards the slightest request from any Azanian as a gross personal imposition.

Prudence Courteney, Sir Samson's daughter and Basil's mistress. She is a silly girl who has but two enthusiasms: sex and the *Panorama of Life*, a written collection of her callow observations. She is fated for an exotic demise, as the main course at a Wanda cannibal feast.

General Connolly, a mercenary in Seth's service. He has wide experience in the internecine wars of Africa. He is an enigmatic man with a mysterious past.

Krikor Youkoumian, Basil's financial secretary in the ministry of modernization. This shrewd, unprincipled, indefatigable Armenian entrepreneur is perfectly fitted for the political and economic life of Azania. While those around him are periodically assassinated or put to flight, he survives each change of regime and turns a nice profit.

William Bland, a junior member of the British legation. His surname is an apt representation of his personality. His tepid romance with Prudence is quickly terminated by Basil's charisma.

Dame Mildred Porch, a formidable Englishwoman who much prefers animals to people. Along with her friend Miss Sarah Tin, she is visiting Azania on behalf of the League of Dumb Chums. Upon discovering a family living with their goats in an abandoned truck, she observes that this arrangement cannot be healthy for the goats.

— Patrick Adcock

THE BLACK PRINCE

Author: Iris Murdoch (1919-   )
First published: 1973
Genre: Novel

Locale: London, England
Time: The 1960's
Plot: Moral

Bradley Pearson, a writer and the narrator of the novel. Bradley, who is middle-aged and solitary, has retired from his job as an inspector of taxes to devote himself to his writing, at which he works painstakingly. His life radically changes when he suddenly realizes that he passionately loves Julian Baffin, whom he idealizes. This love transforms his sterile existence, finally allowing him to write his great book, which he completes while unjustly imprisoned for the murder of Arnold Baffin.

Julian Baffin, the twenty-year-old daughter of Bradley's friends Arnold and Rachel Baffin. Julian has asked Bradley to give her informal tutorials on great books, because she wants to be a writer. It is during her Hamlet tutorial that Bradley realizes that he loves her; later, she tells him that she has admired him since she was a child. She idealizes and romanticizes Bradley, but ultimately their relationship seems to have had little impact on her.

Arnold Baffin, a prolific writer. Bradley encouraged his early efforts and helped to find him a publisher for his first novel; they have been friends ever since. Bradley is often drawn into Arnold and Rachel's domestic quarrels. Ar-

nold is outraged when he learns of Bradley's love for Julian Baffin. Bradley is convicted for Arnold's murder; suggestions of professional jealousy help convince the jury of his motive.

Rachel Baffin, Arnold's wife. A dissatisfied, unfulfilled woman, Rachel attempts to seduce Bradley. She confuses Bradley because her confidences to him often contradict what she has told him previously. She draws Julian away from Bradley by making the attempt at seduction seem Bradley's and not her own. She seems ready to believe that Bradley killed Arnold, although apparently she was the one who hit Arnold with a poker.

Francis Marloe, Bradley's ne'er-do-well former brother-in-law, a doctor who has been dropped from the lists for impropriety in prescribing drugs. Francis arrives at Bradley's flat hoping that Bradley will be able to persuade Christian (Francis' sister and Bradley's former wife) to give him money. Bradley asks Francis to take care of Priscilla, his younger sister, while he is away with Julian. Francis is a drunkard, and Priscilla commits suicide while in his care. Francis later sets himself up as a psychologist, and, in his epilogue, he claims that Bradley was a latent homosexual in love with him.

Christian Evandale, Bradley's former wife and Francis' sister. After her marriage to Bradley failed, she married a wealthy American. She has recently returned from Illinois as a widow. A showy, friendly woman, she helps care for Priscilla, flirts with Arnold, and proposes that she and Bradley remarry. In her epilogue, she denies making the proposal.

Priscilla Saxe, Bradley's younger sister. Desperately unhappy and hysterical, she shows up on Bradley's doorstep after leaving her husband. She tries to commit suicide with her sleeping pills and is successful on her second attempt. Bradley does not leave his tryst with Julian upon her death; when Julian discovers that, she finds it horrifying.

Roger Saxe, Priscilla's husband. Bradley has never liked him and indicts him as cruel and unfeeling when he goes to pick up Priscilla's things. Roger has been having an affair for years; now that Priscilla is gone, he wants to marry his girlfriend.

Marigold, Roger's pregnant girlfriend. She feels sorry for Priscilla and convinces Roger to give Priscilla some of the pretty things about which Priscilla obsesses.

P. Loxias, the editor of the book. He becomes Bradley's friend and teacher in prison and encourages Bradley to write the book. He solicits the comments from Christian, Rachel, Julian, and Francis that form the epilogue of the novel.

— *Karen M. Cleveland*

BLACK ROBE

Author: Brian Moore (1921-   )
First published: 1985
Genre: Novel

Locale: Quebec and a remote Indian village
Time: 1635
Plot: Historical

Father Paul Laforgue, a Jesuit priest and missionary to the Huron Indians. A slight, pale, thin-bearded intellectual, born and educated in France, he dreams of the glory of martyrdom in the wilderness. Fired by religious fervor, he learns the Algonkian and Huron languages and prepares meticulously for work among "the Savages." Confronted with the realities of life among the Indians, he accepts his own misery and physical suffering with courage; he is forgiving of the sins of others but is haunted by guilt for his own human weaknesses. Initially secure in the correctness of his culture and religion, he comes to respect many of the Indian ways and to question his religious certitudes. A man of conscience, he refuses to acquiesce in the religious sophistry of Father Jerome and baptize Indians before they understand and accept the faith. Because his own faith is not absolute, he comes to see himself as unworthy of martyrdom. In the midst of his crisis of faith and unsure of God's will, he dedicates himself to his work in hope of achieving "God's" favor and out of compassion for the Indians as fellow human beings.

Daniel Davost, who accompanies Father Laforgue on his journey to Ihonatiria. Not yet twenty years old, he has been in New France for one year after having promised to serve God for two years in a distant land. Intelligent and adaptable, with a talent for languages, he is thought of highly by the priests. He wants to go with Laforgue not out of religious devotion, as he claims, but to continue the sexual relationship he has secretly begun with the Algonkin girl Annuka. Suffering feelings of guilt and convinced of his own damnation, he is critical of doctrinaire Christianity and is gradually drawn to the Indian way of life. He deserts Laforgue to follow Annuka and asks to marry the girl, declaring the Indians to be his people. He returns with Chomina and his family to help Laforgue, but all are captured by the Iroquois. After their escape, Laforgue agrees to marry Daniel and Annuka. When the couple finally join the priest at Ihona-

tiria, Daniel is dressed and painted like the Algonkin he wishes to become.

Annuka, a beautiful Algonkin girl who is in love with Daniel Davost. Formerly promiscuous, she promises to be faithful to Daniel and wants to marry him, despite her father's objections. After her father's death, she goes with Daniel to live among the Hurons at Ihonatiria.

Chomina, an Algonkin elder and Annuka's father. He acts as a moral conscience for his people and fears that they are becoming greedy and materialistic like the French. Keeping the promise he made to help Laforgue on his journey, he is captured by the Iroquois, who kill his wife and son, torture him and his daughter, and inflict wounds that later prove fatal. He acts with bravery and explains rather than condemns the brutality of his enemies. The principal spokesman for Indian beliefs and attitudes toward life, he engages Laforgue in philosophic debate, rejecting baptism and the Christian belief in a better life after death.

Father Fernand Jerome, one of the Jesuit founders of the mission at Ihonatiria and the man Laforgue is sent to help. At the age of forty-four, he has suffered a series of strokes and has difficulty moving his tall, bulky frame. He has a heavy gray beard and a pale, half-paralyzed face with one eye enlarged and discolored. His assistant, Father Duval, has been murdered by the Indians, and Jerome is drifting in and out of consciousness when Laforgue arrives. With a final burst of what Laforgue sees as misplaced religious zeal, Jerome uses the Indians' superstitions and fears to convince them that they should be baptized. Before he can reap his "harvest of souls," however, he is murdered by a terrified Indian who blames the "Blackrobes" for the fever that is decimating the Hurons.

Neehatin, a powerful and duplicitous Algonkin leader who secretly consults his wife on decisions and stubbornly pursues an explanation for his dreams.

— *Douglas Rollins*

THE BLACK SWAN
(Die Betrogene)

Author: Thomas Mann (1875-1955)
First published: 1953
Genre: Novella

Locale: Düsseldorf, Germany
Time: The 1920's
Plot: Symbolism

Rosalie von Tümmler (fon-TEWM-lehr), a widowed upper-class socialite of fifty who has settled in the city of Düsseldorf following her husband Robert's "heroic" death in a car accident while serving in World War I. She and her two children, Anna and Eduard, live quietly and modestly together. She is a child of nature, a likable, happy, thoughtful, and slightly too chatty woman. She is a good friend of her daughter, Anna, who is unmarried. Rosalie is dismayed at the onset of menopause, saying she is "no longer a woman" but only "the dried out shell" of what she once was. She falls in love with her son's much younger American tutor, Ken Keaton. She begins menstruating again; this is brought on by what her surgeon, Dr. Muthesius, says must be "some kind of stimulation" (though their affair remains unconsummated). She thinks her love of Keaton has rejuvenated her and that her menstrual blood is a sign of the power of this love; in actuality, she has advanced ovarian cancer. Following a massive hemorrhage and unsuccessful surgery, she dies amid narcotic visions of the symbolic black swan, true love, and nature.

Ken Keaton, an American veteran who stayed in Europe following World War I to pursue his amateur interests in history and folk customs. He sustains himself by teaching English to the children of well-to-do Germans. He has all-American good looks and a simple charm. Rumors of Ken's amorous successes with both daughters and mothers in society circles do not dissuade Rosalie from falling for his good-natured manner. Ken has American attributes more connected to 1950 than to 1920.

Anna von Tümmler, Rosalie's single, thirtyish daughter. She pursues fairly serious art in the form of cubist-inspired painting, which her mother finds ugly and confusing. She is rational and detached, and in her objective, critical views of things she shows an affinity to the cultural New Objectivity of 1920's Weimar Germany. Her exceptional determination is rooted in part in her physical deformity—a clubfoot—which has, along with one sad love affair, caused her to re-

nounce intimacy. She and her mother carry on long pseudo-philosophical discussions on art, nature, love, and the nature of womanhood. Anna's especially painful menstrual cramps seem to be a kind of affront to Rosalie's experience of menopause. Anna sees her mother's infatuation with Ken as slightly embarrassing and tries unsuccessfully with Eduard to put an end to it.

Eduard von Tümmler (AY-dew-ahrd), Rosalie's son, who is in his last year of high school. He is being taught English by Ken, whom he finds agreeable enough until Ken and his mother begin their affair. He would like to defend his mother's honor and reputation, which both he and Anna see as compromised by her love for Ken.

The black swans, which are encountered by the family and Ken on an outing to a nearby rococo palace. They symbolize both the round voluptuousness of the woman and the phallic power of the man. Before Rosalie and Ken kiss in a tomblike passage in the palace, they feed dry bread to the swans in the slimy garden lake. The castle and gardens are full of decaying rococo erotic symbols: Pan, nymphs, certain primeval plants, and the black swans, whose blackness is both rare and precious and the color of death. One swan hisses at the group—or at Rosalie alone—perhaps because she nibbled a bit of bread before giving it to the swans. Anna says the swan will not easily forgive her mother. This hissing swan appears again at the end of the story, in Rosalie's dying visions of his "blood-red beak" and the "black beating of his wings."

Dr. Oberloskamp (OH-behr-LOS-kahmp), **Dr. Muthesius** (mew-TEH-zee-ews), and **Dr. Knepperges** (KNEH-pehr-gehs), Rosalie's physician and surgeons. Their scientific medical language contrasts ironically with Rosalie's euphemistic descriptions of aspects of a woman's reproductive system.

Dr. Brünner (BREW-nehr), Anna's only love, who left her after a long courtship, causing Anna to renounce love and live only for herself and her art.

— *Scott Denham*

BLACK THUNDER

Author: Arna Bontemps (1902-1973)
First published: 1936
Genre: Novel

Locale: Henrico County, Virginia
Time: 1800
Plot: Historical

Gabriel Prosser, a slave who leads a slave rebellion. He is the coachman on the Prosser plantation, located near Richmond, Virginia. He is twenty-four years old and the tallest of three uncommonly tall brothers. He is considered by the other slaves to be a "man of destiny" because of the reputation he acquired after defeating Ditcher, a black slave driver, in a fight. After the death of Bundy, a slave, he changes from a silent, dreamy person to one who speaks with quiet dignity and excitement about his revolutionary plans. His rebellion fails because of the treachery of two fellow slaves, and the slaves

are impeded by a devastating storm. Gabriel escapes capture for some time but is finally captured and taken to Richmond for trial. He refuses to give any significant information about the conspiracy before his execution.

Ben, an old, gray-headed house slave, the servant to the elderly slave master Mossely Sheppard. He is one of the traitors of the slave rebellion. Ben does not share the other slaves' love and desire for freedom, and he is distrusted by the other slaves, who do not share their plans for the rebellion with him. At the end of the novel, he is the target of the wrath of the remaining slaves on the plantation after the execution of Gabriel and the conspirators.

Pharaoh (FAY-roh), a slave and the second traitor of the slave rebellion. He wishes to lead a fighting line during the rebellion, but because Gabriel does not trust Pharaoh, Gabriel will not permit this. Pharaoh's anger and resentment turn him into a traitor. After Gabriel's execution, he becomes insane. Upon learning of Gabriel's defeat, other slaves wear Pharaoh down by throwing knives at him at every opportunity. At the end of the novel, he climbs a tree and begins barking like a dog.

Juba, a young slave woman who is in love with Gabriel and who is the only female participant in the slave rebellion. On the night of the revolt, she rides the colt Araby as a signal for the conspirators. She is a strong and defiant person and never cries out, even though she is beaten unmercifully by her slave master for her part in the revolt. She is later sold on the auction block.

Bundy, an elderly, rum-drinking slave who is killed at the beginning of the novel when his master, Thomas Prosser, allows his horse to trample him because Prosser considers Bundy to be useless. Bundy's murder serves as a catalyst for Gabriel's revolutionary plans.

Melody, a free, apricot-colored mulatto with enameled black hair and barbarous hoops in her ears. She is a friend of Biddenhurst and the black conspirators and leaves town after the revolt fails. She aids Gabriel in his flight.

Mingo, a black freeman whose distinctive characteristic is his ability to read. He is a saddle maker and a friend to the slaves; his wife and children are still slaves. He reads to the slaves from the Bible and thereby gives the conspirators inspiration and courage.

Alexander Biddenhurst, a Frenchman who is hopeful about race relations. He is a friend of the mulatto Melody, but he is forced to flee Richmond after the slave rebellion because the whites think that he is one of the authors of Gabriel's plans as well as a fellow conspirator.

M. Creuzot (krew-ZOH), a Frenchman who is a printer of religious pamphlets. He believes that the prospects for the unity of poor whites and blacks are negative. He is forced to flee for his life after the slave revolt because the whites believe that he conspired with the revolting slaves.

Thomas Prosser, Gabriel's master, a cruel and inhumane slave owner who tramples an old slave, Bundy, with his horse.

Mossely Sheppard, an elderly, rich, feeble old white man who is Ben's master. Ben reveals the plans of the rebellion to him.

Ditcher,

General John Scott, and

Criddle, slave participants in Gabriel's revolt.

— *Betty Taylor Thompson*

BLACK VALLEY
(Valle Negro)

Author: Hugo Wast (Gustavo Adolfo Martínez Zuviría, 1883-1962)
First published: 1918
Genre: Novel

Locale: Argentina
Time: Early twentieth century
Plot: Regional

Gracián Palma (grah-see-AHN PAHL-mah), the ward of Don Jesús de Viscarra, to whose estate, Black Valley, he is taken for the summer. He becomes a member of and learns the secrets of Don Jesús' turbulent family and his equally turbulent neighbors.

Don Jesús de Viscarra (heh-SEWS deh bees-KAH-rrah), the guardian of Gracián Palma and owner of Black Valley. Engaged in a lifelong boundary dispute with a neighboring landowner, Don Pablo Camargo, he is shot and killed by his adversary after a lawsuit is decided in Don Jesús' favor.

Mirra (MEE-rrah), Don Jesús de Viscarra's daughter, who is in love with Gracián Palma.

Flavia (FLAH-vee-ah), the sister of Don Jesús. She is the mistress of Don Pablo Camargo and the mother of his daughter, Victoria.

Don Pablo Camargo (kah-MAHR-goh), a neighbor of Don Jesús de Viscarra and his sworn enemy. He kills Don Jesús as the result of a boundary dispute. He is the lover of Don Jesús' sister, Flavia, and the father of her daughter Victoria.

Victoria, the natural daughter of Flavia and Don Pablo. She marries Gracián Palma.

Lazarus, the overseer of Black Valley, who is in love with Flavia and the possessor of the secret of her affair with Don Pablo.

Amoroso (ah-mohr-OH-soh), the devoted servant of Flavia.

Pichana (pee-CHAH-nah), an old beggar woman.

BLACK WATER

Author: Joyce Carol Oates (1938-   )
First published: 1992
Genre: Novel

Locale: An island near Boothbay Harbor, Maine
Time: The 1980's
Plot: Psychological realism

Kelly Kelleher, a bright, young, idealistic political campaign worker. She is a summa cum laude graduate of Brown University with a bachelor's degree in American studies. Born

Elizabeth Anne Kelleher to conventional parents, her nickname points to a second identity. There are aspects of her identity that her well-meaning but conservative parents do not see. Born with a wandering eye that has been corrected, Kelly nevertheless has a side of her that wanders from her parents' straight and narrow path. She becomes active in liberal causes sponsored by the Democratic Party and works on the campaign of presidential candidate George Dukakis. During this campaign, she demonstrates a tendency to get caught up in the romance of things and to not see warning signs of failure or trouble. She is so crushed by the defeat of Dukakis that she suffers a breakdown, a crisis of identity that makes her lose her bearings. Although she has an underlying vulnerability—an inability to be clear about herself that lurks under the surface of her upbeat, optimistic, persona—Kelly rebounds. Although a recent love affair has foundered, Kelly is thrilled when she learns that she and her favorite politician both will be attending a Fourth of July picnic at a friend's home on a small island in Maine. This prestigious senator was the subject of her college senior thesis, and her excitement at the prospect of meeting her hero is ratified by a horoscope she reads with her friends the night before the party. It counsels her to "go for it," to give vent to her wishes and desires, and suggests that she has been cautious for too long. This Scorpio horoscope validates Kelly's image of herself as a modern American girl, entitled to a strong sense of personal agency and to self-fulfillment. The sense of something "in the stars" suggested by the fact that she consults the horoscope anticipates her fate the following day. She is, in fact, involved in something that cannot be stopped. There are hints of a reckless, self-destructive side to Kelly, as if she is giving in to a dark death wish in her unconscious. When she meets the senator at the party, they immediately take to one each other. Even though she is young enough to be his daughter, there is an erotic current between them. Flattered by the fact that the powerful senator is lavishing attention on her, she agrees to leave the party and go away

somewhere with him. Although he has had too much to drink, Kelly is overawed and permits the senator to drive recklessly along an unpaved back road. The car plunges into the brackish black water of the marshland. As the car sinks, she relives her life, filled with hope and expectation. Despairing of rescue by the senator she has seen as a beacon shining in the darkness, she is overcome by the swampy water, and she drowns.

The senator, a powerful, charismatic man widely known as the last, best hope of the progressive wing of the Democratic Party. Flirting with Kelly at the Fourth of July picnic, he seems at first protective and paternal. He is obviously past his peak and encourages Kelly's adulation as a way to boost his flagging sense of self-esteem. To Kelly, however, he remains an impressive figure by dint of both his political prestige and his authority as a mature male. When he is responsible for the automobile accident in which Kelly drowns, he does not behave well. He leaves Kelly trapped in the car to drown and even kicks her in the face to free himself. As he runs from the scene of the accident, he begins to invent a cover story that makes Kelly the culpable agent, but it is clear that the filthy black mud covering him is symbolic of his political future. He will never be nominated by his party and never be elected president; he will be derided and mocked. In the space of one day, the senator has been transformed from a potentially great leader to a libertine, or even to a figure of gothic power whose transgressive behavior has ended in the death of a young woman.

Lisa Gardner, a school friend of Kelly. She instigates a suicide pact with her twin sister, Laura. Lisa's name echoes Kelly's (Elizabeth), and she mirrors Kelly's death wishes and doubleness.

— Margaret Boe Birns

THE BLACKER THE BERRY: A Novel of Negro Life

Author: Wallace Thurman (1902-1934)
First published: 1929
Genre: Novel

Locale: Boise, Idaho; Los Angeles, California; and Harlem, New York
Time: The 1920's
Plot: Satire

Emma Lou Morgan, the extremely color conscious, and therefore self-conscious, protagonist. Because of her very dark skin, young Emma Lou repeatedly has been ostracized and victimized by her fair-skinned family in Idaho, her white high school classmates, fellow students at the University of California, and the people she meets when she flees from Southern California to Harlem. Naïve, intellectually pretentious, and an elitist, Emma Lou has internalized self-hatred; she worships light skin and, ironically, is herself biased against other dark-skinned people, generally finding them ugly and unattractive or too poor and unsophisticated for her. Having left college to work in New York, Emma Lou finds that her color prevents her from obtaining "congenial" jobs. As a maid for a white actress, she learns how white people think that black people act and live in Harlem. Toward the end of the novel, she completes a teacher training program and begins to teach. Because of both the color bias of others and her own excessive color consciousness, she remains largely isolated and alienated from the Harlem community.

Alva, Emma Lou's racially mixed Harlem lover, a charming, though heavy drinking, ladies' man. He is considered attractive largely because of his "high yellow," or parchment, complexion and his sophisticated manners. Alva cynically uses Emma Lou both for sexual gratification and as a means of financial support. He perceives her loneliness and turns it to his advantage by courting her and introducing her to Harlem nightlife despite the laughter of his friends, who mock his attentions to so dark a woman. Eventually, he tires of her heightened color sensitivity and tells her frankly about her own prejudices. Toward the end of the novel, although his charms are considerably dissipated by alcohol and fast living, Alva still is able to manipulate Emma Lou.

Braxton, Alva's roommate and a would-be hustler, gambler, and youthful ladies' man as well. Braxton thinks of himself as a slightly duskier version of the white matinee idol Rudolph Valentino. He is proud, vain, and physically attractive. Braxton never has money because he will not work but cannot successfully make his living off his looks, his women, or his skills at gambling and hustling. He never says anything kind to Emma Lou and has no regard for dark-skinned black women.

Arline Strange, a white actress playing the part of a mulatto in the theater. She employs Emma Lou as her maid and attendant. She and her brother are the first people to introduce Emma Lou to Harlem's more celebrated nightclubs.

Geraldine, Alva's light-skinned girlfriend, whom he marries after she moves in with him, declaring that she is pregnant with his child.

Maria Lightfoot, Emma Lou's maternal grandmother in Boise, Idaho. Conscious of both class and color, Mrs. Lightfoot contributed to the social isolation Emma Lou endured as a child.

Jane Lightfoot Morgan, Emma Lou's mother, whose one act of bravery was marrying a man with ebony skin. Insensitive and ashamed of her daughter because of her dark complexion, she offers Emma Lou very little emotional support.

Joe Lightfoot, Emma Lou's uncle, the only relative who does not belittle her color. He persuades Emma Lou to attend the University of Southern California, thinking that there she could find "a larger and more intelligent social circle" in which the color bias would be less intense.

Jasmine Griffith, a West Indian immigrant renting a room in the same Harlem boarding house as Emma Lou. She functions as a foil to show the mutual suspicion and distrust that

African Americans and West Indian immigrants once shared.

Gwendolyn Johnson, Emma Lou's one friend in Harlem. Educated, helpful, and sensitive to the effects of intraracial prejudice, Gwendolyn attempts to help Emma Lou by introducing her to the proper and respectable Harlem circles and by repeatedly deprecating light-skinned Negroes, despite her own light complexion.

Tony Crews,
Cora Thurston,
Paul,
Truman, and

Aaron, all young artists and intellectuals representing the "New Negro" intelligentsia of the Harlem Renaissance era. Tony Crews is modeled on Langston Hughes; other characters are thinly veiled portraits of authentic members of the Harlem literati.

Clere Sloane, a former actress who employs Emma Lou as her personal maid—almost her companion—when Arline Strange decides to go to Europe without her maid.

Campbell Kitchen, the husband of Clere, a celebrated writer and intellectual. A white liberal with a sincere interest in exploiting Harlem and the Negro vogue of the times, Campbell encourages Emma Lou to read and to go back to school for her teaching certification.

— Sandra Y. Govan

THE BLACKS: A Clown Show
(Les Nègres: Clownerie)

Author: Jean Genet (1910-1986)
First published: 1958
Genre: Drama

Locale: Europe and Africa
Time: The 1950's
Plot: Existentialism

Archibald Absalon Wellington, a black actor in the role of master of ceremonies in a play-within-a-play about the rape and murder of a white woman. He is a man who demands strict obedience to the script as he directs his troupe's performance for five white members of the royal court, who are seated on an upper stage. Archibald's purpose is to present his black actors in the light of the white court's expectations. Because the white audience assumes that black people are liars and thieves, he instructs his actors to play those caricatures. He charges them to manufacture hate and to delete any word or gesture that might suggest love or humanity. At the close of the performance, he thanks his actors and congratulates them on portraying the stereotypes expected.

Dieudonné Village (deeyoo-doh-NAY vee-LAHZH), a black actor who plays the part of a rapist and murderer. He is the only male character to express love, and it is directed toward Vertu, the black whore. His desire to obey Archibald compels him to temper his love with words of despite. He leaves Vertu behind to reenact the slaughter of a white woman and seduces another actor, the black male Diouf, who is dressed as the female victim. He then rapes and strangles her. Although hunted down by the court, he assassinates them one by one. He returns to Vertu with words of love.

Mademoiselle Étiennette-Vertu-Rose-Secrète Diop (ay-tee-ahn-NEHT vehr-TEW rohz seh-KREHT dee-OHP), a black actress and prostitute. She is a woman of reason and balance

and believes that there are bad black people as well as good ones. She is the only female character to express a love interest, which is directed toward Village. Vertu does not participate in the murder of the white girl.

Samba Graham Diouf (dee-OOF), an old black actor who is the voice of order and reason. He seeks moderation and urges the blacks to be conciliatory. He pleads compromise, which falls on deaf ears. When ordered by Félicité to play the part of the slain white girl, Diouf dons a dress, a blonde wig, and a white girl's mask. Immediately prior to his rape, Diouf is aided by Village in giving symbolic birth to five puppets representing the five members of the court. Diouf is then seduced by Village, taken behind a screen, raped, and strangled. He next appears—still as a white girl—on the upper stage, a symbol of the white man's territory. From there, he gives an account to the black people of what it is like to be in the white man's land.

Madame Félicité Gueuse-Pardon (fay-lih-see-TAY guhz-pahr-DOHN), an imposing sixty-year-old black actress often perched on a throne. She displays strength, courage, and wisdom. It is she who orders Diouf to assume the role of the murdered white girl, while she portrays the girl's mother. When confronted with the white queen on her own turf, she executes an eloquent battle of words that she easily wins. In this discourse, she expresses her vision of an all-black world. She directs some of the action.

Madame Augusta Neige (nehzh), a hostile, defiant black actress. She is moody, rebellious, and hatefully envious of white women. She advocates rape and murder but condemns Village, whom she claims felt love for the woman he strangled. She seethes with hatred, even boasting that she will drink the blood of whites. To her, all blacks are good and all whites are bad. In the reenactment of the murder, she plays the white girl's sister.

Mademoiselle Adélaïde Bobo (ah-day-la-IHD boh-BOH), a black actress. She is a calculating, cold-blooded woman who adheres to the script the court wants to see performed. She preaches that the ideas of blacks must spring from hatred. In the murder of the white girl, she plays the victim's neighbor.

Edgar-Hélas Ville de Saint-Nazaire (ehd-GAHR-AY-lah veeyay deh sahn-na-ZAYR), a black actor who, like Diouf, makes an attempt at reason. He appears at intervals during the play to inform the black actors of events taking place outside the theater. There are hints of an antiwhite revolution.

The Queen,
The Governor,
The Missionary,'

The Judge, and

The Valet, all members of the court who are viewing the performance from the upper stage. They are all frauds playing the role of whites; they are actually blacks wearing white masks. They are bigoted figureheads with little power, scanty intelligence, and no passions. As vapid creatures who are not open to the truth, they demand drama from the blacks that fits neatly with their presupposed, stereotypical ideas. They assume that blacks are inhuman rapists and murderers, and this is the only way they will tolerate them being portrayed. In horror, they watch as the blacks rape and strangle a white girl. The heinous crime validates what they already knew to be true, and they go to Africa (the stage below) to avenge the girl's death. Although they give lip service to justice by claiming not to indict all of Africa for one man's crime, they immediately turn around and claim that any black person can be killed to pay the price for the crime. One black is as good—or bad—as another. One by one, the members of the court remove their white masks, and one by one they are assassinated by the blacks.

— *Steven C. Kowal*

BLEAK HOUSE

Author: Charles Dickens (1812-1870)
First published: 1852-1853
Genre: Novel

Locale: London, Lincolnshire, and Hertfordshire, England
Time: Mid-nineteenth century
Plot: Social morality

John Jarndyce, the unmarried, aging owner of Bleak House and a party in the famous and protracted Chancery suit of *Jarndyce vs. Jarndyce*. Generous to a fault, he makes two young cousins, Ada Clare and Richard Carstone, his wards in the hope that they will fall in love and fill his ancestral home with renewed life. He also takes into his home an orphan, Esther Summerson, as a companion to Ada. He himself falls in love with Esther, but when he learns that she is in love with Allan Woodcourt, a young surgeon, he releases her from her promise to him and gives the couple a new Bleak House of their own. He is loyal to his old friend and is always scrupulously fair, even though he calls his library "The Growlery" and retreats there when the winds of adversity blow on him. Admirable in every way, the head of the Jarndyce family creates rather than preserves a family dignity.

Esther Summerson, the orphan whom John Jarndyce takes into his home and later into his heart. She is the natural daughter of Lady Dedlock and a gallant named Captain Hawdon (who dies and is buried under the name of Nemo). Though part of the story is told by Esther, her ingenuousness makes of her less of a heroine and more of a companion and comforter who goes under various motherly terms of endearment. Although she respects and admires her benefactor, she truly loves the compassionate doctor, Allan Woodcourt, who woos her in spite of her disease-ravaged face, the result of a serious illness incurred while nursing Charley, her maid. Her immediate sympathies are aroused by any homeless beings and by those, like Caddy Jellyby, whose homes are friendless and loveless. She finally finds happiness with her husband and two daughters.

Ada Clare, John Jarndyce's cousin and ward. She secretly marries Richard Carstone, her cousin, to protect him from the grinding poverty that lawyers and the courts bring upon him. She manages to keep her loyalties and sympathies divided by remaining with her benefactor while extending her love to Carstone. Beautiful and tractable, she displays evenness of disposition and generous motives that make her a tearful heroine.

Richard Carstone, Ada's cousin and husband. Anything suits this young man, who has already sold his soul to the case of *Jarndyce vs. Jarndyce*. He tries medicine, the law, and the army, only to die of disappointment after the suit in Chancery has been settled and he learns that legal costs have eaten up the whole of his inheritance. John Jarndyce provides for Ada and her infant son.

Lady Honoria Dedlock, secretly the mother of Esther Summerson by Captain Hawdon, a rake to whom she was once engaged. When Tulkinghorn, her husband's legal adviser, threatens to inform her husband of her past, she flees from her home and dies, a victim of shame and exposure, at the gate of the cemetery where her lover has been buried under the name of Nemo. Her body is discovered by Esther Summerson.

Sir Leicester Dedlock, an honorable gentleman of prejudice and pride of family, completely unaware of his wife's guilty secret.

Mr. Tulkinghorn, a conniving solicitor who threatens to expose the secret in Lady Dedlock's past. He is murdered by Lady Dedlock's French maid when he refuses to pay her blackmailing demands and threatens her with imprisonment.

Allan Woodcourt, the surgeon who attends Captain Hawdon at the time of his death and who extends his help to Esther Summerson and Richard Carstone as well. He marries Esther after John Jarndyce releases her from her promise to him.

Mrs. Woodcourt, his handsome mother, proud of her Welsh ancestry.

William Guppy, a lawyer's clerk in the firm of Kenge and Carboy, John Jarndyce's solicitors. Attracted to Esther Summerson, he "files a declaration" of his love. Later, discovering that she has lost her beauty as a result of illness, he regrets his proposal and asks her to make a statement, before a witness, that there was never any formal engagement between them. He also meddles, though in a cowardly and humorous fashion, in Tulkinghorn's intrigue to discover Lady Dedlock's connection with the dead Nemo.

Miss Flite, a Jarndyce relative, half-crazed by the frustrations and delays of the suit in Chancery. Bright, friendly, perceptive of the crushing power of the law, she raises birds for release when the case is settled, and she tries to keep others from her own sad fate.

Miss Barbary, Lady Dedlock's sister and Esther Summerson's aunt and godmother, a good, austere woman.

Mademoiselle Hortense, Lady Dedlock's French maid. She murders Tulkinghorn when he resists her attempt at blackmail.

Inspector Bucket, the police detective who solves the mystery of Tulkinghorn's murder.

Rosa, a villager also employed as a maid by Lady Dedlock. She is engaged to marry Watt Rouncewell.

Mrs. Rouncewell, the Dedlock housekeeper.

Mr. Rouncewell, her son, the father of Watt Rouncewell.

George Rouncewell, another son, a soldier and later the owner of a shooting gallery in London. He is falsely arrested for the murder of Tulkinghorn.

Watt Rouncewell, the young man engaged to Rosa.

Mrs. Rachael, later Mrs. Chadband, a servant to Miss Barbary.

The Reverend Mr. Chadband, her husband, a self-conscious clergyman given to flowery speech.

Mrs. Snagsby, one of his parishioners, a shrew.

Mr. Snagsby, a law-stationer, her mild, henpecked husband.

Captain Hawdon, now calling himself **Nemo**, a law writer, the former lover of Lady Dedlock. After dying in a garret over Krook's dingy shop, he is buried in the Potter's Field.

Jo, also called **Toughey**, a street sweeper, befriended by Nemo. Lady Dedlock pays him two half-crowns to point out Nemo's grave.

Krook, the owner of a rag-and-bottle shop and the landlord of Miss Flite and Nemo. He has in his possession a packet of papers belonging to the former Captain Hawdon. This fact has been ferreted out by Tony Jobling, and William Guppy has agreed to reclaim the papers for Lady Dedlock. On the night that the papers are to change hands, Krook, a habitual drunkard, perishes of spontaneous combustion, and the papers are apparently destroyed in the fire.

Mrs. Smallweed, Krook's sister.

Mr. Smallweed, her husband, a superannuated man of unimpaired and irascible mind.

Bartholomew Smallweed, also called **Chickweed**, their grandson, a sponging friend of William Guppy.

Judy Smallweed, Bartholomew's twin sister.

Tony Jobling, a law writer for Mr. Snagsby and a friend of William Guppy. Calling himself Weevle, he takes lodgings in Krook's establishment and learns that Krook has in his possession a bundle of Captain Hawdon's papers.

Mrs. Jellyby, a plump, strong-minded woman who neglects her house and family while interesting herself in philanthropic projects, one of which is to settle a colony of English poor in Boorioboola-Gha, on the Niger River in Africa.

Caroline Jellyby, also called **Caddy**, Mrs. Jellyby's oldest daughter. Tired of her mother's endless projects, she marries Prince Turveydrop. A close friend of Esther Summerson, Caddy names her first daughter Esther.

Mr. Jellyby, a mild, miserable man who goes bankrupt.

"Peepy" Jellyby, the Jellybys' weak and neglected son.

Prince Turveydrop, named in honor of the Prince Regent. He marries Caddy Jellyby.

Mr. Turveydrop, Prince Turveydrop's father, a model of deportment and a monster of selfishness.

Harold Skimpole, the sentimental, unworldly recipient of John Jarndyce's bounty, a character thought to have been modeled after the poet Leigh Hunt.

Mrs. Skimpole, his sickly wife.

Arethusa Skimpole, the "Beauty" daughter,

Laura Skimpole, the "Sentiment" daughter, and

Kitty Skimpole, the "Comedy" daughter, the Skimpole children.

Lawrence Boythorn, John Jarndyce's friend. His character is modeled on that of the poet Walter Savage Landor.

Mr. Gridley, also called **The Man from Shropshire**, a farmer's son ruined by a suit in Chancery, frequently jailed for contempt of court. While hiding from the law, he dies in a London shooting gallery.

Bayham Badger, a medical practitioner to whom Richard Carstone is apprenticed for a time. He is proud of his wife's two former husbands.

Mrs. Badger, his wife, who brings glory to her present married state because she is the widow of Captain Swosser, an officer of the Royal Navy, and Professor Dingo, a scientist.

Charlotte Neckett, also called **Charley**, Esther Summerson's devoted maid.

Mr. Kenge, nicknamed

"Conversation" Kenge, a member of the law firm of Kenge and Carboy. Through him, John Jarndyce first meets Esther Summerson.

Mr. Vholes, Richard Carstone's solicitor. He helps to bring about the young man's ruin.

Mr. Quale, Mrs. Jellyby's partner in her impractical philanthropic schemes.

Miss Wisk, betrothed to Mr. Quale.

Mr. Tangle, a legal authority on the case of *Jarndyce vs. Jarndyce*.

BLESS ME, ULTIMA

Author: Rudolfo A. Anaya (1937-)
First published: 1972
Genre: Novel

Locale: Guadalupe, New Mexico
Time: 1943
Plot: Bildungsroman

Antonio Márez y Luna (MAH-rehs ee LEW-nah), a child at the threshold of a larger world. Although he is only seven, Antonio's brothers are already fighting in World War II. Before his first day of school, Antonio sees a traumatized veteran killed by an enraged mob. In school, Antonio must master a new language because classes are taught in English. At the end of the year, he is promoted an extra grade. The larger world proves more difficult to master, however. Antonio witnesses the deaths of several people he loves, endures the nauseating fears that beset local children in response to nearby atomic testing, and shares his father's anguish when his brothers return from the war only to wander away again, their cultural roots severed. Finally, he watches as Ultima, his spiritual mentor, dies, defeated by an opponent who hates her healing powers.

Ultima (EWL-tee-mah), an aged *curandera* (healer), trained by el Volaré, the flying man from las Pasturas. Ultima is a friend of Antonio's mother, Maria Luna. In her old age, she is left behind in a village that has lost many members through the war and economic migration. The Márez y Luna family invites Ultima to stay with them. Ultima is loved by a faithful few whom she helped in the past, especially Maria and Narcisco. She is also the object of community mistrust. Even many of those she once healed, including Maria's brothers, the Lunas, refuse to oppose those who seek to harm her. Through Ultima, Antonio finds a path through the morass of injustice, chaos, and dogma that surrounds him. Ultima accepts her death because she has devoted her life's energies to life itself. Ultima shows Antonio that even amid the catastrophic social and economic upheavals that have rent their region since the onset of Spanish colonization, one can contribute to healing within one's community.

Tenorio Trementina (teh-NOH-ree-oh treh-mehn-TEE-nah), an evil *brujo* (witch) who seeks to destroy Ultima.

Tenorio first comes into conflict with Ultima when his daughters place a curse on Lucas, Maria's brother. Although Ultima tells Tenorio that she plans to lift the curse and warns that his daughters will be endangered if he does not order them to lift it, Tenorio remains intransigent, denying that his daughters have caused Lucas' ailment. Tenorio's pride blinds him to his daughters' peril. In refusing to acknowledge his daughters' involvement, Tenorio, in effect, signs their death warrant. When Ultima lifts the curse, the malevolent energies of the Trementina sisters are released, and the sisters are, one by one, consumed by the forces with which they trafficked. As his three daughters sicken and die, Tenorio's chief concern is for his honor. He organizes three initiatives against Ultima, claiming that she has cursed his daughters. In his first attack, Tenorio's eye is gouged out by Ultima's owl. In the second, he kills Narcisco but nearly stands trial for murder. In his third attack, he kills Ultima's owl, and hence Ultima. In attempting to finish his work against the life force Ultima represents, however, he seeks to kill Antonio, and he is shot dead.

Narcisco (nahr-SEES-koh), the town drunk. He is one of a circle of visionary characters who are conscious of a spiritual realm in which the forces of life struggle against the forces of death. Like the other major characters. Narcisco undergoes a sequence of three transformative events. In a series of confrontations, Narcisco argues for calm in the face of riotous passions. In the first of these, Narcisco is ignored, and the demented veteran Lupito is killed. In the second, a confrontation with drunken witch hunters, Narcisco reasons with an angry mob and exorcises the ugly passions that Tenorio has aroused. In the third confrontation, in which Narcisco is caught between two irrational obsessions—Tenorio's passion for vengeance and domination and the addiction of Antonio's brother Andrew to prostitutes—Narcisco gives his life in Ultima's defense.

BLESS THE BEASTS AND CHILDREN

Author: Glendon Swarthout (1918-1992)
First published: 1970
Genre: Novel

Locale: Box Canyon Boys Camp, Arizona
Time: The 1960's
Plot: Social realism

John Cotton, the fifteen-year-old leader of a misfit group of campers called the Bedwetters. The son of a selfish and disinterested mother and numerous stepfathers, Cotton has a rage against the world so deep as to induce catatonia during periods of stress. As misfit children are thrown out of other cabins, Cotton takes them in. Although not a natural leader, he seizes authority, bullying and cajoling the boys into working together. In an abortive raid to capture the trophy of another cabin, Cotton joins the disorganized Bedwetters. His humiliation at their failure reduces him to tears. Ruthlessly, he begins his crusade to save these rejects from society. Setting the horses free from their corral as a ruse to draw away the other campers, Cotton and his Bedwetters capture all the camp trophies. Teft's careful shooting of the trophies, placing a bullet in each, frightens the other campers so badly that Cotton's mission is accomplished: The Bedwetters are given fearful respect. Wheaties, the boys' counselor, insists on stopping at the Roscoe Ranch Buffalo Preserve near Flagstaff to see a buffalo shoot, and the boys are

sickened at the slaughter. Cotton rallies them to bring back Lally 2, who has gone to free the buffalo. Pushing and prodding, Cotton leads the others in a final act of redemption, freeing the penned buffalo. Defiant to the end, he dies while stampeding the herd.

Gerald Goodenow, a sissy and a crybaby who still wets the bed at the age of fourteen. Overly dependent on his mother, he is unable to function normally. A confrontation with Cotton over his breaking the group rules is a turning point in Goodenow's life; he accepts Cotton as his leader. With the others, he has the courage to face the dangers of freeing the buffalo herd and volunteers to open the pens.

Billy Lally, called **Lally 2**, the twelve-year-old brother of Stephen. Deluged with material things but otherwise ignored by his frequently absent parents, Lally 2 is locked in mortal combat with his older brother for their attention. His defense against a psychotic brother and uncaring parents is to withdraw into a world of fantasy. He wets his bed, sucks his thumb, and suffers from severe nightmares. Lally 2's first real love is for Sheba, an elderly mare assigned to him at camp. Upset at the slaughter of the buffalo, he adamantly refuses all orders to return to camp. He is determined to free the buffalo.

Stephen Lally, called **Lally 1**, Billy's fourteen-year-old brother. His hatred of his brother is almost psychotic in its intensity. When frustrated, he sets fires, kills pets, and butts his head against walls. Cold and hungry, he braves the buffalo pens.

Lawrence Teft III, the fourteen-year-old son of affluent parents. Teft's savage inner strife manifests itself in perpetual teeth grinding while he sleeps. His crimes have escalated from petty theft to stealing automobiles, and he has become more self-destructive. During the trophy raid, his shooting of the other teams' trophies brings the Bedwetters a terrified respect.

His expertise at stealing automobiles furnishes the transportation to the buffalo killing grounds.

Sammy Schecker, the twelve-year-old son of a famous Jewish comedian. He has no identity beyond his father's reflected glory. A compulsive eater and whiner, Schecker rattles off his father's routines compulsively. Cotton's confrontation with him over his constant chatter brings Schecker's first triumph, as he overpowers his tormentor. With Goodenow, he has the courage to open the gates for the buffalo herd.

Wheaties, the group's inept nineteen-year-old camp counselor. Their hatred of him is reciprocated. He takes the Bedwetters to the buffalo preserve, where the buffalo are being slaughtered.

— *Inez L. Ramsey*

BLITHE SPIRIT: An Improbable Farce in Three Acts

Author: Noël Coward (1899-1973)
First published: 1941
Genre: Drama

Locale: Kent, England
Time: Late 1930's
Plot: Comedy

Charles Condomine, a novelist in his forties. Charles is bright, sophisticated, articulate, and debonair but somewhat at the mercy of his wives, past and present. His interest in spiritualism as a subject for a novel leads Charles to ask Madame Arcati to dinner and a séance. He is skeptical but becomes a believer when the ghost of his first wife appears—and stays. From then on, poor Charles is a shuttlecock between the women battling for his affections: Ruth, his living wife, and Elvira, his dead one. Charles prefers Elvira.

Ruth Condomine, Charles's second wife. Like her husband, Ruth is witty and sophisticated, and she is quite the society matron. Ruth is a bit stuffy and a little predictable. She is convinced that Charles has lost his mind when Elvira appears, because at first she can neither see nor hear Elvira. Throughout much of the play, Ruth acts as a concerned wife, trying to restore Charles to normalcy.

Elvira, the ghost of Charles's first wife. Elvira is gray from head to toe, and only Charles can see or hear her. In life, Elvira was spirited, outgoing, wild, and carefree. In death, she is no

different; she has cocktails with Genghis Khan. She does love Charles, if somewhat casually, and is jealous of Ruth. Her attempts to monopolize the attention and conversation of Charles after she reappears form the central tension of the play.

Madame Arcati, the local spiritualist and medium. Elderly but spry, Madame Arcati bicycles into the play wearing slightly outlandish clothes and talking to an eight-year-old contact on the other side. As everyone soon finds out, Madame Arcati is no fraud. She truly is in contact with the other world and inadvertently is the "medium" through which Elvira is called back to this one. The problem is that Madame Arcati cannot figure out how to return Elvira to the other side.

Edith, the maid. Edith plays a tiny part in the bulk of the play but turns out to be a central character. Edith, not Charles, has the extrasensory powers that called Elvira back from the dead, and only Edith can make Elvira return.

— *Evelyn Romig*

THE BLITHEDALE ROMANCE

Author: Nathaniel Hawthorne (1804-1864)
First published: 1852
Genre: Novel

Locale: Massachusetts
Time: Mid-nineteenth century
Plot: Psychological realism

Miles Coverdale, a young New England poet, the narrator of the story. He is a highly sensitive young man and an eager observer of the persons he meets at Blithedale Farm, an experiment in communal living that he joins for a time. Three of his fellow experimenters particularly attract his attention: Zenobia Fauntleroy, Priscilla Moodie, and a man named Hollingsworth. As an observer of their lives, Miles is intrigued, caught by his interest in them as human souls and, as well, by his love for Priscilla Moodie, a love he never reveals to her.

Hollingsworth, a dark, powerful man who was once a blacksmith. He has fastened himself to a single project in

obsessive fashion: He desires to set up a philanthropic institution for the reform of criminals and thus to reduce the amount of evil in the world. This project is Hollingsworth's ruling passion, and all else in his life must be subservient to it. He joins the experiment at Blithedale Farm because he sees in the farm a place to erect the buildings to house his reformatory and because he sees in Zenobia, a wealthy young woman of the group, a person who can help his project with her money and influence. Unfortunately for Hollingsworth's project, he falls in love with Priscilla Moodie and thus alienates Zenobia, who is Priscilla's half sister. Zenobia's later suicide weighs heavily on Hollingsworth's conscience, for she left him with a curse. He gives up his idea of reforming other persons until he can assure himself that he is not guilty of crime. His tragedy is that of conscience, for he believes he is responsible for Zenobia's death; he believes he has driven the girl to suicide and so regards himself as her murderer. With this thought weighing upon him, he can no longer consider trying to reform others guilty of crime. Though he marries Priscilla Moodie, he is a broken man.

Zenobia Fauntleroy, a wealthy young woman from another part of the United States. She is attractive both in personality and in appearance. Her vivid presence is always accentuated by her habit of wearing a flamboyant flower in her hair. She is unhappy with woman's lot in life, and her mission is to remake society so that she and her fellow women can take what she regards as their rightful places in the affairs of the world. She falls in love with Hollingsworth and offers her fortune to help him in the establishment of his reformatory, as well as her personal aid in the project. As the months pass, however, she learns that Hollingsworth loves her half sister, Priscilla Moodie. Unhappy Zenobia suffers other shocks. She loses all her wealth in a strange way, apparently to her half sister, and learns for the first time the girl's identity as a relative. These blows unnerve Zenobia, who drowns herself. Her real name is Fauntleroy, although the narrator avoids using any other than her Biblical pseudonym.

Mr. Moodie, an extremely shy and retiring man, a peddler of sorts. He reveals to Miles Coverdale that he was once wealthy and came of good family. He has given up his family name of Fauntleroy, however, and assumed that of Moodie. He has been driven from home by crime, and his wealth has passed to his daughter, the Zenobia of the story, inasmuch as he is supposedly dead. In New England he has remarried, and the daughter of that marriage is Priscilla Moodie, actually Zenobia's half sister. Mr. Moodie puts Priscilla under the protection of Hollingsworth and thus precipitates the tragic chain of events.

Priscilla Moodie, Zenobia's ethereal half sister, who has supported herself and her father for many years by sewing little articles for her peddler father to sell. Though she enters the story as a poor, shadowy excuse for a girl, she develops a personality through her love for Hollingsworth and his affection for her. After Zenobia's suicide, Priscilla marries Hollingsworth and becomes his psychological support in his battle against feelings of guilt.

Mr. Westervelt, a fine-appearing but shallow man who is a promoter and rascal. He has a vague connection with Zenobia, as if they had known each other well at one time. Westervelt comes to dominate Zenobia and uses her in an act on the lyceum circuit, in which she figures as the Veiled Lady. He uses her, perhaps under hypnosis, to make people believe that he can forecast the future. His exploitation of the girl ends when she runs to Hollingsworth for protection during a performance.

THE BLOOD KNOT

Author: Athol Fugard (1932-   )
First published: 1963
Genre: Drama

Locale: Korsten, near Port Elizabeth, South Africa
Time: Early 1960's
Plot: Psychological realism

Morris Pietersen, a "Colored" (mixed race) male of unspecified age who lives with his brother, Zachariah. One of Morris' most important characteristics is the fact that, in contrast to Zachariah, he has light skin, light enough so that he has been able to pass for white. As a result, Morris seems to feel guilty regarding his dark-skinned brother, needing to prove to himself and Zachariah that they do indeed have a "blood knot" and that they are, in fact, tied as brothers in a valued, however troubled, relationship. An essential aspect of Morris' personality is that he seems driven to become closer than he has been to Zachariah. This desire is shown, in part, by Morris taking a servile position to his brother. For example, it is the brother with near-white skin who assumes the domestic chores in the house, such as cooking and preparing Zachariah's foot baths, among other things. Morris dreams that the two of them will move someday to a deserted land to escape other negative aspects of society. A main part of his outlook on existence is improving his relationship with his brother. His desire to be close to Zachariah is sometimes undercut by his absorption in South Africa's racialism. A central part of the plot, for example, is Morris' exhibition of a latent dislike of blacks, as is shown when the two brothers play a game in which Morris pretends to be white, while Zachariah acts as a subservient black man. Morris' inner feelings are shown by the fact that although he is at first unable to enact the role of a white man, he soon is so carried away by the role-playing that he wishes to be abusive to Zachariah, wanting to poke him with an umbrella. Morris, therefore, shows both his inner conflict as well as the tension that lurks below the surface of the two brothers' relationship.

Zachariah Pietersen, a mixed-race male of unspecified age who, in contrast to Morris, who does the domestic work at home, Zachariah works at a park—ironically, keeping blacks from entering. One of his most important characteristics is his dark skin. Unlike Morris, Zachariah has always had to live a life subjected to the laws pertaining to "Coloreds"; he, unlike Morris, is unable to "pass" for white. It is not surprising, therefore, that he is the more reality-bound of the brothers, having little interest in Morris' illusion of a new life in a deserted land. His realistic nature is emphasized even as he and his brother play games of imagination; for example, he tells Morris how to "act white" as the brothers pretend that Morris is a white man and that Zachariah is a black in a submissive role. Another important element is that Zachariah is conflicted in his feelings toward his brother. He recalls bitterly that their mother favored the light-skinned Morris. Zachariah also feels that Morris, who at times seems to push his illusions and opinions on him, is a burdensome brother. Resentment and jealousy, therefore, lurk beneath Zachariah's feelings toward his brother.

— *Jane Davis*

BLOOD MERIDIAN: Or, The Evening Redness in the West

Author: Cormac McCarthy (1933-   )
First published: 1985
Genre: Novel

Locale: Southwestern United States and Mexico
Time: 1833-1878
Plot: Western

Blasarius, known as **the kid**, a scrappy runaway with a taste for violence. At the age of sixteen, he joins an outlaw army with the ostensible goal of "liberating" Mexico but an actual mission of seizing land. After his party is slaughtered by Comanches, he is arrested in Mexico. He and his fellow prisoner Toadvine are freed to join a rabble gang of scalp hunters, led by Captain Glanton and Judge Holden. The kid is initiated into a naturalistic universe in which, according to the judge, war is god. When a gypsy reads the men's tarot cards, the kid draws the Four of Cups, indicating discontent and doubt—the kid has not completely internalized the brutality—but help from a divine source. The mysterious judge then shows special interest in the kid. When the kid and Tobin become separated from the group, the kid, despite Tobin's warnings, cannot shoot the judge, who calls to him that his soul is not like that of the others. Wounded, the kid wanders to San Diego, where the arrow lodged in his thigh is removed. During the ensuing delirium, the judge appears and declares that, although he had loved him like a son, the kid is culpable for all the bloodshed, because he remained uncommitted to the mission: He still retained some modicum of mercy in his heart. Years pass, during which the kid, now isolated, wears David Brown's necklace of human ears and avoids killing when possible. In Texas, he again meets the judge, who warns that the kid's soul will be required that night. Going to the toilet, the kid meets the naked judge, who embraces him in his death.

Judge Holden, an enigmatic figure who seems omnipotent, ubiquitous, and omniscient. He converses expertly on all subjects, speaks all languages fluently, and plays the fiddle and dances. A man of ambiguous morality, pleased with the terrible beauty and violence of creation, he represents the awful neutrality of the universe. Knowing people's destinies without interfering, he shows both kindness and cruelty: He rescues an Apache child from a massacre, indulges it, and then scalps it. An enormous, hairless, eerily pale man with a childlike face, he has tremendous oratorical power. He seems pleased by the idiot, whom he leads around on a halter. After the kid's death, he leads revelers in fiddling and dancing as the dance of life continues.

Louis Toadvine, an earless, branded roisterer who joins forces with the kid after a bloody fighting ritual. When they meet again in prison, he claims that he and the kid are seasoned Indian fighters so that they can join Glanton's army. A man of no thought, he is hanged.

Tobin, a former priest who still believes in a power behind the universe but now believes that power to be malignant. He recognizes the judge as an embodiment of that power and fears his influence on the kid, in whom he senses a special fate. After he and the kid reach San Diego, he disappears.

Captain John Joel Glanton, the leader of the expedition, a hard man without feeling or principles. He kills gratuitously and scalps anyone who can pass for Indian. Incited by weakness and vulnerability, he is completely amoral. In charge of his own destiny, he will pursue his blood lust to the end. He is killed by Indians.

John Jackson, a black horseman and brawler who despises his white *Doppelgänger* of the same name. The white Jackson rides beside the black Jackson and whispers to him until the black Jackson shoots the white one. When the gypsy asks Jackson to draw a card, the judge indicates that in Jackson's fortunes lie all their fortunes. His drawing of the Fool indicates the impulsiveness and folly of their undertaking, embodied particularly by Jackson. He is killed by Indians.

James Robert Bell, an idiot whose brother keeps him naked and filthy, feeds him feces, and pulls him in a cart behind Glanton's army. He is rescued by kindly women who bathe him, show him tenderness, and put him to sleep in comfort. During the night, he wanders into the river, where he would have drowned had not the judge saved him and restored him to his fellows. The judge leads him by a neck halter. He croaks, drools, and dances and seems to possess some secret woe. The kid, seeking him, never finds him again.

David Brown, a skilled, violence-loving killer. A simple man, he considers the judge's ideas "crazy." He wears a necklace of human ears that is appropriated, after Brown's hanging, by the kid.

— *Jo N. Farrar*

THE BLOOD OF THE LAMB

Author: Peter De Vries (1910-1993)
First published: 1962
Genre: Novel

Locale: Chicago, Illinois; a sanatorium in the Rockies; and New York City
Time: 1920's-1950's
Plot: Comic realism

Don Wanderhope, the son of pietistic Dutch immigrants in South Chicago. As a youth, he works for his father, who has a garbage-collection business, and attends the University of Chicago. As his name suggests, he can neither believe nor disbelieve in divine providence. Times of hopefulness and happiness in his life invariably are followed by suffering and loss.

He decides finally on reason, courage, and grace, but insists that the grace is solely humanity's to give, that there is no God to make all things right in the end.

Ben Wanderhope, Don's father, an intelligent but ill-educated immigrant businessman. He wavers between a variety of Dutch Calvinism that allows grace only to the elect and no belief at all. His faith is rekindled when he thinks that he is drowning in a garbage pit and again when profession of belief will lead to reduced fees for Don's treatment at a church-run sanatorium. Finally, he becomes so depressed that he has to be institutionalized for the remainder of his life.

Louie Wanderhope, Don's older brother and hero, who dies while a medical student at the University of Chicago. Always a scoffer, on his deathbed he assures those in attendance that he has "no doubts" whatsoever as to what is to follow. His smile at Don lets his brother know exactly what he means by his statement, though the others are pleasantly misled.

Greta Wigbaldy, a girl from the same milieu as Don, later his wife. Following their marriage, which takes place after his return from treatment for tuberculosis, her personality be-

comes increasingly disordered. She already is the mother, with a married man, of a child given up for adoption. She is unfaithful to Don, drinks too much, and eventually kills herself, leaving to Don her daughter by him.

Carol Wanderhope, Don and Greta's beautiful and precocious daughter. Don's love for his daughter is intensified when he learns that she has leukemia. It is only after her death that he discovers—via a tape recording she made—that she knew for some time what was coming.

Rena Baker, a decent Calvinist girl whom Don meets and loves at the tuberculosis sanatorium in the Rockies. Her piety seems as genuine as her love for Don. Two days after the near consummation of that love, she has to undergo an operation and dies.

— *James H. Bowden*

BLOOD WEDDING
(Bodas de sangre)

Author: Federico García Lorca (1899-1936)
First published: 1935
Genre: Drama

Locale: Castile, Spain
Time: Early twentieth century
Plot: Tragedy

The Bride, a rich man's daughter who was engaged to Leonardo some years ago, when she was fifteen years old. She does not truly love the Bridegroom, but the families consider theirs a good match. She will marry him and try to make the best of it because she can never be with Leonardo. She would like to forget Leonardo and live honorably with her husband, but she is helpless when she hears Leonardo's voice. At the wedding reception, she tells the Bridegroom that she would like to rest a little before they dance. Instead, she rides away with Leonardo on his horse. Fleeing with him, she realizes her mistake and begs Leonardo to run away from her so that she will die alone. Instead, the two men kill each other, and she returns to the church hoping that the Bridegroom's Mother will kill her. The two women reflect on the men they have lost to knives.

The Bridegroom, a rich young man who has bought a valuable vineyard and is now ready to marry a woman he has known for three years. As the wedding approaches, he is happy and eager; he loves the Bride and looks forward to his future as husband, father, and landowner. He dismisses all talk about the Bride's former engagement because it was so long ago and cannot possibly matter now. At the wedding, he is both tender and demanding; the last thing he says to his wife is that she had better be ready to satisfy him sexually that night. When he learns that his wife has run away, he immediately gets on a horse and chases her. In the ensuing fight, he and Leonardo kill each other.

Leonardo Félix, who has been married to a cousin of the Bride for two years. He has never stopped loving the Bride, to whom he was once engaged. They were not permitted to marry

because Leonardo is not wealthy; he and his wife barely have enough money to get by. As the Bride's wedding approaches, he rides by her home more frequently, even in the middle of the night, and one morning he goes to tell her how her marriage will hurt him. As a member of the Bride's extended family, he attends the wedding. He convinces the Bride to run away with him. When the Bridegroom overtakes them, he and Leonardo kill each other with their knives.

Leonardo's Wife, the mother of his baby child. Although she has been married to Leonardo for two years, she is jealous of the feelings she suspects he still has for the Bride. She tells Leonardo that the neighbors have seen him riding far across the plains when he was supposedly out working; the wife suspects, correctly, that he was trying to see the Bride. She is the first to notice Leonardo's disappearance from the wedding. When she next sees him, he has run away with the Bride and been killed.

The Bridegroom's Mother, a widow whose husband and older son were both murdered by members of the Félix family. She has reservations about the upcoming wedding, for reasons she does not fully understand; part of her worry is that when the Bridegroom leaves home, she will be alone. She also fears knives and other weapons. She carries out her role as mother of the groom, advising the Bridegroom on presents to buy for his bride and working out the wedding arrangements. She carries a sense of foreboding throughout. In the end, her remaining son is indeed killed, with a knife, by a member of the Félix family, just as she has always feared.

— *Cynthia A. Bily*

A BLOODSMOOR ROMANCE

Author: Joyce Carol Oates (1938-   )
First published: 1982
Genre: Novel

Locale: Bloodsmoor, a valley in eastern Pennsylvania
Time: 1879-1900
Plot: Alternative history

John Quincy Zinn, a gentleman inventor, fifty-two years old in 1879. John is tall, wide-shouldered, and handsome despite the dagger-shaped birthmark on his left temple. He is the son of a dishonest peddler whom, as a child, he saw tarred, feathered, and burned. John was adopted by a farm family, became a radical schoolmaster influenced by transcendentalism, and finally, after being lionized by Philadelphia society, married into the wealthy Kiddemaster family, which supports his experimental laboratory and large family. Convinced of the inevitability of progress, John believes that inventions will bring the perfectibility of humankind. At his death, he is engaged, under government patronage, in devising weapons of destruction, including the basis of nuclear weaponry. Despite the radicalism of his early years, he regards Deirdre, Constance Philippa, and Samantha as dead when they run away to live their own lives in violation of the conventions of the Kiddemaster class.

Prudence Kiddemaster Zinn, John's wife, who is stout, stern, matronly, and conventional. She once was the highly independent headmistress of a girls' school. Renouncing her independence to pursue John, her spirit is broken by a series of pregnancies, sometimes difficult labors, miscarriages, and occasional deaths. In old age, however, she leaves John to return to militant feminist causes.

Deirdre Louisa Bonner Zinn, an adopted Zinn daughter. She is sixteen years old in 1879, when she is abducted in a mysterious black balloon. Deirdre is dark-haired, pale, and small; she has a marked widow's peak and piercing silvery-gray eyes. She is disliked by the Zinn sisters and unhappy in her adopted home. Spiritual manifestations have plagued her since childhood. After her abduction, she reappears as Deirdre of the Shadows, a distinguished and successful trance medium. When she is investigated by the Society of Psychical Research, her spirits drive three men to their deaths, thus convincing even the most skeptical of the powers that control her. She suffers a breakdown in 1895 and retires. When she returns to Bloodsmoor because of Edwina Kiddemaster's will, she is revealed to be Edwina's daughter by a secret early marriage, and she is named heir to the vast Kiddemaster wealth, which she shares with her adopted family.

Constance Philippa Zinn, later **Philippe Fox**, the oldest Zinn daughter. Twenty-two years old in 1879, she is tall, striking, and satiric. Because her family desires socially impressive marriages, she becomes engaged to a twice-widowed, sinister German baron. On her wedding night, she flees their hotel, leaving her husband to consummate the marriage with a dressmaker's dummy. Going west, she becomes a gambler, journalist, and law officer, among many other things. She undergoes a sex change. When she returns to Bloodsmoor because of Edwina's will, she is the masculine Philippe Fox, who then elopes with a childhood friend imprisoned by her vicious husband and again disappears.

Malvinia Zinn, the daughter who is the family beauty. Twenty years old in 1879, Malvinia is tall, blue-eyed, and vain, with rich, dark hair. Courted by a man of wealth, she runs off with an actor and launches a successful stage career, to her family's horror. After a life of dissipation, marred by the hereditary Zinn Mark of the Beast, she repents, becomes a teacher, and marries a man whose life she had harmed in her childhood.

Octavia Zinn, the Christian and conventional Zinn daughter. Twenty-one years old in 1879, placid and plump, she is a born lady. She has a warm smile, plump cheeks, and brown eyes. She marries a tyrannical and narrow retired Lutheran minister, Lucius Rumford, whose exotic sexual practices she, in her innocence, regards as normal. These practices cause his death. She bears three children; two die young, one perhaps killed by another. She finds a happy second marriage with Sean McInnes, a successful investor, attorney, and U.S. congressman whom she had once adored when he was merely the son of their Irish coachman.

Samantha Zinn, the daughter who serves as John's laboratory assistant. Small, immature, red-haired, and freckled, Samantha frightens off suitors with her intelligence. Pressured by her mother to marry a decadent aristocrat, she runs off with Nahum Hareton, her father's other assistant, a man of dubious background. As a small boy, he had disappeared from a time machine John Zinn had manufactured when a schoolmaster. She is an inventor, focusing on time-saving devices for housewives such as disposable diapers.

Edwina Kiddemaster, Prudence's aunt, the author of more than seventy etiquette books. Enormously wealthy, she is conservative in her writing but less so in her private life. Her will stipulates that the Zinn daughters must be reunited at Bloodsmoor, where Deirdre is revealed to be her daughter by a disastrous marriage.

Sarah Whitton Kiddemaster, Prudence's mother. She is conventionally female, but an autopsy reveals that she has virtually no internal organs. She has sewn an antimacassar 1,358 yards long.

— Betty Richardson

BLOODY POETRY

Author: Howard Brenton (1942-   )
First published: 1985
Genre: Drama

Locale: Switzerland, England, and Italy
Time: 1816-1822
Plot: Historical

Percy Bysshe Shelley, an English Romantic poet. Thin, sallow, sensitive, and neurotic, Bysshe, who passes through his middle and late twenties in the course of the play, champions the cause of workers, though he is the son of an aristocrat. He is a teetotaler and fights for the rights of women, yet he abandons his first wife, Harriet, to prostitution and takes Mary Godwin as his lover. Although he marries Mary after Harriet's suicide, he is never faithful. He sleeps with Claire and, later, a boatman's daughter. Bysshe advocates free love but confesses that he does not feel free. His careless actions cause the death of his first wife and of his daughter Clara. In the end, Bysshe drowns in a boating accident.

George Gordon, Lord Byron, a Scottish Romantic poet. Byron is a talented, flamboyant, and rich profligate in his late twenties and early thirties. He is a priapic bisexual who sleeps with all manner of boys, virginal girls, and married women. He suffers from alcoholism and syphilis. Byron domineers over the other characters in the play, especially the hapless Dr. Polidori. He impregnates Claire, then rejects her. He takes their daughter Allegra away from Claire and places the child in a convent, where she dies. Although Byron causes pain in the life of anyone who cares for him, he is nevertheless energetic, charming, and devastatingly attractive.

Mary Shelley, Bysshe's second wife. Mary, who also is a writer, is nineteen years old when the play begins and only twenty-five when she is widowed. She is the voice of reason in the play, handling all the practical details of life while her husband follows his dreams. She has a son, William, by him and later a daughter, Clara, who dies on a journey to Venice to follow Bysshe. Mary proposes marriage to the reluctant Bysshe after she learns of his first wife's death, even though she knows that he has been sleeping with the pregnant Claire, who is expecting Byron's child. Mary's practical nature causes her to worry about her family's tenuous financial situation.

Claire Clairemont, Mary's half sister and Byron's lover. Only eighteen years old when the play begins, Claire is obsessed by her unrequited love for Byron, and she unsuccessfully tries to get him to marry her by bearing his child. Claire, Mary, and Bysshe share a passionate triangular relationship, though it is Mary who weds Bysshe and bears his children.

Dr. William Polidori, Byron's biographer. Puritanical, jealous, vain, highly strung, and obsessed, Polidori follows Byron and Bysshe all over Europe, alternately fascinated and repulsed by their antics.

Harriet Westbrook, Bysshe's first wife and, later, a ghost. Twenty-one years old, sad, and beautiful, Harriet drowns herself two years after Bysshe abandons her with two children to a life of prostitution. She quotes one of his love poems to her as she throws herself into the Serpentine River. Later, she haunts the stage near Bysshe and comments ironically on his actions.

— *Pamela Canal*

A BLOT IN THE 'SCUTCHEON

Author: Robert Browning (1812-1889)
First published: 1843
Genre: Drama

Locale: Rural England
Time: The eighteenth century
Plot: Tragedy

Thorold, Earl Tresham, a proud English nobleman who is resolved to keep his family's reputation untarnished. Horrified when he discovers that his sister has taken a lover, he traps the man and kills him in a duel. He poisons himself, hoping that his death, his sister's, and her lover's will erase the blot on the family escutcheon.

Henry, Earl Mertoun, the suitor of Mildred, Earl Tresham's sister. He wants to cover up their affair by marrying the girl, whom he truly loves. He is found sneaking into the castle one night, is challenged to a duel, and is killed by Earl Tresham, against whom he does not try to defend himself.

Mildred, Earl Tresham's fourteen-year-old sister, led by her innocence into taking Earl Mertoun as her lover. When he offers marriage, she feels she cannot in honor accept his suit to marry her as though she were truly a virgin. She dies of grief on hearing that her lover is dead.

Guendolen, a cousin of Earl Tresham and Mildred. She tries to help the young girl by convincing Earl Tresham that Earl Mertoun's suit is honorable.

Austin Tresham, Earl Tresham's brother and Guendolen's fiancé. He tries, with Guendolen's help, to save Earl Mertoun's life after he has been wounded. Austin and his bride, Guendolen, inherit the title and estates after Earl Tresham's death.

Gerald, the retainer who informs Earl Tresham of Mildred's affair.

THE BLUE BIRD: A Fairy Play in Six Acts
(L'Oiseau bleu)

Author: Maurice Maeterlinck (1862-1949)
First published: 1909
Genre: Drama

Locale: An imaginary land, France, and Belgium
Time: Late nineteenth or early twentieth century
Plot: Allegory

Tyltyl (teel-teel), a woodcutter's son. Dressed in a light-blue jacket, scarlet knickerbockers, and white knee-length socks, he is innocent and naïve. At the beginning of the play, which takes place during the Christmas season, he notices the abundance of gifts and cakes enjoyed by his rich neighbors. Accepting his situation without rancor and jealousy, he participates vicariously in their pleasures. The Fairy Bérylune appears at night and asks him to seek the Blue Bird needed to cure her ill daughter. Adventurous and courageous, he finds the Fairy interesting and stimulating, and he answers her questions on her grotesque appearance forthrightly and accurately. His good nature prompts him to seek the Blue Bird, and the Fairy arms him with a magic diamond that enables him to defeat possible adversaries. Along with his sister Mytyl, his dog, his cat, and everyday commodities that are anthropomorphized (for example, Bread, Sugar, Fire, Water, and Milk), he undertakes a journey leading to four successive realms. Although he becomes afraid during his encounter with the Oak and the other elements of nature seeking revenge for past human wrongs, he finds the strength and courage to endure pain and to keep his promise to the Fairy. He encourages Mytyl to share the dangers and difficulties of the quest. At the end, he returns to the security of his home. He is realistic and acknowledges his failure to capture the Blue Bird; however, he generously relinquishes his own blue bird to Madame Berlingot, who, in turn, gives it to her daughter. Cured, the neighbor's daughter finds momentary happiness. Just as the Blue Bird eludes capture, however, Tyltyl's bird escapes. Resigned to the situation, Tyltyl recognizes the continual need to seek the bird. By pursuing the quest of happiness, he is prepared again to undertake a voyage to a deeper understanding of life.

Mytyl (mee-teel), Tyltyl's sister. Appearing in a Red Riding Hood costume, she resembles her brother in innocence and purity. She loves her family and expresses joy in being reunited with her deceased grandparents, brothers, and sisters. In undertaking the journey to capture the Blue Bird, however, she lacks Tyltyl's resolve and fortitude. During her encounter with Night, she gives in to anxieties, crying and complaining as Tyltyl is about to open the door to the Forest. In contending with nature's elements, she emits horrifying screams, and unlike her brother, she appears more human than heroic. The search for the Blue Bird reflects a growth of self-understanding and wisdom: She distinguishes the differences of character between the dog and the cat and, like her brother, discovers the secrets of life, the significance of duty and sacrifice, and the elusive and transitory nature of happiness.

Bérylune (bay-ree-lewn), a fairy who appears at the end of the play as **Madame Berlingot** (behr-ling-oh), the woodcutter's neighbor. Initially, she enters crippled and grotesque, walking with a cane and appearing with a conjoining nose and chin. She asks Tyltyl and Mytyl to capture the Blue Bird needed for the recovery of her daughter. She gives them a magic diamond that provides them with a supernatural force to ensure their safety. To convince them to undertake the quest, she uses the enchanted jewel to undergo a self-transformation from a hag to a beautiful princess, then to instill life into the furniture and other inanimate objects. At the conclusion, she reappears as the neighbor, accompanied by her beautiful young daughter, who is lame. Tyltyl's bird brings about a miraculous cure, which, in turn, induces gratitude from Madame Berlingot.

Tylo (tee-loh), a bulldog anthropomorphized during the journey. Instinctively, it opposes the character of Tylette, the cat. Consistently loyal to the children, it fights valiantly during the battle with the elements and often shows excessive affection to its masters.

Tylette (tee-leht), the cat. Constantly wary of Tylo, the dog, it is hypocritical and independent. It attempts to dissuade the children from carrying out their promise of capturing the Blue Bird, and it informs Night of the children's intention. At the same time, it pretends to help them to locate the Blue Bird. Unlike Tylo, it does not defend them in the battle against the elements, and, as a character contrary to the dog, it seeks to confine and denigrate its natural adversary.

Light, the Fairy's assistant, who guides the children on a journey to insight into life's secrets and the meaning of happiness.

— Donald Gilman

BLUE BOY
(Jean le bleu)

Author: Jean Giono (1895-1970)
First published: 1932
Genre: Novel

Locale: The Provence region of France
Time: About 1900-1914
Plot: Bildungsroman

Jean (zhahn), **the Blue Boy**, a boy of about seven when the story opens. He grows to maturity by the end of the book, when he joins the French army in 1914. Jean lives with his mother and father in the Provençal hills at the Italian border. He is the narrator of this fictionalized autobiography, in which he recounts incidents in his own life and the lives of those around him from a boy's point of view, observing grief, sickness, death, and cruelty, as well as joy and delight. An impressionable, imaginative, solitary child, he spends hours watching people from the windows of his parents' apartment, looking into the windows and doors of the neighbors' apartments and down into the sheep pen that forms the "courtyard" of the apartment building. Much of his time is spent in his mother's laundry on the ground floor and in the cobbler's shop of his father on the third floor. Carefully dressed, with a starched white collar and a sky-blue silk tie, he attends the convent school of the Sisters of the Presentation. Much later, when he has become a young man, he gets a job at a bank, where he must wear blue livery. At that job, he feels divided into two parts, one that carries out orders and performs menial tasks, and the inner one, which he calls "Blue Boy." That part has been taught how to escape into the world of poetry, music, and compassion for the suffering of others.

Père Jean (pehr), the Blue Boy's father, a cobbler and a healer, the real hero of the book. The boy sees many people come to his father's workroom seeking help with problems of all kinds, physical and spiritual. The cobbler welcomes them all without question or judgment and does what he can to relieve their suffering and enable them to continue their lives with renewed strength and courage. The father keeps cages filled with songbirds. After a long period of yearning and saving, he buys a small plot of land for a garden, where, as he grows old and ill, he sits under the trees he planted and feeds the rabbits. It is here and in the workroom that Jean and his father have their last conversations. The old man speaks his thoughts about living in order to heal and to comfort through extinguishing wounds and composing poetry. If his son learns these things, the father says, he will become a man.

Massot and his wife, to whom Jean is sent by his father to live for a year, so that the boy can regain his health after a long illness. Massot is a shepherd. Jean plays with their shy little girl, Anne, and he spends the summer with "the dark man," who has also been sent by Père Jean to be healed. The two tend the sheep, talk, and immerse themselves in Homer's *The Iliad*. Both the boy and the man are healed.

Décidément (day-see-day-MAHN) and

Madame-la-Reine (rehn), a violinist and a flutist, respectively. The two brothers share an apartment in the house where Jean lives. Jean's father sends his young son to listen to the musicians, recognizing that for the boy the pleasure of hearing music is greater than the act of performing it. The two musicians are among the most memorable of the myriad characters who people the book. The death of Décidément occurs shortly after Jean returns from his year at Corbieres with the Massots.

— Natalie Harper

THE BLUE MOUNTAINS OF CHINA

Author: Rudy Wiebe (1934-   )
First published: 1970
Genre: Novel

Locale: The Ukraine, Siberia, western Canada, and South America
Time: 1919-1970
Plot: Historical

Jakob Friesen IV, a guilt-ridden exile who abandons his son to escape persecution. A brooding, cynical man, Friesen never recovers from his high-handed betrayal of his son (whom he abandoned in Russia), even while living among the Mennonite community with which he emigrates. As a hardhearted immigrant to western Canada, he spends his life contemplating the paradoxes of the Christian faith and the tenacity it takes to persevere in the midst of suffering and brutality. As one who is losing his faith in humanity and God, Friesen poignantly counsels the younger John Reimer toward the end of the novel, tempering with his introspective realism the wild-eyed, radical idealism of the naïve missionary.

Frieda Friesen, a cousin of Jakob who, with the children of other Mennonite immigrants, attempts to make a new life in western Canada, far away from her parents' native Russia. Her character is revealed solely through the memoirs that help give the novel its thematic structure. Her journal entries burn with a faith that acts as a calming influence on her family and others caught in spiritual turmoil. Her quiet peace in the face of the temptation to be assimilated by a new, worldly culture in the West rests on her boundless perseverance and her unshakable faith in God. Her character exemplifies the core of Mennonite faith, particularly their determination to be faithful until death.

David Epp, a heroic second-generation Mennonite missionary. Epp's spirit is informed by the lofty faith of Frieda Friesen. A warm, unselfish believer, Epp trades his own life, in martyrdom at the Chinese border, for the lives of those who he is helping to emigrate from Russia. Fiercely independent, Epp believes in the impossible; his pioneering, indomitable faith leads him to principle and eternal destiny above earthly comfort and safety. Epp thus becomes a model of missionary fervor to those who immigrate to the West.

Samuel Reimer, an average churchgoer and wheat farmer who suddenly believes he is called by God to be a prophet. After confrontations with the local pastor and his immediate family—who deny that God speaks today—Reimer emerges as a tragicomic figure who defies the more prudent of his family members, who are incredulous at his announced mission to preach peace to war-torn Vietnam. Wounded by their rejection, Samuel dies of a broken heart.

John Reimer, Samuel's brother, a missionary who travels across Canada with a cross on his back. Youthful, naïve, and idealistic, Reimer returns from a missionary training stint in Paraguay intent on taking the Gospel to the secular Canadian culture, with the visual symbol of the cross on his back. His confrontation with the hardened Jakob Friesen IV forms the climax of the novel.

Emily Reimer, Samuel's wife, whose concern for the material prosperity of the household accelerates Samuel's insistence on his own austere prophetic career.

Jakob Friesen V, the only son of Jakob IV. He is abandoned by his father in Russia before he is exiled.

Erna Epp, David Epp's wife and, later, widow.

— Bruce L. Edwards

THE BLUE ROOM
(La Chambre bleue)

Author: Georges Simenon (1903-1989)
First published: 1964
Genre: Novel

Locale: Poitiers and a nearby small town and village in France
Time: Mid-twentieth century
Plot: Detective and mystery

Antonio (Tony) Falcone (fahl-KOHN), a thirty-three-year-old man who is arrested and tried for poisoning his wife, Gisèle. As three officials question him, he reveals the relevant facts of his life. He is proud to have established his own business selling and repairing agricultural equipment. A devoted family man, he appreciates his wife's homemaking, takes his daughter to church on Sundays, visits his aged father regularly, and vacations with his family at the seaside. Tony also takes advantage of sexual opportunities. To him and the women involved, these encounters are isolated incidents that entail no obligations. He maintains this attitude during his passionate affair with Andrée Despierre. She, however, is determined to marry Tony, even though he wants to end their relationship. Andrée murders her husband and Tony's wife, and both she and Tony are sent to prison for life.

Andrée Formier Despierre (ahn-DRAY fohr-MYAY day-PYEHR), the daughter of a local hero, Dr. Formier. She lives with her mother in the chateau in Saint Justin. They are proud provincial bourgeoises who have fallen on hard times; it is obvious that she marries Nicholas Despierre for money. Andrée is a tall, attractive woman, with dark hair that contrasts with her white, translucent complexion. Revealing her sexual aggressiveness, she initiates an affair with Tony Falcone. During their eight meetings at the Hôtel des Voyageurs in the blue room, she expresses intense sexuality and possessiveness. She wants Tony to leave his wife and marry her. After Tony makes it clear that their affair has ended, she sends notes reminding him of their relationship. Driven by passion, she poisons both Nicholas and Tony's wife, Gisèle. She is arrested for the first murder, but Tony is arrested for his wife's death. At his trial, she brazenly states that his passion for her is as strong as hers is for him, and that he intended to get rid of Gisèle in order to marry her. She is triumphant when the jury sentences both of them to life imprisonment: She interprets the sentence as their means of remaining together forever.

Madame Despierre, the most respected and wealthiest citizen of Saint Justin. A mean-spirited woman who always dresses in gray, she spends most of her time working in a grocery store, one of her many properties. She grudgingly retires, however, when Andrée, her son Nicholas' wife, comes to work at the store. She reveals the depths of her malicious nature during Tony Falcone's trial for the murder of his wife. Although he is innocent of poisoning her, Madame Despierre tells the court that only Tony had the opportunity to put strych-

nine into the jar of plum jam. She lies because she wants both the guilty Andrée and the innocent Tony to be punished for her son's death.

Gisèle Falcone (zhee-ZEHL), Tony's wife, a small, quiet, and shy woman. After she marries Tony in Poitiers and moves with him to his village of Saint Justin, she contentedly keeps house and helps with his accounts and bookkeeping. Tony appreciates her devotion and at times feels a profound tenderness toward her that he cannot express. Although the villagers do not know her well, they recognize her kindness and are incensed when they find out that she has been murdered.

Françoise (frahn-SWAHZ), a sturdy peasant woman about thirty years old who has worked in cafés and hotels from the age of fifteen. While employed at Vincente Falcone's Hôtel des Voyageurs, she reveals her bold and adventurous character by challenging Tony to have sexual intercourse with her. Afterward, their relationship reverts to what it had been originally. This incident typifies the sort of sexual relationships Tony has with many other women and contrasts with his liaison with Andrée.

— *Frank Ardolino*

BLUEBEARD
(Blaubart)

Author: Max Frisch (1911-1991)
First published: 1982
Genre: Novel

Locale: The environs of Zurich, Switzerland
Time: Late twentieth century
Plot: Psychological realism

Felix Theodor Schaad (FAY-lihks TAY-oh-dohr shat), a Zurich physician. Schaad is a fifty-four-year-old internist who is accused of brutally murdering his sixth wife, Rosalinde Zogg, by suffocating her and strangling her with his tie. The novel begins three weeks after Schaad has been acquitted of the crime and consists of his reliving the hearing. At the time of the murder, he is divorced from Zogg and is married to his seventh wife, Jutta. The question of whether Schaad is pathologically jealous and capable of violence toward women is continually raised by the prosecuting attorney, but answers are inconclusive. Schaad's philanthropy and public service are pointed out. The doctor emerges as a complex and tormented individual who is perplexed by male-female relationships, particularly in their modern incarnations. After the acquittal, Schaad returns to his medical practice but is unsuccessful in resuming his former life. He tries drink, travel, and billiards, and finally returns to the town where he was born, confesses to the murder, and drives his car into a tree. He recovers from the accident and is told that his confession is false because the murderer, a Greek student named Nikos Grammaticos, has been found and taken into custody.

Rosalinde Zogg (ROH-zah-lihn-deh tsohk), Schaad's sixth wife. After her divorce from Schaad, Rosalinde is supporting herself as a call girl, receiving visitors in her elegant and tastefully furnished apartment. Books scattered about the apartment suggest that she may be intellectually inclined. Schaad believes her to lack self-confidence, because she did not fulfill the expectations her father, a major, had for her. She was raped by an air force captain, and her first mar-

riage occurred when she was nineteen years old.

The prosecuting attorney, about whom no descriptions of personality or references to character traits are provided. The prosecuting attorney is mentally revived by Schaad as the interrogator of witnesses and Schaad during his trial for the murder of Rosalinde.

Herr Pfeifer (PFI-fehr), a friend of Schaad and a witness. Herr Pfeifer states that he once heard Schaad say that he could strangle Rosalinde. Schaad helped Pfeifer complete his studies, supporting him with the sum of twenty-five thousand dollars.

The son, a witness. The son explains that he believes his father to be egocentric but that he is not a murderer.

Lilian Schaad, formerly **Habersack**, a nursery school teacher. Lilian is the mother of Schaad's son. She testifies that Schaad kept notebooks, often writing down his thoughts after marital squabbles. She and all of Schaad's other former wives deny that Schaad was ever violent toward them.

Gisela Schaad (GEE-zeh-lah), formerly **Stamm**, a medical assistant and one of Schaad's wives. Gisela testifies that she and Schaad were closer before their marriage, while Schaad was still married to someone else, than afterward.

Corinne Schaad, formerly **Vogel**, one of Schaad's wives. Corinne complains that Schaad kept her from sleeping with his incessant intellectual lecturing.

Andrea Schaad, formerly **Padrutt**, one of Schaad's wives. She states that Schaad is affectionate but possessive, a trait that led to their divorce. While married to Schaad, Andrea conducted an affair with a married man.

Major Zogg, Rosalinde's father and a witness at Schaad's trial. Zogg testifies that Schaad and Rosalinde wished to remain friends after the divorce.

Herr Zogg, Rosalinde's brother. Zogg often saw Rosalinde with eyes red from weeping.

Herr Rossi, a witness. Schaad saved Rossi, who intended to commit suicide.

Herr Schwander (SHVAHN-dehr), Rosalinde's former husband and a witness. Schwander was a friend of Schaad and was married to Rosalinde when she and Schaad were having an affair.

Helene Mathilde Jetzer (heh-LEH-neh mah-TIHL-deh YEHT-sehr), formerly **Knuchel**, the first wife of Schaad and a witness. Helene appears to be a mature woman who believes the cause of her divorce from Schaad to be mutual disappointment in the marriage. She is the only one of Schaad's former wives to whom he responds with a gesture indicating good will.

Herr Neuenburger (NOY-ehn-bewr-gehr), a friend of Schaad and a witness. Neuenburger, who has known Schaad for at least thirty years, makes derogatory remarks about his friend's, and all physicians', intellectual capacities. He enjoys drinking wine with Schaad.

Jutta Schaad (YEW-tah), Schaad's seventh and present wife and a witness. Jutta is a thirty-six-year-old film editor who does not live with her husband because she had promised herself never again to live with a man. Their marriage ends after Schaad's acquittal, when she announces that she intends to leave him for the cameraman with whom she has been working in Kenya.

— *Helga Stipa Madland*

BLUES FOR MISTER CHARLIE

Author: James Baldwin (1924-1987)
First published: 1964
Genre: Drama

Locale: The American South
Time: The 1960's
Plot: Protest

Meridian Henry, a minister in a small Southern town. Henry, a civil rights activist, had urged his fellow African Americans to adopt a nonviolent posture in response to threats and violence committed against them by whites resisting changes in the status quo. He had placed his faith in God and a liberal white friend to influence others and effect social change. The racially motivated killing of his son causes Meridian to reevaluate his nonaggressive strategy for civil rights. He begins to question God's allowance of the suffering of African Americans and has doubts concerning his white friend's willingness to eliminate the privileged position of whites.

Richard Henry, Meridian's murdered son. Seen in flashback sequences, he is a musician whose attempt to find fame in New York ended bitterly with his incarceration for heroin addiction. In his twenties, he returned to his hometown still resentful of his father's inaction concerning the suspicious death of Richard's mother. To whites, Richard is abrasive, threatening, and too boastful of his sexual prowess, especially in regard to white women. To blacks, he is a proud, bold young man who refuses to suffer quietly the indignities experienced by African Americans in a racist society.

Lyle Britten, a store owner suspected of murdering Richard. He is a lower-class, uneducated white man who speaks crudely. A family man, he has aspirations of expanding his business so that he can better provide the means to care for and educate his infant son. Although he admires his white wife and is proud to be a racist, he prefers sex with black women. Lyle feels threatened by the unwillingness of Richard to acquiesce to the town's racial social order.

Josephine (Jo) Gladys Britten, Lyle's wife. Better educated than her husband, she married Lyle out of love and a desire not to end life having never married. She suspects her husband of infidelity and knows that even before Richard's murder, Lyle had killed a black man (the husband of his mistress). Still, she staunchly defends her husband's virtue and lies about the events leading up to Richard's murder.

Parnell James, the editor of an unpopular town newspaper. Reared in a wealthy household, he is an iconoclastic middle-aged white man. He labels himself as a liberal but enjoys his privileged racial status. He cannot reconcile his private feelings about the exotic nature of African Americans with his public statements claiming no difference between the races. Caught between his friendships with Meridian and Lyle, Parnell claims that he desires the conviction of Richard's murderer. He appears unwilling to divulge evidence, however, that would cast doubt on Lyle's innocence in the crime.

Juanita, a college student and civil rights activist. A black woman of strong convictions, she aspires to be a lawyer and use the judicial system as a means to achieve racial equality. Highly attractive, she is desired by Meridian and Parnell but chooses to become Richard's lover.

Joel Davis, called **Papa D.**, a black owner of a juke joint whom black people consider to be an Uncle Tom. His disclosure that Lyle was the last person to see Richard alive forces the authorities to arrest the white man on suspicion of murder.

Lorenzo,

Pete,

Ken, and

Arthur, black college students and civil rights activists. They distrust the judicial system and have little hope for the conviction of Richard's murderer.

Hazel,

Lillian,

Susan,

Ralph,

Ellis,

the Reverend Phelps, and

George, friends of Lyle, all bigoted and narrow-minded white townspeople. They are adamantly opposed to social change, especially that which promotes racial equality.

— *Addell Austin*

THE BLUEST EYE

Author: Toni Morrison (1931-   )
First published: 1970
Genre: Novel

Locale: Lorain, Ohio
Time: 1940-1941
Plot: Bildungsroman

Claudia MacTeer, the nine-year-old black girl who possesses the most consistent narrative voice in a novel resonant with several different narrative voices, all used to reveal the personal histories of significant characters. Claudia tells the story of Pecola Breedlove as both child narrator, present at critical moments in Pecola's life, and as reflective adult looking back at particular events and signs. Psychologically and emotionally healthy, sturdy, loyal, and compassionate, Claudia and her sister function as dramatic counterparts to Pecola Breedlove. Both girls befriend Pecola, and both apparently are the only characters who can feel sorrow or pity for her.

Pecola Breedlove, the novel's tragic, unassuming protagonist and ultimate victim. At the age of eleven, Pecola, her family, and virtually everyone she meets, except the MacTeers, is convinced of her alleged ugliness. Her lack of self-esteem is generated by the destructive idea that no one values a black child and also by the contempt heaped on her by others. A pathetic figure, abused by her parents, denied by other adults, and the target of vicious attacks from other children, Pecola believes that acquiring blue eyes will lessen her loneliness and cause others to see her in an entirely new and more appreciative light. At the novel's close, she has been raped by her father and driven into madness and into a quest for "the bluest eyes."

Pauline (Polly) Breedlove, Pecola's mother, a maid and frustrated artist who prefers keeping order in the homes of the whites for whom she works rather than attempting to do so in her own home. A complex character suffering from both physical and emotional disabilities, Pauline is still a young woman, in her early thirties, when she is introduced. She works hard and attends church regularly, but just as regularly she initiates arguments that typically degenerate into fights with her husband, Cholly. Seldom deliberately physically abusive, Pauline nevertheless is an emotionally abusive parent who can neither show love nor demonstrate affection or concern for her own children or her husband. The only people she nurtures are the whites who employ her. Convinced of her own ugliness by images from films, Pauline has internalized this belief, acts it out daily, and has transferred it to her family.

Cholly Breedlove, Pecola's father and the father of the child she bears. Although he has committed incest, Cholly is not a one-dimensional villain. A strong young man despite the trauma of his childhood and youth, Cholly took his young wife north in an effort to better their lives. Even in Ohio, however, he finds himself frustrated, burned out, and embittered by the demands of marriage and the social conditions facing black men. He turns to drinking and fighting with Pauline to escape the limitations surrounding him. He can neither be the dependable romantic hero Pauline wants nor the full economic provider his family needs. His first sin is that he causes his family to be placed "outdoors"; his worst sin is the drunken but "tender" rape of his daughter.

Frieda MacTeer, Claudia's ten-year-old sister. She is the more knowledgeable, more mature, and more sophisticated sibling. Frieda knows what menstruation is and is able to explain to Pecola and Claudia that this change in a girl's body permits her to have a baby, as long as the girl has "somebody to love" her. A woman-child, Frieda is the quintessential elder sister who makes most of the decisions about actions and activities she and Claudia undertake. She is also more judicious, knowing when to fight for the protection of another child and what to do when her own rights are about to be violated. Both Frieda and Claudia remain supportive and loyal to Pecola despite her misfortunes.

Micah Elihue Whitcomb, called **Soaphead Church**, a misanthropic odd old man who, despite his antipathy toward humankind, ironically works in professions designed to assist people. Soaphead, so called because of the texture of his hair, emigrated from the West Indies. He collects things and has a tortured family history that includes a brief marriage. Despite perverse sexual leanings (he is a pedophile), Soaphead was an Anglican priest; currently, he makes his living as a psychic reader or spiritual adviser and healer. In this capacity, it is Soaphead Church who, for a fee, grants Pecola's wish for blue eyes by convincing her that she has them and subsequently writes a letter to God indicating why he took this action.

Maureen Peel, a newcomer in the town who creates havoc at school. Well to do and considered pretty because of her relatively light skin and long hair, Maureen upsets relationships between children and has a largely negative psychological impact. She is far more acceptable to most adults, to teachers, and to other students at school than the darker-skinned Pecola. She causes conflicting emotions in the Mac-Teer sisters, who are jealous of her preferred status yet want to be her friend.

— Sandra Y. Govan

THE BOARDING-HOUSE

Author: William Trevor (William Trevor Cox, 1928-   )
First published: 1965
Genre: Novel

Locale: A southwestern suburb of London
Time: August, 1964
Plot: Comic realism

William Wagner Bird, a boardinghouse owner. He dies in the first chapter and leaves his boardinghouse to two difficult boarders, Nurse Clock and Studdy. His diary provides background on the history of the residents. Nothing in the behavior of the new co-owners or the chaos they create provides a clue about why they were chosen.

E. A. Clock, a visiting nurse, resident, and coinheritor of the house. Bilked by a charm school when she was young, she is brusque, efficient, and intrusive. Her major focus is in alleviating the pain of the elderly. To that end, she decides unilaterally to turn the house into a nursing home, ordering "undesirables" to locate elsewhere. She is the central intelligence of the novel, being the only one who realizes the nefarious nature of Studdy.

Studdy, alias **Moran**, a petty crook, blackmailer, resident, and coinheritor of the house. He preys on women, including an invalid from whom he bilks money; a woman who brings the "meals on wheels"; Mrs. le Tor, whom he sees in a tea shop; and Miss Clerricot, a timid secretary. He writes anonymous letters to terrorize victims, not necessarily to obtain money but for the enjoyment of power over people. He dislikes Nurse Clock so much that he wears a pin in his lapel with which to prick her.

Miss Clerricot, a middle-aged secretary and resident of the house. She innocently goes with her employer, Mr. Sellwood, on a business trip to Leeds. When she discovers that he has other ideas, she leaves. Nevertheless, she is tormented by Studdy's claim that her employer's wife is looking for her.

Rose Cave, a middle-aged resident. She is haunted by her dead mother. A gentle soul, Rose often cries out in her sleep. She is flattered that Nurse Clock wants to keep her on as an employee when the house is converted to a nursing home.

Major Eele, a middle-aged resident. His reminiscences about a brief disastrous marriage supply humor. His fantasies about women and Mrs. le Tor in particular are based on his one recreation, viewing pornography in films and magazines.

Thomas Orpen Venables, a forty-nine-year-old resident and office worker. He lives his life in fear of vengeance from the parents of a young woman whom he had gotten pregnant but would not marry. As a result, he suffers severe stomach pains and appears to be dying.

Tome Obd, a Nigerian and a failed law student. For twelve years, he has been bringing flowers and love letters to the closed door of Miss Tonks. When she finally confronts him and spells out her rejection of him, he sets fire to the boardinghouse and commits suicide.

Mr. Scribbin, a resident who is a railroad fancier. His only enjoyment is playing phonograph records of trains. Nurse Clock evicts him because of the noise. Someone, possibly Studdy, breaks three of his records. For the first time, he stands up to people.

Mrs. Slape, the cook, who is dedicated to her work.

Gallelty, the cook's helper, a Manx girl. One day, she had asked Mr. Bird for directions and ended up living in the house, helping the cook.

Mrs. le Tor, a prospective resident. She has a humorous date with Major Eele and is blackmailed by Studdy.

— *Lila Chalpin*

BOESMAN AND LENA

Author: Athol Fugard (1932-   )
First published: 1969
Genre: Drama

Locale: South Africa
Time: Late 1960's
Plot: Protest

Boesman, a "colored" (mixed-race) South African in his fifties. He and his wife, Lena, wander along the mudflats of a South African river after being driven away from their home by white authorities as part of a slum clearance. Boesman's personality is shown in how he reacts to this situation: He accepts his and Lena's bleak life with a hardened demeanor. That this dispossession is the latest in a series of such incidents in Boesman and Lena's lives helps to explain Boesman's cynical personality. His manner is exemplified by his refusal to stop and ponder why he and Lena—or, in fact, South Africa's nonwhites as a group—suffer such a grim fate as his and Lena's. Boesman believes that asking such questions of existence is futile. He believes that it is sufficient to know only the surface of life, merely to endure what life deals, and not to question or complain. For these reasons, Boesman is in conflict with Lena, and that conflict constitutes the major tension of the play. Boesman's rationale for his feelings that he and Lena must concentrate solely on the present and not probe into the reasons for the hardships of their existence is that life is solely the present and that the past—or how he and Lena got to the present—is irrelevant. These beliefs are central to Boesman's and the play's development. The height of both the play's and Boesman's development comes when he reveals why he holds the beliefs he does about his and Lena's condition. He reveals that a main component of his personality is his disillusionment with the powerless life he has led, believing

that his and Lena's lives themselves—and not merely their situation—are futile and meaningless. Thus, the plot of the play hinges on Boesman's reactions to and interpretation of his and Lena's plight and how the two of them clash on these issues.

Lena, Boesman's wife, a mixed-race woman in her fifties. A major aspect of her personality is her compulsion to ask why their situation is as bleak as it is. One of the major aspects of Lena's outlook on life is her belief in questioning: She clearly believes that for life to be worth living, one must examine it. Lena, for example, unlike Boesman, wants to delve into the past, to retrace their steps so she can know how the two of them arrived at their present situation. Another main component of Lena's personality, unlike Boesman's, is that Lena regrets their lack of companionship, in terms of their relationships both with each other and with the outside world.

Old African, a man of an unspecified age who is, according to the author, the quintessence of old age and decay. He meets Boesman and Lena on the mudflats. His presence is important in showing the futility of Lena's desire for communication with others (he speaks only Xhosa, which Lena does not understand) and in making clear the frustrating nature of humanity's desire to overcome loneliness, for he also wishes to communicate with Lena about his exhaustion, the fact that he is lost, and his own impending death. The appearance of Old African heightens the conflict between Boesman and Lena. To Lena, the man is a possible link to humanity; to Boesman, he is merely an anonymous and intrusive old black man. The Old African, therefore, serves two purposes: to show Lena's need for human companionship and to develop the tension and contrast between Boesman and Lena.

— *Jane Davis*

BOGMAIL

Author: Patrick McGinley (1937-   )
First published: 1978
Genre: Novel

Locale: County Donegal, Ireland
Time: The 1970's
Plot: Detective and mystery

Tim Roarty, the proprietor of a pub in the County Donegal village of Glenkeel. Tall, bearded, and bald, he emits an air of pessimism, considering himself a man of action condemned to an idle existence. A former seminarian, he has been impotent since he was twenty-eight. His wife died seventeen years before the time of the story, after giving birth to a daughter, Cecily, to whom Roarty is devoted despite his not being her natural father. When barman Eamonn Eales turns his attentions to Cecily, Roarty sends the girl to London, kills his employee, and buries him in a bog, deeming this murder a triumph of intelligence. His smugness is shattered when he finds himself the victim of a blackmailer who he decides is Kenneth Potter, whom he also attempts to murder. After Roarty accidentally shoots Rory Rua, the dying man reveals that he is in fact the blackmailer.

Kenneth Potter, an Englishman living in County Donegal while working for a mining firm. The introspective Potter has become increasingly lonely since turning forty and losing his ardor for his Irish wife, who remains in Dublin. He finds himself revitalized by Irish village life and his affair with Nora Hession. Attempting to become part of the community, he leads the opposition to Canon Loftus' replacement of the wooden altar in the village chapel with a limestone one, only to have the priest convince the villagers that Potter's company is exploiting them. Fired from his job, he returns to London.

Nora Hession, the housekeeper for the local priest. Intelligent and sensitive, she has been forlorn since being mistreated by a lover seven years earlier. She is transformed by her love for Potter and, when she becomes pregnant, agrees to go away with him. She changes her mind when she discovers that he is married.

Canon Loftus, the priest of Glenkeel. A morose man, he blames the miseries of the world on women. He spends most of the week working on his farm, devoting little time to his parishioners. He has had a new chapel built. The villagers think it is ugly, but it conveys for him the austerity of true spirituality.

McGing, the village police sergeant. Headstrong and obstinate, with an inflated sense of his intelligence, he has waited all his life for a mystery only he can solve. Faced with the murder of Eales, he thinks of himself as Sherlock Holmes locked in a battle of wits with a wily Moriarty, but he always draws the wrong conclusions. He decides that the murderer is Rory Rua after it is too late to arrest him.

Gimp Gillespie, a reporter for the *Donegal Dispatch*. He collects news by sitting and drinking in Roarty's pub. Potter's closest companion in Glenkeel, he betrays his friend by changing sides in the conflict with Canon Loftus and by writing an article for a Dublin newspaper attacking the motives of Potter's firm.

Cor Mogaill Maloney, the village eccentric. A young Marxist, he is thought of as an intellectual because he carries copies of the *Irish Times* and a history of Ireland in his knapsack. His odd behavior includes looking up the exhaust pipes of automobiles. He is the only one to stand by Potter against the priest.

Rory Rua, Potter's landlord, a lobster fisherman. After Roarty ignores his first blackmail note, he cuts a foot off Eales's corpse and sends it to McGing. He uses his blackmail proceeds to purchase a run-down farm that Roarty has been trying to buy for years.

Eamonn Eales, Roarty's barman and victim. Secretive, sharp-tongued, and overconfident, this vagabond ladies' man from Kerry travels with two predatory black cats. Roarty regards him as the personification of evil.

Crubog, a poor elderly pensioner and owner of the farm Roarty covets. After insisting that he will never sell, he enrages the publican when he gives in to Rory Rua.

— *Michael Adams*

THE BOHEMIANS OF THE LATIN QUARTER
(Scènes de la vie de Bohème)

Author: Henri Murger (1822-1861)
First published: 1851; serial form, 1847-1849
Genre: Novel

Locale: Paris, France
Time: Early to mid-nineteenth century
Plot: Sentimental

Rodolphe (roh-DOHLF), an impoverished poet who takes up with Mimi and later writes a successful book, but who is not lucky in love.

Mimi (mee-MEE), "**La Bohème**" (boh-EHM), who becomes the mistress of Rodolphe, and briefly of Paul. She dies grieving for Rodolphe.

Alexander Schaunard (ah-lehk-SAHN-dr shoh-NAHR), a composer and portrait painter, ejected from his studio in the Latin Quarter.

Marcel (mahr-SEHL), a painter who takes over Schaunard's studio.

Mother Cadet (kah-DAY), whose rabbit stew attracts the penniless Bohemians.

Colline (koh-LEEN), a philosopher who shares his stew with Schaunard.

The Uncle of Rodolphe, who wants him to write a manual on stove-making.

Mlle Musette (mew-ZEHT-), the mistress of Marcel, and others, who gives a party for the artists.

The Councilor of State, who jilts Musette.

M. Benoit (beh-NWAH), the landlord of Rodolphe, whose room he rents to Mimi.

Momus (moh-MEWS), the owner of Cafe Momus. He is generous to artists.

Barbemuche (bahrb-MEWSH), who pays for the artists' Christmas Eve in the Café Momus.

M. Maurice (moh-REES), a temporary lover of Musette.

Viscount Paul, a lover of Mimi.

Phémie (fay-MEE), the mistress of Schaunard.

THE BOND
(Bandet)

Author: August Strindberg (1849-1912)
First published: 1893
Genre: Drama

Locale: Sweden
Time: Late nineteenth century
Plot: Social criticism

Baron Sprengel and
Baroness Sprengel, principals in a divorce case. Having agreed between themselves on terms for an amicable settlement of their difficulties, the baron and baroness go to court confident that they will divide between them the care of their child and that the details of their quarrel will not be aired in public. When the husband and wife find that it is the court and not themselves who will decide on the disposition of the child, their fears of losing him and the goading of the court cause them to become overt enemies hurling charges and counter-charges at each other. When the jury places the child in the custody of a peasant couple for a year, the baron suggests that their anguish is a judgment of God.

The judge, a young man taking the bench for the first time. Observing the bitter quarreling of the baron and baroness, he adjourns the court in despair of doing justice. He seeks help from the pastor, who advises him always to stick to the letter of the law and avoid personal involvements if he wants to keep his sanity.

The pastor, the spiritual adviser to the judge.

Alexandersson, a farmer who loses a case in which it is agreed that he is actually right but technically guilty. He later appears as a witness (probably false) against Baroness Sprengel.

Alma Jonsson, Alexandersson's servant, whom he accuses of theft. He loses the case.

THE BONDMAN

Author: Philip Massinger (1583-1640)
First published: 1624
Genre: Drama

Locale: Syracuse
Time: The fourth century B.C.E.
Plot: Tragicomedy

Pisander (pih-SAN-dur), a Theban nobleman disguised as **Marullo**, a bondman. He is diverted by his love of Cleora from taking revenge on Leosthenes, who has jilted his sister. He instigates a revolt of the slaves in the absence of the Syracusan army, his purpose being to obtain Cleora's love. His gracious and generous behavior while he is in power in the city and his fortitude in adversity win her heart. He is much given to verbal heroics.

Cleora (kleh-OH-ruh), the daughter of Archidamus, beloved by Leosthenes and Pisander. Filled with noble sentiments and rhetoric, she is angered by Leosthenes' distrust of her and vows to remain blindfolded and speechless until he returns from the war with Carthage. She becomes further angered when, after fulfilling her vow, she is still distrusted. Finally, she accepts Pisander.

Leosthenes (leh-OS-theh-neez), who formerly was contracted to Statilia. His lack of faith in Cleora and his persecution of Pisander/Marullo alienate her. When confronted with Statilia in the trial scene, he shamefacedly acknowledges her claim and gives up Cleora to Pisander.

Statilia (steh-TIH-lee-uh), Pisander's sister, in disguise as **Timandra**, Cleora's slave. She loves Leosthenes and helps her brother win Cleora for both selfish and unselfish reasons.

Archidamus (ahr-chih-DA-muhs), the praetor of Syracuse, a just and noble-hearted ruler. He dislikes Leosthenes and, after protecting his supposed slave Marullo in the trial, finally welcomes him as a son-in-law in the person of Pisander.

Timagoras (tih-MA-goh-ruhs), Cleora's hot-tempered brother, a friend of Leosthenes. His snobbish, arrogant behavior toward Pisander/Marullo and his angry abuse of his sister for favoring a slave help to strengthen Cleora's growing love.

Timoleon (ti-MOH-leh-on), a Corinthian general aiding the Syracusans against the Carthaginians. He admires Cleora for her inspirational speeches to the soldiers. Undismayed by the slaves who hold Syracuse when he returns from the war, he puts down their rebellion.

Cleon (KLEE-on), a foolish, impotent old man.

Corisca (koh-RIHS-kuh), his wanton second wife. When the army takes away the presentable male citizens, she is too snobbish to take a lover from among the slaves but too lustful to be without a lover; she therefore attempts to seduce her stepson. During the temporarily successful revolt of the slaves, in her suffering and sorrow as a slave of slaves, she acquires self-knowledge and redemption.

Asotus (eh-SOH-tuhs), Cleon's stupid, cowardly son. Left behind when the able warriors go out to battle, he mistreats the slaves and becomes enamored of his stepmother. When the slaves rebel, he is forced to play the ape with a chain around his neck.

Olympia (oh-LIHM-pee-uh), a wanton, rich widow and a friend of Corisca. So man-crazy that she has love affairs with her own slaves when other men are not available, she marries Poliphron while the slaves are in power.

Poliphron (PO-lih-fron), a slave, a friend and confidant of Marullo.

Cimbrio (SIHM-bree-oh), a slave. He becomes drunken and rowdy while the slaves have control but is terrified into submission on the return of the masters.

Gracculo (GRA-kuh-loh), a satirical slave. He makes comical remarks about Cleon, Corisca, and Asotus in asides to the audience. During the rule of the slaves, he leads Asotus around on his chain and makes him do tricks. He is a spokesman for the repentant slaves.

Zanthia (ZAN-thee-uh), Corisca's slave. She takes part in the play-acting scene that Corisca plans for the seduction of Asotus.

THE BONDS OF INTEREST
(Los intereses creados)

Author: Jacinto Benavente y Martínez (1866-1954)
First published: 1908
Genre: Drama

Locale: Italy
Time: Early seventeenth century
Plot: Comedy

Leander (lee-ahn-DEHR), a rogue with gentlemanly qualities who impersonates a rich, mysterious nobleman. Although he is in love with Silvia, he does not want to marry her under false pretenses.

Crispin (krees-PEEN), Leander's accomplice, who pretends to be his servant. He arranges Leander's marriage by playing the self-interest of one creditor against another.

Silvia Polichinelle (poh-lee-chee-NEHL-yeh), a rich young woman who convinces Leander that they are united by the greatest bond of interest, love.

Signor Polichinelle, Silvia's miserly father, who is forced to agree to the marriage and dowry.

Signora Polichinelle, Silvia's mother, who despises her husband as a vulgar tradesman.

Doña Sirena (see-REH-nah), an aristocratic but penniless widow who foresees making money for arranging Silvia's marriage.

Columbine (koh-lewm-BEE-neh), the maid and confidante of Doña Sirena. She is won over by Crispin.

An innkeeper, who is deceived by Crispin's rudeness into thinking that Leander is an important noble.

Harlequin, an impoverished poet in love with Columbine and befriended by Crispin in the name of Leander.

A captain, a down-at-the-heels rogue, also befriended by Crispin.

BONE

Author: Fae Myenne Ng (1956-   )
First published: 1993
Genre: Novel

Locale: San Francisco's Chinatown
Time: The 1960's to the 1980's
Plot: Domestic realism

Leila (Lei) Fu Louie, the narrator. A community relations specialist for a public school, Lei also is the specialist in family relations for the Leong family. She is the "First Girl," the eldest daughter of Dulcie Leong and stepdaughter of Leon Leong, Chinese immigrants who live in San Francisco's Chinatown. As the eldest daughter, she has been her parents' translator and their bridge into contemporary American society.

Dulcie (Mah) Leong, Lei's mother. She has worked most of her life as a seamstress and now owns a children's clothing store. She came to America with her first husband, Lei's father. After he deserted Dulcie and Lei, leaving to seek better opportunities in Australia, she married Leon.

Leon Leong, Lei's stepfather, a retired seaman. Leon entered the United States using false papers and a false name, which he adopted. When ashore, he worked a variety of odd jobs, unable to find anything permanent. He lost his investment in a laundry business when his partner cheated him.

Nina Leong, Lei's half sister. The "End Girl," the youngest daughter in the Leong family, Nina has rebelled against the traditional demands placed on her by her parents. She has escaped by moving across the continent to New York. Her ties to her Chinese heritage remain intact; she leads tours to Hong Kong and mainland China.

Ona Leong, Lei's half sister who recently committed suicide. Lei remembers her as the "forward-looking one," but as the "Middle Girl," Ona was stuck in the middle of family crises. She had fallen in love with the son of Leon's cheating business partner and refused to stop seeing him, despite her father's orders.

Mason Louie, Lei's husband, a car mechanic. Lei is attracted to Mason not only by his lean good looks but also by his relaxed, confident manner. He, more than any other character, seems comfortable spanning the bridge between Chinese traditions and modern American life. Lei sees him as the one person she does not have to worry about; he can take care of himself.

— *Jane Anderson Jones*

THE BONE PEOPLE

Author: Keri Hulme (1947-   )
First published: 1983
Genre: Novel

Locale: New Zealand
Time: The 1970's
Plot: Psychological realism

Kerewin Holmes, the protagonist, a painter. A large-boned woman in her thirties who likes to adorn herself with rings, she lives alone in a tower-house that she built for herself. In her desire to avoid human contact, she has cut herself off even from her own family. She is kind to Simon, however, when he appears in her Tower, and she later comes to love both him and Joe, his foster father. Through her involvement with them, she learns her own need for others. At the end of the novel, she marries Joe and establishes a real home for Simon.

Joseph (Joe) Kakaukawa Gillayley (kah-kow-KAH-wa gihl-LAY-lee), a part-Maori factory worker. A dark-skinned, broad-shouldered man in his thirties, he has a deep, musical voice and an appealing smile. Since the death of his wife, Hana, Joe has indulged in alcohol and in brutality, regularly beating his foster son, even though he loves the boy. During the course of the novel, Joe exorcises his demons and commits himself to Maori traditions, as well as to making a new family with Kerewin and Simon.

Simon P. Gillayley, a child of unknown parentage who was washed ashore from a shipwreck and adopted by Joe and his wife about three years before the time of the novel. A small, thin, sharp-featured boy of about six with a shock of blond hair, Simon cannot speak and communicates by gestures and by writing. His missing teeth and body scars are evidence of the beatings he has endured. Although he is an affectionate child, he is a compulsive thief, and he is given to fits of violence and vandalism. Despite Joe's brutality, Simon loves him deeply. After the earthquake, he runs away from a foster home to find Joe. In Kerewin, for the first time he finds a real mother.

James Piripi (Piri) Tainui (pee-ree-PEE tay-ee-NEW-ee), Joseph's cousin, a Maori. He is a thin, slight man with large, gentle brown eyes. It is he who picks up Simon from Kerewin's Tower when the boy first appears there. He and his parents are deeply concerned about Joe's abuse of Simon, but he hopes that the problem can be resolved within the family.

Marama Tainui (mah-RAH-mah), Piri's mother. A kind, elderly woman, she has deep maternal feelings for both Joe and Simon. Aware that Joe is beating Simon, she takes the child whenever she can, and she continues to urge Joe to let Simon live with her and her husband, Wherahiko. Simon confides to Kerewin that he does not want to go to Marama because she cuddles him and weeps about his father, a reminder to Simon of the brutality that he wishes to keep secret. In the celebration that ends the book, Marama is seen surrounded by all of her grandchildren, who can sleep safely beside her. Thus, she represents the ideal of the close Maori family, an ideal that will be attained by Kerewin and Joe in their new relationship.

Tiakinga Meto Mira (tee-ah-KEEN-gah MAY-toh MEE-rah), an elderly man who considers himself the keeper of the Maori faith. A brittle, shriveled man of seventy-nine, he has lived for sixty years in an isolated place by the sea, guarding the stone and the rotting canoe that mark the home of the old gods. Having inherited his charge from his grandmother, he has been waiting for his successor. When he rescues and nurses Joe after his suicide attempt, Mira realizes that Joe is that successor and passes his charge to him. Mira also tells of his encounter with Simon's father, a heroin addict, who died there. Relieved of his responsibility for the sacred place, Mira dies and is buried by Joe.

— Rosemary M. Canfield Reisman

BONECRACK

Author: Dick Francis (1920-   )
First published: 1971
Genre: Novel

Locale: Newmarket, England
Time: Late 1960's
Plot: Social morality

Neil Griffon, a financial consultant temporarily acting as head of Rowley Lodge stables. At the age of thirty-four, he is attractive and extremely intelligent. He has a highly developed business sense that has allowed him to make a small fortune of his own. He is called on to look after Rowley Lodge stables, where he grew up, after his father is in an automobile accident. His new position puts him in direct confrontation with Enso Rivera, who is obsessed with the idea of having his son Alessandro ride the favorite, Archangel, in the Derby. Despite threats from Enso, including attacks on three horses and having his own collarbone brutally smashed, he manages to avoid giving in to this unreasonable demand. Ultimately, he proves himself a success at managing the stable, and he weans Alessandro away from the insane influence of his father at great personal risk.

Alessandro Rivera, an apprentice jockey. He is young, arrogant, and completely self-centered. He decides almost as a whim that he wants to ride the favorite horse, Archangel, in the Derby, despite the fact that his only experience has been riding in a few amateur races in Europe. By using threats, his father has him taken as an apprentice at the stable where Archangel is trained. He offends everyone at the stable. It is only after his father's thugs destroy two horses that he begins to see that his own actions are unacceptable. Realizing that Alessandro really wants to be a jockey, Neil Griffon is able to teach him to be more human and, in doing so, turns his affections from his insane father. As a result of this shift in affection, Enso takes actions against Griffon that cause the death of another promising horse, his own henchmen, and himself, and ultimately leave Alessandro free to become the outstanding jockey he wants to be.

Enso Rivera, an international fence. He is aging, fat, and, as a result of syphilis, driven by an insane megalomania. Despite being extremely wealthy, he does not spend money when a threat will work as well. He believes that all he has to do is threaten Neil Griffon to ensure that his untrained son will be allowed to ride the favorite horse in the Derby. He is obsessed with the idea of giving his son anything that he wants, no matter what the cost to others. As a result of his obsession, he accidentally sets his own thugs to murder his son: Alessandro is exercising the racehorses, and Enso thinks he is another jockey. He prevents the murder by killing his own men, and in the fight with them, he is killed.

Neville Griffon, Neil's father, the owner of Rowley Lodge stables. At the time of the action, he is hospitalized with a broken leg after an automobile accident. At sixty-seven years of age, he is as cold to his son as he always has been and is convinced that Neil knows nothing about running a stable and will destroy his business. He resents it when Neil makes a success of the racing season, but father and son finally come to an uneasy truce on the subject. He dies suddenly of a pulmonary embolus without ever leaving the hospital.

Etty Craig, the head stable hand at Rowley Lodge. A woman of forty-three, she is the only female head stable hand at Newmarket, and she has held the position for six years. She values horses above humans. It is by using her knowledge and instinct for racing that Neil is able to make a success of the business. At first, she reports everything privately to Neville Griffon, but finally she realizes that Neil knows what he is doing and gives him her full support.

— *C. D. Akerley*

THE BONFIRE OF THE VANITIES

Author: Tom Wolfe (1931-   )
First published: 1987
Genre: Novel

Locale: New York City
Time: The 1980's
Plot: Social realism

Sherman McCoy, a thirty-eight-year-old Wall Street investment banker who earns a million dollars a year trading in bonds. At the peak of his career, he considers himself a "Master of the Universe." Sherman, for all his faults, is one of the entrepreneurs who bring billions of dollars into New York City to feed, clothe, and house its inhabitants. He is married and has a young daughter but maintains an adulterous relationship with a sexy Southern belle. Their affair leads to disaster when they are attacked by two teenage African Americans after they make a wrong turn off the expressway. One of the predators is seriously injured by Sherman's Mercedes while Sherman's panicked mistress is behind the wheel. The media quickly present the incident as if a wealthy white person callously left an innocent black youth to die on the pavement after running him down in his luxury car. This presentation pressures the police into making a major investigation. When Sherman is identified, he is thrown into jail with hardened criminals. He loses his job and his large income because his company is afraid of adverse publicity. He is stripped of his assets while defending himself in a first trial that is thrown out of court and a second trial that ends with a hung jury. The experience toughens him. He has always been protected by money and social status but becomes an impoverished, radical urban guerrilla fighting the justice system and the ignorant masses who are deluded by a black demagogue and the venal press. At the conclusion of the novel, the injured black teenager has died of his injuries and Sherman faces a possible sentence of up to twenty-five years if convicted of manslaughter in his third trial.

Judy McCoy, Sherman's fading wife, who knows he is having an affair and does not care. She fancies herself an artist and interior decorator and manages to keep Sherman broke by spending all of his income on furnishings and meretricious artwork. Like all the characters in the novel, Judy represents a New York type rather than a unique individual. She is a typical first wife who is discarded in favor of a younger, more glamorous woman by a husband who achieves spectacular financial success.

Maria Ruskin, Sherman's mistress, who is married to an elderly multimillionaire and is waiting for him to die. She is spoiled, selfish, and more ruthless than Sherman, who was educated in an Ivy League college and has had his mind filled with liberal ideals. Maria refuses to provide Sherman with an alibi for the night of the accident because she is afraid that her husband would divorce her if he learned she had been out late with another man.

Peter Fallow, an alcoholic English reporter for a New York scandal sheet. He exploits Sherman's case because it makes lurid reading for the ignorant masses who buy his newspaper. He cares nothing about the truth but only about selling papers and holding on to his job. He is chronically in danger of being fired because of his drinking and laziness.

The Reverend Reginald Bacon, a corrupt black minister with dubious credentials. He stages demonstrations to exploit Sherman's case for personal profit. He receives cash payoffs from the white establishment for keeping the underprivileged blacks of New York City from rioting, burning, and looting. He cares nothing about the true facts in Sherman's case but makes the injured black hoodlum seem like a martyr to white prejudice and injustice. The crafty, cynical Bacon knows that whites are not providing welfare for nonwhites out of compassion or idealism but because of their fear of violent revolution.

Lawrence Kramer, an ambitious young assistant district attorney who prosecutes Sherman in his first trial for reckless endangerment. Kramer resents the fact that Sherman earns a million dollars a year and lives in a Park Avenue condominium worth several million dollars. Kramer does not understand that part of his zeal in prosecuting Sherman is motivated by envy. He cares nothing about the facts but wants to win a legal victory and become famous through this highly publicized case.

Judge Myron Kovitsky, a feisty judge who presides over Sherman's first trial and is the only person interested in getting at the truth. He defies media and mob pressure when he throws the case out of court for violation of due process.

Thomas Killian, Sherman's streetwise defense attorney, who teaches Sherman the real facts of life and serves as a spokesman for the author, who believes that whites in America are losing their privileged position because of the influx of nonwhites and will have to learn, like Sherman McCoy, to fight for survival.

— *Bill Delaney*

BONJOUR TRISTESSE

Author: Françoise Sagan (Françoise Quoirez, 1935-   )
First published: 1954
Genre: Novel

Locale: The French Riviera and Paris
Time: A summer and early fall in the 1950's
Plot: Psychological realism

Cécile (say-SEEL), the narrator, a seventeen-year-old girl who is spending the summer in the south of France with her father and his mistress. Just prior to the vacation, she had failed her *baccalauréat*, the state exam that ends the French secondary school cycle and symbolizes a degree of social as well as academic respectability for the student who passes it.

Raymond, the narrator's father, a seductive, forty-year-old widower whose overwhelming charm appears alternately as a strength and a weakness. Cécile loves her father precisely for those qualities that lead him to manipulate, and be manipulated by, women: his emphasis on physical beauty (his own and other people's) and his constant desire to seek validation in the love and admiration of others.

Elsa Mackenbourg, Raymond's mistress, a pale, red-haired woman who lives off of her beauty. Neither a fashion model nor a prostitute, she occupies a gray area between respectability and disrepute. She clearly is the intellectual inferior of the other characters in the novel, especially Anne Larsen.

Anne Larsen, whose arrival at the summer house at the beginning of the novel sets the plot into motion. When Cécile's mother died fifteen years earlier, her father entrusted her to Anne, who was one of the mother's closest friends. As a result, Anne had an enormous impact on Cécile's early childhood, nurturing in her an admiration for cultural sophistication and understated elegance (she works in the fashion industry). She presents a physical contrast (older, darker) as well as an intellectual and spiritual contrast to Elsa.

Cyril, a twenty-six-year-old law student who initiates an innocent summer romance with Cécile, then falls in love with her. Although he is substantially older than Cécile and seduces her rather forcefully into losing her virginity, there is a strong sense that she is superior to him in many respects: more intelligent, a better strategist, and less sentimental.

— *M. Martin Guiney*

THE BOOK OF BEBB

Author: Frederick Buechner (1926-   )
First published: 1979
Genre: Novel

Locale: Florida, Texas, New York City and vicinity, and South Carolina
Time: The 1950's and 1960's
Plot: Fiction of manners

Lion Country, 1971

Antonio Parr, the narrator, in his middle thirties. Antonio and his friend Ellie Pierce gather information to expose Leo Bebb as a fraudulent promoter of religion. Antonio quickly becomes involved with the Bebb family and marries Sharon Bebb.

Leo Bebb, a heavyset, bald Southerner in his late fifties. He operates a diploma mill, called Gospel Faith College, and an ordination mill, called The Church of Holy Love, Inc., in Armadillo, Florida, and later on Red Path Ranch near Houston, Texas. Leo Bebb has all the traits of a charlatan who takes money in exchange for academic and ministerial credentials. His life is littered with scandals such as exposing himself to children, for which he served time, and exposing himself again at Herman Redpath's ordination. This latter event helped restore Herman's potency.

Sharon Bebb, the adopted daughter of Leo and Lucille Bebb. Sharon is a foulmouthed and promiscuous woman who marries Antonio Parr.

Lucille Bebb, the first wife of Leo Bebb. She accidentally killed her first child and attempted suicide out of grief. She spends most of her time trying to drown her sorrows with Tropicana drinks, made of orange juice and gin.

Laverne Brown, called **Brownie**, a former car salesman whom Leo Bebb raised from the dead and promoted to being the dean of Gospel Faith College. As Leo's loyal assistant, Brownie functions like a slavishly dutiful wife, maid, and colleague. Brownie's B.D., S.T.M., Th.D., and D.D. degrees are all from his own correspondence college.

Miriam Blaine, the twin sister of Antonio Parr, the former wife of Charlie Blaine, and the mother of Chris and Tony Blaine. She suffers from myeloma, a cancer of the bone that takes her life.

Charlie Blaine, the hypochondriac former husband of Miriam Blaine who cannot bear to see her before her death and eventually leaves her sons with Antonio and Sharon.

Tony Blaine, the youngest son of Charlie and Miriam Blaine. Tony, along with Chris, comes to live with Antonio and Sharon.

Chris Blaine, the studious elder son of Charlie and Miriam Blaine. He later helps take care of his cousin, Billy, while Sharon and Antonio busy themselves with their careers.

Open Heart, 1972

Antonio Parr, who learns through the deaths of Herman Redpath and Lucille Bebb that Leo Bebb is imperfect but nevertheless changes some people's lives, including Antonio's. Antonio also struggles with the infidelity of his wife.

Sharon Bebb, who gives birth to Billy, her first child. She takes up yoga and has her first affair, with Antonio's nephew, Tony Blaine.

Leo Bebb, who leaves the work of Gospel Faith College and The Church of Holy Love to Brownie following Herman Redpath's death. Leo then starts Open Heart near Stamford, Connecticut. This church proves to be a dismal failure.

Lucille Bebb, who slashes her wrists again out of frustra-tion over all the things she knows about Leo but must keep secret. Her suicide occurs in Texas, away from all family. Only Brownie is with her in the end.

Clarence Golden, a three-hundred-pound former convict who served five years in prison as the cell mate of Leo Bebb. Clarence keeps showing up in Leo's life and appears at Open Heart. He is sometimes described as a man from a flying saucer or as an angel.

Gertrude Conover, the wealthy second wife of Leo Bebb. She is a Theosophist in her late seventies. She claims she has known Bebb in many previous incarnations.

Love Feast, 1974

Antonio Parr, who travels to Europe with Sharon Parr, Leo Bebb, and Gertrude Conover in an effort to escape the failings in Antonio's marriage and at Open Heart. Antonio later sepa-rates from Sharon and has a brief affair with Laura Fleischman, who ironically later marries Tony Blaine.

Sharon Parr, who with Anita Steen opens a health food store called the Sharanita Shop. Anita's lesbian tendencies worry Antonio, and his fight with Sharon about Anita leads to a time of separation. During this time, Sharon has another affair with Tony Blaine, who is the probable father of her second child, Lucille.

Leo Bebb, who returns from Europe to find that Open Heart has burned down. He starts a new work, an event involv-ing eating, drinking, and preaching called Love Feast, in Princeton, New Jersey. He makes one prominent convert, Nancy Oglethorpe, who assists Leo and Gertrude Conover. Leo gets in trouble with the Internal Revenue Service for tax evasion and enlists the help of Clarence Golden. The plane in which they try to escape burns and crashes, but no trace is found of their bodies.

Treasure Hunt, 1977

Antonio Parr, who joins Sharon Parr and Gertrude Conover in a search for Leo Bebb's childhood home in Poin-sett, South Carolina. They discover who Sharon's real parents are and inherit Leo's home. Because Gertrude claims to have found Leo's reincarnation in a blind baby named Jimmy Bob Luby, the Parrs give Leo's home to the poor Luby family. Antonio grows to appreciate Leo as a kind of saint for the way he changes lives for the good.

Babe Bebb, the twin brother of Leo Bebb who rejects his Baptist heritage and operates a place called Uforium that ad-vocates escaping Earth aboard a flying saucer. Like Leo, Babe has perverse tendencies. At night, he roams around Poinsett, South Carolina, doing all kinds of mischief while wearing his wife's wig and dress so that he can spoil her reputation and thereby get even with her for her affair with Leo Bebb.

Bertha (Bert) Bebb, the wife of Babe and the actual mother of Sharon Bebb by her brother-in-law, Leo Bebb. She lost her hair as a result of an experiment conducted by her husband.

Laverne Brown, who loses his faith in what Bebb taught him and instead adopts the teachings of Babe Bebb about life-rays, aliens, and UFOs. He dies in a scuffle with Babe Bebb.

— Daven M. Kari

A BOOK OF COMMON PRAYER

Author: Joan Didion (1934-   )
First published: 1977
Genre: Novel

Locale: Boca Grande, a mythical Central American country
Time: The 1960's
Plot: Parable

Charlotte Douglas, the protagonist. She is an attractive, upper-middle-class woman aged forty who was born in Hollis-ter, California. She is a Westerner, like many of Didion's characters. She spent two years at the University of California, Berkeley, where she met and married Warren Bogart, a non-tenured English instructor. He is the father of her older daugh-ter, Marin. After a divorce, she married her second husband, Leonard Douglas. She has a second daughter late in life. The baby is born with severe health problems and dies on the journey to Boca Grande.

Grace Strasser-Mendana, the narrator. She is a sixty-three-year-old anthropologist who has married into one of Boca Grande's few solvent families. Her husband's death left her in control of most of the arable land and thus in virtual control of decisions affecting the country. She is dying of pancreatic cancer.

Leonard Douglas, Charlotte's second and current husband. He is a prominent San Francisco attorney who specializes in defending radical causes. She leaves him to travel with her first husband, who seems to need her more than does the calm and self-assured Leonard.

Warren Bogart, Charlotte's first husband. He is a charm-ing and sadistic former English instructor whom Charlotte marries, has a child with, and divorces. He is dying and needs

Charlotte, so she travels with him to New Orleans.

Marin Bogart, the daughter of Charlotte and Warren Bogart. Although a minor character in the novel, she plays an important role in her mother's story by deeply affecting her mother's emotional life. Marin comes from a relatively con-ventional, upper-middle-class background and appears to be a rather ordinary teenager. She is strongly reminiscent of Patricia Hearst of the time period of the novel.

— *Betty Alldredge*

THE BOOK OF LAUGHTER AND FORGETTING
(Le Livre du rire et de l'oubli)

Author: Milan Kundera (1929-   )
First published: 1979
Genre: Novel

Locale: Czechoslovakia and France
Time: 1948 through the 1970's
Plot: Political

Milan Kundera (mee-LAHN kewn-DEH-rah), who acts as the narrator. He comments freely about the act of writing, about his own life, about his characters—some of whom are based on real people and some of whom are frankly imaginary—and about the history and fate of his native country, Czechoslovakia.

Mirek (MEE-rehk), a well-known intellectual and television personality, actively involved in the Prague Spring reforms, a campaign of openness, relative freedom, and rich cultural activity initiated in response to long years of Communist oppression in Czechoslovakia. With the invasion in 1968 of Russian tanks and 500,000 Russian troops, the Prague Spring was crushed. Some half a million supporters of the Prague Spring—Mirek among them—are pushed out of their jobs or arrested, and some 120,000 Czechs leave the country as exiles. As the novel opens, Mirek is attempting to recover his youthful love letters, which he wrote to Zdena, who is now, as always, a fervent supporter of Communist rule and the Russian state. Returning from his unsuccessful attempt to recover the letters, Mirek is arrested in his apartment. He, his son, and many of his friends are put on trial and imprisoned for antistate activities.

Zdena, who twenty-five years previously was Mirek's lover. An ugly woman, Zdena has never forgiven Mirek for leaving her and has transformed her unrequited love into an unwavering political loyalty to the state and the Central Committee of the Communist Party.

Karel, who is married to Marketa. He has long lived by the slogan, "As far from Mother as possible." Now that his father has died and his mother is old and alone, however, he feels pangs of guilt and so invites her for a week's visit. Dissatisfied with the sexual restrictions attendant on monogamy, Karel develops a sexual relationship with Eva and convinces her to befriend his wife, Marketa. As the story opens, Marketa has invited Eva for a visit that coincides with that of Mother, who overstays her welcome.

Marketa, Karel's devoted but jealous wife. She has invited Eva, whom she believes she met first and introduced to her husband, to spend the day with her and Karel. A *ménage à trois* ensues.

Mother, an old woman who has trouble keeping her memories straight. Asked to stay only until Saturday, she pretends to have misunderstood and stays until Monday and thus is present for Eva's visit and for some strange goings-on.

Eva, a tall, slender, and sexually adventurous young woman, interested only in friendship and sensuality.

Madame Raphael, a teacher of a summer-school course for foreigners in a small town on the Riviera. She has asked her students to present an analysis of Eugène Ionesco's play *Rhinoceros*.

Gabrielle and

Michelle, American students in Madame Raphael's class. For comic effect, they dress up as rhinoceroses, wearing cardboard cones on their noses as they present their analysis.

R., a shy, delicate, and intelligent editor of an illustrated Prague weekly for young people. She has asked Milan Kundera, who has lost the privilege of working after the Russian occupation, to write an astrology column under a pseudonym. Interrogated by the secret police and compelled to reveal Kundera's identity, she warns him, and he leaves the country.

Tamina, a thirty-three-year-old widow who works as a waitress in a small café in a small Western European town. A Czech exile, she tries to recover memories of her dead husband, who was fired from his job after the Russian invasion. Denounced and slandered after leaving the country, Tamina's husband dies. Unable to return to Czechoslovakia, Tamina tries unsuccessfully to have her cruel mother-in-law in Prague send her old love letters and notebooks.

Hugo, a café regular, a young writer with bad breath who has published only one article. He tries repeatedly but unsuccessfully to impress Tamina, whose mind seems always to be elsewhere.

The student, a young, romantic, and sexually frustrated young poet and student of poetry who conceives a passion for a butcher's wife. Inviting her to spend the night in his Prague attic apartment, the student learns that he in turn has been invited the same night to the Writers' Club, where the country's best poets will meet. Faced with this painful dilemma, he tries to work out a compromise.

Krystyna (krih-STEE-nah), a woman in her thirties, a butcher's wife who has occasional extramarital encounters with a mechanic. Swept off her feet by the charmingly shy student, Krystyna agrees to meet him in Prague.

Voltaire (vohl-TAYR),
Goethe (GUH-tuh),
Lermontov (LYAYR-mon-tof),
Yesenin (yihs-YAYN-yihn),
Petrarch (PEE-trahrk),
Boccaccio (bohk-KOT-choh), and
Verlaine (vehr-LEHN), the names ironically given to the famous poets who argue about women and poetry as they get drunk at the Writers' Club in Prague.

Raphael, an angel who guides Tamina to a boat that takes her to a children's island.

Edwige, the frankly sexual, feminist lover of Jan.

Jan, a forty-five-year-old man who is leaving the country. Before he goes, he wishes to explore the borders of sexuality; he finds sexuality without borders to cross exhausting.

Passer, a tenacious lover of life and of humankind. He is terminally ill but is a table-pounding optimist to the end.

Barbara, a middle-aged woman who presides impatiently at the orgies she throws at her home for twenty or so invited guests.

— Michael Zeitlin

THE BOOK OF LIGHTS

Author: Chaim Potok (1929-   )
First published: 1981
Genre: Novel

Locale: Brooklyn, Manhattan, Boston, Philadelphia, Korea, Japan, and Jerusalem
Time: 1950-1957
Plot: Psychological realism

Gershon Loran, the protagonist, a Jewish chaplain in Korea and a student of Cabala (Jewish mysticism). A shy and melancholy man, unkempt and poorly groomed before his metamorphosis in Korea, he is given to having visions and other mystical experiences. Gershon has a brilliant mind, a fact clear to nearly everyone but himself. His life seems random to him, made up mostly of unlucky chances, and he faces it numbly and without enthusiasm, never really knowing what he wants to do. Keter and Malkuson both want Gershon as a disciple; Keter wins him because Malkuson's Talmud and Bible hold little mystery for Gershon, and Keter sees life as mostly mysterious, mostly posing unpleasant and unanswerable questions. Gershon's unexpected common sense and his willingness to face and accept the dark side of life make him a good chaplain in Korea and a good friend to Arthur Leiden, though Gershon typically does not recognize his own goodness. His successes never remove from him the sense he has throughout the story that he is always waiting.

Arthur Leiden, Gershon's roommate at the Riverside Hebrew Institute and fellow chaplain in Korea, a suave and handsome Bostonian. Arthur's life is dominated by an obsession with his father's role (and, by extension, the role of the Jewish people) in the development of the atomic bomb. His sense of guilt and his wish to atone for it drive him to Korea, whence he can visit Japan. In particular, he wants to see Kyoto, which his mother (an art historian) was instrumental in saving from bombing, and Hiroshima, which his father (a physicist) was instrumental in destroying. Formerly a gifted physics student at Harvard, Arthur has turned to religion out of fear; he sees it as safer than science and as less likely to destroy the world. Emotionally very unstable throughout the novel, Arthur dies in a plane crash while trying to return to Japan. A letter from Arthur received by his parents after his death reveals that he has learned acceptance and new hope from his association with Gershon.

Jakob Keter, a visiting professor of Cabala at the Riverside Hebrew Institute and Gershon's mentor. At fifty-five years of age, Keter is tall, trim, and bald, with a long face, bright eyes, and a humorless teaching style; his typical dress is a dark suit and a red bow tie. Having contemplated a career in mathematics or physics when a young man, Keter has given himself instead to the scientific study of Cabala, because he believes it to be the soul of Judaism.

Nathan Malkuson, a great scholar and Gershon's Talmud professor at the Riverside Hebrew Institute. In his fifties, Malkuson is of medium height, with cold eyes and a disdainful smile. Malkuson considers Cabala foolishness and wants Gershon to become a Talmudist because Talmud, the law, is the mind of Judaism, its rational meaning. After Arthur's death and Gershon's return to New York, Malkuson is Gershon's spiritual adviser.

Karen Levin, Gershon's girlfriend. Karen, who has no illusions about her looks, has single-mindedly devoted her life to academic pursuits. She earns a Ph.D. in philosophy from Columbia and teaches at Barnard and the University of Chicago. She would like to marry Gershon but is prevented by his uncertainty about his own life.

Roger Tat, Gershon's first assistant in Korea. Roger's passions are music and his girlfriend back home. Although urged by Gabriel Rosen to find a Jewish assistant, Gershon keeps Roger, a Mormon, and finds him intelligent, efficient, and forethoughtful. Like John Meron, Roger is a significant non-Jew in Gershon's life, helping him avoid the closed-mindedness he so hates in Gabriel Rosen.

John Meron, an electrical engineer, Gershon's Roman Catholic roommate at the engineering battalion. John finds in Gershon a good friend and travels with him to Japan.

Gabriel Rosen, a Jewish medic, Gershon's assistant after Roger leaves Korea. To Gershon, Gabriel represents "road map" religion, "the smug superiority of those certain of salvation." Gershon dislikes Gabriel and what he represents.

Toshie, a young Japanese woman, a geisha, black-haired and beautiful, whom Gershon meets and befriends in a Tokyo club. Toshie acts as translator for Gershon and Arthur on their tour of Japan, which culminates in Hiroshima. In spite of Gershon's carefully platonic arrangements with Toshie, she is upset by a situation wherein she cannot physically repay his kindness to her. Arthur asks Toshie's forgiveness for his family's role in developing the atomic bomb.

— Jonathan A. Glenn

THE BOOK OF THE COURTIER
(Il libro del cortegiano)

Author: Baldassare Castiglione (1478-1529)
First published: 1528
Genre: Novel

Locale: Italy
Time: March, 1507
Plot: Didactic

Lady Elisabeta Gonzaga (eh-leez-ah-BEHT-ah gon-ZAH-gah), who became duchess of Urbino when she married Duke Guidobaldo in 1488. She organizes the activities at her court during four evenings in March, 1507; discussions begin and end when she says so. Although her husband is on his death-bed and they have no children, she is a gracious hostess, idealized as the model of female virtue and paid many compliments.

Lady Emilia Pia (PEE-ah), the widow of the duke's illegitimate brother and the confidante of the duchess. She is the first to speak in defense of women and has the shrewdest tongue of all the women present.

Count Lewis (Ludovico) of Canossa, a relative and friend of the author. A diplomat visiting Urbino, he leads the discussion on the first evening, during which he and others try to determine the qualities and speech of the ideal courtier.

Sir Frederick (Federico) Fregoso, a courtier, soldier, and diplomat; brother of Lord Octavian. A student of languages and the friend of literary figures such as the author, he leads the discussion on the second evening, explaining how a courtier should behave and speak.

Lord Octavian Fregoso, a native of Genoa, where he was elected doge in 1513. Living in temporary exile at Urbino, he leads the fourth evening's debate about the relationship of the courtier to the prince and about the ideal form of government.

Lord Julian (Giuliano) de Medicis (MEH-dee-chees), the youngest child of Lorenzo de Medici. Like Lord Octavian, he is living in temporary exile at Urbino. He is asked to begin the discussion on the third evening. His subject is the ideal woman at court but extends to the relative merits of women in general. He takes a "separate but equal" view of men and women,

wanting to be manly and women to be womanly and seeing equal potential for virtue in both.

Bernard Bibiena (bee-bee-EH-nah), a courtier (whose true name is **Bernardo Dovizi**) in the service of Lord Julian's older brother Giovanni de Medici (soon to become Pope Leo X). He is a writer and a friend of the author as well as a patron of Raphael. A great wit, he serves as an authority on humor during the discussion on the second evening, telling many funny stories.

Gaspar Pallavicin (pahl-lah-vee-cheen), or **Pallavacino Gaspare**, a native of Lombardy. He is young and sickly. He is the cynic in the group and is especially cynical about women. His comments on the second evening lead to a delightful exchange with Lady Emilia and to the decision that the third evening should be devoted to the qualities desirable in a woman at court. He does not change his opinion, but his opinions are pushed so far to the side that he hardly dares to speak after the third evening.

Pietro Bembo (pee-EH-troh), a poet and courtier associated with the courtly circle at Urbino from 1506 until 1512. Bembo admires the literary style of Petrarch and Boccaccio and delivers the most famous speech in the text. As the fourth evening draws to an end, he describes the ideal of Platonic love.

Francesco Maria della Rovere (roh-VEH-reh), who was appointed prefect of Rome in 1504. He ruled Urbino as a papal fief from 1508, when Duke Guidobaldo died, until 1516, when driven out by the troops of Pope Leo X. He was the author's patron during these years and is described in kind terms, though he does not have a major role in the text.

— *Thomas Willard*

BOOK OF THE DUCHESS

Author: Geoffrey Chaucer (c. 1343-1400)
First published: c. 1370
Genre: Poetry

Locale: Idealized dream landscape
Time: Indeterminate
Plot: Allegory

Dreamer, the narrator. He is dying over the loss—whether through death or through rejection—of his beloved lady. His lovesickness has led to sleeplessness and despair, and he seems unable to imagine any hope. Longing for sleep leads him to reading about loss of love through death, and this in turn leads to a dream in which he confronts that loss. Variously interpreted as naïve and bumbling, inept, or psychologically astute, the Dreamer must come to the point where he can state baldly the nature of his loss and accept that. This he does by taking on the role of a comforter.

The Black Knight, possibly an idealized version of John of Gaunt. He is a representation of the Dreamer's own psychological state. He is young, about twenty-four years old, with few hairs in his beard. His entire life has been given to the service of love, and it has not been an easy service for him. For a long time, he was so fearful of rejection that he only made up songs about his beloved; when he finally did approach her, he was indeed rejected, leading to terrible sorrow for a year. After a time, his beloved perceives his virtue, loyalty, and faithfulness and accepts him. Her death leaves him disconsolate. Some see in him a kind of unreasoning passion that is unproductive in that it leads only to death, the same situation in

which the narrator finds himself in the beginning of the poem.

White, whose name probably is a pun on the name Blanche, the duchess of Lancaster, whose death the poem probably is meant to commemorate. She is portrayed as the ideal lady, the perfect beloved, in both physical and spiritual senses. She is first discovered dancing on a green sward. The Black Knight is struck by her beauty; nature seemingly has made her perfect, with golden hair, laughing eyes, a wondrous visage, and fine and bright skin. Everything about her is perfect in its moderation, for she is long but not overly long, and plump and round but not overly large. Her language is gentle, her joy in life such that dullness is afraid of her, her manner comely and merry. Faithful, good, and marked by understanding, she is the archetypal image of the beloved lady who is the end of the lover's quest.

Alcyon, the queen, the bereft lover about whom the Dreamer reads. She is in the position of John of Gaunt, for her spouse has died. She also is in the position of the Dreamer, in that she is suffering from loss and cannot sleep. Her despair at learning of her husband's death is so extreme that it leads to her own death, a tragedy that is not the course the Dreamer seems to take at the end of the poem.

Ceyx, the king who drowns. He is a flat, undeveloped character who seems to have been the ideal husband. Like White, he does not need to be developed as much as he needs

to be idealized, for it is his loss that spurs the action of Alcyon's story.

— Gary D. Schmidt

THE BOOK OF THE LADIES
(Le Livre de la cité des dames)

Author: Christine de Pizan (c. 1365-c. 1430)
First published: 1405
Genre: Novel

Locale: Paris and the allegorical City of Ladies
Time: Early fifteenth century
Plot: Allegory

Christine de Pizan (pee-ZAWN), the narrator. Christine establishes herself as the author by placing herself in her study reading. She initiates the allegorical narrative by describing how three personified figures appear to help her construct the City of Ladies. The questions that Christine poses to her allegorical guides structure the work and connect the stories of women's lives. Christine ensures that her presence as author receives emphasis by her repetition of the phrase "I, Christine" as she takes up a new question or topic. Although Christine's authorial stance is a strong element, she reveals little about her personality or character in a direct manner. Indirectly, however, the reader learns about Christine's studious habits, her relationship with her mother, her connections to French courtly circles, and her interests in women's issues. Most important, Christine's insertion of her name continuously reinforces her gender and thus her distinctiveness as a female author.

Lady Reason, Christine's first allegorical guide. As Christine contemplates how women have been maligned by the misogynistic attitudes of male authors, a vision of three ladies appears to her. These allegorical personifications are all female because in Latin the gender of the abstract words that they embody is feminine. The only indications about their physical appearance are that they wear crowns and that their faces shine with a brightness that illuminates the room. Reason speaks first to Christine. Reason indicates that she holds a mirror instead of a scepter as an aid to achieving self-knowledge. As with the other two guides, the primary knowledge about Reason's character and purpose is derived from her comments and speeches to Christine. Reason repre-

sents the reasonable. She presents logical arguments against the misogynistic viewpoints advanced by men. The foundations that she helps Christine lay for the City of Ladies are built with the contributions of women in specific realms of knowledge such as the arts and sciences.

Lady Rectitude, the second allegorical guide. When Reason finishes introducing herself to Christine, Lady Rectitude explains her presence. Her attribute is a ruler that separates right from wrong. She explains that she encourages people to follow the path of correct behavior and truth and to defend the rights of the oppressed and the innocent. The ruler, with its capacity for measurement, also reinforces the image of building the city. She is Christine's guide for the second book of the City of the Ladies. Rectitude is a more unusual allegorical figure. She is an advocate for female virtues that are unique to women and thus outside the areas of men's activity. She emphasizes women's prophetic powers, their faithfulness and devotion to their husbands and families, and their nurturing abilities.

Lady Justice, the third allegorical guide. Justice holds a golden vessel as her attribute; it signifies how she measures out the just rewards or punishments to individuals according to their behavior. Justice guides Christine in the third book, in which she fills the high towers of the city with the Virgin and female saints. Their sacrifices for God have earned them the ultimate reward that Justice can dispense: They have been accorded sainthood in heaven. Of the three allegorical figures, Justice is the most remote and ethereal.

— Karen Gould

THE BOOK OF THESEUS
(Teseida)

Author: Giovanni Boccaccio (1313-1375)
First published: c. 1340-1341 (English translation, 1974)
Genre: Novel

Locale: Athens
Time: Antiquity
Plot: Romance

Theseus (THEE-see-uhs), the political ruler of Athens. The episodes in which Theseus is the primary actor are limited to books 1 and 2, in which he goes to war. He marches first against the Amazons in Scythia and then Creon in Thebes. In both instances, he proceeds with the confidence of self-righteousness in his mission against indignities and inhumanities that others had suffered. He demonstrates against Hippolyta, queen of the Amazons, that he enjoys the power to subdue her forces regardless of how valiantly they fight. To Creon, he proves that cruel tyranny can never endure the

sword of one in favor of the gods. These two episodes establish Theseus as an ideal model of the chivalric knight of the Middle Ages, one who exhibits a combination of personal valor earned in military battle and beneficent wisdom granted toward his enemies. Throughout the remainder of the epic, Theseus serves as the standard of honorable behavior by which to judge the actions of the other figures, and he presides over the unfolding of subsequent episodes involving those others.

Arcites, a former enemy of Theseus who fights at Thebes and is taken prisoner. He is one of the two principal antagonists. Arcites is a noble youth who proves his personal valor in military battle at Thebes. As a captured enemy, he is returned to Athens and imprisoned, where he first sees and falls in love with Emilia. The majority of the epic revolves around his quest to win her against similar designs by Palaemon, his competitor as a suitor. Their subsequent contests with each other symbolize conflict between reason and passion. Arcites, owing tribute to Mars, the god of war and personal mental straightness, represents reason. He seeks to contain the competition with his friend within the bounds of civility. He wins the joust to determine who should marry Emilia but is mortally wounded.

Palaemon (PAL-uh-mon), another soldier who fights against Theseus at Thebes and is captured. He also proves his personal qualities on the battlefield of Thebes. He endures prison alongside Arcites and even longer. He is able to escape, but rather than flee the country, he seeks out Arcites in order to fight for Emilia, with whom he, too, has fallen in love. In the ensuing contests, he represents passion. Venus, the goddess of love and sensual appetite, is the one to whom he prays for support. His quest for Emilia's heart is more obsessive than Arcites', though no deeper in intensity. He loses the joust with his friend, but with Arcites mortally

wounded, he follows Arcites' expressed wish that he should marry Emilia.

Emilia, the daughter of Hippolyta. Upon Theseus' conquering of her realm and marriage of her mother, she journeys to Athens with them. While living there, she attracts the interest of Arcites and Palaemon, both of whom fall in love with her. For most of the epic, she serves as the object of their desire and motive for their actions. Arcites and Palaemon, each in his own way, seek to win her heart. Emilia reflects the typical woman of romance epics. Her identity comes in alliance with male characters; she has very little voice of her own as either a figure in the story or through narration. For example, she is unable to form a preference for whom she might desire as a husband. She is won by Arcites but, because of his mortal wounds, marries Palaemon.

Hippolyta (hih-POL-ih-tuh), queen of the Amazons. Chosen as leader by her people, she demonstrates her personal courage in battling Theseus. She also allows her reason to take precedence over her passions by deciding to surrender and to trust Theseus' good intentions rather than to continue the contest beyond the point of hope for victory. She marries Theseus.

— *Alan Cottrell*

BORDERLINE

Author: Janette Turner Hospital (1942-   )
First published: 1985
Genre: Novel

Locale: Boston, Montreal, and places between
Time: The 1980's
Plot: Surrealism

Felicity, an art historian and curator of a private gallery in Boston. Strikingly beautiful, with cornsilk hair and slightly uneven eyes, the thirty-three-year-old Felicity has been a magnet for danger and confusion all of her life. She longs for her dead father, avoids committed relationships, and collects newspaper clippings that confirm her suspicion that reality and unreality are never far apart. She is not easily surprised. When she and Gus stumble upon Dolores Marquez, a Salvadoran refugee, hidden in a carcass of beef, they instinctively help her get across the border. This act brings Felicity into the center of an international intrigue, as mysterious figures on both sides try to locate the refugee. As she tries to cope with being stalked, having her apartment ransacked and her car disabled, and answering conflicting pleas for help, Felicity thinks through her own past and tries to find sense in it. Because she always has been imaginative and introspective, no one takes her story seriously until she disappears.

Augustine (Gus) Kelly, a traveling insurance salesman from Ontario. A middle-aged Catholic with thinning hair and four daughters, Gus drinks too much, talks too much when he is drunk, and is habitually unfaithful to his wife. After he and Felicity smuggle Dolores Marquez over the border, Gus's guilt over his unfaithfulness, his lack of success in business, and his failure to rescue Dolores take over, and he has drunken visions merging imagery of his wife, Dolores, the Virgin Mary, and various saints. Gus's wife mistakes frantic telephone calls from Felicity for calls from a mistress and leaves him. Attempting to contact Felicity, Gus calls Jean-Marc and tells him what he knows of Dolores. To rescue Dolores and save his

marriage, Gus rents a room in Montreal, where he drinks constantly and eventually finds Dolores again. Trying to take her to safety, he is killed, leaving a large insurance settlement for his family.

Jean-Marc Seymour, the narrator, the son of Felicity's former lover. Jean-Marc has hated his father since he was ten years old and yearned for Felicity in a way that none of them understands. He and Felicity have confided in each other and relied on each other, and it is to him that she turns when danger nears. The twenty-five-year-old homosexual piano tuner casts doubt on the story even as he tells it: He admits that he cannot remember the sequence of events, he tells himself different versions of what may have happened, and he raises the possibility that he has imagined the entire thing. Trying to piece together the parts that he can remember (for he never really believed Felicity's story) a year after Felicity has disappeared, he also works through his relationship with his father.

Dolores Marquez, a Salvadoran refugee known also as **La Salvadora**, **La Desconocida**, and **La Magdalena**. She has the face of Perugino's fifteenth century painting, the *Magdalena*, with high cheekbones, long dark hair, and dark brown eyes. This widow of a Salvadoran guerrilla is suspected by both the guerrillas and the government of being a spy. She has suffered the murder of her husband and the death of a child born while she was fleeing her homeland. Dolores is either a victim of oppression whose strongest loyalties are to her mother and two surviving children, or a violent player in a deadly struggle—or both.

— *Cynthia A. Bily*

BORIS GODUNOV

Author: Alexander Pushkin (1799-1837)
First published: 1831
Genre: Drama

Locale: Russia
Time: 1598-1605
Plot: Historical

Boris Godunov (boh-RIHS goh-do-NOHF), a privy counselor who manages to have Tsarevitch Dimitry assassinated without having to take the blame for the murder. As the new czar, Godunov exacts strict obedience from his subordinates, treats the masses cruelly, and puts down ruthlessly any attempt to unseat him. While engaged in a war against a pretender, he is suddenly taken ill and dies, naming his son the new czar before his demise.

Grigory Otrepyev (grih-GOH-rihy oht-REH-pyehf), a young monk turned rebel who pretends he is the late Dimitry. He marshals armies in Poland and, eventually, marches against Godunov. The struggle is bitter, and Grigory, finally triumphant, is disturbed because the populace stands silent when asked to acclaim him.

Basmanov (bahs-MAH-nof), a general interested in military victory, not political complexities. First, he supports Godunov's son as czar; then, persuaded by Pushkin, a Grigory supporter, he leads his troops over to the other side. It is

Basmanov's defection that spells victory for Grigory.

Maryna (mah-RIH-nuh), a girl who holds Grigory's army idle in Poland because Grigory, having fallen in love with her, is loathe to give the order to advance against Godunov. Maryna, although repelled because Grigory is only an unfrocked priest and not Dimitry, as he claims to be, still consents to become Grigory's wife if his armies overthrow Godunov.

Feodor (feh-O-dohr), Godunov's son, who is czar for a short time before, according to the Grigory followers who last saw him, he takes poison.

Pushkin (POOSH-kihn), a Grigory supporter who persuades Basmanov to defect to the pretender's side and who, making a violent speech in the great square, inflames the people against Godunov.

Father Pimen, an old monk, formerly a soldier, who counsels Grigory to put worldly ambitions out of his thoughts.

BORN BROTHERS

Author: Larry Woiwode (1941-   )
First published: 1988
Genre: Novel

Locale: Hyatt, North Dakota; Pettibone, Illinois; and New York City
Time: The 1940's through the 1980's
Plot: Family

Charles Neumiller, the narrator, whose recollections of his youth record a Neumiller family history. He is an alcoholic whose marriage has ended, and his life is a shambles. In his spiritual agony, he admits his loss and readiness for death as he writes his memoirs for his beloved brother Jerome, to whom the title refers. Although the Neumiller family is poor, his remembrances of his childhood in North Dakota are generally happy, the one dark cloud being his mother Alpha's fears that he is too headstrong. A family move to Illinois sets the stage for tragedy. Alpha dies in childbirth. When the boys are in high school, Charles and Jerome's father, Martin, becomes critically ill. Charles is seriously injured in an automobile accident, and Jerome remains steadfast in his devotion to Charles during his long recovery period. In the throes of his blooming sexuality and despite his father's warnings, Charles becomes sexually involved with Bobbi Gilette, who is devastated when he drops her. When Jerome goes off to college, Charles pursues his interest in drama and discovers a talent for writing. He wins a state competition for an original monologue. He follows Jerome to college. His relationship with Rick Purkeet, a homosexual friend, and his romance with Jill Jarvis contribute to his development of a destructive drinking problem. Jill's advances to Jerome lead to the brothers' first real schism. When Jerome goes on to medical school, a rudderless Charles leaves college. Naturally gifted, he builds a successful radio career in New York City, marries Katherine, and has a family. Unable to control his alcoholism, he loses everything but Jerome's love. Hopeless, Charles attempts suicide.

Jerome Neumiller, the oldest child of Alpha and Martin Neumiller, eighteen months older than Charles. Jerome is, from adolescence, a more mature and thoughtful person than his brother. He is the driver of the automobile in which Charles is severely injured. Jerome helps care for and provides strong moral support for his brother. Hardworking and less outgoing than his younger brother, Jerome becomes a doctor, marries, and cares for their aging father until his death.

Martin Neumiller, the husband of Alpha and father of the five Neumiller children. Most of his life is spent as an educator. A devout Catholic, he struggles to support his family. After Alpha's death, he tries to care for the children and provide good advice, which Charles sometimes fails to accept. His interests in drama and coaching forensics influence the boys to participate in public speaking events. Strong and dependable, he attempts to guide his sons through the turbulent days of adolescence. His death is a time of crisis for Charles, who cannot control his addiction.

Alpha Neumiller, Martin's wife. A devoted mother, she is a strict disciplinarian in bringing up her children. With little money and the demands of rearing a large family, her health suffers. A sixth pregnancy, resulting in uremic poisoning, ends her life.

Bobbi Gilette, Charles's high school girlfriend. Their increasing sexual exploration frightens him into cutting off their relationship. Hurt and angry, she leaves school.

Rick Purkeet, a college friend of Jerome and Charles. A homosexual, he makes advances to Charles, who, angered, accuses him of encouraging his drinking.

Jill Jarvis, Charles's girlfriend in college. Immature and demanding, she teases Charles and keeps him agitated and unhappy. When he finds her with Jerome, Charles feels he has been betrayed. His faith in Jerome is dealt a harsh blow.

Katherine Neumiller, Charles's wife and mother of his two children. She loves him but becomes increasingly disillusioned when he continues his heavy drinking. Although they attempt a reconciliation after the death of his father, their marriage ends in divorce.

— *Inez L. Ramsey*

BORN IN CAPTIVITY

Author: John Wain (1925-1994)
First published: 1953
Genre: Novel

Locale: Various English towns and a Sussex country estate
Time: Late 1940's
Plot: Comic realism

Charles Lumley, a job seeker. A young man in his twenties whose appearance is as unimpressive as his university degree, Lumley has no money and no idea what to do with his life. Highly imaginative, he often defends himself by making up outlandish tales. At other times, when pressed, he abandons his usual apologetic manner and gentlemanly self-effacement to become verbally abusive or physically violent. In his attempt to avoid living up to his parents' expectations, he takes jobs as a window washer, a driver, a hospital orderly, a bouncer, and a chauffeur before finally becoming a radio gag writer and, despite his best intentions, a financial success.

George Hutchins, a university fellow. In his early twenties, he has a heavy build and a ruddy complexion. Hardworking, humorless, and ambitious, he is ashamed of his working-class parents. To distance himself from his background, he has imitated his professors, acquiring an upper-class accent, a pipe, and the affectation of modesty. His encounters with Lumley always prove disastrous. When he appears at the Braceweight estate as a tutor, he causes an accident that costs Lumley his job as chauffeur. Later, angry because of some harmless prank telegrams, he frames Lumley for theft.

Veronica Roderick, who sometimes calls herself **Moll Flanders**, Lumley's beloved. A small brunette in her twenties, she pretends to be the niece of her lover, a wealthy businessman. Because of his love for her and his need for money, Charles gets into drug smuggling. Later, even though Veronica has returned to her keeper, Charles's memory of her keeps him from proceeding with his wedding plans. When he becomes prosperous, Veronica comes back into his life.

Edwin Froulish, a would-be novelist. Another university acquaintance of Charles, he is plump, untidy, and nervous. Convinced of his genius, he lives on the allowance of his slatternly girlfriend. For a time, Charles lives with them. After Edwin has succeeded as a radio gag writer, he finds Charles a job with his team.

Ern Ollershaw, Charles's partner in a window-cleaning business. A stocky, middle-aged man with missing teeth and a broad Lancashire accent, Ern makes up for his lack of elegance with his loyal and generous nature. He wins Charles's heart by beating up a bully who has attacked him. Later, while he is being led away by the police for involvement in a car theft ring, he makes sure that Charles gets his proper share of the window-cleaning profits.

Bunder, the head of a drug smuggling gang. A tall, awkward young man with prominent white teeth and a mustache, he dresses expensively. After the police raid his operation, he takes Charles on a high-speed chase. When Charles pulls at the hand brake, Bunder pushes him out of the car. As a result, Charles is badly injured and must be hospitalized for some time.

Mr. Braceweight, a rich chocolate manufacturer. In late middle age, he is pale and thin, with a colorless personality. Hospitalized for a tonsillectomy, he meets Charles, who has taken a job as an orderly, and hires him as a chauffeur. Because he is so kind, Charles is extremely unhappy when Mr. Braceweight loses faith in him as a result of George Hutchins' vicious frame.

Walter Braceweight, the son of Mr. Braceweight. Sixteen years old, he is a mechanical genius. It is the vehicle he invented that crashes into the Daimler. By protecting Walter, Charles loses his job as chauffeur but is therefore free to be employed as a gag writer and to become wealthy.

— *Rosemary M. Canfield Reisman*

THE BOROUGH: A Poem in Twenty-four Letters

Author: George Crabbe (1754-1832)
First published: 1810
Genre: Poetry

Locale: A seaside community
Time: Eighteenth century
Plot: Social realism

Peter Grimes, the best-known character, largely because of the opera *Peter Grimes* (1945), written by Benjamin Britten Evil-tempered and willful, the young Grimes first defies and then abuses his kindly father, a fisherman. Although he repents briefly after his father's death, Grimes is soon his old self, drinking for amusement and fishing and stealing to support himself. A sadist by nature, Grimes takes a poor boy as an apprentice. For his own pleasure, Grimes beats him, starves him, and eventually causes his death. After two other boys in Grimes's care also die, the parish authorities refuse to place others with him. Shunned by his neighbors and haunted by the ghosts of his father and the three dead apprentices, Grimes dies alone. In his opera, Britten changed the monster of this work to an innocent man, misunderstood and slandered by his neighbors.

Abel Keene, a decent, respectable man. Tiring of a

teacher's hectic life, Keene finds an ideal job as bookkeeper for a merchant. Because he yearns for companionship and acceptance, he is easily persuaded to join the merchant's son and his friends in their carousals. Flattered by the attention, Keene cannot see that he is merely the butt of their jokes. When the merchant dies, Keene loses both his job and his supposed friends. In despair, he consults Calvinistic preachers, but they will not guarantee him God's forgiveness, and Keene hangs himself.

Ellen Orford, a trusting, devout woman who is a lifelong victim of men and of society. As a child, she endures her stepfather's cruelty. As a young woman, she gives her heart to a rich young man, but he marries someone of his own class, leaving Ellen with a retarded child. Ellen marries a tradesman, and they have five sons; however, after being converted to a fanatical sect, he comes to loathe Ellen and her daughter, the fruit of sin. After he kills himself, the authorities take away four of Ellen's sons, leaving her with only one sickly boy and the girl. All four boys die, one of them by hanging, and the daughter dies in childbirth, having been seduced by the brother at home. In teaching, Ellen finds an outlet for her loving nature; however, when she goes blind, she is deprived of her position. Because she has never lost her faith in God, she dies in peace and in the expectation of a better life.

Jachin, a parish clerk, a serious, responsible man. Although he can reject alcohol and sex, Jachin falls to greed and the fear of poverty. When his fees decline, Jachin begins giving alms to himself instead of to the poor for whom they are intended. Exposed and dismissed from his job, he feels the contempt of his neighbors and his own bitter consciousness of having sinned. Repenting, he dies alone.

Sir Denys Brand, a proud, wealthy man whose life is based on pretense. Praising temperance, he eats sparingly; actually, he is motivated by stinginess. Similarly, he is charitable only when he will receive some public acknowledgment; he is incapable of secret kindnesses. Because he is essentially unfeeling, he assumes that members of the lower classes cannot feel pain, and he gives refuge in the almshouse only to those who were once members of his own class.

Blaney, a spendthrift and a playboy. During his lifetime, Blaney loses three fortunes: his inheritance from his father, wealth acquired through marriage, and finally a bequest from a distant relative. Initially, Blaney indulges in dissolute pleasures that injure no one but himself, but he becomes so jaded that he must effect the ruin of others. Appointed by Brand to the almshouse, he spends his final years fondly remembering his dissipated past.

Clelia, another inhabitant of the almshouse. A coquette, dedicated to winning the admiration of men, the young Clelia falls easily to a practiced seducer. No longer desirable as a wife, she becomes the mistress of one of her former suitors, an attorney. Later, she is kept by an innkeeper. When he goes bankrupt, Clelia tries to make a living, but without success. Now old, vulgar, and unattractive, she spends her time with Blaney, exaggerating her past triumphs.

Frederick Thompson, a merchant's son. Intelligent but lazy, and badly spoiled by his mother, he will not do what is required of him at college, in an office, on a ship where he has been appointed a midshipman, or even in traveling companies of players. Although he insists that his one desire is to be free, Thompson always slinks back to his parents when he is ill or when he needs money. After being kicked out of the house of prostitution where he is working, Thompson tries to go home again, but when he stops to rest, he dies.

— *Rosemary M. Canfield Reisman*

BOSNIAN CHRONICLE
(Travnička hronika)

Author: Ivo Andrić (1892-1975)
First published: 1945
Genre: Novel

Locale: Travnik, Bosnia
Time: 1806-1814
Plot: Historical

Jean Baptiste-Étienne Daville (zhahn bahp-TEEST-ay-TYEHN dah-VEEL), a French consul in Travnik. As a representative of French power and civilization, Daville has the difficult task of upholding a semblance of civility in a remote Balkan town ruled by the Ottoman Empire. Caught in a constant silent struggle between the other two powers, Turkey and Austro-Hungary, he accomplishes the task adroitly but not without a price to his personal life. He writes an epic poem about Alexander the Great and adores his mentor and idol, Napoleon Bonaparte. Perhaps because of the stifling environment, but more likely because he is not exceptionally clever and gifted, he fails to develop his intellect fully and to embrace new ideas sweeping Europe. His faith in human values, however, which he saw symbolized in Napoleon, helps him to survive the fall of his idol and keep a decor of civility even when it seems out of place. After his tour of duty, he leaves Travnik battered but not defeated, saddened but not bitter, and content with a job well done.

Josef von Mitterer, an Austrian consul in Travnik. Daville's counterpart, von Mitterer is made of a different fiber. Capable and efficient, with an unerring sense of purpose, and polite but unemotional, he accomplishes his task unwaveringly. Even though he realizes that Daville represents Western values similar to his own, von Mitterer seems to enjoy sparring with his French partner. Lacking the inner life and mental agility of his French partner and conditioned by his military upbringing and diplomatic vocation, he sacrifices human qualities to his sense of duty and expediency.

Mehmed-Pasha, the first of the Turkish viziers. A former slave from Georgia who climbed his way to a high position in the Turkish hierarchy thanks to his natural abilities, Mehmed-Pasha never forgets the power that he serves and represents, yet he always shows a friendly face and a smile, which hide his real thoughts and feelings. When Mehmed-Pasha is replaced after an internal struggle at the Turkish court, Daville feels a personal loss of a polite partner with whom he could talk and do business.

Ibrahim-Pasha, Mehmed-Pasha's replacement as a vizier, the exact opposite of his predecessor and much more difficult to work with. He is beset by various illnesses, "a walking ruin," morose and ill-willed most of the time, and surrounded by a similarly dispositioned group of assistants (the local people call them "a museum of monsters"). Under this unpleasant veneer, Daville discovers a very unhappy man with whom he can still work.

Ali-Pasha, the third Turkish vizier, who turns out to be the worst of the three. Upon taking over, he proceeds to execute all the undesirable elements, such as thieves, gamblers, idlers, and political prisoners. Once his rule of iron hand is established, however, he becomes polite and even seemingly friendly with the two Western consuls. At the same time, neither he nor the other viziers ever forget that the power that they serve cannot hold foreign territories without the rule of an iron fist.

Madame Daville, the French consul's wife. Small and frail in appearance, she is a dedicated wife and a determined helper in her husband's difficult task. Her practicality and strong religious beliefs make it easier for her to overcome various misfortunes, such as the loss of a child for lack of medical help. Her gentle nature of simple yet true nobility serves as a beacon of devotion and reason in the midst of a primitive and often hostile environment. She is the most redeeming character in the novel.

Amédée Chaumette des Fossés (ah-may-DAY shoh-MEHT day foh-SAY), Daville's assistant. Des Fossés represents a new breed of French diplomats. Much more flexible and open to changes, practical, and expedient, he is better suited for the rough-and-tumble world of power politics.

César d'Avenat (say-ZAHR dah-veh-NAH), called **Davna**, the vizier's doctor and interpreter. An adventurer and connoisseur of people, Davna is the most colorful, even if a less important, character in the novel. Born in Italy of French parentage, he travels to many places and serves many masters. Travnik, with its plethora of races and its international intrigue, becomes a perfect stage for him.

— *Vasa D. Mihailovich*

THE BOSTONIANS

Author: Henry James (1843-1916)
First published: 1885-1886
Genre: Novel

Locale: Boston, Massachusetts, and New York City
Time: The early 1870's
Plot: Psychological realism

Olive Chancellor, the portrait of the Boston lady. She is won over to the cause of the suffragists but exercises poor taste in attempting to accomplish their goals.

Adeline Luna, her sister. She is a worldly woman who does not subscribe to the concept of the "new woman."

Basil Random, her cousin from Mississippi. A lawyer practicing in New York City, he falls in love with Verena Tarrant's voice, if not her ideas, and is able to persuade her to marry him. He believes that people must excel within their appointed stations in society.

Verena Tarrant, Olive's protégée. An attractive young woman, Verena possesses few ideas of her own but is groomed for the cause of the woman suffrage movement. She is saved from this fate, however, by Basil Random, who carries her off to Mississippi as his bride.

Selah Tarrant, Verena's father, a fake mesmeric healer.

Mrs. Tarrant, Verena's mother. She is the daughter of Boston abolitionists.

Miss Birdseye, an eighty-year-old reformer who is both sincere and ineffectual. Henry James's favorite character, she dies believing that Basil Random has been persuaded of the need for a women's movement.

Dr. Prance, a woman who is a true doctor and who, in her real and practical way, is doing more for the women's rights movement than the suffragists.

Mrs. Burrage, a New York society hostess.

Henry Burrage, her son, a Harvard undergraduate who courts Verena.

Mrs. Farrinder, a suffragist campaigner who is suspicious of Tarrant.

BOTCHAN

Author: Sōseki Natsume (Kinnosuke Natsume, 1867-1916)
First published: 1906
Genre: Novel

Locale: Tokyo and a castle town on the island of Shikoku, Japan
Time: 1894-1895
Plot: Satire

Botchan, a very impulsive, unsophisticated young man from Tokyo. Sometime after the death of his parents, he accepts a job as a mathematics teacher in a junior high school in a small town on the island of Shikoku. His innocence is threatened repeatedly by the school's rambunctious students, devious and fractious teachers, and cravenly weak administrators. His personality and values conflict with those of the small town, and he lasts less than a year at the school. Botchan gets into one scrape after another but leaves with his honor and innocence intact after giving Red Shirt and Clown a well-deserved physical drubbing with the help of his friend, Porcupine.

Kiyo, a longtime servant of Botchan's family who dotes on her young master and wants to keep house for him. She advises Botchan, sends him money, and serves as his mother figure and standard of values.

Badger, the principal of the school. He studiously assumes an air of superiority and encourages Botchan to become a model teacher and mentor. He cannot live up to the ideal he requires of others, however, and is easily manipulated by Red Shirt.

Red Shirt, the school's head teacher, a two-faced man who lies and connives to ruin other teachers and force them out of the school. He engineers Koga's transfer to another school to steal Miss Toyama's love, makes Botchan believe that Porcupine has stirred up the students against him, and involves both Porcupine and Botchan in a student riot to bring about their resignations from the school.

Yoshikawa, nicknamed **Clown** by Botchan, a drawing teacher who slavishly flatters the educational establishment, Badger, and Red Shirt. He connives with Red Shirt to manipulate Botchan into joining their faction.

Hotta, called **Porcupine**, the senior mathematics teacher and Botchan's immediate superior. A physically strong, gruff man with a sense of honor, he befriends Botchan on his arrival but becomes his temporary enemy as a result of the lies of Red Shirt and Clown. His behavior at a faculty meeting earns Botchan's respect, as does testimony about him from Mrs. Hagino.

Koga, a mild-mannered English teacher nicknamed **Hubbard Squash** by Botchan because he is pale and fat. Once betrothed to Miss Toyama (the Madonna), he is tricked into allowing himself to be transferred to another, distant, even more isolated school by Red Shirt, who is courting Miss Toyama.

Ikagin, Botchan's first landlord, a dealer in antique art who constantly, but unsuccessfully, tries to sell bogus artworks to Botchan and Porcupine.

Mrs. Hagino, Botchan's refined, aristocratic landlady, recommended by Mr. Koga. A local gossip, she informs Botchan of Koga's broken engagement to Miss Toyama and that he is unhappy about being transferred.

— *Joseph Laker*

BOUVARD AND PÉCUCHET
(Bouvard et Pécuchet)

Author: Gustave Flaubert (1821-1880)
First published: 1881
Genre: Novel

Locale: France
Time: Nineteenth century
Plot: Psychological realism

Bouvard (boo-VAHR), a middle-class clerk, the protagonist of Flaubert's unfinished, posthumously published novel. He meets Pécuchet beside the Canal Saint Martin one summer afternoon and finds they have many common interests and traits. Upon receiving a bequest from a man he had thought was his uncle but who turns out to be his natural father, he decides, after consultation with his friend, to buy a house and farm far from the desk where he has toiled, and forget his plebeian occupation. In this way, circumstances that have prevented his extraordinary mind from achieving success will be changed. After a round of unsuccessful endeavors and undertakings, he returns to his desk.

Pécuchet (pay-kew-SHAY), his fat friend, who comes to help Bouvard run his farm. Consulting their neighbors, buying all the books and magazines available, they vainly try to make the farm pay, but the livestock runs away or dies. After the wheat field burns, Pécuchet persuades his friend to give up most of the farm in order to concentrate on a beautiful formal garden.

Madame Bordin (bohr-DAHN), who attends the official banquet and opening of the formal garden and finds the dinner a failure and the garden impossible to see in the late evening. When Bouvard begins reading historical romances as a way of understanding psychology, she becomes his romantic interest.

When she suggests that he give her part of his land, she is abruptly dropped.

M. Vaucorbeil (voh-kohr-BEHY), the local doctor. When the experiments of the partners leads them to an interest in medicine, Dr. Vaucorbeil protests their attempts to cure some of his own patients. However, he is avenged when their reading about medical symptoms convinces them that they are suffering from many ailments.

Abbé Jeufroy (zhew-FRWAH), the village priest, who comes into conflict with the pair after their interest in the study of life and the universe turns up geologic findings that contradict the teachings of the Church.

M. Foureau (foo-ROH), the village mayor.

Mélie (may-LEE), the servant of the partners. Pécuchet's romantic interest in her leaves him with an attack of venereal disease.

Victorine (veek-toh-REEN), a girl about to be sent to an orphan asylum. She is adopted by the partners, but she will not learn obedience and is eventually sent away. She is one more of their failures.

Victor, whom the partners think they can salvage from a reformatory. He proves to be an incorrigible delinquent.

Gorju (gohr-ZHEW), a veteran of seven years of African fighting.

THE BOY WITHOUT A FLAG: Tales of the South Bronx

Author: Abraham Rodriguez, Jr. (1961-   )
First published: 1992
Genre: Short fiction

Locale: The South Bronx, New York City
Time: Late twentieth century
Plot: Social realism

The Rodriguez boy (rohd-REE-gehs), a gifted student and would-be rebel in "The Boy Without a Flag." The Rodriguez boy and his friend Edwin have a crush on their young teacher, Miss Colon, and they help her decorate her classroom at Halloween, earning her gratitude. They also defame her by producing and distributing a comic book called "Slut at the Head of the Class." To earn his father's respect, the Rodriguez boy reads voraciously and writes novels and plays. His father, a poet, tries to discourage him, knowing that he will not be able to earn a good living as a writer. Influenced by one of his father's tirades against American imperialism, he decides not to salute the American flag at school.

Nilsa (NEEL-sah), a fiery tomboy in "No More War Games." She loves to play war games and cringes at the thought of giving them up, but her friend Cha-Cha, formerly a tomboy, insists that she must act sexy and feminine if she wants to get a boyfriend. As she stalks her prey in one last battle inside a dilapidated building, she feels powerful and sexy. She imagines herself as a new type of woman, one who can play soldier and dress in tattered clothes and still look beautiful and date boys. When she commands Patchi, her prisoner, to tell her she is pretty, he says, "Yuh all right." His response devastates her. She realizes that boys are not attracted to powerful women.

The narrator, a sixteen-year-old heroin addict in "Babies." Abused as a child, she uses heroin to escape her painful memories. She is torn between a desire to become a mother and the realization that her world is "no place for babies." Her maternal instinct is manifested in her compassion for others. Her abortion signals her surrender to the powerful environmental forces working against her. Like the flame on her birthday candle, she shimmers precariously, about to expire.

Angel, the adolescent narrator of "Birthday Boy." He is physically and mentally precocious and has a sense of humor, which he displays in the police station. For more than eleven years, he enjoyed a happy relationship with his father, but then his father became mean and abusive, blaming him for his mother's infidelity and eventually driving him onto the streets.

Although he steals, he is not a bad person. His refusal to stab his father during a violent beating indicates his morality. He struggles to remain independent of Spider's crack operation. His burglary of an apartment is probably to get money for his pregnant girlfriend, Gloria, and to support himself.

Marty, a railway motorman in "Short Stop." He stops his train to help a suicidal teenager. Unlike the female conductor, who refuses to announce the stops correctly, or the two transit cops, who release the obviously distressed and suicidal teenager, Marty cares about people and his job. His capacity for affection and his desire to nurture are evident in the camaraderie he shares with his fellow motorman, Clint; his fondness for his wife, Melissa; and his yearning to be a father.

Dalia, a junior-high-school student in "The Lotto." She is shy, nervous, and superstitious. When boys talk to her, she averts her eyes. She is especially vulnerable to peer pressure. At her friend's prodding, she has sex with a street boy and later feels guilty about it. Her guilt manifests itself as morning sickness, which she interprets as a sign of pregnancy. Infected by her mother's distorted religious beliefs, she worries that God will reveal her pregnancy to her parents.

Elba, a teenage wife and mother, the title character of the last story. Although she once loved her husband, Danny, she now despises him, so much so that she scrubs her body clean of his unpleasant touch and dries herself off with a "virgin" towel, one not used by him. She views their cramped, roach-infested apartment as a prison cell. Although she tries to be a mature and responsible mother, Danny refuses to cooperate. He frequently comes home drunk and treats her like a whore. Her revulsion for Danny undercuts her affection for their baby, who looks like his father. Elba's act of rebellion takes the form of a symbolic prison break.

THE BOYS IN THE BAND

Author: Mart Crowley (1935-   )
First published: 1968
Genre: Drama

Locale: An East Side apartment in New York City
Time: The 1960's
Plot: Psychological realism

Michael, a guilt-ridden, thirty-year-old homosexual whose sole purpose in life is to avoid his feelings. When unable to cope on a daily basis, he escapes into characterizations of past female screen stars. If reality becomes more threatening, he takes a jet to some distant location, then spends extravagant sums of money he does not have. Until recently, alcohol had been another escape. After selling one unproduced screenplay, he gave up writing. Because he does not have any other source of income, he spends most of his time avoiding creditors. Michael backslides to the bottle when the all-male birthday party he is throwing for his friend Harold is crashed by Alan, his former Georgetown University roommate who is straight and not aware of Michael's homosexuality. Michael's hostility increases, to the point at which he invents an insidious emotional game designed to hurt and demoralize his guests.

Donald, a responsible, hardworking gay man who scrubs floors for a living. At the age of twenty-eight, he views his life as a failure and is committed to therapy. He is an intelligent man and an avid reader. At the birthday party, it is revealed that he had a one-night stand at a bathhouse with Hank's lover Larry.

Hank, a math teacher in superb athletic condition. Thirty-two-year-old Hank has left his wife and children for a relationship with Larry. Deeply in love, he is frustrated by Larry's unwillingness to be faithful. This tension prompts continuous barbs between the two. Hank becomes the only gay man with whom the straight Alan can relate.

Larry, a commercial artist and Hank's twenty-nine-year-old lover. He has a strong sexual appetite and, even though he confesses during Michael's game to loving Hank more than anyone else, he still cannot promise to be monogamous in their relationship. Although he becomes jealous of the attention that Alan is giving to Hank, he continues to flirt with Donald.

Emory, an effeminate, campy interior decorator. The small, frail thirty-three-year-old is a somewhat pathetic character. Shunned by mainstream society, he has found a friend in a member of another minority—Bernard, the black man whom he incessantly derides.

Bernard, an employee of the library's circulation department. Although he has experienced prejudice because he is black as well as gay, he feels more fortunate than the flagrantly effeminate Emory. That is why he allows Emory—and only Emory—to belittle him at times. As proud as Bernard is, Michael manages to humiliate him during his game. He coaxes Bernard into telephoning a white man whom Bernard has loved since the time he and his mother worked for the man's family, when the man was only a boy.

Harold, an unattractive, gay Jewish man. Harold is thirty-two years old, and it is his birthday being celebrated. He is obsessed with his lack of good looks, poor complexion, and fleeting youth. Harold arrives at the party late and intoxicated. He receives a beautiful but moronic male hustler as a gift from Emory.

Alan, a thirty-year-old lawyer with a wife and two daughters. Although Alan is Michael's former roommate from Georgetown University, he is unaware of Michael's homosexuality. When he arrives at the party uninvited, he discovers that he is the only heterosexual present. Someone as effete as Emory is repulsive to him, and Alan physically attacks him. During the game in which he is compelled to participate, Michael tries to extract a homosexual confession from him. Instead, Alan calls his wife and pledges his love to her.

Cowboy, a muscular, good-looking, and vacuous twenty-two-year-old hustler. He is Emory's twenty-dollar birthday present to Harold.

— *Steven C. Kowall*

THE BRACKNELS

Author: Forrest Reid (1875-1947)
First published: 1911
Genre: Novel

Locale: Ireland
Time: Early twentieth century
Plot: Domestic

Mr. Bracknel, an Irish businessman who prides himself on his practicality. He is a tyrannical husband and father, although he believes his family defies him only to displease him. He is disappointed in his wife because she is sickly, in his son Denis because he thinks the boy mad. He also tries to keep his daughters from meeting young men. He dies of a heart attack brought on by an argument with his eldest son, Alfred, a ne'er-do-well.

Mrs. Bracknel, a sickly woman who seems much older than her forty-six years.

Alfred Bracknel, the eldest son, who has a job in his father's business but prefers to devote himself to pleasure. Though he is incompetent, he inherits his father's business, a fact that makes him glad of his father's death.

Denis Bracknel, seventeen years old. He is interested in the mystical and occult. He finds the world too much to bear and commits suicide beside a pagan altar he discovers near his home.

May Bracknel, a healthy, normal person, the eldest of the Bracknel daughters.

Amy Bracknel, a man-crazy, sensual girl who is infatuated with Hubert Rusk. She annoys the tutor, who is oblivious to her, by disturbing his charge's lessons. She even tries to announce her engagement to Mr. Rusk.

Hubert Rusk, Denis Bracknel's tutor, an easy and affable young man hired because he can understand Denis' mental condition. He comes to fear that the boy's mental aberrations are bad for his own mental health, but he stays on the job, in deference to the wishes of the Bracknels' doctor, until the boy commits suicide.

THE BRAGGART SOLDIER
(Miles gloriosus)

Author: Plautus (c. 255-184 B.C.E.)
First performed: c. 200 B.C.E.
Genre: Drama

Locale: Ephesus, in Asia Minor
Time: The third century B.C.E.
Plot: Comedy

Pyrgopolinices (pihr-goh-pol-ih-NI-sees), a vain and stupid braggart and professional soldier. Convinced that all women find him irresistible, he seizes a young Athenian girl, Philocomasium, and carries her off to his house in Ephesus. The slave of the girl's sweetheart is, by coincidence, also in the braggart's household. Pleusicles, the girl's lover, takes up residence in the house of an old man next door to Pyrgopolinices. Pleusicles and his slave, Palaestrio, plot to free the girl. Pyrgopolinices is convinced that the wife of his neighbor is in love with him. A courtesan, playing the part of the wife, tempts Pyrgopolinices and asks him to make room for her in his house. Philocomasium pretends, when Pyrgopolinices tries to send her away, that she is overcome with grief at having to leave him. To get rid of her, the braggart presents her with expensive gifts and allows Palaestrio to accompany her. That night, Pyrgopolinices is escorted into the house next door, where he expects to meet his latest conquest. Instead, he is soundly beaten by the servants of the house, who have been lying in wait for him.

Palaestrio (pa-LEES-tree-oh), Pleusicles' faithful slave. Hurrying by sea to inform his master that Philocomasium had been abducted, Palaestrio had been captured by pirates. His captors presented him to Pyrgopolinices. When Pleusicles arrives in Ephesus, Palaestrio contrives to dig a tunnel between the two houses so that the two lovers can meet. It is Palaestrio who takes the major part in directing the complicated scheme that frees Philocomasium and disgraces Pyrgopolinices.

Pleusicles (PLEW-sih-kleez), a young gentleman of Athens. After Pyrgopolinices has been convinced that the wife of his neighbor is in love with him, Pleusicles appears at the braggart's house in the disguise of a sailor. He introduces himself as an agent of Philocomasium's mother and escorts away both the girl and Palaestrio.

Periplecomenus (pehr-ih-pleh-KOH-meh-nuhs), the old gentleman who owns the house next to Pyrgopolinices, a bachelor who likes to discourse wittily on the joys of celibacy. Periplecomenus enthusiastically cooperates with the plot to reunite the two lovers.

Philocomasium (fihl-uh-koh-MAY-see-uhm), the girl kidnapped by Pyrgopolinices. She is modeled on the type of the "good courtesan." Philocomasium is faithful to Pleusicles.

Sceledrus (SKEH-leh-druhs), the braggart's drunken slave. He accidentally sees Pleusicles and Philocomasium embracing. Before he can report this irregularity to Pyrgopolinices,

Sceledrus is intercepted by Palaestrio, who convinces the latter that the girl he saw is Philocomasium's twin sister.

Acroteleutium (ak-ruh-teh-LEW-tee-uhm), a clever courtesan who impersonates Periplecomenus' wife. She is impudent and quite frank about her depravity.

Milphidippa (mihl-fih-DIH-puh), Acroteleutium's maid, who conducts the braggart into the trap set for him in Periplecomenus' house.

Artotrogus (ahrt-oh-TROH-guhs), Pyrgopolinices' parasite, to whom the braggart displays his vanity and stupidity.

Cario (KA-ree-oh), Periplecomenus' cook, who threatens to torture the braggart after he has been taken in the wrong house.

Lurcio (LUR-kee-oh), Pyrgopolinices' impudent slave boy.

BRAND

Author: Henrik Ibsen (1828-1906)
First published: 1866
Genre: Drama

Locale: The western coast of Norway
Time: The nineteenth century
Plot: Social criticism

Brand, an uncompromising young priest who vows to bring about the cure of the world's triple sickness, as exemplified in the fainthearted, the lighthearted, and the uncontrolled. Demanding of his followers all or nothing, he is faced with the same choice for himself when he is confronted with the possible death of his son and, later, of his wife, Agnes. He makes the sacrifices he feels are required of him and calls on the people to go up the mountain with him to a new life, where every day is dedicated to God. When the way becomes too hard for his followers, they drop by the wayside, and he goes on alone except for Gerd, who sees that his hands are pierced and his brow marked with thorns.

Agnes, Brand's wife, who challenges her husband to make the choice he demands of others: all or nothing—his duty or her life. She rejoices when he chooses his holy work, and soon afterward she dies.

A peasant, a symbol of the fainthearted. He will not give his own life for his daughter's.

Einar, a painter, a symbol of the lighthearted. Engaged to Agnes, he becomes a fanatical missionary after her marriage to Brand.

Gerd, a gypsy girl, a symbol of the uncontrolled. She follows the forsaken Brand up the mountain, where she sees him as Lord and Redeemer.

The mother, who refuses her son Brand's request that she relinquish all her earthly possessions. She dies unrepentant.

The doctor, who reminds Brand that an attempt to save his son's life will require him to belie his demand of all or nothing from his followers.

The mayor,
the dean,
the sexton, and
the schoolmaster, other members of Brand's flock.

BRAVE NEW WORLD

Author: Aldous Huxley (1894-1963)
First published: 1932
Genre: Novel

Locale: London and New Mexico
Time: The future
Plot: Science fiction

Bernard Marx, a citizen of the world in the year 632 A.F. (After Ford), a world in which individuality has long been forgotten, a world dehumanized and organized around the motto "Community, Identity, Stability." Marx, born of a "prenatal bottle" instead of woman, is an anomaly in the community because too much alcohol got into his blood surrogate while he was incubating before birth. He has sensibilities, therefore, similar to those of people living during the time of Henry Ford. Marx conducts an experiment that fails: By studying a savage named John, whom he brings to the new culture, he learns that human emotions produce only tragedy in the brave new world.

Lenina Crowne, an Alpha worker in The Central London

Hatchery and Conditioning Center, who is interested in Marx. She was predestined to her class, as were all citizens of the community, for, depending upon the community work to be done, citizens may come from the bottles as Alpha Plus Intellectuals all the way down through Epsilon Minus Morons. Lenina helps Marx with the experiment, falls in love with the savage, and is whipped to death by him when he attacks her in a fit of passion.

Thomakin, the director of Hatcheries, who years before had abandoned a woman he had taken with him on vacation to the Savage Reservation, a wild tract in New Mexico preserved by the state to advance the study of primitive societies. When it is discovered that Thomakin is the father of the savage whom Marx brings back to London, Thomakin resigns his directorship of the Hatcheries.

John, the savage who is the subject of Marx's experiment and is Thomakin's son. John received his only education by reading an old copy of William Shakespeare's plays. While beside himself with passion, he whips Lenina to death and, in a fit of remorse, hangs himself.

Mustapha Mond, a World Controller responsible in the main for the conditioning of the young to the ways of the brave new world.

Linda, John's mother, the woman abandoned by Thomakin at the Savage Reservation.

BREAD AND WINE
(Pane e vino)

Author: Ignazio Silone (Secondo Tranquilli, 1900-1978)
First published: 1936
Genre: Novel

Locale: Italy
Time: The 1930's
Plot: Social realism

Pietro Spina (pee-EH-troh), a former favorite pupil of Don Benedetto. Despite physical hardships and intellectual disappointments, Spina remains faithful to his concept of justice and thus demonstrates that good men will fight, even if unsuccessful, as long as they exist. He ages his features with iodine and as a priest, "Don Paolo Spada," becomes an antiwar agitator among the mountaineers.

Doctor Nunzio Sacca (NEWN-zee-oh SAH-kah), an old friend who finds and helps Spina.

Matelena Ricotta (mah-teh-LAY-nah ree-KOHT-tah), owner of the mountain inn where Spina hides.

Bianchina Girasole (bee-ahn-KEE-nah jeer-ah-SOH-leh), who considers Spina a saint because he consoled her following an abortion. She seduces Alberto, the brother of her friend Cristina, and becomes a prostitute when sent to Rome by Spina to agitate against the Abyssinian War frenzy.

Cristina Colamartini (krihs-TEE-nah koh-lah-mahr-TEE-nee), whose devotion to God goes beyond reason. She sacri-fices herself to cold and the wolves to carry food to the hidden Spina.

Alberto Colamartini, the brother of Cristina, and socially above any Girasole.

Pompeo (pom-PAY-oh), the son of a Fossa chemist. Once a reformer, he catches the war frenzy and nearly denounces Spina for writing antiwar slogans on walls.

Romeo, head of the antiwar movement in Rome until he is captured.

Uliva (ewl-EE-vah), a disillusioned man who is killed by a bomb he is making to blow up a church filled with government officials.

Murica (mewr-EE-kah), a potential ally in Spina's struggle to put God back in the affairs of man. He is killed by government authorities.

Don Benedetto (beh-neh-DEHT-toh), an old Catholic teacher and Spina's intellectual mentor.

Marta, his faithful sister.

BREAD GIVERS

Author: Anzia Yezierska (1885-1970)
First published: 1925
Genre: Novel

Locale: New York City's Lower East Side
Time: Early twentieth century
Plot: Social realism

Sara Smolinski, the youngest of four daughters of Reb Smolinski and his wife. As early as age ten, Sara is intelligent enough to understand the unhappiness and frustration imposed on her Jewish immigrant family by the poverty and squalor of their Hester Street tenement and the zealous domination of her Old World father. Sara also sees the failure of her sisters to free themselves from the domestic tyranny of their father. With a strong will and sense of purpose, she rebels against the old values and follows her "Americanized" way to personal and social freedom. Her aspirations impel her to leave home and to live on her own wages earned as a laborer in a laundry. She becomes educated and begins her career as a teacher.

Reb Smolinski, referred to as **Father**, a Polish-born despotic zealot and Hebrew scholar who stubbornly applies the literal meaning of the principles of the Torah to life in America. Reb's religious views, which are in obvious conflict with the values of the New World, make him a selfish tyrant. He insists, as the Torah commands, that his daughters work to support him in his studies. Every penny that they make must be turned over to him; every action that they perform must be geared to his comfort and needs as a holy man of God. He is impractical, unable to survive on his own, and completely dependent on his wife.

Mrs. Smolinski, referred to as **Mother**, his wife. She sees the disparity between Reb's ideals and the demands of the new life, but she supports her husband as a dutiful wife. She respects him for his principles, but she is clearheaded about the need for survival and often scolds Reb for his foolishness. Strong and practical (she rents out part of the apartment for income), she is nevertheless sensitive to her daughters' wants, especially to Sara's attempt to succeed.

Bessie Smolinski, the oldest daughter, the first to bear the burdens of "giving bread" (providing financial support) to the family. If she had any aspirations, she has buried them in the selfless performance of her duty. At her father's behest, she marries Zalmon the fish peddler, a widower with a large family. As second mother to the family, she becomes a drudge.

Masha Smolinski, Sara's beautiful sister. At first, Masha's love of finery and an "American" lifestyle keeps her above the squalor of immigrant life, but ultimately she, like Bessie, accedes to Reb's arrangements and marries a dull, loveless parvenu in the garment business. Although Masha initially "escapes" from the Hester Street tenement, she is no more liberated in mind and spirit than Bessie is in body.

Fania Smolinski, the last sister, delicate and childlike. Her life is ruined when she, like all but Sara, marries a man chosen by her father. The husband turns out to be a gambler, and Fania lives on the verge of starvation.

Hugo Seelig, the principal of Sara's school. A quiet, educated man whose parents came from a neighboring village in Poland, he falls in love with Sara, in whom he sees a kindred spirit. He does not believe Reb's accusations of Sara's familial disloyalty. He acquires the old man's respect and approval by becoming Reb's pupil and learning Hebrew. At the novel's end, Hugo and Sara become engaged.

— *Edward Fiorelli*

BREAK OF NOON
(Partage de Midi)

Author: Paul Claudel (1868-1955)
First published: 1905
Genre: Drama

Locale: Far East
Time: Early twentieth century
Plot: Problem

Ysé, a wife and mother. Thirty years old, beautiful, and the mother of two children, Ysé is a bundle of contradictions: She is a pragmatist and a dreamer, she is strong and weak, and she is free and yet easily controlled. Lonely, fickle, passionate, guilty, and driven, she struggles to find her place in the world and yet remains always aware of the unsuitable nature of each choice she makes.

Mesa, the commissioner of customs in China. In his thirties, Mesa is of medium height, rather undistinguished physically, and not particularly handsome. A successful government officer, he is plagued by his awareness of the superficiality of his success. He has attempted to renounce the world to seek spiritual fulfillment but felt rejected by God. A virgin and a loner, he is an unhappy person who has a highly philosophical perspective on life. His meeting with Ysé seems an act of destiny, and the attraction between the two of them is the motivating action for the play.

Amalric, a businessman. Perhaps forty years old, Amalric has no distinguishing physical qualities. He is a realist among a group of dreamers. Though in love with Ysé, he is not controlled by the passion of love. He seeks a means to make money to live comfortably, and he is not controlled by strict ethical or moral codes. In act 3, he is living with Ysé, even though she is legally married to de Ciz and has a child by Mesa.

De Ciz, an adventurer and entrepreneur. Married to Ysé, he is young and adventurous, though without a great sense of personal strength. Although he is intelligent and clever, he is easily manipulated by both Ysé and Mesa because of his need for risk, riches, and success.

— *John C. Watson*

BRENDAN

Author: Frederick Buechner (1926-   )
First published: 1987
Genre: Novel

Locale: Central Ireland and the North Atlantic Ocean
Time: Sixth century A.D.
Plot: Biographical

Brendan, an Irish saint who lives from c. 484 to c. 578 A.D. and is rumored to be the first European explorer to reach the Americas. His birth is marked by a brush fire that, like the burning bush of Moses, leaves no evidence of anything being consumed. From his earliest days, he seeks to live a holy life and to help others do the same. The historical Brendan is known for founding numerous monasteries and convents and for his sailing adventures that may have taken him as far as the New World of the Americas. Brendan is a rough, strong monk who bravely faces the task of winning the Druid chieftains to Christianity. He helps ensure that Hugh the Handsome will become the first Christian king of Cashel, instead of his pagan cousin Hugh the Black. Although Brendan rarely misspeaks, he seems to have spoken rashly to a young monk, who subsequently drowned. Out of penance for having in some way caused this disaster, Brendan sails far and wide in search of Terrestrial Paradise, or Tir-na-n-Og. Upon his return, he slumps into depression for a season, but eventually he recovers to establish more monasteries and even visit Wales and the court of King Arthur to win more converts. Although Brendan is strict in establishing the moral and dietary practices of monks, he is creative in embellishing the tales of his adventures and is highly sought as a storyteller.

Finn, a poor peasant who narrates the novel. Finn is a brave companion of Brendan who sacrifices even the comforts of his own marriage for the sake of helping Brendan with his voyages and efforts to make new converts in Wales. As a result of a hard slap from his father, Finn is deaf in one ear, suggesting that the accounts he gives of Brendan's words may be less than precise.

Briga, Brendan's sister, for whom he builds a convent at Anaghdown. She gives him much encouragement and is with him when he dies.

Bishop Erc, a leader of the monks who trained directly under Saint Patrick. He chooses Brendan for spiritual service.

Jarlath, the abbot under whom Brendan trains after Ita

finishes rearing him to early manhood. Jarlath's monastic order is strict, not allowing the creature comforts of fire to warm the rooms of the monks.

Abbess Ita, the nun responsible for the early training of Brendan, from his first birthday up to early manhood. According to one legend, she suckles him as a child. She serves as a spiritual counselor in later years and encourages his journeys abroad.

Malo, a bitter man who becomes a monk to spite God. Malo blames God for the torturous death of his wife and family at the hands of pagan neighbors who blamed their misfortunes on Malo and his family becoming Christians. At Ita's insistence, Malo serves as the thorn in Brendan's flesh during the last part of his ministry, following the tragic drowning of the young monk. According to legend, Malo later became an important leader in the monastic orders.

Colman, a Celtic bard named **MacLennin** who is renamed Colman upon his baptism. "Colman" means "little dove" in Latin; the name emphasizes the taming influence of the Holy Spirit in his life. Colman sails with Brendan on his first journey and later starts his own order of monks.

Crosan, a court jester who joins Brendan's group after Hugh the Handsome is safely placed on the throne. Crosan is the only individual to join Brendan for both sea journeys. Crosan serves as a lookout for much of the trip, then dies at the far end of the second journey.

Finnloag and

Cara, the father and mother of Brendan. They give up their child at one year of age so that Erc can rear him to be a monk. Brendan discovers that the home of his parents has burned to the ground, but he learns later that they had fled safely and died while he was on his second long journey.

— Daven M. Kari

THE BRICK PEOPLE

Author: Alejandro Morales (1944-   )
First published: 1988
Genre: Novel

Locale: Southern California
Time: The 1890's to the 1940's
Plot: Historical

Octavio Revueltas (ohk-TAH-vee-oh rreh-VWEHL-tahs), a Mexican immigrant who arrives at Simons brickyard during the Mexican Revolution. He becomes an expert brickmaker and learns to gamble in order to supplement his income. When he weds Nana de León in 1926, they begin a family whose children will be first-generation Chicanos and Chicanas, people of Mexican descent born and reared in the United States. Octavio becomes increasingly interested in the union movement because he believes that the Simons family exercises too much control over the workers' lives in what is essentially a company town. During the Great Depression, Octavio makes contact with several unions. The Simons workers strike in 1937, but the strike is broken by scabs, and union solidarity disintegrates. Octavio retreats to his family convinced that working conditions will never improve. His direct experience of exploitation and racism makes him wary of the Anglo-American world outside the brickyard. Unlike his wife, Octavio struggles to resist assimilation into the dominant culture.

Nana de León Revueltas (leh-OHN), a strong and intelligent woman who is determined to establish her family's independence and better its economic situation. As a young woman, she elopes with Octavio Revueltas and moves to her parents' home. For the next few years, much of her energy is spent trying to set up an autonomous existence for her husband and children, away from the extended family and the authority of her mother-in-law; at one point, she actually moves the family without advising Octavio. Nana believes that the stubborn dominance of the Chicano-Mexicano male is a product of his oppression and low self-esteem.

Walter Robey Simons, one of the heirs of the family business, who competes with his brother Joseph until the latter's death. Unlike his brother, Walter is interested in Mexican culture, because he believes that an understanding of his employees' mentality will allow him to maintain control of them. After the death of his first wife, Sara, he marries a classical pianist who compares the adaptability and persistence of the Mexican worker to that of the cockroach. Both the Great Depression and the strike at Simons drive Walter into the role of absentee owner; his business affairs are managed by others as he travels through Europe with his wife. In Paris, he chokes to death on a swarm of brown insects.

Malaquias de León (mahl-ah-KEE-ahs), one of the first workers who challenges the authority of the Simons company and its surrogates. His confrontation with the foreman, Gonzalo Pedroza, sets the stage for his eventual firing and departure from the brickyard. Because he attains a relative economic independence through the sale of horses, he is able to move his family to a nearby barrio; however, he fails to raise the money for the land he had always wanted to own.

Rosendo Guerrero (rroh-SEHN-doh geh-RREH-roh), the first foreman, who helps Joseph Simons learn the brickmaking business and who designs the first brickyard. Rosendo's parents were killed in Mexico during the Napoleonic occupation, and Rosendo escaped to Los Angeles, where he met a Simons cousin who taught him the basic procedures for making bricks. He later becomes friends with Walter Simons, to whom he is close in age, and urges him to travel to Mexico in order to learn more about its culture. His death is mysterious and seems to have been part of a sacrificial ritual linked to ancient American Indian religious practices.

Arturo Revueltas (ahr-TEW-roh), the firstborn son of Nana and Octavio. Arturo experiences racism in the school system and drops out at the age of fourteen. As a young child, he is labeled "retarded" by Anglo-American schoolteachers who are unaware of or uninterested in the problems of bilingual students. During World War II, he is drawn to the young Chicanos known as zoot-suiters, but his mother forbids him to wear the zoot-suiters' distinctive wardrobe. The final scene of the novel finds Arturo listening to his father's memories of the journey north as the two men prepare to build the family's new home.

THE BRIDAL CANOPY
(Hakhnasat kala)

Author: Shmuel Yosef Agnon (Shmuel Yosef Czaczkes, 1888-1970)
First published: 1931
Genre: Novel

Locale: Eastern Galicia and Palestine
Time: Mid-nineteenth century
Plot: Folklore

Reb Yudel Nathanson, a Hasid (member of a Jewish mystical sect) who has devoted his life to the study of the Torah (Jewish sacred literature). An ascetic who has no concern with earthly goods, he wears rags, sleeps on a floor mat, rises early to begin the long day's study and prayer, and eats only to keep body and soul together. At the beginning of the novel, he leaves his town of Brod in Poland to wander far and wide among Jewish villages to seek a bridegroom for his eldest daughter. As naïve as a child, he is exposed by his journey, for the first time, to a vast array of people, each with his own story to tell, and he is involved in continuous adventures and misadventures. He finds a moral and a purpose in all things, and all that he sees and hears draws from him an endless stream of commentary and gloss from Hebrew holy books. He lays all problems in the lap of the Almighty, including his complete ineptitude in fulfilling the goal of his travels. Through a series of coincidences and fortunate accidents, he arranges his daughter's marriage to the son of a very wealthy man, and he happily returns to his life's work of prayer and study.

Nuta, the drayman who takes Yudel on his search. Fat and robust, he is as secular as Yudel is religious. Because he and his wife are constantly quarreling, he is eager to accompany Yudel for as long as possible and finds no greater happiness than to fill his belly with fine food and drink and to listen to the stories of those they meet on their travels. He is not above an occasional minor theft or deception, but after meeting an old man who is a saint, he gradually becomes transformed, establishes a good relationship with his wife, gives up the occupation of drayman, and is appointed inspector of weights and measures.

Frummet, Yudel's long-suffering wife and mother of his three daughters. She and the daughters earn their meager livelihood by plucking feathers to use for pillow stuffing. When her husband disregards her insistence that he must arrange for the daughters' marriages before they are too old, she appeals to the holy Rabbi of Apta, who orders Yudel to fulfill the commandment of the bridal canopy. Near the end of the novel, Frummet discovers the hidden treasure that enables her daughter to match the twelve thousand gold pieces offered by the groom's family as their half of the dowry.

The Old Man, a holy man, one of the Thirty-Six Hidden Saints for whose sake the Almighty preserves humankind. He humbly digs clay for Jewish women to spread on the floors of their homes, and they pay him handsomely in wine, food, and candles. He and his aged wife live in the forest in a booth constructed of the materials of forest and field. His intervention in the decree that prohibits the marriage of minor men allows Yudel's daughter to wed her youthful groom.

Reb Ephraim (eh-FRAH-eem), one of scores of people Reb Yudel encounters in his travels. His former poverty leads him to excess in food and drink following his marriage to a wealthy woman. He soon forswears his gluttony and adopts a spartan diet, interspersed with prolonged fasts. Eventually, he eats only when he can share the bounty of his table with a guest. All travelers and beggars, Yudel among them, are immediately taken to his house. The arrival of a guest is an occasion for rejoicing, for without them Reb Ephraim might have starved.

Reb Vovi Shor, the father of the groom, a wealthy man who is practical, efficient, and decisive in word and action.

Reb Yudel Nathanson, a wealthy man from Brod for whom Yudel the Hasid is mistaken.

— *Lolette Kuby*

THE BRIDE

Author: Bapsi Sidhwa (1938-   )
First published: 1983
Genre: Novel

Locale: Pakistan
Time: 1920-1960
Plot: Domestic realism

Qasim, the protagonist, a tribal Kohistani from the Himalayan mountains. Qasim is unlike his fellow Pakistanis on the plains: His skin is lighter, he is taller, and his facial features are sharper. The greatest contrast lies in his traditions, especially his concept of honor. After the deaths of his wife and children, he moved to the plains but never adjusted or was entirely accepted there. He continues to long for the mountains where he was born until his romanticized memories turn into an obsession, which eventually destroys the person he loves. Although described as a simple man, Qasim develops into a complex character, and he emerges as a sensitive, loving, and generous man who is misguided by his perverse sense of honor.

Zaitoon, Qasim's adopted daughter. After her parents are killed in the partition riots of 1947, three-year-old Zaitoon is rescued by Qasim, who rears her with the assistance of friends. Through most of the novel, Zaitoon, who grows into a beautiful young woman, remains in the background, a sketchily developed character who represents the facelessness of females in Pakistani society. Once she finds herself in a situation of conflict, however, she reacts, draws on a well of strength not revealed before, and develops into a fully realized character.

Nikka, Qasim's friend. Making good use of his powerful wrestler's body and his knack for opportunism, Nikka promotes himself and succeeds as a businessman and political operative in the newly established Pakistan. He is a comic character without scruples and serves as a contrast to his humorless, honor-bound friend Qasim.

Carol, an American married to a Pakistani. In some ways, she typifies women in cross-cultural marriages. At times arrogant and self-centered, frequently bored, and sometimes insensitive to the society into which she has married, the blonde and attractive Carol is far more than a stereotype as she struggles to find her place in a strange world. Her life and

attitudes stand in sharp contrast to the way Zaitoon lives and reacts.

Sakhi, Zaitoon's tribal husband. Although handsome in an unrefined way, Sakhi is depicted as an ignorant, cruel, and primitive man who follows a strict code of honor without thinking. At times, his humanity shines through the crude façade.

— *Robert L. Ross*

THE BRIDE OF LAMMERMOOR: A Legend of Montrose

Author: Sir Walter Scott (1771-1832)
First published: 1819
Genre: Novel

Locale: Scotland
Time: Late seventeenth century
Plot: Gothic

Edgar, popularly called the Master of Ravenswood, even though the Ravenswood estate has passed into the hands of his family's enemy, Sir William Ashton. Edgar and Lucy Ashton fall in love, but tragedy and death prevent the resurgence of the Ravenswood fortunes and the marriage of the lovers.

Sir William Ashton, Lord Keeper of Scotland. He is the new master of the Ravenswood estate and the longtime enemy of the late Lord Ravenswood. He is prevented by his wife from befriending Edgar and bringing about a marriage between him and Lucy, his daughter.

Lucy Ashton, daughter of Sir William and secretly betrothed to Edgar, Master of Ravenswood. Forced to marry Frank Hayston of Bucklaw, she loses her mind and dies the day after the wedding.

Lady Ashton, wife of Sir William. Her cruel persecution and virtual imprisonment of her daughter Lucy drive the girl to madness and, finally, to her death.

Frank Hayston of Bucklaw, a wealthy young nobleman and Lady Ashton's favored contender for the hand of Lucy, who dies the morning after being married to him.

Caleb Balderstone, Edgar's faithful old servant, who tries to keep alive the ancient glories of the Ravenswood family.

The Marquis of A———, Edgar's powerful kinsman.

Alice, a blind tenant on the Ravenswood estate who prophesies that tragedy will result from the union of a Ravenswood and an Ashton. Her ghost warns Edgar of the danger of such an alliance.

Captain Craigengelt, an adventurer-soldier, companion of Frank Hayston.

Young Ashton, Lucy's brother. Believing that Edgar is responsible for his sister's death, he challenges Edgar to a duel. On the way to the duel, Edgar is trapped in quicksand and perishes.

BRIDESHEAD REVISITED: The Sacred and Profane Memories of Captain Charles Ryder

Author: Evelyn Waugh (1903-1966)
First published: 1945
Genre: Novel

Locale: England
Time: The twentieth century
Plot: Social realism

Charles Ryder, a young man who in his days at Oxford meets Sebastian Marchmain and is gradually introduced to the Marchmain family of Brideshead. He becomes an architectural painter and marries the sister of another Oxford friend, but his ties to the Marchmain family persist, and later he falls in love with Sebastian's sister Julia, who is also married. They plan to divorce their spouses and marry each other, and for a while they live together; but Julia's Catholic faith claims her at last, and she gives up Charles.

Lady Marchmain, the stanchly Catholic mother of Sebastian and Julia, who are in revolt from her as well as from their religion. After her death, her rebellious husband and children are drawn back to the values of the Church.

The Marquis of Marchmain, Lady Marchmain's husband and the owner of Brideshead. For many years he has lived with his mistress in Italy. After the death of his wife, he returns to Brideshead with his mistress to spend his last days. Although he is in failing health, he refuses to see a priest: but as he is dying, the priest is brought in, and Lord Marchmain makes the sign of the cross.

Brideshead (Bridey) Marchmain, the oldest of their children. A pompous man, he marries a self-righteous widow with three children.

Sebastian Marchmain, Charles Ryder's friend, an ineffectual though clever and charming young man. His rebellion takes the form of severe alcoholism. After years of aimless wandering, he tries to enter a monastery in Carthage and is refused. Unconscious from drink, he is carried into the monastery by the monks. He plans to stay there as under-porter for the rest of his life.

Julia Marchmain, whose form of rebellion is to marry a rich but socially inferior Protestant of whom her mother disapproves. Though he is willing to be converted, it is discovered that he is divorced, and they are forced to marry in a Protestant ceremony. Later Julia falls in love with Charles and has an affair with him, but, believing that to marry him would only magnify the sin, she gives him up.

Cordelia Marchmain, the youngest of the four children. On returning from Spain, where she worked with an ambulance corps, she tells her family about Sebastian, whom she visited.

Cara, Lord Marchmain's lifelong mistress.

Rex Mottram, Julia's vital and ambitious but ill-bred husband.

Boy Mulcaster and

Anthony Blanche, Oxford friends of Sebastian and Charles.

Celia Ryder, Boy Mulcaster's sister and Charles' wife.

Beryl Muspratt, a widow with three children. Engaged to Bridey, she refuses to come to Brideshead because Charles and Julia are living there in sin. Traveling with Bridey in Italy after their marriage, she meets Lord Marchmain, who dislikes her.

Kurt, Sebastian's roommate and companion in Fez. Kurt is seized by Germans and taken back to Germany. Sebastian follows him, but after Kurt hangs himself in a concentration camp, Sebastian returns to Morocco.

Mr. Samgrass, who is employed in doing some literary work for Lady Marchmain. She hires him also to keep Sebastian away from alcohol, but the plan is doomed to failure.

Father Mackay, the priest whom the Marchmain children and Cara bring to the bedside of the dying Lord Marchmain.

Johnjohn Ryder and

Caroline Ryder , children of Charles and Celia.

THE BRIDGE OF SAN LUIS REY

Author: Thornton Wilder (1897-1975)
First published: 1927
Genre: Novel

Locale: Peru
Time: Early eighteenth century
Plot: Philosophical realism

Brother Juniper (JEW-neh-pehr), a Spanish friar who tries to prove that the collapse of the bridge of San Luis Rey in Peru is an act showing the wisdom of God, who properly sent five persons to their deaths in the accident. For his book, which is condemned by the Church, the friar is burned at the stake.

The narrator, who finds a copy of Brother Juniper's eighteenth century book and reconstructs for the reader the lives of the five persons who died when the bridge collapsed.

The Marquesa de Montemayor (mohn-teh-may-OHR), an ugly woman with a beautiful daughter. She is highly possessive and selfish, first to her daughter and then to Pepita, her maid. By reading a letter from Pepita to an abbess the Marquesa learns her own nature, becomes contrite, and resolves to be a better woman, only to die the next day when the bridge collapses.

Pepita (peh-PEE-tah), maid for the Marquesa de Montemayor, who dies also when the bridge collapses. She is unhappy when she is sent from her convent by the Abbess Madre Maria del Pilar, whom she loves, to serve the noblewoman. Her letter confessing her unhappiness reveals to the Marquesa the noblewoman's thoughtless and self-centered life.

Uncle Pio (PEE-oh), an actor who discovers La Périchole singing in a tavern. He makes a great actress and singer of her, and comes to love her. He is disappointed by the girl, who becomes the mistress of the viceroy and soon is too proud for

her own good. Uncle Pio takes her illegitimate child to rear, but the next day he and the child are victims of the collapse of the bridge.

Jaime (HAY-meh), illegitimate son of La Périchole and the viceroy. He dies when the bridge collapses.

Esteban (ehs-TEH-bahn), a young man whose twin brother gives up his love for La Périchole because of the affection between the two brothers, foundlings reared by the Abbess Madre Maria del Pilar. Manuel dies, and his brother, who becomes a victim of the bridge's collapse, is inconsolable.

La Périchole (PEHR-ee-choh-leh), an actress who is overly proud, especially after becoming the viceroy's mistress. Her pride diminishes when smallpox destroys her beauty. She puts her son in the care of Uncle Pio the day before both of them die.

Manuel, twin brother of Esteban. He hides his love for La Périchole so he will not hurt his brother's feelings, but in a delirium, close to death, he reveals his secret passion.

The Abbess Madre Maria del Pilar (pee-LAHR), who befriends the twin brothers, Esteban and Manuel, as well as Pepita, the girl who becomes the Marquesa de Montemayor's maid. The Abbess is a wise and kindly woman.

Doña Clara, cynical daughter of the Marquesa de Montemayor. She learns too late of her mother's change of heart and inner goodness.

THE BRIDGE ON THE DRINA
(Na Drini ćuprija)

Author: Ivo Andrić (1892-1975)
First published: 1945
Genre: Novel

Locale: Višegrad, Bosnia
Time: 1516-1914
Plot: Historical realism

Mehmed Pasha Sokolli (SOH-koh-lih), a grand vezir at the Ottoman court. When he was ten years old, he was taken away from his Serbian parents as a part of the so-called blood tribute. He is trained in Istanbul to be a janissary, and he becomes a grand vezir, the highest position a non-Turk could attain at the court. To still his nostalgia for his home country, he orders a bridge to be built at his expense across the Drina river at the town of Višegrad, which was the last place he saw his mother, who could not cross the river and follow him any

longer. He appoints his brother Makarije to the highest position in the Serbian Orthodox church. He is stabbed to death by a deranged dervish when he goes to the mosque.

Abidaga (ah-bih-DAH-gah), the first builder of the bridge on the Drina. He is known far and wide as very stern, even cruel, especially when his orders are not fully carried out. He orders a Serb laborer, Radisav, to be impaled at the bridge site because he sabotaged the building of the bridge. Abidaga is replaced when the news reaches Istanbul that he had embezzled the vezir's money and forced laborers to work without pay.

Radisav (rah-DEE-sahv), a Serbian peasant and laborer at the bridge. He is caught destroying at night what had been built during the day, and for this he is impaled at the bridge site as a warning to the opponents of the bridge. The impaling takes place over several days and is watched by the frightened populace. Radisav is admired by the Serbs as a hero and a symbol of their suffering under the Turks.

Fata (FAH-tah), a beautiful young girl from a well-to-do Muslim family. Her father forces her to marry a man she does not love. During a wedding procession, she jumps to her death from the bridge into the Drina. This is one of many dramatic events that takes place on and around the bridge throughout the centuries.

Alihodja Mutevelic (ah-lih-KHOH-djah mew-teh-VEH-lihch), a Bosnian Muslim who was supposed to become a *hodja* but declined and continued managing his father's shop. When the Austrians occupy Bosnia in 1878, he is nailed by his ear to the bridge because he did not believe that the infidels would ever come to Višegrad, yet he did not want to oppose them. When World War I breaks out, the bridge is bombarded. Alihodja dies on the bridge as a symbol of the end of the Turkish reign.

Salko Corkan (SAHL-koh CHOHR-kan), the One Eyed, a powerful young Gypsy who lives off temporary jobs. The whole town feeds him; he belongs to everybody and nobody. He plays the role of the town fool, falling in love with every pretty woman; his love affairs, however, never amount to anything. He embodies the constant yearning for love and happiness that is never fulfilled but is never extinguished.

Lotte (LOH-teh), a young and pretty widow with a free tongue and masculine energy. She is one of many Ashkenazi Jews who came from Galicia to Bosnia to try their luck in business. She builds a hotel next to the bridge and spends many years providing travelers with rest and the townspeople with entertainment. With the passage of time, her fortunes dwindle. She disappears together with the Austrian hold on Bosnia.

— *Vasa D. Mihailovich*

A BRIEF LIFE
(La vida breve)

Author: Juan Carlos Onetti (1909-1994)
First published: 1950
Genre: Novel

Locale: Buenos Aires and Santa María, Argentina
Time: Late 1940's
Plot: Psychological

Juan María Brausen (BROW-sehn), the protagonist, who is suffering an existential crisis at a time when both his vacuous job as a Buenos Aires adman and his marriage are dissolving. Outwardly conventional, cautious, and repressed, he considers his life to be a form of death. Inwardly, though, he lives an artist's fantasy life. To save himself from the outer void, he takes on two new identities: an impersonation that he assumes so as to enter the life of the prostitute who lives in the apartment adjacent to his own, and his fictional surrogate, the protagonist of a film scenario that he is alternately writing and imagining over the course of the novel. All three levels of his identity merge ambiguously at the end of his story. He flees with the young man who has independently carried out the murder of Arce's prostitute and ends up in the imaginary town of Santa María, the setting of the film scenario.

Juan María Arce (AHR-seh), the name under which Brausen moves in with Queca, the prostitute, who is unaware that he lives next door as Brausen. He virtually becomes a kept man. A channel for Brausen's repressed violent instincts, he develops a sadistic relationship with Queca and plans to kill her, essentially as a gratuitous act but also because she taunts him as a perpetual cuckold. When Ernesto murders her for his own reasons on the same night that Arce planned to do the job, Arce adopts a protective, paternal attitude toward the younger man, recognizing that Ernesto is in effect a more active part of himself.

Dr. Díaz Grey (DEE-ahs), Brausen's fictional alter ego, a slim provincial physician with thinning blond hair. Díaz Grey, like Brausen, is middle-aged and repressed. He is a bachelor but is awakened to love by the appearance of Elena Sala in his life. He faithfully accompanies Elena on her quest for a young man whom she wishes to save from desperation. Quite cor-

ruptible, Díaz Grey supplies Elena with regular injections of morphine and, after her death, accompanies her husband to Buenos Aires to procure drugs for illicit trade, without questioning the wisdom of such an endeavor. At the end of the novel, he is newly devoted to Annie Glaeson, a young violinist, and on the verge of being apprehended with Lagos by the police. Díaz Grey is last seen in Buenos Aires, having left behind his fictional habitat, Santa María, and effectively changed places with his creator, Brausen.

Gertrudis (hehr-TREW-dees), Brausen's wife, originally from Montevideo, Uruguay, as he is. She has grown corpulent in her maturity and had a mastectomy just prior to the action of the novel. She is saddened by both her mutilation and the loss of love between herself and her husband. Brausen is put off by her new physical state and also by the routine of marriage that Gertrudis represents. She leaves Brausen and goes to live with her mother in a Buenos Aires suburb. He derives his more seductive fictional character, Elena Sala, from Gertrudis.

Raquel, Gertrudis' younger sister, who is twenty years old and still living in Montevideo. Slender, reddish-haired, and green-eyed, she gives rise to a nostalgic fascination for youth in Brausen, who seduces her on a trip he takes to her city, although she has recently married. Later, naïvely wishing to make a clean break with Brausen, she visits him in Buenos Aires, but he treats her harshly and orders her out of his apartment. Raquel is visibly pregnant by the time of her visit, one of several signs that her youth is behind her.

Enriqueta (Queca) Marti (ehn-ree-KEH-tah KEH-kah mahr-TEE), the diminutive prostitute who lives and works in the apartment next door to Brausen's. Queca's vulgar, chatty vitality paradoxically attracts Brausen-Arce, as do the unreality and inauthenticity of their relationship. She is as insincere as he is, constantly telling him lies about herself. Her only moments of truth and intelligence with him are when she is describing her obsession with "them," invisible spirits who torment her when she is alone. As time goes on, Arce routinely beats Queca, and she verbally abuses him and seems to intuit his desire to kill her.

Ernesto, a tall, bony, dark-haired, impulsive young man, one of Queca's lovers. He finds Brausen-Arce with her in her apartment one night, beats him, and throws him out the door. Eventually, Ernesto kills Queca, and after the murder, Brausen-Arce takes charge of the disoriented young man and attempts to help him escape by going to Santa María.

Elena Sala (eh-LEH-nah SAH-lah), the tall, blonde married woman with a lewd smile who one day shows up in Díaz Grey's office to get morphine. She continues to receive it from the doctor, along with his discreet attentions and his devotion. She controls their curious relationship with her self-possessed manner and quiet determination, right up until the night that she gives herself to him sexually and then dies of a drug overdose. Elena's search for young Oscar may be motivated by love, in addition to altruism.

Horacio Lagos (ohr-RAH-see-oh LAH-gohs), Elena's aging husband, a short, pudgy man, formal and tedious in speech and manner but intelligent and mysterious in his actions. Setting himself up as a cuckold, he indulges Elena's interest in the young Oscar Owen in Buenos Aires, then effectively turns her over to Díaz Grey in Santa María when she embarks on her search for Owen in the Argentine provinces. After her death, Lagos organizes the final drug deal as, in his cryptic words, a revenge and an homage. Díaz Grey initially despises Lagos, but in Buenos Aires he sympathizes with him, even though there is evidence that, because no real escape plan has been made, Lagos' revenge is aimed at his companions and himself.

Oscar Owen, known as the Englishman, a tall, elegant, pipe-smoking young man with a thin face and a cocky look who introduced the Lagoses to drugs and acted as Elena's escort in Buenos Aires. Lagos considers him to be a gigolo and perhaps somewhat effeminate, and he insists to Díaz Grey that Owen did not have a sexual relationship with Elena. Owen participates indifferently as the driver in the drug deal that takes place toward the end of the novel.

Annie Glaeson, a talented teenage violinist whom Díaz Grey meets during the search for Owen and whom Lagos convinces to accompany him, Díaz Grey, and Owen to Buenos Aires for the drug operation. Her motivation for the trip is not specified, but Díaz Grey transfers his affection from the deceased Elena to the young violinist. At the end of the novel, the two of them walk off slowly and happily into the sunrise of the day when they are all likely to be apprehended.

Julio Stein (HEW-lee-oh), Brausen's bantering, alcoholic colleague at the Macleod advertising agency, who prides himself on taking life less seriously than Brausen. Stein suggests that Brausen write a commercially viable film scenario, which Brausen never delivers to him but uses as a projection for his own identity crisis. Stein also warns Brausen that Macleod is about to fire him.

Miriam (MEER-ee-ahm), also called **Mami** (MAH-mee), a sentimental fifty-year-old French prostitute and madam, still beautiful, with whom Stein has been involved since he was twenty and she was thirty-five. Mami is nostalgic for Paris; she sings chansons and pores over a street map of the French capital. One of her songs gives the novel its title: "La vie est breve."

Macleod, the ruddy-faced, sixty-year-old North American owner of the advertising agency where Brausen and Stein work. Almost a caricature of the Yankee businessman, Macleod is religiously devoted to his profession, and when he is dismissing Brausen, he recommends that in the future his erstwhile employee forget about himself and give himself completely to business.

— *John Deredita*

BRIEF LIVES

Author: Anita Brookner (1928-   )
First published: 1990
Genre: Novel

Locale: London
Time: The 1930's to the late 1980's
Plot: Psychological realism

Fay Langdon, the narrator, in her late sixties as she tells the story. A rather ordinary woman, she is intelligent and still pretty, though conscious of aging. She becomes nervous and lonely in the late afternoon, and she fights melancholy. Born Fay Dodworth, she believed in the stories of Hollywood musicals and sang romantic songs on the radio. She yearned for happiness and gave up her work for marriage, then spent much of her life waiting for her husband, Owen—and later her lover, Charlie—to come to her. She was unhappy in love, missing intimacy with Owen and stability with Charlie. She was fascinated by Charlie's wife, Julia, though she never really liked her, and later feared that Julia would discover the adultery. In later life, she attempts to break out of her rut by doing charitable work and seems to be beyond yearning.

Julia Morton, formerly **Margaret Julia Wilberforce**, the wife of Charlie Morton. She has just died, at almost eighty years of age. She was tall, slim, and hard, with heavy eyelids over pale blue eyes. She was sardonic, heartless, restless, and dangerous. She used coarse language but was not sensual. She worked as an aristocratic nightclub comedienne and later dressed in an out of date elegance. After Charlie's death, she became an irritable and demanding recluse. She believed in the right of women to behave capriciously. She became a sterile old lady, and Fay notes that she lost all charitable feelings. Secretly, her true love was her brother Gerald, and she spent her last five years with him in Spain.

Charlie Morton, Julia's husband, who died a decade ago. Bulky, vague, and charming, the lawyer had warm brown eyes and a cheerful expression. He managed Julia's life without complaining and became Fay's lover.

Owen Langdon, Fay's husband. Handsome and attractive, and spoiled by his mother, he was the youngest pilot at the

Battle of Britain. He was Charlie Morton's junior law partner and was ambitious and involved in shady deals. He was only occasionally tender but probably was faithful to Fay; he was "emotionally inarticulate." He died in a car accident in the south of France at the age of fifty-two.

Maureen Luckham, a devoted flunky to Julia who lived in Julia's apartment with her. She was not likable or attractive. She participated in church activities and knitted shapeless sweaters. When she married, she deserted Julia.

Gerald Wilberforce, Julia's unfortunate brother, a car salesman. He inherited the family money and moved to Spain with his lover.

Millie Savage, a singer from Fay's radio days. She was happily married, then widowed. She is a sane and loyal friend to Fay.

Alan Carter, Fay's physician who became her friend, though Fay hoped for more. He is eccentric, blunt, and absolutely unromantic.

— *George Soule*

BRIGHT SHADOW

Author: Joyce Carol Thomas (1938-   )
First published: 1983
Genre: Novel

Locale: Ponca City, Oklahoma
Time: The 1970's
Plot: Domestic realism

Abyssinia (Abby) Jackson, a young woman attending a local college with the intention of earning a degree in science, with a minor in literature, as preparation for medical school. She is the first member of her family to seek an advanced degree. Her parents are extremely intelligent and well-spoken, and they have stressed the virtues of a traditional education and a solid religious (Pentecostal) background. Abby is proud of her African American heritage and enthusiastically curious about both the social milieu and the natural phenomena of the countryside in Oklahoma where she lives. Her relationship with Carl Lee Jefferson, a young man also attending Langston College, is initially complicated by her father's misgivings about Carl Lee's uncertain family background. Abby's love for Carl Lee and the quality of his character eventually lead to parental approval. During the course of the narrative, Abby confronts the presence of evil in a previously secure environment, and she must recognize and accept her gift for visionary insight. With the support of her family and their close friends, and with Carl Lee's love, she is able to weather a crisis of faith and support Carl Lee in his own personal time of deep stress.

Strong Jackson, Abby's father, a hardworking barber with additional skills as a draftsman and carpenter. He is the solid rock on whose strength the family and his community can depend. He is direct in speech, with a colloquial eloquence that is inspiring if a little daunting. He has survived economic distress and the racist tendencies of American society. At first, he is unaccountably angry when Abby begins to become friendly with Carl Lee, suggesting that he is overprotective and even a little jealous of Carl Lee's intentions. His good sense and sound judgment lead him to recognize that Carl Lee is an exemplary young man.

Carl Lee Jefferson, a law student at Langston College who dominates competition as the star of the track team. He is an appropriate match for Abby because his decency, gentleness, and good sense match hers, and his goals are also not limited by any kind of diminished sense of possibility. He has had to struggle with the wayward anger and incipient alcoholism of his father, who reared him. With Abby's help, he perseveres through the trauma of rebellion against his father's viciousness. He and Abby are a source of comfort for each other as each faces a testing time resulting from a family tragedy.

Patience Jackson, Abby's mother, a wise, sensible, experienced woman whose guidance is crucial for Abby as she matures. Patience provides the warmth of a loving home for her family and friends, demonstrating by example how to handle the emotional crisis and offering her skills with domestic and social situations to support and nurture those who need her. Her set of rules to live by, which she calls ten "Laws for Lovers," are an impressive personalization of the Ten Commandments.

Serena Jordan, Abby's aunt, who is married for the first time, at the age of sixty, to a man of the cloth who turns out to be possessed by evil. She is Abby's teacher in nontraditional methods of understanding. A prophet, seer, and spiritual seeker, she transmits to Abby her gifts for visionary experience and seems to reappear after her death in the guise of a cat (named Opia, which means serenity). She is memorialized by Abby, who is able to sing in the choir with a voice that recalls Serena's extraordinary vocal ability.

The Reverend Rufus Jordan, who marries Serena after the death of Serena's sister Sadonia. He is almost a caricature of selfishness and possessiveness. Described as overweight, with a squat body and squinty eyes, he is pompous and vain. These attributes pale in the light of his actions after he is deranged by a kind of demon of evil.

Samuel Jefferson, Carl Lee's father, whose experience of racist actions has left him bitter and confused. Although he loves his son, he is unable to reconcile his paternal concern with a will to dominate. His relationship with Carl Lee's mother, a Cherokee woman seen only on the fringes of society, contributes to his furtiveness and makes Carl Lee, effectively, a "motherless child." Carl Lee learns about his origins only after his father's death.

— *Leon Lewis*

A BRIGHTER SUN

Author: Samuel Selvon (1923-1994)
First published: 1952
Genre: Novel

Locale: Barataria, a village east of Port of Spain, Trinidad
Time: New Year's Day, 1939, to late 1945
Plot: Social realism

Tiger, a Trinidadian peasant of East Indian descent. Curious, ambitious, diligent, and determined to become a man, he moves, after an arranged marriage at the age of sixteen, from a traditional community on a sugar estate to a multiracial village near Port of Spain. Contemplating life's mysteries and dreaming of what education might have afforded him, he sometimes resents the burden of his young family but resolves to understand and control more of his life. Turning from most of the old ways and prejudices toward the ideal of a more integrated society, he learns to read and consciously changes and improves his use of language to prepare for the inevitable changes and opportunities he envisions. He develops a love for his pastoral surroundings but, seeking advancement and contact with a bigger world, obtains employment with the American military, constructing a highway. He is fearful of becoming like Sookdeo, but, tense and culturally confused, he drunkenly beats his pregnant wife, causing her to lose their child. Penance paid, in his early twenties he is mature and responsible, a nascent community leader with an uncertain but optimistic view of his own and his nation's future.

Urmilla, Tiger's wife. Long-haired and frail, with sad black eyes, she is married at the age of sixteen and soon pregnant with a female child. Although she is friendly with her Creole neighbor Rita and would like to laugh and talk with Tiger and share his worries, she is a traditional Hindu wife, passive, obedient, hardworking, and eager to please.

Joe Martin, a laborer and Tiger's Creole neighbor. Born to a prostitute in a Port of Spain slum and reared by his great-aunt, Ma Lambie, he suffered physical abuse, hatred, and hunger until, at the age of sixteen, he finally beat her in return. Big, strong, and without ambition, he works for the Americans and gives his money to Rita, who tries to moderate his tough, slovenly behavior in a suburban setting. Content in his illiteracy and limited knowledge, he is initially against mixing with his Indian neighbors but, as a result of Rita's influence and his own essential good nature, he gradually becomes their friend.

Rita Martin, Joe's common-law wife. Generous, decent, strong-willed, and combative, she lifts Joe and herself above their slum origins and, unable to have children, rears her nephew Henry as her own. Rita ignores racial differences to befriend Urmilla, serving as her midwife and acting as the principal agent in the Indian couple's assimilation.

Ma Lambie, Joe's brutal great-aunt. A large, frowning, ugly black woman with huge breasts, she is a barren former prostitute who seeks comfort in her old age from Joe, a child abandoned at birth. When Joe hits her, she becomes a cringing and obsequious old woman fervently singing for salvation at roadside prayer meetings. After it becomes clear that she will get nothing from Joe, she turns her hostility and sharp tongue on Rita.

Boysie, an East Indian farmer and friend of Tiger. Familiar with both the country and the city, he is an influence on Tiger and introduces him to the cosmopolitan life of Port of Spain and a broader horizon. An advocate of racial mixing and bored by the village ways, he enjoys shocking traditional Indians by showing off his Creole girlfriend. He saves money to leave for England or America after the war.

Sookdeo, an old East Indian farmer who teaches Tiger to read. Misshapen by work, small, and dark, with a gray beard and straggly hair, he is the village drunk and trickster. His comic antics hide feelings of fear and desolation at growing old and never having a son.

Tall Boy, a Chinese shopkeeper with many children. Popular, fair, clever, and generous, he gives his customers credit and has integrated well into the community, adopting local manners and habits. Hardworking, ambitious, and frugal, he sends money to relatives in China.

Larry and

Chief, two white American servicemen with whom Tiger works. Good-humored, enthusiastic, and naïvely secure in the superiority of their own values, they enjoy the superficial introduction to the exotic foods and customs of poor East Indians that Tiger and Urmilla provide. Ignorant of the dislocation their visit already has caused and relaxed by too much rum, they unwittingly encourage the further breaking of taboos; the result is Tiger's drunken beating of Urmilla.

— *Douglas Rollins*

BRIGHTON BEACH MEMOIRS

Author: Neil Simon (1927-   )
First published: 1984
Genre: Drama

Locale: Brighton Beach, a district of Brooklyn, New York
Time: Autumn, 1937
Plot: Comedy

Eugene Morris Jerome, a fifteen-year-old Jewish boy living in Brooklyn, New York. Eugene is an enthusiastic, energetic, and persistent boy with a passion for baseball, especially his hometown Dodgers. Newly aware of girls, he is impatient for sexual knowledge and lusts after his cousin Nora. He is young enough to take life, his family, and all their problems lightly and clever enough to be very humorous in the process. He is blamed for everything and must continually cover his tracks. Behind his innocent cleverness is the sharp and insightful mind of an aspiring writer; storytelling and entertaining are already basic elements of Eugene's highly expressive manner.

Kate Jerome, Eugene's mother. Kate is an optimistic yet realistic forty-year-old woman. Her belief in God and providence and her determination to find the good in all the bad things that happen are balanced with a xenophobic distrust of anything or anyone not immediately familiar. Her generous and nurturing nature can become overprotective; her capacity to worry and dominate sometimes overwhelms the members of her family. Kate works hard to keep them all going but harbors deep anger and resentment for the sacrifices she must make and the trials she must endure.

Blanche Morton, Kate's widowed younger sister. Blanche is a mournful woman who suffers from asthma and headaches and is gradually losing her eyesight from overwork at her sewing machine. She does her best to rear her daughters but feels woefully inadequate and looks to Kate and Jack for help. Her dependence on them—having housed her family under their roof for three years—feeds her feelings of guilt and powerlessness. Not interested in remarriage, she is content to wallow in self-pity over her undeserved tragedy until a fight with Kate inspires her to accept some responsibility for her life.

Nora Morton, Blanche's pretty sixteen-year-old daughter. Nora dreams of being a Broadway dancer and is hungry for independence. She misses her father dearly and has come to resent both Blanche's inability to make parental decisions and the excessive attention paid to her sister Laurie's fragile condition. Headstrong and enthusiastic, Nora says what is on her mind.

Laurie Morton, Blanche's thirteen-year-old daughter. Laurie has a heart flutter that makes the family members treat her like an invalid, and she has learned to indulge herself in their attention and exploit their concern. She studies hard and has no interest in boys yet. Precocious and contrary, she delights in correcting people and meddling tactlessly in their discussions and problems.

Stanley Jerome, Eugene's older brother. Stanley is a sincere and serious young man with a strong belief in principles and a sense of underdog morality. Despite his honesty and good faith, he somehow manages to get himself into trouble, alienating his boss and gambling away an entire paycheck. At the age of eighteen, he is seasoned and wise about teenage lust and is a good adviser to Eugene. For all of his wayward tendencies, Stanley is in awe of his father and generally acts out of selfless devotion to his family's welfare.

Jacob (Jack) Jerome, Eugene's father. Between a day job cutting raincoats and a night job selling party favors, Jack is horribly overworked, and his labors have made him older than his forty-two years. At the end of an exhausting day, he is the authority figure to whom all the family members look for guidance, and he manages to deal patiently and sensitively with their various dilemmas. He has both strong ideals and a businessman's sense of compromise; rather than give orders, he offers advice.

— *B. P. Mann*

BRIGHTON ROCK

Author: Graham Greene (1904-1991)
First published: 1938
Genre: Novel

Locale: Brighton, England
Time: The 1930's
Plot: Psychological realism

Pinkie Brown, called **The Boy**, a frail, seventeen-year-old gang leader. Pinkie's Catholic background haunts him with a growing sense of his eternal damnation; still, he wildly hopes that there is a chance for repentance and salvation. Initially, he sets out with his gang to kill Fred Hale, the man who betrayed Pinkie's mentor to a rival gangster. A sixteen-year-old waitress named Rose sees Spicer, one of Pinkie's men, shortly before Hale's murder. To have her conceal what she knows of the crime, Pinkie pretends an attraction to her, even though he is disgusted by thoughts of sex or physical closeness with Rose or anyone. When he learns from Rose that a woman is inquiring into Hale's death, he acts to solidify his position: He kills Spicer, who was thinking about going to the police, and he arranges a marriage with Rose so that she cannot be forced to testify against him. Increasingly desperate, he takes Rose into the country and tries to talk her into shooting herself by pretending to agree to a suicide pact. A fellow gang member arrives with a policeman, and Rose throws away the gun. Pinkie assumes that he has been betrayed. He smashes a bottle of vitriol, his face steaming as the acid blows on him, and throws himself over a cliff to his death.

Fred Hale, the man who betrayed Pinkie's mentor, Kite, to a rival gang leader, Colleoni. Hale has a deep inner humility but an intense pride in his profession. His job at the moment is to pose as a newspaper's **Kolley Kibber**, a character who leaves cards along a route printed in the newspaper and who pays out cash prizes to people who find the cards and recognize him. Hale is certain that he will be killed during a holiday at Brighton by Pinkie's gang, which is out to avenge Kite's death, but he proudly continues his work nevertheless. As he feared, he is attacked by the gang while he waits for a companion. He dies of a heart attack.

Spicer, a member of Pinkie's gang. Spicer has twenty-five years of experience in the gangs, having begun before Pinkie was even born. He is easily made nervous and opposes trying to kill Hale from the start. He limps because of a corn on his left foot, and the pustules around his mouth are a sign of his nervousness. His job is not to kill Hale but to take Hale's Kolley Kibber cards and leave them along the route to suggest that Hale continued his assigned work. While planting a card at a restaurant, Spicer is spotted by Rose, a new waitress, who later recalls that Spicer's appearance did not match the photograph of Hale printed in the newspaper. Spicer's restlessness makes him expendable, and Pinkie later kills him.

Ida Arnold, who becomes an amateur detective and probes into the murder of Fred Hale. Ida, a fortyish, coarse lover of life, is first seen singing in the public bar, where she meets Hale. Unlike Pinkie, Ida has no sense that there is more to life than the here and now. She operates entirely on a temporal and societal plane, with a better understanding of right and wrong than of good and evil. Because Hale seemed likable—she was his companion at the time of his death—and because a certain mystery surrounds his death, she investigates to see that justice is served.

Rose, a sixteen-year-old waitress. Rose shares Pinkie's fear of eternal damnation, and she offers him an unselfish, redemptive love. She is also aware that their civil marriage constitutes mortal sin. Her love for Pinkie eventually reaches the point where Ida Arnold cannot reason with her and make Rose see that Pinkie intends to kill her. She is perfectly willing to be damned, as long as she can share her fate with Pinkie. She hesitates in killing herself out of a normal fear of death when Pinkie gives her the gun for their suicide pact. This delay allows others to arrive. Rose is spared, and Pinkie falls to his death from a cliff. At the end of the novel, her final illusion about Pinkie is about to be shattered as she walks home to play, for the first time, a phonograph record he made for her, on which he has spoken not of his love, as she thinks, but of his hatred.

— *Glenn Hopp*

BRITANNICUS

Author: Jean Racine (1639-1699)
First published: 1670
Genre: Drama

Locale: Rome, the palace of Néron
Time: A.D. 55
Plot: Tragedy

Britannicus (brih-TA-nih-kuhs), the son of the dead Emperor Claudius. Used as the proving ground in the contest for power between Emperor Néron and Agrippine, he is finally poisoned in the struggle. His murder sets the pattern for the remainder of Néron's reign.

Agrippine (a-gree-PEEN), the widow of Emperor Claudius and mother of Emperor Néron. She wins the throne for her son; then, dominated by her lust for power, she attempts to continue her dominion over him. Fearing the diminution of her influence, she plots to replace Néron with Britannicus. Néron's violent reaction against her causes his first crime, the poisoning of Britannicus, and sets the direction of his destiny.

Néron (nay-ROH[N]), Agrippine's son and the emperor of Rome. Impatient under the yoke of his mother's domination, he learns of her plan to place Britannicus on the throne in his stead and commits the first of his many crimes, the murder of the would-be usurper.

Junie (zhew-NEE), Britannicus' betrothed, abducted by Néron, who falls in love with her and plans to divorce his wife in her favor. Junie remains faithful to Britannicus and becomes a priestess of Vesta after his death.

Narcisse (nahr-SEES), Britannicus' tutor, an opportunist who works on Néron's baser instincts.

Burrhus (BUR-uhs), Néron's tutor, who tries to emphasize the better elements in the emperor's character.

Albina (ahl-bee-NAH), a confidante of Agrippine.

Pallas (PA-luhs), a freedman, a friend and adviser to Agrippine.

Octavia (ohk-tah-VYAH), Néron's wife.

BROAD AND ALIEN IS THE WORLD
(El mundo es ancho y ajeno)

Author: Ciro Alegría (1909-1967)
First published: 1941
Genre: Novel

Locale: Peru
Time: 1912-1926
Plot: Social realism

Rosendo Maquis (rroh-SEHN-doh MAH-kees), mayor of the Peruvian Indian village of Rumi. He fights a losing battle to keep his people from losing their ancestral lands. He is a peaceful man who seeks only justice from the whites. Seeking to recover the village's prize bull, he is imprisoned as a thief. He dies in prison, victim of a brutal beating administered when he is erroneously thought to be responsible for helping another prisoner, Fiero Vasquez, escape.

Bismarck Ruiz (bees-MAHRK rrwees), an unethical lawyer. He is retained by the Indians to help them in court to keep their lands from falling into the hands of Don Amenabar, a white rancher. Ruiz is but half-hearted in his efforts, as he is also in the employ of Don Amenabar.

Don Amenabar (ah-meh-nah-BAHR), a greedy, ruthless rancher. He treats the Indians as an inferior people and robs them of their cattle and lands. He tries, too, to make slaves of them for his mines.

Correa Zavala (koh-RRAY-ah sah-BAH-lah), a zealous young lawyer. He, filled with indignation, undertakes to help the Indians, but his well-meant efforts are unsuccessful.

Fiero Vásquez (FYAY-roh BAHS-kehs), a notorious Peruvian bandit. Implored by an Indian woman from Rosendo's village who loves him, he offers to help the Indians fight eviction by force. The peaceful villagers, knowing violence will not bring them any lasting peace, reject his offer.

Benito Castro (beh-NEE-toh KAHS-troh), successor to Rosendo as the leader of the Indians of the village of Rumi. He is killed by soldiers who evict the poor people from their lands.

La Castelaña (kahs-teh-LAH-nyah), a notorious woman, mistress of the lawyer Bismarck Ruiz.

BROADWAY BOUND

Author: Neil Simon (1927-   )
First published: 1987
Genre: Drama

Locale: Brighton Beach and Brooklyn, New York
Time: 1949
Plot: Autobiographical

Kate Jerome, who is about fifty years old and graying. She is the mother of Eugene and Stanley Jerome, the daughter of Ben Epstein, and the wife of Jack Jerome. After thirty-three years of marriage, she confronts Jack with his extramarital affair; they do not speak to each other afterward. Shortly after the radio broadcast of a show written by her sons, Kate shows her son Eugene how she once danced with George Raft.

The next morning, she discovers that Jack has moved out to be with Audrey, the dying woman with whom he had an affair. Kate is silent at her discovery. Eugene states that Kate never does anything very exciting with the rest of her life, yet she never complains of sacrificing for others. She gave her love freely and rejoiced with the successes of her sons. After all, as Eugene explains at the end of the play, Kate had at one time danced with George Raft.

Eugene Morris Jerome, the twenty-three-year-old son of Kate and Jack Jerome, brother of Stanley Jerome, and grandson of Ben Epstein. Eugene works in the stockroom of a music room and writes comedy skits with his older brother. He is often the narrator of the play and is the cowriter of a CBS radio broadcast.

Stanley Jerome, Kate and Jack Jerome's twenty-eight-year-old son and Eugene's brother. Stanley, the manager of boys' clothing at Abraham and Straus, joins with Eugene to form a comedy writing team. Stan decides that Eugene and he must move out when his father says that he will never forgive his sons for the broadcast, explains that the woman with whom he had an affair was a kind and decent woman, and says that he believes that he has lived out his welcome in his own home. After Stan negotiates a two-hundred-dollar-a-week deal for Eugene and himself with *The Phil Silvers Show*, the brothers finally are able to move into a place of their own. Stan and Eugene later are able to make peace with their father.

Ben Epstein, Kate's seventy-seven-year-old father. Ben lives with Kate and her family. He is a dedicated socialist and, according to Stan, has not laughed since the stock market crash of 1929. He does not move to Florida with his wife in the beginning because he does not want to take money from his son-in-law and because he believes that Kate will need him because of her marital problems. Ben's reaction to the radio broadcast written by his grandsons is that he does not hate it, which is a compliment coming from him. Ben tries to convince Jack not to leave Kate, but Jack leaves anyway. When Eugene and Stan move out, Ben explains that he sometimes had been joking with them when he appeared to be serious; he explains further that he believes that they knew he was pre-

tending. The audience knows that Kate has adjusted to her husband's departure when Eugene says later that the now seventy-eight-year-old Ben moved to Florida to be with his wife.

Jack Jerome, Kate's fifty-five-year-old husband, who admits to having an affair. Jack believes that he recognizes his family in the radio broadcast his sons write and informs them that he will never forgive them. The morning after the broadcast, Jack moves out. He remains with Audrey (the other woman) until her death. Jack makes peace later with Eugene and Stanley, and two years later, he marries again.

Momma Epstein, Kate's mother, who moves to Florida for her health. After the radio broadcast, she calls from Florida to say that she loved the program, recognized some of the characters, and yearns to hear from Ben.

Josie, Eugene's girlfriend. She has been engaged to a Harvard student, and Eugene is able to win her love. Later, they marry, and Eugene professes great happiness.

Blanche Morton, Kate's prosperous sister, who keeps Momma until Momma's move to Florida. There is obvious tension between Kate and Blanche and between Ben and Blanche, which they sometimes seem to try to overcome. Blanche informs Ben (Poppa) that his wife (Momma) must move to Florida for health reasons and that Momma wants him to move with her.

Joe Pinotti, Stan's friend who listens to the radio show written by Stan and Eugene. After the show, Joe calls Stan to say that he thought the show was better than Jack Benny. Like Jack Jerome and Momma Epstein, Joe believes that the characters resemble people he knows.

— *Anita P. Davis*

THE BROKEN JUG
(Der zerbrochene Krug)

Author: Heinrich von Kleist (1777-1811)
First published: 1811
Genre: Drama

Locale: A village in The Netherlands
Time: Late eighteenth century
Plot: Farce

Adam (AH-dahm), the village judge. In an attempted seduction of Eve, a village girl, he is surprised by her betrothed, beaten by him, and forced to jump out of her window to escape recognition by his attacker. In spite of his invention of a series of unlikely stories designed to conceal his identity from the townsfolk and explain away the scars of battle, he eventually is found out, exposed before his court, and forced to flee the village to escape another beating.

Martha Rull (MAHR-teh rool), a village woman. She is in Adam's court carrying a broken jug and furiously demanding justice.

Ruprecht (REWP-rasht), Eve's suitor, who is accused by Martha Rull of breaking her pitcher. Under duress, he finally

testifies that he broke the jug during an altercation with Eve's would-be seducer.

Eve (AY-fa), Martha Rull's daughter, who is engaged to Ruprecht and is the object of Adam's attempted seduction.

Brigitte (bree-GIH-teh), Ruprecht's aunt and a witness to the would-be seducer's hasty retreat from Eve's house. Her appearance in court with a wig dropped by the fleeing lover establishes Adam's identity as the culprit.

Walter (VAHL-tehr), a counselor of the High Court, who is on a tour of inspection, during which he finds Adam's court in a state of chaos.

Licht (lihsht), the clerk of the court.

Veit Tümpel (fit TEWM-pehl), Ruprecht's father.

THE BRONZE HORSEMAN
(Medniy vsadnik)

Author: Alexander Pushkin (1799-1837)
First published: 1837
Genre: Poetry

Locale: St. Petersburg, Russia
Time: 1703 and 1824
Plot: Historical realism

Peter the Great (**the Bronze Horseman**), the historical figure Peter the First, known in the West as Peter the Great. He ruled Russia from 1682 until his death in 1725. An enormous man of vast talents and brutal rages, he set out to make Russia a truly European power by sheer force of will and imperial decree. His reforms affected every aspect of government—military, administrative, and fiscal—and every aspect of society and culture. This meant that, among other changes, centuries-old habits of dress and manner sanctified by religious custom were ordered cast aside in favor of Western styles. The czars hitherto had been perceived as God's righteous, anointed rulers, the embodiment of all that was Orthodox Russia. Such decrees as Peter's therefore led many to believe that he was an impostor, perhaps even the Antichrist himself. No act was more symbolic of the cataclysmic changes Peter brought on Russia than was his founding of a new capital, St. Petersburg, in 1703, the act with which the poem begins. In his role as creator and conqueror, he chooses a site well suited to his strategic and political aims but utterly unsuited to human habitation. The marshy delta of the Neva River is unformed, unstable land, a floodplain that will claim thousands of lives as the capital is being built and later thousands more from disease and natural disaster. What Peter sees is a fortress, a port, an elegant city, a "window hacked through to Europe." One hundred years later, the Bronze Horseman, French sculptor Falconet's equestrian statue that stands on the granite-faced bank of the conquered Neva, takes over for the flesh-and-blood emperor. Commissioned by Catherine the Great as a tribute to Peter, it stands on a single piece of Finnish granite sculpted to suggest a wave. The statue's only flicker of reaction to human concerns comes when crazed Evgeny turns to threaten it, and it descends—or seems to descend—from its pedestal to pursue the man through the deserted city streets for one long terrifying night.

Evgeny, a poor clerk in the machinery of government introduced by Peter. The author gives him no last name, and he might well be no more than an anonymous drudge, like thousands of others in the imperial capital, except that he is descended from an ancient and noble family whose glory days have long since ended, thanks in part to Peter's reforms. Evgeny, however, is neither bitter nor ambitious, though he vaguely regrets not being smarter or better connected. His hopes are much more modest than his lineage, and he dreams of making enough money to settle down with his beloved Parasha and rear a family. Even these humble dreams, however, are swept away by the great flood of 1824. Although Evgeny escapes with his life, the loss of Parasha drives him to madness. His brief spark of rebellion against Peter and his city is quickly extinguished.

Parasha, the girl Evgeny intends to marry. She and her mother live in a tiny house on one of the Neva's many islands, home to the humbler folk of the city. She is neither seen nor heard directly, but both her presence in Evgeny's thoughts and her sudden, shocking absence are crucial. Her disappearance in the flood sends Evgeny into grief and madness.

— *Jane Ann Miller*

BROTHER ASS
(El hermano asno)

Author: Eduardo Barrios (1884-1963)
First published: 1922
Genre: Novel

Locale: A rural town in Chile
Time: Twentieth century
Plot: Psychological realism

Fray Lázaro (LAH-sah-roh), a novice in a Franciscan order in rural Chile. His name in the outside world was Mario. He chose to enter a Franciscan monastery after he was rejected by his girlfriend, Gracia. Although he has spent seven years at the monastery, he hesitates to take life vows as a friar because he worries that his vocation may not be authentic. He believes that he is wasting his youth and his potential (he enjoys writing), and the religious life is not giving him strong personal satisfaction. His daily routine of teaching and work in the monastery's fields is boring and unrewarding. When he meets María Mercedes, Gracia's younger sister, he finds relief from the tedium of his life. Every day, he feels more eager to see her. Fray Lázaro begins to suffer a severe religious crisis when he realizes that he is in love with the innocent woman. Although he struggles against physical attraction to María Mercedes, he recognizes sexual desire in his love for her. His internal debate is interrupted by Fray Rufino's attempt to rape María Mercedes. Fray Lázaro assumes all guilt for the violent act, and the order transfers him to another monastery.

Fray Rufino (rew-FEE-noh), a Franciscan friar, old and feeble. Fray Rufino's reputation as a saint has spread throughout the town, causing people to seek his company and counsel. His miracles include his ability to communicate with animals, his power to cure dying animals, and his restoration of the sight of a blind woman. In order to maintain humility, Fray Rufino takes on a heavy work load, adding to his own chores at the monastery the most menial tasks of his fellow friars. He also punishes his body by flagellation and by other physical ordeals, such as crawling on the stone floors of the church while carrying a heavy wooden cross. During a conversation with Fray Lázaro, Fray Rufino confesses that he is visited by the ghost of a former Franciscan monk. The apparition, Fray Rufino claims, reminds him of his human imperfections and of the animal desires that control his behavior. In a neurotic crisis, Fray Rufino attempts sexual abuse of María Mercedes, who is at the monastery seeking his advice. Fray Rufino blames the apparition of the Franciscan monk for this terrible action, claiming that it was the ghost's idea, not his.

María Mercedes, a young woman living in the small town near the Franciscan monastery. Upon moving to the town and finding out that Fray Lázaro, an old boyfriend of her sister, is a novice in the Franciscan monastery, María Mercedes starts visiting him. She remembers Mario as a man full of life, and she is truly interested in knowing the reasons he chose a religious life. María Mercedes' innocent questions provoke a spiritual crisis in Fray Lázaro. Eventually, María Mercedes falls in love with him. Desperate when her family forbids her visits to the monastery, María Mercedes asks Fray Lázaro to arrange an appointment for her to ask Fray Rufino's advice. It is during that visit that Fray Rufino sexually attacks María Mercedes. Although the young woman tells her family that the attacker is Fray Rufino, they are convinced by the religious administrators that Fray Lázaro is responsible for the assault.

Gracia, a married woman, María Mercedes' older sister. After rejecting young Mario's romantic approaches, Gracia married a musician with an established local reputation. She attempts to stop María Mercedes from seeing Fray Lázaro, and it probably is she who starts the rumors of romance between them.

The Provincial, the superior who directs the monastery. He protects the monastery's reputation by forcing Fray Lázaro to accept the blame for Fray Rufino's attack on María Mercedes.

— *Rafael Ocasio*

THE BROTHERS

Author: Terence (Publius Terentius Afer, c. 190-159 B.C.E.)
First performed: 160 B.C.E.
Genre: Drama

Locale: Athens
Time: The second century B.C.E.
Plot: Comedy

Micio (MEE-shee-oh), an easygoing Athenian bachelor. After adopting Aeschinus, the son of his austere brother Demea, he becomes an indulgent, permissive parent. His wise handling of Aeschinus' escapades finally convinces his brother of the wisdom of ruling by kindness rather than by fear.

Demea (DEE-mee-uh), Micio's unyielding brother, who is dedicated to strict discipline in the upbringing of children. He is the father of Ctesipho, and his severity makes the boy fearful of his parent. Learning through experience the folly of trying to rule by fear, he tries leniency and generosity, to the gratification of all concerned.

Aeschinus (EHS-kih-nehs), the son of Demea adopted by Micio. A report that Aeschinus has entered a house and abducted a woman causes the distressed foster father to be accused of parental overindulgence. When the break-in is finally and satisfactorily explained, the foster father's leniency is justified and Aeschinus is permitted to marry Pamphila.

Ctesipho (TEH-sih-foh), Demea's son. He is in love with a slave girl he cannot afford to buy. Angered by his father's severity, he, with the help of his brother Aeschinus, abducts the girl in defiance of parental restraint. His father, finally realizing the error of his disciplinary methods, gives his approval to Ctesipho's passion.

Sostrata (SOHS-trah-tuh), Pamphila's mother.

Pamphila (PAM-fih-leh), Sostrata's daughter, loved by Aeschinus.

Sannio (SA-nee-oh), a slave dealer.

Hegio (HEE-jee-oh), an old Athenian and a friend of Demea.

Syrus (SIH-ruhs) and

Phrygia (FRIH-jee-uh), slaves freed by Micio.

THE BROTHERS ASHKENAZI
(Di brider Ashkenazi)

Author: Israel Joshua Singer (1893-1944)
First published: 1936
Genre: Novel

Locale: Poland
Time: Late nineteenth and early twentieth centuries
Plot: Historical realism

Simcha Meyer Ashkenazi, the elder of twin brothers. A shrewd schemer, he advances in affluence through successive marriages and unscrupulous dealings. Later, though his fortune is not always spared, he does manage to survive various historical disasters: the trade-union movement, a pogrom against the Jews, World War I, and the Russian revolution.

Jacob Bunim Ashkenazi, his brother, who is popular and extroverted. His rise in the world results from his ebullience and popularity, and parallels Simcha's. At last, returning to Poland from Russia with Simcha, whom he has freed from jail by bribery, he is shot by anti-Jewish border guards because, unlike Simcha, he refuses to grovel and repudiate his religion.

Abraham Ashkenazi, their father, greatly respected in his town of Lodz in Poland. After Simcha connives succesfully to take over his father's position, Abraham counts Simcha among the dead.

Dinah Ashkenazi, Simcha's wife. In love with Jacob, she is betrothed to Simcha at thirteen. He divorces her to marry a rich widow.

Pearl Ashkenazi, Jacob's wife, who is too sickly to keep up with her vigorous husband. She divorces him.

Nissan, the son and pupil of a famous rabbi, and Simcha's fellow student. A reader of secular books, he is betrayed by Simcha and cast out by his father. He becomes a weaver and a revolutionary. Beaten in his capacity as strike leader by Simcha, he avenges himself in Russia after the revolution; his party confiscates Simcha's property.

Tevyeh, a weaver and a fanatical revolutionary. Simcha has him arrested and exiled along with Nissan.

Gertrude Ashkenazi, the daughter of Dinah and Simcha, and Jacob's second wife. He marries her because she reminds him of Dinah.

Ignatz Ashkenazi, Simcha's long-forgotten son. Simcha, returned from Russia and rebuilding his factory, induces Ignatz to come back from France. Simcha suspects darkly that Ignatz' French wife is not Jewish.

Huntze, the German owner of the biggest steam mill in Lodz. Abraham is Huntze's general agent until Huntze's death, after which Huntze's sons dismiss Abraham and appoint Simcha in his place, to repay a favor.

THE BROTHERS KARAMAZOV
(Bratya Karamazovy)

Author: Fyodor Dostoevski (1821-1881)
First published: 1879-1880
Genre: Novel

Locale: Russia
Time: The nineteenth century
Plot: Psychological realism

Fyodor Pavlovitch Karamazov (FYOH-dohr PAHV-loh-vihch kah-rah-MAH-zof), a crude buffoon of a father and the extremist, sensual, materialistic progenitor of a line of doomed sons. As an aging libertine he is brought in competition with his sons over a woman, money, and status, and also by a sheer determination to live and control his destiny without interference. His manners are as threatening as his brooding appearance, and as a sensual his debauchery is extreme, unabated even in his dwindling years. He is crafty, greedy, close-fisted, exhibiting a low cunning which speaks of a special kind of intelligence. His pose is artful; his lust for life and his voluptuousness are phenomenal. Obscene as he is, a malignant joker of low order, he has about him an air of magnificence gone to seed in an aging domestic tyrant.

Dmitri (DMIH-trihy), often called Mitya, his oldest son, who most resembles his father and most despises him for the wrong done the dead mother and himself. Morbidly fearful of his heredity, Dmitri reviles his father not so much for what he has done as a man who has cheated his son of both birthright and lover, but for what he is, a cruel, crafty despoiler of all that is decent. Like his father, he is muscular, though slender, sallow, with large dark eyes. He is a kind of scapegoat, the one on whom the curse of sensuousness falls most heavily, given as he is to strong feelings and actions. He has a brooding Russian personality, an excitability, a violent nature capable of deep emotions and lasting love and antagonisms, though he has also simplicity, natural goodness, an open heart, directness, and awareness.

Ivan (ih-VAHN), his half brother, an intellectual, poet, and atheist, given to visions and flights of fancy, secretiveness, remote aloofness. Five years younger than Mitya, he seems older, more mature, better poised. He has a subtle mind, both skeptical and idealistic, mercurial and unrealistic. Although none of the boys, having been cared for by relatives, is close to their tempestuous father, Ivan is the least known to Fyodor Karamazov and the one he most fears for qualities so remote from his own. Though he wills his father's death, he is greatly shocked at the deed and his part in it, and he suffers a guilt complex so great that it unhinges his dualistic mind. He serves as the author's mouthpiece in the long Grand Inquisitor scene and the account of his private devil. Ivan is loved distantly and respected by his brothers for this very lucidity and clairvoyance. He inherits the lust, the extremism, the egocentricity of his father, but in a refined, inward, though almost as compulsive a way.

Alyosha (ah-LYOH-shuh), also known as **Alexey** (ah-lehk-SAY), Ivan's brother and Dmitri's half brother, the spiritual son who is the peacemaker, the sympathizer, the trusted and beloved brother if not son. Nineteen, healthy, bright, personable, good-looking, Alyosha, out of goodness and love, forms a bond with his unregenerate father and his distrustful brothers. His devotion to the good Father Zossima, his acceptance of his own worldliness at war with his spirituality, and his sheer love of life make him an attractive character, a natural, human person among grotesques.

Grushenka (GREW-shehn-kuh), beloved by father and son, an intemperate temptress, an earthy type who realizes more than she can communicate. She appears a hussy, but she is also devoted, loyal in her own way, and loving. Primitive, independent, free of the petty vindictiveness that plagues her lovers, Grushenka enlivens the story with a wholesome, womanly, even motherly quality.

Katerina Ivanovna (kah-tehr-IHN-uh ih-VAH-nohv-nuh), beloved by Ivan but engaged to Dmitri, an aristocrat and compulsive lover of great force of character. Willing to beg for love, to buy her beloved, she also has a fierce pride that flames up in revenge. Though she is attractive in a more austere way than Grushenka, they share many eternally feminine traits.

Smerdyakov (smehr-DYAH-kof), a half-witted servant, perhaps a natural son of Karamazov, and his murderer. He is scornful and sadistic. As the murderer who cannot live with his guilt, he is seen as more sinned against than sinning, the victim more than the antagonist. He hates his master and Dmitri, but he is curiously drawn to Ivan and in reality dies for him. Smerdyakov hangs himself.

Father Zossima (ZOH-seh-mah), a devout religious ascetic, Aloysha's teacher in the monastery to which the boy retires for a time. Aware of the sensual nature of the Karamazovs, the old priest advises the boy to go back to the world. Because of his holy example, his followers expect a miracle to occur when Father Zossima dies. Instead, his body decomposes rapidly, a circumstance viewed by other monks as proof that the aged man's teachings have been false.

Marfa (MAHR-fuh), a servant in the Karamazov household and Smerdyakov's foster mother.

Grigory (grih-GOH-ree), Marfa's husband.

Lizaveta (lyee-zah-VEH-tuh), the half-witted girl who was Smerdyakov's mother. Many people in the village believed that Fyodor Karamazov was the father of her child.

BROWN GIRL, BROWNSTONES

Author: Paule Marshall (1929-   )
First published: 1959
Genre: Novel

Locale: Brooklyn, New York
Time: During World War II and a few years surrounding the war
Plot: Social realism

Selina Boyce, a young black girl growing up among Barbadian immigrants in a section of Brooklyn. Selina is a sensitive, intelligent child, extremely attached to her free-spirited father and at fierce odds with her strong-willed, practical mother, both recent immigrants from Barbados. Throughout most of the novel, Selina attempts to act as mediator between her beloved but hopelessly idealistic father and her hard, manipulating mother, whose only dream is to buy a home of her own, rather than run the boardinghouse in which the Boyce family lives. The explosive tension within the family is matched by the internal sexual and emotional tension within the adolescent Selina. She watches helplessly as her family disintegrates, and she struggles to escape the destruction through a personal metamorphosis, a transformation from an "invisible" black child into a self-reliant woman in search of her roots.

Deighton Boyce, Selina's father. Deighton's impractical idealism leads him to various dead ends. He chases one grand scheme to achieve fame and financial security after another, only to abandon the projects when success or acceptance is not immediate. Still, Selina adores her free-spirited father and shares his whimsical dreams. When Deighton receives word that he has inherited a piece of land in Barbados, he and Selina begin to spin a dream of a return to the homeland as prosperous landowners. When Selina's mother sells Deighton's land behind his back, Deighton initiates a path of rage and self-destruction.

Silla Boyce, Selina's mother. Silla is a strong, willful woman with one goal: to establish a permanent home for herself and her family in New York. She wants no part of Deighton's dream of a return to their homeland, which she remembers as oppressive and spiritually bankrupt. She covertly sells Deighton's land, and when he wastes the money she received for the land and abandons the family for a religious cult, she reports him to the immigration services and has him deported. All of her actions enrage Selina, with whom Silla engages in an ongoing struggle for control and dominance.

Suggie, a tenant in the Boyce's boardinghouse. Suggie is well known for her sexual adventures, inviting various men up to her room each night. Her bohemian lifestyle attracts the curiosity of Selina, who eventually finds in Suggie a kind of mentor and friend. Suggie encourages the frightened, shy Selina to reach out for life and also assists Selina in discovering her sexual self.

Miss Thompson, a hairdresser and an acquaintance of the Boyces. Miss Thompson serves as a mother figure to Selina, who is able to talk to the hairdresser in ways she finds impossible with her own mother. Miss Thompson walks with a limp as the result of a wound in her leg received in her youth when a young man attempted to rape her. She carries her wound as a reminder to herself and all who see her of the victimization of uneducated, disenfranchised immigrant women.

Clive Springer, Selina's first lover, a twenty-nine-year-old artist and World War II veteran. In addition to initiating Selina into the world of sexual expression, Clive helps her through various racial and social traumas. Despite his important role as Selina's first male mentor other than her father, Clive himself is defeated by the world. The war destroyed much of his sensitivity, and racial and artistic prejudices continue to plague him.

— *Penelope A. LeFew*

THE BROWNING VERSION

Author: Terence Rattigan (1911-1977)
First published: 1949
Genre: Drama

Locale: A public school in southern England
Time: The 1940's
Plot: Problem

Andrew Crocker-Harris, a schoolmaster in an English public school. He is a failure both in his teaching of the classics and in his marriage. "The Crock," as he is dubbed by his pupils, is retiring for health reasons, one year short of qualifying for a pension. He assumes that because there is precedent, he will be granted a pension. With a reputation for giving students grades that are neither more nor less than they deserve, he seems an anachronism in a time when younger masters curry favor with students. Emotionally repressed, he gives no outward sign of his knowledge of his wife's infidelities, the latest involving Frank Hunter, a popular and younger master. On this, his penultimate day at the private school, he experiences for the first time in many years an emotional release that he describes as the twitchings of a corpse. His pupil, Taplow; his colleague, Hunter; and his replacement, Gilbert serve as catalysts for this release. Confronting his personal and professional failure openly, he breaks down his traditional English "stiff upper lip" and makes hard choices: to leave Millie, to take a position at a crammers' school, and to follow rather than precede a popular master in speaking at term-end exercises. In making these choices, he begins to rejoin the human community and gain a self-respect that enables him to face his future with a new dignity.

Millie Crocker-Harris, the unfaithful wife of Andrew. Bitter about his professional failure and their marital failure, she has been involved in a desultory affair with Frank Hunter. She expresses her contempt for her husband in a grippingly climactic moment when, in the presence of Hunter, she taunts Andrew with the fact that she had witnessed Taplow mimicking Andrew. She reacts even more cruelly to Andrew's emotional display when he receives a gift from Taplow—a secondhand copy of Robert Browning's version of Agamemnon. She describes the gift as a few bobs' worth of appeasement for a grade.

John Taplow, a plain boy of about sixteen who wears glasses. Entering the Crocker-Harris flat for a final Greek tutorial, he is soon joined by Hunter, who has arrived for his final farewell to Andrew. The two have an easy, informal exchange, during which Taplow mimics "the Crock." Despite Andrew's reputation for teaching Agamemnon as an exercise in translation, rather than as an exciting story about a woman who murders her husband, Taplow confesses to a sympathy for Andrew. His sympathy is expressed in his inscription in his gift, a quotation from a speech by Agamemnon to Clytemnestra: "God from afar looks graciously upon a gentle master."

Frank Hunter, a ruggedly built younger man with the confident bearing of a popular schoolmaster. Intending for some time to bring his relationship with Millie to an end, he now does so out of anger over Millie's devastating cruelty to Andrew. In an offer of friendship that he convinces the reluctant schoolmaster to accept, Hunter promises to visit Andrew when Andrew is settled in his new position.

Dr. Frobisher, a stereotypical headmaster who conveys to Andrew the rejection of the latter's application for a pension and who only makes matters worse when he attempts to assuage the impact of his disappointing news by suggesting that Andrew precede rather than follow the more popular master as speaker at the end-of-term ceremonies. The latter would be embarrassingly anticlimactic, but Andrew refuses to speak in the earlier position.

Peter Gilbert, the young replacement for Andrew. During his visit to look over the Crocker-Harrises' flat, into which he and his wife will move, he inadvertently lets slip the headmaster's description of Andrew as the Heinrich Himmler of the lower fifth. Even though he apologizes for the unintentional tactlessness of his comment, Gilbert, like Taplow and Hunter, serves as a catalyst for Andrew's confrontation with his failure to communicate with the young boys. The two men reach an understanding and achieve a bond of which Andrew was in need.

Mrs. Gilbert, the young wife of Peter. In a marriage only two months old, she seems superficial and immersed in petty concerns, so that Peter reacts harshly to her inaccurate account of what he describes as their sordid encounter, their first meeting. Their marriage seems destined for a fate not unlike that of the Crocker-Harrises.

— *Susan Rusinko*

BRUNO'S DREAM

Author: Iris Murdoch (1919-   )
First published: 1969
Genre: Novel

Locale: London, England
Time: Mid-1960's
Plot: Farce

Bruno Greensleave, a terminally ill old man. Bruno's illness has disfigured him, so that he looks somewhat like the arachnids he studies; his head seems bulbous and enlarged, but his limbs are wasted and thin. Aware that he is dying, Bruno wishes to make amends for the missteps he has made along the way. He wants to reunite with his estranged son, Miles, and regrets that he did not go to his dying wife when she called for him.

Miles Greensleave, Bruno's son. He has been estranged from Bruno since his first marriage, to an Indian woman, Parvati. He works as a minor civil servant but considers his vocation to be poetry. He married Diana several years after Parvati's death and lives a quiet, contemplative life. He realizes that he loves Lisa, Diana's sister, who lives with them. He idealizes Lisa, and the loss of her enables him again to write poetry.

Danby Odell, Bruno's son-in-law. He has managed Bruno's printing business since his marriage to Gwen, Bruno's daughter, who has been dead for many years. Danby idolized Gwen, to whom he always felt slightly inferior. Danby takes care of Bruno, who lives in Danby's house. Women find Danby charming, and he has been having an affair with Adelaide for some time before he flirts with Diana and then falls in love with Lisa.

Diana Greensleave, Miles's second wife. She first saw Miles in the market and fantasized that she could assuage his pain. Upon their marriage, she creates for Miles a safe haven and does ease his anguish. She accepts her second place in Miles's heart, Parvati being his great love. She returns Danby's flirtation and is greatly hurt when both Miles and Danby fall in love with Lisa. She tends and loves Bruno at the end of his life. By the end of the novel, she becomes a kind of divine figure, bearing others' pain and watching over them benevolently.

Lisa Watkin, Diana's sister. Lisa had a varied career before coming to live with Miles and Diana. After receiving a first-class degree at the University of Oxford, she taught in Yorkshire and joined the Communist Party. Later, she converted to Catholicism and joined the Order of Poor Clares. After leaving the order, she went to Paris and came down with tuberculosis. She teaches school in the East End of London. Lisa always has been considered the emotionally fragile sister, an image belied by her career. She returns Miles's love but refuses to have an affair with him. To shatter Miles's idealization of her, she has a happy, hedonistic affair with Danby.

Adelaide de Crecy, Danby's housekeeper and mistress. She greatly loves Danby and at first would have agreed to an affair even had he not promised to support her. She is devastated when Danby falls in love with Lisa, and eventually she marries her cousin, Will Boase, amid floods of tears.

Will Boase, Adelaide's cousin. Will is a temperamental, out-of-work actor who is given to violent passions. He loves Adelaide but tries to use her position in Danby's household to acquire money. He eventually becomes a great actor.

Nigel Boase, Adelaide's cousin and Will's twin. He works as a nurse to Bruno and is very tender with him. He believes himself godlike and spies on others to acquire knowledge about them. He informs Will of Danby's affair with Adelaide and tells Diana that she will watch over others benevolently.

— *Karen M. Cleveland*

THE BRUSHWOOD BOY

Author: Rudyard Kipling (1865-1936)
First published: 1895
Genre: Novel

Locale: England and India
Time: The nineteenth century
Plot: Fantasy

Georgie Cottar, the character to whom the book's title refers. The Brushwood Boy is a highly imaginative young man of the upper middle class who, alone among his nurse, his father and mother, and a houseful of domestics, dreams dreams. His dreams always begin the same way. There is a pile of brushwood on a beach; there are people, sometimes a policeman; and there is always an adventure, usually a pleasant one. The story takes Georgie from his third year, through public school, to Sandhurst, to the Indian service as an officer in charge of many soldiers, and back to England as a young adult. Each stage of his life is productive of the dream that begins at the brushwood pile. A girl moves in and out of the dreams, but as he gets older, Georgie notices that the girl becomes more consistently the same person. She finally materializes as the girl Georgie hopes to marry and live with in real life.

Miriam Lacy, the young girl Georgie meets when he returns to England on a year's furlough from his regiment. Like the girl in his dreams, she has black hair fixed in a widow's peak, and she speaks with a slight lisp. Strangely, she seems to know all about Georgie's dream, because she sings songs that are summaries of the stories he has dreamed.

Annieanlouise, the name formed by running together Georgie's two favorite female names, Anna and Louise. In the dreams of his childhood, Georgie called the girl he dreamed about by this name. Annieanlouise becomes, of course, the Miriam of Georgie's real world.

BRUT

Author: Layamon (fl. twelfth century)
First published: c. 1205
Genre: Poetry

Locale: Britain
Time: c. 409-689
Plot: Epic

Aeneas (ee-NEE-uhs), the Trojan hero, legendary ancestor of the ancient rulers of Britain.

Ascanius (as-KAY-nee-uhs), his son.

Brutus (BREW-tuhs), his grandson, who colonizes Britain with a group of Trojan descendants. Brave and generous to his followers, he is an ideal leader in the tradition of Beowulf.

Assaracus, the heir of a Greek knight and his Trojan concubine. He is Brutus' companion and military aide.

Corineus, the ruler of a Trojan colony in Spain and, later, of Cornwall. He is a man of violent temper and great bravery.

Geomagog, the giant who rules Logice, the island where Brutus lands.

Locrin, Brutus' successor, who brings chaos upon his country by repudiating his wife, Corineus' daughter, for his mistress, a maiden of his enemies, the Huns.

Camber and

Albanact, his brothers, rulers of Wales and Scotland.

Humber, the king of the Huns, defeated by Locrin and Camber.

Aestrild, Locrin's mistress.

Guendoline, Locrin's rejected queen, who raises an army to defeat her husband and kill her rival.

Leil, a monarch who dies of sorrow at the uprising of his barons.

Ruhhudibras, the founder of Winchester and Canterbury.

Bladud, his heir, whose discovery of hot springs is considered evidence of his consultation with devils.

Leir, the legendary original of William Shakespeare's Lear. He divides his kingdom between two of his daughters but rejects the third for her refusal to flatter him. After suffering persecution from the elder two, he is happily reunited with his youngest child.

Gornuille,

Ragun, and

Cordoille, his daughters.

Aganippus, the king of France, Cordoille's husband.

Gorbodiago, a good king, the model of the title figure in Thomas Norton and Thomas Sackville's *Gorboduc* (1565).

Fereus and

Poreus, his sons, murdered and murderer.

Jadon, their mother, who takes Poreus' life to avenge his killing of Fereus.

Cloten, the duke of Cornwall, the man with the greatest right to Gorbodiago's throne. He lacks wealth and power to claim it.

Donwallo Molinus, his son, the fairest king of England, who brings peace, quiet, and good laws to his people.

Belen and

Brennes, brothers and joint rulers. They conduct successful campaigns against Scandinavian and Roman forces.

Julius Caesar and

Claudius, Roman emperors and rulers of Britain.

Luces, the just monarch in whose reign Christianity reaches England.

Asclepidiot, the ruler who expels the Romans.

Helen, the daughter of Coel, king of Britain, and Constantine's mother, who discovers the Cross of Christ in Jerusalem.

Constantine, her son, who reigns in Britain and expels the tyrant Maxenz from Rome.

Vortiger, a powerful earl, controller of half of Wales. To acquire power, he instigates a plot to place on the throne his king's son Constance, who is a monk and is therefore ineligible to rule.

Constance, a weak king.

Uther, his brother, a fine warrior who, before he becomes king, defeats both the Irish and the invading heathens under Hengest.

Hengest, the leader of the Germanic tribes who joins Vortiger's court at his own request.

Vortimer, Vortiger's son and heir, a Christian ruler who tries to expel Hengest.

Merlin, a magician, "son of no man," who serves as counselor to Uther and Arthur.

Ygaerne, the wife of Gorlois, earl of Cornwall. Uther desires her.

Arthur, the son of Uther and Ygaerne, recalled from his home in Brittany to be a wise and generous king of England and sworn enemy to the Saxon invaders. A fierce warrior, he extends his conquests to Rome itself. Mortally wounded in battle against his treacherous nephew, Modred, he departs for

Avalon to be healed by the fairy queen, promising to return.

Wenhavere (Guinevere), his queen. She betrays him with Modred and retreats to a nunnery after her lover's defeat.

Walwain (Gawain), Arthur's nephew, a noble, virtuous knight, prototype of the hero of Pearl-Poet's *Sir Gawain and the Green Knight* (fourteenth century), who is debased in Sir Thomas Malory's *Le Morte d'Arthur* (1485).

Kay, one of Arthur's trusted knights.

Beduer (Bedivere), Arthur's steward and another of his favorite knights.

Modred, Walwain's treacherous brother.

Luces, the Roman emperor killed by Arthur after he had demanded tribute from the British.

Austin, a priest sent, years later, to introduce Christianity into Britain a second time.

Æthelbert, his royal convert.

Aeluric, his enemy, a Northumbrian king.

Penda, the king of Marcia, who treacherously murders the son of his ally, King Edwine.

Cadwalader, the last of the British kings, beset by plague and famine.

Athelstan, the first English king of all England.

BUCHANAN DYING

Author: John Updike (1932-   )
First published: 1974
Genre: Drama

Locale: Lancaster, Pennsylvania, and Washington, D.C.
Time: The 1860's
Plot: Historical

James Buchanan, the fifteenth president of the United States. This three-act closet drama opens in 1868 with Buchanan, a big man in his late seventies, lying on his deathbed at his estate in Pennsylvania. Because of age and decrepitude, he is in an abnormal mental condition. Most of the people who were important in his life appear in his bedchamber as hallucinations. Among the forty or so characters who make cameo appearances in this biographical pageant are such famous historical figures as Andrew Jackson, Stephen Douglas, James Polk, Jefferson Davis, and Abraham Lincoln. There are also less illustrious people, including relatives and personal friends. Most of those who confront Buchanan accuse him of one fault or another, depending on their individual perspectives and relationships with the former chief executive. Among the many accusations are that he was a cold, selfish, scheming pettifogger who betrayed his country by conspiring with the proslavery faction on the eve of the Civil War and that he was primarily responsible for that tragic conflict. From Buchanan's explanations of his various actions during his long period of public service, it becomes apparent that he was an exceptionally hardworking, conscientious, and circumspect if not brilliant man who was just as concerned as his successor, Abraham Lincoln, with preserving the Union. Buchanan dies a lonely, friendless, disappointed old man but a much more sympathetic figure than generally portrayed in history books.

Harriet Lane Johnston, Buchanan's niece. She appears at different ages throughout the play, at first as a vivacious blonde teenager, later as a mature woman, and finally as a stately matron. Buchanan was the first bachelor to become a U.S. president, and he chose his intelligent, spirited niece to act as his first lady. She was an accomplished hostess and became extremely popular in Washington circles as well as with the American public. In the play, she serves mainly as an interlocutor to Buchanan in order to bring out biographical material in a conversational format.

Anne Coleman, Buchanan's fiancée. This slender, hypersensitive, aristocratic brunette died at the age of twenty-three. Her death was attributed to hysteria resulting from her breaking off her engagement to Buchanan in a fit of irrational jealousy. There were many rumors, however, that she had committed suicide. Her tragic death was the single most important event in Buchanan's life. He told many people that his unrequited love for Anne explained his never having married. Her portrait hangs above the fireplace mantel in the old man's bedchamber. Hostile contemporaries believed he was simply too cold, self-centered, and cerebral a person to engage in matrimony. In the play, he is accused of having been more interested in his fiancée's family fortune than in her person. She appears in his hallucinations to discuss these and other matters of a nonpolitical nature, rounding out the portrait of Buchanan as a human being as well as a politician.

— *Bill Delaney*

BUDDENBROOKS
(Buddenbrooks: Verfall einer Familie)

Author: Thomas Mann (1875-1955)
First published: 1901
Genre: Novel

Locale: Germany
Time: The nineteenth century
Plot: Social realism

Johann Buddenbrook (YOH-hahn BOO-dehn-brohk), the stout, rosy-faced, benevolent-looking patriarch of the Buddenbrook family. He is the wealthy, successful senior partner of a grain-trading firm inherited from his father.

Johann "Jean" Buddenbrook, Jr., called **The Consul**, his serious-looking, aquiline-nosed, blond-bearded first son by his second wife. Jean combines the sentimentalist and the

businessman. He rejoices over a happy family gathering, worries about the alienation of his half brother, Gotthold, from the family, and then advises coolly that Gotthold's request for money be denied because of likely future results to both family and firm. Jean's pietism seems foreign to the other Buddenbrooks, whose religion is superficial and confined to conventional sentiments proper to people of their class.

Antonie (Tony) Buddenbrook (AHN-toh-nee), later **Frau Grünlich** and **Frau Permaneder**, Jean's oldest child. She has ash-blonde hair, gray-blue eyes, and finely shaped but stumpy hands. Impetuous in youth, she becomes conventional in maturity, but to her brother Tom she always remains a child in her reactions to the incidents in her life. She easily adapts herself to any situation; she is not humiliated by the dissolution of her marriage to Grünlich and is proud of the fact that she becomes a person of importance in the family. She adapts as readily to the breaking up of her marriage to Permaneder. As she develops a closer intimacy with her father following her first divorce, she recognizes and establishes closer ties with Tom after the death of their father. She sees the two of them as true Buddenbrooks, for their brother Christian does not really seem one of the family, and young Clara remains an unimportant sister. The retention of dignity for both herself and the family becomes almost a religion with Tony.

Tom Buddenbrook, Jean's older son (modeled upon Thomas Mann's father). A quick-witted, intelligent, even-tempered boy, he becomes a strong, sturdy youth resembling his grandfather Johann. As he matures, he develops a stocky, broad-shouldered figure and a military air. His excessive clothes consciousness seems out of character for a Buddenbrook. An earnest, responsible businessman, he is proud of his burgher ancestry, and he contrasts his own desire to preserve the family name with the lack of imagination and idealism shown by Gotthold, his father's half brother. He is increasingly disgusted with Christian's business irresponsibility and his reputation as a strange kind of clown. He cannot forgive Christian's joking observation in company that all businessmen are swindlers. In his prime, Tom is more aggressive than the earlier Buddenbrooks, but occasionally a little less scrupulous. His participation in public affairs and his interest in culture set him somewhat apart from his ancestors and his business associates. Early in his forties, he becomes increasingly aware that he has grown prematurely old, and he thinks more and more of death. At forty-eight he feels that death is stalking him. He dies not many months later following a fall in a snowy street after the partial extraction of a rotted tooth.

Christian Buddenbrook (KRIHS-tee-ahn), Jean's younger son. A born mimic, he is a moody, whimsical, sometimes extravagantly silly boy. As a youth, he first betrays his weakness for pretty women and his deep interest in the theater. During an eight-year absence from home, principally in South America, he becomes lean and pallid, his large humped nose more prominent, his neck thinner, his hair sparse. Through association with Englishmen abroad, he himself grows to look like an Englishman. His self-absorption and his lack of dignity in his social manners disturb Tom Buddenbrook's sense of propriety. Christian becomes more and more a neurotic and a hypochondriac as he ages. After Tom's death, Christian marries his mistress, who not long afterward has to put him in a mental institution. Like Tom's son Hanno, he symbolizes the decay of the Buddenbrook family.

Frau Consul Elizabeth Kröger Buddenbrook (ay-LEE-sah-bat KROH-gehr), the wife of Jean Buddenbrook. A woman of the world and a lover of life, she becomes well known in her later years for her piety and her numerous charities. After a long life with her family, she dies of pneumonia.

Clara Buddenbrook (KLAH-rah), the fourth and youngest child of Jean and Elizabeth. Hawk-nosed, dark-haired, and firm-mouthed, she is at times haughty. She marries Pastor Tiburtius, a minister from Riga, and dies childless a few years later.

Gotthold Buddenbrook (GOT-hohld), the elder Johann's unambitious son by his first wife. Having angered his father by a disapproved marriage and by becoming a shopkeeper, he is thereafter shunned by the family. He resents the favored treatment accorded his half-brother Jean. After his father's death, Gotthold retires and lives on the income from his inheritance and the sale of his shop. He dies at sixty of a heart attack.

Gerda Arnoldsen Buddenbrook (GAYR-dah AHR-nold-sehn), an aristocratic Dutch heiress who attends school with Tony. Her immense dowry later influences Tom's decision to marry her, though he declares to his mother at the time that he loves Gerda. The marriage is a happy one, but Gerda (perhaps modeled in part on Thomas Mann's mother), with her high degree of refinement, her detached nature, and her intense interest in music, remains somewhat a stranger among the Buddenbrooks.

Little Johann (Hanno) Buddenbrook, the pathetic, sickly son of Tom and Gerda. He shares his mother's love of music, and she thinks him a precocious genius. He dies in his teens of typhoid fever. Like his Uncle Christian, Hanno symbolizes the decadence of the family, and with his death the family itself comes to an end, for no male is left to carry on the Buddenbrook name.

Bendix Grünlich (BEHN-dihks GREWN-lihsh), Tony's first husband, a well-to-do Hamburg merchant and a pink-faced, blue-eyed, golden-whiskered, obsequious flatterer and rascal. His bogus charm takes in Jean, who urges Tony to marry him despite her disgust for him. When his impending bankruptcy later leads him to seek money from Jean, Buddenbrook angrily discovers that Grünlich, even before marrying Tony, had unscrupulously capitalized on his supposed connection with the family. A divorce follows shortly after Tony's return to her parents' home with her daughter.

Morten Schartzkopf (MOHR-tehn SCHAHRTS-kopf), a charming, serious-minded, liberal-thinking but naïve medical student whose brief romance with Tony is broken up when Grünlich reports to Morten's father a prior claim on Tony.

Alois Permaneder (AH-loh-ees PEHR-mah-nay-dehr), Tony's second husband, a bullet-headed, walrus-like, fat-cheeked man of forty, a Munich brewer. Vulgar in speech and desirous of an easy life, he gets no sympathy from Tony regarding his decision to retire from the brewing business to live on his income from rents and investments. After Tony finds him one night drunkenly forcing his attentions on Babette, the cook, she leaves him. When she seeks a divorce, he willingly agrees to it and returns her dowry because he has no need of it.

Erica Grünlich (AY-rih-kah), the daughter of Tony and her first husband. Tall, fresh-colored, pretty, healthy, and strong, she is occasionally inclined to melancholy moods. Her marriage, after the birth of a daughter, ends in disaster.

Hugo Weinschenk (WIN-shank), Erica's husband, a crude, pompous, self-made man, the middle-aged Silesian director of a fire insurance company. Convicted of unscrupulous business practices, he goes to prison. Upon his release and after a brief visit with the Buddenbrooks, he disappears.

Friederick Wilhelm Marcus (FREE-deh-rihk WIHL-hehlm MAHR-kos), Jean's confidential clerk. After Jean's death, he becomes a junior partner in the Buddenbrook firm. His conser-vatism counteracts Tom's occasional tendency to overreach himself.

THE BULL FROM THE SEA

Author: Mary Renault (Mary Challans, 1905-1983)
First published: 1962
Genre: Novel

Locale: Greece
Time: Preclassical Greece
Plot: Historical realism

Theseus (THEE-see-uhs), the protagonist and narrator. He becomes the king of Athens after the death of his father, Aegeus, then begins his attempt to unify Attica and create a strong central government in Athens. His love affair with Hippolyta, queen of the Amazons, ends with her death, but he has already married Phaedra, princess of Crete. He later brings her and their son Akamas to Athens. The tragedy of the relationship among Hippolytus, Phaedra, and Theseus results in the deaths of Phaedra and Hippolytus. Theseus ends his days a lonely, embittered, increasingly powerless old man who chooses to throw himself off the cliffs of the island of Skyros.

Hippolyta (hih-PAH-luh-tuh), the queen of the Amazons and lover of Theseus. When she is brought back to Athens after being beaten in battle by Theseus, she becomes the mother of their son, Hippolytus. She is the great love in Theseus' life, and her death in battle effectively ends Theseus' joy in life. Her courage and honesty sharply contrast with Phaedra, and she remains symbolic of everything Theseus admires in a woman.

Phaedra (FEE-druh), the princess of Crete and wife of Theseus. The younger sister of Ariadne, Phaedra fell in love with Theseus when, as a young child, she watched him in the bull ring. Their marriage is a political alliance only, and her later obsession with Hippolytus causes Theseus to kill her after he discovers that she has lied that Hippolytus raped her. She represents a type of femininity that repels Theseus.

Hippolytus (hih-PAH-luh-tuhs), the son of Theseus and Hippolyta. Hippolytus is as physically beautiful as his mother and, like her, is completely uninterested in the power and politics of Athens. He is drawn to the worship of Artemis and wishes to be a healer. His radical difference in personality from his father causes problems in their relationship, for Theseus does not understand his son's chastity or religious interests. Hyppolytus falls victim to Phaedra's lies about him because he refuses to betray her confidence, and his father never recovers emotionally from his death.

Akamas, the son of Theseus and Phaedra. Akamas is as Cretan as Hippolytus is Greek, but the two half brothers enjoy a close relationship until Hippolytus' death. It is Akamas who tells his father the truth about Phaedra's love for Hippolytus. Akamas shows no leadership abilities and is not favored by Theseus.

Pirithoos (pi-RITH-oh-uhs), the king of the Lapiths and a friend of Theseus. The meeting between these two kings results in a lifelong close friendship. Both men enjoy traveling as pirates in search of plunder, and it is Pirithoos who encourages Theseus to delay marrying Phaedra in order to journey to Scythia, where he encounters and falls in love with Hippolyta.

Aithra, the mother of Theseus and a priestess of Mother Dia (Demeter). Aithra recognizes that her son often angers Mother Dia and insists that he be ritually cleansed after he returns from Crete.

Old Handy, a centaur doctor and teacher. Known as Chiron in Greek mythology, Old Handy lives in the wilds and runs a kind of school for young princes such as Pirithoos and Achilles. Theseus' meeting with him occurs when Pirithoos visits his former teacher.

— *Angela Hague*

BULLET PARK

Author: John Cheever (1912-1982)
First published: 1969
Genre: Novel

Locale: Suburban New York
Time: The 1960's
Plot: Psychological realism

Eliot Nailles, a middle-aged chemist turned advertising man whose current project is the promotion of a mouthwash called Spang. He lives in the "village" of Bullet Park, a suburb of New York City, where he works. He loves his wife and son in a desperate and finally futile way, wishing to impart to them a sense of the blessedness of autumn leaves and thunder but not quite knowing how to do so. He is baffled by the affluence of Bullet Park and the "modern conveniences" of television, liquor, and, finally, drugs. He succeeds in saving Tony, his son, from Paul Hammer's murderous machinations and in bringing about an apparent return to normalcy on the part of his family. In the book's final paragraph, however, he is drugged and blankly "happy."

Paul Hammer, a middle-aged man who is independently wealthy and who moves with his wife, Marietta Hammer, to Bullet Park and becomes a neighbor of the Nailles family. He appears initially to be eccentric and proves finally to be psychotic. He has traveled the world in search of images that will lay to rest a constant malaise that he refers to as his *cafard* and *bête noire*. The most prominent of these images is a yellow room. Hammer eventually occupies such a room somewhere outside the city, but he has it tarnished by his "bewitching" wife, who paints it after Hammer has lost faith in its ennobling powers. Arrived in Bullet Park, Hammer decides to authenticate himself by some bizarre act; he subsequently plans to immolate Tony Nailles on the altar of Christ Church in Bullet

Park. After being thwarted in this attempt by a chainsaw-wielding Eliot Nailles, Hammer is sent to a mental institution.

Nellie Nailles, the middle-aged wife of Eliot Nailles. She is loved by her husband, principally on the basis of her radiant thighs. She appears initially to be the stabilizing influence in the family, but she becomes dislocated after going into the city and attending an avant-garde play featuring a nude scene. Nellie returns to Bullet Park and strives to regain her composure but realizes that her composure is possibly contemptible, depending, as it does, on "shutting doors." Despite her good heart, she is as impotent as her husband is in the matter of helping her troubled son.

Tony Nailles, a high school football player and the son of Eliot and Nellie Nailles. He is addicted to television. After his father flings the television from the house, he develops a mysterious ailment that renders him unwilling to leave his bed. Tony is the only character in the novel who appears to be headed in positive directions after his cure by Swami Rutuola, but he drops out of the book after being healed and returns only at the end as the would-be sacrificial victim of Paul Hammer.

Swami Rutuola, a black man of unspecified age, a self-proclaimed healer. He is the head of the Temple of Light, located in the slums of Bullet Park. Commissioned by Nellie Nailles to try to help her son, he does so by teaching Tony to chant what he calls "place cheers" (sentences that invoke healing images of places) and such words as "valor" and "love."

The swami appears to be sincere in his ministrations, and they work. He refuses pay for his services.

Gretchen Shurz Oxencroft, the mother of Paul Hammer. A gray-haired, fiercely blue-eyed eccentric, she lives in Kitzbuhel and is afflicted by a sense of the overwhelming mystery of life and by a determination that only an act as radical as a crucifixion will wake the world to life's mystery. She tells her son these things, perhaps influencing his attempt at homicide.

Mildred Hoe, an unmarried high school French teacher. Miss Hoe constantly fears that she will be brutally raped and murdered. In a conference with Tony Nailles about his poor performance in French, she is told by Tony that he could kill her if he wished. She screams for help, says that she has been threatened, and presses charges. After several harrowing hours in the police station, Tony is released into his father's custody.

Marietta Hammer, the middle-aged, beautiful, blonde wife of Paul Hammer. She refers to her husband as a "henpecked doormat" and prophesies that he will never find what he is looking for but will, rather, always be lonely.

Emma Hubbard, a thirty-year-old war widow. She meets Tony Nailles at a bookstore, and they subsequently spend a night together. The next day, Mrs. Hubbard and Tony have a rather uneasy lunch with Tony's parents, after which Tony promises his father, in Mrs. Hubbard's absence, never to do anything so unseemly again.

— *Johnny Wink*

BULLIVANT AND THE LAMBS

Author: Ivy Compton-Burnett (1884-1969)
First published: 1947
Genre: Novel

Locale: A country house in England
Time: 1892
Plot: Character study

Horace Lamb, the middle-aged head of a British household of gentry. He is tyrannical, domineering, selfish, ruthless, pompous, and humorless. In the face of his difficulties in supporting a menage of family and relatives, he is avaricious. He has married Charlotte for her money in an effort to preserve his position. He strives to economize to save his estate, while his wife, feeling powerless, pretends not to notice. Meanwhile, Horace denies his household basic material comforts—heat, food, and proper clothing—because his commitment is to the past, his property and heritage, rather than to his future, that is, his children. His conception of serving his dependents involves sacrifice on their part, not on his. Horace is always suspicious of them and their motives. He ostensibly reforms in the wake of three brushes with death and his wife's planned elopement with his own cousin, Mortimer, who shares his household. His change of heart may be genuine and permanent, or it may merely be a strategy to outmaneuver the others.

Charlotte Lamb, Horace's fifty-year-old wife, who has no faith in herself as spouse or mother. She married Horace for love, hoping to fulfill herself. Charlotte is a good woman, and her plan to leave Horace now is motivated more by her desire to provide her children with a happier home than by her love for Mortimer Lamb. On her return from a long voyage, she finds a "reformed" Horace and castigates him for his past behavior.

Mortimer Lamb, Horace's dependent, fifty-four-year-old cousin, a good but ineffectual man. He resents his situation as

well as Horace's harshness and constant efforts to economize, especially by keeping the house chilly to save coal. Mortimer is attracted to Horace despite the latter's tyrannical rule, and he recognizes that he needs his cousin. After his aborted elopement with Charlotte Lamb, he consents to wed Magdalen Doubleday, the sister of the Lamb children's tutor, Gideon Doubleday. Mortimer discovers that Magdalen had deliberately placed a compromising letter in Horace's way, thereby warning Horace of Mortimer's relationship with Charlotte. On learning of her deviousness, Mortimer abandons his plans to marry Magdalen.

Bullivant, the late-middle-aged butler who, with his preaching, cunning, and bullying, dominates the other menials "downstairs" just as Horace Lamb lords it over his household "upstairs." Bullivant is pompous but also humorous, mischievous, curious, and good-hearted, especially to women. His extreme articulateness, with many circumlocutions and clever turns of phrase, is unusual for an individual of his standing and bespeaks verbal skill beyond that of his employers. Although Bullivant holds witty conversations, especially with Mortimer Lamb, he is sententious with the servants. Bullivant is extremely efficient and unruffled by the worst crises. He is fanatically loyal to the Lamb family. Bullivant strives to justify Horace's scrimping, mean-souled tightfistedness. The butler also evidences infinite patients in explaining the meaning of hierarchy and the matter of status to

Miriam Biggs, the kitchen maid at the bottom of the menials' pecking order, and to George, the houseboy. In this endeavor, Bullivant is assisted by the nonconformist, hymn-singing cook, Mrs. Selden.

Miss Buchanan, a taciturn but humorous woman who owns a general store and runs a private post office in the nearby village. She keeps mostly to herself to guard the secret (uncovered by George, the rebellious houseboy) that she is illiterate. Miriam Biggs, the ungainly sixteen-year-old scullery maid, offers to teach Miss Buchanan to read.

George, the houseboy born in the workhouse, an obstreperous youth. Unlike Miriam the maid, George refuses to accept his status. His sole ambition is to rise above his menial station, in any way possible, without necessarily offering anything in return. He steals food and removes the warning sign from a dangerous bridge over a ravine so that Horace Lamb might be killed.

Sarah (aged thirteen),
Jasper (twelve),
Marcus (eleven),
Tamasin (ten), and
Avery (seven), Horace and Charlotte Lamb's children. Horace intrudes into their lives by demanding their obedience to his arbitrary and petty rules. Except for Tamasin, who harbors some affection for her father, the other children fear and despise him. They voice their resentment of Horace's oppression and unfair treatment, even as he portrays himself as a devoted and selfless parent. Although Horace deprives his children of creature comforts, his chosen form of abuse is psychological. Marcus and Jasper fail to warn their father of the defective bridge that Horace is about to cross, speculating that they might be better off if he were dead. Their father, however, escapes harm once again.

— *Peter B. Heller*

THE BULWARK

Author: Theodore Dreiser (1871-1945)
First published: 1946
Genre: Novel

Locale: Dukla and Philadelphia, Pennsylvania; New York City; and Atlantic City
Time: 1890 to the mid-1920's
Plot: Social realism

Solon Barnes, an upright, severe Quaker businessman who raises his children in strict accordance with Quaker moral principles. A family tragedy brings him to the realization that his concern for business and strict standards has obscured for him the central "Inner Light" of the Quaker faith. With the help of his daughter Etta, he regains his serenity during his last days.

Rufus Barnes, Solon's respected Quaker father and the founder of the family fortune.

Hannah Barnes, Solon's upright Quaker mother and the sister of Phoebe Kimber.

Benecia Wallin Barnes, Solon's quiet, religious wife.

Isobel Barnes, Solon's studious, unattractive oldest daughter.

Orville Barnes, Solon's severe, respectable elder son.

Dorothea Barnes, Solon's beautiful second daughter.

Etta Barnes, Solon's sensitive, intelligent youngest daughter. An individualist, she becomes the mistress of an artist, Willard Kane. She leaves her lover when Solon needs her and

becomes her father's mainstay in his last days.

Stewart Barnes, Solon's spoiled, unprincipled younger son. Interested only in the pursuit of lower-class girls, he becomes involved in the death of Psyche Tanzer. Charged with rape and murder, he commits suicide in his jail cell.

Phoebe Kimber, Hannah Barnes's sister.

Cynthia Barnes, Solon's sister.

Volida La Porte, Etta Barnes's unconventional friend.

Victor Bruge and

Lester Jennings, reckless friends of Stewart Barnes charged along with him in the rape and murder of Psyche Tanzer.

Psyche Tanzer, a young girl killed by "drops" administered by Victor Bruge.

Rhoda Kimber and

Laura Kimber, Phoebe's daughters.

Justus Wallin, Benecia Barnes's father.

Hester Wallin, Justus' sister.

Willard Kane, Etta Barnes's artist lover.

THE BURDEN OF PROOF

Author: Scott Turow (1949-   )
First published: 1990
Genre: Novel

Locale: Kindle County and Chicago, Illinois
Time: 1989
Plot: Suspense

Alejandro "Sandy" Stern, a prominent lawyer. Sandy immigrated to America in the 1940's and subsequently romanced and married Clara Mittler, who committed suicide shortly before the action of the novel. Sandy must discover why his wife killed herself and also has to deal with the complicated legal problems of his principal client, Dixon Hartnell. Discovering the reasons behind his wife's death and Dixon's erratic behavior forces Sandy to confront painful truths about his marriage and his family.

Dixon Hartnell, Sandy's brother-in-law, the head of Maison Dixon, a commodity-trading firm. A Korean War veteran, Dixon has used his talent at salesmanship to build his firm. He appears to have made illegal commodities transactions and could be guilty of insider trading. Dixon refuses to explain why Clara Stern gave him a check for $850,000 shortly before her suicide. He periodically avoids subpoenas and refuses to meet with Sandy to discuss his legal problems. Dixon also hides incriminating documents in a safe, which periodically disappears. Eventually, Dixon's motives are revealed, and he is discovered to be more honorable than he appears.

Sonia Klonsky, an assistant district attorney in charge of prosecuting the Hartnell case. She originally aspired to be a writer and became a lawyer in her mid-thirties. At the age of forty-one, Sonia is pregnant with her first child, but her relationship with her husband, Michael, is gradually worsening. At first, she seems very cold and calculating, but eventually she and Sandy become friends, and their friendship blossoms into romance.

Peter Stern, Sandy's son, a doctor. He has always had a difficult relationship with his father, and it worsens as the novel progresses. He occasionally gives his father medical advice.

Marta Stern, Sandy's daughter. She has just gotten out of law school and only recently decided to settle in Kindle County after a career as a Legal Aid lawyer in New York. Her passion and intelligence enable her to serve ably as her father's lawyer at several dramatic hearings in the book's final chapters.

Kate Granum, Sandy's youngest daughter, a quiet and unassertive woman who is closer to her father than either of her siblings.

John Granum, Sandy's son-in-law. He wanted to be a professional football player but was not drafted by a team. After drifting in and out of several jobs, he eventually ended up working for Maison Dixon as a commodity trader. He is quiet and easily manipulated by Dixon.

Nate Cawley, Sandy's next-door neighbor, a doctor. He assisted Clara Stern shortly before her death. His prescriptions and his refusal to tell Sandy that his wife had contracted a disease cause his longtime friendship with Sandy to end.

Margy Allison, the chief operating officer of Maison Dixon. Margy, a redhead from Oklahoma, is Dixon's assistant and has intimate knowledge of Dixon's finances and records. She reveals many of these secrets to Sandy during a brief but torrid affair.

Helen Dudak, a longtime friend of Sandy. She comforts him after Clara's death, and eventually they have an affair.

— *Martin Morse Wooster*

BURGER'S DAUGHTER

Author: Nadine Gordimer (1923-   )
First published: 1979
Genre: Novel

Locale: Johannesburg, South Africa, and Nice, France
Time: 1962-1977
Plot: Psychological realism

Rosemarie (Rosa) Burger, the daughter of white South African Communists, now seeking her own identity. Rosa is a complex, serious young woman who was reared in a household dedicated to the struggle against apartheid. Both of her parents were imprisoned at various times throughout her childhood, and their deaths have now left her emotionally at sea, uncertain whether her identity as "Lionel Burger's daughter" is one she wants or is able to live up to. The book's story is that of her slow journey toward self-knowledge and self-acceptance.

Lionel Burger, Rosa's father, a committed Communist activist. He is a hero of the antiapartheid struggle, a well-known figure in whose home blacks and whites are equally welcome. His final imprisonment ruins his health, and he dies in jail. A kind and intelligent man, he leaves a legacy of idealism that is both stifling and overwhelming for his daughter.

Cathy Jansen Burger, Rosa's mother and Lionel's second wife, also a committed activist. Cathy Jansen was a young union organizer when she met and married Lionel Burger. The couple had two children, Rosa and a son, Tony, who drowned as a boy. Like her husband, Cathy had a life dedicated to the fight against apartheid. She, too, was imprisoned several times before her death after a long illness.

Colette "Katya" Swan Burger Bagnelli, Lionel Burger's first wife, a former dancer. Katya leaves South Africa and the Communist Party after her divorce from Lionel and is a plump older woman living comfortably in the South of France when Rosa meets her. Warm and sunny by nature, she represents for Rosa the possibilities beyond her life in South Africa.

Conrad, a young student who becomes Rosa's lover. Conrad, a dreamer with an unstructured lifestyle, provides Rosa with a refuge, after her father's death, from her responsibilities

as Lionel Burger's daughter. Their conversations force her to reexamine and analyze her childhood.

Bernard Chabalier, a married teacher, Rosa's lover in France. Rosa meets Bernard while she is staying with Katya and falls deeply in love. Although he is married and a father, the two make plans to continue their relationship in Paris, until Rosa decides that she must return to her own country.

Zwelinzima "Baasie" Vulindlela (zway-leen-ZEE-mah bah-see vew-lee-ihn-DLAY-la), a young African boy taken in by the Burgers when Rosa was a child. Although the two were reared for a time as brother and sister, Baasie is an angry and bitter young man. He rejects what Rosa has become when the two meet years later in England.

Marisa Kgosana (koh-SAH-nah), the wife of an imprisoned black leader. A proud and beautiful woman, Marisa has long been a friend of the Burgers.

Fats Mxenge (ihm-KAY-ngay), Marisa's cousin, a boxing promoter. Fats opposes a total boycott of white society, hoping to arrange fights for his black boxers with white opponents.

Richard (Dick) Terblanche and

Ivy Terblanche, friends of the Burgers, also dedicated Communists and antiapartheid activists.

Clare Terblanche, Dick and Ivy's daughter. A plain, awkward girl, she has taken the path of commitment avoided by Rosa.

Flora Donaldson, a wealthy white liberal. Generous in her financial support of the antiapartheid cause and a close friend of the Burgers, she herself is not on the front lines of the struggle.

Brandt Vermeulen, an influential Afrikaner and apartheid supporter. He helps Rosa obtain a passport for her trip aboard.

— *Janet Lorenz*

BURIED CHILD

Author: Sam Shepard (Samuel Shepard Rogers, 1943-   )
First published: 1979
Genre: Drama

Locale: A small Midwestern farm
Time: The 1970's
Plot: Psychological realism

Dodge, who is in his seventies, very thin, and sickly looking, with a chronic cough. He spends most of the play lying on the couch and later on the floor. He gradually weakens throughout the play and dies at the play's end, after willing the house and property to his grandson Vince. Dodge apparently drowned an illegitimate child of his wife, Halie, and then buried the child, possibly conceived through incest, in the backyard, providing the play's title and the source of the family curse. The curse may or may not be expiated by his death and the admission of guilt he makes during the play.

Halie, his wife, about sixty-five years old, with pure white hair. At the beginning of the play, she comes down from her room upstairs, veiled and dressed entirely in black, as if in mourning. She speaks primarily in monologues, seeming not to notice her family. In the last act, returning after spending the night away with Father Dewis, she has changed, perhaps symbolically, into a bright yellow dress, and her arms are full of yellow roses. She is slightly drunk and giddy, and she is more communicative than in the first act. At the end of the play, she returns to her room upstairs.

Tilden, their eldest son, in his late forties. He dresses plainly and has a burned-out expression. Apparently, he has suffered some psychological trauma, only vaguely alluded to but probably the result of either a trip to New Mexico (and thus perhaps related to his son Vince, who is on his way there and apparently comes from there) or his suggested incestuous relationship with Halie (and thus related to the buried child, his other son). During the play, Tilden's primary action is to bring in armloads of vegetables from the backyard. This action, which he performs twice, prepares for the climactic scene at the end of the play, when he carries the freshly exhumed body of the buried child into the house.

Bradley, their next eldest son, an amputee. He is a big man with muscular arms and shoulders, developed from using crutches. His left leg is wooden, having been amputated above the knee, and he walks with an exaggerated, almost mechanical limp, accompanied by a squeaking sound of leather and metal from the harness and hinges of the false leg. At the end of the first act, he cuts off the hair of the sleeping Dodge, weakening him further, and eventually replaces him on the couch. By the end of the play, his leg has been taken away by Shelly, weakening him in turn, and he is replaced on the couch by Vince.

Vince, Tilden's son, a musician about twenty-two years old. He is visiting his family after six years' absence. At first, he is rejected by the family, but by the play's end he has come to fit into their bizarre patterns of behavior and has inherited the family house (though perhaps not the family curse), symbolically replacing Dodge as the patriarch and taking over his position on the couch.

Shelly, Vince's girlfriend, nineteen years old and beautiful. Unlike Vince, she at first seems to fit into the family and to be accepted by them. By the end of the play, having elicited the story of the buried child from Dodge and having witnessed Vince's altered behavior, she rejects the role she has been forced into and leaves.

Father Dewis, a Protestant minister, a distinguished looking, gray-haired man in his sixties. He is evidently having an affair with Halie.

— *William Nelles*

BURMESE DAYS

Author: George Orwell (Eric Arthur Blair, 1903-1950)
First published: 1934
Genre: Novel

Locale: Kyauktada, Burma
Time: The 1920's
Plot: Political realism

John Flory, a timber merchant stationed in the village of Kyauktada in Upper Burma. About thirty-five years old and with a face stained by a prominent birthmark, Flory seems destined to a lonely bachelorhood in the insular company of the few other British subjects of the area. Like them, he spends much of his time living the life of the "pukka sahib," the loyal representative of British values and European styles of living. Also like them, he spends much of his spare time drinking and gossiping at the British Club. Flory is sensitive and observant, however, and, unlike most of his bigoted countrymen in Upper Burma, he has a genuine respect for eastern culture. He counts Dr. Veraswami, an Indian, as one of his closest friends and even proposes him for membership in the British Club. When Elizabeth Lackersteen arrives at the village seeking a husband, Flory hopes that he has found a soul mate. Her rejection of him precipitates his suicide.

Elizabeth Lackersteen, the orphan of a bankrupt drunkard. She has come to Burma to find a suitable husband. At twenty-two years of age, she is pretty and stylish but superficial and self-absorbed. At first, her eagerness to find a mate makes her receptive to Flory's attentions, but she distrusts his interest in native culture. Lieutenant Verrall's interest in her, coupled with rumors of Flory's Burmese mistress, makes her drop him. Heeding her aunt's warnings about the fates of obstinate women who refuse acceptable offers of marriage while in the East, Elizabeth marries Mr. Macgregor when Verrall decamps.

U Po Kyin, the subdivisional magistrate of Kyauktada. A grossly fat man of fifty-six, he has made a career of corruption as a parasite of the British. A lifelong lover of politics and power, during the novel's action his main attention is given to anonymous attacks on Dr. Veraswami and to the secret backing of a native rebellion in Thongwa Village, actions he takes to secure himself an invitation to join the British Club as its first native member. He expects to make himself look like a hero by putting down the rebellion and by discrediting his only serious rival.

Dr. Veraswami, an Indian physician, the only doctor in Kyauktada. He also superintends the jail. The small, plump black man treasures Flory's friendship and maintains a high regard for Europeans in the face of their repeated insults to his race. As a physician who treats Europeans, he is the most likely candidate for native membership in the British Club and thus has become the object of U Po Kyin's slanderous anonymous letters. Flory's death deprives him of his only European friend and defender, as well as the main source of his status. His ruin is thus accomplished, as he has foreseen all along.

Lieutenant Verrall, a polo player and military policeman. Burdened by his debts, Verrall has moved to the Indian army from a British cavalry unit because it is cheaper and less demanding of his time, which he prefers to spend on polo. He despises all things oriental and insults everyone who does not share his regard for physical fitness. His evening rides with Elizabeth become a sort of courtship. He scuttles the relationship when he leaves Kyauktada to escape his debtors.

Ma Hla May, Flory's beautiful Burmese mistress. In her early twenties, she enjoys her life as a European's mistress and the clothes and gifts it involves, even though she has little fondness for Flory. When Flory discharges her to protect his tenuous relationship with Elizabeth, her pride is hurt, and U Po Kyin easily convinces her to try to blackmail Flory.

Mr. Macgregor, the British deputy commissioner to Kyauktada and the model of the pukka sahib. Bulky, humorless, and middle aged, he has a devotion to exercise and proper behavior that stands him in sharp contrast to Flory. After Flory's death, Macgregor marries Elizabeth and becomes more humanized.

— *Ann Davison Garbett*

THE BURN
(Ozhog)

Author: Vassily Aksyonov (1932-   )
First published: 1980
Genre: Novel

Locale: Primarily Moscow, Russia
Time: 1970-1973, with flashbacks
Plot: Phantasmagoric

Pantelei Apollinarievich Pantelei (pahn-teh-LAY ah-poh-lih-NAH-rih-vihch), also called **Pantik**, **Academician**, **Pantelyusha**, and **Pant**, a writer. Forty years old in 1972-1973, he wins at the racetrack, flies to Yalta, and ends up in a sobering-up station. Arrested in Moscow, he shares a dream in jail with the other heroes (Kunitser, Sabler, Khvastishchev, and Malkolmov); their identities merge with one another and with Tolya's.

Aristarkh Apollinarievich Kunitser (ah-rih-STAHRKH KEW-nih-tsehr), also called **Kun** and **Arik**, a forty-year-old physicist and space scientist. He takes Nina Lygher-Cheptsova, his lover, to political meetings at Argentov's.

Samson (Samsik) Apollinarievich Sabler (SAB-lehr), a forty-year-old jazz saxophonist in a Moscow nightclub. He faints during rehearsal and discovers he has emphysema.

Radius Apollinarievich Khvastishchev (RAH-dee-uhs khvah-stih-SHCHEHV), a forty-year-old sculptor. He invites a cloakroom attendant to pose, then learns the attendant is Lygher.

Gennady (Genka) Apollinarievich Malkolmov (geh-NAH-dee MAHL-kohl-mov), a forty-year-old physician who, in 1961, met Masha at a United Nations hospital in Katanga. Summoned to care for the injured Cheptsov, he allows him to die.

Tolya von Steinbock, also called **Tolya Bokov** and **Anatoly Apollinarievich Bokov**, who is seventeen years old in 1949. He is in Magadan, Eastern Siberia, where Tolya lives with his mother and loves Lyudmila Guly. He witnesses his mother's second arrest and Cheptsov's torture of Sanya.

Alisa, a seventeen-year-old Magadan camp inmate in 1949 who is married to Fokusov. She is a sexually promiscuous Moscow beauty with reddish blonde hair in the 1970's. When Pantelei confronts her, she chooses her husband's wealth. Blazer says she is in the KGB.

Sanya Gurchenko (GOOR-chehn-koh), known as **Father Alexander**, a Catholic camp inmate and carpenter who escapes to the West in 1951. He introduced Tolya to the underground world of "Crimea." As Father Alexander, he encounters Pantelei/Khvastishchev in Rome in 1965-1966.

Patrick Thunderjet, an Anglo-American friend of the heroes. He met Malkolmov and Masha in Katanga in 1961. He spends an evening with Khvastishchev, Toma, and Klara. He and Academician win at a Moscow racetrack and fly to Yalta, where he drunkenly requests political asylum. In 1972-1973, he is at the University of Sussex in England.

Stepan Cheptsov, a retired KGB officer who arrested Tolya's mother and Sanya Gurchenko twenty years earlier. Retired to Moscow, he holds menial jobs to support Paulina and his stepdaughter Nina, whom he rapes. He gets drunk and beats his head bloody before he is taken to the hospital.

Nina Lygher-Cheptsova, Lygher's daughter. In Magadan during the Stalinist era, she is adopted by Cheptsov in Moscow, where she lives with him and her mother in 1972-1973. She is Kunitser's lover and types for counterrevolutionaries.

Alik Neyarky (AH-lihk neh-YAHR-kee), a big former ice hockey player. He joins Academician and Patrick Thunderjet at the racetrack and on the flight to Yalta.

Tatyana Nathanovna von Steinbock, Tolya's mother. Arrested in 1937 as a counterrevolutionary, she served ten years in Magadan before being allowed some freedom as housekeeper in an orphanage. In 1949, she is arrested again, by Cheptsov.

Apollinary Ustinovich Bokov (ah-poh-LIH-nah-ree ew-STIH-noh-vihch BOH-kov), Tolya's father, who appears in a dream, in his native village of Fanino.

Martin, also known as **Philip Yegorovich** (yeh-GOH-roh-vihch), a German Catholic political prisoner in Magadan. He lived with Tolya's mother and practiced homeopathic medicine.

Boris Yevdokimovich Lygher (yehv-doh-KIH-moh-vihch LI-gur), a second cloakroom attendant at the National Hotel in Moscow, where Khvastishchev meets him. His name derives from *la guerre*, which is French for "war." His patriotism is suspect.

Paulina Ignatievna (ee-GNAH-tih-yehv-nah), Lygher's wife and Nina's mother. She had been prominent in Magadan society during the Stalinist era. In 1972-1973, she is the mad wife of Cheptsov in Moscow.

Lyudmila Guly, the daughter of a colonel of security forces in Magadan. She scorns Tolya.

Sergeyevich Mukhachov-Bagrationsky (sehr-GEH-yeh-vihch moo-kah-CHOV-bah-grah-TEE-ohn-skee), called **Blazer**, a friend to Pantelei, whom he wants to write screenplays for Western consumption. An honorary member of the Moscow police, he has immunity from arrest.

Vadim Serebyanikov (vah-DEEM seh-reh-BYA-nih-kov), an alcoholic former friend of Pantelei. Once first violin in an orchestra of "new voices," he is now a solid Party member.

Academician Fokusov (foh-KEW-sov), Alisa's husband. He is middle-aged and a famous tractor designer.

Jan Strudelmacher (SHTREW-dehl-mah-chehr), a blond, athletic, joking mercenary. In an attack on the United Nations hospital in Katanga in 1961, he tries to rape Masha.

Marianne Coulagot (kew-lah-GOH), called **Mashka** and **Masha**, a Russian Frenchwoman and Swiss citizen, the beautiful former mistress of Kunitser/Sabler/Malkolmov/Khvastishchev/Pantelei. She meets him (them) while riding the streets of Moscow with Patrick Thunderjet. She first met him/them (as Malkolmov) in the United Nations hospital in Katanga in 1961; she was a Christian Sister of Mercy.

Silvester, who composes music for Sabler's jazz group and helps Sabler to plan a concert in 1973. With his long hair and mustache, he looks like a Western intellectual, though he once had a 1950's-style crew cut.

Zheka Buzdykin (bewz-DEW-kihn), called **Fatface**, a musician who plays jazz with Sabler. Sabler dislikes him because of the Czechoslovakia uprising in 1968.

Marina Vladi (mah-REE-nah VLAH-dih), a woman who was in the audience when Sabler played at Leningrad in 1956. She inspires him to musical invention.

Arina Belyakova (ah-REE-nah beh-LYA-koh-vah), Sabler's young lover in Leningrad, where she studied medicine in 1956. In 1973, she treats him for emphysema.

Klara Khakimova (khah-KI-moh-vah), a rich Asian girl from Uzbek and a student at Moscow University. She was with Sabler in the Blue Bird in 1970.

Tamora Filchenko, called **Toma**, a KGB agent who meets Academician as Khvastishchev at the National Hotel.

Tinatina Shevardina (tih-nah-TIH-nah sheh-VAHR-dih-nah), a female student of Malkolmov. She meets him for a party and a drive through Moscow.

L. P. Fruitozov (frew-ih-TOH-zov), called **Agent Silicate**, who investigates the incident at the Moscow Hotel National.

Silly Zoika (ZOY-kah), a plump, dark, small woman who provides sexual pleasures for Academician, Patrick, and Neyarky at a party in Afanasy's new apartment.

Afanasy Seven-For-Eight, Silly Zoika's fiancé, a songwriter without talent.

Petyusha, a young party official on the plane to Yalta.

Fyodorich (FYOH-doh-rihch), an older companion of Petyusha. He looks like Cheptsov.

Natalya, who is lured to Yalta by hopes of a film career but is raped instead. She meets Academician, who gives her money to throw along the beach.

Vitaly Yegorovich Chuikov (vih-TAH-lee yeh-GOH-roh-vihch CHEWIH-kov), the director of the Party sanatorium and commander of children's war games at Yalta. He is a retired major general who carouses with Patrick, Neyarky, and Academician.

Boris, a Magadan guard who, with Cheptsov, tortures Sanya Gurchenko.

Sergeant Ryumin (RYEW-mihn), who is in charge of prisoners, including Academician and friends, in the Yalta courtroom. He wants more severe punishments.

Aunt Varya, a political prisoner. She is a friend of Tolya's mother in Magadan.

Igor Yevstigneyevich Serebro (yehv-stih-GNEH-yeh-vihch seh-reh-BROH), a sculptor and friend of Khvastishchev. Interviewed on the BBC in 1973 after his defection, he admits he was a KGB agent.

Major Paly (PAH-lee), who accompanied Cheptsov to arrest Tolya's mother the second time, in Magadan.

Zilberantsev (zihl-beh-RAHN-tsehv), a medical colleague of Malkolmov. He knows about the serum, Lymph D.

Nikodim Vasilievich Argentov (nih-koh-DIHM va-see-LYEH-vihch ahr-GEHN-tov), a fellow scientist of Kunitser. In his rooms in 1973, a meeting is held for a new political party in Moscow.

Makkar (mah-KAHR), a twenty-year-old guitarist for Sabler's new group in 1973.

Grisha Koltun (grih-SHAH KOHL-toon), an army major and Nina's new husband. He had participated in the invasion of Czechoslovakia in 1968.

— *Richard D. McGhee*

BURNING WATER

Author: George Bowering (1935-   )
First published: 1980
Genre: Novel

Locale: Vancouver, British Columbia; Guatemala; the Pacific Coast of North America; South America; and Hawaii
Time: Early 1790's and late 1960's
Plot: Magical Realism

George Vancouver, the commander of the British warship *Discovery*. A short, thickset man resembling a bulldog in appearance and temperament, Vancouver is willful, impatient, and unyielding. He is a strict and capable captain and an almost fanatically precise surveyor who does not believe in the existence of a Northwest Passage. A homosexual, he feels great affection for Admiral Quadra as both a father figure and a lover. Toward the end of the *Discovery*'s voyage, he suffers severely from tuberculosis and from the emotional trauma of Quadra's death. He hates Menzies because in him he sees a mirror of his own flaws. He prefers warfare to trade and would rather be fighting the French than expediting commerce in the New World.

Archibald Menzies, a botanist and surgeon traveling as a civilian passenger on Vancouver's ship. He is collecting plants for the Royal Society. When the ship's doctor falls ill and returns to England, Menzies takes over his responsibilities. Witty, argumentative, and intelligent, he is Vancouver's only intellectual equal on board the *Discovery*, which perhaps accounts for the tension between them. Almost despite himself, Menzies cannot seem to refrain from antagonizing and provoking the short-tempered Vancouver. Menzies takes a scientist's interest in the lands they visit and in the customs of the native people, things for which Vancouver has little patience. When a negligent sailor allows Menzies' painstakingly collected plant specimens to be destroyed during a storm, Menzies, infuriated by the commander's indifference, murders Vancouver.

Don Juan Francisco de la Bodega y Quadra, a Peruvian-born nobleman. Quadra is the naval commander of Spanish-held Nootka. Sophisticated, urbane, and a lavish, luxury-loving host, Quadra is also Vancouver's teacher and homosexual lover.

Lieutenant Peter Puget, a blunt, rude officer on the *Discovery*, notable for his fierce dislike of and contempt for the natives he encounters.

Joseph Banks, a member of the Royal Society. He is responsible for placing Menzies on Vancouver's voyage; consequently, he is despised by Vancouver.

John Meares, an unscrupulous trader. He provides Indians with rum and firearms, contrary to British policy. He serves as an emblem of the crass commercialism that motivates much of the exploration of the New World and that Vancouver hates.

First Indian, a young man who fancies himself an artist and visionary. He is eager to be considered a full man of the tribe. Impulsive and imaginative, he initially believes Vancouver's men are a vision, or gods who have sailed from the sun on a giant bird.

Second Indian, who is older and more practical than the first. He likes to tease and deflate the callow and boastful first Indian. He believes the Europeans are ordinary men. The dialogue between the two Indians serves as an objective if not entirely comprehending commentary on the actions of the Europeans.

First Lieutenant Zachary Mudge, a pragmatic and affable sailor on Vancouver's ship. Clever and forthright, he is one of the few men on the ship who can talk back to Vancouver.

Captain James Cook, the commander on Vancouver's early voyages, including one to the Sandwich Isles. Vancouver sees Cook as another father figure. Cook is killed and eaten by Sandwich Islanders.

The author, referred to as **he**, who narrates the portions of the novel taking place at the time of its writing. He travels from his home in Vancouver, British Columbia, to Trieste, Venice, Guatemala, and South America in an attempt to better understand his characters by familiarizing himself with the places in which they lived. Introspective and solitary, he feels a strong though not uncritical affinity with his protagonist.

— *Catherine Swanson*

A BURNT-OUT CASE

Author: Graham Greene (1904-1991)
First published: 1961
Genre: Novel

Locale: The Congo
Time: Mid-twentieth century
Plot: Bildungsroman

Querry, a retired church architect in his mid-fifties who has come to the heart of Africa to escape fame and failure at love. When Querry arrives at a leper colony in the Congo, he decides to stay only because the boat can go no farther. Feeling depressed and spiritually empty, he describes himself figuratively as a "burnt-out case," comparing his lack of emotion to the leprous condition of losing one's fingers and toes to the disease and losing the feeling in one's hands and feet. Soon after his arrival at the colony, Querry is drawn out of his emotional isolation by his friendship with Dr. Colin, the colony's physician, and his affection for his servant, Deo Gratias. Eventually, Querry begins to experience a rebirth of interest in life and humanity. He draws up plans for a new hospital, and he shows Christian charity toward Marie Rycker, the young wife of a factory owner. Ironically, just as Querry begins to enjoy life and discover God, his happiness is cut short by Marie's husband, who kills Querry in a jealous rage, falsely thinking that Querry has had an affair with Marie.

Dr. Colin, the sole physician of the leper colony, also a man in his mid-fifties. Colin can be seen as Querry's opposite: While Querry struggles with his loss of religious faith, Colin is comfortable with his own atheism; while Querry fears and shuns the world around him, Colin embraces all humanity

with loving kindness and compassion. Although he battles almost futilely against the poverty and disease that ravish his patients, and although he has no religious faith to sustain him, Colin never loses his belief in humanity and the power of good works. Colin is the only character who understands Querry's spiritual dilemma, and Querry looks to him for encouragement and advice. Only with Colin's help does Querry experience psychic rebirth and regeneration before his death.

Rycker, the middle-aged manager of a palm oil factory. As a young man, Rycker wanted to be a priest and studied for six years with the Jesuits before dropping his vocation. A bitter and unhappy man, Rycker takes comfort and pride in his "spiritual problems," believing that his struggles with faith make him superior to other men. When Querry, the famous Catholic architect, comes to town, Rycker latches onto him to give his own meaningless life a sense of importance, but Querry shuns him. When Rycker's wife, Marie, falsely claims that Querry is the father of her unborn child, Rycker is eager to believe the lie, and in a final bid for recognition and a sense of importance, he murders Querry in a jealous rage.

Marie Rycker, the pitiful, childlike wife of Rycker, a man old enough to be her father. Schooled in a convent, Marie has little understanding of life or love. Miserably unhappy with her uncaring, domineering husband, she feels empty and isolated from the world. When Querry comes to her house as a guest, she is dazzled by his fame and reputation with women. Later, when Querry befriends her in a time of need, she falls in love with him. In a naïve attempt to escape her life with Rycker, Marie unwittingly destroys Querry's life by claiming that he is the father of her child.

Father Thomas, the young superintendent of the missionary school. Like Rycker, he latches onto Querry in an attempt to bolster his own sagging faith. Thomas is the first to believe the rumor that Querry is the father of Marie's child, thus proving himself a figurative "doubting Thomas."

Montagu Parkinson, an unscrupulous journalist who comes to the leper colony in search of Querry. Eager to maintain the safety and quiet of his new life, Querry begs Parkinson to leave him alone, but Parkinson refuses, taking cruel pleasure in writing false stories about Querry's greatness. Parkinson functions as Querry's double. Like Querry, he has lost his faith and given up his profession; unlike Querry, however, Parkinson is incapable of regeneration. Like Rycker and Father Thomas, Parkinson is eager to exploit Querry for his own gain.

Deo Gratias, a young leper who is assigned to be Querry's servant boy. When Deo Gratias gets lost in the dark jungle, Querry rescues him. Querry's concern and compassion for the young man can be seen as the first stirrings of Querry's emotional rebirth.

— *Karen Priest*

BURR

Author: Gore Vidal (1925-   )
First published: 1973
Genre: Novel

Locale: New York City; Washington, D.C.; and the western states and territories
Time: 1833-1840, and Burr's memoirs, covering 1776-1807
Plot: Historical

Aaron Burr, a Revolutionary War officer, U.S. senator, investor, vice president of the United States under Thomas Jefferson, and killer of Alexander Hamilton in a duel. He was acquitted of charges of treason associated with trying to separate the western states from the Union. The Burr of the plot is seventy-seven years old at its opening. He marries a rich widow who spends the next four years, his last four, suing him. He enjoys life in spite of two strokes and continuing financial disasters, and he mildly enjoys his reputation as "the hellish Aaron Burr [who] meant single-handedly to disband the United States." Colonel Burr, as he is now called, is "an eighteenth-century man," inspired by the words of Voltaire and the deeds of Napoleon I, who, after the trial, refused offers of his service. Burr studiously aided and indulged his young protégé, Schuyler, giving no hint of paternity and skillfully avoiding the furious politicking that sought to deny the election of 1836 to Martin Van Buren by associating him with Burr. The Burr of the memoirs displays a strategy for taking Quebec that was correct and ignored. Even his view of ambivalence on the Constitution was closer to Supreme Court decisions and amendments than Jefferson's position. Burr, in the memoirs, is never wrong. He could have been elected president in 1800 but chose honor over deals. Burr died without regret "that history, as usual, has got it all wrong."

Eliza Bowen Jumel Burr, Burr's second wife. Wealthy and litigious, she hoards treasures and memoirs of a past both sordid and elegant; she claimed intimacy with Napoleon I.

Theodosia Burr Alston, Burr's daughter, named for her mother. A plump, dark girl, she was lost at sea. Eliza said that she was the only person whom Burr truly loved. Intelligent and well educated, she corresponded with Jeremy Bentham, whose economic principle of utility is discussed in the novel. She represents a noble side of Burr's character. She was, Burr told Charlie Schuyler, the cause of the duel.

Charles (Charlie) Schuyler, the narrator of the novel, twenty-five years old in 1833, Burr's law student and a writer for the *Evening Post*. Under the pen name "Old Patroon," he achieves local fame. With blue eyes and yellow hair, he is, he writes, "the caricature of a Dutch lout." He is paid to find proof that Burr is the real father of Van Buren and to write an anonymous pamphlet that will cause Van Buren to lose the election. Burr gives Charlie his memoirs and recollections and, in his way, his love. In 1840, as U.S. consul in Naples, Charlie learns that Burr was his father and is happy.

Helen Jewett, Schuyler's mistress. He wanted to marry her; she refused, miscarried their son, and returned to Mrs. Townsend's, where she was murdered. She was the sad note in Charlie's life.

Rosanna Townsend, formerly "one of the gayest," who had known Burr, Hamilton, Eliza, and "everybody." She ran the famous establishment at 41 Thomas Street where Charlie met Helen, and she tried to educate Charlie in "real life."

William Legett, Schuyler's editor at the New York *Evening Post*. In his thirties, he seemed older as a result of the yellow fever contracted while he was in the navy. He was court-martialed for dueling. Out to destroy Mr. Biddle's bank, promote free trade, abolish slavery, and help workers' unions, he was helpful to Charlie, and Charlie was tolerant of his radicalism.

William Cullen Bryant, the editor of the *Evening Post*, in his forties. He has carved lips and full face whiskers. His New England manner disguised whatever pleasure he found as "America's First Poet."

William de la Touche Clancy, who edited the magazine *America*. He is an unreconstructed Tory and represents the diversity of the New York press.

Thomas Skidmore, an egalitarian machinist who made the embarrassing point that "until we give each man his due, there is no society but a tyranny of the rich." Many sought their "due" in the West, as Burr foresaw.

Martin Van Buren, the eighth president of the United States. Charlie saw a physical and psychological resemblance to Burr. Taciturn to a fault, Van Buren was a key player with Jackson in the stand against the "Virginia Junto" and the South led by Henry Clay. His election is the focus of the novel.

Andrew Jackson, a U.S. general and seventh president of the United States. He supported Burr in his Western adventure in 1806, dining him royally at the Hermitage in Nashville. In the novel, the question is whether Jackson will live until Van Buren's election.

George Washington, the first president of the United States. In his memoirs, Burr finds his commanding officer during the American Revolution inept in war but unsurpassed in courting junior officers and Congress, a headquarters general who made an appropriate "god" for the new Republic.

Thomas Jefferson, the secretary of state under Washington and third president of the United States. Burr referred to him as "my sovereign." He, not Hamilton, is the villain of the memoirs. As presented by Burr, he is an opportunist who slandered as a monarchist anyone who stood in his way. Of brilliant mind, he was more imperialistic than Burr (or Napoleon, whose empire slipped away) and ordered Burr tried for treason so that he could retain complete command of the country. He and Burr argued about the Constitution, with Jefferson insisting on its perfection and Burr ambivalent.

Alexander Hamilton, Washington's aide and the first secretary of the Treasury. As young officers, Hamilton and Burr recognized each other as equals in ambition. Burr regretted killing him because his fortunes were in decline and only death could have made him famous.

James Wilkinson, the commanding general in the western territories. In 1805 he was fat, soft, vain, overuniformed, and in Spanish pay. He urged Burr to lead the West in war against Spain. Later, to save his skin, he became the chief witness against Burr.

John Marshall, the chief justice of the United States who presided over Burr's treason trial. Always suspicious of his cousin Tom, Marshall prevented Jefferson from using the trial to weaken the judiciary.

James Madison, the fourth president of the United States. Burr referred to him as the only true Republican.

Washington Irving, a famous American writer, described as elderly in 1833 though only fifty years old. He was stout and shy, and he favored the Dutch and Van Buren. He was sure that Van Buren could not be Burr's son.

— Frederic M. Crawford

BUS STOP

Author: William Inge (1913-1973)
First published: 1955
Genre: Drama

Locale: Kansas, thirty miles west of Kansas City
Time: The 1940's or 1950's
Plot: Comedy

Cherie, an attractive chanteuse, slightly past her prime, who has been singing in a Kansas City nightclub but is now traveling west, allegedly for a film test at a Hollywood studio. She is hotly pursued by Bo Decker, who, having heard her rendition of "That Old Black Magic" at the nightclub where she entertained, was so completely captivated by her that he ended up losing his virginity to her. Now he insists that she must marry him, presumably to make him an honest man. Unsentimental about her fleeting affair with Bo, Cherie does not want to go off to live on Bo's farm in Montana, although, as she considers her options, the prospect of marrying Bo seems to be a reasonable one for her.

Bo Decker, a young, extremely innocent cowboy whose infatuation with Cherie consumes him. He will not leave her alone and is completely dismayed when she does not want to marry him. More financially secure than most of the men Cherie has met, and certainly not unattractive, Bo is a good catch, but it takes Cherie a while to realize that. Cherie enlists the sheriff's help to keep Bo from pursuing her, but finally she accedes to going to Montana with him.

Virgil Blessing, Bo's surrogate father and traveling companion. Virgil is a lonely man who has devoted himself to rearing Bo, whose parents are dead. When Cherie comes into Bo's life, however, Virgil gives his blessing to their forthcoming union and bows out as they leave together on the bus for Bo's ranch in Montana. Virgil represents pure love, and he ends up literally being left out in the cold when the bus pulls out.

Dr. Gerald Lyman, an egocentric former professor, given to drinking too much, who now spends most of his time on buses traveling aimlessly from one place to another. As the play develops, it becomes clear that his problem is nympholepsy. He tries to arrange an assignation in Topeka with the teenage Elma Duckworth but finally, in a rare moment of conscience, calls it off. Perhaps for the first time in a long while, he does the right thing. Although the audience is never told explicitly that Lyman is in trouble with the law, his concern about getting over the state line as soon as possible suggests that he is running away from something.

Grace, a middle-aged waitress who works long hours at the café where the bus stops. Grace is good-hearted and unattached. During the play, she sneaks off with Carl, the bus driver, for half an hour, taking him to her apartment above the café. As the play ends, Virgil has no place to go and the town is completely closed up, but Grace has had her satisfaction for the night, so she does not invite the forlorn Virgil to share her bed, although to do so would have been to provide a reasonable solution for both of them.

Elma Duckworth, a high school student who loves literature and who romanticizes life. Innocent and nubile, Elma is Grace's helper in the café. When Grace goes off with the bus driver, Elma takes over, going from customer to customer and eliciting information from all the passengers on the bus, serving the function of a one-person chorus. She and Dr. Lyman do a scene from *Romeo and Juliet* and she is almost drawn into his web, but his conscience apparently forestalls their meeting in Topeka.

Carl, the bus driver. Realizing that the blizzard raging outside will make it impossible for him to keep his schedule, he seeks comfort in Grace's bed.

Will Masters, the sheriff, a tall, hefty man with a stubbly beard and a scar on his forehead. Cherie turns to him for protection when Bo's pursuit bewilders her. It is he who first tells Grace that the bus that is about to arrive will not be able to make it to Topeka because the road is blocked by drifting snow. His role essentially is that of a conciliator between Bo and Cherie.

— *R. Baird Shuman*

BUSSY D'AMBOIS

Author: George Chapman (c. 1559-1634)
First published: 1607; revised, 1941
Genre: Drama

Locale: Paris, France
Time: The sixteenth century
Plot: Tragedy

Bussy d'Ambois (bew-SEE dahm-BWAH), an ambitious, unscrupulous commoner. He is brought by Monsieur to court, where he quickly insinuates himself into the king's favor, seduces the woman his patron desires, and wins the enmity of most of his fellow courtiers through his insolence. His quick tongue saves him more than once from hanging. He disregards the warning of devils that he conjures up, and he dies propped on his sword, shot by Monsieur and the duc du Guise.

Henry III, the king of France. He is essentially both just and honorable, but he is too susceptible to Bussy's flattery.

Monsieur (meh-SYUH), the duc d'Alencon, who so desperately desires his brother's throne that he is willing to do almost anything except murder to win it.

Maffe (mah-FAY), his servant, concerned more with serving himself than with serving his master.

Tamyra (tah-mee-RAH), the countess of Montsurry. She scorns Monsieur's advances but arranges, through her friar, secret meetings with Bussy. She betrays her husband with few qualms. When caught, she finally succumbs to torture and writes the letter that takes Bussy to his death. Torn by conflict-ing loyalties to her husband and her lover, she finally begs Montsurry's forgiveness and vows to wander alone until her death.

Montsurry (mahn-sew-REE), Tamyra's devoted husband, who is made almost mad by the knowledge of her infidelity. He, too, is distressed by conflicting emotions of love and honor.

The duc du Guise (dewk deh geez), the king's second brother, Bussy's sworn enemy.

Elenor (ay-lay-NOHR), his duchess, to whom Bussy first pays court.

Barrisor (bah-ree-ZOHR),

l'Anou (lah-NOO), and

Pyrrhot (pee-ROH), courtiers who, enraged by Bussy's presumption, challenge him to a duel and die in the ensuing combat.

A friar, the go-between for Tamyra and Bussy. His ghost warns them of their danger.

Pero (pay-ROH), Tamyra's maid, who betrays her mistress to Monsieur.

BUTLEY

Author: Simon Gray (1936-   )
First published: 1971
Genre: Drama

Locale: A faculty office at London University
Time: Early 1970's
Plot: Psychological realism

Ben Butley, a lecturer in English literature at London University. He is a childish, irresponsible, disorganized cynic who smokes constantly and drinks heavily. Ben frequently quotes Beatrix Potter and T. S. Eliot and ridicules others with his abrasive wit. Separated from his wife, Anne, he lives with his office mate, Joey Keyston, with whom he also lived before his marriage. Ben tells students that he cannot see them because of his administrative burden, but he also declines to speak with his department chairman, claiming to be too busy with tutorials. After a visit by Anne, who reveals that she is going to marry someone else, he learns that Joey also is leaving him. Frustrated at losing both wife and friend, Ben taunts Joey's lover, Reg Nuttall, into striking him.

Joseph (Joey) Keyston, Ben's colleague and roommate, who began his relationship with Ben as his student. He is Ben's opposite: neat, organized, ambitious, and timid. Joey, who is working on an edition of Robert Herrick's poetry, is concerned that Ben's recklessness will interfere with his promotion in the English department. He is too frightened of his friend to tell Ben that he is moving in with Reg. Despite himself, he gets caught up in Ben's cynical games, inventing a stereotyped Yorkshire working-class background for Reg. Joey accuses his mentor of attempting to make a mess of his life just as Ben has done for Anne, charging him with spreading futility.

Reg Nuttall, a London publisher. He invites Ben's ridicule by being knowledgeable about food, proud of his time in the National Service, enthusiastic about the Leeds football club, and sensitive about his homosexuality. In addition to taking Joey, Reg infuriates Ben by agreeing to publish a novel by Ben's rival, Tom Weatherley.

Edna Shaft, an English literature professor in her late forties. She is upset that Ben has encouraged a student, Gardner, to complain to the head of the department about her dull teaching. She irritates Ben by inducing Joey to move into an office near hers and by finally completing the book on Lord Byron on which she has been working for twenty years.

Anne Butley, Ben's estranged wife and mother of their daughter, Marina. Jealous and contemptuous of Joey, she comes to Ben's office to ask for a divorce and to reveal that she plans to marry Tom, whom Ben considers to be the most boring man in London.

Carol Heasman, a student. She forces Ben to listen to the essay she has written about William Shakespeare's *The Winter's Tale* and is humiliated by his sarcastic response.

Gardner, a slovenly student who wears a feathered hat and sandals. He wants to study Eliot under Ben but is rejected as being uninteresting.

— *Michael Adams*

BY LOVE POSSESSED

Author: James Gould Cozzens (1903-1978)
First published: 1957
Genre: Novel

Locale: The New England town of Brocton
Time: A September in the 1950's
Plot: Social realism

Arthur Winner, Jr., a lawyer. He has lived his fifty-four years in Brocton, a small county seat town near the Delaware Valley. He is highly respected in his profession, his church, and his community for his wisdom, capable advice, and willingness to serve. He has been married twice, first at the age of twenty-five to Hope Tuttle, who died in childbirth eight years before the time of the story. Of their children, Warren is dead from a foolish training accident in World War II, Lawrence is a tax lawyer in Washington, and Ann is a teenager living at home under the tutelage of Clarissa, Arthur's second wife, to whom he has been married for four years. He has modeled his life on his deceased father, the "Man of Reason," yet his life is tempered by love of family, friends, and Brocton's institutions. In his legal work and personal relationships, he contends with the circumstances into which his clients have been placed by their inability to control passions and emotions, an inability referred to as their "possessions" by these forces. At the end of the novel, he struggles with the degree of his responsibility for an adulterous affair with Marjorie Penrose, for Helen Detweiler's suicide, and for consequences of his discovery of Noah Tuttle's illegal acts. Though weary, he resolves that he will continue to pit reason and strength against the tangles of passion and to be content with inevitable compromises.

Noah Tuttle, the dean of the local law profession. He is eighty-two years old, grumpy, and failing in health and memory. He strongly resists the moral standards of the present generation. A distinguished scholar of estate and trust management and for forty years the partner of Arthur Winner, Sr., he is now senior partner of the firm of Tuttle, Winner, and Penrose. Because he has been trusted and respected for his administration of many local trusts, it is shocking when it is revealed at the end of the novel that he has commingled money from many trusts with his own account, in personal and well-intentioned, but illegal, attempts to protect from financial disaster those who had trusted him.

Julius Penrose, the third partner in the law firm. Since joining the firm thirteen years earlier, he has become Arthur's closest friend. Although he is thought by many to be hard and cynical, Arthur finds their long legal and philosophical discussions very congenial. His paralysis from polio ten years earlier has increased his bitterness about the course of his life. Arthur admires Penrose's courage and sensitivity when he finally reveals that he has kept secret his knowledge of Noah's embezzlements and Arthur's affair with Marjorie, his wife. He convinces Arthur to join him in concealing Noah's misappropriation of funds and in attempting gradually, with luck and skill, to maintain control of the unsavory tangles.

Marjorie Penrose, the wife of Julius Penrose, possessed by wild emotions, nymphomania, and alcoholism. Her seduction of Arthur soon after Hope Winner's death has led to a guilty fear of death and a conversion to Roman Catholicism to structure her penitence.

Mrs. Pratt, a college friend of Marjorie. After twenty years, she has returned to assist in Marjorie's conversion. Her religious beliefs and vicarious interest in the sexual activities of others are distasteful to Arthur, who must suffer the revelation that she knows of his affair with Marjorie.

Helen Detweiler, a secretary to the law firm. After the accidental death of her parents, she devoted herself to rearing her younger brother and to serving Noah and Arthur. Now twenty-nine years old, she is fearful of unpleasantness and uncertainty. When her brother Ralph demonstrates his incapacity to deal with his life, she commits suicide by poison.

Ralph Detweiler, Helen's brother. At the age of eighteen, he is weak, immature, and spoiled by his sister. He has impregnated one girl, Joan Moore, and is accused of raping another, Veronica Kovacs. Arthur manages his defense and arranges bail. Ralph steals money from one of Helen's boarders and flees.

Clarissa Winner, Arthur's second wife. Formerly the beautiful, athletic director of a summer camp for Brocton girls and now in her mid-thirties, she has taken over the role of mentor to Ann Winner and reintroduced supportive love in Arthur's life.

Ann Winner, Arthur's fifteen-year-old daughter. Her growing sexual and social maturity frequently enters her father's consciousness.

Dr. Whitmore Trowbridge, the new rector of Christ Church. He seeks counsel from Arthur, a vestryman, on many matters, including removing the control of the Orcutt trust (which supports the church) from Noah to a Diocesan Investment Trust.

— *William L. Phillips*

C

THE CABALA

Author: Thornton Wilder (1897-1975)
First published: 1926
Genre: Novel

Locale: Rome
Time: c. 1920
Plot: Fantasy

Samuele, a young American writer and student introduced to the members of the Cabala, a group of wealthy, clever, esoterics in Rome. He becomes involved in many of their varied activities and learns that the Cabalists are the ancient pagan gods, who have become victims of their human-like frailties.

James Blair, a bookish man and friend of Samuele, who introduces his friend to the Cabala. Blair is upset when one of the Cabalists, Alix d'Espoli, falls in love with him and haunts his presence.

The Duchess d'Aquilanera, an Italian noblewoman and a Cabalist. She is a loving mother and is disturbed by the wildness of her teen-age son, Marcantonio.

Marcantonio d'Aquilanera, son of the Duchess. He is a youth of sixteen who already has had a series of love affairs, conduct that threatens to spoil his chances of a good marriage. He loves to drive his expensive cars at high speed, just as he

drives himself. Denounced for his immorality by Samuele, Marcantonio commits suicide.

Cardinal Vaini, a former missionary to China. Though a Cardinal, he speaks derisively of prayer. After having been shot at by a religious fanatic, he resolves to return to China, only to die of a fever en route.

Astrée-Luce de Morfontaine, a religous fanatic whose faith is shaken by Cardinal Vaini's comments. She accuses him of being the devil and tries to kill him with a pistol.

Alix d'Espoli, an Italian princess, a Cabalist. She falls in love with Blair and makes him miserable by pursuing him. Though unintelligent, she appeals to many people because of her charm and beauty.

Elizabeth Grier, an American girl who is a member of the Cabala. She reveals to Samuele that the Cabalists are really ancient gods and goddesses. She disturbs Samuele by saying that he is the pagan Mercury.

THE CABIN
(La barraca)

Author: Vicente Blasco Ibáñez (1867-1928)
First published: 1898
Genre: Novel

Locale: Spain
Time: The nineteenth century
Plot: Realism

Batiste Borrull (bah-TEES-teh bohr-RREWL), a tenant farmer near Valencia, Spain, who vainly fights public opinion.

Roseta (roh-SEH-tah), his daughter, a worker in a Valencia silk mill.

The Bishop, his chubby youngest son, who dies from exposure after being beaten and thrown into a water-filled ditch by his schoolmates.

Pimentó (pee-mehn-TOH), the community bully, fatally wounded by Borrull.

Pepeta (peh-PEH-tah), Pimentó's anemic but hard-working wife.

Barret (bah-RREHT), the previous occupant of the Cabin,

evicted for nonpayment of rent. He murders his landlord, Don Salvador.

Rosario (roh-SAHR-ee-oh), one of Barret's three daughters, all of whom end up as prostitutes.

Don Salvador, a greedy landowner and usurer.

The Sons of Salvador, who continue their father's evil practices.

Joaquín (wah-KEEN), a schoolteacher.

Tonet (toh-NEHT), in love with Rosario.

Old Tomba (TOHM-bah), a blind shepherd and prophet of doom.

CADMUS

Author: Unknown
First published: Unknown
Genre: Short fiction

Locale: Greece
Time: Antiquity
Plot: Adventure

Cadmus (KAD-muhs), the founder of Thebes. Told by his father not to return to Phenicia without Europa, his kidnapped sister, he goes off to found the Greek city of Thebes, aided by five warriors who spring from a dragon's teeth. Harassed by Mars for killing the dragon, he leaves Thebes for the land of the Enchelians. But he finds no peace and is finally changed into a serpent by the gods.

Agenor (ah-JEE-nohr), Cadmus' father, King of Phenicia. He commands his son to bring back Europa when she is stolen by Jupiter.

Europa (yew-ROH-pah), Cadmus' sister. When Jupiter, in the form of a bull, kidnaps her, her brother is sent to find her and bring her back to her father.

Jupiter, king of the gods. Enamored of Europa, he steals her from her family.

Minerva (mih-NUR-vah), the goddess of wisdom, daughter of Jupiter. She tells Cadmus to sow the teeth of a dragon he has slain, from which spring a host of warriors. All but five kill one another in battle; the remaining warriors become Cadmus' servants and help him build the city of Thebes.

Harmonia (hahr-MOH-nee-uh), the daughter of Mars and Venus. She is given by Jupiter to Cadmus to be his wife. Because she loves her husband, she begs to be turned into a serpent when he is transformed into one. The gods grant her request.

Mars, god of war. He seeks revenge for Cadmus' slaying of a dragon and puts a curse on the man and his children. He causes the children to die and harasses Cadmus so relentlessly that he asks to be turned into a serpent.

CAESAR AND CLEOPATRA

Author: George Bernard Shaw (1856-1950)
First published: 1901
Genre: Drama

Locale: Egypt
Time: Autumn 48-Spring 47 B.C.E.
Plot: Comedy

Julius Caesar, the dictator of Rome and conqueror of the world. A middle-aged, rather prosaic man, he meets the childish Cleopatra on a moonlit night in the desert. Although fascinated and rather amused by the beautiful child, he is too practical and detached to be enthralled by her charms. He forces her out of her childishness and teaches her statecraft that makes her truly the queen of Egypt.

Cleopatra, the sixteen-year-old queen of Egypt. An excitable schoolgirl, she is at war with her husband-brother, Ptolemy Dionysus, for the crown. She believes herself to be in love with the elderly Caesar, who forces her to assume her dignity as queen, but she really loves only herself. At the end of the play, she is looking forward to the arrival of the young

and handsome Antony.

Ptolemy Dionysus, Cleopatra's brother, husband, and rival for her crown, killed in battle against Caesar.

Ftatateeta, Cleopatra's bullying and savage nurse, against whom the queen finally revolts, at Caesar's instigation. She is killed by Rufio.

Britannus, Caesar's secretary. The eternal Englishman, conventional and easily shocked, he is doggedly faithful to Caesar.

Rufio, a Roman officer and the slayer of Ftatateeta.

Pothinus, Ptolemy Dionysus' guardian. He plots against Caesar and, at Cleopatra's instigation, is killed by Ftatateeta.

Apollodorus, a Sicilian.

CAESAR OR NOTHING
(César o nada)

Author: Pío Baroja (1872-1956)
First published: 1910
Genre: Novel

Locale: Spain, Italy, and France
Time: Early twentieth century
Plot: Political

Caesar Moncada (SEH-sahr mohn-KAH-dah), who has a highwayman and a cardinal among his ancestors. He turns his back on the Church to become a financial dictator. He adopts the Borgia motto: "Caesar or Nothing." He turns out to be nothing.

Cardinal Fort, formerly Father Vicente de Valencia. He is Caesar's uncle.

Laura, Caesar's sister, who becomes the Marchesa of Vaccarone and a social leader of Rome.

The Abbé Preciozi (preh-see-OH-see), who is sent as Caesar's adviser by Cardinal Fort.

Father Miró (mee-ROH-) and

Father Herreros (eh-RREH-rohs), two priests who might have helped Caesar's scheming if Cardinal Fort had not stopped them.

Archibald Marchmont, who is in love with Laura.

Susanna Marchmont, his wife, who takes a trip with Caesar as Caesar's wife.

Kennedy, an Englishman who tells Caesar about Roman history and the Borgias.

Countess Brenda, an important member of Roman society with whom Caesar has an affair.

Senator Calixto, a political leader of Zamora who offers to put Caesar's name on the ballot whenever he returns to Spain. Don Calixto is Amparo's uncle.

Don Platón Peribáñez (plah-TOHN peh-ree-BAHN-yehs) and

Antonio San Román (sahn rroh-MAHN), political figures in the district of Castro Duro.

Father Martín Lafuerza (mahr-TEEN lah-FWEHR-sah),

another local vote-getter and an opponent of Caesar.

Ignacio Alzugaray (ahl-sew-GAHR-ay), Caesar's school friend.

Carlos Yarza (KAHR-lohs YAHR-sah), a Paris bank employee who interests Caesar in speculation.

García Padilla (gahr-SEE-ah pah-DEE-yah), a political opponent beaten by Caesar in the first campaign. By fraudulent practices, he defeats Caesar in the next election.

Driveller, a ruffian hired by Father Martin to browbeat Caesar's followers.

The Cub-Slut, a female member of the local underworld who warns Caesar of an attempt on his life.

Lengthy, the son of the Cub-Slut. He is killed by Driveller in a political row.

Gaffer, one of Caesar's followers, attacked by Driveller.

Amparo (ahm-PAH-roh), the niece of Don Calixto; she marries Caesar, after some uncertainty.

CAIN

Author: George Gordon, Lord Byron (1788-1824)
First published: 1821
Genre: Drama

Locale: Outside Eden
Time: The period of Genesis
Plot: Tragedy

Adam, the first man. He orders Cain to leave the family after the murder of Abel.

Eve, Adam's wife, the first woman. Because she was bitter at the expulsion from Eden, Cain blames her for his undying bitterness against God and death and claims that this bitterness was transmitted to him before birth.

Cain, Adam's elder son. He refuses to pray because of the expulsion from Eden and is sullen at the loss of immortality. He hates work and doubts God's goodness. Tempted, he follows Lucifer and expresses a wish to remain in Hades. Jealous of his brother Abel, Cain strikes him a blow, killing him. Marked by an angel, Cain leaves his family. Destined to grow

no living thing, he is a bitter man.

Abel, Cain's young brother and victim. He is a good man who worships God sincerely. He is killed for telling Cain that he loves God more than life.

Adah, Cain's wife. She tries to keep her husband from following Lucifer to Hades. When her husband is banished from the family, she accompanies him, taking their children. She is a faithful wife.

Zillah, Abel's wife, a good woman.

Lucifer, the fallen angel. He says he did not appear as a snake to tempt Eve. He exults that Cain shares his misery.

Enoch, the son of Cain and Adah.

THE CAINE MUTINY

Author: Herman Wouk (1915-   )
First published: 1951
Genre: Novel

Locale: New York City, San Francisco, and the Pacific Ocean
Time: 1942-1945
Plot: Bildungsroman

Lieutenant Commander Philip Francis Queeg, the captain of the USS *Caine*. A neurotic officer of mediocre ability, he is not typical of his fellow Naval Academy graduates. He comes to the *Caine* from a somewhat murky background and seems determined, at least initially, to correct whatever happened in the past to make him a below-average officer. Within a few weeks, however, he shows himself to be an incompetent martinet incapable of seeing the big picture. As a result, he evokes in his officers and men reactions ranging from pity to rage and, finally, sincere concern for the safety of the ship. This concern leads to him being relieved during a typhoon and to subsequent disgrace.

Lieutenant Stephen Maryk, an executive officer of the USS *Caine* during the mutiny. A naval reservist, he is an officer of excellent potential, typical of the young men brought into service early in World War II. Solid and dependable, Maryk is torn between the requirement of loyalty to a skipper, even one who seems mentally ill, and what he perceives is best for the ship. When his sea sense tells him that the *Caine* is doomed during a terrible storm, he relieves Captain Queeg of command and saves the ship. Indicted for mutiny, he is acquitted in a dramatic trial but, as is sometimes the way in the service, his career is ruined.

Lieutenant Thomas Keefer, an aspiring novelist and the communications officer of the USS *Caine*. Self-satisfied, witty, and urbane, Keefer is the first to suggest that Captain Queeg may be paranoid. Keefer is a petty intellectual who looks down on all career military men and relishes any opportunity to embarrass them. More than any officer in the *Caine*'s wardroom, he is responsible for the mutiny. Ironically, Keefer becomes commanding officer of the *Caine* after the court-martial and, ultimately, proves that he is a physical as well as a moral coward.

Ensign Willis Seward Keith, a Princeton graduate and volunteer officer. As a young man, he has never been challenged, but there is in his character a core of hardness that emerges under the adversity of combat and a neurotic skipper. He initially falls under the spell of Thomas Keefer, but through hard work and natural ability, he overcomes the mistakes of inexperience and develops into a competent officer. He eventually becomes a party to mutiny, a hero, and the final commanding officer of the USS *Caine*.

Lieutenant Barney Greenwald, a fighter pilot and lawyer. Greenwald, a brilliant attorney in civilian life, plays a small but pivotal role as defense counsel for the mutineers at their court-martial. He quickly realizes that Keefer is the real culprit

THE CALL

Author: John Hersey (1914-1993)
First published: 1985
Genre: Novel

Locale: Upstate New York and northeastern China
Time: 1878-1981
Plot: Historical

David Treadup, a courageous, vital, and self-sacrificing man who devotes his life to Christian and humanitarian missions in the shifting, violent world of China during the first half of the twentieth century. Given to binges of vandalism in his youth, David pursues classical learning to escape the hard life of his parents' farm. Following his religious conversion in 1903, his mind and body thrive. A handsome and large young man, he finds an outlet for his leadership skills and personal magnetism in the campus YMCA. At the age of twenty-seven, he embarks for China with a burning desire to evangelize that land through Gospel preaching. Soon disillusioned with the methods of old-fashioned missions, Treadup looks for another door into the Chinese mind. With his overpowering body and charisma, Treadup mesmerizes millions during his lectures on the gyroscope, airplane, and wireless, convincing listeners that the unseen is real and propelling them toward the modernization of China. He perseveres even during a bout with dysentery, delivering his lectures from a horizontal position onstage. During the early years of communist revolution in China, Treadup develops a hatred of violence. Suffering through years of diabolical Japanese occupation, Treadup experiences uncertainty, loneliness for his wife, deprivation, and a frustrating halt to his work. Confined to a prison camp, he becomes defeated and exhausted, a totally broken man. He ceases his prayers and loses touch with God, eventually coming to believe that there is no God. His unexpected release by the Japanese brings great sorrow to Treadup, for he must leave the work of a lifetime. When Treadup returns to China in a war rehabilitation position, he is arrested by the People's Liberation Army. As their prisoner, he experiences total deprivation. Accused of being an agent of American capitalism, he undergoes the ultimate humiliation: The voices of the Chinese people convict him in an open-air trial. Shortly after his expulsion from the People's Republic of China, he dies in Thornhill, New York, at the age of seventy-two.

Emily Kean Treadup, an attractive, serene woman who brings love and balance into David Treadup's life. During periods of potential fretfulness as his wife, Emily becomes hyperactive in community works, founding the Anti-Footbinding League in Tientsin and working against child labor, opium dens, prostitution, and the horrible working conditions for women in factories. Throughout her life, she grieves for the loss of her baby, Nancy. Usually, she is submissive, but she is self-confident as she rears her three sons on the mission field. Emily is a beautiful woman who remains sensual through her middle years, but when she finally returns to the United States alone during the Japanese occupation of China, she becomes frail and ancient-looking. She dies shortly after David's return to New York, seemingly as a consequence of being relieved of her duties at Thornhill Free Library.

Johnny Wu, an ambitious, American-educated young Chinese man who, with David Treadup's help, develops a program for Chinese literacy. He estranges Treadup by retaining only nationals in the organization after it is off the ground, but the missionary admires his ebullience throughout all of China's woes.

Lin Fu Chen, a Westernized Chinese intellectual, Treadup's most influential friend during his early years in China. He opens Peikai University for the teaching of science, economics, and liberal arts.

James B. Todd, the handsome blond evangelist who directs the YMCA's foreign missions from his elegant office in New York City. Motivated by self-love and overconfidence, he is skeptical and at times even antagonistic toward Treadup's philosophy and programs. He manages, however, to manipulate the missionary, who holds his power and charisma in awe.

Roscoe Hersey, a missions volunteer who relieves the young Treadup in Tientsin. Later, he becomes general secretary of the YMCA. He is devoted to his work and the Chinese and is serious, gentle, and tactful. After working in flood relief, he becomes ill with encephalitis and returns to the United States.

Phineas Cunningham, an irrepressible British physician who becomes Treadup's only English friend in his entire lifetime. A brilliant man of letters and a student of culture and religion, he is an agnostic who chips away at Treadup's Christianity during their work together improvising medical care in Tientsin and in Japanese prison camps.

— *Janie Caves McCauley*

CALL IT SLEEP

Author: Henry Roth (1906-1995)
First published: 1934
Genre: Novel

Locale: New York City
Time: 1907
Plot: Psychological realism

David Schearl, a Jewish boy who leaves Russia with his mother to settle in New York City, where his father has recently established himself. David is extraordinarily sensitive, and it is through his senses and intellect that the life of the immigrant city comes to life. He is fiercely attached to his protective mother and afraid of his harsh father, who scorns David and suspects that his son actually is the offspring of his wife's affair with another man. The curious David makes friends with Leo, an Irish boy, and learns in rather crude fashion about Catholicism and the habits of other immigrant children. David struggles to understand and to articulate his experiences.

Genya Schearl, David's sympathetic and fatalistic mother. She arrives in America with her son and is greeted grudgingly by her suspicious husband. He has had a difficult time settling in this new country and jumps on every word of hers that suggests to him that she is not supportive or understanding of his plight. She is patient and tries to placate him, but he knows that she does not put him first in her heart. It is David to whom she is devoted and David whom she will defend when the frustrated father tries to beat him. She tries to do the best by her husband, but she is unfaithful to him and cannot overcome the estrangement that her husband only worsens by his unforgiving and relentlessly cruel treatment of her and David.

Albert Schearl, an embittered immigrant who flounders from job to job until he lands a milk route, a job that seems to pacify him somewhat. He broods about David, whom he considers a weakling and a spoiled child. In spite of his suspicions about David's parentage, Schearl makes certain that his son gets a Jewish education. Schearl eventually realizes that his own hostility has driven his wife and son away from him.

Leo Dugovka, an Irish boy who befriends David one day and allows him to fly his kite on a rooftop. Leo has seen much more of the city than has David. David covets not only Leo's experiences but also his possessions, such as the rosary that Leo promises to give David if David will introduce him to one of his female cousins. Leo gets David in trouble in a scene that culminates in Mr. Schearl accusing David of adopting the Christian religion. Leo introduces David to a much bolder conception of the city and fulfills David's yearning to grow beyond the fears of his ghetto experience.

Aunt Bertha, Mrs. Schearl's outspoken sister. Like Leo, she provides comedy and good spirits in this otherwise grim novel. She quarrels with Mr. Schearl and goads David's mother into confessing that she did have an affair with another man. Bertha marries Nathan Sternowitz, then opens a candy store with her husband. This is where David and Leo go to meet David's cousin, Esther Sternowitz, and where David begins to fathom some of the mysteries of sex.

— *Carl Rollyson*

THE CALL OF THE WILD

Author: Jack London (1876-1916)
First published: 1903
Genre: Novel

Locale: The Yukon
Time: The 1890's
Plot: Adventure

Buck, the hero of the story, a dog that is part German Shepherd and part Saint Bernard. Buck is abducted from his home in San Francisco to serve as a sled dog. He is abused cruelly by his first masters, but he adjusts admirably to the elemental life of the Yukon. He has to fight several dogs to maintain his place in the pack, and he is called on to perform several extraordinary feats of endurance and courage. He serves his human masters faithfully, but when his final master dies, Buck answers the call of the wild, forsaking civilization and joining a wolf pack, returning to an instinctual mode of life that always has been an incipient factor in his strength and indomitability.

Spitz, the malevolent head of the pack. He attacks Buck repeatedly, sensing Buck's fitness to supplant him as the dogs' leader. Spitz is valued by his masters for his ferocity and intelligence, but the masters concede Buck's superiority when Buck challenges Spitz to a fight to the death and wins.

Perault, Buck's first Yukon master, a hard but fair man who acknowledges Buck's supremacy among the dogs. Perault and Buck drive themselves equally hard, and Perault makes the dogs an extension of his own will.

Francois, Perault's French-Canadian partner, who predicts that Buck will become a great sled dog, perhaps the finest in the Yukon. He treats Buck with enormous respect and knows how to get the best out of the dog.

Hal, Buck's next master, a crude man who ignores the advice of experienced Yukon travelers, whipping his dogs into

a state of exhaustion. As the dogs weaken, he shoots them. He nearly kills the prostrate Buck when he refuses to respond to the whip, and only the intervention of John Thornton saves the dog. The reckless Hal perishes when his overloaded sled breaks through thin ice.

Mercedes, Hal's sister. She accompanies Hal and their brother Charles on the foolhardy Yukon trip. She takes too many unnecessary things that weigh down the sled, and she interferes with the dogs, feeding them too much. Her passiveness and insistence on her helplessness contribute to dooming the journey.

Charles, Mercedes and Hal's brother. He constantly quarrels with Hal as the two men fritter away their food supply and cruelly drive the dogs even when it is apparent that the team is sapped of all energy and of any will to continue.

John Thornton, Buck's last master and his benefactor. Of all Buck's masters, Thornton most obviously recognizes Buck's greatness. He develops an intimate love for the dog that makes Buck perform incredible feats, including breaking out a half-ton sled, frozen in its tracks, and pulling it one hundred yards. Buck repays his master's pride and confidence in him not only through his prodigious work but also through a fierce watchfulness. Only when Thornton is overwhelmed and murdered by a band of Indians does Buck feel released to the wild.

— *Carl Rollyson*

CALM DOWN MOTHER

Author: Megan Terry (1932-   )
First published: 1966
Genre: Drama

Locale: New York City
Time: The 1960's
Plot: Feminist

Woman One,
Woman Two, and
Woman Three, who are on stage as the play begins, clustered together to suggest a plant form while a voiceover tape talks about one-celled creatures floating in the sea. Woman One says she is Margaret Fuller, the noted nineteenth century feminist, and that she accepts the universe. The other two women in unison reply that, as the nineteenth century philosopher Thomas Carlyle said, you had better accept, for life must live while it can. In a later scene, Woman One is angry; she and Woman Two beat Woman Three. They appear again in the final scene, as they singly or in twos or threes repeat the words "bodies," "bellies," and "eggs in bellies" as they touch their breasts and sides and stomachs. They end by turning their backs to the audience as they ask if "eggies in our bellies" are enough. Here, as throughout the play, they imply that there is more to women than their sexual or reproductive functions. For most of the play, these three characters assume the roles of other women. Sometimes the roles are specified—in the second scene, for example, Woman One becomes Sophie—but usually the scenes shift abruptly without the directions saying which woman plays which role. This adds to the thematic suggestion that society often sees women as alike or as merely fulfilling roles rather than being individuals.

Sophie, an elderly woman behind a counter in a Brooklyn delicatessen with her sister Esther. A young girl comes in to buy beer. The girl is in a hurry, but Sophie keeps looking at her hair and wanting to touch it because it reminds her of her mother's hair and of her own when she was young. Sophie regrets the loss of her sense of herself as attractive to men the way her mother had been. At first the girl is sympathetic, but when Esther begins a mocking refrain of Sophie's woes, the girl joins in. Even Sophie joins the lament, and the three women stroke one another's hair until the grief becomes so strong that the girl feels suffocated and flings the others away.

Nancy, a young woman originally from Oklahoma who is visiting her friend Sally in a New York apartment. She is worried about Sally's relationship with an abusive former lover. Nancy is drinking heavily and thinks her life is falling apart. She has helped her sister through a divorce and was the family member who had to settle her grandfather's estate. Her father drinks too much and has had a heart attack. Her mother is dying of bone cancer.

Mrs. Tweed and
Mrs. Watermelon, two old ladies in a nursing home. Mrs. Tweed is more conventional and tries to be stoic, thinking that the days go by endlessly, but Mrs. Watermelon is angry and tired of her confined nonlife. A nurse comes in with a tray of food for them, but she has no sympathy for their condition and does not see them as fellow human beings.

Momo,
Felicia, and
Inez, three call girls who are in their apartment dressing and putting on makeup before they go to work. They continually bicker and complain about one another. Inez claims to have more work experience with men and threatens to tell their pimp, Ricky, that the other two are not giving him enough of the money they make. Momo says she is sick of the other two ganging up on her, but each of them turns her anger and frustration on the other two.

Sue,
Sak, and
Ma, two young women and their mother washing dishes at a tenement sink. Sue is angry about a magazine article that opposes birth control. Sak tells her she should not be taking birth control pills and that she will burn in hell for disagreeing with the priests. Ma does not want to hear the discussion. When Sue keeps defending her position that not all eggs and sperm can possibly become babies anyway and that men should not be the ones to decide about birth control, Ma disowns her as her daughter and tells her to pack her things and get out. Sue says she will go but that she does not need to pack anything, because according to the priests all she needs is the eggs inside her anyway.

— *Lois Marchino*

CAMBRIDGE

Author: Caryl Phillips (1958-   )
First published: 1991
Genre: Novel

Locale: Baytown, West Indies, and England
Time: Early nineteenth century
Plot: Historical realism

Emily Cartwright, the thirty-year-old narrator. Sent to a West Indian plantation for three months before her marriage to Thomas Lockwood, Emily struggles with her feelings of superiority and the abusive treatment of the slaves. Not interested in the attentions of Mr. McDonald or Mr. Rogers, Emily surrenders to Arnold Brown, who she originally thinks is disgusting. Extending her trip three additional months to gather material for a lecture and tour in England, Emily discovers the truth about Mr. Wilson. Emily's happiness is destroyed when Cambridge kills Mr. Brown. Her virtue lost, she delivers a stillborn child in the presence of Stella and Mr. McDonald.

Arnold Brown, a ruddy-complexioned man in his thirties and the abusive overseer/manager of the Cartwright plantation. Brown takes over the Cartwright plantation by overthrowing Mr. Wilson. Carrying a personal vendetta, Brown rapes Christiania and later beats Cambridge in front of Emily. After adjusting his appearance, Brown attracts Emily, and they become intimate during a picnic at Hawthorn Cottage. Cambridge hopes to come to a nonviolent agreement with Brown, but during the confrontation, Brown is killed.

Cambridge, a large, gray-haired black man, called **Olumide** in his home country; Emily refers to him as Hercules. Betrayed by his fellow Guineamen and forced onto a slave ship when he is fifteen years old, Olumide sails to London to his new master's Pall Mall home. On the trip to England, Olumide meets John Williams, who teaches Olumide English and names him Thomas. Tom's master in London sends him to Miss Spencer of Blackheath for a Christian education. Once

Tom completes his education, Miss Spencer names him David Henderson. After falling in love with Anna, a white Englishwoman, David marries. David and his wife tour England as missionaries but are ostracized. During a difficult labor, Anna and her baby die. David returns to Miss Spencer's home and discovers that he has inherited four hundred guineas. Deciding to continue his ministry, David sails to Africa, but his money is stolen, and the ship's captain enslaves him. At the Cartwright plantation, David is named Cambridge. He courts and marries the magical Christiania. After an overseer coup, Cambridge declines the title of head driver. Frequently abused, Cambridge prays for a solution on Christmas Day. He confronts Brown and asks to be treated with some decency. After Brown strikes Cambridge, the two men struggle, and Cambridge kills Brown. Cambridge is hanged.

Mr. McDonald, a lawyer and physician, an intelligent, humane Scotsman. Infatuated with Emily, Mr. McDonald cares for her during several illnesses and desires to be her suitor. After discovering that Emily steps out with Mr. Brown, McDonald asks if he may escort her around town. Emily rejects him, but he continues to care for her whenever she needs him. Without making judgmental comments, Mr. McDonald delivers Emily's child.

Mr. Wilson, who was hired to run the Cartwright plantation but is accused of stealing and banished at gunpoint to another island. Overthrown by Mr. Brown, who believes in cruel oppression, Mr. Wilson leaves the plantation until Emily Cartwright visits. Mr. Wilson returns to Baytown hoping to correct his situation. When Emily says that he has been charged with theft, Mr. Wilson laughs and witnesses that he has never stolen so much as a fruit from a bush. His only crime is caring for the welfare of the slaves.

Christiania, the village obeah and Cambridge's wife. After being mistreated by her first husband, whom she is forced to marry at the age of ten, and after being raped by Mr. Brown, Christiania rejects Christianity and returns to her magical powers. When Emily corrects her for sitting at the table, Christiania casts spells outside Emily's window. Afraid of her powers, the slaves, Brown, and Emily make no effort to retrieve Christiania when she escapes.

Mr. Rogers, a slight, unhealthy, and prejudiced Anglican minister. Mr. Rogers visits Emily with Mr. McDonald. After overeating and indulging in too much drink, Mr. Rogers falls asleep on the veranda. Embarrassed, Mr. Rogers makes Mr. McDonald apologize. Feuding for Emily's favors, Mr. McDonald warns Emily that Mr. Rogers has dishonorable affections for her; however, Emily astutely concludes that Mr. Rogers has never had designs of any kind on a woman.

Isabella, Emily's faithful servant and constant companion for twenty years. Traveling with Emily to Baytown, Isabella becomes ill soon after the voyage begins. Tormented by the fever, Isabella dies and is buried at sea near the Azores.

Stella, a slave who cares for Emily at the Baytown plantation. Although not as civilized as Isabella, Stella dedicates herself to Emily's care.

— *Patricia T. Cheves*

CAMEL XIANGZI
(Lo-T'o Hsiang-tzu)

Author: Lao She (Shu Qingchun, 1899-1966)
First published: 1936
Genre: Novel

Locale: Beijing, China
Time: The 1930's
Plot: Realism

Hsiang-tzu, a Beijing rickshaw puller born and reared in the countryside. Self-confident, brawny, and hardworking, the twenty-year-old orphan enthusiastically adopts the colorful capital of northern China as his lifelong home. Although he pulls rickshaws with exemplary zeal and skill, his rural naïveté and his low position in the social class structure combine to bring him one misfortune after another. Having lost his wife during a breech childbirth and, subsequently, his fiancée through suicide, and having seen his hard-earned life savings repeatedly slip through his fingers, Hsiang-tzu sinks into the urban underclass of shiftless vagrants when his once iron-hard will to better himself finally breaks. He becomes a mere husk of his former self.

Old Liu, the vain and overbearing owner of the rickshaw agency where Hsiang-tzu rooms and works during much of the novel. A former soldier of fortune who, in his younger days, amassed a large nest egg through mobster racketeering, the seventy-year-old man has since settled down to the more mundane occupation of renting out rickshaws to men who cannot afford to buy their own. His only child, a thirtyish daughter who is increasingly fearful of ending her days as a spinster, seduces Hsiang-tzu and tries to persuade Old Liu to accept the lad from the countryside as his son-in-law. Enraged that she would shame the family name by getting engaged to somebody of such humble origins, in a fit of pique Old Liu self-righteously disowns his daughter, abruptly sells the agency, and finally condemns himself to living out his remaining days in grim loneliness.

Hu Niu, Old Liu's daughter, the real brains behind the day-to-day management of the Liu family rickshaw agency. Wily, aggressive, and fiery in temper as well as passions, she presides as the dominant partner in her marriage with Hsiang-tzu. Although she appreciates the crucial role Hsiang-tzu plays in her sex life, his homespun rural attitudes toward work and the family occasionally infuriate her, so much so that she curses him as a bumpkin. Ironically, Hu Niu joins the ranks of the poverty-stricken multitude whom she had always scorned as being improvident and undeserving of compassion: Disinherited by her father and with her modest savings almost gone, she finally lacks the means to secure proper medical care during childbirth and dies in her humble cottage along with her stillborn child.

Mr. Ts'ao, a kindly professor and armchair socialist who twice hires Hsiang-tzu to be his family's private rickshaw man. The modest and orderly household that this fortyish man heads seems to Hsiang-tzu a veritable oasis: Of the many families that hire Hsiang-tzu for a stint as a private rickshaw man, only the Ts'ao family treats Hsiang-tzu as a dignified human being worthy of respect. Unfortunately, Ts'ao's political affiliations get him in trouble with the right-wing government, and he must flee town hurriedly, thus leaving Hsiang-tzu stranded. By the time Ts'ao returns to Beijing, Hsiang-tzu has encountered so many wrenching reversals in his own life that he no longer has the strength of character to maintain his belief in the value of hard work, even in an enlightened residence like that of the Ts'aos.

Hsiao Fu Tzu, the ill-fated fiancée of Hsiang-tzu during the period following the death of Hu Niu. She is a kindly, submissive, and self-sacrificing young woman of barely twenty who is forced into prostitution by her ne'er-do-well father, Old Ch'iang. Hsiang-tzu is about to buy her way out of the brothel where she has been working under duress; he hopes to marry her and take her back to the Ts'ao residence, where he has been offered the job of private rickshaw puller. Hsiao Fu Tzu's suicide at the wretched brothel functions as the final straw and breaks Hsiang Tzu's will to struggle on as a self-respecting manual laborer.

Yuan Ming, a lazy, opportunistic, and chameleonic student who raises a serious political accusation with the government against his teacher, Mr. Ts'ao. Mr. Ts'ao has friends in high places who protect him from being placed on the most-wanted list of left-wing extremists, but this protection does not extend to Hsiang-tzu, whose life savings are confiscated by an unscrupulous police detective during the evening when the Ts'ao family flees their home to lie low for several months. Ironically, Yuan Ming eventually gets involved in a secret plot with bona fide leftist politicos and is betrayed to the police by none other than the increasingly unconscionable Hsiang-tzu, who receives an under-the-table payoff from the police.

— *Philip F. Williams*

CAMILLE
(La Dame aux camélias)

Author: Alexandre Dumas, *fils* (1824-1895)
First published: 1852
Genre: Drama

Locale: France
Time: The nineteenth century
Plot: Sentimental

Camille Gautier (kah-MEEL goh-TYAY), a poor needleworker who becomes a notorious courtesan. She passes up a chance to become mistress to Count de Varville because she loves a younger man, Armand Duval, for whom she leaves the gaiety of Paris to live in the country. For her lover's sake, she finally leaves him because her liaison is hurting his family. He believes until she is dying that she has left him because she is fickle. Her symbol is a camellia.

Count de Varville (vahr-VEEL), a French nobleman in love with Camille. He offers to pay all her debts if she becomes his mistress. He becomes her lover after she leaves Armand Duval.

He and Armand fight a duel, in which the count is wounded.

Armand Duval (ahr-MAHN dew-VAHL), a young man who has nothing but love to offer Camille. They become lovers. He thinks she has deserted him, until on her deathbed she tells him she left him for his own good and that of his family.

M. Duval, Armand's father. He pleads with Camille to leave his son so that Armand and his family will not suffer in their reputations.

Mme Prudence, a milliner, Camille's friend. She introduces Armand to Camille.

Nanine (nah-NEEN), Camille's faithful maid.

CAMPASPE

Author: John Lyly (c. 1554-1606)
First published: 1584
Genre: Drama

Locale: Athens
Time: c. 325 B.C.E.
Plot: Historical

Alexander, the king of Macedon, eager for conquest and glory, but generous and merciful when victorious. Passionately enamored of his captive, Campaspe, he asks Apelles, his court painter, to paint her portrait. He becomes suspicious of Apelles and angrily jealous, but finally he is moved to allow the lovers to marry because, as he says, a man who cannot command himself is unworthy to command the world.

Hephestion (hee-FEHS-tee-uhn), Alexander's chief general. Worried about the softening influence of love on the great warrior, he rejoices when Alexander conquers his desire for Campaspe and returns to military conquest.

Diogenes (di-OJ-eh-neez), a crusty independent philosopher. Scorning luxury and emotion, he lives in a tub. Even

Alexander's glories do not impress him. Alexander is forced to admit that if he were not Alexander he would like to be Diogenes, who has neither wants nor fears.

Apelles (uh-PEHL-eez), Alexander's painter. He loves Campaspe, he thinks hopelessly, for he knows that Alexander loves her also. He wins her love while painting her portrait and finally receives her at Alexander's hands.

Campaspe (kam-PAS-pee), Alexander's beautiful and virtuous Theban captive. At first skeptical of Apelles' love, she later accepts and returns it.

Sylvius (SIHL-vee-uhs), an Athenian citizen who wishes the unwilling Diogenes to instruct his sons.

Manes (MAY-neez), the discontented servant of Diogenes.

CANCER WARD
(Rakovy korpus)

Author: Aleksandr Solzhenitsyn (1918-   )
First published: 1968
Genre: Novel

Locale: An unnamed city based on Tashkent, Kazakhstan, Soviet Union
Time: 1955-1956
Plot: Social realism

Oleg Filimonovich Kostoglotov (fee-lee-MOH-roh-vihch ko-sto-GLOH-tov), a land surveyor. A loner, unmarried and without relatives, fiercely independent, and rebellious by nature, the thirty-four-year-old Kostoglotov is a former army sergeant and inmate from a Stalinist labor camp, arrested for making politically disparaging remarks about Joseph Stalin. Exiled to the remote central Asian town of Ush-Terek, he has been sent to a hospital in another unnamed central Asian city for treatment of stomach cancer. Skeptical of all authority, Kostoglotov clashes with his political opponent, the Stalinist bureaucrat and fellow cancer patient, Rusanov, who defends thought control and police state methods. In medical matters, he confronts Dr. Lyudmila Dontsova and insists on his right to know the exact details of his illness. When he discovers that the hormone injections he is being given may save his life but will result in the loss of his sexual capacity, he persuades Zoya, a nurse with whom he is sexually involved, to discontinue the treatments. Later, on the insistence of Dr. Vera Gangart, with whom he develops a close personal friendship, he resumes the treatment. His cancer is temporarily cured, and he is released from the hospital. Torn between his attraction for Zoya and for Vera, he ultimately ends his relationship with both women, thanking Zoya for their sexual intimacy, which he will always remember, and explaining to Vera that their relationship would be incomplete without the hope of sexual fulfillment. Amid rumors of a forthcoming amnesty for political exiles, Kostoglotov returns to Ush-Terek to live a life of simplicity similar to that of his fellow political exiles, Nikolay and Yelena Kadmin.

Pavel Nikolayevich Rusanov (PAH-vehl nee-koh-LAH-yeh-vihch rew-SAH-nov), a prominent Communist Party bureaucrat. An arrogant, forty-five-year-old careerist and status seeker, Rusanov expects special privileges in the hospital as a result of his party affiliation. He is an authoritarian official who has risen through the bureaucratic ranks by denouncing his coworkers and cooperating with the secret police. His stay in the cancer ward is marked by numerous confrontations and arguments with the democratic Kostoglotov, whom he despises. Apprehensive about the future because of the uncertainty of his medical recovery and the political changes occasioned by the liberalization in Soviet society following the death of Stalin, he nevertheless clings to Stalinist principles. Responsible for the denunciation of innocent citizens during the purge years of 1937-1938, he dreads the reintegration of victims of the purges into Soviet society. Although confronted with death and the ultimate question of the meaning of life, Rusanov learns nothing from his stay in the cancer ward and leaves the ward psychologically unchanged.

Dr. Vera Kornilyevna Gangart (kohr-NIH-lyehv-nah gahn-GAHRT), a radiotherapist. A small, shapely woman in her early thirties, she is shy, naturally kind, idealistic, and seemingly more innocent than a twenty-year-old. Having fallen in love with a schoolboy in her youth, she has remained faithful to his memory after he was killed during World War II. Determined to continue her life, she became a doctor and pledged herself to healing the afflicted. Inspired by the dedication of her mentor, Dr. Dontsova, she has been working as a resident doctor for eight years. When she meets Kostoglotov, she is personally attracted by his strength of character but finds herself in conflict with his insistence on questioning medical authority. A woman of deep inward convictions, she believes explicitly in the established methods of medical treatment. Dedicated to saving lives, she urges Kostoglotov to continue his hormone treatments, even though they will result in the loss of his sexual capacity. Attracted by Kostoglotov's strength of character, she contemplates developing a relationship with him, but he refuses to sacrifice her personal happiness to his sexual inadequacy.

Dr. Lyudmila Afanasyevna Dontsova (lyuhd-MIH-lah ah-fah-NAH-syehv-nah DOHN-tsoh-vah), the head of the radiotherapy department. A hardworking, conscientious, and dedicated doctor, she is nearly fifty years old. Dontsova is referred to affectionately by her younger resident doctors as "Mama." A professional woman, mother, and housewife burdened with both professional and domestic duties, she is frequently weary from overwork but tirelessly pursues her goal of alleviating pain and curing patients. She comes into conflict with the rebellious Kostoglotov when she insists on her right as a doctor to make decisions concerning a patient's treatment without consulting the patient. Ultimately, she convinces Kostoglotov to acquiesce in undergoing hormone treatments, believing that any impairment in a patient's physical condition, including loss of sexual capacity, is justified in order to save the patient's life. Ironically, Dontsova herself is stricken with abdominal cancer. Stunned by this unexpected event, she seeks the medical advice of her mentor, Dr. Oreshchenkov, who together with Dr. Gangart realizes the seriousness of her condition and recommends that she go to Moscow for further tests.

Zoya (ZOH-yah), a nurse. An attractive twenty-three-year-old woman reared in a broken home, Zoya has become independent and self-reliant, working part-time in the hospital to support herself while studying at a medical institute. Cheerful and fun-loving, she enjoys life and has had numerous affairs but is seeking a serious, stable relationship and is consequently attracted by Kostoglotov's perseverance and strength. Sharing his independent spirit, Zoya agrees to Kostoglotov's request for medical information about cancer and provides him with a medical book. When she becomes sexually involved with Kostoglotov, she also agrees to his request to discontinue his hormone injections, because they will result in his sexual impotency. As their sexual attraction for each other wanes, Zoya resumes the hormone injections out of fear of losing her job; Dr. Gangart discovers that Kostoglotov has not been receiving the hormone therapy.

Dyomka (DYOM-kah), a lathe operator, an idealistic sixteen-year-old student whose father was killed in World War II and whose stepfather deserted his sexually promiscuous mother. Dyomka harbors bitter feelings toward his mother for her promiscuity and for abandoning him. He is befriended by Kostoglotov, who encourages him, after his leg is amputated, to learn to use a crutch. Resilient and confident about the future, he resolves to return to work.

Sharaf Sibgatov (shah-RAF sihb-GAH-tov), a young Tartar slowly dying from cancer of the sacrum, a gentle, polite man who endures his suffering meekly and is grateful for the medical attention he receives. He arouses the pity of Dr. Dontsova, who redoubles her efforts to save him but ultimately is unsuccessful.

Alexey Fillipovich Shulubin (ah-lehk-SAY fih-LIH-pohvihch SHEW-lew-bihn), a librarian. An old, idealistic Bolshevik, defeated and despondent, tired of living and guilt-ridden for his complicity in the Stalin purges, Shulubin has lost his self-respect but still believes in socialist ideals. He supports Kostoglotov in Kostoglotov's numerous arguments with the unrepentant Rusanov.

Vadim Zatsyrko (vah-DIHM zah-TSYIHR-koh), a geologist. Handsome, talented, self-sacrificing, and dedicated to hard work, the twenty-six-year-old Vadim passionately desires to make an important geological discovery before he dies of terminal cancer. A Communist Party member, he is contemptuous of his intellectual inferiors and supports Rusanov in Rusanov's ideological arguments with Kostoglotov.

Yefrem Podduyev (yeh-FREHM poh-DEW-yehv), a worker. A hardy, middle-aged man less than fifty years old, he is crude, vulgar, and promiscuous. Yefrem is conscience-stricken after reading Leo Tolstoy's moral tales. Engaged by the precept that human beings should live by Christian love, he is denounced by Rusanov and Vadim for spreading alien religious ideology, but he is vigorously defended by Kostoglotov.

Dr. Dormidont Tikhonovich Oreshchenkov (dohr-mih-DONT tih-KHO-noh-vihch oh-REH-chehn-kov) a general practitioner. A warm, compassionate, seventy-five-year-old family doctor, Oreshchenkov cherishes his private medical practice. He shows kindness and sympathy to his former student, Dr. Dontsova, when she learns that she has cancer. He encourages her to go to Moscow for further tests.

Avieta Pavlovna Rusanova (ahv-YEH-tah PAHV-lohv-nah rew-SAH-noh-vah), a journalist, Rusanov's eldest daughter. Young, intelligent, talented, and energetic, Avieta seeks to follow her father's example and make connections to advance her career. She supports Rusanov in his ideological disputes and defends his role in the purges.

Lev Leonidovich (leh-oh-NIH-doh-vihch), the head surgeon. Nearly forty years old, Lev is a conscientious, dedicated doctor, popular with his patients for his cheerfulness and optimism. He inspires Kostoglotov's respect for his common sense, and Dyomka chooses him to amputate his leg.

Asya, an attractive seventeen-year-old schoolgirl, lively and energetic. Asya, who has been sexually active since the ninth grade, believes that one must live for romantic love. In despair when she learns that she must have a mastectomy, she turns to Dyomka for consolation.

Prokofy Semyonovich (proh-KOH-fee sehm-YOH-noh-vihch), a tractor driver. A strong, young Ukrainian suffering from a tumor of the heart, Prokofy is optimistic about his recovery and eager to return to work. He shows his release papers to Kostoglotov, who, out of compassion, refuses to translate the Latin phrase indicating that Prokofy's tumor is inoperable and incurable.

Elizaveta Anatolyevna (yeh-lih-zah-VYEH-tah ah-nah-TOH-lyehv-nah), an orderly in the radiology department. Not yet fifty years old but prematurely aged, Elizaveta is a former political exile, intelligent and educated, who serves tirelessly and uncomplainingly as a scrubwoman. Agonizing over her memories of the purges, she is urged by Kostoglotov to tell her eight-year-old son the truth about the labor camps.

Rodichev (roh-DEE-chehv), an engineer. A former friend of Rusanov falsely accused by Rusanov of belonging to a counterrevolutionary organization, Rodichev has spent eighteen years in a labor camp. His release from the camp causes Rusanov great anxiety.

Kapitolina Matveyevna Rusanova (kah-pih-TOH-lih-nah mah-TVEH-yehv-nah), Rusanov's wife. A fashionably dressed, energetic, intelligent woman, married to Rusanov for twenty-five years, Kapitolina is a faithful wife and true friend to her husband. Like her husband, she has grown accustomed to privilege and status.

Yura Rusanov (YEW-rah), a lawyer, Rusanov's eldest son. Yura is a disappointment to his father because of his failure to assert his rank and cultivate the proper acquaintances. Unlike his father, Yura is humane, compassionate, and interested in justice.

Maxim Petrovich Chaly (mahk-SEEM peh-TROH-vihch CHA-lee), a black marketeer and speculator, a lively, jovial man. His offer to obtain good automobile tires for Rusanov's new car through the black market is accepted by Rusanov when Rusanov is released from the hospital.

Nikolay Ivanovich Kadmin (nih-koh-LAY ee-VAH-noh-vihch KAHD-mihn), a male obstetrician. He is a lively, sixty-year-old doctor and political exile who lives a simple, unassuming life in Ush-Terek and corresponds with Kostoglotov.

Yelena Alexandrovna Kadmina (yeh-LEH-nah ah-lehk-SAN-drov-nah KAHD-mih-nah), Nikolay Kadmin's wife. She is a warm, compassionate, fifty-year-old political exile in poor health who shares both her husband's friendship with Kostoglotov and his joy in living a simple life.

Auntie Styofa (STYOH-fah), a grandmother, a humble, warm, compassionate Christian who consoles Dyomka and attempts to reconcile him to his fate.

Lavrenty Pavlovich Rusanov (lah-VREHN-tee PAHV-lohvihch), Rusanov's second son. An average student, talented in sports, he was named by his parents in honor of Lavrenty Beria (BAY-ree-ah), the head of Stalin's secret police. Egged on by his father, he maliciously attempts to run down Kostoglotov with his father's automobile when Kostoglotov is released from the hospital.

Maika Rusanova (MAY-kah), Rusanov's youngest daughter. An average pupil unable to achieve good grades on her own, Maika was placed on the honor roll because her teacher knew Maika's parents.

— *Jerome J. Rinkus*

CANDIDA

Author: George Bernard Shaw (1856-1950)
First published: 1897
Genre: Drama

Locale: London, England
Time: 1894
Plot: Comedy

Eugene Marchbanks, an eighteen-year-old poet, the nephew of an earl. Having left Oxford, Marchbanks is found sleeping outdoors by Morell, who brings him home. Marchbanks proceeds to fall in love with Morell's lovely wife, Candida. Marchbanks is slight, effeminate, frightened, and painfully sensitive, but he has the genuine poet's insight into human motivations. He is sure that his own helplessness and inadequacy will prove irresistible to a woman so purely feminine as Candida. He is horrified that Candida must dirty her hands working around the house. Unable to understand what a woman could find to love in Morell, Marchbanks demands that Candida be given a chance to choose between them. When confronted with the choice, Candida says she chooses "the weakest." Marchbanks at once understands why Candida loves Morell: He is even more in need of maternal care and pampering than is Marchbanks. Suddenly a man, Marchbanks leaves to get about his work, after thanking Morell for giving Candida so much opportunity to love.

Candida, the wife of the Reverend James Morell. She is attractive enough to charm men into doing her will, and her use of the feminine advantages is ennobled by dignity and intelligence. Taught by her husband to think for herself, Candida does so, to her husband's distress. She suggests to him that perhaps she should make love to Marchbanks lest some bad woman do it and damage his spirit, but the occasion never arrives. When Morell leaves Candida alone with Marchbanks, the latter is afraid to speak and reads poetry to her.

The Reverend James Mavor Morell, a Christian Socialist

clergyman of the Church of England. Vigorous and handsome, Morell is immensely in demand as a speaker for progressive causes. He is admired by men and adored by women. He is proud of his strength and competence and, until the end of the play, unaware of his absolute dependence on his wife. At last, he realizes that it is Candida, the personification of feminine urges, who is his protector and supporter. Becoming conscious of the true nature of her love for him, Morell avows that he is the product of her love.

Mr. Burgess, Candida's father, a vulgar and ignorant man who has grown rich in commerce. Burgess is instinctively respectful to people of rank. He frightens Marchbanks into near hysterics by trying to be friendly with him. Morell, a good Socialist, detests his father-in-law. Burgess thinks Morell is mad, but Morell's political influence is useful to him, and he is patronizingly polite to his son-in-law.

Miss Proserpine Garnett, Morell's secretary. Efficient and affectionate, Proserpine is in love with Morell. Marchbanks unnerves her by trying to discover what a woman could find to love in a man like Morell. She causes the sensitive Marchbanks to break into tears. When Burgess reprimands her for annoying an earl's nephew, Proserpine calls Burgess a fathead.

The Reverend Alexander (Lexy) Mill, Morell's enthusiastic young curate, newly out of Oxford, who follows Morell about with doglike devotion. He and Proserpine, both teetotalers, get drunk on Burgess' champagne after one of Morell's speeches.

CANDIDE: Or, The Optimist
(Candide: Ou, L'Optimisme)

Author: Voltaire (François-Marie Arouet, 1694-1778)
First published: 1759
Genre: Novel

Locale: Europe and South America
Time: The eighteenth century
Plot: Social satire

Candide (kahn-DEED), a gentle, honest, and pleasant young man, reputed to be the illegitimate son of the sister of Baron Thunder-ten-tronckh. Expelled from the Baron's castle after exploring the mysteries and pleasures of love with Cunegonde, the Baron's daughter, Candide travels all over the world. A dutiful young man who has been taught that this is the best of all possible worlds, Candide searches the globe for proof, meeting old friends and acquaintances in unexpected places and unusual circumstances. During his travels he has many misadventures and endures many hardships and pains. Impressed into the Bulgarian army, he discovers the horrors of war. He lives through the Lisbon Earthquake and is ordered flogged by officers of the Inquisition. He finds and loses his sweetheart Cunegonde. He discovers wealth and loses it. He kills men when he does not mean to do so. All these experiences slowly convince Candide that this is really not the best of all possible worlds. After years of wandering, he retires to a little farm where he lives with a small group of friends and his

wife, Cunegonde, now old and far from pretty.

Cunegonde (kew-nay-GOHND), the beautiful daughter of the Baron Thunder-ten-tronckh. With Candide, she explores love, only to have her young lover dismissed violently from the castle. After his dismissal, she endures much pain and many adventures. She is captured by the Bulgarians, raped, and wounded. She makes her way to Portugal, where she becomes the mistress of two men, a Jew and an officer of the Inquisition. She is reunited with Candide only to be separated from him by another series of unhappy adventures. At last she and Candide are reunited. Married, they settle down on a small farm. By that time, his ardor for her has been cooled by the adventures she has undergone and the effect they have had upon her. She becomes adept as a pastry cook, happy in that humble occupation.

Pangloss (pan-GLOHS), Candide's tutor, a professor of abstract nonsense. Despite the terrible adventures that befall Candide and Pangloss' other friends, he is unwilling to forgo theorizing or to admit that this is not the best of all possible worlds. He settles down with Candide on the latter's farm after undergoing many misadventures, including being hanged unsuccessfully by the Inquisition.

Baron Thunder-ten-tronckh (tewn-DAHR-tehn-TROHNK), Cunegonde's brother, who inherits his father's title. He is a proud young man, even in adversity and poverty, and he refuses again and again to give his consent to a marriage between his sister and Candide. Tired at last of the Baron's refusals, uttered with no regard for what Candide has endured on behalf of Cunegonde or the girl's changed condition, Candide causes the proud Baron to be shipped as a galley slave.

Jacques (zhahk), a kindly Anabaptist who befriends Candide in Holland and travels with him to Portugal, only to be drowned at the time of the Lisbon Earthquake.

Martin (mahr-TAN), a friend Candide meets in Surinam. Accused by the Church of being a Socinian heretic, Martin admits to Candide that he is a Manichee, though none is supposed to be left in the world. Martin travels with Candide on the latter portion of Candide's wanderings and settles down with Candide on a small farm.

Paquette (pa-KEHT), a maid to the Baroness Thunder-ten-tronckh. Loved by Pangloss, she gives him venereal disease.

After many misadventures of her own, she turns up again in Candide's life and becomes a member of the little colony on his farm, where she earns her living by doing embroidery.

Friar Giroflée (jee-roh-FLAY), a discontented friar who falls in love with Paquette during her travels and leaves his order for her sake. Befriended by Candide, he joins the colony on Candide's farm and turns carpenter.

The old woman, Cunegonde's servant. She relates that she was once a beautiful princess, the daughter of the Princess Palestrina and a fictional pope, Urban X. The splendid life she expects is lost when she is captured by Moroccan pirates and condemned to a hard life as a slave. She clings to Cunegonde and Candide and settles with them on Candide's farm.

Cacambo (kah-KAHM-boh), Candide's servant. Separated from Candide in South America, he turns up later in Venice as a slave belonging to the deposed Sultan Achmet III. Through Cacambo's intercession, Candide and his party are allowed to visit Turkey.

A contented old man, who has learned that hard work and minding one's own business are the best means to happiness. He avoids boredom, vice, and need by working a twenty-acre farm. Following his advice, Candide settles with his friends on a farm of his own.

CANE

Author: Jean Toomer (1896-1967)
First published: 1923
Genre: Poetry and short fiction

Locale: Rural Georgia, Chicago, and Washington, D.C.
Time: The early 1920's
Plot: Experimental

Fernie May Rosen, the beautiful, unhappy daughter of a black mother and a white Jewish father. She spends most days listlessly sitting on the porch of her rural Georgia home. She is the object of men's desires. Her remote indifference leads men to abandon her, but ironically they remain under her spell and bring her gifts as signs of their adoration.

Tom Burwell, a black field hand competing with a white man for the attentions of Louisa, a black woman working for his rival's family. A gentle introvert, Tom cannot express his feelings to Louisa. In a rage, he kills her other lover, and he is lynched by a white mob.

Paul Johnson, a Southern black man whose skin is light enough to allow him to pass as white. He is studying at a

Chicago physical education school, where he meets Bona Hale, a white Southerner. She is attracted to him because of his blackness, but his uncertainty about his racial status makes him aloof and inaccessible. His ambivalence and denial of part of his heritage cause Bona to leave him.

Ralph Kabnis, a Northern black teacher of Southern descent who comes to rural Georgia apparently in search of his roots. Sensitive and neurotic, he cannot accept what he sees as submissiveness on the part of other black people. After he loses his teaching job, he becomes an apprentice in a wagon shop, but his spiritual and emotional decline continues. At the end of the novel, he is a childlike, dependent failure.

— Gerald Strauss

CANNERY ROW

Author: John Steinbeck (1902-1968)
First published: 1945
Genre: Novel

Locale: A fishing village near Monterey, California
Time: About 1940
Plot: Sentimental

Doc, the owner and operator of Western Biological Laboratory. He was graduated from the University of Chicago. Doc is small, strong, and wiry, and he loves science, beer, women, classical music, books, and prints. He is a thoroughly civilized man and the acknowledged, but unofficial, "mayor" of Cannery Row in Monterey. He is a fountain of wisdom, philosophy, and sometimes medical and psychiatric advice. Doc has a pointed brown beard and is described as half Christ and half satyr. Doc has a fear of getting his head wet. He is beloved

by all but is nevertheless a lonely and remote man.

Mack and the Boys, a group of unemployed men who live in the Palace Flophouse. They are open, honest, and generous in their way, kind and understanding, and sometimes extremely compassionate. They have no greed, meanness, egotism, or self-interest.

Mack, the leader of the Boys. Once married, Mack is very intelligent and without conventional ambition. To the others, he is mentor, sage, and sometimes exploiter. He leads the frog-hunting expedition and plans Doc's party. It is said that Mack could have been the president of the United States if he had so wanted. Mack loves food, drink, and, sometimes, women and fighting.

Dora Flood, the proprietor of the Bear Flag Restaurant, which actually is a decent, clean, honest, old-fashioned brothel. Dora is probably in her late sixties and, the narrator says, is respected by the intelligent, learned, and kind; she is hated by spinsters and prudish women. She is a large woman with orange hair and a big heart. During the Depression, she paid for groceries for many poor families, and she is a large donator to local worthy causes. During the influenza epidemic, she put her cook to work making soup and her girls to work delivering it.

Hazel, one of the Boys, twenty-six years old and dark-haired. He is not very bright and has no viciousness or guile. He occasionally helps Doc with the collecting of marine life and is good at it. Hazel, who has had four years of regular school and four years in reform school, was named for his great aunt by his exhausted and confused mother, who had borne seven children in eight years.

Eddie, one of the Boys, the understudy bartender at La Ida, from which he brings home jugs full of dregs from all the drink glasses.

Gay, one of the Boys, married to a woman who sometimes beats him while he is asleep. Gay is an excellent auto mechanic but drinks too much and is often in jail.

Lee Chong, a Chinese grocery store owner and owner of the Palace Flophouse. He stands behind the cigar counter, in front of the whiskey shelves, wearing half-glasses and extending credit judiciously. Lee Chong is shrewd but kind and can be generous and sentimental. He is a wise man, sometimes abused but always tolerant.

Henri, a painter, who is not French and whose name is not really Henri. He sometimes paints with chicken feathers, sometimes with nutshells. He loves all things French and all things modern. He is swarthy and morose. Henri has been married twice and has had many other women in his life, but they always leave him because he lives in an unfinished boat, up on blocks and with no plumbing.

Alfred, a bouncer at the Bear Flag Restaurant. He is accepted by the Boys. His talent is for keeping order without actually hurting anyone.

"The Captain," the owner of the frog pond raided by Mack and the Boys. The Captain, whose wife is in politics, is clearly henpecked, but she is away.

Frankie, a mentally retarded and physically uncoordinated eleven-year-old who usually is filthy. Frankie loves Doc absolutely but is unable to function in society.

Wilbur, who used to work for Dora as a bouncer. He wanted to be one of the Boys but was never accepted by them.

Sam Malloy and

Mrs. Malloy, who live happily in a boiler in a vacant lot until Mrs. Malloy gets the urge to decorate with window curtains. Seeing an opportunity to go into business, they rent small pipes to single men.

Mary Talbot, a woman with red hair, golden skin, and green eyes. She is a loving, kind woman of infinite optimism.

Tom Talbot, Mary's husband, an as-yet-unsuccessful writer. Mary cheers him up.

Old Chinaman, a mysterious figure who walks, for years, into the ocean at dusk with a wicker basket. He emerges at dawn. Some people think that he has powers. Some think that he is God; others, death.

— *Donald R. Noble*

THE CANNIBAL

Author: John Hawkes (1925-1998)
First published: 1949
Genre: Novel

Locale: Germany
Time: The twentieth century
Plot: Allegory

Zizendorf, the narrator of parts 1 and 3. He is without a family history and almost without personality as well. Although he shows some affection for Jutta, his female counterpart, he displays little emotion. A Nazi soldier during World War II, he becomes Jutta's lover and the editor of the newspaper *The Crooked Zeitung*. His plot to assassinate Leevey is motivated by a desire for vengeance and power. Although he believes he is a disillusioned rationalist, he is a madman, the cold-blooded killer of Leevey, Herr Stintz, and the Mayor.

Stella (Madam Snow), a singer at the Sportswelt Brauhaus at the beginning of World War I. Bold and vivacious, she is an embodiment of the German Motherland. Although courted by Cromwell, she marries Ernst Snow, a darkly romantic figure to her, scarred from fighting in duels. Although sentimental on the surface, Stella is an opportunist who sides with the Nazis during World War II. Her son is crippled and her grandson is killed in this war. In the present, she consults her cards for signs of things to come. She longs for the Germany of her youth.

Ernst Snow, a morose young man who is dominated and manipulated by his father. He marries Stella. He expresses masochistic tendencies and is scarred frequently in duels with men he consciously identifies with his father. His masochism becomes more extreme in his attempt to escape life through religion. He ultimately identifies with Christ on the cross and longs for death, but his human nature will not be denied. Shortly before he dies, he expresses his long-repressed hatred for his father.

Jutta, Stella's younger sister, a child during World War I. She rejects religious illusions and discovers sex after she is placed in a nunnery following the deaths of her parents. Believing that life "was not miraculous but clear, not right but undeniable" and married to a Nazi soldier during World War II, she is the perfect mate for Zizendorf.

Cromwell, an English Germanophile who claims to have no home. He believes technology is the key to the future and represents dehumanizing order. Although he loses Stella to Ernst during World War I, he wins her, in a sense, when she sides with the Nazis in World War II.

The Census-Taker, a drunk and a voyeur. He watches Zizendorf and Jutta make love. He has no function in the town because its population has neither increased nor declined. Zizendorf refers to him as "my relic-brother," thereby revealing potential weaknesses in himself, which he must repress to carry out his plans.

Herr Stintz, a one-eyed schoolteacher and former tuba player in the orchestra. An honest man, he tells Zizendorf that no one can get away with anything. He takes Selvaggia out to witness the assassination of Leevey. This is a necessary violation of innocence, an act of education. In contrast, Zizendorf tells Selvaggia to go back to sleep. Herr Stintz's condition and fate represent the condition and fate of art and education in the novel.

Selvaggia, Jutta's daughter, who represents the child in everyone, the witness more or less continually violated by atrocity.

Leevey, an American Jew, the overseer of one-third of Germany. He is ironically linked with Zizendorf, his killer, through their mutual association with machines and technology. Zizendorf takes Leevey's watch, which represents dehumanized order. Zizendorf makes love to Jutta on the day of Leevey's assassination; paralleling that, Leevey has sex with a spiteful and diseased German whore.

The Duke, identified only by his title. He pursues Jutta's son throughout the 1945 sections of the novel, finally killing and butchering him, then cooking him and feeding the meal to Madam Snow.

Balamir, the son of the German kaiser of World War I, or so he believes. One of the inmates of the asylum, he represents the Germany of Stella's youth, which she hopes to revive. She abandons her faith in him when he fails to unearth the furniture buried in her basement.

The boy, Jutta's son, who flees from the Duke until he is caught and killed. Like his sister, Selvaggia, he is an image of childhood innocence. He may be identified specifically with the innocence of youth sacrificed in wars resulting from ideals of conquest and heroism.

The Mayor, the cowardly betrayer of the innocent Pastor Miller. He turns away when Miller is executed and sleeps through most of the action. Too blind to tend to the chronicles of history, and with his memory obliterated, he is nevertheless tormented in dreams by images of Pastor Miller. He represents an oblivious political bureaucracy.

— *James Green*

THE CANTERBURY TALES

Author: Geoffrey Chaucer (c. 1343-1400)
First transcribed: 1387-1400
Genre: Poetry

Locale: A pilgrimage road between London and Canterbury
Time: Remote antiquity to the fourteenth century
Plot: Romance

The Knight, a courtly medieval fighting man who has served king and religion all over the known world. Modest in dress and speech, though the highest in rank of the pilgrims to Canterbury, he rides with only his son and a yeoman in attendance. He tells a metrical romance, the first of the stories in the series related by the various pilgrims. His is a tale of courtly love, the story of the love two young Theban noblemen, Palamon and Arcite, have for Emily, the beautiful sister-in-law of Duke Theseus of Athens. The young men compete in a tourney for the girl's hand. Palamon wins but is killed in an accident, so that Arcite eventually has his love rewarded.

The Squire, the Knight's son. A young man of twenty years, he has fought in several battles. Like his father, he is full of knightly courtesy, but he also enjoys a good time. He tells a story of adventure and enchantment in a distant land. The story he leaves unfinished tells of three gifts sent to Canacee, daughter of King Cambuscan. Each of the gifts has magic powers: a ring that enables the bearer to talk to birds, a brass horse that will take its rider anywhere, and a mirror that shows the truth and the future. The ring enables Canacee to learn the story of a lovelorn hawk for the mate who has deserted her.

The Yeoman, the Knight's attendant, a forester who takes excellent care of his gear. He wears a St. Christopher medal on his breast. He does not tell a story.

The Prioress (**Madame Eglentyn**), who travels with another nun and three priests as her attendants to the shrine of St. Thomas Becket at Canterbury. A woman of conscience and sympathy, she wears a curious brooch on which appears the ambiguous statement, in Latin, "Love conquers all." Her story is that of a schoolboy murdered for his religion by Jews. The child's death is discovered by a miracle of Our Lady. Like most of the stories told in the collection of tales, this one fits the personality of its narrator.

The Second Nun, who accompanies the Prioress. She also tells a Christian legend, that of the martyrdom of St. Cecilia. The story is typical of medieval hagiography.

The Nun's Priest, whose name is **John**. He tells the beast epic relating the adventures of the cock, Chauntecleer, and the fox. It is a didactic yet humorous story suitable for the Prioress' father confessor.

The Monk, a fat hedonist who prefers to be out of his cloister. No lover of books and learning, he prefers to hunt and eat. He cites tragedy as being the story of a man fallen from high degree and then offers many examples, including anecdotes of Lucifer, Adam, Samson, Hercules, Balthasar, Ugolino of Pisa, Julius Caesar, and Croesus. His lugubrious recital is interrupted by the Knight.

The Friar, named **Huberd**. He is a merry chap who knows barmaids better than the sick. Having the reputation of being the best beggar in his house, he appears to be a venal, worldly man. His story is a fabliau of a summoner who loses his soul to the devil. The story arouses the discomfiture of the Summoner in the group of pilgrims.

The Merchant, a tight-lipped man of business. Unhappily married, he tells a story of the evils of marriage between old men and young women. It relates how a superannuated husband named January is deceived by his young and hearty spouse named May.

The Clerk of Oxford, a serious young scholar who heeds philosophy and prefers books to worldly pleasures. His tale is an answer to the Wife of Bath's idea that in marriage the woman ought to have dominion. The Clerk's tale is of an infinitely patient wife named Griselda who endures all manner of ill treatment from her husband.

The Sergeant of Law, a busy man who seems busier than he really is. He makes a great show of his learning, citing cases all the way back to William the Conqueror.

The Franklin, a rich landlord who loves to eat and keeps a ready table of dainties. He has been sheriff of his county. His story is an old Breton lay, a tale of chivalry and the supernatural. He apologizes for his story and its telling, saying he is an uneducated man.

The Haberdasher,
the Carpenter,
the Weaver,
the Dyer, and
the Tapestry Maker, each a member of a guild and each rich and wise enough to be an alderman. None of them tells a story.

The Cook, named **Roger**, who was hired by the master workmen to serve them during their journey. He is a rollicking fellow. Pleased by the bawdy tales of the Miller and the Reeve, he insists on telling a bawdy story of his own, one left unfinished.

The Shipman, the captain of the *Maudelayne*, of Dartmouth. He is a good skipper and a smuggler. Like others of the company, he tells a fabliau, a bawdy tale. He relates the misadventures of a merchant of St. Denis, in Belgium, who is cheated of his wife's favors and his money by a sly monk named John.

The Doctor of Physick, a materialistic man greatly interested in money. He knows all the great medical authorities, as well as his astrology, though he seldom reads the Bible. His story, which he attributes to Livy, is the old tale of Appius and Virginia.

The Wife of Bath, named **Alice**, a clothmaker and five times a widow. Apparently wealthy from her marriages, she has traveled a great deal, including three trips to Jerusalem. She is well versed in marriage and lovemaking. Her theory is that the woman must dominate in marriage. To make her point, she tells a tale of a loathsome lady who, when her husband is obedient, becomes fair.

The Parson, a poor but loyal churchman who teaches his parishioners by his good example. Refusing to tell an idle tale to his fellow pilgrims, he tells what he terms a merry tale about the Seven Deadly Sins.

The Plowman, an honest man, the Parson's brother. He tells no tale.

The Miller, a jolly, drunken reveler who leads the company playing on his bagpipes. He tells a bawdy story about a carpenter named John who is cuckolded by his young wife, Alison, and her witty lover, Nicholas.

The Reeve, a slender, choleric man named **Oswald**. Having been a carpenter, he is incensed by the Miller's tale. In retribution, he tells a story about a miller cuckolded by two lusty students who sleep with the miller's wife and daughter.

The Manciple, an uneducated man who is shrewd enough to steal a great deal from the learned lawyers who hire him to look after their establishments. He relates the old folktale of the tattling bird.

The Summoner, a lecherous, drunken fellow who loves food and strong drink. Angered by the Friar's tale about a summoner, he tells a tale about a friar who becomes the butt of coarse humor.

The Pardoner, a womanish man with long, blond hair. He tells a tale of three young men who seek death and find it. His story is actually a sermon on the evils of unnatural love of money. He follows up the sermon with an attempt to sell phony relics to his fellow pilgrims.

Harry Bailey, the host at the Tabard Inn in Southwark. He organizes the storytelling among the pilgrims, with the winner to have a meal at his fellows' cost upon the company's return. He is a natural leader, as his words and actions show.

Geoffrey Chaucer, the author, who put himself into his poem as a retiring, mild-mannered person. He tries to recite the Rime of Sir Thopas, a dreary tale that is interrupted as dull, whereupon he tells the story of Melibee and Dame Prudence.

The Canon, a traveler who joins the pilgrims briefly on the road to Canterbury. He leaves when it is hinted that he is a cheating alchemist.

The Canon's Yeoman, who remains with the pilgrim company and tells an anecdote about an alchemist, a canon like his master, who swindles a priest.

A CANTICLE FOR LEIBOWITZ

Author: Walter M. Miller, Jr. (1923-   )
First published: 1959
Genre: Novel

Locale: Somewhere between Salt Lake City, Utah, and El Paso, Texas
Time: 2500, 3174, and 3781
Plot: Science fiction

Brother Francis Gerard, a young, fresh-faced novice of the Albertian order of Leibowitz. Brother Francis discovers a fallout shelter containing relics of the Blessed Leibowitz (who, apparently, was a scientist in pre-nuclear holocaust America). Francis' discovery causes a stir in the abbey, especially because rumors allege that the pilgrim he saw prior to his discovery was Leibowitz himself.

The pilgrim, who also appears as **Benjamin Eleazar bar Joshua** and **Lazarus**, an old man who may be the Wandering Jew. His figure appears in each of the three sections of the

book, though he is not overtly identified as the same man each time. As the pilgrim, he marks a stone for Brother Francis that leads to discovery of the fallout shelter. As Benjamin Eleazar, he discusses with Dom Paulo the rise of a secular state and waits for a messiah. As Lazarus, he is assigned the role of the man whom Christ raised from the dead and smiles wryly at Abbot Zerchi's hope that there will not be another nuclear holocaust.

Dom Arkos, the abbot of the Leibowitz Abbey in the first section of the book. Arkos attempts to quash the rumors surrounding the man whom Francis met in the desert and turns the examination of the fallout shelter and its contents over to another order. Toward the end of Arkos' tenure, Leibowitz is declared a saint.

Brother Fingo, a man with an unusual pattern of melanin distribution. Fingo carves a wooden statue of Leibowitz that, over the years, vaguely reminds Brother Francis, Dom Paulo, and Dom Zerchi of someone they cannot identify. The implication is that the statue reminds them of the Wandering Jew.

Dom Paulo, the abbot of the Leibowitz Abbey in the second section of the novel. He presides over the abbey during a period in which the secular and religious worlds are beginning to diverge. He refuses to send to the secular capital the ancient manuscripts (the Memorabilia) that the abbey holds, but he allows the secular scholar Thon Taddeo to examine them in situ.

Thon Taddeo Pfardentrott, a brilliant secular scholar. An illegitimate son of the ruling family, he was reared in a Benedictine abbey, which provided him with an excellent education. He nevertheless argues the superiority of secular scholarship and scoffs at religion, saying that science should not be constrained by ethical or religious concerns. Thon Taddeo's abstract work on the nature of electricity leads Brother Kornhoer to construct an electric light.

Brother Kornhoer, a monk at the abbey who constructs a dynamo to generate power for an electric light.

Brother Armbruster, the librarian at the abbey, who sees Brother Kornhoer's work as heretical.

Marcus Apollo, a papal nuncio to the court of Hannegan, the ruler of Texarkana. Apollo tries to warn Dom Paulo about Thon Taddeo's secular loyalties. He is later executed for treason because of his support of New Rome over the political government.

The Poet, a guest at the abbey. He has one removable eye, which he claims enables him to see more clearly. The brothers call it "the Poet's conscience." The Poet, playing the fool, accuses Thon Taddeo of avoiding the responsibility of preventing misuse that should accompany scientific advances. He tells Thon Taddeo, who has picked up the glass eye, that he has need of it.

Dom Jethrah Zerchi, the abbot in the novel's third section. He must confront the certainty of another nuclear holocaust. He tries to defend the faith in a world gone mad and must argue against euthanasia despite its seeming kindness. The shock wave of a nuclear bomb hits the abbey as he hears the confession of Mrs. Grales. As he lies trapped in the rubble, he receives the Eucharist from Rachel.

Mrs. Grales/Rachel, a two-headed woman. Mrs. Grales is confessing her sins when the shock wave of a nuclear bomb hits the abbey. The effects of the bomb apparently kill Mrs. Grales while raising to life Rachel, her previously dormant other head. Rachel seems to Abbot Zerchi to be an incarnation of innocence, perhaps another Mary, mother of Christ.

Brother Joshua, a former astronaut. He leads a group to colonize another planet, escaping the effects of the holocaust. They take with them the Memorabilia, on microfilm.

Dr. Cors, a Green Star worker. He argues with Dom Zerchi about euthanasia, which the doctor has recommended to a young woman and her baby.

— Karen M. Cleveland

CAPRICORNIA

Author: Xavier Herbert (1901-1984)
First published: 1938
Genre: Novel

Locale: Capricornia, Australia
Time: The 1880's to the 1930's
Plot: Social satire

Oscar Shillingsworth, a civil servant and later a cattle rancher. He is a tall, erect, neat man who in his maturity wears a huge mustache. Determined to get on in life, he works assiduously for the government, marries well, and leases a large cattle station in Australia's rough-and-ready Northern Territory (called Capricornia in the novel). At the beginning, he is in his thirties and is somewhat prim and self-interested. His wife runs off, and various other problems of life make him a more generous, concerned man in the long run.

Mark Shillingsworth, Oscar's younger brother, who comes to Capricornia with him to work as a government clerk. He is twenty-two years old and less eager than Oscar to please the society of middle-class clerks and shopkeepers. Almost immediately, he falls in with a happy group of gamblers and drunkards. Tall and handsome, attractive to women, and prone to alcoholic excess, he soon falls out of work and society, has a child with an aboriginal girl, and kills a Chinese merchant in a brawl over money. He disappears and is believed to be dead for much of the novel, but he turns up as a middle-aged man, still prone to getting into trouble but often rather innocently so.

Norman Shillingsworth, Mark's illegitimate son, named **Mark Anthony Shillingsworth** but known in his childhood, while living as a half-caste, as **Nawnim**, an aboriginal version of "No Name," which gradually is anglicized as Norman. His mother dies soon after he is born, and Mark Shillingsworth never takes responsibility for him. Yellow-skinned, black-eyed, and handsome, he lives from hand to mouth until Oscar Shillingsworth takes him into his family and rears him as a white child. He is educated as a draftsman but has natural gifts as a mechanic and ambitions to work on the railroad. He becomes a genial, attractive young man, but he is clearly of mixed blood, which he is told is part Javanese because that is less socially offensive than being part aboriginal. Much of his difficulty in life comes from his ignorance of his past and the reluctance of Australian society to accept him as a full member of a white family.

Heather Poundamore, Oscar Shillingsworth's sister-in-law. A pretty young woman, she falls in love with Mark. Their relationship is stormy because of his drinking and his relations with native women. She takes a job as a barmaid to keep an eye on Mark, and after his disappearance she remains faithful to his memory. She is a kind, sensible woman, careful with money and a good businesswoman. She is a great help to both Mark and Norman when they get into trouble with the law.

Charles Ket, a young laborer from the western coast of Australia. He at first passes himself off under the name of

Harold Carlton and is getting on in Capricornia's white society until it is revealed that he is of mixed white, Oriental, and aboriginal blood. His narrow black eyes and hair betray his Chinese connection, and his swarthy skin gives away his aboriginal lineage. He is a bitter, vicious man and a dangerous enemy, not disinclined to do physical harm up to and including murder. He becomes a great hater of the Shillingsworth family because he had ambitions of marrying Oscar's daughter.

Frank McLash, a big, low-browed twenty-year-old, shaped like a kewpie doll, with an egg-shaped head. From his early years he is prone to getting in trouble with the law. He serves time in a reformatory while in his teens. He is torn between being a thief and a railway engineer, but the latter job repeatedly is torn from his grasp, sometimes by bad luck and sometimes by his own stupidity. He serves in World War I and survives, but after that his life is one disaster after another,

particularly when he teams up with Charles Ket in a short life of crime.

Pansy McLash, Frank McLash's long-suffering, widowed mother. She keeps a kind of hotel, the Siding House. Although she has a strong love for liquor, she has an even stronger love for her feckless son, and she has sacrificed financially and otherwise for him all his life. She can be a good friend but is an enthusiastic enemy.

Tocky, a half-caste who becomes involved with Norman and, in her way, loves him. Beautiful, full-lipped, with long, enticing eyelashes, she brings out the worst in men. She is lively and charming and has survived a life of physical misery by her wits. She rarely does what she is told. When she obeys Norman, it ends in disaster for her and their child.

— *Charles Pullen*

CAPTAIN BLACKMAN

Author: John A. Williams (1925-   )
First published: 1972
Genre: Novel

Locale: Every theater of important American military action
Time: 1971, with dream sequences from 1775 to 2001
Plot: Historical realism

Captain Abraham Blackman, a powerful black man, about forty years old. He is a career soldier who is highly sensitive to the exploitation of black soldiers throughout America's history. He teaches a seminar on black military history to the men in his command (C Company) in Vietnam, a command predominantly composed of African Americans, Puerto Ricans, and "crackers," the detritus of the white world. He is very effective in uniting the allegiances of his men, particularly the black men, who do not seem fully aware of the injustices visited upon them during their tours of duty. While leading a patrol, an activity unusual for one of such high rank, Blackman draws enemy fire to protect the men in his squad and is severely wounded. He enters a dream state and relives a part of each conflict in which the United States has taken part, beginning with the Revolutionary War. Blackman gradually works his way up in rank through his imaginary experiences, beginning as a raw foot soldier in 1775 and finally appearing as a lieutenant in World War II; at the time he is wounded, he is in reality a captain but is promoted to major while he recuperates. Many of his current associates appear in these illusions, playing roles that correspond to their situations in his life. He also encounters historical figures and locations that probably played an important part in his history lessons. Blackman is not aware of his displacement in time during these illusions. He is highly cognizant of the inequities visited on the black soldiers by the whites and of their methods of maintaining control. These visions leads him to devise a comprehensive plan for a black coalition to conquer the white-dominated nation. In the dream at the close of the novel, the scope of his ideas apparently takes the complacent whites totally by surprise, and his plan succeeds.

Mimosa Rogers, Blackman's girlfriend, a member of the U.S. Foreign Service, probably in her late twenties. His female counterpart, she is tall, very attractive, highly intelligent, and devoted to helping Blackman achieve his goals, which she shares. After he is wounded, she is fiercely protective of him. She appears in many of the historical time frames during

Blackman's dream; nearly every encounter is marked by an intense sexual experience.

Ishmael Whittman, Blackman's principal antagonist, a blond, blue-eyed representative of the inferior white person who holds a superior position only by virtue of race. He outranks Blackman despite the fact that Blackman is the better soldier, and both are aware of the relationship. He encounters Blackman several times during their real military careers. Whittman is extremely pleased to hear of Blackman's serious wounds and waits with hope for news of his death. Whittman appears in most of the dream sequences, always as an officer of superior rank to Blackman and as an ineffective leader. His fear of the black man who is more intelligent, braver, and of stronger character is expressed through a desire to eradicate or, failing that, to subjugate that which he fears. Although in the final dream segment Whittman has attained the rank of general, Blackman, through his superior intelligence and ability, is able to defeat Whittman and everything for which he stands.

Robert Doctorow, a white member of Blackman's command. Sensitive to bigotry because of his Jewish heritage, Doctorow joins the black military history seminars, in spite of opposition from the black grunts, at least for long enough to prove that he will not be intimidated by them. An aspiring writer, he keeps a notebook of his experiences as preparation for the book he intends to write. He is committed to influencing social change, a desire exemplified by his role of idealistic volunteer in the Spanish Civil War sequence of Blackman's dream. He is injured slightly in the rocket attack that kills Harrison and Belmont.

Luther Woodcock, a soldier in Blackman's command, white in appearance (except for his enormous "Afro" haircut) but black by heritage. He is a personification of the new black attitude that emerged in the late 1960's and early 1970's. Rather than trying to blend into the white world, Woodcock flaunts his black roots proudly. Woodcock, a medic, administers first aid to Blackman when he is wounded. He appears in the World War I sequence as one of the few black officers and as a friend to Blackman. In the final dream, he is instrumental in the defeat of the whites. He is wounded slightly in the rocket attack on the base.

David Harrison (Little David), a black sergeant in Blackman's Vietnam squad. He is a small man physically, but he is of imposing character and refuses to bend to the idea of white supremacy. This pride leads to his death at the hands of white soldiers in the U.S. Cavalry segment of Blackman's dream. He appears as a dependable close friend in the U.S. Cavalry and Civil War sequences. Harrison is killed in a rocket attack after Blackman's patrol returns to its base on the hostile perimeter and Blackman is placed in a helicopter for transport to a hospital.

Belmont, the black radioman in Blackman's company. His grandfather was a much-decorated flying ace in World War I,

highly respected in France but reduced to a lackey's status upon his return to the United States because of his color. Paul Belmont, the grandfather, is mentioned in the World War I dream. Belmont is killed in the rocket attack on the base.

Johnny Griot, a black soldier of C Company who appears in the War of 1812 sequence. He inspires Blackman to repel a group of drunken whites who try to abuse the sleeping black soldiers in this segment of the dream.

Antoine (Black Antoine), another black soldier in C Company who appears in the War of 1812 sequence. As a result of their actions in this conflict, the black soldiers are granted a section of land, although the government refuses to grant freedom.

— *Mary Johnson*

CAPTAIN HORATIO HORNBLOWER

Author: C. S. Forester (1899-1966)
First published: 1939
Genre: Novel

Locale: Various oceans, Europe, and South America
Time: Early nineteenth century
Plot: Historical

Captain Horatio Hornblower, the commander of HMS *Lydia* and HMS *Sutherland*, British warships of the Napoleonic era. He is brilliant, brave, and skillful, but he is also shy and consumed by self-doubt, and he rigorously disciplines himself against a natural talkativeness. During his many adventures, he sinks the hostile warship *Natividad* while commanding the much smaller *Lydia*, heroically cripples a French squadron at the cost of losing the *Sutherland*, is captured by the French, is reported dead, escapes, seizes a captured English ship, sails to England, is knighted, and is reunited with the widowed Lady Barbara.

Lieutenant William Bush, Hornblower's stolid, capable, fearless first lieutenant. He loses a foot during the battle with the French squadron; captured along with Hornblower, he accompanies him during the long escape from the heart of France. Upon returning to England, Bush is promoted to the rank of captain.

Brown, Hornblower's powerfully built coxswain and personal servant. Though uneducated, he is highly intelligent and adaptable, and he proves invaluable during the escape from France.

Lieutenant Gerard, Hornblower's handsome, rakish second lieutenant.

Don Julian Alvarado (HEW-lee-ahn ahl-vah-RAH-doh), called **El Supremo** (sew-PREH-moh), a megalomaniacal petty tyrant who instigates a rebellion against Spanish rule in Central America. After his rebellion is crushed, he is captured by the Spanish and executed.

Captain Crespo, El Supremo's henchman, the commander of the *Natividad*. Though brutal and apparently primitive, he

proves to be a capable seaman, a clever tactician, and a brave opponent; he chooses to go down with his ship rather than surrender to Hornblower.

Maria, Hornblower's short, dumpy wife, who dies in childbirth while he is a captive in France.

Lady Barbara Wellesley, the beautiful, accomplished, self-possessed sister of the Duke of Wellington. Sailing to England aboard the *Lydia*, she falls in love with Hornblower, but he refuses her because he is married; in a fit of anger, she then weds Admiral Leighton. After the deaths of Maria and Leighton, she adopts Hornblower's child. She and Hornblower are reconciled after his escape from France.

Admiral Sir Percy Leighton, Hornblower's immediate commander and Lady Barbara's husband, a pompous, unimaginative man who owes his rank to his family's political prominence. He is injured in the final destruction of the French squadron crippled by Hornblower, and he later dies of his wounds.

Colonel Caillard (ki-YAWR), an officious, cruel aide to Napoleon assigned to escort Hornblower to Paris.

Comte de Graçay (gray-SAY), the kindly lord of the chateau where Hornblower, Bush, and Brown find refuge during their escape. A charming, cultured scion of the French aristocracy, he disapproves of Napoleon's regime.

Marie de Graçay, his attractive, widowed daughter-in-law, who becomes Hornblower's lover during his stay at the chateau.

Longley, Hornblower's cabin boy aboard the *Sutherland*, killed during the fight with the French squadron.

Polwheal (pohl-WEEL), Hornblower's steward.

CAPTAIN SINGLETON

Author: Daniel Defoe (1660-1731)
First published: 1720
Genre: Novel

Locale: England, Africa, and various oceans
Time: The eighteenth century
Plot: Adventure

Captain Bob Singleton, sailor, explorer, and pirate. Early in life, he becomes accomplished in the arts of navigation and thievery, talents that are to stand him in good stead in his subsequent careers as explorer and pirate. Driven by storm, shipwreck, and mutiny to a trek across Africa, he makes explorations that yield a considerable treasure, which he recklessly spends on his return to England. To recover his losses, he sets sail again, joins a mutinous crew, and becomes a pirate. The pirate crew is joined by a Quaker surgeon, William Walters, under whose influence Singleton begins to feel qualms of conscience about his crimes. Finally, his moral regeneration complete, he marries William's widowed sister and lives the remainder of his life in quiet contentment.

William Walters, a Quaker surgeon. A member of the crew of a captured ship, he joins Singleton and gradually gains a considerable moral influence over him. When the two men decide to abandon piracy, Williams takes command of their ventures and dissuades the conscience-stricken Singleton from suicide so that, together, they may put their illegal fortune to a worthy use.

Captain Wilmot and

Captain Avery, masters of ships in the pirate fleet commanded by Captain Singleton.

THE CAPTAIN WITH THE WHISKERS

Author: Benedict Kiely (1919-   )
First published: 1960
Genre: Novel

Locale: Northern Ireland and Dublin
Time: Late 1940's to early 1950's
Plot: Love

Owen Rodgers, the narrator, in his twenties, a former medical student who eventually becomes a successful hotel manager. An incurable romantic leaning toward alcoholism, he is obsessed with the fall of the Chesney family and haunted by memories of its patriarch, Captain Conway Chesney. He becomes the chaste lover of Maeve Chesney, who represents to him the idealized queen of his dreams, while he becomes the actual and fatal lover of the other Chesney daughter, Greta. He ends up marrying his first love, Lucy, who dies after bearing him three children. He spends his remaining days in Dublin ruefully singing songs in seedy pubs.

Captain Conway Chesney, the head of the Chesney family and patriarchal commandant of Bingen House. He is a hero of the Boer War and Owen Rodgers' mentor. In spite of his death early in the story, his commanding presence remains and persistently manifests itself in the corrosive crippling of his children, both emotionally and spiritually. He is a small man, virulently anticlerical, and willfully vindictive, not only to his children but also to the entire area. His greatest sin is changing the name of his estate from its original Irish name of Magheracolton to its British name, Bingen House, thus severing the natives from their cultural and linguistic heritage.

Maeve Chesney, one of the captain's two daughters. She is lively, beautiful, and sexually desirable. She becomes Owen Rodgers' idealized beloved but in reality is promiscuous, fun-loving, and rather shallow. Owen runs into her again late in the novel, when she is in Dublin with her teenage son, after she has lost much of her allure and most of her memories.

Dr. Grierson, a sophisticated parish priest of the area who holds a doctorate from Louvain. He tends to his priestly duties conscientiously but suffers under the heavy hand of his ecclesiastical superiors, who have exiled him for his intelligence and compassion. He spends most of his time drinking heavily, recovering, and advising young Owen Rodgers. He considers the captain to be irredeemably wicked and possesses little hope for humanity.

Lucy, Owen Rodgers' first girlfriend. She is in her twenties, plumply attractive but rather unimaginative and ordinary. Owen leaves her to pursue both Chesney women, only to return to marry her and take her to Dublin, where she bears him three children and then dies in middle age.

John Rodgers, Owen's cultivated and highly intelligent father. He is fully conscious of the evil effects of the captain's influence, not only on the Chesney family but also on the entire area. A loving preserver of Irish books and music, he hates the captain principally because he has destroyed the cultural coherence of the local area by replacing its Irish names with English ones. He is Dr. Grierson's closest confidant and most sympathetic listener.

Greta Chesney, the hardworking, practical, and quietly attractive daughter of Captain Chesney. She tries unsuccessfully to escape the life-denying effects of her father and commits suicide following a disastrous affair with Owen Rodgers.

Alfred Chesney, nicknamed **Slobber**, the captain's oldest son, brutalized by his father for associating with members of the lower classes. Alcoholic, ugly, and desperate for love, he is arrested for the rape of a minor and sent to prison for a year.

Edmund Chesney, the captain's second son. He is soft, corpulent, and loquacious. He manages to escape to England temporarily but returns home after his father's death, blaming the captain for his older brother's sexual misconduct.

Francis Chesney, the captain's third son, pimply faced and sallow. He manages to escape to study for the priesthood, although he is almost disqualified because of his sister's illegitimate child and Greta's suicide. After returning from studies at Louvain, he becomes increasingly alcoholic and disillusioned and holds scrupulously to the rituals and rules of the church.

— *Patrick Meanor*

CAPTAINS COURAGEOUS

Author: Rudyard Kipling (1865-1936)
First published: 1897
Genre: Novel

Locale: The Grand Banks of Newfoundland
Time: The 1890's
Plot: Adventure

Harvey Cheyne, the fifteen-year-old son of an American millionaire. Washed overboard from the liner he is taking from America to Europe, he is picked up by the *We're Here*, a schooner out of Gloucester bound for the Grand Banks. Young Harvey is forced to live from May until the following September aboard the fishing schooner. He is arrogant and peevish at first, but by the time the ship returns to Gloucester, he has changed. He is now a self-reliant young man who has proved himself in a rigorous environment.

Dan Troop, the son of the schooner's skipper and a boy of about Harvey's age. Dan believes Harvey's account of his family's wealth and influence, but he and the cook are the only people aboard who do accept the story as true. Later in life, Dan becomes mate on one of the fast freighters Harvey owns.

Disko Troop, the owner and skipper of the *We're Here*. He resents Harvey's presence aboard his schooner and meets the youth's insolence with hard discipline. As the voyage continues, Troop learns to respect the boy's quick grasp of the principles of navigation and his good work generally aboard the schooner. When the *We're Here* is first back to Gloucester with a full ship, Troop's respect for Harvey is complete.

Mr. Cheyne, Harvey's father, a wealthy ship owner who has risen from poverty to wealth through sea trade. Mr. Cheyne is delighted to see the change the tour at sea has effected in his son.

Long Jack,

Manuel,

Salters,

Pennsylvania, and

The Cook, crew members aboard the *We're Here*.

THE CAPTAIN'S DAUGHTER
(Kapitanskaya dochka)

Author: Alexander Pushkin (1799-1837)
First published: 1836
Genre: Novel

Locale: Russia
Time: c. 1774
Plot: Historical

Piotr Andreitch Grineff (PYOH-tr ahn-DREH-ihch grih-NEHF), a young officer in a Russian regiment. A kindly and generous young man who falls in love with the commandant's daughter, he goes to great lengths to protect her from harm and fights a duel when a fellow officer criticizes a love poem he has written to her. At first his parents do not approve of the girl, but they later give their consent to the marriage.

Maria Ivanovna (MAH-ryuh ih-VAH-nov-nuh), the Captain's daughter, a lovely girl very much in love with Piotr. When he sends her to his parents for her protection, she so impresses them that they change their minds about not allowing their son to marry her. She saves her lover from exile in Siberia by appealing to the Empress.

Alexey Ivanitch Shvabrin (ah-lehk-SAY ih-VAHN-ihch SHVAH-brihn), an officer in Piotr's regiment. A suitor rejected by Maria, he is jealous of her love for Piotr. When the rebel Pougatcheff takes the Bailogorsk fortress, Shvabrin deserts to the rebel side. He does everything in his power to separate Maria and Piotr. He accuses Piotr of being a spy for the rebels and is responsible for his rival's sentence of exile.

Emelyan Pougatcheff (eh-meh-LYAHN pew-GAH-chehf), a Cossack rebel leader who claims to be the dead Emperor Peter III. He is cruel and ruthless. After the capture of the Bailogorsk fortress, however, he spares Piotr's life and sends him away under safe conduct because the young officer had earlier given the rebel, disguised as a traveler, a sheepskin coat to protect him during a snowstorm.

Savelitch (sah-VEH-lihch), Piotr's old servant, whose intervention saves his master from several predicaments. He is faithful, loyal, and shrewd.

Vassilissa Egorovna (vah-SIH-lih-sah eh-GOH-rov-nah), the captain's wife, a capable woman who runs her household and her husband's regiment with great efficiency. When she protests against her husband's murder by the Cossack rebels, she is killed.

Captain Ivan Mironoff, the commanding officer at the Bailogorsk fortress and Piotr's superior. Captured when Cossacks under Emelyan Pougatcheff seize the fortress, he and his aides are hanged by order of the rebel chief.

Captain Zourin, who rescues Piotr, his family, and Maria from death at the hands of the renegade Shvabrin.

THE CAPTIVES
(Captivi)

Author: Plautus (c. 255-184 B.C.E.)
First performed: The second century
Genre: Drama

Locale: Aetolia
Time: During the war between Aetolia and Elis
Plot: Farce

Hegio (HEE-jee-oh), a rich Aetolian who spends his time negotiating for the return of a son, Philopolemus, who was captured in war by the Elians. Hegio mourns another son, Tyndarus, kidnapped when he was four years old. Prisoner exchanges take place, confessions are made, false identities are put straight, and Hegio's sons are at last reunited with their father.

Tyndarus (TIHN-duh-ruhs), the son who, kidnapped when four years old, is returned to his father because the slave who had stolen the boy is caught and confesses the deed, thus identifying to Hegio the now adult Tyndarus.

Philopolemus (fih-luh-PO-leh-muhs), the captive son who is returned to Hegio in exchange for Philocrates, the wealthy Elian whom Hegio held captive.

Ergasilus (ur-guh-SI-luhs), a parasite who, fearing the loss of favors from his host Hegio, works diligently to straighten out the confusion attendant on the prisoner exchange. Hegio rewards Ergasilus' good work by promising him board for the rest of his life.

Philocrates (fih-LO-kruh-teez), a very rich Elian prisoner of war and Tyndarus' master. He is bought in a lot of prisoners by Hegio when the father is looking for an Elian to exchange for Philopolemus.

Aristophontes (eh-RIHS-toh-FON-teez), a prisoner of war who knows Philocrates. It is Aristophontes who explains to Hegio that a hostage he holds, Tyndarus, is not Philocrates. Ironically, Hegio, not knowing that Tyndarus, posing as Aristophontes, is his son, sends Tyndarus to work in the quarries.

Stalagmus (steh-LAG-muhs), Hegio's former slave, who kidnapped Tyndarus and sold him to the Elians. When he confesses his crime, Tyndarus is brought home to his father's house and Stalagmus, in Tyndarus' chains, takes the son's place in the quarries.

THE CARETAKER

Author: Harold Pinter (1930-   )
First published: 1960
Genre: Drama

Locale: A run-down London flat
Time: The 1950's or 1960's
Plot: Surrealism

Mick, a man in his late twenties, Aston's brother. He is the first character seen onstage in the play, although he does not speak or interact with the other characters until the end of act 1. From the outside, he tries to control the other two. When he does speak, he tends to utter either single lines or long incoherent ramblings about unseen friends and relatives, sprinkled with dozens of London place names, financial terms, and interior decorator's phrases. He owns the derelict building in which Aston has his flat, and he has dreams of converting it into a high-class penthouse, dreams that he has no apparent means to fulfill. He has tried and failed to reconnect with Aston by giving him a home, and he hopes now that he can get to Aston through Davies. Instead, he becomes jealous of Aston's relationship with Davies and turns his anger on them both.

Aston, a man in his late thirties. He lives alone in a run-down flat piled high with old paint buckets, boxes of screws and nails, a shopping cart, and even a detached kitchen sink. A former factory worker, he has been unemployed ever since undergoing electric shock treatments years ago. The treatments left him brain-damaged, and he endures terrible headaches. He rescues Davies from a fight and brings him to his own flat, where he offers him a bed, a bit of tobacco for his pipe, an old pair of shoes, and, eventually, a job as caretaker of the building. Aston is planning to build a wooden shed in the backyard and spends hours planning the materials and tools he will need, but clearly he will never even begin the project.

Instead, he sits on his bed and pokes at a broken plug with a screwdriver to satisfy his urge to work with his hands. He is unable to stay focused on any one idea very long or to form any real human connections. He plans to complete various tasks or talk with people again after he has built his shed. Although he does not recognize his connection to his brother and to his room, they are all he has, and when Davies tries to come between Aston and Mick, Mick rejects him and clings to the security—and isolation—of his life in the flat.

Davies, an old tramp from Sidcup. He is argumentative and paranoid, seeing danger in every brown or black face and hearing a threat in every accent different from his own. When Aston rescues him from a fight with a Scot, Davies reveals that this is not the first time he has brawled with foreigners; he stoutly believes that none of these fights was in any way his fault. He worries about his papers, which he has left with a friend in Sidcup; he believes he must retrieve the papers before he can work or move on, yet he makes no effort to go after them. He fears that the junked gas stove in Aston's flat will kill him, although it is not connected. Frequently, he awakens Aston in the night with the sounds of his dreaming. When he moves in with Aston, he is willing to help out and to assume the unspecified duties of the caretaker, but soon he becomes aggressive and demanding. When he tries to drive a wedge between the brothers, they throw him back on the street.

— *Cynthia A. Bily*

CARMEN

Author: Prosper Mérimée (1803-1870)
First published: 1845
Genre: Novella

Locale: Primarily Seville and Córdoba, Spain
Time: Early nineteenth century
Plot: Psychological realism

Carmen, an attractive, quick-tempered, thieving gypsy girl who seduces, torments, and eventually tries to drop Don José, as she had done with several other lovers before. As a gypsy woman, she is without rights, lives by her own code, and belongs nowhere. This exotic femme fatale leads men, through her fickleness and infidelities, not only to distraction but also to destruction. When she slashes the face of another girl working in the cigarette factory during an argument, she persuades the corporal of the guard, Don José, to let her escape but

allows him to pay the price. She does this shrewdly; having discovered his Basque origin, she addresses him in his own tongue to win his sympathies. Carmen is also a free spirit who cannot be tamed, a girl with a strong sense of independence who cannot commit herself to any single relationship: To her, love, certainly within the bonds of marriage, represents servitude. She therefore refuses Don José's offer to escape with him to America after he kills two men and becomes an outlaw, all on her account. She explains that no one will determine the course of her life. She does so even though she realizes that such refusal and her admission that she no longer loves Don José will lead inevitably to her own death. Remaining true to her nature until the end, she adds up to more than a promiscuous gypsy.

Don José (hoh-SAY), also known as **Don José Lizzarrabengoa** (lee-zah-rrah-behn-GOH-ah) or **Don José Navarro** (nah-VAH-rroh), a handsome, well-born Basque cavalryman from Navarre. At first, he is an innocent, honest, kind, and unadventurous man launched on a promising military career. As punishment for releasing Carmen after the knife incident, he accepts his demotion from corporal to private and a prison term, and he refuses to escape when Carmen sends him a metal file and money in jail. His passion for Carmen drives him to the angry killing of one of his officers, another of Carmen's lovers. With his military career now ruined, Don José deserts the army and joins a band of outlaws, by arrangement of Carmen, who spies for this group. Don José is unhappy in his criminal life, which is out of character for him, and is tor-

mented by his fickle but increasingly compelling lover. In a fit of irrational rage and jealousy, he eventually kills Garcia (gahr-SEE-uh), the one-eyed brutal leader of the smugglers' band, after learning that Garcia is also Carmen's first husband—even though by now Garcia would have been willing to waive any claims on her for a small amount of money. On discovering that, during his absence on plundering and robbing assignments across Spain, Carmen has taken up with Lucas, a bullfighter in Córdoba, Don José follows her and again pleads with her to be faithful to him and to accompany him to America to start a new life. Carmen claims not to love him anymore even while recognizing his right to punish her with death according to gypsy tradition. Don José's final act is to ask a monk to pray for the soul of one about to die. After killing Carmen, Don José turns himself in to the constabulary and awaits execution. He comes through as a weak yet passionate, idealistic, and even honorable man.

— Peter B. Heller

THE CASE OF SERGEANT GRISCHA
(Der Streit um den Sergeanten Grischa)

Author: Arnold Zweig (1887-1968)
First published: 1927
Genre: Novel

Locale: Russia
Time: 1917
Plot: Social realism

Sergeant Grischa Iljitsch Paprotkin (GREE-shah ee-LEECH pah-PROHT-kihn), a Russian soldier held as a prisoner by the Germans in 1917. Though not ill-treated by his captors, he wishes to return to his family, and so contrives an escape. During his lonely wanderings, he begins to lose his humanity, but he recovers it when he becomes the lover of Babka, a woman leading a band of refugees who take him into their midst. Sergeant Grischa assumes the identity of Sergeant Pavlovitsch Bjuscheff, a Russian deserter, so that he can avoid punishment as an escaped prisoner. He is recaptured and, under his assumed identity, sentenced to death as a spy. While his case is fought over by German generals after he has revealed the truth about himself, Grischa remains in prison, hoping the war will end. When his sentence is not revoked he behaves like a brave soldier, even when forced to dig his own grave before being killed.

Babka, a strong-minded, vigorous Russian woman, known affectionately as "Grandmother," who leads a band of homeless refugees. She finds Grischa wandering across the countryside and makes him a member of her band and her lover. When he is sentenced to death, she bravely goes to him, walking

many miles to do so. She hopes to free her lover by poisoning his guards, but he prevents her from carrying out the plan, believing he must meet his fate. After Grischa's death Babka bears his child.

General von Lychow (LI-chov), a Prussian officer of the military caste who is a commander of combat troops. He is jealous of upstart administrative officers who question his authority and authorizes his aide to work on the case of Grischa to save the life of the condemned man.

Ponsanski, General von Lychow's aide, a Jewish lawyer who is interested in the case primarily from the view that it is an interesting instance of legal jurisdiction.

General Schieffenzahn (shee-fehn-ZAHN), an administrative officer who usurps the authority of General von Lychow. He wishes to execute Grischa to demonstrate his power. Although he is persuaded to send a reprieve for the sergeant, a snowstorm prevents delivery of the message.

Lieutenant Winfried, a German officer and friend of Ponsanski.

Lieutenant Wilhelmi, General Schieffenzahn's aide, who recommends the death of Grischa.

CASS TIMBERLANE: A Novel of Husbands and Wives

Author: Sinclair Lewis (1885-1951)
First published: 1945
Genre: Novel

Locale: Grand Republic, Minnesota
Time: The 1940's
Plot: Social realism

Cass Timberlane, district judge in Grand Republic, Minnesota. A good man, he lives a lonely life after his divorce until he is stirred in his forty-first year by a young girl, Jinny Marshland, who is from the lower classes. He marries the girl, despite the objections of his friends and hers. The marriage is

not entirely a happy one, but thanks to the judge's patience and love, the marriage succeeds.

Blanche Timberlane, the judge's ex-wife.

Jinny Marshland, a young girl who marries Judge Timberlane. She finds difficulty in adjusting to her new life. She has an affair with Bradd Criley and, wanting to live in New York, almost breaks up her marriage. When she falls ill and realizes she needs her husband, she goes back to him and the small town in which they live.

Bradd Criley, one of Judge Timberlane's friends. He pursues the judge's wife, as he does every attractive woman, and becomes her lover.

Dr. Roy Drover, one of the judge's friends, a philanderer.

Boone Havock and

Queenie Havock, wealthy but vulgar friends of Judge Timberlane.

Jay Laverick, the rich, drunkard friend of Judge Timberlane. His attentions to Jinny cause gossip.

Chris Grau, a well-to-do, attractive woman in love with Judge Timberlane. She sympathizes with his problems.

Mrs. Higbee, Judge Timberlane's understanding housekeeper.

CASSANDRA: A Novel and Four Essays
(Voraussetzungen einer Erzählung: "Kassandra" *and* Kassandra)

Author: Christa Wolf (1929-   )
First published: 1983
Genre: Novel

Locale: Mycenae, Troy, Athens, and Crete
Time: c. 1200 B.C.
Plot: Psychological realism

Cassandra, the story's narrator, a princess of Troy in Anatolia, a seer, and a priestess of the god Apollo. According to myth, Apollo granted her the gift of prophecy so that she would agree to sleep with him; when she refused, he left her with the gift but added that no one would believe her prophecies. Captured by Mycenaean Greeks under King Agamemnon, Cassandra meditates about her life in the now-ruined citadel of Troy as well as about the terrible future her captors face. Cassandra proudly recalls having been the beloved favorite of King Priam of Troy. Painfully, however, she also recalls how he cast her into prison because she dared to prophesy Troy's imminent doom. She dies rather than go with Aeneus to found a new society.

Priam (PRI-uhm), the proud king of Troy, who chooses not to heed the counsel of seers prophesying Troy's downfall, the chief of whom is his own daughter Cassandra. Noble, wise in many ways, yet stubborn and unyielding, Priam hopes to stave off fate. With his overthrow, he becomes one more Trojan leader to endure defeat in war.

Hecuba (HEH-kyuh-buh), the wife of King Priam. Along with Cassandra and others in the inner court of Troy, Hecuba hates Troy's arrogance while, at the same time, wishing for its success in battle against the Greeks. The bearer of many children, including Cassandra, Hector, Paris, and Troilus, she saves her youngest son from the wrath of the Mycenaeans by sending him abroad to Thrace, where he is subsequently murdered by the Thracian king. Wise to the world's cruel and capricious ways because of the many tragedies she has endured, Hecuba is a thoroughgoing skeptic.

Aeneus (ah-NEE-uhs), a Trojan warrior and lover of Cassandra who, after having taught her about love, vanishes. Cassandra, still dazzled by the intensity of their brief tryst, sees his disappearance as one more legacy of the war between Troy and the Greeks. Aeneus is emblematic of the young heroes who died for a lost cause. He is the son of Anchises.

Hector, a son of Priam and Hecuba. He is a large, rather sluggish young man of few words, admired by his sister Cassandra for engaging in warfare though it goes against his torpid nature to do so. Hector's misfortune is to be chased down and killed by the vengeful Greek warrior Achilles.

Anchises (ahn-CHIH-zees), a Trojan shepherd. From his legendary union with Aphrodite came a son, Aeneus.

Agamemnon (a-guh-MEHM-non), the great, powerful king of the Greek city-state Argos and leader of the Mycenaean forces in the Trojan War. Cruel, resourceful, and cunning, Agamemnon, cuckolded by Paris—who abducted his wife, Helen, to Troy—takes his revenge on the city, razing it and killing or enslaving all of its inhabitants. Among these captives is Cassandra, who, at the novel's outset, is to be killed behind Mycenae's Lion Gate.

Achilles (ah-KIHL-leez), the most famed of the Greek warriors who sacked Troy. Achilles is proud to the point of being haughty, self-directed, and moody in the extreme. He is hated intensely by Cassandra. She particularly detests his brutal nature.

Panthous (PAN-thews), a priest in Apollo's service and Cassandra's overseer in her role as priestess. Cassandra envisions Panthous as an envious and evil-minded man given to craftiness and outright treachery. Nevertheless, she admires some of his actions, such as putting an end to human sacrifices in Troy.

— *John D. Raymer*

CASTE

Author: Thomas William Robertson (1829-1871)
First published: 1878
Genre: Drama

Locale: England
Time: The nineteenth century
Plot: Social criticism

The marquise de St. Maur (sahn mohr), an Englishwoman married to a French nobleman. She is a proud person, conscious of rank and family. Only her son's return from supposed death enables her to accept her lower-class daughter-in-law without reservation.

Captain George D'Alroy, the son of the marquise de St. Maur, who falls in love with a beautiful dancer from the lower classes and marries her despite her origins. He insists that he would rather die or lose his commission than lose her love. His faith in his wife is rewarded, for when he returns from India after having been presumed dead, he finds that she has proved sincere and capable.

Captain Hawtree, D'Alroy's friend, who tries realistically to point out the social chasm between the dancer and his friend, as well as the difficulties that a successful marriage between them must overcome.

Esther Eccles (EHK-ehlz), the pretty young dancer who marries D'Alroy. When her husband is thought to be dead in India, she successfully cares for herself and her child, refus-

ing to be patronized by her proud mother-in-law.

Polly Eccles, Esther's sister, who is satisfied to marry a tradesman. Even when her sister is accepted in aristocratic circles, Polly believes that she is happier than Esther.

Mr. Eccles, the father of Esther and Polly, a ne'er-do-well drunkard. He even squanders money left by D'Alroy to take care of Esther.

Sam Gerridge, Polly's fiancé. He is a good man who contributes to Esther's support when she needs help.

THE CASTLE
(Das Schloss)

Author: Franz Kafka (1883-1924)
First published: 1926
Genre: Novel

Locale: Europe
Time: Unspecified
Plot: Allegory

K., a young man seeking entrance to the Castle. He is both puzzled and irritated by his inability to get to the Castle, where he had thought himself needed as a Land Surveyor. He never reaches the Castle. Kafka intended, in a chapter planned but never written, to relate that K. was to be given permission to live and work in the village though not to enter the Castle itself. K.'s efforts to reach the Castle resemble Christian's struggle in *The Pilgrim's Progress* to reach the Celestial City; however, Christian succeeds, whereas K. does not.

Frieda, a fair-haired, sad-eyed, hollow-cheeked young barmaid who is Klamm's mistress. She becomes K.'s fiancée and stays with him at the Bridge Inn and, later, at the schoolhouse. Jealous of his apparent interest in Olga and Amalia, she rejects K. for Jeremiah.

Barnabas, a white-clad young messenger who brings K. a letter from Klamm and introduces him to Barnabas' family. He is a servant at the Castle.

Olga, his yellow-haired sister, a strapping girl with a hard-looking face. She shows kindness to K. and tells him much about the organization of the Castle and about the village people.

Amalia, another sister who closely resembles both Olga and Barnabas.

Arthur, K.'s assistant, a slim, brown-skinned, jolly young man with a little pointed black beard. He and Jeremiah keep an almost constant watch on K.

Jeremiah, another assistant who looks so like Arthur that K., who says they are as alike as two snakes, calls him Arthur also.

Klamm, a chief at the Castle who is often seen at the Herrenhof. He is plump, ponderous, and flabby-cheeked, and he wears a pointed black mustache and a pince-nez.

Schwarzer, a young man who telephones the Castle to check on K. He is in love with Gisa.

The Superintendent, a kindly, stout, clean-shaven man suffering from gout. He tries to explain to K. the intricacies of the management of the Castle.

Gardana, the landlady at the Bridge Inn. She was once, briefly, Klamm's mistress.

Momus, the village secretary, a deputy of Klamm.

Gisa, the lady schoolteacher.

Sortini, a great official at the Castle who once wrote an obscene letter to Amalia.

THE CASTLE OF CROSSED DESTINIES
(Il castello dei destini incrociati)

Author: Italo Calvino (1923-1985)
First published: 1969
Genre: Novel

Locale: A castle and a tavern
Time: Mythic past
Plot: Fantasy

The first narrator, a traveler (perhaps a knight) who comes upon the castle in the woods and joins the guests, who recount their tales through the medium of tarot cards. Weary from many recent trials and combats, the narrator feels unstable and confused in his perceptions. His confusion contributes, as the story unfolds, to his uncertainty about reading the various stories accurately. The uncertainty of reconstructing stories from emblematic representations, a dominant theme of the book, originates in this state of mind of the narrator.

The alchemist, who selects the King of Cups tarot card to represent himself. He is identified with Faust, and the tale of the bargain with the devil for the secret formula of gold begins

with the alchemist's reading of the Ace of Cups and the Popess cards, which conclude the tale of a knight who narrates before him. The alchemist challenges the others with his elliptical and allusive style in representing his story. The many symbolic possibilities of the cards he employs and the rich complexity of the Faust legend make his audience restless and impatient for clear exposition.

Roland, the mythical knight of the Charlemagne legend, who identifies himself with the King of Swords card. Roland is referred to as gigantic, moving his leaden arms and ironlike fingers slowly. Domineering and threatening, he hoards the most beautiful of the tarot cards for the colorful tale of his going mad in pursuit of Angelica. As he recounts his tale, Roland undergoes a visible transformation. Ending with the card of the Hanged Man, he takes on a serene, radiant expression, from which the narrator infers an acceptance of reason over the paladin's former unrestricted passion that led to his defeat.

Astolpho, the English knight who, in Ludovico Ariosto's *Orlando furioso* (1516), recovers the wits of Roland. The first narrator, longing for further testimony of Roland's adventures, finds this small, humorous, childlike youth among the guests and hands him the Knight of Clubs card. The youth tosses it in the air, and when it lands on the table, he begins the tale of Charlemagne sending Astolpho to the moon to find Roland's reason. His tale maintains the theme of defeat that links the tales of the other guests. The youth ends his tale cryptically, with suggestions of failure and foreboding. Rather than discovering harmony of sense and meanings on the moon, he reports that the moon is a desert, an empty horizon where all poems and discourse begin and end.

The second narrator, who finds himself, like the first narrator, at a banquet with other travelers who are struck mute and communicating their adventures with a tarot deck. The second narrator, like his fellow banqueters, is white haired from the sudden fear at finding himself in the mysterious forest. This narrator sees himself mirrored in three cards: the Knight of Swords, the Hermit, and the Juggler. He describes himself as a writer whose impetuosity and anxiety are akin to those of a warrior. He reads his fate as a writer in the images of famous paintings of Saint Jerome and Saint George. The first, the hermit and saint, represents his solitude and devotion to finding order in chaos; the second, the dragon slayer, depicts his struggle with confronting inner and outer demons. The second narrator thus sees himself as representing the other travelers and all who attempt to recount and interpret the elusive meanings of their lives.

The Queen of Clubs, a woman who identifies herself by beginning with this tarot card. A gigantic maiden of powerful arms and hands, she impels the narrative forward by controlling the cards when others are grabbing wildly, threatening to take control and disarrange the cards. The maiden jostles her fellow travelers and wrests the cards from them until the guests are subdued into watching her unfold her own tale of her giving birth to twins by a prince and controlling his father.

— *Dennis C. Chowenhill*

THE CASTLE OF FRATTA
(Le confessioni di un ottuagenario)

Author: Ippolito Nievo (1831-1861)
First published: 1867
Genre: Novel

Locale: Italy and England
Time: 1775-1852
Plot: Historical

Carlo Altoviti (ahl-toh-VEE-tee), a poor relation in the feudal Fratta family and the narrator. He becomes an honored member of the family and a patriot who lives to see the Castle of Fratta reduced to rubble and the Frattas dispersed. In his old age, he returns to Fratta to write his memoirs.

Giovanni (gee-oh-VAHN-nee), the count of Fratta, the austere head of the Fratta family.

Cleonice (kleh-oh-NEE-chee), the countess of Fratta, Count Giovanni's haughty wife.

Clara, Count Giovanni's grave, beautiful daughter, who finally enters a convent.

Pisana (pee-ZAH-nah), Count Giovanni's fascinating younger daughter, loved by Carlo Altoviti. She eventually becomes his mistress.

Aquilina Provedoni (ah-kwee-LEE-nah proh-veh-DOH-nee), Carlo Altoviti's wife.

Todero Altoviti (toh-DEH-roh), Carlo's father. Deserted by Carlo's mother, he disappears. When he has grown wealthy in trade he returns, hoping to establish a prominent family. His hopes are dashed with the capitulation of Venice to the French.

Monsignor Orlando, a stupid, gluttonous priest, Count Giovanni's brother.

Lucilio Vianello (lew-chee-LEE-oh vee-ah-NEHL-loh), a young doctor. He is in love with Clara Fratta. After the fall of the patricians, she refuses to return from the convent and marry him.

Leopardo Provedoni, Carlo Altoviti's friend.

Antonio Provedoni, Leopardo's father, the mayor of the Commune.

Doretta, the daughter of the chancellor of Venchieredo, Leopardi Provedoni's wife.

Raimondo di Venchieredo (dee VEHN-kee-ehr-eh-doh), Doretta's lover.

The count of Venchieredo, Raimondo's father, sentenced to prison for laying siege to Fratta.

Alberto Partistagno (pahr-tees-TAH-noh), a young nobleman, Clara Fratta's suitor.

Giulio del Ponte (jee-EW-lee-oh), a young poet, another of Clara's suitors, later in love with Pisana Fratta.

Aglaura, Carlo Altoviti's half sister.

Spiro Apostulos (SPEE-roh AHPOHS-tew-lohs), Aglaura's husband.

Mauro Navagero (MAH-ew-roh nah-vah-JEE-roh), an aged Fratta kinsman, Pisana Fratta's husband.

Almoro Frumier (ahl-MOH-roh frew-MEE-ehr), a Venetian senator, a Fratta kinsman.

The Spaccafumo (spah-kah-FEW-moh), a bandit.

Father Pendola, a Jesuit priest and a political intriguer in the Venetian Republic.

Lady Badoer (bah-DOH-ehr), Clara and Pisana Fratta's grandmother, who dies of atrocities committed by the soldiers of Napoleon.

Captain Sandracca, captain of the militia at Fratta.

Amilcare Dossi (ahmeel-KAH-reh DOHS-see), a young political liberal who influences Carlo Altoviti.

Ettore Carafa (eht-TOH-ray kah-RAH-fah), a lover of Pisana Fratta.

Napoleon Bonaparte, the emperor of France.

THE CASTLE OF OTRANTO

Author: Horace Walpole (1717-1797)
First published: 1765
Genre: Novel

Locale: Italy
Time: The twelfth century
Plot: Gothic

Manfred, the prince of Otranto, a usurper. After Manfred's son is mysteriously killed on his wedding day, Manfred plans to divorce his wife and marry the promised bride himself. After much frightening supernatural intervention, Manfred surrenders his claims to Otranto; he and his wife then enter neighboring convents.

Conrad, the fifteen-year-old son of Manfred. On his wedding day, he is found crushed to death beneath a gigantic helmet.

Isabella, the daughter of the Marquis of Vicenza and the fiancée of Conrad. Manfred plans to marry her after Conrad's death, but she escapes him with the aid of the true heir to Otranto, whom she marries after Manfred's abdication.

Theodore, a young peasant and the true heir to Otranto. He is imprisoned and nearly executed by Manfred's order, but with both human and supernatural aid he triumphs, marrying Isabella and becoming the new Prince of Otranto.

Matilda, Manfred's daughter. She gives aid to Theodore. Learning that Theodore is in the chapel with a woman, the jealous Manfred goes there and stabs the woman, only to learn that he has killed his daughter Matilda.

Father Jerome, formerly prince of Falconara, now a priest. Called to give absolution to the condemned Theodore, he discovers that Theodore is his own son, born before he entered the Church.

The Marquis of Vicenza, Isabella's father. Disguised as the Knight of the Gigantic Sabre, he comes to Otranto, bringing with him a huge sword carried by a hundred men. On its blade is written that only Manfred's blood can atone for the wrongs done to the family of the true heir. By betrothing the Marquis to Matilda, Manfred gets his consent to his own marriage with Isabella; however, terrifying omens and warnings cause the Marquis to renounce Matilda.

Prince Alfonso the Good, formerly the ruler of Otranto. It is the helmet of his statue that crushes Conrad. His giant form appears to proclaim Theodore, the son of his daughter, heir to Otranto. He then ascends to Heaven.

Saint Nicholas, who receives Prince Alfonso into Heaven.

CASTLE RACKRENT: An Hibernian Tale

Author: Maria Edgeworth (1767-1849)
First published: 1800
Genre: Novel

Locale: Ireland
Time: The eighteenth century
Plot: Regional

Thady Quirk, known as **Honest Thady**, **Old Thady**, and finally **Poor Thady**, the narrator of the story and a lifelong attendant to a procession of masters of Rackrent Castle in Ireland. Loyal and steadfast, he embodies all the qualities of the true Irish servant. Clothed in his heavy great cloak, he observes the world as he experiences it in terms of the differing characters of his several masters.

Sir Patrick Rackrent, a lusty, generous landowner whose original family name was O'Shaughlin. He is convivial to a fault and friendly to all, and he dies singing while Thady himself is still a lad.

Sir Murtagh Rackrent, the heir. He is a close-fisted lawyer married to a widow of the Skinflint family. The two live on the tenants' "duty" fowls and services so that the castle is almost free of expense on the part of Sir Murtagh. As Thady notes, it is lamentable that knowledge of the law permits Sir Murtagh to take land and property from other people. Sir Murtagh dies fittingly after hearing the cry of a banshee; actually, his death is a result of overstraining his voice in the law courts and in arguments with his wife, who strips the house after the death of her husband.

Sir Kit, Sir Murtagh's younger brother. A warm and friendly person, he is kind to the tenants, yet he turns all Rackrent affairs over to an agent, an Irish "middleman" who is all servility to his master and tyrannical to every wretch beneath him. Sir Kit orders the castle renovated before he brings a Jewish bride from England, an heiress reputed to own many diamonds. She hates Castle Rackrent and the bog in front of it.

Because she insists on her own dietary restrictions and refuses to give up any of her money, Sir Kit imprisons her in her room, where she remains for seven years. Rackrent is heavily mortgaged because of Sir Kit's gambling debts, and he is finally killed in a duel after philandering extensively. His wife returns to England.

Sir Conally (Sir Condy), a member of a remote branch of the family and Sir Kit's successor. Educated at a college in Dublin, he had sat as a child at Thady's knee and heard many family stories. He had also attended grammar school with Jason, Thady's son, who had helped him with his learning. Sir Condy marries Isabella Moneygawl of Mount Juliet's Town; her father cuts her off without money because he disapproves of her marriage. Deeply in debt, Sir Condy wins a seat in Parliament and so keeps from going to jail. His debts mount, and he leaves Castle Rackrent for the Lodge, Thady accompanying him. Here he holds his own wake with the friendly townspeople. His wife leaves him for her father's home, but word comes that she has had an accident and is not expected to live. Poor Sir Condy dies bereft of everything.

Jason Quirk, Thady's son, a lawyer who contrives to take over the Rackrent property by assuming its debts. He aspires to own all that has belonged to Sir Condy, especially when Lady Isabella Rackrent is expected to die also.

Isabella Rackrent, the attractive wife of Sir Condy. She leaves her husband when Castle Rackrent is up for auction. Badly injured in a carriage accident, she recovers and fights for her widow's rights against Jason Quirk.

Judy Quirk, old Thady's grandniece, admired by Sir Condy. Remaining loyal to the Rackrent family, she scorns Jason and his maneuvers and, as the wife of a huntsman, lives on at the Lodge in a manner proper to her station in life. Thady respects and loves her, partly because his own son now travels a different road from that followed by the loyal old retainer.

CASUALS OF THE SEA

Author: William McFee (1881-1966)
First published: 1916
Genre: Novel

Locale: England
Time: Early twentieth century
Plot: Domestic realism

Bert Gooderich, a stolid machinist who falls off a bridge and is drowned.

Mary, his wife, thankful to marry Bert after having been deserted by her lover, a baker's boy, the father of Minnie.

Young Bert, their son, big, strong, and pugnacious, with an ambition to be a soldier. Shortly after his enlistment, he is killed at Pretoria.

Hannibal, another son, a big, inarticulate, bungling lout who becomes a factory worker, a ship's mess boy, and finally a trimmer on the S.S. *Caryatid*. He dies of pneumonia caused partly by inhalation of coal dust and partly by the cough syrup for which Minnie had written advertisements.

Minnie, Mary's daughter, a stubborn, difficult girl, thin and reserved, engaged for a time to a coal clerk. She becomes Captain Briscoe's mistress, later his wife. She is jailed for engaging in a suffragette demonstration. She is also a writer of advertisements for cough syrup.

Captain Briscoe, a ship's captain, Minnie's lover and later her husband.

Nellie, Hannibal's wife, a plump, merry girl. She works in her uncle's tavern and later manages it.

Mrs. Gaynor, an American woman, next-door neighbor of the Gooderich family.

Hiram, her son, a sailor.

Mrs. Wilfley, a greedy woman who organizes a benefit musicale for the Gooderich family and pockets most of the receipts.

Anthony Gilfillan, a middle-aged man who befriends Minnie at a party and later takes her to the Continent with him.

THE CAT
(La Chatte)

Author: Colette (Sidonie-Gabrielle Colette, 1873-1954)
First published: 1933
Genre: Novel

Locale: Neuilly and central Paris, France
Time: Early 1930's
Plot: Psychological realism

Alain Amparat (ah-LAN ahm-pehr-AH), the only son of the Amparats and heir to Amparat et Fils (Amparat and Sons), an old and respected Parisian silk manufacturing firm, which employs him as its figurehead director. Alain carries himself with the arrogant, slightly bored self-assurance that often accompanies both "old money" and natural good looks. He is twenty-four years old, tall, handsome, and very fair, with good teeth, long cheeks, a slightly equine nose, natural waves in his overly thick golden hair, and clear, grayish-green eyes framed by lush dark lashes. He is condescending toward his fiancée, Camille, whom he characterizes pejoratively as a "typical modern girl." His commitment is shallow and perfunctory. He fully accepts and loves only his mother and Saha, his cat, the one thing in his life that he has chosen for himself. Soon after the wedding, Alain begins to feel restless, lose weight, and resent his wife's corresponding heartiness. Because Camille outstrips Alain both sexually and in her ability to live life, he turns from her to Saha, whom he can dominate and who expects no more from him than love and sensuality. Only with Saha, Alain realizes, can he truly be himself. He begins to dread the day when Camille will move into his family home and is relieved when her attempted murder of Saha gives him an excuse to end the marriage and escape back to his childhood paradise with his beloved cat.

Camille Malmert (kah-MEEL mal-MAHR), Alain's fiancée and later his bride, the nineteen-year-old daughter of a newly rich manufacturer of washing machines. Her family has more money but less social status than the Amparats. She is slim, healthy, dark, and attractive, with good teeth, white skin, small breasts, a resonant voice, stubby fingers, and large, almost black eyes surrounded by bluish-looking whites. She seems to Alain to be slightly commonplace because of her lack of modesty, her determination to speak her mind, and her love of jazz, slang, fast cars, and nightclubs. After Alain brings Saha to live with them, Camille views the cat as a rival, especially after Alain begins sleeping on the divan with the cat on his chest. She is both mystified by and jealous of Alain's ability to empathize and communicate with Saha and irritated by his inability to understand and respect her. Her jealousy grows in direct proportion to her husband's increasing indifference toward her. Camille forces a resolution to this strange love triangle by acting rashly. Her unsuccessful attempt to murder Saha by pushing her off their ninth-floor balcony gives Alain the excuse that he is looking for to leave Camille and return to his family home. The end of her marriage does not break Camille's spirit. She leaves Alain, busily making plans for her life without him.

Saha, a three-year-old purebred Russian Blue cat that Alain purchased as a five-month-old kitten at a cat show. She is proud and suspicious, with deep-set golden eyes, big cheeks, a small body, a perfect face, and moonstone-colored fur. To Alain, she represents the nobility of all cats because of her natural dignity, innocence, modesty, and disinterestedness, as well as her ability to accept the inevitable, bear pain in silence, and love both freedom and order. He believes that such cats have affinities only with the finest type of human beings, those who can understand and communicate with them. Saha loves Alain, and she instinctively dislikes and distrusts Camille. After Alain and Camille marry, Saha is left behind at the Amparat family home, where she refuses to eat. Her health deteriorates to such an extent that Alain brings her to live with him and Camille. She eats, but only enough to keep alive. After Camille's attempt to murder her, Saha and Alain return to his maternal home, where she once again begins to play, hunt, and eat normally.

Mme Amparat, Alain's widowed mother, an aging upper-middle-class society matron. She considers Camille her social inferior, judging her to be "not quite our type."

Émile (ay-MEEL), the Amparats' elderly, taciturn family butler, who has oyster-colored eyes and prominent whiskers. He reflects the Amparats' condescending attitude toward Camille.

Mme Buque (byewk), Alain and Camille's housekeeper and cook. She is a large, fat, red-cheeked woman who cooks food well and serves it badly.

M. Veuillet (vyew-YAY), Alain's father's oldest partner. He does most of the decision making at the Amparat silk firm.

Adele (ah-DEHL), another elderly family servant, who exhibits a patronizing attitude toward Camille.

— *Nancy E. Rupprecht*

CAT AND MOUSE
(Katz und Maus)

Author: Günter Grass (1927-   )
First published: 1961
Genre: Novella

Locale: Danzig, Germany
Time: During World War II
Plot: Bildungsroman

Pilenz (pih-LEHNTS), at once the narrator of and a participant in the story. Pilenz often seems to be trying to justify his actions through his narrative. He was an altar boy in his youth, but as he ages he leaves behind his faith, although he continues to be involved with the Roman Catholic church. As a child, he was capable of great cruelty to Mahlke, although he sometimes seemed to admire him as well; Pilenz gave him the nickname "The Great Mahlke." Pilenz went beyond mere childhood pranks to help bring about Mahlke's ultimate undoing. He therefore is in an unusual position: Although he is aware of Mahlke's role as "mouse," he does not act altruistically to help him; rather, he chooses to join the "eternal cat" in persecuting Mahlke.

Joachim Mahlke (yoh-AH-khihm MAHL-keh), who grew up as an only child living with his mother and aunt. Mahlke is an awkward and frail boy who develops an enormous Adam's apple as an adolescent. Portrayed as the eternal victim, Mahlke nevertheless seeks continually to align himself with those forces most likely to destroy him, including the German army, the National Socialist headmaster of his militaristic school, and his cruel and persecuting schoolmates. His Adam's apple, the symbol of his victim status as "mouse," is something of an obsession for Mahlke, as is the Virgin Mary, who becomes an outlet for his adolescent affections.

Waldemar Klohse (VAHL-deh-mahr KLOH-zeh), the headmaster of the Conradium, an elite school for boys in Danzig. A member of the National Socialist party, Klohse enforces a strict school environment in which athletic activity and party loyalty are heavily emphasized. He is most clearly Mahlke's nemesis and is one of the most obvious embodiments of the "eternal cat."

Father Gusewski (gew-ZEHVS-kee), the priest at St. Mary's chapel, a former gymnasium converted to a small Roman Catholic church that is attended by both Mahlke and Pilenz. He is a practical man and generally is kind to the boys, although he ultimately fails to assist Mahlke when he most needs his help.

Tulla Pokriefke (TEW-lah poh-KREEF-keh), a skinny girl who spends a summer with the boys on the minesweeper. An unabashed admirer of Mahlke, she encourages him to compete with the other boys in demonstrations of manliness. She is never embarrassed by the boys' nakedness, and they tolerate her presence. As the boys grow up, she becomes the object of their experimental desires.

Winter, a member of the gang of boys that includes Mahlke, Pilenz, and Hotten Sonntag. When he becomes very nervous, he tends to break down in tears.

Hotten Sonntag (HOT-tehn), another member of the gang of boys that includes Mahlke, Pilenz, and Winter. His sisters are the object of many adolescent fantasies.

— *Kelly C. Walter*

CAT ON A HOT TIN ROOF

Author: Tennessee Williams (Thomas Lanier Williams, 1911-1983)
First published: 1955
Genre: Drama

Locale: A plantation home in the Mississippi Delta
Time: The 1950's
Plot: Psychological realism

Margaret (Maggie) Pollitt, a young woman from a poor background married into a wealthy Southern family. Maggie's hard life has given her the strength and determination to do whatever she must to survive. When she felt threatened by the closeness between her husband, Brick, and his friend Skipper, she accused Skipper of being in love with Brick, then tried to seduce Skipper, leading to Skipper's suicide and Maggie's estrangement from Brick. Because of Brick's alcoholism and irresponsibility, as well as the fact that they have no children, Maggie fears that the Pollitt estate will go to Brick's brother Gooper and his wife Mae, leaving Maggie and Brick at the financial mercy of their relatives. To prevent this, Maggie announces that she is pregnant, then blackmails Brick into sleeping with her by withholding liquor from him.

Brick Pollitt, a young alcoholic former football player. Brick is tormented by guilt over the death of his former teammate and best friend, Skipper. Brick and Skipper shared an intimate and ambiguous relationship. When an emotionally distraught Skipper called Brick to confess his love for him, Brick hung up on Skipper, precipitating his suicide. Brick hates Maggie because she tried to seduce Skipper in an effort to come between the men. Brick is disgusted with the hypocrisy, lies, secrecy, and plotting he sees going on around him in the family. Having lost all ambition, he longs only for the blissful oblivion that sufficient amounts of alcohol can provide. Brick is the only member of the family who does not care about inheriting control of the Pollitt empire. Everyone around him plots and schemes for it, with Brick at the center of their manipulations.

Big Daddy Pollitt, the wealthy and socially prominent patriarch of the Pollitt family. Big Daddy is a tough, vulgar, outspoken man who has always maintained firm control over his twenty-eight-thousand-acre plantation as well as his family. Big Daddy derives his power as much from the raw force of his personality as from his accumulated wealth and influence. At the age of sixty-five, he views himself as beyond social norms, finally able to live the way he wants, regardless of family or social pressures. He reveals his renewed sexual fantasies, as well as his disgust with Big Mama, Gooper, Mae, and all the church and social groups he has participated in throughout his life. He feels affection for Brick and tries to discover the cause of Brick's decline. When Big Daddy is diagnosed with terminal cancer, no one wants to tell him, but Brick accidentally reveals the truth in a moment of anger. Being deceived by his family confirms Big Daddy's belief that the world is full of hypocrisy and liars, and the shock of his impending death horrifies and enrages him.

Ida Pollitt, called **Big Mama**, Big Daddy's wife. Big Mama lives in the shadow of her husband, wanting only to please him and keep the family happy. She endures his harshness and insults because of her love for him, though his verbal cruelty and emotional indifference hurt her deeply. Though essentially a meek person, Big Mama summons the strength of will to resist Gooper and Mae's attempts to take over control of the plantation, choosing instead to place her trust in Brick.

Gooper Pollitt, called **Brother Man**, Brick's older brother. A lawyer in Memphis, Gooper has helped with running the plantation and considers himself the responsible son, the one most capable and deserving of taking over when Big Daddy dies. To further solidify his position, Gooper has fathered five children in a failed effort to please Big Daddy. Gooper is disgusted by Brick's lifestyle and feels superior to both him and Maggie, whom he considers a scheming interloper.

Mae Pollitt, called **Sister Woman**, Gooper's wife. A former cotton carnival queen, Mae is loud and obnoxious. Having given birth to five children and now pregnant with a sixth, Mae has devoted most of her married life to producing grandchildren for Big Daddy in an effort to ingratiate herself with him and to help Gooper acquire control of the estate. Mae, who realizes that Brick and Maggie have not been sleeping together, is furious when Maggie claims to be pregnant, but she is powerless to expose the lie or change Big Mama's mind.

— *Charles Avinger*

CATCH-22

Author: Joseph Heller (1923-   )
First published: 1961
Genre: Novel

Locale: The imaginary island of Pianosa, eight miles south of Elba, and Rome
Time: 1944
Plot: Social satire

Captain John Yossarian, a United States Air Force bombardier who tries to escape World War II by embracing the absurd. He is foiled by the madness and stupidity around him and by the ultimate irony of the rule known as Catch-22: Anyone can be grounded for being insane, but requesting to be grounded means that an individual is sane.

Colonel Cathcart, the group commander, who sends his pilots on increasingly dangerous missions in order to become famous and earn a promotion.

Major Major Major, the commander of the 256th Squadron, who was promoted by a machine.

Lieutenant Milo Minderbinder, the mess officer. He turns his black market operation into a powerful syndicate and is not above aiding the enemy for profit.

Captain Black, the squadron intelligence officer, who constantly requires pilots to swear loyalty oaths.

Doc Daneeka, the flight surgeon. He informs Yossarian about the tenets of Catch-22.

Captain R. O. Shipman, the chaplain, who is accused of tampering with the enlisted men's mail.

General Dreedle, the wing commander, who is engaged in a power struggle with General Peckem.

General Peckem, the commander of Special Services. He is more concerned with appearances than with military strategy.

Clevinger,

Orr,

Kid Sampson,

McWatt,

Aardvark,

Hungry Joe, and

Nately, members of the 256th Squadron.

THE CATCHER IN THE RYE

Author: J. D. Salinger (1919-   )
First published: 1951
Genre: Novel

Locale: Pennsylvania and New York City
Time: Saturday to Monday in a December in the late 1940's
Plot: Social realism

Holden Caulfield, a tall seventeen-year-old with prematurely graying hair. In a California sanatorium where he is undergoing treatment for a physical and mental collapse, he narrates the very subjective account of his almost two-day sojourn in New York City shortly before his breakdown. In the narrative, he flees Pencey, an exclusive boys' preparatory school in Pennsylvania from which he had been expelled, just before the Christmas break. Alienated, lonely, sad, and afraid to go home until the date his parents expect him, Holden roams New York City seeking comfort and understanding from past friends and acquaintances, from strangers, and, stealthily, from his adored little sister, Phoebe. Still mourning his younger brother Allie's death from leukemia three years earlier, Holden nurses a morbid sensitivity behind a façade of adolescent loudmouthed belligerence, bravado, and apathy that has cost him friends and family approval and caused this third expulsion from a school. Longing for emotional support, Holden perversely trusts almost no one. He views his world, not incorrectly, as being full of "phonies"; often, he fantasizes about a solitary life as a self-sufficient deaf-mute. Holden longs for an idyllic world epitomized for him in the words of Robert Burns's "Coming Through the Rye." He wishes himself to be the "catcher," protector of children's innocence, in a kind of sunlit never-never land where life's ugly adult realities—and even death—are kept at bay. He wryly admits, though, that such a world cannot exist. His temporary retreat is the collapse from which he is now recovering by warily recounting his experiences and feelings to a shadowy listener, probably a psychiatrist.

Sally Hayes, Holden's longtime friend in New York City, a little older than he and certainly more worldly. A pretty, vain, wealthy, and self-absorbed social climber, she disappoints Holden's hopes of a comforting and yielding companion when they meet for a Sunday date in downtown New York City. When she rejects Holden's wild scheme for a romantic trip to northern New England, he publicly insults her, and she flounces out of Rockefeller Plaza alone. Holden appreciates her physical charms but ultimately rejects her as shallow and smug.

Phoebe Josephine Caulfield, Holden's wiry, red-haired, and bright ten-year-old sister. Regarding Phoebe as a living copy of all that he loved in Allie, Holden creeps home Sunday night to seek out her loyal companionship and her understanding. He is comforted by Phoebe's jauntiness and vitality; he yearns to protect her from the ugliness he perceives in the world around them. A last coherent memory he has before his breakdown is of a rush of happiness as he watches Phoebe serenely riding the Central Park carousel, a tangible link with much that was joyous in his own childhood.

D. B., Holden's older brother, a successful Hollywood scriptwriter. Holden views D. B.'s life and career as "phoney" and wishes he would return to the "pure" artistry of his short fiction.

Jane Gallagher, a friend, from his summers in Maine, who is Holden's age. Holden and Jane enjoyed an unintimidating, platonic, late-childhood relationship in which each derived comfort from the other, especially when their separate private griefs intruded. At Pencey, when Holden discovers that his roommate, the "sexy bastard" Ward Stradlater, has a blind date with Jane, he is distraught, jealous and repelled by the thought of Jane at the mercy of handsome, conceited Stradlater. His concern precipitates his physical and verbal attack on Stradlater and his flight from Pencey later that Saturday night, marking the start of his odyssey.

Mr. Antolini, a youngish man now married to a wealthy older woman. He was once Holden's English teacher at another preparatory school. Holden has respected Antolini as a teacher and valued him as a compassionate, trustworthy confidant, especially after seeing Antolini's selfless response to a violent student death. In New York City, Holden seeks out Antolini for solace and shelter after he must flee discovery by his parents at home. He finds Antolini welcoming and ready with measured advice, but drinking steadily. Only disquieted when he settles to sleep on the Antolinis' couch, the self-absorbed Holden seems not to perceive the restless cynicism that pervades Antolini's response to his problems and perhaps explains the ever-present highball. Holden flees in panic when he awakes to find Antolini patting his head, a gesture Holden interprets as "perverty," though he later regrets his precipitous flight when he remembers Antolini's previous kindnesses. This betrayal of trust contributes further to Holden's overwhelming sense of depression and alienation. It is perhaps Antolini, above the several other flawed people Holden meets, who most embodies the moral emptiness and irrelevance of Holden's world.

— *Jill Rollins*

CATHERINE CARMIER

Author: Ernest J. Gaines (1933-   )
First published: 1964
Genre: Novel

Locale: Southern Louisiana
Time: The early 1960's
Plot: Psychological realism

Jackson Bradley, a searcher who measures people, places, and events by whether they will contribute to his search or impede it. Returning to Louisiana after completing his college education in California, he no longer feels at home in the rural community of his origins.

Catherine Carmier, a woman divided between her need to fulfill herself as an individual and her powerful attachment to her family, especially to her father. Her relationship with her father has a troubling intensity; she is not sure that she could love any other man as much as she loves him.

Raoul Carmier, a hard, determined man. His extremely light skin has created in him a sense of distance from his darker-skinned neighbors without creating any compensatory sense of closeness to white people. He lives in a kind of self-imposed isolation from the community and insists that his wife and daughter share it with him. His hardness is seen in a more positive light when he stands up to the Cajuns after almost everyone else has surrendered.

Charlotte, Jackson's aunt, sees in him not only the young man she has helped to rear but also the main hope for the future of the community. Her emotional investment in him blinds her to his needs as a separate human being.

Della, Raoul's wife, emotionally estranged from her husband ever since the birth of her son Mark, whose dark skin revealed that Raoul could not be the father. Recognizing her husband's obsession with Catherine, Della waits for her moment, when she can take her rightful place as Raoul's true wife.

Madame Bayonne, Jackson's former schoolteacher, who has a freedom of mind that allows her to understand Jackson's questing nature at the same time that she sees deeply into the powerful emotional entanglements of the local community. Her role is that of confidante to Jackson and of ironic and compassionate commentator on the action.

— *W. P. Kenney*

CATHLEEN NI HOULIHAN

Author: William Butler Yeats (1865-1939)
First published: 1902
Genre: Drama

Locale: A cottage near Killala, Ireland
Time: 1798
Plot: Allegory

Cathleen ni Houlihan, "The Poor Old Woman," who symbolizes impoverished Ireland, seeking independence from British rule. A stranger, she has come to the countryside of Killala to enlist the help of the Irish in retrieving her four stolen fields. She entrances Michael Gillane into leaving his home and joining her cause. His sacrifices and those of others transform her old age into youth. She steps from the Gillanes' door a young queen.

Michael Gillane, a young man scheduled to be married the day after he meets Cathleen ni Houlihan. His life is full of promise; he is engaged to a pretty girl whose parents have given a dowry of one hundred pounds. He rejects domestic bliss, however, to fight for Ireland. In joining the French forces against the British, he risks his life, knowing that death will bring eternal fame.

Peter Gillane, Michael's father, a farmer who is much interested in the dowry brought by his future daughter-in-law. The dowry will make it possible to buy livestock for 10 acres of their land. When he begrudgingly offers Cathleen ni Houli-

han a shilling, he is amazed by her refusal, for money dominates his life.

Bridget Gillane, Peter's wife, who is angered by her husband's remark that she brought no dowry with her. A hard-working, practical woman, she wants the best for her two sons. With Michael about to be married, she begins to plan Patrick's future as a priest. Full of hospitality, Bridget directs Michael to open their door to Cathleen and bids her husband to offer the old woman money.

Patrick Gillane, the Gillanes' twelve-year-old son. He announces the events of the outside world: the approach of the old woman to their neighbors' home, the cheering that greets Cathleen ni Houlihan, the landing of the French at Killala, and their being joined by the Irish. It is Patrick who proclaims the transformation of Cathleen ni Houlihan.

Delia Cahel, the young girl Michael is to marry. She loses the struggle for Michael's affections and their life together; their love is overshadowed by his devotion to Ireland.

— *Jacqueline L. Gmuca*

CATILINE

Author: Ben Jonson (1573-1637)
First published: 1611
Genre: Drama

Locale: Ancient Rome
Time: 62 B.C.E.
Plot: Political

Catiline (KA-teh-lin), also referred to as **Lucius Sergius Catilina** (LEW-shee-uhs SUR-jee-uhs ka-teh-LI-nuh), a patrician traitor. Power-mad, bloodthirsty, venomous, and given to monstrous crimes, he corrupts others and draws them to his party of followers, with which he hopes to control Rome. His inhumanity is disclosed in his sacrifice of a slave and a hideous, perverted communion of the conspirators in which they drink the slave's blood. He is, fortunately for Rome, indiscreet and hasty. Failing to win a consulate by election, he hastens his attempted revolution before his preparations are complete. His death demonstrates his reckless courage.

Marcus Tullius Cicero (MAHR-kuhs TUH-lee-uhs SIH-

seh-roh), a "new man," not an established aristocrat. Able and self-confident, he wins a consulate and uses his governmental position and oratorical powers to save Rome from Catiline's conspiracy. He is willing to use dubious characters as spies, and with information furnished by them he forces Catiline into premature action and consequent defeat. A cautious politician, he does not force the hands of sympathizers with the subversives, and he sends to execution only those active in the conspiracy. Caesar and Crassus thereby survive as threats to Rome's future.

Caius Julius Caesar (GAY-yuhs JEW-lee-uhs SEE-zur), who potentially is more dangerous to Rome than any of the active conspirators. He is too shrewd to make an open break with the republic until he sees how matters are likely to resolve. When Catiline is goaded into premature action by Cicero, Caesar refrains from joining the conspirators openly. He pleads in vain for moderation in punishing the arrested conspirators and prophetically warns Cicero of his fate.

Publius Lentulus (PUHB-lee-uhs LEHN-chew-luhs), a senator formerly ejected from the senate for infamous behavior but later restored. He is filled with family pride and delusions of grandeur. Catiline flatters him with prophecies that a third member of the family Cornelii is to rule Rome, and Lentulus is easily convinced that he is the man intended. He remains in Rome, is arrested, and is executed.

Caius Cethegus (seh-THEE-guhs), a savage, fire-eating conspirator. Indiscreet and tactless, he requires considerable care by Catiline to keep him from disrupting the revolutionary forces. He is hasty, reckless, and chronically angry. He is executed with the rest of the rebels who remain in Rome when Catiline leaves.

Quintus Curius (KWIHN-tuhs KEW-ree-uhs), a former senator also ejected from the senate for infamous behavior. Enslaved by his passion for Fulvia, he rashly betrays himself and the other conspirators to her. Under her influence, combined with fear and greed, he becomes a spy for Cicero. His information enables Cicero to avoid assassination and to expose Catiline's machinations to the senate. Caesar prevents his receiving official reward after Rome is saved.

Fulvia (FUHL-vee-uh), an expensive and extravagant courtesan. She gives her favors where the return is greatest. Suspecting some major plot, she takes back the degraded Curius so that she can wheedle his secret from him. Unwilling to take second place to another woman, she chooses to go over to Cicero rather than to Catiline. Although Cicero feels shame at having to depend on such tools, he skillfully uses Fulvia and Curius to thwart Catiline and thus save Rome.

Sempronia (sehm-PROH-nee-uh), the snobbish wife of Decius Brutus. She is an intellectual feminist, past her prime but still hungry for masculine attention, for which she pays lavishly. She is active in Catilinarian politics but escapes punishment, for Cicero says a government should not show its anger against fools or women.

Marcus Porcius Cato (POHR-shee-uhs KAY-toh), called **Cato the Younger** and "the voice of Rome." A staunch, loyal Roman citizen, he is a strong supporter of Cicero, whom he considers sometimes too mild; however, in general he gives Cicero complete approbation.

Caius Antonius (an-TO-nee-uhs), a candidate for consul in the same election as Cicero and Catiline. He and Cicero win, and Cicero buys his support with a province.

Marcus Crassus (KRA-suhs), a cautious Roman. Like Caesar, he is sympathetic to Catiline but unwilling to risk open commitment.

Petreius (peh-TREE-yuhs), the leader of the Roman forces against Catiline's army. He gives a vivid and poetic account of the defeat and death of Catiline.

Quintus Fabius Sanga (FAY-bee-uhs SAN-guh), Cicero's emissary to the ambassadors from the Allobroges. From them, he gets documentary evidence of the conspiracy for the senate.

Aurelia Orestilla (oh-REE-lee-uh oh-rehs-TIH-luh), Catiline's wife, for whom he murdered his former wife and son. She aids him in his conspiracy by holding a meeting of the feminine auxiliary of the conspirators.

Volturtius (vohl-TUR-shee-uhs), a conspirator captured with the Allobroges. He gives evidence to the senate against the other conspirators.

Quintus Cicero, the brother of the consul. He gathers help to prevent Vargunteius and Cornelius from assassinating his brother.

Sylla's Ghost (SIHL-uh), who in the prologue narrates Catiline's inhuman crimes and invokes terror on Rome comparable to what he himself had brought in the past.

Flaccus (FLA-kuhs) and

Pomtinius (pom-TI-nee-uhs), praetors. Cicero trusts them and calls them in to help prevent his assassination.

Syllanus (sih-LAY-nuhs), a senator. He favors death for the arrested conspirators.

Autronius (oh-TROH-nee-uhs),

Vargunteius (vahr-guhn-TEE-yuhs),

Lucius Cassius Longinus (LEW-shee-uhs KA-see-uhs lon-JI-nuhs),

Portius Lecca (POHR-shee-uhs LEH-kuh),

Fulvius (FUHL-vee-uhs),

Lucius Bestia (BEHS-tee-uh),

Gabinius Cimber (guh-BIH-nee-uhs SIHM-bur),

Statilius (steh-TIH-lee-uhs),

Ceparius (see-PAY-ree-uhs), and

Caius Cornelius, conspirators.

CAT'S CRADLE

Author: Kurt Vonnegut, Jr. (1922-   )
First published: 1963
Genre: Novel

Locale: Ilium, New York, and the Caribbean Republic of San Lorenzo
Time: Early 1960's
Plot: Science fiction

John, the narrator. John, a Cornell-educated journalist, spends the course of the book interviewing the friends and children of Dr. Felix Hoenikker for a book about the day the atom bomb was dropped. John is always perfectly gracious and objective in his interviews, even when his subjects are hostile and impute ulterior motives to his writing. His research takes him to the island nation of San Lorenzo, where he unintentionally becomes president and witnesses the unleashing of ice-nine, which freezes the world.

Dr. Felix Hoenikker, a Nobel Prize-winning atomic scientist and creator of ice-nine. He already is dead as the book opens, but much of his later life is uncovered by the narrator. Fascinated by the puzzles of nature, Hoenikker has very little interest in people. He had no interest in the human implications of the atom bomb he helped create, nor in the potential human harm his invention of ice-nine may cause. The novel ends with Hoenikker's invention freezing, and thus destroying, the entire earth.

Newt Hoenikker, a midget, the youngest child of Dr. Hoenikker. Newt is a cynical young man whose one-week marriage to a Ukrainian midget named Zinka apparently was a ruse designed to obtain the secret of ice-nine for the Soviet Union. An incident from his childhood explains the name of the novel: On the day the atom bomb was dropped on Japan, Dr. Hoenikker dangled a string in the form of a "cat's cradle" in front of six-year-old Newt, causing the boy to cry.

Angela Hoenikker, later **Mrs. Harrison C. Conners**, Newt and Franklin's sister, the eldest of Dr. Hoenikker's children. Tall and homely, Angela dropped out of high school in her sophomore year to take care of her father and brothers after her mother died. Her only diversion was playing the clarinet. After her father died, she lost much of her purpose, until she met Harrison C. Conners, a handsome researcher in her father's lab. They were married shortly after meeting. She paints a storybook picture of her marriage, although Newt asserts that her husband is unfaithful. Franklin implies that Conners married her only to get the secret of ice-nine for the U.S. government.

Franklin (Frank) Hoenikker, the middle child of Dr. Hoenikker. He is a major general and minister of science and progress in the Caribbean republic of San Lorenzo. An immature-looking twenty-six-year-old, Frank went to San Lorenzo after escaping the Federal Bureau of Investigation, which sought him for smuggling cars to Cuba. As an adolescent, Frank was ignored by classmates, who called him "Secret Agent X-9" because he kept to himself. His time alone was spent building models, though near the end of the book he reveals that he had not always been alone: He had an affair with his boss's wife.

"Papa" Monzano, the dictatorial president of San Lorenzo. A native of the island republic, Monzano is the handpicked successor of Corporal Earl McCabe, an American who began the current regime on San Lorenzo in the 1920's. Like McCabe, he pretends opposition to Bokonon. Tiring of a system based on lies, Monzano, now in his late seventies, brought Frank Hoenikker to San Lorenzo as a way of turning to science. Learning from Frank the secret of ice-nine, Monzano commits suicide by swallowing it, thereby freezing himself and, by contact with him, all the water on earth.

Lionel Boyd Johnson, called **Bokonon**, a philosopher and opponent of Monzano. Born on the island of Tobago in 1891, Johnson washed up on the shores of San Lorenzo in 1922, along with U.S. Army Corporal Earl McCabe. McCabe became the island's ruler and, discovering that he could not relieve its poverty, sought to make its people happy with harmless lies. Johnson ("Bokonon" in the native dialect) created a new religion, which McCabe pretended to suppress, playing the evil dictator while Bokonon became the good holy man in the jungle. His religion, Bokononism, is based on the principle that all religions are *foma* (harmless lies), including Bokononism.

— *John R. Holmes*

THE CAUCASIAN CHALK CIRCLE
(Der kaukasische Kreidekreis)

Author: Bertolt Brecht (1898-1956)
First published: 1949
Genre: Drama

Locale: The Soviet Caucasus
Time: Shortly after World War II
Plot: Epic

Grusha, a young, attractive, unmarried, helpful kitchen maid in the family of the governor of a Caucasian city. The governor, returning from Easter Mass, is killed in a political uprising. His wife, concerned about fleeing with her elegant dresses, forgets her baby, and the kindhearted Grusha cares for him. Fleeing for safety to her brother's distant home in the mountains, she protects the child. Grusha's sister-in-law, concerned about an unmarried girl with a baby, has Grusha married to a supposedly dying man who revives immediately after the wedding. Grusha, however, is still loyal to her Easter morning betrothal to Simon, a soldier. When soldiers take the child back to the governor's wife, Grusha pleads in court for the child. The governor's wife needs the son for access to the family estates, but Grusha loves him and is best for him. She wins him and is given a divorce. Her love for Simon also is rewarded.

Azdak (ahz-DAHK) a village scrivener, suddenly elevated, during a time of political chaos, into the role of judge for two years. He is a drunken rascal given to stealing chickens and rabbits. During the political war, he befriended a beggar, sheltering him from the police, only to learn later that it was the grand duke. Azdak, upset at being a traitor to his own class, wants to be tried in court but instead is made judge. His rulings, using a feigned stupidity, reflect sympathy for the poor and weak. When he seems sympathetic to the governor's wife, Grusha berates him, touching off his guilt for betraying his own class. When the birth mother pulls the child from the chalk circle and Grusha refrains, so as not to maim him, Azdak grants her custody of the child.

Simon Shashava, a soldier and a guard at the palace. He has watched Grusha from behind a bush as she went to the river to do the laundry, putting her bare legs in the water. Simon, ordered to accompany the governor's wife into exile, first wins Grusha's promise of marriage, expecting to return in a few weeks. He follows her to her new husband's home in the mountains and then to court. He is willing to accept the child and marry Grusha.

Georgi Abashwili, a governor for the grand duke who is rather lackadaisical about his responsibilities and in recognizing realities. When the palace is captured after Easter Mass, he is killed.

Natella Abashwili, the governor's wife, a whining, superficial, self-centered woman concerned more about her dresses than about her child or the danger of the situation. It is clear that she seeks custody of the child primarily to get control of the governor's large estates.

Michael Abashwili, their child. He is well-behaved and cooperative on the difficult twenty-two-day journey with Grusha. He reciprocates Grusha's love.

Arsen Kazbeki, a fat, two-faced prince who shows deference to the governor and then engineers the palace revolt and kills the governor.

— E. Lynn Harris

CAUGHT

Author: Henry Green (Henry Vincent Yorke, 1905-1973)
First published: 1943
Genre: Novel

Locale: London and the English countryside
Time: 1939-1940
Plot: Social morality

Richard Roe, a widower in his mid-thirties who volunteers for duty in the London Auxiliary Fire Service. He was badly hurt by the death of his wife. Roe, a product of an affluent, cultured home, learns what life holds in store for members of the working class when he signs on as a fireman and lives among them. In his detached way, he loves his son, Christopher, but their relationship grows distant after Roe's sister Dy takes over his duty as parent. In Roe's absence, Christopher is abducted for a short time by the sister of his superior officer, Albert Pye.

Albert Pye, a sub-officer of the London Auxiliary Fire Service station and Roe's superior officer. Pye, a rough man from humble origins, is tormented by memories and represses the fact that when young, he made love to his own sister, an act that propelled her into madness and eventually leads to his suicide in a gas oven.

Dy, Roe's sister-in-law, who cares for his young son, Christopher, when his fire duties call him away from home. Sharp-tempered and snobbish, she detests the fire service personnel and their mean surroundings.

Christopher Roe, Richard's son, who falls under the care and tutelage of Dy. A five-year-old at the novel's outset, Christopher gradually loses interest in his father as a result of his prolonged separation from him. He increasingly adopts the upper-class attitudes of Dy at the same time his father is

shedding his preconceived notions about people of "lower station in life."

Hilly, a fire service driver for Pye who becomes romantically involved with Roe. Hilly's love helps Roe move away from the pain of his wife's death, and he admires her frank, commonsense approach to life.

Prudence, the upper-class lover of Pye who eventually tires of him and dismisses him from her thoughts. She is Hilly's opposite in many ways: She is rich and cultivated, though narrow and bigoted. Her interest in the British working class extends only to brief romantic adventures with firemen.

Arthur Piper, the oldest fireman with London's fire service. He saw duty in World War I. He constantly plays up to his superior officers in an absurd, wheedling fashion.

Shiner Wright, a heroic, rugged fire service veteran who is killed fighting a huge conflagration in the area around London's docks, a blaze set by Nazi bombs.

Trant, Roe and Pye's commanding officer, a stern, rule-bound man with little interest in the men and women in his command.

Mary Howells, a menial worker at the fire service station known for her interest in passing along information about others.

— John D. Raymer

CAVALLERIA RUSTICANA

Author: Giovanni Verga (1840-1922)
First published: 1880
Genre: Short fiction

Locale: A small village in Sicily
Time: Late nineteenth century
Plot: Social realism

Turiddu Macca (tew-REED-dew MAHK-kah), a swaggering youth with an eye for the ladies. He is self-confident, cocky, and convinced of his own sexual appeal. Returning from the army, still wearing the rakish cap of the soldier, he fully expects to continue his relationship with Lola, to whom he considers himself engaged. He learns that she is going to marry the local carter, Alfio. In spiteful bravado he courts Santa, the daughter of a well-to-do landowner. Although he does not really love her, he woos Santa with a kind of rough tenderness and a self-assuredness that expects no refusal. He is capable of real courage and dignity, as in the final scene, when he fights a knife duel with Lola's husband. Although he knows he could be killed—as indeed he is—Turiddu meets the cuckolded carter in the hills at dawn because he is expected, as a man, to play his part in the primitive ritual of honor and to pay with his life for his affair with Lola.

Lola, the daughter of a local farmer. As calculating as Turiddu is headstrong, she marries the carter not for love but for the security he could provide. She knows that marriage to Turiddu cannot offer her the stability and prestige she wants; in fact, she enjoys tormenting Turiddu by sitting on her balcony with her hands folded on her stomach, showing off her rings and jewelry. Even after her marriage, Lola is a temptress. Her awareness of her own sexuality is the equal of Turiddu's and more than a match for his egotism. One night, when her husband is away on business, Lola confidently seduces Turiddu, inviting him into the house, regardless of what the rest of the village might think. She ensnares him, but he willingly becomes ensnared. Lola clearly establishes the theme of the story—treachery. She betrays Turiddu and betrays her husband twice, once by marrying him without love and once by her seduction of Turiddu.

Santa, who falls in love with Turiddu even though she knows the kind of man he is. She is undeceived by his declarations of her beauty. She is a true peasant, strong, clever, and vindictive. When she learns that her Turiddu has been carrying on with Lola, she feels slighted, perhaps even jealous. She comes to hate Turiddu as much as she once loved him. Fearlessly and implacably, she tells Lola's husband about the affair.

Alfio (ahl-FEE-oh), an uncomplicated man. He marries Lola not because he loves her but simply because she is an attractive ornament. When he discovers that Turiddu has cuck-olded him, he unhesitatingly seeks him out. Without emotion, he challenges Turiddu; equally without remorse, he kills him. He is direct, blunt, and instinctual. He is portrayed as stolid and humorless. His challenge to Turiddu is curt and business-like. His animal nature reflects the hardness of the life of the peasant. Ironically, he would have been a good match for Santa, with her brutal honesty. Instead, he becomes an instrument of revenge.

— Edward Fiorelli

CAWDOR

Author: Robinson Jeffers (1887-1962)
First published: 1928
Genre: Poetry

Locale: Carmel Coast Range, California
Time: 1900
Plot: Psychological realism

Cawdor, a fifty-year-old farmer, hard and strong. Drawn to worship Fera's youthful beauty and contrarily to possess her sexually, he bargains to let her father stay in his home if Fera will marry him. Rightly suspecting Fera's later passion for Hood but mistaken in believing Hood guilty, Cawdor seeks confirmation of his suspicions. Burning with jealousy, he believes Fera's lie that Hood raped her in the laurels; enraged, he meets Hood at the high rock and knocks him over the adjacent cliff. When he learns from Fera of Hood's innocence, he blinds himself like Oedipus of old, who put out the eyes that could not see the truth.

Hood Cawdor, his second son, a strong young hunter who has been separated from his father because of a quarrel. Loyal to his father after his return, Hood resists Fera's attempts at seduction by the seashore, in his room, and in the laurels. He is killed anyway by gulled Cawdor.

Fera, Martial's daughter, an intense, bold girl who admires strength and who expects hardness and pride in Cawdor's treatment of her as a wife. She begins a sexual pursuit of Hood almost upon his return home. Inflamed with desire and angry at being rebuffed when she tries repeatedly to seduce him, she goads Cawdor with the lie that Hood violated her in the laurels. Thus, through her duplicity, she accomplishes her re-venge for being spurned. Having failed at seduction, she also fails in attempting suicide and still again in her cruel urging that Cawdor kill himself. Although Fera speaks often of longing for death and of death as a blessing, it is difficult to decide how sincere she is because she lies with such ease. Fera is destructive by nature.

George Cawdor, Hood's brother, a farmer, in contrast to Hood the hunter.

Michal Cawdor, the younger sister of George and Hood. She traps ground squirrels and watches her caged, crippled eagle kill and eat them. At Fera's suggestion, she finally has George shoot the eagle.

Martial, a former schoolmaster, a dreamer, and an abject alcoholic failure. This former enemy of Cawdor was blinded in the explosion of an oil drum during a sweeping brush fire. A pitiful remnant of a man, he slowly declines and dies as the result of his burns and is buried near the graves of Cawdor's wife and child.

Concha Rosas, Cawdor's Indian servant and mistress.

Jesus Acanna, Cawdor's Indian farmhand.

Dante Vitello, a new Swiss farmhand.

Romano, Concha Rosas' young son.

CECILIA: Or, Memoirs of an Heiress

Author: Fanny Burney (Madame d'Arblay, 1752-1840)
First published: 1782
Genre: Novel

Locale: England
Time: The eighteenth century
Plot: Social realism

Cecilia Beverley, a charming, benevolent heiress. To retain the fortune left her by an eccentric uncle, she must marry a man who will take the name of Beverley. During her minority, Cecilia is the ward of three distinct types of men named by her uncle. Her extended love affair with the son of one of the guardians brings her insult, near-poverty, temporary insanity, and finally happiness. Cecilia is the model heroine who reciprocates to those who befriend her, has compassion for those who would harm her, and is benevolent to those who need help.

Mortimer Delvile, her lover and husband. He is a violent admixture of submission to his parents, devotion to Cecilia, and jealousy of others attending to her. Sensitive and un-worldly, Mortimer is always in need of a protector.

Compton Delvile, his father and one of Cecilia's guardians, whose chief objective in life is preservation of the family name. His pride is odious because it is tainted with meanness and incapacity.

Augusta Delvile, his high-spirited and fastidious wife. She loves Cecilia but accepts her as a daughter-in-law with great misgivings because she fears unhappiness for her son in marriage. Her pride is coupled with dignity and generosity of mind.

Mr. Monckton, the self-appointed protector of Cecilia. In love with her, he lies, pries, and spies to avert any attachment between her and any man.

Mr. Harrel, one of Cecilia's guardians. Using her as a perpetual go-between with moneylenders, he draws heavily on Cecilia's funds. His gay, fashionable, splendid way of life eventually drives him to suicide to escape his creditors.

Priscilla Harrel, his helpmate in lavish living. Cecilia provides for her after Harrel's suicide.

Mr. Albany, "the old man in the corner" at various functions. He is silent in groups but articulate with Cecilia in pronouncing his philosophy of benevolence. Through Albany, she provides pensions for the indigent of the countryside.

Mr. Briggs, the third legally appointed guardian, who manages Cecilia's finances during her minority. Rich, eccentric, uncouth, and miserly, Briggs would have Cecilia live in his comfortless home to conserve her money.

Mr. Arnot, Priscilla Harrel's brother. Mild, serious, and comfortable financially, he tries to discipline Priscilla in her spending.

Mr. Belfield, an animated, intelligent young man who gives his time to company, his income to his whims, and his heart to the Muses. Injured in a duel, he is helped secretly by Cecilia, whose kindness to him arouses Mortimer's jealousy.

Henrietta Belfield, his sister, befriended by Cecilia and in love with Mortimer. Through Cecilia, she becomes friendly with Arnot.

Sir Robert Floyer, a vain, supercilious man-about-town. A contender for Cecilia's affection, he involves Belfield in the duel.

Mrs. Charlton, Cecilia's longtime friend and confidante.

Lady Margaret Monckton, Monckton's cold, irascible wife, considerably older than her husband and jealous of Cecilia. Ill most of her life, she dies of apoplexy.

Miss Bennet, Lady Monckton's submissive companion, an accessory to Monckton's schemes to keep Cecilia unmarried.

Mrs. Matt, one of Cecilia's pensioners, hired by Miss Bennet to disrupt Cecilia's wedding.

Mr. Morrice, an officious young lawyer. He keeps Monckton's friendship by spying on Cecilia.

Lady Honoria Pemberton, Compton Delvile's cousin. Volatile and high-spirited, she belies her fashionable education.

Lord Derford, a young nobleman whom Compton Delvile, in his effort to separate Cecilia and his son, urges upon Cecilia.

Lord Ernolf, Derford's father, willing to accept Cecilia as a daughter-in-law because of her income.

Mrs. Wyers, the landlady of the house where Cecilia goes looking for Mortimer. She keeps Cecilia confined, thinking her mentally unsound.

Mrs. Hill, the wife of an injured carpenter, one of Cecilia's pensioners. Her rooming house becomes a rendezvous for Mortimer and Cecilia.

Dr. Lyster, the Delvile family physician, who philosophizes, in describing Delvile, Sr., that people make themselves miserable by seeing only one road to contentment when other channels would serve equally well.

Mr. Biddulph, Mortimer's former schoolmate, who convinces him of Cecilia's devotion.

CELESTINA
(Comedia de Calisto y Melibea)

Author: Fernando de Rojas (c. 1465-1541)
First published: 1499; revised, 1502
Genre: Novel

Locale: Spain, probably Toledo
Time: The fifteenth century
Plot: Tragicomedy

Calisto (kah-LEES-toh), a nobleman who sees and falls in love with Melibea. He hires Celestina to arrange a meeting. He is killed by falling from a ladder while leaving Melibea's garden.

Melibea (may-lee-BAY-ah), a beautiful girl who lets herself be talked into a rendezvous with Calisto and who commits suicide after his death by leaping from her roof.

Celestina (thay-lehs-TEE-nah), an elderly go-between and seller of love charms whose greediness brings about her death.

Lucrecia (lew-KRAY-thyah), Melibea's maid. She warns Melibea's mother against the evil Celestina, but to no avail.

Pármeno (PAHR-may-noh) and

Sempronio (saym-PROH-nyoh), servants of Calisto who

promote Celestina's arrangement with their master and murder her when she refuses them a reward. Apprehended by the police, they are beheaded on the spot for their crime.

Sosia (SOH-syah), another servant of Calisto who helps to plot his master's death.

Areusa (ah-RAY-ew-sah) and

Elicia (ay-LEE-thyah), prostitutes in Celestina's house. Areusa loves Pármeno; Elicia loves Sempronio. The girls hire Centurio to avenge the servants' deaths.

Pleberio (play-BAY-ryoh), the father of Melibea.

Alisa (ah-LEE-sah), the mother of Melibea.

Centurio (thayn-TEW-ryoh), a scoundrel soldier hired to kill Calisto.

THE CENCI
(Les Cenci)

Author: Antonin Artaud (1896-1948)
First published: 1964
Genre: Drama

Locale: Italy
Time: The sixteenth century
Plot: Historical

Count Cenci (chen-chee), the malevolent patriarch of a wealthy Renaissance family. In his late sixties, he is arrogant, blasphemous, and sadistically cruel to all the members of his

family. His primary motivation in practicing evil is that he identifies himself with nature and, therefore, must abandon himself to his desires. After bribing the pope to pardon him for murdering some old enemies, he organizes a luxurious orgy, during which he triumphantly announces the deaths of his two sons and threatens both his wife, Lucretia, and his daughter, Beatrice. After repeatedly raping Beatrice, he is murdered by assassins hired by Beatrice and Lucretia, but not before arranging for their deaths with the pope, to whom he has willed his entire estate.

Beatrice Cenci, a young, beautiful, and highly sensitive virgin. The only daughter of the wicked count, she is terrified of what he has blatantly threatened to do to her and spends half the play trying to avoid him. After her father rapes her, she is forced either to submit to his repeated assaults or to murder him. Her major revelation in the play is that her only choice is to be a victim or a victimizer and that either choice will send her to eternal damnation. Shortly before she is executed by order of the pope, she realizes that her major crime was in being born.

Lucretia Cenci (lew-KREE-chee-ah), the second wife of the count and the stepmother of Beatrice, Bernardo, and Giacomo. A middle-aged beauty, she is alternately terrified and mystified by her husband's unmotivated sadistic behavior. She, Beatrice, Giacomo, and Orsino conspire to have the count murdered by hired assassins. She slips a sleeping potion into her husband's wine to ready him for the murder. She is executed with Beatrice at the play's conclusion.

Bernardo, the younger brother of Beatrice. He is unaware of the murder conspiracy. Because of his sensitive, artistic nature, he has difficulty believing the degradation taking place in the court. The count spares his life because he wants him to be the surviving sufferer. He is forced by the pope to witness the torture and death of his beloved sister and stepmother. He collapses at the end in a paroxysm of agony.

Camillo (kah-MIHL-loh), a cardinal and papal legate. Although he is completely aware of the count's evil projects, he nevertheless arranges a pardon from the pope for some of his earlier atrocities. He maintains his middle position in case the count is overthrown. Once he arranges for the papacy to become sole heir to the count's property and possessions, however, he permits the family drama to play itself out to its inevitably tragic conclusion.

Orsino (ohr-SEE-noh), a prelate, priest, and conspirator in the plot to murder the count. Middle-aged and desperately in love with Beatrice, he initially plans to support Beatrice in punishing her father for his sexual assaults on her. Once she rejects him, though, he helps to arrange the count's assassination knowing full well that it will destroy the family and he will have his revenge on Beatrice.

Giacomo Cenci (jee-AH-koh-moh), one of the count's elder sons. Once he discovers that his father is raping his sister and that the pope is to inherit the count's considerable holdings, he becomes one of the planners of the count's murder, as he has nothing to lose. He escapes punishment by fleeing the country.

— *Patrick Meanor*

THE CENCI: A Tragedy in Five Acts

Author: Percy Bysshe Shelley (1792-1822)
First published: 1819
Genre: Drama

Locale: Rome and the Apennines
Time: 1599
Plot: Tragedy

Count Francesco Cenci (frahn-CHEHS-koh CHEHN-chee), a Roman nobleman who lives to make people suffer. His special target for punishment is his family. He persecutes his sons—two of whom are sent to Salamanca to die—his wife, and his daughter Beatrice, against whom he commits unmentionable crimes. Finally, he is assassinated, but even in death his baleful influence continues: His wife and daughter, though literally innocent, die for his murder.

Count Orsino (ohr-SEE-noh), a nobleman turned priest who is responsible for much of the scheming that takes place in the play. He loves Beatrice but betrays her when she is tried for her father's murder. He hires assassins to kill Cenci and abandons them when they are caught. He betrays Beatrice's brother, Giacomo, to the Roman police. Orsino escapes punishment by disguising himself and fleeing the scene when the officials close in.

Lucretia (lew-KREH-chee-ah), Cenci's wife and Beatrice's stepmother. She helps the assassins by giving Cenci a sleeping potion. After languishing a long time in prison, she is executed for her part in her husband's assassination.

Beatrice, Cenci's daughter, the chief object of his persecution. She loves Count Orsino. She is executed along with her stepmother.

Giacomo (jee-AH-koh-moh), Cenci's son, whose wife's dowry the father takes. After the assassination, Orsino tricks Giacomo, and the son is caught by the police.

Bernardo, Cenci's youngest son, who pleads at the papal court for the lives of his sister and stepmother. His petition is rejected.

Olimpio and

Marzio, assassins hired by Orsino to murder Cenci. After some hesitation, they strangle the sleeping nobleman.

Savella (sah-VEHL-lah), an official of the papal court who comes to arrest Cenci for his crimes. Finding the count dead, Savella launches the investigation that exposes the Cenci family and the assassins as participants in Cenci's murder.

THE CENTAUR

Author: John Updike (1932-   )
First published: 1963
Genre: Novel

Locale: Olinger, Pennsylvania, and its environs
Time: Three days in early January, 1947
Plot: Magical Realism

George Caldwell, a general science teacher at Olinger High School and, at the mythic level, the centaur **Chiron** who is the teacher of the gods. Fifty years old and in physical pain, Caldwell is fearful about death and uncertain about the value of his own teaching. Despite his doubt and self-deprecation, Caldwell shows a deep sensitivity to the needs and fears of others. During the three days depicted in the novel, he and his son, Peter, are forced by car trouble and a snowstorm to spend two nights together away from home. They encounter a world that is realistic in detail yet explicitly mythic in its emotional and spiritual resonance.

Peter Caldwell, George's son, a fifteen-year-old high school student who at the mythic level is **Prometheus**, the Titan who brought fire to humans and was chained to a rock on Mount Olympus as punishment. Chiron accepted death in exchange for Prometheus' freedom. In the period of the novel, Peter is troubled by psoriasis, a skin condition inherited from his mother, and is fearful about his father's illness. Furthermore, Peter is struggling to understand his emerging sexuality and his relationship to the community of his childhood. A promising art student, he contrasts the grimy, uncultured bleakness of Olinger with images of glamour and wealth in New York City. Ironically, as he tells the story fourteen years later, Peter is an abstract expressionist painter in New York City, but his life with his black lover seems to lack the "firm stage resonant with metaphor" that he recalls in depicting his adolescence.

Catherine (Cassie) Caldwell, George's wife and Peter's mother. She is the goddess **Ceres** at the mythic level. No longer a beautiful woman, she is intermittently sharp and tender in her responses to George, Peter, and her father, who lives with them. Her greatest fulfillment is in her love of nature. As a result of her desire to live in the rural farmhouse in Firetown, George and Peter must drive eleven miles to Olinger High School. This journey precipitates their three days of adventure in the novel.

Pop Kramer, Cassie's father, who at the mythic level is the dethroned Titan **Kronos**. He is an aphorism-spouting old man whose certainties contrast with George Caldwell's pained and thoughtful skepticism.

Al Hummel, a skilled mechanic and the owner of a local garage. He is Cassie's cousin. At the mythic level, he is **Hephaestus**, the god of fire and craftsmanship. Hummel's hunched and limping body reflects a childhood accident as well as expressing his dismay at the postwar economy and his grief in his childless marriage to Vera, who is notoriously unfaithful. An understanding friend to George, Hummel helped him to get the teaching job in Olinger. On the second night that George and Peter are stranded in Olinger, they trudge through the snow to Hummel's house, where they sleep together in Peter's great-aunt's bed. The next day, Hummel helps them to shovel out their snowbound car for their return to the farmhouse in Firetown.

Vera Hummel, Al's wife and the girls' basketball coach at the high school. At the mythic level, she is **Venus**, the goddess of love. She is beautiful, amber-haired and slender, with golden skin and clear, delicate features. Her laughter is not, however, simply an expression of spontaneous joy; it is also a release and a consolation for her grief in her marriage to Hummel and, in her role as goddess, for her woe at men's ribald mockery of sexual desire. Her scenes with George and Peter affirm that sexual sensitivity and responsiveness are central issues in Peter's understanding of his father and his own emerging maturity. On the morning after the snowstorm, for example, Vera gives Peter breakfast and talks with him, providing glowing moments of release from the fears and anxieties he has carried throughout the previous three days.

Louis M. Zimmerman, the Olinger High School principal and, at the mythic level, **Zeus**, the ruler of the heavens. Both resented and respected in the small town, he is assertive, lecherous, and impetuous. In his insensitive evaluation of George's teaching, his misappropriation of 140 tickets for a basketball game, and his affair with a woman on the school board, Zimmerman is a major source of George's anxieties about money and his fear of losing his teaching job.

Dr. Harry Appleton, a local medical doctor, a plump, pink, balding man. He is **Apollo**, the god of healing, at the mythic level. Like Peter, Doc Appleton has psoriasis, and his matter-of-fact concern for Peter's skin condition parallels his humane directness in discussing George's symptoms and fears. His telephone call to Cassie reporting the results of George's X rays lifts the dread that has characterized the three days of adventure.

Hester Appleton, Doc Appleton's twin sister and the Olinger High School teacher of French and Latin. At fifty years old, she is plump and virginal, and, at the level of myth, she is the goddess **Artemis**. With her precise, sensitive use of language and her expressions of concern for George, Hester affirms his significance as a teacher and as a person.

Ray Deifendorf, a student at Olinger High School and a successful competitor on the losing swimming team that George coaches. Deifendorf is somewhat lewd and insensitive, but he feels deep affection for George. Years later, Peter learns that Deifendorf has become a high school teacher.

— *Donald Vanouse*

CEREMONIES IN DARK OLD MEN

Author: Lonne Elder III (1931-1996)
First published: 1969
Genre: Drama

Locale: 126th Street, Harlem, New York
Time: Early spring, sometime around the late 1960's
Plot: Psychological realism

Russell B. Parker, a widower who runs a barbershop that has no customers and who lives upstairs with his daughter and two sons. Parker is not an ambitious man, but he is amiable and ordinarily honest, at least until he is talked into going along with Theo's schemes. He loves his children, and his attempts to recover his youth are touching.

William Jenkins, Parker's friend and checkers opponent who finds himself drawn into the crooked dealings that Parker's sons undertake with Blue Haven. He and Parker obviously feel deep affection for each other as they engage in badinage over their checkers games, which Jenkins always wins.

Theopolis Parker, Russell Parker's older son, known as Theo. He teams up with Blue Haven to set up a bootlegging business but finds himself doing all the work while his father dips into the till. Theo is eager to run a con, and he has better judgment than his brother Bobby.

Bobby Parker, Russell Parker's younger son, an expert burglar and shoplifter. As the second son, Bobby resents playing second fiddle to Theo, whose thoughtless insulting descriptions of Bobby probably help compel Bobby to perform reckless criminal acts under the spell of Blue Haven, acts that lead to his being shot by a security guard.

Adele Eloise Parker, Parker's hardworking daughter, who supports the whole family with her office job. Adele is intelligent and conscientious, but the man she is seeing beats her, and she seems doomed to be used by men.

Blue Haven, a tough man of the streets who knows how to get along and exploit weaker men such as Theo and Bobby. In his blue ensembles and dark glasses, carrying his gold-headed cane, Blue Haven can appear menacing.

Young girl, the unnamed pickup with whom Parker becomes infatuated after he gets a few dollars from Theo's till to spread around. She is callous and exploitive, and she is a great disappointment to Parker.

— *Frank Day*

CEREMONY

Author: Leslie Marmon Silko (1948-   )
First published: 1977
Genre: Novel

Locale: Laguna Pueblo, New Mexico
Time: The 1940's, after World War II
Plot: Social realism

Tayo, the protagonist, a half-breed whose mother was a disgrace to the community and whose father was a white man who worked on the highway. After he is orphaned, he is taken in by his aunt, uncles, and grandmother and is reared with his cousin Rocky. Tayo is reminded constantly of his separate status, of his not really belonging. Surviving the war in the Pacific, Tayo returns to the United States, first to a veterans' hospital and finally to the reservation to embark on his journey of healing.

Rocky, Tayo's all-American cousin. A high school football star, he has plans for college. His life will demonstrate to white people that Indians are not unambitious failures. First, though, he will prove himself—and his patriotism—by serving in the war. Alongside Tayo, he fights the Japanese in the Philippines, only to die in the jungle rain.

Auntie, a strict Catholic who has capitulated to the dominant Western culture. She passes those same values to her son, Rocky. Her sister, an alcoholic who slept with white men and preferred the bars of Gallup to the reservation, left Tayo to remind her of the family's shame. Auntie never allows Tayo to forget his mother's disgrace and seems even more unforgiving when Tayo returns from the war and her son does not.

Josiah, Auntie's brother and Tayo's uncle, an important presence in Tayo's life. A rancher, Josiah searches for the perfect breed of cattle to raise in the hard, dry terrain of New Mexico. Rejecting Rocky's confidence in the extension agent, with his books and scientific knowledge, Josiah chooses the Mexican spotted cattle that know how to survive.

Betonie, a spiritual healer, a half-breed medicine man to whose hogan Tayo is brought when Western doctors and the local medicine man can do nothing to heal him. Surrounded by telephone books from every city he has ever visited, by years of Santa Fe Railroad calendars, and by bags of herbs, bones, sticks, and whatever else may provide wisdom and magic, Betonie initiates the ceremony that Tayo must complete to find his spiritual health.

Night Swan, the aging mixed-breed Mexican dancer with whom Josiah has a relationship. The mysterious woman's green eyes, dancing, and sexuality first provide Josiah with needed companionship and later propel Tayo in his journey of self-discovery.

Ts'eh, another mysterious woman Tayo meets in his journey/ceremony as he searches for the spotted cattle. She knows about plants, berries, sticks, rocks, and the skies. She helps Tayo find the cattle and find himself.

Robert, Auntie's quiet husband, whose silence is supportive and reassuring to Tayo.

Emo,

Harley,

Pinky, and

LeRoy, drunken veterans whose best days were in California, where they posed as Italians, hid their Indian identities, and slept with white women. Back on the reservation, they drink and tell war stories, relishing their victimization by white society while they plot yet another way to be compensated through lying, cheating, or stealing. Tayo's "friends" turn out to be the enemies to his and all Indian people's healing.

— *Laura Weiss Zlogar*

CEREMONY IN LONE TREE

Author: Wright Morris (1910-1998)
First published: 1960
Genre: Novel

Locale: Nebraska
Time: The 1950's
Plot: Family

Walter McKee, who is responsible for organizing his father-in-law's ninetieth birthday celebration, held in the prairie ghost town of Lone Tree. Although McKee is tired of the continual presence of Tom Scanlon, his father-in-law, he labors on under a sense of duty. This condition of denial accounts for an emotional decay in McKee, a corrosive element that distances him from his wife, family, and friends. McKee focuses on this lack of understanding, which produces a continual state of perplexity over the most normal circumstances of life. McKee's return to Lone Tree with the Scanlon clan reinforces his sense of isolation in the world. With the quiet death of the old man and the marriage of his niece and nephew, McKee is vindicated in his consistent decency.

Lois McKee, McKee's wife, who long ago abandoned Lone Tree for Lincoln, Nebraska, and exchanged rural hardships for a streamlined existence in the suburbs. With McKee, she builds a life of denial in an attempt to control the present; she maintains a sense of propriety at all costs. Her return to Lone Tree brings a certain foreboding of exposure and humiliation in front of her family, and in many ways this is played out. Lois not only excoriates McKee for the coward that he is; she also demolishes Boyd's pathetic fantasy of unrequited love for her.

Etoile Momeyer, the daughter of Bud and Maxine, a self-assured young teenager. Proud and confident in her physical beauty and spirited individualism, she clashes with her family and in-laws over everything. It is no surprise that Etoile plots to win and marry her cousin Calvin. After a hectic courtship in which she plays the dominating role, they return to Lone Tree as a married couple. Etoile clearly embodies the frontier spirit of her grandfather and is perhaps more at home in the lawless prairie than any of them.

Calvin McKee, the great-grandson and physical embodiment of Tom Scanlon, with the same adventurous spirit. Calvin is given to either wandering off or disappearing on prospecting jaunts. He has no idea how to handle Etoile's attentions. Handicapped by a stutter, Calvin is afraid to express himself verbally, which accounts for his overreliance on physical activity. Calvin eventually marries Etoile after a dramatic buggy rescue on the way to Lone Tree.

Gordon Boyd, McKee's boyhood friend, who arrives from Acapulco with his new girlfriend. Keen on upsetting McKee and exposing all the emotional hypocrisy and shortcomings of his family, Boyd proves himself to be a derelict and a failure. Despite his efforts to drive a wedge between Lois and McKee, he is forced to recognize the pointlessness of his attempts and admit that McKee has a viable life after all.

Tom Scanlon, the founder and final resident of Lone Tree. He is trapped in the past and refuses to enter the twentieth century. His enforced stay with the McKees in Lincoln unleashes a surge of impish behavior, and his return to Lone Tree is accompanied by flashbacks more real than his present life. On the morning of his ninetieth birthday, Scanlon dies quietly, marking the passing of the pioneer era.

Maxine Momeyer, Etoile's mother, the antithesis of her proud sister, Lois McKee. Washed out by a life of drudgery and economic deprivation, Maxine ironically provides the stable center for the Lone Tree ceremony by taking charge of practical matters.

Bud Momeyer, Maxine's husband, who has been a mail carrier for twenty-eight years. He provides a childish light-heartedness at the somber celebration. His playfulness and quirky demeanor contrast with the more conventional aspects of the family.

— *Paul Hansom*

THE CEREMONY OF INNOCENCE

Author: Ronald Ribman (1932-   )
First published: 1978
Genre: Drama

Locale: A monastery on the isle of Wight and a castle in England
Time: Winter, 1012, to Christmas, 1013
Plot: Historical

King Ethelred, the poignantly idealistic, moralistic king of England. Against the wishes of many of his advisers and all of his family, he has signed a truce with the Danes. The plot turns around his dogged but hopeless attempts to stave off the unraveling of the fragile peace. He is a visionary who uses the peace to try to educate the peasants and equip a ship for a voyage of discovery. His ethical sense is rooted in guilt: The one man he idolized in his youth, his pious stepbrother who was ruling the country, was killed by his mother so that Ethelred could take the throne. Perhaps for this reason, he is almost truculent in his refusal to compromise on ethical questions. As the play proceeds, he becomes more and more isolated from his pragmatic advisers, until he is ready to forfeit his kingdom to maintain his purity.

Edmund, Ethelred's son. Edmund is intemperately concerned with his own and his country's honor. Going further than the king's other advisers, who only offer verbal objections to the truce, the headstrong Edmund physically disrupts the new status quo by destroying the possessions of the Danish king's daughter, Thulja, and later by murdering four Danish farmers residing in England. His hot temper and facility with insults cause his downfall when his taunting of the Danish ambassador is met with a dagger.

Alfreda, Ethelred's aged mother. Sharp-tongued, treacherous, and actively evil, she upbraids her son for fearing violence, telling him that keeping a war stirring distracts the populace. She constantly reminds him that his own position was achieved through murder, and it is her murder of Thulja that finally sunders the peace.

Emma, Ethelred's wife, the daughter of the duke of Normandy. She is almost simpleminded in her virulent hatred of the Danes. Her detestation is based on fear and suspicion, and she has little with which to counter the arguments of her husband except a blind loyalty to the brutal practices of her father. She becomes increasingly estranged from her neglectful spouse as he devotes all of his time to his political preoccupations.

Thulja, the fifteen-year-old daughter of King Sweyn of Denmark. She has been left as a hostage at the English court to ensure that the Danes abide by the peace treaty. She is a babe in the woods, uncomprehending of the intrigues and depressed by the rebuffs she suffers from the "war" party, who consider her an irritating symbol of a dishonorable peace. Her purity and ability to extend uncalculating sympathy make her the only person with whom Ethelred can share his dreams. Her murder in the English court precipitates the sundering of the truce.

The earl of Kent, the adviser closest to the king, who is able to see the value of Ethelred's dreams and argue for them pragmatically. Because he has a fourteen-year-old crippled daughter, he feels sympathy for Thulja. He is too practical to follow the king in his pacifism when he believes that it endangers the country.

The earl of Sussex, the main verbal antagonist of Kent. A blunt, angry leader who proclaims that the only worthy morality stems from the point of a sword. Although as bound by honor as Edmund, he is able to curb his feelings when he finds the majority against him.

The bishop of London, a temporizer who holds a middle place between Sussex and Kent. At first, he is committed to peace and economic reconstruction, but he begins to balk when the king tampers with church prerogatives.

King Sweyn, the leader of the Danes. Possessor of the superior army, he is willing to abide by the truce to better conditions for his many countrymen who have settled in England. Although he worries about leaving a daughter among the English, he is cunning enough to order her to spy out their forces during her residence.

Thorkill, a Danish emissary sent to England to learn the facts about the murder of four Danish farmers. Although willing to be mollified by a sufficiently searching inquiry, he is bewildered by the unmannerly behavior of Edmund. He is slow to anger but violent when provoked.

Abbot Oswald, the head of a monastery on the Isle of Wight where Ethelred has sought sanctuary from the mounting pressure to declare war. Isolated from the events of the world, he views the power conflicts surrounding the throne with detachment, coupled with an irritating lack of passion.

— *James Feast*

CÉSAR BIROTTEAU
(Histoire de la grandeur et de la décadence de César Birotteau)

Author: Honoré de Balzac (1799-1850)
First published: 1837
Genre: Novel

Locale: Paris, France
Time: Early nineteenth century
Plot: Naturalism

César Birotteau (say-ZAHR bee-rah-TOH), a self-made man who at the peak of his success mistook it for the beginning, and whose downfall resulted from his lack of judgment of the jackals in the business world. A peasant in appearance and manners, of straightforward honesty and perseverance, César Birotteau is a man in love with his own wife, devoted to his lovely daughter, loyal to his good friends, and gentle even to those who despise and misuse him. His noble character is revealed through adversity, and he dies following his exoneration from the debts of his bankruptcy. As a manufacturer of perfume and as a manager of a business, he is canny, even ingenious, but in dealing with the world of finance he is an infant sustained finally by his brave wife and daughter.

Constance Birotteau, his beautiful and devoted wife, who is not only wiser than her husband but more resourceful as well. Endowed with a fine physique and constitution, Mme. Birotteau manages all of the business for the family and even has a presentiment concerning their over-extended credit. As kind and honest as her husband but with more will power and intelligence, she never succumbs to pride of possession or the desire for prestige in social life. She never fails to back her bungling husband, however, and she works and saves toward this end. In spite of attempts on her honor, she is a heroine of dimensions only hinted at in her husband.

Césarine (say-zah-REEN), their beautiful daughter, who combines in her person all the good traits of her parents. Robbed of her dowry by an ironic blow of fortune, she refuses to be humbled. Instead, she uses adversity as a means to attain her deepest ambitions: the love of a devoted and fine young man, a home free from social pretense, and an independence from all that a large dowry implies of social position and prestige. Her touching sacrifices for her parents, her loving attention to their needs and wishes, and her sincerity in all catastrophes make her a strange contrast to most of Balzac's wealthy daughters, who typically repay devotion with ingratitude.

Anselm Popinot (poh-pee-NOH), Birotteau's son-in-law, a young peasant with a club foot who in a few years elevates himself from the humble position of apprentice to the rank of perfumer by honesty, hard work, imagination, and daring. He has a remarkable character and evenness of disposition that will not allow him to make sentimental errors of such proportions as would have made the Birotteau fortunes irretrievable. At the risk of seeming ungrateful, he refuses to add his small profits to the sinking capital of his benefactor. Instead, he builds a new business into an enterprise that saves both family fortune and honor, and he becomes the husband of Césarine.

Ferdinand du Tillet (dew tee-YAY), a reprobate who as apprentice to César Birotteau makes advances to Constance and steals three thousand francs from the firm. Not content to repay good with evil, he makes it his life's work to ruin the man who so generously forgives him his offenses. A real villain, du Tillet uses his experience in knavery, learned at Birotteau's expense, to seduce and abduct, and he parlays his sins into a fortune and a secure position in corrupt society.

M. Pillerault (pee-yuh-ROH), an ironmonger, the uncle and benefactor of Constance as well as the firm friend and financial adviser of Birotteau. A noble and self-effacing gentleman of the old order, the elderly tradesman remains true to his nephew and other friends who have been ruined by a thieving notary. Admirable in his business principles, he firmly sustains his family.

Roguin (roh-GAN), a dishonest notary, du Tillet's tool in his scheme to ruin César Birotteau. Persuaded to invest in a land-speculation venture, Birotteau turns three hundred thousand francs over to Roguin, but he gets no receipt for his money.

Claparon (klah-pah-ROHN), a dummy banker also involved in du Tillet's plot.

La Belle Hollandaise (ah-lawn-DAYZ), a courtesan loved by Roguin.

Vauquelin (va-kuh-LAN), a chemist who aids Birotteau in the expansion of his business in the days of his prosperity.

THE CHAIN OF CHANCE
(Katar)

Author: Stanisław Lem (1921-   )
First published: 1976
Genre: Novel

Locale: Naples and Rome, Italy; and Paris, France
Time: Late 1970's
Plot: Science fiction

John, the narrator, a laconic fifty-year-old American private detective of French Canadian origin who has been hired to investigate the death of an American named Adams. An unreflective man of action, almost a machine, he seldom becomes nervous or frightened. As an astronaut, he learned how to wait patiently for those moments when quick and decisive action was required, yet he can make quite impulsive decisions, as when he enlisted in the commandos at the age of eighteen and participated in the invasion of Normandy as a glider infantryman. Dismissed from the Mars program because of allergies to grass and dust, he has been hired to investigate the death of a fellow American who was one of twelve victims of the same mysterious cause of death in Naples.

Annabella, a young French girl whom John heroically saves from being killed by a Japanese terrorist's bomb in the Rome airport. Although newspaper accounts of this event describe her as a teenager, she is in fact younger than that. At first, she is apprehensive about John, fearing that he may be part of the terrorist's plot, but she becomes friendly with her protector when he takes her back to her parents.

Dr. Philippe Barth, a distinguished French computer scientist who serves as a consultant to the Sûreté. Because he has been programming a computer to solve problems in which the amount of data exceeds the storage capacity of human memory, John consults him as a last resort to help him unravel the case. Barth introduces John to a number of specialists whose conflicting advice, when taken together, enables him to understand the cause of Adams' death.

Lapidus (LAH-pee-dew), a French pharmacologist. His full-length beard and rather rough appearance make him look as though he has just returned from being marooned on an uninhabited island. He explains to John the scientific reasons for his belief that Adams and the others were the victims of gradual poisoning.

Saussure (soh-SEWR), a French specialist in pure mathematics. Lean and dark, he wears a gold pince-nez that gives him an old-fashioned appearance. Intellectually, he is rather a drifter, and he has recently resigned from a project attempting to calculate the probability of existence of extraterrestrial civilizations. He gives John insight into the "chain of chance" that caused the victims' deaths by showing that they were the result of a random causality.

Mayer, a German statistician. A burly man with curly blond hair, he resembles the cartoon Germans of World War I French propaganda. Because he is an applied mathematician, he serves as a foil to the pure, theoretical mathematics of Saussure.

Inspector Pingaud (pan-GOH), an elderly officer in the Sûreté. He tells John and Barth of a previous case of poisoning by accidental combinations of random elements, leading them to a successful solution of the Adams case.

— *Robert L. Berner*

A CHAIN OF VOICES

Author: André Brink (1935-   )
First published: 1982
Genre: Novel

Locale: Near Cape Town, South Africa
Time: The 1780's-1826
Plot: Historical

Piet van der Merwe (peet fahn derh MEHR-vah), an Afrikaaner farmer and patriarch. Once a strong and forceful man, the aged Piet has become helpless from a stroke. Because the novel is composed solely of monologues by the characters, Piet himself records his part in the events that surround the slave uprising, traces the course of his life to the uprising and his stroke, and reveals his relationships with the other characters. He emerges as a God-fearing, British-hating, racist, self-righteous, and often cruel man who unintentionally destroys his family as he seeks to carry out what he believes to be the will of God. In some ways, he is a stereotypical Afrikaaner of the era.

Alida van der Merwe (ah-LEE-dah), Piet's wife. Aging and worn from her hard life as a farmer's wife on the South African veld, Alida recounts the past years with bitterness: her youth as a beautiful young woman in Cape Town, her stormy marriage, the years of childbirth and hard work, and the disappointments and disillusionment. She has attained a sort of peace, having become reconciled to the destructive force unleashed by her husband and even to her own death, for which she longs.

Ma Rose, an elderly native woman. She is closely connected to the van der Merwe family as servant, mistress to Piet, and nurse to his children. Through her monologues, Ma Rose emerges as the noblest of the characters, endowed with patience, resolve, fairness, and understanding. As she speaks, she enlarges her own character to embrace the long-suffering black race by drawing parallels between the present struggle for freedom with the trials recorded in ancient tribal myths. Of Ma Rose, one of the characters says that her book "was the whole world."

Barend van der Merwe (BEHR-ihnt), Piet's eldest son, a farmer. Like his father, whom he longs to please, Barend develops into a cruel, harsh man who mistreats his wife and slaves. During the slave uprising, he proves himself a coward.

Nicolaas van der Merwe (NIH-koh-lahz), Piet's youngest son, a farmer. Weaker and more sensitive than his father and older brother, Nicolaas destroys himself through his longing to gain their approval. He is his mother's favorite child, but Piet disrupts their relationship.

Galant (gah-LAHNT), a slave. Galant is a handsome and powerfully built black man who was reared with Piet's sons and becomes Nicolaas' slave. Their relationship as slave and master is a subtle, complex one that finally leads to Nicolaas' murder by Galant.

Hester van der Merwe, Barend's wife. An attractive young woman, she finds her marriage to Barend dismal, especially the sexual violence that she is forced to endure. While pretending to be submissive, she nourishes an inner strength that leads her to freedom, in part through her sexual encounter with Galant, then through the courage she shows during the slave rebellion. Along with Ma Rose, Hester evolves into one of the novel's rare sympathetic characters.

Cecilia van der Merwe, Nicolaas' wife. Plain and drab in appearance, she has developed a harsh and cold air to endure not only the oppression that is the lot of Afrikaaner women but also the indifference of a husband who despises her.

Pamela, a slave woman and Galant's chosen wife. She is forced to become Nicolaas' mistress and has a son by him.

Lydia, a simple, childlike slave woman, another of Nicolaas' mistresses.

— *Robert L. Ross*

THE CHAINBEARER

Author: James Fenimore Cooper (1789-1851)
First published: 1845
Genre: Novel

Locale: Upstate New York
Time: c. 1785
Plot: Historical

Mordaunt Littlepage, a young landowner, the narrator of *The Chainbearer*. On a visit to his wilderness tract, Ravensnest, he has a run-in with lawless squatters, who imprison him. He is finally rescued by a posse after a battle with his captors. He marries Chainbearer's niece, Dus Malbone.

Andries Coejemans, also known as **Chainbearer**, an old woodsman and surveyor, Mordaunt Littlepage's devoted friend from Revolutionary War days, when they were both captains. In his attempt to rescue Mordaunt from the squatter outlaws, he is imprisoned with his friend and mortally wounded by his captors. Feeling deeply indebted to Chainbearer for their happiness, the Littlepage family erects a monument in his honor and reveres his memory all of their lives.

Ursula Malbone, nicknamed **Dus**, Chainbearer's orphaned niece, who marries Mordaunt.

Jaap, Mordaunt's loyal black servant.

Aaron Timberman, nicknamed **Thousandacres**, a squatter and illegal operator of a sawmill on Mordaunt's land. He

imprisons Mordaunt and is later slain by the rescuing posse.

Tobit and
Zephanaiah Timberman, Aaron's lawless sons.

Lowiny Timberman, Aaron's daughter. She tries to help the imprisoned Mordaunt and, after his marriage to Dus, becomes their maid.

Jason Newcome, the untrustworthy squire at Ravensnest village.

Frank Malbone, Dus' half brother and Mordaunt's agent at Ravensnest.

Susquesus, nicknamed **Trackless**, an Indian hunter, loyal friend of Mordaunt and Chainbearer.

Cornelius Littlepage and
Anneke Littlepage, Mordaunt's parents.

Kate Littlepage, Mordaunt's sister.

Tom Bayard, betrothed to Kate.

Priscilla Bayard, Tom's sister.

Dirck Follock, Cornelius Littlepage's friend.

THE CHAIRS
(Les Chaises)

Author: Eugène Ionesco (1912-1994)
First published: 1954
Genre: Drama

Locale: An island
Time: Indeterminate future
Plot: Absurdist

Old Man, a "general factotum" aged ninety-five. He is an employee, or assistant, who serves in a wide range of capacities. He, like all the characters in this play, both visible and invisible, is made up of contrasts and contradictions; he is both man and child. His speech is composed of words and logical sentences as well as some nonsense words and syllables and illogical sentences. Although he is a character of flesh and blood, he sometimes appears to be more illusionary than the invisible characters. While awaiting the arrival of guests, he and his wife reminisce about earlier times and play games of

make believe; for example, he sits on his wife's lap like a little child and calls for his mother. Although he says he is bored with it all, he continues to play the same games and tell the same story night after night. He invites a large crowd of both great and ordinary people to hear his great message that will benefit humanity. Believing himself to be inadequate to communicate this message to others, he has hired a professional orator to deliver it. He greets invisible guests as they arrive and talks with these guests while awaiting the Orator. When the Orator finally arrives, the Old Man gives him a wordy ineffectual introduction. Saying that his life is now fulfilled, the Old Man jumps out of the tower window to his death.

Old Woman, the Old Man's ninety-four-year-old wife and "helpmeet." Like the Old Man, she is made up of contrasts and contradictions. She is both mother and wife to the Old Man. At times, she seems stronger and more mature than her husband, telling him that he could have been so much more than what he is if he had had more power in life. At other times, she seems only her husband's shadow as she literally echoes the words that he says. She has heard the same bedtime story for seventy-five years but still asks the Old Man to tell it again. It fascinates her because it is his life, and she purposely makes her mind new, "a clean slate," for him every evening. She helps the Old Man greet their invisible guests and brings chairs for them. She also serves as usher and seller of Eskimo pies and programs. She reveals a hidden personality when she reacts like an old prostitute to one of their guests. She claims that she and the Old Man have a son, but the Old Man says they have no children. Like the Old Man, she is extremely honored that the emperor has come to their house to hear the Orator present her husband's message. She echoes her husband's words and actions about their dying but states that at least a street will be named for them. She jumps to her death from another window to die at the same moment as the Old Man and to be united with him in time and eternity.

The Orator, a deaf-mute between forty-five and fifty years old, dressed in the typical garb of a bohemian artist of the nineteenth century. He is built up by the Old Man as the greatest professional orator of all time, having documents to prove it. He is also called a friend of the Old Man. Although he is the third flesh-and-blood character, he is made to seem more like an invisible character than those who are invisible because he does not speak or react to the Old Man and Old Woman. He signs autographs in an automatic fashion and is impassive and generally immobile until after the double suicide, when he tries in vain to communicate with the invisible audience.

Guests, a cross section of humanity, including the emperor. The guests have come to hear the Old Man's message. All of them are invisible to the audience and are indicated by empty chairs placed on stage for them to occupy and by the speech and gestures of the Old Man and the Old Woman.

— *Bettye Choate Kash*

CHAKA

Author: Thomas Mofolo (1875?-1948)
First published: 1925
Genre: Novel

Locale: Zululand, Africa
Time: Early nineteenth century
Plot: Historical realism

Chaka (SHAH-kah), the most powerful of all Zulu warriors and kings. At first, Chaka is depicted as an undeserving victim in every respect. Because of circumstances of birth, he cannot peacefully ascend to his father's kingship. Moreover, he and his mother, Nandi, are driven from his father's house by the other wives. Chaka is described as having the most painful of childhoods because of this banishment. Even so, he acts the part of the hero-warrior, destroying a lion, hyena, and madman, all enemies of the tribe. Midway through his life, however, Chaka transforms himself from protagonist to antagonist. He sells his being to the control of the witch doctor Isanusi, after which his own moral destruction is assured. Isanusi gives him everything as promised, but the price Chaka must pay is an unquenchable thirst for blood. Chaka conquers all, but to do so he must make medicine from the blood of those whom he loves. He murders, in turn, his son, wife, and mother. Chaka never loses a battle and incessantly conquers more lands and peoples, yet he never attains any satisfaction or happiness in life. He dies alone and to everyone's manifest relief.

Senzangakhona (sayn-zahn-gah-KOH-nah), Chaka's father. King Senzangakhona violates the moral code of his tribe by impregnating Nandi before they are married. The long-awaited son, Chaka, is therefore doomed from the outset. Unable to control the tongues of his wives who would tell that Nandi was pregnant at the time of the secret marriage, Senzangakhona falls to their demands, first banishing Nandi and Chaka, then later ordering them killed.

Nandi (NAHN-dee), Chaka's mother. Nandi loves Chaka unquestionably and uncontrollably. She acts in his behalf on all counts, yet she, too, is murdered by him in his thirst for blood and battle.

Noliwa (noh-LEE-wah), the daughter of Dingiswayo and favorite wife of Chaka. Beautiful, faithful, and faultless, Noliwa never violates any of Chaka's wishes or orders. She, too, is murdered by him when the witch doctor orders her death at the hands of Chaka.

Isanusi (ee-sah-NEW-see), who is known by the sundry titles of "doctor," "sorcerer," and "witch-doctor." Isanusi is evil, and he inflicts evil on all of African humanity by tempting Chaka to become his primary instrument. Isanusi, seemingly, is given all power of life and death in this world. He knows and controls all human activity—if not immediately, at least eventually. He delivers on his promise to give Chaka everything, but his price is total obedience. Chaka keeps his part of the bargain.

Ndlebe (ihn-DLAY-bay) and
Malunga (mah-LEWN-gah), two agents of Isanusi. After Chaka and Isanusi make their initial contract, Ndlebe and Malunga are sent to Chaka to assist him in war and politics. They have supernatural powers they use toward that end.

Dingiswayo (deen-gee-SWAY-oh), a neighboring king who gives refuge to Nandi and Chaka when they are banished by Senzangakhona. Dingiswayo, a good man, is father to Noliwa. Chaka succeeds to the kingship at Dingiswayo's death.

Zwide (ZWEE-day), another neighboring king and enemy to Dingiswayo and Chaka. Zwide is killed in battle by Chaka after the death of Dingiswayo. Chaka becomes king of Zwide's domain.

Nongogo (nohn-GOH-goh), a faithful servant to Chaka. Nongogo is murdered by Chaka on the whim of a moment.

— *Carl Singleton*

316 / *The Chaneysville Incident*

THE CHANEYSVILLE INCIDENT

Author: David Bradley (1950-   )
First published: 1981
Genre: Novel

Locale: Pennsylvania
Time: Late 1970's, 1930-1965, and precolonial days to the twentieth century
Plot: Psychological realism

John Washington, a history professor and scholar. A cynical young black man of about thirty, John returns to his hometown to comfort a dying friend, Jack Crawley, and ends up reevaluating his own life when he finally understands the circumstances surrounding the deaths of his father, Moses Washington, and his great-grandfather, C. K. Washington. The beginning of this insight occurs when, after Crawley's funeral, John is presented with the folio bequeathed to him earlier, in his father's will. The contents of the folio, along with other clues left by Moses, guide John through a historical puzzle and eventually help him find peace and meaning in his own life.

Moses Washington, John's father, a bootlegger with enough information to blackmail all the rich white townspeople, who spurn the impoverished black community banished to the Hill. A powerful man within the district, he is feared by both blacks and whites, even though he keeps to himself, spending most of his time tramping through the Pennsylvania hills and checking on the status of his numerous stills. His suicide, mistaken as a murder, is disguised as a hunting accident to prevent an investigation from accidentally uncovering the folio, believed to contain dangerous evidence incriminating the town officials. Moses, like his son, John, is preoccupied with history and struggles to learn the truth about his ancestors. He possesses his grandfather's diary, but the book ends abruptly, and he becomes obsessed with learning what happened to C. K. Eventually, he learns the truth, and the reality brings about his suicide when John is nine years old.

Brobdingnag C. K. Washington, John's great-grandfather, a runaway slave. A self-educated man, he is literally branded

C. K. by his master as a punishment. He uses his knowledge to forge himself a pass and manages to escape. In Pennsylvania, he falls in love with a free black woman, Harriette Brewer, who shares his dream of helping other slaves become free. On her first attempt, though, she is caught and sold into slavery. C. K. makes numerous trips to the South trying to find her and becomes infamous for the number of slaves he helps, but he is unable to locate her. Eventually, he marries another woman, who gives birth to Lamen, Moses' father. C. K. is finally caught while helping twelve runaways. Rather than return to slavery, the thirteen people kill themselves, believing that they will reach eternal freedom through death. It is at C. K.'s grave that Moses kills himself.

Peter John (Old Jack) Crawley, "the old man with the stories." Jack, one of Moses Washington's only close friends, becomes a surrogate father to John after Moses' death. He teaches John how to coexist with nature, inspires in him a predilection for hot toddies, and keeps alive memories of Moses for the boy. Because of personal experiences with the Ku Klux Klan, he also cultivates within John a deep suspicion of white people. That distrust causes the young academic to lead a lonely and cold life.

Judith Powell, a psychiatrist. Lovely and graceful like a ballerina, she is emotional, persistent, and stubborn. Although she is John's girlfriend, he has a difficult time trusting her because she is white. She follows him to his hometown and badgers him until he confides in her his struggle to understand C. K., Moses, and himself.

— Coleen Maddy

A CHANGE OF HEART
(La Modification)

Author: Michel Butor (1926-   )
First published: 1957
Genre: Novel

Locale: A train traveling between Paris and Rome
Time: 1955 or 1956
Plot: Psychological realism

Léon Delmont (lay-AHN dehl-MOHN), the director of the Paris office of the Scabelli typewriter company. He is successful and well off, but at forty-five years of age, his hair is getting thin and gray. He is a smoker and wears tan shoes and a luminous watch with a purple leather watchband. He is intellectual and anticlerical (he reads *Letters of Julian the Apostate* on the train) and has strong views about what is good and bad art. He is concerned about his family's material welfare, but his relationship with his wife has gone sour, and he yearns for a new life on a new footing—in Paris, but with his Italian mistress, Cécile. He is on a train to Rome to tell Cécile that he has found her a job in Paris and is leaving his wife for her. During the train journey, however, he has dreams, nightmares, and reminiscences. Shortly after noticing a sign saying

"It is dangerous to lean out," he has a dream in which, for the first time, he has a negative image of Cécile, who wears a look of mistrust similar to that so often worn by his wife, Henriette. This thought creates his first doubts and sets in motion his eventual change of heart. He realizes that Cécile, once in Paris, would be different, more like Henriette. The similarity had become apparent during a brief trip to Paris, when she had seemed to share Henriette's contempt for him. If she comes to Paris, he realizes, he will lose her. He decides against following through on his plan.

Henriette Delmont, his wife and the mother of their four children. Her hair, like his, is no longer black. She despises him for letting his professional contacts degrade him, and he perceives her as contemptuous, critical, and petty. Almost three years earlier, she insisted on going with him to Rome, but it was winter and the trip was a failure, possibly making him more open to the affair with Cécile that developed subsequently. She has become suspicious and resentful.

Madeleine Delmont, their eldest child, age seventeen.

Henri Delmont and

Thomas Delmont, their sons, about twelve years old. They are rascals, distrustful of him and aware that their parents' relationship has deteriorated.

Jacqueline Delmont, their youngest child.

Cécile Darcella (say-SEEL darh-seh-LAH), Léon's mistress, a secretary to an attaché at the French Embassy in Rome. She has jet-black hair and wonderful skin with a smooth, silken glow. She shares Léon's anticlericalism and his love for art. To him, she seems like youth preserved; she finds him too bourgeois, anxious, and fettered. She went with him to Paris once, but the trip was a failure: She complained continually of how little she saw him.

Alexandre Marnal (a-lehk-SAHNDR mahr-NAHL), an employee of Léon.

Jean Durieu (dyuh-REEYOO), the director of the Durieu Travel Agency, who has promised a job for Cécile in Paris.

The Intellectual, possibly a law professor. He is tallish, pale, and not over forty. He has gray hair and nails that are bitten and tobacco-stained, and he wears thick-lensed glasses and a wedding ring. His forehead is prematurely baldish, with three deep furrows. He looks timid. He may be going to give a lecture at Dijon. He carries a dark red, ink-stained briefcase.

The Young Marrieds, probably honeymooners. They are perhaps in their twenties. He is fair and she is darker, gracious, and considerate, even apologetic. They eat at the first sitting, as Léon does. They carry large, twin suitcases made of fine pale leather. On their way to Syracuse, they embody the theme of marriage that preoccupies Léon.

The Priest, a man of about thirty or thirty-five, already plumpish, with nicotine-stained fingers, though he is otherwise meticulously clean. He is calm but vigorous, even impulsive. He looks bored, discontented, tense, and dissatisfied. He may be contemplating abandoning his present life, as Léon is. He is associated with the sign "It is dangerous to lean out."

The Englishman, a short, very clean man with a rosy, even florid complexion and small, greedy, fishlike eyes. He may be slightly older than Léon, because he is even more bald. He wears a black raincoat and a derby hat. He is possibly the agent for a London wine merchant.

The Traveling Salesman, a man with a coarse profile and huge hands. He appears to be very strong and wears a wedding ring. His suitcase is made of cheap, reddish-brown, imitation leather.

The Italian, a man of about forty-five who wears a wedding ring, a cobalt-blue scarf, and pointed black-and-white shoes splashed with mud. He carries a traveling bag and is perhaps a salesman representing French products in Italy, the reverse of Léon, for whom he represents an alter ego.

The Worried Little Woman, who has a lined face and is wearing a hat trimmed with a net and big hatpins. She is accompanied by a ten-year-old boy who reminds Léon of his son Thomas when younger.

— *Patrick Brady*

A CHANGE OF SKIN
(Cambio de piel)

Author: Carlos Fuentes (1928-   )
First published: 1967
Genre: Novel

Locale: Mexico City, Xochicalco, and Cholula, Mexico
Time: April 11, 1965
Plot: Experimental

Javier (hah-VYEHR), a middle-aged Mexican harboring aspirations of being a writer. He takes a drive with his American-born wife, Elizabeth; a friend, Franz; and Franz's lover, Isabel, a young Mexican woman. Javier, who met Elizabeth when he was a student in New York City, is at once in love with and bored by her. Because of his ambivalence, he is taken in by the charms of Isabel, though in his imagination he sees her as a vacuous version of his wife. In this surrealistic novel, Javier may or may not have led Elizabeth and Franz to a terrible death inside an Aztec pyramid and may or may not have attempted to strangle Elizabeth and put Franz's body in his car trunk.

Elizabeth, the American-born wife of Javier. Elizabeth, growing restless, finds life with Javier increasingly unfulfilling, sensing as she does that Javier finds her too old for him. She wishes not only that Javier was more attuned to her needs but also that he would become a successful writer rather than an aimless, unproven one.

Franz, a young Czechoslovakian-born friend of Javier who becomes emotionally and sexually involved with Elizabeth while carrying on an affair with lovely Isabel. He incurs Javier's envy because of his youthful energy, wit, and good looks. That envy may have led Javier to murder him. In any event, Franz, at the very least, creates problems for Javier, and these problems create hostility.

Isabel (EE-sah-behl), the youngest and most naïve of the four principal characters. She lacks Elizabeth's worldliness, mental powers, and acerbic wit, but her sexual intensity draws Javier's attentions away from Elizabeth. Whether in fact or only in his imagination, Javier wins Isabel's affections, only to become disgusted by her lack of depth and maturity. For the most part, Isabel is a pawn caught up in the unhappiness of Javier, Elizabeth, and Franz.

Freddy Lambert, the all-knowing and all-seeing, yet thoroughly mysterious, narrator of the story. Lambert not only can overhear dialogue but also can peer deep into characters' minds, capturing their thoughts, dreams, and fantasies.

— *John D. Raymer*

THE CHANGELING

Authors: Thomas Middleton (1580-1627) and William Rowley (1585?-1642?)
First published: 1653
Genre: Drama

Locale: Alicante, a seaport on the eastern coast of Spain
Time: Early seventeenth century
Plot: Tragedy

Beatrice-Joanna (beh-ah-TREES-hoh-AHN-yah), the beautiful daughter of Vermandero, a wealthy government official. Her sudden infatuation for Alsemero, a handsome Spaniard, precipitates her rapid moral degeneration, which culminates in the grotesque irony of her wedding night: She spends it with De Flores, a man whom she loathes, while her servant enjoys the husband for whom she entered on her career of deceit and murder. She proceeds boldly in her villainy and professes love she does not feel to procure De Flores' help in the murder of her fiancé, Alonzo. She is so completely unaware of the implications of what she is doing that she is almost stunned when De Flores demands the fruits of this feigned love as his payment. Dying of the wounds he has inflicted on her, she wonders at the evil influence this strange lover has exerted over her, drawing her into his power in spite of her intense loathing of him.

De Flores (FLOH-rehs), her strange partner in crime, Vermandero's servant. His life revolves around a single obsession, his passion for this young woman who shows him nothing but scorn and loathing. Although he is not convinced of the sincerity of Beatrice-Joanna's blandishments, he sees in her request for help the means to satisfy his desire. Her wishes are, for him, sufficient justification for all of his crimes, and he dies defying the hell into which he has brought himself, satisfied by the few moments when he possessed her.

Vermandero (vehr-mahn-DEH-roh), Beatrice-Joanna's father, the governor of the castle of Alicante. Although he seeks the best possible marriage for his daughter, he sternly expects her to follow his wishes. Struck by the full horror of the crimes of his daughter and De Flores, he sees himself and his companions circumscribed within the hell the guilty pair have created.

Alsemero (ahls-MEH-roh), a Spanish nobleman who falls in love with Beatrice-Joanna at first sight, wins her father's favor, and quickly weds her after Alonzo's strange disappearance. He dabbles in magic and produces a liquid to test the virtue of his betrothed, for he is determined not to marry her unless she can be proved chaste. He, too, is appalled by his wife's villainy and sees only justice in her death. His sympathy is reserved for his father-in-law, to whom he offers himself as a son to replace the lost daughter.

Alonzo de Piracquo (pee-RAHK-kwoh), Beatrice-Joanna's husband, a trusting man who is insensitive to his bride's lack of feeling for him. He goes blindly to his death, completely unaware of De Flores' villainous intentions.

Tomaso (toh-MAH-soh), Alonzo's brother, who perceives at a glance that Beatrice-Joanna is indifferent to Alonzo and warns him of the danger of a loveless marriage. Certain that his brother was murdered, he presses the investigation of Alonzo's death. His instinctive impressions of individuals are invariably accurate. He is overwhelmed with a sense of evil and corruption when he meets De Flores.

Jasperino (hahs-peh-REE-noh), Alsemero's servant, sensitive to his master's moods and watchful over his affairs. It is he who discovers the bizarre liaison between De Flores and Beatrice-Joanna and brings about their deaths.

Diaphanta (dee-ah-FAHN-tah), Beatrice-Joanna's waiting woman, who is virtuous in spite of her witty, worldly-wise conversation. Ignorant of the fate that De Flores has in store for her, she agrees to substitute for her mistress on her wedding night.

Alibius (ah-LEE-bee-ews), a jealous old doctor who keeps his lovely young wife confined at home with his patients, a crew of fools and madmen.

Lollio (LOH-yee-oh), his servant, who is responsible for keeping order among the inmates of the house, watching his mistress as well as the doctor's patients. His sharp eyes quickly see through the disguises of Antonio and Franciscus, but he disregards his master's orders to seek money from the "changeling" and the madman and to try to win a share of his mistress' favors.

Isabella (ees-ah-BEH-yah), Alibius' young wife. She chafes under her virtual imprisonment and welcomes Antonio's profession of love as a happy diversion.

Antonio and

Franciscus, Vermandero's men, who disguise themselves as fool and madman to gain access to Isabella.

Pedro, Antonio's friend, who takes him to Alibius, pretending to be his cousin.

CHANGING PLACES: A Tale of Two Campuses

Author: David Lodge (1935-   )
First published: 1975
Genre: Novel

Locale: Esseph and Rummidge, in England, and Euphoria, in the United States
Time: 1969
Plot: Satire

Philip Swallow, a forty-year-old lecturer in English at the University of Rummidge, a Redbrick college in the English Midlands. At the start of the novel, he lacks confidence, is eager to please, and is very suggestible. Professionally, he lacks ambition and is relatively unknown in scholarly circles, with few publications; however, he is a superlative examiner of undergraduates. A faculty exchange takes him to the campus of the University of Euphoria in the United States and Euphoria's Morris Zapp to Rummidge. Swallow finds his sexual drives rekindled as he has an affair with Melanie Byrd (unknown to him, Morris Zapp's daughter by his first marriage) and with Zapp's estranged wife, Désirée. He also becomes caught up in student protests on the American campus. He is revitalized and acquires self-confidence.

Morris Zapp, a tenured full professor at the University of Euphoria in the United States. He is also forty years old. He published five books (four on Jane Austen) before the age of thirty. His enthusiasm for research was largely a means to an end, and when he became tenured, his enthusiasm for scholarship waned. He is immensely self-confident and assertive, legendary for his sarcasm and intimidating to both students and colleagues. The faculty exchange takes him to a setting where his academic reputation does not count, his colleagues initially ignore him, and students are not impressed by him. His loneliness leads him to attach himself to and then have an affair with Hilary Swallow, Philip's wife. He comes to the fore when his familiarity with student unrest and the politics of academe enable him to solve Rummidge's first problems of student protest. In the end, he is reconciled with Désirée and has become friends with the Swallows.

Désirée Zapp, his wife. At the start of the novel, she feels overwhelmed by Morris' strong personality and wants a divorce but agrees to defer action if he moves out of the house. Freed of his presence when he accepts the faculty exchange, she becomes involved in the early women's liberation movement. She eventually invites Philip Swallow to live with her when the home he is renting is damaged by a hill slide. She and Philip have an affair. Désirée acquires confidence and self-esteem by the conclusion of the novel.

Hilary Broome Swallow, Philip's wife. The two met when Hilary was an English student and Philip was doing postdoctoral work. They married and went to Euphoria on his fellowship. Returning to England, Hilary became a devoted wife and mother to their three children (Amanda, Robert, and Matthew). Their relationship has become very predictable and dull, though Hilary does not realize this. Shocked by Philip's infidelities in Euphoria, she becomes more assertive in her own household and enters into an affair with Zapp. She fully expects Philip to return to her and the children, and at the end of the novel there is hope that their relationship will be better.

Charles Boon, a graduate of Rummidge who is ostensibly pursuing a graduate degree at Euphoria. He is a popular student leader and talk show host in the American college community. He likes Swallow and assists his former tutor in finding acceptance by some of the dissident elements at Euphoria.

Melanie Byrd, Morris Zapp's daughter from his first marriage. She is young, attractive, and part of the youth culture surrounding the American campus community. Swallow rents an apartment in her building and has an affair with her, not knowing her relationship to Zapp. His infatuation helps to open him to new views and feelings.

— Francis J. Bremer

THE CHANGING ROOM

Author: David Storey (1933-   )
First published: 1972
Genre: Drama

Locale: Northern England
Time: The 1960's
Plot: Representational

Harry Riley, a janitor working in the dressing room (changing room) of a professional rugby team in northern England. Of all twenty-two characters in the play, Harry is the only one who seems to share no joy or comradeship in the work performed by the team. He works, he says, only for the team owner, Sir Frederick Thornton, and in twenty years he has never witnessed a rugby game at the stadium. Nevertheless, Harry is the focal point of the play. He asserts that modern living has softened team players, and he maintains that people living with the innovations of "progress" are diminished because they have distanced themselves from hard physical work, which is necessary for a sustaining, substantive life. Harry is a split character, on one hand often superstitious and ill-informed, but on the other able to accurately diagnose a change in team players. Harry is the first character on stage and the last to exit. His regular sweeping motion as he cleans the floor throughout the play is symbolic of the physical work that Harry believes is important.

Ken Walsh, a team forward who earns a measure of respect from other team players and supporters because of his levity. A laborer by profession, Walsh enjoys the comradeship of playing the game and is a main figure in the interaction between characters that makes up the advancement of the play.

Clifford Owens, the team captain, who has a managerial and motivational function on the team. Owens is well liked by his teammates and by the club owner, but his professional approach to the team effort illustrates how team players are responding more and more to the sport as a job rather than an avocation. Owens' accomplishments as an athlete are not in question. His success illustrates that the significance of teamwork is changing among the players over time.

Sir Frederick Thornton, the club owner, whose presence reminds the players of the class difference between themselves and the wealthy. Thornton respects his players and enjoys a brief camaraderie with the team. Philosophically, he places himself between the conservative, backward-looking impulse represented by Harry Riley and the satisfied "progressive" response offered by his assistant, MacKendrick. Thornton's association with the team is more than financial, however, as demonstrated by his distress over a dream in which rugby is played only by robots. Thornton's decision to keep Kendal, even after his injury, indicates that the team owner cares for the well-being of his players.

MacKendrick, the team secretary and accountant. MacKendrick counters Harry's argument that progress diminishes humans by pointing out its substantial benefits, including better housing, modern conveniences, and higher employment. He believes that life is better and offers more than ever before. MacKendrick, like Thornton, is attracted to the team's spirit even though he administers rather than plays with the team.

Kendal (Kenny), an older player whose injury during the game dramatizes the players' very real physical risks. Kendal's injury, like the hard-won game, occurs offstage, emphasizing the interaction among team players and supporters rather than the game itself.

Trevor, a high school teacher who plays on the team. Trevor's presence demonstrates the team's changing composition over time. Players are no longer simply physical men who enjoy the companionship of playing the game, as they were twenty or fifty years ago; more often, they are white-collar professionals who play to supplement their lives emotionally as well as financially.

— Karen Dwyer

THE CHANT OF JIMMIE BLACKSMITH

Author: Thomas Keneally (1935-   )
First published: 1972
Genre: Novel

Locale: New South Wales, Australia
Time: c. 1900
Plot: Social realism

Jimmie Blacksmith, a half-white, half-aborigine man bent on achieving social status and material success through land ownership. He murders the families of two of his previous employers. Educated by a missionary, the twenty-two-year-old is perceptive and intelligent, but he is snobbish toward his aborigine kinfolk and frustrated by expectations of failure from his white employers. After being cheated out of wages on several jobs as a fence-builder and after witnessing and participating in the brutal treatment of an aborigine murder suspect while working as a police tracker, Jimmie explodes in a berserk rage of vengeance, killing the Newby women and children and, eventually, the Healy family. While eluding an extensive manhunt for several months, he discovers that he cannot claim the cultural identity of the Mungindi tribe. Captured, he converts to Christianity before he is hanged, as Australia, so obsessed with bringing him to justice, celebrates its independence.

Mort Blacksmith, Jimmie's half brother, a full-blooded aborigine. Flippant and prone to fits of laughter, the seventeen-year-old Mort embodies innocence and tribal loyalty. Having left his job as a horse-breaker for white farmers, he accompanies his uncle and cousin in a futile effort to convince Jimmie not to marry a white woman, if he is to be considered a Mungindi man. Drawn into Jimmie's violence, he kills a woman; later, during the pursuit of the brothers, he kills a man. Both acts apparently are in self-defense. Attempting to maintain tribal values of love and loyalty, Mort refuses to abandon Jimmie. He is shot to death while trying to save the life of their hostage, McCreadie.

Tabidgi (tah-BIHD-jee), or **Jackie Smolders**, Jimmie and Mort's maternal uncle, a traditional man of the Tullam section of the Mungindi tribe. With his gray beard falling out in tufts, Tabidgi appears ancient relative to his forty-two years. An alcoholic but nevertheless deeply reverent toward his tribe's mystical beliefs, he carries an initiation tooth to Jimmie to remind him of his obligation to marry within the aborigine kinship system. When Jimmie begins his murderous rampage, Tabidgi half-consciously participates out of terror; captured soon afterward, he is hanged along with Jimmie.

Peter Blacksmith, Jimmie's fourteen-year-old cousin who travels with Tabidgi to deliver Jimmie's initiation tooth. Kind and compassionate, he cares for Jimmie's wife, Gilda, after he has beaten her. Left behind after the murder of the Newbys, he is acquitted.

Gilda Howie Blacksmith, Jimmie's wife, a poor white eighteen-year-old girl from Sydney. Frail, sickly, and thin-hipped, she marries Jimmie when she discovers that she is pregnant, but her child was fathered by Mrs. Hayes's cook, a white communist. Jimmie, hoping to acquire status through the marriage, rejects her and the child. Although present at the Newby massacre, she is acquitted with Peter.

Wallace Hyberry, a butcher from Balmain, a Sydney suburb. Incorruptible and aloof from his duties as hangman, he prides himself on his technological expertise but is blind to the larger contexts of Jimmie's crimes. As grand master of his fraternal lodge, he is most concerned that the notoriety of Jimmie's violence and elusive flight will deprive him of royal honors when Australia becomes independent.

The Reverend Mr. A. J. Neville, Jimmie's Methodist teacher. Nurturing Jimmie's aspirations for material success and encouraging him to marry a white woman, the condescending and narrow-minded minister dismisses any validity in aboriginal culture and conveys consistent expectations of Jimmie's inferiority, beating him for truancy when Jimmie leaves the missionary briefly to undergo his tribal initiation ritual.

Senior Constable Farrell, a policeman who employs Jimmie as a tracker. With a love for boar hunting and brutal abuse of aborigines in his district, Farrell uses virility as a mask for his homosexuality. His vicious sodomy of an aboriginal inmate feeds Jimmie's guilt and self-hatred, annihilating any respect for the law that Jimmie might have had.

Mr. Healy and
Mrs. Healy, Irish Catholic farmers who employ Jimmie as a fence-builder. Having cheated Jimmie out of wages, refused him food or a ride to another town, and denied him a letter of reference, because he himself is illiterate, Mr. Healy precipitates the explosion of Jimmie's long-simmering rage. Mrs. Healy becomes a principal target of Jimmie's rage in that she is, for him, the symbol of success: a landowner's wife, the archetype of submission to her husband's power and status.

Petra Graf, a boarder at the Newbys and schoolmistress at nearby Wallah. The stout, aloof, and patronizing young woman is the model of rural propriety. Condescending to Gilda, she fosters the illusions of social status in the rural homestead.

Dowie Stead, Miss Graf's unwilling fiancé, a farmer from Gulargambone. He is secretly romantic and a patron of aboriginal prostitutes but outwardly practical. His brown hair, blue eyes, and passive face are a portrait of Nordic coldness. His relentless pursuit of Jimmie is not so much to avenge the murder of Petra as it is to vent his frustration at discovering that his father has been sharing his black mistress, Tessie.

The Newby family, a fifty-two-year-old farmer near Wallah, his robust and racist wife, and their six children. Given to mocking Jimmie's efforts to succeed and cheating him of wages, Mrs. Newby becomes Jimmie's first victim when she accuses him of lying about a sack of flour. Her two adolescent daughters are also killed with Petra and herself.

Mr. McCreadie, a schoolteacher who becomes Jimmie and Mort's hostage. Asthmatic and sick for much of the time that he is held captive, he is sensitive and empathetic to the frustration of the aborigines. Treated derisively by Jimmie, he leads them to the sacred site of a "rock womb" of the Manning River tribes. They discover that the site has been desecrated by a vacationing rugby team. Succeeding in convincing Jimmie that he must abandon Mort and himself in order to find self-respect, McCreadie is saved from dying of pneumonia by Mort's attempted surrender.

— *Michael Loudon*

CHARLES DEMAILLY
(Les Hommes de lettres)

Authors: Edmond de Goncourt (1822-1896) and Jules de Goncourt (1830-1870)
First published: 1860
Genre: Novel

Locale: Paris, France
Time: Mid-nineteenth century
Plot: Naturalism

Charles Demailly (shahrl deh-mah-YEE), a writer. Burdened with a loneliness and a super-sensitivity that make it difficult, if not impossible, for him to find satisfaction in real life, he falls in love with an ingenue, Marthe Mance, and endows her with the perfection of which he has always dreamed. When, by her shallowness, insincerity, and cruel treatment, she finally destroys his image of her, his creativity is also destroyed, and he sinks into apathy and, finally, into madness.

Marthe Mance (mahrt mahns), an actress and Charles Demailly's wife, who is endowed by her husband with qualities of perfection which, in reality, she has never possessed. Enchanted at first by her husband's play, in which she is the idealized heroine, she begins to show her shallowness and insincerity when the production is unfavorably criticized and she fears for her own success as its leading lady. Step by step, she then destroys Charles's image of her until she has destroyed the man himself.

Nachette (nah-SHEHT) and
Couturat (kyew-too-RAH) , writers for *Scandal*, a journal that thrives on gossip, superficial aesthetic criticism, and sensationalism.

Chavannes (shah-VAHN), Charles Demailly's boyhood friend, who encourages him in his efforts at serious writing.

Remonville (ruh-mohn-VEEL), a writer and Charles Demailly's friend.

Boisroger (bwah-roh-ZHAY), a poet who introduces Charles Demailly to a circle of serious artists.

CHARLES O'MALLEY, THE IRISH DRAGOON

Author: Charles James Lever (1806-1872)
First published: 1841; serial form, 1840-1841
Genre: Novel

Locale: Ireland and Continental Europe
Time: 1808-1812
Plot: Picaresque

Charles O'Malley, an Irish dragoon. He is a big man, an excellent shot and horseman. He goes to Dublin to study law but indulges in too many escapades. He then enters the army as an ensign, serving gallantly in the war against Napoleon in Spain. He returns to Ireland to look after his estates after the death of his uncle, but he returns to war when Napoleon escapes from Elba. He wins the hand of Lucy Dashwood by rescuing her father from execution by the French.

Lucy Dashwood, daughter of General Dashwood, an English girl. She marries Charles after he saves her father from execution.

General Dashwood, an Englishman. When he tries to buy estates in Ireland, he is challenged to a duel by Charles' Uncle Godfrey and Billy Considine. When the general is captured by the French and condemned to death, he is rescued by Charles.

Godfrey O'Malley, Charles's uncle, master of O'Malley Castle in Galway. He is a hard-drinking, hard-riding man who is good to his tenants and to his nephew.

Blake, a distant cousin of Godfrey who refuses to support him when he stands for Parliament. Charles first meets Lucy at Blake's home.

Billy Considine, Charles's good friend, who acts as his second in a duel.

Captain Hammersley, General Dashwood's aide and Charles's rival for the hand of Lucy.

St. Croix, a French officer befriended by Charles in Spain. Later, he helps Charles rescue General Dashwood from the French.

Donna Inez, a Spanish girl who becomes a friend of Charles after he rescues her.

Captain Powers, who prevents a duel between Charles and Hammersley. He marries Donna Inez.

Frank Webber, Charles' roommate at college in Dublin and the ringleader in their escapades.

Michael Free, Charles's faithful servant.

THE CHARTERHOUSE OF PARMA
(La Chartreuse de Parme)

Author: Stendhal (Marie-Henri Beyle, 1783-1842)
First published: 1839
Genre: Novel

Locale: Italy
Time: Early nineteenth century
Plot: Historical

Fabrizio del Dongo (fah-BREE-zeeoh), an Italian nobleman destined to become an archbishop in the family tradition. A romantic youth, devotedly attached to Napoleonic ideals, the sixteen-year-old adventurer abandons the security of wealth and position to engage in the Battle of Waterloo under an assumed name, with the papers and uniform of a deceased hussar, and in complete ignorance of the ways of war and the world. This episode leads him gradually into deceptions of a higher order, an education he does not want, and an ecclesiastical post for which he is unfitted. Gentle and considerate in private friendships and devoted to humanitarian principles, he nevertheless resorts to intrigue and even murder to attain his ends in the Italian court at Parma. Never really in love until the romantic hopelessness of an affair makes him act in an unorthodox way, Fabrizio gains and loses patronage and affection. He spends his declining years in quiet meditation in the Charterhouse of Parma, a monastery.

Clelia Conti (KLEHL-lee-ah KOHN-tee), the beautiful daughter of a traitor count. As a girl, Clelia sets her heart on the handsome and chivalrous young soldier lately home from France. Although she takes a vow never to set eyes on the man who becomes her father's prisoner after his arrest for murder, she finally takes him as her lover in spite of her marriage vows to a marchese whom she cannot love. Clelia is one of the two great beauties of the Parmese court, both enamoured of the young monsignor. She dies soon after the death of the child fathered by Fabrizio, now an archbishop.

Gina Pietranera (pee-eh-trah-NAY-rah), the duchess of Sanseverina, the mistress and later wife of Count Mosca, and the aunt and benefactress of Fabrizio del Dongo. Widowed before she is thirty, the unorthodox and spirited beauty becomes the chief ornament of the court of the prince of Parma. Taking part in political intrigue, Gina effects the escape of her nephew, the discomfiture of the prince, and the devotion of her lover. Though greatly attracted to her nephew, she never pleads the cause of what the whole court assumes to be an established fact, a menáge. Capable of acting under the whim of a moment, Gina is also able to act with cool precision and great foresight.

Count Mosca (MOHS-kah), Gina's lover, a prime minister under two heads of state, and the jealous friend of Fabrizio. The count, against all reason, successfully wooes the penniless Gina, finds her a husband who needs a court accomplice and preferment, and then gives up his portfolio in order to live as her husband in penury. He is an inspired Machiavelli, a generous nobleman, and a clear-headed cynic.

Father Blanés (blan-EHS), a priest-astrologer and a friend of Fabrizio. This ghostly cleric, the surrogate father of the impressionable young mystic whose real father early disowned him, proves to be the awakener of spiritual qualities as well as churchly ambitions in his protégé.

Ludovico (lew-doh-VEE-koh), the trusted servant of the duchess and the great friend and protector of Fabrizio. Valorous and canny, Ludovico protects the headstrong and amorous young man from many intrigues and aids the imaginative poet, Ferrante, who supervised his eventual escape from prison.

Marietta Valsera (mah-ree-EH-tah vahl-SEH-rah), the actress whose jealous lover is killed by Fabrizio. A young and not very talented performer, Marietta unconsciously leads her admirer into an ambush. She redeems herself by protecting her lover's identity even at her own peril. For Fabrizio, she personifies conquest and no more.

Fausta, a beautiful and famous soprano who inspires Fabrizio to imaginative and romantic heights.

Count Conti, the treacherous militia officer and keeper of the prison where Fabrizio is confined. He acquiesces in a plot on the life of his political prisoner.

Rassi (RAHS-see), a plebian but brilliant lawyer of the Parmese court who sells preferment among the nobility to his best advantage.

Giletti (jee-LEHT-tee), Marietta Valsera's rascally protector and lover. Jealous of Fabrizio, he attacks the young man and is killed during the scuffle. His death creates a scandal that leads to Fabrizio's arrest when the young cleric returns to Parma.

A CHASTE MAID IN CHEAPSIDE

Author: Thomas Middleton (1580-1627)
First published: 1630
Genre: Drama

Locale: London, England
Time: Early seventeenth century
Plot: Farce

Yellowhammer, a goldsmith. Eager to see his children rise in the world, he betroths his daughter to Sir Walter Whorehound, giving heed to the man's title but not to his reputation, and arranges for his son to wed the nobleman's supposed niece, who proves to be a Welsh prostitute and Sir Walter's mistress. His harsh refusal to allow Moll to marry her sweetheart, Touchwood Junior, nearly brings tragedy on his family.

Maudlin, his loquacious wife. She scolds her daughter for her sluggishness, regaling the girl with tales of her own gay youth, and she embarrasses her university-trained son by fussing over him before his tutor and many of her friends. She is as distressed as her husband when she learns that her stern treatment of Moll apparently has caused her death.

Moll, their daughter, whose languid attitude is simply a cloak for her love for young Touchwood. She is never quite successful in her attempts to elude her parents long enough to marry, until her clever maid arranges for her feigned death and reunion with her lover.

Timothy, her learned, self-confident brother. He comes home from Cambridge with his tutor to impress his family and friends with his knowledge of Latin. Tricked by Sir Walter into marriage with a prostitute, he is consoled by her wit and physical attractions for the loss of the nineteen Welsh mountains he hoped to acquire as her dowry.

Sir Walter Whorehound, a loose-living gentleman who tries unsuccessfully to bring about at one time his own marriage with Moll, Timothy's with his Welsh mistress, and the christening of his son by Allwit's wife, without having his duplicity discovered. His plans are thwarted. Wounded in a duel with young Touchwood, he learns that he will not be Sir Oliver Kix's heir, and he is promptly deserted by the Allwits.

Allwit, a contented cuckold who allows Sir Walter to bed his wife, father the children who bear his name, and maintain his entire household. Unwilling to lose all his worldly comforts, he judiciously spreads gossip about his patron's character whenever he suspects Sir Walter of considering marriage. Once the knight's fortunes change, Allwit leaves him to his late fate without a qualm, planning with his wife to live comfortably off the possessions Sir Walter has given them over the years.

Mistress Allwit, his wife. She is happy to bear Sir Walter's children and accept the compliments of her friends on their looks and accomplishments, but, like her husband, she has no qualms about deserting her lover when he falls into difficulties.

Sir Oliver Kix and

Lady Kix, a devoted couple who spend much of their time quarreling and making up after their disagreements. Their great source of trouble is their unfulfilled desire for a child. They are completely taken in by the scheme of Touchwood Senior, who ensures that an heir to the Kix fortune is conceived.

Touchwood Senior, a poor but prolific gentleman who is forced to separate from his wife to limit the size of their ever-increasing brood. His good services for Sir Oliver and Lady Kix enable him to be reunited with his family, for Sir Oliver promises to support them.

Mistress Touchwood, his wife, who obligingly agrees to live apart from him, in spite of her fondness for her husband.

A country girl, the mother of one of Touchwood's many children.

Touchwood Junior, Moll's husband to be, a brother of the older Touchwood. He plans his elopement and thoroughly enjoys having his bride's father make the ring with which his daughter intends to deceive him. After his marriage plans have been twice thwarted, he is severely wounded by Sir Walter in a duel and writes to Moll as if he were dying. He is, however, miraculously revived, and, at the third try, his wedding takes place, much to the delight of all concerned.

Davy Dahanna, Sir Walter's servant, a "poor relation" from Wales.

Susan, Moll's maid, who plans the counterfeit death and marriage of her mistress and Touchwood Junior.

A Welsh girl, Sir Walter's mistress, who becomes Timothy's bride. She counters her husband's philosophy with her own wit, arguing that her past is blotted out; her marriage makes her honest.

CHÉRI and THE LAST OF CHÉRI
(Chéri *and* La Fin de Chéri)

Author: Colette (Sidonie-Gabrielle Colette, 1873-1954)
First published: 1920, 1926
Genre: Novel

Locale: Paris and the French countryside
Time: The 1910's
Plot: Psychological realism

Chéri, 1920

Frédéric Peloux (fray-day-REEK puh-LEW), called **Chéri** (shayr-EE), an idle and moody twenty-five-year-old man. He has inherited a fortune. He is an extremely handsome man of medium height, with blue-black hair; dark eyes framed by thick, lustrous lashes; a disdainful but pretty mouth; unblemished white skin; and a hard, darkish chest shaped like a shield. To remove him from his dissipated life in Paris, he has been taken, in late adolescence, to Normandy by a friend of his mother, Léa de Lonval, an aging but still beautiful courtesan. He and Léa become lovers. This idyllic life ends when his mother arranges a marriage for him to Edmée, a wealthy young woman of eighteen. Chéri accepts but has no enthusiasm for the marriage. After a brief period of domesticity, he longs for the old days with Léa, which, to his dismay, he discovers cannot be recaptured. He finally realizes that his only course is to return to his family.

Léonie Vallon (lay-oh-NEE vahl-LAHN), later **Léa de Lonval** (lay-AH deh lahn-VAL), nicknamed **Nounoune** (new-NEWN), a passionate, aging, and still beautiful courtesan who is in love with, and the mistress of, young Chéri. She is forty-nine years old, tall, and blonde, with ruddy cheeks, a beautiful face, a good body, thin-wristed arms, large pure-blue eyes, a proud nose, an opulent bust, an even row of teeth, a good smile, long legs, and a straight back. She has successfully parlayed the gifts from her admirers into a comfortable fortune. During their six-year liaison, Léa teaches Chéri how to live in her world—how to choose friends, wines, food, jewelry, and clothing, as well as how to be the perfect lover. When Chéri is unable to assume the responsibilities of marriage, she realizes that her pampering has caused him to remain a child. Suffering from the loss of a "great love," she flees from Paris to return a year later much aged but still in love with Chéri, who fancies himself still in love with her. When the combination of Chéri's marriage and the Great War alters her world forever, she yearns for Chéri and the past but successfully adapts to the changes.

Charlotte Peloux, Chéri's miserly, gossipy, and inquisitive mother, a wealthy former ballet dancer and courtesan who boldly rears Chéri as a child of the demimonde. Mme Peloux is a small, round barrel of a woman with short legs, tiny feet, large eyes, fair hair, a shrill off-key voice, and a coquettish way of standing with her feet in the fifth position. She chooses

Edmée as wife for her son and arranges the marriage terms. Her primary occupation is afternoon tea with her friends.

Edmée (ehd-MAY), Chéri's wife, the attractive, eighteen-year-old daughter of a beautiful former courtesan, Marie-Laure. She has frightened, secretive eyes; thin arms; small breasts; rosy lips; small, squarish teeth; white skin; and fluffy, ash-brown hair with a slight crimp in it. Although Edmée has a fortune of her own, she is a docile wife to Chéri. Miserable in her marriage with the erratic, heartless Chéri and convinced of his love for Léa, she suggests divorce. Her suggestion is re-jected by her husband as no real solution to the problem. Chéri returns to her when he realizes that he must part from Léa.

Marie-Laure (ma-REE-lohr), Edmée's elegant mother, a spectacular beauty in her day. She is in her forties but dresses as if she were eighteen.

Desmond, a penniless hanger-on who has been Chéri's friend since boyhood. His ugliness contrasts with Chéri's good looks. Like Chéri, he avoids military combat, but, unlike Chéri, he thrives in the postwar era.

The Last of Chéri, 1926

Frédéric Peloux, now thirty years old, with faintly shadowed eyelids and a leaner physique. He is a veteran of World War I, in which he was mistakenly decorated for bravery, even though he finagled military service behind the lines. Chéri refuses to accept the reality of the postwar world; the independent, self-assured woman Edmée has become; impending middle age; or the fact that Léa has grown gracefully into a comfortable old age without him. Unable to work, to recapture the past, to adapt to the present, to relate to his wife and friends, or to accept the loss of Léa and his youth, Chéri spends his time reminiscing about the past with The Pal. Seeing no place for himself in the modern world, he commits suicide with a pistol in her apartment.

Léa de Lonval, who has settled into a happy, chaste old age and adopted a masculine style of dress that gives her an aura of sexless dignity. She stops dyeing her gray hair, cuts it short, and allows herself to become very stout, with a fat neck, sagging cheeks, and a double chin. Her ability to live well and happily without Chéri in the modern world puzzles and saddens him.

Edmée, whose hospital administrative work and separation from Chéri during the war have brought her to the realiza-tion that she enjoys both her career and her independence. She no longer defines herself exclusively in relation to her husband. In the postwar world, her career flourishes. As Chéri withdraws from her, it becomes the most important thing in her life. Moreover, Edmée proves to be a better financial manager than Chéri and takes control of their joint fortune. Perfectly at home in the modern world, Edmée, like Léa, is able to adjust to life with or without Chéri and to thrive.

Charlotte Peloux, who became productively involved with Edmée's hospital during the war. She continues to be produc-tive in the postwar world.

Desmond, who opens a jazz nightclub that becomes a com-mercial success by pandering to what Chéri considers to be the worst elements of modern taste. He is now far too busy and too happy to be at Chéri's beck and call.

The Pal, a contemporary of Léa and Charlotte who has a name so ordinary that nobody ever remembers it. She smokes opium and gives it to others. It is only in her company that Chéri finds peace by reminiscing about the past. He commits suicide in her apartment, thinking of Léa and the war.

CHEROKEE

Author: Jean Echenoz (1949-   )
First published: 1983
Genre: Novel

Locale: Paris and the French Alps
Time: The 1980's
Plot: Detective and mystery

George Chave (shahv), the protagonist. A tall, thin man in his thirties, he is looking for work as a way to please his girlfriend, Veronique, but he soon shifts his devotion to Jenny Weltman. Hired as a detective, he arouses the envy of other employees by finding a lost wife and a lost parrot. As unex-plainable events take place around him, he is pursued by the police, hidden by friends, kidnapped, taken by a cult, and finally united with Jenny.

Fred Shapiro, a mysterious businessman. An expensively dressed man of thirty-eight, he is balding and has a hooked nose. A distant cousin and childhood playmate of George, he had long ago incurred George's dislike when he did not return a rare, borrowed record of "Cherokee." When George encoun-ters him again, Fred is able to suggest a job opening. Later, Fred kills his uncle, Fernand; becomes the leader of the Rayonite cult; seizes George for use in their rituals; and kills a policeman who is storming their stronghold. At the end of the novel, Fred is driving the car containing George and Jenny.

Croconyan (kraw-KAHN-yehn), a thief. A large, short-haired man, he is strong and resourceful. After George aids him in a bar fight, he becomes a loyal friend, first hiding him in Paris and later joining him in the Alpine retreat.

Ferguson Gibbs, a rich, red-haired Englishman involved in business with Fred Shapiro. He abducts George and later be-comes a substitute priest of the Rayonites until they turn against him.

Jenny Weltman, the woman for whom George searches throughout most of the novel. Young and pretty with blue-gray eyes and blond hair, she first meets George in the National Library. She acts as a priestess for the Rayonites but finally is reunited with George.

Fernand, a bookseller. A man of sixty-five, dressed in numerous layers of clothing, he mourns for the writers whom he knew in his youth. After George tries to sell books to him, he suggests that Fred might be able to help him find a job. Fred, his nephew, later kills him.

Christian Ripert (rih-PEHR), a detective. A tall, thin man, he is motivated by envy of George, who solves cases that he and his partner cannot. His pursuit of George does not bring him luck: First, Ripert is injured when George pushes him off of a balcony, then later he is shot and killed by Fred at the Rayonite headquarters.

Martial Bock, another private detective and Ripert's partner. A short, fat man, he dresses as gaudily as a pimp, like Ripert. After kidnapping Veronique from the mountain hideout, he and his partner end up joining the police in the siege of the Rayonite headquarters.

Veronique, George's first girlfriend, an office worker. Although she leaves George for a photographer, she later joins both of them, along with Croconyan, at the photographer's home in the Alps, where George tries to hide. It is Veronique who leads the detectives and the police to rescue George from the Rayonites.

— *Rosemary M. Canfield Reisman*

THE CHEROKEE NIGHT

Author: Lynn Riggs (1899-1954)
First published: 1936
Genre: Drama

Locale: Oklahoma
Time: 1895-1931
Plot: Social realism

Viney Jones (later **Viney Clepper**), a frontier schoolteacher. Given to crudity and ruthlessness, Viney herself is the product of education by whites. She is trained sufficiently to become a teacher of children herself. She resents her Cherokee heritage and eventually abandons it and moves to town, presumably married to a white man. She returns to Claremore Mound to visit her sister, Sarah, who is living in poverty, not so much to help her but to be arrogant in her treatment of her. Viney represents the Cherokees of the younger generation who have given themselves to the materialism and education of the dominant society.

Bee Newcomb, another part-breed Cherokee. As a whore, then a prostitute, Bee represents the physical and sexual decline of the Cherokee. Her worst act, however, is not having sex with clients or even with her half brother Gar; it is tricking Art Osburn, a fellow part-breed, into confessing a murder. This deceit for money is far more damning than having sex for money.

Art Osburn, who murders his wife. Art responds to the controls of the white society with violence. Having married a white woman with children, he finds that he cannot continue life with her because of her ways. When he confesses to the murder, he becomes a victim.

Old Man Talbert, a collector of arrowheads and one of the last remaining true Cherokees. Talbert, who is first thought to be a grave robber, turns out to be searching for something that will revive the dignity of his parents' way of life. Instead, he finds only relics that the younger Cherokees look at with disdain.

Sarah Pickard, Viney's sister. Sarah's qualities as a character are essentially defined by her poverty. Too proud to leave the Indian lands and accommodate a white lifestyle, Sarah remains in the old ways and thus is ridden with poverty and disease. Although morally superior to her sister, she is stubborn to the extent that she is not admirable.

Kate Whiteturkey, an eighteen-year-old Osage Indian woman who is married to Hutch Moree. As owner of three Studebaker cars, Kate has acquired some of the luxury material goods offered by white society. She denies her Indian heritage to herself and to other Indians. She finds meaning in life by boasting that her husband has ten silk shirts and six pairs of cowboy boots.

John Gray-Wolf, one of the last true Cherokees. Gray-Wolf does not appear in the play until the last scene, set in 1895. He is the only character with both integrity and Indian heritage, and he will soon die. He is a remnant of all that was but that is now lost.

Edgar "Spench" Breeden, the father of Gar Breeden and Bee Newcomb. Spench is one of the more flagrant degenerates in the cast. He would steal and kill; moreover, he has fathered children by two women at the same time, only to desert both women. He dies after being chased by white men seeking to punish him for his misconduct.

— *Carl Singleton*

THE CHERRY ORCHARD
(Vishnyovysad)

Author: Anton Chekhov (1860-1904)
First published: 1904
Genre: Drama

Locale: An estate in Russia
Time: Early twentieth century
Plot: Impressionistic realism

Madame Lubov Andreyevna Ranevskaya (lew-BOHF ahn-DREH-ehv-nuh rah-NEHF-skah-yah), a middle-aged woman and the owner of a large estate that has become impossible to maintain because of debts. Madame Ranevskaya is a remnant of the old order of Russian feudal aristocracy being pushed aside by social change. Her estate, her mansion, and especially the cherry orchard exist for her as symbols of her past, her innocent youth, and her formerly carefree life. She cannot reconcile herself to giving them up, she cannot change with the times, and she cannot assume the financial and emotional responsibility demanded of her. The forces that molded her are disappearing from Russian life.

Anya (AHN-yah), Madame Ranevskaya's seventeen-year-old daughter. Although she loves the estate and the cherry orchard, her youth makes it possible for her to bend with the social tide. She reconciles herself to loss and change, to a new Russia of which she will be a part. Her love for Peter Trofimov, a student representative of the intellectual liberal in the new order, influences her toward confidence and hope for the future.

Varya (VAH-ryah), the adopted daughter of Madame Ranevskaya. Having managed the estate for years, she is exhausted by concern: about debts, for the servants, and about the future. Her efforts have come to nothing. She is in love with Lopakhin, a wealthy merchant who is so busy making money that he cannot bring himself to propose to her. Varya's illusions of happiness and peace tempt her to run away to enter a convent. Neither of the aristocracy nor of the rising middle class, but caught between both, she finds that only work can ease her frustration and unhappiness.

Leonid Andreyevitch Gaev (leh-oh-NIHD ahn-DREH-yeh-vihch gah-EHF), Madame Ranevskaya's brother, a restless, garrulous, and impractical dreamer. Bound to the old ways, he tries in vain to save the estate by borrowing or begging the necessary money. Like his sister, he is unwilling to sell the cherry orchard and let it be used for a housing subdivision. Until the last, he cherishes his illusions that they will be saved by a stroke of good fortune.

Ermolai Alexeyevitch Lopakhin (ehr-moh-LIH ah-lehk-SEH-yeh-vihch loh-PAH-khihn), a wealthy merchant whose father was a peasant. Without sentiment for the past, he lives in the present and for commercial opportunism. He redeems the past, literally, when he buys the Ranevsky estate, where his father and grandfather had been serfs. His feelings are calculated in terms of profit and loss, and his love for Varya cannot compete with his commercial zeal.

Peter Sergeyevitch Trofimov (PYOH-tr sehr-GEH-yeh-vihch troh-FIH-mof), an idealistic young student willing to work for the future betterment of humankind. He claims his mission is freedom and happiness, escape from the petty and deceptive elements of life. His love for Anya is confused with social zeal, and his understanding of people is slight.

Boris Borisovitch Simeonov-Pishchik (boh-RIHS boh-RIHS-eh-vihch sih-MEH-ehn-of-PIH-shchihk), a landowner constantly in debt, always trying to borrow money. Unlike the Ranevskys, he has no feeling for the land or his heritage. He eventually leases his land to be torn up for its valuable deposits of clay.

Charlotta Ivanova (shahr-LOHT-teh ih-VAH-neh-vah), the governess to the Ranevskys, a young woman who does not know her parentage. She is classless, ready to be swept by any tide.

Simeon Panteleyevitch Epikhodov (seh-MYOHN pahn-teh-LEH-yeh-vihch eh-pih-KHOHD-of), a clerk in the Ranevsky household. He is in love with Dunyasha, a maid, who does not return his love.

Dunyasha (doo-NYAH-shah), who is in love with the brash young footman, Yasha. She dresses well and pretends to be a lady.

Fiers (fihrs), an old footman, faithful to the Ranevsky family for generations. Concerned only with the well-being of his employers, he is inadvertently left to die in the abandoned house, a symbol of the dying past.

Yasha (YAH-shah), an insolent young footman, Fiers's grandson. Caring nothing for his family, Yasha thrives on cruelty and opportunism. He knowingly leaves his grandfather to die alone.

THE CHEVALIER DE MAISON-ROUGE
(Le Chevalier de Maison-Rouge)

Authors: Alexandre Dumas, *père* (1802-1870), with Auguste Maquet (1813-1888)
First published: 1846
Genre: Novel

Locale: Paris, France
Time: 1793
Plot: Historical

Maurice Lindey (moh-REES la[n]-DAY), a lieutenant in the Civil Guard of France. He rescues a beautiful, unknown woman from a group of drunken volunteers and falls in love with her before she vanishes into the night. Searching for her, he falls into the hands of a group of loyalists disguised as tanners and learns the identity of his beloved. She is Geneviève Dixmer. Maurice is used by the loyalist tanners to further their plot to rescue Marie Antoinette; finally, along with Geneviève and Louis Lorin, he dies on the scaffold.

Geneviève Dixmer (zhahn-VYEHV deeks-MEHR), a beautiful aristocrat and loyalist conspirator loved by Maurice Lindey. Arrested as a suspect in the futile attempts to rescue Marie Antoinette, she dies along with Maurice.

Monsieur Dixmer, the husband of Geneviève Dixmer and manager of a tannery business used as a front for loyalist activities. He is killed by Maurice during a quarrel.

Morand (moh-RAH[N]), the chevalier of the Maison Rouge. He is Monsieur Dixmer's business partner in the tannery, which is used as a cover for Morand's real identity as the chevalier of the Maison Rouge. He is dedicated to the rescue of Marie Antoinette.

Louis Lorin (lwee loh-RA[N]), the faithful friend of Maurice Lindey, with whom he dies on the scaffold as a loyalist suspect.

Héloïse Tison (ay-loh-EEZ- tee-ZO[N]), a young girl who is executed for her aid to the loyalist conspirators.

Simon (see-MOH[N]), a shoemaker and the cruel guardian of the Dauphin.

Marie Antoinette (mah-REE ah[n]-twah-NEHT), the queen of France.

CHEVENGUR

Author: Andrei Platonov (Andrei Platonovich Klimentov, 1899-1951)
First published: 1972
Genre: Novel

Locale: Russia's central provinces and Moscow
Time: Shortly before and during the Russian Revolution
Plot: Satire

Alexander (Sasha) Dvanov (DVAH-nov), an orphan and Red Army soldier. Having been orphaned early and thrown out of his foster parents' home, Sasha becomes a mendicant and later joins the Bolsheviks. As a beggar, he is a failure, because he is not brave enough to beg. He embraces Communism instinctively, at first because everyone else is joining the movement and it is frightening to be left alone again. Later, he learns more about Communism, but his understanding of it remains on a rudimentary level, as he seeks understanding among the simplest and best of people. The nebulousness of his political views is best exemplified by his participation in building, together with a number of similar souls, a city of Chevengur that corresponds to their idealistic notion of brotherly love and comradeship. In the end, he fades away into the foggy future of the city, without any assurance that it would ever work, let alone fulfill his dream of a better life for everyone.

Zakhar Pavlovich (zah-KHAR PAHV-loh-vihch), Sasha's guardian, a railroad mechanic. A progenitor of Sasha's dreamlike attitude toward life, Zakhar is also a dreamer but of a different kind. He is inordinately gifted as a practical man and a mechanic; he is able to make and fix almost anything. He makes things for others, never for himself, and he does so out of curiosity about what makes things what they are and how they work. He lives alone and never needs people, considering machines to be people, and is attracted to unusual projects such as building a wooden clock powered by Earth's rotation. He is able to converse with anyone in a neighborly way. This combination of friendliness and aloofness draws him to the revolution; without subscribing to its political aims, he believes, again instinctively, that it may do some good.

Stepan Kopenkin (steh-PAHN koh-PEHN-kihn), a dedicated revolutionary with some of the strangest notions about Communism. He wants to build a family army to fight the enemies of the poor and common people. He has an obsession with a German revolutionary, Rosa Luxemburg, and carries her picture sewn into his cap. He uses her as a yardstick for measuring a good revolutionary. With his horse, named Proletarian Strength, he resembles Don Quixote more than a fiery Bolshevik. He believes that people would set things right by themselves if they were left in peace and that Rosa, as a symbol of revolution, had thought up everything in advance. Like Sasha and, to some degree, Zakhar, he is vague about the real goals of the revolution. He trusts his instincts, believing that within himself he has the gift of revolution. That, however, is only a mask for his desire to live totally free.

Prokofy (Proshka) Dvanov (proh-KOH-fee), Sasha's foster brother. A revolutionary of a different kind, Proshka is using the revolution for his own ends. Practical and at times cruelly selfish, he operates almost exclusively on the basis of "what's in it for me." Even though he has worked for many people, he is loved by no one. He has acquired a good knowledge of Marx, but his use of Marx depends, for example, on his girlfriend's mood and the objective circumstances. By and large, he is a predator who needs no people and collects property in place of people; he loves no one beyond his own door. The only reason he has survived so far is because he is able to manipulate his comrades and because of the uncertainties of the revolution.

Chepurny (sheh-PUR-nee), called the Jap, a revolutionary and president of Chevengur. Another blind believer in revolution, the Jap calls himself "a naked communist" who has not read a line of Marx but has picked up an idea or two at meetings and now spends his life fighting for it. Because most of the characters are not persons but embodiments of ideas, the Jap and others should be seen as spokespeople of the times, despite their individual idiosyncrasies.

Sonya Mandrova (MAHN-droh-vah), Sasha's childhood friend. Abandoned by her mother at birth, Sonya is caught in the maelstrom of the revolution and becomes one of the millions of simple people who are forced by circumstances to participate in it. Her juvenile love for Sasha disappears in the vagaries of the revolution. She later becomes a cleaner at a factory. She has difficulties in sustaining her attachment to men and refuses to have children, in the belief that if she could have a flower instead of a child, she then would be a mother, thus revealing a poetic nature that the revolution's harshness has arrested forever.

— *Vasa D. Mihailovich*

CHEYENNE AUTUMN

Author: Mari Sandoz (1896-1966)
First published: 1953
Genre: Novel

Locale: The Great Plains, from Indian Territory to the Yellowstone Country
Time: 1878-1879
Plot: Historical realism

Little Wolf, also called Brave Man, the bearer of the Sacred Chief's bundle and one of the Old Man Chiefs. In his prime at the age of fifty-seven, Little Wolf is one of two leaders attempting to take their Northern Cheyenne back to their Montana homeland from the hated Indian Territory. Distrustful of whites, he believes that their promises are no more than "wind on the grass." When the group divides at the Platte River, with Dull Knife hoping to reach safety at Red Cloud's agency nearby, Little Wolf takes his followers to their original destination in the north. His one weakness is his jealousy of Thin Elk.

Dull Knife, also an Old Man Chief. Once a famed warrior, now, in his sixties, he wants only to return north. He naïvely believes that the Army will honor its promise to let the Cheyenne return home from the intolerable southern agency. After their capture and their failed attempt to escape from Fort Robinson, Nebraska, he is embittered, a failure in his own eyes.

Little Finger Nail, a young warrior, sweet singer, and artist. In the absence of older leaders, he leads the tribal remnant in their thirteen-day escape from Fort Robinson. He is killed in their last encounter, at Warbonnet Creek. His book of pictographs recording their trek remains strapped to his back, with two bullet holes in it.

Wild Hog, a headman. Big and broad, standing 6 feet, 5 inches, he is married to a Sioux. When Dull Knife fails to take charge during their capture, he assumes leadership. Later, he attempts suicide, hoping that his family can then be sent to Red Cloud's nearby Sioux agency.

Black Coyote, a prominent subchief, inimical to the whites and a troublemaker for the leaders. After killing Black Crane, he is exiled as a renegade. Later captured and convicted of killing a soldier, he is hanged by whites.

Thin Elk, a joker, a ladies' man, and Little Wolf's nemesis. Once ordered to stay away from the chief's wives, he now flirts with a daughter. After the trek, Little Wolf, forgetting a chief's obligation to ignore personal problems, kills him and forfeits his leadership.

Black Crane, an elder, the experienced camp finder, a strong conservative influence. He is killed during an argument with the violent Black Coyote.

Bridge, the frail old medicine man, who sacrifices his health through fasting and prayer so that the Powers will aid the Cheyenne in their flight. Sometimes they help, but he is killed in the outbreak at Fort Robinson.

Comes-in-Sight, a Cheyenne maiden forced to kill her demented father to prevent him from raping her. Cheyenne law requires that she and her family be exiled, but they closely follow the sympathetic group.

Yellow Swallow, the sickly nine-year-old son of a Cheyenne and General George Custer. Brought on the flight by relatives, he returns south before reaching the Platte River.

Red Cloud, an Oglala Sioux about fifty-five years old. Although made a chief by the whites, he is held a virtual prisoner at his own agency. The Oglalas and Cheyenne are intermarried, but he cannot help his friends.

Brave One and

Enemy, heroic women who survived two massacres before walking the entire distance to Fort Robinson, often carrying small children. They are killed at Warbonnet Creek, northwest of Fort Robinson.

Woman's Dress, a Sioux Army scout. Already considered a traitor to the Sioux Chief Crazy Horse, he leads the Army to the last stronghold of the Cheyenne who are attempting to escape from Fort Robinson.

Captain Little Flying Dutchman (Henry W.) Wessells, the short, light-haired commandant at Fort Robinson. A rigid follower of rules, he locks the Cheyenne into their barracks without food, heat, or water for days, attempting to force them to return to Indian Territory. When they break out, he kills, wounds, or captures more than two-thirds of them.

Lieutenant William Chase, a young officer in charge of the Cheyenne at Fort Robinson. Sympathetic to the Indians, he spends his pay on food and treats for them, but at Warbonnet Creek he aids Wessells in annihilating the remaining Indians.

Lieutenant White Hat (Philo) Clark, an ambitious, experienced Indian fighter. Little Wolf trusts him more than most whites and surrenders to him near Fort Keogh after Clark allows the band to keep their weapons and horses.

Colonel Caleb Carlton, who hunts the Cheyenne through Nebraska's sandhills and captures Dull Knife's people near Fort Robinson.

General Braided Beard (George) Crook, commander of the Department of the Platte. A superb Indian fighter, he nevertheless protests their treatment to Washington, to no avail.

General Bear Coat (Nelson A.) Miles, who is headquartered at Fort Keogh on the Yellowstone. He is an active campaigner against Indians, yet he allows Little Wolf's band to settle on their own reservation in Montana.

Edgar Beecher Bronson, a rancher near Fort Robinson. Sympathetic to the Cheyenne, he later writes a book giving the details of the outbreak.

— Helen Winter Stauffer

CHICKEN SOUP WITH BARLEY

Author: Arnold Wesker (1932-   )
First published: 1959
Genre: Drama

Locale: London's East End
Time: 1936-1956
Plot: Social realism

Sarah Kahn, a small, fiery Jewish woman of European origin, thirty-seven years old at the opening of the play. She lives in the East End of London. She is the wife of Harry, whom she constantly nags, and the mother of Ada and Ronnie. Two features immediately characterize her: her warmhearted but unsentimental dynamism and her total commitment to communism. This commitment is less ideological than intuitive, being based on a sense of community and the need to care, an extension of her strong sense of wider family. It is because of this feeling that she is the one figure who does not become disillusioned as the play progresses. Although personal tragedy overtakes her during the twenty-year span of the play (particularly her husband's physical and mental collapse and the breakup of her own family and the Jewish East End community), she never loses her warmth or her convictions. In this loosely structured chronicle play, she is the one character who holds the play together, as the matriarch in a matriarchal

society and the true essence of socialism: a caring heart that can withstand political oppression, crass materialism, and disillusion. She alone remains unbroken.

Harry Kahn, a Jewish member of the working class, thirty-five years old at the beginning of the play. He is something of a thinker. Although he apparently shares his wife's beliefs, he is almost her complete opposite: physically weak, timid, and a compulsive liar. Their incompatibility leads to frequent quarrels that finish with Harry feeling defeated and guilty. In act 2, he suffers a partial stroke, which makes employment difficult; he more or less gives up. By act 3, he has had a second stroke and is a physical wreck, helpless and incontinent. The play suggests that his physical weakness is an outward sign of his emotional and spiritual weakness.

Ada Kahn, Sarah and Harry's daughter. As the play opens, Ada is fourteen years old and, like her mother, totally and actively committed to communism, especially in the immediate confrontation with the Fascist "Blackshirts." As the play progresses, she loses her youthful zeal because of a long engagement and, after her marriage, an even longer separation from her husband, Dave, caused by the Spanish Civil War and World War II. She also is demoralized by the failure of their utopian scheme to live simply in the country.

Ronnie Kahn, Sarah and Harry's son. In act 1, Ronnie is a child; in act 2, he is a politically committed high school student; and in act 3, he returns from a job in Paris as a chef. In many ways, Ronnie resembles the author, just as the play is the story of the author's own family. Ronnie is shown to be particularly sensitive to his parents' failures. He is terrified of becoming as weak as his father, and he argues fiercely with his mother that communism has failed. The argument leads Sarah to define her socialism of the heart, but Ronnie cannot accept this, at least "not yet."

Cissie Kahn, Harry's sister, a Trades-Union organizer. She is as strong in character as Sarah and is as committed in her beliefs, but she lacks her sister-in-law's humanity and warmth. She prefers confrontational roles, but, as the play proceeds, she finds less and less support among her union members, until she is finally "retired" from her post.

Dave Simmonds, Ada's husband. Among the Jewish teenage boys in his group, Dave is the most attractive and idealistic. He volunteers to fight in the Spanish Civil War against the Fascists. For most of the play, he is only heard of through Ada, who reveals his disillusionment with the working class and the failure of his rural socialist scheme.

Monty Blatt, another of the Jewish teenagers in act 1. He reappears in act 3 with his wife, Bessie, at a reunion with Sarah and Harry. He is now a successful entrepreneur in Manchester and wants to forget his earlier communist leanings, even while continuing to admire Sarah for her commitment.

Prince Silver, the third of the teenagers who participate in the demonstration. He also reappears in act 3, now running a secondhand shop and clearly no longer politically active. He is one of the players in an unsuccessful game of cards that is in stark contrast to the idealistic dialogue of act 1.

Hymie Kossof, Sarah's brother. He makes a dramatic entry in act 1, having been hurt in the demonstration. Like Prince, he settles down in life. He is also in the game of cards and, also like Prince, refuses to wait up with Sarah for Ronnie to return from Paris—a final symbolic act of desertion.

— *David Barratt*

THE CHICKENCOOP CHINAMAN

Author: Frank Chin (1940-   )
First published: 1981
Genre: Drama

Locale: The Oakland district of Pittsburgh, Pennsylvania
Time: Late 1960's
Plot: Comedy

Tam Lum, a Chinese American writer and filmmaker. Tam Lum is a young writer cast loose from his Chinese heritage, displaced from mainstream American culture, and obsessed with creating a unified artistic identity and discovering an appropriate voice and language in which to tell his stories. He is puzzled, cross, mocking, frustrated, isolated, and essentially passive, with a touch of the poet and a gift for telling a story. In the play's major action, Tam Lum journeys to Pittsburgh to interview Charley Popcorn for a documentary film on the life and career of Ovaltine Jack Dancer, a black fighter who had been the childhood hero of Tam Lum and Kenji.

Kenji, sometimes called **Blackjap Kenji**, a Japanese American research dentist who has been Tam Lum's friend since childhood. In his youth, Kenji rejected his cultural and racial heritage, just as did Tam Lum. Together, they found heroes and role models in black men, such as Ovaltine Jack Dancer, and in media heroes, such as the Lone Ranger. Tam Lum stays at Kenji's house in Pittsburgh and renews their friendship while in the city to interview Charley Popcorn. In contrast to Tam Lum, Kenji moves toward assimilation during the play. At the end, Lee will stay with Kenji, as his wife or lover, and Robbie, Lee's son, will have the father he seeks.

Lee, an attractive Eurasian or Chinese American woman whom Kenji has invited to stay in his apartment. Lee is hostile toward men, especially Chinese men. She represents the lack of sympathy in the white, black, and Oriental worlds for any person who attempts to create a new self by amalgamating elements of all three cultures. Lee's hostility toward Tam Lum provides the major conflict of act 1. During the

play, Lee begins to understand Tam Lum and to appreciate the form his rebellion takes.

Tom, Lee's former husband, a Chinese American writer. Tom is a neat, tidy, completely assimilated Chinese American, a man who has denied his Chinese heritage and past to be acceptable to the majority white culture. Tom is the opposite of Tam Lum in many ways. Tom has attempted to blend with the white culture, whereas Tam Lum has resisted assimilation. He represents a white culture that demands too high a price for success: the repudiation of the writer's Chinese heritage. A major scene in act 2 consists of an argument between Tam Lum and Tom over what it means to be Chinese.

Robbie, Lee's twelve-year-old son. Like Tam Lum and Kenji, Robbie is looking for a strong father figure. He represents impressionable youth, which repeats the prejudices of the adult world but neither fully understands nor believes them.

Charley Popcorn, an old black man. Charley is a former boxing trainer who runs a pornographic cinema in Pittsburgh. Tam Lum believes that he is the father of Ovaltine Jack Dancer, but Charley denies it. Tam Lum's major disappointment in the play is his failure to find the father of his childhood hero, who represents to him the ideal father. Charley Popcorn is the object of Tam Lum's quest to Pittsburgh to meet the ideal father.

The Lone Ranger,
Tonto, and
Hong Kong Dream Girl, all fantasy/dream characters who represent Tam Lum's rejection of his Chinese as well as his American heritage.

— *James W. Robinson, Jr.*

CHILD OF GOD

Author: Cormac McCarthy (1933-   )
First published: 1973
Genre: Novel

Locale: Sevier County, Tennessee, in the Appalachian Mountains
Time: The early 1960's
Plot: Social realism

Lester Ballard, a twenty-seven-year-old farmer in Sevier County, Tennessee. After his mother runs away and his father kills himself, Lester is left alone, too brutal and mean to make friends. In later years, his only companion is his rifle, and his only interests are hunting, drinking, and sex. After he loses the family farm for nonpayment of taxes and is badly beaten when he objects, he resolves to avenge himself on the new owner, John Greer. In the meantime, he tries to make a home in a remote, deserted house. All the women he approaches reject him. For companionship, he has to depend on three stuffed animals he wins at a fair; for a sexual outlet, he watches couples in cars or fondles clothing stolen from women. Lester is so preoccupied with his own needs that he has no empathy for others. When one girl turns him down, Lester murders her and sets her house on fire, leaving her retarded child to burn to death beside the body of his mother. Finally, Lester takes as his lover a girl he has found dead in a car. After he loses her body in a fire, he begins killing the women he needs. Although couples and cars keep disappearing, for a long time Lester is not suspected of being involved. Ironically, it is not his sexual obsession but his insistence on getting revenge that leads to his downfall. He tries to kill John Greer but merely wounds him. He is shot, loses an arm, and ends up in a mental hospital, where he is again lonely, alienated from his fellow killers.

Fate Turner, high sheriff of Sevier County. Fate's Christian name is appropriate because, though from one perspective he is merely a human being with human limitations, he is also Lester's nemesis. Fate represents the county when Lester's farm is sold, and although he does not order Lester to be beaten, he does not object. Later, Fate arrests Lester twice for crimes he did not commit. The first time he releases Lester, Fate warns him that the next step on his path is murder. The second time, not realizing that Lester already has killed the young mother, Fate again urges him to change his ways. At the end of the novel, it is Fate who goes down into the sinkhole and brings out Lester's victims for burial, thus closing the case.

John Greer, a man from Granger County who innocently purchases Lester's farm at an auction. Because he is an outsider, he does not realize how dangerous an enemy Lester can be. When he encounters Lester, he is not even sure who he is. Living and working on the farm, he is unaware of the fact that Lester is watching him. When Lester finally attacks, Greer reacts quickly enough to save his own life. To Lester's disappointment, Greer survives.

Reubel, a dumpkeeper. Although he whines about the promiscuity of his nine daughters, he has taken no responsibility for rearing them. On one occasion, Reubel has sexual intercourse with one of his daughters and then is vaguely regretful. In his interest in whiskey and sex, he can be seen as a parallel to Lester; the only difference is that he is more lethargic, or perhaps that he simply has access to what he needs.

— *Rosemary M. Canfield Reisman*

CHILDE BYRON

Author: Romulus Linney (1930-   )
First published: 1981
Genre: Drama

Locale: London, England
Time: November 27, 1852
Plot: Historical

George Gordon, Lord Byron, a famous English Romantic poet, flamboyant society figure, and sexual rebel. Fiery, cynical, passionate, and candid, Byron confronts his daughter, Ada, on the day of her death and attempts to justify his life to her. As a boy, he is a moody, fat, clubfooted poseur. He is introduced to sex at the age of nine by his nurse; as a young man, he has become an internationally acclaimed poet, a superb athlete, and a notorious sexual veteran who has bedded practically everything presented to him but whose most passionate love affair has been with his half sister Augusta Leigh. Exiled for his scandalous behavior once it no longer suits the public fancy, he lives with the Countess Guiccioli, then with the poet Percy Bysshe Shelley. He finally flees to Greece, where he dies in the fight for Greek independence. Throughout his recital of his life and loves, Byron remains contemptuous of public opinion, insisting that society is basely hypocritical. He emerges as a heroic figure, genuinely hurt but proud and clear-sighted about the demands made on an artist by his public. His defiance raises questions about the emotional and artistic costs of fame and about the boundaries between the artist's work and his life.

Ada, the Countess of Lovelace, a mathematician and designer of a calculating machine, the Analytical Engine. She is Byron's daughter by Annabella Millbanke. Thirty-six years old and dying of cancer, Ada cannot finish her will without confronting the father she never knew but whose infamous life nevertheless seems linked to hers. She conjures up Byron's ghost and demands that he justify his life and paternal neglect. Coolly logical, scientifically skeptical, and something of a reasoning machine herself, Ada discovers in the course of her accusations and Byron's explanations that she is in fact very much her father's daughter: The same rebellious spirit animates them both. Each has achieved much, suffered much, been misunderstood and disgraced, and lived with self-exile and self-loathing. Both will be dead at the age of thirty-six.

Annabella Millbanke, Ada's mother and later a formidable bluestocking. A logical and direct provincial girl with mathematical interests, she first charms Byron with her candor, but once married, she is unable to endure what she claims are Byron's perversities, and she demands a separation and custody of their child. She fuels the gossip about Byron's gambling, incest, sodomy, and homosexuality that leads to his eventual exile from England.

Lady Byron, Byron's mother, a coarse, boozy, unstable woman who both indulges and attacks her son.

Chorus of Men and Women, the voices of society that at first overwhelm Byron with rhapsodic adulation, celebrating his scandalous behavior with offers of wine, dinners, and themselves, but later turn vengeful, insisting on his expulsion from their midst as a pervert and criminal.

— *Thomas J. Campbell*

CHILDE HAROLD'S PILGRIMAGE

Author: George Gordon, Lord Byron (1788-1824)
First published: 1812-1818
Genre: Poetry

Locale: Europe
Time: The Middle Ages
Plot: Picaresque

Childe Harold, a wandering young man. The term "childe," in medieval English, denoted a young man of the noble classes, about to enter knighthood. Harold begins the story as a rather desperate young man, engaged mostly in debauchery and drunkenness. He leaves England ("Albion's land") in a quest for truth about the world, or at least about himself. He travels by sea to Portugal, Spain, France, and Germany, and finally Greece and Italy. Throughout the journey, he is bewildered about the truth and never quite finds his way. He begins to find his way in Germany, on the banks of the Rhine. There, he finds a young woman with whom he can have a meaningful relationship, but he decides he is unworthy. He then travels to Greece, where he is astounded by natural beauty once again but is appalled by the decadence to which the once great Greeks have fallen. In Rome, he finds a similar situation, and there he dies. Childe Harold is more of a metaphor than a real human being. He represents Lord Byron in some sense, but more important, he represents the fall of humankind from the glory of ancient times to the decadence

that Byron perceives has befallen his own generation.

Harold's page, whose age is unclear. He is useful in the narrative only as the one person Harold seems to care about seriously as he leaves England. Apparently, though this is unclear, he does not accompany Harold on the journey. His major function in the poem is to suggest that Childe Harold, generally a callous individual, can show real love to a boy, even if he has difficulty showing such love to a grown woman.

Julia, Harold's first love on his travels. Julia is introduced about midway through the poem and is soon gone. She is the first nonsexual love object that Harold encounters, apart from his page. She is described as beautiful, and Harold describes himself as unworthy of her. Her principal task in the narrative is to provide the first platonic love for Harold. Knowing Julia changes him significantly. After he meets Julia, Harold has more to say about the beauties of nature and less to say about the evils of humankind.

— *Marc Goldstein*

CHILDHOOD, BOYHOOD, YOUTH
(Detstvo, Otrochestvo, Yunost')

Author: Leo Tolstoy (1828-1910)
First published: 1852, 1854, 1857
Genre: Novel

Locale: Petrovsk and Moscow, Russia
Time: The 1830's and 1840's
Plot: Bildungsroman

Nikolai Petrovich Irtenev (nee-koh-LAY peh-TROH-vich eer-TEH-nev), a ten-year-old child of a well-to-do Russian family. In this semiautobiographical novel in three parts, he grows into an adolescent and a student at Moscow University. In his formative years, he shows some constant traits: He is self-centered, insecure, sensitive, capricious, and outspoken, with a tendency to philosophize. He also displays some contradictions, depending on circumstances: He is often devious, yet strives for forthrightness; he is stubborn, yet submissive; loving, yet sometimes fickle or even cruel; ambitious, yet at times irresponsible; shy, yet capable of resolute acts; and both confident and self-pitying. His obsessive self-doubts concerning his looks often prevent him from engaging in normal relationships. He is given to daydreaming, and his artistic talent is expressed through his sharp observations as the narrator of the novel. Nikolai's most important character trait is his burning desire to achieve a moral equilibrium that would allow him to orient himself properly in the bewildering period of growing up. He reflects the author's lifelong struggle for moral perfection.

Vladimir Petrovich (vlad-DEE-mihr), Nikolai's older brother, who often is his exact opposite. He has a happy, big-hearted disposition. He is more sensible and practical, much more decisive, less emotional, conscious of his rights, and understanding and forgiving of his brother's youthful outbursts. His relationship to Nikolai is more akin to tolerance than a close emotional tie, and he makes sure that his brother always understands his subordinate position.

Piotr Aleksandrovich (PYOH-tr a-lek-SAN-droh-vich), the boys' father, a Russian country gentleman. He loves his family while remaining aloof from it. He loves his wife but accepts her early death with a remarkable resignation that allows him to remarry soon thereafter. His two chief passions are cards and women. It is questionable whether he has any moral convictions or even whether he needs them. He bears his privileged status as a birthright and always uses connections to get ahead.

Natalya Nikolayevna (nah-TAH-lyah nee-koh-LAH-ehv-nah), Piotr's wife, an exceptionally good-hearted woman with a beautiful smile that stays with her son Nikolai for the rest of his life as a sign of incomparable loveliness and a source of inspiration. Her tender sensitivity is accentuated by her early death, which lends her an aura of sublime tragedy. She is "an angel from heaven" to those around her. She accepts her fate stoically as God's holy will, although not without questioning its fairness, because she had so much love and happiness to give.

Dmitri Nekhlyudov (DMEE-trih nek-LYEW-dov), Nikolai's friend, who satisfies Nikolai's need for a companion during his young manhood. Through him, Nikolai hones and tests his own notions of moral righteousness, especially through Dmitri's refusal to smoke, drink, play cards, or womanize. Dmitri also displays eccentricity in his attachment to an older and homely woman of unusual spiritual capacity that should help him overcome his hot temper and innate wickedness.

Grandmother, a dignified matron of the family, especially after her daughter's death. Nikolai is attached to her and loves her like his own mother. She is especially good at upholding the family's dignified reputation in society.

Natalya Savishna (sa-VEE-shnah), a woman who lived with the Petrovich family for sixty years and whose entire life has been one of pure unselfish love and self-sacrifice. A simple-hearted and affectionate creature, she dies soon after Nikolai's mother, without regrets or fear, steadfast in her faith and having fulfilled the Gospel commandments. She had a powerful and beneficial influence on Nikolai's mind and on the development of his sensibility.

Karl Ivanych Mauer (ee-VAH-nich MAH-ew-uhr), the tutor of Nikolai and Vladimir. A descendant of German immigrants, he uses his knowledge to instruct the Petrovich children in the basics of science and humanities. Despite his being a sad, lonely, and self-pitying figure and at times a strict disciplinarian, he was liked by Nikolai and left an early imprint on his pupil.

— *Vasa D. Mihailovich*

CHILDHOOD'S END

Author: Arthur C. Clarke (1917-   )
First published: 1953
Genre: Novel

Locale: New York City, a Pacific island, and another planet
Time: The 1950's and the twenty-first century
Plot: Science fiction

Rikki Stormgren, the secretary-general of the United Nations, a native of Finland. At the age of sixty, he is widowed with grown children. He devoted his keen mind and diplomatic talents to thirty-five years of public service before being selected by the Overlords as their only liaison with the human race. With a patience born of long experience (and adeptness at poker), he shares mutual trust and faith with the Overlord Karellen, even while kidnapped and held a short time by extremists on Earth. His cleverly arranged glimpse of Karellen does not satisfy his curiosity about the Overlords, and for the ensuing thirty years of his retirement he wonders about their purpose.

Karellen, the supervisor of Earth for the alien race called the Overlords. Immortal by human standards, he and his colleagues act as guardians of the colony Earth for the Overmind of the universe. His, and the Overlords', charge is to act as midwives in the birth and transformation of a new generation of cosmic minds for ultimate union with the Overmind. Mentally gifted but physically barren, they insist only on global justice and order; they act to end wars, South African apartheid, and cruelty to animals. The Overlords all seem to be identical, having the physical form of the legendary Devil and requiring sunglasses because the Earth's sunlight is brighter light than that of their own sun. His mission accomplished, Karellen leaves the dying Earth to visit the next nursery, always probing the mystery of the Overmind.

Jan Rodricks, a University of Cape Town graduate student in engineering physics. Of mixed black and Scottish blood, he is a twenty-seven-year-old romantic and accomplished pianist whose hopes to explore space are dashed by the arrival of the Overlords. Undaunted, he stows away aboard one of their starships, enabling him to visit their home planet and return with them to Earth. He has aged only six months, but the time dilation caused by relativity means that eighty years have passed on his own world. He remains on Earth, transmitting his impressions of the death throes of Earth to the Overlords as they speed away in their starships.

George Greggson, a television studio designer. Devoted to his profession as an art form, he emigrates to the artist colony of New Athens in the South Pacific with his wife of ten years, Jean Morrel, and their two children. Sporting fashionable side-whiskers, he strives to maintain the spark of human creativity in spite of the cultural leveling influence of the Overlords. Instead, he succumbs to their mission when his children become the first embryos of the new cosmic generation. His hopes dashed, he and his wife elect collective suicide with many of their fellow colonists in a nuclear blast.

Jean Morrel, a student and the mate of George Greggson. Individualistic like her husband, twenty-six years old, and platinum blonde, she enjoys dancing and the amenities of modern technological living. She is first Greggson's mate, then his "contracted" wife. Natural psychic powers lead her to a vague fear of the Overlords, who are alerted to them during an early paranormal séance. At New Athens, she endures antiquated housekeeping chores and avoids discussing paranormal matters until the truth becomes known that her own mind was a channel for the timeless knowledge of the universe that emerges in her children. Their loss to the Overmind drives her and her husband closer together than ever.

Jennifer Anne Greggson, the baby daughter of George and Jean. Referred to endearingly as "the Poppet" (a little doll), she does not grow beyond infancy before her mind awakens to the call of the Overmind. Confined thereafter to her cradle, at physical rest with her eyes closed, she has to be left alone while she develops her psychic powers, with which she satisfies her own personal needs. Like an earthly contagion, her powers link with the mind of her brother and then with those of all young children of Earth. Isolated from their elders by the

Overlords, they collectively evolve until their ultimate mental and spiritual power enables them to join the Overmind in the universe and to destroy the Earth physically.

Jeffrey Angus Greggson, Jennifer's brother. A precocious but typical boy of seven, he is intelligent, artistic, and curious about science and the sea. Through dreams, he is the first earthling to be contacted by the Overmind but is bypassed in his evolution by his sister, because he had more acquired mortal habits to unlearn.

Rupert Boyce, a brilliant jungle veterinarian working in Africa. He is gregarious, tactless, and oft-married. A connoisseur of "paraphysics," he lends his immense library on the subject to the Overlords, who therefore assist his veterinary work.

Alexander Wainwright, the head of the Freedom League. Originally a clergyman, he is tall, handsome, and in his late forties. With complete integrity, he admires the peace and prosperity made possible by the Overlords but labors to restore the freedom of choice and creativity they have taken from the human race. He fails.

Rashaverak, an Overlord and anthropologist. He tirelessly pores over Boyce's books on psychic matters to find explanations for mental breakthroughs.

Thanthalteresco, the **Inspector**, an Overlord. Typically inscrutable, he has an insatiable appetite for statistics in probing human behavior to help fathom cosmic knowledge.

Joe, an extremist opponent of the Overlords. Polish, about fifty years old, and weighing some 250 pounds, he belongs to the outlaw group that kidnaps Stormgren. A complex but honest man in the latter's view, he is conservative in his politics and frustrated by the seeming conquest by the Overlords. Once exposed by the Overlords, the activities of Joe and his colleagues are effectively compromised.

— *Clark G. Reynolds*

CHILDREN OF A LESSER GOD

Author: Mark Medoff (1940-   )
First published: 1980
Genre: Drama

Locale: A state school for the deaf
Time: Late 1970's
Plot: Psychological realism

James Leeds, a speech teacher at a state school for the deaf. A sensitive, caring, and charismatic teacher in his thirties, James finds himself challenged by Sarah Norman, a sarcastic and rebellious maid at the school whom the headmaster has asked James to help in his spare time. Matching her sarcasm with his own wit and with unorthodox methods of instruction, James attracts her to him and is in turn attracted by her beauty and intelligence. Engaging in a battle of wits via sign language, they fall in love and get married, against the warnings of the headmaster. Despite his attempts to understand Sarah and her point of view, James insists on trying to make her over, pressuring her to learn to read lips and to speak rather than remain entirely dependent on sign language. When a fellow student, Orin Dennis, engages in a battle with James and tries to recruit Sarah into his militant program of reform, she rejects them both, stating that she is her own person. If James is to win her back, he must accept her on her own terms. He learns the damage his attempts to remake her have caused, acknowledges his love and need for her, and attempts a reconciliation.

Sarah Norman, a twenty-six-year-old maid at a state school for the deaf. Deaf since birth, Sarah is estranged from her mother and rebellious against the world. She is highly intelligent but uses her wits only for sarcastic retorts against anyone who tries to intrude into her privacy. Physically beautiful, she has used her sexuality as a way to communicate with the opposite sex but has found her brief relationships meaningless. When James engages her on her own terms in a battle of wits, she reluctantly falls in love with him and marries him, only to find that he is unable to respect her refusal to learn to read lips and speak and thereby give up what he calls her "angry deaf person's license." When she becomes a battleground between her husband and Orin Dennis in the latter's war against school regulations and organization, she leaves her husband, insisting that she will not be manipulated and will not be "the creation of other people." Only if her husband can let her be the individual that she is, coming into her silence to know her, will she return to him.

Orin Dennis, a student in his twenties at the state school for the deaf. He has some residual hearing and can lip read. Temperamentally militant, Orin is wary of James and hostile to the headmaster. He tries to manipulate Sarah and Lydia into joining his attack on the school organization and authority.

Mrs. Norman, Sarah's mother. Abandoned by her husband when Sarah was a little girl, she has been unable to cope with her daughter's handicap and complex personality, with the result that Sarah ran away when she was eighteen. James helps bring about a tentative reconciliation between them.

Mr. Franklin, in his thirties or forties, the supervising teacher at the state school for the deaf. Alternately pompous and congenial, he is skeptical about James's approach to Sarah and even more skeptical of the success of their marriage, of which he disapproves. A bureaucrat, he bristles when his authority is challenged.

Lydia, in her late teens, a student at the state school for the deaf. A lip reader with some residual hearing, Lydia is infatuated with James and is manipulated by Orin.

Edna Klein, in her thirties, a lawyer recruited by Orin to assist in his attempts to reform the power structure at the state school for the deaf.

— *Robert E. Morsberger*

CHILDREN OF GOD

Author: Vardis Fisher (1895-1968)
First published: 1939
Genre: Novel

Locale: New York, Illinois, and Utah
Time: 1820-1890
Plot: Historical

Joseph Smith, a visionary and mystic, founder of the Church of Latter-day Saints; a poor, handsome, humorless giant who believes himself a prophet of God and who reports the finding of some inscribed golden plates, which he translates into a bible for his followers. Persecuted in New York, Ohio, and Missouri, he is finally killed by a mob in Illinois.

Brigham Young, the strong, able leader of the church after Smith's death. Unsentimental, hardheaded, and unceasingly devoted to the church, he leads his saints to Utah and becomes governor until the territory is made a state. After withstanding many onslaughts, he dies just before being tried for his reputed crimes.

John Taylor, leader of the church after Young's death.

Oliver Cowdery, a schoolteacher, Joseph's first convert, who records Joseph's dictated translation of the Book of Mormon and later becomes a missionary to the Indians.

Heber Kimball, Brigham's close friend and one of his chief aides. He dies of pneumonia after falling from a carriage.

Emma Hale Smith, Joseph's first wife, who complains, among many other things, about Joseph's many wives.

Newel Knight, a convert who introduces Joseph to conditions among his Ohio followers.

Ulysses S. Grant, disgusted president of the United States, who plans to wipe out the Mormon empire.

Bill Hickman, an adventurous former Methodist who becomes a volunteer avenger, scout, and Indian fighter for the Mormons until he finally sours on Mormonism.

Sidney Rigdon, an unpredictable, strong-voiced prophet who, after Joseph's death, is ambitious to head the church and is later excommunicated.

John Bennett, a handsome, sensual adventurer and jack-of-all-trades attracted to Mormonism by Joseph's plural marriage policy.

Jedediah Grant, a zealous preacher, the firebrand of the church, who pleads with Brigham for a casting out of the sinners.

Moroni and

Nephi McBride, grandfather and grandson, leaders of a group of dissident Mormons who leave Salt Lake City after the abolition of plural marriages.

Alfred Cumming, the enormously fat governor of Utah.

Horace Greeley,

Artemus Ward, and

Richard Burton, three visitors to Salt Lake City who later write about the Mormons and their activities.

Wilford Woodruff, Mormon leader after John Taylor. He abolishes plural marriages in an attempt to save the church from destruction.

The Whitmers, a family of early converts.

Moroni, an angel who tells Joseph where to find the golden plates and commands him to translate them.

THE CHILDREN OF HERACLES
(Hērakleidai)

Author: Euripides (c. 485-406 B.C.E.)
First performed: c. 430 B.C.E.
Genre: Drama

Locale: Before the temple of Zeus at Marathon
Time: The age of legend
Plot: Tragedy

Iolaus (i-oh-LAY-uhs), an aged warrior, the former companion and friend of Heracles and the guardian of Heracles' children in their attempt to escape the efforts of Eurystheus, the king of Argos, to destroy them. At the opening of the play, after long wandering, Iolaus has sought refuge with the children before the altar of the temple of Zeus at Marathon. He pleads successfully for their sanctuary before Demophon, the king of Athens, against the arguments of Copreus, the messenger of Eurystheus. The protection offered by the Athenians means inevitable attack from Eurystheus, and the oracles tell Demophon that for him to be victorious, a maiden of a noble house must be sacrificed to Persephone. Because Demophon will not offer up his own child and cannot expect any other citizen to do so, Iolaus offers to give himself up to Eurystheus if the children can be saved. Although made in vain, the suggestion is sincere. The question is resolved by the sacrifice of Macaria, a daughter of Heracles. When a messenger appears with news of the preparation for battle with the Argive host, Iolaus, whose feebleness has been emphasized repeatedly, suddenly insists that he go with him, and he is led off, stumbling in his weakness. In the course of the battle, however, he is rejuvenated temporarily by special gift of the gods and, with the help of Hyllus, a son of Heracles, he captures Eurystheus. Iolaus' character is strangely uneven, and he does not develop into the great and tragic figure he might easily have been.

Demophon (DEE-muh-fon), the king of Athens and son of Theseus. A personification of the spirit of Athens, he exhibits all the qualities attributed to the city: He is noble, brave, dignified, and kind. He offers sanctuary to the children not only because he is a kinsman to Heracles but also because his city is free. He is democratic as a ruler: He will not compel the sacrifice of any citizen and is careful to accept that of Macaria only after she has indignantly rejected any substitution.

Alcmene (alk-MEE-nee), the mother of Heracles. She appears late in the play when she mistakes a messenger, bringing news of the arrival of Hyllus, for an Argive and repels him furiously. She earnestly begs Iolaus not to go into battle; however, when Eurystheus is brought captive before her, the violence of her character is given full play. Although the chorus forbids the murder of a prisoner, she thirsts for the death of her enemy and offers to take the blood-guilt upon herself. She has her way after agreeing to surrender the body to his friends after death. The scene is abrupt and horrible because the reader has not been made to feel the suffering that would lead Alcmene to such violence.

Eurystheus (ew-REHS-thews), the king of Argos and Mycenae. Although spoken of throughout the play, he appears only at the end and then is not villain enough to fit the impression that has been built. He has been spoken of as proud, a bully, and a coward, but he is calm, dignified, and brave before Alcmene and the threat of death. Refusing to plead for his life, he assures the Athenians that because they tried to save him, his spirit will help them against the descendants of the children of Heracles who will later invade Attica.

Macaria (mah-KAYR-ee-uh), the daughter of Heracles who gives her life as a sacrifice for the safety of her brothers and sisters. She has pride of blood but is nevertheless restrained and modest. She is the ideal type of the young virgin.

Copreus (KOP-ree-uhs), the herald of Eurystheus. He attempts to drag the children from the temple of Zeus and attacks Iolaus. Because he is a messenger of Eurystheus, his action accounts largely for the impression of insolent pride that the chorus has of the king.

Children of Heracles, who, though silent, are on the stage from the beginning of the play to the end.

CHILDREN OF THE GHETTO

Author: Israel Zangwill (1864-1926)
First published: 1892
Genre: Novel

Locale: London
Time: The nineteenth century
Plot: Realism

Esther Ansell, a poor Jewish girl adopted and educated by a rich woman. Esther, sensitive and very intelligent, graduates from London University. She writes a novel of Jewish life entitled *Mordecai Josephs.* A shy girl, she hides behind the pen name "Edward Armitage." Despite her success, Esther returns to the ghetto. Later she migrates to New York, drawn by her love for her family, who are already in the United States.

Mrs. Henry Goldsmith, a wealthy Jewess who adopts Esther Ansell and educates her, even sending Esther's family to America to free the girl from ghetto life. Mrs. Goldsmith is a woman who likes intellectuals and is generous to them.

Moses Ansell, a pious, orthodox, unworldly Jew. He is Esther's father. He spends too much time praying and too little time earning a living.

Benjamin Ansell, Esther's young brother, who is placed in an orphanage at his mother's death

Becky Belcovitch, a kindly neighbor of the Ansells in the ghetto.

Malka Birnbaum, cousin of Moses Ansell's dead wife. She tries to help her cousin's family.

Sam Levine, a commercial traveler who through ignorance of the ancient Jewish traditions marries the wrong girl.

Leah Birnbaum, loved by Sam Levine. She gives up her beloved because he is not an orthodox Jew.

Hannah Jacobs, Sam Levine's accidental and temporary wife. She loves David Brandon, who has left the orthodox customs of his people.

David Brandon, Hannah's suitor, whom she loves but finally rejects because of his unorthodoxy.

Reb Shemuel Jacobs, Hannah's indulgent father. He is a rabbi.

Melchitsekek Pinchas, a young, poor Jewish poet and scholar. He becomes editor of a newspaper sponsored by the Goldsmiths.

Raphael Leon, a young journalist of strong moral principles. He loves Esther Ansell and promises to follow her to America.

Sugarman, a marriage broker in the London ghetto.

Wolf, a Jewish labor leader who wants to be sent to Parliament.

Shosshi Shmendrik, a street hawker who marries for money.

Widow Finkelstein, a storekeeper who marries Shosshi.

Bear Belcovitch, a neighbor of Moses Ansell. He wants his daughter to marry Shosshi Shmendrik.

Debby, a poor young seamstress, Esther Ansell's friend.

Leonard James, Hannah Jacob's brother. He is a snobbish, vulgar young Jew who deserts his name and religion.

Rabbi Joseph Strelitski, a rabbi at a fashionable synagogue in London. He sees himself as a hypocrite and leaves his temple to start a new life in New York.

CHILDREN OF VIOLENCE

Author: Doris Lessing (1919-   )
First published: 1952-1969
Genre: Novel

Locale: Africa and London
Time: 1934-2000
Plot: Bildungsroman

Martha Quest, 1952
Martha Quest, the protagonist. Her name is symbolic: "Martha" echoes the biblical character of that name, known for service, and "Quest" represents her search for meaning. The book begins when she is fifteen years old, imagining a "four-gated city" that will be the utopia where all can live happily. She wishes to avoid standard female roles but winds up in a traditional marriage.

May Quest, Martha's mother, who represents what Martha does not want to become: a nagging old woman who tries to live through her children because the sex roles of society have

not given her any opportunity to make anything of herself.

Douglas Knowell, Martha's first husband, who represents Martha's areas of ambivalence. She feels some affection for him but sees him more as an avenue of escape from her parents than as an agent of entrapment in the roles of wife and mother. He seems interesting and imaginative but turns out to be shallow and traditional in his views.

Adolph King, a Jewish radical with whom Martha has her first affair.

A Proper Marriage, 1954

Martha Quest, who gives birth to a daughter but hates her stereotyped role. She decides to leave her husband and child.

Douglas Knowell, Martha's husband, even more a force of oppression and boredom than before, not letting Martha have a life of her own.

Jasmine Cohen, who knew Martha as a teenager. She offers Martha friendship and the opportunity for political activism.

A Ripple from the Storm, 1958

Martha Quest, who seeks meaning in relationships and radical politics.

May Quest, Martha's mother, who disowns Martha for abandoning her supposed responsibilities as wife and mother.

Anton Hesse, a Communist. He attracts Martha by caring for her when she is sick. His nurturing and idealism are counterbalanced by his sexual inabilities and his need to keep Martha in a traditional submissive housewife role. Martha marries him to save him from deportation and regrets having done so. In the end, she falls asleep as he is explaining his heartfelt political views.

Mrs. Van, in some ways a powerful and competent woman who is also involved in politics. She turns out, in her own way, to be as much a prisoner of the maternal role as Martha's mother.

Landlocked, 1965

Martha Quest, who still seeks the good city and a role for herself after having had two unsuccessful marriages. She decides that Africa is not the place for her and prepares to leave for England. She begins to look for spiritual, as well as political, approaches to fulfillment.

Thomas Stern, a Polish Jew who escaped from the Nazis, the most exciting man Martha has yet encountered. He breaks off his affair with Martha, first to fight for Israel, then to work in a small African village, where he suffers an attack of blackwater fever and dies. Martha reads a manuscript he wrote and decides he was in part driven mad by his memories.

The Four-Gated City, 1969

Martha Quest, who finds a vision of her four-gated city. In the wake of a disaster that has all but destroyed Great Britain, children are being born with strange new mental powers. She finds happiness in flight from the city and acceptance of the world as one great organism.

Mark Coldridge, a novelist whose books mirror the chaos of his times. His writings become popular as science-fictional predictions. He hires Martha as his secretary and housekeeper.

Margaret Patten, Mark's mother, a living barometer of social and cultural trends. She has married a homosexual because it is fashionable.

Lynda Coldridge, Mark's wife, who appears to be insane. She is compared explicitly to the madwoman in *Jane Eyre*. She has been institutionalized and lurks in the basement, but she may in fact have found a way of avoiding the traditional female roles. It is suggested that her "insanity" may include telepathic and other psychic powers.

— *Arthur D. Hlavaty*

THE CHILDREN'S HOUR

Author: Lillian Hellman (1905-1984)
First published: 1934
Genre: Drama

Locale: Massachusetts
Time: The 1930's
Plot: Problem

Mary Tilford, a malicious fourteen-year-old schoolgirl. She attends a private girls' school, where she bullies her fellow classmates, disobeys her teachers, and whines when she is not given her way. She has been brought up by an indulgent grandmother who has spoiled her. When two of her teachers, Karen Wright and Martha Dobie, try to discipline her, she retaliates by spreading the rumor that they are lesbians. Although the rumor is untrue, Mary sticks to her charge. Her shocked grandmother then removes her from the school and convinces the parents of the other children to do likewise, thus destroying the school and ruining the teachers' lives.

Amelia Tilford, an influential and wealthy older woman. She dotes on Mary, her grandchild. She knows that Mary is petulant, and she initially scoffs at Mary's attack on the teachers, but she is horrified when Mary whispers her charge that Martha and Karen are lesbians. Blinded by her outrage and unwilling to see through Mary's manipulation of the facts, she succeeds not only in closing the school but also in ostracizing the two teachers. When Amelia finally learns of Mary's deception, she abjectly asks for Karen's forgiveness and searches for a way to rectify the harm she has caused the teachers.

Martha Dobie, an intense woman, twenty-eight years old, devoted to her friendship with Karen and rather jealous of Joe Cardin, Karen's fiancé. When Martha learns of Mary's charge against her, she goes with Karen to confront Amelia Tilford, who thinks that the two women have come merely to brazen things out. Martha and Karen take Amelia to court on charges of libel but lose their case when Martha's Aunt Lily refuses to testify. Feeling guilty about the breakup of Karen and Joe, and suspecting that she has harbored sexual feelings for Karen, Martha kills herself at the end of the play.

Karen Wright, a twenty-eight-year-old teacher who has joined Martha in working hard to establish the Wright-Dobie boarding school. Although she is very close to Martha, she senses a strain between them when she becomes engaged to Joe Cardin, and it may be this strain that Mary is able to manufacture into a lie. Karen is more even-tempered than

Martha, and although she grieves at the failure of their school, she clearly will survive, even though it appears that her fiancé has begun to doubt her and to wonder whether she indeed has a lesbian relationship with Martha.

Dr. Joe Cardin, Karen's fiancé. He tries to expose Mary as a liar, and he intercedes on behalf of Martha and Karen with Amelia Tilford but proves unable to shake Mary's story or to change Amelia's mind. Although he tries to stick loyally by the two women, visiting them when everyone else has shunned them, he eventually succumbs to doubts about the relationship between Martha and Karen and reluctantly accepts Karen's suggestion that they should not marry.

Lily Mortar, Martha's aunt and a teacher at the school. She is proud of her career in the theater and relates to students her experiences on the stage. She is highly critical of Martha and points out that her niece is jealous of Karen and Joe. Her loose talk inadvertently helps Mary in concocting her charges against the teachers. During the trial, when Karen and Martha are trying to establish their innocence, Lily remains out of town and does not answer their pleas for help. She returns when it is too late, thinking only of herself and apparently oblivious to the grave injury she has done to the lives of Karen and Martha.

— *Carl Rollyson*

CHINA BOY

Author: Gus Lee (1946-   )
First published: 1991
Genre: Novel

Locale: San Francisco, California
Time: The 1950's
Plot: Autobiographical

Kai Ting, the seven-year-old son of a Nationalist Chinese Army officer, living in a predominantly African American and poor neighborhood in San Francisco. Kai, the youngest child and only son in his family, is short, skinny, and myopic. Kai leads a sheltered life. His stepmother, Edna, forces him to stay in the street most of the time. Kai's fractured English, gentle manners, and inability to fight earn him the nickname "the China Boy" and make him the punching bag of all the neighborhood boys. He is particularly tormented by Big Willie Mack, a towering twelve-year-old who takes his shoes and his money. His constant battering does not soften the heart of his stepmother, who sends him right back to the street to face the bullies. At the suggestion of a neighbor, Hector Pueblo, Kai's father sends him to the YMCA to learn boxing. His instructors feel sorry for the gentle little boy, who is starved physically and emotionally, and try their best to teach him the basics of self-defense. Kai is a slow learner and continues to be pounded in his neighborhood. After one particularly vicious beating by Big Willie, Kai's instructor, Barney Lewis, realizes that the only way to end this constant terror is to force Kai to fight back. He devises a street attack plan for him. Kai is given step-by-step instructions to draw Big Willie into a confrontation. Kai fights with all of his might. He is beaten badly, but Big Willie, hurt himself, realizes that he cannot continue to pick on him. With the confidence gained by standing up to Big Willie, Kai seems ready to face his stepmother as well.

Edna McGurk, Kai's stepmother. She comes from a wealthy Philadelphia family. After losing her husband in the Korean War, she married Kai's father. She had anticipated living in a sophisticated and wealthy Chinese family and was unprepared for the role of a mother in a household with limited

means. Full of resentment for her stepchildren, she is harsh to Kai and his sister Jenny. Her sole mission seems to be to eradicate all Chinese traces in the family: She allows no words in the Chinese language, no Chinese food, and no Chinese friends.

Toussaint LaRue, a nine-year-old neighborhood boy who befriends Kai. Toussaint's mother, a widow with limited means, has a generous, loving heart. She wipes Kai's tears, cleans his wounds, and encourages her son to help the little boy. Kai sees the real meaning of Christian charity in the LaRue household. Toussaint's lessons in cultural adaptation do not save Kai from Big Willie's beatings, but his friendship keeps Kai alive.

Big Willie Mack, a twelve-year-old bully of the neighborhood. He has no family and no fixed place to stay. He takes what he needs from the younger children and beats them for fun. He targets Kai because of his physique and manner of speaking. He is taken by surprise when Kai stands up to him.

Anthony Barraza, a former Marine who teaches boxing at the YMCA. A gruff, kindhearted man, he is touched by Kai's plight, arranges to have him fed at the cafeteria, and does not give up even when he sees no progress.

Barney Lewis, the chief of instruction at the YMCA. He is responsible for drawing the final battle plan for Kai's confrontation with Big Willie. He goes to Kai's neighborhood and meets Hector Pueblo, a mechanic at a nearby garage who has witnessed the battering of Kai and observed Big Willie's mode of operation. Knowing Kai's limitations in boxing skills, he prepares him emotionally and psychologically for the fight, which becomes a turning point in Kai's life.

— *Leela Kapai*

THE CHINABERRY TREE: A Novel of American Life

Author: Jessie Redmon Fauset (1882-1961)
First published: 1931
Genre: Novel

Locale: Red Brook, New Jersey
Time: 1930-1931
Plot: Social realism

Laurentine Strange, a coprotagonist, a beautiful, middle-class black woman of twenty-four who has quietly and stub-

bornly refused to live fully. When her younger cousin comes to live with her, Laurentine is exposed to a number of new experiences and people that assist her in slowly emerging from a self- and other-created shell. For years, Laurentine and her mother, Sarah, have been the talk of the black community of Red Brook, New Jersey, because Laurentine is the product of Sarah's well-known affair with the married and white Colonel Francis Halloway. It is only when Laurentine meets Dr. Stephen Denleigh, a newcomer to Red Brook who can accept her and her "bad blood," that she begins to participate fully in life.

Melissa Paul, a coprotagonist, Laurentine's sixteen-year-old cousin. She comes to live with the Stranges when her mother, Judy, Sarah's sister, marries and moves from Philadelphia to Chicago. Judy thinks Melissa will be better off with Sarah. Melissa likes the middle-class lifestyle in Red Brook and is immediately popular at school. She makes the Strange household temporarily come alive with people and events. Melissa, a typical flirtatious teenager, has two memorable relationships in the novel, one with Asshur Lane and one with Malory Forten.

Sarah Strange, also called **Aunt Sal**, Laurentine's mother and Melissa's aunt. She is forty-five years old. Somewhat like Laurentine, Sarah has limited her living, but unlike her daughter, she has experienced real love, in her scandalous affair with the late Colonel Halloway. Because Sal has known real love,

she does not let the community's ostracism of her destroy her sense of self.

Dr. Stephen Denleigh, Laurentine's suitor, who is forty years old and an outsider to Red Brook. He falls in love with Laurentine shortly after their first meeting and does not let the community's assessment of the Stranges become his own. He supports Laurentine and urges her to resist the community's assault on her and her family.

Asshur Lane, Melissa's first suitor, a young man who follows the convictions of his heart, not the standards of the community. He is moral, strong, steady, outgoing, and pleasant. He is a "black-next-door-neighbor" type.

Malory Forten, Melissa's second suitor. He is handsome, intelligent, moody, withdrawn, pretentious, and snobbish. When he meets Melissa, he thinks he has at last found his soulmate. Even before the events of the novel reveal that Melissa cannot be the one for him, he finds several "faults" with her.

Millie Ismay, Laurentine's friend and confidante. She helps Laurentine to gain entrance to a group of upper-class blacks who do not hold Laurentine's birth and parentage against her. Mrs. Ismay is Bostonian by birth, married to a doctor, and a bit unconventional.

— *Charles P. Toombs*

THE CHINESE WALL
(Die chinesische Mauer: Eine Farce)

Author: Max Frisch (1911-1991)
First published: 1947
Genre: Drama

Locale: China
Time: Mid-twentieth century and c. 200 B.C.
Plot: Farce

The Contemporary, a modern intellectual who is both the narrator of the play and a central character. He moves back and forth in the play's time structure, introducing the many historical and literary personages, debating with them, and commenting on their role in history and relation to the modern world. The figures represent recurring archetypal characters that populate the modern imagination. The narrator hopes to convince them (and the audience) of the need to break the cycle of their behavior. The return of such tyrants as the Chinese emperor Hwang Ti and France's Napoleon Bonaparte could mean the end of humanity in the atomic age. For his eloquent warnings of a nuclear holocaust, the Contemporary receives an award from Hwang Ti, but he proves to be ineffectual. Neither the tyrants nor the people are deterred by his intellectual arguments, and the cycle of destruction begins anew.

Hwang Ti (hwahng tee), the emperor of China from 247 to 210 B.C., the gentle-looking but ruthless founder of China's first central government. To secure his regime from threats outside China, he orders the building of the Great Wall. To maintain totalitarian rule domestically, Hwang Ti demands the absolute praise and allegiance of his people. While seeking to silence the dissent ascribed to an unseen citizen called Min Ko, "The Voice of the People," the fanatical emperor accuses a mute of being "The Voice of the People" and tortures him,

trying to extract a confession. Hwang Ti is deposed by a tyrannical prince who perpetuates the oppression.

Olan, a Chinese farmer's wife. She and her son have made a pilgrimage to Nanking to see the emperor, and she wonders if the complaints about the emperor are true. When her son is tortured as Min Ko, she refuses to admit the truth, namely that he is mute and unable to register dissent. Her motherly pride prompts her to hail him as "The Voice of the People."

The Mute, Olan's son **Wang**. Because he is the only silent member of a throng cheering the emperor, he is arrested as the traitorous Min Ko, the final enemy in the land.

Mee Lan, the daughter of the emperor. She is dissatisfied with the powerful young princes who court her and seeks instead a defender of truth and intelligence such as the Contemporary. Mee Lan's humanistic inquiry of him ("What do you know about man?") is answered brutally by the revolutionary forces who ravish her.

Wu Tsiang, a Chinese prince who is betrothed to Mee Lan. He is bitter because she, who despises his love of power, refuses to marry him. The prince promises revenge and leads the revolt that topples the emperor.

The Maskers, historical and literary figures promenading in a polonaise, "like figures on a musical clock," symbolizing the recurrent forms of human thought and behavior.

— *Allen E. Hye*

CHIPS WITH EVERYTHING

Author: Arnold Wesker (1932-   )
First published: 1962
Genre: Drama

Locale: England, in a Royal Air Force hut
Time: Mid-twentieth century
Plot: Social realism

Pip Thompson, the protagonist, the lone upper-middle-class recruit among working-class conscripts. He resists the efforts of the officers to enlist him as one of them. His hatred of the class system was catalyzed one day by an accidental experience in a dirty East End café; its tea-stained menu, written in a beautifully foreign hand, read "Chips With Everything." Pip is both envied and criticized as a snob by his fellow draftees. Even the officers regard his sympathy with the working class as a perverse form of snobbery. His revulsion to killing is displayed in his temporary defiance of an order to participate in bayonet practice. Both his rebellion and his leadership ability are evident in a carefully planned and successfully executed raid on a nearby coke pile, undertaken to keep the hut warm. In the surprise ending that evoked ambivalent responses from critics, Pip suddenly dons an officer's uniform. His joining ranks with the "other side," however, is not meant to draw on his middle-class privilege but is instead precipitated by the impending arrest of the entire hut for the men's refusal of an order to take a runaway (Smiler) to the guard room. Pip's new authority allows him to override the Pilot Officer's command to imprison the men. He does so in the name of loyalty—his and the men's—to a higher responsibility in which understanding of the need to protect a fellow serviceman, in this case the much-abused Smiler, is accommodated.

Smiler Washington, a homesick recruit identified by the perpetual smile with which he was born and cannot erase. He becomes the major butt of criticism from his superiors as each one of them commands him to wipe the smile from his face, something he cannot do. Because the "bastards" will not believe him, he reaches a breaking point and runs away. After suffering bleeding feet in his long walk, he is returned to the hut. Rather than imprisonment, his punishment (by Pip) is to be put three weeks back in flight.

Charles (Chas) Wingate, a recruit who both envies and resents Pip's educational advantages. Like Pip, who at first lies about having six brothers, he invents four brothers. They confess and establish a conversational relationship; Charles longs to be able to talk with Pip on equal terms. He constantly asks Pip questions and is fascinated by his tales of history, especially of the French Revolution, at first even accusing Pip of making up stories.

Wilfe Seaford, the first of the recruits to mock Pip's posh background. He sings a bawdy tune and is told by Pip to put his working-class halo away because they will have to put up with one another for the next eight weeks.

Andrew McClure, a Scot and an electrician who rejects the Pilot Officer's advances when the latter places his hands on Andrew's knee. He further defies the Wing Commander's wish for a cheerful or modern piece (such as an Elvis Presley song) by reciting a melancholy Robert Burns poem.

Archie Cannibal, who accuses Dickey (in the bed next to him) of talking so much that he sounds like an adding machine. At the Christmas party, the two men grapple in a physical fight, but they leave together, with Cannibal helping Dickey up from a fall.

Dickey Smith, the eldest of the new conscripts and, therefore, assigned by Corporal Hill to be his assistant. Having attended a technical school, he exercises his verbal superiority over Cannibal, whom he accuses at the Christmas party of "having uttered a syllable of many dimensions."

Dodger Cohen, one of the two smallest recruits. He is assigned to factotum duties for Corporal Hill. A comically realistic character, he tells of his family's pram business that is always short of storage space. He sees every pregnant woman as a potential pram buyer and every building, even the hut, as a potential pram storage place.

Corporal Hill, the fair but stern driller of discipline, particularly in the "square-bashing" of marching techniques.

Wing Commander, the moral disciplinarian for whom honor, along with thrift and respect, is paramount.

Squadron Leader, the legal enforcer of discipline.

Pilot Officer, the overseer of neatness and cleanliness and the most informal of the officers in his relationship with the recruits.

Physical Training, a noncommissioned officer whose aim is to make the men sweat like Niagara Falls until they look like Greek Gods.

— *Susan Rusinko*

CHITA: A Memory of Last Island

Author: Lafcadio Hearn (1850-1904)
First published: 1889
Genre: Novel

Locale: Louisiana coastal waters
Time: The nineteenth century
Plot: Impressionistic realism

Chita, a child rescued from the sea during a storm off the Louisiana coast. She is so young that all she can tell her rescuers on Last Island is that her real name is Lili, her Creole name is Zouzoune, and her mother and father are named Adele and Julien. Called by her new friends Chita, the little girl grows up on the island without knowing any more of her earlier existence.

Dr. Julien La Brierre, a physician from New Orleans who comes to see a patient on Last Island. He falls ill himself, and in his delirium he is reminded of his dead wife by Chita's startling resemblance to the drowned woman. He dies without realizing that the girl is really his daughter.

Feliu Viosca, a fisherman who lives on Last Island. He rescues Chita from the sea and takes her into his home.

Carmen Viosca, the fisherman's wife. She treats the foundling from the sea as though she were her own child.

Laroussel, a Creole who was Dr. La Brierre's rival for his dead wife's hand years before. At one time the doctor and Laroussel fought a duel over Adele, who became the doctor's wife. He questions Chita on Viosca's island and gives her a trinket, but he does not discover that she is Dr. La Brierre's child.

Captain Harris, a sea captain who checks for survivors after the storm. He decides it is best for Chita to remain with the fisherman and his wife, who have given the girl a home.

Captain Abraham Smith, a sea captain who tries to rescue as many people as he can from the hurricane.

Mr. Edwards, the patient whose illness summons Dr. La Brierre to Last Island.

A CHOCOLATE SOLDIER

Author: Cyrus Colter (1910-   )
First published: 1988
Genre: Novel

Locale: At and near Gladstone College in Valhalla, Tennessee
Time: The 1920's to the 1980's
Plot: Psychological realism

Meshach Coriolanus Barry, the narrator, a lonely, obsessive fifty-five-year-old black pastor. A life of professional tragedies as well as accomplishments has led him through prison and mental hospitals. He decides to write the history of his long-dead college friend Cager Lee. For thirty-five years, Meshach has been obsessed with the events leading to Cager's death, and he has mythologized Cager as the "hero" of his tale. Meshach sets himself up as Cager's antithesis, a hypocritical preacher who merely goes through the motions of faith. By writing this history, Meshach hopes not only to define his relationship to Cager but also to understand the meaning of his own life.

Carol Barry, Meshach's daughter, a serious young woman in her late twenties whose relationship with her father has been strained since her teenage years, when, as the narrator hints, he engaged in an incestuous relationship with her. Meshach desperately needs Carol as an audience for his story about Cager, but she has heard this story before and resents her father's need to relive the past. Unable to cope with her father's obsessive need to retell history, she finally rejects him.

Rollo Ezekiel "Cager" Lee, the rebellious, doomed hero of Meshach's narrative, portrayed as a messianic young man whose desire to improve the lives of his fellow African Americans leads him to drop his studies at Gladstone College and attempt to muster an all-black militia. Believing that force is always necessary in the struggle for freedom, Cager idolizes Robert E. Lee as a brilliant military tactician. It is while working as a butler for Mrs. Dabney that Cager learns about a nineteenth century slave rebellion, which stirs him to make the

same type of violent gesture of protest against oppression. After murdering Mrs. Dabney, Cager is lynched by a mob.

Mary Eliza Fitzhugh Dabney, the elderly matriarch of an old Virginia plantation family who divides her time between donating to conservative philanthropic societies and leading organizations celebrating the Confederacy. She employs Cager as a servant and is transformed by his influences. Without realizing the source of her new attitude, she begins to change from a fiery believer in social Darwinism into a generous benefactor of all-black Gladstone College before she is killed by Cager.

Haley Tulah Barnes, a compassionate black professor of history at Gladstone College. When he sees that Cager is doing poorly at school, he works out a plan to get Cager a job with Mrs. Dabney so that the boy will have some time to consider his future goals.

Flo, a beautiful and dignified single mother in her late twenties or early thirties who falls in love with Cager because of his intensity and drive. Flo provides Cager with maternal and romantic affection, but she makes the mistake of thoughtlessly revealing to him that his genitals are severely misshapen. Emotionally wounded, Cager isolates himself from her. In the meantime, Meshach, also smitten with Flo, becomes her new lover. Flo, however, sees through Meshach's preacherly professions of faith to the doubting confused man he really is. Still in love with Cager when he is lynched after killing Mrs. Dabney, Flo flees to New Orleans with her daughter. Years later, she dies there, from tuberculosis.

— *V. Penelope Pelizzon*

THE CHOSEN

Author: Chaim Potok (1929-   )
First published: 1967
Genre: Novel

Locale: The Williamsburg section of Brooklyn, New York
Time: The 1940's
Plot: Fiction of manners

Reuven Malter, a young Orthodox Jew who narrates his experiences during his high school and college days in Williamsburg and Brooklyn, among the Orthodox and Hasidic communities. Reuven's greatest challenge lies in coming to terms with the Hasidic Jews who consider his father's methods of textual criticism of the Talmud to be suspect. They also reject his father's quest to establish a new Zionist nation in

Palestine. Reuven often is tempted to hate the Hasidic Jews for their intolerance toward his father, but Reuven's father continually counsels him to be loving and tolerant even toward those who are not so in return. Reuven and Danny Saunders meet first at a baseball game, during which Danny deliberately tries to hit the ball directly at Reuven's head while Reuven is pitching. The resulting injury nearly blinds Reuven in one eye but leads to a friendship between these two that enables them both to see and learn things they could not understand on their own. Through this friendship, Reuven helps Danny confront his religious community and come to accept his special gifts for helping others through psychology.

Danny Saunders, a brilliant young Hasidic Jew who is expected to take his father's place as the leader of their sect of Russian Hasidic Jews. His photographic memory enables him to be a quick learner, but his quest for knowledge outside his own religious community leads him eventually to pursue a career in psychology instead of the priesthood. His mind functions like a fine machine, but he struggles to learn how to identify with people's feelings. He keeps the Jewish laws of his sect with great care and honors his father's excommunication of the Malters, even though the resulting separation causes Reuven much pain.

Reb Saunders, a spiritual leader of a sect of Russian Hasidic Jews and the father of Danny Saunders. Reb Saunders is a complex man who readily identifies with suffering in the world, especially because his family in Russia had been killed before he led his people to the United States. He rears his son Danny in absolute silence, except when they are studying the Talmud together. Reb Saunders hopes thereby to teach his brilliant son to become spiritually sensitive. When he does choose to speak to Danny, Reb Saunders uses an intermediary such as Reuven Malter, who hates the silence imposed on his friend but comes to respect Reb Saunders' objectives. At one point, Reb Saunders excommunicates Reuven and David Malter because he opposes the establishment of a new Israel by anyone except the Messiah. After Israel becomes a nation, Reb

Saunders suspends the ban on the Malters and resumes his friendship with them.

David Malter, an Orthodox Jewish teacher who is known for his many articles on the Talmud and his efforts to support the establishment of a Zionist nation in Palestine. As a widower, he rears his only son, Reuven, with the help of a Russian housekeeper named Manya. Being a tolerant man, David teaches his son to understand and respect the traditions of the Hasidic community, even though it bitterly opposes much of what David Malter advocates. He also helps Danny in his independent reading of Sigmund Freud and other thinkers not taught at his father's yeshiva or at parochial school. David's crowning achievement is to promote the establishment of a nation of Israel in Palestine, which he does as a means of reestablishing the Jewish community after the Holocaust of World War II. Throughout the novel, David struggles with a heart condition but is determined to promote his faith regardless of the personal price he must pay.

Rav Gershenson, a teacher of Talmud in Samson Raphael Hirsch Seminary and College, which Reuven and Danny attend. As a spiritual leader in his late sixties, he cautions Reuven against using the textual critical methods of his father, especially in class. He, like many others in his community, fears that identifying textual errors in the Talmud will undermine confidence in the authority of Jewish law.

Nathan Appleman, a psychology professor at Samson Raphael Hirsch Seminary and College who teaches Danny to move beyond psychoanalysis and use the newer methods of experimental psychology.

— *Daven M. Kari*

THE CHOSEN PLACE, THE TIMELESS PEOPLE

Author: Paule Marshall (1929-   )
First published: 1969
Genre: Novel

Locale: A mythical island in the Caribbean
Time: The 1960's
Plot: Social realism

Saul Amron, a veteran anthropologist and expert field worker in Third World countries. He leads a research group of Bournehills, on a Caribbean island. Sensitive, caring, and willing to listen, he acquires an understanding of the island people. Recruited from a teaching position at Stanford University, he reluctantly agrees to return to fieldwork; his first wife, a Holocaust survivor, died of a miscarriage in Honduras on his last field trip. In many ways, the Bournehills trip is an attempt to atone for his perceived failures, but he meets with limited success at Bournehills.

Harriet Amron, his wife, heiress to a Main Line Philadelphia family fortune founded on the slave trade and the exploitation of the Bourne Island people. After her divorce from a nuclear scientist, she meets, seduces, and marries Saul, then secures his research post with an organization funded largely by her family fortunes. She functions as the quintessential WASP (white, Anglo-Saxon Protestant), intent on control. Although Saul warns her not to interfere, she does, and then she becomes increasingly isolated. When she learns of Saul's affair with Merle Kinbona, she succeeds in having him recalled to Philadelphia. When he tells her the marriage is over, she commits suicide.

Merle Kinbona, a descendant of the white plantation owner and owner of the only guest house in Bournehills. She witnessed her mother's murder and was educated at her mulatto father's expense in England. She is tormented by her past, her inability to identify her mother's murderer, and the lesbian relationship in England that caused her husband to take their daughter and return to Africa. Her bizarre attire suggests her cultural conflict, and her nonstop talking masks her inner turmoil. She is the unifying force in the novel, the bridge between the Bournehills "little fellas" and the educated "liberals."

Allen Fuso, Saul's assistant, a statistician whose guilt-ridden memories about the death of a friend, Jerry Kislak, render him incapable of action or love. In a state of "atrophy," this "bland amalgam" is drawn to the vitality of Vereson Walkes.

Vereson Walkes, a young Bournehills man who works in the United States for three years and returns to his home to accomplish two goals: to find and punish the woman who neglected and lost their child, and to buy a car he can drive to victory in the Whitmonday Race in Spiretown. He wins the race but dies when his brakes fail.

Lyle Hutson, a Bourne Islander whose local academic success wins for him an education at Oxford, the London School of Economics, and the Inns of Count. In England, he was Merle's lover and a radical socialist; on Bourne Island, he is a wealthy lawyer whose clothes, car, and house reveal that he has sold out and collaborated with progressive schemes that would benefit only the rich.

Leesy, Vere's great-aunt, the epitome of the "little fella" with her half acre of cane, a fear of machines, and household furnishings that tie her to the past.

Ferguson, Bournehills' reciter of stories about rebel hero Cuffee Ned and would-be opponent of the closing of the sugarcane plant. The sight of the plant owner renders him speechless.

Stinger, a hardworking Bournehills resident whose work makes Saul understand the plight of the "little fellas."

Delbert, a store proprietor who resembles a tribal chieftain. He is Saul's primary source of information.

— *Thomas L. Erskine*

THE CHOUANS
(Les Chouans)

Author: Honoré de Balzac (1799-1850)
First published: 1829
Genre: Novel

Locale: Brittany
Time: 1799
Plot: Historical

The Marquis de Montauran (mohn-toh-RAN), fiery leader of the Chouans, rebels against the French Republic. His nickname is Gars, and he is the son of Mme du Gua. He loves Marie de Verneuil, although he is warned that she is a spy. He goes to her home to marry her after she herself has told him that she has been hired to betray him. The morning after the marriage, he is shot and captured; later, he dies in prison, after he tries to escape from her house in Fougéres.

Marie de Verneuil (vehr-nyew-YUH), in love with Montauran. She is the natural daughter of the duke de Verneuil and the former wife of Danton. When Montauran's jealous mother tries to shoot her, Marie seeks revenge, but her love eventually conquers her hate. She marries Montauran hoping they can escape from intrigues and leave France. Her plans fail, and she is shot wearing her husband's uniform while acting as a decoy to help him escape.

Hulot (ew-LOH), an officer in the French Republican Army, sent to put down the rebellious Chouans, an aggregation of aristocrats, smugglers, and Breton peasants. He is utterly disgusted by the capture and death of Montauran and Marie de Verneuil.

Mme du Gua Saint-Cyr (gwa sahn-SEHR), jealous mother of Montauran. She knows of her son's rebellious activities and supports him in them. When she discovers Marie's love for her son, she tries to shoot Marie.

Corentin (koh-rahn-TAN), a spy for the French Republic. It is he who employs Marie as a lure to trap Montauran and bring the Chouan leader to his death.

Francine (frahn-SEEN), former sweetheart of Marche-à-Terre. She is Marie's maid.

Marche-à-Terre (mahr-shah-TEHR), one of the rebellious Chouans. A fierce and rapacious villain, he leads the rebels in forays of thievery and violence.

Galpe-Chopine (galp-shoh-PEEN), a peasant who helps Marie in many ways.

Barbette, the wife of Galpe-Chopine.

CHRIST STOPPED AT EBOLI: The Story of a Year
(Cristo si è fermato a Eboli)

Author: Carlo Levi (1902-1975)
First published: 1945
Genre: Novel

Locale: Gagliano, a small town in southern Italy
Time: 1935-1936
Plot: Social realism

Carlo Levi (LAY-vee), a physician and political prisoner, the narrator and protagonist of the story. Kind, contemplative, artistic, and observant, he has a deep compassion for those who are poor, ill, and disadvantaged. A painter by vocation, he would prefer merely to observe without becoming directly involved, but he cannot. His political imprisonment involves being sent to live in a small and remote southern Italian village, where he is watched closely at all times. He records the experiences and the impressions of his sojourn.

Luigi Magalone (lew-EE-gee mah-gah-LOH-neh), the mayor. Smug and self-satisfied, the Fascist mayor enjoys the power and the prestige of his position. He gives orders to the prisoners for the sheer pleasure of seeing his requests enacted and is particularly zealous in the literal and unwavering application of Fascist laws and regulations in his village.

Giulia Venere (jee-EW-leeah veh-NEH-rah), Carlo Levi's housekeeper. She is a middle-aged woman who is hardworking, unemotional, and strong. She is ignorant but is naturally intelligent and practical. Her life is linked to superstitions and traditions. Despite her natural wisdom and knowledge of life, she firmly believes in the magical powers of curses, potions, and incantations. The world has no secrets for her and no illusions, but she holds in great reverence and fear the realm of the spiritual and of the intangible. It is from her that Carlo learns much about the traditions and folklore of the village, and about the villagers themselves.

Don Giuseppe Trajella (jee-ew-SEHP-peh trah-EHL-lah), the parish priest. Old and ailing, his most visible characteristics are those of rancor and bitterness toward the entire village. Although bright and cultured, he has no interest other than venting and feeding his anger and his unhappiness. He has been in the parish for many years, having been assigned there as punishment for misconduct. The entire village ridicules, persecutes, and torments him.

Dr. Milillo (mee-LEEL-loh), an elderly physician and uncle of the mayor. He is a man whose seventy years of age have made his movements slow and his voice shaky. A gentle and well-intentioned man, he remembers very little about medicine and is ill-equipped to tend to the sick. He feels threatened by Dr. Levi's arrival and is reassured by the latter that his place will not be usurped.

Dr. Gibilisco (jee-bee-LEE-skoh), a physician. Like Dr. Milillo, he too is an elderly practitioner. A meticulous dresser and man of imposing presence, he projects an image of confidence that conceals a profound ignorance of the medical profession. An exacting and mistrusting man, he demands payment from even the poorest of patients. His profession, in his view, makes him superior to the rest of the villagers and assigns him control over their life and death.

Donna Caterina Magalone Cuscianna (kah-tehr-EE-nah mah-gah-LOH-nay kew-SHEEAH-nah), the head of the local Fascist Party and sister of the mayor. She is open, cordial, hospitable, and maternal. In addition, she is clever, calculating, and powerful. From her privileged position as sister of the mayor and head of the Fascist Party in the village, she has as much to say about what happens in town as Magalone himself. Her driving force is hatred toward certain women in the village, in particular the pharmacist's daughter, whom she believes to be her husband's lover.

— *Susan Briziarelli*

A CHRISTMAS CAROL

Author: Charles Dickens (1812-1870)
First published: 1843
Genre: Short fiction

Locale: London
Time: The nineteenth century
Plot: Ghost

Ebenezer Scrooge, a grasping, covetous, flinty old pinchpenny. With his pointed nose, shriveled cheeks, and stiff gait, he is repulsive to all his acquaintances. Drop by drop, he has squeezed all vestiges of humanity from his shriveled soul.

Bob Cratchit, Scrooge's destitute clerk. Although overworked and underpaid by Scrooge, Cratchit still retains his goodness and generosity.

Tiny Tim, Bob Cratchit's youngest son. Tiny Tim, crippled and frail, seems doomed to an early death unless there are improvements in the family fortunes. Weak in body but not in spirit, he does not die; instead, he lives to enjoy the generosity of a regenerated Ebenezer Scrooge.

The Ghost of Christmas Past, With a strong beam of light streaming from his head, this is the first of three phantoms who are to attempt the difficult task of converting Scrooge.

The Ghost of Christmas Present, A huge, jolly figure, this specter, bearing a glowing torch, takes Scrooge to many homes, among them Bob Cratchit's.

The Ghost of Christmas Yet to Come, This is the most fearful sight of all. Shrouded in black, this ghost conducts Scrooge to many cheerless scenes, including a view of his own neglected grave.

Jacob Marley, Scrooge's former business partner, who appears to him in spectral form. In life, he had been as ruthless as Ebenezer; in death, he is compelled to wander far and wide searching for spiritual salvation.

Fred, Scrooge's jovial nephew.

Fezziwig, Scrooge's former employer, a prosperous man of good will, whom he sees with the aid of the Ghost of Christmas Past.

CHRONICLE OF A DEATH FORETOLD
(Crónica de una muerte anunciada)

Author: Gabriel García Márquez (1928-   )
First published: 1981
Genre: Novel

Locale: A Colombian village on the Caribbean coast
Time: Early twentieth century
Plot: Detective and mystery

Santiago Nasar (sahn-tee-AH-goh nah-SAHR), a member of the Arab community, slim and pale, with dark curly hair. He is killed in front of his own house at the age of twenty-one. A handsome bachelor, he is described as having had a love for horses, falconry, and church pomp; his other characteristics included flirtatiousness, valor, merriness, peaceableness, and prudence. Normally dressed in khaki with riding boots, he donned unstarched white linen pants and shirts on special occasions. Inheritor of the Divine Face cattle ranch and a firearms enthusiast, he carried a .357 magnum with armored bullets as he traveled in the country. Although he is killed as the deflowerer of Angela Vicario, his innocent behavior up to the moment of his death suggests that he was wrongly accused of the act.

Angela Vicario (AHN-heh-lah vee-KAHR-ee-oh), the youngest and prettiest daughter of a poor family. She resists the prospect of marriage to Bayardo San Román and unsuccessfully attempts to pass as a virgin on their wedding night. After Bayardo takes her back home, she is beaten by her mother, Purísima (Pura) del Carmen Vicario. Questioned by her brothers, she names Santiago as the man responsible for deflowering her. In the aftermath of the murder, she grows from a hapless spirit to a mature and witty woman. Previously uninterested in Bayardo, she becomes obsessed with him and remains unmarried, writing hundreds of letters to him in the years after their separation.

Bayardo San Román (bay-AHR-doh sahn rroh-MAHN), who captures the imagination of the villagers when he arrives in town wearing clothing ornamented with silver. About thirty years old, he has a slim waist, golden eyes, and tanned skin. A drinker, he seems to lack a steady occupation but exhibits familiarity with railway engineering, telegraphy, frontier illnesses, card games, and swimming. Soon after seeing Angela, he courts her and proposes to her. When he discovers on their wedding night that she is not a virgin, he carries her to her mother. Afterward, he is found in a state of severe intoxication and carried out of the town by members of his family. Although he never opens any of Angela's letters, he saves them and eventually returns to her.

Pedro Vicario and

Pablo Vicario, brothers of Angela, identical twins who support their family by slaughtering pigs. Both presented themselves for military service at the age of twenty, but Pablo, six minutes older than Pedro, stayed home to support the family. Pedro entered service, where he contracted a case of blennorrhea (excessive mucus discharge). Told that Santiago has dishonored their sister, the brothers undertake to stab him to death. Although they are unrepentant after the deed is done, the narrator notes that they seemed reluctant to carry it off: By informing more than a dozen villagers of their intent, they seem to have been hoping to be stopped. In jail, they are haunted by an odor of Santiago that lingers after his death. Pablo, who suffers a severe case of diarrhea in confinement, becomes a goldsmith upon his release. Pedro, whose chronic pain prevents him from sleeping for eleven months, is cured of his disease while behind bars. After he is freed, he rejoins the military and disappears on a mission.

The narrator, a friend of Santiago. Returning to his hometown, he investigates Santiago's murder twenty-seven years after its occurrence. The narrative summarizes the results of his efforts.

Clotilde Armenta (cloh-TEEL-deh ahr-MEHN-tah), a milk vendor who appeals to the Vicario twins to refrain from killing Santiago. In an effort to prevent the crime from taking place, she asks all the people she sees to warn Santiago of the danger he is in, attempts to intoxicate the brothers, unsuccessfully tries to restrain Pedro, and shouts a warning to Santiago.

Don Rogelio de la Flor (roh-HEH-lee-oh), Clotilde Armenta's husband.

Colonel Lázaro Aponte (LAH-sah-roh ah-POHN-teh), the mayor. He and Don Rogelio disappoint Clotilde because they do not take strong measures to prevent the murder from occurring. Don Rogelio dies from shock after seeing Santiago's bloody corpse.

Purísima (Pura) del Carmen (pewr-EE-see-mah), Angela's mother, who beats her daughter harshly after Bayardo returns her.

Luis Enrique (lew-EES ehn-REE-keh), the narrator's brother and a friend of Santiago.

Cristóbal (Cristo) Bedoya (krees-TOH-bahl bay-DOY-ah), another friend of Santiago. Luis, Cristo, Santiago, and the narrator had been drinking companions of Bayardo.

Luisa Santiaga (lew-EE-sah sahn-tee-AH-gah), the narrator's mother, who was Santiago's godmother and a blood relative of Pura. She is initially impressed with Bayardo, but her regard for him gradually ebbs. On the day of the murder, she tries to warn Santiago of the threat to his life but is told that she is too late.

— *David Marc Fischer*

THE CID
(Le Cid)

Author: Pierre Corneille (1606-1684)
First published: 1637
Genre: Drama

Locale: Seville, Spain
Time: Eleventh or twelfth century
Plot: Tragedy

Don Roderick (dohn roh-deh-REEK), the **Cid**, the leading warrior in the cause of the king of Spain against the Moors. He is faced with the major conflict of the drama: his filial obligation to vindicate the honor of his father, who has been insulted by Don Gomez, against his love for Don Gomez's daughter, Chimène. Roderick is brave, the fiercest and most valiant soldier in the kingdom. His love for Chimène, on the other hand, shows his gentle nature. When he is confronted with his conflict between love and honor, between personal happiness with Chimène and preservation of his family honor at the cost of his love, he chooses honor. After he has killed Chimène's father, Roderick offers himself as a sacrifice to Chimène's vengeance. By the end of the drama, he has defeated the Moorish army, has fought a duel, and has received the king's permission to wed Chimène.

Chimène (shee-MEHN), Roderick's lover, the daughter of Don Gomez, who insulted the honor of Roderick's father. Like her lover, she endures the main conflict of the drama. Her love for Roderick clashes with her duty as a daughter of Don Gomez to seek revenge on his killer. Although she loves Roderick deeply, she must subdue that emotion and act as reason dictates and the social code demands. That code requires that she hate Roderick and pursue a means to seek his death. Thus, she defiantly holds love at bay. Like Roderick, she gives up her personal happiness for the cause of honor and filial responsibility. She pleads with the king to arrange a duel between Roderick and Don Sanche, a young knight who loves her. Hoping that the young knight will kill Roderick—yet hoping also that he does not—she promises to marry the winner. When Roderick returns victorious, having spared the life of his opponent, Chimène's conflict is at its pitch: She is happy that Roderick has survived, yet as a daughter of the slain count, she spurns Roderick's love and his final offer to surrender himself to her. The play ends with Chimène refusing to marry Roderick as she proclaims her anguish over her conflicting desires.

Doña Urraque (dohn-YAH ur-RAHK), infanta of Castile. She also endures the thematic conflict of love and honor. She loves Roderick, yet she knows that because he has no royal blood, she must not think of marrying him. Like the historical

Queen Elizabeth I of England, the infanta must put the demands of the country and the court before her own desires. With this resolve, she hides her love for Roderick and encourages his own love for Chimène, thus deepening her anguish and the anguish of the lovers themselves. She is Chimène's confidante, her other voice, a kind of alter ego who insists that Chimène should renounce her vengeance and marry Roderick.

Don Gomez (dohn GOH-mehs), the count of Gormaz, Chimène's father. He is a vain, self-important courtier whose preference by the king prompts him to insult his rival, Roderick's father. Although Don Diègue is a much older man, the count slaps him, boasting of his own valor and strength. When Diègue, in disgrace, exhorts his son Roderick to vindicate him, Roderick confronts the count and offers battle. Although boastful and hotheaded, the count is no coward. He fights Roderick and meets his death honorably.

Don Diègue (dohn dyehg), Roderick's father, once Spain's greatest warrior. Old and enfeebled, he feels slighted by the king's preference for Don Gomez. His injured pride provides a key to the motive of revenge and is the source of the conflict between love and honor.

Ferdinand, (fehr-dee-NAHN), the first king of Castile. He understands the conflict between love and honor facing the characters. As head of state, he seeks to mediate the problems in the interest of Spain. His emotions have little to do with his actions. He is thus a voice of reason, calling for order and stability.

— Edward Fiorelli

THE CIDER HOUSE RULES

Author: John Irving (1942-   )
First published: 1985
Genre: Novel

Locale: Maine
Time: The 1880's to 1900 and the 1920's to the 1950's
Plot: Social realism

Wilbur Larch, an obstetrician and abortionist. As a young doctor, he decides to forge a medical career helping desperate, helpless, and usually poor young women terminate their pregnancies in supportive surroundings or, if they choose, deliver children whom he will try to place in proper foster homes. He has accepted as the burden and blessing of his life the administration of St. Cloud's orphanage, which he operates as a kind of home to an extended family of life's victims. He is completely and unselfishly committed to his chosen task as a healer in the largest sense, and he accepts his responsibilities as a sort of symbolic father to the inhabitants of the orphanage. In the tradition of the practical New Englander, he sees his life goal as "being of use" to humanity. His experiences have shown him that the laws and conventions of society often are diametrically opposed to the requirements of human need, so that he is willing to resist unjust rules in accordance with his own firm moral standards. In spite of his deep convictions, he is understanding and tolerant of others' opinions. His ultimate goal is to provide a "family" of some kind—a center of love and respect—for all those who have not had the good fortune to be born into satisfactory circumstances. Through his long and productive life, he epitomizes the qualities that a true practitioner of the healing arts must possess: a heartfelt concern for human suffering, a vital capacity to share the tribulations of his patients, a rage against the pain he cannot cure, and a warmth that radiates the spiritual decency his life represents. Known appropriately as "St. Larch" by his admiring colleagues, he is an organizer of a community of compassion that is both a family and a kind of temple to serve the needs of humanity.

Homer Wells, an orphan who can never satisfactorily leave the home at St. Cloud's. He is Larch's surrogate son and successor. Although he disagrees with Larch's position on abortion, arguing from an ethical stance that regards all forms of life as sacred, he loves Larch and recognizes that difficult decisions sometimes compel choices that are far from ideal but that best suit the needs of suffering humans in an imperfect world. He is aware of his isolation as an orphan and is motivated by a desire to establish a deep connection with people he loves, but his path is strewn with obstacles, and his relationships with the people he loves are complicated by situations he can only suffer through. He demonstrates his suitability as Larch's successor when he is able to combine his own needs with an awareness of the requirements of the people he cares for and the institution he wishes to sustain. By becoming "Dr. Fuzzy Stone," he returns to St. Cloud's to fulfill the destiny he accepts as inevitable.

Candy Kendall Worthington, Homer's closest friend, then the one true love of his life and the mother of their son, Angel Wells. She is the daughter of a solid New England family who discovers her real capabilities as a person when her essentially sheltered, protected life is disrupted by an unplanned pregnancy and the inadvertent consequences of a genuine love for Wells and for her fiancé, Wally Worthington.

Melony, also called **Melody**, an unadoptable, perpetually angry young woman who meets Wells when they are both awaiting placement in foster homes. Her inability to feel comfortable in any home setting is the result of dark impulses born of loneliness and mistreatment. Wells is haunted by her in memory during the years that he is searching for an independent identity and gratefully accepts her donation of her body to the medical facilities at St. Cloud's after her death, as a gentle conclusion to a life of desperate wandering.

Wally Worthington, the son of a privileged, wealthy family. He is the polar opposite of Melony, perpetually hopeful and cheerful in spite of experiences in World War II that leave him in a condition of physical disability. He is Candy's husband and Homer's friend. His acceptance of the somewhat unusual family situation is an example of human adaptability and innate decency.

Olive Worthington, Wally's mother, an example of the best kind of old New England manners and morals. Her wealth has not made her a snob or bigot, and she is the closest person to an older, mothering presence in the course of the narrative.

Arthur Rose, the chief of a crew of African American orchard workers. His daughter Rose Rose becomes Angel Wells's wife.

— Leon Lewis

CINNA
(Cinna: Ou, La Clémence d'Auguste)

Author: Pierre Corneille (1606-1684)
First published: 1643
Genre: Drama

Locale: Rome
Time: c. 10 C.E.
Plot: Tragedy

Cinna (SIH-nuh), the grandson of Pompey. In love with Amelia, he seeks to win her hand by avenging her father's death through the murder of Emperor Augustus, whom he regards as a tyrant. He is finally led to remorse for his evil intentions by the emperor's display of forgiveness, mercy, and generosity.

Amelia, who is loved by Cinna. She asks, as a provision of their marriage, that he avenge her father by murdering Emperor Augustus. Long remorseless in her demands for revenge, she is finally won over by the emperor's nobility and clemency, takes blame for the plot on herself, and gives her friendship to Augustus.

Augustus, the emperor of Rome. He discovers, among those he loves and trusts, a plot to take his life. The emperor, through his mercy and forgiveness, causes remorse among the conspirators and wins their admiration and friendship.

Livia, the empress of Rome. She commends her husband's generosity and mercy to all future rulers.

Maximus, Cinna's friend and fellow conspirator.

Fulvia (FOOL-vee-uh), Amelia's friend and confidante.

Evander (eh-VAN-dur), Cinna's freedman.

Euphorbus (ew-FOHR-buhs), Maximus' freedman and fellow conspirator.

Polyclitus (pol-ih-KLI-tuhs), Augustus' freedman.

CINQ-MARS

Author: Alfred de Vigny (1797-1863)
First published: 1826
Genre: Novel

Locale: France
Time: The seventeenth century
Plot: Historical

Henri d'Effiat (ahn-REE dehf-FYAH), marquis of Cinq-Mars (sah[n]-mahr), a real-life character in France's first historical novel. He serves the king through his hatred of Cardinal Richelieu and his desire for permission to marry Marie de Gonzaga. As a conspirator, he signs a secret treaty providing for help from Spain, then tells Marie about it in the presence of the priest, a spy, who affiances them. He is beheaded.

Cardinal Richelieu (ree-sheh-LYEEUH), who, to maintain power with the king, has the messenger with Cinq-Mars' treaty killed at the Spanish frontier. He resigns as minister of state in order to force the helpless King Louis XIII to increase his power.

King Louis XIII (lwee), who makes Cinq-Mars an officer in his guards. After Richelieu's resignation, he is unable to handle the affairs of the kingdom alone, and he reappoints Richelieu, giving him permission to kill the conspirators.

Marie de Gonzaga (gohn-ZAH-gah), duchess of Mantua, who loves Cinq-Mars though she is destined to become queen of Poland.

Anne of Austria, who tries to protect the king and their son, the future Louis XIV, from the ambitious Richelieu.

François August de Thou (frahn-SWAH oh-GEWST deh tew), a friend of Cinq-Mars, beheaded as a conspirator.

The Duke de Bouillon (bew-YOHN), estranged from the king by Richelieu.

Gaston d'Orléans (gas-TOHN dohr-lay-AHN), brother of the king, banished by Richelieu.

Marshal Bassompierre (ba-sohn-PYEHR), an enemy of Richelieu arrested at the home of Cinq-Mars.

Urbain Grandier (ur-BAN grahn-DYAY), a monk of Loudun, executed as a magician by order of Richelieu.

The Abbé Quillet (kee-YAY), Cinq-Mars' former tutor, who defends Grandier.

A judge, Richelieu's agent at the trial of Grandier. Cinq-Mars strikes him in the face with a red-hot cross that had been given to Grandier to kiss.

THE CIRCLE

Author: W. Somerset Maugham (1874-1965)
First published: 1921
Genre: Drama

Locale: Dorset, England
Time: 1919
Plot: Comedy of manners

Arnold Champion-Cheney, a member of Parliament and owner of a country estate, Aston-Adey. About thirty-five years of age, he is tall and good-looking, fair complexioned with a clean-cut and sensitive face. Impeccably dressed, he is an example of the prim and proper upper-class Englishman. Although politics is his career, his primary interest appears to be collecting antique furniture. Although he loves his wife of three years, he lacks passion and has little interest in sex; he has no inkling that he stands on the verge of losing her. As a gentleman, he shows himself capable of generosity but is averse to self-sacrifice.

Elizabeth Champion-Cheney, Arnold's wife, a charming, pretty woman in her early twenties. Taken for granted by her husband, she is a romantic at heart, idealizing human love relationships. She is truthful, frank, tolerant, and witty, a good hostess. Her husband's career and enthusiasm for antiques leave her cold.

Clive Champion-Cheney, Arnold's father, formerly a member of Parliament, now an affluent upper-class Englishman living in retirement. A single man in his early sixties, he is tall with gray hair, dresses carefully, and bears himself with dignity. Highly intelligent, he is a man of the world. His ample wit turns toward the caustic and at times sarcastic. His unexpected arrival at the Champion-Cheney estate creates an awkward situation because the invited guests include Kitty, his former wife. Highly analytical, he essentially is a man of reason rather than emotion.

Lady Catherine (Kitty) Champion-Cheney, Champion-Cheney, ArnoldArnold's mother and Clive's former wife. For thirty years, she has been the mistress of Lord Porteous. She is a gay, small woman with dyed red hair and painted cheeks. She is vain, preoccupied with retaining a youthful appearance. Her mistakes in the play make her appear an object of humor and sympathy, yet she remains a romantic at heart. She is both talkative and sentimental and obviously is dependent on her long-standing relationship with Lord Porteous, whom she seeks to possess.

Lord Porteous, called **Hughie**, a former member of Parliament and former associate of Clive, normally living in exile with Kitty. A bald, elderly gentleman, he is gruff and somewhat snappish, but underneath a crusty exterior he reveals a sentimental streak. He gave up his chance to be prime minister for the love of Kitty and harbors some bitterness that his life has not turned out well, though he would never express this sentiment.

Edward (Teddie) Luton, a youthful manager of a rubber plantation in the Federated Malay States. He recently was discharged from the English army, following World War I. He is pleasant, athletic, well-mannered, and ambitious. Desiring a wife to accompany him back to the Far East, he boldly declares his love for his hostess, Elizabeth. His masculine directness and competitive nature contrast with Arnold's passive and prim character.

Anna Shenstone, a guest at the Champion-Cheney home, a pleasant and elegant woman of forty. She has a small role in the play, serving to focus the dialogue. In partnership with Teddie Luton, she wins at bridge against Kitty and Lord Porteous.

— *Stanley Archer*

THE CIRCLE OF CHALK
(Hui-lan ji)

Author: Li Xingfu
First performed: The thirteenth or fourteenth century
Genre: Drama

Locale: Nanking and Peking
Time: Before the thirteenth century
Plot: Comedy

Chang-hi-tang, a beautiful sixteen-year-old girl who has been sold to a house of ill repute to keep her family from starving. Immediately befriended by a wealthy man, the delicate and talented young girl is brought as second wife into a childless household. Her sweet demeanor and her ability to bring forth a son cause the first wife to vow revenge. Hi-tang, above reproach, follows her mentor's directions in all things, even to serving the tea with which the elder wife poisons her husband. Hi-tang is accused of the murder by the elder wife, who also claims that Hi-tang's son is really her own. The wise emperor devises a test. He orders the child placed in a chalk circle, from which each wife may try to pull the child and claim him. Because of her true mother love, Hi-tang refuses to try pulling her son away from the other woman across a chalk circle, for fear of hurting him. She thus proves her innocence. She is made empress when it is revealed that the new emperor is the true father of her child. Hi-tang had always thought that the prince had come to her only in a dream.

Ma Chun-shing, the duped husband whose first wife is unfaithful and treacherous while his second is always loving and trustworthy. He elevates in his heart the beautiful young wife and thereby brings down the wrath of the barren Mrs. Ma. On one occasion, the victim of jealousy, he believes his young wife has given away jewels and robes to a lover, but he discovers that the man is her unfortunate brother. When Mr. Ma considers divorcing his first wife so that he may elevate Hi-tang to the position of first wife, Mrs. Ma poisons him.

Mrs. Ma, the vindictive first wife of Ma Chun-shing, who claims Hi-tang's son as her own and contrives with a lover to poison her generous husband. She is unable to find fault or complain against the model second wife for many years, but a plot of revenge finally reaches fruition. With bribery and mendacity, the evil woman wins the trial, has Hi-tang imprisoned, and thus keeps the young son and the fortune of the family. When she is called to a high tribunal by the new emperor, her evil deeds are revealed and her fate is sealed.

Chang-ling, Hi-tang's brother, a young scholar embittered by the duplicity and oppression of the government's representatives. Arrested for expressing doubts that the new emperor will improve the lot of the common people, he is taken before the same high tribunal as his sister. The new emperor is in sympathy with his ideas of reform, however, and Chang-ling is not only pardoned but also made a judge in place of the evil Chu-chu.

Chow, a clerk in the local court, the lover and accomplice of Mrs. Ma. This despicable man cruelly watches virtue suffer and vice triumph as he carries on him the poison his mistress finally asks of him. Calculating and brutal, he conspires to rig the trial and bribe witnesses until he at last is brought to justice.

Chu-chu, a judge of the local court who accepts a bribe to find Mrs. Ma innocent and Hi-tang guilty. He sentences Hi-tang to death, but before the sentence is carried out, all involved are called before the new emperor for an investigation. Chu-chu's decision is then overruled, and he loses his judgeship to Chang-ling.

Prince Po, one of the old emperor's sons and later the new emperor. As a dashing young prince, he had fallen in love with

Hi-tang, and on her wedding night he had stolen through her window and made love to her as she slept. Thus, her child is actually his, not Mr. Ma's. When Hi-tang is brought before him, he recognizes her, and after learning the truth in the case he metes out justice to the evildoers and makes Hi-tang empress.

THE CITADEL

Author: A. J. Cronin (1896-1981)
First published: 1937
Genre: Novel

Locale: Two small towns in Wales, London, and a town in southwestern England
Time: First third of the twentieth century
Plot: Social realism

Andrew Manson, the central character. Coming from a background of poverty, he attends the University of Dundee with the help of an academic prize and graduates as a medical doctor. He accepts a position as an assistant to Dr. Edward Page in the coal-mining community of Blaenelly in Wales. He is the latest in a series of assistants who actually are expected to run the practice for Page for little remuneration. Manson is idealistic and works hard despite his growing sense of being exploited. He forms a close friendship with Philip Denny, a talented physician in the community, whose tendency to drink excessively makes him less than respectable. After Christine's death, it is with the support of Denny that Manson is able to pull himself together, and they open a clinic for the treatment of lung disease.

Christine Manson, née **Barlow**, a schoolteacher in Blaenelly. She meets Manson when he enters her schoolroom to protest her allowing an ill child to return to school. They are attracted to each other and marry. She tutors Andrew in languages to help him prepare for his advanced degrees. Throughout their marriage, she works to keep him committed to the ideals of his youth. Estranged when he is tempted by wealth and status, they are reconciled, but she dies in a street accident.

Edward Page, an elderly physician in Blaenelly. He has suffered a stroke and knows that he will never practice again, but he is dominated by his wife, who maintains the fiction that

he will recover. He likes Manson but is incapable of protecting the young doctor from his wife's exploitation.

Blodwen Page, Dr. Page's wife. A short, plump woman about forty years old, she has a domineering personality. She will not admit to the miners in her husband's practice that he will never work again and recruits assistants such as Manson to do all the work. She pays these assistants meagerly and feeds them as cheaply as she can.

Philip Denny, a bright, idealistic physician who assists Dr. Lewis in Blaenelly. He welcomes Manson and finds in him a kindred spirit. Although prone to overindulgence in drink, Denny is a more than capable physician with an unconventional approach to life. He helps Manson in Blaenelly and in finding a new position. Later, he persuades Manson to set up a lung clinic and helps his friend overcome the death of Christine.

Freddy Hampton, a former classmate of Manson who makes good in London. He has an elaborate practice dedicated to soaking rich patients and develops a circle of acquaintances who call one another in for consultations as a further means of enriching themselves. Hampton seems the epitome of a successful physician to Manson, and Manson is persuaded to join with him. Manson breaks with Hampton when he realizes that the latter has no true concern for patients.

— *Francis J. Bremer*

CITIES OF SALT
(al-Tīh)

Author: Abdelrahman Munif (1933-)
First published: 1984
Genre: Novel

Locale: Saudi Arabia
Time: World War I to 1953
Plot: Naturalism

Miteb al-Hathal, a Bedouin tribesman with a special passion for the Wadi al-Uyoun desert oasis, where he and his family live. The appearance of Americans, who were invited by the Arabian government to explore and drill for oil, changes Miteb's previously stoic and optimistic attitude toward life. With characteristic boldness and candor, he warns people about impending disaster and even stands up to the regional emir, but no one heeds him. When the Americans level the orchards and gardens to force people to leave what will henceforth be an oil-drilling site, Miteb mounts his Omani camel and disappears for good. Reports of his visitations come from various parts of the region.

Ibn Rashed, a man from Wadi al-Uyoun who acquiesces to the American presence and decides to join the forces of change. He encourages the local population to relocate and

becomes a personnel recruiter for the Americans, bringing Bedouins from all over to Harran with promises of good salaries and homes. The workers find only dehumanizing tents and later barracks. He loses his struggle against Dabbasi for local influence and power and comes to fear paranoically the specter of Miteb al-Hathal. He dies a broken man, an example of an Arab who has broken his ties and traditional fidelity to tribal values.

The Americans, oil workers at Wadi al-Uyoun and Harran, and at the pipeline camps in between. These one-dimensional characters, almost caricatures of American workers and managers abroad, seem superficially interested in local culture and customs but are quick to defend and implement company policy in the face of local traditions and concerns.

Bedouin workers at Harran, people lured by the promise

of good wages, houses, and a future for their families. These people come from all over to work for the Americans. Hard workers and good Muslims, but unaware of the facts of life in the modern world beyond their personal experience, they seem simple and uncouth animals to the Americans and Westernized Arab company men.

Harrani townspeople, generous, uncomplicated people unaware of much that is transpiring in the modern world beyond their region. Some accede to Ibn Rashed's entreaties that they sell their land to the Americans; however, Dabbasi convinces some of them to hold onto their land at least, in the face of the foreign takeover of their community.

Naim Sh'eira, the Americans' Arab translator, who, like other Arab company men, learns American disdain for his fellow Arab Bedouins.

Emir Khaled al-Mishari, a middle-aged, heavyset, and dark-skinned man who replaces an earlier emir who had refused to stay in Harran once he saw changes and the Americans there. Ignorant, indecisive, timorous, and self-indulgent, Khaled is fascinated by a succession of such modern gadget gifts as a telescope, a radio, and a telephone. The climactic workers' strike and the community uprising lead to his mental breakdown. People see him yelling into his unconnected telephone in his car, speeding from Harran with his entourage.

Fawaz, Miteb al-Hathal's eldest son, somewhat responsible for the family after his father's disappearance. Feeling the youthful Bedouin urge to travel, however, he leaves home on a brief trip, during which he has a vision of Miteb in a storm. On a second trip, he accepts Ibn Rashed's offer of a job in Harran. At the novel's end, he leads a charge of striking workers and Harranis toward the American compound.

Dabbasi, a round-faced man with a small beard, in his mid-fifties. He comes to Harran and there wins the hearts of the emir and the populace. He marries a Harrani and marries his son Saleh to one as well. His own wedding party is the social event of the day. He eventually defeats Ibn Rashed in their competition for local power and influence.

Abdu Muhammad, Harran's first baker, who falls pathetically in love from a distance with one of the American women brought by boat to the Americans in Harran.

Hajem, a boy assigned with his elder brother, Mizban, to sea-rock cutting in the Harran port expansion project because they are the only Bedouin workers who can swim. After Mizban drowns by catching his foot on an underwater rock, Hajem becomes simple-minded and unable to communicate. The crowd at Mizban's funeral displays community desperation, sadness at their own plight, and their sense that the Americans are responsible for all untoward events. Terminated from his employment, Hajem is sent back inland by Ibn Rashed to his uncle, who later comes to Harran to demand justice and compensation. The uncle is astounded by the disrespectful and untraditional treatment he receives. Their detainment by the deputy emir upsets the workers, which leads ultimately to Ibn Rashed's downfall. The uncle takes his nephew back inland without fanfare and without compensation.

Akoub, a short, middle-aged Armenian truck driver from Aleppo who dies in his truck in Harran some time after newer vehicles and more commercial operations have driven him out of business. All of Harran goes to Akoub's funeral, his death marking the end of an older and more personal way of transporting people and things.

Raji, Akoub's fellow truck driver, a tall, skinny, bald, contentious man, quick to anger but good-hearted. He and Akoub eventually become best friends. Akoub's death devastates him. At the novel's end, Raji carries the wounded in his old truck from Harran to Ujra.

Mufaddi al-Jeddan, a traditional practitioner of medicine, a dervish who treats people for free and seeks only such goods as sandals, other clothing, and food as he needs them.

Dr. Suhbi al-Mahmilji, a physician who has lived in Tripoli and Aleppo and has also served as a hajj pilgrimage physician before coming to Harran. Suhbi becomes a favorite of the emir, who chooses him to give the welcoming speech for Crown Prince Khazael, the sultan's deputy, on the occasion of the opening of the Wadi al-Uyoun-Harran pipeline.

Johar, one of the emir's bodyguards. Later, as the chief security officer for the emir, he establishes a paramilitary organization and terrorizes Bedouin workers and townspeople. He is assumed to have ordered or committed the murder of Mufaddi al-Jeddan.

Khazna al-Hassan, a Bedouin midwife and healer who treats women and children and thinks of Mufaddi al-Jeddan as her brother. She worries about him when he is arrested, cares for him after he is beaten, and is disconsolate at his death.

— *Michael Craig Hillmann*

THE CITY AND THE HOUSE
(La città e la casa)

Author: Natalia Ginzburg (1916-1991)
First published: 1984
Genre: Novel

Locale: Rome and countryside near Perugia in Italy, and Princeton, New Jersey
Time: Late 1970's or 1980's
Plot: Domestic realism

Giuseppe Guaraldi (jew-SEHP-peh gwah-RAHL-dee), a writer and scholar, approaching age fifty, who has just ended a long love affair with Lucrezia, a married woman. He sells his apartment against the advice of his friends, leaves his job, and moves to Princeton, New Jersey, to live with his older brother. He imagines an idyllic life with his brother that will provide him with the security he needs after the end of his affair. Instead, he finds that, shortly before his arrival in Princeton, his brother has married Anne Marie, a colleague from the scientific institute where he works. Giuseppe views the marriage as an intrusion and begins writing a novel to keep himself from being lonely. At first, he dislikes Anne Marie immensely, but, upon the sudden death of his brother, he begins to feel an affinity for her that eventually leads to marriage. Although he and Lucrezia had a child together, Giuseppe has never acknowledged his son and concentrates on the child of his previous marriage, Alberico, and on Anne Marie's daughter, Chantal, and her husband, Danny. When Alberico is murdered by drug dealers, Giuseppe returns to Italy for the funeral and realizes how little he has been connected to his life there.

Lucrezia (lew-KREH-zee-ah), Giuseppe's former lover. Although she has been married to Piero for many years and they have five children together, Lucrezia has had a number of affairs. At the end of her relationship with Giuseppe, she begins an affair with Ignazio Fegiz, an annoying know-it-all with whom she becomes obsessed. She feels restless after her long-term relationship with Giuseppe and uses Ignazio as the means to extricate herself from the country house her friends have used as a symbol of stability in their relatively rootless lives. She is an unsatisfied woman for whom the role of wife and mother has paled, although, in the eyes of her friends, she has performed it beautifully. After she leaves Piero, she finds a dark and unattractive apartment in Rome where she lives with her five children. She discovers that Ignazio is totally committed to another woman and that he is far from being the love of her life. Lucrezia finds herself living alone in Rome, an observer of the disintegration of her friends' lives as well as her own.

Alberico Guaraldi (ahl-behr-EE-koh), Giuseppe's homosexual son. Alberico has spent most of his adult life away from his father, who thinks of him as a dilettante. He lives in various countries and pursues his career as a filmmaker. When he succeeds in making a critically acclaimed film, he is as surprised as anyone. He and his father have not been close, less because of his homosexuality than because Alberico is financially independent through an inheritance from his mother's family. He owns an apartment at a time when his father and his father's friends are practically homeless, frequently moving from one apartment to another. While the so-called adults of his family are wandering and searching for meaning in their lives, he has found a creative calling and establishes a family for himself. Alberico, his lover, and their friend Nadia, who comes to live with Alberico when she discovers that she is pregnant by another man, form a domestic partnership of relative stability. After Nadia has her child, Alberico and his lover take on the parenting role that she refuses. Their lives revolve around filmmaking, the baby, and drugs. The drugs eventually result in the violent deaths of all three.

Anne Marie Guaraldi, the widow of Giuseppe's brother and Giuseppe's wife after his brother's death. Anne Marie is a humorless and rather cold woman who pursues scientific interests. She was married before she met Giuseppe's brother and has a daughter, Chantal, from that marriage. She is not a motherly woman and rarely sees her daughter. Chantal comes to live with her mother when her husband, Danny, and she separate, but it is Giuseppe who consoles her. Anne Marie does not want to be bothered with the mess of relationships. After Anne Marie marries Giuseppe, they settle into a convenient silence. He writes his Italian novel in his study, and she continues her employment at the scientific institute and socializes with her coworkers. Because Anne Marie refuses to give of herself in a relationship, Giuseppe and Chantal take comfort from each other and have a short love affair. Anne Marie has had three marriages, all of which she considers successful in comparison to her daughter's, yet her first marriage ended in divorce, her second husband died early in the relationship, and she sees her marriage to Giuseppe as a convenient way to continue living in the same house. She needs little from her familial relationships, which makes her somewhat of a puzzle to Giuseppe, who feels his disconnectedness acutely. It is this puzzling aspect and her lack of warmth, in comparison to the motherly and nurturing Lucrezia, that attracted Giuseppe to her after his brother's death. She seems serene to him at first; he later recognizes that this serenity is really a lack of interest.

— *Stephanie Korney*

THE CITY AND THE PILLAR

Author: Gore Vidal (1925-)
First published: 1948
Genre: Novel

Locale: Rural Virginia, Seattle, Beverly Hills, New Orleans, the Yucatán, and New York City
Time: Late 1930's to mid-1940's
Plot: Social realism

Jim Willard, a homosexual youth, roughly seventeen years old and a high school junior at the beginning of the novel. He is tall and handsome, an athlete who has played both baseball and tennis, with short blond hair. In high school, Willard already has formed a sexual attraction to a male friend, Bob Ford, with whom he has his first sexual encounter while the two are on a summer camping trip. Willard is a romantic about love, regularly looking back in time to recapture the magic of his first idealized love, even in later affairs with a novelist, a Hollywood film star, and a woman. In his early adulthood—first at sea, later in California, Mexico, the Army, and New York—he pursues the illusion that he has created of his high school friend, Ford.

Bob Ford, a tall, lean, and muscular high school athlete, with red, curly hair and blue eyes, who is Willard's first love. Ford flees high school after graduation by joining the Merchant Marine. Later, he returns to his Virginia hometown to marry a high school girlfriend, Sally Mergendahl, with whom he fathers a child. Unlike Willard, Ford is a heterosexual who merely engaged in one homosexual experience, and his eventual reunion with Willard is a hostile confrontation.

Collins, a short, squarely built seaman, twenty years old, with dark, curly hair, whom Willard encounters when he ships out to try to find Ford. Collins is egotistical, particularly about his success with women sexually, and he takes Willard to a brothel in Seattle. Willard is repulsed by the situation.

Otto Schilling, a half-Austrian, half-Polish tennis instructor at a Beverly Hills hotel where Willard gets an assistant's job teaching tennis. It is through this job connection that Willard meets Hollywood actors who are homosexual, in spite of the censorious advice of Schilling not to become involved in such liaisons.

Ronald Shaw, a "disturbingly handsome" Hollywood actor of Jewish origins (his real name was George Cohen) with whom Willard begins a homosexual affair shortly after their meeting at a party at Shaw's estate. Shaw is thirty-five years old, with dark, curly hair, a classic profile, and light-blue eyes. He is a highly successful film star often featured in period costume epics. His homosexuality is rumored but not publicly known.

Paul Sullivan, a novelist who is disillusioned with screenwriting. At twenty-eight years of age, he has written critically approved but financially unremunerative novels. Sullivan, reared as a Catholic, left the church after discovering his homosexuality and after an attempt at marriage. The sandy-haired Sullivan also is something of a masochist about his life, one of those who prefers to be unhappy much of the time and who masks that unhappiness with a cynical, bitter attitude toward the world in general. Sullivan and Willard begin an affair that separates Willard from film actor Ronald Shaw and takes the pair on travels first to New Orleans and later to Mexico and Guatemala, where the pair meet Maria Verlaine.

Maria Verlaine, a dark, exotic, smartly dressed woman given to affairs with artists and frequently attracted to homosexual men as companions (or as would-be lovers). She is worldly-wise, divorced from a French gigolo. In middle age, she has become increasingly interested in younger men, espe-

cially blonds. Although she attempts a physical relationship with Willard, he is unable to respond to her, and their intense encounter is essentially an unconsummated love affair while Willard, Paul Sullivan, and she are at her plantation in the Yucatán.

Sergeant Kervinski, a homosexual noncommissioned officer in Special Services in the Army Air Corps whom Willard encounters when he enlists during World War II. Kervinski is attracted to him, but Willard is unresponsive to the sergeant. Kervinski is slim, dark, fast-talking, and given to making leading suggestive remarks about the sexiness of women to test soldiers' potential as homosexual conquests. Ultimately, Kervinski becomes involved with a young Army corporal whom Willard had tried to seduce in the barracks.

Ken Woodrow, an Army corporal from Cleveland, Ohio, aged twenty-one and the graduate of a secretarial college. Woodrow is a dark-haired young man with gray eyes and a small, slim body. Although initially friendly to barracks buddy Willard, Woodrow resists Willard's attempt to seduce him one evening but later responds to similar overtures from Sergeant Kervinski.

— Jere Real

THE CITY BUILDER
(A városalapító)

Author: George Konrád (1933-   )
First published: 1977
Genre: Novel

Locale: An unnamed provincial city in Hungary
Time: The 1970's
Plot: Psychological realism

The narrator, an aged city planner and former professor in a central Hungarian town. He has been awarded many degrees and diplomas and honored for his role in the technical progress of his city in the early days of socialism. Keenly aware of his own physical and moral degeneration, he at times seems obsessed with death and guilt as he lives alone with his memories in an apartment stuffed with an accumulation of useless objects. In the city all around him, he sees reminders in concrete of the errors of his life, errors that can be erased only by dynamite. As a city planner, he mapped out for society a future that has become an almost unbearable present in a state ruled by power-hungry bureaucrats, chosen for their cynicism and idle chatter and protected by the organizational system. Born into a wealthy bourgeois family, he became a member of another privileged class, the intelligentsia, after private property was abolished. Although, as an idealistic builder of the city following the devastation of war, he attempted to abolish social stratification, in reality he created a modified system of inequalities to replace the former political structure. Once he repeated mindless slogans and believed the hierarchical military to be the most efficient of all organizations. He perfunctorily eulogizes his superior, a former Gestapo spy with thirty-two years in the movement who has committed suicide. Reflecting on the dead director, the city builder admits his own lust for power. Later, he inspects an earthquake-torn city, where, he believes, his own son lies buried in the rubble. Finally, he joins a noisy crowd in the town square on New Year's Eve. All greet one another in a friendly manner, and all expect to live until the year's end. The narrator has lingering

doubts about the survival of either himself or his society.

The narrator's wife, an attractive, socially active woman who at the age of forty was killed when her car crashed into a tree. The city builder is haunted by memories of her life and death. He sees her lying on a pathologist's marble slab after the fatal accident. He relives her cremation. He recalls divorce proceedings in which both he and she stated that they could not live without each other. He remembers her indefatigable sensuality, her fragrance, her shrieks, and her endless activity. She often arrived home late in the evening, laden with intriguing parcels and exuding fascinating stories. She could be vindictive and stealthy. Nevertheless, the city builder is plagued with guilt for his infidelity while she was alive.

The narrator's son, an apprentice city builder, student of philosophy, and radical intellectual who often violently disagreed with his father's political position. The city builder recalls that from the day his son entered his life, he was a touchy tyrant who usurped the attention of the city builder's wife and, indeed, the whole household. An amateur man of the theater, the son was arrested at the age of twenty-two for insulting a state inspector who suspected him of subversion. While serving six months in prison, he fought the guards who abused him, and he sustained permanent injuries to the face and eyes. He was gifted in argumentation but emotionally unstable, alternating between states of frenzy and stupor. His father ultimately believes him to be an earthquake casualty but is unable to find his body.

The narrator's father, a private builder and architect and an alderman who enjoyed wealth and power as the head of the third generation to occupy the fashionable family estate. His greatest professional accomplishment was the designing of the city's neo-Romanesque power plant, a kind of castle for machines rather than people. An authoritarian father given to violence, he paid lip service to religion but reveled in slander and sexual debauchery. His sudden death profoundly affects the city builder, who longs to know what lies on the other side of life.

— *Janie Caves McCauley*

CITY OF NIGHT

Author: John Rechy (1934-   )
First published: 1963
Genre: Novel

Locale: El Paso, New York, Los Angeles, San Francisco, and New Orleans
Time: The 1950's
Plot: Bildungsroman

The narrator, the nameless protagonist, of Mexican American background. His ethnicity does not play a significant role during his years as a male prostitute, but subconsciously it manifests itself in a sense of guilt, fostered by his mother's fervent Catholicism and by his father's death. Much of the narrator's career is a rebellion against his family background and religious promises of eternal life and redemption. The death of his dog and his mother's claim that dogs do not go to heaven push the narrator into a crisis of faith that he acts out through open rebellion and emotional withdrawal. This pattern repeats itself throughout the narrator's wanderings through the homosexual underground. On one hand, the narrator thrives on the life of the streets and the desire that other men express for his body; on the other hand, he rents rooms away from this environment so that he can always have an emotional refuge. The need to have his body adored by as many people as possible stems from his loss of religious faith. If there is no afterlife, no possibility of redemption and resurrection, as he often tells himself, then his youthful body is his only weapon against the forces of time; thus as long as he is young and desirable, he engages in an orgy of desirability. Despite his intent to kill compassion in himself and wear a mask of insensitivity, the narrator cannot do so. He thus becomes a confessor figure to his clients, because there is an aura about him that other male prostitutes do not possess.

Pete, a typical young male prostitute who initiates the narrator into the life of the streets. Despite his tough exterior, he is vulnerable and lost. His one display of affection toward the narrator serves to separate the two, because they feel that they have violated the code of toughness their trade demands.

The Professor, a client. Despite his ability to deceive himself through a torrent of words, he is as lonely and craves love as much as all the narrator's customers.

Jeremy Adams, a man who empathizes with the narrator's psychological dilemma. He makes the narrator realize that there is no real difference between prostitute and client; both are symbiotically linked through shared loneliness.

THE CIVIL WARS: a tree is best measured when it is down

Author: Robert Wilson (1941-   )
First performed: Various sections, 1983-1985
Genre: Drama

Locale: The United States, Europe, Japan, and a jungle
Time: Indeterminate
Plot: Minimalism

Abraham Lincoln,
Mrs. Lincoln,
Robert E. Lee,
Mrs. Lee,
John Wilkes Booth,
Mathew Brady, and
American Civil War soldiers, some of the historical and fictional personages, resembling animated wax figures on display, who populate the work's arresting scenarios. They are derived from a series of "free associational" thoughts, sparked by reflections on the American Civil War. Because the playwright also considered his central concept of civil war to be applicable to a wide variety of confrontations, including family conflicts, the family of Frederick the Great and an American *fin de siècle* family appear as well. The international scope of the project (originally scheduled to premiere at the 1984 Summer Olympic Games) is reflected in the use of figures (for example, a Japanese sun goddess, William the Silent, and Giuseppe Garibaldi) who may be identified with the countries that participated in the venture. The appearance of Hercules in the final act is perhaps in recognition of the ancient origin of the Games.

— *David Marc Fischer*

CLARISSA: Or, The History of a Young Lady

Author: Samuel Richardson (1689-1761)
First published: 1747-1748
Genre: Novel

Locale: England
Time: Early eighteenth century
Plot: Sentimental

Mr. Harlowe, a domineering man who cannot understand how his children can disobey him. He arranges a loveless marriage for his daughter Clarissa. When she refuses to obey his commands, he locks her in her room, with only an insolent servant allowed to see her. After her elopement with Robert Lovelace, her father disowns her and will not let her have clothes or money. Not until she is dying does he lift his ban and seek a reconciliation.

Clarissa Harlowe, his young and beautiful daughter, who accepts Lovelace's attentions as a way of escaping from her father's demands. Thinking that he is taking her to the home of Lord M———, his kinsman, she flees with Lovelace, only to be put into a house of ill repute where, for fear of being tracked down by her father, she claims to be Lovelace's wife. Once she escapes, only to be dragged back, drugged, and raped. Escaping again, she is caught and jailed for debt. She is freed but goes into a physical decline and buys her casket, inscribed with her death date: the day she left the Harlowe home. Though the repentant Lovelace now wants to marry her, she refuses him. Despite letters from her contrite family—for the whole novel is told in letters—she dies, to the grief and remorse of all.

Arabella, the older Harlowe daughter. She hates Clarissa for attracting her own suitor, Robert Lovelace.

James Harlowe, Clarissa's older brother, selfish and domineering, like his father. Having known and disliked Lovelace at Oxford University, he starts rumors that Lovelace is a profligate. He is also jealous of Clarissa because she is the heiress of their wealthy grandfather.

Robert Lovelace, a young Englishman of noble family. Brought by an uncle to the Harlowe home as suitor of Arabella, he falls in love with Clarissa. Because of his choice, he is spurned by the whole family. In revenge for their insults, he determines to seduce Clarissa and gets her to run away with him under promises of marriage, only to break his word. Finally, when he discovers he really loves her, he vainly offers her marriage. After her death, he goes to France, where he fights a duel with Clarissa's cousin, Colonel Morden, and is killed. He dies repentant of his crimes.

John Belford, a friend of Lovelace who frees Clarissa from jail by proving that the charges of debt against her are false. He receives from Lovelace letters that narrate the course of his courtship and his perfidy.

Roger Solmes, a rich, elderly, but uncouth man chosen as Clarissa's husband by her father. When Clarissa writes to him begging him to end their relationship, he refuses.

Mrs. Sinclair, the keeper of the London bawdy house where Clarissa is kept prisoner.

Colonel William Morden, Clarissa's cousin, who tries first to reconcile Clarissa and her family and then to persuade her to marry Lovelace. He finally avenges her death when he kills Lovelace in a duel.

Miss Anna Howe, the friend and confidante of Clarissa; through their interchange of letters, most of the story is told.

Aunt Hervey, who wants Lovelace to marry Arabella.

Uncle Harlowe, who brings Lovelace to the house.

Mr. Mennell, who manages the affairs of Mrs. Fretchville and wants to rent her apartment to Clarissa.

Hannah, Clarissa's faithful servant.

Mr. Diggs, the surgeon who looks after James Harlowe's wound after he and Lovelace duel.

Elizabeth Lawrence, Lovelace's aunt, who wants to meet his "wife."

Charlotte Montague, a cousin of Lovelace.

Dorcas Martindale, who tries to help Clarissa escape.

F. J. de la Tour, who writes the final letter describing the duel and death of the chevalier Lovelace.

CLAUDIUS THE GOD AND HIS WIFE MESSALINA

Author: Robert Graves (1895-1985)
First published: 1934
Genre: Novel

Locale: Rome
Time: A.D. 41-54
Plot: Historical

Tiberius Claudius Drusus Nero Germanicus (ti-BIH-ree-uhs KLOH-dee-uhs DREW-suhs NEE-roh jur-MA-nih-kuhs), emperor of Rome. Popularly supposed at the beginning of his rule to be a cripple, a stammerer, and an idiot, he is in reality a planner of governmental, financial, and social reforms, including the abolition of many of the previous emperor Caligula's cruel decrees. Busy with state affairs, he is long ignorant of Messalina's depravities. He is deified as a result of his planning of the great Roman victory in Britain at Brentwood Hill. After a wholesale execution of Messalina's immoral associates and following his marriage to Agrippinilla, he takes little interest in governmental affairs and is finally poisoned by his wife.

Messalina (meh-suh-LI-nuh), his third wife. Though she is director of public morals, she herself pursues a life of debauchery, licentiousness, political intrigue, bribery, cheating, and murder. After her divorce from Claudius, her remarriage to Silius, and Claudius' discovery of her debaucheries, she is killed by the colonel of the palace guard.

Calpurnia (kal-PUR-nee-uh), Claudius' mistress, who finally reveals to Claudius the truth about Messalina.

Agrippina (ag-rih-PI-nuh), called **Agrippinilla**, Claudius' fourth wife, whom he marries for political reasons. She poisons him so that Nero may succeed him. She is killed by soldiers sent by Nero to murder her.

Lucius Domitius (LEW-shee-uhs doh-MIH-shee-uhs), later called **Nero**, Agrippinilla's son and Claudius' grandnephew. Adopted by Claudius and appointed joint heir with Britannicus, he becomes emperor through his mother's plotting. After a reign marked by debauchery and murder, he is killed at his own request by a servant.

Herod Agrippa (HEH-ruhd uh-GRIH-puh), Claudius' friend since his youthful days. He is imprisoned by Tiberius for treasonous sentiments but is released by Caligula and given control of Judea, Samaria, and Edom by Claudius. His plan to set up a Jewish kingdom with himself as Messiah collapses with his death.

Brittanicus (brih-TA-nih-kuhs), Claudius' son, whom Claudius suspects of having been fathered by Caligula; he is poisoned in A.D. 55.

Octavia (ok-TAY-vee-uh), Claudius' supposed daughter,

believed by Claudius to have been fathered by the commander of the Germans under Caligula. Married to Nero, she dies violently.

Varus (VAH-ruhs), a general.

Caractacus (keh-RAK-ta-kuhs) and

Togodumnus (toh-guh-DUM-nuhs), brothers and joint rulers of Britain. Togodumnus is slain in battle; Caractacus is captured, brought to Rome, and then generously freed by Claudius.

Aulus Plautius (OH-luhs PLOH-shee-uhs), the leader of Claudius' invasion forces against Britain.

Barbillus (bahr-BIH-luhs), an astrologer who predicts Claudius' death.

Silius (SIH-lee-uhs), Messalina's former husband, whom she remarries.

Antonia (an-TOH-nee-uh), Claudius' daughter, married to Pompey. After his death, she marries Faustus.

Pompey (POM-pih), a homosexual murdered, by Claudius' orders, in bed with his slave Lycidas.

THE CLAYHANGER TRILOGY

Author: Arnold Bennett (1867-1931)
First published: 1910-1915
Genre: Novels

Locale: Five Towns, England
Time: The 1870's-the 1890's
Plot: Social realism

Clayhanger, 1910

Edwin Clayhanger, who wants to continue school and become an architect. Because Edwin's father will not allow him to continue his education, Edwin begins work at his father's printing shop. He heroically saves the building from collapsing. After moving to Bleakridge, Edwin meets Hilda Lessways and falls in love. Disappointed that she marries another, Edwin remains single. After hearing of the death of Hilda's husband, Edwin visits Hilda in Brighton and helps financially. When Hilda returns to Bleakridge, Edwin discovers the truth about George Cannon, Hilda, and her child.

Darius Clayhanger, Edwin's relentless father. Extremely proud that he survived poverty and his experience in the Bastille, Darius conservatively manages his shop, money, and children. He refuses to acknowledge Edwin's dreams and forces him to work in the printing shop. After an illness, Darius reluctantly relinquishes the control of his company. He dies and leaves the company to Edwin.

Hilda Lessways, the mysterious friend of the Orgreaves. Arriving in Bleakridge with Janet, Hilda meets Edwin. Hilda sneaks out of the Orgreave house and questions Edwin about his beliefs. After saving Mr. Shushions at St. Luke's Square, she kisses Edwin in the printing shop. Hilda confesses her love to Edwin but leaves Bleakridge and writes to Janet that she has married another man. During her son's illness, Hilda returns to Bleakridge and reveals that she was married to George Cannon and pregnant when she kissed Edwin.

George Edwin Cannon, George Cannon and Hilda Lessways' illegitimate child. George comes to Bleakridge with

Janet Orgreave, and Edwin befriends him. When George develops the flu, Hilda returns to Bleakridge and bares the truth about George's birthright.

Clara Clayhanger, Edwin's younger sister. Clara marries Albert Benbow, a shifty businessman. Edwin becomes disgusted with Clara's purpose in life, to have children.

Maggie Clayhanger, Edwin's unmarried older sister. Maggie manages the Clayhanger household.

Aunt Clara Hamps, Edwin's mother's sister, whose constant moralizing Edwin deplores. Aunt Clara, a visiting nuisance, imparts useless advise.

Big James Yarlett, the large-framed, gentle, and sensitive foreman of D. Clayhanger, Printer and Stationer. Big James dedicates his life to the Clayhangers.

Janet Orgreave, Charlie's elegant, mannered sister and Edwin's neighbor at Bleakridge. Janet sets her marital goals toward Edwin, but he is not interested. Janet remains unmarried and becomes the caretaker of her parents.

Charlie Orgreave, Edwin's good-humored childhood friend. Charlie continues school and becomes a medical doctor. He returns to Bleakridge with Hilda and cares for George during the flu epidemic.

Mr. Shushions, the superintendent of the Sunday school and childhood benefactor of Darius Clayhanger. When Darius' family is thrown into the Bastille, Mr. Shushions secures the family's release. Destitute and starving, Mr. Shushions dies in the Bastille before Darius can rescue him.

Hilda Lessways, 1911

Hilda Lessways, who learns about life through bad decisions. After arguing with her mother, Hilda consults George Cannon. Persuaded to study shorthand, she works for Cannon's newspaper. Hilda's mother dies suddenly, and Hilda helps Sarah Gailey in London with Cannon's boardinghouse. Janet Orgreave invites Hilda to Bleakridge, where she meets Edwin Clayhanger. Returning to London, Hilda follows Sarah to Brighton. Hilda marries George Cannon, becomes pregnant, and discovers that the marriage is illegal. When she discloses the truth, Edwin forgives her, which secures her future as Clayhanger's wife.

George Cannon, practices law illegally behind the façade

of Q. Karkeek. Never completely honest in his financial endeavors, George invests Hilda's money after their marriage. He is imprisoned for fraud and bigamy.

Sarah Gailey, George Cannon's sister. Unable to teach dancing, Sarah manages George's boardinghouse in London. When George sells the residence, Sarah goes to Brighton. Sarah confirms the truth about her brother's first marriage.

Edwin Clayhanger, who remains in love with Hilda. After hearing of George Cannon's death, Edwin locates her in Brighton and pays her boardinghouse debt. Edwin is shocked when he discovers the truth about Hilda during young George's illness.

Louisa, a maid at the Brighton boardinghouse who shouts out that George Cannon has another wife in Devonshire.

Florence (Florrie) Bagster, who is hired to work for Mrs. Lessways at the age of thirteen and rehired to work for Hilda

at Brighton. Florrie runs away with Mr. Boutwood, a resident of Cannon's boardinghouse. Florrie tells Louisa that George Cannon is already married.

These Twain, 1915

Edwin Clayhanger, who vacillates between his happiness and misery. Unable to control Hilda, Edwin contemplates his decision of marriage. No matter how strongly he resists Hilda's antics, Edwin always gives in to her desires.

Hilda Clayhanger, who manipulates Edwin to acquire possessions. Disillusioned with her inequality in marriage, Hilda schemes to get her way even when Edwin refuses to comply with her wishes.

George Edwin Cannon Clayhanger, who becomes an intelligent young man. George hopes to join the firm of Johnnie Orgreave in London.

George Cannon, who is released from prison after serving two terms. George returns to his first wife. Unable to tolerate his living conditions, George leaves his wife and borrows money from Edwin to escape to America. As prom-

ised, George repays Edwin.

Tertius Ingpen, an industrial inspector and Edwin's friend. Ingpen, a bachelor, believes that women are not equal, yet he helps Hilda scheme against Edwin to acquire what she wants. After Ingpen injures his groin, he asks Edwin to destroy some photographs. Edwin discovers that Ingpen has been having an affair with a married woman.

Aunt Clara Hamps, who bequeaths her estate to Clara's children because she realizes that the Benbows will not provide for them.

Maggie Clayhanger, who inherits the Bleakridge house. Maggie sells the house to Hilda and Edwin and moves in with Aunt Clara until Clara's death. She then moves into the Benbow home to care for the children.

— *Patricia T. Cheves*

CLEAR LIGHT OF DAY

Author: Anita Desai (1937-   )
First published: 1980
Genre: Novel

Locale: The suburbs of Old Delhi
Time: Summer, 1947, and about fifteen years before and after
Plot: Psychological realism

Bim Das, a history teacher. The unmarried, eldest Das daughter, now over forty, still lives in the decaying family home situated on the outskirts of Old Delhi. Slightly heavy and turning gray, Bim is not particularly attractive and makes little effort to be so. Her energy and capability, along with her keen understanding, compensate for whatever she lacks physically. Shown through flashbacks in her younger years, Bim has always been at peace with herself and managed to convey that quality to others. She represents the old India: spiritual, peaceful, unselfish, unhurried, and sure of life. In some ways, though, she has not come to grips with the present and melded it with the past, and therein lies her flaw.

Tara, Bim's sister, an Indian diplomat's wife. Altogether the opposite of her older sister, Tara is attractive, sophisticated, and worldly, having accompanied her husband to various overseas posts. To an extent, her poise is merely an exterior quality, in spite of her seemingly successful marriage, her two teenage daughters, and her role as hostess and wife in diplomatic circles. Representing the new India that was created after independence in 1947, Tara finds herself torn between the past and the present, especially when she visits Bim at the family home and dredges up memories of another time, when life seemed surer and more settled.

Baba Das, Bim and Tara's retarded brother. Although he is in his thirties, Baba is like a child, innocent and unaffected by

events around him. He is fat, lethargic, and dependent on Bim, who caters to his every wish. For most of the day, he plays English-language records from the late 1940's. Like his sisters, he is caught in the web of the past, even in his mindless state.

Bakul, Tara's husband and a diplomat in the Indian foreign service. Handsome, successful, and aggressive, Bakul considers the family's obsession with the past foolish and tedious. He has left the old India behind and entered the larger world, even though he gives lip service to the idea of Mother India as home.

Raja Das, the eldest son of the Das family. During the flashbacks to the gaining of independence in 1947 and the partition riots, Raja appears as a kind of romantic hero. He reads and writes poetry, dreams of heroics, and possesses the total devotion of his sister Bim, who nurses him to health during a long illness. Coming from a traditional Hindu family, he breaks tradition by marrying a Muslim woman, then leaves Delhi for Hyderabad, where he becomes a rich businessman. Although he does not appear in later sections of the novel, he is described by Bim as having become excessively fat, arrogant, and pretentious.

Mira-masi, the aunt of the Das children. A traditional Indian woman, she served as their nurse during childhood.

— *Robert L. Ross*

CLIGÉS: A Romance
(Cligés: Ou, La Fausse morte)

Author: Chrétien de Troyes (c. 1150-c. 1190)
First published: c. 1164
Genre: Poetry

Locale: England, Brittany, Germany, and Constantinople
Time: The sixth century
Plot: Romance

Alexander, a prince of Greece. Ardently desiring knight-hood in King Arthur's court, he goes to Britain. After performing many brave deeds in Arthur's service, he is knighted by the king. He marries Soredamors, and they become the parents of Cligés.

Cligés, the son of Alexander and Soredamors. He fulfills his father's wish that he be knighted by King Arthur. In love with Fenice, he engages, with her, in an elaborate scheme to deceive her husband, Alis. On Alis' death, the lovers succeed, as husband and wife, to the throne of Greece.

Soredamors, Alexander's wife and the mother of Cligés. She is the sister of Sir Gawain and the niece of King Arthur.

Fenice, Alis' wife. With her lover Cligés, she deceives her husband. On Alis' death, she marries Cligés and becomes empress of Greece.

Alis, Alexander's brother and the regent for Cligés. He breaks his vow never to marry, weds Fenice, and is deceived by her and her lover Cligés, who assumes the throne on his uncle's death.

Thessala, a sorceress whose potions assist Fenice in deceiving her husband.

John, a stonecutter who provides a trysting place for the lovers Cligés and Fenice.

Arthur, the king of Britain.

Guinevere, King Arthur's queen.

Sir Gawain, a knight of the Round Table and Cligés' uncle.

Count Angreè, a traitor to King Arthur.

Sagremore,

Lancelot of the Lake, and

Perceval of Wales, knights of the Round Table who are defeated in tournaments by Cligés.

The duke of Saxony, a contender for the hand of Fenice.

A CLOCKWORK ORANGE

Author: Anthony Burgess (John Anthony Burgess Wilson, 1917-1993)
First published: 1962
Genre: Novel

Locale: England
Time: Indeterminate future
Plot: Dystopian

Alex, the narrator, who speaks in "nadsat" (a teenagers' slang incorporating elements of Elizabethan English and modern Russian). At fifteen years of age, he is the leader of a gang made up of himself and three "droogs" (*droog* is Russian for "friend"), each a year or two older than he. Three years later, he will lead three droogs, each younger than he. His pleasures consist of violence—theft, mugging, vandalism, and rape—and classical music, especially that by Mozart and Beethoven. His droogs—Georgie, Pete, and Dim—become disaffected under his leadership and betray him by leaving him to be captured by the police. He spends two years in prison, where he undergoes psychological conditioning (the Ludovico Technique) that leaves him physically incapable of violence and enjoyment of music. Unable to make a moral choice—that is, to choose either good or evil—and capable only of acting in accordance with what society considers good, he is released from prison. He is victimized and abused by society until, restored to his true self at the age of eighteen, he undergoes a transition to responsible maturity.

F. Alexander, the middle-aged author of a sociological work titled *A Clockwork Orange*, referring to the modern world's tendency to translate humans into vegetable-like automata. His wife dies after being beaten and raped by Alex and his gang. He takes in and cares for Alex after his release, when Alex has been severely beaten by police thugs: He is unaware at first that Alex is the person who had brutalized his wife. When he learns the truth, he seeks to kill Alex.

The prison chaplain, called "charlie" or "charles" in nadsat. He tries to dissuade Alex from accepting the Ludovico Treatment as the price of early release from prison. He and F. Alexander, in their turn, uphold the necessity of moral choice.

Dim, a member of Alex's first gang. He is slow-witted, huge, and strong. He wields a chain and flails Alex across the eyes with it when the gang deserts their leader at the scene of the crime for which Alex is imprisoned. The crime is the fatal beating by Alex of a middle-aged woman, who cares for a menagerie of cats, in the course of robbing her house. Dim later becomes a policeman and is one of the police thugs who trounce Alex.

Dr. Brodsky, a fat, curly-haired practitioner of behaviorist psychology. He subjects Alex to the Ludovico Technique, which ensures that Alex will become intolerably nauseated and ill at thoughts or acts of violence or at the sound of classical music.

Georgie, a member of Alex's first gang who seeks to supplant Alex as its leader. His death occurs while Alex is in prison.

Pete, a member of Alex's first gang. He is the least averse to Alex, although he participates in the gang's betrayal of their leader. He later marries and leads the life of a good citizen.

Alex's father, a caring but weak-willed parent who is dominated by his son. As a workingman, he conforms to the soulless society of which he is a part.

Alex's mother, a weepy, weary, well-meaning woman who is as ineffectual as her husband.

Billyboy, the leader of a gang in rivalry with Alex's gang. Beaten by Alex in a brawl, he reappears in two years as a policeman and, along with Dim, brutally beats his former enemy.

P. R. Deltoid, Alex's postcorrective adviser. He tries unsuccessfully to deal with Alex's truancy and, after Alex is arrested, spits in his face.

Jack, an elderly professorial man who is beaten by Alex and his gang but, two years later, leads a group of elderly library patrons in administering a beating to the behavioristically conditioned and consequently unresisting Alex.

Dr. Branom, the zealous and sycophantic assistant of Dr. Brodsky.

Joe, a workingman in his thirties. As a lodger, he preempts the room and usurps the filial position of the imprisoned and then released Alex. Eventually, he surrenders his lodgings after a run-in with the police for loitering.

Bully, a member of Alex's second gang. Like Georgie, he aspires to the leadership held by Alex. Like Dim, he is big and strong.

Rick, a member of Alex's second gang. He has a face "like a frog's."

Len, a member of Alex's second gang.

Z. Dolin, a political activist seeking to make a case against the incumbent party by exposing the inhumanity of Alex's conditioning. He is aided in his efforts by F. Alexander.

Something Something Rubinstein, a colleague of Z. Dolin.

D. B. da Silva, a colleague of Z. Dolin.

Rex, a policeman and the driver of the car Dim and Billy-boy use to take Alex out into the country to be beaten.

Georgina, Pete's wife, well groomed and attractive. She is amused by Alex's garbled (nadsat) language.

— *Roy Arthur Swanson*

THE CLOISTER AND THE HEARTH: A Tale of the Middle Ages

Author: Charles Reade (1814-1884)
First published: 1861
Genre: Novel

Locale: Holland, Germany, France, and Italy
Time: Fifteenth century
Plot: Historical

Gerard Eliason, an artist. He goes to Rome, where he becomes a Dominican monk named Brother Clement. Believing his fiancée is dead, he returns to his homeland to find she is alive and has borne him a son. After becoming a parson at Gouda, he lives apart from Margaret, his beloved, but allows her to help him in his religious work.

Elias, Gerard's father, a Dutch cloth and leather merchant. He does not want his artist son to marry Margaret Brandt and has him imprisoned; however, Elias is finally reconciled to her.

Katherine, Elias' wife. Like her husband, she does not want her son to marry Margaret.

Margaret Van Eyck, sister of the famous painter Jan Van Eyck. She is Gerard's teacher.

Reicht Heynes, Margaret Van Eyck's servant, who encourages Gerard as an artist.

Peter Brandt, an old man befriended by Gerard.

Margaret Brandt, Peter's daughter. She is betrothed to Gerard and bears him a son. When he returns to Holland as a monk, she helps him in his religious work.

Gerard, son of Gerard and Margaret Brandt, who grows up to be Erasmus, the famous scholar.

Ghysbrecht Van Swieten, burgomaster of Gerard's village. He is an evil man who cheats his people and makes life difficult for Gerard and Margaret.

Giles, Gerard's dwarf brother, who helps Gerard escape from prison.

Kate, Gerard's crippled sister, who helps Gerard escape from prison.

Denys, a Burgundian soldier who befriends Gerard on his way to Italy. Denys is a worldly but loyal man. He finds Margaret Brandt and befriends her for Gerard's sake.

Martin, an old retired soldier who procures a pardon for Gerard after the young man's escape from prison.

Hans Memling, a messenger who takes false word to Gerard that Margaret has died.

Pietro, a young artist in Rome with whom Gerard works for a time.

Fra Colonna, a classical scholar for whom Gerard works in decorating manuscripts.

Luke Peterson, a suitor for Margaret Brandt's hand in marriage.

THE CLOSED GARDEN
(Adrienne Mesurat)

Author: Julien Green (1900-1998)
First published: 1927
Genre: Novel

Locale: France
Time: 1908
Plot: Psychological realism

Adrienne Mesurat (ah-DRYEHN meh-zew-RAH), a highly impressionable French girl of sixteen. She falls in love with Dr. Maurecourt when he tips his hat to her. Her peculiar actions, including stealing out of the house to watch Maurecourt's house, arouse suspicions in her sister and even the neighbors. After her sister has left home for a hospital, Adrienne accidentally kills her father by knocking him down a flight of stairs. Alone in the world, robbed by Mme. Legras, Adrienne goes mad.

Germaine Mesurat (zhehr-MEHN), Adrienne's older sister, an invalid. She suspects Adrienne of having a lover. When Germaine's father refuses to acknowledge her illness, she

leaves for a hospital after taking some of her sister's dower money.

M. Antoine Mesurat (ahn-TWAHN), a retired teacher living with his two daughters in the placid little French town of La Tour l'Eveque, leading a quiet life. He never thinks that his two daughters may be unhappy sharing his tranquil existence. Thinking the girls superior to any proposals they have, he repulses their suitors. He is accidentally killed when Adrienne knocks him down a flight of stairs.

Dr. Denis Maurecourt (deh-NEE moh-reh-KOOR), a physician. He tips his hat to Adrienne, by that action unknowingly causing her to fall in love with him. When she tells him of her infatuation, he informs her that he is ill and has only a short time to live.

Mme Legras (leh-GRAH), a temporary neighbor to the Mesurats. She is a prying woman who tries to find out if Adrienne has a lover and if M. Mesurat's death was truly accidental. She assumes the role of protectress to Adrienne in order to pry into the girl's life. When she has a chance, she steals all of Adrienne's valuables and disappears.

CLOSELY WATCHED TRAINS
(Ostře sledované vlaky)

Author: Bohumil Hrabal (1914-1997)
First published: 1965
Genre: Novel

Locale: A railroad station in German-occupied Czechoslovakia
Time: Winter, 1945
Plot: Impressionism

Miloš Hrma (MEE-lohsh HUHR-mah), the narrator, an apprentice train dispatcher. Inexperienced and innocent at the age of twenty-two, Miloš views the bizarre and brutal events around him with morally noncommittal curiosity. Following his first sexual encounter, which is a failure, he attempts suicide. Although rescued, he remains preoccupied by doubts regarding his manhood until drawn into a plot to blow up a Nazi ammunition train. In acting deliberately, he finds the answer to his persistent question, "Am I a man?"

Ladislav Hubička (hew-BIHCH-keh), the senior dispatcher. Hubička, whose name means "nice lips," draws Miloš' envy and admiration with his success with women. He is under investigation for imprinting all the station's rubber stamps on the bare buttocks of the female telegraphist late one night. A fearless nonconformist, he is a key figure in the plot to blow up the munitions train.

Lánský, the stationmaster. Lánský takes great pride in his Venetian armchair, Persian carpet, and marble clock. Hot-tempered and exacting as a boss and as a husband, he dissipates his rages by bellowing into a heating vent. Although careful to conform outwardly to Nazi rule, he symbolically protests the brutal takeover of neighboring Poland by killing all of his Nuremberg pigeons (a German breed) and replacing them with Polish silver-points.

Virginia Svatá, the station telegraphist. An attractive, fun-loving young woman, Virginia willingly participates in Hubička's lascivious escapade and refuses to incriminate him during the investigation.

Masha, a conductor, Miloš' girlfriend. Young and exuberant, Masha easily forms a mutual attachment to Miloš while they are painting a fence together. Blaming her own inexperience for their sexual fiasco, she sticks by Miloš after his suicide attempt, making a date with him shortly before the sabotage is to be carried out.

Viktoria Freie, a member of the Czech resistance. The name of this well-endowed beauty means "victorious freedom" and is probably a code name. Viktoria not only delivers the bomb that is to be used in the sabotage but also provides Miloš with an unforgettable sexual initiation that dispels his self-doubt and inspires him to act courageously.

Councillor Zednicek, the head of a commission to determine whether a criminal charge should be lodged against Hubička for his indiscretion. Zednicek has a son in the German army and is himself an opportunistic collaborator with the Nazis.

Slušný (SLEWSH-nee), the traffic chief who arrives at the station with Councillor Zednicek. He enjoys exercising his authority and intimidating the subordinate employees of the railroad.

Mrs. Lánský, the stationmaster's wife. Although her tender care of her geese and other animals seems contradicted by the ease with which she slaughters them, she is still respected by Miloš, who seeks her tutelage in lovemaking.

Countess Kinská, an equestrienne whose family castle stands as a reminder of Czech aristocracy. She stops at the station on her rides and converses with Lánský while Hubička weaves erotic fantasies about her.

Miloš' father, a train engineer who retired early. He collects and salvages all kinds of scrap.

Miloš' grandfather, a circus hypnotist, killed in an attempt to turn back German tanks by means of hypnosis.

Miloš' great-grandfather, a veteran who was wounded at the age of eighteen during a student uprising. He flaunted his disability pension by drinking rum in front of people hard at work and finally died from one of the many beatings he provoked.

Miloš' mother, a nurturing maternal figure who polishes the buttons on Miloš' uniform and watches for him from behind a window curtain.

Great-Aunt Beatrice, a nurse who takes care of dying burn victims and is well acquainted with death.

— *Marian Price*

CLOTEL: Or, The President's Daughter, a Narrative of Slave Life in the United States

Author: William Wells Brown (1815-1884)
First published: 1853
Genre: Novel

Locale: Richmond, Virginia; New Orleans, Louisiana; Natchez and Vicksburg, Mississippi; and Dunkirk, France
Time: 1817-1842
Plot: Historical

Clotel, an attractive quadroon, sixteen years of age at the opening of the novel. She is Currer's older daughter. She is purchased by Horatio Green, becomes his concubine, and gives birth to Mary. Clotel later is sold. She commits suicide after she escapes from her new owners and is captured by slave catchers in Washington, D.C.

Currer, a forty-year-old mulatto woman. Currer is the former housekeeper of Thomas Jefferson, who, according to the novel, fathered her two daughters. Currer and her daughters are sold in Richmond, Virginia. Separated from her daughters, Currer later dies of yellow fever in Natchez, Mississippi.

Althesa, the younger of Currer's daughters, fourteen years old when the novel opens. Sold in the slave market of New Orleans, she marries Henry Morton and has two children, Ellen and Jane.

Horatio Green, the white Virginian who purchases Clotel as his concubine.

The Reverend John Peck, the Methodist parson of Natchez who purchases Currer.

Georgiana Peck, the Reverend Peck's daughter. She believes in abolition and manumits her servants before her death.

Mary, Clotel's daughter and a servant of Horatio Green and his wife. She eventually marries George Green.

George Green, a mulatto servant of Horatio Green who passes as white. He becomes romantically attached to Mary. After a separation, they reunite and marry in France.

— *Joseph McLaren*

CLOUD NINE

Author: Caryl Churchill (1938-   )
First published: 1979
Genre: Drama

Locale: A British colony in Africa, and London
Time: Late nineteenth century and 1979
Plot: Comedy of manners

Clive, a British administrator stationed in Africa. A stereotypical Victorian, Clive constantly cites his duty to God, the British Empire, the queen, and his family as motivation for his behavior. Like the other characters, Clive is a caricature who is both humorous and a painful reminder of social problems. As a Victorian colonialist, he is narrow-minded, hypocritical, and blind to the injustice done to the native Africans on whom his comfort depends. He continues to dominate his family and the natives only with difficulty, however, and act 1 ends with Clive's son watching silently as the faithful native servant raises a rifle to shoot Clive. Apparently Clive is not killed, however, because he reappears briefly at the end of act 2 to lament the fall of the British Empire. Clive's Victorian system of colonial repression parallels the system of sexual repression in the 1970's of act 2.

Betty, Clive's wife. In act 1, Betty "is played by a man because she wants to be what men want her to be." She identifies her duty as waiting patiently for Clive and the other men to order and control the world. In act 2, Betty, who has left Clive, is played by a woman, because she is coming to know herself better. At the play's close, Betty from act 1 reappears and the two Bettys embrace, indicating how far Betty has come in achieving wholeness and promising a world of reconciliation.

Joshua, Clive's black servant, "played by a white man because he wants to be what whites want him to be." Joshua separates himself from other natives and serves as Clive's spy. An unspoken pact with Clive permits Joshua the minor rebellion of impertinence to Betty, as long as he remains absolutely subservient to Clive. His raising of the rifle against Clive at the end of act 1 suggests a native effort to break free of British imperialism.

Edward, Clive's nine-year-old son, played in act 1 by a woman to highlight Clive's effort "to impose traditional male behavior on him." Edward is a lying, sneaking, sniveling child who blames others for his failures and escapes punishment for misbehavior by mouthing all the manly platitudes in which Clive believes. Edward is the product of Victorian colonialism, but his incipient homosexuality indicates that he, too, is about to break out of control. In act 2, Edward, now thirty-four years old, works as a gardener in England. His bisexuality indicates

his general uneasiness in the world, but he has grown into a mature appreciation of home, children, and settled relationships.

Victoria, Clive's two-year-old daughter, played in act 1 by a dummy, which is what her good Victorian parents expect her to be. In act 2, Victoria, now twenty-seven years old, is played by a woman because she is beginning to realize her own identity. She confronts all the women's issues of the 1970's, seeking to balance career, marriage, parenting, and new sexual relationships. She even begins to deal with her mother, moving from calling her "Mummy" to calling her "Betty."

Maud, Clive's mother-in-law, who lives with him and provides a constant reminder of the good old days when Victorian ideals were more firmly in control.

Ellen, Edward's governess, who has difficulty making him behave as Clive wishes. She is in love with Betty, but at the end of act 1 she marries Harry Bagley.

Harry Bagley, an explorer and a friend of Clive. Betty is attracted to him, and they carry on a flirtation, but Harry is really a homosexual. His socially acceptable marriage to Ellen denies both individuals' sexual preferences and represents repressive Victorian control over sexual behavior. Harry reappears briefly and silently in act 2, when Gerry picks him up for a homosexual encounter.

Mrs. Saunders, a widow who is having an affair with Clive. She is played by the actress who plays Ellen to indicate the parallels between their characters. Clive finds her as dark and mysterious as the continent, and her freedom of thought and behavior hints at the eventual emancipation of Victorian women.

Martin, Victoria's husband in act 2. He works to be helpful and supportive of his emancipated wife but has as much difficulty creating new patterns of behavior as do the women and occasionally continues to dominate Victoria.

Lin, Victoria's lesbian friend in act 2, whose professed hatred for men highlights Victoria's more moderate position.

Cathy, Lin's daughter, whose desire to carry a rifle and wear pink dresses indicates the uneasiness of sexual roles in the 1970's. Cathy is played by a man "partly as a reversal of Edward being played by a woman" and partly to indicate the "emotional force of young children."

Gerry, Edward's homosexual lover, who is as inconsiderate, manipulative, and insensitive to Edward as Clive was to Betty in act 1.

Soldier, the ghost of Lin's brother, who was killed while serving with the British army in Northern Ireland, where the colonialism of act 1 is playing out its bitter end.

— Helen Lojek

THE CLOUDS
(Nephelai)

Author: Aristophanes (c. 450-c. 385 B.C.E.)
First performed: 423 B.C.E.
Genre: Drama

Locale: Athens
Time: The fifth century B.C.E.
Plot: Social satire

Strepsiades (strehp-SI-eh-dees), an old, plodding, and stolid citizen of Athens who is hounded by creditors and burdened with debts incurred partly through the excesses of his horse-loving son, Phidippides. Resolving to cure his financial troubles, he sends his son to study the new science, taught by Socrates in the Thoughtery, a plan Strepsiades believes will guarantee the confutation of his creditors and the preservation of his fortune. His son, however, refuses to be tutored. Strepsiades resolves to attend the Thoughtery himself, but he proves himself a bumbling pupil, exhausting the patience of Socrates. Strepsiades then convinces his son to sit under Socrates. Socrates calls up the Just and Unjust Discourses to instruct Phidippides. In a violent dialogue, the Unjust Discourse wins and converts Phidippides to a modern position. After returning home, Phidippides demonstrates that he has been an apt pupil of the Sophists. He beats his father unmercifully, justifying himself by his new learning. Outraged at Socrates and his disciples, Strepsiades, with the help of a servant, burns down the Thoughtery.

Phidippides (fihd-DIHP-eh-dees), the son of Strepsiades, converted from his lethargic, spendthrift ways by the Sophists into a man who discovers the joys of defying established laws. By subtle reasoning, he justifies beating his father and declares that he intends to beat his mother as well.

Socrates (SOK-ruh-tees), a philosopher and teacher of the new science, and owner of the house called the Thoughtery. Approached by Strepsiades to teach Strepsiades the new ways, he is found suspended in a basket "contemplating the sun." Socrates, attempting to teach Strepsiades that the clouds are the genii of the universe, invokes them with prayers and praises. The clouds, he says, control human thought, speech, trickery, roguery, boasting, lies, and sagacity. This play lampoons the new science, but in portraying Socrates as a caricature of the new scientist it perverts Socrates' true convictions. Socrates rejected the natural sciences, had refused to organize a school of philosophy, rejected the Sophists, never took pay for his teaching, and affected not omniscience but ignorance.

Disciples of Socrates, who relate to the newly arrived Strepsiades examples of the new science, which is ridiculed through the examples and through the disciples.

Just Discourse, a defender of the old ways, including silence as a rule for children, respect for elders, physical fitness, and modesty. He is defeated by Unjust Discourse in the debate.

Unjust Discourse, a critic of the old ways. He celebrates deception, disrespect, slovenliness, immorality, and sexual promiscuity. His students become accomplished Sophists.

Pasias (pas-I-uhs) and

Amynias (a-mihn-I-uhs), moneylenders who visit Strepsiades to collect their due. The little that Strepsiades learned in the Thoughtery enables him to confute them and drive them away empty-handed.

A Chorus of Clouds, which sing praises to the Sophists for their acumen. They advise Socrates to take advantage of the ignorant and the stupid and extol the power of the clouds over the lives of men. In the parabasis, the Chorus berates the Athenians for having treated the play scornfully and recommends highest awards for the play.

THE CLOVEN VISCOUNT
(Il visconte dimezzato)

Author: Italo Calvino (1923-1985)
First published: 1952
Genre: Novel

Locale: Terralba, a small state on the Italian coast
Time: Late eighteenth century
Plot: Fable

Viscount Medardo of Terralba, a young Italian nobleman from a small principality on the coast of Italy. Fighting against the Turks, he is split in two by a cannonball; one surviving half is saved by doctors, and he returns home. Once there, he displays a perverted and evil nature, shown especially in his penchant for splitting things—such as fruits, frogs, and mushrooms—into two parts. His courtship of the peasant girl Pamela further reveals his sadistic inclinations. The other part of Medardo, which also survived and was healed by hermits, returns to Terralba; this portion of the viscount is all virtue and makes his presence known by a series of good deeds, many of which inevitably require redressing the harm done by his evil half. The people of Terralba are oppressed and terrified by the bad portion of the viscount and soon find themselves harassed and limited by the good portion. These opposing parts become known to the people of Terralba as "The Bad 'Un" and "The Good 'Un." Inevitably, the two sides come into a conflict that can be resolved only by their reunion.

The narrator, Medardo's nephew, seven or eight years old. A shrewd and observant child with much common sense, he serves as a generally accurate and unbiased witness of events. Left mostly to himself by his family, he is free to roam the hills and coasts of Terralba and so follow the other characters throughout the novel.

Dr. Trelawney, a shipwrecked English physician living in Terralba. In his sixties, Dr. Trelawney is a short man with a face lined like an old chestnut and long, thin legs. He wears an old coat with fading trimmings, a tricorn hat, and a wig. He has traveled the world, including voyages with the famous Captain Cook, but knows nothing of the globe because he remained in his cabin playing cards the whole time. He is immensely fond of *cancarone*, the harsh and heavy local wine, and he practices very little medicine, seeming to be afraid of the body and disease. There is some doubt as to whether he is actually a medical doctor. Instead of healing, he conducts implausible scientific research, such as his attempts to capture will-o'-the-wisps and preserve their essence in bottles.

Ezekiel, a large, bearded, dour man, leader of the exiled Huguenots who live on a hilltop in Terralba. Although banished because of their religion, the Huguenots have lost all outward traces of its form or content and live a bleak existence best expressed in Ezekiel's frequent oath: "Famine and plague."

Esau, the youngest son of Ezekiel. He smokes, drinks, steals, and cheats at dice and cards. He is ignorant of religion and indifferent to the threats of his father.

Galateo, one of the lepers who lives in the village of Pratofungo on the coast of Terralba. Exiled because of their physical condition, the lepers have given themselves up to a life of revelry, merriment, and debauchery, hiding their deformities under garlands of flowers.

Pamela, a young peasant girl, plump and barefoot. She tends goats and ducks and lives in a small cottage with her animals and family. Although naïve and unschooled, she is clever enough to recognize the dangers in the courtship of "The Bad 'Un" and hides in a cave in the mountains until discovered by "The Good 'Un." Sensibly, she refrains from marriage to either half of the viscount, instinctively preferring a complete husband.

Sebastiana, the old nurse of the Medardo family. She has seen generations of them come and go, and perhaps because of this knowledge she is exiled by "The Bad 'Un" to live with the lepers in Pratofungo.

— *Michael Witkoski*

THE CLOWN
(Ansichten eines Clowns)

Author: Heinrich Böll (1917-1985)
First published: 1963
Genre: Novel

Locale: Bonn, Germany
Time: 1945-1960
Plot: Psychological realism

Hans Schnier (shneer), a professional clown. All events in this first-person novel are seen through the eyes of Hans, the twenty-seven-year-old son of a wealthy industrialist. He is not, however, the typical son of a rich businessman. As a youth, he showed little aptitude for school, and he has never had any interest in business. Instead, Hans has the character traits and temperament of an artist: He is spontaneous, impulsive, creative, naïve, and innocent, and he cannot feign feelings that he does not possess. Nor can he, as someone once urged him, "be a man." To "be a man," he would have to become like everyone else, which he cannot and will not do. Similarly, he cannot act on his father's criticism that he lacks the very quality that makes a man a man: the ability to accept a situation. Hans, unlike most of his friends and acquaintances, does not want to accept the past and gloss it over, nor does he want to be merely swept along by the new tide of democracy. These qualities make him a misfit and an outsider. The loss of Marie destroys his primary link to the real world. Without her, he turns more and more to drink and ends up alone, playing his guitar and singing for a few coins from passersby at the train station.

Marie Derkum (DEHR-kuhm), the young woman whom Hans considers to be his wife, although they are not legally married. Sweet, trusting, and religious, Marie is in many ways the antithesis of Hans: She is from a very poor background, performed well in school, and is a devout Catholic. In time, her desire to return to the good graces of the church and to have a conventional, church-sanctioned marriage overcomes her love of Hans, and she leaves him to marry Prelate Züpfner.

Alfons Schnier, the director of a coal-mining company and father of Hans. When Hans was growing up, his mother was the dominant personality in the family. Hans also has vivid memories of his father, such as how he courageously defended Hans when, as a boy of about ten, he called Herbert Kalick a "Nazi swine." Schnier is now a handsome, distinguished-looking man in his sixties who has recently discovered that he has a talent as a television talk-show guest. He offers his son financial assistance, but only on the condition that Hans take formal training from the best teacher. Hans does not accept his father's offer.

Mrs. Schnier, Hans's mother, a homemaker and socialite. Hans considers her to be stupid, stingy, and hypocritical. During the war, she was a staunch racist and a fanatical German nationalist. She even sent her only daughter, sixteen-year-old Henrietta, to fight (and die) on the home front. Now Mrs. Schnier is president of the Executive Committee of the Societies for the Reconciliation of Racial Differences. Hans has never forgiven his mother for the death of his beloved sister, and he has not seen her since he left home to live with Marie and become a professional clown, more than five years earlier.

Heribert Züpfner (HEHR-ih-behrt ZEWPF-nehr), a Catholic prelate, about the same age as Hans. Züpfner, who as a youth was kind to Hans and occasionally went out with Marie, is one of several prominent young Catholics among Hans and Marie's friends, including Sommerwild and Kinkel. By convincing Marie to leave Hans for him, he shatters Hans's world.

Herbert Kalick (HEHR-behrt KAH-lihk), a recent recipient of the Federal Cross of Merit for his work in spreading democratic ideas among young people. When he was a youth of fourteen, Kalick, while serving as the leader of Hans's Hitler Youth group, was responsible for the death of one small boy and for the persecution of another lad who could not prove his Aryan background. Now a shining light in the new democratic movement, Kalick has recently invited Hans to his house to ask forgiveness for his past mistakes. Hans, however, cannot forgive and strikes him before leaving without accepting the offer of reconciliation.

Leo Schnier, Hans's younger brother, who became a Catholic and is now a seminary student. He is generous, unde-

manding, and generally supportive of his brother.

Martin Derkum, Marie's father, a not very successful shopkeeper. He is an intellectual and thought by many to be a Communist. Kind, generous, and not the typical chameleon of the times, changing with each new situation, he is one of the few men Hans respects.

— *H. J. Weatherford*

COCK-A-DOODLE DANDY

Author: Sean O'Casey (John Casey, 1880-1964)
First published: 1949
Genre: Drama

Locale: The parish of Nyadnanave in Ireland
Time: Shortly after World War II
Plot: Tragicomedy

Michael Marthraun (MAR-thrown), a grasping and stingy man in late middle age who has the good fortune to own some peat bogs that will increase his modest fortune. Eager to squeeze every ounce of profit from his peat, Michael bitterly resists Sailor Mahan's efforts to raise the price of hauling the peat to town, an act that would allow Mahan to pay his drivers a more respectable wage. Michael has recently remarried, but he resents his young wife, Lorna, especially when she dares to disagree with him and support the drivers' pleas for higher wages. He is even more suspicious of the modern ways of his lovely daughter, Loreleen, whose short dresses, nylons, and cosmetics make her a disturbing presence in the parish. Michael is particularly bedeviled by the mysterious enchantments of the mythic rooster, or cock, a symbol of sexuality.

Sailor Mahan (MAY-an), at one time a sailor but now the owner of a fleet of lorries (trucks). He is a middle-aged man whose experience in various seaports has made him less puritanical than Michael. Though more tolerant of Loreleen than are Marthraun and the priest, he is also a hypocrite and a lecher. When Loreleen desperately needs a loan to leave the parish, he arranges a meeting with her but uses the occasion to attempt to seduce her; she is given a reprieve by the intervention of an angry mob. Mahan is another person bedeviled by the appearances of the mysterious demoniac rooster.

The Mysterious Cock, a magical black rooster that appears and disappears somewhat capriciously. Representing the power of sexuality, he bothers and torments the puritanical men of the parish of Nyadnanave, causing them to hear strange sounds and see frightening sights, such as whiskey boiling and dishes being thrown about. His most important moment comes when he causes a tremendous wind in scene 3.

Lorna Marthraun, Michael's pretty young wife. She is a woman of spirit who supports her stepdaughter, Loreleen, and finally rebels against Michael's mean-spirited stinginess. Lorna apparently married Michael only because her paralytic sister, Julia, needed money for a trip to Lourdes, where she hoped she would find a miraculous cure. At the end of the play, Lorna decides to leave the parish when she sees that Loreleen has been driven away.

Loreleen Marthraun, Michael's daughter by his first marriage. Loreleen is a lovely young woman of about twenty who has adopted more modern manners and clothes as the result of living in London. Her makeup, short skirts, and nylons make her a bewitching presence in the dour parish of Nyadnanave.

Many of the people, including her father and the priest, consider her to be so disturbing that they begin to believe that she is a witch. After a mob led by Father Domineer tries to stone her for alleged sexual immorality and after Sailor Mahan tries to seduce her, she packs her belongings and leaves on foot, without shoes.

Marion, the maid in the Marthraun household, a saucy and pretty young woman of about twenty-five. She is a familiar character type who comments satirically on the action, and her charms contribute to the sexual confusion of the puritanical males. She is loved by the Messenger and loves him in return; however, this romance is not sufficient to keep her in the parish. She follows Loreleen and Lorna into exile at the end of the play.

The Messenger, Robin Adair, the bringer of news and telegrams who serenades Marion on his accordion. A jaunty young man, he is sometimes more like an incarnation of the Greek god Hermes than a real person; however, he can merely observe the foolish behavior of the men of the parish, not change it. Robin comforts Loreleen when she is persecuted by the villagers and shows the ability to control the demoniac cock with ease. At the end of the play, he pronounces judgment on Michael Marthraun and prepares to follow Marion to a more tolerant environment, leaving the parish to its folly.

Father Domineer, the parish priest of Nyadnanave. The priest is a harsh and brutal man who views Loreleen, with her modern manners and clothes, as the veritable incarnation of Satan. A middle-aged bigot and reactionary, he strikes one of Mahan's truck drivers and kills him, merely because the man is living out of wedlock with a local woman. After leading an angry mob that abuses Loreleen, he confronts her and demands that she repent and abandon her liberated ways. Father Domineer sees the demoniac cock as his mortal enemy and tries to exorcise the unruly rooster from the parish.

Shanaar (shah-NAR), an elderly itinerant sage who travels about the parish spreading suspicion and dark peasant superstitions. Full of pagan fears of mysterious forces, Shanaar advises Michael to ignore whatever he cannot understand or finds frightening.

One-Eyed Larry, an ignorant peasant youth who follows Father Domineer around and tries to assist him at the exorcism.

The Sergeant, a beefy middle-aged man who represents the civil authority of the parish. He pursues the demoniac rooster across the country but is embarrassed by losing his trousers in the mighty wind conjured up by the cock's supernatural power.

Julia, Lorna's younger sister, a paralytic girl without much time to live. In desperation, she sets out on a trip to Lourdes, hoping for a miraculous cure by the Virgin. Despite Father Domineer's blessing, she returns home in despair with her condition unchanged. As she faces a bleak future, the Messenger counsels her to have courage.

— Edgar L. Chapman

THE COCKTAIL PARTY

Author: T. S. Eliot (1888-1965)
First published: 1950
Genre: Drama

Locale: London, England
Time: Mid-twentieth century
Plot: Comedy of manners

Edward Chamberlayne, a middle-aged lawyer. Faced with the prospect of having to meet people without the aid of his wife, who has just left him, he discovers that he cares nothing for the young woman with whom he has been having an affair and that he definitely wants his wife to return. Later, after he thinks he has had a nervous breakdown, he sees a psychiatrist and comes to realize and accept the fact that he is a mediocre man who is afraid that he is incapable of really loving anyone. From this point, he begins to build a happy life.

Lavinia Chamberlayne, his wife. Having put herself under the care of a psychiatrist, Lavinia is allowed to believe that she has been to a sanatorium and been cured. After she has returned to her husband, the psychiatrist unexpectedly brings them together in a new and revealing relationship. Lavinia finally realizes that she has always been afraid that she is completely unlovable. She, too, can then adjust and build a satisfactory life with Edward.

Julia Shuttlethwaite, a friend of the Chamberlaynes. Although she gives the impression of being a meddlesome old woman with only a few of her wits about her, she is the one who contrives to have the Chamberlaynes take the action that they do.

Celia Coplestone, a sensitive young poet. Having fancied herself in love with Edward Chamberlayne, she is somewhat shocked when she realizes his true character. She is also led by Julia and Alex to the psychiatrist and finds her purpose in life through him. After a short period of training, she enters a religious order and becomes a nurse on an island in the East, where she is killed by the natives.

Peter Quilpe, a shy young man in love with Celia. He also has had an affair with Lavinia. When he realizes that Celia does not care for him, he goes to California and makes a success of himself in the film industry.

Alexander (Alex) MacColgie Gibbs, another friend of the Chamberlaynes who, like Julia, gives the impression of being meddlesome. He is also a part of the conspiracy between Julia and the psychiatrist that ultimately straightens out the lives of the Chamberlaynes and Celia.

Sir Henry Harcourt-Reilly, who at first is known only as an unidentified guest at a cocktail party in the Chamberlaynes' flat. He is later revealed to all as the psychiatrist who helps them to solve their problems. He sets up, with Julia and Alex, the conspiracy involving the Chamberlaynes.

A COFFIN FOR DIMITRIOS

Author: Eric Ambler (1909-1998)
First published: 1939
Genre: Novel

Locale: Istanbul, Athens, Sofia, Geneva, and Paris
Time: 1922-1938
Plot: Spy

Charles Latimer, an English writer of detective stories in his early forties. Formerly, Latimer was a professor of political economy at a minor English university; the success of his stories freed him from academe. On a visit to Istanbul in 1938, Latimer meets Colonel Haki, an admirer of detective novels, who in passing gives Latimer the opportunity to view a body that the Turkish police have identified as that of Dimitrios Makropoulos, known to them since 1922. Latimer, on a whim and as an exercise in detection, decides to trace Makropoulos' career. In Paris, he discovers the real Makropoulos and only narrowly avoids being murdered by him.

Dimitrios Makropoulos, also known as **Talas**, **Taladis**, **Rougemont**, and **Monsieur C. K.**, a murderer, thief, spy, pimp, drug dealer, and businessman. Makropoulos, of Greek extraction, was born in 1889. Coming to the attention of the Turkish police in 1922, in subsequent years he engaged in various illegal activities in several European countries. By 1938, he is a director of the Eurasian Credit Trust. It is not Makropoulos' body that is discovered floating in the Bosporus

but that of Manus Visser, who had been blackmailing the Greek. Makropoulos killed Visser and disguised the corpse, making it appear to be the body of the long-sought Makropoulos. Makropoulos is blackmailed again, and he and his new blackmailer kill each other in a shootout.

Mr. Peters, also known as **Frederik Petersen**, a drug dealer and former convict. A fat and unhealthy-looking Dane of fifty-five, Peters first knew Makropoulos in the late 1920's in Paris, where Peters owned a nightclub. Makropoulos persuaded Peters, along with several others, to work for him in what became a widespread and profitable drug operation. Eventually, Makropoulos absconded with the profits, but he first turned Peters and the rest over to the police. Later learning of Makropoulos' new identity, Peters decides to blackmail Makropoulos. He joins forces with Latimer because the latter had seen the "fake" Makropoulos. The two confront Makropoulos, who pays the blackmail, but the next day Makropoulos traces his blackmailers to the house in Paris owned by Peters and formerly used by Makropoulos.

There, Makropoulos and Peters kill each other.

Colonel Haki, the head of the Turkish secret police. Haki, a fan of detective fiction, meets Latimer at a party in Istanbul and offers Latimer the plot for a future story. When Haki is summoned to the morgue to examine a recently retrieved body identified as that of Makropoulos, Latimer accompanies him. Haki, ruthless and assured, has no doubt that the body is that of Makropoulos.

Dhris Mohammed, a black Muslim fig-picker in Smyrna. In 1922, Makropoulos and Mohammed robbed and killed a moneylender. Mohammed was later arrested, but before he was hanged he blamed the murder on Makropoulos, who already had escaped. It was on this occasion that Makropoulos first came to the attention of the police.

N. Marukakis, a middle-aged Greek journalist in Sofia, Bulgaria. Latimer, following the career of the supposedly dead Makropoulos, turns to Marukakis for information regarding an attempted political assassination that occurred in 1923 and that involved Makropoulos. Latimer learns that the incident had been financed by the Eurasian Credit Trust, a shadowy bank registered in Monaco. Marukakis also introduces Latimer to Irana Preveza.

Irana Preveza, the madam of a Sofia nightclub and brothel. A former prostitute, Preveza knew Makropoulos in 1923. She had loaned him money that he never repaid, and fifteen years later, Preveza is still bitter and angry. She is the first person interviewed by Latimer who actually knew Makropoulos.

Wladyslaw Grodek, a master spy. Living in Switzerland and now retired at the age of about sixty, Grodek tells Latimer about the time he employed Makropoulos, in Belgrade in 1926. Makropoulos, using a combination of blackmail and force, was successful in obtaining secret naval plans for Grodek but then turned on Grodek, who was working for the Italians, and sold the plans to the French government instead.

Bulić, a low-level Yugoslav bureaucrat in the ministry of marine. A dissatisfied man in his forties with a younger wife, Bulić allows himself to become compromised by Grodek and Makropoulos in a crooked gambling affair and provides the naval plans. He is later arrested and sentenced to prison.

Manus Visser, a drug dealer. A Dutchman, Visser was part of Makropoulos' drug operation in Paris and served time in prison in 1931 after Makropoulos informed the police of the names of his former associates. Years later, Visser discovered Makropoulos' new identity as Monsieur C. K. and blackmailed him. Visser, however, eventually was murdered by Makropoulos, who disguised Visser's body as his own. It is thus Visser's body that Colonel Haki identifies as that of Makropoulos.

— *Eugene S. Larson*

THE COFFIN TREE

Author: Wendy Law-Yone (1947-   )
First published: 1983
Genre: Novel

Locale: Burma, New York City, and Chicago
Time: The 1960's
Plot: Psychological realism

The narrator, a young Burmese woman who immigrates to the United States. The daughter of a revolutionary, she is reared in a financially secure but emotionally deprived environment. Her mother died when she was born, and her father is rarely home. When she is twenty, the narrator and her half brother are sent from Burma to New York City because a government coup has made their safety uncertain. Friendless, they struggle to adapt to a new climate and culture but sink into a degraded state of poverty and isolation. When the brother is beset with mental illness, the narrator cares for him until his death. A year later, she attempts suicide. During her stay at a mental hospital, she struggles to cope with her past and find a reason to continue living.

Shan, the narrator's half brother. The son of a tribal woman who goes mad, he is tended by village women until adolescence. He is physically abused by his father and grows into an idle dreamer who is obsessed with looking for treasure. He is kind to his half sister, who is ten years younger. Once in America, he is unable to hold a job and lives increasingly in a fantasy world of threatening enemies and delusions of glory and power.

Auntie Lily and

Auntie Rosie, older cousins of the narrator's mother who bring up the narrator in the family home. In their sixties, they are girlish and ignorant of the world but blossom under the hardships caused by the government coup.

The narrator's father, leader of the guerrilla People's Army in the Hill States of Burma. He is an impatient, brutal man who provides for his children but is too absorbed in his political cause to give them the attention and nurturing they need.

The narrator's grandmother, a bitter woman who dies when the narrator is young but whose tyrannical influence continues to be felt. She blames her daughter's death in childbirth on her granddaughter.

Morrison, a friend of the narrator's father who lives in New York. He and his callous wife fail to provide financial assistance or emotional support when the narrator and her brother arrive in the United States.

Benjamin Lane, a journalist in New York. He and his wife take the narrator and her brother into their household for a year.

Colonel Morgan, the narrator's elderly neighbor. His misunderstanding of her effort to befriend him prompts her suicide attempt.

Paddy, a patient at 3 East whose mental illness reminds the narrator of Shan's. Paddy withdraws more and more but writes long notes to the narrator describing his feelings.

Sarah, a wisecracking, cynical patient at 3 East.

Helga, a patient whom the other residents at 3 East like to tease.

Dr. Friday, the narrator's psychiatrist. The narrator is discouraged to discover that he has limitations, just like the patients.

— *Patricia L. Watson*

A COIN IN NINE HANDS
(Denier du rêve)

Author: Marguerite Yourcenar (Marguerite de Crayencour, 1903-1987)
First published: 1934
Genre: Novel

Locale: Rome, Italy
Time: 1933
Plot: Social realism

Marcella Ardeati Sarte (mahr-CHEHL-lah ahr-DEHAH-tee SAHR-teh), Dr. Alessandro Sarte's wife. She is separated from him and living with Massimo Iacofleff. She declares herself as realizing her vocation in her revolt against authority, law, and justice, as established by rulers such as Julius Caesar and Benito Mussolini. Marcella's true vocation is to feel allied to all those who are humiliated, oppressed, and committed to rebellion. She is demoniacally bound to her mission of assassinating Mussolini. Her harshness is in response to that dictator's authoritarian willfulness. Destruction fascinates Marcella, and Dr. Alessandro Sarte repeatedly sees her as a medusa or a vampire.

Dr. Alessandro Sarte, a famous surgeon and the husband of Marcella. He has failed in both of his functions, however, as he cannot heal Lina Chiari's breast cancer and he cannot understand his wife. The doctor hides behind the mask of social success and exploits his patients financially. He seems to be cold, hard, bitter, and distressed. He likes hunting for deer with royalty and driving beautiful sports cars to attract women. For him, all women are interchangeable. Dr. Sarte, who sees the film *Sir Julius* while sitting next to Angiola, makes love to her but despises her.

Ruggiero di Credo (rew-gee-EHR-oh dee KRAY-doh), the former Italian consul to Biscra. He married a vulgar Jewish Algerian woman, and they have two children, Rosalia and Angiola. His baroque domain of Gemera, in Sicily, which he inherited, is decaying. Faithful to the Bourbons, he disdained the dynasty of the Savoys; living in Sicily, he had no interest in the fall of papal Rome to the north. His hats resemble either halos or helmets. When he joins the army for four years, his wife betrays him. The splendor of Gemera remains but a dream for him and his family, and after it is destroyed, they leave for Rome, in the hope of exploiting his aristocratic ancestors and relatives. Life has stolen his dreams, but it is Ruggiero's constant misinterpretation of reality that leads to his isolation in an asylum, then death.

Rosalia di Credo, the uneducated daughter of Ruggiero di Credo who becomes a votive candle vendor in Rome. Rosalia remains devoted to the dream of her past, to Gemera, and to both her father and her sister, Angiola. Her own wishes are seldom granted, and her solitary destiny without love and happiness is her immediate reality. Rosalia and Angiola propose two opposed ways of understanding life. While Rosalia takes care of her father until she has to put him into an asylum, she continues to weep for all the sorrows of love, and she suffers for both her father and her sister. Her life is sustained by the hope that her sister will return to her, when, in fact, Angiola will destroy herself in many love affairs.

Angiola (ahn-gee-OH-lah), Rosalia's sister. Although educated in a fashionable school run by aristocratic nuns in Florence, Angiola takes lovers and marries men from all classes, from tailor to maharaja. She is unfaithful to all of them—even to her husband Paolo Farina, who pays the mortgage for Gemera until she leaves him.

Paolo Farina (pa-OH-loh fah-REE-nah), a young lawyer. He is married to Angiola, but she leaves him for another lover. Paolo then immediately hopes to possess Lina Chiari.

Lina Chiari (LEEN-ah kee-AH-ree), a prostitute. She soon realizes that true love cannot be bought. When Lina discovers that she has breast cancer, her future seems to be stripped of all hope. Her lipstick and artificial smile cover her despair.

Old Giulio Lovisi (jee-EW-lee-oh loh-VEE-see), the owner of a cosmetics store and a villa in Ostia. He is married to Giuseppa, and their daughter, Giovanna, is married to the writer Carlo Stevo, a socialist whom Giulio would like to "own." Carlo disappears while in jail for crimes against the state. Giulio often lights votive candles and says his prayers in an incoherent and automatic way. He remains enslaved to money worries and family problems, and he realizes the irreversible decline of his feelings for his wife, whose corpulence, sour disposition, and many shortcomings can only worsen. When a wish is granted to Giulio, his agony of hoping is perpetuated.

Carlo Stevo (STEH-voh), the husband of Giovanna. He is a writer and inspires Marcella's assassination attempt. Carlo dies in jail.

Giovanna Lovisi-Stevo, Carlo's wife and Giulio's daughter. She takes care of their crippled child in the hope of seeing her husband again. The angelic and golden world of the church is the antithesis of Giovanna's life. Giovanna is embittered, solitary, and prone to temptations while waiting in vain for the return of her husband.

Miss Jones, Giulio's salesgirl. When fired from her job because of Giuseppa's jealousy, she says her prayers in the hope of returning to England and regrets her madness in having come to Italy, where none of her dreams has come true. Small miseries make up the lives of Giulio and Miss Jones. Their prayers sustain their hopes, which are the only things that give meaning to their lives.

Old Mother Dida of Ponte Porzio, the wife of Fruttuoso. She has faced a ruthless fate in her husband, a good-for-nothing man who had given her many children and poverty, and she is now filling her life with routine and habit. Selling flowers near the film theater and the Conti Palace, she has outlived her husband, a king, and three popes. Indifferent to politics and religion, she loves Father Cicca and his organist without any religious faith. Despite her stinginess, she offers the ten-lira coin received from Dr. Sarte to the exhausted Clément Roux.

Clément Roux (klay-MAHN rew), a French artist about seventy years old. He has no interest in the modern architectural and political world of Rome. He meets with Massimo Iacofleff, but their ensuing conversation is completely at cross purposes, as neither listens to the other.

Massimo Iacofleff (mahs-SEE-moh ee-AH-koh-flehf), a double agent. He is introduced as a lover of Lina Chiari. He tells Clément about his complicity with Marcella, when they traded in false passports in Vienna, and how he is now worried that Marcella might have despised him when she died alone during her failed assassination attempt. He is one of the two main witnesses to the assassination attempt. He expresses admiration for Marcella's heroism and Carlo's commitment.

— *Marlies Kronegger*

COLD COMFORT FARM

Author: Stella Gibbons (1902-1989)
First published: 1932
Genre: Novel

Locale: London and Sussex, England
Time: Early twentieth century
Plot: Parody

Flora Poste, a recently orphaned young woman, nineteen years old. She is left with an endowment of one hundred pounds a year. Because her expensive education has not prepared her to earn a living, she decides to leave London and stay with relatives until she finds someone she chooses to marry. She stays with the Starkadders, an aunt and various cousins who reside at Cold Comfort Farm in Howling, Sussex. Her relatives and the farmhands are a rude, filthy, and quarrelsome bunch; the farmhouse is deteriorating, and the livestock are neglected. Flora hears there is a mysterious curse on the farm that keeps the Starkadders in squalor and emotional turmoil, and she decides to tidy up her relatives' lives. With unfailing good manners, plentiful help from her London friends, hard work, and her book of common sense, Flora manages to achieve her goal and her heart's desire.

Ada Doom Starkadder, the sister of Flora's deceased mother and acknowledged head of the Starkadder family. She lives in one of the farmhouse's upper rooms, which she rarely leaves, and controls the entire family with threats of having an "attack" if any member leaves the farm. As a child, Ada saw "something nasty in the woodshed" and has convinced the others that she never recovered from the shock. Her madness takes the form of demanding to know everything that goes on, and she has an attack unless she goes over the farm's books twice a week. Her attacks escalate when the family members start to leave, one by one, but Flora convinces Aunt Ada to give up her miserable life and seek happiness.

Judith Starkadder, Flora's cousin. She is married to Amos Starkadder, and they have a son, Seth, on whom she dotes, although he is rude and indifferent to her. Two hundred photos of Seth decorate her room, where she spends most of her time weeping and moping. When he leaves, she drapes all the photos in black. She is remarkably indifferent to her other two children, Reuben and Elfine. She has abandoned all hope of happiness and takes a fatalistic view of life, but she gives herself up to the care of a psychiatrist, and her prognosis is good.

Amos Starkadder, Judith's husband, a deeply religious man filled with the spirit of hellfire and damnation. He finds fulfillment in preaching twice a week at the Church of the Quivering Brethren. Flora suggests that he might serve the Lord even better by traveling around the country to preach. Although Amos suffers from the same curse as the rest of his family and thinks he cannot leave the farm, the idea grows on him. He finally defies Ada and sets out on his mission. When last heard from, he has had such success in London that he is setting out for America to spread the word.

Seth Starkadder, a handsome, virile, and libidinous man. Incapable of seeing any woman as anything but a sex object, he has fathered the hired girl's four children as well as many others. He considers Flora as simply another female, but she sees him as another problem to be solved. Tied to the farm by the family curse, his great passion is the "talkies" that he sneaks off to see in the nearby town. When Flora introduces him to a producer friend from Hollywood, the producer immediately recognizes Seth's magnetism and offers to put him in films. Seth is last seen on the silver screen about a year later, starring in *Small Town Sheik*.

Reuben Starkadder, the only true farmer in the family. He loves farming and has a sensuous, almost lecherous feeling for the land. He is suspicious that Flora is trying to wrest ownership of the farm from the family. Although Reuben wants desperately to inherit the farm from his father, Amos believes Reuben is eager for his death and threatens to leave the place to Adam Lambsbreath, the hired hand. When Flora convinces him she has no interest in the farm, Reuben becomes her ally and eventually proposes to her, but she suggests someone more suitable. After Amos finds his true vocation of preaching worldwide, he finally leaves the farm to Reuben.

— *Sheila Golburgh Johnson*

COLD STORAGE

Author: Ronald Ribman (1932-   )
First published: 1978
Genre: Drama

Locale: New York City
Time: 1977
Plot: Existentialism

Joseph Parmigian, a dying cancer patient in his sixties. He is of Armenian background, is married, and owns a fruit and vegetable store in Greenwich Village. He is still hungry for experience and knowledge. An opinionated smart aleck who, with brass, sarcasm, and broad humor, smashes through the reserved shell of Landau, a fellow patient in a New York City hospital. Parmigian, prodding and provoking, demands that Landau reveal his dreams. Parmigian has never felt settled or satisfied with life, and his wacky exuberance is balanced by a bleak vision of the ultimate meaninglessness of things and contradictory subcurrents, typified by his revelation of "the best time to commit suicide, when you're in a good mood." In the end, though, it is not so much this out-of-place, deathbed Rabelaisianism that inspires Landau to break his reticence but Parmigian's confession that he is at the end of his tether in trying to face up to his approaching death.

Richard Landau, a man in his mid-forties who is in the hospital for "exploratory" surgery. He is a Jewish investment adviser who recommends art and antiques to wealthy clients; he is married, with two daughters. He is vaguely discontented with the whirl of modern life and seeks solace in the eternal verities as they are offered by fine china and antique furniture. He is quietly self-possessed, alternately tantalized and scandalized by Parmigian's verbal antics. Although he is drawn into the conversation by the older man's ability to reconstruct, without knowing him, the general contours of his life, Landau skillfully parries efforts to get him to reveal himself. When he does reveal himself, he discloses an obsession that proves sobering to Parmigian. Landau is searching, through psychiatry and introspection, for a clearer memory of his parents, who gave him to another family in Nazi Germany to save him from the concentration camps in which they perished. This inward, backward quest has stopped Landau from living in the present, though his self-confrontation in the hospital brings about his spiritual rebirth, ironically midwifed by a man on the brink of death.

Miss Madurga, the young, attractive Hispanic private-duty nurse of Landau. She was formerly Parmigian's nurse. She appears briefly at the opening of act 1, to serve as a bridge to begin the conversation between the two patients, and at the close of act 1, to wheel Landau away. There is no nonsense about her.

— *James Feast*

THE COLLECTOR

Author: John Fowles (1926-   )
First published: 1963
Genre: Novel

Locale: London and Sussex, England
Time: Early 1960's
Plot: Psychological realism

Fredrick Clegg, a clerk in the Town Hall Annexe in Southampton, England, until he wins seventy-three thousand pounds in a lottery and quits his job. He is painfully diffident and ashamed of being a member of the uneducated working class of British society. When Clegg wins the lottery at the age of thirty-seven, he has both the determination and the financial power to realize his greatest ambition: He wants to possess Miranda Grey, the daughter of a doctor and a member of England's cultured, educated upper class. Believing that once Miranda spends time with him she will see that he is worthy of her interest and affection, Clegg purchases a secluded house several miles outside Lewes, England, decorates it the way he mistakenly thinks Miranda would like it, and remodels the cellar and equips it with plumbing and electricity so it will be habitable. He next purchases clothes, records, and books, and he places these in the cellar apartment—not for himself but for Miranda. After he kidnaps her, the cellar of his house becomes her prison for two months, until she dies of pneumonia, at which time Clegg buries her body in his backyard. Throughout his retrospective account of his time with Miranda, he frequently assures the reader that he never meant to harm her, that his interest in her was nonsexual, and that he would have gotten a doctor for her if she had not proved herself to be unworthy of his trust and admiration. What he never says directly but shows by his actions and attitudes is that he hates women; if they arouse his otherwise repressed sexual desire, he perceives them as disgusting and worthless whores. He ultimately views Miranda as such a woman, consequently allows her to die, and then, after burying her, begins to stalk his next victim, a young woman who physically resembles Miranda.

Miranda Grey, a second-year art student at the Slade Art School in London. Twenty years old when Clegg kidnaps her, Miranda begins writing a diary that makes up approximately half of the novel's narrative. In her diary entries, she attempts to analyze Clegg and her predicament as his prisoner as well as to understand her religious faith, her sexuality, her talents as an artist, and her relationships with her family and various men in her life, most specifically with George Pastan. Pastan was an artist twice her age whom she had begun to view as her mentor but whom she had refused as a lover; her ongoing analysis of this relationship serves as a significant means by which Miranda is able to unveil and embrace the person she is instead of the person, according to her society, she should be. When Clegg captures her, Miranda is a pacifist who believes in nonviolence at any cost; although she strays from her belief in pacifism when she physically attacks Clegg several weeks after her abduction, she is filled with disgust at herself for stooping to his level and letting herself down. She realizes with certainty that she is a moral person unashamed of being moral. She also discovers that her morality should not preclude a sexual relationship with her mentor-friend George Pastan.

— *David A. Carpenter*

THE COLLEGIANS

Author: Gerald Griffin (1803-1840)
First published: 1829
Genre: Novel

Locale: Ireland
Time: Late eighteenth century
Plot: Domestic

Hardress Cregan, a wealthy, spirited young man of the upper classes. He lives for sports and a good time. Though a courageous man, he is shy around women. Disdainful of the lower classes, he nevertheless marries Eily O'Connor, a lower-class girl. He is afraid to let his family know of the alliance. He regrets his marriage when he comes to love his cousin, Ann

Chute. His servant murders Eily, and Hardress plans to marry Ann; however, the servant confesses to his crime and implicates Hardress, and Hardress is sent into exile as a criminal.

Kyrle Daly, a middle-class young man, a friend of Hardress during and after their college days. He loves Ann Chute and marries her after Hardress is exiled.

Eily O'Connor, a ropemaker's daughter, secretly married to Hardress. She is a beautiful girl. When her husband falls in love with Ann Chute, Eily is willing to go to Canada to be out of the way, but she is murdered by her husband's servant.

Ann Chute, a beautiful upper-class girl, Hardress' cousin. She loves Hardress and wants to marry him. After his crime is discovered, however, she marries Kyrle, realizing at last that he is much the better man.

Mrs. Cregan, Hardress' mother. Not knowing her son is already married, she throws him and Ann together and tries to make a match between them.

Danny Mann, Hardress' devoted servant, a cruel hunchback. He kills Eily to get her out of her husband's way. When he confesses his crime to avenge a beating by Hardress, he is found guilty and hanged.

COLOMBA

Author: Prosper Mérimée (1803-1870)
First published: 1840
Genre: Novel

Locale: Corsica
Time: Early nineteenth century
Plot: Adventure

Colomba della Rebbia (koh-LOHM-bah dehl-lah REHB-bee-ah), who demands the death of her family's blood enemy, Barricini, for the murder of her father. She considers the evidence of his innocence faked. She vainly tries to rouse her brother to murder him. Later, she learns from the broken Barricini that he had indeed faked the proof of his innocence. She feels no sympathy for him in his adversity; instead, she finds satisfaction in the belief that her father's blood is thus avenged.

Lieutenant Orso della Rebbia, of Napoleon's army, Colomba's brother. He refuses to murder Barricini as his sister demands. He is accused of murdering two sons of Barricini,

but he is cleared when Colonel Nevil testifies that the sons first ambushed Orso. He marries Lydia.

Lawyer Barricini (bahr-ree-CHEE-nee), the mayor of the village and the suspected murderer of Orso's father.

Two sons of Barricini, who ambush Orso but are shot by him.

Colonel Sir Thomas Nevil, an Irish officer who has come to Corsica to hunt. He testifies that Orso's shooting of Barricini's sons was in self-defense.

Lydia Nevil, his daughter, who wants to leave the settlement of crime to the law.

COLOR OF DARKNESS: Eleven Stories and a Novella

Author: James Purdy (1923-   )
First published: 1957
Genre: Short fiction

Locale: Various
Time: Contemporary
Plot: Surrealism

Fenton Ridgeway, a nineteen-year-old orphan in "63: Dream Palace." He has come to the big city from West Virginia after his mother's death, bringing along his sickly thirteen-year-old brother, Claire. Fenton is torn between caring for his brother—which keeps him trapped in an abandoned, rotting house, where Claire reminds him of family duty, God, and his mother—and involving himself with the dissolute, effete Parkhurst Cratty and the rich, alcoholic widow, Grainger, who are fascinated by his rough manners and good looks. He can be dull, oafish, and violent, but he also has clear insights into his own personality as well as the character of those around him. He describes himself as sick where his soul is supposed to be.

Parkhurst Cratty, a writer in "63: Dream Palace" who does not seem to write anything. He is fascinated by Fenton Ridgeway from the moment he meets him in the park. Cratty, who is supported by his wife, is looking for subject material. Cratty is, at first, determined to keep Ridgeway to himself, away from Grainger, the rich widow with whom he shares a drunken, almost surrealistic existence in her home, the "Dream Palace." Eventually, when he does take Fenton there, Grainger verbally attacks Cratty while attempting to fit Fenton into the clothes, and the role, of her former husband.

The father, a cold, self-absorbed man in "Color of Darkness" whose wife has left him because he has time only for his work. He has left his son to be reared by the housekeeper, Mrs. Zilke. His isolation is so complete that he cannot even remember the color of his son's eyes, despite the fact that his son looks just like him. He is unable to say the word "son" without a sense of nausea.

Paul, a sickly child in "Why Can't They Tell You Why?" who is forced to call his physically and verbally abusive mother Ethel, rather than Mama. His only comfort in life comes from eavesdropping on her telephone conversations with a friend and in looking through a box of photographs of the father he never knew. When his mother, resenting this interest, threatens to send him to an asylum unless he destroys the pictures, he desperately tries to protect them, crouching over them while a thick, black substance spews forth from his mouth.

Lois Klein, a middle-aged woman in "Don't Call Me By My Right Name." She is dissatisfied with her six-month marriage because she dislikes her husband's last name. After drinking too much at a party, she publicly demands that he change his name. Even after her husband becomes violent, hitting her repeatedly when she keeps on arguing, her main grievance against him remains the shallow, superficial fact that he refuses to change his name.

Mahala, a middle-aged African American woman in "Eventide" who mourns the fact that her son left home more than a month ago. She is an overly possessive mother, preserving his dirty clothes in the closet, kissing and smelling them to keep his memory and presence with her. Although her sister, Plumy, lost her son when he was only four, Mahala had never had any sympathy for her. Now that she realizes her own son is lost to her, involved with a white woman in the world of jazz clubs, she begins to feel some identification with Plumy.

Mrs. Farebrother, a woman in "Sound of Talking" who is trapped in a marriage with a paraplegic husband. His suffering is so intense at times that it is difficult for her even to look at him. Both she and her husband are filled with resentment because of the charades they must endure. He insists that she talk to him to relieve his boredom, although they both know her conversation will only irritate him in the end. She forces herself to invent tales to meet his incessant questions. When he finally offers to buy her the raven she has been telling him about, she displays a rare honesty and admits that she does not want it. In fact, she is devastated to discover that she does not really want anything anymore.

Mrs. Zeller, who in "Cutting Edge" dominates her family until her grown artist son returns home for a visit. When he refuses to shave off his beard at her insistence, she reveals the emptiness and lack of love in the family.

— *Mary E. Mahony*

THE COLOR PURPLE

Author: Alice Walker (1944-   )
First published: 1982
Genre: Novel

Locale: Georgia, Tennessee, and Africa
Time: 1920's-1940's
Plot: Social realism

Celie, a survivor of sexual and physical abuse who writes intimate letters to God and to her sister Nettie. She is the owner of Celie Folkpants, Unlimited. Described as black, poor, and ugly, she is fourteen years old at the beginning of the story. Celie is a terrorized and passive girl with little belief in herself who undergoes a major transformation in attitude and becomes an outrageous, audacious, courageous, and willful woman who enjoys her lesbian sexuality. She gives birth to two children, conceived while she is being raped repeatedly by Alphonso, whom she believes to be her father. Both children are quickly taken from her by him. Celie is married off to Albert but falls in love with Shug Avery, a former lover of her husband. After Celie nurses Shug through an illness, they become lovers; later, they move to Memphis, where Celie starts a pants company. Celie returns to Georgia when she inherits her parents' house.

Nettie, Celie's younger sister, a missionary in Africa. Considered to be very pretty and very clever, Nettie loves Celie and remains devoted to her throughout her life. During a separation of some twenty years, she writes to Celie regularly, telling Celie of her experiences in Africa. Nettie helps take care of and watches over Celie's two children, who have been adopted by the missionary couple whom Nettie accompanied to Africa. Nettie eventually reunites the family.

Albert, a poor farmer. Abusive and dissatisfied with himself and his life, Albert is in love with Shug, but, because he is incapable of disobeying his father, he married another woman. He beats Celie, his second wife, because she is not Shug. He conceals all the letters that Nettie sends to Celie. Albert thinks little of treating Celie as less than human until she stands up to him and then leaves, at which point he becomes physically and spiritually ill, recovers, begins to lead a moral life, and becomes friends with Celie.

Shug Avery, whose real name is **Lillie** and who also is called **The Queen Honeybee**, a blues singer. Confident, flamboyant, and independent, Shug is considered to be immoral by some church folk but is nevertheless popular and admired as a performer. She is wise in the cultural values of the black community, and her presence has a transforming effect, especially on Celie but also on others. Shug moves in with Celie and Albert; she is first Albert's and then Celie's lover. She marries Grady, becomes lovers with a young blues flutist named Germaine, and eventually returns as Celie's lover.

Harpo, the owner of a juke joint, Albert's oldest son. As a young man, he is very tall, skinny, and dark-skinned. He is insecure in his manhood and frustrated by his inability to make his wife do as he commands. When his wife leaves him because she is exasperated by his attempts to beat her, he turns their house into a juke joint that provides Shug Avery and others with a place to sing the blues.

Sofia Butler, the defiant wife of Harpo. Big, strong, and ruddy looking, her personality is that of a fighter, and she refuses to be pushed around by anyone. When the mayor's wife sees her on the street and asks her to be her maid, Sofia curses, responds to the mayor's slap by knocking him down, and is then beaten severely by the police. She is sentenced to jail for twelve years but spends most of that time as maid to the mayor's wife.

Alphonso, called **Pa** by Celie, who is mistaken by Celie and Nettie as their father but really is their stepfather. He is a mean man who has sexual relations with a number of young girls, some of whom he marries. When he rapes Celie, he tells her to say nothing to anyone but God; thus, her subsequent letters are addressed to God.

Mary Agnes, called **Squeak**, Harpo's lover and a late-blooming blues singer. Described as yellow-skinned, Mary Agnes facilitates Sofia's release from prison into the service of the mayor's wife by calling on her white uncle, the prison warden, who rapes her during this visit. She leaves Harpo to go with Celie and Shug to Memphis to start a singing career. She becomes lovers with Shug's husband and moves to Panama with him, then returns to Memphis and her singing career.

Grady, Shug's husband, who moves to Panama with Mary Agnes in order to run a marijuana plantation.

Olivia, Celie's daughter and oldest child, an independent thinker who is reared in Africa by Samuel and his wife, Corrine, both missionaries.

Adam Omatangu, Celie's son, a thoughtful and sensitive young man who writes verses and loves to sing. Adam obtains the second name of Omatangu when he marries an African woman.

Tashi Omatangu, Adam's wife, one of the Olinka people who joins the *mbeles* to fight against white colonialists in Africa but is persuaded by Adam to become married to him and return with him to the United States.

— *Leslie W. Lewis*

COLOURS IN THE DARK

Author: James Reaney (1926-   )
First published: 1969
Genre: Drama

Locale: Canada
Time: The 1960's
Plot: Mythic

Pa, the father, who can read palms and tell the color of things even while blindfolded. He also plays the man initiated into an understanding of his own life during the Sundog ritual. He is the cruel schoolmaster who whips the children for their faults in spelling, the wealthy and powerful executive who is the first to die in the Dance of Death, and the grocer who pulls a customer backward and forward through time by the string attached to her parcel. He recites the poem on the Royal Visit. He plays the teacher of the writing class and the student who baby-sits for the limbless young man.

Ma, the mother, who blindfolds the child suffering from the measles. She is the lawyer at the trial of the cruel schoolmaster and the announcer of the significance of the colors at the beginning of the "color" acts. She is the waspish antisuffragist mistress of the Winnipeg boardinghouse and also a girl boarder at the same boardinghouse. She is the Wind Lady, who dances with her rain doll, and the rich young lady whose swimming pool and vacations in Antigua cannot save her from the Dance of Death.

Gramp, the grandfather, the bear who threatens to eat the small berry-picking girl. He is also James McIntyre, the Ingeroll cheese poet. He is Mr. Winemeyer, the wise sculptor hermit. He is the aggressively pedantic Professor Button, who decries religious faith but whose knowledge of languages is no match for Bible Sal's ability to speak in tongues. He plays

Tecumseh in the schoolmaster's trial, the Minister at the Christening, and the Death King in the Dance of Death scene.

Gram, the grandmother, a Sundog and the lady who initiates the father into a knowledge of himself at the Sundog ritual. She is Granny Crack and the old beggar woman who wanders the countryside and hangs out all the clothing of her life on a line. She is the music teacher, the old farm wife who ladles out horse soup, and the girl at the Winnipeg boardinghouse. She is also the Death Lady in the Dance of Death.

Son, the son, one of the boys on a bicycle trip who meets the reclusive Mr. Winemeyer and the judge at the trial of the cruel schoolmaster. He is the grocery boy, the accuser at the Sundog ritual, and the university student who is a friend of Bible Sal. He is also a boarder at the Winnipeg boardinghouse. He plays the young man with no arms and no legs who yearns for someone to accept and love him.

Niece, the daughter, the girl, and the Bride. She is also Bible Sal, whose religious devotion drives her to attempt to copy out the entire Bible. Bible Sal visits the lecture of Professor Button, a teacher of Old Testament studies at University College, University of Toronto. She counters his cynical faithlessness with a display of her ability to speak in tongues, a gift she did not previously know she had. She is also the maid at the Winnipeg boardinghouse.

— *Catherine Swanson*

COME BACK, LITTLE SHEBA

Author: William Inge (1913-1973)
First published: 1950
Genre: Drama

Locale: A Midwestern college town
Time: Late 1940's
Plot: Psychological realism

Doc Delaney, a chiropractor in a Midwestern city. This outwardly gentle, courteous, and patient man in his early forties seethes inside because of his frustrating life. He felt compelled to drop out of medical school about twenty years earlier and marry Lola because he had made her pregnant. Married to a woman who is his social and intellectual inferior, and disappointed in his ambitions and by the fact that Lola was rendered sterile by the botched delivery of their stillborn first child, Doc became an alcoholic who was nearly homicidal when intoxicated. He squandered all the money he had inherited and allowed his practice to go to ruin. For the past eleven months, he has belonged to Alcoholics Anonymous and is trying to rebuild his shattered life.

Lola Delaney, a housewife. Married to Doc at the age of eighteen, Lola has remained mentally an adolescent for the past twenty years. In contrast to her shy, introverted husband, she has no internal resources and is completely dependent on other people. She has let herself become fat, and she neglects her housekeeping, along with her personal appearance. At the age of eighteen, she had been strikingly attractive and much sought after by young men. Because this was the only area in which she ever experienced success and satisfaction, she has never gotten over her youthful illusions about romantic love. Her small lost dog, Little Sheba, symbolizes for her, on an unconscious level, her own lost youth and beauty, which she hopes somehow will come back to her.

Marie, a college student who boards with the Delaneys. At the age of eighteen or nineteen, she is pretty, cheerful, sprightly, and friendly, a ray of sunshine in this unhappy household. Both Doc and Lola project their fantasies onto this fairly ordinary girl. Doc sees her as pure and almost saintly. Lola sees her quite simply as herself at that same age. Marie's passionate relationship with Turk, in which Lola takes a strong vicarious interest, triggers Doc's repressed rage and leads directly to the violent climax of the play. Through their emotional involvement with Marie, both Doc and Lola eventually come to realize their mistaken illusions about the glamour of youth.

Turk, a college athlete, good-looking, aggressive, muscular, and narcissistic. Although only nineteen or twenty years old, he has been in the military service and has acquired a superficial sophistication. His attitude toward young women is predatory; he is interested only in sex. Although Marie is strongly attracted to him on this level, she knows he is not a suitable prospect as a spouse. Doc hates him because he is sensual and uninhibited, everything Doc is not. When Doc realizes that the two young students are sleeping together under his roof, he gets roaring drunk and threatens to kill Turk as well as Lola, whom he blames for acting as a pander in the illicit affair.

Bruce, Marie's fiancé, who lives in another city. This intelligent, ambitious, and well-mannered young man comes from an upper-middle-class family and is already making headway in the business world. Marie regards him as a good catch, but he does not fire her blood the way Turk does. When she and Bruce go off to get married at the end of the play, it is clear that they will have a conventional middle-class marriage without any physical excitement.

Mrs. Coffman, a housewife, the Delaneys' next-door neighbor. This middle-aged mother of seven children serves as a contrast to the slovenly, irresponsible Lola. Mrs. Coffman speaks with a German accent and has the hardworking, no-nonsense attitude often associated with members of that ethnic group. She is kindhearted, however, and proves helpful to Lola in her hour of need.

— *Bill Delaney*

THE COMEDIANS

Author: Graham Greene (1904-1991)
First published: 1966
Genre: Novel

Locale: Haiti and the Dominican Republic
Time: Early 1960's
Plot: Tragicomedy

Brown, the narrator, a part-Englishman from Monaco who has inherited a hotel in Haiti. Jaded, cynical, and detached, Brown has returned to Haiti in his late fifties because he has no real home and the hotel is all he owns. After run-ins with François "Papa Doc" Duvalier's secret police and after he has betrayed his friend Jones and his mistress Martha through his misplaced suspicion of them, he escapes from the fear-ridden country to the Dominican Republic, where he becomes a partner in a mortician's concern.

"Major" Jones, a former theater manager in his late forties who pretends to have been a war hero. A man sought by the police in several countries, he is nevertheless very likable, because he has a kindness about him and always makes people laugh. Tricked by Brown into joining the cause of the resistance against Papa Doc, he dies heroically in an effort to allow his fellow rebels to escape.

William Abel Smith, an elderly, idealistic vegetarian who has come to Haiti because he believes that avoidance of meat will neutralize destructive passions and because he wishes to start a Haitian vegetarian institute. Having run on the vegetarian ticket in the 1948 election, he is accepted as a former presidential candidate by the naïve authorities and even granted some credibility. His attempts to help people usually backfire disastrously, as when he gives beggars money that is immediately snatched by the secret police, but he is instrumental several times in helping Brown.

Mrs. Smith, Smith's wife, as idealistic as her husband. She is devoted to Smith and is even more likely than he to take immediate, direct action when she perceives injustice.

Martha Pineda (pih-NAY-dah), Brown's mistress. Married to a South American diplomat who knows about the affair and tolerates it, she is torn between her love for Brown and her attachment to her son Angel. As emotional and committed as Brown is restrained and detached, Martha is pulled back and forth between commitments until the end of the novel, when it becomes clear that she will follow her husband, who has been transferred, and will no longer see Brown.

Dr. Magiot, an elderly Communist doctor who is committed to people rather than causes. He reappears throughout the action to do what he can to alleviate suffering, but at the end he too is betrayed and killed by the supporters of Papa Doc. His last letter, received by Smith after Magiot's death, urges Smith to join the committed, not to "abandon all faith."

Captain Concasseur, an officer in the Tonton Macoute, Papa Doc's secret police. Like his colleagues, he wears black sunglasses to maximize his effect of terror. Concasseur enjoys torturing and destroying, but his fun terrorizing Brown is broken up by the Smiths. Concasseur eventually is killed by the rebels, before they are killed by other members of the Tonton Macoute.

Henri Philipot, the young nephew of a slain Haitian minister. He gives up his writing of obscure verse to join the rebels. He survives to tell of the death of Jones and the others.

— *Janet McCann*

THE COMEDY OF ERRORS

Author: William Shakespeare (1564-1616)
First published: 1623
Genre: Drama

Locale: Greece
Time: The first century B.C.E.
Plot: Farce

Antipholus of Syracuse (an-TIHF-oh-luhs), the son of Aegeon and Aemilia. Separated from his twin brother in his childhood, he meets him again under the most baffling circumstances. Shortly after he and his servant, Dromio of Syracuse, land in Ephesus, the whole series of comic errors begins. Antipholus meets his servant's lost twin brother, who is also bewildered by the ensuing conversation. Thinking this Dromio to be his own servant, Antipholus hits the mystified man on his head with great vigor. Finally, at the end, this puzzle is solved when he recognizes that he has found his identical twin.

Antipholus of Ephesus (EHF-eh-suhs), the identical twin brother of Antipholus of Syracuse. Equally bewildered by his mishaps, he is disgruntled when his wife locks him out of his house. She is blissfully unaware of the truth—that the man at her house is not her husband. In addition, a purse of money is received by the wrong man. Never having seen his own father, or at least not aware of the relationship, he is even more amazed when the old man calls him "son." By this time, the entire town believes him to be mad, and he, like his twin, is beginning to think that he is bewitched. It is with great relief that he finally learns the true situation and is reunited with his family.

Dromio of Syracuse (DROH-mee-oh), the twin brother of Dromio of Ephesus and attendant to Antipholus of Syracuse. He is as much bewildered as his master, who, in the mix-up, belabors both Dromios. To add to his misery, a serving wench takes him for her Dromio and makes unwanted advances. Much to his chagrin, she is "all o'er embellished with rubies, carbuncles, sapphires." In addition, she is "no longer from head to foot than from hip to hip. She is spherical, like a globe."

Dromio of Ephesus, who was separated from his identical twin at the same time that the two Antipholuses were separated, during a shipwreck. As is his brother, he is often belabored by his master. In this case, if his master does not pummel him, his mistress will perform the same office. During all this time, he is involved in many cases of mistaken identity. Sent for a piece of rope, he is amazed when his supposed master knows nothing of the transaction.

Aegeon (ee-JEE-on), a merchant of Syracuse. Many years before, he had lost his beloved wife and one son. Since then, his other son has left home to find his twin brother. Now Aegeon is searching for all his family. Landing in Ephesus, he finds that merchants from Syracuse are not allowed there on penalty of death or payment of a large ransom. When Aegeon is unable to raise the ransom, the duke gives the old man a one-day reprieve. He finds his sons just in time, the ransom is paid, and the family is reunited.

Adriana (ay-drih-AY-nuh), the wife of Antipholus of Ephesus. When her husband denies his relationship to her, she (unaware that he is the wrong man) thinks he is insane. Already suspicious of her husband because of supposed infidelities, she suspects him even more.

Aemilia (ee-MIHL-ee-uh), the wife of Aegeon and abbess at Ephesus. In the recognition scene, she finds her husband, who has been separated from her for many years.

Solinus (soh-LI-nuhs), the duke of Ephesus.

Luciana (lew-shee-AH-nuh), Adriana's sister, wooed by Antipholus of Syracuse.

Angelo, a goldsmith.

Pinch, a schoolmaster and "a hungry lean-fac'd villain, a mere anatomy."

THE COMFORTERS

Author: Muriel Spark (1918-   )
First published: 1957
Genre: Novel

Locale: London and the surrounding countryside
Time: The 1950's
Plot: Satire

Caroline Rose, a woman of about thirty with a Cambridge education. She is thin, angular, sharp, and inquiring, well-dressed and good-looking. After converting to Catholicism, she renounces sex, stops living with her lover, Laurence Manders, and goes on a religious retreat. When she hears ghostly voices and a typewriter, she thinks that she is mad but soon guesses that the typewriter is typing the novel of her life and the lives of others. She wonders if this mysterious "author" is a figure from some other dimension—perhaps a soul from purgatory, perhaps Satan himself. She breaks her leg when she and Laurence have a serious automobile accident. More and more, her thoughts influence the novel; she senses its approaching end. At a climactic picnic, she falls into the river with Georgina Hogg, struggles free, and saves herself. She seems to envision a happy ending, though whether in fiction or in reality is unclear.

Laurence Manders, a man of about thirty, a lapsed Catholic who works as a sports commentator for the British Broadcasting Corporation. Despite the fact that Caroline leaves him, he still loves her, and he worries about her sanity. At the end, he discovers Caroline's notes for her novel and protests that

she misrepresents him. Perhaps he is rewarded by a happy ending.

Georgina Hogg, a woman of about fifty, the cousin and first wife of Mervyn Hogg and the mother of Andrew. She is sanctimonious, bullying, self-centered, and universally hated. Her hair is white, her pale-blue eyes have no lashes, and her bosom is tremendous. She was Laurence's nursery governess and now works at a religious retreat center. There are hints that she is not a real person; on the way to a picnic that plays a crucial part in the plot, she falls asleep in the car and disappears like a witch. Later, she struggles with Caroline in the river and apparently drowns. No body is recovered.

Louisa Jepp, who is seventy-eight years old. She is the daughter of a gypsy, the mother of Lady Manders, and the grandmother of Laurence. Short and fat, she is a determined woman; her thin black hair frames a lined face with deep-set spectacled black eyes. Her home, "Smuggler's Retreat," is aptly named, for she runs a diamond-smuggling gang. She ends up marrying one of her partners in crime, J. G. L. Webster.

Mervyn Hogg, or **Mervyn Hogarth**, Andrew's father. He is a bigamist, having married both Georgina Hogg and Eleanor

Hogarth. Mervyn is about fifty and is a thin, colorless, cynical little man. As part of Louisa's smuggling operation, he takes his son to Continental shrines and returns with diamonds encased in plaster statuettes and rosary beads.

Willi Stock, known as **The Baron**, who is fifty years old and was born in the Congo; he is a naturalized British citizen. He may have African blood, and he may be a real baron. Amused and aloof, he runs an intellectual bookshop, befriends Caroline, and spreads stories about her. He is Louisa's London contact, receiving jewels from Webster and selling them. He becomes obsessed with the idea that Mervyn is "the foremost diabolist in these islands." He is present when Georgina disappears and is at the picnic. Near the end of the novel, he is committed to a mental hospital.

Eleanor Hogarth, a woman of about thirty. She is a dancer, Mervyn's wife, Willi's mistress, and Ernest Manders' business partner. She was at Cambridge with Caroline, married soon thereafter, and left when she discovered Mervyn's bigamy. She calls Georgina a witch.

Lady Helena Manders, the daughter of Louisa, wife of Sir Edwin, and mother of Laurence. A convert to Catholicism, she builds religious retreat centers. Although she hates Georgina,

she charitably finds work for her. She is in the car when Georgina disappears.

Sir Edwin Manders, a lifelong Catholic, Lady Helena's husband and Laurence's father. He manufactures Manders Figs in Syrup. He is often at a retreat but wonders if his disengagement is proper.

Ernest Manders, a dancer, Sir Edwin's brother and Eleanor's business partner. Although he is in most ways a good Catholic, he is homosexual and is effeminate. When he inadvertently blackmails Mervyn, Georgina thinks that the Manders suspect something. His revelations to Helena help precipitate the ending.

Andrew Hogg, or **Andrew Hogarth**, the son of Mervyn and Georgina, about twenty-five years old. He is confined to a wheelchair. He helps his father smuggle diamonds. When the smuggling stops, he is cured (some say miraculously) and goes to Canada to lecture.

J. G. L. Webster, a man of seventy-seven years, with white hair and a mustache. He bakes the loaves in which the diamonds are conveyed from the Hogarths to Louisa and is her messenger to Willi. Ultimately, he marries Louisa.

— *George Soule*

COMING UP FOR AIR

Author: George Orwell (Eric Arthur Blair, 1903-1950)
First published: 1939
Genre: Novel

Locale: A London suburb and a rural English town
Time: Early 1900's and 1938
Plot: Social realism

George Bowling, a forty-five-year-old insurance representative. Fat and sentimental, with a mouth full of false teeth, George is in every way the lower-middle-class Englishman, even to his love of reading and his nostalgia for an Edwardian, pre-World War I past that can no longer be found, except perhaps in memory. In order to escape the increasingly bland routine in his London suburban home, as well as his complaining wife and children, George fantasizes about taking a trip to his childhood home of Lower Binfield, a small town in rural Oxfordshire. He discovers, however, that one cannot go home again, for Lower Binfield, as many towns have, has become devoid of individuality as a result of "progress." The childhood carp pool George dreams about fishing in again, for example, has become a rubbish dump in the middle of a housing tract of fake Tudor homes. George's family home and the family business of Samuel Bowling, Corn & Seed Merchant has been reduced to Wendy's Tea-Shop. George is a sentimentalist who gets teary over primroses, a middle-aged man who fantasizes about women without being able to do anything about them. He wants only peace and an authentic England, and he is right in his predictions about the start of World War II and about what will happen to England after the war: It will become even more standardized. George is a fleshy, three-dimensional character who is both a sentimental-

ist about the past and a prophet of the future. The other characters in the novel pale in comparison to him.

Hilda Bowling, George's wife of fifteen years. Hilda has been worn down by marriage and by trying to rear two children on George's limited income. She no longer shares any of George's dreams and walks through her days with a "perpetual brooding, worried look in her eyes." It is largely because of Hilda—if only in reaction to what their married life has become in fifteen years—that George's adventures take place.

Elsie Waters, George's first lover. George romanticizes his relationship with Elsie, which occurred years before in Lower Binfield. When he finally sees her in the present, however, he discovers that she has become a shapeless old woman.

Joe Bowling, George's brother, with whom George shared many childhood adventures, particularly fishing, an activity which in his present fantasies has taken on almost epic proportions. Joe is dead now, as is the past that George hoped to find in Lower Binfield.

Porteous, a retired English public-school master and an old friend of George. George respects "old Porteous" but is shocked to realize how out of touch the older man is. The retired schoolteacher recognizes neither the real threat of Adolf Hitler nor the impending doom of England after the war.

— *David Peck*

COMPANY

Author: Samuel Beckett (1906-1989)
First published: 1980
Genre: Novel

Locale: The mind of the creator
Time: Unspecified present, probably the 1970's
Plot: Experimental

A **Voice**, seemingly speaking in a dark room, unidentified, addressing the Hearer about his past life and present situation. The Voice seems to move about in the unlit space, sometimes far off, sometimes very close to the Hearer; the Voice is tonally flat on all occasions. Sometimes there are long periods in which the Voice is silent. When it is heard, it is always very soft.

The **Hearer**, as he is called, who is unidentified by name (although he is given a name, only to have it immediately taken away). He is clearly a male and is lying on his back in the dark. He is a very old man, immobile save for the opening and closing of his eyes. The anecdotes of his childhood indicate that he was born and brought up in Ireland. He does not speak, and it is made clear that he has never been very active intellectually. At first, he is not sure if the Voice is really speaking to him. It seems that he has been in the darkened space for a very long time before the Voice begins to speak. The Voice provides some company for him, and the third-person narrator allows the reader to know how he reacts to the Voice.

The **Narrator**, called the **cankerous other** and sometimes the **Deviser**, who is able to record the words spoken by the Voice and to enter the mind of the Hearer to reveal how the Hearer responds to what is being said about him. The technical device of third-party narration is given character of a kind. The Narrator is described as the Deviser devising the Voice and the Hearer to keep himself company. There is a vague suggestion that he is really telling a tale of his own life. He possesses a talent for telling witty and sometimes heartfelt anecdotes.

The **Commentator**, the voice behind it all, who claims to have invented the narrative voice, the Voice, and the Hearer.

He provides a running critical commentary on the story, breaching the credibility of the tale and continually considering other ways of telling it and of changing the nature of the characters, physically and in terms of character and action. The box-within-a-box of normal third-party narration is opened up in this way to critical comment and to the possibility that there may be another writer, perhaps the real writer, behind this voice.

The **Hearer's father**, who is unnamed and appears in some of the anecdotes told about the Hearer's life as a child. A ruddy, round-faced man, wearing a thick mustache, he is a reader of *Punch*, likes egg sandwiches and long walks, and is off walking in the rugged countryside at the time of his son's birth. After his death, he occasionally reappears to his son, but as the son gets older, these appearances cease.

An old beggar woman, another character out of the Hearer's childhood. Half blind, stone deaf, and not quite sane, she thinks she can fly, and, on one occasion, throws herself out a second-story window. The Hearer was kind to her.

Mrs. Coote, a friend of the Hearer's mother, a small, thin, pessimistic woman. She was having tea one day with his mother while he was busy climbing a huge fir tree in the garden and throwing himself down through the branches.

The Hedgehog, an animal found wandering one day by the young Hearer. He put it in a hat box with a supply of worms but made sure that the animal was free to come and go. Some time later, he found the rotting corpse of the Hedgehog in the box. This anecdote, as well as many of the others that the Voice relates, may have been based on incidents in the author's childhood.

— *Charles Pullen*

THE COMPANY OF WOMEN

Author: Mary Gordon (1949-　　　)
First published: 1981
Genre: Novel

Locale: New York City and western New York State
Time: August, 1963; Winter, 1969-1970; and 1977
Plot: Social realism

Felicitas Maria Taylor, a bright and articulate but sheltered Catholic girl. In the beginning of the novel, she is an early adolescent coming to recognize her special relationship to Father Cyprian among the women who make up his "company"; he has special regard for her intellectual and spiritual potential. Felicitas' talent at Latin and Greek lead her to a classics major at Columbia University. There, at the height of the Vietnam War protests, she meets and eventually moves in with a radical political science professor, Robert Cavendish, the man who may be the father of her child. Shocked by her unplanned pregnancy, Felicitas nevertheless rejects abortion. Instead, she returns to her mother and they, along with the other members of the company, move to the country to rear the child near Father Cyprian, whose guidance has marked all of their lives.

Charlotte Taylor, Felicitas' widowed mother. Her husband died when Felicitas was six months old. Being the oldest of thirteen children has taught her realism, toughness, and self-reliance in a demanding world, but those qualities do not diminish her devotion to her daughter or to the other women of the company. She is powerless to help in her daughter's painful romance, but she is quick to plan the move to the country to

accommodate Felicitas and Linda. At the novel's end, at the age of sixty-seven, she is planning a new insurance business with a neighbor.

Father Cyprian Leonard, a brilliant, acerbic, and conservative Roman Catholic priest. He organized the retreats that evolved into the company of Charlotte, Elizabeth, Mary Rose, Clare, and Muriel, the company that continues to surround him each summer for a retreat. Having struggled up from an impoverished rural background, he uses his sharp mind and tongue to try to direct Felicitas into orthodoxy and away from the sentimentality of popular Catholicism. His conservative politics cause her to clash with him over the Vietnam War. At the end of the novel, however, his love for her daughter, Linda, makes him pray (to his surprise) for the church to reverse its stand on the ordination of women when Linda tells him that she intends to become a priest.

Elizabeth McCullough, a genteel schoolteacher and lover of literature. In the 1930's, her husband abandoned her with a small child, who died young. Quiet and sensitive, she introduces Felicitas to the novels of Jane Austen and is unsure whether her own religion is of the spirit or of literature.

Mary Rose Costello, the simplest member of the "company," formerly a night club dancer. Father Cyprian helped her during her naïve marriage to a dangerously unbalanced man by having the man committed to a mental hospital; that aid left her as Father Cyprian's disciple. Now she works in a film theater owned by her friend Joe Siegel, where she worries about the X-rated films and indulges her uncomplicated and generous nature in befriending first Felicitas and then Linda. After her first husband's death, she marries Joe Siegel.

Clare Leary, a businesswoman who has high regard for excellence. She has always recognized good quality in the leather goods in which she deals. She had hoped to enter a convent but instead took over her father's business after his death. She appreciates the quality of Father Cyprian's character and helps to finance his work and retirement. Her life outside his "company" is marked by detachment and noninvolvement. At the novel's end, she of all the women most misses the city.

Muriel Fisher, Father Cyprian's housekeeper, an unloving and unlovable woman. Little in her meager life has prepared her to be otherwise. She recognizes her limitations and the animosity the others often feel toward her pettiness (which often springs from her jealous guarding of Father Cyprian). When Felicitas was in the hospital, Muriel's gift to her was a packet of religious tracts.

Robert Cavendish, a radical professor of political science at Columbia. He uses the rebellion of the 1960's to indulge his selfishness; he has rejected his privileged background and marriage for sex, drugs, and radical politics. Felicitas fails to notice his clichés and superficiality because she is caught up in the romance of his attentions, his unconventionality, and his good looks. He lives with two of his cast-off lovers and a variety of other drifters, who move through his apartment in a haze of drugs and political rhetoric. His interest in Felicitas is almost entirely sexual.

Linda, Felicitas' child, seven years old at the novel's end. She tells Father Cyprian that she intends to become a priest, having satisfied herself that the fact that Jesus' twelve disciples all were male is irrelevant to the priesthood.

Leo Byrne, a quiet outdoorsman. Felicitas plans to marry him at the novel's end.

— Ann Davison Garbett

THE COMPLETE TALES OF UNCLE REMUS

Author: Joel Chandler Harris (1848-1908)
First published: 1955
Genre: Short fiction

Locale: The American South
Time: The nineteenth century
Plot: Folklore

Uncle Remus, the principal raconteur in the Uncle Remus books. This old black man tells all but eighteen of the antebellum folktales. In "Songs," in which he is introduced, he is nearly eighty years old, telling a story to a seven-year-old white boy called Pinx by his mother, Miss Sally. Miss Sally and her husband, Mars John, own the plantation in central Georgia on which Uncle Remus works, living by himself in a cabin only a few yards from the "big house." The black people on the plantation consider him their leader, and its owners think of him as a "family confidant." A gentle and dignified man, he does not put up with much nonsense, even from Miss Sally and her family, for whom he feels great affection. A master storyteller, his principal themes are the dangers of acting "biggity," too full of oneself, and the state into which the world has fallen because of people acting as if they know no more of morals than do animals. At times dictatorial, jealous, and even petty, he never remains thus for long, being at heart and most often a strong, generous man who is humble in the best sense of the word but never subservient. His greatest challenge comes in his waning years, in the form of Pinx's son, an overly proper and adult little boy whose long-dormant childhood Uncle Remus, at Miss Sally's unspoken request, undertakes to awaken, primarily by telling him folktales.

Brer Rabbit, the clever protagonist of two-thirds of the tales and a supporting character in most of the rest. He is probably the best-known trickster in American literature and also the most loved, despite the fact that during the course of the tales in which he appears he lies to, steals from, injures, mutilates, betrays, murders, and humiliates virtually every other animal and human being in the "settlement," except members of his own family, Brer Terrapin, and Miss Meadows

and her "gals." Sometimes he deceives and harms others because they will not leave him and his family alone; other times, he does so because he is a born troublemaker who simply cannot stand it when things are too peaceful and who simply cannot pass up any opportunity to play one of his "pranks" and laugh himself sick at its results, some of which are ghastly. Readers actually like Brer Rabbit because Uncle Remus always presents him as a cheerful, ingenious little scamp, not without friends, who is mischievous rather than malicious and whose pranks are hilarious, though absolutely not to be imitated.

Brer Fox, a southern gray fox. He is Brer Rabbit's chief nemesis and most frequent dupe. Despite the fact that in at least three tales he is presented as a fairly clever creature, Brer Fox manages to trick Brer Rabbit only twice. Every other time he comes into contact with Brer Rabbit—or Brer Terrapin—he ends up being "outfoxed" and at the very least humiliated; sometimes he also ends up robbed, injured, or dead. A hothead as well as a dupe, he is the only animal who ever breaks the sacrosanct peace of Miss Meadows' house.

Brer Wolf, who, next to Brer Fox, is Brer Rabbit's most frequent adversary; next to Cousin Wildcat, he is the most dangerous. He is the only animal who eats any animals other than frogs, chickens, or cows. Among his victims are some of Brer Rabbit's children. He seems to be the only animal with a hint of conscience or religion. In one story, he dies because his guilt causes him to fail a trial by fire; in another, he agrees to pray before killing Brer Rabbit.

Brer Possum, a genuinely hapless creature who twice is an absolute innocent who gets burned to death for something Brer Rabbit has done. The first time, in fact, it is Brer Possum himself who suggests the trial by fire that he cannot possibly win.

Cousin Wildcat, the only animal who lives outside the community. He is thoroughly unsociable and unresponsive to greetings. He is also the most deadly and most sinister character. In one tale, he slashes Brer Wolf nearly in half with one swipe; in another, he drops silently out of a tree to seize Brer Rabbit and then whispers threats in a chilling, barely audible voice.

Miss Meadows, an enigmatic woman about whom readers know only three things: that she and her "gals" often entertain Brer Rabbit and "de gang" at her house; that Brer Rabbit successfully courts one of her gals; and that Daddy Jack considers her a "noung leddy," but most emphatically not a "werry nice noung leddy." Some critics now consider her a "madam."

— *Viktor R. Kemper*

THE COMPROMISE
(Kompromiss)

Author: Sergei Dovlatov (1941-1990)
First published: 1981
Genre: Novel

Locale: Tallinn, the capital of the Estonian Socialist Republic
Time: November, 1973-October, 1976
Plot: Satire

Sergei Dovlatov (sehr-GAY doh-VLAH-tov), a journalist in his mid-thirties, formerly a camp guard. Educated as a philologist, he is talented, very tall, and an alcoholic. Something of a dissident (he is part Jewish), he works for an Estonian newspaper. He is separated from his wife and behind in his alimony payments. In telling the reader the truth behind several apparently innocuous "compromising" human interest stories he had written for his newspaper, the narrator presents himself as the center of a kind of novel that ends with the reporter's return to his family in Leningrad. It is Dovlatov as author who in fact recalls the events behind the stories, but the narrator appears to be fictional, if for no other reason than that his surname is almost never mentioned or, if it is, usually is rendered incorrectly by one of the characters, as Dolmatov, Dokladov, Zaplatov, or some other variation.

Mikhail (Misha) Borisovich Shablinsky (boh-RIH-soh-vihch shah-BLIH-skee), a reporter for the "industry desk" at the newspaper, an excellent but cynical writer who is ruthlessly successful with women. He finally decides to get married and therefore breaks up with Marina, who in turn takes up with Dovlatov. Shablinsky is an established journalist and a member of the Communist Party; the narrator, though a superior writer, is not a Party member.

Marina (mah-REE-nah), one of the secretarial workers at the newspaper. She is around thirty years old and single. She smokes, is well-informed, and is somewhat bitter about men. She sees Dovlatov as pensive, polite, and honest, in keeping with his pattern of being liked by cast-off women. The narrator

is inclined to view their relationship as one of intellectual intimacy, with shades of animosity and sex. To Marina, this is love, and she weeps over Dovlatov in frustration.

Henry Franzovich Turonok (FRAHN-zoh-vihch tew-ROH-nok), the editor-in-chief of Dovlatov's newspaper and an important member of the Communist Party. He continually accuses Dovlatov of political myopia, for not understanding, for example, that in a list of socialist countries Hungary should follow East Germany, because in Hungary there was an uprising. When he assigns Dovlatov to do a story on the birth of the 400,000th inhabitant of the city of Tallinn, he rejects first a newborn Ethiopian baby and then a Jewish child, finally allowing Dovlatov, by then very drunk after waiting around the hospital all night, to write about a 100 percent Russian infant and the infant's parents.

Mikhail Vladimirovich Zhbankov (vlah-dih-MIH-roh-vihch ZHBAN-kov), an alcoholic photographer for the newspaper. He makes a number of disconcerting anti-Semitic remarks but later turns out to be Jewish himself. He is occasionally assigned to work with Dovlatov on stories. A typical such story is the achievement of an Estonian milkmaid, Linda Peips, in extracting a record-breaking amount of milk out of one cow. Dovlatov and Zhbankov drive to the collective farm and interview the girl, who does not even speak Russian. They stay on for two days, however, drinking excessively and having sexual intercourse with their young Party hostesses.

— *Donald M. Fiene*

COMRADES
(Kamraterna)

Authors: August Strindberg (1849-1912) with Axel Lundegård (1861-1930)
First published: 1888
Genre: Drama

Locale: Paris, France
Time: Late nineteenth century
Plot: Comic realism

Axel, an established artist. Married to Bertha, a feminist, he has agreed to live with her not as a husband but as a comrade, each partner with equal rights and freedom to achieve artistic expression in his or her own way. Finally, disgusted by Ber-

tha's demanding self-assertiveness and conniving, he leaves her for a "womanly woman."

Bertha, an aspiring artist and ardent feminist married to Axel, with whom she lives as a comrade with equal rights.

Less gifted than her husband and envious of his talent, she attempts to assert herself and humiliate him. She finally succeeds in losing him to a more feminine woman.

Dr. Östermark, Axel's friend and the divorced husband of Mrs. Hall.

Mrs. Hall, Dr. Östermark's divorced wife. She seeks the help of Bertha in planning revenge on her former husband.

Abel, Bertha's mannish female friend. An ardent feminist, Abel is in league with Bertha to humiliate Axel.

Willmer, Bertha's effeminate author friend.

Carl Starck, Axel's happily married friend, an army officer.

COMUS

Author: John Milton (1608-1674)
First published: 1637
Genre: Drama

Locale: The kingdom of Neptune
Time: Antiquity
Plot: Allegory

Comus (KOH-muhs), the sorcerer son of Bacchus and Circe who transforms men into animals' shapes with a magic potion and leads this herd of beasts in nightly revels and rites of Hecate. He captures the Lady and tries to lure her into his control by persuasively and eloquently urging her to emulate the generous, unstinting bounty of nature by permitting the enjoyment of her beauty while she is young.

The Lady, a young noblewoman. Separated from her brothers in a wood, she is frightened by the sounds of Comus' revels, by "beckn'ing shadows dire, and airy tongues that syllable men's names on Sands and Shores and desert Wildernesses." She places her trust in Providence and in her own virtue. She counters Comus' plea that she make the most of her beauty while it lasts with her own view of nature as a power that bestows its blessings according to "sober laws and holy dictate of spare Temperance." She finds her strongest defense in "the sublime notion and high mystery that must be utter'd to unfold the sage and serious doctrine of Virginity."

The Elder Brother, her companion, who is, like his sister, convinced of the supernatural power of virtue and wisdom as defenses against all evils. Explaining his inclination to be hopeful, rather than afraid, after the Lady's disappearance, he speaks rhapsodically of the divine nature of chastity, which purifies the mind and brings it to the refined state of the immortal soul. He is ready for action as well as philosophy, and he valiantly attacks Comus and breaks his magic glass.

The Second Brother, a far more fearful young man. He sees his sister's beauty as a great temptation to every evil creature and finds little comfort in his brother's "divine philosophy." Following the advice of the Attendant Spirit, he joins the attack on Comus to free the Lady.

The Attendant Spirit, a being dedicated to the preservation of the true servants of virtue. He disguises himself as Thyrsis, a shepherd, to warn the brothers of Comus' presence in the wood and to lead them to the place where their sister is fastened motionless in the sorcerer's enchanted chair. He calls up the nymph Sabrina to free the Lady, because he is powerless after Comus' magic glass has been broken.

Sabrina, the nymph who lives in the Severn River, the legendary King Locrine's daughter, who drowned herself to escape her stepmother's fury. Called up from her underwater home, she sprinkles the Lady with clear water from her stream and releases her from enchantment.

CONCLUDING

Author: Henry Green (Henry Vincent Yorke, 1905-1973)
First published: 1948
Genre: Novel

Locale: A government training institute in England
Time: Indeterminate future
Plot: Satire

Mr. Rock, the central character, a seventy-six-year-old man who is white-haired, hard of hearing, and bespectacled. As a young man, he made a great scientific discovery, and now he is being considered for election to the Academy of Sciences. He enjoys living in his cottage on the grounds of a state school for girls with his granddaughter, whom he loves. He is gruffly kind to the schoolgirls who are fond of his pets: a cat, a goose, and a pig. Moira often comes to visit him. Rock is concerned when two of the girls are missing and searches for Mary when others cover up her absence.

Miss Mabel Edge, one of the two principals of the Institute, a state school for girls. Short, thin, and white-haired, with white hands, she schemes to get rid of Rock to have his cottage for a still-to-be hired handyman. Miss Edge is a spinster who angers Miss Marchbanks with her high-handed ways. At a break from the annual dance, Miss Edge, stimulated by ciga-

rettes, indirectly asks Rock to marry her. She is furious when, on the way out, he laughs. Feared by all the staff, Miss Edge has only one friend, Miss Baker.

Miss Hermione Baker, the other principal of the school, a short, fat woman. Like Miss Edge and some of the other bureaucrats, she fears that some complaint will be made against them, and perhaps they will be forced to leave the beautiful estate on which the school is situated. Miss Baker and Miss Edge are colleagues and confederates in the scheme against Rock, but Miss Baker is more restrained and less frantic. She talks often about the farm she knew as a child.

Elizabeth Rock, Rock's thirty-five-year-old granddaughter. She is recovering from a nervous breakdown. She is having an affair with Sebastian Birt and wants to marry him and live with him in her grandfather's cottage. She does not accept the fact that because of state regulations, Sebastian will be reassigned if they marry. Elizabeth will not allow Sebastian to criticize her grandfather, and she will not allow Rock to criticize Sebastian. At the dance, she plasters herself against Sebastian, not realizing how shocking this is to the principals, who call it a display of animalism.

Sebastian Birt, a first-year economics tutor at the school. Fat and very short, he loves Elizabeth. Like all the other adult characters, he is worried about keeping his job, keeping his living quarters, and avoiding the censure of the principals. Sebastian is also loved by Miss Winstanley, another teacher, whom he ignores. He worries that Rock will make trouble, for example by reporting Mary's disappearance to a state bureaucrat, Swaythling.

Moira, one of the senior students. She has strong blue eyes, an apricot neck and face, golden legs, and short, curly hair. She likes to talk to Rock. When Miss Marchbanks thinks she has Merode isolated in a bathroom, Moira talks to her through a ventilator shaft. Moira takes Rock to the girls' secret clubhouse, and she kisses him on the lips, but Rock only wants to get away.

Merode, an orphan at the school. She is missing but is then found in the woods, in her pajamas and coat, with a scratched knee. She cries and will not explain how she got there. Moira tells Rock that the junior girls meet George Adams at night. Merode and her aunt say that she was sleepwalking. When she is found by Sebastian and Elizabeth, she has a white face and painted toenails.

Mary, who usually is a steady girl but is missing the same day as Merode is. Rock and some of the girls fear that she has drowned in the lake. The principals have preferred her as an orderly to wait on them. Mary's divorced parents are in Brazil, and she is substantially alone. The other girls finally conclude that Mary ran away because she was overworked as a waitress and pressured to make good grades in her final exams. At the end of the novel, Mary still has not been found.

George Adams, a woodman whose wife died the previous winter. He thinks that people, including Rock, are scheming to get him out of his cottage. To confound his supposed enemy, he writes an anonymous letter to Miss Edge about the Rock household and "furnicating." The night of the dance, he gets into a rage when Rock walks by, but he refuses to come out and face Rock.

Miss Maggie Blain, the cook at the school, a woman with green eyes and an enormous bosom. She is kind enough to give Rock breakfast each day and to give him swill for his pig. She is touchy, however, and cannot be pushed. She is concerned about her girls and angry that no one told her that Mary was missing.

Miss Marchbanks, who is left in charge when the principals go to London for a day to attend a meeting. She is kind to Merode when she is found but is unable to get a coherent story from the girl, who faints when she is pressed. Miss Marchbanks tries to put Alice, Rock's Persian cat, on Merode's lap to soothe her, but it does not work. Miss Marchbanks has brown eyes and spectacles. She tries to suggest fir trees as decorations for the dance, but her idea is squashed by the principals, who want everything to remain the same from year to year.

Mrs. Manley, Merode's aunt, a middle-aged woman with a fruity voice. When she arrives at the school, she insists on seeing Merode, which is against the rules. She also suggests that the principals might be at fault in the girl's disappearance. Mrs. Manley insists that Merode was sleepwalking, and, to save themselves trouble, Miss Edge and Miss Baker seem ready to accept that excuse.

— *Kate M. Begnal*

CONCRETE
(Beton)

Author: Thomas Bernhard (1931-1989)
First published: 1982
Genre: Novel

Locale: An estate in Austria and the Canary Islands
Time: Early 1980's
Plot: Philosophical

Rudolph, the narrator of the story, a scholar and musicologist who is obsessed with writing a monograph on composer Felix Mendelssohn. A neurotic and sickly man who is dependent on medication, he lives alone on his country estate in Peiskam. Rudolph is an extreme perfectionist and is highly vulnerable to the slightest distraction. Although he thinks constantly about his monograph, he never seems to get to writing it. He is interrupted occasionally by visits from his vivacious socialite sister. Her domineering personality causes him great difficulties and destroys his concentration. He travels to Palma, Mallorca, at the beginning of the novel when, after one of her visits, he cannot concentrate on his work. There, he remembers the tragic story of a young woman whom he met two years earlier, on a previous journey to the island. Her fate plunges him into a depressed state, and he contemplates death and the meaninglessness of his life.

Rudolph's sister, an outgoing and vital woman who leads an active social life in the capital city of Vienna. A successful businesswoman who is involved in all the mundane activities of life, she is clearly the opposite of her sickly and isolated brother. She torments the narrator about his lack of success and his inability to write his treatise. Her visit at the beginning of the novel prompts him to travel to Mallorca.

Anna Härdtl, the young German woman whom the narrator meets on one of his trips to Mallorca. She is married and operates a small business with her husband in Munich. The business is not going well, and they decide to take their savings and take a vacation in Palma. One morning, she discovers that her husband has fallen (or thrown himself) from the balcony of their hotel room and is dead. The narrator befriends her, but he learns, after a brief trip away from Palma, that she has committed suicide. She is buried under a simple concrete slab.

— *Thomas F. Barry*

THE CONCUBINE

Author: Elechi Amadi (1934-   )
First published: 1966
Genre: Novel

Locale: The eastern Nigeria village of Omakachi
Time: Mid-nineteenth century
Plot: Folklore

Ihuoma (ee-hew-OH-mah), Emenike's twenty-two-year-old wife, married to him for six years. Before her marriage and move to Omakachi, she lived in the nearby village of Omigwe, where her parents, Ogbuji and Okachi, still reside. She spends the majority of her time caring for her three children and her husband. Emenike dies suddenly of "lock-chest," and Ihuoma is left a lonely widow with her husband's land to tend and few future marriage prospects. Her beauty, strength, and kind nature endear her to everyone, especially a young man named Ekwueme. At first, she fights off his advances, knowing that he has been promised to someone else. The village medicine man, Anyika, tells Ekwueme that Ihuoma had inhabited the spirit world as the Sea King's wife until she preferred to live with mortals; the Sea King becomes jealous when any man loves her, killing the man and leaving her forever alone on Earth. This fate proves to be true for Ihuoma when she finally gives in to Ekwueme after his promised wife, Aruhole, "poisons" him with a love potion. Ihuoma nurses him back to health with her presence, but her son accidentally shoots Ekwueme with an arrow, killing him and again leaving Ihuoma without a husband.

Ekwueme (ay-KWEW-ay-may), the son of Adaku and Wigwe. He is an accomplished trapper and is well-liked in Omakachi. After Emanike's death, he realizes his fondness for Ihuoma and begins to visit her regularly. Although an arranged marriage with an Omigwe woman, Aruhole, looms in his future, Ekwueme pursues Ihuoma and eventually asks her to be his wife. Ihuoma's refusal on the grounds of tradition crush him, but he still hopes to change her mind until his parents convince him otherwise; they remind him of his duty and obligation to uphold family honor. Ekwueme submits, marrying Aruhole, an overly emotional and often irrational mate. He languishes in this unhappy marriage until Aruhole administers a love potion that drives him to passivity and then to the brink of insanity. The connection he feels with Ihuoma and an antidote prepared by Anyika bring him back to his senses. His wife has long since fled, and Ekwueme is free to marry Ihuoma. Before the marriage, Anyika warns him of his lover's past life as the Sea King's wife, but Ekwueme resolves to continue with the ceremony after they perform protective ritual appeasements to the gods. Before completing the rituals, he is fatally wounded by Nwonna, Ihuoma's son.

Emenike (ay-MAY-nee-kay), Ihuoma's first husband, well respected in Omakachi as the "ideal young man" because of his striking appearance and intelligence. During a journey through the forest near the village, he encounters Madume, a man he had recently quarreled with over rights to a piece of land. They wrestle, and Madume's sheer bulk overpowers Emenike, who is thrown against a tree stump and seriously injured. He survives only to die of "lock-chest" days later.

Aruhole (ah-REW-hoh-lay), a young Omigwe woman, the daughter of Wagbara and Wonuma, betrothed to Ekwueme at birth. She has a lovely appearance and a fair amount of intelligence, but she experiences unprovoked fits of crying and hysterics. Although her parents and peers consider Ekwueme a fine match for her, she has unexplainable doubts about him and about marriage in general. Trapped in the prearrangement, she follows through with the marriage, and her emotional outbursts become more frequent. Aruhole begins to feel insecure and fearful because of Ekwueme's increasing disdain for her. She consults a medicine man in another village, who gives her a love potion to slip into Ekwueme's food. When the potion fails to elicit the expected results, and instead endangers her husband's mental state, she flees Omakachi, returning to her parents' home.

Madume (mah-DEW-may), an Omakachi villager who wrestles with Emenike over a land dispute. He proposes to Ihuoma after Emenike's death but receives a cold and bitter "no" from the widow. Soon after his confrontation with Ihuoma, on the land he wrongly considers his own, he is blinded by a spitting cobra and shamed in the eyes of the villagers. In response to loss of face, he hangs himself.

Wakiri (wah-KEE-ree), the Omakachi village gossip who provides comic relief for Ihuoma, Ekwueme, and other villagers. A gentle character accompanies his wit. He helps Ihuoma take care of affairs after Emenike's death; he also provides Ekwueme with advice and support.

Anyika (ah-NYEE-kah), the Omakachi medicine man. He knows the ways of the village gods, and villagers consult him for rituals of healing or appeasement. He recognizes Ihuoma's spiritual origins and predicts the fates of the young men who love her.

Nnadi (ihn-NAH-dee), Emenike's brother and protector of Ihuoma after her husband's death. He defends her honor and aids in maintenance of her home and lands.

— *Elizabeth Vander Meer*

A CONFEDERACY OF DUNCES

Author: John Kennedy Toole (1937-1969)
First published: 1980
Genre: Novel

Locale: New Orleans, Louisiana
Time: Early 1960's
Plot: Farce

Ignatius J. Reilly (ihg-NAY-shuhs), a blowsy, flatulent, thirty-year-old, obese, self-styled "philosopher." He always wears a green hunting cap. He is hobbled by phobias and has a dyspeptic pyloric valve that closes at any provocation. He is obsessed with his bodily functions, though he is asexual, and is disdainful of the "corrupt twentieth century." Reilly languishes at home, criticizing his widowed mother and her friends, refusing to find work, watching television (especially the shows he considers "offenses against taste and decency"), and, on his Big Red tablets, writing a journal of his "travels" and his medieval world vision. Eventually he is forced to work, first in the office at Levy Pants, which he almost ruins by discarding the company files and organizing the black workers in what he calls a "Crusade for Moorish Dignity." He then finds a job with Paradise Vendors selling "weenies" from a pushcart, all the while eating more hotdogs than he sells. He becomes the catalyst for all the chaotic action in the novel and is the intersection point for the characters in the several subplots. His picaresque tour of New Orleans reveals Reilly's complete self-indulgence, his philosophical inconsistencies as he sates himself on the very things he abhors in food and entertainment, and his negative, unfeeling attitude toward all around him. Only at the end of the novel, when his mother finally recognizes that Reilly is coldhearted, selfish, and beyond emotional redemption and therefore attempts to commit him to a mental ward, does Reilly show a hint of warmth, as Myrna Minkoff spirits him away.

Irene Reilly, the widowed mother of the protagonist. She is lonely and unwilling to see her son as a failure, because he has a master's degree. She suffers from a drinking problem, low self-esteem, a bad elbow, and Reilly's incessant demands and verbal abuse. As her circle of friends enlarges and as she acquires a suitor in Claude Robichaux, however, she becomes increasingly disenchanted with her son and finally moves to free herself from his lethargy and criticism.

Myrna Minkoff, a New York "radical," Reilly's nemesis and erstwhile girlfriend. Through her preaching of a politics of sexual liberation and Reilly's own need to prove himself to Minkoff by taking action, Minkoff becomes Reilly's foil and fantasy, but in the end his savior.

Claude Robichaux, Mrs. Reilly's elderly suitor. He believes that nearly everyone and everything is "communiss."

Angelo Mancuso, a bungling policeman and Reilly's nemesis. An aspiring detective relegated to "undercover" work in restrooms and in disguises on the street, Mancuso befriends Mrs. Reilly and later becomes a hero by chancing to uncover a pornographic distribution operation at the Night of Joy bar.

Lana Lee, the owner of the Night of Joy bar. Of chiseled body and stony heart, Lee distributes pornographic cards to schoolchildren when she is not overtaxing her employees, Burma Jones and Darlene, at her lowlife bar.

Burma Jones, the self-styled "colored dude" and low-paid black floor sweeper at the Night of Joy bar. Fearful of Lee's threats to turn him in to the police for vagrancy, he effects his own emancipation and earns a reward by leading Mancuso to Lee's hidden pornography.

Darlene, a B-girl at the Night of Joy bar. Her intellectual fare is *Life* magazine, and her life's ambition is to stage a striptease act with her pet cockatoo.

Gus Levy, the owner of Levy Pants. Disdainful of running a company he inherited from an unloving father, Levy thinks little of management (thus the opening for Reilly) and much of baseball.

Mrs. Levy, Levy's wife. She nags Levy to keep Miss Trixie employed and the Levy daughters in high style.

Mr. Gonzales, the manager of Levy Pants. He struggles to keep alive the business that Levy cannot abide, and he becomes the victim of Reilly's dreams to "save" Levy Pants by prettying up the office while discarding office files.

Miss Trixie, a senile bookkeeper at Levy Pants. She wants only to retire and receive the Easter ham long due her from Levy, but she is forced to stay on because of Mrs. Levy's misguided notion that work is good for her.

Mr. Clyde, the owner of Paradise Vendors. In his desperation to find vendors for hotdogs and in his pity for Reilly, he outfits Reilly and sends him out into the Dantesque world of the French Quarter.

— *Randall M. Miller*

A CONFEDERATE GENERAL FROM BIG SUR

Author: Richard Brautigan (1935-1984)
First published: 1964
Genre: Novel

Locale: San Francisco and Big Sur, California
Time: The 1960's
Plot: Fantasy

Lee Mellon, an unemployed, twenty-three-year-old iconoclast who claims to be a descendant of a Confederate general. Assertive, apolitical, unreflective, and hedonistic, Lee is an existential rebel, a "rebel without a cause," who pursues independence and pleasure with the energetic determination of a military campaign. Amoral and self-centered, Lee manages to survive by panhandling, stealing, extorting, and generally taking advantage of the people he meets. Because none of these techniques is very successful, Lee often must rely on his considerable ability to endure material deprivations. After spending a depressing year in an abandoned house in Oakland, a period in which his only triumph is tapping into the local utility's gas line, Lee travels to Big Sur, where he camps out in some ill-built shacks on borrowed land. There he lives from day to day, battling the frogs that keep him awake at night, courting Elizabeth, and contending with Johnston Wade's neurotic antics.

Jesse, the novel's narrator and the chronicler of Lee Mellon's exploits. After a disappointing love affair with a girl named Cynthia, Jesse leaves San Francisco and joins Lee at Big Sur. A sensitive and passive opposite to Lee, Jesse describes himself as an unemployed minister. In the absence of a spiritual calling or a firm basis for belief, he retreats into an absurdist minimalism—represented by his careful enumeration of the punctuation marks in Ecclesiastes—and a fatalistic acceptance of the world as he finds it. Jesse meets Elaine in a Monterey saloon, and she returns with him to Big Sur. Their affair eases Jesse's lingering sorrow over Cynthia, but it does nothing to fill his spiritual emptiness. His growing passivity and alienation threaten to develop into emotional paralysis, as his sexual impotence suggests.

Elizabeth, a part-time prostitute and Lee's sometime companion at Big Sur. She is an idealized combination of whore and mother who works as a highly skilled and highly paid Los

Angeles prostitute for three months out of the year, then returns to her modest house at Big Sur, where she rears her children as vegetarians and refuses to kill even the rattlesnakes.

Elaine, an intelligent and attractive young woman who meets Jesse in a Monterey saloon and becomes his lover. A product of a middle-class background, Elaine is an example of bourgeois alienation. Attracted to the unconventionality of Jesse and Lee, Elaine buys them supplies and drives them back to their Big Sur encampment. There she enjoys the rebellious pleasures of marijuana and sex.

Johnston Wade, a rich, unstable insurance executive whom Lee dubs "Roy Earle" after the Humphrey Bogart character in the film *High Sierra*. Johnston arrives at the Big Sur encampment driving a new Bentley, in hysterical flight from his upper-middle-class family. He carries a briefcase containing $100,000. An exaggerated vision of the destructive power of money, Johnston spends a night chained to a log by Lee. By the next day, he has regained his composure, if not his sanity, and he leaves to return to his business and family.

— *Carl Brucker*

CONFEDERATES

Author: Thomas Keneally (1935-   )
First published: 1979
Genre: Novel

Locale: Virginia, Maryland, and North and South Carolina
Time: 1862
Plot: Historical

Usaph Bumpass, a Confederate soldier serving in the regiment of the Shenandoah Volunteers. Malnourished, bedraggled Usaph is a veteran of the war at the age of twenty-three. A poorly educated farmer, he is secretly envious of his two educated friends, Danny Blalock, a schoolmaster, and Gus Ramseur, a music teacher. Usaph constantly worries about the danger of his lovely wife feeling lonely on their farm and being unfaithful to him. When he receives a letter from her, delivered by Decatur Cate, he is sure that Ephie and Cate are lovers.

Ephephtha (Ephie) Bumpass, the beautiful wife of Usaph, reared in the swamps of the Carolinas. She was raped when young, then became accustomed to but not charmed by men's demands on her. When Usaph takes her from the swamps to Virginia, she thinks that she has been saved, but then Usaph goes to war, and she is convinced that she is being punished for loving him too much. The worldly Decatur Cate represents refinement to Ephie. She is torn between running off to California with him and remaining faithful to Usaph.

Decatur Cate, a Union sympathizer conscripted into Bumpass' regiment. Gangling, hollow-cheeked, and twenty-five years old, Cate is an introspective former portrait painter forced to join the army when Usaph's Aunt Sarrie has him arrested. While painting Ephie's portrait, Cate convinces her to become his lover and go to California. Aunt Sarrie intervenes, and Cate is sent to Usaph's regiment, where he delivers a letter from Ephie. Usaph immediately suspects the worst, and Cate becomes his nemesis.

Thomas "Stonewall" Jackson, a Confederate general and actual historical figure. He is called "Stonewall" for not letting the Union get around his troops. A tall, lean, and handsome West Point graduate, Jackson acts as if time is limited. All the other characters' fates depend on his military maneuvers.

Lafcadio Wheat, the commanding colonel of the Shenandoah Volunteers. Tall, black-whiskered, and thirty-three years old, Wheat is a former lawyer fond of inspiring his men with jokes and personal stories. Usaph becomes his runner and is with him when he dies.

Gus Ramseur, a Confederate soldier and Bumpass' best friend. A gentleman and a music scholar, golden-bearded Gus is the only man Usaph considers worth saving. Ramseur wants to write an overture of military music after the war.

Horace Searcy, an English war correspondent and Union spy. The daring Searcy is an abolitionist who detests the South. He has a secret commission from U.S. Secretary of War Edwin Stanton to gather intelligence. Because of his reputation as a world-renowned war journalist, Searcy has letters of introduction and safe passage from both the Union and the Confederacy. Searcy's identity is discovered after he relays some vital information to the North about the South's military strategy. He is given passage out of the country on a ship. Before leaving, he tries to persuade Dora Whipple to marry him.

Dora Whipple, a Confederate widow who becomes Searcy's lover and accomplice. Mrs. Whipple already was a Union spy working in a military hospital in Richmond when she met Searcy. After becoming the matron at the military hospital in Orange, she sneaks to Searcy's room at night. An accomplice of hers is caught, and her name appears on a list of spies. She is tried and refuses to deny being a spy. Accepting her fate and wishing to join her late husband in death, she refuses Searcy's offer to become his wife and save herself by leaving with him for England.

Aunt Sarrie Muswell, Usaph's aunt who takes care of Ephie during the war. Aunt Sarrie hires Cate to paint Ephie's portrait, then realizes that Ephie is impressed by Cate's worldliness. She arranges for Cate to be conscripted into the military in spite of his limp. She then arranges for Ephie to visit an herbalist when Ephie becomes pregnant.

Danny Blalock, a schoolmaster and fellow Confederate soldier in Bumpass' regiment. Danny and Ash Judd are fond of leaving the regiment to find women. Danny dies at Gettysburg, as a major.

Ash Judd, a farmer and fellow Confederate of Bumpass. Twenty years old, he looks up to Danny Blalock. Ash is superstitious and believes that a witch has put a spell on him that will protect him throughout the war. He drowns in his own blood.

— *Sandra Willbanks*

THE CONFESSION OF A FOOL
(Die Beichte eines Toren *and* Le Plaidoyer d'un fou)

Author: August Strindberg (1849-1912)
First published: 1893 and 1895
Genre: Novel

Locale: Stockholm, Sweden
Time: The 1870's and 1880's
Plot: Psychological realism

Axel, the narrator of the novel and its protagonist. At the book's outset, he is in his late twenties, and his narrative, an autobiographical account of his first marriage, follows him through his early forties. Axel is a librarian at the Royal Stockholm Library, as well as an aspiring, and eventually successful, playwright. A small but intense man, he is interested primarily in scientific and aesthetic pursuits. He also may suffer from acute paranoia, and thus his chronicle forces the reader to question whether the novel is an accurate presentation of the facts or the lunatic ravings of a man who is, or is going, insane. Axel's problems begin when he is introduced to Marie, a baroness with whom he immediately becomes obsessed. At first he idealizes her, imagining her to be a chaste, Madonna-like figure, and he shuns the thought of any romantic inclinations toward her. As it becomes clear that the baroness is unhappy in her marriage to Baron Gustav—even so far as to condone the baron's illicit affair with her young cousin, Matilda—Axel finds himself sexually attracted to her. He becomes so infatuated with her that the thought of living without her drives him to attempt suicide. Fortunately, or perhaps unfortunately, the attempt fails, the baroness's marriage collapses, and she and Axel become lovers and marry. Axel idealizes the beginning of their marriage just as he initially idealized the baroness herself. His romantic bliss is soon shattered, however, when he begins to suspect that Marie had ulterior motives for marrying him. She has ambitions of becoming an actress, and because Axel has had some success as a playwright, he wonders if she married him simply to further her career. Furthermore, he imagines that she may have married him for what little money he has, because the baron, despite his noble title, is in fact broke. These suspicions lead Axel to believe that Marie does not love him and that, therefore, she must be unfaithful. He becomes jealous of anyone or anything to which she devotes her time, even her dog. Axel is able, for very brief intervals, to cast aside his suspicions and to picture Marie as a loving and devoted wife. His doubts finally become so intense that he suspects Marie, who is conscious of his passionate love for her as well as his pathological jealousy, of trying to drive him mad with her constant flirtations. By the novel's conclusion, Axel's paranoia reaches such a crescendo that his marriage dissolves, and he resolves upon completion of his memoir to commit suicide.

Marie, a baroness who leaves her husband to marry Axel. She is a petite, beautiful woman in her early thirties. If Axel's early narrative is to be trusted, she has an angelic quality. She is unhappy with her marriage to Baron Gustav because he is both poor and unfaithful but especially because she wishes to pursue her consuming passion to be an actress. Her marriage to Axel allows her to pursue this career, which falters either because she cannot act or because Axel, afraid of losing her and resentful of her success, does not offer sufficient help. If Axel's narrative is to be trusted, and this is doubtful, she is an adulteress, fickle to the extreme, a spendthrift, an unfit mother, and a bisexual. Moreover, he claims that she is intent on driving him insane with her flirtations. It appears that she really does care very little about motherhood and that she may have had one affair (among the hundreds of which she is accused), but given Axel's state of mind, it is impossible to be certain.

Gustav, a baron, Marie's first husband. At thirty years of age, he is disappointed with his life and seems intent on dissipating in drinking, gambling, and womanizing. A baron in title only, he has lost his fortune. He maintains his marriage to Marie merely for the sake of appearances; he is having an affair with Matilda, Marie's eighteen-year-old cousin. Marie eventually divorces him and marries Axel.

Matilda, Marie's pretty but empty-headed young cousin. When Axel is first invited to the home of the baron and baroness, he supposes that Matilda is Marie's companion. He eventually learns, however, that Matilda is invited there to continue her affair with the baron, who has lost interest in his wife.

— *Matthew K. Davis*

CONFESSIONS OF A MASK
(Kamen no kokuhaku)

Author: Yukio Mishima (Kimitake Hiraoka, 1925-1970)
First published: 1949
Genre: Novel

Locale: Tokyo and its environs
Time: The 1920's to the late 1940's
Plot: Psychological realism

Kochan, a student. Born in 1925, Kochan is a sickly child who is subject to periodic bouts of illness. As a result, he is excluded from close personal relationships with boys of his age and grows up with little understanding of what normal boys are like. He is latently homosexual and aware of his attraction for other males at a very early age. He makes attempts, nevertheless, to be like those around him, even going as far as convincing himself that he is in love with Sonoko. It is only when her brother asks if he intends to marry her and after he fails to have any physical response to a prostitute that he finally accepts that he can never be like other men, even though he must put on a public act that he is the same as everyone else.

Omi, a student. A young man in his early teens, he is several years older than the students in his class and as a result is more physically developed than they are. The combination of his physical attractiveness and the fact that he is considered wicked and therefore a loner attracts Kochan, who falls in love with Omi. Omi is arrogantly superior to the students around him but not unkind to Kochan, although he is aware of the passion Kochan feels for him. Omi is expelled from school during the summer break, and Kochan never sees him again.

Sonoko, a student. Younger than Kochan, she is the sister of one of his few friends, Kusano. She is a proper Japanese girl, unschooled in love and secluded from life, who slowly develops a deep feeling for Kochan. He quickly convinces himself that he feels the same way about her. After she and her family leave Tokyo to avoid the air raids, he goes to visit, and in his attempt to appear normal, he kisses her. It is obviously the first time she has been kissed. When Kochan politely rejects the idea of marrying her, she marries another man. She and Kochan meet after her marriage, and they spend a year secretly meeting each other, though they do nothing more than talk. She is aware of the danger in their meeting, and her thoughts remain fixed on her husband.

— *C. D. Akerley*

CONFESSIONS OF FELIX KRULL, CONFIDENCE MAN: The Early Years
(Bekenntnisse des Hochstaplers Felix Krull: Der Memoiren erster Teil)

Author: Thomas Mann (1875-1955)
First published: 1954
Genre: Novel

Locale: Germany, Paris, and Lisbon
Time: Early twentieth century
Plot: Picaresque

Felix Krull (FAY-lihks krewl), alias **Armand**, a hotel employee; alias the **Marquis de Venosta**. Impressed at a theatrical performance by the ease with which the actors create various impressions, Felix himself becomes an actor. From that time on he plays a variety of roles in life. As Armand, the waiter in a hotel, he leads a double life on the proceeds from the sale of jewels he steals from a guest, Mme Houpflé; impersonating the Marquis de Venosta, he sets out on a trip around the world.

Müller Rose (MEW-lur ROH-suh), an actor whose performance inspires Felix Krull himself to become an actor.

Madame Houpflé (HEWPF-lay), a guest at the hotel where Felix Krull, alias Armand, is employed. She becomes Armand's mistress, and, to complete her humiliation, she begs him to rob her of all her valuables.

The Marquis de Venosta (vay-NOH-stah), a nobleman. In despair because his parents plan to send him around the world, thus separating him from his mistress Zaza, he engages Armand (Felix Krull) to impersonate him and make the journey in his stead.

Dom Antonio José Kuckuck (ahn-TOH-nyoh ho-SEH KEW-kewk), a Portuguese museum director whom Felix Krull, alias the Marquis de Venosta, visits in Lisbon.

Dona Maria Pia Kuckuck (mah-REE-ah PEE-ah), the wife of Dom Antonio José Kuckuck. She falls in love with Felix Krull, alias the Marquis de Venosta, while he is attempting to seduce her daughter.

Susanna "Zouzou" Kuckuck, their daughter.

Engelbert Krull (ahng-GEHL-burt) and

Frau Krull, Felix Krull's parents.

Olympia Krull, Felix Krull's sister.

Herr Schimmelpreester (shih-MAL-pray-stur), Felix Krull's godfather.

Lord Strathbogie, a guest at the hotel where Felix Krull, alias Armand, works.

Zaza (sah-sah), the Marquis de Venosta's mistress.

THE CONFESSIONS OF NAT TURNER

Author: William Styron (1925-   )
First published: 1967
Genre: Novel

Locale: Southeastern Virginia
Time: Early 1800's to November, 1831
Plot: Psychological realism

Nat Turner, the narrator and protagonist, a black slave and preacher who is slightly more than thirty years old at the time of narration. Born a slave to the somewhat socially enlightened Turner family, the precocious Nat is educated by the Turners after they discover his attempt to read a book that he stole from the family's library. This and other acts of benevolence during his youth raise Nat's expectations without altering his prospects, thus creating a bind from which Nat never escapes. After his dreams of the freedom promised him by the Turners fail to materialize, Nat endures a series of degrading hardships at the hands of the various white people to whom he is sold. These experiences bond Nat with his own race, although he consistently expresses contempt for their subservient actions and mannerisms. The educated slave becomes a pariah, a lonely man belonging neither to the blacks nor to the whites. Bolstered by the early assurances of his mother and by a later mystic vision that he has been preordained to accomplish great things, Nat becomes a preacher, a comforter of those—black and white—who suffer the oppression of the closed Southern society. His observations of and personal experiences with the slave system lead him to understand the depth of the blacks' hatred of the whites. Nat also intuits that despite white people's power over black people, fear of the slaves pervades even the strongest bastions of the white community. This understanding of the dynamics of the society in which he lives, coupled with his mystic vision of his role in life, leads Nat to form an elaborate plan of "annihilation and escape" designed to free blacks from white domination. This plot results in a slave rebellion that ends in the deaths of fifty-five whites and approximately two hundred blacks. The insurrection fails because Nat's "soldiers" are more intent on avenging themselves against the whites than on escaping their subservience. Nat evades the Virginia authorities for nearly two months but eventually is captured, tried, and hanged for his crimes. Nat's confession reveals a highly complex character who attempts to live in both the black and white worlds and who undergoes a radical transformation from educated preacher to slave champion to murderer as a result of the irresolvable tension between those worlds.

T. R. Gray, the court-appointed lawyer who records Nat's confession. In attempting to understand Nat's motives, Gray asks the central question of the novel: How could the slave have been so cruel to those who were as kind to him as the system allowed? The attorney treats Nat in a condescending manner, especially when explaining the court system and expressing his opinion that Nat's fellow insurrectionists have made him the scapegoat for their own crimes. Nevertheless, Gray does demonstrate concern for Nat, bringing him a Bible, having his chains loosened, and requesting warm clothing for the prisoner. In admitting to Nat that his trial is a sham, Gray interprets society's final insult for Nat, that is, that other rebel slaves have been tried and released solely to protect rights of property. Gray thus becomes the chief spokesman for the society that confounds Nat Turner.

Mr. Trezevant, the commonwealth's attorney who prosecutes Nat.

Judge Jeremiah Cobb, the man who passes the death sentence on Nat yet demonstrates an understanding of the cruelty of slavery. Nat had come to respect the judge during their conversation before Nat's rebellion.

Lou Ann, Nat's mother, a slave in the Turner household who was reared in the Turner home and who in turn rears her son there. In her position as family cook, she enjoys a favored status accorded by both whites and blacks. She is convinced that her son is intended for greatness and encourages him in this notion. She dies when Nat is fifteen years old.

McBride, Turner's cruel overseer, who rapes Lou Ann while young Nat watches.

Samuel Turner, the slave owner who rears Nat. A truly benevolent man, Turner plans to have Nat educated and freed once he is assured that the precocious slave could make his own way in the world. Turner is deeply troubled by the effects of slavery, such as the separation of families and the cruelty inflicted on adults and children alike. Financial troubles, however, prohibit Turner from carrying out his grand scheme of liberation for Nat. He entrusts his plans for Nat to others who fail to adhere to them. In this respect, he proves to be a very poor judge of character.

Nell Turner, Samuel's wife. Mrs. Turner is impressed with Nat's intellect and teaches him to read, treating him almost as a pet in her home.

Louisa Turner, the daughter of Samuel and Nell. Louisa befriends Nat and assists with his education.

The Reverend Eppes, a Baptist preacher, Nat's second owner, who promises Samuel Turner that he will arrange for Nat's continued education and eventual emancipation. In reality, Eppes uses Nat as his sexual pawn and contributes much to Nat's growing hatred of whites.

Tom Moore, Nat's third master, who buys the young slave from Eppes.

Sara Moore, the wife of Tom and, after his death, the wife of Joseph Travis. Sara is kind to Nat, and although he is fond of her, she is the first victim of the rebellion.

Joseph Travis, Nat's last owner. The Travis family is destroyed in Nat's insurrection.

Willis, a slave of the Turner family and an early friend of Nat. The two boys experience together many of adolescence's rites of passage. Turner's selling of Willis and Nat's unwitting complicity in the business deal fuel Nat's steadily increasing disillusionment with white people.

Hark, born **Hercules**, a later friend of Nat who participates in the rebellion. Hark's harsh treatment by the Travis family and their overseer poignantly establishes the cruelty of slavery.

Nelson,

Henry, and

Sam, slaves who with Hark form the inner circle of Nat's strike force in planning and executing the rebellion.

Isan, a rebellious slave whose anger and rage, along with the effects these emotions have on Tom Moore, plant the idea of an uprising in Nat's mind.

Ethelred T. Brantley, a fifty-year-old white former plantation overseer in trouble with the law. Brantley hears Nat preach and, because he has been rejected by the white Christian community, turns to the black preacher for salvation. Nat baptizes himself and Brantley in front of his own followers and a crowd of forty to fifty whites who pelt the two with rocks. This episode further solidifies plans for rebellion against white oppression.

Margaret Whitehead, a young white girl who befriends Nat. Margaret, with her fine education and profound unawareness of the true plight of Nat and his people, epitomizes the gap between blacks and whites. She is the one person who could have kept Nat from fulfilling his "mission." He kills her when the rebellion breaks out as a means of maintaining his leadership of the rebel slaves. Margaret regards Nat as asexual, but his feelings for her are clearly human and physical. She, more than any other character, represents promised but unfulfilled dreams.

— *Lagretta T. Lenker*

CONFESSIONS OF ZENO
(La coscienza di Zeno)

Author: Italo Svevo (Ettore Schmitz, 1861-1928)
First published: 1923
Genre: Novel

Locale: Trieste, Graz, and Lucinico, Austria
Time: The 1880's-1916
Plot: Psychological realism

Zeno Cosini (ZEH-noh koh-SEE-nee), an Italian businessman in Trieste (then part of Austria). The book is supposed to be a narrative that Zeno prepared for Dr. S., his psychoanalyst. Zeno first discusses his attempts to stop smoking, in which he

displays his usual pattern of taking a "health-giving bath of good resolutions" that are never carried out. The same irresolution appears in the two most important aspects of Zeno's life: sex and business. He wins his plain but affectionate wife after proposing in vain to two of her sisters (a third has pronounced him quite mad). Although he comes to love his wife, all of his baths of good intentions cannot keep him from taking a mistress, Carla, a music student. He is generally content to leave his family business in the hands of the manager, Olivi. Even when he joins his brother-in-law, Guido Speier, in a separate venture, he mostly watches passively, until Guido dies, leaving his affairs in a disastrous state; then Zeno steps in and by some lucky speculations recovers part of the losses. When war between Italy and Austria separates him from his family and Olivi, he again asserts himself and proves adept at profiting from wartime shortages. The references to psychoanalysis in the novel invite a Freudian interpretation of Zeno, which is supported by Zeno's extreme hypochondria and his troubled memories of his father. Zeno himself likes to analyze life in terms of health and disease, especially Basedow's disease. The name Zeno recalls two Greek philosophers, one a paradoxical skeptic and the other a stoic.

Giovanni Malfenti (jee-oh-VAHN-nee mahl-FEHN-tee), a successful businessman with four daughters. Zeno takes him as a role model and resolves to marry one of his daughters, whom he has never seen.

Guido Speier (GWEE-doh speh-EE-ehr), a young man set up in business by his father in Trieste. Initially, he makes a good impression, especially in contrast with Zeno; he is handsome and plausible and plays the violin very well, whereas Zeno plays it very badly. He wins Ada where Zeno failed. It is after they go into business together that he reveals his depth of incompetence in undertakings far beyond any Zeno would consider; it is Zeno who tries to protect Guido's father's interests and who manages to save some of Guido's estate for Ada. It is Guido's final folly to feign suicide twice to get money from Ada; the second time, he miscalculates and kills himself.

Ada Malfenti Speier, the eldest and most beautiful daughter, who wisely rejects Zeno and unwisely accepts Guido Speier. She loses her beauty through Basedow's (Graves') disease, a form of goiter. After Guido's death, she goes to live with his relatives in Argentina.

Augusta Malfenti Cosini, Zeno's wife. Although not beautiful, she is patient and understanding.

Alberta Malfenti, an intellectual whom Zeno courts briefly.

Anna Malfenti, the youngest sister, who believes Zeno is completely mad.

Olivi (oh-LEE-vee), the manager who conducts the Cosini business with the prudence and industry that Zeno lacks but without Zeno's "inspirations."

Carla, a music student. Zeno is first her patron and somewhat incompetent adviser, then later her lover. Carla deserts him to marry her teacher.

— *John C. Sherwood*

THE CONFIDENCE MAN: His Masquerade

Author: Herman Melville (1819-1891)
First published: 1857
Genre: Novel

Locale: The Mississippi River
Time: The nineteenth century, before the Civil War
Plot: Social satire

The Confidence Man, masquerading, in turn, as a deaf-mute beggar; as a crippled beggar named Black Guinea; as John Ringman; as a solicitor of funds for the Seminole Widow and Orphan Society; as Mr. Truman, president of the Black Rapids Coal Company; as an herb doctor; as a representative of the Philosophical Intelligence Office; and as Francis Goodman, world traveler. By means of his glib tongue and show of sympathetic camaraderie, he succeeds in duping the passengers on board the *Fidele* even as a placard offering a reward for the impostor is posted on the steamship's deck.

Mr. Roberts, a kindly, gullible merchant swindled by the confidence man.

An Episcopal Clergyman, an officious demander of references who is blandly gulled out of alms for "Black Guinea" as well as a contribution to the Seminole Widow and Orphan Society.

Pitch, a misanthropic frontiersman inspired by the confidence man's glib tongue to hire a boy through the impostor's "employment agency."

Charles Noble, a garrulous passenger who succeeds in evading the confidence man's appeals for a loan.

Mark Winsome, a mystic philosopher who accuses Charles Noble of being the confidence man.

Egbert, a disciple of Mark Winsome. He disgusts the confidence man by relating a long story concerning the folly of making loans between friends.

THE CONFIDENTIAL CLERK

Author: T. S. Eliot (1888-1965)
First published: 1954
Genre: Drama

Locale: London, England
Time: Mid-twentieth century
Plot: Comedy of manners

Sir Claude Mulhammer, a successful middle-aged financier who lives in London with his wife, Lady Elizabeth, and illegitimate daughter Lucasta. He has just employed his illegitimate son Colby Simpkins as his new confidential clerk. His wife is not aware of the existence of this son; Sir Claude hopes to have her accept him as his clerk (and possibly grow fond of him) before divulging Colby's real identity to her. Sir Claude trusts his former confidential clerk, Eggerson, explicitly and asks his help to sort out the delicate situation at home. Through his conversations with Eggerson and Colby, readers learn that Sir Claude had aspired in his youth to be a potter and was therefore a disappointed artist, though successful in the profession he took up to please his father. He is a sentimentalist and dreams of bringing Colby into the house in his true status as son. In a series of farcical situations and revelations, Sir Claude is both pleasantly surprised and then distressed. His wife welcomes Colby as the new clerk, and it is revealed that Colby is not his son after all. Sir Claude learns through these experiences and is both sad and happy at the end, sad to lose the son he longed for but happy to form a new family unit with Lacasta and Kaghan.

Eggerson, Sir Claude's former confidential clerk, the soul of discretion and trustworthiness. Although he has retired from his position at the Mulhammers', he remains their friend and consultant through family crises. Sir Claude depends on him to undertake the most delicate of operations to negotiate a peaceful existence with Lady Elizabeth. Eggerson is a quiet and intelligent man who is entrusted with the responsibility of conducting the investigation that will reveal the true identities of Colby and Kaghan. He has found an inner balance between reality and spirituality. Apart from helping out the Mulhammer household when called on to do so, he spends his days peacefully tending his garden in a suburb of London.

Colby Simpkins, Sir Claude's new confidential clerk and apparently his illegitimate son. Sir Claude has supported his upbringing at the home of his aunt, Mrs. Guzzard. He considers himself a failed musician and has turned unwillingly to a clerk's profession instead of following his true desires to fulfillment. He is uneasy with the idea of joining the Mulhammer family as their son and apprehensive of Lady Elizabeth's reactions to him. He is a deeply spiritual young man who is searching for a way to integrate his public and private lives; he cannot accept that this can be achieved in the affluence of his new position. Colby is relieved when it is revealed that his aunt, Mrs. Guzzard, is actually his mother and that he is the son of another disappointed musician. The revelation of his identity allows Colby to resolve to follow his dreams for

whatever they are worth. Eggerson shrewdly conjectures that his ultimate calling lies with the church.

Lucasta Angel, Sir Claude's illegitimate daughter, who often pretends to be a little crazy. As is discovered in her conversation with Colby, she too is searching for some inner truth and is afraid to reveal her innermost thoughts and desires to the world. Engaged to the businessman B. Kaghan, she finds herself troubled by her attraction to Colby but realizes that he does not really need a close human relationship, as she desires. Kaghan understands her well, and she is relieved formally to announce her impending marriage to him. When the truth about the identities of Colby and Kaghan are revealed, she and Kaghan sincerely promise to build a meaningful family unit with the Mulhammers.

B. Kaghan, a businessman who is Lucasta's fiancé. He is revealed to be Lady Elizabeth's long-lost illegitimate son, whom she gave up in his youth. He is embarrassed and confused by his new identity but appears to be sincere and affectionate.

Lady Elizabeth Mulhammer, Sir Claude's wife, an idiosyncratic lady with a good and sympathetic heart. She spends her time exploring concepts of mind control and spiritual healing. She shows a surprising depth of intelligence in a conversation with her husband, during which she deduces that they have not tried to understand each other and others. She vows that they should do so in the future.

Sarah Guzzard, who reared Colby with Sir Claude's financial help. She is revealed to be Colby's mother. A dignified and intelligent woman, she is most important for solving the play's mysteries by revealing the true identities of Colby and Kaghan.

— *Brinda Bose*

THE CONFORMIST
(Il conformista)

Author: Alberto Moravia (1907-1990)
First published: 1951
Genre: Novel

Locale: Rome, Italy, and Paris, France
Time: 1920-1945
Plot: Social realism

Marcello Clerici (mahr-CHEHL-loh klehr-EE-chee), the protagonist, a man dominated by psychological tendencies that are reflected in the title of the novel. Since childhood, Marcello has desired to be recognized as being normal. As a young boy, he had several haunting experiences with guilt (the presumed consequence of social abnormality); these follow him into adulthood. One involved pleasure in killing small animals, then trying to convince himself, through others, that his actions were not abnormal. A second event was his traumatic violent experience with a homosexual stranger. When Marcello receives a special assignment to aid in the assassination of his former professor, a Paris-exiled critic of the Fascist regime, he initially assumes that he can maintain a separation between his "normal" life and the brutal world of Fascist politics. This attempt at psychological compartmentalization fails when Marcello decides to combine his honeymoon with the espionage assignment to Paris. Marcello's thwarted quest to achieve normalcy carries through after his return to middle-class existence in Italy during the war. Although he seems to

have overcome the trauma of Lina's death, his discovery that Lino did not die from the gun wounds Marcello inflicted on him as a youth rekindles the nightmare of the futility of his actions: He had carried feelings of guilt and suffered psychologically for years for something that did not happen.

Lino (LEEN-oh), a homosexual chauffeur who attempted to lure the young Marcello by promising to give him a real revolver, something Marcello sought as a means toward establishing his credibility among friends and enemies alike. Lino's treachery leads Marcello to seize the gun and shoot his amorous and confused assailant. Lino's pitiful state is reflected in his invitation to the youth to kill him if he cannot possess Marcello.

Lina (LEEN-ah), the young and voluptuous French wife of the aging Professor Quadri. Her body is described as strong but lithe, like that of a gymnast or dancer. When the newly wed Clericis arrive unannounced at Quadri's Paris residence, Lina remains aloof, if not openly hostile. Like her husband, Lina knows that Marcello's supposedly friendly visit to his former professor is a cover for a Fascist espionage mission. Although the professor appears sincere in his desire to win over Marcello from Fascism, Lina's interest in their Italian visitors is dominated by a lesbian attraction for Giulia.

Orlando, the least-developed character in the novel. A Fascist secret police agent who has served in many countries, he is assigned with Marcello to carry out the assassination of Professor Quadri. Marcello's view of Orlando is somewhat condescending: He characterizes Orlando's face as that of a petty bureaucrat, tenant farmer, or, at most, a small landowner. Orlando's carnal baseness is demonstrated several times; for example, when Orlando is assured that the "official" contacts and formal instructions for the espionage mission have been taken care of, he indulges his lust immediately with a prostitute.

Professor Quadri (KWAH-dree), a man who is considered to be a traitor because of his abandonment of the Fascist cause. The formerly eccentric and bookish professor is portrayed as having adjusted well to his orderly and visibly comfortable life in exile. Although Quadri is engaged in an international network for anti-Fascist propaganda, his character emerges mainly in personal interaction with his young but sexually imbalanced wife, Lina, and with Marcello, who is the only person with whom he carries on a sustained dialogue. Quadri seems not to condemn Marcello for the political choice he has made. He focuses his efforts on trying to dissuade him from his Fascist beliefs. He apparently does not even suspect that Marcello is torn between his duty to carry out Rome's assassination orders and the temptation to abandon his mission to pursue what he perceives (erroneously) to be Lina's amorous attachment to him.

Giulia Clerici (jee-EWL-yah), the twenty-year-old daughter of a deceased government official who is heir to the "twin divinities of respectability and normality." Although these characteristics are things sought by Marcello, her strong devotion to Catholicism is difficult for him to accept. She is largely unimaginative but possesses a sensual vivacity that clearly attracts masculine attentions. Before meeting Marcello, she suffered the humiliation of having love forced on her by an older married man. Once married to Marcello, and despite the circumstances of their honeymoon, Giulia tries to impress Marcello with the enthusiasm of her love, yet it is her predictable normalcy that attracts him most. When Giulia finds herself to be the object of Lina's lesbian desires, she becomes very uncomfortable. It is her (normal) unwillingness to respond to Lina's overtures—despite Marcello's attempts to use this very situation as a way to get Lina away from the assassination target and, supposedly, into a liaison with him—that makes Lina decide to travel from Paris with Quadri, with whom she meets her senseless death.

— *Byron D. Cannon*

CONINGSBY: Or, The New Generation

Author: Benjamin Disraeli (1804-1881)
First published: 1844
Genre: Novel

Locale: England and Paris
Time: 1832-1840
Plot: Bildungsroman

The Marquis of Monmouth, a British nobleman opposed to reform, especially the Reform Bill of 1832.

Harry Coningsby, a liberal-minded young English nobleman, grandson of the Marquis of Monmouth. Disinherited for defying his grandfather on political grounds, he is eventually elected to Parliament. He marries Edith Millbank, and after the death of his grandfather, he inherits the marquis' fortune indirectly.

Edith Millbank, the beautiful but shy daughter of a wealthy industrialist. Harry Coningsby falls in love with her, but her father refuses at first to permit the marriage. Later he relents, and she is married to Coningsby.

Oswald Millbank, Edith's father. A wealthy manufacturer, he thinks England should be governed by an aristocracy of talent rather than by a hereditary aristocracy. He was at one time the fiancé of Coningsby's mother.

Oswald Millbank, the son of the industrialist of the same name. He is one of Coningsby's close friends and Edith's brother.

Lucretia, a young Italian noblewoman. She tries to attract Coningsby and his friend Sidonia. Failing in these attempts, she settles for marriage with the Marquis of Monmouth for his wealth. Her husband sends her away when she proves to be unfaithful.

Princess Colonna, Lucretia's stepmother. She is a strong supporter of young Coningsby in his early relations with his grandfather.

Sidonia, a wealthy young Jew, a friend of Coningsby. He is also a friend of the Millbank family. He is suspected, wrongly, by Coningsby of being a rival for Edith's hand in marriage.

Flora, a young actress befriended by Coningsby. She turns out to be the natural daughter of the Marquis of Monmouth. The marquis leaves her his fortune, but she in turn wills it to Coningsby when she dies.

Mr. Rigby, a member of Parliament who is supported by the Marquis of Monmouth. He is young Coningsby's caretaker.

Lord Wallinger and

Lady Wallinger, relatives of Edith who take her to Paris, where Coningsby renews his acquaintance with Edith and falls in love with her.

THE CONJURE-MAN DIES: A Mystery of Dark Harlem

Author: Rudolph Fisher (1897-1934)
First published: 1932
Genre: Novel

Locale: Harlem, New York
Time: The 1930's
Plot: Detective and mystery

John Archer, a medical doctor in his middle thirties. He assists homicide detective Perry Dart in solving the "murder" of the conjure-man. He is tall, slender, light-skinned, usually composed, intellectual, and a student of science and human nature.

Perry Dart, a homicide detective in his middle thirties, with a very dark complexion. He is the first of only ten African American members of Harlem's police force to be promoted to detective. He is a Harlem native and knows its lowest dives and loftiest temples. He is small in stature but makes up for his size with the power of his investigative mind and insights. Like John Archer, he is a keen student of human nature.

N'Gana Frimbo, a psychist and conjure-man, educated at Harvard. He is a philosopher and an avid reader of a wide range of philosophical and metaphysical texts. He is mysterious and apparently offers the sort of counseling and advice that his clients need, for he has many clients even though he does not advertise. He is a major player in solving his own murder. He, Dr. Archer, and Perry Dart have one thing in common, despite the apparent differences of their professions: They are all students of human nature.

Bubber Brown, a would-be private detective and codiscoverer of the body of the conjure-man. He is short and a little overweight. He provides much of the novel's humor and other light touches. He knows much of what goes on in Harlem and would like to be Perry Dart's partner in solving the crime. In his conversations with his friend Jinx, he exhibits a real and easy facility with words. He often plays the dozens, engaging in battles of insults.

Jinx Jenkins, Bubber's friend, codiscoverer of the body, and for a time the chief suspect in the murder. He is in many ways the opposite of Bubber. He is tall, thin, and serious, a bit less outgoing and more suspicious of other people's views of him. Like Bubber, he likes to use words, and he expertly plays the dozens with Bubber. He had come to see Frimbo for help in getting a job.

Spider Webb, a murder suspect and number runner. He works for a major criminal figure in Harlem and visits Frimbo for advice.

Doty Hicks, another murder suspect, a drug addict who needs counseling from Frimbo.

Samuel Crouch, an undertaker who rents the upstairs of his building to Frimbo.

Martha Crouch, Samuel's wife. She is present when the murder takes place because she has come to collect the rent from Frimbo.

Easley Jones, a friendly railroad man who seeks advice from Frimbo.

Aramintha Snead, a devoted church worker. The tall, thin, poorly dressed woman wants Frimbo to stop her husband from drinking.

— *Charles P. Toombs*

THE CONJURE WOMAN

Author: Charles Waddell Chesnutt (1858-1932)
First published: 1899
Genre: Short fiction

Locale: North Carolina
Time: The post-Civil War period
Plot: Regional

The narrator, a grape farmer from Ohio who settles in North Carolina because of his wife's ill health, buying a dilapidated plantation which has an old vineyard. He hires Uncle Julius and is regaled by the old man with stories of witchcraft. The narrator learns by experience that the stories are usually told for a purpose, most often to the benefit of the old servant.

Annie, the narrator's wife, whose ill health causes her husband's removal from Ohio to North Carolina.

Uncle Julius, an elderly black man who tries to prevent the narrator from buying the plantation because he has been selling the grapes from the untended vineyard. He becomes the narrator's coachman and loyal employee, but he often tells stories of witchcraft to prevent his employers from taking some action detrimental to his own well-being.

Aunt Peggy, the black "conjure woman" of Uncle Julius' stories. Her generally beneficent supernatural powers are used to place "goophers," or spells, on people, places, or things.

Mabel, the narrator's sister-in-law, who is persuaded by one of Uncle Julius' stories to cease being jealous of a rival and to marry her fiancé.

Becky, a slave in one of Uncle Julius' stories. She is helped by the powers of the conjure woman when her infant is traded by her owner for a horse.

Sandy, a slave in one of Uncle Julius' stories who is turned into a tree by the conjure woman. She turns him into a tree so that their owner cannot take Sandy, whom she loves, away from her.

A CONNECTICUT YANKEE IN KING ARTHUR'S COURT

Author: Mark Twain (Samuel Langhorne Clemens, 1835-1910)
First published: 1889
Genre: Novel

Locale: New England and England
Time: The sixth century and the nineteenth century
Plot: Social satire

Hank Morgan, called **the Connecticut Yankee**, an ingenious man who is struck on the head during a quarrel in a New England arms factory in the year 1879. He awakes in England, in June, 528, and is taken prisoner. About to be burned at the stake on the twenty-first of June, he remembers that there was a solar eclipse on that day. By prophesying the eclipse, he saves his life and discredits Merlin. Later, he is named "The Boss" and decides to raise the status of the common people through a variety of programs and innovations to be implemented over the next several years. His innovations include schools, a telephone system, soap, and gunpowder. He points out to King Arthur the grave injustices of the feudal system while accompanying him on a tour of his realm. He marries Alisande. When their little daughter becomes ill, he takes her to France to recuperate. While he is away, the church orders that all of his improvements in England be destroyed. When he returns, he destroys some of his equipment so that it cannot be used, and he undertakes an apocalyptic war with the knights. Merlin casts a spell on him that will cause him to sleep for thirteen hundred years.

Clarence, a foppish page who becomes Morgan's chief assistant in his efforts to modernize the land and improve the lot of the common people.

King Arthur, a kind and courageous ruler who does not realize the inequities that exist in the social structure of his kingdom. He is killed in a battle with Sir Launcelot over Queen Guenever. His death is the signal for the church to move against and destroy the social progress brought about by Morgan's democratic innovations.

Sir Kay, the seneschal who first captures Morgan.

Sir Sagramour la Desirous, who challenges Morgan to a joust and is aided by Merlin, until Morgan kills him.

Merlin, the court sorcerer whose magic power cannot match Morgan's nineteenth century knowledge. After Morgan supplants him, Merlin plots his revenge.

Alisande, also called **Sandy**, a damsel whom Morgan helps and whom he finally marries.

Hello-Central, their daughter, whose convalescence in France gives the church a chance to unite feudal power and destroy Morgan's power.

THE CONNECTION

Author: Jack Gelber (1932-   )
First published: 1960
Genre: Drama

Locale: New York City
Time: Late 1950's
Plot: Existentialism

Cowboy, a sensible, practical, calm, and honest heroin dealer. In the second act of the play, he arrives in Leach's New York apartment, where the other characters have been waiting for him impatiently. He gives them heroin injections in Leach's bathroom while the unsuspecting Sister Salvation looks around the apartment. Cowboy is weary of the dangers of dealing heroin. When Leach takes an overdose, Cowboy saves his life, but he refuses to be considered the play's hero.

Leach, a clearly discontented heroin addict and the occupant of the apartment in which the play takes place. Trying to dominate the other characters, he gets into an argument with Ernie, who refuses to abide by Leach's rules and who accidentally breaks the boil on Leach's neck. He pays for heroin to be given to the play's author and to the two photographers hired to film the play within the play, so that these three people can lose their conventionality. Feeling cheated by Cowboy when he does not get high on the heroin, he overdoses on stage but probably will survive.

Solly, an educated, conciliatory heroin addict. He is the mouthpiece for the play's philosophy and comments on the antisocial attitude of the twentieth century, on the fascination with warfare in the twentieth century, and on waiting, the heroin addicts' main occupation, which often leads to suicide. He and Leach involve the play's author and its producer as well as the two photographers in the action. Solly is a good storyteller and argues that addiction to heroin is no worse than more conventional addictions to money or clothes.

Ernie, a dissatisfied heroin addict and musician. He is not trusted by any of the other characters because of rumors that he may have killed another addict. Although he announces that he has been hired to play his trumpet, he will not be able to take the job because he had to trade in his instrument at a pawnshop. All he has left is the useless mouthpiece, which he blows time and again while insulting other characters and the audience. When Leach overdoses, Ernie leaves out of fear.

Sam, an uneducated, good-natured, and lethargic heroin addict. Sam dozes on stage during much of the performance and complains that Leach does not let him sleep. He tells long stories and takes Solly as his mentor, asking him many questions, such as why heroin is illegal.

Sister Salvation, an unsuspecting, lonely Salvation Army sister, whom Cowboy takes to Leach's apartment to evade the police. She seems not to notice that Cowboy is giving the other characters heroin, suspecting only that the men have been drinking alcohol in the bathroom. When Solly asks her to leave as long as they are getting along well, she is reluctant to go because she fears loneliness and her approaching death.

Jim Dunn, the seemingly superior producer of the play within the play, for which he hired the other characters and musicians. Dressed in a suit, he introduces the players and the play's theme of narcotics, announces the intermission, and expresses his discontentment with the performance. He is unable to keep out of the play within the play and interacts with the players. He tries to control the performances and to execute his sensationalist views of what drama should do.

Jaybird, the author of the play within the play whose staging he, Jim Dunn, two photographers, and the audience watch. He lived with heroin addicts for several months so that he could write an outline for an experimental play on narcotics. This experience and the performance of his play transform him from a "square" into a more open-minded person who also tries heroin. He cannot be an experimental playwright wholeheartedly, however, because he wants to remain in control of his play. He also considers heroism the basis of Western drama, although the play as a whole denies the possibility of heroism.

— *Josef Raab*

THE CONSCIENCE OF THE RICH

Author: C. P. Snow (1905-1980)
First published: 1958
Genre: Novel

Locale: England
Time: Early twentieth century
Plot: Psychological realism

Lewis Eliot, a young lawyer from a working-class family. During an internship year in London, Lewis becomes a close friend of Charles March and a frequent guest in the family home. Lewis' primary function in the novel is that of observer. Although he is an outsider, Lewis earns the trust of all the members of Charles's immediate family and becomes their confidant. Lewis sometimes tries to play a more active role in the lives of the Marches, but he fails in his attempt to avert the scandal that threatens them, and he also fails to effect desired reconciliations, first between Charles and his father, then later between Charles and his sister Katherine. Lewis, however, remains friendly with all the members of the family.

Charles March, a young lawyer from a wealthy Jewish family. Although he performs well in his first case, Charles decides to leave his profession, which he believes will restrict him to the company of wealthy Jews. Ironically, it is a Jewish girl, Ann Simon, with whom he falls in love and eventually marries. Once Charles realizes that the source of his unhappiness is not his Jewish background but the guilt he feels because of his sadistic impulses, he can proceed with his life. He marries Ann and, despite his father's disapproval, becomes a doctor. His loyalty to Ann causes his father to reject him and costs him his inheritance, but he finds happiness with her and fulfillment in service to others.

Leonard March, Charles's father, a member of one of the wealthiest and most powerful Jewish families in England. Although he is friendly toward the friends his children bring home, even Gentiles from a mediocre background such as Lewis, Leonard expects his children to marry within their circle and to make him proud of them. He is disappointed when Katherine marries a Gentile, but he is furious when Charles, who he admits is his favorite, not only leaves the law but also marries a girl who, though Jewish, is a Communist, and then, at her suggestion, becomes a doctor. Leonard at-tempts to bend Charles to his will by exerting emotional pressure and by threatening to withdraw financial support. When he has to make good his threats, Leonard loses his son.

Katherine March, Charles's vivacious younger sister. Like her brother, Katherine is determined to break out of the narrow circle within which Leonard has confined his children. She is also intimidated by her father. For that reason, she conceals the seriousness of her relationship with a Gentile, Francis Getliffe, until the two are engaged. To Katherine's surprise, Leonard's reaction is fairly mild, and he is soon planning the wedding. When the family is threatened with scandal, both Katherine and Francis side with Leonard against Charles and Ann. Their third child is named for Leonard.

Ann Simon, a doctor's daughter and a committed Communist who works with a radical, antigovernment newspaper. Because of her political views and her influence over Charles, Leonard loathes Ann and opposes his son's marriage to her. When she contracts pneumonia, Leonard hopes that she will die. Ann loves Charles so much that she would do anything for him. She offers him a chance to destroy the newspaper and thereby end the threat to the family, but Charles refuses to do so.

Francis Getliffe, a scientist and a member of the Cambridge University faculty. An easygoing man and a traditionalist, he soon seems more at home in the March family than does Charles. He supports Leonard's belief that Charles should put the good of the family first.

Sir Philip March, Leonard's brother and the head of the March family. After becoming a parliamentary secretary, he is accused of making money from his inside knowledge of government policies. Although he is innocent, he is forced out of his office and loses his hopes for a ministry.

— *Rosemary M. Canfield Reisman*

THE CONSCIOUS LOVERS

Author: Sir Richard Steele (1672-1729)
First published: 1723
Genre: Drama

Locale: London, England
Time: Early eighteenth century
Plot: Sentimental

Young Bevil, a gentleman of means who is in love with one girl but engaged to another, who in turn loves another man. After many complications of plot, the lovers are properly paired off.

Lucinda Sealand, who is engaged to young Bevil, who has sent her a letter permitting her to break the engagement. Her thankful letter of reply raises a misunderstanding and almost results in a duel between young Bevil and his friend Mr. Myrtle, whom Lucinda plans to marry.

Indiana Danvers, a girl whom young Bevil has befriended and whom he wishes to marry. She is the daughter of a British merchant who disappeared in the Indies some time before.

Mr. Sealand, Lucinda's father. Learning that young Bevil is paying Indiana's bills, he wrongly suspects that she is his mistress. Going to investigate before breaking off Lucinda's engagement to Bevil, he finds that Indiana is his long-lost daughter and he agrees to her marriage with Bevil.

Mr. Myrtle, young Bevil's friend, who is in love with Lucinda. Hoping to frustrate Mrs. Sealand's plan to marry Lucinda to Mr. Cimberton, Myrtle goes in disguise to the Sealand house. Finally, when all is cleared up, he reveals his identity and claims his bride.

Sir John Bevil, young Bevil's father, at whose request young Bevil is engaged to Lucinda. Later, after discovering that Indiana is Mr. Sealand's daughter, he is pleased that she will marry his son.

Mrs. Sealand, Lucinda's mother, a foolish woman who is eager to marry Lucinda to a rich man.

Mr. Cimberton, a peculiar and wealthy suitor for Lucinda's hand, favored by Mrs. Sealand. He looks over Lucinda as if he were buying a prize mare. Learning that Lucinda will have only half her father's fortune, he leaves in a huff.

Tom, young Bevil's artful servant.

THE CONSERVATIONIST

Author: Nadine Gordimer (1923-   )
First published: 1974
Genre: Novel

Locale: Transvaal, South Africa
Time: The 1960's
Plot: Psychological realism

Mehring, the protagonist, a wealthy South African industrialist and amateur farmer. A large, middle-aged man with graying sideburns, Mehring is attractive to women and a popular addition to dinner parties. He is a frequent international traveler and knows much about base metals but nothing about art, music, or poetry. He has many acquaintances but no close relationships or real friends in his life: His wife left him eight years ago, his son and he have nothing to say to each other, his mistress has left South Africa, and the black laborers on the farm largely ignore him. What he does have is a 400-acre farm, which he bought intending to use it for rendezvous with his mistress, who visited the farm only once. Mehring attempts to control his land, to keep it organized and perfect, in the face of unconquerable natural and political forces.

Antonia Mancebo, Mehring's mistress. In her thirties, she has an olive complexion and straight dark hair with only one or two strands of gray, which she does not bother to pluck. She does not, Mehring says, have a beautiful body. Antonia is married to a professor who is often away, but she has close ties to her friends, who include blacks and revolutionaries. She frequently marches in antiapartheid demonstrations and has close brushes with the law. Antonia taunts Mehring for his conservative beliefs, his power, and his money. She cannot understand why he does not leave the farm as it is rather than trying to shape it into his image of what it should be. Finally, she leaves South Africa rather than condone its policies.

Terry, Mehring's son. Sixteen years old, tall and thin with long blond hair, Terry attends a boarding school, where he experiments with leftist politics and homosexuality. He wears tattered jeans and no shoes, and he gives his spare clothes away to the blacks on the farm. Mehring has had custody of Terry since his divorce, but as Terry gets older he shows less and less interest in his father, the farm, and the wealth he stands to inherit. During his last school vacation, Terry hitchhikes to Namibia instead of going home to be with his father. Rather than face conscription into an army whose politics he cannot support, Terry wants to live with his mother in New York.

Jacobus, the black chief herdsman on Mehring's farm. Jacobus is middle-aged or perhaps older, with long and callused hands and blackened teeth. He has been on the farm since before Mehring bought it, and he will be there after Mehring has gone. He has learned how to deal with the white owners who come and go. When Mehring is around, Jacobus calls him Master and speaks briefly and haltingly. When Mehring is not on the farm, however, Jacobus speaks expansively and articulately, comes and goes as he pleases on Mehring's tractor, and has the run of the farmhouse. By playing Mehring carefully, Jacobus is always able to get what he wants.

Bismillah, an Indian shopkeeper living on a compound near the farm. The middle-aged Bismillah talks very little, except to his family and Jacobus. He is constantly aware of the threats posed by white bureaucrats, whom he bribes to be allowed to keep his business, and blacks, whom he keeps out with a high, barbed-wire fence and guard dogs. He runs his shop under the supervision of his father and has been successful enough to send his son away to be educated. Three generations live in his home, and several blacks live and work in the compound. Bismillah's existence depends on his ability to remain inoffensive to the various groups struggling in South Africa, and he is able to speak Hindi, English, Afrikaans, mine pidgin, and farm pidgin.

— *Cynthia A. Bily*

CONSUELO

Author: George Sand (Amandine-Aurore-Lucile Dupin, Baronne Dudevant, 1804-1876)
First published: 1842-1843
Genre: Novel

Locale: Venice, Bohemia, and Vienna
Time: The eighteenth century
Plot: Historical

Consuelo (kohn-SWAY-loh), a gifted singer who, before her mother dies, promises to marry a young musician named Anzoleto. Consuelo is a charming and beautiful woman, in addition to being a fine artist. After she finds that her betrothed is untrue to her, she becomes a companion to Amelia, the niece of Count Rudolstadt. The count's son, Albert, falls in love with her and tells her that she is the only person who can save him from insanity. She helps her rival, Corilla, give birth to an illegitimate child the girl has by Anzoleto. Just before Albert dies, she marries him, but she refuses any of the fortune that comes to her as a result. She goes to Berlin and becomes the idol of Frederick the Great.

Niccolo Antonio Porpora (NEE-koh-loh ahn-TOH-nee-oh pohr-POH-rah), Consuelo's music teacher and godfather. He is determined to make a great artist out of her and, by his duplicity, manages to keep her away from Albert until it is too late for her to help him.

Count Albert Rudolstadt, the son of a nobleman, who

calls Consuelo by name the first time he hears her sing, although no one has told him her true name. He is convinced that Consuelo is his salvation and that no one else can save him from the curse of insanity. When Porpora writes to tell Albert that he will never consent to Consuelo's marriage to the young nobleman, Albert weakens and dies, after begging Consuelo to marry him so that his soul can find peace.

Anzoleto (ahn-zoh-LEH-toh), the poor young musician whom Consuelo has promised to marry. When Consuelo's success becomes greater than his, he tries to assure his position in the theater by pretending to be in love with her rival, Corilla. Porpora dislikes Anzoleto, and he contrives to have Consuelo find Anzoleto and Corilla together. Anzoleto

fathers Corilla's child and is never heard from again.

Count Rudolstadt, a Bohemian nobleman, Albert's father. He is willing to consent to Consuelo's marriage to Albert in order to save his son.

Corilla (koh-REEL-lah), a singer and Consuelo's rival, both in the theater and in Anzoleto's affections. Corilla does not know that Consuelo, who was disguised as a boy at the time, had helped her with the birth of her child.

Joseph Haydn, the composer, whom Consuelo meets on the road to Vienna. She takes him along to be a pupil of Porpora.

Amelia, the niece of Count Rudolstadt. Betrothed to Albert, she fears him because he is thought to be mad.

CONTENDING FORCES

Author: Pauline Hopkins (1859-1930)
First published: 1900
Genre: Novel

Locale: Bermuda, North Carolina, Boston, and New Orleans
Time: The 1790's and the 1890's
Plot: Social morality

Sappho Clark, a beautiful mulatto woman. Sappho is abducted by a white uncle when she is fifteen years old. She is placed in a brothel, where she remains for three weeks before she is rescued and carried to a convent, where she gives birth to a son. Later, she moves to Boston to start a new life. There, she meets Will Smith, whom she marries after a series of difficulties.

Will Smith, a black civil rights activist. An intellectual and philosopher, Will is a leader in his community. He meets Sappho in his mother's boardinghouse and courts her, continuing the courtship despite many difficulties. They are married at the conclusion of the novel.

Dora Smith, a spirited, independent black woman. At the beginning of the novel, she is engaged to John Langley, who

betrays her because of his desire for Sappho Clark. Dora turns her attention to a childhood friend, Arthur Lewis, whom she eventually marries.

John Langley, an ambitious black lawyer. An unscrupulous, self-centered man, John focuses his every move on satisfying his needs, ambitions, and desires. He alienates all who care for him and meets a dreadful death seeking gold in the Klondike.

Arthur Lewis, the president of a technical college for black people in the South. He has long loved Dora, whom he eventually marries. His career goals are focused on the betterment of black people.

— *Rennie Simson*

THE CONTRACTOR

Author: David Storey (1933-   )
First published: 1970
Genre: Drama

Locale: Yorkshire, England
Time: The 1960's
Plot: Naturalism

Ewbank, the title character, a self-made owner of a tent-erecting business. He is a hardworking, bustling Northerner, very much the boss, with a sharp tongue and a fondness for his tipple. He is affectionate with his wife and daughter (who is marrying "above" the family) but rather lost with his son. Ewbank is more at home with his sleeves rolled up among his all-male "family" of workmen, whose language he speaks. The high point of the wedding celebrations (the wedding itself takes place offstage) comes when he shares cake and a toast with the men. He treats Glendenning like a son, buying him chocolate when he cries. He provides the marquee, the erection and the dismantling of which constitute the action of the play, for his daughter's wedding reception, which is held at his house. His separate worlds of home and work thus come into collision, bringing him to reflect briefly on the ephemeral, or "nomadic," quality of his life as an erector of tents.

Paul, Ewbank's university-educated son, well-intentioned and kindly but restless and overly thoughtful, with little sense of self-worth and less of direction, which gives him the ap-

pearance of an ineffectual lounger. Paul is the playwright's surrogate in the play: a young man out of tune with his family because he has been educated out of his class. In this play, in which work is the focus of dramatic attention and the index of value, it is inevitable that he should find a brief sense of belonging by joining in the erecting of the tent. He refuses his father's offer to hand the business over to him and decides to leave, destination unknown, at the end of the play.

Kay, Ewbank's foreman, a taciturn, efficient former convict. Kay can be needled for a long time before he finally loses his temper, which he does with Fitzpatrick. The play as a whole focuses not on individual characters (though they are sharply individualized) but on the work and on the dynamics of the group relationships it brings about. Kay quietly orchestrates this work.

Fitzpatrick, an Irish workman. An inveterate scrounger, work-shy, and the most loudmouthed of Ewbank's five-man gang of misfits, Fitzpatrick forms a "double act" with another Irish workman, Marshall, playing games with words in the working-class music hall tradition of nonstop patter and the "turn." His humor is aggressive, provoking one confrontation with Bennett (rapidly defused) and another with Kay, who sacks him. Ewbank reinstates him.

Bennett, a rather colorless workman. Bennett harbors a grudge against Kay, who he thinks picks on him, and so reveals to the others the fact that Kay has done a "stretch" in prison. In act 3, when the tent is dismantled, it is revealed that his wife has left him.

Glendenning, a mentally retarded workman. Glendenning is shy and affectionate, stammers when he speaks, and is quick to come to tears. He works honestly and hard while enduring needling from his crude fellow workers.

Old Ewbank, Ewbank's long-retired and senile father, once a ropemaker. Old Ewbank wanders on and off clutching a short and useless piece of rope, with old Mrs. Ewbank in tow, like his keeper. As a decrepit spokesman for the Northern work ethic and the value of craftsmanship, he unintentionally parodies what he preaches.

— *Joss Lutz Marsh*

CONVERSATION IN THE CATHEDRAL
(Conversación en la catedral)

Author: Mario Vargas Llosa (1936-   )
First published: 1969
Genre: Novel

Locale: Lima, Peru
Time: Late 1940's and early 1950's
Plot: Social realism

Santiago Zavala (sahn-tee-AH-goh sah-VAH-lah), also known as **Skinny** and **Superbrain**, who is progressively transformed from the favorite son into an aspiring Communist and finally into a columnist in a dead-end newspaper job. He is the novel's protagonist, and much of the narrative is rendered in his voice and from his perspective. He is a disillusioned intellectual and self-disinherited son of the bourgeoisie who is determined to forge an authentic existence. When he is unable to break with his past, however, he slowly sinks into despair and cynicism. His preoccupation throughout the novel is with how both the nation and the individual have been betrayed by the same degrading and corrupt political forces.

Ambrosio Pardo (ahm-BROH-see-oh PAHR-doh), a *zambo* (part black and part Indian), first a chauffeur for Santiago's father, then a worker at a dog pound. His particular mixture of blood carries an implicit tension that is externalized in the novel. He is both an innocent victim of Peru's social order and a victimizer who adapts to a corrupt system to survive. Ambrosio's inability to break the social, political, and economic bonds that shackle him illustrates one of the novel's major themes: how society, especially a politically corrupt society, can succeed in shaping and determining its members in perverse and inhuman ways.

Trinidad Lopez (tree-nee-DAHD), a textile worker and political fanatic. Although he appears to be an activist who is aware of the political reality of his time, the narrative raises serious doubts concerning the validity of his assertions. He is constantly in and out of jail, and his activities with his comrade Pedro Flores lead to his final arrest and death. Never really understanding the deeper implications of the *aprista* movement for which he fights, he is nevertheless beaten, tortured, and finally killed for his revolutionary activities. His death,

therefore, is completely meaningless.

Amalia Cerda (ah-MAH-lee-ah SEHR-dah), a servant, later the wife of Trinidad Lopez, then of Ambrosio. Although politically naïve, she is curious about the activities of Trinidad. Both she and Trinidad are portrayed as victims of the political process: Neither understands the functions of their institutions, yet the lives of both are determined by those very institutions.

Don Fermín Zavala (fehr-MEEN), Santiago's father, a wealthy Peruvian industrialist. He has strong ties with the Odría regime and is deeply involved in deals with the government strongman, Cayo Bermúdez. His are the middle-class values against which his son revolts. He is involved in a homosexual relationship with Ambrosio.

Don Cayo Bermúdez (KI-oh behr-MEW-dehs), the minister of security and right-hand man of Peru's dictator, General Manuel Odría. He represents evil in its most sordid aspects, taking charge of the regime's dirty work and permitting those who are allied with the dictatorship to acquire a certain amount of respectability. He is without guilt or conscience. He functions both as the chief instrument of corruption and as one of its victims.

Hortensia (ohr-TEHN-see-ah), a wealthy prostitute and the mistress of Cayo Bermúdez. She and Queta, another prostitute, engage in homosexual relations for the voyeuristic enjoyment of Cayo Bermúdez. She is murdered by Ambrosio to protect Don Fermín from the possibility of blackmail. She intended to blackmail Don Fermín because of his homosexual relationship with Ambrosio. This act of murder becomes a turning point in the novel because it forever dooms Ambrosio to his marginal social status and forces a confrontation between Santiago and his father.

— *Genevieve Slomski*

COONARDOO: The Well in the Shadow

Author: Katharine Susannah Prichard (1884-1969)
First published: 1929
Genre: Novel

Locale: Wytaliba, a cattle station in Australia
Time: Late nineteenth century to the 1920's
Plot: Social realism

Coonardoo, an aboriginal housemaid at Wytaliba station (homestead) in the north of Western Australia. She has dull golden hair, a thin, reedy voice, pretty hands and feet, and firm, pointed breasts. She is long-legged and wiry and is "as spirited as an unbroken filly." A year older than Hugh Watt, she is devoted to him and exhibits a devouring love for him.

Intelligent and authoritative in the uloo (aboriginal camp), she is patient and gracefully submissive in the homestead. She generously gives herself to Hugh when directed to do so by her husband but has the air of a faithful, deserted animal when he later shuns her and abuses her. She is "of more than usual intelligence" and is the nexus between the white and black characters.

Bessie Watt, a former schoolteacher who married Ted Watt, a good-looking, good-natured, feckless, and illiterate drunk who owned the million-acre station Wytaliba and died just after Hugh's birth. The aborigines call her Mumae (father); she understands their culture and is insightful, shrewd, and unsentimental, yet kind and practical. She is a manly, small woman with eyes "hard and blue as winter skies"; she is frugal and manages to pay off a large mortgage. She appreciates the value of education and sends Hugh to a school in Perth. She sees the unsuitability of Jessica as a station wife and forbids Coonardoo's marriage as a child. She is an admirable, hardworking outback person.

Hugh Watt, Bessie's son, who succeeds her as owner of Wytaliba. As a child, he is "a boy with a swag of ideals"; he has a sharp and scratchy voice, is blue-eyed and very assured and bossy, and plays with Coonardoo, learning her tribal lore. He has his mother's work ethic and fortitude, but he lacks her insight and flexibility. Restrained and reserved, he reads the *Iliad* and values honor and courtesy. Although he has habits of independence and solitude and has occasional fits of anger and dejection, he is generally high-minded, kindly, courteous, and gentle. He marries in a purely practical manner and does not understand the roots of loneliness in his family and himself. He is tormented by having had sex with Coonardoo, yet he truly loves their son, Winni. He is jealous of Sam Geary's lifestyle and success and is tormented by his abuse of Coonardoo. In most ways, he is "a good, ordinary little man."

Jessica Haywood, Hugh's fiancée, who visits Wytaliba when Hugh returns from Perth at the age of twenty. She is a very pretty, delicate, and blossomy creature who plays the piano. She is upset by unshaven men, aborigines, and the isolation of the bush; she returns, disillusioned, to the city.

Mollie Watt, Hugh's wife and formerly a maid-of-all-work in her aunt's boardinghouse in Geraldton. She enters marriage not for romance but in expectation of social advancement. She has five daughters in five years. She is a small woman with straight dark hair; her face is round and plump, belying her rasping nature. Although she is a good cook and household manager, she cannot get along with aborigines, especially after she concludes that Hugh and Coonardoo are the parents of Winni. Although she gives evidence of being a commonsense person, she has "all the obstinacy of a small mind." To her credit, she lasts ten years in the bush, but her extravagant social life in Perth (and the consequent financial drain on Hugh) results in the bank's foreclosure and the loss of Wytaliba to Sam Geary. Hugh's early praise for her is a premature evaluation that he later regrets.

Warieda, the principal stockman and horsebreaker on Wytaliba, where he is the imperious leader of the aborigines. A proud upholder of traditional ways, he "lends" his wife, Coonardoo, to Hugh while Hugh is grieving over Bessie's death. Warieda is tall and handsome, arresting, and magnetic; his wild, bright eyes are challenging; and his dark, sinewy arms are like tree branches. Although reared under the aegis of the Watts, he succumbs to the traditional "pointing the bone" by a tribal magician and wanders off and dies.

Sam Geary, the unprincipled, opportunistic, and sensual whiskey-loving owner of a neighboring cattle and sheep station. He is brash and brutish and has a jaunty bearing that goes with his feeling that he is always master of the situation and the business superior of Hugh. He is bowlegged, sunscorched, bullock-shouldered, and slouched; his eyes are bulbous and pale blue; he has straight, fair eyelashes; and tufts of hair protrude from his nostrils. He has a number of aboriginal gins (women) as consorts, though Sheba is his primary one; he teases Hugh for not taking black women for his pleasure and for working so hard. Eventually, he becomes the owner of Wytaliba.

Phyllis, the oldest daughter of Hugh and Mollie Watt. She leaves for the coast at the age of nine and returns a decade later, tired of city social life and determined to carry on the tradition of her grandmother, Bessie, as the wife of an optimistic stockman, Bill Gale.

— *Marian B. McLeod*

THE COPPERHEAD

Author: Harold Frederic (1856-1898)
First published: 1893
Genre: Novel

Locale: New York state
Time: The 1860's
Plot: Regional

Abner Beech, a farmer and a violent Anti-Abolitionist in the equally violent Abolitionist community of Dearborn County, New York. His political sentiments earn for him the name "Copperhead" (a Northerner with Southern sympathies) and the enmity of his neighbors, who plan to tar and feather him. When Abner's house is ignited and burned by the bonfire for the tarring, the neighbors recover their senses, ask his forgiveness, and offer to restore his property. Goodwill reigns again among the folk of Dearborn County.

Jee Hagadorn, Abner Beech's Abolitionist neighbor and enemy.

Jeff Beech, Abner Beech's son, a Union soldier in love with Esther Hagadorn.

Esther Hagadorn, Jee Hagadorn's daughter and the sweetheart of Jeff Beech.

Ni Hagadorn, Jee Hagadorn's son.

Jimmy, an orphan boy who lives with Abner Beech.

Hurley, Abner Beech's Anti-Abolitionist hired man.

Warner Pitts, Abner Beech's former hired man, an officer in the Union army.

Byron Truax, a fellow soldier of Jeff Beech.

M'rye, Abner Beech's wife.

Janey, a hired girl.

Avery, the local squire.

CORIOLANUS

Author: William Shakespeare (1564-1616)
First published: 1623
Genre: Drama

Locale: Rome, Corioli, and Antium
Time: The third century
Plot: Tragedy

Caius Marcius, afterward **Caius Marcius Coriolanus** (KAY-yuhs MAHR-shuhs kohr-ee-oh-LAY-nuhs), a great warrior of the Roman Republic, a man of immense valor and equally great pride. He does not desire public acclaim for his achievements; his own knowledge of their worth is sufficient. He violently resents having to beg for the voices of the common people, whom he has watched flee from the battlefield in fear, and he is ultimately unable to stifle his contempt long enough to win the consulship. For his arrogance, he is banished from Rome. His alliance with Aufidius to avenge the wrongs he has received from Rome is a manifestation of his fierce pride. The dominant force in his life is the personality of his mother, who has shaped him into the confident, arrogant, and single-minded man he is. Although he cannot obey her injunction to betray himself to win the favor of the people, he is ultimately broken by her will and agrees to make peace between the Volscians and the Romans. There is, after this submission, no course for him but death, and he perishes, branded a traitor by both nations and taunted as "boy" by the Volscians.

Volumnia (vohl-LUHM-nee-uh), his mother, a noble Roman matron who has instilled in her son a strong sense of personal pride, integrity, and a streak of brutality. She dominates both Coriolanus and his wife and speaks proudly of the ruthlessness of her young grandson. Apparently oblivious to the effects of her pressure on her son, she rejoices in having saved Rome from a bloody destruction.

Menenius Agrippa (meh-NEE-nee-uhs uh-GRIHP-uh), a witty Roman senator who uses his reputation as something of a buffoon to communicate with the people and their tribunes. He loves Coriolanus like a son, and the younger man almost breaks his heart when he sends him unheeded from the Volscian camp.

Tullus Aufidius (TUHL-uhs oh-FIHD-ee-uhs), the Volscian general and Coriolanus' great rival, who welcomes him as an ally when he appears at the Volscian camp. He comes to regret his decision when he finds the allegiance of his army transferred to the Roman who had defeated him each time they met on the battlefield. Coriolanus' submission to his mother enrages him, for he had hoped to march victorious through Rome. He conspires to have Coriolanus killed as a traitor to the Volscians; however, he pays tribute to the nobility of his adversary as he stands over his body at the end of the play.

Cominius (ko-MIHN-ee-uhs), a general of the Roman army, a man of dignity and wisdom who recognizes and praises the great gifts of Coriolanus, to whom he is devoted. He mourns his banishment and offers to accompany him into exile.

Virgilia (vehr-JIHL-ee-uh), Coriolanus' gentle wife, whom he calls "my gracious silence." She avoids her husband's public triumphs when she can, but she joins her mother-in-law at the Volscian camp to seek the salvation of Rome.

Sicinius Velutus (sih-SIHN-ee-uhs veh-LEW-tuhs) and

Junius Brutus (JEWN-yuhs BREW-tuhs), the tribunes of the people, possessive of their prerogative and fearful of the effects of Coriolanus' pride and power on those they represent. Disregarding the advice and the pleas of Menenius and Cominius, they initiate the popular uprising that results in the great soldier's banishment.

Titus Lartius (TI-tuhs LAHR-shuhs), another of the Roman generals.

Young Marcius, Coriolanus and Virgilia's son, who has inherited his father's intense, amoral valor.

Valeria (va-LIHR-ee-uh), a noble lady, Virgilia's sympathetic friend.

Nicanor (ni-KAY-nohr) and

Adrian (AY-dree-ehn), representatives, respectively, of the Romans and the Volscians. They meet between Rome and Antium and discuss the probable results of Coriolanus' banishment.

THE CORN IS GREEN

Author: Emlyn Williams (1905-1987)
First published: 1938
Genre: Drama

Locale: A remote village in Wales
Time: Late nineteenth century
Plot: Melodrama

Miss Lily Christabel Moffat, the founder of a school for miners' children in Wales. An unmarried, middle-aged Englishwoman, Miss Moffat is characterized by her direct, honest, and friendly manner. She is well-educated, well-read, intelligent, and tireless. Her unsentimental, businesslike approach to life makes her an anathema to the local squire, who, along with the other locals, opposes her idea of educating the illiterate children of the village. Miss Moffat wins over the community through her sincere concern and energetic devotion to the students, even manipulating the squire into supporting her efforts to win a scholarship to Oxford for Morgan Evans.

Morgan Evans, a young coal miner. Fifteen years old at the beginning of the play, Evans is the quick, impudent ringleader of the young miners who come to Miss Moffat's school. He proves himself to be an extraordinarily gifted student and becomes the focus of Miss Moffat's obsession with bettering the lot of the village children. His strong spirit rebels against Miss Moffat's strict control, and his career is almost ruined by a brief liaison with Bessie Watty.

Miss Ronberry, a Welsh gentlewoman of no particular occupation. Entrapped by her own ideas of the proper role of a woman, at the age of thirty Miss Ronberry is still seeking a husband from among the suitable male gentry, and her looks are becoming sharp and hard. Her genteel observance of class distinctions (as signaled by speaking English instead of Welsh), her sentimental view of life, and her traditional attitudes about women put her in the squire's camp, yet she is so overwhelmed by the strong will of Miss Moffat that she cannot refuse to become involved in teaching the children.

John Goronwy Jones, a churchgoing village handyman. Even though he claims to be saved by his religion, Jones remains gloomy, intense, and discontented. Born the son of a grocer, Jones has been educated at the local grammar school but still cannot surmount class distinctions, so that he belongs neither to the gentry nor to the working class. Even though he resents English domination of Wales and retains his native language, he responds eagerly to Miss Moffat's idea of a school and teaches the younger children.

The squire, an Englishman and the most prominent citizen of the village. A handsome gentleman of forty, the squire enjoys his social superiority and power over the lower classes (miners and women). He is deeply offended by Miss Moffat's ideas and manner and uses his influence to thwart Miss Moffat's school. In spite of his vanity and stubbornness, however, he is kind and generous. Miss Moffat cleverly appeals to his pride and wins his support.

Mrs. Watty, Miss Moffat's housekeeper, a middle-aged Cockney woman with an illegitimate daughter and a questionable past. She bustles about taking care of Miss Moffat with efficiency and kindness. She is an enthusiastic convert to The Militant Righteous Corps.

Bessie Watty, the fourteen-year-old illegitimate daughter of Mrs. Watty. Plump and pretty, Bessie aspires to be ladylike, without success. She loathes the country school life she is forced to lead and longs for her former tawdry London life. She seduces Morgan Evans, becomes pregnant, and is bought off by Miss Moffat.

— *Jean McConnell*

THE CORNERSTONE
(La Pierre Angulaire)

Author: Zoé Oldenbourg (1916-   )
First published: 1953
Genre: Novel

Locale: France and the Holy Land
Time: Early thirteenth century
Plot: Historical

Ansiau (ahn-see-OW), the old lord of Linnières in Champagne. Returning from the Crusades half-blind and ill, grieving for the son who died in the Holy Land, and troubled about his ungovernable illegitimate daughter, he finds that he no longer has the force to govern. He resigns his fief to his son Herbert and sets out on a pilgrimage to Acre and Jerusalem. Eventually, he becomes totally blind and thus especially vulnerable to the marauders in battle-torn southern France. His piety and his kindly nature win him the respect of strangers and the loyalty of three companions. Although he fails to locate his son's grave in Acre and falls into the hands of Muslims before he can reach Jerusalem, he is venerated by his captors as a holy man. He dies at peace with God.

Herbert le Gros (groh), Ansiau's son, the new lord of Linnières, a huge man with huge appetites. He is a wife abuser, a womanizer, and a glutton, but his primary interest is in acquiring land, money, and power. He values his son and heir, Haguenier, as someone who can help him achieve those goals, and he becomes furious whenever Haguenier fails to live up to his expectations. Although licentious, Herbert is calculating; only once does he lets his passions run away with him: By sleeping with his half sister, he risks criminal prosecution, damnation by God, and the disapproval of his mother. Although he is cursed both by her and by his rejected lover, the immediate cause of his death is his own brutality. When Herbert attacks his unfaithful wife, Haguenier fights against him, and Herbert's back is broken. Herbert forgives his son and is forgiven by his mother before he dies, but he also makes sure that the future is arranged as he wishes it to be.

Haguenier (ah-geh-NYAY), Herbert's son and heir, an idealistic nineteen-year-old who is particularly susceptible to women. After meeting Lady Marie de Mongenost, he decides to spend his life making her happy. His sympathy toward women causes him to defy his father, as when he balks at divorcing his wife. Tragically, by protecting his stepmother, he causes Herbert's death. Guilt-ridden, he accedes to his father's deathbed demands. Haguenier arranges the marriage of his infant daughter, turns over his property to his baby daughter's husband, and becomes a monk.

Lady Marie de Mongenost (mohn-geh-NOHST), a self-centered beauty who amuses herself by toying with men's affections. She sees the idealistic Haguenier as a perfect subject for her experiments in power, which are supposedly based on the tenets of courtly love. Her skill in deceiving Haguenier is shown by the fact that he orders his motherless daughter to be reared by Marie.

Eglantine (ehg-lahn-TEEN), Ansiau's illegitimate daughter. Her wildness is a continuous reproach to the father, who loves her dearly. By sleeping with her brother, she feels that she has confirmed her status as an outcast from the Christian community. His rejection leaves her completely isolated. She aborts her child and dedicates him to a pagan goddess, whom she thinks will help her to destroy Herbert. Eglantine's spells result in her own death. Believing that she has cursed the land, the peasants murder her.

Ernaut (ehr-NOH), the bastard son of Herbert by a peasant girl. He becomes one of Haguenier's best friends. Even though he has been knighted and given property by his father, because of his low birth Ernaut is refused the hand of the woman he loves. When she marries someone else, he hangs himself.

Lady Alis (ah-LEE), Ansiau's loving wife. A devout, strong-minded woman, she is respected and feared by her son, Herbert. Because of his dissolute lifestyle, she refuses to live in his castle. After learning about his affair with Eglantine, she curses him, an act she later regrets.

Auberi (oh-beh-REE), a twelve-year-old boy, Ansiau's servant. Although initially he bewails his lot, soon he is so devoted to his master that the Muslims who capture them think they are father and son. At Ansiau's insistence, he escapes and makes his way back to the Christian community

Riquet, a runaway monk who joins Ansiau on his pilgrimage. A strong, resourceful young man, he protects and provides for his companions. After staying behind to pursue a girl, he rejoins them in Marseilles and arranges for their passage to the Holy Land. Ansiau last sees him marching off into slavery.

Gaucelm of Castans (gow-SEHLM, kas-TAHN), also called **Bertrand**, a traveling companion of Ansiau, who has been blinded for a heresy he did not embrace. His wife and their daughters have been killed, so his only remaining hope is that his son has survived. When he finds the boy bent on martyrdom, Bertrand subsides into bitterness and despair. After he is captured, he courts death and is decapitated.

— Rosemary M. Canfield Reisman

CORONATION
(Coronación)

Author: José Donoso (1924-1996)
First published: 1957
Genre: Novel

Locale: Santiago de Chile and Valparaiso, Chile
Time: The 1950's
Plot: Social realism

Andrés Abalos (ahn-DREHS ah-BAH-lohs), the middle-aged, neurotic heir of a proud Chilean family now in decline. Rich and free of any strong familial ties or occupational obligations, he devotes himself to the reading of French history, his collection of walking sticks, and the avoidance of any type of emotional entanglement or commitment. His complacency changes to panic when he realizes that, after his grandmother's death, he will be left entirely alone, without any links to the past and no promise for the future. This psychological crisis is exacerbated by his growing obsession with the servant girl Estela, whom he sees as a symbol of youth and hope. His final humiliation at her hands leads him to accept madness as the only escape from a sordid, meaningless world.

Misiá Elisa Grey de Abalos (mee-see-AH eh-LEE-sah greh), Andrés' regal nonagenarian grandmother. Once known for her beauty and modesty, she now poisons the atmosphere of her household with the obscene delusions of her madness. Her sexual taunts and accusations insidiously compel Andrés to admit his attraction for Estela.

Estela (ehs-TEH-lah), a young peasant girl who is taken from her family to be the companion and nursemaid to Misiá Elisa. At first, submissive and uncomplaining, Estela seems overwhelmed by the big city of Santiago, until she meets and falls in love with Mario. She lies and steals for him to prove her love and, finally, must choose between blind devotion and self-respect. She is desired by Andrés and Mario; their passion for her forces each man to reevaluate the direction of his life.

Mario, Estela's lover. Young, handsome, and carefree, Mario is known for his dalliances with many women, but the innocence and adoration of Estela quickly break down his defenses. The promise of his life is darkened by the haunting fear that he will be unable to overcome the cycle of poverty and will be drawn into the criminality and despair of his brother René's world. This fear becomes reality when, trapped by circumstances seemingly beyond his control, he accepts the inevitable and joins with René. He agrees to the plot to rob the Abalos mansion even though it means betraying and humiliating Estela.

René (rreh-NEH), Mario's manipulative half brother. Always looking for his big opportunity and blaming everyone else for his failures, he leads a life that is a series of scams and petty frauds. He yearns to escape from a wife and family he despises so that he can enjoy himself, free from all responsibility. Envious of his brother, he deliberately tries to ruin Mario's future prospects and sets out to turn him against Estela.

Dora, René's pitiful wife, beaten down by the harshness of her life and the ridicule of René. The pathetic love she retains for her husband is her only hope.

Carlos, a doctor, Andrés' friend and confidant. He has sacrificed his ideals for money and reputation. His self-satisfied comparison of his full life to the vacuum of his friend's precipitates Andrés' psychological trauma.

Adriana (ah-dree-AH-nah), Carlos' wife. Disillusioned by her husband's constant infidelity, she has converted herself into the perfect wife and mother. This façade is her protection against any emotional participation.

Lourdes (LOOR-dehs), Estela's aunt and longtime servant to the Abalos family. Aging and without any life outside the mansion, she, along with Rosario, lives in the past and devotes herself to the care of her mistress, whom she considers a saint.

Rosario (rroh-SAHR-ee-oh), the longtime cook for the Abalos family. Her life also revolves around the gratification of any whim of Misiá Elisa and Misiá Elisa's grandson, Andrés, whom the servants still treat as a child.

— Charlene E. Suscavage

CORRECTION
(Korrektur)

Author: Thomas Bernhard (1931-1989)
First published: 1975
Genre: Novel

Locale: Altensam, an estate in Austria
Time: Early 1970's
Plot: Philosophical

The narrator, a sickly individual who is obsessed with reconstructing his friend Roithammer's unfinished literary work. He is a middle-aged, highly intellectual, and introspective individual plagued by chronic lung infections. The narrator becomes so involved with his late friend's life that he moves into his former apartment and seems to reach a similar point of suicidal despair.

Roithammer, the narrator's friend who has committed suicide. Roithammer was a brilliant intellectual and scholar whose wide-ranging interests included philosophy, mathematics, architecture, and modern music. For a time, he had been a promising student and tutor at the University of Cambridge. He returned, however, to his family estate of Altensam but was stifled by the petty and provincial atmosphere of the surrounding community. This sensitive and highly introspective man was considered an eccentric by the local people. When Roithammer received an inheritance from his father, he planned to design and construct a special round building for his beloved sister. She died soon after its completion.

Roithammer then spent a short time in England and returned to Altensam to write an account of his childhood and life in Altensam. He moved into a small attic apartment and worked on ever more succinct versions of his work. Unable to finish his work, he became increasingly depressed and committed suicide.

Höller, a taxidermist from whom Roithammer rents an attic apartment. He later rents it to the narrator and tells him about his friend's last weeks of life.

— *Thomas F. Barry*

CORREGIDORA

Author: Gayl Jones (1949-   )
First published: 1975
Genre: Novel

Locale: Lexington, Bracktown, and Versailles, Kentucky; Cincinnati, Ohio; and Brazil
Time: 1947-1969
Plot: Psychological realism

Ursa Corregidora, the narrator, a twenty-five-year-old blues singer at Happy's Café in a small town in central Kentucky. She is a beautiful, light-skinned black woman. Ursa must undergo a hysterectomy as a result of injuries sustained when her drunken husband pushed her down some steps; she was pregnant at the time. Her consequent inability to bear children ineffably traumatizes her: It makes her feel like less of a woman and also contributes to her sense of guilt that she is somehow failing the generations of women who were her ancestors, because the women in her family have always been told to "make generations" to bear witness to their former slavery under Corregidora, a Brazilian plantation master. Her despair at being the last of the line prolongs her recovery, and she apathetically allows herself to be taken care of by Tadpole, her boss at Happy's, whom she soon marries. Her indifference to him is exemplified in her inability to show love for him; later, she admits a resentment toward all men. Her deep-seated pain finds expression in her singing voice, now richer with the exquisite anguish she has experienced. When Tadpole reacts with the same jealousy as her first husband, Ursa leaves him to sing in another club, the Spider, where she is protected from the advances of men not only by a bodyguard but also by her now instinctive aversion to them. Twenty-two years later, still nursing a reserve of hatred toward him mixed with resignation, she reunites with her first husband.

Mutt Thomas, Ursa's first husband, for whom she feels a strong sexual attraction. He becomes increasingly hostile toward her as a result of jealousy: He wants her to sing only for him. In private, he uses sex as a weapon to punish her; in public, he threatens and embarrasses her. He feels guilty about the consequences of his violence and wants to make amends, waiting abjectly night after night outside the café because he has been forbidden entrance, but Ursa refuses to see him. He disappears for more than twenty years, showing up again at the

Spider to take Ursa home.

Tadpole McCormick, the owner of Happy's Café, who becomes Ursa's second husband. He is initially patient and loving to Ursa, solicitous of her physical and mental health. At first, her reticence in expressing affection does not bother him. He eventually runs out of patience at the lack of real intimacy in their relationship and turns for solace to a new teenage singer he has hired for the bar. Finally, he and Ursa are divorced.

Mama, Ursa's mother. An independent, close-mouthed woman, she has tried to discourage the young Ursa from singing the blues, calling it the devil's music. She relates much of the Corregidora background of lust, brutality, sadism, and incest, and she finally confides to the adult Ursa the sad story of her own tragic marriage.

Catherine (Cat) Lawson, a fortyish, attractive, worldly hairdresser and former maid who lives across the street from Happy's. She mothers Ursa and gives her perceptive advice. When Ursa discovers Cat's lesbianism, she retreats from their friendship, despite the older woman's attempts to explain herself. As a result, Cat moves back to her hometown, where she loses her hair in a factory accident.

Jeffrene (Jeffy), a fourteen-year-old lesbian who has an affair with Cat Lawson. When Jeffy tries to seduce Ursa in bed one night, Ursa knocks her to the floor in revulsion.

Jim, Mutt's cousin. He acts as Mutt's advocate to the wounded Ursa, who repels his pleas for a reconciliation. His reappearance at the end of the novel foreshadows Mutt's.

Corregidora, Ursa's incestuous great-grandfather, long dead at the time of the story. A psychosexually abusive Brazilian slaveholder, he rapes the women of Ursa's family, using his daughters to breed generations of slave women whom he prostitutes to other wealthy slaveowners.

— *Caren S. Silvester*

THE CORSICAN BROTHERS
(Les Frères corses)

Author: Alexandre Dumas, *père* (1802-1870)
First published: 1844
Genre: Novel

Locale: Corsica and Paris
Time: 1841
Plot: Adventure

Madame Savilia de Franchi (sa-vee-LYEEUH deh frahn-SHEE), the kind, indomitable, aristocratic Corsican hostess of the narrator. Although widowed and reduced to lesser means from former affluence, Madame de Franchi takes great pride in hospitality at her Sullacaro estate and is honored to have as a guest an eminent novelist. The mother of Siamese twins who had been separated successfully, she learns of her absent son's health through the report of the psychic twin at home. As a family, she explains, the de Franchis have had an interesting history; she and her husband, with guns kept prominently on display, managed to settle an ancient vendetta by killing simultaneously two enemy brothers. One son received from her his ability to fight and manage; the other was more scholarly and introspective. Gracious and dignified, she impresses the author as the epitome of Corsican traits.

Lucien de Franchi (lew-SYAHN), her outgoing sportsman son, who has remained with his mother to manage the family estate and provide for her welfare. Something of a diplomat, the hardy and handsome Lucien succeeds in settling another vendetta carried on for years between rival families living nearby. As the host of the author, Lucien takes his guest along to witness the truce, discusses his love of his native mountains, and displays his skill in hunting. He explains also that he and his brother Louis are completely devoted to each other in spite of their sharp differences in tastes, abilities, interests, and appearances—strange differences for identical twins who seem to share in part their nervous systems. Some months later in Paris, the loyal brother avenges the death of his scholarly twin. No vendetta results, but his vengeance is complete when he kills his antagonist in a duel, just as Louis had been killed. Only then is the young Corsican able to give vent to his grief for the loss of a part of himself.

Louis de Franchi (lwee), the scholarly twin, a somewhat effete young man who nevertheless possesses the feelings of pride and honor of his illustrious family. He also plays host to the narrator in Paris and reveals that he is distraught over a love affair, the reason why his brother Lucien has recently felt depressed. His deep love for Emelie, concealed from his good friend, her husband, forces him to defend her honor even though he knows the result will be his death. Hoping to conceal the truth from his mother and brother, he entrusts to his new friend a letter in which he says that he is suffering from a brain fever. The narrator acts as Louis' second in the duel. As he feared, Louis is killed. Lucien learns of the tragedy by intuition, for Louis died of a bullet wound below his sixth rib and Lucien carries the stigmata. In spite of the fact that Louis wished no more Corsican violence, his death is courageously avenged.

Emelie, the beautiful but unfaithful wife of a sea captain and the friend of Louis, in whose trust she is placed. Herself in love with a married man and beloved by her loyal friend, she resents the young man's intrusion into her intrigue. Being made the sport of the lover, she turns to Louis in order to save face.

M. de Chateau-Renaud (sha-TOH reh-NOH), Emelie's lover, who humiliates her at a supper party attended by the narrator and his Corsican friend. Having compelled Emelie to accompany him on a wager, he challenges her defender to a duel. He responds just as bravely to the challenge from the murdered man's brother, who kills him.

The narrator, **Alexandre Dumas**, the Corsican traveler. With all the romantic flamboyance of his nature, Dumas reveals himself as an admirer of the Corsican spirit, the pride of birth, family, country as well as independence, bravery, and loyalty. Purportedly recounting a historic tragedy, the narrator really embellishes a legend.

Orlandi (ohr-lahn-DEE), a Corsican bandit, and

Colonna (koh-lohn-NAH), the heads of two families whose vendetta was caused by a quarrel over a chicken. Lucien de Franchi is the mediator in settling the feud.

Griffo, the servant of Lucien de Franchi.

D———, the narrator's friend, the host at the supper party at which M. de Chateau-Renaud appears with Emelie.

COSMOS
(Kosmos)

Author: Witold Gombrowicz (1904-1969)
First published: 1965
Genre: Novel

Locale: Poland
Time: The 1960's
Plot: Philosophical realism

Witold (VEE-tohld), the narrator, a student from Warsaw who does not get along with his parents. He is obsessed with interpreting the random events and objects in his environment. He and a fellow student rent a room in the mountain resort of Zakopane in Poland as a place to study for their examinations. On their first day at the resort, they come across a dead sparrow that has been left hanging by a wire, and Witold ponders whether it is meant to be some kind of message or sign. They begin to discover what appear to be other signs or clues, including more objects left hanging. Witold is also fixated on the physical features of those around him (such as their hands) and grows obsessed with the mouths of two women who live in the rooming house. He becomes increasingly compelled to look for connections and links between events as if there were some kind of plot or mystery to be unraveled. He is never sure whether the objects they find really do have significance or he has merely interpreted them so. Witold begins to lose his control of reality and creates his own mystery by killing a cat and hanging it. He eventually finds the body of a man hanging in a tree.

Fuchs (fewks), a fellow student and friend of Witold. He often seems bored and vacant. He assists Witold in his efforts to resolve the mystery of the puzzling objects.

Kulka Wojtys (KEWL-kah VOY-tihsh), the somewhat plump housewife who rents a room to the two friends.

Leo Wojtys, Kulka's husband. He is a short, bald man who is a retired banker.

Lena, Kulka's daughter, an attractive woman with a virginal appearance. Witold is obsessed with her freshness and the innocent eroticism of her mouth. It is her cat that Witold throttles.

Louis, Lena's husband. He is tall, well built, and intelligent looking and has well-shaped hands. Witold finds him hanging in a group of trees, an apparent suicide.

Katasia (kah-TAH-syah), Kulka's poor relative who helps in the kitchen. She has a lip disfigurement that gives her a somewhat sensual and reptilian look. Witold becomes transfixed by the erotic suggestiveness of her mouth and lips.

— *Thomas F. Barry*

THE COSSACKS
(Kazaki)

Author: Leo Tolstoy (1828-1910)
First published: 1863
Genre: Novel

Locale: The Caucasus
Time: The nineteenth century
Plot: Psychological realism

Dmitri Andreyevitch Olyenin (dih-MIHT-rihy ahnd-RAY-ehv-ihch ohl-YEHN-ihn), a young man of noble birth attached to a Russian military company. Stationed in a Cossack village, Olyenin feels a strong sympathy for these wild and happy people so different from the effete, useless society that he knew at home. An idealistic young man, he lives in the home of a beautiful Cossack girl who is alternately affectionate and disdainful toward him. In his somewhat confused idealism, he at first believes that "happiness consists in living for others." He decides to renounce self and find happiness in the love of beautiful, proud Maryanka. Later, realizing the vast cultural gulf between them, he rides sadly out of the village, his going barely noticed by the young girl.

Maryanka (mah-rih-AHN-kuh), the attractive daughter of a Cossack ensign, a man of property and position in the village. The girl has no objection to a temporary connection with Olyenin, but he is unable to hold her affections for long because she loves Lukashka, a vigorous warrior. At the last, she drives Olyenin off with loathing and scorn. She is not to be won by a lover who is not a Cossack.

Lukashka (loo-KAHSH-kuh), the young Cossack who is to marry Maryanka if he can quit carousing long enough for the ceremony. During his infrequent leaves from guard duty, the brave Lukashka makes love to his mistress, pursues Maryanka intermittently, drinks vast quantities of wine in the village streets, and still manages to keep a clear head. He becomes a leader in his Cossack company when he kills the savage captain of a raiding mountaineer band. His reputation is enhanced after Olyenin generously gives him a horse, a real status symbol for the aspiring Cossack. As the novel ends, Lukashka lies badly wounded. Perhaps, unlike Uncle Yeroshka, he will not live to enjoy his fame as a bravo.

Uncle Yeroshka (yeh-ROHSH-kuh), an aged but still powerful Cossack. From Yeroshka's own lips, Olyenin learns of the hardy old man's feats as a warrior and a hunter. Like most of his countrymen, Uncle Yeroshka can drink great quantities of wine and vodka and is still able to hunt game all day after a night of drunkenness. Now about seventy, he becomes a good friend to young Olyenin and teaches him much about hunting wild game and ferocious mountaineers, who come out of the Caucasus to rob and kill.

Dame Ulitka (oo-LIHT-kuh), Maryanka's virago of a mother. At first she is rude to Olyenin, who is boarding in her home. She thinks of him as another Russian outsider until she learns that he is a wealthy nobleman.

Prince Byeletsky (bee-LEHT-skihy), "who believes in taking all the good the gods may give, and thus in a week's time becomes hail fellow well met with everyone in the stanitsa." A merry young man, this friend of Olyenin soon enjoys great popularity in the village.

Ensign Ilya Vasilyevitch (ihl-YAH vah-SIH-leh-vihch), Maryanka's father. A man of forty, he is passionately interested in acquiring money and property, even if he must use his brother to get them.

Vanyusha (vah-NEW-shuh), Olyenin's friend and servant. He never quite approves of the drunken Cossack life.

THE COUNT OF MONTE-CRISTO
(Le Comte de Monte-Cristo)

Author: Alexandre Dumas, *père* (1802-1870)
First published: 1844-1845
Genre: Novel

Locale: France
Time: The nineteenth century
Plot: Historical

Edmond Dantès (ehd-MOHN dahn-TEHS), a young man unjustly imprisoned in the grim Château D'If. He escapes fourteen years later, after he has learned where a vast fortune is amassed. He secures the fortune and assumes the title of Count of Monte-Cristo. He then sets about avenging himself on those who were instrumental in having him imprisoned.

M. Morrel, a merchant and shipowner, the friend of young Dantès, and the benefactor of Edmond's father. He is later saved by Monte-Cristo from bankruptcy and suicide.

M. Danglars (dahn-GLAR), an employee of M. Morrel. He helps to betray Edmond Dantès to the authorities because of professional jealousy. He later amasses a fortune, which Monte-Cristo causes him to lose. He is further punished by being allowed to starve almost to death as he had allowed Edmond's father to starve.

Mercédès (mehr-say-DEHZ), the betrothed of young Edmond Dantès. Believing him to be dead, she marries his rival, Fernand Mondego. In the end, she leaves her husband's house, gives his fortune to charity, and lives on the dowry Edmond had saved for her in his youth.

Louis Dantès (lwee), Edmond's father. He dies of starvation after his son is imprisoned.

Gaspard Caderousse (gahs-PAHR ka-deh-ROOS), a tailor, innkeeper, and thief. One of Edmond's betrayers, he is killed while robbing Monte-Cristo's house.

Fernand Mondego (mohn-deh-GOH), the count de Morcerf (mohr-SEHRF), a fisherman in love with Mercédès. He mails the letter that betrays Edmond to the authorities. He later marries Mercédès and becomes a soldier and a count. Monte-Cristo later brings about the revelation that Fernand got his fortune by selling out the pasha of Janina to the enemy. His wife and son leave him, and he commits suicide.

The Marquis de Saint-Méran (sahn-may-RAHN) and
The Marchioness de Saint-Méran, the father and mother of M. Villefort's first wife, poisoned by his second wife.

Renée (reh-NAY), the daughter of the marquis and marchioness de Saint-Méran. She marries Villefort.

M. Villefort (veel-FOHR), a deputy prosecutor, later attorney general, and a royalist. He causes Edmond to be imprisoned because he fears involvement in a Napoleonic plot. Monte-Cristo later discovers an attempted infanticide on the part of Villefort and causes this secret to be revealed publicly at a trial Villefort is conducting. After this public denunciation and the discovery that his second wife has poisoned several members of his household, her son, and herself, Villefort goes mad.

The Abbé Faria (fah-RYAH), Edmond's fellow prisoner, who dies of a stroke after educating Edmond and revealing to him the whereabouts of the vast lost fortune of the extinct family of Spada in the caverns of the isle of Monte-Cristo.

Emmanuel Herbaut (ehr-BOH), a clerk in Morrel's business establishment. He marries Julie Morrel.

Julie Morrel, the daughter of the merchant Morrel. She finds the purse in which Monte-Cristo had put money to repay the loan that Morrel had given his father, old Dantès, and thus saves her own father from bankruptcy. She later marries Emmanuel Herbaut.

Maximilian Morrel, the son of the merchant, a soldier and a loyal friend of Monte-Cristo. He marries Valentine de Villefort.

Viscount Albert de Morcerf (mohr-SEHRF), the son of Fernand and Mercédès. He leaves his disgraced father's house, gives his fortune to charity, and seeks his own fortune as a soldier.

Baron Franz d'Épinay (day-pee-NAY), the friend of Albert, about to be betrothed to Valentine de Villefort when the betrothal is called off after Franz discovers that her grandfather had killed his father.

Luigi Vampa (LWEE-jee VAHM-pah), a Roman bandit and friend of Monte-Cristo. He kidnaps Albert but frees him at Monte-Cristo's order. Later he also kidnaps Danglars, robs, and almost starves him.

Peppino (pay-pee-NOH), also known as **Rocca Priori** (roh-KAH pree-oh-REE), one of Vampa's band. Monte-Cristo saves him from being beheaded.

Countess Guiccioli (GWEET-choh-lee), the friend of Franz and Albert in Rome and later in Paris.

Giovanni Bertuccio (joh-VAHN-nee behr-TEWT-chyoh), the steward of Monte-Cristo, who reveals to his master Ville-fort's attempted infanticide. Unknown to Villefort, he saves the child's life.

Lucien Debray (lew-SYAHN deh-BRAY), a friend of Albert, secretary to the Internal Department, and the lover of Mme Danglars.

M. Beauchamp (boh-SHAHN), Albert's friend, a newspaper editor.

Count Château-Renaud (sha-TOH reh-NOH), another of Albert's friends.

Eugénie Danglars (ew-zhay-NEE), the daughter of Danglars, about to be betrothed, first to Albert, then to Andrea Cavalcanti. She later runs away with her governess to go on the stage.

Assunta (ah-sew-TAH), Bertuccio's sister-in-law. She claims Villefort's child from the foundling home where Bertuccio had placed it.

Benedetto (bay-nay-DAY-toh), also known as **Andrea Cavalcanti** (kah-vahl-KAN-tee-), the illegitimate son of Villefort and Mme Danglars. He does not know who his parents are, and they believe him to be dead. He is a forger, a thief escaped from the galleys, and the murderer of Caderousse. He discovers that Villefort is his father and reveals this fact at the trial. It is implied that the court will find "extenuating circumstances" in his new trial.

Haidée (eh-DAY), the daughter of Ali Tebelen, pasha of Janina and Basiliki, captured and sold as a slave by Fernand Mondego after he betrays her father. She is bought by Monte-Cristo, and they fall in love.

Baptistin (bah-tees-TAN), the servant of Monte-Cristo.

Hermine Danglars (ehr-MEEN), Danglars' wife and the mother of Benedetto and Eugénie.

Héloïse de Villefort (ay-loh-EEZ), the second wife of Villefort. She poisons the Saint-Mérans and tries to poison Noirtier and Valentine so that her son may inherit their vast wealth. Her guilt discovered, she kills her son and herself.

Edouard de Villefort (ay-DWAHR-), the spoiled, irresponsible son of Héloïse and Villefort. He is killed by his mother.

Valentine de Villefort (vah-lahn-TEEN), the daughter of Villefort and Renée Saint-Méran Villefort. She is poisoned by the second Mme Villefort but is saved by Noirtier and Monte-Cristo after being given a sleeping potion that makes her appear dead. After her rescue, she marries Maximilian Morrel.

Noirtier de Villefort (nwahr-TYAY), the father of Villefort and a fiery Jacobin of the French Revolution. Completely paralyzed by a stroke, he communicates with his eyes.

The Marquis Bartolomeo Cavalcanti (bahr-toh-loh-may-OH), the name assumed by a man pretending to be Andrea Cavalcanti's father.

Barrois (bah-RWAH), a faithful servant of old Noirtier, poisoned by drinking some lemonade intended for Noirtier.

Ali Tebelen (al-LEE- tayb-LAN), the father of Haidée, betrayed by Fernand.

Louise d'Armilly (dahr-mee-YEE), the governess to Eugénie Danglars. They run away together in hopes that they can go on the stage as singers.

Lord Wilmore and
Abbé Busoni (byoo-ZOH-nee), aliases used by the count of Monte-Cristo.

THE COUNTERFEITERS
(Les Faux-monnayeurs)

Author: André Gide (1869-1951)
First published: 1925
Genre: Novel

Locale: Paris, France
Time: Early 1920's
Plot: Psychological realism

Edouard (ay-DWAHR), a novelist who resembles André Gide. He is a close observer of and a commentator on the other characters and their actions, and he is a connecting link in their stories. He believes it is a person's duty to be himself regardless of consequences, though the difference between the real and the counterfeit self may sometimes be hard to discern. His interest in Olivier is homosexual but on a higher level than Passavant's.

Olivier Molinier (oh-lee-VYAY moh-lee-NYAY), his thoughtful, reserved nephew, jealous of Edouard's interest in Bernard, which he thinks is erotic. He temporarily falls under Passavant's malign influence but escapes. He attempts suicide but is revived by Edouard.

George Molinier, Olivier's younger brother, a passer of counterfeit coins. The coins are symbolic of the false selves that people reveal in society. Boris' shocking death has a sobering effect on him.

Vincent Molinier, Olivier's tall, handsome older brother, a friend of Passavant; Laura's lover and father of her child. He becomes insane after Lady Griffith's death, which he may have brought about.

Bernard Profitendieu (proh-fee-tahn-DYEW), Olivier's friend and Edouard's bold, unscrupulous, impudent secretary and disciple; an illegitimate son.

Laura Douviers (doo-VYAY), Edouard's friend and Vincent's discarded pregnant mistress, whom he met while both were patients in a sanatorium.

Felix Douviers, Laura's generous husband, willing to forgive her and accept the child as his own.

Comte Robert de Passavant (pah-sah-VAHN), a cynical libertine, homosexual, and dilettante writer. He symbolizes aristocratic decadence.

Armand Vedel (ahr-MAHN veh-DEHL), Laura's younger brother and Olivier's friend; he succeeds Olivier as editor of Passavant's journal and apparently as sexual partner also.

Rachel, Laura's older sister, manager of the Vedel School.

Sarah, Armand's submissive sister in whom Bernard is briefly interested sexually.

Lady Lillian Griffith, a friend of Passavant. She and Vincent elope to Africa, where she is drowned.

Albéric Profitendieu (ahl-bay-REEK), Bernard's foster father, a magistrate who is concerned about the counterfeiters' operations. He is disliked by Bernard, who runs away after discovering his illegitimacy.

La Pérouse (pay-ROOZ), an old music teacher, a friend of Edouard.

Boris, his young grandson. In a school initiation into boys' secret society, he shoots himself after a real pistol bullet has been substituted for a dummy.

The Vedels, Laura's family, close friends of Edouard's. They are symbols of bourgeois decadence.

Oscar Molinier, Edouard's brother-in-law, a magistrate.

Pauline, his wife, Edouard's unhappy half-sister.

THE COUNTERLIFE

Author: Philip Roth (1933-)
First published: 1986
Genre: Novel

Locale: New York City, New Jersey, Israel, and London
Time: 1978
Plot: Metafiction

Nathan Zuckerman, a Jewish writer based to some extent on the author. A tall, dark man in his mid-forties, he is the supposed author of the novel as well as a character in it. In the second of five chapters, he goes to Israel at the request of Carol, Henry's wife, who wants Nathan to convince Henry to return home. In chapter 4, he is impotent as a result of cardiac drugs, the same condition ascribed to Henry in chapter 1. The events of chapter 4 are background to earlier chapters. In chapter 4, Nathan meets Maria, who moves into his building with her husband and small daughter, Phoebe. Soon, they are engaged in an affair of sorts, with him giving her sexual satisfaction. He says that he wants to have a child with her, and she says that he desires this only because it is impossible. He turned down the chance to have children with his three former wives, all shiksas, like Maria. In this version of events, he has a coronary bypass operation and dies, like Henry did in chapter 1. In the concluding chapter, he is married to Maria, who is pregnant with his child; it is not clear whether he ever was

impotent or had the operation. He has just returned from seeing Henry in Israel. He says that he married Maria because he wanted to break away from his old life and his own examination of it. After arguing with Maria about anti-Semitism and Jewish identity, he realizes that living in England with her has made him more of a Jew.

Henry Zuckerman, Nathan's thirty-nine-year-old brother, a dentist. He is tall, with an athletic physique, and has dark good looks but is shy. The first chapter describes him as being impotent as a side effect of drugs he takes for a coronary condition. Years earlier, he had a brief affair with a woman named Maria, who returned to her home in Switzerland. He decides to have a coronary bypass operation so that he can stop taking the drugs and resume a sexual relationship with Wendy, his dental assistant. He dies during the operation. In chapter 2, Henry survives the operation and goes to Israel because he now feels his Jewish identity and believes that his life in New Jersey smothered it. He calls himself Hanoch and has become a follower of Mordecai Lippman, an Israeli extremist. In later chapters, Henry denies the events of chapter 1, and in chapter 4, it is Nathan who has the operation and dies. In that version of the story, Nathan has written a draft of the novel in which they are all characters. Henry finds the novel after Nathan's death, and he destroys part of it as well as pages out of Nathan's private journal so that no one will suspect him of being an adulterer.

Maria, a tall, charming, twenty-seven-year-old English-woman. In chapter 4, she meets Nathan in New York City and they have an affair while she is married to the political aide to the British ambassador at the United Nations. Nathan dies in that chapter, and she goes to his apartment one last time. She reads the final chapter of his novel in progress (Henry already having destroyed some earlier chapters). She claims that he distorted all the characters except her daughter, Phoebe. Maria leaves the book intact, even though she is identifiable in it and it mentions their affair. She detests the women in history who destroyed great writers' letters and memoirs, and she thinks that the book perhaps will be her salvation by leading to a divorce. In the final chapter, she has been married to Nathan for four months, and she is pregnant with his child. They have moved to England because Maria's former husband threatened to sue for custody of his daughter, Phoebe, if he was not allowed to exercise visitation rights conveniently. Maria and Nathan fight after Nathan meets her family and discovers its members' anti-Semitism. They argue about English anti-Semitism in general and Jews' need to keep proclaiming their identity. She writes a note to Nathan saying that she is leaving him and his book, explicitly recognizing herself as a character in the book and criticizing him for killing both his brother and himself.

Mordecai Lippman, an ardent Israeli settler. He has wide-set eyes and a smashed nose, and his leg was mangled in the 1967 Six-Day War. He has white hair even though he is not much older than fifty. Lippman hates Shuki Elchanan for pandering to the ideas of Westerners and believes that Jews should never give ground. He thinks there will be a purging of Jews in America.

Shuki Elchanan, a friend of Nathan. They met on Nathan's previous trip to Israel, in 1960. Shuki lost his hearing in one ear and sight in one eye during the Yom Kippur War. Shuki wants Israel to sign a peace treaty with the Arabs and believes that Mordecai Lippman is a gangster. Knowing that Nathan uses his own life and experiences as material for books, he warns Nathan not to become wrapped up in Lippman's comic possibilities and write about him, because that would help Lippman spread his ideas.

Jimmy Ben-Joseph, a tall, young Israeli who dreams of being a baseball player. He meets Nathan in Israel, at the Wailing Wall, and follows Nathan onto the plane as Nathan leaves the country. He tells Nathan that he intends to hijack the plane and shows him a note demanding closure of Jerusalem's Holocaust memorial; he believes that Jews need to live for the present. After admitting that his hijacking story was a joke and stating admiration of Nathan for standing up to him, he shows a grenade. Security officers attack and beat him, as well as detaining Nathan as a suspected accomplice.

— *A. J. Sobczak*

THE COUNTESS CATHLEEN

Author: William Butler Yeats (1865-1939)
First published: 1892
Genre: Drama

Locale: Ireland
Time: Indeterminate
Plot: Allegory

Countess Cathleen, an Irish noblewoman who has been away from home for many years. In a time of famine, she has returned to her castle, seeking shelter within its walls from the evils of the outer world. Her desire to retreat is undermined by repeated encounters with the starving peasantry, whose pleas for assistance cause her to empty her purse before she can rediscover the lost way to her castle. She resists the urging of her poet-lover Aleel to retreat yet further, embracing instead her duty to her dependents. Concluding that no place is safe from the world, she vows to open her castle to those in need and to empty her treasury to supply them with food. When even this plan is foiled by the theft of her treasury, she is tempted to personal despair but continues to assert publicly that God will provide. Her sense of duty ultimately brings her to imperil her own soul by offering it to the devils in exchange for money enough to feed the poor and the return of all the souls previously purchased; her Christlike acceptance of responsibility for the sins of others results in a similarly Christlike ascent into heaven.

Aleel, the poet-lover of the Countess Cathleen, who accompanies her to lighten her burden with his music and his stories of fairyland. He is fiercely protective of her, quarreling with Oona and nearly fighting with Shemus when they interrupt his efforts to distract Cathleen. His most successful effort tells the story of a mortal who died from unrequited love for the queen of the fairies; now, he says, she weeps not because she has realized his love too late, but because he was so unimportant that she no longer remembers his name. This is Aleel's fear for himself, and it seems to come true when Cathleen dismisses him from her company to find the peace he urges for her. He wanders the woods forlorn, freely offering his soul to the devils because it can do him no good, but he is refused because he already has given his soul away. As a poet, Aleel experiences numerous visions of a higher reality. Even though he is at heart a pagan, he is granted a final transcendent vision of the battle between angels and demons and of Cathleen's ascent into heaven.

Oona, Cathleen's childhood nurse and adult companion. She shares Aleel's fierce loyalty to her mistress but is too preoccupied with the concerns of the world to distract her effectively. Oona forces her mistress' recognition of the castle when they finally reach it, and it is she who discovers that the treasury has been robbed. She lacks the imagination to comprehend Aleel's visions, concerning herself with Cathleen's physical comfort more than her emotional state. She remains with the countess but is kept from knowledge of Cathleen's decision to sell her soul until it is too late. Her lifelong charge taken from her, Oona provides a final note of sorrow, bemoaning Cathleen's loss even though reassured that her mistress is in heaven.

Shemus Rua, a rough and materialistic peasant, so beset by the famine that he no longer believes in anything. He is unsuccessful both in hunting and in begging for food, and he curses the world for his state. Desperation makes him ungrateful for Cathleen's aid, and the need to assert himself drives him to beat his wife and to call on supernatural forces in which he only half believes. Because he does not believe in the soul, he has no compunction about selling his, and he finds a kind of joy in despair when he does so, becoming a willing lieutenant in the scheme to buy other souls.

Mary Rua, another peasant, whose values are more conventionally Christian than her husband's. She resists compromise with the evil of the times, insisting on proper gratitude to the Countess Cathleen and a holy respect for the supernatural. She will have no dealings with the demons, preferring to subsist on weeds rather than eat what is provided by their money. She dies in her bed, having preserved her soul at the expense of her body.

The demons, who disguise themselves as merchants, although many people have seen them in the form of human-faced owls and similar monsters. They will commit any dishonest act to further their goal of acquiring the souls of the desperate. They particularly value the immaculate soul of Cathleen.

— *A. Waller Hastings*

THE COUNTESS DE CHARNY
(La Comtesse de Charny)

Author: Alexandre Dumas, *père* (1802-1870)
First published: 1853-1855
Genre: Novel

Locale: France
Time: 1791
Plot: Historical

Countess Andrée de Charny (ahn-DRAY deh shahr-NEE), the wife of Count Olivier de Charny. As a young girl, she was raped by a peasant who later becomes Dr. Gilbert; as a result, she bore a son, Sebastian. Fearful lest her early misfortune become known to her beloved husband, she maintains a distant marriage relationship that mystifies him. When her secret is finally revealed by Dr. Gilbert himself, husband and wife are happily united.

Dr. Gilbert (zheel-BEHR), Louis XVI's physician and trusted friend. As a humble peasant, years before, he had attacked a young woman, later to become Countess Andrée de Charny. As Dr. Gilbert, he seeks to expiate his crime by deeds of charity.

Count Olivier de Charny (oh-lee-VYAY), an aide to King Louis XVI and devoted to the cause of the monarchy. He is the husband of Countess Andrée de Charny.

Sebastian (seh-bas-TYAHN), the illegitimate son of the Countess Andrée de Charny and Dr. Gilbert.

Louis XVI, king of France.

Marie Antoinette (ahn-twah-NEHT), queen of France.

The Marquis de Favras (fah-VRAH), a trusted aide of Louis XVI.

Count Alessandro di Cagliostro (ah-leh-SAN-droh dee kah-glee-OH-stroh), or **Joseph Balsamo** (zhoh-ZEHF bahl-sah-MOH), an Italian adventurer involved in the intrigues surrounding Louis XVI and Marie Antoinette.

Gamain (gah-MAN), locksmith to Louis XVI.

Honoré Mirabeau (oh-noh-RAY mee-rah-BOH), a French statesman with revolutionary sympathies with whom Dr. Gilbert advises Louis XVI to join forces.

The Marquis de Bouille (boo-YEH), a French general involved in the abortive plan for the escape of Louis XVI.

M. de Malden (mahl-DAHN) and

The Marquis de Choiseul (shwah-ZOHL), a trusted nobleman in the cause of Louis XVI.

Jean Drouet (zhahn droo-AY), a revolutionary patriot who informs the nationalist troops of the attempted escape of Louis XVI.

THE COUNTRY DOCTOR
(Le Médecin de campagne)

Author: Honoré de Balzac (1799-1850)
First published: 1833
Genre: Novel

Locale: Southern France
Time: Early nineteenth century
Plot: Naturalism

Dr. Benassis (beh-nah-SEE), the self-appointed godfather to a remote and dying mountain village, where he revitalizes the economy and administers to physical and spiritual needs. A hundred years ahead of his time, the benevolent despot removes a dying line of cretins, imposes a regimen of self-sacrifice and good works on village officials, and surrounds himself with vital workers who in eight years carry out a reform program of health and welfare. He devotes his life to anony-

mous good works because of heavy burdens on his conscience: a lost fortune, the betrayal of a loved one who died, and the loss of his son by his mistress. As a doctor, he practices psychology and even recognizes the psychosomatic bases of many illnesses. As a mayor, he genially dispenses the village's wealth as well as his own in order to make the helpless self-sufficient. His death leaves the populace devastated but inspired.

Colonel Pierre Joseph Genestas (zheh-nehs-TAHS), one of Napoleon's finest soldiers, who has seen the political tide go against him and who comes to see the doctor for a purpose. Posing as a Captain Bluteau, the colonel observes the physician on his rounds of mercy and administration before asking him to care for his foster child, a sixteen-year-old weakling. Knowing the old man to be sublime, he vows to return to the village and carry on the doctor's good works in appreciation of his son's recovery.

Adrien (ah-DRYAHN), his adopted son, the child of an army officer and a Polish Jewess, who has ruined his health through his intensive study and lack of exercise. A sensitive, beautiful child, Adrien responds splendidly to the doctor's prescriptions: a milk diet and hardy exercise in hunting and mountain climbing. More fortunate than a young consumptive, Jacques, Adrien recovers fully, but the other boy dies shortly after his benefactor's death. Adrien, deeply appreciating the efforts of his foster father and the doctor, returns kindness for kindness.

La Fosseuse (foh-SEWZ), the ward of the doctor, who has been despised and rejected by society for her inability to work or produce. The beautiful young girl, a kind of poetess of nature, after a very sad childhood is cared for by the aging doctor.

Jacquotte (zhah-KOHT), the doctor's faithful servant and housekeeper.

Curé Janvier (zhahn-VYAY), the enlightened village priest.

A COUNTRY DOCTOR

Author: Sarah Orne Jewett (1849-1909)
First published: 1884
Genre: Novel

Locale: Oldfields, Maine
Time: Mid-nineteenth century
Plot: Bildungsroman

Nan Prince, a young girl who wants to become a doctor. As a child, she is mischievous but likes to care for animals. She assists the local doctor, who rears her after her mother's and grandmother's deaths. The girl attends medical school, despite pressure from her relatives and her suitor. Upon completing her medical education, she returns to the town to assist the doctor and eventually to take over his practice.

Adeline Thacher Prince, Nan's mother. She returns home to Oldfields to die, bringing her infant daughter. She is a wild, rebellious woman who reputedly is addicted to drink. She resents her husband's family because they opposed her marriage.

Mrs. Thacher, Nan's maternal grandmother, who cares for the child until her own death.

Dr. Leslie, the doctor in Oldfields. He looks after Nan and rears her in his own home after her grandmother's death. He encourages her study of medicine.

Miss Nancy Prince, a wealthy spinster, Nan's aunt. She is shocked at Nan's seemingly unladylike ambition to be a doctor and tries to dissuade the girl from studying medicine. She also tries to interest Nan in a young man, George Gerry, in hopes that Nan will marry and abandon her ambition to practice medicine.

George Gerry, a young friend of Miss Nancy Prince. He and Nan fall in love, as Nan's aunt hopes, but George cannot persuade Nan to marry him and abandon medicine.

THE COUNTRY GIRLS TRILOGY AND EPILOGUE

Author: Edna O'Brien (1930-   )
First published: 1986
Genre: Novels

Locale: Rural Ireland, Dublin, and England
Time: 1930's-1960's
Plot: Psychological realism

The Country Girls, 1960

Caithleen (Kate) Brady, a young Irish country girl. At the age of fourteen, Kate finds romance in the person of Mr. Gentleman. That year, however, her mother dies, and Kate finds herself homeless. Kate spends three relatively happy years at a convent school after winning a scholarship to go there. When she is expelled, she loses her chance to attend college. Instead, with her friend Baba, she goes to Dublin, where she works in a grocery store. When Mr. Gentleman breaks off their love affair, Kate thinks her life is over.

Bridget "Baba" Brennan, a pretty, spoiled young woman. As a child, she uses Kate as a target for her cruelty; at the convent, she finds Kate to be a useful confidante and confederate. Selfishly, Baba decides to get Kate, as well as herself, expelled so that the two of them can move to Dublin. In Dublin, she enrolls in a business course, but she is really interested only in men and what she can get out of them. After contracting tuberculosis, Baba leaves for a sanatorium.

Mrs. Brady (Mama), Kate's mother, a loving, devout woman. When she learns that her husband is about to lose the farm, she goes out to borrow money. On her way home, she is accidentally drowned.

Mr. Brady (Dada), Kate's father, an irresponsible, abusive drunkard. He sells his property to pay his debts.

Jacques de Maurier, called **Mr. Gentleman**, a wealthy, middle-aged French solicitor. After courting Kate for years, he breaks off with her without ever consummating their relationship.

Martha Brennan, Baba's mother, an attractive woman who is bored with her husband. She amuses herself by drinking and flirting. Martha is kind to Kate, giving her a home after the death of her mother.

Mr. Brennan, Baba's father, a veterinarian. He sometimes hints to Kate that he wishes Baba were more like her. When Kate's father hits her, Mr. Brennan throws him out of the house.

The Lonely Girl, 1962

Caithleen (Kate) Brady, , who, after two years in Dublin, meets Eugene Gaillard. Dragged home by her father, Kate escapes and goes to live with Gaillard at his country house. When her father's second attempt to reclaim her fails, Kate settles in, pretending to be Gaillard's wife. The lovers quarrel constantly. Finally, Kate leaves Gaillard and moves to London.

Girls in Their Married Bliss, 1964

Bridget "Baba" Brennan Durack, who is now living in London with her husband. Over his protests, she keeps going to Kate's rescue. When she finds herself pregnant after a one-night stand, Baba turns to Kate for advice, tells Frank, and has the baby.

Frank Durack, Baba's husband, a wealthy contractor. He sees the unstable Kate as the real danger to his marriage and social standing. He has to face the fact that his wife is pregnant by another man. He agrees to accept the child as his but takes refuge in alcohol.

Caithleen (Kate) Brady, who became pregnant during a second involvement with Gaillard. They were married. The

Epilogue, 1986

Bridget "Baba" Brennan Durack, who during the past twenty years has had a daughter and seen her turn out as defiant as her mother. Baba has never been faithful to Frank, but since his stroke, she has nursed him devotedly. After being out of touch for many years, she and Kate again became friends. Baba is fulfilling her final obligation

Eugene Gaillard, a film director who is separated from his wife. Though charmed by Kate's youth and innocence, Gaillard is too controlled not to be annoyed by her emotional outbursts. He is also concerned about his wife's threats to deny him future contacts with their daughter. When Kate leaves, he does not pursue her.

marriage, however, is a failure. Kate has an affair, Gaillard finds out, and she leaves him, taking their son, Cash. Emotionally fragile, she lives for Cash. After Gaillard takes him away, she has herself sterilized so that she will have no more children.

Eugene Gaillard, Kate's husband. Although he loves Cash, he hates Kate bitterly. To get him away from his mother, he snatches Cash from school and takes him to Fiji.

Cash Gaillard, the son of Kate and Eugene Gaillard, a pawn in the conflict between them.

Maura, a young girl employed by the Gaillards who takes Kate's place. She goes to Fiji with Eugene and Cash.

to her friend, taking her in a casket to be buried.

Caithleen (Kate) Brady Gaillard, who won her legal battle to have Cash returned to England but lost him again when he went to Harvard. After being rejected by another married man, she killed herself.

— Rosemary M. Canfield Reisman

THE COUNTRY HOUSE

Author: John Galsworthy (1867-1933)
First published: 1907
Genre: Novel

Locale: England
Time: Early twentieth century
Plot: Social

Horace Pendyce, a British landholder of the late nineteenth century whose conservative opinions represent promulgation of traditional social attitudes and actions. When his son seeks his fortune at race tracks and, furthermore, is named in a divorce action, Pendyce feels his world slipping away from him. His efficient but unobtrusive wife takes the situation in hand, however, and after extricating her son from his involvement with a married woman, she persuades the injured husband to drop his divorce suit naming young Pendyce. Aristocratic tradition is again secure, and life at the country estate of Worsted Skeynes becomes serene once more.

Margery Pendyce, Horace's wife. She takes prompt action when her husband threatens to disinherit their son for not arranging his social affairs to his father's liking. She leaves Horace, takes her son George in hand in London, and persuades a husband not to press proceedings in a divorce action in which the husband has named her son.

George Pendyce, the irresponsible heir to Worsted Skeynes, the Pendyce country estate. Unconventional, he refuses to conform to the sort of behavior society expects of him. Helen Bellew and his gambling indebtedness create problems that distress his conservative father.

Mrs. Helen Bellew, a rash young woman, judged by the standards of late nineteenth century English country society.

She falls in love with George Pendyce when she is not divorced from her husband, of whom she has grown tired. She tires of George, too, and tells his mother so. Her conduct, generally, is a portent, Galsworthy implies, of the role English women of the future will assume.

The Reverend Hussell Barter, a typical parish rector of the era. His views are ultra-conservative, and his opinions appreciably influence the direction society takes. When he discovers George and Helen kissing at a social affair, he considers it his duty to inform the husband. He is a stanch defender of traditional morality.

Captain Jaspar Bellew, Helen's husband, who does not love her. He initiates divorce proceedings because his pride has been injured, but he is persuaded by Mrs. Pendyce to drop the action.

Gregory Vigil, Helen's cousin and guardian, who himself is in love with her. Despite advice to the contrary, he attempts to start divorce action on behalf of his ward. Captain Bellew, at last aware of his wife's flirtatious ways, begins proceedings before Vigil can act.

Edmund Paramor, Vigil's lawyer, who advises him not to start the divorce action, primarily because it would cause social embarrassment.

THE COUNTRY OF THE POINTED FIRS

Author: Sarah Orne Jewett (1849-1909)
First published: 1896
Genre: Novel

Locale: The seacoast of Maine
Time: Late nineteenth century
Plot: Social realism

The Boarder, a woman writer who comes to Dunnet Landing, Maine, to work in seclusion. Here she meets many people and finds friendly, interesting characters.

Mrs. Almira Todd, a friendly widow who accepts the writer as a boarder. She is also an herb doctor, growing herbs in her garden and searching out others in the fields.

Captain Littlepage, an elderly, retired sea captain who tells the writer a yarn about his own shipwreck and a town of ghosts near the North Pole, where souls await their passage to the next world.

Mrs. Blackett, Mrs. Todd's aged mother. She lives on an island with her son William and does her own housework.

William Blackett, Mrs. Todd's brother, a bashful man. He loves Esther Hight and finally is able to marry her when he is in his fifties.

Mrs. Fosdick, a friend of Mrs. Todd. She comes often to visit with her friend and to tell stories about the local folk.

Mr. Tilley, an old fisherman. He is reserved with strangers, but he accepts the writer as a friend and shows her the house he has kept for eight years the same as it was when his wife died.

Esther Hight, a woman loved by William Blackett. She supports herself and her elderly mother by tending sheep. After her mother's death, she is free to marry William.

COUNTRY PLACE

Author: Ann Petry (1908-1997)
First published: 1947
Genre: Novel

Locale: Lennox, Connecticut
Time: Post-World War II
Plot: Social realism

Johnnie Roane, the protagonist, a young man who returns home from World War II with idealized expectations of a happy reunion with his wife, Glory, and a happy return to his hometown, Lennox. A sensitive and artistic man, Johnnie has squelched dreams of becoming an artist and moving to New York in order to keep Glory. His long-distance deification of Glory helped him to endure the war.

Mrs. Bertha Laughton Gramby, the wealthiest woman in town. Her advanced years, fortune, and race have granted her status as an icon in the predominantly white town. A living embodiment of New England tradition, Mrs. Gramby blindly idealizes the past. Her status as a widow has compelled her to subordinate her son Mearns's youthful ambitions and marital prospects in order to keep him in Lennox, yet she is disappointed by his later lack of ambition and his poor choice of Lil as a bride. His marriage, in middle age, will bear no heirs to the Gramby estate.

Glory Roane, Johnnie's beautiful and promiscuous young wife. She lives in a state of illusion, spurred by fantasies drawn from films and by fear of the realities she will face. Discovering her pleasure at the independence she acquires after Johnnie's departure, Glory is reluctant to succumb to the boredom and drudgery of domestic duties, turning instead to the glamour she finds at her job at Perkins' store, where she receives much attention from the men in town.

Lillian Gramby, a woman whose hawklike appearance denotes her hunger for wealth as a means of obtaining security and status. As Glory's mother, she worked as a seamstress to rear her daughter alone. After Glory's marriage, Lil, a manipulative and class-conscious woman, plots to marry Mearns Gramby, the town's most eligible bachelor. To her growing resentment and dismay, Lil discovers that the marriage is not what she had expected. Unable to find status and prestige as Lil Gramby, Lil temporarily finds refuge in an affair with Ed Barrell. She ends the relationship when she finds that she receives no benefit other than sexual relations, which she detests.

The Weasel, an observant, meddlesome outsider to Lennox. His malevolent manipulations of the townspeople's affairs lead to violence and upheaval. The Weasel speaks for Lennox as a representation of the ugly truths hidden beneath the town's tranquil surface; the Weasel gleefully brings these truths to light.

Pop Fraser, the town's pharmacist. He presents a compassionate point of view regarding Lennox. Pop justifies his status as storyteller with his intimate, detailed knowledge of the townsfolk, his customers. He claims to be able to tell them what they loved and what they hated, what they hoped for and what they feared, although he hastens to admit to an inherent prejudice against women.

— Michele Mock-Murton

THE COUNTRY WIFE

Author: William Wycherley (1641?-1715)
First published: 1675
Genre: Drama

Locale: London, England
Time: The seventeenth century
Plot: Comedy

Mr. Horner, a man with a reputation for lewdness. Newly returned from France, he finds an excellent method of duping unsuspecting husbands. With the aid of a quack, he

spreads the fictitious information that he is no longer sexually potent. Foolish husbands, needing someone to escort and amuse their wives, invite the clever Mr. Horner to their homes.

In this way, he finds his way to the bedchambers of many high-born ladies who no longer have to fear the tarnishing of their reputations if they associate with a man because this one is impotent.

Mr. Pinchwife, who, like Sparkish and Sir Jasper Fidget, is a cuckold who helps to bring about the very thing he fears most, the seduction of his naïve wife. He is right when he says that cuckolds are generally the makers of their own misfortune. Dour, humorless, and exceedingly jealous, he takes every precaution to keep his wife from falling into the predatory hands of Horner. Foolishly, he is the very instrument that brings about this event.

Mrs. Margery Pinchwife, his country wife. She is little aware of London's pleasures until she is informed of them inadvertently by her husband. Little by little, she loses some of her innocence until, finally, she meets Horner. After this brief interlude, she learns what a dullard her husband is. Cleverly, she manages to send a love letter, carried by her unsuspecting husband, to Horner.

Mr. Sparkish, a boring idiot who desires, more than anything else, to be a wit. He is called "a bubble, a coward, a senseless idiot" and is outraged. Credulously, he is duped by all he meets, always feeling, however, that he is a wit, even to the very end.

Sir Jasper Fidget, the husband of Lady Fidget. Almost the equal of Sparkish in stupidity, he unsuspectingly begs Horner to be an escort for Lady Fidget. Even when he is in the next room from the lovers, he is unaware that his wife and Horner are doing anything other than looking for china plates.

Lady Fidget, a woman who wants to protect her reputation for virtue at all costs. In public, she raves about her chastity; in private, however, she tells bawdy jokes, drinks wine, and, in her boudoir, finds the indefatigable Horner a delightful and stimulating companion.

Alithea, a comely young woman, the sister of Pinchwife and the mistress of Sparkish. At first, she remains true to her witless lover. Later, however, she finds Harcourt a much more interesting person.

Mr. Harcourt, a friend of Horner. Clever and somewhat unscrupulous, he gulls the would-be-wit, Sparkish, by pretending to be a good and faithful friend.

Lucy, Alithea's maid, who is clever enough to help Mrs. Pinchwife meet Horner. At the end of the play, she convinces Pinchwife and Sir Jasper that there has been no intrigue between their wives and Horner.

Mrs. Dainty Fidget, who, like Lady Fidget, is infatuated with Horner, particularly when she can associate with him without endangering her reputation.

Mrs. Squeamish, another of the many women surrounding Horner. In the end, she learns, as do the others, that she must share him with several women.

A quack, through whose professional status Horner is able to convince the gulls of his impotency. The quack helps him by spreading this information through the city. He is amazed when the scheme works so well.

Mr. Dorilant, Horner's friend and a man about town. During Horner's dalliance with Mrs. Pinchwife, Dorilant shows considerable interest in Lucy.

THE COUP

Author: John Updike (1932-   )
First published: 1978
Genre: Novel

Locale: Kush, a fictional African country; and Franchise, Wisconsin
Time: 1973, with flashbacks to 1954-1958
Plot: Political

Colonel Hakim Félix Ellelloû (hah-KEEM fay-LEE ehl-lay-LEW), the forty-year-old, self-effacing president of Kush, a sub-Saharan African state. After the 1968 coup against French colonial authorities, he became minister of defense, then president after the assassination of his predecessor. Previously, as a student at conservative McCarthy College in Wisconsin, he had his strict Muslim Marxist beliefs confirmed by what he considered to be capitalist greed and consumerism. He has brought back Candace from the United States but keeps her muffled in purdah. Having visited his people in disguise, he blames their poverty on corrupt King Edumu. A purist, he has the king tried and executed, hoping that rains will then come to the arid desert and end a five-year famine. He is hostile to imperialists of both the United States and Russia; he believes they would subvert Kush's peanut and cattle culture as surely as Arabs, centuries before, sold West Africans into slavery. He is equally hard on himself and considers his humiliation in the tasteless, bourgeois Bad Quarters well-deserved, especially because the rains soon follow. He agrees to be exiled in southern France and to leave Kush to its fate.

King Edumu IV (ay-DEW-mew), a blind, old rebel against French colonialism. He supports Ellelloû's political rise be-

cause he respects the colonel's love for Kush. He is imprisoned and finally decapitated for failing to end his people's poverty and considering trade with the West.

Donald Gibbs, a U.S. official trying to insinuate American influence into Kush affairs by offering crates of processed, famous-brand cereals. When a stack of these is set afire, he dies like a martyr at its pinnacle.

Angelica Gibbs, Donald's wife. She hardly remembers his name but comes to claim his ashes. Refusing to return to a wintry climate, she offers herself to Ezana, who has replaced Ellelloû.

Klipspringer, a State Department representative who has no real knowledge of nor interest in Kush.

Colonel Sirin, the strict head of a Soviet intercontinental ballistic missile site in the desert. His underground bunker is decorated in czarist comfort.

Michaelis Ezana (mihk-AY-lihs ay-ZAH-nah), a former minister of the interior in Kush. Infatuated with Western materialism, he is eager to make financial deals with the World Bank or any wealthy foreign country. He betrays the nomadic desert economy by helping to build an industrial city and an oil refinery along the Libyan border. He weds the widowed Angelica Gibbs.

Dorfû (DOHR-few), a young opportunist who, in conspiracy with Ezana, organizes the coup against Ellelloû. Originally, he was an underling, a police guard whose sole function was to read the Koran to the blind king. He evacuates the inhabitants of the small villages, now zoned for agribusiness.

Kutunda (kew-TEWN-da), an impoverished companion to a company of traveling well-diggers. After briefly serving as Ellelloû's mistress, she joins the coup against him. Her greed makes her a bloodthirsty minister of the interior. She becomes sister-mistress of Dorfû.

Sheba (SHEE-bah), the childlike, petite fourth wife of Ellelloû. She joins him in the caravan heading toward Libya. In a constant dreamlike state, she plays music to overcome the desert delirium but disappears at the end of their quest.

Kadongolimi (kah-dohn-goh-LEE-mee), the earthy first wife of Ellelloû, fat as a queen termite. Her age allows her to mother Ellelloû and temper his rigorous views with common sense. She dies after he is overthrown.

Candace (Candy) Cunningham, Ellelloû's second wife, who rebelled against her Wisconsinite father's racism. In her desire to prove herself to be a liberated woman, she spends several years in Ellelloû's harem, completely shrouded. There she develops a robust coarseness but is not insensitive to his feelings of a mission failed when she finally leaves him to return to the United States.

Sittina (siht-TEE-nah), the sophisticated third wife of Ellelloû. Educated in Alabama, she is a dress designer and semiprofessional painter. The wife most compatible with the larger world of art that transcends power struggles, she accompanies Ellelloû when he goes into exile in France.

Mr. Cunningham, Candace's father, who would like to see all "undesirables" placed in concentration camps.

— Leonard Casper

COUP DE GRÂCE
(Le Coup de grâce)

Author: Marguerite Yourcenar (Marguerite de Crayencour, 1903-1987)
First published: 1939
Genre: Novel

Locale: Kratovitsy, a Baltic estate
Time: The years following World War I and the Russian Revolution
Plot: Existentialism

Erick von Lhomond (loh-MOHN) a Prussian soldier who fought with the White Russians against the Bolsheviks during the Russian civil war. He later became a soldier of fortune, engaged in civil conflicts in central Europe, the Chaco, Manchuria, and Spain. Tall, lean, blue-eyed, and tanned, he retains his youthful elegance at forty, his age when he narrates the story of his relationship with Conrad and Sophie de Reval twenty years earlier. His narrative begins when he returns to Kratovitsy, his boyhood home, after his training as a White Russian soldier. When he returns, he lives on an old, overrun estate that belongs to the de Reval family: Conrad de Reval; his retarded, unmarried aunt; a gardener; and Conrad's sister, Sophie. He had lived with the family before, when he was sixteen years old. During that idyllic time on the estate, which was like paradise, Erick and Conrad became best friends. Since that time, Erick's overriding passion has been his love for Conrad. He is indifferent to other people and to political causes and believes that this detachment is the primary reason for his effectiveness as a soldier. He is cold and detached, "morally impotent." When Sophie, Conrad's sister, falls in love with him, his unspoken love for Conrad dooms this relationship to a tragic denouement. After Conrad's death, Erick's rightist political affiliation forces a mortal confrontation with Sophie, who joined the Reds when she realized Erick's feelings for her brother. Erick's emotional and moral detachment determines the outcome of their final meeting.

Conrad de Reval (reh-VAHL), a young Prussian aristocrat engaged in the cause of the White Russians during the Russian Revolution. He is physically very much like Erick, but his hair is fairer. He combines poetic sensitivity and boyish shyness with daredevil courage. It is his ardent desire to be a writer like Rainer Maria Rilke, but his main occupation in the novel is that of a soldier fighting on the side of the Whites against the Reds. Conrad's primary importance in the novel is that he is a passive catalyst in Erick and Sophie's story. It is Erick's and Sophie's separate and individual love for Conrad that is at the center of their own ambiguous and tragic relationship.

Sophie de Reval, a young Prussian aristocrat who, dressed as a boy, fights with the Reds during the Russian Revolution. She is a romantic figure who possesses strange, wild grace. She is possessed by an obsessive love for Erick and is unaware that his feelings for her brother go beyond friendship. She is confused by his behavior toward her and mistakes his friendship for romantic love. When he rebuffs her, she enters into a series of sexual liaisons, and when she finally realizes that it is Conrad whom Erick loves, she is driven to flee her home and family and join the Reds. When Erick sees her for the last time, she has been taken prisoner by the Whites. She has been fighting for the Reds disguised as a boy, and in masculine garb she looks remarkably like Conrad. When Erick is ordered to execute Sophie, he is forced to confront his own feelings for both the brother and the sister.

Volkmar, a soldier fighting for the White Russian cause. He is Erick's rival. He is in love with Sophie, and Erick has never liked him. After Erick rejects Sophie's romantic advances, she becomes involved with Volkmar. Erick reacts violently to her public displays of affection for Volkmar, and these reactions mislead Sophie to believe that Erick is in love with her.

Gregory Loew, a Jewish bookstore clerk who also was in love with Sophie. He enables her to flee her home in Kratovitsy and join the Reds by lending her his clothes, in which she disguises herself as a man.

— Anne Callahan

COUPLES

Author: John Updike (1932-   )
First published: 1968
Genre: Novel

Locale: Tarbox, Massachusetts
Time: 1963-1964
Plot: Social morality

Piet Hanema (peet), a builder and partner in the firm of Gallagher and Hanema, Real Estate and Contracting. A muscular, restless, red-headed, thirty-four-year-old Korean War veteran whose Dutch parents died in an auto accident, he worries about damnation and the aimlessness of his life. An insomniac and a womanizer, he has dreams that are often morbid, and his lusty heterosexuality is a subversive influence on the other Tarbox couples. Hired by Ken and Foxy Whitman to repair their house, he becomes the pregnant woman's lover and later impregnates her himself. After others find out about Foxy's subsequent abortion, Piet separates from his wife, marries Foxy, and moves to San Diego.

Angela Hanema, Piet's wife, a kindergarten teacher. A sweet, serene, stately thirty-four-year-old with tiny feet and a dolphinlike body, the angelic Angela has a bland, languid opacity that makes her somewhat boring and frigid. She is shaken out of her comfortable domesticity by the consequences of her husband's infidelities. She agrees to sleep with Freddy Thorne as payment for his arranging Foxy's abortion. In return, Piet agrees to let her start psychotherapy. After divorcing Piet, she becomes a full-time teacher and invites her father to move in with her and her two daughters.

Ruth Hanema, the eldest daughter of Piet and Angela. A placid, stoic nine-year-old whose bedroom decorations include pictures of Jacqueline Kennedy, Queen Elizabeth, the Beatles, and a naked Nigerian bride, she thinks most people are "retardates" and is the object of subtle parental neglect of her emotional needs. Piet sees her as a burgeoning replica of his wife.

Nancy Hanema, the youngest daughter of Piet and Angela. A thumb-sucking worrier, she is obsessed with her own negative self-image and the demise of her hamster, the First Family's infant, and various wild animals whose carcasses she comes upon. Her insecurities mirror Piet's fears about mortality and God's mysterious ways.

Elizabeth "Foxy" Whitman, the wife of Ken and lover of Piet. A vain, amber-eyed, five-foot, nine-inch Radcliffe graduate from Maryland, she is in her late twenties and trapped in a cold marriage. Somewhat of a tart, she is seen as bitchy and manipulative by those envious of her. Her habits can be slovenly, as evidenced by accumulation of unwashed dishes and her use of a piece of dry bacon as a bookmark. After her abortion and estrangement from Ken, she goes to the Virgin Islands, awaiting Piet's decision whether to marry her.

Ken Whitman, a thirty-two-year-old research biologist interested in starfish and photosynthesis. He is a sullen, self-righteous man with icy eyes, a zombielike personality, a grimacing mouth, and hair beginning to gray at the temples. Unhappy in mid-career, he fears that Jewish and Asian colleagues are more brilliant and original. Incapable of deep feelings toward his wife or son, he demands a divorce after finding out about Foxy's affair and abortion. Although he hates Piet, he expresses the hope that Piet will marry Foxy. At the end of the book, he takes up with Janet Appleby.

Constance Fox Roth, Foxy's mother. A jolly, divorced busybody, generally well preserved, she is partial to her poodle, cocktail dresses, and red-tipped filter cigarettes. She likes being called Connie and bears little resemblance to the mother Foxy remembers from childhood. Visiting her daughter and grandson, she is not shocked by Foxy's marital problems but urges her to hold on to Ken.

Freddy Thorne, a dentist and spiritual guru of the Tarbox couples. A plump, bald, unathletic cynic with soft, clammy skin, a sickly mouth, and a green toenail, he has a dentist's preoccupation with decay, an appetite for dirty truths, and a conspiratorial distrust of others' intentions. Although he is androgynous, he collects Japanese erotica and is working on a pornographic play. His revenge for Piet's sleeping with his wife is a night with Angela, whom he has long found alluring in a rather nonsexual way.

Georgene Thorne, Freddy's wife and Piet's first lover. A short, healthy-looking banker's daughter with a narrow nose, green eyes, a freckled chin, and graying hair, she is a practical, sporting woman (good at tennis) who makes the best of a dreary marriage. Angry at finding Piet with Foxy after the abortion, she jealously informs Ken of his cuckoldry. When her loss of Piet's companionship proves irrevocable, she becomes closer to her children, Whitney and Martha.

Matt Gallagher, Piet's partner. Matt is a straitlaced, judgmental Irish Catholic whose opaque morality makes him critical of Piet's affairs. Prim and proper, he is unadventurous and unethical, preferring dull rectitude to joyous spirituality. Disdainful of those who attend the Thornes' party on the night of John F. Kennedy's assassination, he advises Piet not to leave Angela for Foxy.

Terry Gallagher, Matt's wife. A tall, willowy, long-haired woman with a Celtic appearance, she dabbles with pottery and the lute. Amiable and amoral, she has an affair with a sculptor and tells Ken Whitman that he should try to save his marriage now that he has a son.

Roger Guerin, a wealthy businessman and frequent golf partner of Piet. Swarthy and dark-browed, with an incongruously small mouth, he has an inheritance that allows him to use his office primarily as a place from which to arrange luncheon and squash dates. Uncomfortable with women and having suppressed homosexual tendencies, he draws closer to his wife, Bea, after suffering a sudden financial setback.

Bea Guerin, Roger's wife. A small, barren woman, she is competitive on the tennis court, flirtatious when drunk at parties, and malicious toward imagined rivals. She gives other women little affectionate pats and allows men to get rough with her in bed. After Piet slaps her, she admits that her husband has done the same thing and that Eddie Constantine has twisted her wrists. She finally finds joy by adopting a black child, thereby integrating Tarbox.

Frank Appleby, a trust officer in a bank. A florid Harvard University graduate and Shakespeare buff with a bilious smile and an ulcer, he sees life as a series of investments. He takes up with Marcia Smith and, realizing that his wife is similarly engaged with Marcia's husband, suggests that the two men switch bedrooms during a ski trip. The two couples become so close that others call them the Applesmiths.

Janet Appleby, Frank's wife, a petulant, plump-faced, big-breasted daughter of a Buffalo businessman, with an addiction to sleeping pills. She fears that others find her common and uncultured, and she vacillates between self-conscious modesty and voluptuous displays. She initiates an affair with Harold Smith after convincing him of their spouses' affair, and she finds a measure of self-confidence from twice-weekly therapy sessions. Attracted to Ken Whitman, she offers her body to him after Foxy leaves Tarbox.

Harold Smith, a thirty-eight-year-old broker. A political reactionary, he is a Princeton University graduate who dances adroitly, enjoys classical music, and uses French expressions to emphasize points, almost as a linguistic tic. Orderly, private, and sexually experienced from frequent liaisons with call girls during business trips, he finds his trysts with Janet Appleby a lively addition to his weekly routine.

Marcia Smith, Harold's thirty-six-year-old wife, the black-haired daughter of a psychiatrist whose brittle personality alternates between a nervous corruptibility and a fragile cheerfulness.

Eddie Constantine, an airline pilot. A crude, perverse, beer-drinking, fast-driving teller of dirty jokes, he has an adolescent, macho personality that perhaps disguises homosexual feelings toward Ben Saltz. After he and Ben purchase a boat, the two couples become so close that they are called the Saltines.

Carol Constantine, Eddie's wife. A lithe, hip, thin-waisted painter of Greek ancestry, she dyes her hair orange and occasionally displays a cruel streak. As Piet's final lover before he settles down with Foxy, she proves to be an ardent sexual partner.

Ben Saltz, an aerospace engineer on the Mariner Venus probe. A doleful, bearded Jew with a rabbinical demeanor, he has an eclectic mind and a ponderous manner. His experiment in hedonism with the Constantines ends with his losing his job.

Somewhat ostracized as a result, he takes a new position in Cleveland, Ohio.

Irene Saltz, Ben's wife and head of the Tarbox Fair Housing Committee. An earnest, efficient do-gooder whose causes range from conservation to civil rights, she likes bird-watching and arguing with right-wingers, and she rails against vestiges of anti-Semitism in Tarbox. Having battled with school authorities over the staging of a Christmas pageant, she almost wins election to the school board.

John Ong, a Korean-born nuclear scientist employed at the Massachusetts Institute of Technology. A small, sober, bony, smiling man whose dainty tennis strokes contrast with his acumen at chess, he speaks with an accent barely comprehensible to the other Tarbox couples.

Bernadette Ong, John's wife. A gregarious and somewhat exotic woman of Japanese and Portuguese ancestry, she enjoys the company of the other Tarbox couples but is somewhat of an outsider.

Dan Mills, the proprietor of the Tarbox boatyard. A dissolute, alcoholic World War II veteran, he once presided over the boatyard crowd until they fell out of fashion and scattered. With his business going bankrupt, he separates from his wife and moves to Florida. His tranquil daughter Merissa becomes the Hanemas' baby-sitter.

The Reverend Horace Pedrick, the pastor of Tarbox Congregational Church. A hairy-eared, skeletal sixty-year-old whose sentiments never stray far from money, he is less a holy man than a pitiful ignoramus. When lightning incinerates his church, Pedrick's first reaction is to inquire how much the repairs will cost.

Leon Jazinski, a construction foreman for Gallagher and Hanema. A smug Pole from New Hampshire without subtlety or respect for tradition, Leon is an ambitious social climber. His pontifications are as unprofound as his professional work is unaesthetic. Ultimately replacing Piet as Gallagher's junior partner, he moves with his wife to a more stylish abode and becomes a Unitarian.

— *James B. Lane*

THE COURTESAN
(La cortigiana)

Author: Pietro Aretino (1492-1556)
First published: 1534
Genre: Drama

Locale: Rome, Italy
Time: Early sixteenth century
Plot: Satire

Messer Maco (MAH-koh), a wealthy fool who is in Rome to become a cardinal. He is deluded into the notion that he must first become a courtier.

Maestro Andrea (ahn-DRAY-ah), a charlatan. Hoping to fleece Messer Maco, he promises to transform him into a courtier and gives him lessons in blaspheming, gambling, slandering, and related arts.

Signor Parabolano (pah-rah-boh-LAH-noh), a nobleman enamored of the virtuous matron Livia.

Valerio (vah-LEH-ree-oh), Parabolano's loyal chamberlain, who defends his master against the jeers of the groom Rosso.

Rosso (ROHS-soh), Parabolano's groom, a rascal and the sworn enemy of Valerio. He plots to pander to his master's lust, win his favor, and thus take revenge on Valerio.

Alvigia (ahl-VEE-jee-ah), a procuress in league with Rosso to secure Livia for Parabolano.

Togna (TOH-nyah), a baker's wife substituted for the inaccessible Livia in a nocturnal assignation with Parabolano. She steals away to the tryst in her husband's clothes.

Arcolano (ahr-koh-LAH-noh), a baker, the husband of Togna. He catches his wife in her disguise and follows her, dressed in her clothes, to the house of the procuress, where Parabolano discovers the ruse.

Livia (LEE-vee-ah), a virtuous matron and the object of Parabolano's lust.

Camilla (kah-MEEL-lah), a courtesan beloved by Messer Maco and used by Andrea to make a fool of him.

THE COURTSHIP OF MILES STANDISH

Author: Henry Wadsworth Longfellow (1807-1882)
First published: 1858
Genre: Poetry

Locale: Plymouth, Massachusetts, and its environs
Time: 1620-1621
Plot: Sentimental

Miles Standish, a captain and protector of Plymouth against the Indians. He is short, broad-shouldered, muscular, and middle-aged; his manners are rough but he is kind. His ancestors were English gentry, and he has led soldiers in notable battles. His favorite author is Julius Caesar. His wife has died, and he wishes to wed Priscilla. Because he believes that he lacks the skill with words to ask her to marry, he begs his friend John Alden, in the name of their friendship, to do so for him. When John reports that Priscilla prefers him to Standish, the captain is enraged and charges John with betrayal. His rage continues at the village council meeting, at which he answers an Indian challenge; he then marches out with his soldiers to fight the Indians. After he sees their crafty preparations for an ambush and hears the Indians' taunts, he kills one warrior (Pecksuot), leads his men to victory, and brings the head of another Indian back to Plymouth, to the joy of the townspeople. Months later, he is reported killed by an Indian poisoned arrow, but after John and Priscilla are married, he returns, asks John's forgiveness, and makes a gallant and sincere speech to Priscilla, one worthy of an English gentleman.

John Alden, a fair, blue-eyed scholar, the youngest person to have come to America on the *Mayflower*. He is a pious man, a writer, and a composer of fanciful phrases, and he is silently in love with Priscilla. When Standish asks him to propose to Priscilla on his behalf, John is dismayed, but in the name of their friendship, he agrees. He makes an eloquent appeal, but Priscilla tells him to speak for himself. When Standish becomes enraged that Priscilla prefers John, the pious John is tormented by guilt for betraying his friend. He believes that God is angry with him and decides to leave Plymouth on the *Mayflower*, which is preparing to sail from Plymouth Rock. As he is about to get on board, he sees Priscilla in the crowd and suddenly has a revelation that he cannot leave her. He and Priscilla agree to be friends. In the months that follow, John builds a house and becomes closer and closer to Priscilla, so close that when he hears of Standish's death, he proclaims that

the restraint imposed by their friendship is over. He and Priscilla are married. When Standish appears, all are reconciled.

Priscilla, a modest, sweet, patient, and strong young woman who works industriously at her spinning. Because her parents and brother have died, she is lonely and dreams of returning to England. When John communicates Standish's proposal, she is stunned and rejects it, saying that Standish's warlike virtues do not attract her. She then implies that John himself might be accepted. When she sees that John did not sail on the *Mayflower*, she seeks him out and asks forgiveness for her frankness. She tells him that because women are supposed to be silent, they often go through life in mute pain. She explains that she could not be silent and proposes that they be friends. When she hears the report of Standish's death, she willingly weds John Alden and then accepts the returned Standish's gallant compliments. She rides to Alden's house through the streets of Plymouth on the back of a white bull.

The Elder of Plymouth, a white-haired old religious man. At the village council, he advocates peace with the Indians. Later, he blesses the marriage.

The Magistrate, the chief secular official of Plymouth, who presides at the wedding.

The Master of the Mayflower, an impatient man who is glad to sail away from the poor town of Plymouth and all of its preaching.

Pecksuot, an Indian warrior at the encampment, seemingly friendly but actually treacherous. His boasts and insults provoke Miles Standish into stabbing him fatally.

Wattawamat, an Indian warrior at the encampment who also is treacherous. He boasts elaborately of his epic birth and is killed by gunshot in the melee that follows Pecksuot's stabbing. Standish takes his head back to Plymouth.

Hobomok, an Indian friendly to the people of Plymouth who acts as interpreter.

— *George Soule*

COUSIN BAZILIO
(O primo Basílio)

Author: José Maria Eça de Queiróz (1845-1900)
First published: 1878
Genre: Novel

Locale: Lisbon, Portugal
Time: The 1870's
Plot: Satire

Luiza (lew-EE-sah), the blonde, beautiful wife of Jorge. During Jorge's prolonged absence, she has an affair with her cousin Bazilio. When she discovers that her maid has stolen some of their love notes and letters, she wants to escape to Paris with him. She refuses at first to accept money from Bazilio to pay off Juliana. To keep Juliana from revealing her secret, Luiza grants Juliana her every wish, even to the point of doing her work for her. Luiza's love for Bazilio turns to hate, and she longs for Jorge's return. The strains of hiding her affair and dealing with Juliana's constant demands break her health.

In desperation, she writes to Bazilio to send her money so she can extricate herself from the intolerable situation. Before she receives a reply from him, however, Jorge returns. After Luiza recovers from a long illness precipitated by Juliana's death, Jorge confronts her with Bazilio's reply to her letter, causing her sudden relapse and death from brain fever.

Jorge (HOHR-heh), Luiza's devoted and rather conventional husband, a government mining engineer. He has accepted an extended assignment in the Alentejo, a mining region in southern Portugal. After his return, Juliana's behavior infuriates him, and he wants Luiza to fire her. He is consumed with jealousy when he intercepts Bazilio's letter to Luiza and realizes that she might have been unfaithful to him. He nurses her back to health from one fever, only to cause her final collapse by demanding an explanation for the contents of Bazilio's letter.

Bazilio de Brito (bah-SEE-lee-oh deh BREE-toh), Luiza's wealthy, handsome, and worldly cousin. He carefully orchestrates Luiza's seduction and rents a seedy room for their rendezvous. When Luiza threatens to end their affair because he has become inconsiderate and indifferent, he cynically introduces her to new sexual sensations to change her mind. He contrives to leave the country immediately after Luiza runs to him with the news of Juliana's knowledge of their romance. His answer to her written request for hush money is intercepted by Jorge. Upon his return to Lisbon, he hopes to resume his liaison with Luiza. The news of her death, however, does not grieve him. He only regrets that his current mistress has not accompanied him to Lisbon.

Juliana Conceiro Tavira (hew-lee-AH-nah kohn-SA-roh tah-VEE-rah), Luiza's ugly, ailing, bitter, and manipulative maid. She steals incriminating notes and letters from Luiza in the hope of extorting enough money from her for a comfortable retirement. The prospect of extracting a large sum is dashed by Bazilio's departure, so she elects to demand favors of Luiza. After Luiza has given her everything she wants, Juliana refuses to work. When Jorge demands that she be fired, she forces Luiza to fire Joanna, the cook, instead. Enraged by

Sebastian forcing her to surrender Luiza's letters, she dies of a heart attack.

Sebastian, Jorge's best friend from childhood. He suspects Luiza's romance with Bazilio. When Luiza requests that he deal with Juliana for her, he retrieves the stolen letters and never betrays Luiza's trust in him.

Leopoldina (leh-oh-pohl-DEE-nah), Luiza's unhappily married school friend. Jorge has forbidden Luiza to see her because of her bad reputation. She fascinates Luiza with tales about her many lovers.

Ernestinho Ledesma (ehr-nehs-TEEN-oh leh-DEHS-mah), a playwright and cousin of Jorge. In the original version of his successful play about adultery, the wife is killed by the offended husband. When Ernestinho complains about being forced to change the ending so that the unfaithful wife is forgiven, Jorge insists vehemently that an unfaithful wife should be killed.

Juliao Zuzarte (hew-lee-OW sew-ZAHR-teh), a dour physician friend of Jorge. He attends Luiza in her final illness.

Joanna, Luiza's loyal cook. She returns to serve Luiza after Juliana's death.

Felicidade de Noronha (feh-LEE-see-dahd deh nohr-OHN-ah), a buxom, heavyset lady who is a friend of Jorge and Luiza. She has never married, although her infatuation with Councilor Accacio has never diminished.

Councilor Accacio (ah-KAH-see-oh), an old-fashioned, dignified bachelor and a friend of Jorge's father.

— *Evelyn Toft*

COUSIN BETTE
(La Cousine Bette)

Author: Honoré de Balzac (1799-1850)
First published: 1846
Genre: Novel

Locale: Paris, France
Time: Early nineteenth century
Plot: Social realism

Baron Hector Hulot d'Ervy (ehk-TOHR ew-LOH dehr-VEE), a councilor of state, an officer of the Legion of Honor, and a hopeless profligate whose rise in government circles has been accompanied by a series of scandals bringing distress to members of his family. After some years of happy married life, he turned from his beautiful, devoted wife and began to associate with the most notorious courtesans in Paris; now he is incorrigible. Not only does he dissipate the family fortune in his gradual degradation, but he also sullies the family honor and causes the deaths of his honorable brother and his wife's uncle as the result of unwise speculations and the misappropriation of state funds. His great charm, wit, and good manners go for nothing finally; when he returns to his family, he seduces a kitchen maid and marries her after his wife's sudden death. Within the course of the novel, his conquests number six—an actress, a singer, the wife of a vile traducer, two young girls, and the peasant whom he finally marries.

Baroness Adeline Hulot (ahd-LEEN), née **Adeline Fischer**, Baron Hulot's devoted, long-suffering wife. In spite of her husband's many offenses, she trusts in God and the mystery of His ways. She maintains her dignity under compromising circumstances, even to the extent of enlisting the aid of one

of her husband's mistresses at a time of crisis. Her final blow is her discovery that her husband has promised to make a kitchen servant a baroness as soon as his ailing wife dies. The shock kills her.

Lisbeth Fischer (leez-BEHT), called **Cousin Bette**, the cousin of Baroness Hulot and the family old maid. Although envious of her cousin's place in the world, she hides her avariciousness and resentment so well that the Hulots often turn to her for comfort in times of trouble. Although she insists that she is proud of her independence and financial security as an employee of a firm of embroiderers, she is nevertheless a lonely person, and she takes as her lover a talented young Polish sculptor, Count Wenceslas Steinbock, whom she has saved from suicide. When Steinbock falls in love with Adeline's daughter, charming Hortense Hulot, and marries her, Cousin Bette plans a subtle revenge. Her malice leads her to introduce Steinbock and Baron Hulot to her friend Madame Valérie Marneffe. Her plan succeeds when both men become infatuated with that beautiful but heartless woman. Though her spite and scheming are undone in the end, Adeline and Hortense are never aware of the plot she has set in motion to destroy their happiness, and she remains good-hearted Cousin Bette, the family eccentric.

Victorin Hulot (veek-toh-RAN), the son of Baron Hulot and his wife. His father's escapades and disgrace turn Victorin into a man of responsibility and integrity, and he rebuilds the family fortune.

Célestin Hulot (seh-lehs-TA[N]), the wife of Victorin Hulot and the daughter of Monsieur Crével, a wealthy retired perfumer.

Monsieur Crével (kray-VEHL), a wealthy man who admires and imitates the manners of Napoleon. Smarting because Baron Hulot has stolen his mistress, he attempts to seduce Adeline Hulot but is repulsed. Later, he disrupts the marriage that has been arranged between Hortense Hulot and Counselor Lebas when he reports that Baron Hulot will not be able to give his daughter a proper dowry. Through Cousin Bette, he also meets Valérie Marneffe and becomes the Baron's rival for the coquette's charms. He marries Valérie after her husband's death, but his happiness as the husband of so charming a woman is short-lived; he and his wife die a short time later of a mysterious disease.

Valérie Marneffe (vah-lay-REE mahr-NEHF), the illegitimate daughter of a marshal of France and the wife of an obscure government clerk. Unfaithful to her husband, she is as famous for her infidelities as she is for her beauty. At first a pawn in Cousin Bette's scheme to be revenged on the Hulot family, she soon takes matters into her own hands and cleverly plays one lover against another, as when she informs Baron Hulot, Steinbock, Crével, and her cuckold husband that each is the father of the unborn child whose real father is the dashing Baron Montès Montejanos. After the deaths of her stillborn child and her husband, she marries Crével; her scheme is to inherit the retired perfumer's fortune and then marry Montejanos. Not aware of her intentions and wildly jealous, Montejanos apparently causes the death of the Crévels by infecting them with a loathsome and incurable tropical disease.

Monsieur Marneffe, a minor government clerk. An acquiescent cuckold, he never interferes in his wife's affairs, but he is not above using her infidelities to advance himself in his work. His death leaves her free to marry a wealthy widower.

Baron Montès Montejanos (moh[n]-TEHS moh[n]-teh-zhah-NOH), a gallant Brazilian nobleman, the only man Valérie Marneffe truly loves. Not knowing that she hopes to secure a fortune by marrying Crével, he is greatly disconcerted on hearing the news and swears revenge against Valérie for her supposed infidelity to him.

Le Maréchal Hulot (mah-ray-shahl), Baron Hulot's older brother, a man of distinguished military service and great personal honor. Cousin Bette gains his confidence and becomes his housekeeper. A short time later, the banns for their marriage are published. Although the government scandal involving his brother is hushed up, the old man insists on making restitution by paying his entire fortune into the state treasury. He then takes to his bed and dies three days later. His death is a blow to Cousin Bette, for it is the indirect result of her own intrigue involving Baron Hulot and Valérie Marneffe, and it ends her hope of outranking through marriage her Cousin Adeline's position in society.

Johann Fischer (zhoh-AHN), Adeline Hulot's uncle and her husband's accomplice in his scheme to defraud the government. Arrested for his dishonest activities, Fischer commits suicide.

Josepha (zhoh-zeh-FAH), a singer at the Opera and at one time Crével's mistress. When Baron Hulot takes the beautiful young Jewess away from him, Crével tries to seduce the baron's wife.

Dr. Bianchon (byah[n]-SHON), the physician who attends the Crévels during their fatal illness.

Agathe Piquetard (ah-GAHT pee-keh-TAHR), the kitchen maid whom Baron Hulot marries after his wife's death.

Counselor Lebas (leh-BAH), a lawyer at one time betrothed to Hortense Hulot. To get revenge on the Hulots, Crével causes the engagement to be broken off when he tells Lebas that the baron cannot supply an adequate marriage portion for his daughter.

Carabine (ka-rah-BEEN), the demimondaine at whose intimate supper party Baron Montès Montejanos learns Valérie Marneffe is to marry Crével.

COUSIN PONS
(Le Cousin Pons)

Author: Honoré de Balzac (1799-1850)
First published: 1847
Genre: Novel

Locale: Paris, France
Time: The 1840's
Plot: Naturalism

Sylvain Pons (seel-VAN pohns), usually called **Cousin Pons** but sometimes referred to as "The Parasite," an elderly musician whose twin passions are art and food. Born ugly, with a massive head and a huge nose, he was at one time a composer of popular songs and several operas; he now makes a modest living as an orchestra conductor and music teacher. He dresses shabbily and constantly dines out at the tables of his distant relatives in order to save money for the purchase of new objects for his valuable art collection. Naïve, greedy in his love of food, perfectly harmless, and shyly affectionate, he plans to leave his collection to Cécile Camusot, the daughter of a cousin-in-law once removed. Denied his relatives' house after he proposes an unfortunate match for his favorite, he takes to his bed, never to recover. While dying, he learns the

ways of the world. He tries to thwart his selfish relatives and grasping housekeeper by making a false will leaving his entire collection to the state, with a provision that Schmucke, his only true friend, will receive from the government a lifetime pension. His plans fail because Schmucke, who by another will is his only heir, innocently allows himself to be defrauded of his inheritance. A brilliant collector and amateur art connoisseur, Cousin Pons is the victim of a campaign carried on by his doctor, a rascally lawyer, his relatives, his housekeeper, and a rival art collector.

Herr Schmucke (shmewk), a pianist, the only close friend of Cousin Pons. Unselfish in his devotion, he becomes the victim of the greedy Camusots, who, bringing a suit to break their relative's will, break the old musician's spirit also and put him in his grave. Schmucke possesses such delicacy of manner and personal integrity that he will not fight to claim the fortune that is rightfully his.

Monsieur Camusot de Marville (kah-mew-zoh deh marh-VEEL), Cousin Pons's cousin-in-law and one of the presiding judges of the Royal Court of Justice in Paris, who has added the name of the family estate to his own in order to distinguish him from his father. A just man, he is ungenerous in his treatment of his distant relative only because his wife, who detests Cousin Pons, blames the old musician for their daughter's loss of a suitor. He willingly joins in the plan to get possession of Pons's estate because it will provide a handsome dowry for the daughter and add considerably to the family fortune. He is one of the few who understands the true nature of Cousin Pons, and on one occasion he attempts to effect a reconciliation after his wife, daughter, and servant have insulted the elderly musician.

Madame Amélie Camusot de Marville (ah-may-LEE), an ambitious, socially proud woman who receives Cousin Pons at her table with great reluctance. During one of his calls, she and her daughter plead a previous engagement and insultingly tell him that he will be compelled to dine alone. Her attitude toward the old man softens somewhat when Cousin Pons introduces to the household a wealthy German banker, Frédéric Brunner, whom he has proposed as a possible match for Cécile Camusot; however, the banker, who considers Cécile a nonentity and her mother a dry stick, is not impressed by the Camusots and refuses to consider an alliance with them. Mme Camusot, convinced that Cousin Pons has planned the whole affair to humiliate his relatives, becomes more virulent than ever in her attitude toward him and forbids him her house.

Cécile Camusot (say-SEEL), the red-haired, plain-spoken, but not unattractive daughter of the Camusots, still unmarried, to her mother's distress, at the age of twenty-three. In an attempt to please his relatives, Cousin Pons suggests a match between her and Frédéric Brunner, a young millionaire banker of German descent, but Brunner is cautious and critical and refuses to consider Cécile as his wife. After all legal entanglements have been resolved, she inherits the fortune represented by Cousin Pons's art collection. She marries Vicomte Popinot.

Madame Cibot (see-BOH), the portress at Cousin Pons's lodgings and his housekeeper. Called in to nurse Cousin Pons during his last illness, and inspired by tales of legacies left by bachelor lodgers to deserving housekeepers, she plans to secure a part of Pons's art collection for herself after she has heard a report of its value. Her scheming involves her with Monsieur Frasier, a rascally lawyer; Dr. Poulain, Pons's physician; Remonencq, an unscrupulous dealer in bric-a-brac, and Elie Magus, a famous art collector who buys some of Pons's most valuable paintings at ridiculously low prices after she is able to convince innocent Schmucke that funds are needed to provide for his sick friend. When Pons rallies sufficiently to realize what has happened, he makes two wills in an effort to outwit Madame Cibot. In the first, she is mentioned as one of his heirs. In the other, the collection is left to his friend Schmucke without reservation. Offered one hundred thousand francs to destroy the first will, Madame Cibot tries unsuccessfully to do so. Remonencq, also eager to share in Pons's estate, helps to poison Cibot as a step toward marrying the widow. The dealer also dies after drinking a glass of vitriol intended

for his wife, and Madame Remonencq becomes the sole proprietress of an art shop.

Monsieur Remonencq (reh-moh-NANK), a rascally dealer in curios and cheap art objects. Taken into Madame Cibot's confidence, he helps Elie Magus, a celebrated art dealer, swindle Schmucke in the purchase of eight paintings from Pons' art collection. Hoping to carry his partnership with Madame Cibot a step farther, he poisons her invalid husband's barley water and marries the widow. He himself dies after drinking a glass of vitriol he intended for his wife.

Monsieur Frasier (freh-ZYAY), the shyster lawyer who directs the legal wrangle that follows the death of Cousin Pons. A cadaverous, ailing, unscrupulous man, he makes Madame Cibot his tool while working in the interest of the Camusot family. He persuades Madame Camusot de Marville to contest the will on the ground that Schmucke had exercised undue influence over his sick friend. Brokenhearted by this accusation, Schmucke lets the estate go unchallenged to the Camusots and dies a short time later. Frasier is appointed to the post of justice of the peace as his reward for handling the legal battle with shrewdness and dispatch.

Dr. Poulain (poo-LAN), the physician who attends Cousin Pons during his last illness. Having heard that the sick man's art collection is extremely valuable, he repeats this information to Madame Cibot and advises her to feather her nest while there is time. He sends her to consult his legal friend, Monsieur Frasier, and thus draws the conniving lawyer into the affair. Frasier tells him that he will be made the head of a hospital if Pons dies intestate.

Elie Magus (ay-LEE mah-GEWS), an impassioned amateur art collector covetous of Cousin Pons' art treasures. His desire to corner the art market causes him to join in the plot to swindle Schmucke and buy some of Pons' best pictures at a low cost.

Comte Popinot (poh-pee-NOH), a prominent figure in political circles. He treats Cousin Pons kindly, and the old musician frequently dines at his house.

Vicomte Popinot, a hero of the July Revolution. Though not enchanted by Cécile Camusot's charms, he eventually marries her and shares in Cousin Pons' legacy.

Frédéric Brunner (fray-day-REEK brewn-EHR), called **Fritz**, a wealthy young German banker. Cousin Pons proposes him as a possible husband for Cécile Camusot, but nothing except the resentment of the girl's mother results from his attempt at matchmaking.

Gaudissart (goh-dee-SAHR), the proprietor of the theater where Cousin Pons conducts the orchestra. He tries without success to protect Schmucke's interests in the matter of the contested will.

Topinard (toh-pee-NAHR), a supernumerary at the theater to whom Cousin Pons had given five francs every month. He takes Schmucke into his own poor lodgings after Frasier has evicted him and nurses the German until his death.

Madeleine Vivet (vee-VAY), a scrawny spinster, lady's maid, and housekeeper to Madame Camusot. Ambitious to become Madame Pons, she is disappointed when he pays no attention to her charms or her savings. She never misses an opportunity to ridicule the old man or play malicious tricks on him.

THE COWARDS
(Zbabelci)

Author: Josef Škvorecký (1924-   )
First published: 1958
Genre: Novel

Locale: Kostelec, Czechoslovakia
Time: 1945
Plot: Social realism

Danny Smiricky (SMIH-rzhihts-kee), an eighteen-year-old jazz saxophone player in a provincial town in Czechoslovakia. As the narrator of the novel, Danny reveals that he is less concerned with the major political upheavals occurring around him during the final days of the Nazi occupation in his town in May, 1945, than with his own personal future. Infatuated with a girl named Irena, Danny fantasizes about the kinds of heroic deeds he could perform to win her heart. Arrested for a cavalier act of defiance in the face of the Nazi forces, Danny is saved from serious reprisal by Dr. Sabata, a friend of his father and an important figure in the town. Danny joins a group of young partisans, in part out of a simple desire to take possession of a gun, but the partisan unit is pressed into service as part of a newly founded local militia. Danny becomes caught up in a fleeting battle with the retreating Nazis. He then spends the day consoling Irena, who is distracted by a lack of news concerning her lover, Zdenek. Frustrated once again, Danny joins his jazz band to take part in a celebration in honor of the Soviet army, which has entered the town to replace the Germans. As the novel closes, Danny pours into his music his mingled feelings of regret over the passing of his youth and his hope for new joy with some as-yet-unknown girl in the future.

Irena, Danny's would-be girlfriend. Although flattered by Danny's attention, Irena has her heart set on the mountainclimber Zdenek. She serves mainly as the foil for Danny's adolescent longings and desires.

Prema (PREH-mah), the fearless leader of the band of partisan rebels that Danny joins. He and Danny set up a machine gun and stop a file of German soldiers maneuvering with a tank on the outskirts of town.

Benno, a member of Danny's band who spent time in a concentration camp because he is of Jewish ancestry. During a brief battle with the retreating Germans, he flees in an ignominious yet comical fashion into the woods.

Bertie Moutelik (MEW-teh-lihk), a young photographer who industriously takes pictures of the local political and military authorities. He takes a picture of Danny proudly displaying a submachine gun.

Dr. Sabata, a local official who has managed to get along smoothly with the occupying Germans yet is ready to greet the newly arrived Soviet forces with equal zeal.

Dr. Bohadlo, the ineffectual leader of Danny's military patrol.

Mrs. Heiserova, the wife of the general director of a textile mill. When Danny asks her to provide temporary housing for some newly released prisoners of war, she initially balks, until she learns that the men are English, not Russian.

Mitzi, a maid who serves as the object of one of Danny's unsuccessful flirtations.

Haryk, one of the members of Danny's band.

Lucie, Haryk's girlfriend, with whom Danny flirts in his ceaseless quest to secure romantic attention.

— *Julian W. Connolly*

THE COXCOMB

Authors: Francis Beaumont (c. 1584-1616) and John Fletcher
    (1579-1625)
First published: 1647
Genre: Drama

Locale: England and France
Time: Early seventeenth century
Plot: Comedy

Antonio, the coxcomb, a ridiculous parody of the conventional friend. He insists that his traveling companion, Mercury, visit his home. Finding that Mercury is infatuated with his wife, he decides to become immortal as a famous friend. He appears in various disguises attempting to persuade Maria to commit adultery with Mercury.

Maria, Antonio's beautiful but heartless wife. She sees through Antonio's disguises and thwarts him several times, finally having the disguised Antonio accused of murdering the real Antonio. At last, she becomes so irritated with him that she commits adultery with Mercury.

Mercury, Antonio's traveling companion. Overwhelmed with Antonio's fatuous friendship and horrified at his own passion for Maria, he strives to avoid temptation, but Maria breaks down his resistance. After the adulterous affair,

he loses interest in her.

Viola, a lovely and virtuous young girl. After running away from home to marry Ricardo, she finds him drunk, rowdy, and dangerous. Fleeing from him, she suffers various perils and hardships. Moved to tenderness by his repentance, she forgives him and consents to marry him.

Ricardo, Viola's sweetheart. On his proposed wedding night, he is drunk and mistakes Viola for a harlot, terrifying her into flight. Repentant, he devotes himself to finding her. When he does find her as a servant of Mercury's mother, he confesses his unworthiness and begs forgiveness.

Valerio, a married man who befriends Viola but attempts to make her his mistress. Ricardo persuades him to help in her discovery.

CRACKING INDIA

Author: Bapsi Sidhwa (1938-   )
First published: 1991
Genre: Novel

Locale: Pakistan
Time: 1944-1948
Plot: Historical realism

Lenny, the protagonist and narrator. Lenny is eight years old in 1947, at the time of the partition of India that creates Pakistan. The protected and pampered daughter of a wealthy Parsee family in Lahore, she not only observes the violence that engulfs the city but also witnesses and participates in the consequent upheaval that affects both her family and her circle of friends. As the events unfold and the horror that the partition creates encroaches on her childhood, she gains a fuller understanding of her own nature and the adult world.

Ayah, Lenny's nursemaid. This beautiful Hindu woman, simply called Ayah—the Urdu word for nursemaid—serves as Lenny's link to the outside world and provides her with the warmth her aristocratic mother fails to give. Ayah attracts a variety of male admirers, whom she treats for the most part with disdain. Ayah's circle offers Lenny a firsthand view of two important factors in Asian society: the subtleties informing male-female relationships and the conflicts created by religious differences.

Godmother, another of Lenny's mainstays. She possesses admirable strength, stability, and wisdom, as well as a keen understanding of human nature. Lenny depends on these qualities as the events of partition crack her once-secure world. Not only does Godmother, who remains nameless like Ayah, represent the finest qualities of womanhood, but she also emerges as a richly comic character, especially in her relations with her husband and sister, known as Slavesister.

Ice-Candy-Man, one of Ayah's admirers. When the novel was first published, it took this character's name as its title. Even though he does not play a major role in the conventional sense, he hovers over the action. His name comes from his occupation as a seller of flavored ice, a favorite confection in Pakistan. He represents the uncaring male world that, through its cold, political calculation, unleashed the destructive forces of partition and carried out the associated violence.

Cousin, Lenny's relative and companion. Another nameless character, this typical young Asian male has recently reached puberty and attempts to explain the mysteries of sex to Lenny. The narrator's stormy yet comic relationship with Cousin enriches the domestic side of the novel, showing how day to day life plays out alongside historical events of magnitude.

Electric-aunt, Cousin's mother. A nervous, energetic woman, she appears at first to be vacuous and silly. Once faced with the challenges of partition, however, she and Lenny's mother show their mettle when they smuggle gasoline to Hindus.

— *Robert L. Ross*

THE CRADLE SONG
(Canción de cuna)

Authors: Gregorio Martínez Sierra (1881-1947) and María Martínez Sierra (1874-1974)
First published: 1917
Genre: Drama

Locale: A cloister of a convent in Spain
Time: Early twentieth century
Plot: Comedy

The Prioress, the forty-year-old spiritual leader of the Dominican sisters in an enclosed Catholic convent in Spain. Wise and loving, she permits the young novices a relaxation of the strict rules of silence as they celebrate her birthday. Her birthday takes an unusual twist when an infant is left at the convent door. She, with the aid of the old doctor, determines in the name of God to rear the abandoned infant in the convent. Eighteen years later, in the second act, she gives the child, Teresa, her blessings as the young woman leaves the convent to marry.

The Vicaress, a forty-year-old sister. She fears any relaxation of the convent's strict rules. Stern and unbending, she is sometimes scandalized by the actions of the novices and fears that the prioress is too forgiving of their minor transgressions. She questions the propriety of taking the child of an unwed mother into the convent. Softened by her love for Teresa, she joins the others in seeking to protect their ward as she leaves for her marriage.

Sister Joanna of the Cross (hoh-AH-nah), an eighteen-year-old novice. She is torn between her desire to remain at the convent and her great love for her younger brothers and sisters, whom she has left at home. She devotes her loving care to the infant Teresa over the years. Caring for the child fulfills a deep need in her heart. Ultimately, Teresa recognizes her as her mother.

Teresa (teh-REH-sah), a foundling left at the convent by her unwed mother. Teresa's singing is a constant joy to the sisters. Unspoiled and loving, she becomes a unifying force within the convent as all grow to love and cherish her. Her upcoming marriage and departure from the country are a source of great stress to the sisters, who are determined to protect her.

Don Jose (hoh-SEH), a sixty-year-old doctor, the only male permitted in the convent. Pragmatic and sometimes testy, he plots to save the foundling by adopting her and leaving her with the sisters to rear. His love for Teresa equals that of the sisters. He determines that Teresa's suitor, Antonio, is an honorable man and supports the proposed marriage. He assures the nuns that their beloved child will be treated well and respected in her marriage.

Antonio, Teresa's suitor. His plan to take Teresa to South America for their marriage is a source of great stress to the nuns. An honorable man, he loves the young woman for her goodness and spirituality. His good humor and apparent love assuage the sisters' fears, and they give their blessings to the union.

Sister Marcella (mahr-SEH-yah), a nineteen-year-old novice. Disposed to melancholy, she sometimes desires the freedom of the birds to leave their cage, a metaphor for the cloistered life. She is frequently in trouble as a result of her sharp tongue. As an older woman, she confesses that she has found release for her passions by catching sunbeams and flying them across the ceiling like birds.

The Poet, the speaker during the interlude between the acts. His poem spans the period between the two acts. His verse suggests that life within the cloistered nest will change as these chaste women of God are moved by the cradle song, the motherhood every woman carries in her breast. Teresa, their child from God, loves Heaven but will seek a different path.

The Mistress of Novices, a kindly woman who supports the young novices. She forcefully argues for keeping the foundling at the convent.

Sister Sagrario (sah-GRAH-ryoh), an eighteen-year-old novice. She is suspected of telling the Mistress of Novices of the minor infringements of rules by others.

Sister Tornera (tohr-NEH-rah), a thirty-year-old nun. Although she is scandalized by the doctor's views on finding a husband, she is among the first of the sisters to speak in favor of keeping the child.

Sister Inez (ee-NEHS), a fifty-year-old nun. She frequently criticizes others but is reduced to tears if they make disparaging remarks about her. As Teresa prepares to leave, the sister is happily sewing fashionable clothing for her trousseau.

Sister María Jesús (mah-REE-ah heh-SEWS), a nineteen-year-old novice. When told that she suffers from bouts of melancholy, the doctor delights in shocking the sisters with his views on the role of marriage in a woman's life. She is immersed in the latest fashions as she helps prepare Teresa's trousseau.

— *Inez L. Ramsey*

CRANFORD

Author: Elizabeth Gaskell (1810-1865)
First published: 1851-1853
Genre: Novel

Locale: England
Time: Early nineteenth century
Plot: Domestic realism

Mary Smith, a young Englishwoman who narrates the little affairs of the spinsters living in the village of Cranford.

Miss Deborah Jenkyns, a domineering spinster. She makes all the decisions for herself and her fifty-five-year-old unmarried sister Matilda, called Matty. They are the daughters of a rector. When Deborah dies, her sister finds it difficult to make decisions for herself.

Miss Matilda (Matty) Jenkyns, who, though she has a better mind than Deborah, allows herself to be dominated by her sister. As a young woman, she had rejected a suitor in order to remain with her mother. When her financial situation becomes grave, her greatest concern is that she will be too poor to be included in the society of the village spinsters. She sets up a small shop and sells tea.

Thomas Holbrook, Matty's rejected suitor.

Lady Glenmire, Mrs. Jamieson's sister-in-law. She upsets the little community by marrying a doctor, whom many regard as no better than a tradesman.

Mrs. Jamieson, a friend of Matty. She becomes the social leader of Cranford's spinster population upon the death of Deborah. She upsets her friends by not including them among the people she invites to meet her sister-in-law, Lady Glen-

mire. She later drops her sister-in-law when Lady Glenmire marries a doctor.

Mr. Hoggins, the doctor whom Lady Glenmire marries.

Miss Pole and

Mrs. Forrester, friends of Matty.

Peter Jenkyns, the long-lost brother of Matty and Deborah. He returns to the village to care for Matilda when she is in financial straits.

Martha, Matty's faithful maid.

Captain Brown, a semi-retired man who is crude but whom the spinsters learn to accept because he is kind and considerate to them. He has two unmarried daughters.

Mary Brown, Captain Brown's older daughter, who is dying of an incurable illness.

Jessie Brown, Captain Brown's younger daughter. After the death of her father and sister, she marries a suitor of long standing.

Major Gordon, who marries Jessie.

Mr. Smith, the narrator's kindly father. He becomes Matty's adviser.

Betsy Barker, the owner of a famous cow.

THE CREAM OF THE JEST

Author: James Branch Cabell (1879-1958)
First published: 1917
Genre: Novel

Locale: Virginia
Time: The twentieth century
Plot: Satire

Felix Kennaston, a successful, highly romantic author. He is writing a novel about Ettarre, an ageless woman, and his plot centers around a broken round medallion with mysterious symbols, which he calls the sigil of Scoteia. In his dreams, he talks with Ettarre and accompanies her to historical places and

times; when he tries to touch her, however, the dream invariably ends. One day in his garden he finds a shiny broken disc which, giving full play to his romantic imagination, he chooses to believe is the real sigil of Scoteia. He finds the other half of the disc in his wife's bathroom and wonders about her relation to Ettarre. After his wife dies, he shows his two magic pieces to his neighbor Harrowby, who readily identifies them as the broken top of a cosmetic jar. Disillusioned at last, Felix prepares to face the realities of middle age.

Kathleen Kennaston, his wife (née Eppes). She is thin and capable, and she treats her husband with polite boredom. Though she is a good wife, Kennaston finds her unexciting and a dull conversationalist. She dies in her sleep.

Richard Harrowby, Felix's neighbor, who admits he cares little for Kennaston, whose story he tells. Harrowby manufactures toilet preparations and, for a hobby, studies the occult. He is both entertained and sometimes annoyed by Kennaston's romanticism.

Ettarre (eht-TAHR), a woman in Kennaston's novel and in his dreams. His ideal (and the ideal of all men), she is similar to, and the younger sister of, Dorothy la Désirée in Cabell's *Jurgen*. Ettarre accompanies Kennaston in his nightly dreams, in which the two are present on important dates in many widely separated ages. When he is about to touch her, how-ever, his dream always ends.

Horvendile (ohr-vehn-DEEL), a clerk, a character in Kennaston's novel with whom the author identifies himself. The names Horvendile and Kennaston are often used interchangeably to suggest that they are two sides of one personality.

Muriel Allardyce (al-lahr-DEES), one of Kennaston's former loves.

Count Emmerick, a character in Kennaston's novel, the brother of Ettarre.

Dame Melicent (meh-lee-SAHN), a character in Kennaston's novel, Count Emmerick's elder sister.

Comte Perion de la Forêt (peh-RYOHN deh lah foh-RAY), Count Emmerick's a character in Kennaston's novel, Melicent's husband.

Maugis d'Aigremont (moh-GEE da-greh-MOHN), a character in Kennaston's novel, a master villain, a brigand slain by Horvendile in Ettarre's bedroom.

Sir Guiron des Rocques (gee-ROHN day rohk), a character in Kennaston's novel, Ettarre's betrothed.

CRIME AND PUNISHMENT
(Prestupleniye i Nakazaniye)

Author: Fyodor Dostoevski (1821-1881)
First published: 1866
Genre: Novel

Locale: Russia
Time: Mid-nineteenth century
Plot: Psychological realism

Rodion Romanovitch Raskolnikov (ROH-dyon roh-MAH-noh-vihch ras-KOL-nih-kov), called **Rodya**, a psychologically complex young law student who murders not for wealth but as an experiment, to see if he is one of those who can circumvent society's restrictions. Impoverished and weakened by illness and hunger, he decides to rid society of a worthless person in order to preserve his genius for posterity, to relieve his devoted mother and sister from compromising themselves, and to prove that he is above conscience. He kills Alonya Ivanovna, a miserly old crone, and her sister. Later, in his loss of illusions, of peace of mind, and of the wealth he sought, he learns through suffering. Important changes result from acceptance of his inward punishment. His humanitarian instincts are brought out; his deep love of family and friends is revealed, and his belief that life must be lived is renewed. The study of his psychoses from the time he conceives his mad theory to his attempt at expiation in Siberia provides a masterly characterization of a tormented mind and shattered body.

Pulcheria Alexandrovna (pewl-CHEH-ryah ah-lehk-SAHN-drov-nah), his long-suffering mother, whose faith in her son sustains her but whose mind gives way under the strain of his deed and guilt. A handsome, middle-aged woman of distinction, a widow who has supported her family and urged her son to make his way in life, Pulcheria is a study of motherhood thwarted, a woman tortured by her inability to fathom her favorite's depravity.

Avdotya Romanovna (ahv-DOT-yah roh-MAH-nov-nah), called **Dounia** (DEW-nyah), her daughter and the younger sister who has aided in her mother's effort to make something of her brother through working and skimping. A mirror of her mother's fortitude and faith, Dounia is the beautiful, impoverished, clear-sighted savior of her family.

Dmitri Prokofitch Razumihin (DMIH-tree proh-KOH-fihch rah-zew-MEE-hihn), Raskolnikov's devoted friend. Enamored of Dounia, he is the savior of the family honor. Like Dounia, he has all the normal responses of a generous nature and works unceasingly to discover and repair the tragic situation of his friend. Affianced to the beautiful Dounia, he founds a publishing company to aid the hapless girl, mother, and brother. He is one of the few characters with a sense of humor; his good deeds lighten a psychologically gloomy and depth-insighted plot.

Piotr Petrovitch Luzhin (pyohtr peh-TROH-vihch LEW-zhin), a minor government official betrothed to Dounia, a man filled with a sense of his own importance. Raskolnikov objects to his suit. Dounia herself loses interest in him after she meets Razumihin, whom she later marries.

Sofya Semyonovna Marmeladov (soh-FYAH seh-MYOH-nov-nah mahr-meh-LAH-dov), called **Sonia**, the daughter of a drunken clerk and stepdaughter of the high-strung Katerina Ivanovna. It is her father who brings the luckless prostitute to Rodya's attention and whose funeral the unstable student finances. From gratitude, the benevolent though soiled child of the streets comforts the murderer and supports him in his transgressions so that he finally will confess. Forced to support her father, her stepmother, and their three children, she remains unsullied, and her spirit transcends these morbid conditions. With great depth of character and faith, Sonia follows the criminal to Siberia, where she inspires the entire prison colony with her devotion and goodness.

Marmeladov, an impoverished ex-clerk and drunkard, Sonia's father. He is killed when struck by a carriage. Raskolnikov, who witnesses the accident, gives Marmeladov's wife some money to help pay for his friend's funeral expenses.

Katerina Ivanovna (kah-teh-RIH-nah ee-VAH-nov-nah), Marmeladov's wife, slowly dying of tuberculosis. She collapses in the street and dies a short time later.

Arkady Ivanovitch Svidrigailov (ahr-KAH-dee ee-VAH-noh-vihch svih-drih-GAY-lov), the sensualist in whose house Dounia had been a governess. He is both the would-be seducer and savior of Dounia, and through her of Sonia's orphaned half sisters and brother, when he gives her money as atonement for his conduct. A complicated character, sometimes considered, with Raskolnikov, one of the alter egos of the writer, he is obsessed by guilt and driven by libido.

Porfiry Petrovitch (pohr-FIH-ree peh-TROH-vihch), a brilliant detective more interested in the rehabilitation than the prosecution of the murderer. Somewhat disturbed and neurotic himself, Porfiry seconds Sonia's influence and causes Raskolnikov to confess his crime and thus begin his redemption.

Alonya Ivanovna (ah-LOH-nyah ee-VAH-nov-nah), a miserly old pawnbroker and usurer murdered by Raskolnikov.

Lizaveta Ivanovna (lee-zah-VYEH-tah), a seller of old clothes and Alonya Ivanovna's sister, also killed by Raskolnikov.

THE CRIME OF SYLVESTRE BONNARD
(Le Crime de Sylvestre Bonnard)

Author: Anatole France (Jacques-Anatole-François Thibault, 1844-1924)
First published: 1881
Genre: Novel

Locale: France
Time: The nineteenth century
Plot: Domestic

Sylvestre Bonnard (seel-VEHS-tr voh-NAHR), a shy philologist who has a penchant for getting involved in other people's lives. A bachelor, Bonnard befriends a poor widow and, later, an orphan girl who is the daughter of Clementine, Bonnard's love in his youth. He lives a good life among books and is happy in his late years because a young couple he has helped return his affection.

M. Coccoz (koh-KOHZ), a poverty-stricken bookseller from whom Bonnard buys no books. Out of compassion for the poor man and his wife and child, he sends logs to their attic room to keep them warm. Coccoz soon dies, leaving his wife and child to face the world alone. His beautiful widow eventually marries Prince Trépof, a wealthy Russian.

Prince Trépof (tray-POHF) and
Princess Trépof, who had married after M. Coccoz's death. The prince, inordinately wealthy, travels the world expanding his matchbox collection. Princess Trépof, remembering the kindness Bonnard had shown her and her first husband, obtains for Bonnard the *Golden Legend*, a manuscript he had given up hope of ever owning.

Jeanne Alexandre (zhahn ah-lehk-SAHN-dr), the shy daughter of Clementine, Bonnard's early love. She is befriended by Bonnard; when she marries, he sells his library, except for a single volume, to provide money to give the young couple a start in life.

Signor Polizzi (poh-lee-ZEE), a slippery jack-of-all-trades

who owns the manuscript of the *Golden Legend*. Polizzi allows Bonnard to travel from Paris to the Polizzi place in Sicily to read the manuscript. Arriving there, Bonnard discovers that the manuscript had already been sent to the Paris bookstore of Polizzi's son.

M. de Gabry (gah-BREE) and
Mme de Gabry, a couple who invite Bonnard to their country estate to catalog their extensive library. While there, Bonnard discovers Jeanne and learns that she is the de Gabrys' ward.

Henri Gélis (ahn-REE zhay-LEES), a student who, while receiving help for his thesis from Bonnard, falls in love with Jeanne, who is now Bonnard's ward. They marry and have a baby, Sylvestre, who dies. Bonnard knows, however, that since they are young, they will eventually raise a family.

Maître Mouche (MEH-tr moosh), Jeanne's guardian while she is the de Gabrys' ward. When Mouche disappears after embezzling some money, Bonnard becomes Jeanne's legal guardian.

Mlle Préfère (pray-FEHR), Jeanne's teacher in the select school the girl attends. At first, Mlle Préfère has hopes of marrying Bonnard. When her affection is not returned, however, she grows hostile toward him.

Thérèse (tay-REHZ), Bonnard's maid, whose firm hand keeps her master's domestic affairs in order.

CRIMES OF THE HEART

Author: Beth Henley (1952-   )
First published: 1981
Genre: Drama

Locale: Hazlehurst, Mississippi
Time: Fall, 1974
Plot: Comedy

Lenore (Lenny) MaGrath, the oldest MaGrath sister. The play is set on and around her thirtieth birthday. Lenny is a thoughtful, self-conscious woman who remains concerned about her critically ill grandfather and her own impending spinsterhood. She is protective of her sisters and eventually puts Chick in her place after Chick's vitriolic attack on the MaGrath family. By the play's end, she is encouraged to

resume a relationship with Charlie Hill, a man who replied to Lenny's advertisement in the personal section of a periodical. Her fear that he would reject her because of her missing ovary proves to be unfounded.

Meg MaGrath, the middle MaGrath sister, twenty-seven years of age. Meg moved to Hollywood to pursue her singing career, abandoning her lover, Doc Porter, who was injured in a hurricane accident. She returns to be close to her sisters after Babe's shooting of her husband. Although she is the most outgoing of the three sisters, she relates to Doc that her life in Hollywood had once led to a nervous breakdown and that she has lost her singing voice. One of the consequences of her return to Hazlehurst is a rekindling of her romance with Doc; another is the return of her singing voice.

Becky (Babe) Botrelle, the youngest MaGrath sister, at twenty-four years of age. Babe is the reason for most of the play's dynamics. She shot her husband, Zackery Botrelle, after he discovered that she had been having an affair with Willie Jay, a fifteen-year-old black boy who came to Babe's house to see the dog she tended for him. Babe is the most fragile of the sisters and thus most like their mother, who scandalously hanged herself and her cat years before the action of the play. Babe's shooting of her husband is resolved in her favor, after Zackery circulates incriminating pictures and after Willie Jay is forced to leave town. Babe later attempts suicide with a rope and with gas. She discovers, as her mother did, that suicide is a lonely act and is relieved by her failure to succeed.

Chick Boyle, the twenty-nine-year-old first cousin of the MaGrath sisters. She has yellow hair, shiny red lips, and a brassy disposition. She is ashamed of Babe's alleged crime and voices her shame frequently and indiscriminately. Chick finally goes too far when she berates Babe as a murderer and refers to all the MaGrath sisters as "trash." Lenny drives her out of the house with a broom and forces her to climb the mimosa tree.

Doc Porter, the thirty-year-old former boyfriend of Meg. Doc comes over to inform Lenny that her twenty-year-old horse, Billy Boy, had died from being struck by lightning. Doc remains infatuated with Meg, even after his marriage to another woman and the birth of his two children. They spend their first date after Meg's return reminiscing about the past.

Barnette Lloyd, Babe's twenty-six-year-old lawyer. Barnette is a graduate of the Old Miss law school who returns to Hazlehurst to open his own firm. Meg remains dubious of Barnette's competence when she first meets him, but Barnette has a personal vendetta against Babe's husband, formerly a state senator from Copiah County. Barnette hopes to uncover all of Botrelle's criminal dealings. Barnette also remains fond of Babe and hopes to save her from her abusive husband and from any criminal charges.

— *Hardin Aasand*

THE CRISIS

Author: Winston Churchill (1871-1947)
First published: 1901
Genre: Novel

Locale: Missouri and Virginia
Time: The 1860's
Plot: Historical

Stephen Brice, a young Boston lawyer who migrates to St. Louis in 1858. He falls in love with Virginia Carvel and, influenced by Abraham Lincoln, becomes an active Republican. Enlisting in the Union army, he serves in the Civil War. His saving of Clarence Colfax's life and his outstanding qualities enable him to marry Virginia despite the fact that she is an ardent Southerner.

Judge Whipple, Stephen's friend. He helps the young man get started in a political career.

Mrs. Brice, Stephen's widowed mother, who migrates with him to St. Louis.

Virginia Carvel, an ardent Southerner. Though her partisan loyalties conflict with Stephen's, she comes to love him and, eventually, marries him.

Colonel Carvel, Virginia's father. He serves in the Confederate forces.

Abraham Lincoln, the president of the United States, who is an influence in Stephen's life. He makes Stephen and Virginia realize they must forgive and forget their sectional loyalties.

Clarence Colfax, a young Southerner, a rival for Virginia's love. His life is twice saved by the intervention of Stephen.

Ulysses S. Grant, the famous Union general. Stephen meets him at the outbreak of the war, before Grant gets a command. Near the end of the war, Stephen, now a major, is sent to Virginia to report to General Grant on Sherman's campaigns.

William T. Sherman, famous Union general. Stephen meets him early in the Civil War and later serves as a member of the General's staff.

Eliphalit Hopper, an unscrupulous carpetbagger.

THE CRITIC: Or, A Tragedy Rehearsed

Author: Richard Brinsley Sheridan (1751-1816)
First published: 1781
Genre: Drama

Locale: London, England
Time: Late eighteenth century
Plot: Satire

Mr. Dangle, a wealthy Londoner who is stagestruck and brings into his house a constant parade of musicians, actors, critics, and other theatrical types. He is one of the witnesses to the rehearsal of Mr. Puff's new play.

Mrs. Dangle, Mr. Dangle's wife, who objects to the stream of theatrical callers who clutter up her house. She discusses the theater and drama with Mr. Sneer, who comes to call, and also rescues her husband from some musicians who cannot speak

English but want him to get jobs for them.

Mr. Puff, a playwright as well as a press agent who praises things for a price. He has several categories of "puffs" that he writes in praise of anyone or anything when he is well paid. His play is the one being rehearsed, and he quarrels with the actors and the under-prompter because they have cut his lines and scenes and because the scenery has not been made. Mr. Puff is very proud of his playwriting ability.

Mr. Sneer, Mr. Dangle's friend, with whom he discusses the theater. He is one of the group who watch the rehearsal of Mr. Puff's play.

Sir Fretful Plagiary, a dramatist who cannot stand any kind of criticism of his work. He brushes aside any critical remarks about his new play and holds forth at great length against those who say anything unflattering about his playwriting.

THE CROCK OF GOLD

Author: James Stephens (1882-1950)
First published: 1912
Genre: Novel

Locale: The Irish countryside
Time: Indeterminate
Plot: Fantasy

The Old Philosopher, living in the center of a pine wood. Many come to seek his advice.

Another Old Philosopher, who lives with the first philosopher. When he decides that he has learned all he is capable of learning, he spins around in the room until he falls dead.

The Grey Woman, the wife of the second philosopher. She spins herself to death because of her grief over her husband's demise. These two bodies are buried under the hearthstone by the Thin Woman. The finding of them later results in the first philosopher's arrest.

The Thin Woman, the wife of the first philosopher. After his arrest, she goes to seek help from Angus Og, who with all the other gods comes to bring happiness to the people. The charges against the philosopher are forgotten, and he is freed.

Seumas, the son of the first couple.

Brigid, the daughter of the second couple. For a while they are lured away by the vengeful and troublemaking leprechauns, but they are freed because the leprechauns fear the Thin Woman.

Meehawl MacMurrachu, who, in following the philosopher's advice to steal the leprechauns' crock of gold because they stole his wife's washboard, rouses the ire of the leprechauns.

Caitilin, Meehawl's daughter. The leprechauns send Pan to steal her away.

The Great God Pan, god of the beast that is in every man. He lures Caitilin away and teaches her the meaning of hunger and pain.

Angus Og, an early Irish god. Petitioned by the philosopher, he forces Caitilin to choose between Pan and him. He is Divine Inspiration. She chooses Angus Og and so is saved from the beast in man. At the story's end, the birth of Angus Og's and Caitilin's child is awaited.

The Most Beautiful Man,
The Strongest Man, and
The Ugliest Man, "the Three Absolutes," gods whose questions the Thin Woman must answer on her way to seek Angus Og's aid for her husband.

CROME YELLOW

Author: Aldous Huxley (1894-1963)
First published: 1921
Genre: Novel

Locale: England
Time: The 1920's
Plot: Social satire

Henry Wimbush, the owner of Crome, a country house in England. He is the host for the house party that brings together the unusual group of people who are characters in the novel. Wimbush is so interested in Crome that he has been writing its history for thirty years. He frequently calls his guests together to read to them choice portions of his account.

Denis Stone, a young poet, almost a symbol in the novel for artistic ineffectuality, who loves Anne Wimbush, old Henry's niece. Stone is disturbed by the other guests at the party, particularly by Scogan, a very rational man. Stone's suit is never realized, though Anne has decided she will accept him if he proposes. The indecisive Stone makes one decision in the novel: He arranges to have sent a fake telegram recalling him to London. Ironically, his one decisive action separates him from Anne.

Anne Wimbush, a young woman, four years Stone's senior, who looks on his suit for her affection first with scorn, finally with sympathy. She, unlike Stone, thinks life should be accepted as it unfolds; Stone attempts to carry personally all the troubles of the world on his shoulders.

Mr. Scogan, Stone's opposite. Scogan is rational to the degree that Stone is sentimental. Scogan's cold-blooded intelligence annoys Stone.

Mrs. Priscilla Wimbush, a rather scatterbrained woman, Henry's wife, who studies the stars. She is enthusiastic because she has picked a winner at a horse race with information she divined from the movements of the celestial bodies.

Gombauld, an artist who is invited to Crome to paint Anne's picture. He expresses his love for Anne and is repulsed.

Jenny Mullion, a young deaf woman who makes up for her lack of hearing by observing very accurately the people at the party. She draws sketches of them in a book she carries, and she writes her impressions of life primarily for her own amusement.

Mary Bracegirdle, a woman remembered for her repressions and Freudian dreams. She is anxious most of the time and given to discussing her psychological ills with anyone who will listen. She decides first to pursue Stone and then Gombauld and manages to talk with each man at the wrong time, when he is occupied with other interests. She does attract a painter of ghosts and spirits, Ivor Lombard, but after visiting her once, Lombard leaves Crome and sends her only a postcard with a terse message. She becomes convinced her life is a ruin.

CROTCHET CASTLE

Author: Thomas Love Peacock (1785-1866)
First published: 1831
Genre: Novel

Locale: England
Time: Nineteenth century
Plot: Fiction of manners

Ebenezer Mac Crotchet, the elderly squire of Crochet Castle, whose ability to make money and translate it into a fake family background is his chief attribute. He fancies himself to be a guardian of ideas and holds long sessions with pseudo-intellectuals discussing science and philosophy.

Young Crotchet, Ebenezer's son, who inherits his father's talent for making money. Young Crotchet's business ethics, however, are shady, and his personal relationships are founded primarily on monetary considerations. When he loses his money, he goes to America to join a banker who, having absconded with a bank's funds, has set up business across the Atlantic.

Susannah Touchandgo, the girl whom Young Crotchet abandoned when her father took the bank's money and went to America, leaving her penniless. She keeps body and soul together by teaching a farmer's children, but finally she marries a gentleman of some means.

Lady Clarinda Bossnowl, a girl betrothed to Young Crotchet because she has a title. When Crotchet goes bankrupt and leaves the country, she is happy to marry a young army officer who has a small but stable fortune.

Mr. Chainmail, an antiquarian who yearns for the olden days of iron clothing. When he discovers that Susannah Touchandgo was gently reared, he happily marries her.

Captain Fitzchrome, a young man who pines for Lady Bossnowl and who finally has the good fortune to win her.

Lemma Crotchet, Ebenezer's daughter, who marries Lady Bossnowl's brother.

THE CRUCIBLE

Author: Arthur Miller (1915-   )
First published: 1953
Genre: Drama

Locale: Salem, Massachusetts
Time: 1692
Plot: Historical

Abigail Williams, a strikingly beautiful seventeen-year-old. She is willful and a flirt. Her rebellion against society is expressed in her wayward behavior, which she transforms into a witch scare by going into fits and stimulating and coercing her girlfriends to do likewise. Abigail senses that the community of Salem, Massachusetts, is uneasy, that it suffers from societal tensions, and that it is prepared to believe that its internal divisions are the result of witchcraft. Abigail and her minions charge many of the most prominent people in Salem with practicing witchcraft.

Tituba, a black servant from Barbados who introduces Abigail and her friends to certain superstitious practices. It is her confession that leads to the witchcraft scare.

The Reverend Samuel Parris, a stiff, intolerant man who is at first nonplussed by the eccentric behavior of the girls. Soon, however, he turns their antics into an indictment of the community. Interpreting their hysterical fits as sure signs of witchcraft, he exploits them to whip his congregation into line. Finding the witches becomes a way for this pious and credulous man to assert his authority.

John Proctor, a man who had a brief affair with Abigail. He does not believe that her fits are caused by the devil. Although he is estranged from his wife, who knows of his liaison with Abigail, Proctor resists Abigail's advances, knowing that the consequence will be that he and his wife will stand accused of witchcraft.

Elizabeth Proctor, John's estranged and unforgiving wife. Although her husband has admitted his lapse into sin and is thereafter faithful to his wife, his relationship with Abigail always stands between them. As husband and wife, however, they maintain their integrity and refuse to confess to the false accusation of witchcraft, even though their protestations of innocence result in a death sentence.

Giles Corey, one of Salem's prominent citizens who opposes the charges of witchcraft and then is accused himself. Rather than admitting to a false accusation, he endures the torture of being crushed to death.

The Reverend John Hale, an expert in matters of witchcraft. He comes to Salem to set up the trials.

Thomas Putnam, a prominent Salem citizen and an argumentative man who turns his quarrels with his neighbors into a hunt for witches.

Mary Warren, one of Abigail's friends. She tries to tell the truth, that the girls were only feigning possession by witches, but she loses courage when Abigail intimidates her.

Rebecca Nurse, one of the most devout residents of Salem. Despite her piousness, she is accused of witchcraft. Her conviction illustrates how widespread the hysteria and paranoia of the community have become.

Judge Hathorne, the hanging judge of the Salem witchcraft trials. Hathorne has little sympathy for the accused and takes his responsibility quite seriously.

— Carl Rollyson

THE CRUISE OF THE CACHALOT

Author: Frank T. Bullen (1857-1915)
First published: 1898
Genre: Novel

Locale: Various, on board the *Cachalot*
Time: Late nineteenth century
Plot: Adventure

Frank T. Bullen, a British seaman, eighteen years old. He has sailed from London frequently. He ships out from New Bedford, Massachusetts, on the whaler *Cachalot*, for his first American sea experience. He is intelligent and is the only crew member to bring reading material aboard. He also is level-headed and pragmatic, aware that his chosen occupation will never make him rich; he is nevertheless eager to steep himself in what he loves, the sea and whaling. A naturally curious person, quick to comply with regulations, he surprises the crew early on by catching a 5-foot, 35-pound fish. Along the cruise, he sights and hauls in a number of whales, lives through ravaging sea storms and infuriating calms, is horrified by the sighting of a Malay *prahu* with thirteen corpses aboard, and delights in viewing ocean phosphorescence and a "milk" sea. Reverent and temperate, he is a solid crew hand. He survives a harrowing ride on the back of a whale after his whaleboat is destroyed. His wonder at and appreciation of creatures of the deep and of the sea itself are evident in the quality and quantity of the extended descriptions and detail. He becomes fourth mate when Mr. Jones dies and thus is the captain's harpooner, the promotion increasing his pay by a third.

Mr. Jones, the fourth mate, a huge black man who becomes Bullen's friend and whom Bullen nicknames "Goliath." A "pure African," he was enslaved with his mother as a child; she escaped into Liberia. She was a powerful Obeah-woman who prophesied that her son would die suddenly and violently at the hand of a white man who would die at his hand. Gracious and communicative, Jones instructs Bullen in the natural history of whales and nurtures an uneasy relationship with the skipper. Jones and the skipper come to blows in a nasty struggle in which they are cast overboard in the Sea of Okhotsk, in the North Pacific; they drown, and their bodies are not retrieved.

Captain Slocum, a grim, demanding, morose, and sullen commander whom Bullen compares to the devil. He is smart and runs a tight ship, but he is tight-lipped, seems to have little curiosity or optimism, and is ill-humored toward the crew, insulting them and sneering at them. He dies in a fight with Mr. Jones.

Mr. Count, the first officer, a good whaleman, a good seaman, and a gentleman. He is considerate enough of the crew to allow them time off during a gam with other whalers off the coast of Formosa. He assumes command of the ship after the skipper is drowned. His natural kindliness and thoughtfulness lead him to giving the crew Sundays off, unlike Slocum. He is a particular friend of Bullen.

Mr. Cruce, the second mate, a Portuguese man about forty years old. He is a better whaleman than a seaman and, when angered, becomes a perfect fiend. He kills the first whale and becomes first mate after Mr. Jones's death.

The third mate, an angry, waspish man with a quick temper, a bitter and impulsive "Yankee with a face like an angry cat." He is cruel to the greenhands on first leaving port, tries to avoid contact with whales, and foolishly attempts to "save" a crew that is in no danger. He becomes second mate when Mr. Jones dies.

Louis Silva, the captain's favorite harpooner. Calm and resourceful, he knows what to do in rough circumstances. He becomes third mate after the captain's death.

Abner Cushing, a farmer from Vermont who steals potatoes and molasses from the ship's stores in order to make beer. His punishment is being suspended with fishline by his thumbs in the weather rigging and receiving two dozen lashes with an improvised cat-o'-nine-tails. Later, he is awarded the coveted bounty of twenty pounds of tobacco, which he generously shares all around, for sighting the first "useful" whale captured. After nourishing a premonition of his death, he dies in the South Pacific when a towline becomes wrapped around his neck, throwing him overboard.

Bamberger, a German baker and tub oarsman. He dies in the Mozambique Channel when Mr. Count fires at an approaching whale.

Samuela, a Kanaka from Honolulu. He gets his chance to serve as harpooner in Bullen's whaleboat when a knee injury prevents the skipper from accompanying Bullen.

"Tui Tongoa," or **"King of Tonga,"** an African American who is enlisted as harpooner and interpreter for the natives aboard.

Captain "Paddy" Gilroy, the genial skipper of the *Chance*, which is encountered by the *Cachalot* in the South Pacific. His marvelous seamanship and excellent knowledge of the New Zealand coast are illustrated by his successfully bringing a whale through rough seas.

— *Jill B. Gidmark*

CRUSOE'S DAUGHTER

Author: Jane Gardam (1928-)
First published: 1985
Genre: Novel

Locale: A marshy coastal area in northern England
Time: 1898-1985
Plot: Psychological realism

Polly Flint, the bright, inquisitive, solitary heroine of the novel. She is brought to live in a remote seaside village with two maiden aunts at the age of eight. Polly identifies early on with Robinson Crusoe, feeling herself to be similarly marooned. As a teenager, she visits the home of Arthur and Celia Thwaite, where she meets a number of "artistic" houseguests, including the young poet Paul Treece. Initially attracted to him, she soon grows impatient with his callowness and boundless enthusiasm. She has a brief affair with his friend Theo Zeit, but her impassioned letters to him while he is fighting in

World War I apparently frighten him off. She is heartbroken for a long period and becomes an alcoholic in middle age. She sets herself the task of translating *Robinson Crusoe* into German, then begins to write critical material on the novel. She also becomes a teacher for the local boarding school. The novel ends with Polly in her eighties, about to be interviewed by a local reporter.

Aunt Frances Younghusband, one of Polly's aunts on her mother's side. Small, gentle, and sweet, she has an "understanding" with the local vicar, Father Pocock. They marry and embark on a mission to India. He dies en route, and later Polly receives a photo from Frances, apparently taken after Pocock's death, showing her with a group of people on board ship, all dressed as Pierrots. It seems that all of her life Frances had a taste for adventure, which she is now indulging. She dies of dysentery soon thereafter.

Aunt Mary Younghusband, Polly's other aunt. Polly thinks of her at first as the "ice maiden" because she seems so remote and austere. On the day of Frances' wedding, though, she amazes Polly by looking radiantly beautiful. It develops that she was at one time going to marry Arthur Thwaite, but her sister prevented it somehow. In later life, she has become very religious and frequently goes on retreat at the local convent. She dies soon after Frances.

Theodore (Theo) Zeit, an upper-class young man of Polly's age. His family is from Germany originally and is Jewish. His father owns the factory that overshadows the seaside village. Theo is good-natured and confident, and he gives Polly the impression of being completely happy and at ease in the world. They have an affair of sorts, but after he leaves the village to fight in World War I, he marries Delphi Vipont, a pale blonde beauty who lived near the village. He returns to the village briefly after the war but decides to live in Germany. Later, during World War II, he sends his two daughters to Polly in England to escape the Holocaust. Ultimately, he returns to the village a frail and wasted man.

Charlotte, the maid for the Younghusbands. Frumpy and somewhat dirty in her personal appearance, she is a quiet and rather bad-natured woman. She holds great affection for her nephew Stanley, who comes for tea every Wednesday. After he dies of influenza, it is revealed that he is actually her son. Wounded by the Younghusband sisters' lack of sympathy for her grief, she flees the house abruptly, never to return.

Agnes Woods, a pale-complexioned, bitter woman who always wears black and carries black knitting with her. She has a secret, unspecified, and admiring relationship with Aunt Frances. After Frances leaves, she suffers a stroke and is virtually incapacitated. When Mary dies, Polly and Alice have an unpleasant time caring for Agnes until she dies.

Captain Flint, Polly's father, a jolly, irresponsible, roving man. Polly remembers little of him except that he shared a meat pie with her in the first-class train compartment on their journey up to the aunts' home and that he sang and danced for the aunts at their home. He used to leave Polly in the care of various people while he went off traveling by sea. He died when his ship sank, going down with the ship while sipping from a large stone bottle of gin.

Arthur Thwaite, a quiet, elderly friend of the Younghusband sisters who visits annually. He has a drooping mustache and wears a monocle. He hardly speaks, except to comment on the weather, but Polly nevertheless is drawn to him. He turns out to be Polly's grandfather; he had once been romantically involved with Aunt Mary, but he also had an affair with Polly's grandmother (the aunts' mother), and from that union Polly's mother was born.

Paul Treece, an energetic, amiable, and very talkative young poet. Paul, a student at Cambridge, meets Polly while they are both guests at the Thwaite home. Paul is one of the "artistic" people Celia has invited to stay. Restless and excitable, Paul is callow but nevertheless a talented poet. He is infatuated with Polly and sends her long letters from the front after he eagerly enlists to fight in World War I. He is killed in France.

Alice, a serving girl of about the same age as Polly. Formerly the vicar's maid, she comes to the Younghusbands when Charlotte leaves. Initially mousy, quiet, and tired-looking, she gradually develops a strong personality and becomes a good friend to Polly. She takes over the running of the boarding-house when Polly succumbs to alcoholism. She ends up marrying Mr. Benson, the schoolteacher who boards with them.

Celia Thwaite, Arthur's sister. An old, garishly painted woman, Celia is a poet who takes enormous pride in the fact that her family at one time knew and entertained people such as Alfred, Lord Tennyson and Virginia Woolf. She likes to surround herself with artistic people and generously opens her house to them. Polly thinks her vain and full of machinations. She may have been responsible for breaking up the relationship between Arthur and Mary years ago.

— *Catherine Swanson*

CRY, THE BELOVED COUNTRY

Author: Alan Paton (1903-1988)
First published: 1948
Genre: Novel

Locale: South Africa
Time: Mid-twentieth century
Plot: Social realism

The Reverend Stephen Kumalo (kew-MAH-loh), a Zulu who is an educated man and an Anglican priest. He lives in the country and is unused to the ways of the city and its people. Even so, he goes to Johannesburg to help his sister and find his son. He does his best, which is not enough, to help his relatives. When his son is executed, he cries out for help—for his land and his people as well as for his son.

Gertrude, the clergyman's sister. She has become a prostitute and dealer in illegal liquor in Johannesburg.

John, the clergyman's brother in Johannesburg, a practical man and a successful merchant. As a native politician, he is disturbed by the police and kept under their surveillance. He is a selfish man; he has also abandoned the Christian faith.

Absalom, the clergyman's son. He is a country boy ruined by white ways in the city. He drinks, commits adultery, and steals, at last killing a man who is an activist for the natives, trying to help them improve their condition. Found guilty of the crime, Absalom is sentenced to hang. His one act of goodness is to marry the woman who carries his unborn child.

Arthur Jarvis, Absalom's victim, a young white man who works hard to help the natives improve their lot in Africa. There is irony in his death at the hands of one of the natives he wants to spend his life helping.

Msimangu (ihm-see-MAHN-gew), a native Anglican clergyman in Johannesburg. He is a good man who tries to help Stephen Kumalo find his people and understand them.

Mr. Jarvis, Arthur Jarvis' father. He carries on his son's work for the natives by bringing milk for their children, farm machinery, an agricultural demonstrator, good seed, and a dam to provide water for irrigation. He even becomes Kumalo's friend after they have both lost their sons, one a murderer and the other his victim.

THE CRYING OF LOT 49

Author: Thomas Pynchon (1937-   )
First published: 1966
Genre: Novel

Locale: Primarily San Francisco, California
Time: Early 1960's
Plot: Satire

Oedipa Maas, a suburban California housewife and Young Republican who is the coexecutrix of the huge estate of Pierce Inverarity, her former lover. An attractive woman of twenty-eight with long hair, she is intelligent and dissatisfied. Feeling imprisoned even before she got married, she looked for liberation through Pierce, but he died, leaving her the job of sorting out his legacy and character. This challenge becomes a mock religious quest. She is a whiz at interpreting texts, but in this case the more information she accumulates, the more difficult it all is to evaluate and the more paranoid she becomes. The focus of her quest for information is The Tristero, or Trystero, a secret countercultural postal system whose symbol is a muted post horn. Every access she discovers to the Trystero can be traced to the Inverarity estate, so it appears that the dead capitalist owned even the counterculture and controlled Trystero. In the course of her quest, Oedipa insulates and desensitizes herself against a predatory environment. Consequently, she is not sensitive enough to communicate with Maxwell's Demon, a spirit in a box, and is overcome by the entropy she discovers in herself and in America. She sees life as a void, becomes suicidal, loses her bearings, and takes a man's name, Arnold Snarb, imposed on her by a stranger. At the end, in paranoia she hopes for a saving revelation at an auction of Inverarity's stamp collection.

Pierce Inverarity, a dead real estate mogul with headquarters in San Narciso, somewhere in Southern California. A "founding father," he seems to possess all of America. He does many impersonations, including The Shadow, and becomes a haunting, ambiguous, demonic god figure to Oedipa. His manipulations are represented by his defense plant, Yoyodyne, and his values by his tacky new housing development, Fangoso Lagoons, which features an artificial lake called Inverarity, with real human skeletons at the bottom. Oedipa fell in love with Pierce, though she may have meant no more to him than another stamp in his collection.

Wendell "Mucho" Maas, Oedipa's husband, a disc jockey for teenagers at radio station KCUF. Mucho is not macho, calls his wife Oed, and is very sensitive. He had to quit his former job as a used-car salesman because he felt sorry for the customers. As he and Oedipa become less able to communicate, he seduces teenage girls and takes drugs. Gradually, he loses his integrity, his ego dissipates, and he merges with the masses and becomes generic.

Metzger, a coexecutor of Inverarity's will, a lawyer and former child motion picture star who performed under the name of Baby Igor. Now thirty-five years old, he is so good-looking that Oedipa promptly sleeps with him after a game of Strip Botticelli. He is too artificial to be sure of his sexual orientation and blames his lack of character on a domineering mother and a cowardly father. Oedipa strikes him as one of "these lib, overeducated broads with the soft heads and bleeding hearts." He leaves her to run off with the very young girlfriend of a member of a rock band called the Paranoids.

— Michael Hollister

THE CRYSTAL WORLD

Author: J. G. Ballard (1930-   )
First published: 1966
Genre: Novel

Locale: The Cameroon Republic in West Africa
Time: c. 1966
Plot: Science fiction

Dr. Edward Sanders, the assistant director of a leper hospital. A gray-haired, unkempt man of forty, he has spent fifteen years in Africa, ten at the leper hospital. Uneasy because of a mysterious letter from his former mistress, Suzanne Clair, Sanders goes to Mont Royal to check on her. There, he risks death from violent men as well as from a rapidly spreading plague that crystallizes all living things. Although he escapes with the help of a jeweled cross, he eventually returns to the crystal forest, where he had for the first time felt whole.

Suzanne Clair, the wife of Max Clair and formerly the mistress of Sanders. A tall, dark woman in her thirties, she had been beautiful. When Sanders finds her, she bears the unmistakable signs of leprosy. She is nevertheless ecstatically happy in the crystal forest, where she leads a train of followers.

Dr. Max Clair, Suzanne's husband, formerly a colleague of Sanders. A small, plump man in early middle age, he now acts erratically, turning away lepers from his hospital at Mont Royal so that they will become crystallized and die.

Louise Peret, a French journalist. A broad-hipped, beautiful girl in her twenties, with dark hair and gray eyes, she looks much like a younger Suzanne. Although she becomes Sanders' mistress and cares for him in his illness, she does not share his enthusiasm for the crystal forest and finally breaks off their affair.

Ventress, a former architect, the cabin mate of Sanders on the trip to Port Materre. A slight, dark man of forty, he is restless and violent. Desperately searching for his wife, he escapes death repeatedly and even incidentally rescues Sanders. After killing Thorensen, he disappears, probably to die in the forest.

Thorensen, a tall, blond mine owner. He is selfish and possessive. After freeing Ventress' wife, he imprisoned her in his own luxurious, isolated home. After a number of skirmishes, he is shot by Ventress.

Serena Thorensen, the former wife of Ventress and the object of his search. A girl in her twenties with long blonde hair, she is emaciated from tuberculosis. When Sanders last sees her, she is only half conscious, lying beside the dead Thorensen.

Captain Radek, a doctor in the army medical corps. The tall, slim man first explains the crystallization phenomenon to Sanders. Later, when he is looking for Sanders, he becomes

partially crystallized. When Sanders rescues him and tries to tear off the crystals, Radek rebukes him and begs to go back into the forest.

Father Balthus, an apostate and priest from Mont Royal. A pale, nervous man, he first meets Sanders on the boat to Port Materre. Later, he nurses Sanders while he recovers from crystallization and gives him a cross that will enable him to return to safety.

— *Rosemary M. Canfield Reisman*

CUDJO'S CAVE

Author: John Townsend Trowbridge (1827-1916)
First published: 1863
Genre: Novel

Locale: Tennessee
Time: 1861
Plot: Historical

Penn Hapgood, a young Quaker schoolmaster in a Tennessee town. It is 1861, and Penn's antislavery convictions make him unpopular among the Secessionists. He steadfastly defends his convictions and aids others with antislavery and Unionist leanings, though his reversals include being tarred and feathered, having to hide out in a secret cave, undergoing capture and just missing hanging, and being captured again and almost bayoneted. At last, his chief enemy is taken and forced to sign a safe-conduct pass for Penn and his party. Reaching Pennsylvania by way of Ohio, Penn enlists in the Union Army; his heroism earns him the name "The Fighting Quaker."

Mr. Villars, a blind clergyman who shelters Penn and thus incurs the enmity of the Secessionists. His trials include imprisonment. He escapes and is guided to the cave, where he hides with the others. The safe-conduct pass gets him to Ohio.

Salina Sprowl, Mr. Villars' older daughter. Her vacillating attitude toward her estranged Secessionist husband constantly puts her friends in jeopardy.

Lysander Sprowl, Salina's worthless husband. Her weakness informs him that the antislavery group is safe in hiding. In order to undo her mischief, she has to set fire to her father's house to create confusion. Later, she makes it possible for Sprowl to escape from the cave where he is held prisoner. Returning with an attacking force, he is shot by his wife. She is bayoneted by Confederate soldiers.

Virginia Villars, the younger daughter of Mr. Villars and loved by a Secessionist planter whom she rejects. She too hides in the cave; in the end, she reaches Ohio with her father.

Augustus Blythewood, a planter in love with Virginia. He is the relentless leader of the Secessionists. In the attack on the cave, he captures Virginia and takes advantage of the opportunity to plead his suit again. She spurns him; captured in turn, he signs a safe-conduct pass for all of Penn's group.

Carl, a German boy and a friend of Penn. He is accepted in the Confederate Army in place of Penn, who was faced with the choice of volunteering or hanging. As a Confederate soldier, Carl has many opportunities to help his friends in escaping. He goes with them to Ohio and thence with Penn to Pennsylvania, where they enlist in the same regiment.

Farmer Stackridge, a staunch Unionist. He befriends Penn and later brings a band of Unionists to the cave, which they fortify and help to defend.

Toby, a freed slave in the minister's household and a loyal friend to Penn and his fellow Unionists.

Pomp, a magnificent and heroic slave, owned by Blythewood. Reaching the North with the others, he serves the Union as a scout.

Cudjo, a fellow runaway slave. He and Pomp hide and befriend Penn in a cave previously known only to escaping slaves. Cudjo's body is left in the cave.

Silas Ropes, a bully and the leader of a Secessionist mob. He causes much trouble before the attack on the cave in which he and Cudjo kill each other.

Dan Pepperill, a poor white man who befriends a slave and is flogged in consequence. Penn's aiding him is instrumental in making Penn unpopular.

Mrs. Sprowl, Penn's landlady and Lysander's mother.

CUPID AND PSYCHE

Author: Unknown
First transcribed: Unknown
Genre: Novel

Locale: Greece
Time: Antiquity
Plot: Mythic

Cupid, a god, Venus' son. He falls in love with Psyche and becomes her lover. When Psyche tries to see him, against his command, he kills her sisters, who had encouraged her action. He also abandons Psyche to the world. His love conquers his will, however, and he takes Psyche back again, petitioning Jove, king of the gods, to let her become immortal.

Psyche, a Greek princess. An oracle tells her father to leave her exposed upon a mountain to prevent the destruction of his people. Because of her beauty, Psyche arouses the jealousy of Venus. After being abandoned by Cupid, her lover, Psyche wanders the earth and finally becomes Venus' slave. With supernatural help, she completes the otherwise insurmountable tasks assigned by Venus and wins back Cupid's love. Upon drinking ambrosia given her by Jove, Psyche becomes immortal.

Venus, goddess of love. Jealous of Psyche, she makes the girl her slave and assigns her four tasks: to separate an immense pile of mixed seeds, to gather the golden fleece of Venus' sheep, to fill a jug with water from a stream that feeds the rivers Styx and Cocytus, and to collect some of Proserpine's beauty in a box.

Zephyrus, god of the south wind. He carries Psyche to Cupid's palace. He also delivers Psyche's sisters there when Cupid grants Psyche their company in her loneliness.

Mercury, the messenger god who conducts Psyche to the presence of Jove.

Jove (Jupiter), king of the gods. He grants immortality to Psyche so that she and Cupid can be together forever.

CURSE OF THE STARVING CLASS

Author: Sam Shepard (Samuel Shepard Rogers, 1943-   )
First published: 1976
Genre: Drama

Locale: California
Time: The 1970's
Plot: Mythic

Wesley Tate, the young son of a lower-middle-class, rural California family. Feeling strong ties to his family and to the land, Wesley maintains the farm after the others have given up. He sees the sale of the land to real estate developers as having significance far greater than the loss of a mere house. At times, Wesley loses patience with his family members, as evidenced by his lack of sympathy for his sister's ruined 4-H project, to which he responds by urinating on her charts and suggesting that his sister do something truly useful. He is also contemptuous of his mother's attorney friend, to whom he is very rude and accusatory. Although Wesley does not get along with his father, he does feel certain responsibilities toward his family. He cleans up the mess left after one of his father's frequent drunken binges and begins to replace the door the old man has beaten down. Wesley also is aware of some inherited traits, especially his father's passionate temper. Failing to experience the rebirth of spirit his father prescribes, Wesley dons his father's discarded old clothes. Wesley and his mother are the only family members left at the end of the play.

Ella Tate, Wesley's mother. Coming from a higher-class background, Ella feels like an outsider among the members of her own family. She feels abandoned by her husband and fears that he might try to kill her in one of his drunken rages. Ella insensitively cooks the chicken that her daughter plans to use in an important 4-H project. She also fills her young daughter's mind with an obsession about germs and with false information about the girl's physical maturity. Longing for the more prestigious lifestyle of the rich, Ella has become involved with an attorney and plans to sell the property and run away to Europe. After returning from jail to visit her daughter, Ella sleeps on the kitchen table. When she awakes, both her husband and her daughter have left, but, confused by Wesley's attire, she repeatedly calls her son by her husband's name.

Emma Tate, Wesley's sister. Outspoken and rebellious, Emma reaches physical maturity on the day the play takes place. She is outraged that her mother has cooked the chicken she has raised and prepared for her 4-H project, so she begins to make plans to run away to Mexico. Emma, who is somewhat loyal to her father, does not like her mother's attorney friend and tells him so. Emma is arrested for riding her horse through the bar her father frequents and shooting the place full of holes. She is released, however, when she makes sexual overtures to the police sergeant. Resolved to embark on a life of crime, Emma takes money and car keys from her mother's purse and leaves just before the car explodes.

Weston Tate, Wesley's father. An alcoholic with a violent temper, Weston is unable to hold a steady job, continues to drive even though his license has been revoked, and is in debt to some rough characters. He secretly sells the property to the owner of the Alibi Club for fifteen hundred dollars. When the family refrigerator is empty, Weston simply buys a bag of artichokes. After passing out on the kitchen table, Weston awakes with a sense of being reborn. He uncharacteristically bathes and shaves, discards his dirty old clothes, and does the laundry and cooks breakfast for the family. Although Weston decides to stay and work the farm, Wesley reminds him that he is still in trouble and encourages him to flee to Mexico.

Taylor, an attorney who speculates in real estate. Taylor has already cheated Weston out of five hundred dollars by selling him a worthless piece of desert real estate; now he is taking advantage of his intimate relationship with Ella to purchase the Tate property without the permission of Weston, whom Taylor has had declared mentally incompetent.

Ellis, the owner of the Alibi Club. Wearing a shiny yellow shirt, tight pants, shiny shoes, many rings, and a gold necklace, Ellis is a burly man whose arms are covered with tattoos. Ellis has taken advantage of Weston's drunkenness and indebtedness to purchase the Tate property for a mere fifteen hundred dollars.

Emerson, a small man who, by blowing up the Tates' car, reminds Weston of the consequences of not paying his debts.

Slater, the man who accompanies Ellis on his threatening visit.

Sergeant Malcolm, a highway patrol officer who notifies Ella that Emma has been arrested. He will take no action against the other criminals, however, because that is not within his jurisdiction.

— *Lou Thompson*

THE CUSTOM HOUSE

Author: Francis King (1923-   )
First published: 1961
Genre: Novel

Locale: Kyoto, Japan
Time: The 1950's
Plot: Social realism

Professor William Knox, a British university professor teaching in Kyoto, Japan. Equally impatient with the reticence and formality of the Japanese and the intrusiveness of foreigners, the forty-four-year-old phonetics expert acts as a somewhat weary and ironic commentator on the rapidly changing culture of post-World War II Japan. A widower, he falls in love with his neighbor Setsuko, who, for various reasons, cannot return his love. Knox's stay in Japan ends when he flies out of the country with the disgraced missionary Welling. At the novel's end, he is in Greece, his favorite country, where he learns that Setsuko has left Japan.

The Reverend Michael C. Welling, an Australian missionary. He is physically attractive yet emotionally weak, as is revealed early in the novel, when he tries to drive away without aiding a woman whom he sideswipes with his car. Welling's cowardice is also revealed through his own remembrances of how he failed to aid his brother during a shark attack and how he conducted himself during the war. His general unhappiness with his work is ameliorated temporarily when he falls in love with Sanae. The married missionary's frequent interaction with his beautiful student, however, soon leads to gossip and controversy. When Sanae is found murdered, the innocent and naïve Welling becomes the primary suspect. Characteristically, he chooses to flee the country rather than to face a prolonged trial and likely conviction.

Setsuko, an American-educated chemist who works in a nuclear weapons lab. The daughter of a Japanese father and a Russian mother, she considers herself to be an outsider in all cultures. Her unusual physical features, American education, and unfortunate relationship with her rich and powerful Japanese uncle all combine to alienate her from Japan and the Japanese. Although she enjoys Knox's company, she cannot return his love. Eventually, she flees Japan under the suspicion of having stolen atomic secrets for the Communists.

Sanae, a young, beautiful Japanese stripper. An orphan reared by missionaries in Hiroshima, she is both perceptive and determined. Her affair with Furomoto ends when, characteristically, he tires of her, but she uses her pregnancy by Furomoto to threaten blackmail. Suspecting Setsuko of having gone through her things on several occasions, Sanae ransacks Setsuko's room, taking some incriminating papers with her

when she leaves. Later, Sanae is found murdered. Whether Sanae is killed because of these secret papers or because of her threat to blackmail Furomoto is left unclear.

Furomoto, a rich and powerful Japanese businessman and artist. Insensitive and, at times, ruthless in both his business and his private affairs, he elicits antipathy in almost everyone with whom he interacts in the novel. His affairs with Sanae and Setsuko, his niece, have tragic consequences for both women. His desire to have Sanae disposed of is made clear; whether his wishes are acted on remains ambiguous.

Aileen Colethorpe, an American artist who rooms with Sanae. Colethorpe is under Furomoto's patronage until she angers him by resisting his artistic dicta. She and Sanae move in with Setsuko and her aunt after Furomoto stops providing the American and her friend with free housing. After Knox has left Japan, she writes him in Greece to tell him about Setsuko's flight from Japan.

Ed Schneider, an American journalist. Cynical, boorish, and brilliant, he has seen his reputation irreparably damaged by his alcoholism. He speaks Japanese fluently and understands the Japanese people better than any other foreigner.

Asai, a poor student. Although driven by his hatred both of Western intrusions into his country and of the Japanese lack of resolve, he chooses to strike out at the representatives of Western ideology. In Welling's Bible class, he ridicules Christian beliefs and goads Welling by telling him that he and the others are taking the class only to practice their English. His anarchism leads him to attempt to kill Furomoto, but the bungled bombing results only in his own death and the death of Furomoto's servant. Setsuko's respect for Asai is an early indication of her political sympathies.

The Reverend Harry Ambleside, the English director of the mission. He is admired by Welling, who notes the mix of altruism and ambition that drives Ambleside. Although Welling's lack of courage bothers Ambleside, he nevertheless tries to help out his fellow missionary once the scandal breaks. Ambleside's generally unruffled attitude toward both religion and the Japanese contrasts sharply with Welling's troubled outlook on both.

— *Tom Rash*

THE CUSTOM OF THE COUNTRY

Author: Edith Wharton (1862-1937)
First published: 1913
Genre: Novel

Locale: New York City and Paris
Time: Late nineteenth century
Plot: Social realism

Undine Spragg (uhn-DEEN sprag), an insatiably ambitious young woman whose beauty gains for her a place in society, four marriages, each more materially profitable than the last, and, finally, a desire for a fifth marriage to which she cannot attain because of her divorces.

Elmer Moffatt, Undine's vulgar, outspoken first husband. Forced by Undine's parents to get a divorce early in his marriage, Moffatt goes to New York, where he becomes a significant financial figure. Later, as one of the richest men

in the city, he remarries Undine and becomes her fourth husband.

Ralph Marvell, Undine's second husband. Disillusioned by his wife's ruthless desire for money and her insatiable social ambitions, he takes his own life.

Raymond de Chelles (shehl), a French comte and Undine's third husband. When he begins to neglect her, she divorces him and remarries the now-wealthy Moffatt.

Jim Driscoll, American ambassador to England and an old

society acquaintance of Undine. She aspires to become his wife.

Peter Van Degen, Undine's lover, who deserts her in Paris when he learns of her callous treatment of Ralph.

Paul Marvell, son of Undine and Ralph.

Laura Fairford, Ralph's sister.

Clare Dagonet (da-goh-NAY), Ralph's cousin and the wife of Peter Van Degen.

Mr. Spragg, Undine's father. He is forced by Moffatt to invest money to further Moffatt's early financial career.

THE CUTTER

Author: Virgil Suarez (1962-   )
First published: 1991
Genre: Novel

Locale: Cuba and the United States
Time: 1969
Plot: Bildungsroman

Julian Campos, the main character, a twenty-year-old university student. He longs for freedom and attempts to attain it legally, but he eventually realizes that he will never be allowed to leave Cuba. Although Julian's parents were deeply distressed about having to leave their son behind when they left the country, they made the choice to leave. Despite Julian's own desperation to leave Cuba, he never forgives his parents for leaving for the United States without him. Julian is a good, responsible young man. He cares deeply for his ailing grandmother Bernarda and for Carmina, Bernarda's housekeeper and nursemaid. Julian tries to do what is right and obtain his freedom legally, but he suffers for his efforts.

Bernarda Del Rio (RREE-oh), Julian's grandmother. She represents that group of people who believed in the system but became disillusioned after the repressive government began to retaliate against those who opposed the revolution. After Julian's father, Ernesto, was imprisoned for organizing "antirevolutionary activities," Bernarda renounced Cuba and the revolution. She longs for a reunion with her son in the United States.

Carmina (kahr-MEE-nah), Bernarda's faithful housekeeper and friend. She nurses Julian's grandmother until she dies, then cares for Julian after his return from a work camp. Although Carmina sympathizes with Julian's desire to leave Cuba and assists him in his efforts, she refuses to leave. Cuba is her home, and Carmina suggests that she has a kind of freedom there.

Blancarosa Calderon (blahn-kah-ROH-sah kahl-deh-ROHN), a former classmate of Julian. She inspires no sympa-

thy, for she betrays her friends. Although government officials and party sympathizers call Julian a *gusano*, a traitor, it is clear that Blancarosa is the only traitor in the novel: She deliberately deceives those who entrust their lives to her.

Ofelia (oh-FEH-lee-ah), Julian's neighbor. She tells Julian about a planned escape from Cuba. Ofelia believes herself to be in love with Julian and is jealous of Blancarosa, toward whom Julian seems to have romantic inclinations.

Fermin (fehr-MEEN), Ofelia's father. Fermin goes to the cane fields with Julian to serve as a "voluntary" worker as a means of earning the right to emigrate. He and Julian spend time together in the camp jail cell. At the camp, Fermin is caught buying *aguardiente*, an illegal alcoholic drink. Fermin, who drinks to ease his frustration, tells Julian, while they are in detention, that he wants to die drunk. Fermin dies mysteriously, apparently getting his wish.

Nicanor (nee-KAH-nohr), a Communist Party cadre. Nicanor is in charge of *El Comite*, "the community watchdog." He is the only major black character. He is a widower who lost his pregnant wife in a fire ten years before the action of the novel. Before the revolution, Nicanor was unemployed. He refuses a chance to flee Cuba after the revolution, vowing to attain a position in which he is powerful enough to "get even" for his wife's death. Nicanor watches Julian carefully and suspects, near the end of the novel, that Julian plans to leave Cuba illegally. Nicanor represents the repressive, ruthless government. He is clearly responsible for thwarting Julian's attempts to leave Cuba legally.

THE CUTTLEFISH: Or, The Hyrcanian Worldview
(Mątwe: Czyli, Hyrkaniczny światopogląd)

Author: Stanisław Ignacy Witkiewicz (1885-1939)
First published: 1923
Genre: Drama

Locale: Unspecified
Time: The 1920's
Plot: Surrealism

Paul Rockoffer, a disillusioned artist. In a time of increasing dehumanization and mechanization of society, Rockoffer finds the pursuit of art meaningless. Forty-six years old, the fair-haired artist, dressed in black, mourns the waste of his life and the isolation and futility of his existence as an artist. In the face of eternal gray boredom, Rockoffer succumbs to the enticements of bourgeois contentment in his engagement to Ella. He is, however, torn by past yearnings as represented by the sensual statue. At the same time, Pope Julius II offers him a life of total devotion to art and Hyrcan IV attempts to convince him of the possibilities of absolute power. Despite his waverings between a life of art and a life of power, Rock-

offer (having killed Hyrcan IV), as Hyrcan V, intends to create a reality in which art, philosophy, love, and science will become "one huge mishmash," thereby fulfilling the Nietzschean notion of the artist as superman.

Julius II, a sixteenth century pope and patron of the arts. A projection of Rockoffer's mind, he is a visitor from the past and represents Renaissance values of strength, intelligence, commitment, and belief in individualism. As a patron of the arts in his support of such artists as Raphael and Michelangelo, Julius II believes that art transcends all ideological absolutes. Dressed in the Renaissance robes from his portrait by Titian, he serves as a reminder of the waning of Humanism and individualism. At times, his viewpoint is caricatured; in the face of contemporary choices, he chooses a more pragmatic point of view.

Hyrcan IV, the king of Hyrcania. Hyrcan IV is the ruler and creator of the imaginary kingdom of Hyrcania, constructed to justify his synthetic philosophy of power. An ultimate pragmatist and believer in the absolutes of power, Hyrcan IV represents the coming age of numbing dictatorship over individual creativity. His costume projects the trappings of power: He appears carrying a sword and wearing a purple cloak and a helmet with a red plume; underneath the cloak, a golden garment glimmers. As he throws off these garments in the last scene and appears in a well-tailored cutaway, the sham of his Hyrcanian worldview is revealed as yet another ideology that pragmatically suits selfish desires.

Alice d'Or, the statue. Dressed in a tight-fitting dress, the fabric of which resembles alligator skin, the blonde, twenty-six-year-old statue reclines on a pedestal on her stomach. As Rockoffer's former mistress, she attempts to entice him by recalling their former sensuality; however, at this point she exists only as a symbol of his atrophied desire.

Ella, Rockoffer's eighteen-year-old fiancée. Ella represents bourgeois domesticity; she comes in carrying parcels to furnish their small apartment, with its small gold sofa where their matrimonial bliss will be lived out in the daily rituals of meals and pleasantries. She is the play's cuttlefish, an insidious predator who clouds perspective by diffusing an inky substance. In the last scene, she sheds her bourgeois limitations, showing the courage to join Rockoffer in his attempt to build a new Hyrcania.

Two Matrons, one of them Ella's mother, the other Hyrcan's. Both mothers project the sentimental belief in the right of mothers to be taken care of by their children. Both are taken along to Hyrcania by Rockoffer: Hyrcan IV's mother, as Rockoffer's adopted mother, and Ella's, as mother-in-law.

Two Old Gentlemen, Ella's uncles. They are minor characters representing bourgeois complacency in the face of social change.

Grumpus, the footman. He is old and wears a gray livery coat with large silver buttons and a gray top hat. In his acceptance of the transition of power lies a suggestion that there is no essential change as far as he is concerned.

— Christine Kiebuzinska

CYCLOPS
(Kyklōps)

Author: Euripides (c. 485-406 B.C.E.)
First performed: c. 421 B.C.E.
Genre: Drama

Locale: Mt. Etna in Sicily
Time: Antiquity
Plot: Mythic

Odysseus (oh-DIHS-ews), the crafty king of Ithaca. On his way home from the sack of Troy, he lands at Etna, in Sicily, the home of the Cyclops. Seeking food, he is captured by the Cyclops Polyphemus but manages to escape by blinding the giant after giving him wine. The story is taken from book 9 of Homer's *The Odyssey*, but Euripides has changed both some details of the original story and the character of Odysseus. Odysseus and his men do not escape by clinging to a ram's belly, nor does the Cyclops block the entrance to his cave with a boulder. The change in the character of Odysseus is more important. He is the son not of Laertes, but of Sisyphus, the famous sinner of Corinth, a cheat and a thief. Odysseus becomes in the play a representative of civilized brutality. His speech for mercy before the Cyclops is filled with sophistry, and the sympathy that he arouses at the beginning of the play, when he is weak and oppressed, is reversed by the brutality of his blinding of the Cyclops who, drunk, becomes a decadent but rather likable buffoon.

The Cyclops (SI-klops), called **Polyphemus** (pol-ih-FEE-muhs), the son of Poseidon. The one-eyed giant of the Homeric legend, he is the exponent of egoism and immoral application of might and right. To Odysseus' argument that the Cyclops should spare him and his men because the Greeks have preserved the temples of his father Poseidon and saved Hellas, the giant replies that he has no respect for the gods; his religion consists of his belly and his desires. He disregards morality through an appeal to nature and believes mercy a mere convention of the weak. The gory description of his cannibalism (he has two of Odysseus' men for his meal) does

much to justify Odysseus' revenge, but he changes as he drinks. He becomes a decadent buffoon who loathes war and tries to rape Silenus. Blinded, he is comic because of his repeated assertion that "Nobody," the name Odysseus has used, has done him in. As Odysseus leaves, having revealed his true identity, the Cyclops prophesies that Odysseus will be forced to wander the seas before returning to his home.

Silenus (si-LEE-nuhs), a follower of Dionysus. Shipwrecked on Etna while searching for Dionysus, who had been captured by Lydian pirates, he was taken by the Cyclops and has remained his slave. He is the "father" of the satyric chorus and a standard part of satyric convention. A lewd, fat, bald, boastful, cowardly, and drunken old man, he freely offers to trade Odysseus food for wine; however, when the Cyclops appears, he says that Odysseus has stolen the wine. He continues to drink throughout the play and is given in mock marriage to the Cyclops.

The Chorus of Satyrs, also a standard part of satyric convention. They are "horse-men," lewd in appearance, speech, and action. They exhibit a strong streak of cowardice. They offer to aid Odysseus in blinding the Cyclops, but when the time for action arrives, they excuse themselves on the grounds that they have become lame while standing still. Their only real interest is in resuming the worship of Bacchus.

Coryphaeus (coh-RIHF-ee-uhs), the leader of the Chorus.

The companions of Odysseus, members of his crew. They remain silent throughout the play. They help Odysseus blind the Cyclops.

CYMBELINE

Author: William Shakespeare (1564-1616)
First published: 1623
Genre: Drama

Locale: Britain, Italy, and Wales
Time: The first century B.C.E.
Plot: Tragicomedy

Cymbeline (SIHM-beh-leen), the king of Britain. On the whole, he is more a conventional figure made to help the plot than a complex human being. Quick-tempered, arbitrary, and unreasonable, he is naturally well-meaning and generous. His second wife influences him far more than he realizes. His forgiveness of his enemies and his son-in-law at the end of the play is an example of his essential goodness.

Imogen (IHM-oh-jehn), Cymbeline's daughter by his former queen; she is disguised for part of the play as **Fidele** (fih-DAYL), a boy. She is the most admired character in the play, and many critics believe it has small excuse for being except as a vehicle for her. She is a faithful wife, independent and courageous. She escapes her father's court, her husband's plot to have her murdered, her wicked stepbrother's attempt to violate her, and her evil stepmother's plot to poison her. Disguised as a boy, she finds her unknown brothers in the forest. She forgives her husband for his lack of trust.

Posthumus Leonatus (POS-tew-muhs lee-oh-NAY-tuhs), Imogen's husband, a gentleman of good lineage but poor fortune; he is unacceptable to Cymbeline as a son-in-law. Banished for marrying Imogen, he goes to Italy. There, carried away while praising his wife, he makes an unwise wager with the evil Iachimo that his wife's chastity will withstand any temptation. She lives up to his faith, but Iachimo presents such strong circumstantial evidence that she has been unfaithful that Posthumus sends orders to his servant to kill her. He receives undeserved forgiveness from her and is reunited with her.

Cloten (KLOH-tehn), the queen's repulsive son. Ignorant and stupid as well as vicious, he clothes himself in Leonatus' garments and follows Imogen, intending to violate her. He meets and threatens Guiderius, who promptly chops off his head. Finding his headless corpse in the familiar garments, Imogen thinks that her husband is dead.

The queen, the second wife of Cymbeline, whom she deceives and manages. The typical stepmother of folktales, she endeavors to destroy Imogen with a supposed restorative that she has poisoned. She is largely responsible for the strife between Rome and England. She dies before her villainies are discovered, but they are exposed after her death.

Iachimo (YAH-kih-moh), an Italian villain. Irritated by Posthumus' praise of Imogen, he wagers that he can seduce her. After he fails in his attempt, he hides in a trunk that is conveyed into her room, observes her sleeping, steals a bracelet from her, and memorizes her bedroom furnishings. With this circumstantial evidence and sworn lies, he deceives Posthumus. He becomes remorseful, and when captured by Cymbeline's forces and questioned by Fidele/Imogen, he confesses all, repents, and is included in the general forgiveness.

Belarius (beh-LAY-ree-uhs), a banished lord, disguised as Morgan. Having been unjustly accused of treason, he has kidnapped the sons of Cymbeline and has reared them in a Welsh forest as his own sons. When Rome sends forces against England, he and the two youths come to the aid of the English forces. He discloses the identity of the young men to Cymbeline and receives forgiveness in the general rejoicing.

Guiderius (gwih-DEE-ree-uhs), who is living in the forest as Polydore but is the elder son of Cymbeline. Although rough and untutored, he has a bold and royal nature. After his heroic deeds in the battle, he confesses to Cymbeline that he has killed Cloten and that he would be delighted to do so again if Cloten were still alive. He is condemned to death by Cymbeline but is pardoned when his true identity is revealed.

Arviragus (ahr-vih-RAY-guhs), who is living in the forest as Cadwal but is the younger son of Cymbeline. He and his brother welcome the homeless Fidele as a brother and grieve deeply at his supposed death. They rejoice when they learn that their supposed brother is actually their sister and that her apparent death was only a drugged sleep.

Caius Lucius (KAY-yuhs LEW-shee-uhs), a general of the Roman forces. He finds Fidele mourning over the body of the supposed Posthumus and offers his protection as a father rather than as a master. After the battle, he is spared by Cymbeline's generosity.

Pisanio (pee-ZAH-nee-oh), Posthumus' loyal, intelligent servant. He disobeys his master's command to kill Imogen and falsely reports her death, but both disobedience and falsehood are higher-level loyalty than literal obedience would have been. He confuses Cloten with false information, which happily leads to the violent death of the villainous prince. He gives the queen's drug to Imogen, thinking it a restorative.

Cornelius (kohr-NEE-lee-uhs), a physician. Mistrusting the queen, he gives her not the poison she asks for but a harmless drug that gives a temporary appearance of death. The drug deceives Belarius and the brothers into thinking Fidele dead. At the play's end, Cornelius exposes the queen's evil plot to Cymbeline.

Philario (fih-LAH-ree-oh), an Italian friend of Posthumus. He introduces Posthumus to Iachimo, thereby making the wager plot possible.

Helen, a lady attending Imogen.

Sicilius Leonatus (sih-SIHL-ee-uhs lee-oh-NAY-tuhs), the father of Posthumus. His ghost, along with those of his wife and two dead sons, appears in the masquelike vision of Posthumus in prison.

Jupiter, who also appears in the vision and promises a happy outcome for Posthumus.

THE CYPRESSES BELIEVE IN GOD
(Los cipreses creen en Dios)

Author: José María Gironella (1917-   )
First published: 1953
Genre: Novel

Locale: Gerona, Catalonia, in northeastern Spain
Time: 1931-1936
Plot: Historical realism

Matías Alvear (mah-TEE-ahs ahl-veh-AHR), a telegrapher with the government postal service and patriarch of the Alvear family. Mildly anticlerical, he shuns politics, preferring to go to the Neutral Cafe for games of dominoes with his friends. His involvement with the tragic events of the Spanish Civil War mainly concerns the telegrams he sends or receives. Originally from Madrid, he has to learn Catalan or be transferred.

Carmen Elgazu (ehl-GAH-sew), his wife, a Basque. She is deeply religious. She ensures that her three children receive a strong religious upbringing and is aided by the priests who advise her, especially Mosén Alberto. She deplores the secularizing tendencies of the Spanish Republic but is not active politically.

Ignacio Alvear (eeg-NAH-see-oh), their oldest son, the central figure of the novel. He enters the seminary as a boarding student but after a few years decides he does not want to become a priest. He begins working as an office boy in the Arús Bank, and associates with his coworkers. After he passes the examinations for his high school studies (undertaken at night), he is promoted. While on vacation at the seashore, he meets his first sweetheart, Ana Maria, but on his return to Gerona he fails to answer her letters and becomes involved with the prostitute Canela, who gives him a venereal disease. His recovery from this illness leads him to make a thorough confession and to be reconciled with his family. He later becomes romantically involved with Marta Martínez de Soria, the major's daughter, who is a Falangist like his classmate Mateo Santos. Although Ignacio is involved in a minor riot, his participation is instigated by his anarchist cousin José from Madrid, and he remains uninvolved in politics.

César Alvear (SEH-sahr), Ignacio's younger brother, who takes Ignacio's place as a seminarian. He is overly ascetic, is in weak health, and has to be monitored by Mosén Alberto lest he engage in too many privations. During the summers, he works with the poor in the slum district, barbering the sick and old and teaching the children who are too poor to afford school. During the general strike, he is forced to leave the seminary because the peasants will not supply the school at Collell if the seminarians remain. He returns to Gerona. When he tries to resume teaching the children in the poor quarters, he is actively discouraged by the residents. He is executed by the Communists after the military insurrection in Gerona is suppressed.

Pilar Alvear (pee-LAHR), the youngest of the Alvear family. She grows into young womanhood and becomes the sweetheart of Mateo Santos, who is a classmate of Ignacio and the son of the tobacconist who is Matías' partner in dominoes. Mateo later organizes a Falangist cell.

Julio Garcia (HEW-lee-oh gahr-SEE-ah), the chief of police in Gerona and an important figure in the local Masonic lodge. He takes a sardonic view of the political changes in Spain. He joins the movement for autonomy of Catalonia, for which he temporarily loses his job and is even threatened with execution. When the Popular Front wins the election of 1936, he is restored as police chief. He accepts the surrender of Major Martínez de Soria after the unsuccessful coup and protects the prisoners from the Communists and anarchists.

Dr. Relken, a German-Jewish archaeologist. He is the authorial mouthpiece for addressing the shortcomings of Spain through foreign eyes. He is beaten up by Mateo and other Falangist youths.

Major Martínez de Soria (mahr-TEE-nehs de SOH-ree-ah), a veteran of the African war. He becomes the military commander of Gerona after the senior major is killed while suppressing the Catalan autonomy movement. He and his daughter Marta frequently ride their horses in the city. Although he is an autocrat and a martinet, he is a deeply patriotic monarchist and leads the insurrection against the Popular Front.

Cosme Vila (KOHS-meh VEE-lah), who works with Ignacio at the bank. He quits to become head of the local Communist Party. He organizes bombings and executions as a way of cold-bloodedly gaining control.

David Pol, a Socialist, a teacher, and a moderate. He and his wife, Olga, are made commissioners of education for Gerona after the Popular Front victory.

Olga Sol, David's wife, a modern woman with short hair who smokes cigarettes and wears slacks. Because she was one of Ignacio's teachers, she agrees to shelter Marta after the military insurrection fails and the families of the participants are imprisoned.

Mosén Alberto (moh-SEHN ahl-BEHR-toh), a conservative priest, the spiritual guide of the Alvear family. Curator of the Diocesan Museum, he is able to flee into exile when the Communist executions begin.

Mosén Francisco, a young, reform-minded priest who is able to reach Ignacio and guide his spiritual life. During the executions, he disguises himself as a militiaman and gives those killed the last rites of the church.

— *R. M. Longyear*

CYRANO DE BERGERAC

Author: Edmond Rostand (1868-1918)
First published: 1898
Genre: Drama

Locale: France
Time: The seventeenth century
Plot: Tragicomedy

Cyrano de Bergerac (see-rah-NOH deh behr-zheh-RAHK), a historical poet, playwright, and soldier who, as a contemporary of the three famous musketeers, creates an image of romance considerably heightened by his lines in the play. Although the possessor of an enormous nose, which its owner declared was a symbol of generosity and independence, Cyrano has a romantic heart and a gifted tongue as well as a spirit of fierce independence. He chooses as his symbol a white plume of unsullied integrity, never lowered for expediency's sake. Although he appears boastful in the braggart warrior tradition, he actually is shy and diffident, especially when confronting beauty in any form. As the accomplice in a love plot, he never speaks for himself until wounded mortally. His name stands not only for an ugly handicap for which compensation must be made but also for all that is good, true, loyal, and fine in human nature. Such integrity is in the great tradition of Don Quixote, whom Cyrano admires because tilting at the windmills of pomposity and philistinism, although it may throw the challenger down, more often elevates.

Christian de Neuvillette (krees-TYAHN deh new-vee-YEHT), Cyrano's protégé in love, who never learns the language of sentiment. Often mistaken for a silent lover, the young soldier has greater depths of feeling and finer sensibilities than he can express. He is undoubtedly handsome and generous, but his valor in battle is offset by this morbid shyness in love, and although he acts the dupe of his mentor, he resents very much his own inadequacies. He dies bravely, knowing that another man has won his wife but realizing that he will not be betrayed by his beloved friend.

Roxane (rohk-SAHN), or **Madeleine Robin**, who as *precieuse* seems the prototype of thoughtless love but who as suffering widow becomes the ideal of womanhood. Bright, beautiful, gay, and youthful, Roxane is the symbol of beauty that all men desire. She insists that the amenities and conventions of love come before the character of the lover, only to learn that there is no substitute for sincerity of feeling and expression. She is also a romantic and somewhat silly heroine who becomes wise and thoughtful only after revelation.

Ragueneau (rah-geh-NOH), a pastry cook/poet who, as a bard of the oven, befriends the hero and holds a salon for destitute artists. This tippling pretender suffers the scorn of his wife and the appetite of his poets. He is loyal to an ideal and constant in his loyalties.

Le Bret (leh bray), the friend and counselor of Cyrano and the author's commentator who interprets the brave soldier's heart. Steadfast in his regard for the hero, Le Bret is the only one permitted to speak directly to him of his inconsistencies. He always proves loyal and devoted.

Montfleury (mohn-flew-REE), a famous actor whom Cyrano will not permit to play because of his lack of refinement and sensitivity to language. As the pompous idol of his day, the actor represents popular tastes, a symbol of decadence that Cyrano cannot tolerate.

The comte de Guiche (geesh), who woos Roxane without success and who has his revenge when he sends Christian, her husband, into battle and to his death. Although a representative of civil and military power, he displays some redeeming features even while he plays the villain of the play. He is a step above the fops and dandies, and he admires the bravery of Cyrano against the odds of life.

CYROPAEDIA
(Kyro paideia)

Author: Xenophon (c. 431-c. 354 B.C.E.)
First published: After 371 B.C.E. (English translation, 1560-1567)
Genre: Nonfiction

Locale: The Median kingdom
Time: Antiquity
Plot: History

Cyrus, the hero, whose education for kingship is the subject of the story. Cyrus is presented as the ideal leader and king, aware of the art of statesmanship as well as its practical politics. Cyrus has great strength of character but always puts the state's interests before his own. Cyrus is born a prince in the minor kingdom of Pars, which is but a small part of the great Median realm of the king Astyages. Cyrus is the son of the Persian prince Cambyses and of Mandane, the daughter of Astyages himself. His father, a firm man, gives him vigorous instruction in the arts of war. He is also tutored by Astyages and is particularly inspired by his grandfather's love of horses. The obvious talents possessed by Cyrus spur court observers to predict great achievements for him in the future; these prophecies are given concrete force by omens and oracles. When Cyaxares succeeds Astyages and discovers that the Median kingdom has been attacked by Assyrians, he summons Cyrus to his aid. Cyrus helps vanquish the Assyrians and later conquers Babylon on his own. Advised by Chrysantas, Hystaspas, and Pheraulus, Cyrus becomes the most powerful leader the world has ever known. He even supplants Cyaxares as king of the Medes and marries Cyaxares' daughter. Rather than directly confronting opponents such as Cyaxares and Croesus, he tries to co-opt them into his own political framework as much as possible. At once victorious general, wise administrator, and heroic paragon, Cyrus sums up the best of which humanity is capable in his time.

Chrysantas (krih-SAN-tuhs), a counselor of Cyrus who is his chief deputy in practical and administrative matters.

Hystaspas (hihs-TAS-pahs), a loyal friend and counselor to Cyrus, renowned for his intelligence and wit.

Pheraulus, a Persian commoner who often mediates between Cyrus and the people whom he rules. Pheraulus is among Cyrus' most trusted advisers.

Cyaxares (si-AK-suh-reez), the brother of Mandane and son of Astyages. As king of Media, he helps Cyrus conquer Assyria. He later gives his daughter to Cyrus in marriage. There is some rivalry between Cyrus and Cyaxares, but in general they work in concert as friends and allies.

Astyages (as-TI-uh-jeez), the grandfather of Cyrus and king of the Medes. Unlike other writers, who portray Astyages as jealous of Cyrus, Xenophon presents him as a loving and encouraging grandfather.

Artabazes (ahr-tuh-BAY-zuhs), a Mede who admires Cyrus and convinces the rest of the Medes to accept Cyrus as their king.

Gobyras and

Gadatas, Assyrian prisoners of war who help Cyrus make his conquest. Their sad personal stories provide variety and contrast in the composition of the work.

Croesus (KREE-suhs), a famous and wealthy king of Lydia who is unexpectedly conquered by Cyrus and becomes a prisoner in Cyrus' court.

Cambyses (kam-BI-seez), Cyrus' father. He gives Cyrus early instruction in the arts of war

Mandane, Cyrus' mother, daughter of Astyages, and sister of Cyaxares. Mandane helps cement the connection between the Median and Persian royal families that helps Cyrus unite the two peoples.

— Margaret Boe Birns

D

DA

Author: Hugh Leonard (John Keyes Byrne, 1926-)
First published: 1973
Genre: Drama

Locale: South Dublin, Ireland
Time: May, 1968
Plot: Comedy

Charlie Tynan, a London playwright. Charlie is Da's foster child. At the age of forty-two, he has returned to Ireland to bury his deceased father. He is a troubled man who is unable to exorcise Da's presence from his memory. Charlie's earlier abjuration of Da's rustic sensibility is a source of shame for him, as is his perception of his father as boorish and obstinate. His father's posthumous visitations to Charlie's mind are reflections of Charlie's fixation on Da and the remarkable impressions he left on Charlie throughout their embattled relationship.

Nick Tynan, called **Da**, a longtime gardener for the Prynne family. Da is eighty-three years old at his death but appears in the play at various ages from his fifties to the time of his death. Da is a cantankerous man, even when younger, yet he is proud of his fifty-eight years of diligent service as a gardener for the Prynne family. Although he is contrary to people like Drumm, his insistence on haunting Charlie is a reflection of his forceful personality and dominant role in shaping Charlie's life.

Margaret (Mag) Tynan, often called **Mother**, Da's wife and Charlie's mother. She is in her late seventies at her reported death, but the play presents her during her late fifties. Mag is devoted to both Da and Charlie and exhibits pride in her rearing of Charlie after his natural mother abandoned him. Her one act of defiance is to accept an invitation to tea from an old friend and thus to alienate Da.

Mr. Drumm, a clerk. He is a priggish, arrogant man in his mid-fifties in one flashback, in which Charlie remembers his first job, when he was seventeen. He is a bookish man who appreciates Charlie's literary interests but strongly dislikes Da's antagonistic, perverse treatment of him when he first arrives to hire Charlie. He admonishes Charlie about embracing any of life's opportunities. He returns to Charlie's house after Da's funeral and admits his own shortcomings.

Young Charlie, Charlie as a seventeen-year-old. He is slightly naïve and seeks to break away from his parents' influence, especially that of Da. He is excited about his employment at Drumm's clerical office and somewhat cynical about the elder Charlie when the two exchange words. The elder Charlie must often put his younger incarnation in his place.

Oliver, Charlie's childhood friend. Oliver is in his early forties and appears at the house after Da's funeral. His childish perspective on life belies his strictly mercenary interest in the now-empty house and his hopes to acquire it. He also appears later in the play, during a flashback of Charlie's departure for London.

Mary Tate, a twenty-five-year-old woman from Charlie's past. Mary appears once in the play and is notable for her effects on Charlie's libido. Described as the "Yellow Peril" by Charlie, Mary is an aloof, lonely young woman who teases Charlie when he flirts with her. Her mysterious reputation as a bad girl is quickly stripped from her by Da when he meets her and Charlie on a park bench. Da reveals that she is really a young girl from Glasthule whose father abandoned her and her family. Her identity restored, she no longer is the conquest Charlie had hoped for.

Mrs. Prynne, the daughter of Jacob Prynne, owner of the garden that Da has tended for more than fifty-eight years. She is fifty years old and apparently prim. Although she is kind in her words to Da, her pension contribution to Da of twenty-six pounds per year is viewed as miserly by young Charlie. Unaware of the slight she has given Da, she exacerbates it further by giving Da a mounted set of fused spectacles from the great fire of the San Francisco earthquake—one of her father's keepsakes.

— *Hardin Aasand*

DADDY WAS A NUMBER RUNNER

Author: Louise Meriwether (1923-)
First published: 1970
Genre: Novel

Locale: Harlem, New York
Time: June 2, 1934, to the fall of 1935
Plot: Bildungsroman

Francie Coffin, the twelve-year-old narrator of this novel of initiation, who witnesses the disintegration of her Harlem family over the course of a year. She has or finds the skills to survive in this world of poverty, violence, and sexual abuse.

Francie is bright, loyal, and enterprising.

Henrietta Coffin, Francie's mother, the person who holds the Coffin family together. She goes to work part-time, later full-time, for a white woman, applies for welfare against the wishes of her husband, and somehow manages to save her shrinking family.

James Adam Coffin, Francie's "beautiful" father, who is a numbers runner in his Harlem neighborhood. He can barely support his family in the bottom of the Depression, even working as a janitor in exchange for rent and with occasional piano jobs. In the end, the pressures of his family get to him, and he leaves to move in with Mrs. Mackey.

James Junior, Francie's older brother, fifteen years old. He is impatient with the pace of his life, joins the Ebony Earls, a youth gang, and drops out of school to work for Alfred, a Harlem pimp. Later, he lives with Belle, a prostitute.

Sterling, Francie's fourteen-year-old brother, who graduates from junior high school. He also is impatient with his family's poverty, and he leaves school to go to work for an undertaker. Sterling watches out for his younger sister and becomes the father figure to the family by the novel's end.

Sukie Maceo, Francie's best friend, a girl with much anger that comes out in fights with Francie. Sukie's sister is China Doll, a prostitute. By the novel's close, Francie realizes that Sukie is headed for the same awful end.

Maude Caldwell, another good friend of Francie. She and the other members of her West Indian family live next door to the Coffins.

Aunt Hazel, Henrietta Coffin's sister, a successful single domestic worker who is always able and willing to lend money to Francie's struggling family.

— *David Peck*

THE DAHOMEAN: An Historical Novel

Author: Frank Yerby (1916-1991)
First published: 1971
Genre: Novel

Locale: Africa
Time: The nineteenth century
Plot: Historical realism

Nyasanu (nyah-SAH-new), the second son of a village chief in Dahomey. Nyasanu is thrust into prominence by fate. He is content with his life, but after his father's death in battle, he assumes the mantle of chief of his village and begins a steady climb to political prominence and wealth. It becomes apparent that Nyasanu is trapped: The more he controls, the less he is able to control. He is aware of the pitfalls of his position but is powerless to change it. He owes his ultimate allegiance to King Gezo. When Gezo tells him to marry his daughter, Princess Yekpewa, Nyasanu must, and this act leads to his downfall. Nyasanu accepts his fate, which is to be captured and sold into slavery. He stoically comments that "no man is powerless who is prepared to suffer the consequences of his actions."

Gbenu (geh-BAY-new), the father of Nyasanu and chief of an important Dahomean village. A high-ranking vassal of King Gezo, Gbenu is a wise leader and brave warrior. These qualities are inherited by his son. After Gbenu's death, Nyasanu assumes the title of village chief and becomes responsible for his father's widows.

Gbochi (geh-BOH-chee), the homosexual brother of Nyasanu and eldest son of Gbenu. He is prevented from succeeding his father because he lacks the necessary leadership skills. Gbochi becomes embittered and plots his brother's downfall.

Gezo (GAY-zoh), the king of the Dahomeans. After Nyasanu defeats the combined enemy forces of the Maxi and the Auyo, Gezo rewards Nyasanu for his bravery by granting him the hand of his daughter in marriage. This royal influence succeeds in obtaining further recognition for Nyasanu; he is awarded the position of provincial governor.

Princess Yekpewa (YAYK-pay-wah), the daughter of Gezo and wife of Nyasanu. Proud of her royal rank, scornful of Nyasanu's other wives, and unwilling to submit to Nyasanu's authority, Princess Yekpewa schemes with Gbochi and her half brother Prince Atedeku to overthrow Nyasanu.

Kpadunu (keh-pah-DEW-new), a friend of Nyasanu who intends to become a sorcerer. Kpadunu has long discussions with Nyasanu and explores the philosophical implications of traditional Dahomean magic and statecraft. Designated as Nyasanu's first friend, Kpadunu has special obligations to Nyasanu and sacrifices his own life in battle to protect his friend.

— *Joe Benson*

DAISY MILLER: A Study

Author: Henry James (1843-1916)
First published: 1878
Genre: Novella

Locale: Vevey, Switzerland, and Rome
Time: Mid-nineteenth century
Plot: Psychological realism

Daisy Miller, the charming and unconforming American tourist whose inattention to decorum (she walks unchaperoned with an Italian suitor in the daytime) results in her ostracism by the Europeanized Americans in Rome. In defiance, she visits the Colosseum at night with the same young man and later dies of a fever contracted there.

Frederick Winterbourne, an American expatriate from whose point of view the story is told. At first puzzled by Daisy,

he soon becomes convinced that she is immoral. After her death, however, he realizes that he loved her, and that her manners indicated only a native American freedom.

Giovanelli, the young Italian whose companionship causes the scandal involving Daisy. An adventurer interested primarily in Daisy's money, he admits to Winterbourne after her death that she never would have consented to marry him.

Mrs. Walker, an American expatriate. Because Daisy rejects Mrs. Walker's efforts to preserve her from scandal, Mrs. Walker cuts her at a party, thus beginning Daisy's complete ostracism.

Randolph Miller, Daisy's young and spoiled brother. His impudence also shocks the American expatriates.

Mrs. Costello, Winterbourne's aunt. She refuses to meet Daisy because she is convinced that the Millers are common.

Eugenio, the Millers' courier and servant. That the Millers treat him almost as a member of the family also causes talk among the American expatriates.

DAME CARE
(Frau Sorge)

Author: Hermann Sudermann (1857-1928)
First published: 1887
Genre: Novel

Locale: Germany
Time: The nineteenth century
Plot: Domestic realism

Max Meyerhofer (MI-ehr-hoh-fehr), a violent and brutal man given to grandiose but unsuccessful schemes for making money. He loses the family estate and sinks constantly deeper into poverty. He dies of a stroke as he is about to burn Mr. Douglas' barn.

Frau Elsbeth Meyerhofer, his long-suffering wife; after years of patience, her spirit is broken, and she dies a lingering death.

Paul Meyerhofer, their third son, born at the time the estate is lost; he is reared in poverty. His father ridicules him, but his mother is loving. After his father attacks a servant wildly, Paul overpowers him and from that day takes over. By hard work, he becomes a man of substance. Suspecting his father's intention to burn Mr. Douglas' barn, he attempts to distract him by setting fire to his own house and barn. Seriously burned, Paul recovers and spends two years in prison. Having lost everything, he feels free from his nemesis, Dame Care.

Mr. Douglas, the new owner of the Meyerhofer estate. Sympathy for Paul causes him to agree to join in one of Max's schemes. Max becomes violent when Douglas objects to having his name used in borrowing money—but Douglas remains steadfast in his friendship to Paul.

Mrs. Douglas, his wife, a kindhearted woman, fond of Frau Elsbeth. She acts as godmother to Paul.

Elsbeth Douglas, their daughter. Engaged to marry her cousin, she loves Paul. After he is burned, she stays by his bed, and her wedding is called off. When he is released from prison, Elsbeth and the family estate are to be his.

Katie and

Greta, Paul's younger twin sisters. Learning that they have been dishonored by his old tormentors the Erdmann boys, Paul forces the Erdmanns at pistol point to swear they will marry the sisters.

Levy (LAY-vee), a sharp trader who dupes Max in a money-making scheme.

Michel (MEE-khehl), a servant. Attacked by Max, he gets revenge by burning the Meyerhofer barn.

THE DAMNATION OF THERON WARE

Author: Harold Frederic (1856-1898)
First published: 1896
Genre: Novel

Locale: New York State
Time: The 1890's
Plot: Social realism

Theron Ware, a young Methodist minister whose religious training and faith are too frail to support the stresses of his life. Unhappy as a small-town minister, he decides to write a book about Abraham, only to find that his learning is too slight on this or any intellectual subject. He learns that his Catholic acquaintances have a great deal more culture than he. As his faith totters, he becomes suspicious of people and alienates his friends and his wife. He proves unfit for the ministry and becomes a real-estate agent.

Alice Ware, a friendly, cheerful young woman, Theron's wife. Though she is accused by her husband of being unfaithful, she is loyal to him. When he falls ill, she nurses him back to health and helps him prepare for a new career.

Celia Madden, a pretty Irish-Catholic girl who becomes friendly with Theron and helps him discover that his prejudices are groundless. Her cultural interests also show him how thin the culture of his own people is. She is wrongly and outrageously accused by Theron of being in love with Father Forbes. For a time, Theron thinks he is in love with her, but he alienates her by saying that he is afraid of scandal

if he is seen talking to her.

Father Forbes, a Catholic priest who becomes Theron's friend until Theron alienates him by talking slightingly about Dr. Ledsmar, the priest's friend, and by following the priest and Celia to New York.

Dr. Ledsmar, a friend of Father Forbes and Theron. He is alienated when Theron suggests that there is a scandalous relationship between Father Forbes and Celia.

Mr. Soulsby, a professional revivalist. He tries to convince the young minister that his sales approach to religion is not hypocritical. When Theron falls ill and leaves the ministry, Mr. Soulsby proves to be a true friend.

Mrs. Soulsby, Mr. Soulsby's wife, a practical woman who with her husband helps Theron make a new start in life as a real estate agent.

Mr. Gorringe, a trustee of Theron's church, the man whom Theron suspects of having an affair with his wife.

Michael Madden, Celia's brother. Taking a dying man's privilege, he tells Theron how others see the young minister.

A DANCE IN THE SUN

Author: Dan Jacobson (1929-   )
First published: 1956
Genre: Novel

Locale: A farm in the Karroo, South Africa
Time: Early 1950's
Plot: Domestic realism

The narrator, a university student who hitchhikes with his friend Frank from Lyndhurst (probably modeled on Kimberley) to Cape Town. Marooned in a small, isolated Karroo village, he finds lodging for the night at Fletcher's home. A student of literature, he is humane in his attitude toward Africans, in part because of his fond memories of his family's African servants; he cannot, however, entirely escape the attitudes that are inevitable in a member of a socially superior caste. Essentially innocent when they arrive at the Fletcher residence, he and Frank feel as if they have grown up after spending the night there.

Frank, the narrator's friend, a medical student. A tall and rather awkward boy who dresses carelessly, he is shy and even timid, but he is a careful observer of people with a lively and almost clinical interest in human behavior. Described by the narrator as a clever boy in school, he is quite witty. Because he is not a racist, he makes fun of Fletcher's racism and his grandiose ideas of "world order" with sardonic remarks that are too subtle for Fletcher to understand. In the novel's plot, he is a more important character than the narrator because he is present in the confrontation between Fletcher and Ignatius Louw.

Fletcher, a British South African. Rather animal-like in bearing and movement, with a large head and bright, staring eyes, he seems younger than he is. He is verbose and jovial, but he tends to shout at everyone and is the sort of person who insists that everyone agree with him. He is arrogant in his assumptions about his own cleverness, and he is above all a raging racist who rants to the narrator and Frank his apocalyptic predictions that civilization is being destroyed by the "inferior" races and their liberal supporters. In fact, he is the victim

of paranoia, exaggerated in his case by his fear that he will lose the estate that he acquired by marriage.

Mrs. Fletcher, his wife, an Afrikaner. Thin and faded, she is the proud daughter of a Boer pioneer whose accomplishments were formidable; she therefore believes that she lowered herself by marrying Fletcher. More quietly racist than her husband, she committed a crime against Joseph's sister and her child because of pride and a desperate concern for the reputation of her family.

Ignatius "Nasie" Louw (NAH-see), Mrs. Fletcher's young brother. Essentially weak-willed and morally bankrupt, he is nevertheless likable. During the night that the narrator and Frank stay with the Fletchers, he returns. He seems to have committed miscegenation with Joseph's sister as an act of defiance against his society, his family, and his Boer father. Now he is consumed with guilt for abandoning her and their child and is enraged at Fletcher for encouraging him to do so. In the end, he runs away.

Joseph, an old African laborer, the brother of Louw's mistress. A tall, well-muscled man, physically scarred by his hard life, he was not willing to remain a servant of the Fletchers and left to see the world. Now, because his sister has disappeared and her "yellow" baby is missing, he asks help from the narrator and Frank. His sense of family loyalty is as great as Mrs. Fletcher's, and he wants desperately to find the child that is his family's only link to the future. On the other hand, he is quite capable of using his painful situation to his own advantage, and at the end of the novel he has blackmailed Fletcher into giving him a job.

— Robert L. Berner

THE DANCE OF DEATH
(Dödsdansen)

Author: August Strindberg (1849-1912)
First published: 1901
Genre: Drama

Locale: An island military fortress off Sweden
Time: Late nineteenth century
Plot: Psychological realism

Part I

Edgar, a captain of the coast artillery. He and his family live in a fortress on a removed island, physically and emotionally isolated from others. His marital tyranny makes his wife a prisoner and her life miserable. He continually battles for dominance, not only with her but also with everyone, because he is contemptuous of all others. Convinced of his own superiority, he refuses to buy food, pay his bills, or hire servants and pay them. Subsequent attacks of a severe illness convince him that there is life after death. Malicious by nature, he previously instigated Curt's divorce, which resulted in the loss of Curt's money and family, yet he clings to Curt during the most severe of his attacks. He threatens to divorce his wife to keep her under his power but resigns himself to being with her after learning that he has not long to live.

Alice, his wife, a former actress. She wants freedom from her domineering husband, who constantly humiliates her. Without servants or money, she does the best she can. Kept in isolation from even her children, Alice has learned secretly to communicate by telegraph to keep in contact with the world. Praying that her husband's illness will be fatal, she allows him to see her making romantic advances toward her cousin, Curt. After he threatens her with divorce, she enlists Curt to help her discredit her husband with charges of embezzlement. After Curt rebuffs her advances, she is relieved when the case is dropped. Hopeless, she stops dyeing her hair and resigns herself to her existence.

Curt, the master of quarantine and Alice's cousin. He introduced Edgar and Alice. He has survived divorce and bankruptcy but still believes in the essential nobility of humanity. Newly assigned to the island as subordinate to Edgar, Curt comforts him during his illness. Curt even forgives Edgar for plotting the divorce that ruined him. Curt manages to resist Alice's blandishments but attempts to aid her in discrediting Edgar, who despises him. Curt is the personal and moral antithesis to Edgar.

Part II

Edgar, who sets out to destroy Curt by taking away his son, belongings, and reputation. He takes Curt's ideas and writes articles claiming them as his own, gives Curt bad financial advice, and runs against Curt for public office. He even takes up a public subscription for Curt without his knowledge or permission. He buys Curt's possessions at public auction and schemes to send Curt's son, Allan, to a far-off garrison. Edgar believes his is the upper hand because the colonel wants to marry Edgar's daughter, Judith. When Edgar learns that Judith has refused the colonel in favor of Allan, he suffers a fatal attack.

Alice, who despises Edgar more than ever but is totally in his power. She attempts to use Judith to her own ends and encourages her to fall in love. After Edgar's death, she remembers her first love for him and all that made him as he was.

Curt, who manages to survive his ruin with dignity. He has,

Jenny, a maid. She quits, leaving Alice to do her work.

Old woman, a resident of the poorhouse. Although she has no material possessions, she has good will.

The sentry, a soldier. He is seen throughout the entire play, pacing back and forth. His presence emphasizes the prisonlike atmosphere.

at last, been reunited with his son, only to have the boy taken over by Edgar, his captain. This is an insult he cannot forgive. On the captain's demise, Curt and Alice console each other with positive memories.

Judith, Edgar and Alice's daughter. Returned to the island after finishing school, Judith is secure in her future as the colonel's lady. Never in love, she enjoys tormenting her two suitors. When she realizes the intensity of her love for Allan, she turns her back on her father and the colonel and gives her entire trust to Allan.

Allan, Curt's son. Allan, who is in love with Judith, is used as a pawn by Edgar to hurt Curt. Inadvertently, he causes the captain's destruction.

The lieutenant, an officer, Allan's rival for Judith. The two become friends through their misery.

— *H. Alan Pickrell*

A DANCE OF THE FORESTS

Author: Wole Soyinka (1934-   )
First published: 1963
Genre: Drama

Locale: Nigeria
Time: Indeterminate
Plot: Mythic

Forest Father or **Forest Head**, the chief god who controls the universe of this play. In the pantheon of Yoruba gods, he is called **Osanyin** (oh-SAH-nyihn). He is the supreme arbiter who rules both humans and lesser gods. Because he represents the divine qualities of justice and mercy, he despairs of the continuous evil of humanity's history but believes that humankind may be improved if mortals can be made to admit the consequences of their acts as part of history. He designs the dance to expose past and present wickedness. He is concerned and sympathetic but all-powerful, reserving his supreme power to restrain and ultimately decide the outcome of the dance and therefore the outcome of the world. In his mortal guise, he masquerades as Obaneji, who leads the party into the forest.

Aroni (ah-ROH-nee), "the Lame One" who opens the play. He is the messenger of the great Forest Head, and it is he who selects the dead man and woman who reflect the violent past that lives on in the grim practices of the present-day characters.

Eshuro (ay-SHEW-roh), one of the aspects of Oro, god of the dead, who has qualities of the Yoruba god of mischief, Eshu. He is spiteful and antagonistic to humankind and demands from Forest Head vengeance against Demoke. He becomes the "figure in red" who controls the "bloody triplets" who, at the point of potential reconciliation, snatch the half-child representing the human future. It is his final chance to destroy the human race, as he so bitterly desires.

Agboreko (ahg-boh-RAY-koh), an Elder of the Sealed Lips who exists as a soothsayer between the two existences. He is

an intermediary between the living people on Earth and the spirits in the Forest.

Rola (ROH-lah), the eternal whore, queen in the ancient court of Mata Kharibu, also called **Madame Tortoise** because of the image that once on her back, she will not turn herself over. She is woman as tormentor and sexual sadist. She demands the attentions and subjugation of all men. In one evidence of her cruel nature, she orders the passivist army captain (the Dead Man) to be castrated for rejecting her sexual overtures. Now reduced to an actual prostitute, she continues her sexual scandals in modern times when two of her lovers die, one by murder and one by suicide. She is the female black widow spider in human form.

Adenebi (ah-day-NAY-bee), a corrupt official, indifferent to decency and principle, concerned only with being paid for his patronage. He now has the position of council orator and uses pompous rhetoric. In early times, he was the court historian and cruelly sent innocent men to their deaths. He repeats similar iniquities in the present when he corruptly licenses the overloading of a truck, which crashes, burning sixty-five people to death. He exemplifies political immorality.

Demoke (day-MOH-kay), a figure who represents the artist as a potent force within society. He was a poet in the ancient court and is now a carver. His apprentice, Oremole, was killed by falling from the tree that they were both carving in honor of the celebration for which the play was written. His act provokes an intense soul-searching. He is not sure that others who accuse him of killing Oremole out of jealousy may not be right. As an articulate and self-aware artist, Demoke represents the nature of humans at a profound level. In a painful moment of self-interrogation, he is forced to admit that he did in fact destroy Oremole. In spite of this crime, for him redemption is possible. He catches the half-child and, by allowing its birth, ensures the future for humanity. Demoke is the redeemer within society because he is an artist.

The Dead Man, a character who is revived from his earlier existence as a captain in the army of the dead emperor Mata Kharibu. He has refused to serve in the emperor's unjust wars.

As a punishment, he is sold into slavery and castrated on the instructions of the jealous empress.

The Dead Woman, his wife. She is equally dirty, ragged, and squalid, a far cry from the visions of lovely opulence from the other world that were anticipated to arrive. She was killed while pregnant. If her child can now be brought to birth, it will establish the future of the human race. In her crude way, she supplies the continuity of life that derives from motherhood and offers life even under degraded conditions.

— *John F. Povey*

A DANCE TO THE MUSIC OF TIME

Author: Anthony Powell (1905-   )
First published: 1976
Genre: Novel

Locale: Primarily London, England; various other places in Great Britain; and Venice, Italy
Time: 1914-1971
Plot: Social realism

Nicholas Jenkins, the narrator, a sympathetic and contemplative, yet oddly detached, man. Jenkins begins as a schoolboy, the son of a mid-level army officer, who encounters his longtime associates Stringham, Templer, and Widmerpool in an aristocratic milieu. Jenkins goes on to university and then to the bare beginnings of a literary career in London. He develops a new, more bohemian circle of friends, including such men as Barnby and Moreland, and has a passionate, adulterous love affair with Jean Templer, who eventually leaves him to go to Latin America. Jenkins begins to lose touch with Templer and Stringham as they diverge on their own separate paths. He then marries Isobel Tolland and concurrently sees his novelistic career begin to blossom. Volunteering for the army with the onset of World War II, Jenkins is stationed with a Welsh regiment in Northern Ireland before moving on to more useful work as a liaison officer between Britain and the other Allied powers. After the war, Jenkins feels dislocated by the death of so many of his friends. He manages to maintain an equilibrium that few of his friends possess. This enables him to survive in situations in which men like Widmerpool undergo a calamitous fall. It is when Jenkins learns of Widmerpool's death that he has a final meeting with Jean Templer and glimpses the lost possibilities of his early love.

Kenneth Widmerpool, Jenkins' schoolmate, foil, and alter ego. Widmerpool is mocked and bullied at school, especially by Stringham, but by the time he reaches London and goes into the business world, he has earned increasing respect. Widmerpool pushes his way to the top, despite several mishaps and botched love affairs. During the war, he rises to become Jenkins' superior and marries Pamela Flitton. He is named a Life peer but is ruined by his wife's misbehavior.

Eventually, he becomes entangled in a sordid cult during the 1960's, and he dies ignominiously.

Charles Stringham, a sensitive, aristocratic boy who is Jenkins' best friend at school. Troubled by his parents' divorce and by alcoholism, Stringham leads a sad life until rising to heroism while imprisoned by the Japanese at Singapore, where he loses his life.

Peter Templer, an outgoing, likable boy who is friendly with Jenkins and Stringham. Templer never fulfills his potential and dies tragically helping the Yugoslav resistance in World War II.

Hugh Moreland, a composer and conductor, the representative of art and the aesthetic in the novel. He becomes Jenkins' closest friend when both men are in their early adulthood in London. Moreland marries Matilda Wilson, the mistress of Sir Magnus Donners, and is devastated when she leaves him to go back to Donners. His life continues on in disrepair until his premature death during the 1950's.

Jean Templer, Peter's sister. During her first marriage, she has an affair with Nicholas Jenkins.

Pamela Flitton, the aggressive, mentally disturbed niece of Stringham. She grows up to have numerous affairs with men during wartime, eventually marrying Widmerpool. She is unfaithful to him on a massive scale and eventually drags him to defeat and ruin.

Sir Magnus Donners, a prominent industrialist who marries Matilda after her divorce from Moreland.

X Trapnel, a talented young novelist who meets an early and tragic death.

— *Margaret Boe Birns*

DANCING AT LUGHNASA

Author: Brian Friel (1929-   )
First published: 1990
Genre: Drama

Locale: County Donegal, Ireland
Time: Summer, 1936
Plot: Psychological realism

Kate Mundy, a parochial grade-school teacher in Ballybeg (Irish for "small town"), County Donegal. She is the only steady wage earner in the family, which includes her fallen-priest brother, Jack; her four younger sisters, all unmarried;

and her illegitimate nephew, seven-year-old Michael. She is the stabilizing economic and social force holding the family together. Her dismissal from her teaching position because of Father Jack's heterodoxy is another straw added to the weight of community dissolution. She winds up tutoring privately in the family of Austin Morgan, the proprietor of a local store. She was once associated with him romantically, but he married a younger woman. Kate is a silent, solo dancer.

Maggie Mundy, Kate's sister, who is responsible for the outside work and the housekeeping chores in the family. Her bootlaces are always untied, reflecting her openness. She plays with and encourages young Michael with his kites, and she plays imaginative language games with him. She is a singer and a "dervish" dancer, full of exuberant energy. When the family breaks up, she carries on, adding her absent sisters' tasks to hers, pretending to believe that nothing has changed.

Agnes Mundy and

Rose Mundy, Kate's sisters. They have a glove-knitting contract that is taken away from them. Agnes, the best of the dancers, looks out for her sister Rose, who is "simple." The naïve Rose's date with the married Danny Bradley at a pagan Lughnasa (pronounced lew-na-sah) gathering in the hills terrifies the protective sister. When income from their knitting disappears, the pair go to England, where for more than twenty years they do menial jobs. Agnes dies of exposure by the Thames, and Rose dies in a hospice for the destitute.

Chris Mundy, Michael's single mother. He, just started in school, has been her primary responsibility because his absent, insouciant father's visits have been sporadic. The youngest of the sisters by at least six years, she is the only one still vain about her physical appearance. Chris loves dancing and dances beautifully with Gerry, but she knows he would be unreliable as a husband and refuses to agree to marry him. Such a decision is a courageous one in such a traditional society. After the dissolution of the family, she works the rest of her life in the knitting factory, hating every day of it. She never learns, the adult Michael says, of Gerry's marriage and children in Wales.

Gerry Evans, Michael's father, a slick verbalizer, flatterer, con man, unsuccessful itinerant gramophone salesman, and former dancing teacher. His involvement in the Spanish Civil War is a comedy of errors; his war wound is suffered in a fall from his motorcycle. He can, however, always make Chris laugh. After three years, his visits to Ballybeg and his promises cease. About twenty years later, in the mid-1950's, he dies in Wales among his new family members.

Jack Mundy, the only son and eldest in the family. He is an ordained Catholic priest who has returned home, terminally ill, from a mission among lepers in Uganda. Apart from a brief stint as a chaplain in the British army, the ceremonial uniform from which he has kept, all of his overseas time has been spent among native Africans. He has evidently misplaced his Christian mission and become something of a convert to an African religion. He endorses "love children"—the more the better—and sacrifices Rose's pet rooster. He has only a year to live and try to integrate his African dance experience and his own "distinctive spiritual search," as Kate puts it, into the unreceptive world of Ballybeg.

Michael, the invisible focus of several scenes with the women. Twenty-five years later, he speaks his lines as a child and comments neutrally, as an adult who got out, on the present and future of the family ensemble.

— *Archibald E. Irwin*

DANGEROUS ACQUAINTANCES
(Les Liaisons dangereuses)

Author: Pierre Choderlos de Laclos (1741-1803)
First published: 1782
Genre: Novel

Locale: Paris
Time: Mid-eighteenth century
Plot: Psychological realism

The Marquise de Merteuil (mehr-TYOO-ee), a fashionable and unscrupulous matron. Abandoned by the Comte de Gercourt, she seeks vengeance for her wounded vanity by a series of manipulations that bring disaster or death to all who become involved with this dangerous acquaintance.

The Comte de Gercourt (zhehr-KEWR), betrothed to Cécile de Volanges. After he deserts the Marquise de Merteuil in favor of Madame de Tourvel, his humiliation becomes the object of the malicious marquise's ruinous machinations.

Cécile de Volanges (say-SEEL duh voh-LAHNZH), a young woman betrothed by her mother to the Comte de Gercourt. She becomes a pawn in the Marquise de Merteuil's scheme of revenge on Gercourt.

The Vicomte de Valmont (val-MOH[N]), an unscrupulous libertine and ally of the Marquise de Merteuil in her scheme to humiliate the Comte de Gercourt.

The Chevalier Danceny (dahns-NEE), a tool of the Marquise de Merteuil and the Vicomte de Valmont. Encouraged by them to form a liaison with Cécile de Volanges, Danceny is to make a laughingstock of the Comte de Gercourt.

Madame de Tourvel (tewr-VEHL), a judge's wife for whom the Comte de Gercourt deserts the Marquise de Merteuil. She becomes the mistress of the Vicomte de Valmont.

Madame de Volanges, the mother of Cécile de Volanges.

Madame de Rosemonde (rohz-MOHND), the aunt of the Vicomte de Valmont.

Sophie Carnay (soh-FEE kahr-NEH), Cécile de Volanges' friend and confidante.

DANGLING MAN

Author: Saul Bellow (1915-   )
First published: 1944
Genre: Novel

Locale: Chicago, Illinois
Time: December 15, 1942, to April 9, 1943
Plot: Psychological realism

Joseph, an unemployed man dangling between civilian life and his final draft call into the U.S. Army, his induction delayed by bureaucratic red tape. A tall, handsome, flabby, well-educated man of introspective and philosophical habits of mind, he keeps a journal of his feelings and musings, growing more bitter, dispirited, and demoralized as he assesses the damage inflicted on his sense of self-identity by the seven-month delay. The major anxiety he feels is existential, such as how to keep his sense of being intact and unencumbered and how to keep his balance between his personal desires and the coercions of society. The problem of freedom is crucial for Joseph, as he clearly recognizes the environmental pressures toward conformity that threaten his personal freedom: the sorrowful, ugly cityscape of Chicago; the stigma of poverty; the demands of his mistress; and the relationships with his wife, family, and friends, all of whom urge him to make something of himself and behave respectably. In a secular age with no deep structure of belief or a priori models of conduct, he is haunted by the question of how to live as a good man. He becomes more peevish, irritable, and quarrelsome as the weeks go by, his life an unrelieved tedium of idleness in the single room he and his wife are renting until his departure. Joseph broods about the avidity of his friends and about his own limitations and sense of mortality. He becomes increasingly disappointed in others, separate, distrustful, and alienated. Feeling constantly badgered by the public conscience, he clings desperately to the one true virtue of preserving oneself: deciding what one can decide and recognizing what is beyond one's control. After quarreling with his wife over his refusal to cash her paycheck and with Captain Briggs, the landlady's son-in-law, about the annoying, alcoholic behavior and petty thievery of a fellow roomer named Mr. Vanaker, Joseph decides to give up his struggle and requests that the draft board expedite his induction. Summoned to report to the Army, Joseph has now placed his destiny in the hands of others and no longer feels accountable for himself. His journal ends on an ambiguous note: Having volitionally canceled his freedom and self-determination, he seems to embrace the life of regimentation that lies ahead.

Iva, Joseph's wife. A quiet, dutiful, circumspect woman, she tries to enable Joseph to enjoy his liberty before he leaves for the Army. Since he quit his job at the travel agency, she has fully supported him. Joseph has dominated her for the six years of their marriage, trying to form her taste and intellect, but she resists his efforts, succumbing instead to the conventional appeals of fashion magazines, clothes, furniture, and radio entertainment. Concerned about appearances and desiring the good opinion of others, she is easily embarrassed by Joseph's behavior. Growing somewhat rebellious, she becomes quick to defy or quarrel with him. She discourages talk (they do not confide in each other), yet she complains that Joseph neglects her. When she nurses him through a minor illness, she becomes less critical and more endearing to Joseph. Hurt by his failure to consult her in his decision to ask the draft board for an early summons, she wishes Joseph would show more grief at the prospect of their long separation. Against Joseph's wishes, she decides to stay with her parents while he is in the Army.

Kitty Daumler, Joseph's mistress, a simple, uncomplicated, down-to-earth woman whom Joseph met when he arranged a tour for her. She confidently sets out to seduce him. Although she is careless, messy, unkempt, and somewhat gross, she is sensually attractive, a lively, plump, solid, worldly presence. Irritated by Iva's nagging and pettiness, Joseph visits Kitty's apartment regularly, drawn by her affectionate and generous nature, yet determined to keep the relationship on the level of amiable talk. Inevitably, he succumbs to desire and the relationship becomes sexual. The affair lasts for two months, until Kitty hints that Joseph should leave Iva. Sobered by the consequences of his own unlimited desire, he attempts to return the relationship to its earlier, friendly but nonsexual, basis. One night, after quarreling with Iva, Joseph visits Kitty to retrieve a book and feels vaguely resentful and insulted to find her with a man. Several weeks later, Kitty sends Joseph a note asking him to drop by. He is surprised to find that he no longer thinks about her.

— *Clifford Edwards*

DANIEL DERONDA

Author: George Eliot (Mary Ann Evans, 1819-1880)
First published: 1876
Genre: Novel

Locale: England and Continental Europe
Time: Mid-nineteenth century
Plot: Social realism

Daniel Deronda, the ward of Sir Hugo Mallinger and a noble, well-educated gentleman. At Cambridge University, he helps a poor student, Hans Meyrick, to pass a scholarship examination. He rescues a young Jewish woman, Mirah Lapidoth, from drowning in the Thames, helps to start her on a singing career, and later marries her. He spends a great deal of time wondering about his parentage and searching for some knowledge of his past in the Jewish East End of London. At the end of the novel, before his marriage, he is pleased to learn that he is Jewish.

Gwendolen Harleth, an impoverished beauty who feels that she must marry a wealthy man in order to live the elegant life she desires. After rejecting several dull suitors, she marries Henleigh Mallinger Grandcourt, a wealthy heir, despite the

fact that she knows Grandcourt has deserted the mistress who has borne him four children. She marries him after her widowed mother has lost all their money in a stock failure. The marriage is unhappy because Gwendolen is secretly in love with Daniel Deronda. After Grandcourt drowns in a yachting accident, Gwendolen feels guilty because she might have done much more to save him and had previously wished him dead. She confesses as much to Daniel, who has always disapproved of her gambling, recklessness, and love of finery. Hoping to marry Daniel, she is disappointed when he tells her about Mirah. She resolves to reform and to live for others.

Mirah Lapidoth, the young Jewish woman whom Daniel saves from suicide and later marries. Because she has been abandoned, Daniel takes her to the home of some friends. She recovers, has a successful singing career, and is reunited with her brother Mordecai before marrying Daniel.

Henleigh Mallinger Grandcourt, the nephew and heir of Sir Hugo Mallinger. He deserts his mistress after nine years and marries Gwendolen Harleth. A cold, supercilious man, he succeeds in breaking Gwendolen's spirit. After he drowns, his will reveals that he has left his property to his illegitimate son and has provided for his mistress better than he has for Gwendolen.

Sir Hugo Mallinger, the intelligent and benevolent owner of Diplow Hall. He has brought up Daniel Deronda and is enormously fond of him. He feels that Daniel is an English gentleman and objects when Daniel wishes to acknowledge the fact that he is Jewish; however, the two remain close friends.

Lady Mallinger, his wife, whom he did not marry until after he had adopted Daniel.

Ezra Lapidoth (Mordecai), Mirah's brother, a consumptive, learned young Jew who lives with the Cohens and gives lessons to Cohen's son. He also works in a bookshop. Abandoned by his father, he has known poverty and hardship. Daniel finds him, discovers his relationship to Mirah, and reunites the two. Much of Daniel's feeling of identification with Jews comes through his conversations with Mordecai. Mordecai dies at the end of the novel.

Ezra Cohen, a crafty but generous East End shopkeeper with whom Mordecai boards. He first introduces Daniel to life in the Jewish section of London.

Mrs. Lydia Glasher, an attractive woman who had left her husband, an Irish officer, and son to become Grandcourt's mistress. She has four illegitimate children by him. She tells her story to Gwendolen because she believes that Gwendolen should morally refuse Grandcourt's offer of marriage.

Hans Meyrick, a Cambridge student. Daniel Deronda helps him win a scholarship when Hans's eyes are temporarily useless as the result of an accident. Hans falls in love with Mirah, but she rejects him. He becomes an artist and something of a dilettante.

Mrs. Fanny Davilow, Gwendolen's widowed mother. She is constantly ruled by headstrong Gwendolen.

The Reverend Henry Gascoigne, formerly Captain Gaskin, the rector of Pennicote, near Offendene.

Mrs. Nancy Gascoigne, his wife, Mrs. Davilow's sister. She tries to help Fanny, her less fortunate sister, and she introduces Gwendolen to eligible young men, but she cannot resist letting everyone know of her generosity.

Rex Gascoigne, their son, reading for the law. He is in love with his cousin Gwendolen.

Anna Gascoigne, his rather plain and meek sister, who tries to help Gwendolen.

Warham Gascoigne, her brother, who goes to India.

Herr Julius Klesmer, a German-Jewish musician who is hired as a tutor at Quetcham Hall, the home of the Arrow-

points. He helps to launch Mirah's singing career and becomes important in the London musical world.

Catherine Arrowpoint, a talented and attractive young woman, Gwendolen's only rival in the social world near Pennicote. She falls in love with her tutor, Julius Klesmer, and marries him despite her parents' objections.

Mrs. Arrowpoint, Catherine's mother. She had hoped that her daughter would make a more socially acceptable match.

Mr. Arrowpoint, her husband, a hospitable gentleman.

Thomas Lush, Grandcourt's scheming follower and companion.

Mrs. Meyrick, Hans's mother, who takes in and nurses Mirah when Daniel brings her to the Meyrick home. A poor and kind woman, she dotes on Daniel.

Kate Meyrick, her oldest daughter, who sews and embroiders.

Amy Meyrick, the second daughter.

Mab Meyrick, the youngest daughter, talented musically.

Alice Davilow, Gwendolen's rather plain half sister.

Bertha Davilow and

Fanny Davilow, also half sisters, both "whisperers."

Isabel Davilow, another half sister, a listening child.

Miss Merry, governess to the four Davilow girls.

Mr. Middleton, the curate at Pennicote, in love with Gwendolen.

Lady Brackenshaw, the social leader of Pennicote.

Lord Brackenshaw, her husband.

Mrs. Vulcany, a Pennicote gossip.

Princess Leonora Halm-Eberstein, Daniel's mother, a singer and actress who had given Daniel to Sir Hugo Mallinger in order that her son might be brought up a gentleman and not be aware of his Jewish origin. Sir Hugo, in love with her at the time, had agreed. She reveals herself to Daniel in Genoa.

Joseph Kalonymos, a Mainz banker and a friend of Daniel's grandfather. Daniel visits him to learn more about his heritage.

Mr. Lapidoth, Mirah's father, an unsuccessful actor and singer who had deserted his children and absconded with their money. He reappears, and his children forgive him.

Mrs. Addy Cohen, Ezra Cohen's wife.

Mrs. Cohen, Ezra's mother, who helps in the shop.

Jacob Alexander Cohen, Ezra's precocious son, whom Mordecai tutors.

Adelaide Rebekah Cohen, Ezra's attractive, dark-eyed daughter.

Eugenie Esther Cohen, a baby.

Mr. Ram, owner of the East End bookshop where Mordecai works and where Mordecai and Daniel meet.

Baroness von Langen, Gwendolen's hostess when she is gambling at the Casino in Leubronn.

Baron von Langen, her husband.

Mr. Vandernoodt, a wealthy and social gentleman staying at Leubronn.

DANIEL MARTIN

Author: John Fowles (1926-   )
First published: 1977
Genre: Novel

Locale: Hollywood, England, Egypt, and Syria
Time: Mid-1970's, with flashbacks
Plot: Autobiographical

Daniel (Dan) Martin, a British playwright turned Hollywood screenwriter. Dan is a forty-five-year-old man in emotional and artistic exile. Reared as a vicar's son in Devon and educated at the University of Oxford, Dan is a comfortable atheist, a tentative socialist, and a skilled dialogue technician. He sees life through the distorting and limiting eyes of a filmmaker, objectifying or reinventing reality to fit his needs. Accordingly, he can be quick and clever (and often evasive and patronizing) in real emotional situations; after a failed marriage, he has had numerous satisfying but double-edged romances. He is very self-aware and senses his alienation and the echoes of his past. In going to the deathbed of his estranged friend Anthony, Dan faces that past (what Anthony, Jane, Nell, and he meant to one another) and rediscovers lost honesty and passion, his love of nature, and his belief in meaningful art. In subsequent travels in England and the Middle East, he falls back in love with Jane, the one with whom he suspects he should have spent his life.

Jane Mallory, Dan's former sister-in-law. A forty-five-year-old widow, Jane emerges from years of unfulfilled marriage to Anthony a withdrawn, confused, and defensive woman. She is intelligent, well-spoken, and newly interested in Marxism and sociopolitical reform, but these sentiments cloak the internal battle to accept responsibility for the subterfuges of the past and to find a new direction in life. Jane is a deeply intuitive woman, responsive less to logic than to "right feeling" and as expressive in silence as in words. By accepting Dan's concern and, ultimately, his love, she becomes strong, open, and trusting once again.

Jenny McNeil, Dan's girlfriend. Jenny is a twenty-five-year-old British actress learning the ways of Hollywood. She is a shrewd and challenging woman who loves both Dan and the games and repartee their relationship entails. Modern and independent, with a sense of perspective and humor, Jenny turns bitter and sardonic when Dan ends their relationship.

Caroline (Caro) Martin, Dan and Nell's twenty-two-year-old daughter. Caro is a sensible, straightforward young woman who, though less sophisticated than she seems, is ready for the challenges of mature womanhood. She feels awkward with Dan but treasures the chance to grow closer; she has mixed feelings toward Nell and needs to establish her independence. She knows that her affair with her boss, Barney, could hurt her deeply, but she is willing to accept all risks and lessons.

Anthony Mallory, Dan's former best friend. Anthony is a brilliant philosopher and academic who faces death from cancer at the age of forty-five. A dogmatic Catholic, he broke with Dan years before over a play Dan wrote but has since come to a more sober, generous, and responsible view of life. After settling his conscience in a final interview with Dan about their shared history and his widow Jane's future, Anthony abruptly and mystifyingly takes his own life.

Nell Randall, Jane's sister and Dan's former wife. Nell, forty-four years old and happily remarried, is a woman of leisure and society. At base insecure, she thrives on propriety and decorum and needs to feel involved and in control of those around her.

Barney Dillon, an acquaintance of Dan from Oxford, now Caro's boss and lover. Barney is a British television personality who has grown bored with his marriage, cynical about his Fleet Street milieu, and disillusioned with his own transparent achievements.

Andrew Randall, another of Dan's Oxford acquaintances, now Nell's husband. Andrew is a supercilious aristocrat whose naturally hearty manner is often a welcome relief in tense family situations.

Rosamund (Roz) Mallory, Anthony and Jane's older daughter. Roz, a twenty-three-year-old research assistant with the British Broadcasting Corporation, is a self-possessed, levelheaded, compassionate, and mature young woman.

Paul Mallory, Anthony and Jane's son, a withdrawn and taciturn schoolboy whose only apparent passion is for English field systems.

Nancy Reed, Dan's first love. Nancy is a chubby, blue-eyed Devon farm girl who loves adventure and delights in secret pleasures with Dan. Later, she reappears as a stout matron.

Abe Nathan, an older Jewish man, apparently lugubrious and obscene but essentially wise and bighearted. He is a veteran of the film industry. He and his wife, Mildred, lend Dan and Jenny their guest cottage in Los Angeles.

Mildred Nathan, his quietly supportive wife.

Ben and

Phoebe, the simple, provincial old couple who inhabit and maintain Thorncombe, Dan's Devon farmhouse retreat.

Parson Martin, Dan's father, a rigid and humorless country vicar who loved gardening and opposed the display of emotion.

Millie Martin, Dan's simple, old-fashioned unmarried aunt and surrogate mother.

Professor Kirnberger, a brilliant, sensitive German Egyptologist whom Dan and Jane befriend on their Nile cruise.

Jimmy Assad, Dan's urbane Egyptian film contact and guide.

— *B. P. Mann*

DANTON'S DEATH
(Dantons Tod)

Author: Georg Büchner (1813-1837)
First published: 1835
Genre: Drama

Locale: Paris, France
Time: Spring, 1794
Plot: Tragedy

Georges Danton (zhohrzh dan-TOH[N]), the first passive protagonist in German drama. The author makes it amply clear that Danton might have avoided imprisonment and subsequent death by escaping the Jacobins in time. In contrast to the traditional tragic hero, who comes to see the world as ominous only when he realizes that his own doom is inevitable, Danton has no illusions about the world from the play's beginning and quietly wills his doom. Tantalizingly and ambiguously, the author never clarifies whether Danton's failure to save his life is a consequence of his weary worldview or a rationalization of a psychological paralysis or depression that precludes any meaningful action on his part. It is not clear whether Danton expects his refusal to flee to result in his arrest, or whether he actually believes his statement, thrice made, that the Committee of Public Safety would not dare arrest a prominent revolutionary leader like himself. By leaving these possibilities open, the playwright establishes both Danton's nihilism and boredom and his reckless nonchalance and laziness. Danton does show vitality and occasional bursts of energy, but they are focused not on purposeful deeds but on poetic evocations of his disillusionment with human nature and witty banter with his companions. His closest dramatic peer is Hamlet, with whom he shares melancholy, morbidity, sensuality, irony, verbal ingenuity, introspectiveness, and resignation to the world's nullity.

Robespierre (roh-behs-PYEHR), Danton's political antagonist and temperamental opponent. He is an ascetic, austere, humorless dogmatist, a fanatically rigid zealot in behalf of his program for revolutionary extremism. His self-righteous convictions cause him to regard anyone who disagrees with him as an enemy of the French people, to be vilified and executed. He chastises men for weaknesses he considers crimes, and he sees those who fail to follow him unreservedly as conspirators, subverters of the public weal. Called the Incorruptible, Robespierre feels he must destroy any sign of doubt in others until there is nothing left that might pollute revolutionary principles as he understands them. He is a psychopath who projects his vengeful, aggressive impulses in the political arena.

Saint-Just (sah[n]-ZHEWST), Robespierre's leading deputy and his only trusted confidant. Even more of a zealot than his chief, he urges Robespierre toward increasingly violent repressive measures.

Camille Desmoulins (kah-MEEL day-mew-LAN), Danton's closest friend. He tries to persuade him to lead a counterattack against Robespierre's faction. Like Danton, Desmoulins is Epicurean, witty, and warmly humane.

Marion (mahr-ee-AH[N]), a sympathetically drawn prostitute who is generous and open with her feelings. Her autobiographical monologue is noteworthy for its direct naturalness of language and worship of the body, in implied contrast to Robespierre's inflated rhetoric and refusal to admit any personal needs.

— *Gerhard Brand*

DAPHNIS AND CHLOË
(Poimenika ta kata Daphnin kai Chloen)

Author: Longus (fl. third century C.E.)
First transcribed: Third century C.E.
Genre: Novel

Locale: The Island of Lesbos
Time: Indeterminate
Plot: Pastoral

Daphnis (DAF-nihs), found as a baby by Lamo and reared by him. Though finally discovering that he loves Chloë, Daphnis is unable to ask for her in marriage until he finds a purse of silver. He is discovered to be Philopoemen, lost son of Dionysophanes.

Chloë (KLOH-ee), found as an infant girl by Dryas in the Cave of the Nymphs, on Lesbos. She is discovered to be Agele, the daughter of Megacles.

Lamo (LA-moh), a goatherd of Lesbos and the foster father of Daphnis.

Myrtale (MIHR-tuh-lee), his wife, who hides the purple cloak and ivory dagger found with Daphnis.

Dryas (DRI-uhs), a shepherd and the foster father of Chloë.

Nape (NA-pee), his wife, who brings up Chloë.

Dorco (DOHR-koh), a fisherman who wants to marry Chloë and tries to kidnap her. He later saves Daphnis after he has been captured by pirates.

Lampis (LAM-pihs), another suitor of Chloë, who steals her.

Gnatho (NA-thoh), Astylus' parasite, who rescues Chloë.

The Methymneans (meh-THIHM-nee-ehns), who carry off Chloë but, frightened by Pan, return her.

Lycaenium (li-SEE-nee-uhm), a woman who teaches love to Daphnis.

Megacles (MEH-gehk-leez), of Mitylene, the father of Chloë.

Dionysophanes (di-oh-nih-SO-fuh-neez), owner of Lamo and the father of Daphnis.

Astylus (as-TI-luhs), the son of Dionysophanes and the young master of Lamo.

Eudromus (yew-DROH-muhs), Astylus' page.

THE DARK CHILD
(L'Enfant noir)

Author: Camara Laye (1928-1980)
First published: 1953
Genre: Novel

Locale: Kouroussa, a village in French Guinea; and Conakry, the capital of Guinea
Time: Mid-1930's to mid-1940's
Plot: Bildungsroman

Camara Laye (kah-mah-rah LAH-yeh), a young Guinean boy from a highly respected family of the Malinke people. Although somewhat timid, he is curious, intelligent, affectionate, and sensitive. As he moves from early childhood through adolescence, his advancement through the colonial French school system takes him away from his home in Kouroussa to Conakry (the capital of Guinea) and, finally, sends him to Paris to continue his studies. Through recounting his childhood memories, he seeks to preserve, defend, understand, and, perhaps, mourn the passing of the traditional way of life of his

The Dark Half / 447

youth. These vignettes include observing his father's mysterious familiarity with a small, black snake ("the guiding spirit of our race"), watching his father and mother at work, experiencing the seasonal rhythms of his grandmother's farming village, and participating in various traditional ceremonies of initiation, including that of circumcision. Laye's departure for Paris at the end of the novel contrasts the anguish of leaving traditional Africa with the attraction of the unfamiliar Western culture.

Camara's father, a blacksmith, goldsmith, and sculptor. Steeped in the traditional ways of his people, he has powers that can be described only as supernatural. These powers are most clearly seen in his relationship with a small, black snake and in the spirituality, craftsmanship, and theatricality he exhibits while working with gold. Although he clearly regrets that much of his traditional wisdom and knowledge will not be passed on to his son, he recognizes that the boy's destiny is different from his own: The Africa of the future will need citizens with technical skills and Western education. When the boy is harassed by older students at the local school, the father is willing to come to blows with the school's principal to defend his son's rights. At other moments, when Camara is tempted to abandon his educational project, his father urges him to persevere.

Camara's mother, a member of another respected Malinke family. She also possesses magical powers. Because the crocodile is her totem, she is able to draw water from the river without fear of these animals. On one occasion, she alone is able to revive a horse who appears to be under a spell. The provider of food, discipline, and, above all, unqualified love, she is not always able to accept the fact that her son is growing up. She suffers greatly each time an event in his life (whether a move to a new school or a traditional African rite of passage) threatens to distance him from her.

— *Janet L. Solberg*

THE DARK HALF

Author: Stephen King (1947-   )
First published: 1989
Genre: Novel

Locale: Maine
Time: 1988
Plot: Horror

Thad Beaumont, a novelist and professor of creative writing at the University of Maine. At eleven years of age, Thad began to suffer blackouts, preceded by the sound of sparrows. When neurologist Hugh Pritchard operated, he removed the fetus of a twin that had been absorbed into Thad's head while both were still embryos. As an adult, Beaumont has published novels that were praised by critics but not widely read. To cure a writing block, Thad writes, under the pseudonym George Stark, violent novels about Alexis Machine, a sadist who kills evildoers. These are so popular that Thad becomes independently wealthy. When a law student, Frederick Clawson, tries to extort money by threatening to expose Thad's identity as Stark, Thad admits responsibility in an interview for *People* magazine and announces that he will write no more Stark books. Shortly after the article appears in *People*, Thad again has blackouts and hears sparrows. When a resident of Castle Rock, Maine, is brutally murdered and Thad's fingerprints are found at the scene, the Castle Rock sheriff, Alan Pangborn, confronts Thad, but he becomes convinced that he is innocent. Soon, other people are murdered, including Clawson, the people associated with the *People* magazine story, and the agents and editors involved with the publication of the Stark novels. Thad tries to convince Pangborn that his pseudonym has come to life. Through the psychic bond that links them, Thad learns that his double is physically disintegrating. Thad intuits that, should he write another Machine novel, his pseudonym would become whole and he himself would deteriorate. Meanwhile, huge numbers of sparrows have gathered. Thad learns from a folklore professor that sparrows are "psychopomps" who conduct souls to the land of the dead. When Stark threatens Liz and the Beaumonts' twins at the Beaumonts' Castle Rock summer house, Thad comes to their rescue. There, he and Stark begin the new Machine novel. The sparrows invade the house and carry Stark away. With the help of Sheriff Pangborn, Thad burns the house and all evidence that Stark ever existed.

George Stark, the pseudonym under which Thad Beaumont writes the Alexis Machine novels. He becomes a separate being when his creator symbolically kills him. Stark is the reincarnation of a fetal twin removed from Thad's brain. He represents Thad's "dark half," the destructive impulses that the writer has repressed. Near Castle Rock's cemetery, where he comes to life, Stark bludgeons an old man to death. He is responsible for the other murders as well. Stark is psychically linked with Thad, but he is unaware of the sparrows gathering around his double. Stark is decomposing and will die unless Thad resumes writing as Stark. Stark takes Liz and the babies hostage, drives to the Beaumonts' summer home in Castle Rock, and threatens to harm them unless Thad begins a new Machine novel. When Thad arrives and begins to write, Stark's sores start to heal. Stark takes over the story, unaware that he is inserting the word "sparrow" more and more frequently into the text. Sparrows invade the house and carry Stark back to hell.

Alan Pangborn, the sheriff of Castle Rock. Pangborn has a keen analytical mind, is almost preternaturally agile, and can assess honesty and character intuitively. Because fingerprints at the crime scenes match Thad's, Pangborn at first suspects Thad, but he comes reluctantly to accept a supernatural explanation. Pangborn tracks down Dr. Pritchard, who operated on Thad's supposed tumor. When the surgeon tells Pangborn that he had removed a fetal twin from the child's brain, Pangborn realizes that Thad's double has come back to life as Stark. When a Castle Rock farmer reports that a black Toronado, matching Thad's description of Stark's car, has emerged from his garage, Pangborn drives to the Beaumont summer house and is captured by Stark. When the sparrows invade the Beaumont house, Pangborn shelters Liz with a blanket. He helps

Thad burn the house and the Toronado to remove all evidence of Stark's existence.

Liz Beaumont, Thad's devoted wife and the mother of Wendy and William. Liz feared the man her husband became when he wrote the Machine novels. When Stark holds her and the twins hostage, Liz conceals household objects that might be used as weapons.

William Beaumont and

Wendy Beaumont, the Beaumonts' twin babies. They treat

the monstrous Stark as their father.

Hugh Pritchard, a retired surgeon who removed the fetal twin from the brain of the eleven-year-old Thad.

Rawlie DeLesseps, a professor of folklore and a colleague of Thad. Rawlie tells Thad that sparrows are "psychopomps," associated with the living dead. He loans Thad a car when Thad seeks to escape police surveillance.

— *Wendy Bousfield*

THE DARK JOURNEY
(Leviathan)

Author: Julien Green (1900-1998)
First published: 1929
Genre: Novel

Locale: France
Time: Early twentieth century
Plot: Psychological realism

Paul Guéret (pohl gay-RAY), an incompetent, prematurely aged tutor. Tired of his wife, he tries to take up an affair with Angèle, a young laundress who is also a prostitute. Disturbed when he learns that Angèle is a prostitute, he beats the girl and disfigures her for life. Still in a passion, he shortly after kills a feeble old man. Guéret is trapped by his employer's wife, who locks both of them in a room and then shoots herself, dooming Guéret to capture.

M. Grosgeorge (groh-ZHOHRZH), Guéret's employer. Realizing Guéret's frustrations, he suggests a mistress and, not knowing of Guéret's infatuation with Angèle, reveals his own relationships with her.

Mme Grosgeorge, M Grosgeorge's wife. She is a woman of twisted emotions who nags her husband, beats her son, and humiliates her son's tutor. She seems only to rejoice when Guéret disfigures his and her husband's mistress. She finds

Guéret, takes him home, and hides him, though she despises him. When he wants to leave, she locks both of them in a room and calmly shoots herself.

Angèle (ahn-ZHEHL), a little laundress forced by her aunt, Mme Londe, to be a prostitute. She is loved by Guéret, who both attracts and repels her. She is beaten and disfigured by Guéret when he learns that she is a prostitute.

Mme Londe (lohnd), Angèle's aunt, a restaurant owner. She seeks power over other people through the knowledge of their guilt and vices learned from Angèle.

Fernande (fehr-NAHND), a twelve-year-old girl turned into a prostitute by Mme Londe when Angèle refuses to continue her practices.

André Grosgeorge (ahn-DRAY), the boy whom Guéret is hired to tutor. He is a backward lad.

DARK LAUGHTER

Author: Sherwood Anderson (1876-1941)
First published: 1925
Genre: Novel

Locale: Old Harbor, Indiana
Time: The 1920's
Plot: Psychological realism

Bruce Dudley, born **John Stockton**, who revolts against the rational sterility that characterizes modern technological society. Dudley wanders around the country taking various jobs. He travels from Chicago to New Orleans to Old Harbor, Indiana, the town where he grew up. He is a reporter, an auto worker, a gardener. His love affair with Aline Grey, as well as his flight with Aline toward an unknown destination, are for Anderson facets of the conduct to be expected of two people who love each other but who are unable to reconcile their values with a society dedicated only to material manipulation and acquisition.

Aline Grey, the unhappy wife of an automobile factory owner. She is attracted to Dudley and encourages his love, though she knows her behavior is likely to cause comment in the small Indiana town where she lives. Her affair with Dudley ruins her husband's life.

Fred Grey, practically an Anderson symbol for blind devo-

tion to technology. Grey is incapable of dealing with any situation that depends for its resolution on a knowledge of human nature. When Dudley and Aline leave, Grey becomes completely confused. Not knowing whether to use a revolver on himself, on Dudley and Aline, or simply on Dudley, he fires a wild shot into the river. Confused, desperate, ineffectual in the knowledge of his wife's desertion, Grey is scorned by the easy laughter of some uneducated domestics, for whom his problem is childishly simple.

Sponge Martin, a worker in the Grey factory. He loves the simple things: fishing, sipping moonshine whiskey, making love to his carefree wife. Martin is used in the novel to lend authority to Dudley and Aline's love affair.

Rose Frank, an acquaintance of Aline. It was at Rose's apartment in Paris, just after World War I, that Aline met a man she wanted in much the same way she was to want Dudley years later in Old Harbor.

DARKNESS AT NOON

Author: Arthur Koestler (1905-1983)
First published: 1940
Genre: Novel

Locale: Russia
Time: The 1930's
Plot: Social realism

Nikolai Rubashov (nih-koh-LI rew-BAH-shof), a political prisoner, a former commissar once politically powerful but now in disfavor and accused of crimes he did not commit. He broods over his actual deeds for the Party and attempts to rationalize them. After publicly denouncing his supposed errors, he is executed. He resembles such old Bolsheviks as Leon Trotsky and Nikolay Bukharin, who wielded ruthless power for supposedly good ends in the early years of the Soviet Union and who were then liquidated by an even more ruthless dictator, Joseph Stalin.

Ivanov (ih-VAH-nof), a prison official, Rubashov's old college friend and former battalion commander. After interrogating Rubashov on two occasions and persuading him to renounce his opposition to Party policies and to acknowledge his errors, Ivanov is executed for negligence in conducting Rubashov's case. Like Rubashov, Ivanov resembles the old Bolsheviks whom Stalin regarded as dangerous enemies. Ivanov may also be compared to Fyodor Dostoevski's Stepan Verhovensky.

Gletkin (GLEHT-kihn), another official who represents the new Party policy of practical application of theoretical principles. He believes in the power of brute force and the instilling of fear to maintain control and order in the state. He is reminiscent of Stalin's police-state aides, of Dostoevski's Pyotr Ver-

hovensky, and of George Orwell's O'Brien.

Mikhail Bogrov (mih-ha-IHL bohg-ROHF), another prisoner, long a close friend of Rubashov. Frightened, beaten, and whimpering, Bogrov is dragged past Rubashov's cell and shot.

Kieffer, called **Hare-Lip** , an informer, the son of a former friend and associate of Rubashov. After being tortured in a steam bath and later used to testify that Rubashov plotted to have him poison Number 1, Hare-Lip is executed.

Number 402, an anonymous prisoner with whom Rubashov exchanges many tapped-out conversations through the wall that separates their cells.

Number 1, the Party dictator who resembles Joseph Stalin and George Orwell's Big Brother.

Richard, a young man arrested in Germany while Rubashov headed the Party Intelligence and Control Department.

Arlova (ahr-LOH-vuh), Rubashov's former secretary and mistress, who was executed after Rubashov shifted a charge of treasonable activities from himself to her.

Little Loewy, a Party worker who hanged himself after being denounced as an agent provocateur.

Rip Van Winkle, a little old man, the inmate of cell 406 and a veteran of twenty years' imprisonment.

DARKNESS VISIBLE

Author: William Golding (1911-1993)
First published: 1979
Genre: Novel

Locale: London and Greenfield, England; and Australia
Time: After World War II
Plot: Moral

Matty "Septimus" Windrave, also called **Windrove** or **Windgrave**, the protagonist, a branded victim of the London firebombing. His past a blank slate, his body horribly burned, and his mind psychologically scarred, Matty Windrave remains an outcast throughout his life because of his monstrous condition—a limp, a two-toned face, a half-bald skull, and a ghastly ear. At the Foundlings School at Greenfield, despite his high-minded craving for knowledge, he is rejected by schoolmasters and classmates alike, a rejection that leads to his quest for spiritual meaning to explain his fate and to point the way toward his destiny. Introspective and enduring, he works as a laborer in Australia (always with superior testimonials) until a mystical experience leads him to write a journal of his mission and directs him back to Greenfield and the beautiful, clever Stanhope twins. Back in Greenfield, he redeems himself by once again being consumed by fire, in this case, a firebomb that burns down his old school. Thanks to Matty, the fire fails to harm the kidnapped Arab child whom he frees. Whether he is a mystic-seer or deluded fanatic, Matty sacrifices himself for an innocent.

Sebastian Pedigree, a pitiable pederast who taught in the boys' school Matty attended. His deviant inclinations lead to a child's suicide, his own dismissal, a series of imprisonments,

and his moral and economic decline. He meets Matty's unspoken pleas for friendship with horror and rejection, blaming him for the tragic pattern of his life. The slightly built and graying Pedigree cannot control the tide of passion that overtakes him in waves, and he relies on a multicolored ball to attract young boys to his center of existence, the public toilets. For all of his sins, he understands suffering and guilt. He is the final witness to Matty's return from the dead. Whether that return is a hallucination or a beatific vision, it is the last thing Pedigree ever sees, as he prays for an end to his surging tide of impulses.

Sophy Stanhope, a wholesomely beautiful child and then young lady whose affected innocence hides her evil twist. Having tortured animals as a child, she continues to delight in breaking conventional taboos by lying, stealing, and prostituting herself. She becomes a thrill-seeking sexual sadist, joining forces with a perverse and amoral thief (Gerry), repeatedly stabbing her sexual conquest (the narcissistic, athletic Fido), and exploiting the knowledge and position of others to further her plot to kidnap and slowly torture and kill a wealthy young Arab prince from Wandicoot School. Her failure to achieve that end leads to perjury and unsuccessful attempts to blame those around her. Her belief that she and her riences cruelty and tyranny when his young widowed mother marries stern Mr. Murdstone, and he quickly forms emotional alliances with the underprivileged and the victimized. His loyalties are sometimes misplaced, as in the case of Steerforth, his school friend who seduces Little Em'ly, but his heart remains sound and generous toward even the erring. As he passes from childhood to disillusioned adolescence, his perceptions increase, though he often misses the truth because he misreads the evidence before him. His trust is all the more remarkable when one considers the recurrence of error that leads him from false friends to false love and on to near catastrophe. Finally, unlike his creator, David finds balance and completion in his literary career, his abiding friendships, and his happy second marriage.

Clara Copperfield, David's childlike but understanding and beautiful mother, destined to an early death because of her inability to cope with life. Strong in her own attachments, she attributes to everyone motives as good and generous as her own. Misled into a second marriage to an unloving husband, she is torn between son and husband and dies soon after giving birth to another child. Mother and child are buried in the same coffin.

Edward Murdstone, Clara Copperfield's second husband and David's irascible stepfather, who cruelly mistreats the sensitive young boy. Self-seeking to an extreme degree, Murdstone has become a synonym for the mean and low, the calculating and untrustworthy. His cruelty is touched with sadism, and his egoism borders on the messianic.

Jane Murdstone, Edward Murdstone's sister. Like her brother, she is harsh and unbending. Her severe nature is symbolized by the somber colors and metallic beads she wears. Her suspicious mind is shown by her belief that the maids have a man hidden somewhere in the house.

Clara Peggotty, Mrs. Copperfield's devoted servant and David's nurse and friend. Cheerful and plump, she always seems about to burst out of her clothing, and when she moves buttons pop and fly in all directions. Discharged after the death of her mistress, she marries Barkis, a carrier.

Daniel Peggotty, Clara Peggotty's brother, a Yarmouth fisherman whose home is a boat beached on the sands. A generous, kind-hearted man, he has made himself the protector of a niece and a nephew, Little Em'ly and Ham, and of Mrs. Gummidge, the forlorn widow of his former partner. His charity consists of thoughtful devotion as much as material support.

Ham Peggotty, Daniel Peggotty's stalwart nephew. He grows up to fall in love with his cousin, Little Em'ly; on the eve of their wedding, however, she elopes with James Steerforth, her seducer. Some years later, during a great storm, Ham is drowned while trying to rescue Steerforth from a ship in distress off Yarmouth beach.

Little Em'ly, Daniel Peggotty's niece and adopted daughter, a girl of great beauty and charm and David's first love. Though engaged to marry her cousin Ham, she runs away with James Steerforth. After he discards her, Daniel Peggotty saves her from a life of further shame, and she and her uncle join a party emigrating to Australia.

Barkis, the carrier between Blunderstone and Yarmouth. A bashful suitor, he woos Peggotty by having David tell her that "Barkis is willin'!" This tag-line, frequently repeated, reveals the carter's good and simple nature.

Mrs. Gummidge, the widow of Daniel Peggotty's fishing partner. After he takes her into his home, she spends most of her time by the fire, meanwhile complaining sadly that she is a "lone, lorn creetur."

Miss Betsey Trotwood, David Copperfield's great-aunt, eccentric, sharp-spoken, but essentially kind-hearted. Present on the night of David's birth, she has already made up her mind as to his sex and his name, her own. When she learns that the child is a boy, she leaves the house in great indignation. Eventually, she becomes the benefactress of destitute and desolate David, educates him, and lives to see him happily married to Agnes Wickfield and established in his literary career.

Richard Babley, called **Mr. Dick**, a mildly mad and seemingly irresponsible man befriended by Miss Trotwood. He has great difficulty in keeping the subject of King Charles the First out of his conversation and the memorial he is writing. Miss Trotwood, who refuses to admit that he is mad, always defers to him as a shrewd judge of character and situation.

Dora Spenlow, the ornamental but helpless "child-wife" whom David loves protectively, marries, and loses when she dies young. Her helplessness in dealing with the ordinary situations of life is both amusing and touching.

Agnes Wickfield, the daughter of Miss Trotwood's solicitor and David's staunch friend for many years. Though David at first admires the father, his admiration is soon transferred to the sensible, generous daughter. She nurses Dora Copperfield at the time of her fatal illness, and Dora on her deathbed advises David to marry Agnes. The delicacy with which Agnes contains her love for many years makes her an appealing figure. Eventually, she and David are married, to Miss Trotwood's great delight.

Uriah Heep, the hypocritical villain who, beginning as a clerk in Mr. Wickfield's law office, worms his way into the confidence of his employer, becomes a partner in the firm, ruins Mr. Wickfield, and embezzles Miss Trotwood's fortune. His insistence that he is a very humble person provides the clue to his sly, conniving nature. His villainy is finally uncovered by Wilkins Micawber, whom he has used as a tool, and he is forced to make restitution. After Mr. Wickfield and Miss Trotwood refuse to charge him with fraud, he continues his sharp practices in another section of the country until he is arrested for forgery and imprisoned.

Wilkins Micawber, an impecunious man who is "always waiting for something to turn up" while spending himself into debtors' prison, writing grandiloquent letters, indulging in flowery rhetoric, and eking out a shabbily genteel existence on the brink of disaster. David Copperfield lodges with the Micawbers for a time in London, and to him Mr. Micawber confides the sum of his worldly philosophy: "Annual income twenty pounds; annual expenditure nineteen, nineteen, six—result happiness. Annual income twenty pounds; annual expenditure twenty pounds nought six—result misery." He tries a variety of occupations in the course of the novel and is for a time employed by Uriah Heep, whose villainy he contemptuously unmasks. Miss Trotwood aids him and his family to emigrate to Australia, where he becomes a magistrate. A figure of improvidence, alternating between high spirits and low, well-meaning but without understanding of worldly ways, Mr. Micawber is one of Dickens' great comic creations.

in the world. Much like Michael, she risks her life to help people, especially in war-torn regions. Several times, she comes and helps Ilana Davita's family, and she prays for them to become Christians. She is the only family member of the Chandals who continues to associate with Michael.

— Daven M. Kari

A DAY IN THE DEATH OF JOE EGG

Author: Peter Nichols (1927-   )
First published: 1967
Genre: Drama

Locale: A southwestern suburb of London
Time: Mid-1960's
Plot: Black humor

Brian (Bri), a thirty-three-year-old schoolteacher in Bristol, England. Bri is an adept comedian, jokester, and mimic who has found that humor is the only escape from or cure for the reality of living with a spastic child. He loves his wife, Sheila, and their daughter, Joe, but feels that circumstances (an unexpected pregnancy and ensuing medical malpractice) have thrown him into an untenable situation. He is moody, emotionally spontaneous, and deeply jealous of Joe for usurping Sheila's attention. An aspiring painter who has lost the creative drive and taken solace in drinking, he dislikes and is ineffective in his job as a schoolteacher. To him, God is a manic-depressive rugby player. Bri is very cynical and will not tolerate false hopes about Joe's condition. Although he propels the elaborate farce that he and Sheila enact to fulfill their life with Joe, he cannot understand why Joe must live, and finally he acts on his impulse to commit euthanasia.

Sheila, Bri's thirty-five-year-old wife. Sheila is an industrious and warm-hearted woman who loves living things; besides looking after Bri and Joe, she cares for a menagerie of pets and houseplants. A decade of hard work and frustrated motherhood have left her weary and somewhat humorless. She thinks carefully about human behavior and believes in psychology and the power of the subconscious. She harbors deep guilt about Joe's condition and feels that her earlier promiscuity and the fear of motherhood it gave her caused her to inhibit Joe's birth and thus damage the child. Although Sheila has no patience for Bri's self-pity, she plays along with his humor and farcical approach to their shared tragedy. In her heart, however, she resents his cynicism and clings to her faith, dreaming that she will someday see her daughter miraculously become a full human being.

Josephine (Joe), a ten-year-old spastic girl. Joe is a pretty child who looks physically normal but is spastic, epileptic, multiplegic, and almost totally incapable of willful human expression or activity. Her limbs are stiff, and she must be propped up; she is susceptible to illness and seizures; and her feeding, medication, and bodily functions require constant care and attention. At best, she looks about vacantly and moans feebly. She spends her days at a school for spastics.

Freddie Underwood, Bri's college friend, now an affluent industrialist, a socialist, and a director of amateur theater. Freddie is hearty and hale and seems older than his thirty-three years. Likable and good-spirited, he is eager to help Sheila and Bri. Freddie is a cautious rationalist who clings to law and order, however, and he considers Bri's and Sheila's play-acting with Joe to be an unhealthy and destructive response to the child's condition. He argues theoretically with Bri against euthanasia.

Pamela Underwood, Freddie's wife. Pamela is a postured and fashionable woman who is obsessed with propriety and appearances. She detests anything "N.P.A." (not physically attractive) and therefore feels no compassion, merely disgust, for Joe, to whom she refers as the "weirdie." Pamela is irritable and impatient and cannot fathom Freddie's desire to help Bri and Sheila. A basically self-centered woman, she devotes all of her attention, with great pride, to her husband and their three beautiful children.

Grace, Bri's mother, a sixty-five-year-old widow. Grace is a fastidious suburbanite who appreciates her routine and the small diversions that fill her life. She chatters freely and cheerfully but, like her son, is subject to moods of gloom and self-pity. She is proud of the sacrifices she made for her husband and son, and she considers Sheila to be inadequate as a wife for Bri and mother for Joe.

— B. P. Mann

THE DAY OF THE LOCUST

Author: Nathanael West (Nathan Weinstein, 1903-1940)
First published: 1939
Genre: Novel

Locale: Hollywood, California
Time: The 1930's
Plot: Social realism

Tod Hackett, a set and costume designer and Yale graduate. His friends say he sold out to Hollywood, but he hopes to prove them wrong by becoming a serious artist. When not doing his hack work at the dream factory, he concentrates on his painting of Los Angeles aflame. Large and awkward, Tod appears void of artistic talent; however, he has intelligence and a complex personality. This protagonist encounters an odd assortment of grotesques—a scriptwriter, prostitutes, bit-part actors, a vaudevillian, a retired bookkeeper, and a gambler. His obsession with Faye Greener prevents his being a totally ob-jective observer of the Hollywood scene. In his masterpiece painting *The Burning of Los Angeles*, Tod depicts these dream makers and consumers as having been cheated by Hollywood's promises of glamour, sex, power, and wealth. At the end, he is rescued by police before being crushed to death by mob violence and expresses his anguish in hysterical laughter and screaming.

Claude Estee, a successful Hollywood screenwriter. He lives in a replica of an antebellum mansion, impersonates a Civil War colonel, and amuses guests by having a rubber horse submerged in his pool. A little man who flaunts his power and money, Claude becomes what he pretends to be, parodying Hollywood's artificiality to control it. He remains Tod's closest friend, and Tod asks the police to take him to Claude's at the end.

Faye Greener, a would-be actress who manufactures dreams. At seventeen, she has had one line (spoken badly) in a film and has acquired a hardened outlook. Her seductive smile shows a lack of intelligence, yet she is a beautiful *femme fatale*—tall, with wide shoulders, long legs, and long, platinum hair. Her sensuality is not of pleasure but of struggle. Although she attracts men with her dazzling sexuality, she treats them cruelly once they have satisfied her needs. Determined to love only handsome, wealthy men, she rejects Tod's advances yet tantalizes him. After her father dies, she moves into Homer Simpson's home but continues her relationships with other men. Tod eventually realizes that like a floating cork, she will survive.

Harry Greener, Faye's ailing father, a vaudeville clown for forty years. His biggest stage success came as a bedraggled harlequin, kicked about by acrobats. While peddling his bogus homemade polish, he collapses in Homer Simpson's home. He has a strangely sadomasochistic relationship with his daughter: He taunts her with maniacal laughter, which she quiets by hitting him hard in the mouth with her fist. Harry goes into his comic routines like a windup mechanical toy, and his masklike face has a repertoire of theatrical expressions. When he dies, Faye resorts to prostitution to pay for his funeral, which turns into a spectacle for curiosity seekers.

Homer Simpson, a retired bookkeeper who has come to California to die. At forty, he is lonely and miserable; his life has been without variety or excitement. Although he is large and muscular, he is impotent, and his peculiarly unruly hands show his oddity. Like a poorly made machine, he worked mechanically with impersonal detachment for twenty years; now he has difficulty relating to people. After Harry dies, he takes Faye in, supports her, and suffers her cruelty in silence. When she leaves him, Homer heads home to Iowa, walking catatonically with suitcases. Before Tod can get a taxi for him, Homer retaliates against Adore Loomis and, in turn, is attacked by the frenzied mob.

Adore Loomis, a would-be child star. Dressed like a little man and performing sexually suggestive lyrics and gestures, eight-year-old Adore is a perverted child forced into adulthood. His merciless attack on Homer pushes the crazed man over the edge of sanity.

Abe Kusich, a dwarf, gambler, and low-life hustler. Tod first sees Abe sleeping in a hotel hallway, having been thrown out without his clothes by a prostitute. He looks grotesque with his slightly hydrocephalic head; moreover, he acts depraved, whether starting a drunken brawl or handling a fighting gamecock.

Earle Shoop, a cowboy who works occasionally in low-budget Westerns. More than six feet tall, Earl wears a ten-gallon hat and high-heeled boots that add another eight inches. Although he is stupid, Earle attracts Faye with his good looks.

Miguel, a Mexican who raises gamecocks. Like Earle, he satisfies Faye's lust for sexuality. He pairs off with her at the end.

— *Laura M. Zaidman*

DAYS OF THE TURBINS
(Dni Turbinykh)

Author: Mikhail Bulgakov (1891-1940)
First published: 1926
Genre: Drama

Locale: Kiev, the Ukraine
Time: November, 1918-January, 1919
Plot: Tragicomedy

Alexei Vasilyevich Turbin (ah-lehk-SAY vah-SIH-lyeh-vihch TEWR-bihn), an artillery colonel in the Russian army. He is serving a Ukrainian hetman in Kiev and collaborates with the Germans against other Ukrainian nationalists and the Bolsheviks. Alexei understands the precariousness of his position, as he is neither a dedicated nationalist nor a friend of the Germans; he only wants to do what he is trained for: to serve as an officer with honor and dignity. When his honor and dignity are threatened, he refuses to continue fighting for a cause that has lost its rationale, preferring to pay for his mistake with his life—not before, however, he absolves everyone serving under him of any obligation to fight to the last along with him. Alexei is a gentleman officer and an idealist, contrary to the official Soviet view of any opponents of the Bolsheviks as morally bankrupt hirelings.

Nikolai Turbin (nih-koh-LAY), his brother, a cadet. Nikolai worships his older brother and, like him, has a high sense of duty. These two sentiments compel him to refuse his brother's command to leave before the final attack, during which he is badly crippled. In this sense, he is an extension of Alexei, with one difference: Alexei is adamantly anti-Bolshevik, whereas Nikolai's reaction to the coming of the Bolsheviks is not as clear.

Yelena Vasilyevna Talberg (yeh-LEH-nah vah-SIH-lyehv-nah TAHL-buhrg), their sister. Yelena is an intelligent woman of excellent upbringing, married to a high officer in the hetman's army. A red-haired beauty with whom everyone seems to fall in love, she shows the dignity of her brothers, never losing moral decorum. She handles the advances of her many suitors with benign firmness and never allows any relationship to sink below the proper level. Consequently, she firmly dissolves her marriage when her husband fails to uphold the standards of moral decency.

Vladimir Robertovich Talberg (vlah-DIH-mihr roh-BEHR-toh-vihch), a General Staff colonel and Yelena's husband. Talberg, also an active officer, is the direct opposite of Alexei: selfish, unscrupulous, insincere in his marriage, vain, jealous, and ready to go to any length in furthering his own cause. He has no qualms in leaving Yelena behind to face complete uncertainty when he flees to Berlin. For this striking conglomeration of negative traits, he "looks like a rat" in the eyes of at least two of his companions.

Viktor Viktorovich Myshlaevsky (VIHK-tohr vihk-TOH-roh-vihch mi-SHLAH-yehv-skee), a captain in the artillery. A good-hearted, loud, and, at times, rowdy officer, as well as a heavy drinker but faithful friend, Myshlaevsky serves his country loyally but only to a point. Once he realizes that the cause he has been serving is falling apart, he changes without much soul-searching and without really knowing to what he is changing.

Leonid Yuryevich Shervinsky (lee-oh-NIHD YUHR-yeh-vihch shehr-VIHN-skee), a lieutenant, the hetman's personal aide-de-camp. Shervinsky's driving force in life is his love for Yelena, for whom he is ready to sacrifice everything. His loyalty to the side for which he is fighting is weak; he does not betray it because of his preoccupation with Yelena and his lack of strong beliefs. He has little difficulty adapting to the Bolsheviks, thanks to his beautiful singing voice and to an uncanny ability to stay afloat in every situation.

Alexander Bronislavovich Studzinsky (broh-nih-SLAH-voh-vihch stew-DZIHN-skee), a captain in the hetman's army. Of all the officers except Alexei, Studzinsky is the most loyal to the struggle against the Bolsheviks, even when it seems hopeless. In this aspect, he shows a remarkable strength of character.

Lariosik (lah-rih-OH-sihk), a cousin of the Turbins, from Zhitomir. A young man who comes to the Turbins to study in Kiev at the time of street fighting, Lariosik adapts quickly to the new situation, perhaps as a result of his falling in love with Yelena. Painfully polite, bashful, and awkward (he always breaks something), often managing to say the wrong thing, he is still liked by all and seems to fit into the chaotic scene into which he has stumbled. His naïveté is refreshing during the period of somber mood and mortal danger for the Turbins.

— *Vasa D. Mihailovich*

THE DEAD

Author: James Joyce (1882-1941)
First published: 1914
Genre: Short fiction

Locale: Dublin, Ireland
Time: 1904
Plot: Ironic

Gabriel Conroy, an unfulfilled teacher and favorite nephew of the Morkan sisters, who live in Dublin, Ireland. A stout, nervous, sensitive man who wears his black hair parted in the middle and glasses with gilt rims, he writes a literary newspaper column and considers himself superior in culture to everyone at the annual Christmastime dance given by his aunts, but he feels like a failure. His after-dinner speech is a sentimental affirmation of traditional Irish character and customs, yet he feels sick of his country. Dutiful but restless, he has insulated himself from life, wears galoshes, and has never been passionately in love. His marriage to Gretta is dull. After the dance, with his wife in their hotel room, he feels a strong desire for her. She weeps and confesses that she is thinking of Michael Furey, a young lover who died for her; then she falls asleep. Gabriel accepts his failure and feels a generous compassion for his wife. Gazing out the window at the falling snow, he identifies himself in humility with all the dead.

Gretta Conroy, Gabriel's wife, a country girl from western Ireland. She has rich bronze hair and frail shoulders, and she suggests grace and mystery. At the dance, she is moved by a sweet Irish song that reminds her of Michael Furey, leading to the confession to her husband that she once had romance in her life.

Lily, the caretaker's daughter and housemaid of the Morkan sisters. A pale, slim, growing girl, she makes Gabriel feel like a failure when he cheerfully inquires whether she will be getting married soon to her young man and she replies with great bitterness that men nowadays are merely out for what they can get.

Kate Morkan, an elderly piano teacher who is Gabriel's aunt and the chief hostess. She is a feeble yet vivacious lady, with old-fashioned braided hair that has not lost its ripe nut color and a face like a shriveled red apple. She fiercely defends the rights of her sister, Julia Morkan, against the pope and is said by Gabriel in his laudatory speech to have too good a

heart, though he actually feels trapped by the culture she represents.

Julia Morkan, Kate's sister, a leading soprano. Gray-haired, dim of mind, and near death, she sings a bridal song with innocence of irony and is excessively praised by Freddy Malins, who is drunk. At the end of the story, she inspires Gabriel's pity in his meditation on the dead.

Mary Jane, a young organist and piano teacher, the only niece of the Morkan sisters and the main prop of the household. With her aunts, according to Gabriel, she is one of the Three Graces of the Dublin musical world.

Molly Ivors, a friend and a teacher colleague of Gabriel, dedicated to Irish nationalism. A frank, challenging woman with a freckled face, prominent brown eyes, and a brooch on her collar bearing an Irish symbol and motto, she irritates Gabriel by accusing him of being unpatriotic. He sees her as a rude propagandist who represents a new generation that lacks the virtues of the Morkan sisters and Mary Jane. She asserts her independence and leaves the dance early.

Freddy Malins, a houseguest given to drink and indecorum. A man of about forty, with coarse features, protruding lips, disorderly and scanty hair, and a sleepy look, he comes late, is drunk, and laughs excessively but proves himself to be a decent fellow by defending a black singer and by paying back a loan from Gabriel.

Mrs. Malins, Freddy's mother, who is visiting from Glasgow. An ineffectual old woman with white hair and a stutter, she has made her son take a pledge not to drink.

Mr. Browne, a non-Catholic guest who knows opera. A swarthy man with a stiff, grizzled mustache, he is forward and offensively common.

Bartell D'Arcy, a conceited and second-rate tenor. He begins to sing an Irish song, moving Gretta to recall Michael Furey, who used to sing the same song, but he breaks it off because he has a dreadful cold.

Michael Furey, the romantic passion of Gretta, a Galway boy who died at the age of seventeen. Very delicate and gentle, with big dark eyes, he was poor and employed in the gasworks, but Gretta thoroughly enjoyed his company. When she was about to move away from Galway, he was ill, yet he came and stood in her garden in the rain; he caught his death.

— *Michael Hollister*

THE DEAD CLASS: A Dramatic Séance
(Umarła Klasa)

Author: Tadeusz Kantor (1915-1990)
First published: 1979
Genre: Drama

Locale: Poland
Time: Early twentieth century, around 1914
Plot: Surrealism

Old Students, eight elderly people, fellow students of the Old Man Repeater, the Old Man with a Bike, the Old Man in the Loo, and the Old Man Exhibitionist. They are dressed in black, with black bowlers; they have grayish faces and dead, staring eyes. Each student carries a child puppet on his back, dressed in school uniform, as an effigy of lost childhood and imprisonment in the past.

The Old Man in the Loo, a student. He sits in the school lavatory, engrossed in endless accounts and quarrels with God. This repetitive action suggests an eternal regression into the anal stage.

The Old Man with a Bike, a student. He never parts with the beat-up remnant of childhood and ceaselessly rides the bike around the desks, adding yet another symbolic action to the eternal imprisonment in repetition of the members of the dead class.

The Old Man Exhibitionist, a student. His fellow students drag him to the privy and pull his pants down. He exposes his backside, remaining in that pose for the duration of the lesson on Solomon.

The Old Man Repeater, a miserable looking student who is taunted and bullied by the others. He stubbornly recites his grammar lesson while the rest talk and squirm in complete indifference. As the Obituary Distributor, he displays his bent for repetitive action by distributing and reading in a droning monotone the endless list of the dead class.

Charwoman, who cleans up the classroom. Her function extends from sweeping up notebooks, paper, and the debris of the dead class to the ritual washing of the cadavers of the dead class, thereby extending her symbolic function to Charwoman-Death. In the final scene, she is transformed into a nightmarish brothel keeper who bumps and grinds while the activities in the classroom continue in automatic and repetitive patterns.

The Woman with a Mechanical Cradle, who is wheeled in, strapped to what looks like a combination of a gynecologist's table with stirrups and an instrument of torture. Each one of the movements of opening and closing her knees is synchronized to the rocking of the coffinlike Mechanical Cradle, with its rattling wooden balls, in a travesty of the birth-death cycle.

The Woman Behind the Window, who carries the frame of a window, always looking in from the outside in a symbolic action of her separation from life.

Somnambulist Prostitute, the town harlot. She struts shamelessly around the leering oldster students, baring her breasts in an automaton-like action.

The Beadle, the preserver of order. He sits passively in his chair, coming to life only to sing the Austrian Empire's national anthem.

Tadeusz Kantor, the creator and director of the play. He remains on stage during the duration of the performance, directing the action by indicating climaxes, musical passages, entrances, exits, and the speeding up or slowing down of action. As a result of his presence, the actions do not always occur in a particular order and sometimes change from performance to performance.

— *Christine Kiebuzinska*

DEAD MAN LEADING

Author: V. S. Pritchett (1900-1997)
First published: 1937
Genre: Novel

Locale: Brazil and London, England
Time: c. 1930
Plot: Psychological

Harry Johnson, a timber merchant and adventurer who relishes solitude. He is about thirty years old, strong, muscular, and awkward. He has big brown eyes, a crinkled forehead, immensely broad shoulders, and a gentle, aloof manner. He is the son of a missionary who disappeared in the same Brazilian forest that Johnson is about to explore along with his two friends, Gilbert Phillips and Charles Wright. Before leaving England, he had a brief love affair with Wright's stepdaughter, Lucy Mommbrekke. Obsessed with the fear that she may be having a child and that he will be chained to her, he falls ill on the launch that is taking him and Phillips upriver to rendez-vous with Wright. He longs to talk to his friends but cannot bring himself to risk their saying that he has lost his nerve. When he recovers from his illness, he and Silva leave in a canvas canoe without telling Phillips and Wright, who overtake them. Johnson is punishing himself and Wright because he feels guilty and wants to be alone. Eventually, he forgets the other men and thinks only of his father, the dead man of the title. He is extremely brave: He makes a tremendous but unsuccessful effort to save Wright's life, and, after weeks of cutting through the jungle, he staggers off to find water for Phillips and disappears.

Gilbert Phillips, an English journalist. He is about thirty years old, tall, and fair as a Dane. Since boyhood, he has been Johnson's friend, and he is a former lover of Lucy. He is highly impressionable and is a worrier who believes that his safety is tied to Johnson. He wallows in self-pity. After Wright's death, he follows Johnson for many miles through almost impenetrable jungle because he is afraid to turn back alone. After Johnson's departure in search of water, Phillips is saved by rain. Terrified of being alone, he stumbles along until rescued by some Germans.

Charles Wright, a former army doctor who is now an explorer. He is trim, erect, and capable, with a wiry strength. He is indignant when he, the leader, feels obliged to follow Johnson, particularly after it becomes evident that the young man is taking a dangerous course differing from the one on which they agreed. Pity prompts him to go hunting with Johnson and try to reason with him. When he is accidentally shot by his own gun, he is carried by Johnson back to the boat, where he dies.

Lucy Mommbrekke, a rather short, soft-bodied, lazy, and sensual girl. She has black, closely curling hair above a very white forehead and dark, lively eyes. After initiating a love affair with Johnson, she appears to become his adoring slave. Like him, she is unsure in social relationships, and she knows that a marriage between them could not be successful. She begs Phillips to look after Johnson on the expedition. Soon after the men's departure, she marries to free herself from her wild, intolerable love of Johnson.

Calcott, a lank, wasted, bald, dirty Cockney of fifty who owns the house from which the expedition is to start. He has spent thirty years in the country and has a Brazilian wife, whom he beats, and seven children. His acute sense of inferiority makes him suspect every visiting Englishman of snubbing him. His conversation is filled with dire prophesies of the horrid fates that befall travelers in the jungle. He was the last person to see Johnson's father.

Silva, a fat Portuguese man in miniature. He is intelligent, discreet, and greedy for gold. He and Calcott conduct spiritualist séances, although he does not believe in spirits. He arranges for the table-tapping to indicate that Johnson's father is not dead and has found gold. Greed is his motive for accompanying Harry.

— *Dorothy B. Aspinwall*

DEAD SOULS
(Myortvye Dushi)

Author: Nikolai Gogol (1809-1852)
First published: 1842 (part 1), 1855 (part 2)
Genre: Novel

Locale: Russia
Time: Early nineteenth century
Plot: Social satire

Pavel Ivanovitch Tchitchikov (PAH-vehl ih-VAH-nuh-vihch CHEET-chee-kof), an adventurer of early nineteenth century Russia. He buys "dead souls," that is, the names of serfs who have died since the last census but who still continue to cost their owners taxes until they can be written off in the next census. Using their names, he plans to get from his uncle's estate the money refused him in the old man's will by mortgaging his own "estate," with its dead souls, to the Trustee Committee. To find dead souls, he rides from village to village visiting landowners and exerting his charm to obtain the names of dead serfs. The villagers begin to talk and, unable to guess what he is up to, accuse him of all sorts of crimes. He has an encounter with the law and is arrested. He is finally released by an unscrupulous lawyer who brings to light all the local scandals, so that the villagers are glad to get Tchitchikov out of town.

Selifan (SEH-lih-vuhn), Pavel's coachman, through whose mistake about roads he visits Madame Korobotchkina. They are put onto the right road by her twelve-year-old maid, Pelageya.

Nastasya Petrovna Korobotchkina (nahs-TAH-syuh peht-ROV-nuh koh-roh-BACH-kee-nuh), an overnight hostess who sells Pavel eighteen of her dead souls for fifteen rubles each.

Petrushka (peht-REWSH-kuh), Pavel's valet, who shares his adventures.

Nozdryov (NOHZ-dryof), a gambler and liar who meets Pavel at an inn and finally denounces him to the police as a spy and forger. He himself is arrested for assaulting a friend, Maximov.

Manilov (mah-nih-LOHF), a genial landowner who offers hospitality to Pavel and gives him his first dead souls.

Lizanka (lih-ZAHN-kuh), the wife of Manilov.

Themistoclus (teh-MIHS-to-kluhs), one of Manilov's two children.

Mihail Semyonovitch Sobakevitch (mih-hah-IHL seh-MYOH-no-vihch soh-BAH-keh-vihch), a landowner who at first demands a hundred rubles apiece for his dead souls but finally settles for two and a half rubles apiece.

Plyushkin (PLEWSH-kihn), a miser who haggles fiercely over 120 dead souls and seventy-eight fugitives. He finally gives Pavel a letter to the town president.

Ivan Grigoryevitch (ih-VAHN grih-GOH-ryeh-vihch), the town president, who transfers Pavel's purchased dead souls to the adventurer's imaginary estate in the Kherson province and makes the transactions legal.

Ivan Antonovitch (ahn-TOH-no-vihch), a minor clerk who must be bribed to record the purchases.

The Governor, who entertains at a big ball.

The Governor's Daughter, with whom Pavel is supposed to be eloping. His coach had previously collided with hers.

Captain Kopeykin (koh-PAY-kihn), a legendary soldier of the War of 1812, turned bandit. Some think he has returned disguised as Pavel.

Andrey Ivanovitch Tyentyelnikov (ahn-DRAY ih-VAH-no-vihch tyehn-TYEHL-nih-kof), a thirty-three-year-old bachelor who plays host to the adventurer. Pavel aids him in his suit for a neighbor's daughter.

General Betrishtchev (beht-RIHSH-chehf), a neighbor of Tyentyelnikov who gives the young landowner his daughter in marriage and sells more dead souls to Pavel.

Ulinka (ew-LIHN-kuh), the general's daughter, in love with Tyentyelnikov.

Vishnepokromov (vihsh-nyeh-POHK-ro-mof), who tries to prevent Ulinka's engagement.

Pyetukh (PEH-tewk), a generous glutton who entertains Pavel.

Platonov (PLAH-to-nov), a young friend who accompanies Pavel on his travels and introduces him to his sister and his brother-in-law.

Konstantin Skudronzhoglo (kohn-stahn-TIHN skew-drohn-ZHOH-glo), a prosperous landowner and the brother-in-law of Platonov. He lends Pavel ten thousand rubles to buy an estate.

Hlobuev (hloh-BEW-ehf), a spendthrift whose land Pavel wants to buy. By forging a will, Pavel tries to help him claim an inheritance from a rich aunt, but he forgets to cancel in it all earlier documents.

Alexy Ivanovitch Lyenitzyn (ah-lehk-SAY ih-VAH-neh-vihch leh-NIH-tsewn), a public official who discovers two wills of the old woman, one contradicting the other. He has Pavel jailed on a charge of forgery.

Ivan Andreitch (ahn-DRAY-ihch), the postmaster of "N."

Samosvitov (sah-MOHS-vih-tof), who offers to get Pavel out of jail for thirty thousand rubles.

Murazov (mew-rah-ZOHF), the shrewd, unscrupulous lawyer who gets Pavel freed by raking up scandals against all those who have accused his client.

THE DEAN'S DECEMBER

Author: Saul Bellow (1915-   )
First published: 1982
Genre: Novel

Locale: Bucharest, Chicago, and California
Time: The 1970's
Plot: Comic realism

Albert Corde, a journalism professor and dean at a university in Chicago. Caught between his intellectual, idealistic belief in morality and the pragmatic, relativistic demands of the modern world, Albert seeks balance in his life. In the past, he abandoned journalism for the relative seclusion of the academy, but two events draw him back into direct consideration of the world beyond the university: Rick Lester's murder and the death of Albert's mother-in-law in Romania. Rick Lester's death leads Albert into an examination of the morally corrupt and destructive environment of Chicago, the doomed lives of its lower class, and the moral obtuseness of its leaders. In Romania, Albert struggles with a political system that is determined to limit human possibilities. In the end, Albert resigns his academic post and decides to return to a kind of intellectual journalism, striving for a balance between the sterile isolation of the academic life and the cynical pragmatism of the capitalists and communists he encounters.

Minna Corde, Albert's Romanian wife, an astronomy professor at the same university. Minna is Albert's complement. As an accomplished pure scientist and an emotional innocent, Minna contrasts with her husband's speculative humanism and worldly experience. Brilliant but uncomplicated, Minna provides her husband with an emotional touchstone that helps him survive.

Valeria Raresh, Minna's mother, who is dying in Bucharest. She is a former Communist Party member, a former minister of health, and a founder of the Communist Party Hospital. Her quiet support for political reform and Minna's defection cost Valeria her position and her privileges, but she is a strong and selfless woman who spends her life doing for others: protecting her daughter by engineering Minna's escape to the West, caring for her younger sister Gigi, upholding the medical ideals of her late husband, and providing quiet leadership for other oppressed medical people in Romania.

Elfrida Zaehner, later **Sorokin**, Albert's sister. Elfrida is wealthy and somewhat ostentatious in her expenditures. Loving her as deeply as he does keeps Albert in sympathetic contact with the genteel world of privilege and prevents him from too readily dismissing the humanity of the upper classes.

Alec Witt, the provost and Albert's superior at his university. Witt is the ultimate pragmatic bureaucrat, superficially polite and considerate but devoid of human compassion or understanding. He loses respect for Albert when he realizes that the dean does not understand or is unwilling to play the "game." Angered by Albert's advocacy in the Lester case, Witt gladly accepts Albert's resignation.

Dewey Spangler, a famous journalist and Albert's boyhood friend. Aging and ill, Spangler persists in pursuing his boyhood rivalry with Albert, embarrassing Albert by reprinting his private remarks in a syndicated column.

Mason Zaehner, Elfrida's deceased husband. Intelligent but determinedly anti-intellectual, he derides Albert's academic life as useless escapism.

Mason Zaehner, Jr., Elfrida's son and Albert's nephew. Mason reacts against the privilege of his upbringing by espousing radical political ideas. His support of Leroy Ebry, who is accused and eventually convicted of murdering Rick Lester, a university student, brings him into angry confrontation with Albert.

Max Detillion, a disreputable lawyer and Albert's cousin. Max cheats the gullible Albert out of thousands of dollars and conducts a shrill, self-serving legal attack against Albert as Leroy Ebry's defense attorney.

Rick Lester, a graduate student at Albert's university who is murdered by Leroy Ebry. Albert becomes deeply involved in the pursuit of Lester's murderer, feeling particularly protective toward Lester's widow, Lydia.

Tanti Gigi, Valeria Raresh's sister, who has always depended on the protection of her older sister. Valeria's death leaves Gigi to face the barrenness of Romanian life alone.

Rufus Ridpath, a black prison warden who is dismissed from his position because of charges of misconduct. Albert defends Ridpath, seeing him as a victim of a corrupt political system and an unusual example of a man of courage and principle.

Traian, a Romanian driver who helps the Cordes through the complex process of bribes necessary to navigate the Romanian bureaucracy.

Ioanna, the concierge in Valeria's building and a police informant. Treated as one of the family although everyone knows that she is an informant, Ioanna exemplifies the odd divided loyalties that exist under the Romanian system.

— *Carl Brucker*

DEAR BRUTUS

Author: Sir James M. Barrie (1860-1937)
First published: 1923
Genre: Drama

Locale: England
Time: Midsummer Eve
Plot: Fantasy

Will Dearth, who in the drawing room is a shaky, watery-eyed relic of what was once a good man. An artist at one time, he and Alice Dearth had loved madly. In the woods, he is a successful artist and the father of a daughter named Margaret. He claims credit for all of his daughter's charm, except her baby laugh; this she lost when he allowed her to lose perfect faith in him. Back in the drawing room, he grants that he is not the man he thought he was. The Dearths, probably the only ones to gain by their revelation, may be able to breast their way into the light.

Alice Dearth, Will's wife. In the drawing room, she is a woman of fierce, smoldering desires. Hers is a dark but brave spirit, a kiss-or-kill personality. In the woods, she becomes a vagrant woman, a whimperer who warns Dearth to take good care of Margaret, for her kind is easily lost. Returned to the drawing room, she lies about what happened in the woods. Although she resents losing her might-have-been station as "the Honorable Mrs. Finch-Fallowe" and her husband's contentment with a might-have-been daughter, Mrs. Dearth shares his present interest in painting. She will try for compatibility, despite her avowal that her husband will not get much help from her.

Margaret, who in the woods is a beautiful and bewitching young girl. Her knowledge that "they" will take Dearth away stands between her and Dearth, to cloud their joy.

Mabel Purdie, in the drawing room a good companion for her philandering husband. Feigning other interests, she is apparently indifferent to his affair with a woman of their set. In the woods, she becomes a charmer who carries on passionately with her husband. Again in the drawing room, she sees her husband for what he is. Indifferent, she pledges to stay by him as long as she cares to bother.

Jack Purdie, in the drawing room a brilliant, intellectual man accepted—in fact, liked—despite his unfaithfulness to his wife. In the woods, he walks alone. No woman can plumb the well of his emotions. Once more in the drawing room, he sees himself objectively; he is a philanderer with no prospect of change in store for himself.

Joanna Trout, in the drawing room a woman attractive in face and figure but dull and humorless in love. She imagines herself the natural mate for the strong-hearted Purdie. In the woods, married to Purdie, she is drab and complaining because he is unfaithful. Back to the here and now of the drawing room, she recalls the might-have-been experience sufficiently to realize that she and Jack are hardly worth sorrow.

Matey, in the drawing room the perfect butler, a general favorite among those who know him, despite his being a pilferer. In the woods, he becomes James Matey, a dishonest business tycoon, and the husband of the disdainful Lady Caroline. Among his real satisfactions is being called "Jim" by Lady Caroline. Back in the drawing room, although he returns reluctantly to normality, he makes the full change quickly. Confronted by a coffee tray, he picks it up and goes to the pantry.

Lady Caroline Laney, in the drawing room a snobbish aristocrat, not so taken as others are by the thieving Matey. In the woods, she cavorts, uninhibited, with her handsome, brawny husband, Matey, answering gladly to his "Caroliny." In the drawing room, like Matey, she retains her role into the return and is shocked when her Jim picks up the coffee tray. She then assumes her former manner.

Emma Coade, an elderly, rounded woman called "Coady," as is her husband. She is the most congenial of the ladies gathered at the scene. Mrs. Coade did not go to the woods, but she knows that the others did. She senses that Lob, their host, is behind these fantastic happenings. The fact that she is Mr. Coade's second wife adds to her sadness when she learns of her husband's second-chance experience.

Mr. Coade, in the drawing room a gracious, older man with a gentle smile. Comfortably well-to-do, he has always meant to write a book but is always conveniently distracted. In the woods, he becomes a jolly, ne'er-do-well old bachelor. Later, in the drawing room, he is still gentle with Mrs. Coade in the same empty way; he sees himself as a genial, lazy old man who gained nothing by his second chance.

Mr. Lob, the wizened, ageless host to his guests, all of whom want a second chance. He is Puck from William Shakespeare's *A Midsummer Night's Dream* in disguise, and he introduces his guests to the Midsummer Eve of what might have been.

DEAR DIEGO
(Querido Diego, te abraza Quiela)

Author: Elena Poniatowska (1933-   )
First published: 1978
Genre: Novel

Locale: Paris, France, and Mexico City, Mexico
Time: The 1920's and 1935
Plot: Epistolary

Angelina Beloff (ahn-gahl-EE-nah BEH-lof), called **Quiela** (kee-EH-lah), a Russian painter of landscapes, still lifes, and portraits who also works as an engraver, lithographer, and book illustrator. She is Diego Rivera's lover in Paris from 1910 to 1920. After he leaves her, she writes to him for a period of nine months until she realizes that he is neither coming back nor sending for her. More than ten years later, she travels to Mexico, where he has gone, but she does not look for him.

Diego Rivera (dee-EH-goh ree-VEH-rah), a Mexican painter who lives with Beloff in Paris. He returns to Mexico in the wake of the Mexican Revolution. His ten-year relationship with Beloff (Quiela for him) is portrayed in *Dear Diego*, but as a character he appears only through her letters. He is judged in the novel because he leaves her and never writes back to her; he merely sends money once in a while. He represents the freedom of expression in contemporary Latin American art that Beloff lacks as a result of her European background.

DEAR RAFE
(Mi querido Rafa)

Author: Rolando Hinojosa (1929-   )
First published: 1981
Genre: Novel

Locale: The Rio Grande Valley of southern Texas
Time: Mid-1950's to early 1960's
Plot: Social realism

Jehu Malacara (HEH-ew mah-lah-KAHR-ah), the head loan officer at Klail City First National Bank, the center of Belken County politics. A Mexican American with a military background, he has chosen to work his way up into the Texas Anglo-American world of politics and money, but he finds himself unable to live with the underhanded games played by the Anglo-American power brokers. Despite his efforts in support of the Texas Mexican struggle to achieve higher economic and political status, he proves a disappointment to the Mexican American community. He quits his job at the bank; at the book's end, it is not known why he leaves the valley.

Noddy Perkins, a self-made man and bank owner who thrives on controlling the politics of Belken County. He is behind the Anglo-American power plays to keep the area's real estate out of the hands of Texas Mexicans. The reader is led to believe that he wants to exploit Jehu, his chief loan officer, by using him in the same manner as he does Ira Escobar. Although his sinister intentions do not bear fruit, Noddy is able to manipulate and control other important characters in his political schemes, even breaking off a love affair between his daughter, Sammie Jo, and Jehu.

Ira Escobar (EE-rah EHS-koh-bahr), a Texas Mexican employed at the Klail City First National Bank who falls prey to the political exploitation of Noddy Perkins. His desire to be a county commissioner makes him vulnerable to exploitation, and he becomes a pawn in Noddy's political schemes. Ira never understands why Jehu ever got a job at the bank or why he leaves this post.

Becky Caldwell-Escobar, the daughter of a prominent Mexican American family. She marries Ira Escobar, who is also from a prominent Mexican American family in Belken County. Their union creates a strong political bond between the two influential families. She is allowed to become part of the social circles of Anglo-Texan women. This achievement does not make an impression on her people, but her affair with Jehu does. In the end, she breaks off her relationship with Jehu and is devoted to her husband. The members of the Mexican American community, however, never accept her affair with Jehu, which they see as a negative reflection on their social values.

Sammie Jo Perkins-Cooke, Noddy's spoiled daughter. Her social activities are essential to the Anglo-Texan power brokers. Although she has good reason to have an affair with Jehu (her husband is having a homosexual affair), her actions are unacceptable to the Anglo-Texan society of the valley. After she breaks off her relationship with Jehu, she goes back to her husband. She will not jeopardize the security and the economic welfare of her father for the fulfillment of their own personal needs; hence, she is a reflection of Anglo-Texan values.

Rafe Buenrostro (RRAH-feh bwehn-ROHS-troh), the silent sounding board for messages sent to him in letters by Jehu Malacara. The author's life reflects that of Rafe: Both lived in and left the Rio Grande Valley at about the same time, both went to the University of Texas, and both fought in the Korean War.

DEATH AND THE KING'S HORSEMAN

Author: Wole Soyinka (1934-   )
First published: 1975
Genre: Drama

Locale: Oyo, Nigeria
Time: The 1940's
Plot: Tragedy

Elesin Oba (ay-LAY-sihn OH-bah), the chief horseman of the recently deceased king of a Nigerian village. Full of vitality, Elesin enjoys women, singing, and dancing. Despite his great thirst for life, he is a man of honor and wisdom. He must, therefore, adhere to native laws and customs that mandate that he kill himself prior to the king's burial so as to accompany his master to heaven. Although he has an abundance of wives and is in his final hours on Earth, his eyes wander to a young

woman who has been promised to another man; as a result of his stature, the girl is given to him in marriage. Regardless of having yet another reason to live, he is prompted by honor to pursue his death ceremony. When the critical rite is interrupted by the British colonial forces and his suicide is prevented, Elesin is disgraced and humiliated. His son, whom he had previously disowned for abandoning the tribe to attend school in Europe, now disowns him. Elesin is repudiated by friends and tribesmen and is held in prison by the British as a means of protecting his life. After witnessing his son's suicide to right his wrong, he strangles himself with his own shackles.

Praise-Singer, a man who follows Elesin around only to sing praises of him. Although his love for Elesin is great, he knows that the world demands the death of his master. During the death ritual, he takes on the role of the deceased king to speak with Elesin. He, too, is disgraced by Elesin failing to complete the ceremony, thereby disrupting the order of the universe.

Iyaloja (ee-yah-LOH-jah), the "mother" of the marketplace. Despite her lofty position above the other women, she is subservient to men and is terrified of offending Elesin, a man of such prominence. Her respect of his mission is so great that she willingly gives her son's fiancée to him in marriage. When Elesin's death is stalled, she scorns him, even calling his seed an abomination.

Simon Pilkings, an English colonialist and district officer of the territory. He is insensitive and impatient of beliefs foreign to him, especially tribal superstition. He does not respect religion (even his own) and often offends people. By seeing things from only his vantage point, he disrupts the order of the tribe's universe, which leads not only to the death of Elesin (whom he was attempting to save) but also to the destruction of Elesin's honor and of his eldest son.

Jane Pilkings, Simon's wife. Although shallow and ignorant, she has educated herself concerning the tribal customs and tries not to denigrate them. She is more compassionate than her husband and is the buffer between Simon and the people he tends to offend.

Sergeant Amusa (ah-MEW-sah), a black man absorbed into the white man's order, including Her Majesty's government service. He is despised by his people for denying his heritage and is considered less than an equal by the British. Although he converted to the Muslim religion, he remains superstitious regarding his own primitive beliefs. Amusa is sent to arrest Elesin to prevent his suicide. He is humiliated and chided by the native girls as a white man's eunuch.

Joseph, Simon Pilkings' native houseboy. He takes his conversion to Christianity seriously and is disturbed by Pilkings' sacrilegious speech.

Bride, the young virgin desired by Elesin. Although she is promised to Iyaloja's son, Iyaloja proudly gives her to the honored Elesin before his valiant death. The bride is impregnated by Elesin, but her unborn child is later cursed by Iyaloja after Elesin fails in his mission of death. The bride remains outside Elesin's jail cell after his incarceration, and it is she who closes his eyes after his suicide.

The Prince of Wales, the visiting English prince to the native colony.

The Resident, Simon Pilkings' superior. He is an arrogant, silly, and ignorant man who is not at all in touch with the natives. His lack of substance is displayed in his fascination with surfaces such as uniforms and tassels.

Aide-de-camp, an assistant to the resident. He is rude and bigoted and much like his superior.

Olunde (oh-LEWN-day), the eldest son of Elesin. Despite his father's renunciation of him for leaving the village, Olunde traveled to London to become a doctor. In his four years among the English, he has learned that they have no respect for what they do not understand. He returns to the village to warn Pilkings not to interfere with his father's suicide. Olunde rejects his father when he learns of Elesin's failed mission. To redeem his people, he takes on his father's task and kills himself.

— *Steven C. Kowall*

DEATH COMES FOR THE ARCHBISHOP

Author: Willa Cather (1873-1947)
First published: 1927
Genre: Novel

Locale: New Mexico and Arizona
Time: The last half of the nineteenth century
Plot: Historical realism

Father Jean Marie Latour (zhahn mah-REE lah-TEWR), a devout French priest consecrated as vicar apostolic of New Mexico and bishop of Agathonica in partibus in 1850. With Father Vaillant, his friend and fellow seminarian, he journeys from his old parish on the shores of Lake Ontario to Santa Fé, seat of the new diocese in territory recently acquired from Mexico. In those troubled times, he finds many of the old missions in ruins or abandoned, the Mexican clergy lax and unlearned, the sacraments corrupted by native superstitions. The travels of these two dedicated missionary priests over a desert region of sand, arroyos, towering mesas, and bleak red hills, the accounts of the labors they perform and the hardships they endure to establish the order and authority of the Church in a wild land, make up the story of this beautifully told chronicle. Father Latour is an aristocrat by nature and tradition. Intellectual, fastidious, reserved, he finds the loneliness of his mission redeemed by the cheerfulness and simple-hearted warmth of his old friend and by the simple piety he often encounters among the humblest of his people; from them, as in the case of old Sada, he learns lessons of humility and grace. For years he dreams of building a cathedral in Santa Fé, and in time his ambition is realized. By then, he is an archbishop and an old man. In the end, he decides not to return to his native Auvergne, the wet, green country of his youth that he had often remembered with yearning during his years in the hot desert country. He retires to a small farm outside Santa Fé; when he dies, his body rests in state before the altar in the cathedral he had built. Father Latour's story is based on the life of a historical figure, Jean Baptiste Lamy, the first archbishop of Santa Fé.

Father Joseph Vaillant (vay-YAHN), Father Latour's friend and vicar. The son of hardy peasant stock, he is tireless in his missionary labors. If Father Latour is an intellectual aristocrat, Father Vaillant is his opposite: a hearty man of feeling, able to mix with all kinds of people and to move them as much by his good humor and physical vitality as by his eloquence. Doctrine, he holds, is good enough in its place, but he prefers to put his trust in miracles and the working of faith. When the gold rush begins in Colorado, he is sent to Camp Denver to work among the miners. There he continues his missionary labors, traveling from camp to camp in a covered carriage that is both his sleeping quarters and an improvised chapel. Borrowing and begging wherever he can, he builds for the Church and for the future. When he dies, he is the first bishop of Denver, and there is not a building in the city large enough to hold the thousands who come to his funeral. Like Father Latour, Father Vaillant is modeled after a real person, Father Joseph P. Machebeuf.

Padre Antonio José Martínez (ahn-TOH-nee-oh hoh-SEH mahr-TEE-nehs, the vigorous but arrogant priest at Taos credited with having instigated the revolt of the Taos Indians. A man of violence and sensual passions, he has lived like a dictator too long to accept the authority of Father Latour with meekness or reason. When Father Latour visits him in Taos, he challenges his bishop on the subject of celibacy. After the bishop announces his intention to reform lax practices throughout his diocese, Padre Martínez tells him blandly that he will found his own church if Father Latour interferes with him. As good as his promise, he and Padre Lucero defy Father Latour and Rome and try to establish a schism called the Old Holy Catholic Church of Mexico. Until his death a short time later, Padre Martínez carries on his personal and ecclesiastical feud with Father Taladrid, who is appointed by Father Latour to succeed the old tyrant of Taos.

Padre Marino Lucero (mah-REE-noh lew-SEH-roh), the priest of Arroyo Hondo, who joins Padre Martínez in defying Father Latour's authority. Padre Lucero is said to have a fortune hidden away. After he repents of his heresy and dies reconciled to Rome, buckskin bags containing gold and silver coins valued at almost twenty thousand dollars are found buried under the floor of his house.

Padre Gallegos (gah-YEH-gohs), the genial, worldly priest at Albuquerque, a lover of whiskey, fandangos, and poker. Although Father Latour likes him as a man, he finds him scandalous and impossible as a priest. As soon as possible, he suspends Padre Gallegos and puts Father Vaillant in charge of the Albuquerque parish.

Manuel Lujon (mahn-WEHL lew-HOHN), a wealthy Mexican. During a visit to Lujon's rancho, Father Vaillant sees and admires a matched pair of white mules, Contento and Angelica. The priest praises the animals so highly that Lujon, a generous, pious man, decides to give him one of them. Father Vaillant, though, refuses to accept the gift, saying that it would not be fitting for him to ride on a fine white mule while his bishop rides a common one. Resigned, Lujon sends the second mule to Father Latour.

Buck Scales, a gaunt, surly American at whose house Father Latour and his vicar stop on one of their missionary journeys. Warned away by the gestures of his frightened wife, they continue on to the next town. The woman follows them to tell that in the past six years her husband has murdered four travelers as well as the three children she has borne. Scales is arrested and hanged.

Magdalena (mahg-dah-LEH-nah), the Mexican wife of Buck Scales, a devout woman who reveals her husband's crimes. After her husband's hanging, she lives for a time in the home of Kit Carson. Later, Father Latour makes her the housekeeper in the establishment of the Sisters of Loretto in Santa Fé. She attends the old archbishop in his last days.

Kit Carson, the American trapper and scout. He and Father Latour become friends when they meet after the arrest of Buck Scales.

Jacinto (hah-SEEN-toh), an intelligent young Indian from the Pecos pueblo, often employed as Father Latour's guide on the priest's missionary journeys. On one of these trips, the travelers are overtaken by a sudden snowstorm. Jacinto leads Father Latour into a cave that has obviously been used for ceremonial purposes. Before he builds a fire, Jacinto walls up an opening in the cave. Waking later in the night, Father Latour sees his guide standing guard over the sealed opening. He realizes that he has been close to some secret ceremonial mystery of the Pecos, possibly connected with snake worship, but he respects Jacinto's confidence and never mentions the matter.

Don Antonio Olivares (oh-lee-VAH-rehs), a wealthy ranchero who has promised to make a large contribution to Father Latour's cathedral fund. He dies suddenly before he can make good his promise, leaving his estate to his wife and daughter for life, after which his property is to go to the Church. Two of his brothers contest the will.

Doña Isabella Olivares (ee-sah-BEH-yah), the American wife of Father Latour's friend and benefactor. After her husband's death, two of his brothers contest the will on the grounds that Doña Isabella is not old enough to have a daughter of the age of Señorita Inez and that the girl is the child of one of Don Antonio's indiscreet youthful romances, adopted by Doña Isabella for the purpose of defrauding the brothers. Father Vaillant convinces the vain woman that it is her duty to tell the truth about her age in order for her and her daughter to win the case. Much against her will, Doña Isabella confesses in court that she is fifty-two years old and not forty-two, as she has claimed. Later, she tells Father Vaillant and Father Latour that she will never forgive them for having made her tell a lie about a matter as serious as a woman's age.

Señorita Inez (ee-NEHS), the daughter of Doña Isabella and Don Antonio Olivares. Her age and her mother's are questioned when the Olivares brothers try to contest Don Antonio's will.

Boyd O'Reilly, a young American lawyer, the manager of Don Antonio Olivares' affairs.

Sada, the wretched slave of a Protestant American family. One December night, she escapes from the stable where she sleeps and takes refuge in the church. Father Latour finds her there, hears her confession, blesses her, and gives her a holy relic and his own warm cloak.

Eusabio (eh-ew-SAH-bee-oh), a man of influence among the Navajos. Though he is younger than Father Latour, the priest respects him greatly for his intelligence and sense of honor. Father Latour grieves when the Navajos are forced to leave their country and rejoices that he has been able to live long enough to see them restored to their lands. When the old archbishop dies, Eusabio carries word of his death to the Indians.

Bernard Ducrot (dew-KROH), the young priest who looks after Father Latour in his last years. He becomes like a son to the gentle old man.

Padre Jesus de Baca (heh-SEWS deh BAH-kah), the white-haired, almost blind priest at Isleta. An old man of great innocence and piety, he lives surrounded by his tame parrots.

Trinidad Lucero (tree-nee-DAHD lew-SEH-roh), a slovenly young monk in training for the priesthood whom Father Latour meets in the house of Padre Martinez. He passes as Padre Lucero's nephew, but some say he is the son of Padre Martinez. When Padre Martinez and Padre Lucero proclaim

their schism, Trinidad acts as a curate for both.

Padre Taladrid (tah-lah-DREED), the young Spanish priest whom Father Latour appoints to succeed Padre Martinez at Taos.

A DEATH IN THE FAMILY

Author: James Agee (1909-1955)
First published: 1957
Genre: Novel

Locale: Knoxville, Tennessee
Time: Summer 1915, and May 15-20, 1916
Plot: Domestic realism

Rufus Follet, a six-year-old who loves his father and mother but is otherwise fearful about the world of grown-ups. That world is a confusing place where older children ridicule his name (his mother tells him it is a fine old name), adults often use words he does not understand, and his beloved father dies suddenly in a car accident. Rufus compensates for his fears by bullying his little sister. It is a mark of his intelligence that he sometimes understands his motives and usually feels remorseful for tyrannizing her.

Jay Follet, the young husband and father who is killed as he returns home from the bedside of his own mortally ill father. Jay loves his wife, for whom he does many kindnesses, and his children, but he resents his drunken brother Ralph's weak reliance on him for emotional support. Jay had been a heavy drinker in the past but for the sake of his wife left that behind. A family friend tells Rufus that his father grew up in poverty and against hard odds but turned out to be a man of great kindness and generosity. The priest who conducts the funeral nevertheless notes that Jay was never baptized and thus is not entitled to the full burial rites of the church.

Mary Follet, Jay's young wife, loving, pious, and naïve. She must begin to face the demands that her new status as widow will place on her. During the few days between her husband's death and the funeral, Mary leans heavily on her family and her faith as a devout Roman Catholic, but she also exhibits her own strength of character at crucial times. She asks her Aunt Hannah Lynch to spend the first night of her widowhood with her instead of asking her mother, whose deafness makes conversation nearly impossible. She refuses to let Ralph Follet, an undertaker, supervise the funeral, knowing that Ralph's drinking would surely cause problems. Although she has a tendency toward prissiness and sometimes offers simplistic solutions to Rufus' problems, she also can call on a psychological toughness that—with the help of her

loving family—will see her through the difficult future.

Hannah Lynch, Mary Follet's aunt, her mother's unmarried sister. She is direct, intelligent, and devoted to her niece and the Follet family. Before Jay's death, she takes Rufus shopping for a cap, knowing that his mother considers him too young for this item of grown-up headgear, even though Rufus desperately longs for it. Even before the news of Jay's death is confirmed, she guesses the seriousness of the accident and exhibits her customary sensitivity and restraint as she waits with Mary for the worst to be confirmed, knowing instinctively that Mary must come to understand the loss in her own way.

Ralph Follet, Jay's alcoholic brother, weak and self-pitying. Ralph's rivalry with his brother for their mother's affections extends back into childhood. In a few moments of honesty, however, he recognizes the pain that his drinking and womanizing cause his mother and his wife, Sally. He acknowledges that they truly love him despite his weaknesses.

Andrew Lynch, Mary Follet's brother, a skeptic who loves his sister even though he doubts the value of her faith. After the funeral, he invites Rufus for a walk, during which he confesses to the boy his rage at what he considers to be the priest's smug dismissal of Jay Follet's worth.

Walter Starr, a simple but sensitive family friend of the Lynches. He goes with Andrew to bring Jay's body home. The children spend the time of the funeral with him. During that time, he gently chastises Rufus for bullying his little sister and makes sure that the children have a chance to watch the funeral procession. He tells Rufus that his father was like Abraham Lincoln.

Catherine Follet, Rufus' little sister, four years old. She is almost overwhelmed by the mystery and upheaval brought about by events she cannot understand.

— *Ann Davison Garbett*

DEATH IN VENICE
(Der Tod in Venedig)

Author: Thomas Mann (1875-1955)
First published: 1912
Genre: Novel

Locale: Italy
Time: Early twentieth century
Plot: Symbolic realism

Gustave von Aschenbach (GEW-stahf fon AH-shehn-bahch), a middle-aged German writer. Small, dark, his bushy gray hair, which is thinning on top, is brushed back on his overlarge head. His mouth is large, his cheeks lean and fur-

rowed, and his prominent chin slightly cleft. He wears rimless gold glasses on his thick, aristocratically hooked nose, and his eyes are weary and sunken. A widower, he has one child, a married daughter. Precocious, Aschenbach early longed for fame, which he has achieved through several works acclaimed by the general public and the critics. He is not a born artist but has made himself one through rigorous discipline and unwavering dedication. A solitary man, he has only a superficial, limited knowledge of the real world. In cultivating his intellect, he has denied his feelings. His passion for Tadzio is symbolic of his narcissism, which first degrades and then destroys him. Aschenbach is a symbol of the artist in modern society.

Tadzio (TAHD-tsee-oh), a Polish boy of fourteen who possesses a classic beauty of face and form. To Aschenbach, his beautiful head seems that of Eros and the boy himself the essence of beauty. When Aschenbach almost touches Tadzio and then draws back in panic, the action symbolizes the artist's fear of giving way to an emotion. Sometimes the artist sees in Tadzio the youth Hyacinth, who died as the victim of the rivalry of two gods. When, after many days, Tadzio finally smiles at Aschenbach, the smile is that of Narcissus looking in the pool, and the artist whispers his love. Tadzio's is the last face the artist sees before he dies.

A Stranger, thin, beardless, snub-nosed, red-haired, freckled, and exotic-looking, he seems to Aschenbach to be bold, domineering, even ruthless.

Another Stranger, an old man masquerading as a youth on an old, dingy Italian ship. He is flashily dressed; his face and eyes are wrinkled, his cheeks rouged, his brown hair and yellow teeth false, and his turned-up mustaches and imperial are dyed. He becomes disgustingly drunk before the ship reaches Venice. When Aschenbach's desperate passion for Tadzio consumes him, he, like the painted stranger, tries foolishly to hide his age.

A Strolling Player, a pale, thin-faced, snub-nosed, red-haired man of slight build whose singing is entertaining but obscene and who carries with him an odor of carbolic acid.

A Gondolier, undersized and brutish-looking. An expert boatman, he is gruff and rude, and he disappears before Aschenbach returns with change to pay him. The gondolier represents Charon, and the artist's ride in the gondola portends his death in Venice.

THE DEATH OF A BEEKEEPER
(En biodlares död)

Author: Lars Gustafsson (1936-   )
First published: 1978
Genre: Novel

Locale: The countryside in the Swedish province of Västmanland
Time: The 1970's
Plot: Domestic realism

Lars Lennart Westin, a retired elementary school teacher living in virtual isolation in the Swedish province of Västmanland. A lean, spent man, he is thirty-nine years old but looks much older. Intensely self-absorbed, he keeps a series of notebooks that record the mundane facts of his life, his imaginative explorations of past and present, and the course of his fatal disease, cancer of the spleen. As the novel begins, he has received a letter from a local hospital, probably containing test results and the diagnosis of his ailment. He burns the letter, unopened. As his story unfolds, he reveals his obsession with pain, the deception and lack of communication that have marked most of his relationships, his desire to understand himself, his resolution never to give up in his various struggles, and his terrible conclusion that his life was real only during his last few months of terminal suffering.

Margaret, Westin's wife for ten years until their divorce, around 1970. The pale and thin daughter of an intensely bourgeois family dominated by a tyrannical father, Margaret initially shared with Westin an aversion to a hypocritical and uncaring society and a desire for independence. As he reviews their uneventful, unsuccessful marriage, Westin discovers that deception, guilt, and Margaret's need to control him were the foundations of their relationship. He refuses to notify her of his disease.

Ann, a large blond doctor in her late thirties or early forties. She radiates motherliness, a quality that Westin craves and that forms the basis of their love affair in the last year of his marriage. When Margaret learns of the affair, the two women become allies and give Westin a strange, yet real, sense of peace.

Uffe and

Jonny, two young boys who meet Westin during the course of his illness. He treats them with affectionate warmth and writes for them the first episode of a science-fiction adventure story, in which the hero must locate and destroy a source of great pain created by the evil Emperor Ming.

Sune Jannson, Westin's uncle, a clever storekeeper and operator in the black market during World War II. Westin admires him as a cunning and persistent individualist and recounts a wartime incident in which Uncle Sune outwitted a contingent of local bureaucrats.

God, who is imagined by Westin—during a temporary cessation of his pain—as a mother who awakes after twenty million years and begins to answer the prayers of human beings. At first, the answers seem wonderful, but because the motherly God grants all wishes indiscriminately, the process soon leads to the dissolution of all human relationships and institutions, and of language itself.

Nicke, a boyhood friend of Westin who died in 1952, after a short life of reckless yet successful adventures. Nicke is the last significant character to appear in the novel, in a flashback that reminds Westin to begin again and never to give up. In Westin's flashback, the fearless young Nicke dives deep into the whirlpool of a dangerous canal lock to retrieve a golden fishing lure. He emerges from the water with a different treasure from the bottom: a unique gold coin.

— *Terry Lass*

DEATH OF A HERO

Author: Richard Aldington (1892-1962)
First published: 1929
Genre: Novel

Locale: England
Time: During World War I
Plot: Political

George Winterbourne, a young Englishman for whom the world goes awry. After an unhappy childhood he turns to dabbling in writing, painting, and sex. Becoming an officer in World War I, he finds himself regarded as a failure by his superiors. Discouraged by opinion, as well as by the lives and characters of his father, mother, wife, and mistress, he stands erect during shelling by German guns and is killed.

Elizabeth Winterbourne, young George's promiscuous wife. She is a would-be intellectual who as a young woman is infatuated by the idea of free love. When she thinks she is pregnant, she forces a marriage with George. Although she remains promiscuous afterward, she is angered by her best friend's becoming her husband's mistress.

Fanny Welford, Elizabeth's best friend and George's mistress. A blasé creature, she spends George's last night in En-

gland with him, but she is not interested enough to arise from bed, or even awaken fully, when he leaves her the following morning.

Mr. George Winterbourne, young George's father. He marries to escape a domineering mother, only to find that he hates his promiscuous wife. Being a sentimental man, he prays for his wife's soul and awaits her pleasure when sent to a hotel while she entertains one or another of a string of lovers.

Mrs. George Winterbourne, young George's mother. She is an elderly wanton who is proud of having had in her life a series of twenty-two lovers. She lavishes a kind of love upon her son and, when he dies, plays a role as the mother bereft of a hero son.

DEATH OF A SALESMAN

Author: Arthur Miller (1915-   )
First published: 1949
Genre: Drama

Locale: New York and Boston
Time: The 1940's
Plot: Tragedy

Willy Loman, a sixty-three-year-old traveling salesman who has begun to dwell on the past and not to know where he is. In the last two days of his life, his past rolls before him. He is a father who loves his sons and wants them to have worldly success, although he does not know how to help them achieve it. His last gesture for his son Biff is to commit suicide so that the son can have the insurance money.

Biff Loman, Willy's thirty-four-year-old son, who is still trying to find himself. A high-school athlete, he gets nowhere after graduation. When he is refused a loan to start a business, he steals a cheap fountain pen. Angry and defeated, he curses his father as a fool and a dreamer, though he loves the man.

Happy Loman, Willy's younger son, modestly successful in life as a clerk in a store. He is a woman chaser and a seeker after pleasure.

Charley, Willy Loman's friend and neighbor. He lends Willy money and offers him a job.

Bernard, Charley's son, a successful lawyer whose own success is an accusation to Willy's sons.

Linda Loman, Willy's wife, a fearful but patient woman who loves her husband despite his failures.

Howard Wagner, the son of Willy's boss. He lets Willy know that he is finished as a salesman.

Uncle Ben, Willy's brother. He goes out into the jungle and in a few years returns from the diamond mines a rich man. His success is an accusation to Willy.

The woman, an unnamed character whom Biff, as a teenager, finds in a hotel room with his father.

THE DEATH OF ARTEMIO CRUZ
(La muerte de Artemio Cruz)

Author: Carlos Fuentes (1928-   )
First published: 1962
Genre: Novel

Locale: Mexico
Time: 1889-1959
Plot: Social realism

Artemio Cruz (ahr-TEH-mee-oh crews), a wealthy, corrupt landowner in postrevolutionary Mexico. He remembers significant episodes of his seventy years of life while on his deathbed. In his memories, related out of chronological order, he searches for his own identity, which is, like the Mexican national identity, based on the rape of the mother. Cruz joins the Mexican Revolution determined to fight against the landowners and for the rights of the peasants who work on the land. He associates himself with the winning faction of Gen-

eral Álvaro Obregón and, during the first years of the revolution, meets Regina. After she is brutally killed, he becomes a selfish opportunist who never opens his heart to anyone. Two years later, he is captured. While awaiting execution, he discusses the meaning of life and revolution with Gonzalo Bernal. Cruz saves himself by offering to turn traitor. Later, he introduces himself to Gonzalo's wealthy family and marries Gonzalo's sister Catalina. That marriage gives him a ticket to the upper class. He comes to epitomize the class that he fought in the revolution. He abandons all morals and has a series of mistresses. He dies as an extremely prosperous man, surrounded by the people who despise him, lovers and business partners who want to use him, without any real friends and without any ideals.

Gonzalo Bernal (gohn-SAH-loh behr-NAHL), a young idealist who joins the revolution in order to fight against the establishment represented by his rich father. He dies disillusioned, in solidarity with other prisoners, realizing that the revolution will not bring desired changes. He exemplifies honesty and spiritual strength.

Lorenzo Cruz, the son of Artemio Cruz. He is faced with situations similar to those of his father, but he always chooses an honorable solution. In that sense, he can be seen as a redeemer of his father's spiritually and morally wasted life. Lorenzo dies in the Spanish Civil War.

Regina (reh-HEE-nah), Cruz's first love. She is hanged by Cruz's opponents at the beginning of the revolution. With her dies a romantic, open, and honest side of Artemio Cruz.

Catalina (kah-tah-LEE-nah), Cruz's wife and Gonzalo's sister. She and Cruz never open up to each other because she sees herself as property given to him by her father. Neither will she forgive the betrayal of her brother. Although Cruz claims that his love for her is genuine and honest, he has several mistresses during their marriage and stays with her only because of social status and the political implications of a breakup.

THE DEATH OF BERNADETTE LEFTHAND

Author: Ron Querry (1943-   )
First published: 1993
Genre: Novel

Locale: New Mexico and Arizona
Time: The 1990's
Plot: Suspense

Bernadette Lefthand, a beautiful and talented young woman. She is a resident of Dulce, New Mexico, the center of the Jicarilla Apache reservation. The daughter of a Jicarilla father and a Tiwa mother from Taos Pueblo, as a teenager Bernadette was a champion fancy-dancer at Indian powwows. She went to the Indian School in Santa Fe, where she fell in love with a Navajo rodeo rider named Anderson George. In her late teens, she married Anderson and bore a son named Anthony. She works for an Anglo woman named Starr Stubbs as a means of supporting her husband. Bernadette's brutal murder is reported in the first pages of the novel; the story of what led to her death takes up the rest of the novel. She was killed after a ceremonial dance at which she was honored for her achievements as a dancer; the dance was disrupted by her drunken husband and his friends.

Gracie Lefthand, Bernadette's less attractive sister, the narrator of much of the novel. She is content to live in her sister's shadow, taking care of the baby when necessary and going along with Bernadette, Anderson, and Anderson's brother Tom to rodeos and festivals on the Navajo and Hopi reservations when they are all young.

Anderson George, a Navajo rodeo rider whose skills diminish as he gets older and becomes more devoted to liquor. He works for a while looking after Starr Stubbs's horses, but he is unreliable. When Bernadette is brutally murdered, all the evidence points to Anderson, and he is arrested. Convinced that he must have killed her in a drunken rage, he hangs himself in a jail cell.

Tom George, Anderson's quiet and sober younger brother. He helps Anderson in his rodeo contests and looks after Gracie when the four young people go on trips, but he is not Gracie's lover. He tries but fails to convince Anderson to moderate his drinking.

Starr Stubbs, a white woman who befriends Bernadette Lefthand and gives her employment as a kind of housekeeper. Starr lives on a large ranch near Dulce that her country singer husband bought as a retreat from the demands of his career. Starr also hires Anderson, trying to help Bernadette save her marriage by restoring some of Anderson's pride. Starr has read many books on American Indians and is genuinely sympathetic to Bernadette, but she represents well-meaning white people who cannot truly understand Indians. She shows her ignorance by laughing at Bernadette's belief in shamanistic healing and by trying to arrange for Anderson to be cured by a white doctor.

Emmett Take Horse, an embittered Navajo who knew Bernadette and Anderson at the Indian School. At one time a successful jockey in the informal horse races staged at Navajo festivals, Emmett suffered seriously crippling injuries in a racing accident. He develops a strong hatred for Bernadette, whom he has loved, and for Anderson. He takes lessons from a Navajo witch, despite his fear of the evil he is learning, and pretends friendship for Anderson while encouraging him in his increasingly destructive drinking. He hacks Bernadette to death and arranges matters so that Anderson appears to be the guilty party.

— *John M. Muste*

THE DEATH OF EMPEDOCLES
(Der Tod de Empedocles)

Author: Friedrich Hölderlin (1770-1843)
First published: 1826
Genre: Drama

Locale: Agrigentum and Mount Etna
Time: The fifth century B.C.E.
Plot: Tragedy

Empedocles (ehm-PEHD-eh-kleez), the legendary philosopher and savant, portrayed as a healer and magician intent on

committing suicide for different reasons, depending on which of the three versions of the text is under discussion. Two versions focus on his tragic flaw of hubris. In the first, Empedocles has the powers of the magician to heal and to move the elements, but his desire to be reunited with the gods causes him to disregard his people's pleas that he return to them from exile, and ultimately to commit suicide. In the second version, before the action of the play begins, Empedocles wishes to share his understanding of the universe with his people. He realizes that his solitude is a result of his own exceptional powers as well as of his hubris in believing himself to be much closer to them than he ought. His first speech shows him imploring the gods and the forces of nature to consider him in his solitariness. In contrast to these versions, in which Empedocles' death is a personal matter, in the fragmentary third version and the author's notes to it, his death becomes universal. He is embittered, but he realizes that his death is necessary for the revival of the civilization of which he has been a part. Initially a tragic hero who falls through hubris, he is transformed into a Romantic hero with superhuman powers who is willing to merge with the elements for the good of humanity.

Hermocrates (hur-MAHK-ruh-teez), a priest of Agrigentum who advocates and participates in the downfall of Empedocles. He opposes Empedocles because of the radical nature of Empedocles' religious vision as well as his own fears of Empedocles' abilities to influence the people in the realm of religion and belief. In the second version, he changes from the flat character of the evil adversary to a relatively sympathetic character who has some capacity for understanding and empathy. He believes that Empedocles has inappropriately disclosed to the people divine secrets not meant for the masses. It is for this reason that he takes part in Empedocles' fall. Hermocrates curses Empedocles and anyone who would befriend him, and he is instrumental in Empedocles' exile.

Kritias, the representative of secular authority. He is the archon, the ruler of Agrigentum. His fear is that through their adulation of Empedocles and their reliance on his powers, people have come to ignore their own laws and customs.

Mecades, who is in the second version a revision of Kritias, although younger and less worldly. As in the first version, in discussing the stature of Empedocles among the citizenry of Agrigentum, Mecades, as representative of secular authority, and Hermocrates, as representative of religious authority, agree that Empedocles has overreached.

Strato (STRAY-toh), a significant addition to the third version of the drama, the king of Agrigentum and brother of Empedocles. He is representative of an amalgamation of religious and secular authority set in opposition to Empedocles and his influence over the masses. His introduction increases dramatic tension through the tension between brothers.

Pausanias (paw-SAY-nee-uhs), a student of Empedocles who follows him into exile as a great supporter and admirer. When Empedocles shares with him his understanding of his own downfall, Pausanias bids him to take courage and exclaims that he refuses to allow it. He is overwhelmed by Empedocles' pessimism as well as his will. In the third version, he follows Empedocles into exile and is twice called by him the "too loyal" one. In the third version, Pausanias glorifies Empedocles in his decision to commit suicide.

Panthea, who expresses the dichotomy between the gods and nature, proclaiming that it was nature rather than the gods who gave Empedocles his lofty soul. She supports Empedocles in his decision to take his own life. With his death, Panthea moans, the hearts of humanity draw away from nature and from "the holy all." She closes with the comment, "For we who are blind/ Needed a miracle once."

Delia, who in the third version provides the impetus for questioning the moral implications of Empedocles' suicide. In the second version, she comments on the death of Empedocles in lines that bemoan the transitory nature of existence. In anguish, she implores, "O Nature, why do you/ Make it so easy/ For your hero to die?"

Manes (MAY-neez), who appears in the third version only. He is the former teacher of Empedocles who forces Empedocles to come to terms with the moral importance and implications of his suicidal plans. He informs Empedocles that only a rare kind of individual, in only cosmically significant circumstances, can legitimately take his own life.

— *Donna Berliner*

THE DEATH OF IVAN ILYICH
(Smert Ivana Ilicha)

Author: Leo Tolstoy (1828-1910)
First published: 1886
Genre: Novel

Locale: St. Petersburg, Russia, and nearby provinces
Time: The 1880's
Plot: Psychological realism

Ivan Ilyich Golovin (ih-VAHN ihl-YIHCH goh-LOH-vihn), a prominent judge. A genial and conscientious lawyer, the popular Ivan Ilyich hides from reality under a cloak of decorum. Obtaining an excellent appointment in St. Petersburg, he finds there a house and an ordered routine exactly to his taste. He feels that life is, at last, just as it should be. Then he learns that he is the victim of a fatal disease. Facing death, he is forced to look, for the first time, at the truth about his life. Only as he becomes aware of the real meaning of his past decisions does he free himself from the fear of death.

Praskovya Fedorovna Golovina (prahs-KOH-vyah FYOH-do-rov-nah goh-LOH-vih-nah), Ivan Ilyich Golovin's wife. Dissatisfied with the role her husband has chosen for her, she becomes demanding and quarrelsome and, finally, isolated from him. Only in death does her husband become aware of her as a person deserving pity and forgiveness.

Gerasim (geh-RAH-sihm), Ivan Ilyich Golovin's peasant servant boy. In his candid admission of the reality and naturalness of death, and with his honesty and clean young strength, Gerasim comforts and cares for his master through his last illness.

Peter Ivanovitch (ih-VAH-no-vihch), Ivan Ilyich Golovin's colleague. Under a show of observing the proper protocol, Peter hides his true feelings about the dying and dead Ivan Ilyich.

DEATH OF THE FOX

Author: George Garrett (1929-   )
First published: 1971
Genre: Novel

Locale: The British Isles, continental Europe, and various oceans
Time: The reign of Henry VIII to the reign of Charles I
Plot: Historical

Sir Walter Ralegh, captain of the guard under Queen Elizabeth and a leading Elizabethan courtier. Ralegh has been a soldier, seafarer, explorer, and counselor to the queen as well as an amateur scientist and engineer, antiquarian, historian, and poet. Known to enemies and friends as the Fox for his shrewd pursuit of public and personal ambitions, Ralegh is now an old man under suspended sentence of death for leading a pro-Spanish plot against King James I fifteen years earlier, in 1603. He is innocent of that charge. Although Ralegh had been proud, headstrong, and lusty as a young man, his years in prison have deepened his meditative and philosophical nature; he reflects on his life as he awaits sentencing and then execution on Lord Mayor's Day, October 29, 1618. Reared to eminence and great wealth under Elizabeth, Ralegh was banished from court in 1592 after his affair with Elizabeth Throckmorton, later his beloved wife Bess. He discovered Guiana for England in 1595, however, and was the old queen's most loyal courtier in her declining years. He was brought to trial by King James shortly after the latter's succession in 1603, and his self-defense at Winchester confounded the king's own lawyers. Imprisoned thereafter in the Tower of London, he was released in 1617. His subsequent disastrous expedition to Guiana, which resulted in an unsuccessful attack on a Spanish stronghold and the death of his son, led to his reimprisonment by the king. He is unjustly sentenced to execution at Westminster by Henry Yelverton, James's attorney general. He is visited by his wife Bess and a scholar friend, Thomas Hariot, on the last night of his life, and is examined spiritually in the morning and justified by Robert Tounson, dean of Westminster. Ralegh defends himself publicly before the crowd gathered for his public beheading, affirming his loyalty to King James as well as to the deceased Elizabeth, going to his death freely, nobly, and courageously.

James Stuart, the king of England and of Scotland. Physically unattractive but possessed of a powerful if pedantic intellect, the king is a complex blend of virtues and vices: humorous and festive yet somewhat degraded in his personal behavior; tenacious and shrewd in pursuing his policies yet self-righteous and arbitrary; and fatherly toward his subjects, friends, and family, yet vengeful and petulant toward those who oppose him. Uncomfortable among the masses in London and almost pathologically fearful of assassination, the king has begun to find the burdens of the crown wearying and frustrating and prefers the companionship of his favorite, George Villiers ("Steenie"), and the pleasures of hunting and extravagant court entertainments. When his chief policy goals (keeping England at peace and arranging a dynastic marriage with England's old enemy, Spain) are frustrated by Ralegh's Guiana expedition, he has the old Elizabethan courtier executed, against the advice of his dying queen. He leaves the affair to his Lord Chancellor, Francis Bacon, and the London civic authorities while he takes a holiday at his estate at Theobalds and the royal lodge at Royston. By disposing of the troublesome Ralegh, James hopes to regain his influence with Spain's ambassador, Count Gondomar, but he also destroys the last living embodiment of the Elizabethan regime.

Elizabeth Tudor, the queen of England, James's predecessor as monarch. She was the greatest of the Tudor monarchs and Ralegh's much-beloved and admired sovereign. Moderately attractive, gifted intellectually and artistically, and supremely skillful in choosing and using ambitious and talented subordinates to carry out her policies, she sacrificed personal happiness for the welfare of the nation that she loved beyond any individual. The success of her reign, which began in crisis and instability, rested on her ability to acquire and maintain the trust and admiration of all of her people; this success was furthered by the use of open public spectacles financed by her wealthier subjects. She made herself the embodiment of her nation both before and after the climactic defeat of the Spanish Armada in 1588, and as Ralegh relives that earlier age in his imagination, it seems a splendid dream. Although her final years were marked by economic and social difficulties in England and a hardening of her personality and her policies, they were eased by Ralegh's loyal and assiduous service during the rebellion by the earl of Essex in 1601, the final crisis of the regime.

— Mark Allen Heberle

THE DEATH OF THE GODS
(Smert bogov: Yulian Otstupnik)

Author: Dmitry Merezhkovsky (1865-1941)
First published: 1896
Genre: Novel

Locale: Rome
Time: Fourth century
Plot: Historical

Caesar Constantius (SEE-zur kon-STAN-shee-uhs), emperor of Rome, who rose to power through assassination.

Julian Flavius (JEW-lee-uhn FLAY-vee-uhs), cousin of Constantius, a young man learned in the pagan philosophies. At twenty, he travels to Asia Minor as a Christian monk, and he is secretly won over to paganism. Later, he fights a successful campaign as a general in Gaul and is hailed as emperor. He becomes embittered when his wife leaves him to become a nun, and he denounces Christianity and reinstates paganism in the Roman Empire. He is ridiculed for his scholarly studies and undertakes a campaign against Persia, believing a victory will win respect for him and for paganism. He is mortally wounded in battle and dies saying that Christ has defeated him.

Gallus Flavius (GA-luhs), Julian's younger brother, an effeminate young man. He is made co-regent with Constantius for a brief time before he is assassinated.

Arsinoë (ahr-SIH-noh-ee), a young woman who delights in paganism. She tells Julian that he must believe in himself rather than in any gods. Later, she disappoints Julian by be-

coming a Christian. Although he wants to make her his empress, she refuses Julian's offer of love and marriage. Just before Julian dies, Arsinoë visits him and tries unsuccessfully to win him back to Christianity.

Publius Porphyrius (PEW-blee-uhs pohr-FIH-ree-uhs), who takes Julian to a wrestling arena to watch the ancient Greek games. There he sees Arsinoë, a young pagan, for the first time.

THE DEATH OF THE HEART

Author: Elizabeth Bowen (1899-1973)
First published: 1938
Genre: Novel

Locale: London and Seale, England
Time: After World War I
Plot: Psychological realism

Portia Quayne, a confused and demanding sixteen-year-old girl who lives with her stepbrother. Through her affection for Eddie, she loses some of her childish idealism and sense of the simplicity of human affairs.

Thomas Quayne, Portia's stepbrother, a partner in a London advertising firm. He takes his stepsister into his home, though he scarcely knows her. Because he and his wife have no children of their own, Portia is disturbing to them.

Anna Quayne, Thomas' wife. Her friendship for Eddie arouses a confused jealousy in Portia. Anna becomes upset when she learns, by reading the girl's diary, that Portia is unhappy in her home.

Eddie, a callow, self-assured twenty-three-year-old employee at Thomas Quayne's office. He is both demanding and disdainful of Portia's affection for him. He upsets her by

showing fondness for Daphne Heccomb.

Mrs. Heccomb. Anna's old governess, who takes care of Portia when the Quaynes go to Capri for an extended holiday.

Daphne Heccomb, Mrs. Heccomb's stepdaughter, who is friendly to Portia.

Major Brutt, a retired officer. Portia runs away from home to him, offering to marry him and polish his boots. The major tactfully sends her back to her stepbrother.

St. Quentin Miller, an author and close friend of the Quaynes. He is Anna's confidant, to whom she pours out her problems with respect to young Portia.

Matchett, the Quaynes' housekeeper. A possessive person, she resents Portia's affection for Eddie.

Miss Paullie, one of Portia's teachers.

Lilian, an inquisitive school friend of Portia.

THE DEATH OF VIRGIL
(Der Tod des Vergil)

Author: Hermann Broch (1886-1951)
First published: 1945
Genre: Novel

Locale: Brundisium (Brindisi, Italy)
Time: 19 B.C.E.
Plot: Philosophical

Virgil (**Publius Vergilius Maro**) (VUR-gihl; PEWB-lee-us vur-JIH-lee-uhs may-roh), the dying Roman poet who, returning to Rome with Augustus Caesar, takes a long look into his own soul and sees his life as hypocrisy. In his devotion to poetry, he has denied love and has thus served death rather than life. He insists that his *Aeneid*, because it lacks this perception, should be destroyed, but he finally agrees to preserve the poem at Augustus' bidding. Knowing, at the last, the salvation that is self-knowledge, the poet dies.

Plotia Hieria (PLOH-shee-uh hih-OO-ree-uh), a woman whose love Virgil had renounced long ago. She appears to the

dying poet in the visionary world of his hallucinations and beckons him on to the renunciation of poetry for love.

Augustus Caesar (oh-GUHS-tuhs SEE-zur), emperor of Rome, whose glory is revealed to the dying Virgil as a hollow majesty. The emperor persuades the poet not to destroy the *Aeneid*, because the poem's true owner is the Roman people.

Lysanias (lih-SA-nee-uhs), a young boy who attends the dying Virgil, sometimes in reality, sometimes in the poet's hallucinations.

DEATH ON THE INSTALLMENT PLAN
(Mort a crédit)

Author: Louis-Ferdinand Céline (Louis-Ferdinand Destouches, 1894-1961)
First published: 1936
Genre: Novel

Locale: Primarily Paris, France
Time: 1900 to World War I
Plot: Social realism

Ferdinand (fehr-dee-NAHN), a doctor and aspiring writer who narrates the novel. Personally as well as professionally

disillusioned, he cares for his patients although he believes most human beings are not worth saving and are, in fact, better off dead. The reasons for Ferdinand's deep-seated pessimism are evident in his account of his childhood and adolescence. Beaten and abused by his petit bourgeois father, exploited by his employers, and disenchanted with women and love, he finds little to admire in his fellow humans and becomes increasingly cynical and cruel as the novel progresses.

Auguste (oh-GEWST), Ferdinand's father, an insurance clerk and amateur painter. Handsome, vain, pompous, and cruel, he is well educated but emotionally insecure. A failure both personally and professionally, he frequently criticizes his wife and son for their shortcomings while failing to recognize his own. Given to violent outbursts, he constantly abuses his wife and son verbally as well as physically when things do not go his way professionally. He reveals his reactionary politics by blaming his woes on the Freemasons and Jews.

Clémence (klay-MAHNS), Ferdinand's mother, a shopkeeper. Well intentioned but physically and emotionally fragile, she spends most of her time unsuccessfully attempting to keep the peace between her husband and her son. Ambitious for Ferdinand, she helps him find jobs (which he never holds) and convinces Auguste to let him go to study at Meanwell College in England. As the novel progresses, Clémence's health eventually is destroyed through overwork and the beatings administered by Auguste.

Caroline, Ferdinand's maternal grandmother and, like her daughter, a shopkeeper by profession and a tireless worker. One of the novel's few admirable characters, she is devoted to her daughter and grandson, whom she teaches to read. She protects both of them from Auguste, whom she detests. In her efforts to provide for her family's needs, Caroline maintains two workers' cottages. After repairing the plumbing at one of these cottages, she catches pneumonia and dies.

Uncle Édouard (ay-DWAHR), Clémence's brother who owns a hardware store and is an amateur inventor. Intelligent,

successful, and modest as well as kind, Édouard is Ferdinand's benefactor. He intervenes quietly in family crises to protect his nephew, pays for his schooling in England, and gets him his job with Courtial des Pereires. At the end of the novel, when Ferdinand is completely down on his luck, Édouard takes him in, cares for him, and encourages him to start again.

Roger-Martin Courtial des Pereires (roh-ZHAY-mahr-TAN kewr-TYAHL day pehr-AYR), an inventor, editor of *Genitron* (a journal for inventors), hot air balloon pilot, and, later, experimental farmer and schoolmaster. An eccentric genius with a weakness for horse racing and prostitutes, Courtial is at once generous, egotistical, sophisticated, and naïve. He is a shrewd businessman as well as a hopeless financial manager. He employs Ferdinand as his secretary at *Genitron*. After the journal's failure, the two, along with Courtial's wife, go to the country to start a school for lower-class children and an experimental potato farm. When Courtial's methods for growing new and better potatoes fail, he commits suicide.

Nora Merrywin, the wife of the headmaster of Meanwell College. Nora is beautiful, kind, and modest, and she quickly inspires Ferdinand's passion. As Meanwell College gradually loses most of its students to a new school nearby, Nora grows increasingly despondent. In despair, she seduces Ferdinand and then, riddled with guilt and shame, she drowns herself. Although he is nearby and could save her, Ferdinand chooses to watch her die.

Irène (ee-REHN), Courtial's wife and a former midwife by profession. Although she was attractive as a young woman, she has become physically repugnant as a result of bodily changes brought on by a hysterectomy. A devoted supporter of her husband, she nevertheless chastises him regularly for his infidelities and gambling. She accompanies him in all of his misadventures and is devastated by his suicide.

— *Richard J. Golsan*

THE DEATH SHIP
(Das Totenschiff)

Author: B. Traven (Berick Traven Torsvan, 1890?-1969)
First published: 1926
Genre: Novel

Locale: Europe and the Mediterranean Sea
Time: Early 1920's
Plot: Social morality

Gerald Gales, an American seaman without a passport who wanders through Europe in the period following World War I and eventually joins the crew of a "death ship." He arrives in Antwerp, Belgium, as a plain sailor on the *SS Tuscaloosa* out of New Orleans, Louisiana. When his ship makes an early departure while he spends a night ashore, Gales discovers that in the aftermath of the war, European authorities have no interest in assisting an undocumented working-class alien, and he is pushed from Belgium to Holland to France and finally to Spain, spending some time in custody in each country. His appeals to American consuls prove fruitless: Paradoxically, he must have proof of his American citizenship for a consul to assist him in obtaining proof of his American citizenship. In Barcelona, Spain, Gales is enticed into signing on as a "coal-drag" on the *Yorikke*, a battered freighter. Occupying the lowest, most dangerous, and most strenuous position on this miserable ship, Gales finds one compensation in his friendship

with Stanislav Koslovski, his fellow coal-drag. The *Yorikke* sails the Mediterranean Sea and the Atlantic Ocean off Africa, smuggling munitions and other goods. During a call in the African port of Dakar, both Gales and Koslovski are kidnapped by the crew of the *Empress of Madagascar*, a ship whose owners have decided that their profit lies in sinking their vessel for its insurance value. When the *Empress of Madagascar* finally breaks up against a reef, only Gales and Koslovski survive. They live together on the floating wreckage until Koslovski drowns, and Gales alone survives to tell the story.

Stanislav Koslovski, the only important named character other than the narrator, Gales. When Gales discovers himself trapped on the *Yorikke*, his fellow coal-drag, Koslovski, emerges as his ally and supporter. Born in Poznan, a city whose nationality has shifted between Germany and Poland, Koslovski is another stateless itinerant worker who stoically accepts the hard work, low pay, and essential homelessness of his status. As a coal-drag, he is responsible for shoveling coal into the *Yorikke*'s furnaces, repairing the grates, and hauling the ashes. Although this brutal labor is necessary for the steamship to move, Koslovski does not expect or receive recompense for his efforts. He resists violently when he and Gales are abducted onto the *Empress of Madagascar*, but once aboard that ship, he works diligently as a fireman. Marooned with Gales on that ship's wreckage, Koslovski finally loses his sanity and leaps into the sea, believing that he is rejoining the *Yorikke*.

The consul, a type rather than an individual. Both Gales and Koslovski seek the assistance of consuls (American for Gales, German and Polish for Koslovski) in their journeys around Europe. Their uniform experience is that the consuls happily assist the wealthy citizens of their respective nations but present unhelpful, bureaucratic faces to undocumented workers who make appeals to them.

The skipper, another type, embodied in the two captains of the *Yorikke* and the *Empress of Madagascar*. Both are dedicated to money; their own personal profit and the profit of their ships' owners. Unlike seamen such as Gales and Koslovski, who come to love the ships on which they suffer, the comfortable captains have no regard for their men or their vessels. The skipper of the *Yorikke* tolerates inhuman working conditions, and the skipper of the *Empress of Madagascar* is willing to sabotage his own ship.

— *J. K. Van Dover*

DEATHWATCH
(Haute Surveillance)

Author: Jean Genet (1910-1986)
First published: 1949
Genre: Drama

Locale: A prison
Time: Indeterminate
Plot: Absurdist

Green Eyes, a handsome, twenty-two-year-old, condemned murderer. He is the leader of the cell and revered in the prison for his insidious crime of seducing a girl and then strangling her during sex. His chief rival is a black murderer named Snowball, whom he has secretly befriended and actually admires. Whereas the prisoner Lefranc lauds a black criminal, Snowball, as the god of the prison, Maurice, another cellmate, worships Green Eyes. This creates endless contention between Maurice and Lefranc; twice Green Eyes is forced to pull Lefranc from Maurice's throat. Being illiterate, Green Eyes needs Lefranc's help in corresponding with his girlfriend on the outside, even though Green Eyes accuses Lefranc of trying to steal her. Green Eyes is at first obsessed with his girlfriend, as evidenced by her face being tattooed on his chest. Realizing that he probably will be executed in two months, he instructs his companions to kill her when they are released from prison. When the guard comes to inform Green Eyes that his girlfriend has arrived for a visit, he refuses to see her. Instead, he gives the guard permission to make a play for her. The third time Lefranc lunges at Maurice, Green Eyes passively stands by to watch the slaughter. Although he does nothing to stop it, he is repulsed by Lefranc's willful murder of Maurice and calls for the guard.

Georgie Lefranc, an insolent twenty-three-year-old convict who is about to be released. He does not have the status of a hard-core killer; his crime is only burglary. Lefranc is envious of Green Eyes' popularity and position but finds a condemned black murderer more worthy of his praise. He bickers incessantly with Maurice, whom he has tried to pulverize a number of times, each time being stopped by Green Eyes.

Lefranc is Green Eyes' link to his girlfriend: Green Eyes is illiterate and must rely on Lefranc to write all of his letters. Lefranc is coerced by Maurice into an admission of trying to steal Green Eyes' girl. In retaliation, Lefranc taunts Maurice about his homosexual infatuation with Green Eyes. Although Lefranc's jail term is due to expire in three days, he foils his release by strangling Maurice in a fit of rage. He does not acquire the respect for this murder that he assumed he would. Green Eyes is repulsed that Lefranc chose his crime instead of allowing the crime to choose him, as Green Eyes claims was true of his murder.

Maurice, an effeminate seventeen-year-old crook. He worships Green Eyes and despises Lefranc because the latter will not recognize Green Eyes as the head of the prison. His constant needling of Lefranc prompts Lefranc to attack Maurice; twice he is saved by Green Eyes' intervention. Maurice feels the distrust that Green Eyes has of Lefranc, especially in regard to his girlfriend. When Maurice learns of Green Eyes' secret friendship with Snowball, he is heartbroken. He still loves Green Eyes but in a different way. He even speaks of pitying his hero. His relentless taunting of Lefranc brings on a third attack, and this time Green Eyes allows him to be strangled to death.

The guard, a stern but conscientious and fair prison guard. He dislikes Lefranc for his impertinence and threatens to throw him back into the guardhouse. He is friendly with Green Eyes, even delivering a warm message and cigarettes from Snowball. He is grateful when Green Eyes gives him permission to have a chance at his girl.

— *Steven C. Kowall*

DEBIT AND CREDIT
(Soll und Haben)

Author: Gustav Freytag (1816-1895)
First published: 1855
Genre: Novel

Locale: Germany
Time: Early nineteenth century
Plot: Social realism

Anton Wohlfart (AHN-tohn VOHL-fahrt), a young middle-class German. Intelligent and attractive, he wins the esteem of his employer, T. O. Schröter, whom he later antagonizes by becoming the agent of Baron von Rothsattel. After bringing order out of the chaos of the baron's affairs, he marries Sabine Schröter and becomes a partner in T. O. Schröter's firm.

T. O. Schröter (SHREH-tehr), an honorable German businessman and the employer of Anton Wohlfart.

Sabine Schröter (zah-BEE-neh), T. O. Schröter's sister, who marries Anton Wohlfart.

Baron von Rothsattel (ROHT-zaht-tehl), a German nobleman. His chaotic business affairs are put in order by Anton Wohlfart, whom the baron insults and finally dismisses because of a misplaced sense of rank.

Lenore von Rothsattel (leh-NOH-reh), Baron von Rothsattel's beautiful daughter, who persuades Anton Wohlfart to become her father's agent and retrieve the baron's ruined estates. She marries Fritz von Fink.

Hirsch Ehrenthal (hihrsh EH-rehn-tahl), an unscrupulous usurer who plots the financial ruin of Baron von Rothsattel.

Veitel Itzig (VI-tehl IHT-zihg), an employee of Hirsch Ehrenthal. With his knowledge of Ehrenthal's affairs and by means of a dishonest manipulation of documents, he plots to acquire Baron von Rothsattel's estates. He is drowned in his attempt to escape arrest.

Fritz von Fink, an Americanized German nobleman and friend of Anton Wohlfart. He is instrumental in saving Baron von Rothsattel's Polish estates and marries Lenore von Rothsattel.

Eugen von Rothsattel (OY-gehn), Baron von Rothsattel's gallant but impractical son.

THE DEBUT

Author: Anita Brookner (1928-)
First published: 1981
Genre: Novel

Locale: London, England, and Paris, France
Time: The 1970's
Plot: Ironic

Ruth Weiss, a scholar who is writing a multivolume study on the women in Honoré de Balzac's novels and teaching a literature seminar. Caught in appearance and character halfway between the nineteenth and twentieth centuries, forty-year-old Ruth has beautiful long red hair (often worn in a classical chignon) and a slight hesitation in her walk. Scrupulous, passionate, thoughtful, and introspective, she is extreme in everything and feels that her life has been ruined by literature. As the novel opens, Ruth is living alone and seeing her publisher once every six months for dinner. The novel recounts her past: her irregular home life with her parents and grandmother, her growing scholarly interests, and her romantic encounters in London and Paris, especially with Richard Hirst and Professor Duplessis. Her ultimate conviction is that moral fortitude is not enough to succeed in life; it is better, and easier, to be engaging and attractive.

George Weiss, a dealer in rare books. Gregarious, affable, and inaccessible to his daughter Ruth, George is glossy, cheery, and a bit of a dandy; he wears smart tweed suits, uses a cigarette holder, and sports a ready smile. In truth, he is somewhat unhappy, with vaguely unrealized dreams. He adores his wife yet is unfaithful to her with his assistant Miss Moss and then with the widowed Sally Jacobs. After his wife learns of the affair with Jacobs, George has a stroke and is nursed back to health by Ruth.

Helen Weiss, an actress. Beautiful, successful, and thin even into middle age, Helen is girlish and outrageous, not interested in being a mother to Ruth. When she is not working, Helen spends most of her time in bed, smoking and talking with Maggie Cutler and becoming increasingly listless. After the discovery of George's latest affair, Helen refuses to stay under the same roof with him; she dies in a taxi with Ruth on the return from an abortive trip to Molly Edwards' house.

Mrs. Weiss, the aging grandmother of Ruth and mother of George. Aware of the irresponsibility of her son and his wife, Mrs. Weiss tries to maintain a normal household for Ruth. She dies after a stroke and three months of being bedridden.

Mrs. Maggie Cutler, the spry, chain-smoking, sloppy housekeeper for the Weisses who becomes Helen's confidant. Maggie finds a husband through a matchmaking agency and leaves Oakwood Court for his company in Folkestone. The Weisses, especially Helen, are outraged at her behavior.

Miss Parker, a teacher. She is one of the first people to take an interest in Ruth. She encourages her to go to university and be a scholar.

Anthea, a college friend of Ruth. Beautiful and popular, Anthea needs Ruth for an acolyte. Anthea's concerns are boys and her appearance. She schools Ruth in these subjects, appalled at her ignorance, and encourages her to move away from her parents. Later, Anthea makes a conventional marriage with Brian and becomes a housewife and mother.

Richard Hirst, a psychologist. With unblemished blond good looks and many charms, Richard attracts women of all kinds. Eager for crises, Richard is blissfully unaware of obligations. He treats a dinner invitation from Ruth with casual nonchalance, arriving hours late, oblivious of her hunger and her feelings.

Mrs. Sally Jacobs, a woman who buys George's rare book shop when he retires. A widow who loves to cook for men, Sally tolerates George's disruption of her orderly flat and thinks she wants him to marry her. When Helen dies, however, Mrs. Jacobs retreats to her sister's house in Manchester and leaves her flat to her nephew Roddy.

Professor Alain Duplessis (doo-pleh-si), a middle-aged, married, and rather heavy professor at the Sorbonne who is somewhat famous. Professor Duplessis makes friends with Ruth in Paris. The friendship promises to turn more romantic when Ruth rents the Dixons' flat and invites him to dinner, but it ends when Ruth is called back to London to care for her ailing parents.

Hugh Dixon, an art dealer in Paris who befriends Ruth and gives her advice about cutting her hair and buying more fashionable clothes.

Jill Dixon, a travel agent and Hugh's wife. Jill tolerates his friendship with Ruth because she does not consider Ruth a threat and because she takes a lover herself.

Molly Edwards, a Christian Scientist and a particular friend of Helen Weiss. The Weisses spend their last vacation together with Molly at her place at Hove.

Humphrey Wilcox, a writer and friend of George Weiss.

Ruth's landlord at her first place in Paris, Humphrey spies on her when she takes her daily bath.

Rhoda Wilcox, Humphrey's wife. She is dedicated to keeping things quiet so that her husband can write.

Roddy Jacobs, a rare book dealer who succeeds his aunt at the shop formerly run by George Weiss. Plump and conventional, he gets along so well with George after Sally Jacobs' departure to Manchester that Ruth agrees to marry him. Only six months later, Roddy is killed in a car accident.

— *Patricia Clark*

THE DECAMERON

Author: Giovanni Boccaccio (1313-1375)
First transcribed: 1349-1351
Genre: Short fiction

Locale: Italy
Time: Antiquity and the Middle Ages
Plot: Story-within-a-story

The narrator, a calculated, controlled voice, sensitive and seemingly genuine, that speaks directly to the reader. In the preface and introduction, the narrator establishes the narrative framework, describes the Florentine Black Plague of 1348, and introduces the ten storytellers. In the prologue to the fourth day, he defends himself against criticism. In the conclusion, he defends himself against charges of obscenity, slandering the clergy, and frivolity.

Pampinea (pahm-pee-NAY-ah), the storyteller who conceives the idea of the excursion into the countryside, which provides the framework for the story as a whole. She also is the one to suggest the rotation of group leadership duties. Pampinea is wise, self-possessed, and the most mature of the group, having often been in love.

Dioneo (dee-oh-NAY-oh), the wittiest, most attractive, and most self-willed of the three young men to participate in the excursion. He is the first to insist on forgetting the cares left behind in Florence and tells the first of the stories to have sexual content. He tells the last story on each of the last nine days, without regard for the topic established for that day.

Filomena (fee-loh-MAY-nah), a wise and discreet woman who seconds Pampinea's suggestion to bring men along on their excursion, relying on truth to protect her honor and reputation should it be questioned later. She is passionate and amorous.

Elisa (eh-LEE-sah), a very young woman characterized by a powerfully passionate nature.

Fiammetta (fee-ahm-MEHT-tah), who is generous in giving love and desirous of being loved but fearful of the pain of losing love.

Ser Cepparello (sehr chehp-pa-REHL-loh), a character in a story told by Panfilo. Known, because of his small stature, as Ciappelletto, he was perhaps the vilest man to ever live. A notary known for his dishonesty, he was chosen by a wealthy merchant to deal with the treacherous Burgundians. While in Burgundy, he took ill and was confessed by a gullible but pious priest, whom he tricked into thinking he was a very godly man. When Cepparello died, the priest convinced his brothers to regard him as a saint, after which many miracles were said to have been performed in his name.

Abraham, a character in a story narrated by Neifile. He is a Jew, harassed by his Christian friend to become a member of the Catholic church. He went to Rome to see how the Holy Father and the cardinals deported themselves. Their wickedness and profligacy were such that Abraham became convinced that the foundation of the church of Rome must truly be God in order for it to prosper and grow, because it obviously was not the piety of its leaders. He converted to Catholicism.

Alatiel (ah-lah-tee-ehl), a character in a story narrated by Panfilo. She is the beautiful daughter of the sultan of Babylon and is promised as a wife to the king of Algarve. On her way to the wedding, she is shipwrecked on Majorca. Her beauty and courage bring her, through a series of nine abductions in various lands over four years, back to her father, who still believes she is chaste. She is finally wed to the king and lives serenely in well-earned peace and honor with him.

Brother Alberto, a character in a story narrated by Elisa. He convinces a woman that the archangel Gabriel is in love with her; then, disguising himself, he takes advantage of her several times. Finally, fearing reprisal from her relatives, he runs away and is given refuge by a poor man, who unwittingly leads him to capture the next day by his brother monks.

Isabetta (ee-zah-BEHT-tah), a character in one of Filomena's stories. After her brothers kill her lover Lorenzo, she is visited by his spirit, who tells her where he is buried. In secret, she exhumes his head and places it in a pot of basil, which she waters daily with her tears. After her brothers discover her secret and take the pot away from her, she dies of grief.

Madonna Usimbalda (ew-seem-BAHL-dah), a character in one of Elisa's stories. She is an abbess who is called from her bed to judge one of her nuns, who is accused of being unchaste. In her haste, the abbess, who had herself been in bed with a priest, mistakes the priest's pants for her veil and wears them on her head into the chamber where the accused nun is to be examined. Madonna Usimbalda's harshness is mitigated when the accused nun points out the abbess' unusual headdress.

Griselda (gree-ZEHL-dah), a character in a story narrated by Dioneo. She is the peasant wife of the Marquis of Saluzzo. Her constancy and firmness are tested by her husband when he takes her two children at birth and pretends to have them killed, meanwhile secreting them. When Griselda bears this with fortitude and mildness, Saluzzo tells her that she has displeased him and pretends to take another wife, driving Griselda out of the house in nothing but an undergarment. He then brings their daughter into the house as his new bride.

After Griselda endures these trials, he restores her as his wife and abundantly honors her as marchioness.

— *Andrew B. Preslar*

DECLINE AND FALL: An Illustrated Novelette

Author: Evelyn Waugh (1903-1966)
First published: 1928
Genre: Novel

Locale: England and Wales
Time: The twentieth century
Plot: Social satire

Paul Pennyfeather, an inoffensive divinity student at Oxford University who is wrongly dismissed for indecent exposure after he is made the victim of a prank. He teaches at a school in Wales and is hired as vacation tutor for one of his pupils. He becomes engaged to the boy's mother, Margot Beste-Chetwynde; just before the wedding, however, he is arrested and later is convicted of operating the international white-slave trade she runs. After she has arranged for his successful escape from prison, Paul is officially declared dead. Disguised by a heavy mustache, he returns to his college at Oxford to continue his interrupted study for the Church.

Sir Alastair Digby-Vaine-Trumpington, whose prank results in Paul's dismissal from Oxford. Later, as Paul's former fiancée's boyfriend, he assists in Paul's escape from prison.

Dr. Augustus Fagan, the head of the inadequate Llanabba Castle school where Paul teaches. Fagan forsakes education for medicine and becomes the owner of the nursing home where Paul's death certificate is signed by a drunken doctor.

Peter Beste-Chetwynde, one of Paul's pupils.

Margot Beste-Chetwynde, his mother and Paul's fiancée. Paul is convicted of her crimes. He spends the interval between his prison escape and his return to Oxford resting up at her villa on Corfu.

Mr. Prendergast, a master at Llanabba Castle school. Later he turns up as chaplain at Blackstone Gaol, where Paul is a prisoner. Prendergast is killed by a crazed inmate.

Captain Grimes, a scoundrel who is periodically in difficulties. To get out of trouble, he marries one of Fagan's daughters and later fakes a drowning. He appears as Paul's fellow prisoner. He is subsequently believed to have perished in the swamp while trying to escape, but Paul believes that the escape was successful.

Arthur Potts, whom Paul knew at Oxford. Working for the League of Nations, he shows an interest in Margot's business affairs. He is chief witness for the prosecution at Paul's trial.

Flossie Fagan, one of Fagan's daughters, a vulgar young woman who wants to be married and is consequently useful to Grimes in getting out of trouble.

Diana Fagan, another of Fagan's daughters, who economizes in sugar and soap.

Philbrick, the butler at Llanabba Castle and a confidence man. He tells varying stories about himself, claiming, among other things, that he is really Sir Solomon Philbrick, a millionaire shipowner. He flees Llanabba as he is about to be arrested on charges of false pretenses. At Blackstone Gaol, Paul finds Philbrick employed as a trusty.

Lord Tangent, a pupil at Llanabba. Acting as starter during an annual field sports meet, Prendergast accidentally shoots Lord Tangent in the heel. Lord Tangent dies of the infection.

Lady Circumference, Lord Tangent's rude mother.

Lord Pastmaster, Margot's impoverished brother-in-law, from whom she buys her country house, King's Thursday.

Otto Silenus, an eccentric designer who changes King's Thursday from the finest example of Tudor domestic architecture in England into a structure of concrete, glass, and aluminum.

Sir Humphrey Maltravers, minister of Transport; later Lord Metroland and the home secretary. He is Paul's rival for Margot's hand. First refused because Margot's son Peter prefers Paul, he is accepted after Paul's conviction. He is involved in the arranging of Paul's escape from prison.

DEEPHAVEN

Author: Sarah Orne Jewett (1849-1909)
First published: 1877
Genre: Novel

Locale: Deephaven, a small town on the coast of Maine
Time: The nineteenth century
Plot: Regional

Helen Denis, the narrator.

Kate Lancaster, the narrator's friend, who asks Helen to spend a summer at Deephaven with her in the house left to her mother by her great-aunt, Katherine Brandon. She and Helen are made welcome by those who have known the Lancaster family through several generations.

Dick Carew, a retired East India merchant, one of Deephaven's leading citizens.

Mrs. Carew, his wife, a social leader in Deephaven.

Mr. Lorimer, a minister in Deephaven.

Mrs. Lorimer, the minister's wife.

Mrs. Kew, wife of the keeper of a lighthouse near Deephaven. She becomes a great friend to Kate Lancaster and Helen Denis.

Captain Lant, a retired sailor who tells the girls about Peletiah Daw and Peletiah's wild nephew Ben.

Danny, a silent, weather-beaten sailor who tells the girls about his pet cat.

Captain Sands, another old seafarer who befriends Helen and Kate.

Mrs. Bonny, an unconventional woman who lives near Deephaven. She reminds the girls of a friendly Indian.

Miss Chauncey, an aristocratic old lady who lives, mildly insane, in an unfurnished old mansion.

THE DEERSLAYER: Or, The First War-Path, a Tale

Author: James Fenimore Cooper (1789-1851)
First published: 1841
Genre: Novel

Locale: Northern New York State
Time: 1740
Plot: Historical

Natty Bumppo, called **Deerslayer**, a skilled, modest, honorable, and brave young hunter. He has been brought up by Delaware Indians and taught by Moravian pietists; he embodies a natural innocence and nobility. Arriving at Lake Glimmerglass, he allies himself with Hurry Harry March and the Hutter family, at the same time trying to help his Indian friend Chingachgook rescue his betrothed from hostile Iroquois. He is soon forced to kill his first man, an Indian. He ransoms the captured Harry and Hutter after their capture during a raid on an Iroquois camp, but he himself is caught while assisting Chingachgook. The Iroquois respect his word and give him leave to offer his friends terms of surrender. When these are rejected, he goes back to be tortured. He escapes but is recaptured. His torture is stopped only by the timely arrival of Chingachgook and Hurry Harry with British troops. Unresponsive to Judith Hutter's charms, he leaves to join the Delaware tribe.

Hurry Harry March, a ferocious, greedy, swaggering frontiersman. Captured with Hutter during a raid for Indian scalps, he is released only by Deerslayer's bargaining. His impulsive shooting of an Indian girl endangers his companions. Large and handsome, he is nevertheless refused by Judith Hutter, who favors Deerslayer. He redeems himself by leading the British soldiers to the Indian camp, thus saving Deerslayer's life.

Chingachgook (chihn-GACH-gook), a Delaware chief. A noble savage, he is as adept in woodcraft and warfare as his friend Deerslayer. He manages to escape with his beloved, Wah-ta!-Wah, when Deerslayer is captured. Later, he saves Hurry Harry in an ambush at Hutter's "castle," and he cuts Deerslayer's bonds just before the British rout the Iroquois. Years later, he revisits Lake Glimmerglass with his son Uncas and his friend Deerslayer.

Tom Hutter, a predatory former pirate who became a trapper in order to escape the law. Living with his two adopted daughters in Muskrat Castle, a hut built on a shoal, he makes his trapping rounds on the lake in a houseboat. As avaricious as Hurry Harry, he joins him on an ill-fated raid, and both are made prisoners by hostile Indians. After being ransomed, he joins Harry on another raid. Returning to his hut, he is scalped in an ambush and buried in the lake by his daughters.

Judith Hutter, his gay, coquettish, shrewd young daughter, who prides herself on her clothes and appearance. Having been seduced by Captain Warley, she is cautious about men and refuses Hurry Harry. Deerslayer, however, resists her attractions and declines her offer of marriage. Having no relatives left when her sister dies, she goes to the British fort, possibly to become Warley's mistress.

Hetty Hutter, Judith's simple-minded sister. She embodies a pure Christian simplicity unalloyed by a sense of expediency. The Indians are in awe of her and allow her to pass unmolested as she serves as a kind of messenger between the captured and uncaptured. Her naïve love for Hurry Harry remains unrequited when she is accidentally shot in the final battle with the Indians.

Wah-ta!-Wah, Chingachgook's beloved, a Delaware maiden captured by Iroquois. A practical child of nature, she condones scalping but deplores Hurry Harry's wanton killing. Although she escapes with Chingachgook, she returns to the enemy camp with Judith and Hetty in an effort to save Deerslayer.

Captain Warley, head of the troop that saves Deerslayer and routs the Indians. A man of the world, his interest in Judith revives when he sees her in the camp in a stunning gown.

Rivenoak, the enemy Iroquois chief, a fierce foe but honorable in character. He offers to let Deerslayer live if he will marry the widow of the brave he killed.

Le Loup Cervier (le lew sayr-VYAY), an Indian, the first person Deerslayer has ever killed. In dying, he names Deerslayer "Hawkeye."

Sumach, his wife, whom Deerslayer refuses.

The Panther, an Indian who attempts to kill the captured Deerslayer but is himself killed instead.

Catamount, a brave who unsuccessfully taunts captured Deerslayer.

THE DEFENSE
(Zashchita Luzhina)

Author: Vladimir Nabokov (1899-1977)
First published: 1929
Genre: Novel

Locale: Russia and Germany
Time: The 1910's and 1920's
Plot: Philosophical realism

Aleksandr Ivanovich Luzhin (ee-VAH-noh-vihch LEW-zhihn), a world-class chess player. Growing up in an aristocratic Russian household, the solitary Luzhin develops into a brilliant chess prodigy. Estranged from his parents, who do not understand his unique talent, he travels extensively to compete in chess tournaments in Europe. After several years, he becomes so immersed in a cerebral world of chess strategies that he loses contact with everyday reality and suffers a mental breakdown during the final match of a major tournament in Berlin. Although he recovers from this breakdown with the assistance of his fiancée, who tries to keep him away from any reminders of chess, he gradually falls prey to a new obsession:

He believes that the events of his life are manipulated by an invisible chess opponent. Trying desperately to foil the relentless control of this unknown opponent, Luzhin increasingly acts in irrational and unpredictable ways. Frustrated by his inability to escape the snares of his opponent, Luzhin commits suicide by jumping from his bathroom window. His last vision is of a vast chessboard, which he takes to be a sign of his future existence.

Mrs. Luzhin, a young woman with an independent mind and a compassionate spirit. She meets Aleksandr at a German resort and finds him so unusual that she decides to accept his abrupt and unmannered marriage proposal. She nurses him carefully after his breakdown, but because he never shares his inner fears with her, she remains unable to help him resist his suicidal anxiety.

Ivan Luzhin, Aleksandr's father, a writer of children's books. Although concerned for his son's well-being, Ivan does not know how to communicate with him. He had hoped that his son would turn out to be a musical prodigy, and he finds his son's chess genius unsettling. The senior Luzhin also has a difficult relationship with his wife, and he causes her pain when he enters into an adulterous affair. After the 1917 Bolshevik Revolution, Ivan lives alone as an émigré in Berlin. He plans to write a novel based on his son's life, but he dies with his plans unfulfilled.

Valentinov (vah-lehn-TIH-nov), Aleksandr's manager during the youth's rise to international fame. A shameless promoter, Valentinov exploits Aleksandr's talent when he is still young, then returns at the end of the novel, causing Aleksandr to take his paranoid suicide leap.

Aleksandr's aunt, a coquettish young woman who enters into an adulterous relationship with Ivan and introduces Aleksandr to the mysteries of chess.

Turati (tew-RAH-tih), Aleksandr's opponent in the climactic championship match that triggers Aleksandr's mental breakdown.

Mrs. Luzhin's parents, Russian émigrés living in Berlin. Mrs. Luzhin's mother disapproves of her daughter's marriage to the eccentric chess player, but her husband provides financial resources to support the couple after their marriage.

A lady from the Soviet Union, a garrulous visitor who visits the Luzhin household in Berlin during the period of Aleksandr's recuperation from his mental breakdown. Her comments about Aleksandr's aunt crystallize his anxiety about being attacked by an invisible opponent, and her presence prevents Mrs. Luzhin from paying full attention to her distraught husband.

— *Julian W. Connolly*

DEIRDRE

Author: James Stephens (1882-1950)
First published: 1923
Genre: Novel

Locale: Ireland
Time: The Heroic Age
Plot: Folklore

Conachur mac Nessa, king of Ulster, strong and willful, beloved by his people. Pride forces him to ignore a prophecy that the infant Deirdre will bring destruction upon Ulster. She is brought up as his ward. Seeing her, he determines to make her his queen. After her escape to Scotland, he resorts to treachery in an attempt to lure her back.

Nessa, the Ungentle, the mother of Conachur. Daughter of a king of Ulster, she was called Assa, the Gentle, until she set forth to seek vengeance on the murderer of her tutors.

Cathfa, a magician, Conachur's father. He forces Nessa to marry him as an alternative to death, but she later leaves him. It is he who makes the direful prophecy about Deirdre.

Fergus mac Roy, king of Ulster, who, at eighteen, is so in love with the still-beautiful Nessa that, to get her to marry him, he temporarily abdicates his throne to the sixteen-year-old Conachur. The abdication proves permanent, and Fergus becomes one of Conachur's most trusted followers.

Clothru, the daughter of the high king of Connacht, and Conachur's first wife. She is killed by her sister Maeve.

Maeve, the sister of Clothru. Claiming to avenge Clothru's death, Conachur instead falls in love with Maeve and marries her against her wishes. Much later, when she leaves him, her unforgiveness is such that she goes to great lengths to take back every bit of the riches she brought with her.

Deirdre, Conachur's ward, brought up to see only women servants and the ugliest guards in Ulster. Evading them, however, she finds three youths around a campfire. She falls in love with the eldest and, to escape Conachur, persuades them to take her away. Brought back from Scotland by Conachur's pretense of friendship and promise of safety, she escapes him again in death.

Lavarcham, Conachur's conversation-woman. In charge of Deirdre's upbringing, she decides to groom her to be queen. She reports on Deirdre to Conachur and in turn tells Deirdre all she needs to know about the king, but she cannot succeed in making Deirdre want him as a husband.

Naoise, who is a brave and handsome youth of nineteen when first seen by Deirdre. She loves him and lives six years with him and his brothers in Scotland. Tricked into returning with her, he is killed.

Ainnle and

Ardan, Naoise's brothers, also killed as a result of Conachur's treachery.

Felimid mac Dall, Conachur's storyteller and Deirdre's father.

Uisneac, Conachur's brother-in-law and father of Naoise, Ainnle, and Ardan.

mac Roth, Maeve's spy, who makes possible her secret preparations to leave Conachur.

DEIRDRE

Author: William Butler Yeats (1865-1939)
First published: 1907
Genre: Drama

Locale: Ireland
Time: Antiquity
Plot: Tragedy

Deirdre (DEER-druh), a young queen. The drama's tragic conclusion seems unalterable, but Deirdre struggles valiantly against it. At first apprehensive of King Conchubar's false offer of safety, she is quick to discover that she and Naoise have been snared in a trap. She attempts to rouse Naoise to flight, to no avail, then to persuade Conchubar, her captor, to release them. When that proves useless, she begs him to free Naoise. Finally, confronted by Naoise's murder and her imminent vassalage as a captive queen, she pretends to accede to Conchubar's desires, only to gain a moment of privacy in which to take her life. Her suicide is presented as a victory of the transcendent imagination over spiritual defeat.

King Conchubar (KAWN-chew-bahr), a crafty, ruthless, patient, and vengeful old king out of the province of Uladh (ancient Ulster). He is based on a character from Celtic literature. Conchubar is first memorably represented in the words of the First Musician as a jealous old man, apparently constructing a sensual bridal chamber to share with Deirdre, whose betrothal to Naoise he allegedly has countenanced. Acting duplicitously in the thrall of lustful passion, Conchubar seems a figure of dread, a projection of Deirdre's and Naoise's fears. Although he is no warrior, Conchubar easily manipulates Naoise and Fergus, demonstrating his superior, and perhaps unassailable, power. His cold-blooded execution of Naoise similarly demonstrates his single-minded, lawless passion. Although he looms as an undefeatable adversary for Deirdre, a personification of her unforgiving destiny, Conchubar also suggests a balance for her: His passion rivals her own, and Deirdre's tragedy, an act of self-transcendence, is made possible only through Conchubar's instigation. Finally, his concluding sorrow resonates with Deirdre's and thus emphasizes the magnitude of her sacrifice.

Fergus (FUR-guhs), a weak and foolish old man who clings to the sentimental illusion that supposing men to be virtuous will make them so. In an older version of the Deirdre story, Fergus betrays Naoise and Deirdre to Conchubar's

vengeance. He serves primarily as a dramatic foil, at first to emphasize that the skepticism of the First Musician is justified. In opposition to Deirdre's lyrical and heroic embrace of tragedy, Fergus embodies the ordinary impulse to shrink from great passions. His is essentially a modern temperament, based on a classical faith in moderation and altruism. Hopelessly inept in Yeats's vision of heroic literature, Fergus in his feebleness lends greater stature to the passions of Deirdre and Conchubar.

Naoise (na-OH-shee), Deirdre's young lover, in Celtic legend one of the three sons of Usna. Naoise's salient characteristic is the youthfulness of his judgment, which leads him to subdue his natural apprehensiveness in favor of Fergus' hollow assurances and to mistake Conchubar's craftiness at first for honor and then for cowardice. If Naoise demonstrates a lack of patience and guile—the qualities that distinguish Conchubar—he embodies insolence, passionate devotion, and youthful nobility. His death represents the tragedy of unfulfilled promise.

First Musician, a woman of about forty years, knowledgeable in the wisdom "of the roads," experienced in love, and skeptical. She establishes the play's context by rehearsing the relevant action preceding it. In several ways, she indicates how the play will conclude. She first encapsulates Deirdre's fate by saying that she has too much beauty for good luck. By describing the bridal chamber that Conchubar has constructed, the First Musician conveys an image of the king's covert, lascivious intentions. In her exchange with Fergus, by reiterating the conventional wisdom that old men are jealous, she imparts to the audience the knowledge that Conchubar's overt change of heart is counterfeit. She thus shifts the audience's concern from plot to the character of Deirdre. Perhaps most important, Deirdre, in her furtive exchange with the First Musician on the subject of love, learns what Conchubar has in store for her and thus prepares to struggle against her fate.

— *Michael Scott Joseph*

DEIRDRE OF THE SORROWS

Author: John Millington Synge (1871-1909)
First published: 1910
Genre: Drama

Locale: Ireland
Time: The legendary past
Plot: Tragedy

Deirdre (DEER-druh), a Gaelic legendary heroine foretold to bring trouble into the world. Loved by King Conchubor, she, in turn, loves Naisi, with whom she flees. After seven years of happiness, the lovers are lured back to the king's castle, where Naisi is slain. In her sorrow, Deirdre kills herself to join her lover in another world.

Naisi (NAY-shee), a Gaelic legendary hero. Winning Deirdre's love, he takes her from King Conchubor. After seven

happy years with his bride, he is tricked into a meeting with the king and is slain.

Conchubor (kon-KEW-bohr), the lonely king of Ulster. In love with Deirdre, whom he has resolved to marry in spite of the prophecy that she is born for trouble, he loses her to Naisi. Eventually, he tricks the lovers into a meeting at which Naisi is slain. After Deirdre commits suicide in her grief, the king is led away, old and broken.

Lavarcham (lah-VAHR-kahm), Deirdre's nurse.

Fergus, King Conchubor's friend. In good faith, he brings King Conchubor's peace offering to Deirdre and Naisi. When he learns of the lovers' betrayal, he burns the king's castle.

Owen, King Conchubor's friend and spy. In despair over his hopeless love for Deirdre, he destroys himself.

Ainnle (AYN-luh) and

Ardan, Naisi's brothers, slain with him by King Conchubor's warriors.

DELIA'S SONG

Author: Lucha Corpi (1945-   )
First published: 1989
Genre: Novel

Locale: Berkeley and the San Francisco Bay area in California
Time: Late 1960's to mid-1970's
Plot: Bildungsroman

Delia Trevino (DEH-lee-ah treh-VEE-noh), a Mexican American student at the University of California, Berkeley. A freshman from a Mexican background, Delia becomes an activist for Third World liberation, participates in campus revolution, and falls in love with one of the idealistic heroes of the revolution.

Jeff Morones (moh-ROH-nehs), also a young activist at the University of California, Berkeley. He is the object—and ultimate winner—of Delia's affections.

Roger N. Hart, alias "James Joyce." Hart is a marine biologist around whom Delia's fantasies turn after an erotic encounter at a Day of the Dead costume party at a friend's home.

Professor Mattie N. Johnson, Delia's mentor. Mattie is a sociologist and activist and is influential in Delia's intellec-

tual, political, and personal growth.

Marta Trevino de Ciotti (chee-OH-tee), Delia's beloved aunt. Delia lives with Aunt Marta in Monterey after leaving Berkeley; Aunt Marta serves as Delia's connection with her Mexican heritage and provides family background.

Samuel Corona, a graduate student in sociology. The intellectual leader of the student revolution, Samuel wins Delia's trust, but he crumbles into alcoholism after the political riots.

Julio Singer, a conga-playing poet. A member of the student activist group with which Delia becomes associated, Julio later becomes a published poet.

Sara Gonzalez (gohn-SAH-lehs), Delia's roommate and a member of the liberation movement in Berkeley.

A DELICATE BALANCE

Author: Edward Albee (1928-   )
First published: 1967
Genre: Drama

Locale: The living room of a large suburban house
Time: October, in the mid-1960's
Plot: Absurdist

Agnes, a handsome wife and mother in her late fifties. Haunted by the possibility of losing her mind, which she defines as a kind of "drifting," whereby she would become a stranger in the world, she attempts to maintain order, a "delicate balance," in her world. She deals with the emotional withdrawal of her husband and the "embarrassment" of her sister by taking the verbal initiative to judge and thereby control them. She comes to realize that her hold on reality depends more on them than she has been willing to admit, and that frightens her.

Tobias, her husband, a few years older. An emotionally repressed and withdrawn man, he covers his deepest fears with a mask of self-control and quiet, and he suppresses them with alcohol. Forced by Agnes to make a decision about whether Harry and Edna will stay, he breaks down under the weight of trying to be honest about how he really feels, not only about them but also about his own family. He has a hysterical fear of death and of being alone, and this allows him to tolerate demands of his family.

Claire, Agnes' alcoholic younger sister. Called an ingrate and one of the walking wounded by Agnes, she is nevertheless the most honest person in the family. She does not hide her feelings or her dark side. She uses her drinking to annoy and embarrass Agnes; to amuse Tobias, with whom she might have

had an affair; to prick Julia's pretensions; and to thumb her nose at society. She is a weary, but tough, survivor.

Julia, Agnes and Tobias' thirty-six-year-old daughter, recently separated from her fourth husband. Returning home with a sense of failure and with raw emotions, she is like a younger version of Claire, for whom she has much admiration and affection. She needs her childhood room, which symbolizes a measure of order in her chaotic emotional life; the fact that it is occupied by her godparents causes her to become hysterical. She realizes that her arrival will necessitate changes in the alliances that have held Agnes, Tobias, and Claire in their uncomfortable triangle.

Harry and

Edna, Agnes and Tobias' best friends and godparents to Julia. Frightened by a "terror" that remains unnameable, they are "intruders" in the household. Like the plague, their fear is contagious; each character reads his or her own personal agony into it. The women of the house want them to go; Tobias begs them to stay. In leaving by their own choice, they force the family to confront and acknowledge their personal fears. The terror seems to be existential in nature, a glimpse into the passage of time, death, and alienation.

— Lori Hall Burghardt

DELIVERANCE

Author: James Dickey (1923-1997)
First published: 1970
Genre: Novel

Locale: Georgia
Time: Late twentieth century
Plot: Bildungsroman

Ed Gentry, the vice president of his own advertising firm. Ed's boredom frightens him enough to take the trip to the wilderness. He is tempted several times to stay home or to go home rather than to deal with the problems that arise during the canoe trip. Ed's philosophy of life is called "sliding," which is continually taking the path of least resistance. Ed, however, is dying emotionally, and he knows it. This insufficiency or void in the middle of his existence is more frightening than the potential terrors of the wilderness. On the trip, he discovers what has been lying deep in his unconscious, namely, his potential to become one with nature and to abandon the laws of civilization. When he is forced to become the hero or die with the others in the woods, Ed is able to find the strength of will to kill another man. He is also able to cover up the murder when questioned at length by the police. Ed's life is changed by the experience he has on the trip, but the changes remain internal. The river stays with him in his dreams and finds expression in his art. After this experience, he is no longer bored because he can see himself in a mythological way.

Lewis Medlock, a survivalist who earns his living managing rental property. Ed, Drew, and Bobby are ambivalent about going down a river without any experience or knowledge, but Lewis, who functions as both herald and helper for the trip, is adamant. He preaches the value of the wilderness and survival. Lewis would welcome the apocalypse and would see it as a challenge for which he has been preparing for years. He is a man of two worlds who is often misunderstood and incomprehensible. Lewis' heart is in the wilderness. His values are the inverse of those of his companions. He lives in the world of artificiality, but his real life is in the wilderness, in struggle and survival.

Bobby Trippe, an incompetent, annoying insurance salesman. He is sodomized on the trip and becomes a victim who needs to be saved. Bobby is the opposite of Lewis. He is fat and lazy and feels right at home in the world of superficiality. Bobby sells insurance—a way to keep risks at bay. Bobby is the perfect representative of the everyday world. He whines and complains the entire trip, and although he actually enjoys the run through the first rapid, he is ready to leave the next morning. Bobby did not understand what he was getting into when he agreed to go on the trip.

Drew Ballinger, a bluegrass guitarist and soft-drink company executive. Drew is, like Bobby, a man of the everyday world. A large part of his existence is wrapped up in his job as a sales supervisor. He keeps a copy of the company history on his coffee table and sees things from the perspective of business. Drew has something that Bobby does not, and that is the gift of music. Drew's music has the ability to go beneath the superficiality of civilization and to connect with something in the wilderness as well. Drew has the potential to be a hero in the mythological sense, but he loses his opportunity by clinging to the laws of civilization. In another sense, Drew is a hero because he sacrifices himself for the others.

— *Gregory Salyer*

DELPHINE

Author: Madame de Staël (1766-1817)
First published: 1802
Genre: Novel

Locale: France
Time: Late eighteenth century
Plot: Epistolary

Delphine d'Albemar (dehl-FEEN dahl-beh-MAHR), the tragic heroine of this sentimental epistolary novel. Intellectually and financially independent upon her widowhood at twenty, she gives away part of her fortune to enable Matilda de Vernon, the daughter of a friend, to marry an unseen Spanish nobleman. When Delphine herself falls in love with the young nobleman, she is maligned and deceived by Matilda's mother in order that the proposed marriage may take place. Always virtuous but never an adherent to convention, Delphine constantly finds her reputation in jeopardy. Deceived into taking vows as a nun, she renounces them to marry her lover, now a widower. Yet because public opinion is against her, she refuses to marry him, not wishing to make his life miserable. Ultimately, she takes poison and dies on his execution ground. The lovers, kept apart in life, are buried side by side.

Madame de Vernon (vehr-NOHN), her close friend, a treacherous woman. On her deathbed, she confesses that she lied about Delphine.

Matilda de Vernon (mah-TEEL-dah), Madame de Vernon's daughter. Her marriage to the man who loves Delphine is doomed to unhappiness. When her death frees her husband, he and Delphine are still unable to find happiness.

Léonce Mondeville (lay-OHNS mohn-deh-VEEL), a Spanish nobleman, Matilda's fiancé. In love with and loved by Delphine, he is tricked by Matilda's mother into going ahead with the marriage to Matilda. After Madame de Vernon, on her deathbed, clears Delphine's name, he and Delphine decide to continue seeing each other. Their affair is not immoral, but it is assumed to be so. At last, having joined the royalist forces, he is captured and sentenced to death by the republican French government. After Delphine's suicide at the spot where he is to be executed, the soldiers refuse to shoot him, but he taunts them until they do.

Madame d'Ervin (dehr-VAHN), a friend of Delphine, at whose house she meets her lover. In keeping Madame d'Ervin's presence in the house a secret, Delphine finds that